T0181090

Lecture Notes in Computer Science 12694

More information about this subseries at http://www.springer.com/series/7407

Pedro A. Castillo ·
Juan Luis Jiménez Laredo (Eds.)

Applications of Evolutionary Computation

24th International Conference, EvoApplications 2021
Held as Part of EvoStar 2021
Virtual Event, April 7–9, 2021
Proceedings

 Springer

Editors
Pedro A. Castillo 🆔
ETSIIT-CITIC
University of Granada
Granada, Spain

Juan Luis Jiménez Laredo 🆔
Université Le Havre Normandie
Le Havre, France

ISSN 0302-9743 ISSN 1611-3349 (electronic)
Lecture Notes in Computer Science
ISBN 978-3-030-72698-0 ISBN 978-3-030-72699-7 (eBook)
https://doi.org/10.1007/978-3-030-72699-7

LNCS Sublibrary: SL1 – Theoretical Computer Science and General Issues

This Springer imprint is published by the registered company Springer Nature Switzerland AG
The registered company address is: Gewerbestrasse 11, 6330 Cham, Switzerland

Preface

This volume contains the proceedings of *EvoApplications 2021*, the *International Conference on the Applications of Evolutionary Computation*. The conference was part of *Evo**, the leading event on bio-inspired computation in Europe, and was held on-line due to the COVID-19 pandemic, between Wednesday, April 7 and Friday, April 9.

EvoApplications, formerly known as EvoWorkshops, aims to bring together high-quality research with a focus on applied domains of bio-inspired computing. At the same time, under the *Evo** umbrella, *EuroGP* focused on the technique of genetic programming, *EvoCOP* targeted evolutionary computation in combinatorial optimization, and *EvoMUSART* was dedicated to evolved and bio-inspired music, sound, art, and design. The proceedings for all of these co-located events are available in the LNCS series.

EvoApplications received this year 78 high-quality submissions distributed among the main session *Applications of Evolutionary Computation* and eight additional special sessions chaired by leading experts on the different areas: Applications of Bio-inspired Techniques on Social Networks Learning, Applications of Deep Bioinspired Algorithms, Applications of Nature-inspired Computing for Sustainability and Development, Evolutionary Computation in Image Analysis, Signal Processing and Pattern Recognition, Evolutionary Machine Learning, Machine Learning and AI in Digital Healthcare and Personalized Medicine, Parallel and Distributed Systems, and Soft Computing applied to Games. We selected 34 of these papers for full oral presentation, while a further 17 works were presented in short oral presentation and as posters. All contributions, regardless of the presentation format, appear as full papers in this volume (LNCS 12694).

Obviously, an event of this kind would not be possible without the contribution of a large number of people.

- We express our gratitude to the authors for submitting their works and to the members of the program committee for devoting their selfless efforts to the review process.
- We would also like to thank Nuno Lourenço (University of Coimbra, Portugal) for his dedicated work with the submission and registration system and Sérgio Rebelo (University of Coimbra, Portugal) for his important graphic design work.
- We are grateful to José Francisco Chicano García (University of Málaga, Spain) for managing and maintaining the *Evo** website and João Correia (University of Coimbra, Portugal) handling publicity did an impressive job.
- We credit the invited keynote speakers, Darrell Whitley (Colorado State University, USA) and Susanna Manrubia (Spanish National Centre for Biotechnology, CSIC, Spain), for their fascinating and inspiring presentations.
- We would like to express our gratitude to the Steering Committee of EvoApplications for helping with the organization of the conference.

- We are grateful for the support provided by *SPECIES*, the Society for the Promotion of Evolutionary Computation in Europe and its Surroundings, and its individual members Marc Schoenauer (President), Anna I. Esparcia-Alcázar, (Secretary and Vice-President), and Wolfgang Banzhaf (Treasurer), for handling the coordination and financial administration.

Finally, we express our continued appreciation to Anna I. Esparcia-Alcázar, from SPECIES, Europe, whose considerable efforts in managing and coordinating *Evo** helped towards building a unique, vibrant, and friendly atmosphere.

Pedro A. Castillo
Juan Luis Jiménez Laredo
Giovanni Iacca
Doina Bucur
Carlos Cotta
Paco Fernández
Valentino Santucci
Fabio Caraffini
Pablo Mesejo
Harith Al-Sahaf
Penousal Machado
Wolfgang Banzhaf
Stephen Smith
Marta Vallejo
Antonio Mora
Pablo García Sánchez
Alberto P. Tonda
J. J. Merelo Guervós

Organization

Organizing Committee

EvoApplications Conference Chair

Pedro A. Castillo   Universidad de Granada, Spain

EvoApplications Publication Chair

Juan Luis Jiménez Laredo   Université Le Havre Normandie, France

Local Chair

Federico Divina   Universidad Pablo de Olavide, Spain

Publicity Chair

João Correia   University of Coimbra, Portugal

Applications of Bio-inspired Techniques on Social Networks

Giovanni Iacca   University of Trento, Italy
Doina Bucur   University of Twente, The Netherlands

Applications of Nature-inspired Computing for Sustainability and Development

Valentino Santucci   University for Foreigners of Perugia, Italy
Fabio Caraffini   De Montfort University, UK

Evolutionary Computation in Image Analysis, Signal Processing and Pattern Recognition

Pablo Mesejo   Universidad de Granada, Spain
Harith Al-Sahaf   Victoria University of Wellington, New Zealand

Machine Learning and AI in Digital Healthcare and Personalized Medicine

Stephen Smith   University of York, UK
Marta Vallejo   Heriot-Watt University, UK

Soft Computing applied to Games

Alberto P. Tonda	Université Paris-Saclay, INRA, France
Antonio M. Mora	Universidad de Granada, Spain
Pablo García Sánchez	Universidad de Granada, Spain

Applications of Deep Bioinspired Algorithms

Carlos Cotta	Universidad de Málaga, Spain
Francisco Fernández de Vega	Universidad de Extremadura, Spain

Parallel and Distributed Systems

Juan Julián Merelo Guervós	Universidad de Granada, Spain
Juan Luis Jiménez Laredo	Université Le Havre Normandie, France

Evolutionary Machine Learning

Penousal Machado	University of Coimbra, Portugal
Wolfgang Banzhaf	Michigan State University, USA

EvoApps Steering Committee

Stefano Cagnoni	University of Parma, Italy
Anna I. Esparcia-Alcázar	SPECIES, Spain
Mario Giacobini	Universitá degli Studi di Torino, Italy
Paul Kaufmann	Johannes Gutenberg Universität Mainz, Germany
Antonio M. Mora	Universidad de Granada, Spain
Günther Raidl	Technische Universität Wien, Austria
Franz Rothlauf	Johannes Gutenberg Universität Mainz, Germany
Kevin Sim	Edinburgh Napier University, UK
Giovanni Squillero	Politecnico di Torino, Italy
Cecilia Di Chio Rossiter (Honorary Member)	University of Southampton, UK

Program Committee

Ahmed Kattan	Umm Al-Qura University, Saudi Arabia
Aladdin Ayesh	De Montfort University, UK
Alberto Tonda	INRA, France
Aleš Zamuda	University of Maribor, Slovenia
Alessandra Scotto di Freca	Università degli studi di Cassino e del Lazio Meridionale, Italy
Alessandro Niccolai	Politecnico di Milano, Italy
Amir Dehsarvi	University of Aberdeen, UK

Anabela Simões	Coimbra Institute of Engineering, Portugal
Anca Andreica	Babeş-Bolyai University, Romania
Anders Christensen	University of Southern Denmark, Denmark
Andrea Tettamanzi	Université Côte d'Azur, France
Andres Faina	IT University of Copenhagen, Denmark
Andrew Turner	Freelance Researcher, UK
Anil Yaman	Korea Advanced Institute of Science and Technology, Korea
Anna Paszyńska	Jagiellonian University, Poland
Anthony Clark	Pomona College, USA
Antonio Fernández Ares	University of Granada, Spain
Antonio Mora García	University of Granada, Spain
Antonio Córdoba	University of Seville, Spain
Antonio Della Cioppa	University of Salerno, Italy
Antonio González	Universidad Rey Juan Carlos, Spain
Antonio J. Fernández Leiva	Universidad de Málaga, Spain
Arkadiusz Poteralski	Silesian University of Technology, Poland
Bernabé Dorronsoro	University of Cádiz, Spain
Bing Xue	Victoria University of Wellington, New Zealand
Carlotta Orsenigo	Polytechnic University of Milan, Italy
Cédric Buche	CNRS CERV - Centre Européen de Réalité Virtuelle, France
Changhe Li	China University of Geosciences, China
Chien-Chung Shen	University of Delaware, USA
Clara Pizzuti	CNR-ICAR, Italy
Daniel Hernandez	Data Frontier/Instituto Tecnológico de Tijuana, México
Daniele Gravina	University of Malta, Malta
David Megías	Universitat Oberta de Catalunya, Spain
David Pelta	University of Granada, Spain
Dávid Melhárt	University of Malta, Malta
Diego Perez Liebana	Queen Mary University of London, UK
Doina Bucur	University of Twente, Netherlands
Edoardo Fadda	Politecnico di Torino, Italy
Enrico Schumann	University of Basel, Switzerland
Ernesto Tarantino	ICAR-CNR, Italy
Evelyne Lutton	INRAE, France
Fabio Caraffini	De Montfort University, UK
Fabio D'Andreagiovanni	CNRS, Sorbonne University - UTC, France
Federico Liberatore	Cardiff University, UK
Federico Divina	Pablo de Olavide University, Spain
Fernando Lobo	University of Algarve, Portugal
Ferrante Neri	University of Nottingham, UK
Francesco Fontanella	Università di Cassino e del Lazio Meridionale, Italy
Francisco Chávez	Universidad de Extremadura, Spain
Francisco Luna	Universidad de Málaga, Spain
Francisco Chicano	University of Málaga, Spain

Contents

Applications of Evolutionary Computation

On Restricting Real-Valued Genotypes in Evolutionary Algorithms   3
*Jørgen Nordmoen, Tønnes F. Nygaard, Eivind Samuelsen,
and Kyrre Glette*

Towards Explainable Exploratory Landscape Analysis: Extreme Feature
Selection for Classifying BBOB Functions   17
Quentin Renau, Johann Dreo, Carola Doerr, and Benjamin Doerr

Co-optimising Robot Morphology and Controller in a Simulated
Open-Ended Environment   34
Emma Hjellbrekke Stensby, Kai Olav Ellefsen, and Kyrre Glette

Multi-objective Workforce Allocation in Construction Projects   50
Andrew Iskandar and Richard Allmendinger

Generating Duplex Routes for Robust Bus Transport Network by Improved
Multi-objective Evolutionary Algorithm Based on Decomposition   65
Sho Kajihara, Hiroyuki Sato, and Keiki Takadama

Combining Multi-objective Evolutionary Algorithms with Deep Generative
Models Towards Focused Molecular Design.   81
Tiago Sousa, João Correia, Vitor Pereira, and Miguel Rocha

A Multi-objective Evolutionary Algorithm Approach for Optimizing Part
Quality Aware Assembly Job Shop Scheduling Problems.   97
Michael H. Prince, Kristian DeHaan, and Daniel R. Tauritz

Evolutionary Grain-Mixing to Improve Profitability in Farming
Winter Wheat   113
Md Asaduzzaman Noor and John W. Sheppard

Automatic Modular Design of Behavior Trees for Robot Swarms
with Communication Capabilites   130
Jonas Kuckling, Vincent van Pelt, and Mauro Birattari

Salp Swarm Optimization Search Based Feature Selection for Enhanced
Phishing Websites Detection.   146
*Ruba Abu Khurma, Khair Eddin Sabri, Pedro A. Castillo,
and Ibrahim Aljarah*

Real Time Optimisation of Traffic Signals to Prioritise Public Transport 162
   Milan Wittpohl, Per-Arno Plötz, and Neil Urquhart

Adaptive Covariance Pattern Search 178
   Ferrante Neri

Evaluating the Success-History Based Adaptive Differential Evolution
in the Protein Structure Prediction Problem 194
   Pedro Henrique Narloch and Márcio Dorn

Beyond Body Shape and Brain: Evolving the Sensory Apparatus
of Voxel-Based Soft Robots.................................. 210
   Andrea Ferigo, Giovanni Iacca, and Eric Medvet

Desirable Objective Ranges in Preference-Based Evolutionary
Multiobjective Optimization.................................. 227
   Sandra González-Gallardo, Rubén Saborido, Ana B. Ruiz,
   and Mariano Luque

Improving Search Efficiency and Diversity of Solutions in Multiobjective
Binary Optimization by Using Metaheuristics Plus Integer
Linear Programming.. 242
   Miguel Ángel Domínguez-Ríos, Francisco Chicano, and Enrique Alba

Automated, Explainable Rule Extraction from MAP-Elites Archives 258
   Neil Urquhart, Silke Höhl, and Emma Hart

Applications of Deep Bioinspired Algorithms

EDM-DRL: Toward Stable Reinforcement Learning Through Ensembled
Directed Mutation... 275
   Michael H. Prince, Andrew J. McGehee, and Daniel R. Tauritz

Continuous Ant-Based Neural Topology Search 291
   AbdElRahman ElSaid, Joshua Karns, Zimeng Lyu,
   Alexander G. Ororbia, and Travis Desell

Soft Computing Applied to Games

Playing with Dynamic Systems - Battling Swarms in Virtual Reality....... 309
   Johannes Büttner, Christian Merz, and Sebastian von Mammen

EvoCraft: A New Challenge for Open-Endedness 325
   Djordje Grbic, Rasmus Berg Palm, Elias Najarro, Claire Glanois,
   and Sebastian Risi

A Profile-Based 'GrEvolutionary' Hearthstone Agent. 341
    Alejandro Romero García and Antonio M. Mora García

Machine Learning and AI in Digital Healthcare and Personalized Medicine

Modelling Asthma Patients' Responsiveness to Treatment Using Feature
Selection and Evolutionary Computation 359
    Alejandro Lopez-Rincon, Daphne S. Roozendaal, Hilde M. Spierenburg,
    Asta L. Holm, Renee Metcalf, Paula Perez-Pardo, Aletta D. Kraneveld,
    and Alberto Tonda

Bayesian Networks for Mood Prediction Using Unobtrusive Ecological
Momentary Assessments 373
    Margarita Rebolledo, A. E. Eiben, and Thomas Bartz-Beielstein

A Multi-objective Multi-type Facility Location Problem for the Delivery
of Personalised Medicine 388
    Andreea Avramescu, Richard Allmendinger, and Manuel López-Ibáñez

Evolutionary Computation in Image Analysis, Signal Processing and Pattern Recognition

RDE-OP: A Region-Based Differential Evolution Algorithm Incorporation
Opposition-Based Learning for Optimising the Learning Process
of Multi-layer Neural Networks 407
    Seyed Jalaleddin Mousavirad, Gerald Schaefer, Iakov Korovin,
    and Diego Oliva

Estimation of Grain-Level Residual Stresses in a Quenched Cylindrical
Sample of Aluminum Alloy AA5083 Using Genetic Programming 421
    Laura Millán, Gabriel Kronberger, J. Ignacio Hidalgo,
    Ricardo Fernández, Oscar Garnica, and Gaspar González-Doncel

EDA-Based Optimization of Blow-Off Valve Positions for Centrifugal
Compressor Systems 437
    Jacob Spindler, Rico Schulze, Kevin Schleifer, and Hendrik Richter

3D-2D Registration Using X-Ray Simulation and CMA-ES 453
    Tianci Wen, Radu P. Mihail, and Franck P. Vidal

Lateralized Approach for Robustness Against Attacks in Emotion
Categorization from Images 469
    Harisu Abdullahi Shehu, Abubakar Siddique, Will N. Browne,
    and Hedwig Eisenbarth

Evolutionary Machine Learning

Improved Crowding Distance in Multi-objective Optimization for Feature
Selection in Classification   489
    Peng Wang, Bing Xue, Jing Liang, and Mengjie Zhang

Deep Optimisation: Multi-scale Evolution by Inducing and Searching
in Deep Representations.   506
    Jamie Caldwell, Joshua Knowles, Christoph Thies, Filip Kubacki,
    and Richard Watson

Evolutionary Planning in Latent Space.   522
    Thor V. A. N. Olesen, Dennis T. T. Nguyen, Rasmus B. Palm,
    and Sebastian Risi

Utilizing the Untapped Potential of Indirect Encoding for Neural Networks
with Meta Learning.   537
    Adam Katona, Nuno Lourenço, Penousal Machado, Daniel W. Franks,
    and James Alfred Walker

Effective Universal Unrestricted Adversarial Attacks Using
a MOE Approach   552
    Alina Elena Baia, Gabriele Di Bari, and Valentina Poggioni

Improving Distributed Neuroevolution Using Island Extinction
and Repopulation   568
    Zimeng Lyu, Joshua Karns, AbdElRahman ElSaid, Mohamed Mkaouer,
    and Travis Desell

An Experimental Study of Weight Initialization and Lamarckian Inheritance
on Neuroevolution.   584
    Zimeng Lyu, AbdElRahman ElSaid, Joshua Karns, Mohamed Mkaouer,
    and Travis Desell

Towards Feature-Based Performance Regression Using Trajectory Data   601
    Anja Jankovic, Tome Eftimov, and Carola Doerr

Demonstrating the Evolution of GANs Through t-SNE   618
    Victor Costa, Nuno Lourenço, João Correia, and Penousal Machado

Optimising Diversity in Classifier Ensembles of Classification Trees   634
    Carina Ivaşcu, Richard M. Everson, and Jonathan E. Fieldsend

WILDA: Wide Learning of Diverse Architectures for Classification
of Large Datasets   649
    Rui P. Cardoso, Emma Hart, David Burth Kurka, and Jeremy Pitt

Evolving Character-Level DenseNet Architectures Using
Genetic Programming   665
    Trevor Londt, Xiaoying Gao, and Peter Andreae

Transfer Learning for Automated Test Case Prioritization Using XCSF   681
    Lukas Rosenbauer, David Pätzel, Anthony Stein, and Jörg Hähner

On the Effects of Absumption for XCS with Continuous-Valued Inputs.   697
    Alexander R. M. Wagner and Anthony Stein

A NEAT Visualisation of Neuroevolution Trajectories.   714
    Stefano Sarti and Gabriela Ochoa

Evaluating Models with Dynamic Sampling Holdout.   729
    Celio H. N. Larcher Jr and Helio J. C. Barbosa

Parallel and Distributed Systems

Event-Driven Multi-algorithm Optimization: Mixing Swarm
and Evolutionary Strategies   747
    Mario García-Valdez and Juan J. Merelo

TensorGP – Genetic Programming Engine in TensorFlow   763
    Francisco Baeta, João Correia, Tiago Martins, and Penousal Machado

**Applications of Nature-Inspired Computing for Sustainability
and Development**

A Novel Evolutionary Approach for IoT-Based Water
Contaminant Detection.   781
    Claudio De Stefano, Luigi Ferrigno, Francesco Fontanella,
    Luca Gerevini, and Mario Molinara

Evolutionary Algorithms for Roughness Coefficient Estimation in River
Flow Analyses   795
    Antonio Agresta, Marco Baioletti, Chiara Biscarini, Alfredo Milani,
    and Valentino Santucci

EA-Based ASV Trajectory Planner for Pollution Detection
in Lentic Waters   812
    Gonzalo Carazo-Barbero, Eva Besada-Portas, José M. Girón-Sierra,
    and José A. López-Orozco

Author Index   829

Applications of Evolutionary Computation

On Restricting Real-Valued Genotypes in Evolutionary Algorithms

Jørgen Nordmoen[1(✉)], Tønnes F. Nygaard[1], Eivind Samuelsen[1],
and Kyrre Glette[1,2]

[1] Department of Informatics, University of Oslo, Oslo, Norway
jorgehn@ifi.uio.no
[2] RITMO, University of Oslo, Oslo, Norway

Abstract. Real-valued genotypes together with the variation operators, mutation and crossover, constitute some of the fundamental building blocks of Evolutionary Algorithms. Real-valued genotypes are utilized in a broad range of contexts, from weights in Artificial Neural Networks to parameters in robot control systems. Shared between most uses of real-valued genomes is the need for limiting the range of individual parameters to allowable bounds. In this paper we will illustrate the challenge of limiting the parameters of real-valued genomes and analyse the most promising method to properly limit these values. We utilize both empirical as well as benchmark examples to demonstrate the utility of the proposed method and through a literature review show how the insight of this paper could impact other research within the field. The proposed method requires minimal intervention from Evolutionary Algorithm practitioners and behaves well under repeated application of variation operators, leading to better theoretical properties as well as significant differences in well-known benchmarks.

Keywords: Evolutionary algorithms · Bounce-back · Real-value · Restricting · Genome

1 Introduction

Evolutionary Algorithms (EAs) are a class of optimization algorithms that take inspiration from nature [5]. By taking inspiration from biological concepts such as *hereditary traits, genotype - phenotype distinction, mutation,* and *survival of the fittest,* EAs have been used to solve many challenging problems [3]. Many different encodings can be used to implement a genotype [18], among them is the real-valued genotype—a vector in $\mathbb{R}^n$ [8]. One often overlooked aspect of real-valued genotypes is the necessity to restrict the values to task specific bounds [21]. Restricting the values is fundamental since very few problems have infinite domains and because restrictions makes the search space feasible to explore [20]. Other considerations, such as the proclivity of generating invalid solutions [12], also make genotype restriction an important topic within the field.

© Springer Nature Switzerland AG 2021
P. A. Castillo and J. L. Jiménez Laredo (Eds.): EvoApplications 2021, LNCS 12694, pp. 3–16, 2021.
https://doi.org/10.1007/978-3-030-72699-7_1

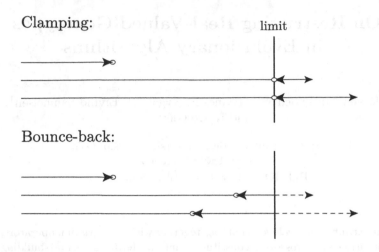

Fig. 1. By clamping the values in a real-valued genome the values will tend towards the limits of the bounds. The proposed *Bounce-back* function reflects values that exceed the limits back inside the bounds, resulting in a uniform distribution inside the bounds.

In this paper, we demonstrate the challenges of restricting real-valued genotypes and the effect these limitations have on the distribution of values in the genome. We start by introducing the theoretical problem and how restriction can affect the distribution. We then show that this problem is not simply a theoretical possibility; by optimizing benchmark functions we show that results diverge by solely varying the restriction function. We also look at the literature to gain an impression of how this problem could affect other EA practitioners.

The contribution of our paper is a better understanding of how value restriction affects real-valued genotypes in EAs. In addition we show that this is a topic deserving of more scrutiny by the wider EA community through a literature overview of both well known EA frameworks and a review of conference proceedings. By showing both the theoretical as well as the practical side of this challenge, we hope that other researchers become aware of the need for better restriction functions for real-valued genotypes and can utilize the results presented here in future research.

2   Background

When designing a restriction function[1] for real values, it is intuitive to create some form of a clamp method which ensures that a value does not exceed desired bounds[2]. Although restricting the values of genomes is nothing new [19], few contemporary articles take a conscious choice when it comes to restricting genomes.

---

[1] Other names include *repair operator* or simply *repairing the genome*.
[2] Like the 'Clamp' method introduced in .NET Core: https://docs.microsoft.com/en-us/dotnet/api/system.math.clamp?view=netcore-2.0 - accessed 18.05.2020.

In [1] the authors compare different restriction methods on the result of evolving with Differential Evolution (DE) and showed that the results are impacted by the choice of restriction function. The paper [21] extended on this work by understanding which type of inheritance model functioned with different restriction functions and as a by-product illustrated how these different restriction functions can alter the search landscape. A larger review of different components that contribute to the evolutionary process in DE were undertaken in [20], in this review article the authors showed that the choice of restriction function can have a significant impact on the results, a result backed by a very comprehensive comparison on different benchmark functions. However, even with these articles, that show significant impact on results solely on the basis of the restriction function, it is our impression that few EA practitioners heed these warnings and make appropriate accommodations in regards to restricting real-valued genotypes.

To gain insight into the practises of restricting real-valued genotypes within the wider EA community, we conducted a limited literature review. We first began with identifying some of the larger open-source frameworks for implementing EAs to see how value restriction is implemented.

DEAP [6] is one of the more popular[3] Python based frameworks for implementing EAs. Looking through the source code of this framework, two functions implement genome value restriction, 'cxSimulatedBinaryBounded' and 'mutPolynomialBounded'. Both of these functions utilize the *Clamped* function to limit real-valued genomes. SFERESv2 [14] is another well-known framework implemented in C++. It too implements value restriction for real-valued genotypes as can be seen in the genotype definition in 'evo_float.hpp'. The restriction function is implemented in 'put_in_range' and is equivalent to the *Clamped* function. Both of these frameworks cite the same source when it comes to their implementation of real-valued genomes and restriction, NSGA-II, a widely used Multi-Objective Evolutionary Algorithm [4]. Consulting the source-code[4] of this algorithm, it can be seen that this too implements restriction through the *Clamped* function.

To evaluate whether or not the observations about evolutionary frameworks are representative for the community, we conducted a small review of the main proceedings from GECCO 2019 and the 2019 and 2020 EvoAPPS proceedings. To evaluate if the results of a paper could be susceptible to the challenges, identified in this paper, we first identified experiments utilizing real-valued genotypes[5], we then tried to identify if the authors discuss their strategy for value restriction or if anything could be discerned from the source of the experiments. The summary of our results can be seen in Table 1.

From the overview, we can see that real-valued genotypes are used in a large fraction of papers in these previous conferences. However, of those that could be identified to use some form of restriction only four papers in GECCO'19, three papers in EvoAPPS 2019 and one paper from EvoAPPS 2020 were found. Of the

---

[3] Based on citations.

[4] Source code available here: http://www.iitk.ac.in/kangal/codes.shtml - accessed 06.04.2020.

[5] Note that papers utilizing Particle Swarm Optimization were excluded.

Table 1. Overview of real-valued genomes and limitation function in previous conference main proceedings.

	GECCO'19	EvoAPPS 2019	EvoAPPS 2020
Total number of papers	173	42	44
Uses real-valued genotype	37 (21%)	11 (26%)	10 (22%)
Comments on value restriction	4	3	1

four papers in GECCO'19 two used strategies that can mitigate the challenges identified in this paper [7,15], with one of those being our contribution, while the other two papers used the *Clamped* function. Of the three papers identified in EvoAPPS 2019 two would not be affected, one not using Gaussian mutation [10], another is our previous contribution using the methods proposed here [16], while the last one used the *Clamped* method. From EvoAPPS 2020, one paper was identified to not be susceptible [17] by only using uniform random mutation between allowable bounds instead of Gaussian mutation.

3   Methods

Several possible functions can be devised for limiting individual genes in real-valued genotypes [1]. The easiest and most straight forward limitation function is to clamp the value to the given bounds. The function is defined as follows:

$$clamp(v, min, max) = \begin{cases} min \text{ if } v < min \\ max \text{ if } v > max \\ v \text{ otherwise} \end{cases} \tag{1}$$

where v is the value to limit and $[min, max]$ are the bounds to apply for the value. This function will be used as the baseline to compare against the proposed *Bounce-back* method as it can be seen as the default when limiting real numbers[6] and is the only one implemented in the EA frameworks reviewed. We will refer to this function as *Clamped* for the remainder of this text.

The proposed limit function, which we will call *Bounce-back* restriction (also known as *reflection* [1] or the *internal reflection rule* [19]), is defined as follows:

$$bounce\text{-}back(v, min, max) = \begin{cases} min + (min - v) \text{ if } v < min \\ max - (v - max) \text{ if } v > max \\ v \text{ otherwise} \end{cases} \tag{2}$$

where, again, v is the value to limit and $[min, max]$ are the bounds to apply for the value. The effect of the *Bounce-back* function is to redirect out-of-bounds

---

[6] Method included in C++17: https://en.cppreference.com/w/cpp/algorithm/clamp - accessed 15.04.2020.

values by the amount that the value is outside of the limits. The effect is illustrated in Fig. 1. The function is independent of both mutation and crossover operators and can be applied in-between or after variation to ensure the genome is within given bounds. Compared to other restriction functions, such as *wrapping*, *re-initialization* and *re-sampling* [1], the *Bounce-back* function results in values in the current vicinity of the solution while also having minimum computational impact. The computational impact can be seen in contrast to *re-sampling* which depending on the variational operators can be computationally more costly to apply. The *wrapping* restriction function would share the same properties in regard to distribution as the *Bounce-back* function, however, the act of wrapping around can lead to discontinuous jumps in genotype space which could slow down the optimization process.

One thing to note about the *Bounce-back* function, as defined in Eq. 2, is that it is not guaranteed to result in values within the given bounds. This can happen when the value $v > max + (max - min)$ or $v < min - (max - min)$. This can either be solved by continued application of the restriction function until the value is within bounds or limiting the difference in Eq. 2 with the *Clamped* function. The later solution was utilized when limiting the distribution in Fig. 2.

To demonstrate the unwanted properties of the *Clamped* function and how these properties are not present in the *Bounce-back* function, we will first take an empirical approach to restricting real-valued genotypes with Gaussian perturbation.

4   Empirical Analysis

To understand why using the *Clamped* function with real-valued genomes can be problematic we will begin by looking at how the function affects the Gaussian distribution. In Fig. 2 the result of applying the two limiting functions to the Gaussian distribution is shown. The grey area shows the original Gaussian distribution while the colored areas represent the respective limitation functions as applied. This example is akin to mutating a value that is on or near the bound with Gaussian perturbation before restricting the value to be less than the bound. As can be seen from the figure, the *Bounce-back* function result in a distribution that is equivalent with the Gaussian distribution. Applying the clamping function results in a distribution that is heavily biased towards the 'limit'. This shows the problem with simply clamping a value to the desired bounds, the value will be skewed towards the bounds because all values above the limit is restricted to become exactly the limit, as illustrated in Fig. 1.

To visualize how the two limitation functions will affect a real-valued genome we created Algorithm 1 which simulate how repeated application of Gaussian perturbation and restriction creates different distributions of values dependent on the limit functions. Figure 3 shows the distribution of values after running Algorithm 1 with n equal to 50000, *cycles* set to 100 and $\sigma = 0.1$. In the figure it can be seen that the distribution of the *Clamped* function is heavily skewed

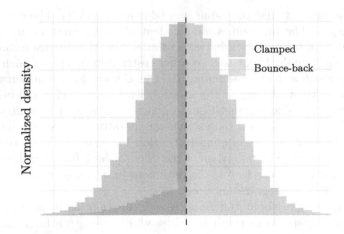

Fig. 2. The resulting distributions of applying the limit functions to a Gaussian distribution, in grey, with mean equal to the 'limit' value marked with a dashed line. This is analogous to mutating a value at 'limit' with Gaussian mutation and then restricting the value to be less than the 'limit'. The *Bounce-back* distribution follows the Gaussian distribution while the *Clamped* distribution is skewed towards the 'limit'.

Algorithm 1. Simulating mutation and value restriction of real-valued genotypes. *'restrict'* is either the *Clamped* or *Bounce-back* function.

1: **input** n ▷ Number of values in genome
2: **input** *cycles*   ▷ Number of times to simulate mutation
3: **input** σ ▷ Standard deviation of Gaussian perturbation
4: *genome* $\leftarrow \mathcal{U}(0,1)^n$ ▷ Create a vector of $\mathbb{R}^n$, uniformly distributed
5: **for** $n \leftarrow 0$ **to** cycles **do**
6:      **for** $i \leftarrow 0$ **to** n **do**
7:          $genome_i \leftarrow \mathcal{N}(genome_i, \sigma)$ ▷ Apply Gaussian mutation
8:          **if** $genome_i < 0.0$ **or** $genome_i > 1.0$ **then**
9:              $genome_i \leftarrow restrict(genome_i)$ ▷ Apply restriction, if outside bounds
10:         **end if**
11:     **end for**
12: **end for**
13: **return** *genome*

---

towards the bounds while the *Bounce-back* function has a much more uniform distribution.

To ensure that the distribution of the *Bounce-back* limitation is uniformly distributed, we performed a One-sample Kolmogorov-Smirnov test [13] comparing the two distributions in Fig. 3 with a uniform distribution. The results show that the *Clamped* distribution is statistically significant different from a uniform distribution, $p \ll 0.005$, while the *Bounce-back* distribution is not significantly different, $p > 0.1$.

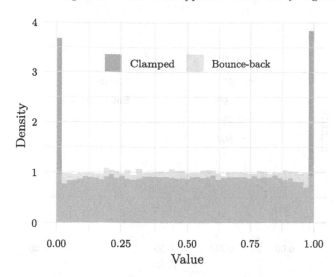

Fig. 3. The resulting distributions of generating 50000 uniform values between $[0, 1]$, perturbing each value with a Gaussian, with $\sigma = 0.1$, and then limiting the value to the range $[0, 1]$. The perturbation-limitation cycle was run 100 times.

To understand how the input parameters of Algorithm 1 impact the output, we varied the two parameters, *cycles* and σ. We will postulate that the number of reals, n, will not impact the underlying distribution and the effect of changing this parameter is to give a better or worse impression of the underlying distribution. The results of changing the input parameters are shown in Fig. 4 and Fig. 5, for number of *cycles* and varying the standard deviation respectively. Changing the number of *cycles*, shown in Fig. 4, does not have an effect on the resulting distribution which is as expected. Since the probability of the Gaussian mutation going out- or staying inside the bounds is symmetrical, the number of times mutation is applied should not affect the resulting distribution. For the standard deviation, shown in Fig. 5, the results are slightly different. Here we can see an effect of increasing σ, which can be explained as a larger part of the initial uniform distribution having a probability of going out of bounds. For the *Clamped* function this results in more values restricted at the bounds as the standard deviation of the mutation increases. On the other hand, we can see that the *Bounce-back* function is not affected by changes in mutation and continues to be uniformly distributed.

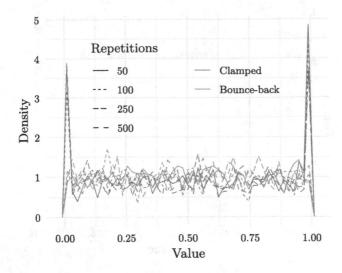

Fig. 4. A comparison of how the number of repetitions of the perturbation-limitation cycle affects the resulting distribution. The distribution in the figure were generated from 1000 uniform random values and perturbed by a Gaussian with $\sigma = 0.1$.

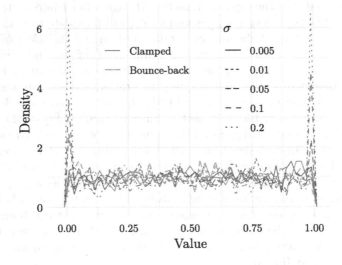

Fig. 5. A comparison of how the standard deviation, σ, of the Gaussian affects the resulting distribution. The distribution in the figure were generated from 1000 uniform random values and perturbed 100 times.

5   Benchmark Functions

To illustrate the potential impact of the limitation function, we applied the two limitation functions to a selection of benchmark problems [22]. All functions were optimized with a single objective $(\mu + \lambda)$ EA using tournament selection, Gaussian mutation, and no crossover operator. The benchmark problems are included to illustrate the challenge of limiting the genome to a specific range outside of theoretical considerations, as demonstrated in the previous section.

The following four functions are used as benchmark problems:

$$\frac{1}{4000} \sum_{i=1}^{N} x_i^2 - \prod_{i=1}^{N} \cos\left(\frac{x_i}{\sqrt{i}}\right) + 1 \tag{3}$$

$$10N + \sum_{i=1}^{N} x_i^2 - 10\cos(2\pi x_i) \tag{4}$$

$$\sum_{i=1}^{N-1} \left(x_i^2 + x_{i+1}^2\right)^{0.25} * \left[\sin^2(50 * (x_i^2 + x_{i+1}^2)^{0.10} + 1\right] \tag{5}$$

$$418.9828872724339 * N - \sum_{i=1}^{N} x_i \sin\left(\sqrt{|x_i|}\right) \tag{6}$$

where N is the size of the genome and x_i is the value of gene i in the genome. We will refer to Eq. (3) as Griewank, Eq. (4) as Rastrigin, Eq. (5) as Schaffer and Eq. (6) as Schwefel. The genotype was encoded as a vector of reals with a range of $[0, 1]$, before being transformed into the range required by each benchmark task. Genotypes are randomly initiated based on a uniform distribution. To generate data, we first optimized the parameters for each function, selecting the best mutation rate σ, tournament size and probability of applying Gaussian mutation to gene i - $P(M|i)$. The final parameters used to generate data are shown in Table 2.

Table 2. Algorithm parameters for each benchmark function. Parameters marked with '†' were taken from [2].

	Griewank	Rastrigin	Schaffer	Schwefel
Generations†	2000			
$(\mu + \lambda)$†	100 + 100			
Size - n†	30			
Repetitions	50			
Tournament	10			
$P(M|i)$	0.05			
Mutation - 'σ'	0.005	0.05	0.05	0.2
Range	±600	±5.12	±100	±500

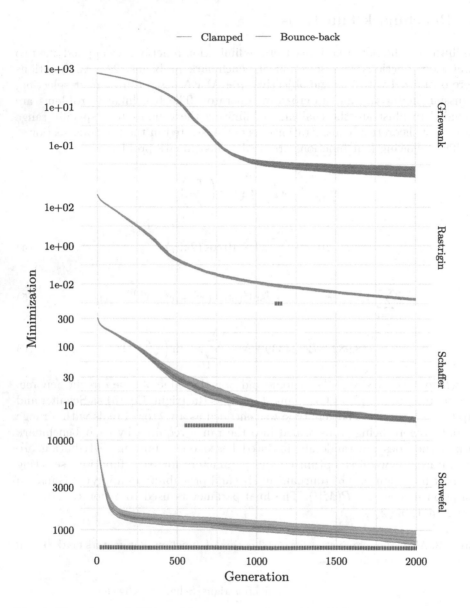

Fig. 6. The mean and 95% confidence interval for the population minimum aggregated over 50 runs of each benchmark function. Differences are marked at the bottom of each graph in black, the difference is statistically significant using a Wilcoxon Rank Sum test over an interval of 10 generations adjusted for the number of tests using Holm correction.

Figure 6 shows the mean and 95% confidence interval of the population minimum for each benchmark function. Statistical significant differences between the two limitation functions are marked in black at the bottom of each plot and is the result of applying the Wilcoxon Rank Sum test on intervals of 10 generations. To correct the p-value for the number of successive tests performed per row, Holm correction [9] was applied. The result show that only one benchmark function is sufficiently affected to lead to different results, however, both Rastrigin and Schaffer show diverging results at some points before converging. Based on the individual search parameters, shown in Table 2, we can also observe that larger σ seems to induce larger differences.

6   Discussion

From the empirical analysis performed, it can be seen that the *Clamped* function skews the distribution of values towards the bounds of the range, as shown in Fig. 2 and Fig. 3. This property can be challenging when the genotype is based on real values that are translated into task applicable ranges during the phenotype conversion. The proposed *Bounce-back* function did not exhibit these properties resulting in no alteration of the underlying value distribution. When experimenting with different facets of mutation, Fig. 4 and Fig. 5, it was shown that the magnitude of the standard deviation had the most effect on the resulting value distribution. This can be understood as expanding the range of the Gaussian distribution applied at each value. As more values have the potential of being mutated near the bounds, more values will be restricted and end up at the extremities of the limit with the *Clamped* function. This leads to the observation that using a larger standard deviation in the mutation operator require more careful thought to which restriction function to apply.

The results in Fig. 6 shows that the choice of restriction function can have an effect on benchmark problems, and is not just a theoretical problem. The effect of the restriction function followed closely the magnitude of the standard deviation used for mutation, detailed in Table 2, and illustrates the challenge that it can be difficult a priori to know the effect of the restriction function on any given task. One thing to point out about the benchmark tasks is that, except for *Schwefel*, the target value for all genes is $x_i = 0$, which is in the middle of the range, away from the bounds. As the target value moves closer to the bounds, we would expect the effect of the restriction function to grow, which could also explain the larger difference observed with the *Schwefel* benchmark function. With real-world tasks where the optimal value is difficult or impossible to confirm, it is even more challenging to a priori predict the effect and interactions of the restriction function, making it paramount that the restriction function has minimal impact on the optimization process.

The literature review conducted showed that two popular EA frameworks utilizes the *Clamped* function for restriction, and that while many papers published at GECCO'19 and EvoAPPS 2019 and 2020 utilized real-valued genotypes, few papers discussed their use of restriction functions. A deeper dive into the source of NSGA-II, a foundational algorithm within the Multi-Objective Evolutionary Algorithm literature, also revealed the use of the *Clamped* function which could affect re-implementations. Although limited, the literature review does underscore how the findings in this paper could impact the broader research field. As shown previously, the restriction function is not guaranteed to lead to significantly different results, however, it is difficult to predict the effect beforehand.

The results shown in this paper has focused on restricting real-valued genotypes in EAs. One interesting direction to take this work in the future is to apply the same *Bounce-back* technique on particles in Particle Swarm Optimization (PSO) [11]. Because of the additional velocity attribute present in PSO the restriction function should take this into account when limiting so that the particles do not keep moving towards the bounds. In the same vein, it would be interesting to know if PSO is sensitive to the challenges presented in this paper, or if the collective behavior can mitigate the boundary effect shown in this paper.

7   Conclusion

In this paper we have shown that one of the most used functions for restricting real-valued genotypes—clamping values to strictly lie between a minimum and maximum—can bias the genome to the extremities of the bounds under repeated application of the variation operators. We therefore suggest a different function which result in a uniform distribution of values within the genome. The *Bounce-back* function is shown both empirically and in practice to lead to a uniform distribution without bias towards the bounds and requires minimal intervention from existing Evolutionary Algorithm implementations, while having a minimal computational impact. We also conducted a limited literature review which illustrated that other practitioners in the field of Evolutionary Algorithms could be susceptible to the complications detailed in this paper. We hope that by illuminating this problem other researchers will become aware of the requirements for restricting real-valued genotypes, and can hopefully mitigate it with minimal effort in future work.

Acknowledgement. This work is partially supported by the Research Council of Norway through its Centres of Excellence scheme under grant agreements 240862 and 262762.

References

1. Arabas, J., Szczepankiewicz, A., Wroniak, T.: Experimental comparison of methods to handle boundary constraints in differential evolution. In: Schaefer, R., Cotta, C., Kołodziej, J., Rudolph, G. (eds.) PPSN 2010. LNCS, vol. 6239, pp. 411–420. Springer, Heidelberg (2010). https://doi.org/10.1007/978-3-642-15871-1_42
2. Brest, J., Greiner, S., Boskovic, B., Mernik, M., Zumer, V.: Self-adapting control parameters in differential evolution: a comparative study on numerical benchmark problems. IEEE Trans. Evol. Comput. **10**(6), 646–657 (2006)
3. Chiong, R., Weise, T., Michalewicz, Z.: Variants of Evolutionary Algorithms for Real-World Applications. Springer, Berlin Heidelberg (2012). https://doi.org/10.1007/978-3-642-23424-8

4. Deb, K., Agrawal, S., Pratap, A., Meyarivan, T.: A fast elitist non-dominated sorting genetic algorithm for multi-objective optimization: NSGA-II. In: Schoenauer, M., et al. (eds.) PPSN 2000. LNCS, vol. 1917, pp. 849–858. Springer, Heidelberg (2000). https://doi.org/10.1007/3-540-45356-3_83
5. Floreano, D., Mattiussi, C.: Bio-Inspired Artificial Intelligence: Theories, Methods, and Technologies. Intelligent Robotics and Autonomous Agents. MIT Press, Cambridge (2008). http://infoscience.epfl.ch/record/118584
6. Fortin, F.A., De Rainville, F.M., Gardner, M.A., Parizeau, M., Gagné, C.: DEAP: evolutionary algorithms made easy. J. Mach. Learn. Res. **13**, 2171–2175 (2012)
7. Glasmachers, T.: Challenges of convex quadratic bi-objective benchmark problems. In: Proceedings of the Genetic and Evolutionary Computation Conference. GECCO 2019. pp. 559–567. Association for Computing Machinery, New York (2019)
8. Herrera, F., Lozano, M., Verdegay, J.L.: Tackling real-coded genetic algorithms: operators and tools for behavioural analysis. Artif. Intell. Rev. **12**(4), 265–319 (1998)
9. Holm, S.: A simple sequentially rejective multiple test procedure. Scand. J. Stat. **6**(2), 65–70 (1979)
10. Iacca, G., Caraffini, F.: Compact optimization algorithms with re-sampled inheritance. In: Kaufmann, P., Castillo, P.A. (eds.) EvoApplications 2019. LNCS, vol. 11454, pp. 523–534. Springer, Cham (2019). https://doi.org/10.1007/978-3-030-16692-2_35
11. Kennedy, J., Eberhart, R.: Particle swarm optimization. In: Proceedings of ICNN 1995-International Conference on Neural Networks, Perth, WA, Australia, vol. 4, pp. 1942–1948. IEEE (1995)
12. Kononova, A.V., Caraffini, F., Bäck, T.: Differential evolution outside the box. arXiv preprint arXiv:2004.10489 (2020)
13. Massey Jr., F.J.: The Kolmogorov-Smirnov test for goodness of fit. J. Am. Stat. Assoc. **46**(253), 68–78 (1951)
14. Mouret, J.B., Doncieux, S.: SFERESv2: evolvin' in the multi-core world. In: Proceedings of Congress on Evolutionary Computation (CEC), Barcelona, Spain, pp. 4079–4086. IEEE (2010)
15. Nordmoen, J., Nygaard, T.F., Ellefsen, K.O., Glette, K.: Evolved embodied phase coordination enables robust quadruped robot locomotion. In: Proceedings of the Genetic and Evolutionary Computation Conference. GECCO 2019. pp. 133–141. Association for Computing Machinery, New York (2019)
16. Nygaard, T.F., Martin, C.P., Torresen, J., Glette, K.: Evolving robots on easy mode: towards a variable complexity controller for quadrupeds. In: Kaufmann, P., Castillo, P.A. (eds.) EvoApplications 2019. LNCS, vol. 11454, pp. 616–632. Springer, Cham (2019). https://doi.org/10.1007/978-3-030-16692-2_41
17. Pontes-Filho, S., et al.: EvoDynamic: a framework for the evolution of generally represented dynamical systems and its application to criticality. In: Castillo, P.A., Jiménez Laredo, J.L., Fernández de Vega, F. (eds.) EvoApplications 2020. LNCS, vol. 12104, pp. 133–148. Springer, Cham (2020). https://doi.org/10.1007/978-3-030-43722-0_9
18. Rothlauf, F.: Representations for Genetic and Evolutionary Algorithms, 2nd edn., pp. 9–32. Springer, Heidelberg (2006). https://doi.org/10.1007/3-540-32444-5
19. Schaefer, R.: Foundations of Global Genetic Optimization, vol. 74. Springer, Heidelberg (2007)

20. Tanabe, R., Ishibuchi, H.: Review and analysis of three components of the differential evolution mutation operator in MOEA/D-DE. Soft. Comput. **23**(23), 12843–12857 (2019). https://doi.org/10.1007/s00500-019-03842-6
21. Wessing, S.: Repair methods for box constraints revisited. In: Esparcia-Alcázar, A.I. (ed.) EvoApplications 2013. LNCS, vol. 7835, pp. 469–478. Springer, Heidelberg (2013). https://doi.org/10.1007/978-3-642-37192-9_47
22. Yao, X., Liu, Y., Lin, G.: Evolutionary programming made faster. IEEE Trans. Evol. Comput. **3**(2), 82–102 (1999)

Towards Explainable Exploratory Landscape Analysis: Extreme Feature Selection for Classifying BBOB Functions

Quentin Renau[1,2]([✉]), Johann Dreo[1], Carola Doerr[3], and Benjamin Doerr[2]

[1] Thales Research and Technology, Palaiseau, France
quentin.renau@thalesgroup.com
[2] École Polytechnique, Institut Polytechnique de Paris,
CNRS, LIX, Palaiseau, France
[3] Sorbonne Université, CNRS, LIP6, Paris, France

Abstract. Facilitated by the recent advances of Machine Learning (ML), the automated design of optimization heuristics is currently shaking up evolutionary computation (EC). Where the design of hand-picked guidelines for choosing a most suitable heuristic has long dominated research activities in the field, automatically trained heuristics are now seen to outperform human-derived choices even for well-researched optimization tasks. ML-based EC is therefore not any more a futuristic vision, but has become an integral part of our community.

A key criticism that ML-based heuristics are often faced with is their potential lack of explainability, which may hinder future developments. This applies in particular to supervised learning techniques which extrapolate algorithms' performance based on exploratory landscape analysis (ELA). In such applications, it is not uncommon to use dozens of problem features to build the models underlying the specific algorithm selection or configuration task. Our goal in this work is to analyze whether this many features are indeed needed. Using the classification of the BBOB test functions as testbed, we show that a surprisingly small number of features – often less than four – can suffice to achieve a 98% accuracy. Interestingly, the number of features required to meet this threshold is found to decrease with the problem dimension. We show that the classification accuracy transfers to settings in which several instances are involved in training and testing. In the leave-one-instance-out setting, however, classification accuracy drops significantly, and the transformation-invariance of the features becomes a decisive success factor.

Keywords: Exploratory landscape analysis · Feature selection · Black-box optimization

1 Introduction

Evolutionary algorithms and other iterative optimization heuristics (IOHs) are classically introduced as frameworks within which a user can gather some

© Springer Nature Switzerland AG 2021
P. A. Castillo and J. L. Jiménez Laredo (Eds.): EvoApplications 2021, LNCS 12694, pp. 17–33, 2021.
https://doi.org/10.1007/978-3-030-72699-7_2

modules to instantiate an algorithm. For instance, the *design* of an evolutionary algorithm requires to choose the population size, the variation and selection operators in use, the encoding structure, fitness function penalization weights, etc. This highly flexible design of IOHs allows for efficient abstractions but comes at the burden of having to solve an additional (meta-)optimization problem. *Automated design* of heuristics aims at solving this problem by providing data-driven recommendations which IOH shall be employed for a given optimization problem and how it shall be configured. Automated IOH design has proven its promise in numerous applications, see [3,7,9,12,20] for examples and further references.

A common critique of machine-trained automated algorithm design is its potential lack of explainability. That is, the general fear is that by relying on automated design approaches, we may be loosing intuition for *why* certain recommendation are made – a key driver for the development of new optimization approaches. This fear is not without any reason: the vast majority of automated algorithm design studies fall short in this explainability aspect.

Our Contribution. Our work aims at providing paths to narrowing this important gap, by studying which information the trained models actually need to achieve convincing performance. As testbed we chose the automated classification of optimization problems through exploratory landscape analysis (ELA). We show that very small feature sets can suffice to reliably discriminate between various optimization problems and that these sets are robust with respect to the classifiers and function instances.

Apart from the explainability aspect, our findings have important consequences also for the efficiency of automated algorithm design: smaller feature sets are faster to compute and they can drastically reduce the time spent in the training phase. Another advantage of feature selection is that the classification or regression accuracy can *increase*.

Background and Motivation. ELA was introduced in [17] with the objective to gain insights about the properties of an unknown optimization problem. Instead of relying on expert knowledge, the keystone of ELA are computer-generated *features* that are based on sampling the decision space. With the purpose of enhancing the effectiveness of this approach, several additional features have been introduced since. A good selection of these features are automatically computed by the R package *flacco* [14], see Sect. 2 for more details.

We chose classification as task, because it offers a very clean setting in which the results are easily interpretable. Classification has a straightforward performance measure, the *classification accuracy*, i.e., the fraction of items that are classified correctly. Additionally, the classification accuracy is a good way of estimating the expressiveness of ELA feature sets, i.e., their ability to discriminate between different problems [26]. A proper classification furthermore plays an important role also in many other ML tasks, including the selection and configuration of algorithms, so that a good classification accuracy can be expected to provide good results also for these tasks.

Related Work. Given the mentioned speed-up and the better performance that one can expect from smaller feature sets, feature selection is not new, but rather standard in automated algorithm design. However, most related works still use a relatively large number of features, hindering explainability of the trained models. Among the ELA-based applications in EC, the following ones have used the smallest feature portfolios.

Muñoz and Smith-Miles [19] compute the co-linearity between landscape features with the idea that if two features are strongly co-linear, they carry the same type of information about the landscape. Applying this procedure, nine features were kept for further analysis: the adjusted coefficient of determination of a linear regression model including interactions [17], the adjusted coefficient of determination of a quadratic regression model [17], the ratio between the minimum and maximum absolute values of the quadratic term coefficients in the quadratic model, the significance of D-th and first order [29], the skewness, kurtosis and entropy of the fitness function distribution [17], and the maximum information content [22].

Another method to perform feature selection is the use of search algorithms. In their work, Kerschke and Trautmann [12] compare four different algorithms, a greedy forward-backward selection, a greedy backward-forward selection, a $(10 + 5)$-GA and a $(10 + 50)$-GA. The smallest feature sets considered in their algorithm selection setting have a size of eight features: three features from the y-distribution feature set [17] (skewness, kurtosis, and number of peaks), one level set feature [17] (the ratio of mean misclassification errors when using a linear (LDA) and mixed discriminant analysis (MDA)), two information content features [22] (the maximum information content and the settling sensitivity), one cell mapping feature [13] (the standard deviation of the distances between each cell's center and worst observation), and one of the basic features (the best fitness value within the sample). This result is still considerably larger than the sets we will identify as promising in our work.

Saini et al. [28] and Lacroix and McCall [15] also use reduced feature sets, but do not expand on how these have been derived.

Availability of Our Data. All our project data is available at [27].

2   Problem Classification via Majority Judgment

Our primary objective is to analyze the number of features that are needed to correctly classify the 24 BBOB functions from the COCO benchmark environment and their robustness across several dimensions and sample sizes. We describe in this section the benchmark set, the experimental procedure, and the classification scheme.

The 24 BBOB Benchmark Problems. A standard benchmark environment for numerical black-box optimization is the COCO (**CO**mparing **C**ontinuous

Optimizers) platform [6]. From this environment, we consider the BBOB suite, a set of 24 noiseless problems. For each BBOB problem, several instances are available, which are obtained from a "base" function via translation, rotation and/or scaling transformations [6]. Each problem instances is a real-valued function $f : [-5, 5]^d \to \mathbb{R}$. Problems scale for arbitrary dimensions d. In our experiments, we consider six different dimensions, $d \in \{5, 10, 15, 20, 25, 30\}$, and we focus on the first five instances of each problem (first instance in Sect. 3. In abuse of notation, we shall often identify the functions by their ID $1, \ldots, 24$.

Computation of Feature Values via Flacco. For the feature value approximation, we sample for each of the 24 functions f a number n of points $x^{(1)}, \ldots, x^{(n)} \in [-5, 5]^d$, and we evaluate their function values $f(x^{(1)}), \ldots, f(x^{(n)})$. The set of pairs $\{(x^{(i)}, f(x^{(i)})) \mid i = 1, ..., n\}$ is then fed to the *flacco* package [14], which returns a vector of features. The *flacco* package covers a total number of 343 features [9], which are grouped into 17 feature sets. However, some of these features are often omitted in practice because they require adaptive sampling [2,12,18,24], while other features have previously been dismissed as non-informative for the BBOB functions [13,26]. After removing these sets from our test bed, we are left with six feature sets: *dispersion* (disp [16]), *information content* (ic [22]), *nearest better clustering* (nbc [10]), *meta model* (ela_meta [17]), *y-distribution* (ela_distr [17]), and *principal component analysis* (pca [14]). But even if this selection reduces the number of features to 46, a full enumeration of all subsets for all sizes $c \leq 46$ would still be computationally infeasible (since we need to train and test a classification model for each such set). We therefore need to reduce the set of eligible features further. To this end, we build on the work presented in [26], in which we studied the *expressiveness* of these 46 features. Based on this work we select four features. We add to this selection another six features, one per each of the feature set mentioned above (to ensure a broad diversity of features) and again giving preference to the most expressive ones and to features invariant to BBOB transformations [30]. This leaves us with the following ten features. We indicate in this list by ✓ and - whether or not a feature is considered invariant under transformation according to [30] (first entry) and according to our data (second entry), respectively. Note here that the setting used in [30] is slightly different from the instances used in BBOB, mostly due to different ways to handle boundary constraints. The assessment can therefore differ.

1. **disp.ratio_mean_02** [✓,✓] (disp) computes the ratio of the pairwise distances of the points having the best 2% fitness values with the pairwise distances of all points in the design.
2. **ela_distr.skewness** [✓,✓] (skew) computes the skewness coefficient of the distribution of the fitness values. This coefficient is a measure of the asymmetry of a distribution around its mean.
3. **ela_meta.lin_simple.adj_r2** [✓,✓] (lr2), which computes the adjusted correlation coefficient R^2 of a linear model fitted to the data.

4. **ela_meta.lin_simple.intercept** [$\checkmark$,-] (int), the intercept coefficient of the linear model.
5. **ela_meta.lin_simple.coef.max** [-,-] (max), the largest coefficient of the linear model that is not the intercept coefficient.
6. **ela_meta.quad_simple.adj_r2** [$\checkmark$,$\checkmark$] (qr2), the adjusted correlation coefficient R^2 of a quadratic model fitted to the data.
7. **ic.eps.ratio** [-,$\checkmark$] ($\varepsilon_{\text{ratio}}$), the half partial information sensitivity.
8. **ic.eps.s** [-,$\checkmark$] (ε_s), the settling sensitivity.
9. **nbc.nb_fitness.cor** [$\checkmark$,$\checkmark$] (nbc), the correlation between the fitness values of the search points and their indegree in the nearest-better point graph.
10. **pca.expl_var_PC1.cov_init** [$\checkmark$,$\checkmark$] (pca), which measures the importance of the first principal component of a Principal Component Analysis (PCA) over the sample points in the whole search space.

Normalization of Feature Values. The value of each feature is normalized between 0 and 1 where 0 (resp. 1) correspond to the smallest (resp. largest) value encountered in the approximated feature values. This normalization is performed independently for each dimension, each sample size, and each classifier used in this paper.

Sampling Strategy. Based on an extension of the preliminary experiments reported in [25] we use a quasi-random distribution to sample the points $x^{(1)}, \ldots, x^{(n)}$ from which the feature values are computed. More precisely, we use Sobol' sequences [32], which we obtain from the Python package *sobol_seq* (version 0.1.2), with randomly chosen initial seeds.

We sample a total number of 100 independent Sobol' designs, which leaves us with 100 feature value vectors per each function. Figure 1 provides an impression of the distribution of these feature values. Plotted are here approximated values for the lr2 feature. The comparison shows that the dispersion slightly decreases with the dimension, which is quite surprising in light of the lower density of the points in higher dimensions. We also see that the median values are not stable across dimensions. Some functions (F5 of course, which is correctly identified as a linear function, but also F16, F19, and F20, for example) show a high concentration of feature value approximations, whereas other functions show much larger dispersion within one dimension (e.g., F12, F15, F17, F18) or between different dimensions (F2, F11, F24).

Sample Size. To study the effect of the sample size on the number of features needed to correctly classify the 24 BBOB functions, we conduct experiments for seven different values of n, namely $n \in \{30d, 50d, 100d, 250d, 650d, 800d, 1000d\}$. We note here that a linear scaling of the sample size is the by far most common choice, see, for example, [3,11,12].

Feature Selection. We apply a *wrapper method*, i.e., we actually train a classifier for every considered subset of features. For a given sample size and a given dimension, we train and test all $\binom{10}{c}$ possible subsets of size c starting with $c = 1$. If none of these size-c subsets achieves our target accuracy, we move on to the size $c + 1$ subsets. As soon as a sufficiently qualified subset has been identified, we continue to evaluate all size-c subsets, but stop the selection process thereafter. This full enumeration of all possible feature combinations for a given size c allows us to investigate the *robustness* of the feature selection. Ideally, we would like to see that the feature sets achieving our 98% accuracy threshold (this will be introduced below) are stable across the different sample sizes. Robustness with respect to the dimension is much less of a concern to us, since the problem dimension is typically known and can be used for the choosing the feature ensemble that shall be applied to characterize the problem.

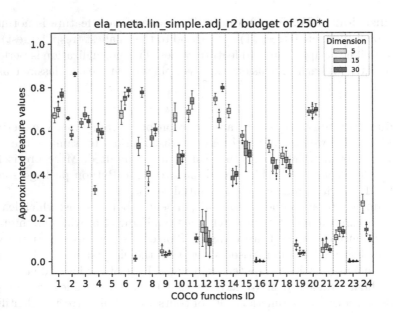

Fig. 1. Distribution of the feature values for the `lr2` feature for different dimensions. Each feature value is computed from $250 \times d$ samples and each boxplot represents results of 100 independent feature computations.

Validation Procedure and Target Classification Accuracy. In our experiments, we use 80 randomly chosen feature vectors (per function) to train a classification model, and we use the remaining $24 \times 20 = 480$ feature vectors for testing. For each of these 480 test cases we store the true function ID (i.e., the ID of the function that the feature value originates from) and we store the ID of the function that the classifier matches the feature vector to. From this data we compute the *overall classification accuracy*.

We repeat this procedure of splitting the set of all feature vectors into 80 training and 20 test instances 20 times; i.e., we repeat 20 times a **random sub-sampling validation**. We require that the overall classification accuracy for each of the 20 validations is **at least 98%**. That is, a feature set is eligible if, in each of the 20 random sub-sampling validation runs, it misclassifies at most 10 out of the 480 tested feature vectors. Feature combinations achieving a smaller classification accuracy in one of the validation runs are immediately discarded.

Classification Model. In the main part of this work, we use a Majority Judgment classifier [1]. A cross-validation with decision trees and KNN classifiers will be presented in Sect. 4.

The Majority Judgment classifier works as follows. Let $\Phi = \{\varphi_1, \ldots, \varphi_k\}$ be the set of features for which we want to know whether it achieves our 98% target precision requirement. We consider one of the independent subsampling validation runs. That is, for each function we randomly select 80 out of the 100 feature vectors. Denote by $\varphi_{i,j,r}$ the r-th estimated value for feature φ_i for the j-th BBOB function, the set $\{(\varphi_{i,j,r}, j) \mid i = 1, \ldots, k, j = 1, \ldots, 24, r = 1, \ldots, 80\}$ describes the full set of training data. From this data we compute for each of the 24 functions $j = 1, \ldots, 24$ and for each feature $\varphi_i \in \Phi$ the median value

$$M(i,j) := \mathbb{M}\left(\{\varphi_{i,j,r} \mid r = 1, \ldots, 80\}\right).$$

This gives us a set of $24k$ values $M(i,j)$ and concludes the *training step*.

Table 1. Example for the Majority Judgment classification scheme with three features. The values in the table are the distances of the measured feature value ζ_i to the median feature values $M(i,j)$ of the training set. The median values are reported in the last line. The ID of the function minimizing this median distance D_j is the output of the Majority Judgment classifier.

	Function ID (index j)			
	1	2	...	24
Feature φ_1	0	0.7	...	0.7
Feature φ_2	0.2	0.6	...	0.5
Feature φ_3	0.6	0.8	...	0.2
Median distance D_j	0.2	0.7	...	0.5

In the *testing step* we apply an *approval voting mechanism* [4] to each of the 480 test instances. Approval voting mechanisms are single-winner systems where the winner is the most-approved candidate among the voters. From this class of approval voting mechanism we choose *Majority Judgment* [1]—a voting techniques which ensures that the winner between three or more candidates has received an absolute majority of the scores given by the voters.

To apply Majority Judgment to our classification task, we do the following. We recall that the task of the classifier is to output, for a given feature vector $\zeta = (\zeta_i)_{i=1}^{k}$, the ID of the function that it believes this feature vector to belong to. To this end, it first computes for each of the k features i and for all 24 functions j the absolute distances $d_{i,j} := |\zeta_i - M(i,j)|$. Table 1 presents an example for what the distances may look like. We then compute for each function the median of these distances, by setting $D_j(\zeta) := \mathbb{M}(\{d_{i,j} \mid i = 1, \ldots, k\})$. The cells with these median values are highlighted with a blue background in Table 1, and the values $D_j(\zeta)$ are reported in the last line. The classifier outputs as predicted function ID the value j for which the distance $D_j(\zeta)$ is minimized. This cell is highlighted in yellow background color.

Computation Time. To give an impression of the computational resources required for our experiments, we report that the computation of the 100 5-dimensional feature vectors requires around 6 CPU hours, whereas the computation of the 25-dimensional feature vectors takes about 1221 CPU hours. Training and testing the classifier takes between 1 s and 3 h, depending on the setting. In total, we have invested around 432 CPU days for computing the data presented in this work.

Table 2. Feature combination size achieving 98% classification accuracy in all 20 runs.

Dimension	Sample size						
	30d	50d	100d	250d	650d	800d	1000d
5	–	–	–	4	4	–	2
10	–	–	–	4	1	2	1
15	–	–	6	4	2	2	2
20	–	–	6	2	1	1	2
25	1	1	1	1	1	1	1
30	–	6	2	1	1	2	2

3   Feature Sets Achieving 98% Classification Accuracy

The portfolios of features for which we obtained the desired 98% classification accuracy for each of the 20 random sub-sampling validation runs are presented in Table 3. For convenience, their sizes are summarized in Table 2.

Our first, and most important, finding is that we can actually classify the BBOB functions with very few features. However, we also see that the existence of such portfolios requires a sufficient sample size. For $d \in \{5, 10, 15, 20\}$, none of the 2^{10} possible portfolios based on size-30d and size-50d feature approximations could achieve the 98% accuracy threshold.

Table 3. Feature combinations achieving the 98% classification accuracy threshold in all 20 runs. Features with the same symbol (X, O, H, V) belong to the same combination. Results are grouped by dimension d and by the sample size n used to approximate the feature values. Blank rows are for (d,n) settings for which all 2^{10} feature sets failed. M = missing data (due to coronavirus measures in France, we have lost access to cluster and data.)

d	n	int	lr2	qr2	max	ε_s	$\varepsilon_{\text{ratio}}$	disp	skew	pca	nbc
5	30d										
	50d										
	100d										
	250d		X	X			X				X
	650d		X	X			X				X
	800d										
	1000d		X				X				
10	30d										
	50d										
	100d										
	250d		XO	XO			XO			O	X
	650d	X									
	800d			X			X				
	1000d	X									
15	30d										
	50d										
	100d	X	X		X		X	X			X
	250d		X		X		X			X	
	650d		X		H	O	XH			O	
	800d						X				X
	1000d						XO	X		O	
20	30d										
	50d										
	100d	X	X		X		X	X			X
	250d			X			X				
	650d	X									
	800d						X				
	1000d			X			XO			O	
25	30d	X									
	50d	X									
	100d	X									
	250d	X									
	650d	X					O				
	800d	X									
	1000d	X							M		
30	30d										
	50d	X	X		X		X	X		X	
	100d		X				XO			O	
	250d	X									
	650d	X									
	800d		O	X			XO	M			
	1000d		O	X	H		XOHV	M			V

We also see that, as expected, the size of the minimal portfolio achieving the target precision decreases with increasing sampling size. A few exceptions to this rule exist:

- No combination in $d = 5$ with $n = 800$ samples achieved the target precision.
- In $d = 10$ we see that a single feature, the intercept feature `int`, suffices to classify with 98% accuracy when the sampling size is $650d$ and $1000d$. For $800d$, however, this feature does not achieve the threshold. A detailed analysis of the classification accuracy achieved with this feature will be given in Fig. 2.
- In $d = 15$, the $\varepsilon_{\text{ratio}}$ information content feature classifies properly when the sample size equals $n = 800d$, but for $n = 1000d$, one additional feature is needed to pass the 98% accuracy threshold.
- In $d = 20$ a single feature suffices for $n = 650d$ and $n = 800d$, but for $n = 1,000d$ an additional feature is needed to achieve the target accuracy.

Overall, we see that for ten settings a single feature suffices for proper classification. An additional seven cases can be solved by a combination of two features. It seems counter-intuitive that in almost all cases the size of the smallest admissible portfolio decreases with increasing dimension. However, as already discussed in the context of Fig. 1, the dispersion of some feature values *decreases* with increasing dimension – an effect that is interesting in its own right. Without going into much detail here, we note that this effect is further intensified when using a properly scaled sampling size that maintains the same sampling density across dimensions.

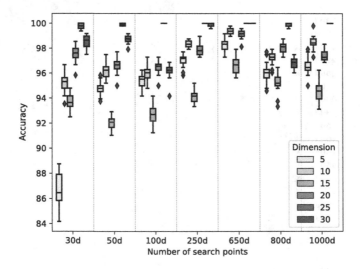

Fig. 2. Distributions of intercept feature accuracy by dimension and sample size

Robustness of the Feature Combinations with Respect to Dimension and Sample Size. Looking at the robustness of the selected combinations over the dimensions and the sample sizes, we observe the following.

One feature, the intercept feature int, is involved in 15 out of the 28 (d, n) pairs for which a successful feature portfolio could be found. This feature, in contrast, is rarely present in other combinations of size $|c| > 1$. To shed more light on its expressive power, we present in Fig. 2 the distributions of the classification accuracy for the various (d, n) combinations. Aggregated over all dimensions and all sample sizes, the median accuracy of the int feature is 96%. Even if the feature does not always reach our threshold of 98%, it is worth noting that its performances is almost always above 90%. Therefore, this feature is very expressive, and this across all tested dimension and sample sizes. Another interesting observation from Fig. 2 is that the classification accuracy is not monotonic in the dimension. In all but one case ($n = 30d$), the $d = 15$ results are worse than those for the other dimensions. As already seen in Table 3, for $n = 250 \times d$ we always have very good classification accuracy.

The most frequent feature is $\varepsilon_{\text{ratio}}$, which is present in almost all combinations of size $|c| \geq 2$. We count 21 successful combinations of size $|c| \geq 2$ and $\varepsilon_{\text{ratio}}$ appears in 20 of these combinations regardless of the dimension and the sample size. In total, it appears in successful portfolios for 17 out of the 28 (d, n) combinations for which a successful subset had been found. The $\varepsilon_{\text{ratio}}$ feature is very useful for our classification task.

The skewness feature *skew*, in contrast, does not appear in any of the portfolios of the smallest size.

Classification Accuracy When Using All Flacco Features. We compare the results presented above with the classification accuracy achieved by the Majority Judgment voting scheme using the whole set of 46 features described in Sect. 2. We perform the same sub-sampling validation as above. Interestingly, none of tests performed on the pairs (d,n) with $n \in \{30d, 50d, 100d, 250d, 650d, 1000d\}$ and $d \in \{5, 10, 15, 20, 25, 30\}$ met our required target precision of 98% for each of the 20 runs. We can thus conclude that, in addition to the gain in explainability, the selection of features for supervised-ELA approaches provide better performances, and – as we shall discuss below – also come at a much smaller computational cost.

4 Robustness with Respect to the Classifier

Having identified feature portfolios that reliably classify the BBOB functions with at least 98% accuracy when using Majority Judgment (MJ), we now investigate how robust this accuracy is with respect to the choice of the classifier. To this end, we apply the same classification routine as above, but now using *decision trees* (DT) and *K Nearest Neighbors (KNN)* as for classification. We use off-the-shelf implementations from the *scikit learn* Python package [23, we use version 0.21.3]. Our goal being in investigating robustness, we do not perform any hyper-parameter tuning for these two classifiers. For the KNN classifier we use $K = 5$. For all classifications with a reduced portfolio of features, if multiple combinations are available, only the one marked with X in Table 3 will be used.

Both KNN and decision trees perform as well as our classifier when trained and tested with the small portfolios from Table 3, i.e., they both reach at least 98% classification accuracy in every run except for the decision trees trained with only one feature, for which the accuracy drops to around 62% in every run. Figure 3 summarizes the classification accuracy of the three classifiers for the case that features are based on $n = 250d$ samples, for the portfolios described in Table 3. Performance is indeed very robust with respect to the classification mechanism.

Running Time. While training and testing were made in around 4 s for the DT and for the MJ voting scheme, the KNN classifier needed around 12 s to complete the 20 sub-sampling validation runs.

Gain Over Full Feature Set. We now study how much we gain in terms of computation time when we compute, train, and test the three classifiers (MJ, DT, and KNN) on the selected feature sets only.

To quantify this gain, we train all three classifiers with the full set of 46 features mentioned in Sect. 2. We first observe that the decision tree classifier has the best performances among the three classifiers in terms of accuracy. It achieves at least 99% classification accuracy. For KNN, in contrast, performances drops below our 98% threshold precision on several runs, resulting in a median classification accuracy (over all tests) of around 97%. The results for KNN align,

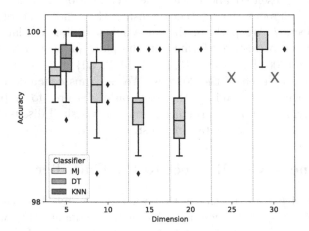

Fig. 3. Classification accuracy for the feature portfolios from Table 3 for budget 250d. Results are sorted by dimension and classifier and are for 20 random sub-sampling validation runs. Training and testing is done on the first instance of each function only. The X corresponds to settings that did not achieve the 98% threshold.

as already briefly touched upon in Sect. 3, with those obtained using MJ, where none of the tests produced 20 runs in which the threshold was reached.

In terms of computation time, we observe significant differences between the small feature portfolios and the full *flacco* set. As already commented in Sect. 2, the computation of the feature values can be very time-consuming. Reducing the number of features therefore reduces the running time of the feature extraction. However, the savings are even bigger when comparing the cost of training (and testing) the classifiers. For decision trees, the execution of the whole classification pipeline takes 3000 times longer than with the small portfolios – around 3 CPU hours instead of a few seconds. For KNN, the total cost is comparable, also around 3 CPU hours for training and testing the classifiers for the 20 sub-sampling validation runs. For the MJ classifier, the overall running time is only around 35 CPU minutes – which is still way above the time needed for the small portfolios.

Thus, overall, the reduced portfolios resulted not only in much faster computation times, but achieved also better classification accuracy.

5 Robustness with Respect to the Problem Instances

The discussion above focused on classifying the first instance of the BBOB functions, and we now investigate how robust the selection is with respect to different instances of the same problems. Concretely, we investigate classification accuracy when performing the same random sub-sampling validation routine as above to the set of features computed for the first five instances of the BBOB functions. In this experiment, we keep 80% of feature values for each instance for training

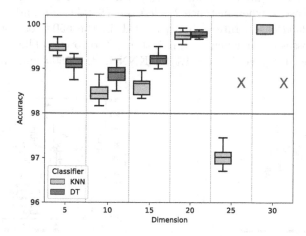

Fig. 4. Classification accuracy of DT and KNN classifiers when applied to the first five instances of the 24 BBOB functions. Feature values are computed from 250d samples, for the portfolios marked by an X in Table 3. Cases with poor performance are marked by a red X. (Color figure online)

the classifier, and we test on the remaining ones. In a second step we then test transferability, by performing a *leave-one-instance-out (LOIO) cross-validation*. In this setting, the classifiers are trained on four instances of each function and tested on the remaining one. We use the portfolios marked by an X in Table 3, and compare to classification accuracy when using all ten features. In the following, MJ voting is excluded as, by design, it is not suited to work with multiple distributions coming from different instances. Hence, only DT and KNN classifiers will be used in this section.

Figure 4 aggregates the results obtained for the first classification task, where we take feature values from each or the first five instances. As in Fig. 3, DT performs badly in $d = 25$ and $d = 30$, where classification is only based on the intercept feature. For these cases, the median accuracy is 45% and 62%, respectively. Since the intercept feature is not invariant to fitness function transformations, the worsened performance is no surprise. In contrast, the median classification accuracy is above 98% for all portfolios with at least two features. We also note that KNN in dimension $d = 25$ does not reach our 98% threshold, but still achieves good performances with an average 97% accuracy.

Figure 5 presents the classification accuracy achieved by KNN and DT in the LOIO setting. Figure 5a is for features lr2, qr2, ε_{ratio}, and nbc computed from $650d$ samples in $d = 5$ and the Fig. 5b is for the two features qr2 and ε_{ratio} computed from $250d$ samples in $d = 20$. For comparison, we also plot the classification accuracy achieved when using all ten features listed in Sect. 2. For most settings, the accuracy obtained with the set of ten features is better than that achieved for the smaller portfolios. For the $650d$ setting, this is the case for all instances. For the $250d$ setting, DT performs better with the smaller portfolio when instance 1 or instance 3 is left out. The performance loss when using the reduced feature set is particularly drastic for KNN when instance 1 is left out (both cases), when instance 2 is left out ($650d$ case), and when instance 4 is left out ($250d$ case). Interestingly, for DT in the $650d$ setting, the largest performance losses occur when leaving instance 2 or 5 out. The average loss in classification accuracy is 5% and 4% for KNN in the $650d$ and the $250d$ case,

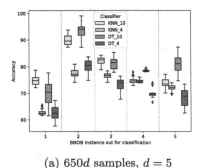

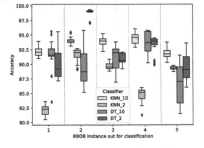

| (a) 650d samples, $d = 5$ | (b) 250d samples, $d = 20$ |

Fig. 5. Classification accuracy of KNN and DT in the leave-one-instance-out setting. The subscripts _2, _4, and _10 refer to the size of the feature portfolio.

respectively. For DT, the average loss in the $650d$ case is 10% and the average gain in the $250d$ case is 2%.

We conclude that the feature selection is robust when studying different instances, except for those portfolios which consist only of a single feature. For the (arguably more interesting) LOIO setting, however, classification accuracy drops, but non-homogeneously for the different instances. We recommend using the larger feature portfolio in this case.

6   Conclusions

Our ambition to build small feature sets is driven by the desire to obtain models that are (at least to some degree) human-interpretable. While our study certainly has several limitations, as only one test bed is considered, it nevertheless shows that the number of features needed to successfully classify the BBOB functions is surprisingly low. Our main direction for future work is an application of the small feature sets to automated algorithm design tasks. [8] shows promising performance of the selected feature portfolio presented in Sect. 2 for automated performance regression and per-instance algorithm selection, results that we wish to detail further based on the results presented in Sect. 3. Our next important goal will then be to uncover *how* the performance of a given solver depends on the selected features, by taking a closer look at the trained regression models. With small feature sets, there is reasonable hope that we can identify meaningful correlations.

We are targeting, in the mid-term perspective, classifiers and automated algorithm design techniques that work well on highly constrained problems and which can cope with discontinuities. Extending the results of this work to such problems forms another important next step.

Other interesting directions for future work include the investigation of new features recently proposed in the literature, (such as, for example, the SOO-based features [5]). We also plan on a closer inspection of the classification results presented above, particularly with respect to the mis-classifications. Functions that are wrongly classified more often than others (a preliminary investigation showed that these mis-classification rates depend on the dimension. In dimensions $d = 10$, for example, function 17 is confused with function 21 in 30% of the tests even when a sample size of $n = 10,000$ is used.) Such data can be used, in particular, for training set selection, but also for the *generation* of new problem instances for which the algorithms show some behavior not observable on other instances of the same collection [21,31].

Acknowledgments. We thank Cédric Buron, Claire Laudy, and Bruno Marcon for providing the implementation of the Majority Judgment classifier.

References

1. Balinski, M., Laraki, R.: Judge: don't vote!. Oper. Res. **62**(3), 483–511 (2014)

2. Belkhir, N., Dréo, J., Savéant, P., Schoenauer, M.: Surrogate assisted feature computation for continuous problems. In: Festa, P., Sellmann, M., Vanschoren, J. (eds.) LION 2016. LNCS, vol. 10079, pp. 17–31. Springer, Cham (2016). https://doi.org/10.1007/978-3-319-50349-3_2

3. Belkhir, N., Dréo, J., Savéant, P., Schoenauer, M.: Per instance algorithm configuration of CMA-ES with limited budget. In: GECCO, pp. 681–688. ACM (2017)

4. Brams, S., Fishburn, P.: Approval Voting, 2nd edn. Springer, New York (2007). https://doi.org/10.1007/978-0-387-49896-6

5. Derbel, B., Liefooghe, A., Vérel, S., Aguirre, H., Tanaka, K.: New features for continuous exploratory landscape analysis based on the SOO tree. In: FOGA, pp. 72–86. ACM (2019)

6. Hansen, N., Auger, A., Ros, R., Mersmann, O., Tušar, T., Brockhoff, D.: COCO: a platform for comparing continuous optimizers in a black-box setting. Optim. Methods Softw. 1–31 (2020)

7. Hutter, F., Kotthoff, L., Vanschoren, J. (eds.): Automated Machine Learning. TSSCML. Springer, Cham (2019). https://doi.org/10.1007/978-3-030-05318-5

8. Jankovic, A., Doerr, C.: Landscape-aware fixed-budget performance regression and algorithm selection for modular CMA-ES variants. In: GECCO, pp. 841–849. ACM (2020)

9. Kerschke, P., Hoos, H., Neumann, F., Trautmann, H.: Automated algorithm selection: survey and perspectives. Evol. Comput. 27(1), 3–45 (2019)

10. Kerschke, P., Preuss, M., Wessing, S., Trautmann, H.: Detecting funnel structures by means of exploratory landscape analysis. In: GECCO, pp. 265–272. ACM (2015)

11. Kerschke, P., Preuss, M., Wessing, S., Trautmann, H.: Low-budget exploratory landscape analysis on multiple peaks models. In: GECCO, pp. 229–236. ACM (2016)

12. Kerschke, P., Trautmann, H.: Automated algorithm selection on continuous blackbox problems by combining exploratory landscape analysis and machine learning. Evol. Comput. 27(1), 99–127 (2019)

13. Kerschke, P., et al.: Cell mapping techniques for exploratory landscape analysis. In: Tantar, A.-A., et al. (eds.) EVOLVE - A Bridge between Probability, Set Oriented Numerics, and Evolutionary Computation V. AISC, vol. 288, pp. 115–131. Springer, Cham (2014). https://doi.org/10.1007/978-3-319-07494-8_9

14. Kerschke, P., Trautmann, H.: Comprehensive feature-based landscape analysis of continuous and constrained optimization problems using the R-package flacco. In: Bauer, N., Ickstadt, K., Lübke, K., Szepannek, G., Trautmann, H., Vichi, M. (eds.) Applications in Statistical Computing. SCDAKO, pp. 93–123. Springer, Cham (2019). https://doi.org/10.1007/978-3-030-25147-5_7

15. Lacroix, B., McCall, J.A.W.: Limitations of benchmark sets and landscape features for algorithm selection and performance prediction. In: GECCO, pp. 261–262. ACM (2019)

16. Lunacek, M., Whitley, D.: The dispersion metric and the CMA evolution strategy. In: GECCO, p. 477. ACM (2006)

17. Mersmann, O., Bischl, B., Trautmann, H., Preuss, M., Weihs, C., Rudolph, G.: Exploratory landscape analysis. In: GECCO, pp. 829–836. ACM (2011)

18. Morgan, R., Gallagher, M.: Sampling techniques and distance metrics in high dimensional continuous landscape analysis: limitations and improvements. IEEE Trans. Evol. Comput. 18(3), 456–461 (2014)

19. Muñoz, M.A., Smith-Miles, K.: Effects of function translation and dimensionality reduction on landscape analysis. In: IEEE CEC, pp. 1336–1342. IEEE (2015)

20. Muñoz, M.A., Sun, Y., Kirley, M., Halgamuge, S.K.: Algorithm selection for black-box continuous optimization problems: a survey on methods and challenges. Inf. Sci. **317**, 224–245 (2015)
21. Muñoz, M.A., Villanova, L., Baatar, D., Smith-Miles, K.: Instance spaces for machine learning classification. Mach. Learn. **107**(1), 109–147 (2017). https://doi.org/10.1007/s10994-017-5629-5
22. Muñoz, M., Kirley, M., Halgamuge, S.: Exploratory landscape analysis of continuous space optimization problems using information content. IEEE Trans. Evol. Comput. **19**(1), 74–87 (2015)
23. Pedregosa, F., et al.: Scikit-learn: machine learning in Python. JMLR **12**, 2825–2830 (2011)
24. Pitra, Z., Repický, J., Holena, M.: Landscape analysis of Gaussian process surrogates for the covariance matrix adaptation evolution strategy. In: GECCO, pp. 691–699 (2019)
25. Renau, Q., Doerr, C., Dreo, J., Doerr, B.: Exploratory landscape analysis is strongly sensitive to the sampling strategy. In: Bäck, T., et al. (eds.) PPSN 2020. LNCS, vol. 12270, pp. 139–153. Springer, Cham (2020). https://doi.org/10.1007/978-3-030-58115-2_10
26. Renau, Q., Dreo, J., Doerr, C., Doerr, B.: Expressiveness and robustness of landscape features. In: GECCO (Companion), pp. 2048–2051. ACM (2019)
27. Renau, Q., Dreo, J., Doerr, C., Doerr, B.: Exploratory Landscape Analysis Feature Values for the 24 Noiseless BBOB Functions (2021). https://doi.org/10.5281/zenodo.4449934
28. Saini, B., López-Ibáñez, M., Miettinen, K.: Automatic surrogate modelling technique selection based on features of optimization problems. In: GECCO (Companion), pp. 1765–1772 (2019)
29. Seo, D., Moon, B.R.: An information-theoretic analysis on the interactions of variables in combinatorial optimization problems. Evol. Comput. **15**(2), 169–198 (2007)
30. Skvorc, U., Eftimov, T., Korosec, P.: Understanding the problem space in single-objective numerical optimization using exploratory landscape analysis. Appl. Soft Comput. **90**, 106138 (2020)
31. Smith-Miles, K., Bowly, S.: Generating new test instances by evolving in instance space. Comput. OR **63**, 102–113 (2015)
32. Sobol', I.: On the distribution of points in a cube and the approximate evaluation of integrals. USSR Comput. Math. Math. Phys. **7**(4), 86–112 (1967)

Co-optimising Robot Morphology and Controller in a Simulated Open-Ended Environment

Emma Hjellbrekke Stensby[1(✉)], Kai Olav Ellefsen[1], and Kyrre Glette[1,2]

[1] Department of Informatics, University of Oslo, Oslo, Norway
emmaste@ifi.uio.no
[2] RITMO, University of Oslo, Oslo, Norway

Abstract. Designing robots by hand can be costly and time consuming, especially if the robots have to be created with novel materials, or be robust to internal or external changes. In order to create robots automatically, without the need for human intervention, it is necessary to optimise both the behaviour and the body design of the robot. However, when co-optimising the morphology and controller of a locomoting agent the morphology tends to converge prematurely, reaching a local optimum. Approaches such as explicit protection of morphological innovation have been used to reduce this problem, but it might also be possible to increase exploration of morphologies using a more indirect approach. We explore how changing the environment, where the agent locomotes, affects the convergence of morphologies. The agents' morphologies and controllers are co-optimised, while the environments the agents locomote in are evolved open-endedly with the Paired Open-Ended Trailblazer (POET). We compare the diversity, fitness and robustness of agents evolving in environments generated by POET to agents evolved in hand-crafted curricula of environments. Our agents each contain of a population of individuals being evolved with a genetic algorithm. This population is called the agent-population. We show that agent-populations evolving in open-endedly evolving environments exhibit larger morphological diversity than agent-populations evolving in hand crafted curricula of environments. POET proved capable of creating a curriculum of environments which encouraged both diversity and quality in the populations. This suggests that POET may be capable of reducing premature convergence in co-optimisation of morphology and controllers.

Keywords: Evolutionary algorithms · Evolutionary robotics · Open-endedness · Co-optimisation · Environments

1 Introduction

Finding a morphology and controller for a robot, that allows the robot to efficiently complete its task, is a difficult endeavour. Creating and programming

© Springer Nature Switzerland AG 2021
P. A. Castillo and J. L. Jiménez Laredo (Eds.): EvoApplications 2021, LNCS 12694, pp. 34–49, 2021.
https://doi.org/10.1007/978-3-030-72699-7_3

robots by hand is feasible when the robots' working environment is predictable, such as in a factory or warehouse. However, it becomes almost impossible when the robots are acting outside in a constantly changing world. When a robot needs to adapt to a variety of new environments, evolutionary algorithms can be used to automatically optimise both morphology and controllers [1,14,16].

When simultaneously evolving the controller and morphology of a robot the controller has a tendency to specialise in the current morphology [3]. If the morphology is changed the controller might no longer work. The morphology and controller are strongly connected, and when the morphology changes it is like the interface between them has been scrambled. This connection between controller and morphology can cause the morphological search to stagnate: When the controller has adapted to the morphology, the morphology may stop changing, as changes will be likely to lower the individual's fitness. Approaches to tackle this problem include directly or indirectly protecting individuals that recently experienced change in their morphology [4], or optimising for morphological novelty in addition to fitness in a multi objective search [12]. However, we believe it might be possible to increase the exploration of morphologies by evolving the agents in changing environments.

Inspired by minimal criterion co-evolution [2], Wang et al. invented the Paired Open-Ended Trailblazer (POET) [22]. In POET, environments evolve open-endedly, while agents are optimised to solve them. A minimal criterion ensures that the environments are appropriately difficult for the agents, increasing in complexity as the agents learn more efficient behaviours. Wang et al. show that the environments are used as stepping stones, enabling the agents to learn new skills, and escape local optima. We modify the part of the algorithm that optimises the agents within their environments, in order to allow POET to modify the agents' morphologies as well. The flow of POET, and the genetic algorithm we use, can be seen in Fig. 1. We explore whether the effect that enabled the controllers evolved with POET to escape local optima, can reduce the problem of premature convergence of morphologies.

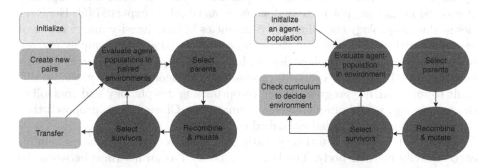

Fig. 1. Left: Illustration of our genetic algorithm when used with POET. **Right:** Illustration of our genetic algorithm when used with a curriculum of environments. (Note that in this context the term agent-population refers to a population of 192 individuals)

Our agents are tested in the OpenAI Gym environment Bipedal Walker [17], Fig. 2. We compare the performance and diversity of the agents evolved with POET to agents evolved in two handcrafted curricula of environments. There are two main contributions in this paper: 1) We show that the environments and algorithm structure of POET encourages morphological diversity, and 2) We show that the agents evolved in our handcrafted curriculum with rapid environmental change generalise well to many new environments, while the agents evolved in POET generalise to environments somewhat similar to the ones the agents have seen previously.

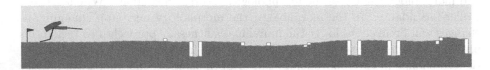

Fig. 2. The Bipedal walker hardcore environment, adjusted to allow for morphological changes.

2   Background

In 1994 Karl Sims published a study, "Evolving Virtual Creatures" [20], which showed virtual creatures evolving in an artificial world with simulated physics. In this artificial evolution the creatures evolved both their bodies and their behaviours simultaneously, and solved various tasks such as walking, swimming and competing against each other. Inspired by Sims' work, many researchers took interest in creating robots that can evolve both their morphology and controller at the same time [3,4,7,8,10], and the field of co-optimisation of robot morphology and controller emerged. Although computing power has increased significantly since Karl Sims' study was published, the morphological complexity of evolved agents has not increased as much as could be expected [5]. Deficiencies in the morphology encodings [9], deficiencies in the diversity maintenance of search algorithms [12], and that the environments used are not complex enough to encourage complex morphologies [1], have been suggested as sources for this problem. In 2012 Cheney et al. [3] proposed their theory on why it was so difficult to make further progress. When co-optimising morphology and controller, the morphology would often converge prematurely. Cheney et al. proposed that this is due to an effect called embodied cognition.

Embodied cognition is a theory stating that how a creature behaves is influenced heavily by their body. The body can be seen as an interface between the controller and the environment, and if the body changes, even just a little, it is as if the interface between body and controller has been scrambled. The controller adapts to its specific morphology, and when the morphology changes, the controller will have to re-adapt before it can manage to locomote with the new body. Cheney et al. [4] continued their research, and studied how explicitly protecting individuals that had just experienced morphological change affected the evolution of morphologies. They showed that when giving the controllers time to adapt to their new bodies, controllers that normally would have been discarded due to low fitness were kept, as they surpassed the previous elites during the time they were protected.

Several algorithms that reduce the problem of embodied cognition, without explicitly protecting novel morphologies, have also been proposed. One such algorithm is ALPS [8], where reproduction is only allowed between candidates that have experienced approximately the same number of earlier reproduction steps. This restriction divides the population into layers based on their age, and lowers the selection pressure on young candidates. Jelisavcic et al. [10], also take a more indirect approach to protecting new morphologies. In their work all controllers adapt to their morphologies, before being evaluated, through lamarckian evolution. Lehman et al. [12] do not allow the controllers time to adapt to their morphologies, but rather increase morphological diversity by optimising for morphological novelty in addition to performance with a multi-objective evolutionary algorithm.

2.1 POET

In traditional evolutionary algorithms it is common to optimise for better performance, but this approach can easily lead the algorithm to converge to a local optimum prematurely. One way to increase the chance of finding good optima is to increase diversity in the population, with methods such as fitness sharing [6,18], speciation [21] or crowding [13]. However, open-ended algorithms such as novelty search [11] have also proven efficient. In the field of open-endedness, the focus is not to move towards solutions with better performance, but to create novel and interesting solutions [19], often by optimising for diversity instead of performance. Counterintuitively, searching for novelty alone can sometimes lead to better solutions than what can be found by optimising directly for performance, as demonstrated by Lehman et al. [11].

The Paired Open-Ended Trailblazer, POET, is an open-ended algorithm created by Wang et al. [22]. POET has a population of pairs, where each pair consists of one environment and one agent. The agents are optimized within their paired environment, and the environments are evolved with an open-ended algorithm optimising for novelty. As the environments increase in complexity, the agents learn increasingly complex behaviours. Wang et al. tested their algorithm in the OpenAI bipedal walker environment [17], and observed that the agents used the environments as stepping stones to learn behaviours and gaits they would otherwise not find. The pairs share their knowledge through agent transfers, helping each other escape local optima.

The POET algorithm starts by initialising one environment-agent pair. This first pair always has a very simple environment, such as flat ground. The main flow of the POET algorithm has three steps: Creating environments, Optimising agents in their paired environments and Transferring agents between environments. For the optimisation step Wang et al. use an evolutionary strategy. The two remaining steps are described in detail below.

Creating Environments. The environment creation step of POET is executed periodically, with a set number of generations between each execution. This step starts off by checking all pairs against a minimal criterion for reproduction. All environments that have a paired agent with fitness higher than the minimal criterion are marked as eligible to reproduce. If there are no eligible environments the creation of environments is skipped. The new environments are then generated by randomly selecting and mutating qualified environments.

The newly created environments then need to be assigned an agent to become a pair. All agents are tested in the new environments, and the environments are assigned a copy of the agent that performed best in them. The new pairs are then checked against a second minimal criterion, the minimal criterion of difficulty. This minimal criterion has an upper and lower boundary for agent fitness, and ensures the environment is not too difficult nor too easy for its agent. The new pairs that do not meet this minimal criterion are removed.

The remaining new pairs are then sorted by environment novelty. The novelty of the environment is found by comparing it to an archive of all environments that have existed throughout the run. The novelty measure is the euclidean distance to the five nearest neighbours in the archive. If a child environment already exists in the archive, it is removed from the list of child pairs. The most novel child pairs are added to the population until the maximum number of children that can be added each generation is reached, or until there are no more children left to add. The POET population has a maximum population size. When the population size exceeds this limit the oldest pairs are removed.

Transferring Agents Between Environments. In the transfer step, all agents are cross tested in all environments. If any of the agents performs better in an environment than the environment's paired agent, the paired agent is removed, and is replaced by a copy of the agent that performs best.

There are two types of transfer, direct and proposal transfer. In direct transfer the agents are tested directly in the other pairs' environments, while in proposal transfer the agents are first trained in the other pairs' environments before they are tested. Transferring of agents allows skills learned in one environment to be used in another environment, and in this way, the pairs trade experiences.

3   Methods

We evolve environment-agent pairs with POET, and compare this approach to evolving agents in hand-crafted curricula of environments.[1] We have substituted

---

[1] Source code can be found at https://github.com/EmmaStensby/poet-morphology.

the agent optimisation step of POET with a genetic algorithm. While the optimisation step used by Wang et al. [22] in POET only evolves the agent controllers, our optimisation step evolves the morphologies of the agents as well, allowing us to look at the effect POET has on morphological development in agents. The flow of the algorithm can be seen in Fig. 1. In order to reduce the computation time of POET we only use direct transfer, and not proposal transfer. Table 1 summarises the values we use for parameters required by POET.

Table 1. POET parameters.

Parameter	Value
Pair population size	20
Transfer frequency	Every 5 generations
Create env. frequency	Every 40 generations
Reproduction criterion	200
Difficulty criterion	50–300
Child environments created	20
Child pairs admitted	2

The environments the agents are evaluated in can contain various features: stumps, pits, rough terrain and stairs. In POET's environment creation step the environments' features are mutated to create new environments. The parameters for the environment mutation are summarised in Table 2.

Table 2. Environment mutation parameters.

Feature	Minimum value	Mutation value	Maximum value
Terrain roughness	0	Uniform(0,0.6)	10
Pit gap	[0,0]	[±0.4,±0.4]	[10,10]
Stump height	[0,0]	[±0.2,±0.2]	[5,5]
Stair height	[0,0]	[±0.2,±0.2]	[5,5]
Stair steps	0	±1	9

3.1 Genetic Algorithm

This section describes the genetic algorithm we use to co-optimise controllers and morphologies. The setup and parameters of the genetic algorithm were decided through initial experiments aiming to find values that efficiently evolved high-quality agents. The genetic algorithm keeps a population of 192 individuals, where each individual consists of a neural network and a morphology, see

Fig. 3. The neural network and morphology controls the behaviour and body of a bipedal walker agent. We will use the term *individual* to refer to a pair consisting of a neural network and a morphology, and the term *agent-population* to refer to a population of 192 individuals being evolved with our genetic algorithm. We use the term agent in agent-population to emphasise that this is the agent part of a POET environment-agent pair. The term *bipedal agent*, is used to refer to the walking figure in the bipedal walker environment.

Controller. The bipedal agent is controlled by a neural network inputting state variables such as joint angles, speed, and ground contact sensors, and outputting force to apply to the leg joints, thus forming a type of closed-loop control architecture. The neural network has an input layer with 24 nodes, two hidden layers with 40 nodes each, and an output layer with four nodes. This gives a total of 2720 weights. The activation function used is the identity function. This network structure has been used in two other studies that also evolved agents locomoting in the bipedal walker environment [7,22]. This design choice was made to reduce the extent of the parameter search. However, it would be interesting to explore whether the same performance could have been reached with a smaller network. The neural network weights are initialised to random values, drawn uniformly between −1 and 1. Mutations can never increase the weights above 30, or decrease them below −30.

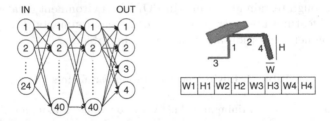

Fig. 3. Overview of the genotype. The genotype for an individual contains a matrix with the weights of the neural network controller, and a vector with the leg sizes.

Morphology. The bipedal walker agent has two legs, each consisting of two segments. The morphology is a vector of eight floats describing the widths and heights of the bipedal agent's four leg segments. The sizes are constrained to values within ±75% of the leg sizes in the original bipedal walker environment. These constraints have previously been used by Ha et al. [7]. The morphology values are initialised to random values drawn uniformly between the minimum and maximum possible size.

Individual Evaluation. To evaluate the fitness of an individual it is tested in a bipedal walker environment. The individual receives positive reward each time step for how far the bipedal agent moved forward, and negative reward for how much force it applied to the joints. It also receives negative reward if the bipedal agent's head touches the ground. The simulation ends when the bipedal agent's head touches the ground, it reaches a flag at the end of the course or 1000 time steps is reached. The reward an individual gets in an environment is not deterministic, and can be unstable. To make the fitness function more stable the individuals are evaluated four times. The fitness is the mean of the reward received in the four evaluations. The negative reward received from applying force to the joints or falling can sometimes exceed the positive reward earned from walking forward, causing individuals to have negative fitness.

Parent Selection. The parents are selected by tournament. Five individuals are chosen at random from the population, and compete with their fitness to become a parent. This is repeated until 192 parents have been chosen. The same individual can be chosen as a parent multiple times. The parents are then separated into 96 pairs, and the two parents from each pair are recombined to create two children.

Recombination and Mutation. The parents are recombined using uniform crossover. For each neural network weight, or morphology value, the parent contributing the value is chosen at random, with equal probability between the two parents. The first child gets the chosen values, and the second child gets the remaining values. After recombination the children are mutated using two types of mutation: replacement and modification. In replacement mutation, neural network weights, and morphology values, are chosen with a probability of 0.0075. The chosen values are replaced with new values. The new values are determined in the same way as initial weights and morphology values were determined at individual initialisation. In modification mutation, neural network weights, and morphology values, are chosen with a probability of 0.075. An offset is added to the chosen weights and values. The offset is a random float drawn uniformly from $(-x, x)$. For the neural network weights x is 0.2. For the morphology values x is 16% of the difference between the minimum and maximum values for the size of the respective leg segment.

Survivor Selection. To create niches of different solutions in the population, and to slow down convergence, deterministic crowding [13] is used when selecting survivors for the next generation. The difference between two individuals is the L1-norm of the individuals' morphologies. We compare only the morphologies, and not the neural networks, to encourage the niches in the population to explore different morphologies.

3.2 Environment Curricula

We use two handcrafted curricula of environments in our experiments. The genetic algorithm used to evolve the POET agent-populations is also used to evolve agent-populations in the curricula. The first curriculum is *Static*, which only contains one flat featureless environment. Static is used as a baseline, and has no environmental change. The second curriculum is *Round Robin Incremental* (RRI), this curriculum consists of five environments. The agent-populations are trained for five generations in each of the environments. When training has finished in the last of the five environments, it starts over again at the first environment. The five environments consist of one flat featureless environment, and four environments with features. Each environment has only one feature. The environments with features appear in the following order: Pits, Rough terrain, Stumps, Stairs. The features start out simple. When an individual in the agent-population reaches 150 or higher fitness in any of the last four environments the difficulty of that environment is increased.

4 Results

In our experiment we want to find out how effective POET is in creating an environment curriculum that maintains both quality and morphological diversity in a population. We evolve agent-populations in the dynamically changing environments of POET, and in the two curricula Static and RRI, with a budget of 384000 evaluations per run. An evaluation being one individual evaluation as described in Sect. 3.1. The experiments were performed on a 40 core node on the UNINETT Sigma2 Saga supercomputer, and each run took about 1895 cpu hours to finish. Ten runs are performed in each of the Static, RRI and POET setups. If POET is effective in maintaining both morphological diversity and quality at the same time, we expect the algorithm to find high fitness solutions for many different morphologies.

4.1 Morphological Differences

Figure 4 shows the morphological diversity throughout the runs, for agent-populations evolved in Static, RRI and POET, as well as the morphological diversity of the populations in the final generation. The population diversity of POET in these graphs is measured only for the first POET pair, meaning that we follow an agent-population evolving in a flat environment. However, the POET agent is sometimes switched due to agent transfers, see Sect. 2.1. The morphological diversity of an individual is measured as the average distance from that individual to the other individuals in the population, and the population diversity of an agent-population is the average diversity of all the individuals in the population. POET has higher population diversity than Static and RRI throughout the whole run, and in the resulting populations at the end of the runs (p < 0.01).

Figure 5 shows morphological feature maps and quality-diversity feature maps for Static, RRI and POET. To create the feature maps we project the morphological search space into two dimensions. In our case the dimensions are

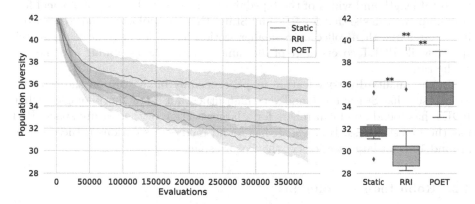

Fig. 4. Left: Morphological diversity through evolution. The graphs shows the mean of five runs, and the scratched area shows the standard deviation. **Right:** Morphological diversity in the final populations. Four to one asterisks indicate respectively $p < 0.0001$, $p < 0.001$, $p < 0.01$ and $p < 0.05$ (Mann-Whitney U test with Bonferroni correction).

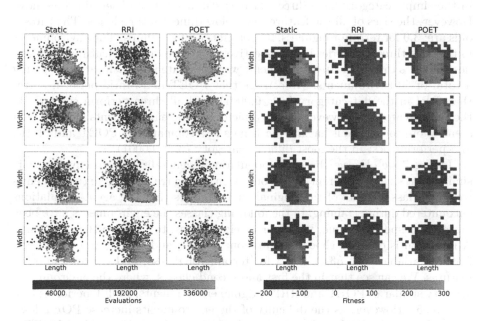

Fig. 5. Each map is from a separate run of one of the algorithms, and shows the total width and the total length of the legs of all individuals encountered throughout the run. **Left:** Morphological feature maps. Every morphology that appears throughout the run is represented as a circle. The color of the circle represents when in the search the morphology appeared. **Right:** Quality-Diversity feature maps. The feature space is divided into a grid, and the color of each cell represents the highest fitness found in that region throughout the run. (Color figure online)

the total length and width of the bipedal agents' legs. In the morphological feature maps we can see that for RRI and Static the morphologies tend to start out in one area and then collect in a smaller section in the lower right of the search space, while POET covers more of the same areas at the beginning and the end of the runs.

In the quality-diversity feature maps, especially in the run on the top row, we can see that Static has found very high fitness for a few morphologies, while POET has found good controllers for a larger section of the feature space. RRI has the lowest fitness. However, it has found mediocre solutions (fitness values around 100) for large sections of the feature space.

4.2   Robustness of Solutions

Next we tested the robustness of the agent-populations by looking at their performance in environments they had not seen during training. This is shown in Fig. 6. We divided the environmental search space into five categories based on difficulty. The environment difficulty is based on the definition used by Wang et al. [22]. The first category has flat featureless environments. The environments in the simple category have three features: stumps, pits and terrain roughness. However, the sizes of all the features are below difficulty thresholds. The thresholds are: 3.0 for terrain roughness, 2.5 for pits, 1.5 for stumps. The environments in the next three categories have respectively one, two or three features with values above its threshold. 10 environments were generated for each category, giving a total of 50 environments. We can see that POET and Static perform better than RRI in the flat category ($p < 0.0001$), and all three perform similarly in the simple category. However, as the difficulty of the environments increase RRI seems more robust, as it has a lower fitness loss compared to POET and Static, and performs best in the most difficult category ($p < 0.0001$).

In Fig. 7 we observe the agent-populations' generalisation to environments similar, but slightly different, to the ones seen during training. Here the first environment class consists of the original environments that the agent-populations encountered during training. In the following classes the environments have been mutated, respectively one, two, four or eight times, to increase their difficulty. A mutation is done by choosing a random feature, and adding an offset to the feature variable. The offset is 2.4 for terrain roughness, and 0.8 for the other features. We can see that in the first and second classes, where the environments are very similar to POET and RRI's original environments, POET performs best ($p < 0.05$). However, as the difficulty of the environments increase POET loses fitness faster than RRI, and in the last class RRI performs better than POET($p < 0.05$).

5   Discussion

POET seems to explore approximately the same areas of the morphological feature space in the beginning and end of the evolution, as we saw in Fig. 5.

This suggests that morphologies that are not easy to exploit are kept by POET even if the algorithm does not quickly find a good controller for it. From the feature maps it looks like the Static and RRI agent-populations quite quickly discard morphologies that do not have a good controller, leading to the large purple sections in the morphological feature maps. These maps, together with the high morphological diversity observed for POET in Fig. 4, lead us to believe that the POET agent-populations have slower morphological convergence than the Static and RRI agent-populations.

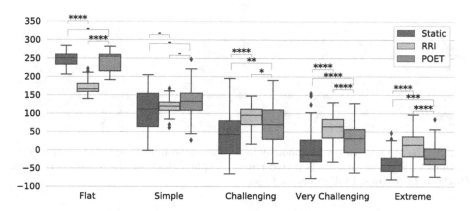

Fig. 6. The agent-populations tested in randomly selected unseen environments of increasing difficulty. Four to one asterisks indicate respectively p < 0.0001, p < 0.001, p < 0.01 and p < 0.05 (Mann-Whitney U test with Bonferroni correction).

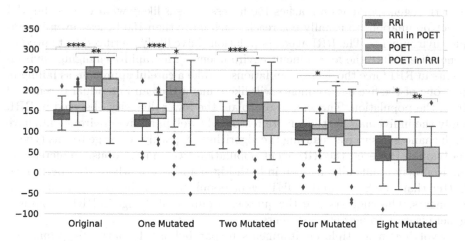

Fig. 7. The agent-populations tested in randomly selected environments from the vicinity of the agent-populations' original environments, with increasing difficulty. Four to one asterisks indicate respectively p < 0.0001, p < 0.001, p < 0.01 and p < 0.05 (Mann-Whitney U test with Bonferroni correction).

We think this may be caused partly by the environmental change, as the RRI agent-populations also have slightly larger yellow areas in the feature maps compared to the Static agent-populations, but also by POET's population size gradually increasing as new environment-agent pairs are added. The pairs can act as niches, exploring different sections of the search space. An example demonstrating the morphological development in a Static and POET agent-population throughout a run can be seen in Fig. 8. We see that in this run the Static agent-population converged to long thin legs while the POET agent-populations' legs were still evolving.

Fig. 8. The top performing morphology in the flat environment captured every 40 generations for 880 generations. **Top two rows:** Morphologies from the Static curriculum. **Bottom two rows:** POET morphologies.

As seen in Fig. 6 the RRI agent-populations have lower fitness in the flat environment than the agent-populations from Static and POET. However, four out of five of the environments in the RRI curriculum increase in difficulty whenever the agent-population reaches 150 fitness. This is likely what causes the RRI agent-populations to usually not reach much more than 150 fitness, even in simple environments. The RRI agent-populations have likely sacrificed gait speed to generalise well to the four difficult environments. The rapidly changing environments in RRI force the agent-populations to take a careful approach, as failing in just one of the five environments will likely mean that an individual is removed from the population. This can also explain the lower diversity observed in RRI. Only the individuals that locomote reasonably well in all five environments have high chances of survival, causing the algorithm to quickly converge to this type of individual. However, the RRI agent-populations were more robust to increase in environmental difficulty, as seen in both Fig. 6 and Fig. 7, where RRI performed better than the Static and POET agent-populations in the most difficult environments. This suggests that the quick environmental change in RRI encourages generalisation to new environments.

Evolving in multiple environments in parallel should naturally promote a diverse set of morphological strategies. This can be observed in the quality-diversity maps: we see that POET tends to have larger high-fitness areas compared to RRI and Static, meaning that POET has found high fitness for a larger variety of morphologies. In Fig. 4 we saw that, although POET and RRI both differ from static in that they experience several different environments, POET had increased population diversity, while RRI had decreased population diversity. RRI likely had decreased diversity due to the difficult nature of its rapidly changing environments, leading RRI to quickly exploit the solutions that were the most robust. The population diversity for POET in this graph is the diversity within the population of a single pair, so the increased diversity is not due to the pairs acting as niches and thus being different from each other. Rather, we believe that this increased diversity is due to the transfer mechanism in POET. The morphologies that are best for the agents current environment may not be best for some other environment. Agent-populations with diverse populations may therefore be more likely to be transferred, as diversity may increase its chances of being a good fit for a new environment. When an agent is transferred it is duplicated, thus increasing its presence in the population. Further experiments would be necessary to confirm this.

6   Conclusion

In our experiments we compared agent-populations evolved in a static environment, in a curriculum of environments and in POET. We observed that the agent-populations evolved in POET had higher morphological diversity than the agent-populations evolved in a static environment, or in a curriculum of environments. This correlation suggests that evolving agent-populations with POET causes increased exploration of morphologies. This property could be promising for tackling the challenging problem of stagnation in co-optimisation of morphology and control in robotics, and suggest that POET could be applied to this domain.

We also compared the robustness of agent-populations when they encountered unseen environments. We conclude that the agent-populations evolved in the hand crafted curriculum, RRI, were most robust to environmental change. The agent-populations evolved in RRI performed best in the most difficult environments, but their fitness values were relatively low across all environments. The POET agent-populations had high fitness values in their original environments, and generalised quite well to environments slightly different from these.

POET requires a lot of time and computation power to reach the most difficult environments. Due to limited time, the environments POET found in our runs were not very difficult. It would have been interesting to see how the diversity, robustness and morphological convergence developed if the algorithms were allowed to run longer.

In future work it would be interesting to test our approach in a complex domain, where the morphologies could evolve more freely, such as on modular robots. We used the bipedal walker environment in order to be able to compare to previous research using this environment [7, 22]. However, the differences in morphologies might have been more prominent had we used an environment with more complex morphologies. It would also be interesting to look at how environment curricula could be created to most efficiently promote both high quality, robust individuals and exploration of morphologies. This could be explored either by looking at how features in hand crafted curricula affect the search, or by attempting to create an algorithm similar to POET that is more computationally efficient, and encourages more frequent environmental change. Perhaps this could be achieved by using information about the progress of the search, or the morphological diversity of the agent-populations, when choosing the next environment. We would also like to compare this approach to other approaches that increase morphological diversity, such as protection of individuals that have experienced morphological change [4], NSLC [12] or map-elites[15].

Acknowledgments. This work was partially supported by the Research Council of Norway through its Centres of Excellence scheme, project number 262762. The simulations were performed on resources provided by UNINETT Sigma2 - the National Infrastructure for High Performance Computing and Data Storage in Norway.

References

1. Auerbach, J.E., Bongard, J.C.: Environmental influence on the evolution of morphological complexity in machines. PLoS Comput. Biol. **10**(1), 17. e1003399 (2014). https://doi.org/10.1371/journal.pcbi.1003399, http://infoscience.epfl.ch/record/195214
2. Brant, J.C., Stanley, K.O.: Minimal criterion coevolution: a new approach to open-ended search. In: Proceedings of the Genetic and Evolutionary Computation Conference, GECCO 2017, pp. 67–74. Association for Computing Machinery (2017). ISBN 9781450349208, https://doi.org/10.1145/3071178.3071186
3. Cheney, N., Bongard, J., Sunspiral, V., Lipson, H.: On the difficulty of co-optimizing morphology and control in evolved virtual creatures. Artif. Life Conf. Proc. **28**, 226–233 (2016). https://doi.org/10.1162/978-0-262-33936-0-ch042
4. Cheney, N., Bongard, J., Sunspiral, V., Lipson, H.: Scalable co-optimization of morphology and control in embodied machines. J. R. Soc. Interface **15**(143), 20170937 (2018). ISSN 17425689
5. Geijtenbeek, T., Pronost, N.: Interactive character animation using simulated physics: a state-of-the-art review. Comput. Graphics Forum **31**(8), 2492–2515 (2012). ISSN 0167–7055
6. Goldberg, D.E., Richardson, J.: Genetic algorithms with sharing for multimodal function optimization (1987)
7. Ha, D.: Reinforcement learning for improving agent design. Artif. Life **25**(4), 352–365 (2019). ISSN 1064–5462
8. Hornby, G.S.: Alps: the age-layered population structure for reducing the problem of premature convergence. In: Proceedings of the 8th Annual Conference on Genetic and Evolutionary Computation, GECCO 2006, pp. 815–822. Association for Computing Machinery (2006). ISBN 1595931864. https://doi.org/10.1145/1143997.1144142
9. Hornby, G.S., Lipson, H., Pollack, J.B.: Evolution of generative design systems for modular physical robots. In: Proceedings 2001 ICRA. IEEE International Conference on Robotics and Automation, vol. 4, pp. 4146–4151. IEEE (2001). ISBN 0780365763
10. Jelisavcic, M., Glette, K., Haasdijk, E., Eiben, A.E.: Lamarckian evolution of simulated modular robots. Front. Robot. AI **6**, 9 (2019). ISSN 2296-9144. https://doi.org/10.3389/frobt.2019.00009

11. Lehman, J., Stanley, K.O.: Abandoning objectives: evolution through the search for novelty alone. Evol. Comput. **19**(2), 189–223 (2011). ISSN 1063-6560. https://doi.org/10.1162/EVCO_a_00025

12. Lehman, J., Stanley, K.O.: Evolving a diversity of virtual creatures through novelty search and local competition. In: Proceedings of the 13th Annual Conference on Genetic and Evolutionary Computation, GECCO 2011, pp. 211–218. Association for Computing Machinery (2011). ISBN 9781450305570. https://doi.org/10.1145/2001576.2001606

13. Mengshoel, O.J., Goldberg, D.E.: The crowding approach to niching in genetic algorithms. Evol. Comput. **16**(3), 315–354 (2008). https://doi.org/10.1162/evco.2008.16.3.315

14. Miras, K., Ferrante, E., Eiben, A.E.: Environmental influences on evolvable robots. PloS One **15**(5), e0233848 (2020)

15. Nordmoen, J., Veenstra, F., Ellefsen, K.O., Glette, K.: Map-elites enables powerful stepping stones and diversity for modular robotics. arXiv preprint arXiv:2012.04375 (2020)

16. Nygaard, T., Martin, C., Samuelsen, E., Torresen, J., Glette, K.: Real-world evolution adapts robot morphology and control to hardware limitations. In: Proceedings of the Genetic and Evolutionary Computation Conference, GECCO 2018, pp. 125–132. ACM (2018). ISBN 9781450356183

17. Oleg, K.: Bipedalwalkerhardcore-v2 (2016). https://gym.openai.com

18. Oliveto, P.S., Sudholt, D., Zarges, C.: On the benefits and risks of using fitness sharing for multimodal optimisation. Theor. Comput. Sci. **773**, 53–70 (2019). ISSN 0304-3975

19. Packard, N., et al.: An overview of open-ended evolution: Editorial introduction to the open-ended evolution ii special issue. Artif. Life **25**(2), 93–103 (2019). ISSN 1064–5462

20. Sims, K.: Evolving virtual creatures. In: Proceedings of the 21st Annual Conference on Computer Graphics and Interactive Techniques, SIGGRAPH 1994, pp. 15–22. ACM (1994). ISBN 0897916670

21. Trujillo, L., Olague, G., Lutton, E., de Vega, F.F., Dozal, L., Clemente, E.: Speciation in behavioral space for evolutionary robotics. J. Intell. Robot. Syst. **64**(3–4), 323–351 (2011). ISSN 0921–0296

22. Wang, R., Lehman, J., Clune, J., Stanley, K.O.: Poet: open-ended coevolution of environments and their optimized solutions. In: Proceedings of the Genetic and Evolutionary Computation Conference, GECCO 2019, pp. 142–151. Association for Computing Machinery (2019). ISBN 9781450361118, https://doi.org/10.1145/3321707.3321799

Multi-objective Workforce Allocation in Construction Projects

Andrew Iskandar[1]($\boxtimes$) and Richard Allmendinger[2]

[1] ASGC UAE, Business Bay, Bay Square, Building 13, 13164 Dubai, UAE
[2] The University of Manchester, Oxford Rd, Manchester M13 9PL, UK
`richard.allmendinger@manchester.ac.uk`

Abstract. Managing construction projects is a complex, resource-intense and risky task that involves the organization and management of people skilled in the design and completion of construction projects. Embarking on a construction project means to plan the allocation of resources and labour, while ensuring that the output (e.g. a new building) meets a certain quality, and is delivered in time and within budget without breaching contractual obligations. We formulate a simplified version of this task as a constrained multi-objective optimization problem, and then use a non-dominated sorting genetic algorithm to tackle the problem. In addition to providing a formal definition of the problem, further contributions of this work include the validation of the methodology using real data of construction projects varying in scale and resource-utilisation; the use of real data is scarce in the construction project management area. We also perform a scenario-based analysis to understand how the approach reacts to changing environmental parameters (such as availability of resources). Finally, we discuss practical implications. Our empirical analysis highlights that the proposed approach improves significantly in terms of project budget, quality, and duration targets, when compared with the industry standard.

Keywords: Multi-objective optimization · Evolutionary algorithms · Workforce allocation · Resource allocation · Construction project management

1 Introduction

Construction project management is a management task that involves the planning, scheduling and allocation of resources to different activities involved in the design and completion of a construction project. With the participation of different stakeholders in a construction project comes the presence of different and often competing goals, related to, for example, budget, cost and quality targets. This paper will simulate and address such multi-objective problems using real construction project data.

On the ground, the delivery of a construction project requires different trades, such as carpenters, painters, plasterers, to work together to build a building, be it

© Springer Nature Switzerland AG 2021
P. A. Castillo and J. L. Jiménez Laredo (Eds.): EvoApplications 2021, LNCS 12694, pp. 50–64, 2021.
https://doi.org/10.1007/978-3-030-72699-7_4

a hospital, hotel, or something else. Each trade has a (limited) labour resource, which may be divided further into skill levels varying in salary, and expected productivity and quality. The amount of labour resource required depends on properties of the construction project at hand, such as scale, type of building, purpose, etc. The core of the decision making problem considered in this work is about deciding how much labour of each skill level should be employed to deliver a construction project resource-efficiently, as quickly as possible, and to the highest possible quality. There are limitations on the number of labour available per skill level, and the labour may need to be shared across several concurrent projects. This problem can be seen as a multi-objective resource allocation problem (MORAP) [6] though they are similarities to other classical problems, which we discuss later on in the paper.

One can find in the literature a range of exact and heuristic methods developed for the MORAP (e.g. [6, 15, 27]). Our intention here is not to research the more efficient algorithm to tackle the particular problem at hand. Instead, our motivation is more profound and driven by practice: We want to understand how the construction problems at hand can be formulated formally into an mathematical problem, and whether multi-objective optimization (MO) can serve as a tool to gain insight into the trade-offs between the multiple objectives to consequently support business decision making.

The construction community is no stranger to the MO literature. The community has considered problems with a mix of conflicting objectives related to, for example, time, cost, resource, cash flow, environment, and quality criteria. Problems of up to four objectives have been studied [12, 23]. Typically the MO problems considered are concerned with scheduling of activities and allocation of resources (see e.g. [2, 12, 17, 23]), and the focus of much research is around proposing new mathematical models and methods to solve these.

The contribution of this paper is to complement existing research by formally defining and solving a MO allocation problem based on real construction data, which we will make available to the community. We analyze the trade-offs between objectives and relationships between decision variables, and then discuss practical implications. Furthermore, we experiment how changes in the problem constraints (e.g. different resource capacities) reflect the relationships between the objectives studied. We begin in the next section by providing a formal problem definition of the MORAP considered here. Following this we introduce and explore the real construction data used in this study, and explain the MO approach used to tackle the MORAP.

2   Problem Statement

This work is motivated by a real MORAP faced by a construction contracting company. Given a set of construction projects, the company needs to decide how to allocate labour (workforce) from different trades (e.g. painters, carpenters, and masons) and skill levels (grades) to each of the projects. The varying skill levels within each trade lead to different productivity rates (speed of work), cost rates (salaries, equipment and materials used), and quality of work. The productivity rate has a knock-on effect on the duration of completing an activity carried out by a trade, and the cost has an impact on the profit of the company. Hence, our objectives are to perform the workforce allocation such that the total project duration (T) and total project cost (C) are minimized, and the project quality (Q) maximized (or, equivalently, the inverse of the project quality minimized). Formally, we can define our MORAP as follows:

$$\min \quad T = \sum_{i=1}^{n} t_i = \sum_{i=1}^{n} \frac{N_i}{(p_{Ai} \times x_{Ai}) + (p_{Bi} \times x_{Bi}) + \ldots + (p_{Mi} \times x_{Mi})}$$

$$\min \quad C = \sum_{i=1}^{n} t_i \times ((r_{Ai} \times x_{Ai}) + (r_{Bi} \times x_{Bi}) + \ldots + (r_{Mi} \times x_{Mi}))$$

$$\max \quad Q = \sum_{i=1}^{n} w_i \times ((q_{Ai} \times x_{Ai}) + (q_{Bi} \times x_{Bi}) + \ldots + (q_{Mi} \times x_{Mi}))$$

$$\text{subject to} \quad 0 \leqslant x_{Ai} \leqslant R_{Ai}, \ 0 \leqslant x_{Bi} \leqslant R_{Bi}, \ \ldots, 0 \leqslant x_{Mi} \leqslant R_{Mi}$$

$$x_{Ai}, x_{Bi}, \ldots x_{Mi} \in \mathbb{Z},$$

(1)

where the decision variables, $x_{Ai}, x_{Bi}, \ldots, x_{Mi}$, are the workforce sizes of the M grades available within trade (or activity) $i = 1, \ldots, n$. $R_{Ai}, R_{Bi}, \ldots, R_{Mi}$ are the total available workforce for each grade and trade, t_i is the duration (in days) that trade i needs to complete its activity, N_i the total quantity or size of activities to be carried out by trade i, and w_i the economic value of a trade's contribution in the project relative to the total contract value of the project. The parameter sets, $\{p_{Ai}, \ldots, p_{Mi}\}$, $\{r_{Ai}, \ldots, r_{Mi}\}$ and $\{q_{Ai}, \ldots, q_{Mi}\}$, represent the daily productivity rate (measured in quantity), daily cost rate (measured in cost units), and the quality rate (measured in percentage) associated with the different trades and their skills levels (grades). The daily cost rates are specified by the market, while the productivity and quality rates are obtained by experience gathered over many years from real onsite activity inspections. The assumption is that trades work in sequence, there is no setup time between trade transitions, there is a one-to-one mapping between trades and an activity, and labour associated with one trade cannot be used for other trades.

The MORAP defined above is linear in its objective functions and constraints, thus could be solved using multi-objective variants of the simplex algorithm (e.g. [3]). We will be using a MO evolutionary algorithm (MOEA) [8] due to two reasons: Analyzing and visualizing a MOEA's convergence behaviour provides insights into the complexity of a problem, and a MOEA will be easier to adapt to non-linear, dynamic versions of the problem (which is part of our future research).

Table 1. Details about activities and their objective values for a real construction project. The trade acronyms stand for CR-carpenter, SF-Steel fitter, CA-Caster, MA-Mason, TM-Tile Mason, PA-Painter, PL-plasterer.

Activity i	Quantity N_i (Unit)	Weight w_i (%)	Trade	Grade A x_{Ai}	Grade B x_{Bi}	Grade C x_{Ci}	Productivity (Unit/day)	Duration T (days)	Cost C (Cost Unit)	Quality Q (%)
1	61,368	16.9	CR	8	39	61	456.50	134	4,923,863	10.5
2	2,142	27.4	SF	7	15	22	8.19	261	8,134,800	16.9
3	25,099	30.5	CA	3	5	15	59.00	425	8,642,970	13.2
4	8,871	3.9	MA	3	11	27	143.50	61	1,017,971	2.4
5	16,153	8.0	TM	3	9	24	105.00	153	2,261,384	4.0
6	75,010	6.3	PA	2	4	30	1524.00	49	865,318	2.1
7	34,431	6.6	PL	5	19	23	436.00	78	918,519	3.9

3   Construction Project Data

To validate the MORAP introduced in the previous section we consider data related to 11 real construction projects that were delivered by a construction contracting firm between 2015 and 2019. The labor resources in the firm comprise several resource trades, each trade constrained to execute a particular type of activity. Additionally, each trade is divided into three grades identifying their skill level: grade A, grade B and grade C, with grade A representing highly skilled, less skilled, and least skilled labour, respectively. The rate at which a labor resource belonging to a particular trade and grade executes an activity is referred to the productivity rate. This rate and the amount of work a trade needs to do (indicated by Quantity in Table 1) dictate an activity's duration; the greater the productivity rate (something we can affect by allocating more or fewer highly skilled labour to a trade) and/or the smaller the workload (the load is fixed), the shorter the duration of completing an activity. The execution cost of an activity covers three cost categories (labor, equipment and material) and the total cost of a project is the cumulative sum of the cost of all activities in the project. The profit associated with an activity is the difference between the cost of execution and the amount paid by the client to the construction firm to execute the activity, otherwise referred to as the Contract Value. Table 1 shows the set of activities for one of the 11 real projects. The values of the objectives, project duration, cost and quality in Table 1, are obtained using the workforce grade specific data shown in Table 2 and Eq. (1).

The 11 construction projects considered are diverse in nature and purpose including the construction of hotels, residential buildings, cultural and educational institutions, commercial buildings, healthcare facilities and social infrastructure. Thus the type, standard and materials used for finishing vary across the projects. The projects vary also in scale and execution methods including high-rise, low-rise, structural steel and concrete buildings. Table 1 shows the activities of one project and the data for the remaining 10 projects studied in this research is available upon request.

Table 2. Per individual pay, productivity and quality details for each skill level and trade.

Activity i	Trade	Pay rate (Unit/month)			Productivity (Unit/day)			Quality (%)		
		A	B	C	A	B	C	A	B	C
1	CR	1900	1350	900	6.00	5.0	3.50	99	79	47
2	SF	1900	1200	1000	0.27	0.2	0.15	96	77	40
3	CA	1500	1100	900	8.00	4.0	1.00	99	62	26
4	MA	1836	1696	1312	6.60	5.6	2.30	99	75	55
5	TM	1896	1673	1233	7.00	4.0	2.00	95	59	42
6	PA	1593	1463	1261	60.00	51.0	40.00	98	81	23
7	PL	1800	1400	1100	14.00	12.0	6.00	98	79	35

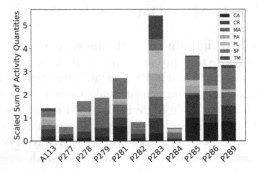

Fig. 1. Normalized workloads of trades for different construction projects.

Figure 1 shows the distribution of quantities (workloads) for the different trades across the 11 construction projects. For ease of comparison, we have normalized the quantities for each trade to be within 0 and 1. It can be seen from the figure that not all projects make use of all trades, and that workloads vary widely across trades and projects, highlighting the diversity of projects. For instance, project P283 involves all trades with each having large workloads. This was a large residential construction project focused on creating a green community area. On the other hand, project P282 and P284 were small projects focused on the construction of a transportation command & control centre, and a school, respectively.

Figure 2 shows the cumulative profit (left plot), duration (middle plot) and quality (right plot) achieved by the various construction projects. It is difficult to make up trends across the three metrics indicating their conflicting nature. The short durations of projects P277, P282 and P284 are due to the lower workloads required by these projects (see Fig. 1 for the workload distribution). If projects have long project durations but low quantities, such as A113 and P278, then this may indicate that there is scope for improvement via a better allocation of labour. With regards to profit generated, there is a spread in the percentage of profits generated, illustrating that there are possible inconsistencies in execution methods of the trades. In terms of quality, there is less fluctuation across the projects. However, the average cumulative quality delivered in all projects is 53.6%, further implying scope to improve the quality achieved by the various trades.

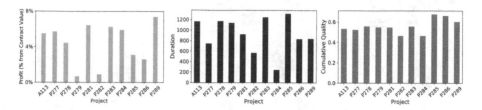

Fig. 2. Project profit (left), duration (centre) and quality (right) achieved by the workforce for the different construction projects.

4 Methodology

To tackle our MORAP, we will employ NSGA-II [9], a popular MOEA that will allow us to discover a set of trade-off solutions in one run. Our NSGA-II optimizes three objectives (project cost, duration and quality) by tuning the number of labour to be employed at each of the three skill levels (grades A, B and C) for each of the trades needed by a project. We use binary tournament selection for parental selection, and uniform crossover (crossover probability of 70%) and polynomial mutation for generating new solutions. The mutation probability is 1/#decision variables; the maximum number of decision variables for a project is #skill levels × #trades, which is 21 if all 7 trades are being used (since we have 3 skill levels) but not all projects use all trades.

We compare the performance of NSGA-II against random search and the actual workforce allocation used to deliver a project. Any results of NSGA-II shown are obtained using a population size of 40 and 30 generations (these values were determined by preliminary experimentation), and 30 independent runs. We will be investigating the algorithmic performance visually and also numerically using the hypervolume indicator [4]. The reference point to compute the hypervolume was obtained by first normalizing

Important to note is that although the workforce allocation is done separately for each project, there is a shared workforce pool and all concurrent projects draw from that pool. The more projects are done concurrently, the smaller the per-project workforce, which in turn defines the total workforce available for each grade and trade (or $R_{Ai}, R_{Bi}, \ldots, R_{Mi}$). In this study each concurrent project is allocated a workforce that is proportionate in size to its contract value.

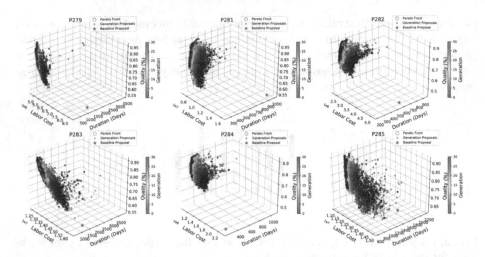

Fig. 3. Trace plots across 30 independent NSGA-II runs, each involving 30 generations and a population size of 40, for 6 selected construction projects. Each plot shows also the overall best trade-off solutions, i.e. the approximated Pareto front, and the baseline solution, which was the actual configuration used in the projects.

5   Results

Our experimental study covers an investigation of the algorithm convergence, followed by an analysis of the impact of the workforce size on algorithm performance, and a discussion of practical implications. In this section we show results for 6 diverse projects selected from the pool of 11 construction projects. Limiting the analysis to a subset of projects allows us to present a more in depth analysis on these projects rather than giving a high level analysis across all of the 11 projects. Results of the remaining projects are available upon request.

5.1   Algorithm Convergence

Figure 3 illustrates the convergence of NSGA-II in the objective space for 6 out of the 11 projects. The performance of NSGA-II is also compared against the performance of the actual workforce configuration used in the project; this configuration (referred to also as baseline here) was derived by an experienced engineer. It can be observed that the baseline solution is very far from the Pareto front discovered by NSGA-II for all objectives but in particular the cost and quality objective. This indicates that there is significant scope for improvement, which is good news. The baseline is not doing as badly (though worse than NSGA-II) in terms of the project duration, which may indicate that getting projects done quickly was important for these projects.

Taking a closer at the convergence behaviour, it is apparent that NSGA-II reaches the Pareto front within around 20 generations. Also, comparing projects

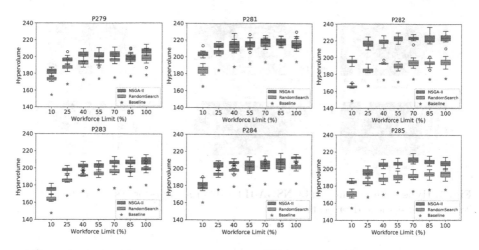

Fig. 4. Hypervolume achieved by NSGA-II, random search and the baseline method for different workforce sizes and 6 selected projects.

P285 and P283 with say P279 and P282 it is apparent that the initial population is closer to the Pareto front for P279 and P282 and the convergence trace is within a narrower band, indicating that some projects (small-scale projects and/or projects with fewer trades and thus decision variables) are easier to optimize than others.

5.2 Sensitivity Analysis for Varying Workforce Size and Productivity Rates

Figure 4 investigates the hypervolume achieved by NSGA-II and random search at the end of an optimization run for different workforce sizes. For reference, the hypervolume achieved by the baseline approach is included here too, but this hypervolume is computed based on one solution only so it cannot be compared against the performance of NSGA-II and random search. A workforce size of 100% implies that the entire workforce can be allocated to that project, whereas a workforce size of say 10% would simulate, for example, a scenario where ten projects all of the same economic value are run concurrently (thus each of the projects has access to 10% of the workforce only).

The pattern observable in the hypervolume plots is in alignment with what we have seen in the trace plots discussed earlier (Fig. 3). In general, an increase in the workforce improves performance. This is as expected because the optimization algorithms are given a larger search space to identify better trade-off solutions. However, there is a sweet-point beyond which a further increase in the workforce is of no benefit. This is because the improvements gained in the project duration are not able to compensate the losses in costs, with quality improvements being minimal with increasing workforce size as they are bounded to 100%. The sweet-point is around 40% for many projects but seems to shift

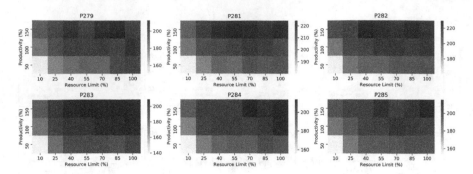

Fig. 5. Hypervolume achieved by NSGA-II for different workforce sizes and productivity rates for 6 selected projects.

to larger workforce sizes (around 70%) for more complex projects, such as P285. The performance difference between NSGA-II and random search is significant, especially for projects P282 and the more complex project P285. This result may imply that NSGA-II needs a smaller workforce size than random search to identify a set of workforce allocations (solutions) of equal quality.

Both NSGA-II and random search outperform the baseline but, remember, that the baseline represents a single solution only so the hyervolume values are not directly comparable.

Figure 5 investigates the impact of varying the workforce size and productivity rates of each of the skill levels by ±50%. The results associated with a productivity level of 100% are identical to the results shown in Fig. 4. A pattern is apparent indicating that the hypervolume and thus performance improves as the workforce size and/or the productivity rate increases. This is not surprising in itself. However, being able to quantify this improvement means that an organisation can now use the insights to decide, for example, how best to invest into upskilling the workforce, and who to upskill to achieve a certain quality target.

5.3   Tangible Benefits

Finally, we want to analyze the gains for selected solutions (workforce allocations) identified by NSGA-II compared to the baseline solution. This is important because ultimately we would be selecting only one solution from the Pareto front to be implemented in reality. We select the three extreme solutions representing the best solution discovered in terms of cost, duration and quality. Figure 6 illustrates the improvements of the extreme solutions relative to the baseline reference shown in Fig. 2. It is obvious that the extreme solutions provide an improvement to the baseline approach for all projects. In terms of generated profit, the optimized solutions have lower costs associated with them, yielding a higher value for project profit. In terms of project duration and cumulative quality, a substantial improvement is shown too. For almost all projects, time has been reduced to more than 50%, and the average cumulative quality has been increased to 90%. Note that in project P284, the baseline duration is slightly better than the optimized duration indicating that the algorithm was not able to find better solutions than the baseline solution.

6 Related Work

6.1 Resource Allocation Problem

In construction project management, resources include individuals, material, equipment and capital, of which individuals are often the most important as they are the highest determinant of several Key Performance Indicators (KPIs) of an activity [28]. Our study is a classical example of a multi-objective resource allocation problem (MORAP) [22] where resources are allocated to various activities to optimize several objectives, namely time, cost and quality in our case. This can be modelled as an extension to a generalized assignment problem (GAP) [20], where a construction project activity is a task and the resources allocated to perform the activity are the agents assigned to the task with the objective of performing the task with the least cost, thereby maximizing profit. Similarly, the flexible job shop scheduling problem (JSP) [7] is very similar to our research, where the jobs assigned to a machine to minimize the make span of the jobs are represented by the resources allocated to the activities within a project to minimize their execution duration. Also, our research can be considered as a multi-objective multiple knapsack problem (MMKP) [25], where labor of different skills are the items (to be packed), and the constructions projects the multiple knapsacks.

Resource allocation optimization has found extensive application in areas such as finance, product allocation, and time allocation [6,27]. In terms of workload allocation, studies have been carried out, for example, in the legal sector [5], where legal staff was assigned to legal cases with the objective of reducing tardiness. In fact, the presence of different skill-levels is something that has been considered in [5] too, but in a different context as we do here.

6.2 Workforce Allocation in Construction Projects

Workforce and resource allocation has also been considered within the construction sector. For example, in [1,11,26,29], resources to be allocated to an activity serve as the decision variables, and the combination of resources are referred to as construction methods. For example, in [11,29] each activity may be executed by different methods to optimize the time, cost and quality of an activity, and consequently the overall project. For each method proposed, a value for time, cost and quality is derived. Similarly, in [1] each activity may be executed by different resource options, each yielding a value for an activity's time, cost and quality. The composition of a method according to [11] is the combination of material alongside labor crews allocated to perform the activity. Although these studies point out that different methods yield different values for the objectives

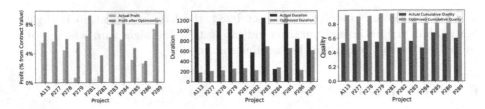

Fig. 6. Improvements in profit, duration and quality of extreme solutions selected from the Pareto front relative to the baseline solution.

outlined, they do not explain in detail the calculation behind how the value of a certain objective is obtained based on a particular method. Hence, one is unable to identify whether a reduction in the duration of an activity, for instance, is due to the use of a labor crew having a higher productivity rate, or whether different skill levels or trades exist within a labor crew. In [14], the workforce allocation in the construction sector was tackled by optimizing the allocation of partially skilled workforce. Although this model incorporated a detailed analysis of the choice of decision variables, which included allocating a pool of workers with predefined skill levels, it did not involve calculating the impact of this on the overall project in terms of cost, duration or quality. Furthermore, according to the literature, most studies involve optimizing a single project of which project particulars are often unknown, including activity quantities, contract values, project background and purpose. Hence, one is unable to distinguish between the performance of the optimization algorithm used for projects that differ considerably in scale, value, activity diversity and execution strategies.

6.3 Multi-objective Optimization in Construction Project Management

In construction project management, several resources are utilized to deliver a project serving the needs of many users including residencies, hotels, schools, healthcare facilities, road and transport facilities etc. Each project is typically made up of several tasks, each generally referred to as an *activity* [28], that is executed by a set of resources. In a limited resource environment, among the difficulties concerned with construction projects are time constraints, budget limitations, safety matters, level of quality etc. which therefore serve as the goals of a project that are often conflicting.

The literature incorporates a variety of trade-off problems in the construction sector including time-cost-resource trade-off and time-cost-environmental impact trade-off. In time-cost-resource trade-off problems, the allocation of resources is a vital determinant of a project's duration and cost, because often expenditure include material and equipment costs and labor wages [24]. One of the earliest attempts to carry out multi-objective optimization in the construction sector was proposed in [16]; here, a genetic algorithm based model was used to solve a two-phase time-cost trade-off problem by allocation in the first phase and levelling in the second phase. The limitation of this model was its inability to simultaneously incorporate the two objectives. To overcome this, an NSGA-II based model was proposed to optimize the two objectives simultaneously, which was later extended to account for resource constraints and activity pre-emption [13,18]. In time-cost-environmental trade-off problems, the environmental impact is considered together with time and cost. This included pollution levels [19] and later greenhouse gas levels [10]. Nonetheless, the incorporation of resource allocation was not proposed by these models.

Of particular relevance to our work is research considering the objectives, project time, cost and quality in construction projects. According to [2,21,28], among the goals that emphasize a project's efficiency and value, and those highly demanded by experts in the field are cost, time and quality, yet this combination has been rarely studied in detail in the literature. These objectives (with the addition of an environmental objective) were considered in [30], however, using a weighted sum approach. The three objectives, cost, time and quality, were considered in [1,11,26,29], and the resulting problems were solved using swarm intelligence methods, such as ant colony and particle swarm optimization. In [29], the time-cost-quality metrics were estimated for each activity based on various options of construction methods upon investigation of past similar projects, after which the total time-cost-quality metrics of the project is obtained based on the weight of each activity by calculating a weighted sum for each objective. Nonetheless it is not clear what the weight of the activity represents—one is unable to identify whether the weight of an activity is determined based on the activity's contract value, its relative quantity or importance score, for instance. The calculation of the quality objective presented in [11] involves a deeper more accurate representation. Here, the quality of an activity is based on the weight of quality indicators derived from performance-based models that reflect the long term performance of the end product of an activity, including compressive strength, flexural strength, and ride quality. Although the quality indicators in this study accurately takes into account the performance of the end product, they do not consider workmanship related quality indicators such as alignment, finishing or aesthetics, for example. In this study, an activity's cost and time are calculated based on the cost and productivity rates of an activity, however a construction method is referred to as a resource option labelled with a crew assigned to execute the activity, and hence one is unable to accurately identify what constitutes a crew. Finally, there is a lack in the construction community of publicly available data than can be used to benchmark different optimization algorithms, and it is also not clear what solution was implemented in reality. Our research aims to advance this area to allow other researchers to benchmark their algorithms.

7   Conclusions and Future Research

This paper has considered a real multi-objective workforce allocation problem encountered by a construction company. Given multiple trades and skill-levels of workers, the problem considered was to decide how many workers from any particular skill-level to allocate to complete a trade's job such the overall project duration, cost and quality are optimized.

We have formulated this problem formally as a constrained multi-objective resource allocation problem, and then used NSGA-II to solve the problem. Data from several real construction projects was used to validate the performance of NSGA-II and a random search algorithm. The performance of the two algorithms was also compared with the actual workload allocation (baseline) used in the projects.

Our experimental study showed that the projects considered are diverse in complexity, and affect search performance in different ways. NSGA-II outperformed random search and the baseline approach significantly in terms of final solution quality. We have also shown that the performance of the three solution approaches increases with the workforce size and the productivity rate of the workforce. Finally, a more in-depth inspection of some of the solutions indicated significant improvements over the baseline solution in terms of profit, project duration and quality. These insights can be used to make better decisions about allocating human resources to construction projects but also inform other business areas of a construction company, such as the company's upskilling strategy.

As pointed out earlier, the problem considered here is a simplified version of the real problem. We formulated the problem as a linear problem. However, in reality, the problem is subject to uncertainties, there may be complex constraints governing the order of activities to be carried out, decisions may need to be made on the fly, and workers may not always be available to do the job they have been allocated to. Moreover, it would be interesting to extend the mathematical model to support investment decisions, such as how best to invest in upskilling of labour. Future research will look into expanding the problem formulation with these additional challenges, and then adapting the optimization algorithms to cope with them. Ensuring that the methodology finds its way into practice to actually drive real-time decision making in construction projects is crucial too.

Acknowledgement. The authors would like ASGC for supporting this study and providing real-world construction data available for the analysis.

References

1. Afshar, A., Kaveh, A., Shoghli, O.R.: Multi-objective optimization of time-cost-quality using multi-colony ant algorithm. Asian J. Civ. Eng. **8**, 113–124 (2007)
2. Alothaimeen, I., Arditi, D.: Overview of multi-objective optimization approaches in construction project management. In: Multi-criteria Optimization - Pareto-optimal and Related Principles. IntechOpen (2019)
3. Armand, P., Malivert, C.: Determination of the efficient set in multiobjective linear programming. J. Optim. Theory Appl. **70**(3), 467–489 (1991)
4. Auger, A., Bader, J., Brockhoff, D., Zitzler, E.: Hypervolume-based multi-objective optimization: theoretical foundations and practical implications. Theoret. Comput. Sci. **425**, 75–103 (2012)

5. Ayodele, M., Allmendinger, R., Papamichail, K.N.: Heuristic search in LegalTech: dynamic allocation of legal cases to legal staff. In: Nicosia, G., et al. (eds.) LOD 2020. LNCS, vol. 12566, pp. 326–338. Springer, Cham (2020). https://doi.org/10. 1007/978-3-030-64580-9_28
6. Chaharsooghi, S., Meimand Kermani, A.H.: An effective ant colony optimization algorithm for multi-objective resource allocation problem. Appl. Math. Comput. **200**(1), 642–656 (2008)
7. Davis, L.: Job shop scheduling with genetic algorithms. In: Proceedings of an International Conference on Genetic Algorithms and their Applications, vol. 140, pp. 136–140 (1985)
8. Deb, K.: Multi-objective Optimization Using Evolutionary Algorithms, vol. 16. Wiley, Hoboken (2001)
9. Deb, K., Pratap, A., Agarwal, S., Meyarivan, T.: A fast and elitist multi-objective genetic algorithm: NSGA-II. IEEE Trans. Evol. Comput. **6**(2), 182–197 (2002)
10. Deniz, G.O., Zhu, Y., Ceron, V.: Time, cost, and environmental impact analysis on construction operation optimization using genetic algorithms. J. Manag. Eng. **28**(3), 265–272 (2012)
11. El-Rayes, K., Kandil, A.: Time-cost-quality trade-off analysis for highway construction. J. Constr. Eng. Manag. **131**(4), 447–486 (2005)
12. Elbeltagi, E., Ammar, M., Sanad, H., Kassab, M.: Overall multi-objective optimization of construction projects scheduling using particle swarm. Eng. Constr. Archit. Manag. **23**(3), 265–282 (2016)
13. Ghoddousi, P., Eshtehardian, E., Jooybanpour, S.: Multi-mode resource-constrained discrete time-cost-resource optimization in project scheduling using non-dominated sorting genetic algorithm. Autom. Constr. **30**, 216–227 (2013)
14. Gomar, J.E., Haas, C.T., Morton, D.P.: Assignment and allocation optimization of partially multi-skilled workforce. J. Constr. Eng. Manag. **128**(2), 103–109 (2002)
15. Kwan, D.W., Lo, E.S., Schober, R.: Multi-objective resource allocation for secure communication in cognitive radio networks with wireless information and power transfer. IEEE Trans. Veh. Technol. **65**(5), 3166–3184 (2015)
16. Leu, S.S., Yang, C.H.: GA-based multi-criteria optimal model for construction scheduling. J. Constr. Eng. Manag. **125**(6), 420–427 (1999)
17. Li, Q., Tao, S., Chong, H.Y., Dong, Z.S.: Robust optimization for integrated construction scheduling and multiscale resource allocation. Complexity **2018**, 1–17 (2018)
18. Ma, W., Che, Y., Ke, H.: Preemptive multi-mode resource-constrained discrete time-cost-resource optimization via non-dominated sorting genetic algorithm. In: Qi, E. (ed.) Proceedings of the 6th International Asia Conference on Industrial Engineering and Management Innovation, pp. 719–728. Atlantis Press, Paris (2016). https://doi.org/10.2991/978-94-6239-145-1_68
19. Marzouk, M., Madany, M., Abou-Zied, A., El-said, M.: Handling construction pollution using multi-objective optimization. Constr. Manag. Econ. **26**(10), 1113–1125 (2008)
20. Nauss, R.M.: Solving the generalized assignment problem: an optimizing and heuristic approach. INFORMS J. Comput. **15**(3), 249–266 (2003)
21. Oke, A.E., Aghimien, D.O.: Drivers of value management in the Nigerian construction industry. J. Eng. Des. Technol. **16**, 270–284 (2020)
22. Osman, M., Abo-Sinna, M., Mousa, A.: An effective genetic algorithm approach to multi-objective resource allocation problems. Appl. Math. Comput. **136**(2), 755–768 (2005)

23. Panwar, A., Jha, K.: A many-objective optimization model for construction scheduling. Constr. Manag. Econ. **37**(12), 727–739 (2019)
24. Senouci, A.B., Eldin, N.N.: Use of genetic algorithms in resource scheduling of construction projects. J. Constr. Eng. Manag. **130**(6), 869–877 (2004)
25. Soylu, B., Köksalan, M.: An evolutionary algorithm for the multi-objective multiple knapsack problem. In: Shi, Y., Wang, S., Peng, Y., Li, J., Zeng, Y. (eds.) MCDM 2009. CCIS, vol. 35, pp. 1–8. Springer, Heidelberg (2009). https://doi.org/10.1007/978-3-642-02298-2_1
26. Tareghian, H.R., Taheri, S.H.: On the discrete time, cost and quality trade-off problem. Appl. Math. Comput. **181**(2), 1305–1312 (2006)
27. Tofan, S., Allmendinger, R., Zanda, M., Stephens, O.: Heuristic allocation of computational resources. In: Proceedings of the Genetic and Evolutionary Computation Conference, pp. 1256–1263 (2017)
28. Walker, A.: Project Management in Construction. Wiley, Hoboken (2015)
29. Zhang, H., Xing, F.: Fuzzy multi-objective particle swarm optimization for time-cost-quality trade-off in construction. Autom. Constr. **19**(8), 1067–1075 (2010)
30. Zheng, H.: The bi-level optimization research for time-cost-quality-environment trade-off scheduling problem and its application to a construction project. In: Xu, J., Hajiyev, A., Nickel, S., Gen, M. (eds.) Proceedings of the Tenth International Conference on Management Science and Engineering Management. AISC, vol. 502, pp. 745–753. Springer, Singapore (2017). https://doi.org/10.1007/978-981-10-1837-4_62

Generating Duplex Routes for Robust Bus Transport Network by Improved Multi-objective Evolutionary Algorithm Based on Decomposition

Sho Kajihara[✉], Hiroyuki Sato, and Keiki Takadama

The University of Electro-Communications, Chofu Tokyo, Japan
kaji_sho@cas.lab.uec.ac.jp, h.sato@uec.ac.jp, keiki@inf.uec.ac.jp

Abstract. This paper proposes the duplex route generation method to evolve the bus route network which is robust to environmental changes and aims at investigating its effectiveness through the experiments. In this study, the "duplex route" corresponds to the alternative route and it has the advantage of not requiring to modify the route network in the environmental changes. To generate the duplex routes, this study employs MOEA/D as the base optimization method and introduces the following two operations in MOEA/D to increase the duplex routes while improving the fitness: (1) the crossover operation to generate the duplex routes, which is improved from the crossover operation in SEAMO2 [9] that evolves unique routes, and (2) the priority solution update operation in the enhanced MOEA/D [4] to maintain a diversity of the routes which contributes to improving the fitness. The experiments on Mandl's benchmark problem has revealed: (1) the proposed crossover operation can generate many duplex networks as compared to the original crossover operation; (2) the priority solution update operation improves the fitness, i.e., a minimization of the passenger transportation time and the number of buses; and (3) integration of the two operations improves both the number of duplex routes and fitness, which is hard to be achieved by either operation.

Keywords: Route network optimization · Robust transport network · Evolutionary computation · Duplex route · MOEA/D

1 Introduction

The mass transportation system plays a major role in our society. Among many kinds of transportation systems, the bus is highly demanded in a disaster situation as shown in the Great East Japan Earthquake [8], in comparison with the railway because the railway did not work in such a situation. However, various environmental changes such as the collapse of bus stops and road destruction occur during a disaster, which makes it difficult for the ordinary bus route network to be kept to cope with such changes. For this issue, Majima proposed

© Springer Nature Switzerland AG 2021
P. A. Castillo and J. L. Jiménez Laredo (Eds.): EvoApplications 2021, LNCS 12694, pp. 65–80, 2021.
https://doi.org/10.1007/978-3-030-72699-7_5

the route network optimization method that can change the routes according to environmental changes [6]. In detail, each route includes or excludes the bus stops selfishly according to the number of passengers which changes according to environmental changes. As the different approach, Kitagawa built the *"robust"* route network that can minimize to suffer from a change in road conditions (*i.e.*, minimize the route modification) [5]. Concretely, this method creates the clusters of the bus stops and evolves the route in each cluster in order not to generate the long-distance route because such route is affected in a high probability by a change of road conditions (*i.e.*, the probability of being affected in the long-distance route is larger than that in the short-distance). Although these methods can cope with environmental changes, they require route modification depending on the disaster situation, which confuses the passengers.

To tackle this problem, this paper proposes the concept of the "duplex route" and introduces it to generate the robust bus route network that has the potential of coping with environmental changes *without modifying* the route network. In this study, "duplex route" corresponds to the alternative route including the transfer bus stops that belong to two or more routes, does not simply mean the duplicated routes (*i.e.*, the same two or more routes). To understand the duplex route, let us show Fig. 1, where the four lines (*i.e.*, the red, blue, green, and orange lines) indicate the four routes and the number indicates the bus stop number. When the road from the bus stop 2 to 5 is damaged which affects the blue route, for example, the green route including the bus stops 2, 4, and 5 can transport passengers from 2 to 5 instead of the blue route. When the bus stop 9 is a half-destroyed (which means that the number of buses that can stop at the bus stop 9 should be half or less), as another example, the green route can be deleted because passengers can go to any destination with the other three routes. Here, the blue route from the bus stop 2 to 5 and the green route are regarded as the duplex routes.

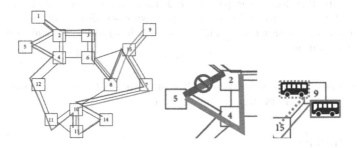

Fig. 1. The merit of duplex route.

To generate the duplex routes, this study employs MOEA/D (Multi-objective Evolutionary Algorithm based on Decomposition) as the base optimization method and introduces the following two operations in MOEA/D to increase the duplex routes while improving the fitness (*i.e.*, a minimization of the passenger transportation time and the number of buses in this paper): (1) the crossover operation to generate the duplex routes, which is improved from the crossover operation in SEAMO2 [9] that evolves the unique routes, and (2) the priority solution update operation in the enhanced MOEA/D [4] to maintain a diversity of the routes which contributes to improving the fitness. The two types of operations are integrated into the proposed method because the only operation (1) is not enough and an increase of the duplex route generally decreases the fitness (e.g., an increase of the buses), which means that the other method, the operation (2), is needed to improve the fitness.

The remainder of this paper is organized as follows. Section 2 describes the basic framework of generating a route network. Section 3 proposes the duplex route network generation method. Section 4 conducts the computational experiments to validate the proposed method, and Sect. 5 analyzes the generated route network. Finally, the conclusion is given in Sect. 6.

2   Basic Framework of Generating Route Network

2.1   Problem Formulation

The transit route network design problem (TRNDP) is a research area to build an efficient route network that minimizes the user cost (e.g., the passenger travel time) and the operator cost (e.g., the route length, the number of buses) under the given conditions of the passenger demand and infrastructure network. TRNDP is a combinatorial optimization problem characterized by NP-hard, which needs a meta-heuristics to find near-optimal solutions. In TRNDP, many researchers employed evolutionary algorithms to optimize the route network. Mumford proposed an initial solution generation method, crossover, repair, and mutation for TRNDP [9]. They also proposed a new benchmark problem since there is only one benchmark problem and it is difficult to compare studies. Buba proposed a route network optimization method using DE [2]. They employed the method proposed by Mumford for initial solution generation, and proposed mutation and crossover for DE so that DE can be applied to TRNDP. They also incorporated a mechanism to repair infeasible solutions on the DE framework. Their experiment using Mandl's benchmark problem shows that when the maximum number of nodes is set in the range of 8–11, the quality of transportation service (percentage of zero transfers) of the resulting route network is high, while the quality is not high when the number of nodes is 12 or more. Thus, it shows that increasing the length of the route is not sufficient to improve the quality of the route network.

TRNDP needs the following data as the inputs to generate the route network: the location of bus stops, the road network that suitable for a bus trip, the demand matrix from origin to destination, and the travel time matrix. The solution of TRNDP is composed of the pair (R, F) where R is a set of the routes and F is a set of frequency in the routes. The passengers are distributed in the routes of R and determine their routes according to the passenger assignment model (e.g., shortest-path assignment model, frequency share-rule [1]). After the passenger assignment, the user and operator costs are evaluated. This paper evaluates the passenger travel time as the user cost and the number of buses as the operator cost.

2.2 Generate Route Network

Majima's method [6] is employed to generate the route network that is improved towards the duplex route network by the method proposed in this paper. This method generates the route network to minimize not only the passenger's travel time but also the number of buses. The algorithm of this method is outlined as follows, each of which is described in detail later.

Step 1: Multiple initial route network generation
Step 2: Route network generation by merging multiple route networks
Step 3: Assign passengers to routes
Step 4: Route modification by bus stop inclusion/exclusion

Step 1 Multiple Initial Route Network Generation: Figure 2 shows how the initial multiple routes are generated under the condition that the destination of all bus stops is set 0. Considering the connection from bus stop 3, the three types of the routes can be generated: (i) Route 0 connecting the bus stop 0 from 3; (ii) Route 1 connecting the bus stop 1 from 3; and (iii) route 2 connecting the bus stop 2 from 3. For routes 1 and 2 which does not directly connect the bus stop 0, the following two types of connection are conducted: (a) the additional type as shown in Fig. 2 left and (b) the absorption type as shown in Fig. 2 right. To determine which route should be selected from the five ones (*i.e.*, the route 0, the route 1 based on the connection type (a) and (b), the route 2 based on the connection type (a) and (b)), Eq. (1) is calculated as the fitness to select the route with the smallest value, where Z is the fitness value; $T_{i,j}$ is the required total time between bus stops i and j; $D_{i,j}$ is the demand from bus stops i to j; w_1 is the weight coefficients; B_k is the number of buses on route k. Note that the weight w_1 in Eq. (1) determines the balance between the user and operator costs. The smaller/larger weight w_1, the less user/operator cost, which means that the generated route network changes according to the weight w_1.

$$\min Z = \sum_{i \neq j} T_{i,j} D_{i,j} + w_1 \sum_k B_k = f_1 + w_1 f_2 \qquad (1)$$

The total passenger travel time is calculated by the following equation, where t_v is the passenger in-vehicle time, t_w is the passenger waiting time, and t_p is the passenger penalty time (transfer time).

$$T = t_v + t_w + t_p \qquad (2)$$

The number of buses in the route k in the addition and absorption types are respectively calculated by Eqs. (3) and (4) where t_{r_k} is the round trip time in the route k; D_{i_k} is the demand from bus stop i to all bus stop on route k; C is the capacity; B_l is the number of buses in the route l before being absorbed; and t_{r_l} is the round trip time in the route l before being absorbed. In particular, the item1 of Eqs. (3) and (4) indicates the number of buses which can meet the demand from bus stop i to all bus stops in the route k, and the item2 of Eq. (4) indicates the required number of bus stops to maintain the arrival interval in the route l before being absorbed. Equation (4) has a role in shortening or maintaining the arrival frequency.

$$B_k = \lceil t_{r_k} D_{i_k}/C \rceil \qquad (3)$$

$$B_k = \lceil t_{r_k} D_{i_k}/C + B_l t_{r_k}/t_{r_l} \rceil \qquad (4)$$

Following to the above procedure, one route network where the destination of all bus stops is 0 is generated. By changing the destination from 0 to others, the BS number of the route networks are generated when the number of bus stops is BS.

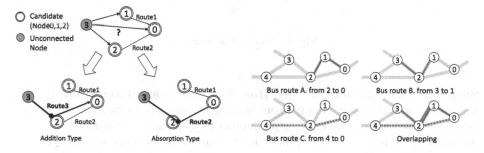

Fig. 2. Connect nodes to create a route   Fig. 3. Overlapping the route

Step 2 Route Network Generation by Merging Multiple Route Networks: The multiple routes generated in step1 are merged to generate the route network as shown in Fig. 3. Considering the three simple routes A, B, and C (*i.e.*, route A composed of the bus stops 0, 1, and 2, the route B composed of the bus stops 1, 2, and 3, the route C composed of the bus stops 0, 2, and 4) instead of the route networks for easy understanding, the route network is generated by merging the routes A, B, and C with allowing the overlapped section(s) in the route.

Step 3 Passengers' Route Selection: The passengers select the shortest path from candidate routes. The shortest path is determined by calculating t_v, t_w, and t_p. To analysis these times, the route network consists of the road links, the boarding link, and the alighting link as shown in Fig. 4. For example, when the bus stop 1 belongs to the route A and B, the bus stop a1 and b1 is virtually generated. The road link has an in-vehicle time t_v, the boarding link has a waiting time t_w and the alighting link has no time (*i.e.*, it is 0 min). When the passenger transfers any routes, the transfer time t_p is calculated as 5 min per transfer. By introducing the transfer time, the passengers can select the path with few transfers in the case of multiple paths with equal passenger travel time. The Dijkstra algorithm is employed to calculate the shortest path according to the cost (time) of all links. After the passenger routes are determined, the unused routes are deleted.

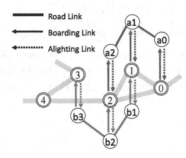

Fig. 4. Analysis network.

Step 4 Route Modification by Bus Stop Inclusion/Exclusion: In the route network, all routes modify their own routes selfishly to increase the profit calculated by Eq. (5), where R_k^n is the number of passengers in the route k at the iteration n, B_k^n is the number of buses in the route k at the iteration n, w_2 is the weight coefficients between the user and operator costs. The w_2 determines the balance between the number of passengers and buses. In particular, the item1 of Eq. (5) corresponds to the user cost and item2 corresponds to the operator cost. The smaller/larger w_2, the longer/shorter route length to "increase the number of passengers"/"decrease the number of buses". B_k^n is calculated by the following equations, where $d_{i,j}^n$ is the number of the passengers from i to j at the iteration n. Note that the variables i and j represent not only the bus stop but also the link. If i is bus stops and j is a route, for example, $d_{i,j}$ represents the number of passengers who board on a bus at the i-th bus stops in the j-th route.

$$P_k = R_k^n - w_2 B_k^n \tag{5}$$

$$B_k^n = \lfloor \max(B_{min}^n, B_{opt}^n, 1) \rfloor \tag{6}$$

$$B_{min}^n = \max_{i,j \in k}(d_{i,j}^n) t_{r_k}^n / C \tag{7}$$

$$B_{opt}^n = \sqrt{t_{r_k}^n R_k^n / 2\omega_1} \tag{8}$$

Equation (7) indicates the minimum number of buses to meet the passenger demand, where $\max_{i,j \in k}(d_{i,j}^n)$ is the maximum number of passengers between adjacent bus stops. The number of buses calculated by Eq. (8) minimizes fitness value Z (Eq. (1)) when only route k is considered [3]. Equation (8) is derived as follows. Considering the only route k, the total passenger travel time T can exclude the in-vehicle time t_v and the transfer time t_p because the in-vehicle time t_v does not depend on the number of buses and the passenger cannot transfer in only one route k. This enables us to consider the waiting time t_w in the total passenger travel time T. The t_w is $t_r/2B$ because the half of the bus operation interval t_r/B is the expected value of the waiting time. From these procedures, Eq. (1) is rewritten as $Z = t_{r_k}R_k/2B + w_1B$. To minimize Z, the following equation should be solved.

$$\frac{dZ}{dB} = 0 \iff B = \sqrt{t_{r_k}R_k/2\omega_1} \tag{9}$$

This is Eq. (8). To increase the profit calculation, the route is modified by the following two types: (i) Inclusion of bus stops (*i.e.*, Include one bus stop that belongs to other routes); and (ii) Exclusion of bus stops (*i.e.*, Exclude one bus stop that belongs to the own route). These inclusion and exclusion operations are applied to all possible bus stops, and the modified route with the highest profit's increase is selected to replace the original route with it. After that, it returns to the passenger's route selection (step3) and repeats this cycle as long as the profit increases. If the profit decreases, a new route is selected to be modified. This cycle is terminated when all routes cannot increase their profits.

3 Duplex Route Network Generation Method

3.1 Architecture: MOEA/D with Crossover in SEAMO2 and Priority Solution Update in Enhanced MOEA/D

The duplex route network generation method is designed by integrating Multi-objective Evolutionary Algorithm based on Decomposition (MOEA/D) [10] with the following two operations as shown in Fig. 5: (1) the crossover operation to generate the duplex routes, which is improved from the crossover operation in SEAMO2 [9] and (2) the priority solution update operation in the enhanced MOEA/D [4]. The reasons why we employ MOEA/D and the mechanisms of SEAMO2 and the enhanced MOEA/D are summarized as follows: (i) MOEA/D evolves the solutions from the neighborhood solutions, which is very important from the viewpoint of the route network generation, because the neighborhood solutions (which have the similar network topologies) have a high probability of inheriting the duplex route(s) in the parent(s) by keeping the similar network topologies, while the far solutions are hard to inherit it/them by varying the network topologies; (ii) the crossover operation in SEAMO2 evolves the unique routes to prevent from evolving the routes that have the same section between them (note that the same section in the routes is not the "duplex" route but the "duplicated" route which cannot be alternative route); and (iii) the priority solution update operation with $n_r = 1$ (see Sect. 3.4) contributes to maintaining the diversity of the routes (which needs to improve the fitness). For the above reasons, the duplex routes have the potential of being evolved by the mechanism in SEAMO2 and can be kept by MOEA/D, while the fitness can be improved by the mechanism in the enhanced MOEA/D. However, SEAMO2 does not have the explicit mechanism of evolving the duplex routes (i.e., the duplex routes are accidentally evolved but not intentionally evolved) and the priority solution update operation does not consider the duplex routes, both of which should be improved to increase the duplex routes.

3.2   Base Optimization Method in the Proposed Method

MOEA/D: MOEA/D is the evolutionary algorithm for multi-objective optimization. MOEA/D distributes the weight vectors in search space to divide the multi-objective optimization problem into the single-objective optimization problems and promotes the solutions to search the direction of their weight vectors. The optimal solutions of these problems approximate the Pareto front of the multi-objective optimization problem. The left side of Fig. 5 shows the flow of the algorithm.

In the initialization phase, (1–1) the N number of the weight vectors $\lambda^1, \ldots, \lambda^N$ which determine the search direction of the solutions are generated; (1–2) the T number of the weight vectors which are near from λ^i is determined as the neighborhood vectors of λ^i by computing all combinations of Euclidean distances between weight vectors. Note that λ^i itself is included in its neighborhood vectors of λ^i; (1–3) an initial population is generated; and (1–4) the reference point z^* is calculated by Eqs. (10) and (11), where $f_j(x)$ is the value of the j-th objective function of the solution x and X is the feasible area in the decision variable space.

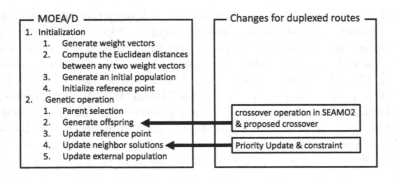

Fig. 5. Changes from original MOEA/D for duplex route network

$$z^* = (z_1^*, \ldots, z_k^*) \tag{10}$$

$$z_j^* = \max\{f_j(x) | x \in X\} \tag{11}$$

In the genetic operation phase executed after the initialization phase, (2–1) the two weight vectors are randomly selected from the neighborhood vectors of

λ^i, and two solutions that are near from the selected weight vectors are selected as the parents; (2–2) the parents generate the offspring through the crossover, mutation, or local search; (2–3) the offspring are evaluated and the reference point z^* is updated; (2–4) the offspring is compared with the solutions of the neighborhood vectors, and the solution is replaced by the offspring if the offspring is superior to the solution from the viewpoint of the scalar fitness value. This study employs the Tchebycheff scalar fitness function computed by Eq. (12). (2–5) the offspring is added to the external population if it is non-dominated solutions, and the solution in the external population is deleted if it is dominated by the offspring.

$$g^{te}(x|\lambda^j, z^*) = \max_{1 \le i \le k} \{\lambda_i |f_i(x) - z_i^*|\} \tag{12}$$

Finally, MOEA/D provides the external populations as the output of the solutions when the stopping criterion is satisfied.

3.3 Crossover Operation for Duplex Route

Crossover Operation in SEAMO2: To generate the unique routes as many as possible, the crossover operation in SEAMO2 [9] selects the routes that have not yet selected as the children routes. Figure 6(a) shows the brief algorithm, which is summarized as follows: (1) after selecting the two route sets as Parents 1 and 2 in the parent selection, one route is selected randomly from Parent 1 and is added to the route pool (i.e., the route 3 in this figure); (2) the route of Parent 2 that at least one bus stop is a common with the bus stops in the route pool is selected to ensure a connection between the selected route and the route in the route pool (i.e., such a connection needs to transfer at the bus stops). If more than one route can be selected from Parent 2, the route with the highest different ratio between the routes in the route pool and the route of Parent 2 (described below) is selected (i.e., the route D in this figure); (3) return to (2) with the other parent (i.e., the route of Parent 1 is selected as the same manner of (2)) until the number of the routes in the route pool becomes the same number of the routes in the parent.

Regarding the different ratio, let give the example. If the bus stops in the route pool are [1, 2, 4, 6, 8] and those in the route D selected from the parent are [1, 2, 3, 6, 8, 10, 13], then the different ratio between the route pool and the route D is approximately 0.43 ≈ 3 (i.e., the number of the bus stops that are only included in the route D: 3, 10, 13)/7 (i.e., the number of the bus stops in the route D). The selection of the route with the highest different ratio contributes to generating the unique routes by reducing the duplicated/overlapped section in the routes.

Proposed Crossover Operation: To increase the number of the duplex routes, the proposed crossover operation changes step(2) in the crossover operation in SEAMO2 as shown in Fig. 6(b). Concretely, the proposed crossover operation adds the following mechanism at the end of step(2), i.e., the selection of

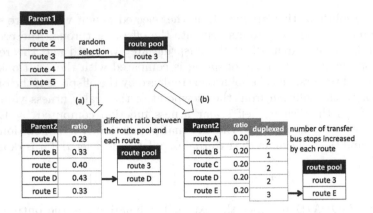

Fig. 6. (a) crossover operation in SEAMO2; (b) proposed crossover operation

the route that increases the number of the common bus stops when the different ratio of all routes selected from the parent is the same (note that the crossover operation in SEAMO2 randomly selects the route in such a case because of the same value of different ratio). For example, if the bus stops of the two routes in the route pool are [[1, 2, 4, 6, 8] (route 3), [1, 2, 3, 6, 8, 10, 13] (route D)] and those in the route E selected from the parent are [1, 2, 5, 4, 12, 11, 10, 13], then the number of the transfer bus stops increased by selecting the route E is 3 (*i.e.*, the new transfer bus stops when selecting the route E are 4, 10, 13 while the transfer bus stops in the route pool are 1, 2, 6, 8). This selection contributes to generating the new alternative routes from the route E to either route in the route pool (which becomes the duplexed routes).

3.4   Priority Solution Update for Diversity

Priority Solution Update Operation: Figure 7 respectively show the solution update operation in the original MOEA/D and the priority solution update operation in the enhanced MOEA/D [4]. The former operation might decrease the diversity of the solutions because the multiple solutions are replaced by one offspring if the offspring is better than the solutions in scalar fitness value as shown in Fig. 7(a), while the latter operation can keep the diversity of the solutions because only one solution is replaced by one offspring by setting the parameter $n_r = 1$, which determines the number of solution replacement (update) as shown in Fig. 7(b). The brief algorithm of the priority solution update is summarized as follows: (1) the solution is selected among the neighbor vectors in the order of the short distance to the target vector (*i.e.*, the solution of the target vector is firstly selected, the solution of the neighbor vectors (which is close to the target vector) is secondly selected, and the solutions are continued to be selected in the same manner) and it is replaced by the offspring if the solution is inferior to the offspring; and (2) return to (1) until the number of the solution replacement becomes n_r, which maximum number is the number of neighbors T.

In the case of $n_r = 1$ which employed in this paper, the offspring is not compared with any other neighbor after one solution is replaced by the offspring.

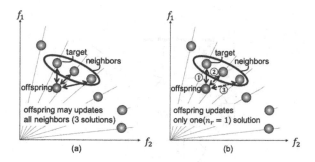

Fig. 7. (a) solution update in MOEA/D; (b) priority solution update in enhanced MOEA/D

Proposed Priority Solution Update Operation: To increase the number of the high duplex route network, this study adds the condition for the solution replacement (update). Concretely, the solution is replaced by the offspring if (i) the offspring is superior to it and (ii) the number of the transfer bus stops in the offspring is greater than or equal to the solution.

4 Experimental Results

4.1 Experimental Setting

To investigate the effectiveness of the proposed method, this paper compares it with the other methods as shown in Table 1, where DC, DU, and DCU means the MOEA/D with the proposed crossover operation, the proposed priority solution update operation, and both of them, respectively. Note that the initial solutions are generated by Majima's method described in Sect. 2.2 and they are evolved by DC, DU, or DCU. As the evaluation criteria, this study evaluates (i) TBS (the number of the transfer bus stops) of all route networks, (ii) the number of solution updates, and (iii) Hypervolume (HV) which measures the fitness of the non-dominated solutions. All experiments are conducted in Mandl's benchmark

Table 1. Tested methods

Name	Description
DC	MOEA/D + proposed crossover
DU	MOEA/D + proposed priority solution update
DCU	MOEA/D + proposed crossover and proposed priority solution update

problem [7] as TRNDP. Figure 8 and Table 2 show the infrastructure network and the OD (origin and demand of passengers) matrix, respectively. The experimental parameters are set as shown in Table 3. In Table 3, w_1 takes a value every 0.05

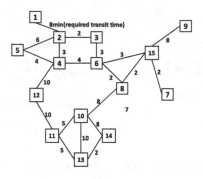

Fig. 8. Infrastructure network and travel time

Table 2. Origin and destination demand

ST	1	2	3	4	5	6	7	8	9	10	11	12	13	14	15
1	0	400	200	60	80	150	75	75	30	160	30	25	35	0	0
2	400	0	50	120	20	180	90	90	15	130	20	10	10	5	0
3	200	50	0	40	60	180	90	90	15	45	20	10	10	5	0
4	60	120	40	0	50	100	50	50	15	240	40	25	10	5	0
$\vdots$															
14	0	5	5	5	0	10	5	5	0	200	15	10	45	0	0
15	0	0	0	0	0	0	0	0	0	0	0	0	0	0	0

Table 3. Experimental parameters

TRNDP parameter	Value
Transfer penalty	5 min/transfer
Bus capacity	50 passengers
Maximum number of allowable transfers	2
w_1	$\{0.10 \leq w_1 \leq 0.90 | w_1 = 0.05j, j \in \mathbb{Z}\}$
w_2	5
MOEA/D parameter	Value
Population size	17
λ_i	$\{0.10 \leq \lambda_i \leq 0.90 | \lambda_i = 0.05j, j \in \mathbb{Z}\}$
T	[3, 4, 5, 6]
n_r	1
Generation	20
Run	15

in order not to generate the same or very similar solution by Majima's method and this coefficient becomes λ_1 of the weight vector.

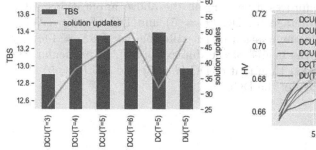

Fig. 9. Average of TBS and solution updates

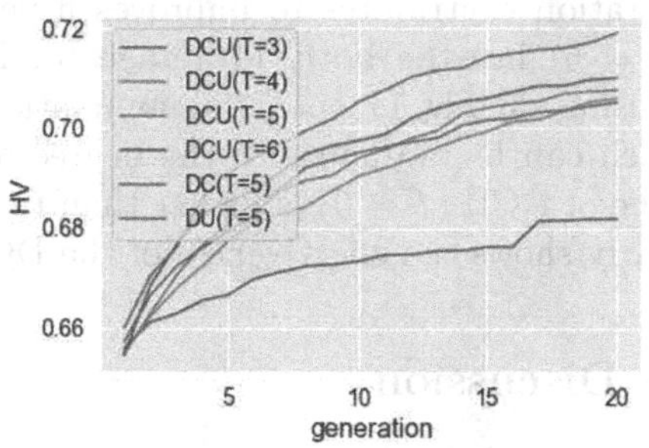

Fig. 10. Hypervolume of all tested methods

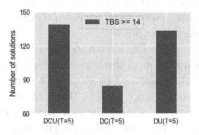

Fig. 11. Histogram of non-dominated solutions at $TBS = 14$ and 15

4.2 Results

Figure 9 shows the average of TBS and the number of solution updates, where the horizontal axis indicates the different methods with the different T while the vertical axis indicates their values. Figure 10 shows HV, where the horizontal axis indicates the generation while the vertical axis indicates HV. Figure 11 shows the histogram of TBS in the solutions (stored in the external population) of all run, where the horizontal axis indicates the summation of $TBS = 15$ and 14 which means the maximum number and maximum number -1 of the transfer bus stops and while the vertical axis indicates the number of solution.

Among DCU, Fig. 9 suggests that TBS of DCU ($T = 5$) is better than DCU with the other T, and thus we compare TBS among DCU ($T = 5$), DC ($T = 5$), and DU ($T = 5$). Figure 9 shows that (i) TBSs of DC ($T = 5$) and DCU ($T = 5$) are higher than that of DU ($T = 5$) and (ii) the number of updates of DU ($T = 5$) and DCU ($T = 5$) are higher than that of DC ($T = 5$). Related to (ii), HV in Fig. 10 shows the same tendency found in Fig. 9, meaning that HVs of DU ($T = 5$) and DCU ($T = 5$) are larger than that of DC ($T = 5$). These results suggest that the proposed crossover operation contributes to increase the number of transfer bus stops, while the proposed priority solution update operation contributes to improves fitness. From the above implications, DCU ($T = 5$) has the both advantages of DC ($T = 5$) and DU ($T = 5$). When focusing on Fig. 11 (*i.e.*, the summation of the solutions at $TBS = 14 and 15$ which can be evaluated as the degree of the duplex routes), in particular, the value of DCU ($T = 5$) is higher than that of DC ($T = 5$) and DU ($T = 5$). This clearly shows the effectiveness of the DCU.

5   Discussion

This section discusses the reason why DCU is better than DC and DU by analyzing the topology of the evolved route network with $T = 5$. Figures 12, 13, and 14 respectively show the route network of DC, DU, and DCU, each of which shows the pair of parents 1 and 2, and the evolved offspring through the crossover operation. In these figures, the colored lines indicate the routes, the orange/white nodes indicate the transfer/not-transfer bus stops, the number in the node indicates the bus stop number. Note that each solution (*i.e.*, the route network) belongs to one of the weight vectors λ^i.

The duplex route network in DC shown in Fig. 12 is good from the viewpoint of the duplex route network because the non-transfer bus stops (*i.e.*, 9, 14) in the parents 1 and 2 become the transfer bus stops in the offspring. This is because $\lambda^6(\lambda = 0.35)$ of the parents 1 and $\lambda^5(\lambda = 0.30)$ of the parent 2 is close (*i.e.*, the topology of two parents is similar), which enables the offspring to inherit the transfer bus stops of the parents while changing the transfer bus stops from the non-transfer ones through the mutation. However, this network is bad the viewpoint of fitness because a lot of buses are needed due to the fact of many overlapped routes (*e.g.*, the five routes in the section between the bus stop 6 and 8 are generated by inheriting the four routes of the parent 1 and the three routes of parent 2). Next, the duplex route network in DU shown in Fig. 13 is good from the viewpoint of fitness and bad from the viewpoint of the duplex route network because of the opposite reasons of DC. Concretely, many overlapped routes are reduced (*e.g.*, the five routes in the section between the bus stop 1 and 2 in the parent 2 become the four routes in the offspring), which decreases the number of buses (*i.e.*, an increase of the fitness), while the number of the transfer bus stops decreases by not inheriting the transfer bus stops 5, 12, 13 of the parents 1 or 2 (*i.e.*, a decrease of the duplex route network). In comparison with DC and DU, the duplex route network in DCU shown in Fig. 14 is good from both viewpoints of the duplex route network and fitness. This is because the number of the transfer bus stops increases (*e.g.*, all bus stops become the transfer bus stops) while decreases the number of the buses (*e.g.*, the three routes in the section between the bus stop 2 and 4 in the parent 1 become the two routes in the offspring) by the integration of DC and DU.

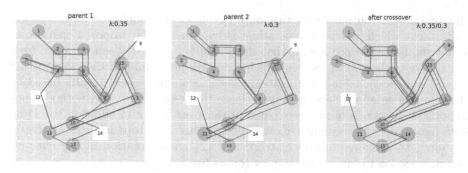

Fig. 12. Evolved route network by DC

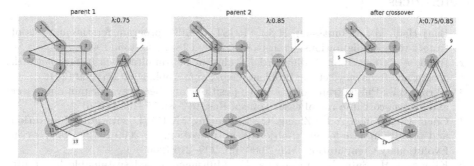

Fig. 13. Evolved route network by DU

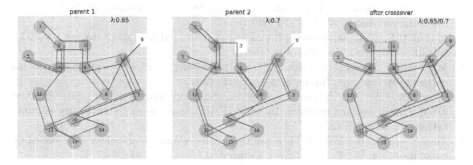

Fig. 14. Evolved route network by DCU

6   Conclusion

This paper proposed the duplex route generation method to evolve the bus route network that increased the robustness to environmental changes by introducing (1) the proposed crossover operation to generate the duplex routes and (2) the proposed priority solution update to improve the fitness. The experiments on Mandl's benchmark problem revealed that the proposed method generated the effective duplex route network that improved both the number of duplex routes and fitness, which was hard to be achieved by either of the proposed operations. What should be noticed here is that these results have only been obtained from the simple testbeds, *i.e.*, the Mandl's benchmark problem, and therefore further careful qualifications and justifications, such as an analysis of results based on the real bus data, are needed to investigate the feasibility of our method. Such important directions must be pursued in the near future in addition to (1) an investigation of the passenger movement to other bus stops in disaster (corresponding to a change of OD matrix); and (2) an exploration of the effective parent selection to inherit the duplex routes from the parents.

References

1. Baaj Hadi, M., Mahmassani, H.S.: TRUST: a LISP program for the analysis of transit route configurations. Transp. Res. Rec. **1283**, 125–135 (1990)
2. Buba, A.T., Lee, L.S.: A differential evolution for simultaneous transit network design and frequency setting problem. Exp. Syst. Appl. **106**, 277–289 (2018)
3. Byrne, B.F.: Public transportation line positions and headways for minimum user and system cost in a radial case. Transp. Res. **9**(2–3), 97–102 (1975)
4. Chen, C.M., Chen, Y.P., Zhang, Q.: Enhancing MOEA/D with guided mutation and priority update for multi-objective optimization. In: 2009 IEEE Congress on Evolutionary Computation, May 2009, pp. 209–216 (2009)
5. Kitagawa, H., Sato, K., Takadama, K.: Multiagent-based sustainable bus route optimization in disaster. J. Inf. Process. **22**(2), 235–242 (2014)
6. Majima, T., Takadama, K., Watanabe, D., Katuhara, M.: Characteristic of passenger's route selection and generation of public transport network. SICE J. Control Measur. Syst. Integ. **8**(1), 67–73 (2015)
7. Mandl, C.E.: Evaluation and optimization of urban public transportation networks. Eur. J. Oper. Res. **5**(6), 396–404 (1980)
8. Mayumi, S.: The rise of NGOs/NPOs in emergency relief in the great east Japan earthquake. Jap. Soc. Innov. J. **2**(1), 26–35 (2012)
9. Mumford, C.L.: New heuristic and evolutionary operators for the multi-objective urban transit routing problem. In: 2013 IEEE Congress on Evolutionary Computation, pp. 939–946 (2013)
10. Zhang, Q., Li, H.: MOEA/D: a multiobjective evolutionary algorithm based on decomposition. IEEE Trans. Evol. Comput. **11**(6), 712–731 (2007)

Combining Multi-objective Evolutionary Algorithms with Deep Generative Models Towards Focused Molecular Design

Tiago Sousa, João Correia, Vitor Pereira^(⊠) , and Miguel Rocha

Centre of Biological Engineering, University of Minho - Campus Gualtar,
Braga, Portugal
pg38283@alunos.uminho.pt, mrocha@di.uminho.pt

Abstract. Recent advances in applying deep generative learning to molecular design have led to a large number of novel approaches to the targeted generation of molecules towards specific features and applications. In this work, we expand on the latent space navigation approach, where molecules are optimized by operating in their latent representation inside a deep auto-encoder, by introducing multi-objective evolutionary algorithms (MOEAs), and benchmarking the proposed framework on several objectives from recent literature. Using several case studies from literature, we show that our proposed method is capable of controlling abstract chemical properties, is competitive with other state-of-the-art methods and can perform relevant tasks such as optimizing a predefined molecule while maintaining a similarity threshold. Also, MOEAs allow to generate molecules with a good level of diversity, which is a desired feature.

Keywords: Molecular design · Deep generative models · Multi-objective evolutionary algorithms

1 Introduction

Developing new chemical compounds with some desired properties, also known as *de novo* molecular design, is an arduous and expensive task. The difficulty mainly arises from the massive space of viable molecules (10^{33} - 10^{80}) within which only a small fraction have the desired properties [28]. Meanwhile, the large costs associated with synthesizing and testing new molecules mean that the development of a single compound can reach 2.8 billion dollars. These problems have long motivated the development of computational tools that have become a valuable and integral aid in various steps of chemical design [8].

Departing from more traditional approaches, generative deep learning (GDL) has recently emerged as a promising development in *de novo* molecular design. Several deep generative architectures have been introduced over recent years, and these have also found use in molecular generation tasks. A rather straight

© Springer Nature Switzerland AG 2021
P. A. Castillo and J. L. Jiménez Laredo (Eds.): EvoApplications 2021, LNCS 12694, pp. 81–96, 2021.
https://doi.org/10.1007/978-3-030-72699-7_6

forward approach is to represent molecules as Simplified Molecular Input Line Entry System (SMILES) and then generate them as a sequence of tokens using stacked Recurrent Neural Networks (RNNs), which are specially suited to handle sequential data. A different approach are Generative Adversarial Networks (GANs) [9], where two networks, the generator and the discriminator, are trained in competition with one another. Here, the generator is trained to produce real looking data capable of fooling the other network, while that network, the discriminator, is trained to distinguish between synthetic and real samples.

An alternative is to leverage auto-encoders (AEs). AEs are neural networks trained to copy their input into the output, with restrictions imposed so that they do not merely learn the identity function. They are normally viewed as two separate networks, an encoder that transforms the input into a more compact latent state, and a decoder that reconstructs the input from this representation. Once trained, novel molecules can be obtained by decoding new points in latent space.

Variational Auto-Encoder (VAEs) [16] are AEs where the encoder outputs two multi-dimensional vectors, which are interpreted as the means and the standard deviations of a multi-dimensional distribution. A single point is then sampled from this distribution and fed into the decoder part of the model to reconstruct the input. Besides being trained to minimize reconstruction errors, a VAE is also trained to keep the parameters encoded close to the normal distribution $N(0, I)$, where I is the identity matrix. Combining the stochastic sampling process with the restriction on encoded parameters to match the normal distribution gives rise to a continuous and structured latent space, suitable for later optimization tasks.

Adversarial auto-encoders (AAE) [22] are a different approach to obtaining a well structured latent space, where instead of introducing a constraint on the encoded parameters, a separate network is trained to distinguish between the output of the encoder and samples from a prior distribution. The encoder is then alternatively trained to minimize the reconstruction error and to fool the new network, in a similar scenario to GANs.

Alongside these new architectures and methods for generating various molecule representations, several approaches have also been proposed for controlling the properties of generated molecules. These include fine-tuning a model on a set of molecules with the desired properties, biasing the generation process [36], employing Reinforcement Learning to directly optimize a model towards those properties [31,40], conditioning a model with explicit inputs detailing the preferred characteristics [30], and as also approached in this work, navigating the latent space of a chemical AE with optimization algorithms [21]. This last method is best employed when the latent space is smooth and well structured, allowing for stable optimization runs. Several algorithms have been considered in this setting, such as Bayesian Optimization and Gradient Ascent [3,14].

Evolutionary Algorithms (EAs) have also been applied to the design of new molecules since the 1990 s [7], and despite the advances of deep learning in the *de novo* drug discovery, they continue to provide good alternative approaches.

One of the main advantages of EAs over ML/DL approaches is that they can introduce a greater diversity of solutions. Indeed, generative DL models are usually trained on reduced datasets of molecules sharing common descriptors or using RNNs, transfer learning, or Conditional AEs to guide the generative models towards desired properties. These strategies, although able to deliver new molecules, narrow the search space of possible solutions. ML models are better suited for optimizing properties within the known range of accessible behavior than for the discovery of new molecules with extreme behavior.

In this context, ChemGE [39] uses grammatical evolution to optimize a population of strings that follow a SMILES context-free grammar. At each iteration, λ individuals are mutated at a single random position obtaining new offspring SMILES representations. Although able to introduce diversity into the population, ChemGE often leads to invalid SMILES, hindering the evolutionary process.

Graph-based Genetic algorithms are also a good prospect to evolve a population of molecules represented as topological graphs where nodes and edges model atoms and bonds. Different types of operators may be used to evolve molecular graphs. Some are atom-based and consist of adding, removing, or substituting atoms or bonds to modify input structures and generate new ones. Other operators are fragment-based which replace or add whole groups of atoms at once. In [20] the author performs the optimization of molecular properties starting solely from the methane molecule using atom-based mutation operators. In [4], the authors propose a Multi-objective Genetic Algorithm to evolve novel topological molecules from a set of user-defined atoms, molecular fragments, or a combination of both by applying atom and fragment-based mutation operators. Additionally, a multi-point crossover, that may occur both at non-ring and ring bonds, and subgraph crossover based on pattern recognition, disconnect two parents into subgraphs and exchanges at least one of the subgraphs between the parents.

Operators may also be reaction-based and generate new compounds by applying rules from a list of encoded chemical transformations to a library of reactants. AutoGrow4 [37] follows such an approach and evolves an initial population of compounds by performing chemical mutations based on a library of 94 reactions. AutoGrow4 also considers a crossover operator that merges two compounds from previous generations by finding the largest substructure shared by both progenitors, and generating a child randomly combining their decorating moieties.

ML models have also been combined with EAs for the optimization of molecular descriptors. Neural-network-evaluated genetic algorithms use ML to assess individuals fitness within a genetic algorithm [23]. Other approaches, such as artificial-neural-network-biased genetic algorithm, employ the data progressively generated by a genetic algorithm that performs fitness evaluations via simulation or experiment to continuously train an artificial neural network (ANN) and introduce into each generation of the genetic algorithm the best-projected candidate identified by the ANN [27].

Sattarov et al. [35] used a Genetic Algorithm to explore the latent space of their SMILES based seq2seq AE. Setting as goal optimizing molecules for activity towards the adenosine A2A receptor, they reported the generation of libraries enriched with actives and novel scaffolds. Winter et al. [38] explored a similar latent space for the optimization of molecular properties resorting to Particle Swarm Optimization.

Both ML/DL and EA approaches on their own exhibit, so far, some limitations for the optimization of molecules with targeted properties. Combining DL with EA allows to overcome some of those limitations, enabling the pursuit of two main objectives: increase the number of valid molecules, which is one of the limitations of pure EA approaches using operators that are not reaction-based, and, at the same time, take advantage of the exploratory capabilities of EAs, specially in large search spaces such as the chemical one, allowing to find molecules targeting specific focuses.

Evolutionary algorithms, and in particular multi-objective ones, have the added advantage to streamline the optimization of distinct chemical properties, which is a common need in this field. For instance, in drug discovery, desired molecules may be the ones that have the desired functionality over the biological target(s), but also avoid toxicity to cells, can be synthesized, are highly soluble, among many other properties.

In this work, we propose to develop flexible multi-objective evolutionary algorithms (MOEAs), which allow defining different objective functions for the novel molecules being evolved. One of our approach's central concepts is viewing the latent space of a chemical VAE as a continuous and reversible molecular representation, a concept introduced by Gómez-Bombarelli et al. [12]. An EA is then used to evolve molecules operating in this continuous representation. This approach avoids the complexity and limitations of directly evolving discrete molecular representations, such as graphs or line notations like SMILES. The MOEAs are benchmarked on several objectives from recent work on the state-of-the-art and also perform a brief comparison between single-objective (SO) and multi-objective (MO) algorithms.

In the remaining of the paper, we first explain our proposed architecture and its modules and explain the case studies used to provide for its validation, followed by the results obtained in each. The paper finishes with conclusions and suggestions for further work.

2   Proposed Method

2.1   Framework Overview

In the EA proposed in this work, each individual, a molecule, is represented as a vector of real numbers. The initial population is obtained by passing known molecules through the encoder of the generative model. The EA then selects individuals and applies its operators to produce a new generation. Each individual is then reconstructed back into a molecule, using the VAE decoder, and evaluated against each problem-specific objectives. The molecules with the best fitness are subsequently selected to integrate the new population. The process is repeated until the stopping criterion is met. Figure 1 outlines the overall procedure. The optimization framework uses PyTorch [26] for the DL generative models and jMetalPy [1] to implement the EAs.

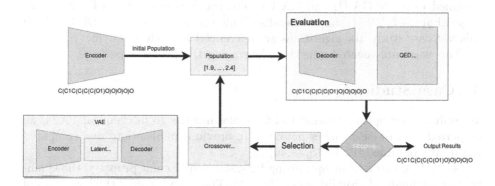

Fig. 1. The proposed method, combining a EA with a chemical VAE. Here, the encoder is used to construct the initial population of latent space representations. After each new generation is created, the decoder is used to reconstruct the individuals into molecules for evaluation.

2.2   Deep Generative Model

For the deep generative model, we implemented and trained a SMILES based VAE following the architecture present in [29]. In this model, the encoder receives one-hot-encoded SMILES and outputs two vectors with length 128, and, after sampling, the decoder reconstructs the original one-hot-encoded SMILES. The encoder was composed of an embedding layer, followed by a single recurrent layer with 256 GRU units, followed by two parallel dense layers. The decoder was composed of an embedding layer and a dense layer, followed by three recurrent layers with 512 GRU units, dropout p = 0.5, and followed by another dense layer.

2.3   Evolutionary Algorithms and Their Configuration

Molecules are represented in the latent space as vectors of 128 real numbers varying in the range [−10,10]. The EAs encode individuals using the same representation, evolving a population of 100 individuals, subsets of the latent space. Our approach uses a standard one-point crossover and two mutation operators:

– Gaussian mutation, which consists of adding a random value from a standard Normal distribution to elements of an individual's vector. Each element has a 10% probability of being mutated.
– Random mutation: one randomly selected element of the vector representation is substitute by a random real value within the range [−10,10].

The proposed architecture allows for both single and multi-objective optimization. While single objective optimizations are assured by an elitist generational GA, denoted 'Ours (SO)', the multi-objective optimizations resort to the Non-dominated Sorting Genetic Algorithm III (NSGA-III) [6] and are denoted 'Ours (MO)'. In a particular case study, we also include a comparison of results obtained using NSGA-III and GA but also the Strength Pareto Evolutionary Algorithm (SPEA2) [41] and Generalized Differential Evolution (GDE3) [17]. In this last case study, the algorithms are referenced by their acronym.

This was implemented in python, leveraging the jmetalpy package.

3   Case Studies

To evaluate our optimization model for molecular design in chemical VAEs, we employed a set of case studies presented in previous publications and compared the results obtained [12,14,15,38,40].

As such, we started by optimizing for a single molecular property, the Quantitative Estimate of Druglikeness (QED) [2]. Then, we targeted the logarithm of the octanol-water partition coefficient (logP) penalized by synthetic accessibility and the presence of unusually large rings (PlogP). Next, this objective is also optimized, while constrained to be similar to an initial set of molecules, and finally, we target a more pragmatic objective by jointly optimizing the predicted activity towards the Dopamine Receptor type D2 (DRD2), the QED, and the predicted non-toxicity. Next, we further detail each of the case studies.

Diversity

Throughout some of the case studies we also discuss the diversity of the molecules being generated. As defined by [14], we considered molecular diversity as the average pairwise Tanimoto distance between each molecule in given set of compounds, as follows:

$$diversity_A = \frac{\sum_{x,y \in A} 1 - sim(x,y)}{|A|} \tag{1}$$

where $sim(x,y)$ is the Tanimoto similarity between the Morgan Fingerprints [33] with radius 2 of two molecules.

Drug-Likeness (QED)

Drug-likeness is a key consideration when selecting compounds during the early stages of drug discovery. The QED [2], along with most of the metrics computed in this work, is obtained from the molecular structure using the open-source cheminformatics software RDKit [19]. This single value reflects the underlying distribution of molecular properties, including molecular weight (MW), the logP, topological polar surface area, number of hydrogen bond donors and acceptors, the number of aromatic rings and rotatable bonds, and the presence of unwanted chemical functionalities.

Solubility Penalized by Synthetic Accessibility and Large Rings (PlogP)

The octanol-water partition coefficient serves as a measure between lipophilicity (fat solubility) and hydrophilicity (water solubility) of a molecule. Molecules with a positive logP are lipophilic, while molecules with a negative logP are hydrophilic. The penalized logP (PlogP) is defined as:

$$PlogP(m) = logP(m) - SA(m) - cycle(m) \qquad (2)$$

where $SA(x)$ is the molecule synthetic accessibility score, and $cycle(m)$ counts the number of atoms over six in the largest ring. In the MO optimizations, each term in Eq. 2 is taken as a separate objective.

Penalized Solubility Constrained by Similarity to Set of Molecules

The constrained PlogP extends the previous by enforcing a similarity constraint to a given starting molecule, that is, $sim(x, y) \geq \delta$. The experiments consider a set of 800 molecules obtained from [14] (selected for having the worst score in their dataset) and constrains $\delta \in \{0, 0.2, 0.4, 0.6\}$. Similarly to the computation of diversity in Eq. 1, $sim(x, y)$ is taken as the Tanimoto similarity between the Morgan Fingerprints with radius 2 of molecules x and y. The constraint, formulated as a new optimization objective, is defined as:

$$constraint = \begin{cases} sim(x, y) + 200, & \text{if } sim(x, y) \geq \delta \\ sim(x, y) * 100, & \text{otherwise} \end{cases} \qquad (3)$$

where δ is the defined threshold and $sim(x, y)$ is the aforementioned similarity between the solution being considered and a given starting molecule. This was designed to provide a clear signal, both guiding the algorithm towards meeting the constraint when it is not yet met and distinctively marking when the constraint has been satisfied.

DRD2 Activity and Drug-Likeness Penalized by Toxicity

This case study's main goal is to find molecules with increased activity against a biological target, the dopamine type 2 receptor DRD2. To assess molecules' activity probability, we use the vector machine (SVM) classifier with a Gaussian kernel proposed in [25].

Two additional objectives are considered, the QED and the non-toxicity of the compound. The last one is predicted using a multi-target deep neural network trained in house on the Tox21 dataset [13]. With this model, a molecule is considered toxic, and given an evaluation of 0.0, if it scores over 0.5 in two or more endpoints. However, if it does not score over 0.5 for any endpoint, it is considered non-toxic and evaluated as 1.0. When a molecule scores over 0.5 in one or two endpoints, it is evaluated with the average of the scores.

4   Results

In this next section, we report and discuss the results for each of the case studies. Each experiment was conducted on a system with two Intel Gold Xeon Gold 6138 CPUs, 750 gb of memory, and a single GPU. Each case study took on average 4 h to fully execute, except for the constrained PlogP that required close to 100 h for the higher thresholds. All experiments were run without parallelization as only one GPU was available.

4.1   Training the DL Model

The training of the VAE was conducted with a subset of the ChEMBL database of approximately 1.7M molecules, 1.5M for training, and 170K for testing. The second term of the objective, restricting encoded parameters close to normal, was annealed, i.e., it was multiplied by a variable weight that started at zero and gradually increased during training. This technique improved reconstruction accuracy by allowing the model to learn the more difficult task of reproducing its input before restricting the latent space.

Furthermore, teacher forcing was also employed to ease the training of the output layer of the decoder. With teacher forcing, the previous time-step output, which would typically serve as the the current step input, is replaced with the ground truth. Despite helping with reconstruction accuracy, the model may become overly reliant on this signal, which will not be present during the actual use of the network, and as such, negatively impact performance. Therefore, the frequency of teacher forcing, or how often the output was replaced with the ground truth, was gradually reduced during training.

Early stopping was also employed, stopping the training process once no further improvements were identified. In practice, the network was trained with a batch size of 512 and the Adam optimizer with default parameters for 40 epochs, with the last epoch with significant improvement, epoch 20, being chosen *a posteriori*. Figure 2 illustrates the progress of the validation loss with training. The model was implemented with pytorch and training performed on a single NVIDIA RTX2080ti.

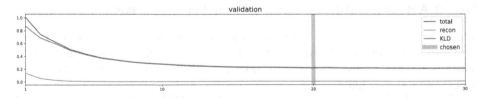

Fig. 2. Validation loss when training the VAE used. Weights were saved after each epoch, with our experiments using the weights from epoch 20. The orange line, labeled 'recon', shows the reconstruction loss, the green line, labeled 'KLD', shows the latent regularization loss and the blue line, labeled 'total', shows the sum of the previous two terms.

4.2 QED

Optimizing QED serves as a first test of whether our method can effectively optimize molecules in the latent space of a chemical VAE. For this task, we performed single-objective optimization with a GA, stopping after 500 generations and executing 30 runs. As with previous methods, we report the 3 best molecules found and the 95% confidence interval for the mean of the best score in each of the 30 runs. Our results alongside the baselines are outlined in Table 1.

Most previously reported methods already saturated this score, plateauing at 0.948. Likewise, our framework achieved a very similar performance, with the worst of all runs scoring 0.9475. Furthermore, the best molecules found between all runs were also novel and diverse, featuring 0.812 calculated diversity. These results, therefore, indicate that our framework can indeed optimize abstract molecular properties while also generating several distinct solutions.

Table 1. Baselines and our results for the optimization of QED reporting the scores for the three best molecules. (* is reported by You et al. [40])

Method	QED			
	1st	2nd	3rd	Mean
Guimaraes et al. [11]*	0.896	0.824	0.820	–
Popova et al. [31]	0.948	0.948	0.947	–
Jin et al. [14]*	0.925	0.911	0.910	–
You et al. [40]	0.948	0.947	0.946	–
Winter et al. [38]	0.948	–	–	–
Ours (SO)	0.948	0.948	0.948	0.9481 ± 0.0001

4.3 PlogP

The penalized logP aimed to be a more realistic and demanding objective, seeking to produce molecules that are not only highly hydrophobic but also easy to synthesise and lack unusual ring structures. However, as reported previously [38,40], this objective can be trivially solved with long aliphatic chains that lack rings and are hydrophobic and easily synthesised.

For this task, we performed both SO and MO optimization with a GA and NSGAIII, respectively. The algorithms were allowed to run for 500 generations and were executed 30 times. Like previous methods, we report the 3 best molecules found and the 95% confidence interval for the mean of the best score in each of our 30 runs. Our results, presented in table 2, were similar to [38], with optimization yielding long aliphatic chains.

Besides the jarringly high final scores, a brief comparison can be established between the SO and the MO case. In the first, out of the 30 runs, the algorithm converged to the same exact molecule in all but 2, resulting in a mean diversity among runs of 0.007. In contrast, the MO case found several different high scoring compounds, and each run resulted in large sets of unique molecules, with a mean diversity among runs of 0.44.

As our scores were consistent with previously reported work, we determine that our framework could successfully complete this case study and even achieving higher absolute values. Furthermore, this experiment also highlighted distinct performances between SO and MO, with the later achieving slightly superior best scores while maintaining a higher diversity of solutions.

Table 2. Baselines and our results for the optimization of logP penalized by synthetic accessibility and the presence of large rings. ([a]reported in a earlier version of their work; *reported by You et al. [40])

Method	PlogP			
	1st	2nd	3rd	Mean
Gómez-Bombarelli et al. [12][a]	5.02	4.68	–	–
Kusner et al. [18]	2.94	2.89	2.80	–
Dai et al. [5]	4.04	3.50	2.96	–
Jin et al. [14]	5.30	4.93	4.49	–
Samanta et al. [34]	2.83	2.48	2.30	–
Winter et al. [38]	26.1	–	–	–
Popova et al. [31]	10.34	10.19	10.14	–
You et al. [40]	7.98	7.85	7.8	–
Guimaraes et al. [11]*	3.63	3.49	3.44	–
Bresson and Laurent [3]	5.24	5.10	5.06	–
Griffiths et al. [10]	4.01	–	–	–
Ours (SO)	32.21	22.01	–	22.35 ± 0.67
Ours (MO)	32.57	25.74	24.30	22.64 ± 0.73

4.4   Constrained PlogP

By constraining solutions to be similar to a specific starting molecule, the trivial result discussed previously is no longer feasible. Therefore, this case study is inherently more challenging as it includes an additional objective (Eq. 3), while remaining a relevant problem. The added difficulty results from drastically reducing the number of viable solutions, thus hindering the optimization process. Still, it is of great importance as optimizing a molecule to be similar to a given one is a common problem faced in drug design.

For this task, each of the 800 compounds was independently optimized for each of the thresholds. Furthermore, an "early" stopping criterion was also employed where, after a minimum of 250 generations, the optimization was allowed to end once a valid solution was found or reach 2500 generations, otherwise.

Following previous work, we report the success rate, the percentage of molecules for which a valid improvement was found, and within those, the mean and standard deviation of the best improvement and corresponding similarity to the initial molecule. As such, only methods with similar success rates should be directly compared. Table 3 outlines our results and Table 4 the baselines. For both the first and second threshold, 0.0 and 0.2, we outperformed all baselines while maintaining equivalent success rates. Of note, the threshold of 0.0 is identical to the unconstrained case, and, as such, the trivial solution emerges again. For the threshold of 0.4, our success rate is placed between the methods of Bresson et al. [3] and Maziarka et al. [24], surpassing both in terms of average improvement. The last threshold of 0.6 has a success rate just slightly below that of the approach of Maziarka et al. [24], but with a bigger average improvement.

Table 3. Our results for the constrained PlogP case study, using either single-objective or multi-objective algorithms, with 2500 maximum generations.

δ	Ours (SO)			Ours (MO)		
	Improvement	Similarity	Success	Improvement	Similarity	Success
0.0	25.73 $\pm$ 2.43	0.02 $\pm$ .02	100.0%	25.91 $\pm$ 1.99	0.02 $\pm$ 0.01	100.0%
0.2	7.50 $\pm$ 1.85	0.22 $\pm$ 0.03	98.37%	6.96 $\pm$ 2.18	0.23 $\pm$ 0.03	99.75%
0.4	4.04 $\pm$ 1.53	0.42 $\pm$ 0.02	72.12%	3.81 $\pm$ 1.63	0.43 $\pm$ 0.03	67.12%
0.6	2.42 $\pm$ 1.41	0.62 $\pm$ 0.02	17.25%	2.39 $\pm$ 1.34	0.63 $\pm$ 0.03	17.87%

Table 4. Baselines for success rates and improvements in the constrained PlogP case study.

δ	Bresson et al. [3]			Maziarka et al. [24]			You et al. [40]		
	Improv.	Similarity	Success	Improv.	Similarity	Success	Improv.	Similarity	Success
0.0	5.24 $\pm$ 1.55	0.18 $\pm$ 0.12	100.0%	8.30 $\pm$ 1.98	0.16 $\pm$ 0.09	99.75%	4.20 $\pm$ 1.28	0.32 $\pm$ 0.12	100.0%
0.2	4.29 $\pm$ 1.57	0.31 $\pm$ 0.12	98.60%	5.79 $\pm$ 2.35	0.30 $\pm$ 0.11	93.75%	4.12 $\pm$ 1.19	0.34 $\pm$ 0.11	100.0%
0.4	3.05 $\pm$ 1.46	0.51 $\pm$ 0.10	84.0%	2.89 $\pm$ 2.08	0.52 $\pm$ 0.10	58.75%	2.49 $\pm$ 1.30	0.47 $\pm$ 0.08	100.0%
0.6	2.46 $\pm$ 1.27	0.67 $\pm$ 0.05	40.1%	1.22 $\pm$ 1.48	0.69 $\pm$ 0.07	19.25%	0.79 $\pm$ 0.63	0.68 $\pm$ 0.08	100.0%

A separate metric to consider in this case study, as introduced by [15], is the diversity of the valid solutions found for each molecule. Table 5 outlines the results and baselines used in [15] alongside our results. The diversity attained by our methods is slightly worse but still in line with the baseline. Furthermore, the MO case, again, mostly outperformed the SO case in this regard, except for the 0.6 threshold.

The last consideration is the stopping criterion. Figure 3 illustrates the mean number of generations each algorithm took for each threshold. A positive correlation trend is apparent, with higher thresholds requiring, on average, more generations to find viable solutions. This result is expected as the higher the

Table 5. Results and baselines used in [15] and our results regarding the diversity of solutions for each molecule in the target set.

δ	VJTNN Jin et al. [15]	MMPA baseline	VSeq2Seq baseline	Ours (SO)	Ours (MO)
0.0	–	–	–	0.334	0.722
0.2	–	–	–	0.553	0.655
0.4	0.480	0.496	0.471	0.416	0.451
0.6	0.333	0.329	0.331	0.298	0.256

threshold, the more it reduces the viable solution space, and therefore optimizing gets more challenging. Although no difference is evident between SO and MO in terms of generations used, the first achieved slightly better mean improvement with a higher or comparable success rate. We attribute this to our implementation of the constraint which, in the MO case, allowed the algorithm to focus on invalid solutions as it operated as an independent objective. Meanwhile, in the SO case, solutions not satisfying the constraint were heavily penalized, helping the algorithm focus on viable solutions.

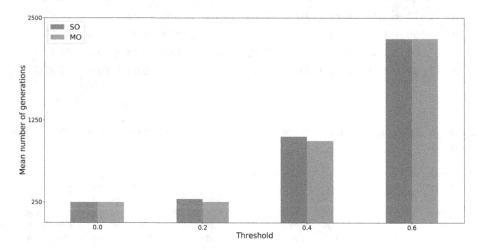

Fig. 3. Mean generations taken by the SO and MO for each of the thresholds. The minimum was set as 250 and the maximum 2500. Should the algorithm find a viable improvement during this interval it was allowed to terminate.

4.5 DRD2 Activity and Drug-Likeness Penalized by Toxicity

The DRD2 activity problem encompasses the simultaneous maximization of three objectives: DRD2, QED, and non-toxicity (nonTox). To address this problem, we considered a GA and three commonly used MOEAs: NSGAIII, SPEA2, and GDE3. Besides allowing the evaluation of the proposed approach in a more pragmatic problem, we also aim to compare the performance of the EAs. For the GA, the objective function is the aggregated sum of all three objectives, which is also used as a comparison score in Table 6. The values for DRD2, QED and nonTox vary in the range [0, 1]. We show the 95% confidence interval for the mean of the best aggregated score along with the value of its respective individual objectives for the 30 repetitions.

Table 6. Optimization results for DRD2 activity and Drug-likeness penalized by toxicity.

Algorithm	Score	DRD2	QED	nonTox	Diversity
GA	2.877 ± 0.026	0.969 ± 0.020	0.908 ± 0.014	1.0 ± 0.0	0.775
NSGAIII	2.882 ± 0.031	0.960 ± 0.020	0.922 ± 0.014	1.0 ± 0.0	0.754
SPEA2	2.902 ± 0.014	0.976 ± 0.012	0.926 ± 0.009	1.0 ± 0.0	0.748
GDE3	2.935 ± 0.002	0.995 ± 0.002	0.940 ± 0.002	1.0 ± 0.0	0.519

The results indicate that GDE3 performs best with the highest aggregated score. However, this performance does not extend to the diversity metric, where GDE3 delivered molecules with the lowest diversity. On the other hand, the GA found molecules with the overall worst score but with the highest diversity. To further assess the MOEAs performance in this optimization task, we include in Table 7 three of the most commonly used Quality Indicators [32], notably, the *Hyper Volume* which measures the size of the portion of objective space that is dominated by a set of solutions, a Pareto Front (PF); the *Generational Distance* which is used to access the convergence of the solution by measuring the distance from the solution PF to the best PF approximation determined by combining non-dominated points from all MOEA solutions; and the *Epsilon (ϵ)* indicator which measures the smallest value to be added to any point in the solution PF to make it non-dominated by some point in best PF approximation. All three indicators point to a better performance of GDE3.

Table 7. Quality indicators for the MOEAs.

Algorithm	ϵ-indicator	Generational distance	Hypervolume
NSGAIII	0.0446	0.1127	0.9111
SPEA2	0.0359	0.1188	0.9356
GDE3	0.0082	0.0927	0.9451

5   Conclusions and Further Work

With the results from the presented experiments, it is apparent that the proposed framework is capable of controlling abstract chemical properties of generated molecules and performing tasks relevant to molecular design, such as optimizing given molecules and generating possible leads for biological receptors. Regarding the scoring on the several benchmarks from the state-of-the-art, the framework mostly outperformed, or at least matched, results from previous work, presenting itself as a viable alternative. Throughout the various experiments, the use of MO algorithms often led to more diverse solution sets. This result is an important advantage over the SO case as having a diverse set of leads is paramount for early *de novo* chemical design. Lastly, a better implementation of the similarity constraint in the constrained PlogP case study may enable the MO algorithm to match and even surpass SO's performance.

In this work, we present a framework combining MOEAs with a chemical VAE for controlling the properties of molecules being generated. We could match or exceed previous approaches in several objectives. In future work, we propose improving the framework by including different deep generative models and multi-objective algorithms. Also, the presented architecture may be validated in real drug discovery scenarios with other objectives.

Acknowledgements. This project has received funding from the European Union's Horizon 2020 research and innovation programme (grant agreement number 814408).

References

1. Benítez-Hidalgo, A., Nebro, A.J., García-Nieto, J., Oregi, I., Ser, J.D.: jmetalpy: a python framework for multi-objective optimization with metaheuristics. Swarm Evol. Comput. **51**, 100598 (2019)
2. Bickerton, G.R., Paolini, G.V., Besnard, J., Muresan, S., Hopkins, A.L.: Quantifying the chemical beauty of drugs. Nature Chem. **4**(2), 90–98 (2012)
3. Bresson, X., Laurent, T.: A Two-Step Graph Convolutional Decoder for Molecule Generation. arXiv:1906.03412 [cs, stat] (2019)
4. Brown, N., McKay, B., Gilardoni, F., Gasteiger, J.: A graph-based genetic algorithm and its application to the multiobjective evolution of median molecules. J. Chem. Inf. Comput. Sci. **44**(3), 1079–1087 (2004)
5. Dai, H., Tian, Y., Dai, B., Skiena, S., Song, L.: Syntax-directed variational autoencoder for structured data. arXiv preprint arXiv:1802.08786 (2018)
6. Deb, K., Jain, H.: An evolutionary many-objective optimization algorithm using reference-point-based nondominated sorting approach, part i: Solving problems with box constraints. IEEE Trans. Evol. Comput. **18**(4), 577–601 (2014)
7. Devi, R.V., Sathya, S.S., Coumar, M.S.: Evolutionary algorithms for de novo drug design - a survey. Appl. Soft. Comput. **27**, 543–552 (2015)
8. DiMasi, J.A., Grabowski, H.G., Hansen, R.W.: Innovation in the pharmaceutical industry: new estimates of R&D costs. J. Health Econ. **47**, 20–33 (2016)
9. Goodfellow, I., et al.: Generative adversarial nets. In: Advances in Neural Information Processing Systems, pp. 2672–2680 (2014)
10. Griffiths, R.R., Hernández-Lobato, J.M.: Constrained Bayesian optimization for automatic chemical design using variational autoencoders. Chem. Sci. **11**(2), 577–586 (2020)

11. Guimaraes, G.L., Sanchez-Lengeling, B., Outeiral, C., Farias, P.L.C., Aspuru-Guzik, A.: Objective-Reinforced Generative Adversarial Networks (ORGAN) for Sequence Generation Models. arXiv:1705.10843 (2017)
12. Gómez-Bombarelli, R., et al.: Automatic chemical design using a data-driven continuous representation of molecules. ACS Central Sci. **4**(2), 268–276 (2018)
13. Huang, R., et al.: Tox21challenge to build predictive models of nuclear receptor and stress response pathways as mediated by exposure to environmental chemicals and drugs. Frontiers Environ. Sci. **3**, 85 (2016)
14. Jin, W., Barzilay, R., Jaakkola, T.: Junction tree variational autoencoder for molecular graph generation. In: International Conference on Machine Learning. pp. 2323–2332. PMLR (2018)
15. Jin, W., Yang, K., Barzilay, R., Jaakkola, T.: Learning multimodal graph-to-graph translation for molecular optimization. arXiv:1812.01070 [cs, stat] (2019)
16. Kingma, D.P., Welling, M.: Auto-encoding variational bayes. arXiv preprint arXiv:1312.6114 (2013)
17. Kukkonen, S., Lampinen, J.: Gde3: the third evolution step of generalized differential evolution. In: 2005 IEEE Congress on Evolutionary Computation. vol. 1, pp. 443–450 (2005)
18. Kusner, M.J., Paige, B., Hernández Lobato, J.M.: Grammar variational autoencoder. In: Proceedings of the 34th International Conference on Machine Learning, vol. 70, pp. 1945–1954. JMLR. org (2017)
19. Landrum, G.: Rdkit: open-source cheminformatics software (2016)
20. Leguy, J., Cauchy, T., Glavatskikh, M., Duval, B., Da Mota, B.: Evomol: aflexible and interpretable evolutionary algorithm for unbiased de novomolecular generation. Cheminform **12**(55) (2020)
21. Liu, Q., Allamanis, M., Brockschmidt, M., Gaunt, A.: Constrained graph variational autoencoders for molecule design. In: Advances in Neural Information Processing Systems, pp. 7795–7804 (2018)
22. Makhzani, A., Shlens, J., Jaitly, N., Goodfellow, I.: Adversarial autoencoders. In: International Conference on Learning Representations (2016). http://arxiv.org/abs/1511.05644
23. Marim, L., Lemes, M., Dal Pino Jr, A.: Neural-network-assisted genetic algorithm applied to silicon clusters. Phys. Rev. A **67**, 033203 (2003)
24. Maziarka, Ł., Pocha, A., Kaczmarczyk, J., Rataj, K., Danel, T., Warchoł, M.: Mol-cyclegan: a generative model for molecular optimization. J. Chem. **12**(1), 1–18 (2020)
25. Olivecrona, M., Blaschke, T., Engkvist, O., Chen, H.: Molecular de novo design through deep reinforcement learning (2017)
26. Paszke, A., et al.: Pytorch: An imperative style, high-performance deep learning library. In: Wallach, H., Larochelle, H., Beygelzimer, A., d'Alché-Buc, F., Fox, E., Garnett, R. (eds.) Advances in Neural Information Processing Systems, vol. 32, pp. 8024–8035. Curran Associates, Inc. (2019)
27. Patra, T.K., Meenakshisundaram, V., Hung, J.H., Simmons, D.S.: Neural-network-biased genetic algorithms for materials design: Evolutionary algorithms that learn (2017)
28. Polishchuk, P.G., et al.: Estimation of the size of drug-like chemical space based on GDB-17 data. J. Comput.-Aided Mol. Des. **27**(8), 675–679 (2013)
29. Polykovskiy, D., et al.: Molecular sets (MOSES): a benchmarking platform for molecular generation models. Frontiers Pharmacol. **11**, 565644 (2020)
30. Polykovskiy, D., et al.: Entangled conditional adversarial autoencoder for de novo drug discovery. Mol. Pharm. **15**(10), 4398–4405 (2018)

31. Popova, M., Shvets, M., Oliva, J., Isayev, O.: MolecularRNN: Generating realistic molecular graphs with optimized properties. [cs, q-bio, stat] arXiv:1905.13372 (2019)
32. Ravber, M., Mernik, M., Črepinšek, M.: The impact of quality indicators on the rating of multi-objective evolutionary algorithms. Appl. Soft. Comput. **55**, 265–275 (2017)
33. Rogers, D., Hahn, M.: Extended-connectivity fingerprints. J. Chem. Inf. Model. **50**(5), 742–754 (2010)
34. Samanta, et al.: NeVAE: a deep generative model for molecular graphs. In: Proceedings of the AAAI Conference on Artificial Intelligence, vol. 33, pp. 1110–1117 (2019)
35. Sattarov, B., Baskin, I.I., Horvath, D., Marcou, G., Bjerrum, E.J., Varnek, A.: De novo molecular design by combining deep deep autoencoder recurrent neural networks with generative topographic mapping. J. Chem. Inf. Model. **59**(3), 1182–1196 (2019)
36. Segler, M.H., Kogej, T., Tyrchan, C., Waller, M.P.: Generating focused molecule libraries for drug discovery with recurrent neural networks. ACS Central Sci. **4**(1), 120–131 (2018)
37. Spiegel, J.O., Durrant, J.D.: AutoGrow4: an open-source genetic algorithm for de novo drug design and lead optimization. J. Cheminformatics **12**(1), 1–16 (2020). https://doi.org/10.1186/s13321-020-00429-4
38. Winter, R., Montanari, F., Steffen, A., Briem, H., Noé, F., Clevert, D.A.: Efficient multi-objective molecular optimization in a continuous latent space. Chem. Sci. **10**(34), 8016–8024 (2019)
39. Yoshikawa, N., Terayama, K., Sumita, M., Homma, T., Oono, K., Tsuda, K.: Population-based de novo molecule generation, using grammatical evolution. Chem. Lett. **47**(11), 1431–1434 (2018)
40. You, J., Liu, B., Ying, Z., Pande, V., Leskovec, J.: Graph convolutional policy network for goal-directed molecular graph generation. Adv. Neural Inf. Process. Syst. **31**, 6410–6421 (2018)
41. Zitzler, E., Laumanns, M., Thiele, L.: Spea 2: Improving the strength pareto evolutionary algorithm for multiobjective optimization. Evol. Methods Des. Optim. and Control Appl. Ind. Probl. **3242**, 95–100 (2001)

A Multi-objective Evolutionary Algorithm Approach for Optimizing Part Quality Aware Assembly Job Shop Scheduling Problems

Michael H. Prince[✉], Kristian DeHaan, and Daniel R. Tauritz[✉]

BONSAI Lab, Auburn University, Auburn, AL 36830, USA
{mhp0009,kzd0054}@auburn.edu, dtauritz@acm.org

Abstract. Motivated by a real-world application, we consider an Assembly Job Shop Scheduling Problem (AJSSP), with three objectives: product quality, product quantity, and first product lead time. Using real-world inspection data, we demonstrate the ability to model product quality transformations during assembly jobs via genetic programming by considering the quality attributes of subparts. We investigate integrating quality transformation models into an AJSSP. Through the use of the de facto standard multi-objective evolutionary algorithm, NSGA-II, and a novel genotype to handle the constraints, we describe an evolutionary approach to optimizing all stated objectives. This approach is empirically shown to outperform random search and hill climbing in both performance and usability metrics expected to be valuable to administrators involved in plant scheduling and operations.

Keywords: Assembly Job Shop Scheduling · Evolutionary algorithm · Genetic programming · Manufacturing · Multi-objective evolutionary algorithm

1 Introduction

The real-world scenario motivating this research involves scheduling the production of complex, low-quantity, mechanical and electrical components with exceedingly strict quality requirements. These products are constructed at a trusted foundry and often involve time-intensive additive manufacturing techniques. As a consequence, when a product fails to meet said requirements, it often must be rebuilt. This incurs a relatively significant delay due to the low quantity of products produced. Often times, an initial sample of the product must be sent off for early inspection and minor design modifications. This scenario motivates the three primary objectives for this optimization problem:

© Springer Nature Switzerland AG 2021 and Honeywell Federal Manufacturing & Technologies, LLC
P. A. Castillo and J. L. Jiménez Laredo (Eds.): EvoApplications 2021, LNCS 12694, pp. 97–112, 2021.
https://doi.org/10.1007/978-3-030-72699-7_7

- Increasing quality of parts produced.
- Reducing time required to produce a defined quantity of parts (makespan).
- Reducing the lead-time of the first produced part.

The first contribution of this work is the modeling of quality, and integration of quality based constraints in the Assembly Job Shop Scheduling Problem (AJSSP). In assembly jobs, we propose that the quality attributes of the produced part can be determined by a non-linear combination of the quality of its subparts. With real-world intermediate inspection data, we demonstrate that accurate quality models may be constructed. We describe the techniques used to produce the quality models, the systems required to integrate this new constraint into the AJSSP, and how this constraint may be utilized to produce optimization objectives relevant to our real-world scenario.

The second contribution of this work is the formulation of a multi-objective evolutionary algorithm (MOEA) approach to optimize the AJSSP under the new constraints and objectives, particularly in the genotype design and operation. The genotype utilizes koza-style genetic programming (GP) trees to select subparts for assembly and a directly evolved schedule to control the order in which parts are assembled. This algorithm is compared against baselines to empirically gage performance. Finally, other attributes of the produced solutions, such as fitness range and distribution, are compared.

2 Background

The AJSSP is a variant of the JSSP with an added job dependency constraint. In the traditional JSSP, a series of jobs must be assigned to a limited number of machines with the typical goal of reducing makespan. The AJSSP adds an extra constraint on top of the traditional JSSP: parts produced from the jobs must be assembled to create the final product. This constraint restricts the number of valid schedules, since assembly is impossible if the sub-parts have not been manufactured. An example of this is shown in Fig. 1. However, like the JSSP, the AJSSP is still considered an NP-hard problem [15]. We find that the AJSSP closely matches our real-world scenario's constraints. Additionally, the AJSSP's consideration of intermediate products and inventory provides a natural integration point for the quality modeling.

2.1 JSSP and AJSSP Literature

The JSSP is a widely studied and relevant problem to the manufacturing industry and operations research. Within the field of evolutionary algorithms (EAs), as indicated by the following surveys, the JSSP has been extended many times to consider multiple objectives [10]. Similarly, many different constraints have been considered such as resource limitations and uncertain processing time [9]. While some works, such as Al-Hinai et al. [2] and Wang et al. [18], consider machine disruptions impacting scheduling, failed products due to quality thresholds is an area that has seen little coverage.

The Assembly Job Shop Scheduling Problem

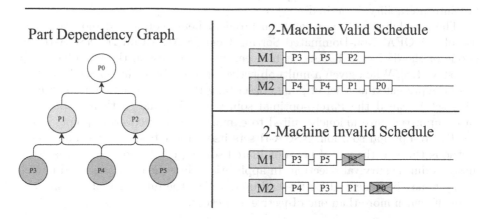

Fig. 1. A visualization of the AJSSP. In this part dependency graph, at a minimum, seven assembly steps must be taken to produce a single output product. Six of those manufacture unique parts, but P4 must be assembled twice for parts P1 and P2. In the invalid schedule, P4 is only assembled once and therefore P2 and P0 can't be produced.

Presently, research into the AJSSP is significantly less common than research into the JSSP. However, some approaches have been attempted. Lu et al. explores the use of combining order review and release mechanisms with dispatching rules [12]. Thiagarajan et al. also considers the use of dispatch rules along with balancing multiple objectives via a weighted sum [17]. In the evolutionary space, Wong et al. compares genetic algorithm and particle swarm approaches using a chromosome to directly encode job sequencing [20]. Previous work from this group [3,19], considers different genetic algorithm techniques to solve the AJSSP and a resource constrained AJSSP respectively. Lv et al. combines the previously mentioned dispatch rules with Koza-style genetic programming (GP) [13]. Pareto-front multi-objective optimization appears to be particularly sparse in this space. In a recent work, Zhang et al. use ant colony optimization to simultaneously optimize makespan, tardiness, and workload [22].

2.2 Evolutionary Methods

Our problem necessitates two separate optimization methods: one to create the transformation models and one to optimize the scheduling and dynamic part selection. For creating part transformation models, GP was selected. GP has had success modeling non-linear scientific processes [4]. By evolving Koza-style trees, GP can create accurate and human-interpretable mathematical models. Traditional mathematical techniques struggle with non-linear and multivariate modeling since it is difficult to design model structure beforehand. Neural network techniques, while accurate, are exceedingly difficult to interpret once models have been trained [21]. For these reasons, GP carries the characteristics valued by small-scale, high-consequence manufacturing, where not only accuracy, but interpretability, is desired.

The scheduling and part selection problem being considered motivates the use of a MOEA. Non-Dominated Sorting Genetic Algorithm II (NSGA-II) [6] is one of the de facto MOEAs. It has seen much success in the manufacturing industry [1,8]. When given a multi-objective optimization, the optimal solution can be represented as a set of points describing the tradeoff between objectives. This set is called the Pareto-optimal solution. EAs, due to their population based approach, are uniquely suited to exploring and discovering points along the Pareto-optimal solution. NSGA-II sets itself apart from other evolutionary methods through the use of non-dominated sorting combined with a clustering analysis during survival selection. In applications like the ones presented in this work, it may be beneficial for the end users to see the full range of options and tradeoffs when more than one objective is present.

3   Modeling of Quality Transformations

At small-scale, high-consequence production facilities, due to the quality requirements, subparts entering assembly and machining processes are often inspected before assembly begins. While the current inspection process weeds out defective parts at a single stage, we were curious if this system could be used to predict quality at a granular level, potentially identifying and preventing compounding errors as higher level assemblies are manufactured.

In order to construct a proof of concept, we obtained 70 instances of real-world product data, including the inspected attributes of all subparts and final assemblies. Initial analysis of the data showed that non-linear transformations were required in order to capture the relationships between the part and assembly attributes. The following sections detail the processes required to produce these models.

3.1   Data Sanitization

In some examples, input part data were missing. Data holes like these are common in real-world data. Normal data cleaning methods such as replacing gaps with the mean of existing data [16] were not used due to the small number of examples available. Instead, data gaps in input data were replaced with zeros. This allows the model's section pressure to favor features that are available in all examples, while retaining the ability to leverage the incomplete data.

3.2   Evolving Models

Due to the non-linearity of the data, and a desire to produce models with high readability, GP was selected to model the transformations. Koza style tree-based GP [14] is employed, with the tree output representing a single expected quality attribute. A standard set of binary functions and terminals, detailed in Table 1, were used to evolve the models. Quality attributes are injected into the model via the attribute terminal.

Table 1. GP primitives

Primitive type	Primitives
Binary functions	+, -, *, /
Terminals	Constant, Quality attribute

The fitness of each genotype is calculated by comparing the model's outputs with the expected data on several real-world parts. A granular and fair accuracy calculation must be constructed to handle variations in part attribute values. Our accuracy calculation scales the accuracy relative to the attribute size. This equation is described in Eq. 1 with α representing the expected value and β representing the model's value. When determining the fitness of a model, accuracy is calculated for multiple parts. The smallest of these values is selected as the fitness. This method was chosen over mean or mode to prevent the optimization algorithm from ignoring outliers.

$$fitness = \log(\frac{1}{\frac{|\alpha-\beta|}{|\alpha|}}) \tag{1}$$

The evolution process is detailed in Algorithm 1. The initial population is generated using the ramped half and half method, a classic GP initialization technique [11]. Each solution is evaluated and assigned a fitness at creatio n time. Unlike Koza-style GP, the children are created through mutation *or* recombination. First, parents are chosen from the population. During recombination, two parents are chosen and a random node from each tree is swapped. During mutation, a random node is selected and regenerated from the single parent. A strategy parameter, *MutationRecombinationRatio*, controls the ratio of children generated by recombination and mutation. The children are merged with the population. Then, using a selection method, the surviving solutions are chosen and move on to the next generation. In order to support fair comparison against baselines, the algorithm is terminated after a set amount of fitness evaluations. Within a few rounds of hand-tuning, the algorithm was able to reach a sufficiently high fitness with a 95% accuracy compared to the ground truth. As such, no more tuning was required. All strategy parameters are listed in Table 2.

4   Integrating Quality into the AJSSP

The AJSSP is well suited for integration of the quality transformation models. Under the AJSSP, the series of assemblies naturally provides a scenario where

Result: Quality Tranformation Model
while *Evaluations* < *Max Evaluations* **do**
    Children = [];
    for $i \leftarrow 0$ **to** λ **do**
        if $U(0..1)$ < *Mutation Recombination Ratio* **then**
            Parent1 = Parent Selection(Population);
            Children.append(Sub-TreeMutation(Parent1));
        else
            Parent1 = Parent Selection(Population);
            Parent2 = Parent Selection(Population);
            Children.append(Sub-Tree Recombination(Parent1, Parent2));
        end
    end
    Population = Population + Children;
    Population = Survival Selection(Population);
    Evaluations += λ;
end

Algorithm 1: The primary loop of the part modeling EA. It is assumed that $MaxEvaluations - \mu$ is evenly divisible by λ for clean termination. Of note, children are created by either recombination or mutation. In the case of mutation the second selected parent is unused.

Table 2. GP configuration

Strategy parameter	Value
Population management	$\mu + \lambda$
μ	200
λ	50
Parent selection	Fitness proportionate selection
Survival selection	K-tournament selection (k = 20)
Max depth	10
Mutation and recombination operators	Koza-style
Mutation recombination ratio	0.2
Initialization	Ramped Half-and-Half (md = 5, d = 10)
Termination	Max evaluations
Max evaluations	10,000

compounding quality shifts can occur. The AJSSP framework also allows for the tracking of final product assembly time and quantity.

Rather than counting the number of parts available at a given timestep or using a validation method to check schedule correctness, we choose to perform something more akin to a factory floor simulation. Each part produced has its quality calculated on the fly with the transformation model. For this AJSSP, all machines producing the same assembly share the same quality transformation model. If a part has multiple quality attributes, multiple models are used to produced the qualities of the assembly, one for each attribute. After a part is produced, it is placed in a "bin" with other parts of the same type. When an assembly job is run, the sub-parts required for the assembly are removed from the bins, and their attributes are fed into the assembly's quality transformation model(s). This system of bins and part tracking allows for part quality to be modeled and recorded throughout the problem, from the lowest level sub-assemblies to the final product.

At the lowest level, base parts must exist to create the initial assemblies. At the modeled facility, many of the lowest level parts are ordered ahead in bulk or are stockpiled on site. To mirror this situation, at the beginning of the AJSSP, a large amount of "supplied parts" are placed in their respective bins. For the supplied parts, in order to maintain consistency, the number of supplied parts and the attributes of said parts are the same for all experiments. These parts were created with a Gaussian distribution of part qualities.

Some more common AJSSP constraints were added to more closely fit the real-world scenario. First, we chose the traditional JSSP over the flexible JSSP: a machine may only run a certain subset of assembly jobs. Second, not all assembly operations take the same amount of time. Finally, it should be noted that the AJSSP simulation contains no stochastic elements. The supplied parts are identical and the machines and quality models are entirely deterministic.

4.1 Objective Calculations

The simulation environment produces three different fitnesses, one for each objective. For simplicity and visualization, each of the fitnesses are designed to be positive and ranked in increasing order. The simulation terminates if the schedule has produced a set amount of deliverable products above a specified quality threshold, emulating a typical single order of products. If a final product fails to meet the quality threshold, it is discarded. A max time is imposed to save computational resources.

The first objective, the makespan, is calculated by taking the difference between the max allowed time, and time when the schedule has produced the required quantity of parts. If the schedule fails to produce the required quantity of parts in the max time, it is assigned a fitness of zero. The next fitness monitors the first part lead time. In order to rank this fitness in increasing order, this is calculated by taking the difference between the max time and the first deliverable product that meets requirements. The last fitness measures part quality. The quality metric of the passing final products are averaged together to form this fitness. Naturally, as a byproduct of these objectives, failed deliverable products are minimized. Creating a failed part wastes machine time that could have been used to create a part that meets requirements.

5 MOEA Solution Method

The stated problem and objectives can be broken down into two primary actions: scheduling jobs on machines, and selecting subparts to use in part creation. Since these problems are so closely related, we choose to bundle both solutions into a single genotype with two distinct components. A visualization of this genotype, as well as a single assembly operation is shown in Fig. 2. The first is a schedule which describes the order and machines jobs are run on. The second component, called the part rankers, is a series of GP trees which are used to select the parts used in the jobs. With the same functions and primitives as the quality models, listed in Table 1, the GP tree uses the part attributes to generate a value. The bins are sorted using the trees' calculated values. When a part is built, the subparts with the highest values are consumed.

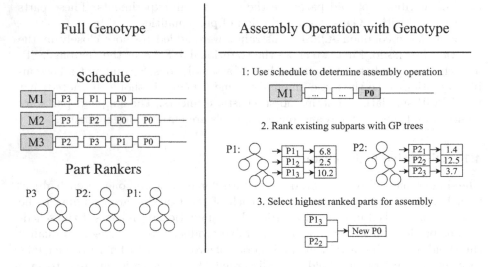

Fig. 2. A visualization of the genotype and the operation of a single assembly step. In practice, the ranking of the subparts is calculated and stored at the subparts' assembly time to prevent unnecessary re-ranking, but the displayed operation produces the same logical outcome.

5.1 Initialization

For the part rankers, unlike the modeling process, initialization is performed completely at random. At each node above the maximum depth, a random leaf or branching node is chosen. At one less than the max depth of the tree, a random leaf node is forced. Schedule initialization is a bit more complex due to the job dependencies. In order to randomly initialize a valid schedule, at every decision point, when a machine is not running an assembly, a random assembly is selected from the set of valid assemblies. The valid set of assemblies is determined from the state of the part bins.

5.2   Mutation and Recombination

The two different components of the genotype must be mutated in separate ways. For the GP trees, a random set of trees are mutated, controlled by the *TreeMutationRate* parameter. For each tree that undergoes mutation, a random node is selected and regenerated using the initialization technique. The schedule is mutated by selecting a random decision point and regenerating the schedule through the initialization technique. The *ScheduleMutationRate* parameter determines the likelihood that the schedule will undergo mutation if the genotype is selected for mutation.

Likewise, different techniques must be used to perform recombination for the two different components. For the GP trees, in recombination, controlled by *TreeSwappingRecombinationRatio*, either the whole tree can be swapped, or a random node of one tree may be swapped with a node of another tree. Similar to mutation, a random subset of trees is selected for recombination via the *TreeRecombinatoinRate*.

Crossover of the schedule always occurs during recombination. For schedule recombination, a random time is selected as the crossover point. The first schedule is copied up to that point. From then on, the second schedule is used as a guide to complete the new schedule. If the next decision of the guide schedule is possible, then it is added. However, if it is not, due to subpart dependencies, a random decision is selected from the set of available decisions, similar to initialization.

5.3   Evolutionary Process

These genotypes are systematically evolved in order to search for new solutions. First, an initial population of genotypes is initialized and ranked based on Pareto optimality as in NSGA-II. The lowest set split during truncation is first sorted via NSGA-II fitness clustering, and the least clustered members are selected for survival. The highest ranking members of the population are selected into a parent set for mutation and recombination. From this set, λ child genotypes are created. Similar to the modeling evolutionary process, *MutationRecombinationRatio* determines the ratio of children created through recombination or mutation. These children are added to the population and all members are re-ranked. Finally, the population is culled via truncation. From there the next set of parents are selected, and the process repeats.

All of the MOEA configuration parameters, including the parameters noted above in the mutation and recombination section, are listed in Table 3. The parameters were optimized with random search. A set of parameters is run five times to capture consistency. The optimal config, observing both relative performance and consistency, was hand-picked. We can observe that, in general, the parameters favored high rates of change, picking above 0.8 for schedule, ranking mutation, and recombination rates. The algorithm, in general preferred recombination to mutation. When given the option to swap trees entirely between genotypes, the algorithm landed on traditional node-based crossover most of the

Table 3. MOEA configuration

Strategy parameter	Value
μ	500
λ	500
Population management	$\mu + \lambda$
Parent selection	Fitness proportionate selection
Survival selection	Truncation with NSGA-II Clustering
Mutation recombination ratio	0.24
Schedule mutation rate	0.88
Tree mutation and recombination operators	Koza-style
Max tree depth	6
Tree mutation rate	0.93
Tree swapping recombination ratio	0.26
Tree recombination rate	0.82
Tree initialization	Random
Termination	Max evaluations
Max evaluations	50,000

time. Other than the high rate of change, the discovered parameters are fairly typical.

6 Scheduling Baselines

In order to evaluate our algorithm's performance, we constructed two baselines using the same genotype configuration as our EA. Random search was performed by repeatedly initializing the genotype structures. These solutions were ranked by Pareto non-domination. For the second baseline we implemented a form of hill climbing designed to operate in a multi-objective environment. The hill climber is seeded with a single initialization of the genotype. At each step, a new genotype is generated via the mutation operator, re-evaluated, and added to the population using the mutation method described in the above section. Afterwards, all genotypes are ranked via Pareto non-domination. Any members not in the Pareto frontier are removed from the population. In order to save on compute resources, the Pareto front is shuffled and truncated if it grows to more than 500 members. The next member to be mutated is selected from the remaining population.

7 Modeling Experiments and Results

Since both the modeling GP and baseline were run 30 times, they can be statistically compared with the student's t-test. K-fold cross validation, specifically 30-fold cross validation with a 20%/80% test-train split, was used to prevent overfitting. First, by conducting a F-test, we determine that the variances are unequal between the two algorithms. Next, a two-tailed t-test was run assuming unequal variances. The t-test confers a confidence interval beyond 0.99 showing a statically significant difference in performance. With GP's higher mean of 95.06%, compared to the random search mean of 68.79%, in the test set, we can conclude that GP outperformed the baseline. Full details of the calculation can be found in Table 4. In the vast majority of instances, GP was able to find more accurate models than the random search baseline.

Table 4. Statistical analysis results

Test or parameter	GP	Random search
Samples	30	30
Mean fitness	95.06%	68.78%
σ	1.4%	0.04%
T-Test, Unequal Variances, 2-Tailed	$1 - p = 4.7 \times 10^{-8}$	

8   Factory Simulation Experiments and Results

Due to the high computational cost, it was infeasible to compare the three algorithms run to convergence. Instead, in order to perform a fair empirical comparison, we opted to provide each of the algorithms the maximum feasible computational time: 50,000 evaluations. Each algorithm was run 30 times with different seeds to capture consistency and provide a more robust comparison. All algorithms were run with the same factory and assembly configuration. This configuration consists of a single deliverable part, D, which is constructed from two subparts: A and B. These subparts are constructed from supplied parts. A is constructed from supplied part SPA and B is constructed from supplied part SPB. The factory has three machines: $M1$, $M2$, and $M3$. $M1$ can produce parts D and A. $M2$ can produce A and B. $M3$ can produce D and B. For this proof of concept, and due to the nature of parts created at our facility, the part models used in our experiments were randomly generated.

8.1   Empirical Comparison

We first compare the performance of the three algorithms by observing Pareto-dominance between fronts. Each run was compared against another through a series of binary comparisons. The comparisons are performed by combining the Pareto-fronts of two runs and re-sorting the genotypes. Since each algorithm was run 30 times, 900 sets of comparisons are performed for each permutation of the comparison. If only one run's solutions appear in the most dominant front, we declare that run to have dominated the other. If both runs' solutions appear in the most dominant front, then we declare the two runs to have tied. When the algorithms tie, we note the number of elements which contributed to the final best Pareto front. If more elements of that front were contributed by a single algorithm, the comparison is labeled a "greater tie". If both algorithms contributed equally to the final front, the result is labeled a "true tie". For each algorithm we performed several runs and compared each run individually. For example, if each algorithm had 30 runs, we recorded 900 different comparisons. The results of these comparisons can be seen in Table 5.

Table 5. Empirical comparison of algorithms

Alg A	Alg B	A Doms	B Doms	A greater ties	B greater ties	True ties
MOEA	Random	710	0	190	0	0
MOEA	Hill	641	0	259	0	0
Hill	Random	190	61	186	423	40

From the results gathered shown in Table 5 we can see that a significant number of solutions tied, but MOEA performed demonstrably better than the baselines. Looking at the complete front dominations, the MOEA solver outperformed random search and hill climbing around roughly 75% of the time. In the case of a tie, the MOEA always contributed more members to the combined Pareto front. Comparing the two baselines, we see an interesting patten. While the hill climber is able to dominate random search more often, random search generally contributed more members to ties. We will explore this more when we discuss aspects of the solution quality. The distribution of fitnesses, shown in Fig. 3 backs up the performance metrics. Observing the top row of plots, the best-performing fitnesses in a run, the MOEA was able to consistently produce solutions with better time savings and part qualities. All three algorithms were able to find the best possible lead time, which was a single optimal permutation of jobs to produce the first part.

8.2   Comparison of Solution Quality

With multiple objectives, more metrics and figures may be derived than front domination. To gather more empirical data about solution qualities, the size of the front and the range of solution fitnesses were chosen as metrics. The data is aggregated in Table 6. The MOEA method was, on average, able to produce solutions with five times the members of both random search and hill climbing. In this context, more solutions would provide greater decision options to the end users of this optimization. This may also explain the discrepancy between the best and merged fitness distributions of solutions produced by the MOEA. The MOEA was able to generate Pareto fronts of wider rangers, bringing down the averages of the merged solutions. The MOEA had the greatest range in time, but only by a small amount. Random search showed significantly more range in part

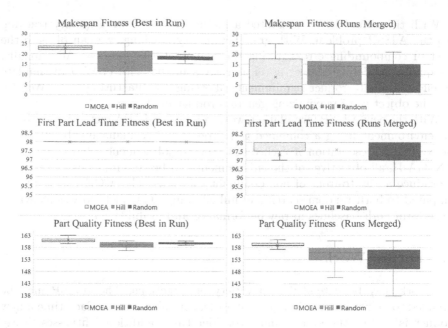

Fig. 3. The distributions of the fitnesses. The top series of charts display the distributions of the best fitnesses for each of the 30 runs. The bottom charts display the fitness distributions of all 30 runs' members merged.

Table 6. Comparison of solution quality

Algorithm	Front size	Makespan	Part quality	First part
MOEA	49.6	18.4	5.98	4.5
Random search	11.0	17.93	22.47	10.0
Hill climbing	9.06	14.36	12.33	1.0

*Makespan, Part Quality, and First Part are the mean ranges of their respective fitnesses.

quality and first part lead time. Considering random search's raw performance, we suspect this is caused by the poorer quality of solutions produced by random search. As solutions approach their maximums, observed in the best in run lead times, the general range of non-dominated solutions tends to close.

9   Conclusion

Inspired by a real-world scenario, we have introduced a new method of modeling quality through the use of intermediate inspection data. Using GP, real-world assembly quality attributes may be reliably and accurately predicted. Confirmed by statistical analysis, GP outperforms random search when generating these models.

With these models, we presented a method of integrating quality tracking into the AJSSP problem. With granular quality tracking, we can observe the effect of compounding errors during the manufacturing process. Additionally, this quality modeling enables novel objectives in the AJSSP. We can simulate the effect of final product requirements affecting manufacturing time. We also gain the objective of maximizing general product quality.

With the new AJSSP formulation, we developed a MOEA method to optimize this environment using a combined genotype of GP to manage sub-assemblies and a direct representation of a schedule to control job sequence. Through the use of NSGA-II, all objectives of the environment can be simultaneously optimized to produce a Pareto-front of non-dominant solutions. The MOEA method was compared to both random search and hill climbing. This method was shown to outperform both baselines in raw performance and usability metrics.

10 Future Work

This work may be extended in a variety of directions. The AJSSP may be extended to delivering multiple product orders simultaneously. Each time a new product is added, the system must consider three additional fitnesses. Early experiments with multiple products shows that NSGA-II is not able to optimize well due to the abundance of non-dominant solutions. Variations and modifications on NSGA-II [7] have been shown to be effective at solving many-objective problems, especially the non-dominant solution issue. Another alternative may be to swap out the NSGA-II optimizer with the NSGA-III optimizer [5], specifically designed to handle such issues.

While this work primarily operates in the empirical domain, further work could be done to create a more rigorous mathematical analysis of the quality-aware AJSSP problem and optimization method. Such a model may provide critical insights into provably optimal solutions and novel solution methods.

This algorithm can be used to analyze how adding or removing machines or suppliers affects the various objectives, as well as the tradeoff between objectives. While the current work may help with short to medium term planning through scheduling, observing how the optimization changes under factory modifications may help inform medium to long term decisions such as purchasing equipment, hiring operators, or expanding floor space. Taking this concept into the adversarial space, this manipulation of factory structure may be linked to another EA forming a competitive co-evolution problem. One agent is trying to maximize factory objectives while the other is attempting to minimize said objectives by sabotaging select parts, machines, or other factory processes. Through this proposed system, critical manufacturing components may be identified.

Acknowledgements. This work is funded by the Department of Energy's Kansas City National Security Campus, operated by Honeywell Federal Manufacturing & Technologies, LLC, under contract number DE-NA0002839.

References

1. Ahmadi, E., Zandieh, M., Farrokh, M., Emami, S.M.: A multi objective optimization approach for flexible job shop scheduling problem under random machine breakdown by evolutionary algorithms. Comput. Oper. Res. **73**, 56–66 (2016). https://doi.org/10.1016/j.cor.2016.03.009
2. Al-Hinai, N., ElMekkawy, T.Y.: Robust and stable flexible job shop scheduling with random machine breakdowns using a hybrid genetic algorithm. Int. J. Prod. Econ. **132**(2), 279–291 (2011). https://doi.org/10.1016/j.ijpe.2011.04.020
3. Chan, F.T., Wong, T., Chan, L.: A genetic algorithm-based approach to job shop scheduling problem with assembly stage. In: 2008 IEEE International Conference on Industrial Engineering and Engineering Management, pp. 331–335. IEEE (2008). https://doi.org/10.1109/IEEM.2008.4737885
4. Dabhi, V.K., Chaudhary, S.: Empirical modeling using genetic programming: a survey of issues and approaches. Natural Comput. **14**(2), 303–330 (2014). https://doi.org/10.1007/s11047-014-9416-y
5. Deb, K., Jain, H.: An evolutionary many-objective optimization algorithm using reference-point-based nondominated sorting approach, part i: Solving problems with box constraints. IEEE Trans. Evol. Comput. **18**(4), 577–601 (2013). https://doi.org/10.1109/TEVC.2013.2281535
6. Deb, K., Pratap, A., Agarwal, S., Meyarivan, T.: A fast and elitist multiobjective genetic algorithm: NSGA-II. IEEE Trans. Evol. Comput. **6**(2), 182–197 (2002). https://doi.org/10.1109/4235.996017
7. Elarbi, M., Bechikh, S., Gupta, A., Said, L.B., Ong, Y.S.: A new decomposition-based NSGA-II for many-objective optimization. IEEE Trans. Syst. Man Cybern. Syst. **48**(7), 1191–1210 (2017). https://doi.org/10.1109/TSMC.2017.2654301
8. Frutos, M., Olivera, A.C., Tohmé, F.: A memetic algorithm based on a nsgaii scheme for the flexible job-shop scheduling problem. Annal. Oper. Res. **181**(1), 745–765 (2010). https://doi.org/10.1007/s10479-010-0751-9
9. Gao, K., Cao, Z., Zhang, L., Chen, Z., Han, Y., Pan, Q.: A review on swarm intelligence and evolutionary algorithms for solving flexible job shop scheduling problems. IEEE/CAA J. Automatica Sinica **6**(4), 904–916 (2019). https://doi.org/10.1109/JAS.2019.1911540
10. Gen, M., Lin, L.: Multiobjective evolutionary algorithm for manufacturing scheduling problems: state-of-the-art survey. J. Intell. Manuf. **25**(5), 849–866 (2014). https://doi.org/10.1007/s10845-013-0804-4
11. Koza, J.R.: Genetic Programming: On the Programming of Computers by Means of Natural Selection, vol. 1. MIT Press, Cambridge (1992)
12. Lu, H., Huang, G.Q., Yang, H.: Integrating order review/release and dispatching rules for assembly job shop scheduling using a simulation approach. Int. J. Prod. Res. **49**(3), 647–669 (2011). https://doi.org/10.1080/00207540903524490
13. Lv, H., Han, G.: Research of assembly job shop scheduling problem based on modified genetic programming. In: 2017 10th International Symposium on Computational Intelligence and Design (ISCID), vol. 2, pp. 147–151. IEEE (2017). https://doi.org/10.1109/ISCID.2017.120
14. Poli, R., Langdon, W.B., McPhee, N.F., Koza, J.R.: A Field Guide to Genetic Programming. Lulu. com (2008)
15. Potts, C.N., Sevast'Janov, S., Strusevich, V.A., Van Wassenhove, L.N., Zwaneveld, C.M.: The two-stage assembly scheduling problem: Complexity and approximation. Oper. Res. **43**(2), 346–355 (1995). https://doi.org/10.1287/opre.43.2.346

16. Rahm, E., Do, H.H.: Data cleaning: problems and current approaches. IEEE Data Eng. Bull. **23**(4), 3–13 (2000)
17. Thiagarajan, S., Rajendran, C.: Scheduling in dynamic assembly job-shops to minimize the sum of weighted earliness, weighted tardiness and weighted flowtime of jobs. Comput. Industr. Eng. **49**(4), 463–503 (2005). https://doi.org/10.1016/j.cie.2005.06.005
18. Wang, Y.M., Yin, H.L., Da Qin, K.: A novel genetic algorithm for flexible jobshop scheduling problems with machine disruptions. Int. J. Adv. Manuf. Technol. **68**(5-8), 1317–1326 (2013).https://doi.org/10.1007/s00170-013-4923-z
19. Wong, T.C., Chan, F.T., Chan, L.: A resource-constrained assembly job shop scheduling problem with lot streaming technique. Comput. Industr. Eng. **57**(3), 983–995 (2009). https://doi.org/10.1016/j.cie.2009.04.002
20. Wong, T.C., Ngan, S.C.: A comparison of hybrid genetic algorithm and hybrid particle swarm optimization to minimize makespan for assembly job shop. Appl. Soft. Comput. **13**(3), 1391–1399 (2013). https://doi.org/10.1016/j.asoc.2012.04.007
21. Zhang, Q.s., Zhu, S.C.: Visual interpretability for deep learning: a survey. Frontiers Inf. Technol. Electron. Eng. **19**(1), 27–39 (2018)
22. Zhang, S., Li, X., Zhang, B., Wang, S.: Multi-objective optimisation in flexible assembly job shop scheduling using a distributed ant colony system. Eur. J. Oper. Res. **283**(2), 441–460 (2020). https://doi.org/10.1016/j.ejor.2019.11.016

Evolutionary Grain-Mixing to Improve Profitability in Farming Winter Wheat

Md Asaduzzaman Noor$^{(\boxtimes)}$ and John W. Sheppard$^{(\boxtimes)}$

Gianforte School of Computing, Montana State University, Bozeman 59717, USA
mdasaduzzaman.noor@student.montana.edu, john.sheppard@montana.edu

Abstract. This paper focuses on adapting and applying a genetic algorithm (GA) and differential evolution (DE) to solve the grain (wheat) mixing problem. The proposed algorithms explore a search space that aims at finding a quality mixing of wheat from grain bins that produce the maximum profit at a grain elevator. The experimental results demonstrate that mixing bins provide more profit than not mixing, and that the evolutionary approaches lead to consistently higher profits than the non-evolutionary methods.

Keywords: Grain mixing · Blending problem · Profit maximization · Genetic algorithm · Differential evolution

1 Introduction

Agriculture and agricultural products are essential in sustaining lives on the planet. To feed the population on the Earth efficiently, considerable planning is required. Issues, such as crop rotation or mixed cropping techniques, optimal seeding and fertilizing, proper irrigation, and efficient harvest and distribution are all required for agriculture to meet the needs of most people.

In this paper, we consider an important component of the food supply chain, referred to as grain mixing. The grain considered in our case is wheat that has been stored in different bins in preparation for being sent to a local grain elevator for dissemination. The farmers load the grain from these bins into trucks and sell the wheat at the nearest elevators/markets. The price they get from the elevators depends on the quality (protein level) of the wheat.

Several factors play an essential role when determining the profit from wheat production. One of the critical elements determining the price of a bushel of wheat is protein content, which is affected by several environmental factors, including temperature during the growing season, soil nitrogen levels, genetics, timing, and precipitation. Due to the resulting variation, protein content might change, not only from year to year but also from crop to crop. The technology is available to track the protein content in a bushel of wheat on site; however, it is expensive, making it inaccessible to several smaller farmers. Consequently, most wheat producers end up taking their harvest to the closest elevators and collecting whatever amount is paid.

P. A. Castillo and J. L. Jiménez Laredo (Eds.): EvoApplications 2021, LNCS 12694, pp. 113–129, 2021.
https://doi.org/10.1007/978-3-030-72699-7_8

The purpose of this project was two-fold. First, we investigated if mixing grain increases the profitability of the farmers. The general approach involved comparing a naïve strategy for delivering grain, as if no protein tracking were done, to that of using the protein content to determine a quality mix for delivery. Constrained evolutionary algorithms: specifically a Genetic Algorithm (GA) and Differential Evolution (DE), was used to optimize the mixing of the grain. These methods were also compared to a greedy mixing strategy to determine if the added complexity is beneficial. The final goal was to see if it is worth investing in the technology and infrastructure needed to track the protein level and mix the wheat on site.

The remainder of this paper is structured as follows. In Sect. 2, we discuss work related to ours. In Sect. 3, we present the grain mixing problem. We then present the formal problem statement in Sect. 4. The data collected for this study is introduced in Sect. 5 followed by our methodology and experimental design in Sects. 6 and 7 respectively. We present our results in Sect. 8, followed by a discussion of those results in Sect. 9. The paper ends with future work and our conclusions in Sects. 10 and 11.

2   Related Work

The grain mixing problem studied in this paper relates to the classical blending optimization problem. The blending problem seeks to find blends of materials by mixing them to meet specific requirements that lower overall production cost. It is possible to solve the classical blending problems by linear programming (LP) methods if both the objective function and the constraints are linear [9]. There exist a few works that attempted to solve the decision version of the grain mixing problem (also known as wheat blending) with linear programming. Hayka and Cakmalki utilized LP methods capable of predicting the optimal wheat blend ratio for a targeted final quality to produce a bread making flour [6]. Haas used the simplex algorithm to find the optimum blend that satisfies the customer's specific solvent retention capacities (SRC) [5]. In our case, the objective function is non-linear and there is no specific targeted wheat quality, which makes it challenging to solve the problem by only using LP.

Mixed-integer linear programming (MILP) is often used to solve many real-world blending problems [14]; however, MILP is known to be NP-hard. Bilgen and Ozkarahan proposed a MILP model to optimize the cost for the wheat supply chain (blending, loading, transportation, and storage), where the model used a specific blending formula for the mixing [3]. MILP has also been used in the blending of oil [12], water [15], gasoline [8], and chemical fertilizer [2].

Xiang et al. proposed a Hybrid-Evolutionary method to solve the wheat blending problem in Australia [10]. Their method used a GA with a heuristic method and a liner-relaxed version of the simplex algorithm to solve the blending problem. Their work closely relates to our mixing problem; however, the problem formulation differs based on the US wheat market. In our problem, there is an added constraint on the capacity a truck can carry, and the farmers have the

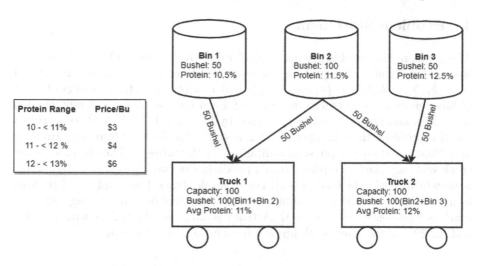

Fig. 1. Grain mixing example

choice of delivering wheat to multiple elevators. Evolutionary approaches have also been used for blending gasoline [4] and composite laminates [1].

Most of the work for the wheat blending problem in the US market has been done in the milling companies to produce client-specific bread making flour. To the best of our knowledge, our approach is the first to address the grain-mixing problem to increase the profitability of the farmers.

3   Grain-Mixing Problem

The objective of this study was to develop a method for farmers to maximize their profit when selling wheat at local grain elevators. When selling wheat, the price per bushel of grain varies based on a range of protein levels. For example, if the protein level is 10–11%, the price might be $3 per bushel where it might increase to $4/bu with protein levels of 12–13%. The overall profit of a truck depends on the number of bushels and the average protein level. At times, there are many cases where the protein level of a bin is short of reaching a higher price range; therefore, it might be possible to mix grain from a high-quality (in terms of protein level) bin with a low-quality bin to make a better overall profit.

Figure 1 illustrates the grain-mixing process. In the example, there are three bins with different numbers of bushels and protein levels. The table presents elevator prices for different quality grains. Without mixing, the profit obtained from all the bins would be $(50*\$3+100*\$4+50*\$6) = \$850$. However, if we mix grain as shown in the figure, the overall profit would be $(100*\$4+100*\$6) = \$1000$, which increases the profit by $150. There are other factors like mixing cost and delivery cost involved in the overall profit. Only the effect of protein content is shown for simplicity.

4   Problem Statement

The grain mixing problem aims to determine the optimal mix of wheat from storage bins to maximize profit when sold to a set of elevators. More formally, let $B = \{b_1, b_2, ..., b_n\}$, $E = \{e_1, e_2, ..., e_m\}$,and $T = \{t_1, t_2, ..., t_l\}$ represents the set of bins, elevators, and trucks respectively. Each bin contains a different number of bushels and protein levels represented by b_i^{Bu}, and b_i^{Pr} $\forall b_i \in B$ respectively. For this problem, the mixing of wheat is restricted to drawing from only two bins at a time based on the physical limitations of the farmers. Therefore, a loaded truck will only contain bushels from a maximum of two bins (or one bin if there is no wheat left in the second bin). For example, truck 1 may mix bushels from b_1 and b_5 but not from the combination of b_1, b_5, and b_7. The mixing ratio of a truck is represented by $\alpha \in [0, 1]$. A truck mixing bins b_1 and b_5 with $\alpha = 0.2$ will fill 20% of the truck with bushels from b_1 and 80% from b_5.

4.1   Cost Model

Let C denote the total number of bushels a truck can carry. If a truck t_i mixes grain from two bins b_j and b_k with a mixing ratio α, the total number of bushels in the truck is computed as follows.

$$t_i^{Bu} = b_{i,j}^{Bu} + b_{i,k}^{Bu}$$

where, $b_{i,j}^{Bu}$ represents $(C \times \alpha)$ bushels drawn from b_j to t_i and $b_{i,k}^{Bu}$ represents $(C \times (1-\alpha))$ bushels drawn from b_k to t_i. The remaining bushels of b_j^{Bu} and b_k^{Bu} is updated by subtracting the used amount respectively. Moreover, by mixing grain from two bins, the weighted average protein level of t_i is computed as

$$t_i^{Pr} = \alpha \cdot b_j^{Pr} + (1 - \alpha) \cdot b_k^{Pr}.$$

Finally, the revenue of truck t_i depends on the elevator/market prices and the average protein level in the truck. The revenue of truck t_i going to elevator e_j is computed as

$$t_{i,j}^{Rev} = \left[e_j^{b\_price} + \left(\left| \frac{|t_i^{Pr} - e_j^{b\_Pr}|}{e_j^{up/down\_Pr}} \right| \right) \times e_j^{up/down\_price} \right] \times t_i^{Bu}$$

where, $e_j^{b\_price}$ is the base protein price of the elevator, t_i^{Pr} is the truck's protein level per unit bushel, $e_j^{b\_Pr}$ is the base protein level of the elevator, $e_j^{up/down\_Pr}$ is the up or down protein level, $e_j^{up/down\_price}$ is the up or down price, and t_i^{Bu} is the total number of bushels in the truck.

To calculate the profit of a truck t_i, the associated mixing cost and delivery cost need to be deducted from the final revenue of the truck. The mixing cost $(t_i^{mix\_cost})$ is associated with the mixing difficulty of the two bins used in the truck, and the delivery cost depends on the cost to deliver the grain to the elevators. The delivery cost is represented as $t_{i,j}^{del\_cost}$ for t_i going to the elevator e_j. The individual profit for truck t_i is then calculated as

$$t_i^{Profit} = \max_j \{t_{i,j}^{Rev} - (t_i^{mix\_cost} + t_{i,j}^{del\_cost})\} \tag{1}$$

A maximum of l trucks are loaded until there are no bushels left in the respective bins. A truck may contain a single bin if there are no bushels left to fill the second bin. In that case, the truck protein level would be the same as the single bin and there will be no mixing cost. Finally, the objective is to maximize the total profit from l trucks given by

$$\text{maximize} \left(\sum_{i=1}^{l} t_i^{Profit} \right) \tag{2}$$

The constraints involved in the optimization problem are as follows:

- For a truck t_i with $b_{i,j}^{Bu}$ bushels drawn from b_j and $b_{i,k}^{Bu}$ bushels drawn from b_k, the total bushels of the truck cannot exceed maximum capacity C.

$$t_i^{Bu} = b_{i,j}^{Bu} + b_{i,k}^{Bu} \leq C \qquad \forall t_i \in T, \forall j, k \in B$$

- The bushels from bin b_j loaded in multiple trucks cannot exceed the total bushels in that bin.

$$\sum_{i=1}^{l} b_{i,j}^{Bu} \leq b_j^{Bu} \qquad \forall b_j \in B$$

- For all trucks and bins,

$$t_i^{Bu} \geq 0 \qquad \forall t_i \in T$$
$$b_j^{Bu} \geq 0 \qquad \forall b_j \in B$$

4.2 Hypothesis

Our goal is to find the best set of bin pairs and the mixing ratios α for l trucks that yield maximum profit. Several optimization techniques will be considered to assess the solution quality. The *NoMix* algorithm will be used to obtain the baseline profit when the trucks contain grain from a single bin to assess if it is better to mix bins in the first place. The *GreedyMix* algorithm will mix grain based on a lookup profit table by taking all the pairwise combinations of bins and α and greedily fill the trucks based on the maximum profit combination (see Sect. 6.2 for more details). We also apply a genetic algorithm (GA) [7] and differential evolution algorithm (DE) [16] as alternative optimization methods.

We hypothesize that the *GreedyMix* algorithm will yield a higher profit than the *NoMix* algorithm as the expectation is that mixing bins provide a better solution. We hypothesize further that the GA and DE algorithms will yield higher profit than the *GreedyMix* as they provide a more comprehensive search of the search space. For the proposed GA and DE algorithm, both algorithms have been adapted to fit the problem definition (constraint validation), and we hypothesize that both algorithms will yield similar solution quality.

Table 1. Wheat distribution across 16 bins

Year	Tot bush	Max Bu/Bin	Min Bu/Bin	Avg Bu/Bin
2016	114284.8	14836.8	1712.7	7142.8
2017	112417.5	14836.8	2985.3	7026.1
Year	Tot prot	Max Prot/Bin	Min Prot/Bin	Avg Prot/Bin
2016	191.3	13.3	10.1	12.0
2017	190.1	13.8	10.1	11.9

Table 2. Market price for different elevators

Year	Market	BasePrice	BaseProtein	upPrice	upProtein	downPrice	downProtein
2016	1	3.32	11.25	0.03	0.75	−0.06	0.75
	2	3.84	11.75	0.25	0.50	−0.30	0.50
	3	3.54	12.00	0.50	0.60	−0.40	0.30
2017	1	4.42	11.50	0.05	0.50	−0.10	0.50
	2	4.47	12.00	0.25	0.50	−0.30	0.50
	3	4.39	12.20	0.50	0.60	−0.40	0.30

5   Dataset

The dataset used in this project was collected from a local Montana farmer who tracks the protein level of his wheat. The data collected is for wheat harvested in 2016 and 2017. All of the wheat was distributed among various bins. For our problem, a bin entry includes the bin id, the average protein level of wheat in that bin, the number of bushels stored, and the site number where the wheat was harvested. Our farmer used 16 bins with different numbers of bushels and protein levels in each bin (Table 1).

The data used also includes a list of elevators that provide the market price for selling wheat. An entry in the elevator list contains the base protein level, the price for the base protein level, the payment added to the base price for higher protein level (upPrice), and the payment deducted from the base price for lower protein level (downPrice). We collected information on three elevators for both years. The market price for different elevators is shown in Table 2.

Figure 2 illustrates the cost function for elevator 3 for year 2017. The orange dot shows the base protein level and base protein price for that elevator. As shown, the price of protein changes as a step function, and the step size differs based on the upProtein (or downProtein) levels from the base protein level.

Multiple trucks, each with a fixed capacity of 8000 bushels, were used to carry the wheat to the elevators. A delivery cost was charged for a fully loaded truck, ranging from $960 to $2000 based on the distance between a bin site and an elevator. Moreover, mixing the wheat from multiple bins to change the protein level incurs a mixing cost, ranging from $8 to $800. The mixing cost also depends on the site number of the bins; mixing two bins from the same site is less expensive than mixing bins from different sites.

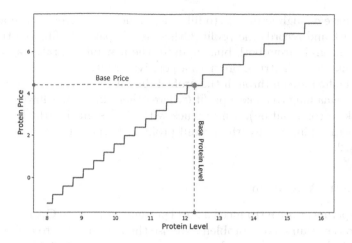

Fig. 2. Cost function of elevator 3 for 2017 dataset

6   Methodology

6.1   No Mixing

The *NoMix* algorithm calculates the overall profit without any bin mixing. The algorithm takes one bin at a time and fills the trucks with the wheat from that bin. If there is not enough wheat to load a truck fully, the algorithm checks if the partially filled truck provides a positive profit. If the profit of a partially filled truck is positive, it takes the truck to the elevator. If not, the grain in that truck is discarded without penalty, and the truck is freed up for use on another bin. The algorithm fills up to l trucks, and the total profit is calculated using the sum in Eq. 2.

6.2   Greedy Mix

The *GreedyMix* algorithm first generates a profit table by taking all of the possible combinations of two bins and the mixing ratio α. The value of α is selected from a discrete set of values in increments of 0.1: $\{0.1, 0.2, ..., 0.9\}$ to generate a finite combination set. When generating the lookup table, we compute the profit of a fully loaded truck using Eq. 1 based on the selection of two bins and the mixing ratio. The dataset contains a total of 16 bins so there are $\binom{16}{2} = 240$ ways to select two bins maintaining the order. Then there exist 9 discrete values for α which provides a total combination of $240 \times 9 = 2160$ unique truck entries in the profit table. Notice that the combinations $((1, 2), \alpha = 0.5)$ and $((2, 1), \alpha = 0.5)$ provide a different profit since delivery cost only depends on the distance between the second bin and the elevator. Therefore, the table contains an entry for 2160 mixing combinations.

To find a solution, the algorithm sorts the profit table in descending order of mixing profit and traverses it from the top. For any particular combination, if both bins have enough grain left to fill a new truck at a given α, the algorithm fills the truck and records the profit. Otherwise, it partially fills the truck with the remaining grain from both bins, updates the new mixing ratio, and includes it in the solution if the truck provides a positive profit.

After the first sweep through the profit table, if there exists a bin with sufficient grain remaining to make a profit (where other bins do not have any bushels left to make a combination), a new truck with id 0 is filled with the remaining grain from that bin. Finally, the overall profit of l trucks is obtained using the sum in Eq. 2.

6.3   Genetic Algorithm

For this experiment, we introduced a novel permutation-based GA representation to apply to the grain mixing problem. We use the permutation to determine how to fill the trucks so as to ensure the constraints remain satisfied. Here, we discuss our specific implementation of the GA.

Population: An individual in the population of the GA algorithm contains a list of candidate trucks. The number of available trucks is set to be sufficiently large to transport all of the grain, and each candidate truck contains a random entry from the profit table (total 2160 mixing combination) defined for the *GreedyMix* algorithm. Therefore, for an individual, the gene contains the tuple $(truck\_id, bin\_pair, \alpha)$, and the list of genes (candidate trucks) represents the chromosome. Each gene in the chromosome represents a unique tuple (a *truck_id* is going to appear exactly once), which ensures a feasible solution in the search space. Finally, to evaluate the fitness of an individual, the candidate truck list is used in the *IndividualMix* method. The *IndividualMix* method traverse the candidate trucks in order and load trucks fully/partially based on grain availability. For an individual I with list *candidateTrucks*, the fitness is determined as follows.

$$fitness(I) = IndividualMix()$$

Note that the candidate trucks only provide the bin-pair combination with the mixing ratio; however, the *IndividualMix* generates the final solutions by assigning bushels based on the bin-pair combinations without violating any constraints. *IndividualMix* skips a particular combination in the candidate trucks if both the bins are already empty and then move to the next combination. Therefore, for a candidate truck size of m, only l trucks are used in the final solution $(l < m)$ returned by the *IndividualMix* method.

Selection: The GA uses tournament selection [11] to select parents from the current population to generate new offspring for the next generation. A tournament consists of s randomly selected individuals from the population, and the individual with the highest fitness (tournament winner) is sent to the mating pool to generate new offspring.

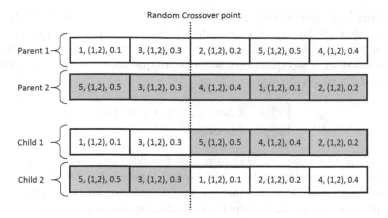

Fig. 3. Crossover operator example

Crossover: After selecting the parents, the GA generates offspring using a variant on the ordered crossover (OX) operator [13], which ensures that the new offspring contains a valid permutation of unique genes in its chromosome. To generate the offspring from two parents, a random crossover point is selected from parent 1. Then the offspring copies genes from parent 1 up to the crossover point. Then the offspring sweeps through the genes of parent 2 and copies the gene if it is not already in the gene sequence. The process stops when the sequence is full. Figure 3 shows an example of the crossover operator with five trucks in a pair of chromosomes. The fitness of the new offspring differs due to different truck order in the chromosome.

Mutation: Our mutation operator takes a gene sequence (bin-pair combinations) and randomly swaps the genes of an individual depending on the mutation probability. The operator replaces a gene of a randomly chosen individual with an entry from the profit table that is not already present in the gene sequence.

6.4 Differential Evolution (DE)

The computational steps for our implementation of DE resemble that of the GA so as to limit the differences in performance to the mechanics of the algorithm alone. The initialization of the population and the fitness function used in DE is the same as the GA. The major difference lies in the *selection, crossover,* and *mutation* operators.

Selection: The selection operator selects the better individual by comparing the fitness of the trial vector $u_{i,g}$, and the target vector $x_{i,g}$. The selected vector replaces the current vector individual for the next generation as follows.

$$x_{i,g+1} = \begin{cases} u_{i,g}, & \text{if } f(u_{i,g}) \le f(x_{i,g}) \\ x_{i,g}, & \text{otherwise} \end{cases}$$

Crossover: The crossover operator closely follows the standard DE crossover operator. After the mutation phase, the crossover operation is applied on the target vector $x_{i,g}$ and the mutant vector $v_{i,g}$ to obtain the offspring/trial vector $u_{i,g}$. The following is a common crossover technique known as binomial crossover to obtain the trial vector $u_{i,g}$.

$$u_{i,j}^g = \begin{cases} v_{i,j}^g, & \text{if } rand(0,1) \le CR \text{ or } j = j_{rand} \\ x_{i,j}^g, & \text{otherwise} \end{cases}$$

where CR represents the crossover rate: a user defined parameter ranges in $[0,1)$. j_{rand} represents a random value in the vector dimension $[1,D]$. The trial vector $u_{i,g}$ takes the jth real-value of either the target vector or mutant vector based on the condition specified above. Our implementation uses this process to generate a new trial vector; however, the trial vector first copies the chromosome of the mutant vector $v_{i,g}$ and replaces the gene with the target vector $x_{i,g}$ if it is not already present in the trial vector and $(rand(0,1) \le CR$ or $j = j_{rand})$ condition is satisfied, as in the OX operator. Here, CR represents the probability of the crossover rate.

Mutation: The algorithm uses the "DE/Best/1" strategy to create the mutant vector. The first donor vector represents the best individual in the current generation, the second donor vector is a random individual selected from the current generation, and the third donor vector is selected randomly from the profit table to add diversity in the population. All of the donor vectors are mutually exclusive.

The chromosome representation is not real-valued and therefore the standard mutation equation had to be changed to adapt to the problem representation. The new mutant vector copies genes from the three donor vectors based on the mutation factor F. In this case, the mutant vector copies genes from the first donor vector (generation best) with probability F and from either the second or third donor vector with probability $(1 - F)$. It excludes genes if they already exist in the gene sequence to maintain a valid permutation. The process is similar to the GA crossover (Fig. 3), but instead of two parents, the operator uses the three donor vectors to create a mutant individual.

7   Experimental Design

Twelve additional datasets along with the two real datasets were created to evaluate the performance of all algorithms. Among the twelve datasets, two datasets were created by flipping the elevator prices of the real dataset (using 2017 elevator data with 2016 bin data and vice-versa). The remaining ten datasets were created by randomly varying the number of bushels and the protein levels of each bin in the original datasets. Therefore, there are five simulated datasets for the year 2016 and five for the year 2017.

The results of the *NoMix* and *GreedyMix* algorithms are deterministic; however, GA and DE are stochastic. Therefore, to evaluate the performance of the

Table 3. Parameter settings for GA and DE algorithms.

Algo	Population	#Iteration	Tournament	Mutation
GA	100	500	5	0.2
Algo	Population	#Iteration	CR	Mutation
DE	100	500	0.9	0.5

stochastic algorithms, we ran 10 experiments for each dataset and recorded the average overall profit.

The GA and DE implementations create random individuals by taking a small subset of the profit table entry for the initial population. The intuition is that for a small subset of the profit table, the *IndividualMix* method returns a different result than the *GreedyMix* algorithm based on the few choices of bin combinations, and the goal of the GA and DE algorithms is to find the best sequence from the profit table for which the profit is maximum. Therefore, the subset size (candidate trucks) plays an important role in the overall solution. The subset has to be selected in a way so that it contains enough bin combinations to empty all the bushels of the bins. If the subset is too small, then it may not contain an entry for a particular bin; therefore, all of the bushels of that bin may be unused in the solution. If the subset is too large, then it will perform like the *GreedyMix* algorithm with all the choices of filling a truck.

To select the subset size, random individuals were created with subset size ranges from 50 to 150, increasing by 10 on each experiment. Then the solution returned from the individual was checked to see if they collected all of the wheat available. For a subset size of 100, more than 90% of the individuals returned solutions collecting all of the wheat; therefore, the number of candidate trucks was fixed to 100. Even if an individual fails to utilize all the bushels and excludes a significant portion of the wheat, the intuition is that the individual will be replaced by others with higher fitness. And sometimes excluding a small portion of wheat might increase the overall profit because the cost of using an extra truck for that small amount might decrease the overall profit.

The hyperparameters used in the GA and DE algorithms were tuned manually. Table 3 shows all the parameter values used in the GA and DE algorithms for all test cases. These sets of parameters provided the highest average profit for the real datasets.

To evaluate the effectiveness of the evolutionary algorithms further, we also introduced a *Random* algorithm that creates 100 random individuals from the profit table and returns the solution from the best individual. The *Random* algorithm helps us assess if the evolutionary algorithms are exploring the search-space efficiently to provide a better solution than random search. Due to stochastic nature, the *Random* algorithm was also run 10 times, and the average overall profit was recorded.

8 Results

Table 4 shows the overall profit obtained from the different algorithms for each of the test cases studied. The notation R_year denotes the real dataset for respective years and RF_year denotes the flipped version of the real dataset. A^*_year denotes the artificial dataset for respective years. The stochastic algorithm's results are the average of 10 runs. The column "Profit" shows the average best profit in thousands of US dollars, and "TR" shows the average number of trucks used in the solution. The bold values represent the best profit obtained for a dataset, and the underlined values represent a substantial profit increase (more than $5000) comparing with the base value ($NoMix$ results)[1]. Unfortunately, we do not have the cost associated with the production (harvesting) that would be necessary to provide a more complete estimate of profit.

Table 4. Algorithm performance ($Profit$ in thousands of dollars).

Dataset	GA		DE		Random		Greedy		NoMix	
	Profit	TR	Profit	TR	Profit	TR	Profit	TR	Profit	TR
R_2016	**435.8**	19	435.4	19	428.9	19	430.5	20	424.5	18
R_2017	496.2	18	**497.0**	18	491.2	18	491.6	20	487.1	19
RF_2016	**506.2**	19	505.9	19	501.9	19	499.9	21	499.7	18
RF_2017	**428.9**	18	427.8	18	421.2	18	423.1	19	418.0	19
A1_2016	415.7	19	**416.0**	19	407.6	19	394.5	19	395.4	20
A2_2016	562.0	22	**562.4**	22	550.8	22	533.1	23	545.4	23
A3_2016	**591.1**	24	589.0	27	569.8	26	543.9	31	570.0	25
A4_2016	**573.9**	24	571.0	26	558.0	25	520.4	29	539.9	25
A5_2016	533.8	25	**534.0**	25	517.6	25	496.9	23	512.2	24
A1_2017	**621.5**	22	617.9	24	599.2	23	581.7	20	608.9	23
A2_2017	**537.0**	20	536.8	21	522.0	20	515.8	18	520.6	22
A3_2017	**676.0**	25	672.5	26	664.3	26	655.8	25	643.9	24
A4_2017	450.5	16	**452.5**	17	443.5	16	435.6	16	430.1	18
A5_2017	**685.4**	24	**685.4**	25	672.4	24	656.0	25	663.5	23

For all test cases, the evolutionary algorithms performed significantly better than all other methods. For real datasets (including the flipped versions), the $GreedyMix$ and $Random$ algorithms always performed better than the $NoMix$. However, for the artificial datasets, $GreedyMix$ failed to outperform $NoMix$ 80% of the time, and the $Random$ algorithm failed to outperform $NoMix$ 20% of the time. The performance of the evolutionary algorithms shows that grain mixing always provides a higher profit than no mixing at all.

---

[1] Note that statistical hypothesis testing was not done since $NoMix$ and $GreedyMix$ only yield a single, deterministic solution.

Table 5 shows an example of one complete solution obtained from the GA algorithm for the R_2017 dataset. In the table, the column name "Bin_Pair" shows the pair of bins mixed to fill the truck, "Pair1_Bu" and "Pair2_Bu" show the number of bushels taken from each bin in the pair, "Protein" shows the weighted average protein level, "Load" gives the total amount of wheat loaded in the truck (max 8000) and "Elevator" identifies the elevator where the truck gets the highest profit.

All of the grain-mixing algorithms provide a similar solution format but with different bin-pair mixing. A complete solution shows a farmer how to load each truck with bushels from respective bins to accomplish the solution's overall profit.

Table 5. Best solution from the GA algorithm for dataset R_2017.

Bin_Pair	MixRatio	Pair1_Bu	Pair2_Bu	Protein	Load	Elevator	Profit
(1, 2)	0.20	1600.0	6400.0	13.49	8000.0	3	41992.0
(15, 2)	0.77	2985.3	892.5	13.50	3877.8	3	20147.5
(9, 12)	0.89	6539.8	800.0	13.03	7339.8	2	35378.0
(3, 12)	0.80	6395.3	1600.0	12.57	7995.3	2	36538.5
(6, 12)	0.90	7200.0	800.0	12.52	8000.0	2	36240.0
(8, 12)	0.38	2400.0	3889.7	11.52	6289.7	2	27228.0
(11, 7)	0.74	4921.3	1712.7	11.85	6634.0	2	28658.8
(1, 4)	0.60	4800.0	3200.0	11.93	8000.0	2	34552.0
(1, 4)	0.23	1600.0	5325.5	11.57	6925.5	2	29911.2
(1, 5)	0.60	4800.0	3200.0	11.74	8000.0	2	34480.0
(1, 5)	0.46	2036.8	2400.0	11.54	4436.8	2	19122.6
(16, 6)	0.93	7200.0	503.7	11.48	7703.7	1	32124.3
(14, 5)	0.98	5600.0	113.4	12.11	5713.4	2	24110.4
(14, 8)	0.63	3057.4	1792.7	11.61	4850.1	2	20224.8
(13, 10)	0.68	5050.0	2400.0	10.60	7450.0	1	30470.5
10	1.00	4892.5	0.0	10.11	4892.5	1	19765.7
16	1.00	6309.0	0.0	11.40	6309.0	1	26308.5
Total					112417.5		497252.8

9   Analysis and Discussion of Results

In most of the cases, the results obtained from the experiments supported the hypothesis. The proposed GA and DE algorithms yielded higher profits than the *NoMix* algorithm for all test cases, demonstrating their efficiency and effectiveness in grain mixing. The *GreedyMix* algorithm, however, did not appear to be an obvious choice as its profits degraded than that of the *NoMix* algorithm in case of the artificial datasets only.

At first glance, it may appear that the *GreedyMix* algorithm should provide the optimal results as it creates all possible combinations of mixes and greedily selects the mix based on the maximum profit. This claim might be true if there existed an infinite number of bushels in all of the bins. But, in the real world, our problem contains a different number of bushels for the different bins, and filling a truck greedily based on profit may not be always possible if there are no bushels left in a specific bin. Furthermore, the truck might be partially filled based on the remaining bushels of bins giving a lower profit than the actual one. Therefore, for all the test cases, *GreedyMix* not only failed to provide optimal results but also gave a lower profit (in the artificial test cases) than the *NoMix* algorithm. The evolutionary methods do suggest, however, that taking a sub-optimal bin-pair combination can yield a higher overall profit than the greedy optimal choice due to the varying bin sizes.

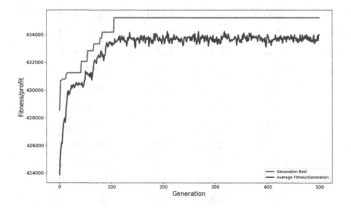

Fig. 4. Convergence example of the GA algorithm (R_2016)

The example solution in Table 5 contains two trucks with a single bin (bin 10 and 16). These trucks suggest that after the first sweep in the candidate trucks list, grain remained in bin 10 and bin 16. This indicates that the candidate trucks do not have any truck entry with bin pair (10, 16). Therefore, the solution loads the truck by separately taking bushels from each bin (no mixing cost incurred). Even without bin pair (10, 16), this solution returned the best profit for the dataset.

To check the convergence of the GA and DE algorithms, the best individual in each generation, and the average fitness of the total population in each generation were tracked. If the generation best individual did not change for more than 100 consecutive iterations, the algorithm was determined to have converged to a solution. Figure 4 and Fig. 5 shows the convergence of the GA and DE algorithms respectively for a test run with R_2016 dataset.

The average population fitness in Fig. 4 is a spiked curve because the crossover and mutation operator in the GA may create a new individual with a lower/higher fitness giving a lower/higher average profit. However, for DE, Fig. 5 shows the average population is a smooth curve since DE always replaces a current individual with a better-fit individual and improving the average population fitness for each generation. The results obtained from the *Random* algorithm also suggest that the evolutionary algorithms are efficiently exploring the search-space for finding a better solution.

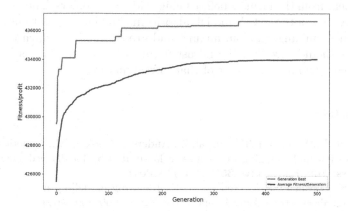

Fig. 5. Convergence example of the DE algorithm (R_2016)

10 Future Work

This work has considered several approaches to determining how to maximize the profit of wheat production by mixing different numbers of bushels to change the protein level contained in a truck being delivered to an elevator. The price of a bushel of wheat depends on its protein level as measured at the elevator. The idea is to see if mixing different protein levels can yield a mix such that the farmer will receive more profit than taking them separately. This work makes certain assumptions for the problem representation like mixing only two bins at a time and used a discrete mixing ratio α for mixing two bins. The effect of using more than two bins in the mixing and using a continuous value for mixing ratio $\alpha \in [0,1]$ will be considered as future work. In addition, using different mutation operators for the DE algorithm and the crossover operator for the GA algorithm and their impact on the overall solution quality will be considered. It is also our intent to explore the suitability of comparing to an MILP model; however, the inherent nonlinearity of the objective function would seem to suggest optimization quality would be limited. Furthermore, a more realistic cost model that includes the production cost associated with harvesting, cost of the protein device and supporting infrastructure, and alternative representations of the model will be considered.

11   Conclusion

In this paper, we evaluated two different evolutionary algorithms—the genetic algorithm and differential evolution—to solve the grain (wheat) mixing problem. The algorithms explore a search space that aims at finding the best mix of wheat that will produce the maximum profit on a farm. This wheat is usually stored in grain bins and are subsequently delivered to elevators for sale. These elevators buy the wheat from the farmers before being sold to customers. The experimental results show that both the GA and DE algorithms find better solutions (increased profit) than no mixing, random mixing, and greedy mixing, which implies that the farmers should invest in the infrastructure of grain mixing as long as the profit exceeds the amortized cost of that infrastructure.

References

1. Adams, D.B., Watson, L.T., Gürdal, Z., Anderson-Cook, C.M.: Genetic algorithm optimization and blending of composite laminates by locally reducing laminate thickness. Adv. Eng. Softw. **35**(1), 35–43 (2004)
2. Ashayeri, J., van Eijs, A., Nederstigt, P.: Blending modelling in a process manufacturing: a case study. Eur. J. Oper. Res. **72**(3), 460–468 (1994)
3. Bilgen, B., Ozkarahan, I.: A mixed-integer linear programming model for bulk grain blending and shipping. Int. J. Prod. Econ. **107**(2), 555–571 (2007)
4. Chen, X., Wang, N.: Optimization of short-time gasoline blending scheduling problem with a DNA based hybrid genetic algorithm. Chem. Eng. Process. **49**(10), 1076–1083 (2010)
5. Haas, N.: Optimizing Wheat Blends for Customer Value Creation: A Special Case of Solvent Retention Capacity. MS Thesis, Kansas State University, USA (2011)
6. Hayta, M., Cakmalki, U.: Optimization of wheat blending to produce breadmaking flour. J. Food Process. Eng. **24**, 179–192 (2001)
7. Holland, J.H.: Adaptation in Natural and Artificial Systems. University of Michigan Press, Ann Arbor (1975)
8. Jia, Z., Ierapetritou, M.: Mixed-integer linear programming model for gasoline blending and distribution scheduling. Ind. Eng. Chem. Res. **42**(4), 825–835 (2003)
9. Vanderbei, R.J.: Convex programming. Linear Programming. ISORMS, vol. 285, pp. 433–443. Springer, Cham (2020). https://doi.org/10.1007/978-3-030-39415-8_25
10. Li, X., Bonyadi, M.R., Michalewicz, Z., Barone, L.: A hybrid evolutionary algorithm for wheat blending problem. Sci. World J. **2014**, 967254 (2014)
11. Miller, B., Goldberg, D.: Genetic algorithms, tournament selection, and the effects of noise. Complex Syst. **9**, 193–212 (1995)
12. Moro, L.F.L., Pinto, J.M.: Mixed-integer programming approach for short-term crude oil scheduling. Ind. Eng. Chem. Res. **43**(1), 85–94 (2004)
13. Oliver, I.M., Smith, D.J., Holland, J.R.C.: A study of permutation crossover operators on the traveling salesman problem. In: Proceedings of the Second International Conference on Genetic Algorithms and Their Application, pp. 224–230 (1987)
14. Pochet, Y., Wolsey, L.A.: Production Planning by Mixed Integer Programming, 1st edn. Springer, New York (2010)

15. Randall, D., Cleland, L., Kuehne, C.S., Link, G.W.B., Sheer, D.P.: Water supply planning simulation model using mixed-integer linear programming "engine". J. Water Resour. Plan. Manage. **123**(2), 116–124 (1997)
16. Storn, R., Price, K.: Differential evolution - a simple and efficient adaptive scheme for global optimization over continuous spaces. Technical report TR-95-012, International Computer Science Institute, Berkeley (1995)

Automatic Modular Design of Behavior Trees for Robot Swarms with Communication Capabilites

Jonas Kuckling⬥, Vincent van Pelt⬥, and Mauro Birattari(✉)⬥

IRIDIA, Université Libre de Bruxelles, Brussels, Belgium
mbiro@ulb.ac.be

Abstract. In this work, we develop a set of behavioral and conditional modules for the use with behavior trees. We present AutoMoDe-`Cedrata`, an automatic modular design method that automatically assembles and fine-tunes these modules into behavior trees that control robot swarms. We test `Cedrata` on three missions and, to gain further insights on its effectiveness, we design control software for the same missions using AutoMoDe-`Maple`, another automatic design method, and by a group of human designers. Results show that the proposed modules allow for well-performing behavior trees. Yet, `Cedrata` had difficulties automatically generating control software that performs similarly well as the one generated by human designers, especially when involving communication.

Keywords: Swarm robotics · Automatic design · Behavior trees

1 Introduction

Swarm robotics is the combination of robotics and swarm intelligence, a field inspired by social insects such as bees or ants [3]. In swarm robotics, a set of relatively simple robotic agents are designed to solve collectively a task without any central control [4]. One difficulty of designing control software in such a setting is predicting the collective behavior emerging from the local interactions. Multiple approaches to the design of robot swarms have been studied and can be classified in two categories: manual and automatic design. In this work, we are interested in *fully automatic off-line design* [1,2]. In automatic off-line design, the problem of designing control software for a robot swarm is transformed into an optimization problem. The optimization problem is then solved without any human intervention. The software, generated by the optimization process in simulation, is then uploaded to the robots that operate in the real world.

JK and VvP contributed equally to this work and should be considered as co-first authors. The experiments were designed by JK and VvP and performed by VvP. The paper was drafted by JK and edited by MB; all authors read and commented the final version. The research was directed by MB.

© Springer Nature Switzerland AG 2021
P. A. Castillo and J. L. Jiménez Laredo (Eds.): EvoApplications 2021, LNCS 12694, pp. 130–145, 2021.
https://doi.org/10.1007/978-3-030-72699-7_9

Francesca et al. [6] proposed AutoMoDe (automatic modular design), a promising automatic off-line design approach, that assembles and fine-tunes pre-defined modules into control software. Different versions of AutoMoDe have been proposed, that investigate different aspects of the design process, such as new modules based on communication [8] or colors [7], different optimization algorithms, such as Iterated F-race [5], iterated improvement [17], or simulated annealing [18], or different control architectures, such as behavior trees [21].

AutoMoDe flavors traditionally assemble their pre-defined modules into probabilistic finite-state machines. AutoMoDe-Maple [15,21] introduced behavior trees [23] as a control software structure. Behavior trees have been originally developed for video games [11] but recently found application in other fields of research, such as swarm robotics [12,13,24]. A behavior tree is a tree structure that contains multiple types of nodes. The root node generates a *tick* with a fixed frequency. This tick is propagated through the tree. A node that receives the tick activates, and either distributes the tick to one or multiple of its children, or it can return the tick to its parent, along with a return value out of *success*, *failure*, or *running*. The inner nodes of the tree are called *control-flow nodes*. These nodes determine how the tick is propagated through the tree. Leaf nodes are either *condition nodes* or *actions nodes*, that respectively test sensor input or execute a unitary task. For a formal definition of the node types, see Marzinotto et al. [23]. Behavior trees offer several advantages over finite-state machines, such as modularity, two-way control transfers and improved human understandability. In one-way control transfer systems control can only be transferred in one direction, making it akin to the "goto" statement in programming [26]. In two-way control transfer systems, control can be transferred in both directions, that is the receiver can return the control to its predecessor along with information about the execution, similar to functions and their return values. Maple makes use of modules that have been originally designed for finite-state machines and that therefore do not allow the use of return values. As a result, the behavior trees created by Maple could not use the two-way control transfers.

Here, we propose a new set of modules that explicitly provide these return values and therefore enable two-way control transfers. We present AutoMoDe-Cedrata, an automatic modular design method that assembles these modules into behavior trees. We test Cedrata on three missions. To better appraise the effectiveness of Cedrata, we asked human designers in swarm robotics to perform manual designs within the constraints of Cedrata. No automatic design method exists for designing behavior trees for robot swarms that is based on the same reference model of Cedrata. The closest alternative, in terms of reference model, is AutoMoDe-Maple [21]. We therefore include Maple in our study. However, as Maple and Cedrata do not share the same reference model, any direct comparison of performance is meaningless. Instead, we will use the behavior trees generated by Maple to understand better the quality of those of Cedrata.

2   Related Work

Behavior trees have received little attention in swarm robotics so far. Jones et al. [12] used genetic programming to evolve behavior trees in a foraging mission for a swarm of kilobots. The authors were able to generate control software that performed satisfactorily in the mission. They could show that the generated control software was easily human readable. In another work, Jones et al. evolved behavior trees onboard a swarm of Xpucks in a cooperative transportation mission [13]. The authors showed that the generated control software performs satisfactorily, and that even though the evolved behavior trees may contain many modules, they can easily be reduced into a concise representation.

Ligot et al. have investigated the use of behavior trees in automatic modular design [21]. They proposed AutoMoDe-Maple, which assembles modules into a restricted behavior tree architecture. However, the modules for Maple were originally conceived to be used in finite-state machines. These behavioral modules could not provide any return values, instead they were conceived to run indefinitely. The authors restricted the allowed behavior tree structures to make use of these modules. The results of their experiments show, that for smaller design budgets, the restricted behavior trees perform similar as finite-state machines. For higher budgets, the restricted behavior tree architecture proved to be too limiting, and finite-state machines could generate control software that could not be represented within the restricted behavior tree architecture.

Hasselmann and Birattari proposed AutoMoDe-Gianduja, an automatic modular design method able to design control software for a swarm of e-puck robots that have local communication abilities [8,10]. The modules of Gianduja could send and receive different messages that had no prior assigned semantic. The authors showed that the design process could generate control software that meaningfully used the communication capabilities of the modules.

3   AutoMoDe-Cedrata

3.1   Behavior Tree Structure

In Cedrata, the optimization process can create a tree that has a maximum of three levels and a maximum of three children per node. The top-level node needs to be a control-flow node. Nodes of the second level can be either control-flow nodes, action nodes or condition nodes. If it is an action node or a condition node, then it can have no children itself. Not all branches are forced to have the same depth: the top-level node could have some children that are control-flow nodes and some that are action or condition nodes. Nodes on the third level can only be action nodes or condition nodes. The structure of such trees is depicted in Fig. 1a. The optimization process can choose any control-flow node type to be either a sequence, sequence*, selector or selector* node. For a formal definition of these nodes, see Marzinotto et al. [23]. The tree is allowed to have at most four action nodes and four condition nodes. The constraints on the depth and on the number of children implicitly impose that the tree contains no more than four control nodes. These constraints have been chosen to allow similar numbers of action and condition nodes as in `Maple`.

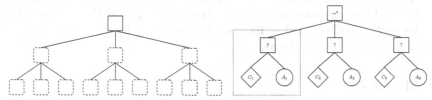

(a) Behavior tree structure for `Cedrata`. (b) Behavior tree structure for `Maple`.

Fig. 1. The possible behavior tree structures for `Cedrata` and `Maple`. In `Cedrata`, the top-level node can be any control-flow node. Underneath it the tree can have between one and three nodes, chosen among control-flow nodes, action nodes and condition nodes. If a control-flow node is chosen, then it can have between one and three children, which are either action nodes or condition nodes. In `Maple`, the top-level node is fixed to sequence* node. Underneath it the tree can have between one and four selector subtrees (highlighted by the dotted border). Each selector subtree consists of one selector node with exactly two children, a condition node (with associated condition C_i) and an action node (with associated behavior A_i).

3.2 Reference Model RM2.2

Table 1. The E-puck reference model RM2.2 used by `Cedrata` [9].

Sensors	Variables
Proximity	$prox_i \in [0,1]$, $\angle q_i$, with $i \in \{1,2,...,8\}$
Ground	$gnd_i \in \{0,0.5,1\}$, with $i \in \{1,2,3\}$
Range-and-bearing	$n \in \mathbb{N}$
	$r_m, \angle b_m, s_m \in \{0,1,...,6\})$, for $m \in \{1,2,...,n\}$
Actuators	Variables
Signal broadcast	$s \in \{0,1,...,6\}$
Wheels	$v_l, v_r \in [-v,v]$, with $v = 0.16\text{m/s}$
Control cycle period: 100 ms	

The reference model RM2.2 is shown in Table 1 [9]. The robot has access to eight proximity sensors, three ground sensors and one range-and-bearing board for sensing. It has access to two sets of actuators: the range-and-bearing board to send messages and two wheels with differential drive. A robot always sends a signal value s, that can be equal to 0, which is a special value that means *no signal* and that is sent by default, or an integer in $\{1, ..., 6\}$. Signal values do not have a particular semantic, instead it is the role of the design process to assign semantics to the signals. The reference model also provides access to the number of neighboring robots n and for each neighboring robot m, it provides a three-tuple of the estimated distance r_m, the angle $\angle_m$ and the received signal s_m. The control cycle period is 100 ms, that is, every 100 ms the sensors and the control software are updated.

3.3   Modules

In the following descriptions of the signal-based conditions and behaviors, the set of signals $\{1, ..., 6\}$ will be denoted S. Some modules can use a special value *any* that is activated if any of the signals in S is received. The set $S^* = S \cup \{any\}$ will denote the sets used by these modules.

Conditions. The set of conditions is shown below. Conditions are associated to condition nodes and check an aspect of the environment. The condition nodes return *success*, when their condition is met, or *failure*, otherwise.

Black Floor. When all grounds sensors detect a black floor, the condition returns *success* with probability β, where β is a tunable parameter.

Grey Floor. When all grounds sensors detect a grey floor, the condition returns *success* with probability β, where β is a tunable parameter.

White Floor. When all grounds sensors detect a white floor, the transition is enabled with probability β, where β is a tunable parameter.

Neighborhood Count. Returns *success* with probability $z(n) = \frac{1}{1+e^{\eta(\xi-n)}}$ where n is the number of robots in the neighborhood, $\eta \in [0, 20]$ and $\xi \in \{0, 1, ..., 10\}$ are tunable parameters.

Inverted Neighborhood Count. Same as Neighborhood Count but with probability $1 - z(n)$.

Fixed Probability. Returns *success* with probability β, where β is a tunable parameter.

Receiving Signal. Returns *success* if the robot has perceived a neighbor sending $s \in S^*$ in the last 10 ticks, where s is a tunable parameter.

Behaviors. The new set of behaviors is shown below. Behaviors are associated to action nodes and allow the robot to interact with the environment. The action nodes can return *success* or *failure*, if the behavior ends in a state that it considers to be a success or a failure. Otherwise, they return *running*.

Exploration. The robot performs a random walk strategy. It moves straight until it perceives an obstacle in front of itself. Then the robot turns on the spot for a random number of ticks in $\{0, ..., \tau\}$, where $\tau \in \{1, ..., 100\}$ is a tunable parameter. This behavior always return *running*.

Stop. The robot stays still. This behavior always return *running*.

Grouping. The robot tries to get closer to its neighbors by moving in the direction of the geometric center of its neighbors. If the number of neighbors becomes greater than N_{max}, the behavior returns *success*, where N_{max} is a tunable parameter. If the number of neighbors becomes smaller than N_{min}, the behavior returns *failure*, where N_{min} is a tunable parameter. Otherwise, it returns *running*. The speed of convergence is controlled by the tunable parameter $\alpha \in [1,5]$. The robot moves in the direction $w = w' - kw_0$, where w' is the target component and kw_0 is the obstacle avoidance component. If robots are perceived, then $w' = w_{r\&b} = \sum_{m=1}^{n}(\frac{\alpha}{r_m}, \angle b_m)$, otherwise $w' = (1, \angle 0)$. kw_0 is the obstacle avoidance component, with k being a constant fixed to 5 and w_0 defined as $w_0 = \sum_{i=1}^{8}(prox_i, \angle q_i)$.

Isolation. The robot tries to move away from its neighbors by moving in the opposite direction of the geometric center of its neighbors. If the number of neighbors becomes smaller than N_{min}, the behavior returns *success*, where N_{min} is a tunable parameter. If the number of neighbors becomes greater than N_{max}, the behavior returns *failure*, where N_{max} is a tunable parameter. Otherwise, it returns *running*. The speed of divergence is controlled by the tunable parameter $\alpha \in [1,5]$. The Isolation behavior use the same embedded collision avoidance than in Grouping, but with w' defined as: $w' = -w_{r\&b}$ if robots are perceived, where $w_{r\&b}$ is defined as in the Grouping behavior. Otherwise $w' = (1, \angle 0)$.

Meeting. The robot listens for a signal $s \in S^*$ emitted by other robots and moves towards the geometrical centre of the emitters. The behavior returns *success* if the distance between the robot and the geometrical centre is smaller than a distance d_{min}, where d_{min} is a tunable parameter. The behaviors returns *failure* if the robot does not perceive any robot sending the expected signal. Otherwise, the behavior returns *running*. The Meeting behavior uses the same embedded collision avoidance as in Grouping, but with w' defined as: $w' = w_{r\&b} = \sum_{m \in S_r^*}(\frac{\alpha}{r_m}, \angle b_m)$ if robots are perceived, where S_r^* is the set of robots that emit the signal s. Otherwise $w' = (1, \angle 0)$.

Acknowledgement. The robot sends a signal $s \in S$ and waits for an answer in the form of the same signal, where s is a tunable parameter. The behavior returns *success* if the signal is received or *running* if not. After t_{max} ticks, the behavior returns *failure* if the signal is still not received, where t_{max} is a tunable parameter. This behavior also sets the velocity of both wheels to zero.

Emit Signal. The robot sets its emitted signal to $s \in S \cup \{0\}$ for the current tick, where s is a tunable parameter. This behavior always returns *success*. This behavior also sets the wheel velocity to zero.

3.4 Optimization Algorithm

`Cedrata` uses Iterated F-race [22] as the optimization algorithm. Iterated F-race works over multiple iterations, each of them reminiscent of a race. In each iteration, a set of candidate solutions is sampled. The candidate solutions are compared over an increasing number of instances. Once a candidate solution performs significantly worse than another, it is eliminated from the race, freeing up the budget for evaluations of more promising candidates. If only one candidate remains, or the budget for this iteration has been exhausted, new candidate solutions will be generated by sampling around the surviving candidates. These new candidates form the set of candidate solutions for the next iteration of the algorithm. For Cedrata, a candidate solution is a behavior tree, with the structure and modules as defined above. The optimization algorithm is free to choose any combinations of nodes, modules, and tunable parameters within these constraints. These behavior trees will be evaluated on the same mission, but with different initial starting positions and headings.

4   Experimental Setup

4.1   Missions

We consider three missions: FORAGING, MARKER AGGREGATION and STOP. All missions take place in a dodecagonal arena (see Fig. 2) and last 250 s.

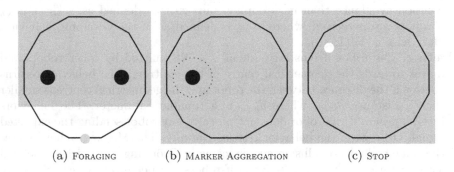

(a) FORAGING   (b) MARKER AGGREGATION   (c) STOP

Fig. 2. Layouts of the arena for the missions considered.

In FORAGING (see Fig. 2a), the robots are tasked to perform an abstracted foraging task. That is, the the robots must bring as many items from the black sources inside the white nest. As the e-puck robot does not have gripping capabilities, we assume it picks up an item when it enters a black area and that it deposits a carried item when it enters the white area. The objective function for this mission is the number of recovered items: $F_{For} = \#items$.

In MARKER AGGREGATION (see Fig. 2b), the robots must aggregate within the dotted area. The area itself is not perceivable to the robots. Instead, a black spot is placed in the middle of the aggregation area that can serve as a marker. The objective function for this mission is the cumulative time that the robots spend within the aggregation area: $F_{MA} = \sum_{i=0}^{2500} N_A^i$, where N_A^i is the number of robots in the aggregation area at time step i.

In STOP (see Fig. 2c), the robots must find a white spot and then stop as quickly as possible. A robot is considered moving, if it has travelled more than

5 mm in the last time step. The objective function for this mission is reduced for each robot that is not moving at any given time step before the white spot has been found and for each robot that is moving after the white spot has been found and additionally for the time that the swarm needed to discover the white spot: $F_{Stop} = 100000 - \left(\bar{t}N + \sum_{t=1}^{\bar{t}} \sum_{i=1}^{N} \bar{I}_i(t) + \sum_{\bar{t}}^{2500} \sum_{i=1}^{N} I_i(t) \right)$, where $\bar{t}$ is the time step during which the white spot was discovered, $I_i(t)$ is an indicator that a robot i has moved in time step t and $\bar{I}_i(t)$ is an indicator that a robot i has not moved in time step t.

4.2   Design Methods

In this work, we study the effectiveness of Cedrata. To gain further insights on the quality of the generated control software, we also design control software using Maple. Additionally, we asked a set of human designers to manually design control software using the set of modules and the tree structure of Cedrata.

For a definition of Cedrata see Sect. 3. Maple [21] is another automatic modular design method that assembles the modules into behavior trees. It has access to six conditions (Black Floor, Grey Floor, White Floor, Neighborhood Count, Inverted Neighborhood Count, and Fixed Probability) and six behaviors (Exploration, Stop, Phototaxis, Anti-Phototaxis, Attraction, and Repulsion). As the behaviors have been originally defined for finite-state machines, they can only return *running*. To allow the use of these behaviors in behavior trees, Maple restricts the structure of the generated trees and can only generate trees in the shape shown in Fig. 1b. Underneath a top-level sequence* node are between one and four selector sub-trees. The first selector sub-tree in the example is highlighted using a dotted box. Each selector sub-tree consists of one selector node with a condition node as its first child and an action node as its second child. Maple uses Iterated F-race [22] as its optimization algorithm.

For the manual designs, a human designer builds the control software of the robot using the same constraints (modules and behavior tree structure) as Cedrata. For the design process, the designers have access to a visual interface that allows them to visualize and manipulate the trees and to directly launch simulations of the control software. They have access to the value of the objective function as automatic methods and to a visual representation of the arena and the behavior of the swarm for inspection. The human designers chosen have expertise in swarm robotics, but do not have prior knowledge of behavior trees or the specific module set of Cedrata.

4.3   Protocol

The automatic designs are conducted according to the following protocol. For each mission, Cedrata is executed with different budgets: 20 000, 50 000, 100 000 and 200 000 simulation runs. After this number of simulations, the automatic design process is halted and it returns the best control software produced. For each budget, 10 runs of the methods are run, leading to 10 instances of control software. Additionally, 10 runs of `Maple` with a budget of 200 000 simulation runs will be performed. The manual design will be done by four human designers per mission, with a maximum design duration of 4 h.

Table 2. Design and pseudo-reality noise models

Sensor/actuator	Design model	Pseudo-reality model
Proximity	0.05	0.05
Light	0.05	0.90
Ground	0.05	0.05
Range-and-bearing	0.85	0.90
Wheels	0.05	0.15

Simulations are performed in the ARGoS simulator [25], a realistic and physics-based simulator. In accordance with the consensus in the literature, a realistic noise model is applied to the simulation (see Table 2). The generated instances of control software of all designs methods are assessed in pseudo-reality to investigate the impact of the reality gap. Ligot and Birattari [20] showed that the effect of the reality gap can be mimicked in simulation-only environments, by testing the control software with a different noise model than it was originally designed for.

4.4   Reference Designs

Besides the behavior trees created by the manual designs method, we will define a *reference* tree for each mission. These reference designs are not part of the experimental protocol and are designed by people with knowledge of the study. They are built using the same constraints on the tree structure as the manual designs, but without time constraints. These designs serve to highlight particular strategies that we expected to be discovered in each mission. They were not known to the human designers prior to their manual designs. By comparing the results of `Cedrata` to the reference designs and the manual designs of the human designers, we can gain insights on the effectiveness of `Cedrata`. Furthermore, by comparing the results of the human designers to the reference design, we can make statements about the general usability of behavior trees, as no human designer had prior experience with behavior trees.

Foraging. This mission was initially conceived for a reference model, which had access to the light sensor. As such, a light was placed behind the nest area to guide robots in their search. However, `Cedrata` does not have any light detection capabilities, therefore preventing use of this information not only for the automatic design but also for a human designer. The reference design for this mission is available in the supplementary material [16]. In this design, robots make use of the signal framework to send indications about the location of the food sources to their neighbors. When a robot finds a food source, it emits a signal. Robots that are in search of a food source can then receive the signal to attract them to it.

Marker Aggregation. This mission was designed to encourage the design process to make use of the signal framework. The reference design for this mission is available in the supplementary material [16]. In this design, robots explore the arena until they find the marker. Then, using the signal framework, they will attract their neighbors to the aggregation area.

Stop. The reference design for this mission is available in the supplementary material [16]. In this design, robots will send and forward signals to their neighbors to transmit the information that the white spot has been discovered. If a robot received a signal, it stops; if it does not receive any signal, it explores the arena to find the white spot.

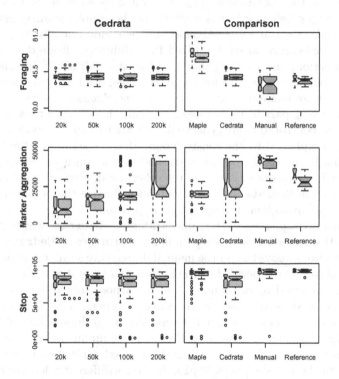

Fig. 3. Results for all conducted experiments. Each row contains all experiments for a particular mission. The first column shows the development of `Cedrata` with increasing budgets. The second column contains a comparison between `Cedrata`, `Maple` (both for a budget of 200k), the manual, and the reference designs. Results are shown both in the design context (thin boxes) and pseudo-reality context (thick boxes).

5 Results

In the following sections, methods are often claimed to "perform significantly better" or "outperform" another method. It implies that a Wilcoxon rank sum test has been performed with a confidence of 95%.

Foraging. The performance of the design methods on the FORAGING mission is shown in Fig. 3. All plots include the results in both design and pseudo-reality environments. The plots show, that for Cedrata despite increasing budgets the performance remains similar. A detailed inspection of the created behavior trees shows that the adopted strategies of Cedrata are the same regardless of the budget. For Cedrata, all the generated behavior trees contain an Exploration behavior which make the robot explore until the end of the mission. Eventually, the robot will pass over a food source and then over the nest. The fact that these strategies do not evolve with the budget size implies that finding them is not a difficult task for the optimization process, as it does so even with low budgets. A typical example behavior tree is available in the supplementary material [16]. In this example, we can see an Exploration behavior but also two conditions that could have been removed: the Fixed Probability condition does not trigger a particular action, and the Neighborhood Count condition is, in this case, too high to ever return *success*. As for the shown tree, a lot of generated instances of control software contain what we can call *superfluous* modules, i.e., modules that do not play a part in the strategy. We can also observe these superfluous modules in the control software generated with Maple, but in a more limited way. This could be explained by the constraints on the tree structure: Maple imposes sub-trees that have exactly one condition and one action node, leaving few possibilities to add extraneous nodes. On the other hand, a superfluous module can easily be added in Cedrata and, as it will not influence the performance of the swarm, be kept throughout the optimization process.

The human designers used the same strategy as Cedrata, which is based on the Exploration behavior, achieving similar performance as Cedrata. Although the strategies from Cedrata and the manual designs are similar, the performance of the control software generated by the human designers shows a wider variance. This is mainly caused by one human designer, whose control software does not seem as fine-tuned as the one by the other designers. This shows one of the major drawbacks of manual design, the dependance on the specific abilities of the human designer. Contrary to our hypothesis, the communication-based reference design does not outperform the exploration-based strategies found by either Cedrata or the human designers. Maple, due to its different reference model, can make use of the light source to forage more efficiently than the other designs. When assessed in pseudo-reality, Cedrata, the manual designs, and the reference design only suffer from small drops of the performance. This is indication that Cedrata could also demonstrate to be resistant against the reality gap.

Marker Aggregation. The performance of the design methods on MARKER AGGREGATION is shown in Fig. 3. All plots include the results in both design and pseudo-reality environments. The performance of Cedrata clear improvements with the size of the budget. **Cedrata** develops two primary strategies: one that uses communication to indicate the position of the black spot, similar to the reference design, and one that only explores until the black spot is found, without explicitly communicating its position. The total performance of the automatic design is influenced by how many strategies of each kind are generated. In this experiment, the designs generated with the lower budget sizes 20 000 and 50 000 contain only behavior trees using the second strategy. The experiment with a budget of 100 000 simulations produced one behavior tree using a reference-like strategy. When the budget increases to 200 000 simulations, this amount increase to four designs finding that strategy. This increasing proportion of reference-like strategies seems to be linked to the budget size. As communication-based strategies usually require two matching modules sending the same signal, this could be an indication that the generation of communication-based strategies benefits from a more thorough exploration of the search space, as opposed to simple exploitation of previously found solutions. The generated behavior trees also contain superfluous modules, as already seen in FORAGING. An example of a behavior tree using the pure exploration strategy is available in the supplementary material [16]. This behavior tree contains some modules that are not useful: the two Emit Signal behaviors send signals that will never be perceived, as no other signal-based modules are present; and the sequence* sub-tree will always only execute its first child because the Stop behavior will always return *running*. This can be explained using the same reasoning that we have proposed for the FORAGING mission, which is that **Cedrata** is flexible regarding the tree structure and therefore allows more choices for placing superfluous modules.

The manual designs use a strategy similar to the one used in the reference design. Yet the human designers where able to find better fine-tuned instances of control software than the reference design. When compared to **Cedrata**, the designs generated by the human designers seem to outperform **Cedrata**. If the comparison is however restricted to the four reference-like designs that **Cedrata** produced for a budget of 200 000 simulation runs, then both design methods perform similarly. With no access to communication through its reference model, **Maple** only generates behavior trees similar to the behavior trees of the communication-less strategy found by **Cedrata**. When comparing the generated behavior trees, **Cedrata** also leads to more variety in the trees than **Maple**: for the same strategy, trees with different topologies can be created. Also in this mission, **Cedrata**, the manual designs, and the reference design successfully manage to mitigate the effects of the pseudo-reality gap.

Stop. The performance of the design methods on the STOP mission is shown in Fig. 3. All plots include the results in both design and pseudo-reality environments. As in FORAGING, **Cedrata** shows similar performance and uses the same strategy for all budget sizes, meaning that the strategy is easily discovered by the optimization process. **Cedrata** uses the following strategy: robots isolate from each other. The swarm expands and covers all the arena, giving a high probability for a single robot to move over the white spot in the process. As a robot that moves slower than 5 mm per second is considered to be not moving by the objective function, and robots in the Isolation behavior often pass under this threshold when they are far away from other robots, the resulting performance is relatively good. Some trees have an Exploration behavior for when robots do not detect neighbors, one such example is available in the supplementary material [16]. This tree contains again some superfluous modules, especially the three Receiving Signal conditions for signals that can't be sent, which is very common for control software generated with Cedrata. In this mission, Cedrata does not exploit the communication abilities of the modules. Following the discussion of the mission MARKER AGGREGATION, this could be attributed to a lack of exploration of the search space. The simplicity of the isolation strategy might lead to the optimization process prematurely converging around these solutions. The human designers used strategies that are similar to the one used in the reference design. As we hypothesized, the correct use of communication leads to behavior trees that outperform those that do not use communication (in this case the ones generated by Cedrata and Maple). Maple finds a strategy where the robots randomly explores the arena until it finds a sufficient number of neighbors to stop. This strategy could have also been discovered by Cedrata, as it only makes use of the modules Exploration, Neighborhood Count, and Stop, which are available to both design methods. This could be another indication that the optimization process of Cedrata converged prematurely towards a too simplistic solution, which was not available for Maple. For all methods, some simulation runs, either in the design or in the pseudo-reality environment, show very low results (almost equal to zero) compared to the other simulation runs. These results correspond to some experiments where no robot finds the white spot or the spot is found within the last seconds of the experiment. As in the previous two missions, Cedrata, the manual designs, and the reference design showed to be resistant against the pseudo-reality gap.

6   Conclusion

In this work, a new flavour of AutoMoDe called Cedrata has been introduced to pursue the work started with a previous one called Maple, which introduced behavior trees. Maple uses modules from earlier flavours, which have been designed for finite state machines. This forces the behavior tree to adopt a particular structure. Cedrata introduces a new set of modules that are specifically designed for behavior trees and allow the tree to have a more flexible structure. We tested Cedrata on three different missions. For each mission we included designs by Maple, manual designs, done by human designers, and reference designs, created with the objective of serving as examples. Multiple observations can be extracted from the results. The modules and behavior tree structure for Cedrata allow for well-performing instances of control software. Indeed, in two of the three considered missions, designs following on Cedrata constraints are able to outperform Maple, which had no access to communication capabilities. In the third mission, Maple outperforms all design methods operating within the constraints of Cedrata. This is because Maple has access to an ambient clue (the light) that was not available for `Cedrata`. We hypothesized that communication-based strategies might offset this disadvantaged, but our results showed that there was no gain in performance for this particular mission. The manual designs performed, in average, as well as the reference ones. This indicates that, under the experimental conditions, designers with no prior knowledge of behavior trees are able to understand and use them to solve missions efficiently. This highlights the human understandability, one of the often claimed advantages of behavior trees.

While behavior trees are convenient to design for human designers, it seems to be more difficult for automatic design processes. In this work, `Cedrata` was unable to reach as good performances as the manual or reference designs on some missions. Based on the MARKER AGGREGATION mission results, we could presume that it is only a matter of budget, and that `Cedrata` should provide better results as soon as we allocate enough budget. However, the results in the other two missions do not support this hypothesis, since we cannot observe any significant improvement of performance over the budget. An important reason, why higher budgets still may lead to improved control software is the size of the search space, which is larger in `Cedrata` than it is for example in `Maple`. Furthermore, due to the flexible structure of the trees, the search space contains a lot of control software with superfluous modules. As the optimization algorithm cannot distinguish between necessary and superfluous modules, parts of the budget will be spent on trying to tune these superfluous modules, even though they have no influence on the performance. Additionally, communication-based strategies seem to be difficult to automatically design. This could be explained by the fact, that most communication-based strategies require at least two modules that are tuned to the same signal value. If Iterated F-race does not randomly sample a solution that already is tuned to the correct signals, the signal-based modules are without worth for the performance, and the design process might converge on solutions that do not make use of communication. In order to counteract this convergence, the optimization algorithm might need to allow for more exploration.

`Cedrata` introduces both a new set of modules and a new tree structure and the results provided make it impossible to attribute specific observations to one of the changes. For example, in the STOP mission, `Cedrata` had the possibility to outperform `Maple`, as evidenced by the manual and reference designs; however `Cedrata` led to lower performing results than `Maple`. The problem may reside in the set of modules, the flexibility of the tree structure, or both of them. Without further experiments, it is difficult to attribute the results to one of the proposed causes. Another observation drawn from the results is that `Cedrata` includes more superfluous modules in its architecture than `Maple`. This leads to the hypothesis that the number of such modules is related to the freedom given on the control structure. Further experiments could try to verify this hypothesis, by either investigating architectures of different freedom or by actively pruning unused modules during the design process. More generally, Iterated F-Race, the optimization algorithm used by `Cedrata`, seems to be unable to efficiently explore the control software space. There are different parameters, such as the budget or the number of iterations, that could influence the strategies discovered by the design process. Further experiments into these parameters and their influence might provide better insights on how control software in the form of behavior trees can effectively be designed. Another idea would be to assess the use of other optimization algorithms, like or simulated annealing [14] or novelty search [19] that is a divergent algorithm that promotes exploration.

Acknowledgements. JK and MB acknowledge support by the FNRS. The project has received funding from the European Research Council (ERC) under the European Union's Horizon 2020 research and innovation programme (DEMIURGE Project, grant agreement No 681872) and from Belgium's Wallonia-Brussels Federation through the ARC Advanced Project GbO–Guaranteed by Optimization.

References

1. Birattari, M., et al.: Automatic off-line design of robot swarms: a manifesto. Front. Robot. AI **6**, 59 (2019). https://doi.org/10.3389/frobt.2019.00059
2. Birattari, M., Ligot, A., Hasselmann, K.: Disentangling automatic and semi-automatic approaches to the optimization-based design of control software for robot swarms. Nature Mach. Intell. **2**(9), 494–499 (2020). https://doi.org/10.1038/s42256-020-0215-0
3. Dorigo, M., Birattari, M.: Swarm intelligence. Scholarpedia **2**(9), 1462 (2007). https://doi.org/10.4249/scholarpedia.1462
4. Dorigo, M., Birattari, M., Brambilla, M.: Swarm robotics. Scholarpedia **9**(1), 1463 (2014). https://doi.org/10.4249/scholarpedia.1463
5. Francesca, G., et al.: AutoMoDe-chocolate: automatic design of control software for robot swarms. Swarm Intell. **9**(2–3), 125–152 (2015). https://doi.org/10.1007/s11721-015-0107-9
6. Francesca, G., Brambilla, M., Brutschy, A., Trianni, V., Birattari, M.: AutoMoDe: a novel approach to the automatic design of control software for robot swarms. Swarm Intell. **8**(2), 89–112 (2014). https://doi.org/10.1007/s11721-014-0092-4
7. Garzón Ramos, D., Birattari, M.: Automatic design of collective behaviors for robots that can display and perceive colors **10**(13), 4654 (2020). https://doi.org/10.3390/app10134654
8. Hasselmann, K., Birattari, M.: Modular automatic design of collective behaviors for robots endowed with local communication capabilities. PeerJ Comput. Sci. **6**, e291 (2020). https://doi.org/10.7717/peerj-cs.291
9. Hasselmann, K., et al.: Reference models for AutoMoDe. Technical report, TR/IRIDIA/2018-002, IRIDIA, Université libre de Bruxelles, Belgium (2018)
10. Hasselmann, K., Robert, F., Birattari, M.: Automatic design of communication-based behaviors for robot swarms. In: Dorigo, M., Birattari, M., Blum, C., Christensen, A.L., Reina, A., Trianni, V. (eds.) ANTS 2018. LNCS, vol. 11172, pp. 16–29. Springer, Cham (2018). https://doi.org/10.1007/978-3-030-00533-7_2
11. Isla, D.: Handling complexity in the Halo 2 AI. In: Game Developers Conference. vol. 12 (2005)
12. Jones, S., Studley, M., Hauert, S., Winfield, A.: Evolving behaviour trees for swarm robotics. In: Groß, R. (ed.) Distributed Autonomous Robotic Systems. SPAR, vol. 6, pp. 487–501. Springer, Cham (2018). https://doi.org/10.1007/978-3-319-73008-0_34

13. Jones, S., Winfield, A., Hauert, S., Studley, M.: Onboard evolution of understandable swarm behaviors. Adv. Intell. Syst. **1**(6), 1900031 (2019). https://doi.org/10.1002/aisy.201900031

14. Kirkpatrick, S., Gelatt, Jr., C.D., Vecchi, M.P.: Optimization by simulated annealing. Science **220**(4598), 671–680 (1983). https://doi.org/10.1126/science.220.4598.671

15. Kuckling, J., Ligot, A., Bozhinoski, D., Birattari, M.: Behavior trees as a control architecture in the automatic modular design of robot swarms. In: Dorigo, M., Birattari, M., Blum, C., Christensen, A.L., Reina, A., Trianni, V. (eds.) ANTS 2018. LNCS, vol. 11172, pp. 30–43. Springer, Cham (2018). https://doi.org/10.1007/978-3-030-00533-7_3

16. Kuckling, J., van Pelt, V., Birattari, M.: Automatic modular design of behavior trees with communication capabilities: supplementary material. http://iridia.ulb.ac.be/supp/IridiaSupp2020-011/ (2020)

17. Kuckling, J., Stützle, T., Birattari, M.: Iterative improvement in the automatic modular design of robot swarms. PeerJ Comput. Sci. **6**, e322 (2020). https://doi.org/10.7717/peerj-cs.322

18. Kuckling, J., Ubeda Arriaza, K., Birattari, M.: Simulated annealing as an optimization algorithm in the automatic modular design of robot swarms. In: Beuls, K., (eds.) Proceedings of the Reference AI & ML Conference for Belgium, Netherlands & Luxemburg, BNAIC/BENELEARN 2019. CEUR Workshop Proceedings, vol. 2491, CEUR-WS.org, Aachen, Germany (2019)

19. Lehman, J., Stanley, K.O.: Abandoning objectives: evolution through the search for novelty alone. Evol. Comput. **19**(2), 189–223 (2011). https://doi.org/10.1162/EVCO_a_00025

20. Ligot, A., Birattari, M.: Simulation-only experiments to mimic the effects of the reality gap in the automatic design of robot swarms. Swarm Intell. **14**(1), 1–24 (2019). https://doi.org/10.1007/s11721-019-00175-w

21. Ligot, A., Kuckling, J., Bozhinoski, D., Birattari, M.: Automatic modular design of robot swarms using behavior trees as a control architecture. PeerJ Comput. Sci. **6**, e314 (2020). https://doi.org/10.7717/peerj-cs.314

22. López-Ibáñez, M., Dubois-Lacoste, J., Pérez Cáceres, L., Birattari, M., Stützle, T.: The irace package: iterated racing for automatic algorithm configuration. Oper. Res. Perspect. **3**, 43–58 (2016). https://doi.org/10.1016/j.orp.2016.09.002

23. Marzinotto, A., Colledanchise, M., Smith, C., Ögren, P.: Towards a unified behavior trees framework for robot control. In: IEEE International Conference on Robotics and Automation, ICRA, pp. 5420–5427. IEEE, Piscataway, NJ, USA (2014). https://doi.org/10.1109/ICRA.2014.6907656

24. Neupane, A., Goodrich, M.: Learning swarm behaviors using grammatical evolution and behavior trees. In: Kraus, S. (ed.) Twenty-Eighth International Joint Conference on Artificial Intelligence (IJCAI-19), pp. 513–520. IJCAI (2019). https://doi.org/10.24963/ijcai.2019/73

25. Pinciroli, C., et al.: ARGoS: a modular, parallel, multi-engine simulator for multi-robot systems. Swarm Intell. **6**(4), 271–295 (2012). https://doi.org/10.1007/s11721-012-0072-5

26. Ögren, P.: Increasing modularity of UAV control systems using computer game behavior trees. In: Thienel, J., et al. (eds.) AIAA guidance, navigation, and control conference 2012, pp. 358–393. AIAA Meeting Papers (2012). https://doi.org/10.2514/6.2012-4458

Salp Swarm Optimization Search Based Feature Selection for Enhanced Phishing Websites Detection

Ruba Abu Khurma[1], Khair Eddin Sabri[1], Pedro A. Castillo[2(✉)], and Ibrahim Aljarah[1]

[1] The University of Jordan, Amman, Jordan
[2] ETSIIT-CITIC, University of Granada, Granada, Spain
pacv@ugr.es

Abstract. Internet-connected devices are increasing rapidly. This facilitates transferring most of the real-world transactions to the cyber world. It follows that eCrime is growing continuously. Phishing is a cyber-attack carried out by intruders. They aim to deceive the users of the Internet to achieve their malicious goals. Therefore, experts have developed different approaches to protect financial transactions and personal login information of the users. Their primary concern is to detect the security breaches for online use of the Internet channels (e.g. emails, SMS, webpages, and social platforms). In this paper, we propose a new phishing detection system based on the Salp Swarm Algorithm (SSA). The main objective is to maximize the classification performance and minimize the number of features of the phishing system. Different transfer function (TF) families: S-TFs, V-TFs, X-TFs, U-TFs, and Z-TFs are used to convert the continuous SSA into binary. Sixteen different binary versions of the SSA algorithm are produced based on different TFs. A comparison analysis is performed to pick up the best binarization method. The phishing system is validated by comparing it with three state-of-the-art algorithms. The results show that BSSA with X-TFs achieved the best results in terms of the used evaluation measures.

Keywords: Phishing · Salp Swarm Algorithm (SSA) · Transfer Function (TF) · Feature Selection (FS) · Wrapper · Classification

1 Introduction

Big data is the fuel of modern technologies such as the Internet of things (IoT), Blockchain, and Data Science. Going by the trend requires dealing with a tremendous amount of data that is rapidly increasing. Raw data may have missing data, non-standardized data, and large numbers of noisy features. High dimensionality affects negatively the knowledge discovery methods (e.g. classification and clustering). It causes overfitting, generating complex models, and needs a

© Springer Nature Switzerland AG 2021
P. A. Castillo and J. L. Jiménez Laredo (Eds.): EvoApplications 2021, LNCS 12694, pp. 146–161, 2021.
https://doi.org/10.1007/978-3-030-72699-7_10

long learning time. Therefore, data pre-processing is a necessary step in knowledge discovery to extract useful knowledge and reduce the noise in data. Feature selection (FS) is a commonly used data pre-processing technique to reduce the dimensionality of a dataset by removing redundant features and irrelevant features.

FS is an optimization problem that involves a complex search process. Generating all the possible feature subsets to select the best feature subset is time-consuming. Recently, stochastic methods based on swarm intelligence (SI) paradigms have been immensely used to mitigate the exponential time complexity.

Salp swarm optimization algorithm (SSA) is a recent SI algorithm [21]. SSA has many properties that motivated us to select it in this study including firstly, it follows a population-based model that allows it to initialize many solutions to explore the search space. This can play a major role in alleviating the premature convergence toward local minima. Secondly, it has only one parameter that controls the gradual convergence toward the best solution. Thirdly, it selects the best solution at each step of the optimization process to guide the rest of the swarm. Fourthly, it has been examined with the FS problem and proved its efficiency in several studies [3–5,12]. Fifthly, it was not used before to tackle security problems such as phishing detection.

Phishing is a common cyber-security threat for users of the Internet. It is a kind of social engineering methods that happens online by deceptive websites, which act as legitimate websites. They aim to steal important financial and personal information from users such as log-in information, credit card information, business secrets, etc. There are many Internet applications such as E-commerce, Internet banking, social networks, and Software-as-a-Service (SAAS) that allow the user information more vulnerable to attackers. According to Anti-Phishing Working Group (APWG) statistics, phishing attacks are continuously increasing [24]. Therefore, there is primary need to develop new methods that can detect the phishing problem and reduce the losses.

Several methods have been proposed in the literature to distinguish the phishing websites from the legitimate websites. Some of these methods depicted a threshold to find the similarity between the suspicious and original website. These methods are not effective because they require to determine a suitable threshold value to increase the security level [8]. On the other hand, feature-based methods use the website components for detection such as the URL, logo, images, and text included in the website. Different machine learning techniques have been used to address the phishing attack based on training model on labeled samples, then examine these models on unlabeled samples [6]. Neural networks and filter methods have been used to detect phishing websites [2]. However, filter methods evaluate each feature of the phishing websites independently without involving a learning algorithm which affect the classification accuracy level [29]. To address these issues, in this paper a wrapper based method using SSA algorithm as a search algorithm and k-NN as a classifier are used to build a cyber-security system to increase the detection accuracy of the phishing websites.

SSA originally was designed as a continuous optimizer to solve real optimization problems. However, discrete/binary problems such as FS problem requires specific handling to adjust the optimizer to work in the feature space. This is commonly performed using transfer functions (TFs). TFs define a probability for switching the elements of the solution between the "0" and "1". The most common TFs are S-shaped and V-shaped TFs. Those were proposed in [10, 25]. Then, they were used for generating binary versions of a number of optimizers [12, 17–19]. It was shown that TFs play a critical role in the binarization process and affects the entire optimization process. Therefore, in this study, we will use novel TFs such as Z-TFs, U-TFs, and X-TFs and compare their effects with the S-TFs and V-TFs. The main objective is to enhance the performance of SSA algorithm when used as a wrapper FS in the phishing detection system.

The main contributions of this paper can be summarized as follows:

- Different binary versions of SSA are generated for optimizing the FS problem.
- Different TF-shaped families are used and compared to determine the best binarization method of the SSA.
- The proposed methods are evaluated on a phishing dataset.

The paper is structured as follows: Sect. 2 provides a background about phishing problem. Section 3 presents the SSA algorithm, system architecture and the use of SSA to solve FS problem. Section 4 discusses different binarization methods to convert SSA from real optimizer into binary. Section 5 discusses the results. Finally, Sect. 6 concludes the paper and highlights some future works.

2   Related Background

In the literature, the researchers have proposed different methods for phishing detection including Blacklist, Heuristic, Visual Similarity (VS), and Machine Learning (ML) [24].

The blacklist method is the traditional method for phishing detection. It is based on preparing a list of illegitimate websites. The shortcoming of the blacklist method is that the accuracy is not high. This is because the list may not be updated frequently so it is impossible to reach a zero-phishing day.

The heuristic method creates a general URL pattern from the websites that were previously classified as phishing websites. The degree of similarity between a new website and this pattern can indicate its classification either it is phishing or legitimate site. This method is more accurate than the blacklist, but it is more vulnerable to attack. It needs direct access by a user to a website.

In the visual similarity method, the classification of a website is based on comparing its images with the images of the original website. This approach needs more time because it may require a 3rd party service.

The machine learning method examines the contents of emails or websites to determine their features. These features are used then to train a classifier and the generated model used in the test phase. The features related to websites can be further categorized into two main groups: content-based and URL based features [20]. The former one is based on the contents of web pages features such as passwords, links, spelling errors, text, images, sounds, animation, videos, applications, and forms. All these features are examined dynamically by running a website so they make the system insecure and slow.

The latter method is based on the uniform resource locator(URL) features such as the length of the web address, the presence of special characters, web traffic, IP address, etc. Analyzing URL features are performed by dealing with the whole URL string or dividing it into its components [9].

Large datasets are another aspect when building a phishing detection system. Large datasets need specific machine learning algorithms to deal with them. In the literature, different algorithms have been used to deal with phishing problems. In [32], a Bayesian phishing classification approach was proposed to detect suspiciously URL. The weakness of this approach is that there was an accuracy degradation because of the conditional independence of the target class. The authors in [28], identified the phishing websites based on the WHOIS database. The illegitimate website was removed from the host server by sending a notification message. In [16], the authors used the Support Vector Machines (SVM) classifier and the lexical and structural components of the URL to detect malicious URL. However, SVM classification results are affected by the values of hyperparameters so they need to be initialized carefully to produce better results. Different algorithms including wrapper methods and Correlation Features Set were used in [7]. However, this approach used a large number of features that consumed large time. In [23], a clustering method was used to gather relevant features. This approach was unable to handle the bias in the imbalance dataset. ANN-Multilayer Perceptron and Random Forest were used to detect phishing webpages in [13,31] respectively. Natural language processing (NLP) achieved high results across a large dataset in [26].

Other machine learning methods proved their effectiveness in detecting phishing websites [11]. Filter methods have been used as a feature-based method. For example, the ranking method is used to determine the significance of a feature subset. The absence of the classifier training process and evaluating a feature subset independently from other features may affect the performance results. Wrapper-based FS methods incorporate a learning algorithm to evaluate a feature subset in the FS process. They have been used recently in a number of studies to efficiently detect phishing websites [8,24,27,29]. In this paper, a wrapper based FS approach is proposed based on an SSA algorithm and k-NN classifier.

3   SSA Based Feature Selection

3.1   SSA

Salp Swarm Algorithm (SSA) is a recent SI algorithm that was proposed in [21]. It mimics a marine animals called salps. Salps live as a chain in sea and oceans. They have specific behavior in locomotion and foraging. The first salp in the chain is the leader of the swarm which guides other salps towards the food source. Other salps in the swarm are followers. They move dynamically with respect to other salps. Thus, the positions of follower salps change either directly or indirectly towards the leader salp. Figure 1 shows the swarm of salps and the individual salp.

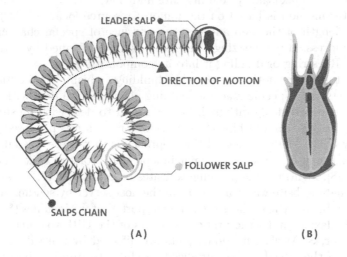

Fig. 1. (A) Swarm of salps. (B) Individual salp.

In SSA algorithm a swarm X of n salps is represented by a two-dimensional matrix as shown in Eq. 1. F in the search space represents the food source which is the target of the salps chain.

$$X_i = \begin{bmatrix} x_1^1 & x_2^1 & \cdots & x_d^1 \\ x_1^2 & x_2^2 & \cdots & x_d^2 \\ \vdots & \vdots & \vdots & \vdots \\ x_1^n & x_2^n & \cdots & x_d^n \end{bmatrix} \tag{1}$$

Following the salps chain model, the position of the leader salp is formulated as in Eq. 2

$$X_j^1 = \begin{cases} F_j + c_1((ub_j - lb_j)c_2 + lb_j), & c_3 \geq 0.5 \\ F_j - c_1((ub_j - lb_j)c_2 + lb_j), & c_3 < 0.5 \end{cases} \tag{2}$$

where x_j^1 and F_j are the positions of leaders and food source in the j_{th} dimension, respectively. c_1 is a variable that is gradually decreased over the course of iterations, and calculated as in Eq. 3, where l and L are the current iteration and the maximum number of iterations, respectively. The other c_2 and c_3 variables in Eq. 2 are two random numbers randomly selected from the interval $[0, 1]$. The variables c_2 and c_3 are very important parameters in SSA as they direct the next position in j_{th} dimension towards $+\infty$ or $-\infty$ as well as determining the step size. The ub_j and lb_j are the upper and lower bounds of j_{th} dimension.

$$C_1 = 2e^{-(\frac{4l}{L})^2} \tag{3}$$

$$X_j^i = \frac{1}{2}(x_j^i + x_j^{i-1}) \tag{4}$$

In 4, $i \geqslant 2$ and x_j^i represents the position of the i_{th} follower at the j_{th} dimension. The pseudocode of the basic SSA is presented in Algorithm 1.

Algorithm 1 Pseudo-code of the SSA algorithm

Input: n (number of salps), d (number of dimensions)
Output:Approximated global solution (**F**)
Initialize the salp population x_i $(i= 1, 2, \ldots, n)$ considering ub and lb

    while (end condition is not satisfied) **do**
        Calculate the fitness of each search agent (salp)
        Set **F** as the best search agent
        Update c_1 by Eq.3
        for (each salp x_i) do
        if $l == 1$ **then**
            Update the position of the leading salp by Eq.2
        else
            Update the position of the follower salp by Eq.4
        end if
        Update the salps based on the upper and lower bounds of variables
    end while
    return F

3.2 Binary SSA for Feature Selection

A solution in FS problem is represented by a binary vector in which a '0' indicates that a corresponding feature is not selected and '1' indicates the selection of the corresponding feature. Besides, a feature subset is evaluated using a fitness function that tries to optimize two conflicting objectives simultaneously. These objectives are the number of features in the dataset and the performance of the classification algorithm. In this study a k-NN classifier with k = 5 [19] is used to evaluate the selected feature subsets. Equation 5 formulates the FS problem where $\alpha\gamma_R(D)$ is the error rate of the classification produced by a classifier, $|R|$ is the number of selected features in the reduced data set, and $|C|$ is the number of features in the original data set, and $\alpha \in [0, 1]$, $\beta = (1-\alpha)$ are two parameters for representing the importance of classification performance and length of feature subset based on recommendations [5].

$$Fitness = \alpha\gamma_R(D) + \beta\frac{|R|}{|C|} \tag{5}$$

3.3   System Architecture

Figure 2 depicts the block of the proposed phishing detection method.

The initial step is to pass the training part phishing dataset into the wrapper-based FS framework. Then, the binary SSA explores and exploits the feature search space to find the best feature subset (F). K-NN evaluates each feature subset internally based on the proposed fitness function. F is the best feature subset that is evaluated with the maximum performance, and the minimum number of features after the stopping criterion is met. In the last step, F uses K-NN to classify the testing part of the phishing dataset using different evaluation measures.

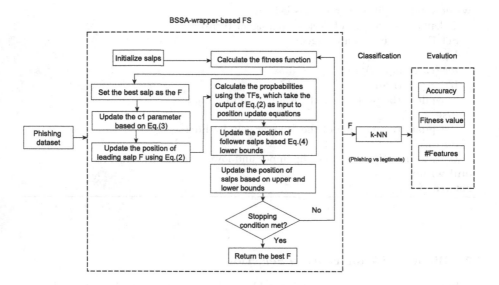

Fig. 2. BSSA-based Phishing detection system

4   Binarization Methods

4.1   S-TFs

In the aforementioned discussion, TFs have a major role in the binarization process of the optimizers. They identifies the probability of updating the position of a solution by switching its value from 0 to 1 and vice versa. In S-Shaped functions, the positions are updated based on Eq. 6

$$X_i^d(t+1) = \begin{cases} 1, & \text{if } rand \leq S\text{-}TF(X_i^d(t+1)) \\ 0, & \text{else} \end{cases} \tag{6}$$

Table 1 shows the mathematical formulas of the four S-TFs used in this work. Figure 3 shows their corresponding graphs.

Table 1. S-shaped TFs

Name	S-TF
S1	T1(x)=$1/(1+e^{-2x})$
S2	T2(x)=$1/(1+e^{-x})$
S3	T3(x)=$1/(1+e^{-x/2})$
S4	T4(x)=$1/(1+e^{-x/3})$

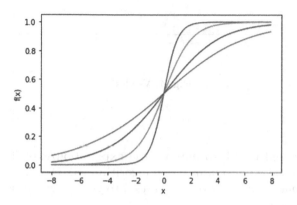

Fig. 3. S-TFs

4.2   V-TFs

In V-Shaped functions, the positions are updated based on Eq. 7. Table 2 shows the mathematical formulas of the four V-TFs used in this work. Figure 4 shows their corresponding graphs.

$$X_i^d(t+1) = \begin{cases} \sim X_i^d(t), & \text{if} \quad rand < V\text{-}TF(X_i^d(t+1)) \\ X_i^d(t), & \text{else} \end{cases} \tag{7}$$

Table 2. V-shaped TFs

Name	V-TF
V1	T5(x)=$\lvert erf(\sqrt{\Pi}/2 * x)\rvert = \lvert\sqrt{2}/\Pi \int_0^{(\sqrt{\Pi}/2)^x} e^{-t^2}\,dt\rvert$
V2	T6(x)=$\lvert tanh(x)\rvert$
V3	T7(x)=$(x)/\sqrt{1+x^2}$
V4	T8(x)=$\lvert 2/\Pi arc(tan((\Pi/2)*x))\rvert$

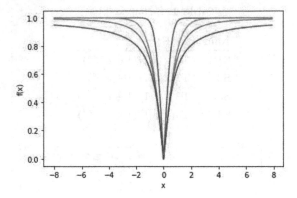

Fig. 4. V-TFs

4.3   X-TF

X-TF was proposed in [14] to improve the exploration/exploitation processes of the binary Social mimic optimization algorithm (SMO). The proposed X-TF uses two components and crossover operation to get a new solution. Table 3 and Fig. 5 show the X-TF.

Table 3. X-shaped TF

Name	X-TF	BSSA version
X_1	T9(x)=$1 + e^x$	BSSAX
X_2	T10(x)=$1 + e^{-x}$	

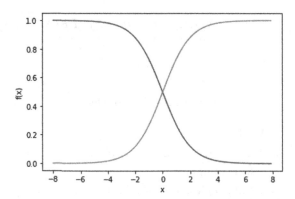

Fig. 5. X-TF

$$y_i^d(t+1) = \begin{cases} 1, & \text{if } rand1 \leq X_1(y_i^d(t+1)) \\ 0, & \text{else} \end{cases} \tag{8}$$

$$z_i^d(t+1) = \begin{cases} 1, & \text{if } rand2 \leq X2(z_i^d(t+1)) \\ 0, & \text{else} \end{cases} \tag{9}$$

where, y_i and z_i are the binary versions of salp(i) generated by equations T9(x) and T10(x) respectively, and $rand1, rand2 \in [0; 1]$ are random numbers.

$$x_i'(t+1) = \begin{cases} y_i, & \text{if } fitness(y_i) < fitness(z_i) \\ z_i, & \text{if } fitness(y_i) \geq fitness(z_i) \end{cases} \tag{10}$$

If $fitness(x_i'(t+1)) < fitness(x_i(t))$ then $(x_i(t+1)) = (x_i'(t+1))$. Otherwise, crossover operation is performed on $(x_i(t+1))$ and $(x_i'(t+1))$.

4.4   Z-TFs

Z-TFs was proposed in [15] to improve the BPSO algorithm. Table 4 and Fig. 6 show the proposed Z-TFs. There are four BSSA versions proposed to map continuous SSA into binary SSA to solve FS problem. The positions of the salps are updated based on a generated random number that is compared with the value generated from the Z-TF for the current salp as in Eq. 11.

Table 4. Z-shaped TFs

Name	Z-TF	BSSA version
Z1	$T10(x) = \sqrt{1 - 2^x}$	BSSA-Z1
Z2	$T11(x) = \sqrt{1 - 5^x}$	BSSA-Z2
Z3	$T12(x) = \sqrt{1 - 8^x}$	BSSA-Z3
Z4	$T13(x) = \sqrt{1 - 20^x}$	BSSA-Z4

$$X_i^d(t+1) = \begin{cases} \sim X_i^d(t), & \text{if } rand < Z\text{-}TF(X_i^d(t+1)) \\ X_i^d(t), & \text{else} \end{cases} \tag{11}$$

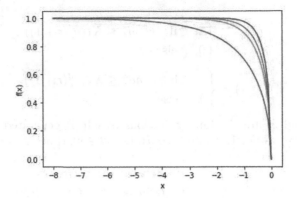

Fig. 6. Z-TFs

4.5   U-TFs

U-TFs was proposed in [22]. The U-TFs have been designed with alterable control parameters α and β. The parameters, α and β determine the slope and the width of the basin of the U-TF respectively.

In this study, we set up the values of α and β as in Table 5. The positions of the salps are updated as in Eq. 12. These values are in the original paper to study the performance of U-TFs on BPSO in [22]. This set of U-TFs is selected to study their effect on the performance of BSSA in the discrete feature space. Therefore, there are three generated binary versions of BSSA using U-TFs as in Table 5 (Fig. 7).

Table 5. U-shaped TFs

Name	U-TF		BSSA version
U1	T14(x)=$\alpha|x^\beta|$	$\alpha = 1, \beta = 2$	BSSA-U1
U2	T15(x)=$\alpha|x^\beta|$	$\alpha = 1, \beta = 3$	BSSA-U2
U3	T16(x)=$\alpha|x^\beta|$	$\alpha = 1, \beta = 4$	BSSA-U3

$$X_i^d(t+1) = \begin{cases} \sim X_i^d(t), & \text{if } \quad rand < U\text{-}TF(X_i^d(t+1)) \\ X_i^d(t), & \text{else} \end{cases} \tag{12}$$

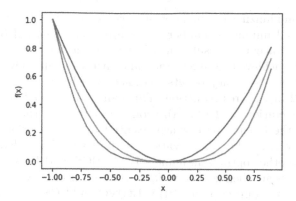

Fig. 7. U-TFs

5 Experiments and Results

The dataset used in this paper was composed by authors in [8]. They collected the dataset using the Phishtank website [1]. The number of community-confirmed URLs in the dataset is 88,647. These URLs contained 30,647 phishing websites URLs and 58,000 legitimate website URLs. They have extracted a total of 111 features based on the address-basr and the domain of the URLs. The target class in the dataset contains binary classes (phishing and legitimate). A detailed description of the dataset is available in [30].

All the experiments were executed on a personal machine with AMD Athlon Dual-Core QL-60 CPU at 1.90 GHz and memory of 2 GB running Windows7 Ultimate 64 bit operating system. The optimization algorithms have been all implemented in Python in the EvoloPy-FS framework [19]. The maximum number of iterations and the population size were set to 100 and 10 respectively. The applied training and testing methodology is simple split with 67% of the dataset is used for training and 33% is used for testing. This division was repeated 30 to statistically significant results. The final statistical results represent the average of 30 independent runs. Three optimization algorithms are used in the experiments as wrapper-based methods to validate the obtained results. GWO with $\alpha \in [2, 0]$, BA with Qmin Frequency minimum = 0, Qmax Frequency maximum = 2, A Loudness = 0.5, r Pulse rate = 0.5, and CS with pa = 0.25, $\beta = 3/2$. Three evaluation measures are used to evaluate the proposed binary methods: classification accuracy, fitness value, and number of selected features in a feature subset.

Table 6 shows the results of experiments performed using SSA algorithm with different binarization methods: S-TFs, V-TFs, X-TFs, Z-TFs, and U-TFs. The results show that the accuracy, fitness value, and number of selected features vary based on the applied TFs. Among the S-TFs, S1 and S3 achieved better accuracy results than S2 and S4. At the same time, S1 and S3 achieved more features reduction compared with both S2 and S4. For the V-TFs, V2 achieved the best accuracy result then came V3. On the other hand, V1 and V4 were better in minimizing the number of selected features. For the Z-TFs, the best accuracy and minimum number of features were achieved by Z1. Z2 and Z3 achieved close accuracy results but Z3 was much better in features reduction. The U-TFs achieved close accuracy and fitness results. Overall, The best accuracy and fitness accuracy results were achieved by X-TF. Also, it was the second after U2 in features reduction. This can be explained that the embedded crossover operation in the binarization step enhanced the exploration and exploitation in the binary space which resulted in better performance results. Because X-TF was the best binarization method with SSA algorithm, it was used to binarize other optimizers namely BBA, BCS, and BGWO. The results of these optimizers are then used to validate the results of BSSA-X. It appears in Table 6 that BSSA-X outperformed BBA, BGWO and BCS in terms of accuracy, fitness value and number of selected features. Furthermore Fig. 8, illustrates the convergence behavior of all the studied binary versions of SSA algorithms. It appears that BSSA-X was the best in achieving the minimum fitness values at the final stages of the optimization process. This can be noticed from the tail of the convergence curve of BSSA-X. Other optimizers their convergence behavior during the learning stage indicates that they fell in the local optima such as BBA-X, BCS-X, and BGWO-X. It appears also that whatever the applied TF with BSSA, the convergence results are much better than other optimizers.

Table 6. Comparison between different versions BSSA and other optimizers

TF-family	Algorithm	Accuracy	Fitness value	No features
S-TFs	BSSA-S1	0.9484	0.0835	57
	BSSA-S2	0.9476	0.0806	67
	BSSA-S3	0.9481	0.0822	52
	BSSA-S4	0.9472	0.0824	71
V-TFs	BSSA-V1	0.9477	0.0824	52
	BSSA-V2	0.9498	0.0809	78
	BSSA-V3	0.9482	0.0827	61
	BSSA-V4	0.9475	0.0840	54
X-TF	BSSA-X	0.9507	0.0798	49
Z-TFs	BSSAZ1	0.9491	0.0820	55
	BSSA-Z2	0.9488	0.0822	79
	BSSA-Z3	0.9489	0.0819	61
	BSSA-Z4	0.9474	0.0812	59
U-TFs	BSSA-U1	0.9480	0.0811	53
	BSSA-U2	0.9482	0.0812	46
	BSSAU3	0.9480	0.0811	53
	BBA-X	0.8904	0.1621	78
	BGWO-X	0.9373	0.1037	53
	BCS-X	0.9476	0.0825	52

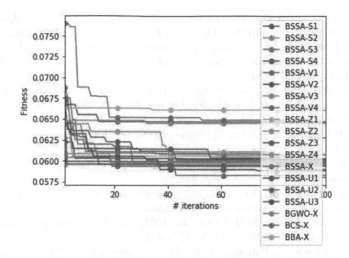

Fig. 8. The convergence curves of different versions of BSSA and other optimizers

6   Conclusion and Future Works

In this work, a new phishing detection system is proposed. The system uses the SSA algorithm as a search algorithm in the wrapper-based FS framework. Sixteen binary versions of SSA algorithm are generated using different TFs. The effect of different TFs are studied and analyzed to determine the most efficient SSA binary version. The results show that the different binary versions of SSA algorithm produce different results in terms of accuracy, fitness values, number of selected features and convergence behavior. This implies that the binarization method (mappers) affects the optimization process in different ways. BSSA-X with embedded crossover operator achieved the best results compared with other BSSA versions. Furthermore, X-TF was used with other optimization algorithms and it showed that BSSA-X outperformed their performance.

For future work, we plan to use TFs to binarize other set of metaheuristic algorithms to solve new optimization problems.

Acknowledgment. This work has been partially funded by project. TIN2017-85727-C4-2-P (Ministerio español de Economía y Competitividad).

References

1. Opendns: Phishtank data archives. https://www.phishtank.com/. Accessed 21 Feb 2019
2. Abad, E.A.G., Ferrer, J.R.A., Naval Jr. P.C.: Phishing website classification using features of web addresses and web pages
3. Ahmed, S., Mafarja, M., Faris, H., ljarah, I.: Feature selection using salp swarm algorithm with chaos. In: Proceedings of the 2nd International Conference on Intelligent Systems, Metaheuristics & Swarm Intelligence, pp. 65–69 (2018)

4. Aljarah, I., et al.: A dynamic locality multi-objective salp swarm algorithm for feature selection. Computers & Industrial Engineering, p. 106628 (2020)
5. Aljarah, I., Mafarja, M., Heidari, A.A., Faris, H., Zhang, Y., Mirjalili, S.: Asynchronous accelerating multi-leader salp chains for feature selection. Appl. Soft Comput. **71**, 964–979 (2018)
6. Alkawaz, M.H., Steven, S.J., Hajamydeen, A.I.: Detecting phishing website using machine learning. In: 2020 16th IEEE International Colloquium on Signal Processing & Its Applications (CSPA), pp. 111–114. IEEE (2020)
7. Basnet, R.B., Sung, A.H., Liu, Q.: Feature Selection for Improved Phishing Detection. In: Jiang, H., Ding, W., Ali, M., Wu, X. (eds.) IEA/AIE 2012. LNCS (LNAI), vol. 7345, pp. 252–261. Springer, Heidelberg (2012). https://doi.org/10.1007/978-3-642-31087-4_27
8. Brezočnik, L., Fister, I., Vrbančič, G.: Applying differential evolution with threshold mechanism for feature selection on a phishing websites classification. In: Welzer, T., et al. (eds.) ADBIS 2019. CCIS, vol. 1064, pp. 11–18. Springer, Cham (2019). https://doi.org/10.1007/978-3-030-30278-8_2
9. Buber, E., Demir, Ö., Sahingoz, O.K.: Feature selections for the machine learning based detection of phishing websites. In: 2017 International Artificial Intelligence and Data Processing Symposium (IDAP), pp. 1–5. IEEE (2017)
10. Eberhart, R., Kennedy., J.: Particle swarm optimization. In: Proceedings of the IEEE International Conference on Neural Networks, vol. 4, pp. 1942–1948. Citeseer (1995)
11. El-Alfy, E.S.M.: Detection of phishing websites based on probabilistic neural networks and k-medoids clustering. Comput. J. **60**(12), 1745–1759 (2017)
12. Faris, H.: An efficient binary salp swarm algorithm with crossover scheme for feature selection problems. Knowl.-Based Syst. 154, 43–67 (2018)
13. Ferreira, R.P., et al.: Artificial neural network for websites classification with phishing characteristics. Social Networking **7**(02), 97 (2018)
14. Ghosh, K.K., Singh, P.K., Hong, J., Geem, Z.W., Sarkar, R.: Binary social mimic optimization algorithm with x-shaped transfer function for feature selection. IEEE Access (2020)
15. Guo, S., Wang, J., Guo, M.: Z-shaped transfer functions for binary particle swarm optimization algorithm. Computational Intelligence and Neuroscience (2020)
16. Huang, H., Qian, L., Wang, Y.: A svm-based technique to detect phishing urls. Inf. Technol. J. **11**(7), 921 (2012)
17. Khurma, R.A., Aljarah, I., Sharieh, A.: An efficient moth flame optimization algorithm using chaotic maps for feature selection in the medical applications. In: ICPRAM, pp. 175–182 (2020)
18. Khurma, R.A., Aljarah, I., Sharieh, A.: Rank based moth flame optimisation for feature selection in the medical application. In: 2020 IEEE Congress on Evolutionary Computation (CEC), pp. 1–8. IEEE (2020)
19. Khurma, R.A., Aljarah, I., Sharieh, A., Mirjalili, S.: EvoloPy-FS: An Open-Source Nature-Inspired Optimization Framework in Python for Feature Selection. In: Mirjalili, S., Faris, H., Aljarah, I. (eds.) Evolutionary Machine Learning Techniques. AIS, pp. 131–173. Springer, Singapore (2020). https://doi.org/10.1007/978-981-32-9990-0_8
20. Korkmaz, M., Sahingoz, O.K., Diri, B.: Feature selections for the classification of webpages to detect phishing attacks: a survey. In 2020 International Congress on Human-Computer Interaction, Optimization and Robotic Applications (HORA), pp. 1–9. IEEE (2020)

21. Mirjalili, S., Gandomi, A.H., Mirjalili, S.Z., Saremi, S., Faris, H., Mirjalili, S.M.: Salp swarm algorithm: a bio-inspired optimizer for engineering design problems. Adv. Eng. Softw. **114**, 163–191 (2017)
22. Mirjalili, S., Zhang, H., Mirjalili, S., Chalup, S., Noman, N.: A Novel U-Shaped Transfer Function for Binary Particle Swarm Optimisation. In: Nagar, A.K., Deep, K., Bansal, J.C., Das, K.N. (eds.) Soft Computing for Problem Solving 2019. AISC, vol. 1138, pp. 241–259. Springer, Singapore (2020). https://doi.org/10.1007/978-981-15-3290-0_19
23. Mohammad, R.M., Thabtah, F., McCluskey, L.: An assessment of features related to phishing websites using an automated technique. In: 2012 International Conference for Internet Technology and Secured Transactions, pp. 492–497. IEEE (2012)
24. Priya, S., Selvakumar, S., Leela Velusamy, R.: Gravitational search based feature selection for enhanced phishing websites detection. In: 2020 2nd International Conference on Innovative Mechanisms for Industry Applications (ICIMIA), pp. 453–458. IEEE (2020)
25. Rashedi, E., Nezamabadi-Pour, H., Saryazdi, S.: Gsa: a gravitational search algorithm. Inf. Sci. **179**(13), 2232–2248 (2009)
26. Sahingoz, O.K., Buber, E., Demir, O., Diri, B.: Machine learning based phishing detection from urls. Expert Syst. Appl. **117**, 345–357 (2019)
27. Saravanan, P., Subramanian, S.: A framework for detecting phishing websites using ga based feature selection and artmap based website classification. Procedia Comput. Sci. **171**, 1083–1092 (2020)
28. Shah, R., Trevathan, J., Read, W., Ghodosi, H.: A proactive approach to preventing phishing attacks using pshark. In: 2009 Sixth International Conference on Information Technology: New Generations, pp. 915–921. IEEE (2009)
29. Suleman, M.T., Awan, S.M.: Optimization of url-based phishing websites detection through genetic algorithms. Autom. Control. Comput. Sci. **53**(4), 333–341 (2019)
30. Vrbancic, G.: Phishing dataset (2019). https://github.com/GregaVrbancic/Phishing-Dataset. Accessed 23 May 2019
31. Weedon, M., Tsaptsinos, D., Denholm-Price, J.: Random forest explorations for url classification. In 2017 International Conference On Cyber Situational Awareness, Data Analytics And Assessment (Cyber SA), pp. 1–4. IEEE (2017)
32. Zhang, H., Liu, G., Chow, T.W.S., Liu, W.: Textual and visual content-based anti-phishing: a bayesian approach. IEEE Trans. Neural Networks **22**(10), 1532–1546 (2011)

Real Time Optimisation of Traffic Signals to Prioritise Public Transport

Milan Wittpohl[1]([✉]) [ID], Per-Arno Plötz[2] [ID], and Neil Urquhart[1] [ID]

[1] Edinburgh Napier University, Edinburgh, Scotland, UK
hello@milanwittpohl.com
[2] Free and Hanseatic City of Hamburg, Germany

Abstract. This paper examines the optimisation of traffic signals to prioritise public transportation (busses) in real time. A novel representation for the traffic signal prioritisation problem is introduced. The novel representation is used within an evolutionary algorithm that supports safe solutions which comply with real-world traffic signal constraints. The proposed system finds near-optimal solutions in around 20 s, enabling real-time optimisation. The authors examine a specific junction in Hamburg, Germany, based on real-world traffic data a variety of different problem scenarios ranging from low to exceptional traffic saturations are generated. In collaboration with domain experts, a fitness function is defined to reduce the journey time of a bus while maintaining an overall stable traffic system. Candidate solutions are evaluated using the microscopic traffic simulator SUMO allowing for precise optimisation and addressing of the flow prediction problem. The results show good scaling of the proposed system, with more significant improvements in more congested scenarios. Given the results, future research on bigger and multiple road junctions is motivated.

This work contributes to the field in four ways. Firstly, by defining a real-world problem containing the actual intersection layout and traffic signal parameters. Secondly, by presenting a software design that integrates highly efficient SUMO simulations into an evolutionary algorithm. Thirdly, by introducing a novel representation that allows unconventional solutions while ensuring compliance with traffic signal regulations at all times. Lastly, by testing the suggested approach on various problem scenarios of the real-world problem.

Keywords: Traffic signal prioritisation · Real-Time traffic simulation · Flow prediction problem · SUMO · Real-World application

1 Introduction

Traffic signals represent one of the most crucial parts of urban infrastructure, uniquely, in comparison to other mechanisms, they control when people stop or move. Traffic signal sequences are planned by traffic engineers, planning in this context refers to programming an advanced logic that controls at what time signals switch between red and green to maximise traffic efficiency. The job of traffic engineers is becoming increasingly challenging. The boom of the automotive industry through the 1970s pushed civil

© Springer Nature Switzerland AG 2021
P. A. Castillo and J. L. Jiménez Laredo (Eds.): EvoApplications 2021, LNCS 12694, pp. 162–177, 2021.
https://doi.org/10.1007/978-3-030-72699-7_11

planners to favour motorised traffic when (re)planning city districts [1]. However, this approach heavily collides with the increasingly popular approach of favouring green spaces, pedestrian-friendly areas and mass transit [1] which leads to less available road space for motorised traffic. Additionally, the rise of urbanisation results in bigger, denser cities all over the globe [2]. In total, increasingly more people have to move through relatively less space to get from point A to B. Solving this problem is immensely important to improve life quality as well as economic value.

Traffic signals are highly regulated [3] and require safe systems, as a high amount of trust is globally established. This makes the adoption of new approaches challenging and requires close attention to real-world constraints.

The increasing priority of public transportation presents an additional problem. Over time, several approaches to prioritisation have been proposed which vary in their levels of modification to the existing road infrastructures. Dedicated bus lanes require a substantial change in behaviour from existing traffic. Not as extreme, but similar are dedicated traffic signals. In terms of minimising the adjustment of existing infrastructure, simply prioritising the bus through modified green times presents the most efficient approach [4]. When planning signals, engineers need to take driving patterns, average speeds and legal restrictions into account their decisions being based on punctuated data. Public authorities may count traffic during different times of the day to obtain low, average and high traffic saturations. Depending on the existing infrastructure a logic based on limited data can be programmed by the traffic engineers. However, they can never account for all possible traffic scenarios. Instead, assumptions must be drawn and a program that works well for most scenarios is developed. However, a system that needs to work well in a large variety of circumstances can rarely perform optimally in a particular scenario. That is true, even if dedicated programs are designed to regulate traffic at certain times within a week. Additionally, the task of planning and testing traffic signals is very time consuming. The task to prioritise public transportation makes this task even more challenging and rather impossible to account for all possibilities.

Through the use of real-time traffic data, it is possible to build intelligent traffic signal systems incorporating prioritisation. The data allows optimising signal plans in real time to improve overall traffic efficiency as well as prioritising public transport. However, to provide significant improvements, novel signal sequences need to be generated without any restrictions and their quality needs to be validated. Most importantly, the improved signals need to be safe as road users put trust in traffic lights. As well as being safe, the improved signals need to increase efficiency. This raises the question of how real-time traffic data can be used to find optimised, yet safe signals in real time?

The field of traffic signal optimisation generally consists of Traffic Signal Control (TSC) and Traffic Signal Prioritisation (TSP). Whereas TSC aims to optimise the traffic in general, TSP aims to prioritise individual traffic members. In both fields, computational intelligence and in particular evolutionary algorithms have shown much promise in recent years. Additionally, for both fields, but especially for TSP, it is crucial to validate that the adjusted traffic signal program has the desired effect. Otherwise, the optimisation might lead to a negative effect, which is commonly known as the flow prediction problem [5, 6]. Furthermore, most of the recent approaches only make small adjustments to the existing signal plan and often neglect real-world traffic signal constraints.

This research seeks to answer the following research questions:

1. How can an evolutionary algorithm prioritise public transportation in real time while taking the flow prediction problem and real-world traffic regulations into account?
2. How can the impact of such a system be measured?

In this paper, a novel approach is proposed to integrate the microscopic traffic simulator SUMO into an evolutionary algorithm in order to allow for real-time traffic signal prioritisation. The proposed algorithm is referred to as EA-FC. This work contributes to the field by:

1. Defining a real-world problem (intersection layout & traffic signal parameters)
2. Presenting a software design that integrates highly efficient SUMO simulation into an evolutionary algorithm
3. Introducing a novel representation that allows unconventional solutions while ensuring compliance with traffic signal regulations at all times
4. Testing the suggested approach on various problem scenarios of the real-world problem.

The focus of this work lies in the novel concept which requires additional refinements in future work.

2 Literature Review

Traffic Signal Control (TSC) adjustments modify the parameters of traffic signals. Research on TSC algorithms started in the mid 20th-century [7]. TSC remains a research field receiving close attention [7, 8]. Due to advancements in sensor-technology, TSC methods can utilise real-time traffic data [7]. Approaches utilising real-time traffic data (e.g. induction loops, cameras) differ from classic, passive TSC approaches and are classified as adaptive [6].

Even though adaptive TSC and TSP approaches are able to respond to current traffic scenarios, research is disunited if a passive or adaptive approach works better and is more likely to actually contribute in the real-world. In recent years Alba *et al.* focused on passive approaches, stating, "real time control of traffic-lights is not feasible because of various reasons (legal, technical, etc.), and we must instead find a highly-reliable global schedule of traffic-lights that works well in the dynamic and uncertain traffic system" [9]. Adaptive TSC approaches vary in their time criticality. While some systems might make fluent adjustments to account for traffic changes (e.g. unusual traffic caused by a sport event), others might need to react in a very short amount of time (e.g. to prioritise an emergency vehicle). In order to effectively prioritise an approaching bus, the signal needs to adapt to the current traffic situation immediately, resulting in little computational time. Of the research on traffic system control and prioritisation, only a small portion operates under short time constraints. As cycles are usually not longer than 90 s, short time constrains refers to adjustment calculated within one cycle. Established commercial systems (e.g. SCOOT [10], SCATS [11], RHODES [12]) are able to prioritise public transportation under short time constrains, but the modifications to the signal plan are slight. Additionally, due to their commercial nature little to no detail on the computation of improved traffic signals is known. To the best of the authors knowledge, and indicated by an extensive study [13], the most widely used commercial systems do not use any kind of evolutionary algorithms.

Adaptive approaches derive traffic information from sensors. Depending on the distance between the sensors and the traffic signal, additional assumptions about the behaviour of the recognized vehicles must be made. Minimising the error between reality and projection will become significantly more difficult, the further away the sensors are placed. This problem is commonly referred to as flow prediction problem and is one of the main reasons why adaptive TSC/TSP approaches fail or might even worsen the signals efficiency [6]. Even if the inconsistencies between real life traffic and the simulation could be minimised, it would remain extremely demanding to build a system capable of optimally adapting to any traffic scenario [14].

In passive approaches, candidate solutions are often validated through the use of well-established traffic simulators [9, 15, 16]. However, to the best of the authors knowledge, traffic simulators have not been integrated into real-time adaptive TSP approaches, presenting a gap in current research. Recent research in adaptive TSC/TSP often focuses on rule-based approaches that limit the possible adjustments to the current signal plan.

Zhang *et al.* propose an approach that uses predefined signal plans, by making only limited adjustments [17]. Another rule-based approach was proposed by Ma *et al.* [18] who utilise dynamic programming for solving the TSP as a multi-stage decision problem [18]. Ahmed & Hawas introduced a virtual queue to account for passenger load in another rule-based TSP approach [19]. Instead of a rule-based approach, Stevanovic et al. introduced a genetic algorithm to optimise cycle length, green splits, offsets and phase sequences [20]. However, the algorithm does not operate in real time and can therefore not adequately conform to current traffic situations.

Current research often neglects real-world traffic signal constraints. Whereas constraints like minimum/maximum green times are often taken into account, more advanced rules such as realistic intergreen times, an early green signal for pedestrians and other, often country-specific, regulations are disregarded. Evolutionary algorithms and computational intelligence-based approaches have proven to be highly suitable for TSC and TSP problems. However, the reviewed TSC and especially TSP approaches often

- do not account for real-world traffic signal constraints, especially advanced rules like realistic intergreen times
- do not validate candidate solution through well-established microscopic simulators in real time, which would make the systems more trustworthy and would allow visualisation of solutions easily
- lack the possibility to drastically change the signal program. Instead, less disruptive methods, like green extension are used
- are based on pre-defined rules which disallows unconventional solutions.

These findings motivate this research to explore the use of evolutionary algorithms to generate (disruptive) signal plans in real time, which are validated through the use of a microscopic simulator.

3   Methodology

This chapter starts with the presentation of a real-world intersection in Hamburg, Germany. Section 3.2 gives a short introduction to the traffic SUMO simulator which is integrated into the evolutionary algorithm using the representation presented in Sect. 3.3.

3.1   Problem Instance

In collaboration with public authorities (domain experts) in Hamburg a simple, yet highly frequented intersection was identified. The junction consists of a main road towards the centre of Hamburg and a less used side street with residential buildings (see Fig. 1).

To model this intersection in a traffic simulator, the intersection layout files, provided by the city of Hamburg, is used. The layout files contain important information such as the lane width and the exact position of the traffic signals. Additionally, traffic signal parameters (e.g. intergreen times) are given. Therefore, the intersection portrays a realistic problem instance for the proposed approach. The intersection layout is also publicly available for future research [21].

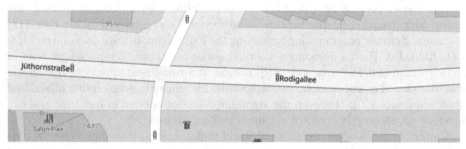

Fig. 1. Real-world junction Rodigalle/Jüthornstraße – Kielmannseggstraße © OpenStreetMap contributors

3.2   Microscopic Traffic Simulation with SUMO

Throughout the literature, researchers frequently use SUMO (Simulation of Urban Mobility) [22, 23]. SUMO is a highly performant, open-source, deterministic, microscopic traffic simulator written in C++ and developed by the Institute of Transportation Research (IVF) at the German Aerospace Centre (DLR) [22]. Due to its performance and wide acceptance in similar research SUMO is chosen for this research. In this work, the use of a traffic simulator aims to tackle the flow prediction problem by validating the impact of a particular traffic signal plan. Traffic simulators are classified by their level of detail, typically researchers mainly distinguish between macroscopic and microscopic models. Macroscopic simulators are more abstract as they simulate traffic flows, rather than individual vehicles [24]. A macroscopic simulator aims to answer questions about the general traffic flow, rather than providing information about individual vehicle movements. Significantly more accurate are microscopic simulators, which simulate the movement and behaviour of every vehicle at every time step. The model calculates the vehicle's movement based on the vehicles physical abilities (e.g. acceleration rate) and the behaviour of the driver (e.g. reaction time, aggression level). SUMO is a microscopic traffic simulator which therefore enables realistic simulations.

A traffic simulation in SUMO consists of three input files: a network file that defines the road layout, a route file that defines the trips taken by users and an additional file that can be used to place detectors or define additional signal plans [25].

For this research, the network and routes are static for a given scenario. The network file is created using the official intersection layout files provided by the city of Hamburg. The route file contains the traffic volumes as defined in Sect. 3.3. The additional file is used to represent the signal plan (candidate solution) to evaluate.

3.3 Design of the Evolutionary Algorithm

This section describes the integration of SUMO in an evolutionary algorithm for real-time traffic signal prioritisation. In collaboration with domain experts, two problem scenarios for traffic signal prioritisation are defined. These problem scenarios are used for the first experiment, presented in Sect. 4.1. Additionally, in Sect. 4.2 a range of problems is generated from these problem scenarios to gain further insights.

In the first problem scenario a relatively low, realistic traffic volume is defined. For the second problem scenario, the network is deliberately congested (e.g. due to roadwork or a sport-event). The purpose of this is to examine how the proposed algorithm performs in drastically different situations. In both cases, the algorithm is tasked to prioritise a single bus that entered the simulation after 20 s and would take about 10 s to reach the intersections in ideal conditions. In contrast to other similar approaches, the improved, generated signal plan runs for a couple of minutes and does not end with the bus reaching its destination, but rather when the last vehicle reaches its destination. This way, the algorithm can heavily prioritise the bus before giving priority to other connections.

Fitness Function

Previous researchers have previously attempted to minimise the average delay per vehicle/passenger [14, 26] or minimise the overall journey times [16]. In this research the journey time for the bus should be minimised as much as possible while maintaining a functional traffic system, meaning that other vehicles should still be able to reach their destination in a reasonable time. In collaboration with the domain experts, the fitness function presented by Eq. 1 is defined, which the algorithm is tasked to **minimise**. The fitness

$$F = 0.7 \times A_B + 0.3 \times A_{LV} \tag{1}$$

is mainly affected by the arrival time of the bus (A_B) but also by the overall simulation for a certain number of vehicles, where A_{LV} represents the time of the last vehicle to reach the destination. The weights 0.7 and 0.3 were set through informal experimentation. Exploring different values for A_B and A_{LV} is not part of this research but will be explored in future work to examine how the weight effects the resulting traffic conditions. In a real-world use case, these parameters could be tuned by public authorities to easily change the priority of different traffic members and therefore enable parameterizable traffic regulation.

Solution Representation

A candidate solution comprises a signal plan consisting of n phases each with a distinct duration and a state. The state has a fixed number of signals which have to be (semi-) compatible to ensure traffic safety[1]. In SUMO a phase is represented by a phase tag with a duration and state attribute. The state represents the shown signals for all traffic lights at the intersection over the given duration. Therefore, the signals do not change throughout a phase, they change when transitioning to the next phase. The state attribute consists of a list of signals. r represents a red light, u a red & yellow light (used in Germany when switching from red to green), y an amber (yellow) light, g a green light with no priority (e.g. left-turning traffic) and G a green light with priority (e.g. straight traffic). The signal is mapped to the traffic signal index of the junction, as shown in Fig. 2 [28].

A candidate solution is defined by the number of phases as well as the durations and states for each phase. As pointed out most prior research tries to reduce journey times while minimising the changes to the signal plan. This approach, however, aims to find disruptive solutions through maximising the novelty of solutions. Instead of limiting the possible adjustments to the signal plan by the algorithm, the search space is significantly extended to allow for substantially different signal plans, hence maximising evolutionary creativity. The number of phases and phase durations can take any integer value between an according minimum and maximum value. For the states, the proposed system picks signals from a set of available states with only (semi-)compatible signals. This way it is

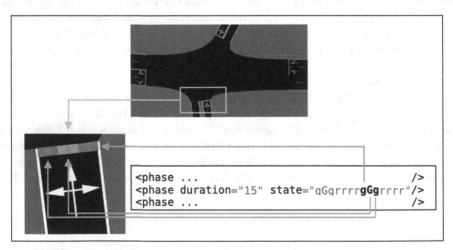

Fig. 2. Signal plan representation in SUMO where the state of a phase is mapped to specific lanes of the given intersection

---

[1] The connections of compatible signals do not cross. Semi-compatible signals may share the same conflict area, but priority must be clearly regulated (left-turning vehicles vs. oncoming vehicles) [27].

ensured that all signals are (semi-)compatible, without limiting the creativity. Ensuring safety is crucial as unsafe solutions could potentially produce (lethal) accidents.

The proposed, novel representation consists of two lists of integers. These lists must always have the same length as they represent the number of phases. The first list represents the durations ([5, 10]). The second list represents the (semi-)compatible states to use ([0, 1]). The values of the second list represent the index of a list of predefined phases with only (semi-)compatible states. Figure 3 illustrates the representation in a simplified manner.

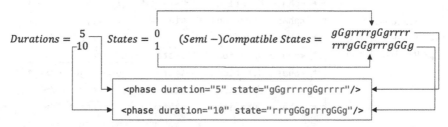

Fig. 3. Solution representation (simplified) where the states refer to a list of predefined phases with only (semi-)compatible states

Both durations and states are simultaneously optimised as they depend on another. Additionally, intergreen times need to be considered. Intergreen times represent the yellow and red times to transition to the next green phase and are dependent on the road layout and not on traffic conditions. Therefore, the algorithm only evolves the durations and states that are not part of a signal change (intergreen times).

For every state change, a transition strategy is defined. The values of the transition strategy represent:

- the duration of the phase before switching to a specific state (fixed value, not optimised by the algorithm)
- a placeholder for the green time duration (dynamic value, optimised by the algorithm, represented by the placeholder of -1)
- the duration of the yellow phase after the green phase and the duration of the red phase (fixed value, not optimised by the algorithm)

The SUMO signal plan is generated, and the duration of the green phases are replaced by the chromosome duration values. This allows for precise configuration per intersection while given the algorithm maximum creativity, see Fig. 4.

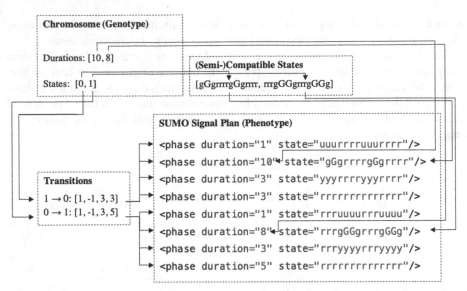

Fig. 4. Genotype to phenotype conversion where intergreen times are inserted for every transition

Search Space

Given the proposed solution representation the search space $\mathbb{S}$ is defined as

$$\mathbb{S} = \sum_{n=P_{min}}^{P_{max}} s \times (s-1)^{n-1} \times d^n$$

where P_{min} and P_{max} represent the minimum and maximum number of phases, s the number of valid states and d the number of possible phase duration. No split-second durations are considered as these are not supported by traffic signals in Germany.

Given the problem instance, the number of phases is set to a minimum of four (P_{min}) and a maximum of eight (P_{max}). The phase durations are set to be between five[2] and 60 s ($d = 56$). In addition to the two valid states of giving east/west and north/south a green signal, four addition valid signals are defined ($s = 6$). These states give each direction exclusively a green signal and could usually not be considered by a traffic engineer as they are only valuable in very few scenarios. Based on the parameters a search space with 4.5499×10^{19} possible solutions, demonstrating exploring even one per cent of the search space will be too computational expensive given the goal of real-time prioritisation. Therefore, a fast converging evolutionary algorithm is needed.

Evolutionary Algorithm Parameterization

Based on similar research and to quickly converge to good solutions, the following parameters and operators are used. The population size is set rather low to allow for a high number of generations within the 20 s time limit. The initial population is generated randomly. The algorithm is referred to as EA-FC throughout the paper (Table 1).

---

[2] In Germany the minimum green time per phase is five seconds [27].

Table 1. Parameters for EA-FC

Parameter	Value
Population size	50
Time limit	20 s
Number of children	10
Selection operator	Tournament selection
Tournament size	5
Number of parents	2
Crossover rate	1
Crossover operator	One point crossover
Mutation rate	0.5
Mutation operator	Swap mutation
Replacement operator	Worst child with probability replacement
Replacement probability	0.5

Over the course of this research four additional evolutionary algorithms were defined that favoured exploration over exploitation. Furthermore, two particle swarm optimisers were tested. Overall, the presented EA-FC performed best in a variety of experiments, hence other algorithms are not presented here.

Evaluation Process and Software Architecture
Ideally, the proposed system would be compared to existing bus prioritisation systems. However, this is not possible for this research. Instead, the algorithm is compared to the real-world fixed-time signal plan as well as a standard adaptive signal plan in SUMO that utilises on-road detectors. Future work should address the issue of neither plans prioritising the bus. The experiments presented here do however provide a valuable starting point.

The proposed system is programmed in Java. The entire code is publicly accessible on GitLab [21]. One virtual server with 6vcpus (approx. 3 GHz per core), 16 GB of RAM and an SSD is used. This configuration drastically exceeds what is possible locally at the traffic controller but could easily be achieved on a central server. While not examined in this work, running an optimised version of the proposed approach locally at the traffic controller is considered to be possible and should be examined in future work. As the algorithm is limited by time and the solution space is tremendously large, the number of solutions that can be evaluated is key for the overall performance. The most computationally expensive tasks are the evaluation of a single chromosome, the evaluation of the entire population and the creation of a new child. These tasks are executed simultaneously in multiple threads. The number of threads equals the number of chromosomes to evaluate/children to create.

3.4 Reproducibility

As previously noted, the intersection layout and traffic data modelled in SUMO is publicly available on GitLab. Additionally, the source code, a runnable java application and information for reproducing the presented experiments can be found in the repository [21].

4 Results

Two experiments are conducted. The first experiment demonstrates the performance of the proposed algorithm in the two problem scenarios. The second experiment explores the robustness of the algorithms.

4.1 Algorithm Performance

As evolutionary algorithms are non-deterministic, EA-FC is executed 100 times per problem scenario. In the first scenario a relatively low traffic volume is used. The results are shown in Fig. 5. EA-FC is sometimes able to find solutions better than the fixed/adaptive signal plan. At best, the algorithm's fitness is approximately one per cent better and at worst, approximately three per cent worse than the fixed/adaptive plan.

Fig. 5. First scenario with relatively low traffic volumes

Noticeably, the journey time of the bus could not be optimised, therefore the fitness improves due to slight reductions of about three seconds for the overall journey time (A_{LV}). The results show that the proposed algorithm does work but is limited to minor improvements.

In the second scenario, a scenario with deliberate high traffic volumes is defined. The results, as presented in Fig. 6. The fixed plan has a fitness of 685.5 and the adaptive plan of 373.5. EA-FC significantly outperforms the fixed plan by up to 78% and the adaptive plan by up to 55%. The journey time of the bus could be reduced by up to 472 s for the fixed and up to 214 s for the adaptive plan. Additionally, the overall journey time could be improved by up to 677 s for the fixed and up to 119 s for the adaptive plan. The results demonstrate that with increasing traffic volumes more significant improvements can be achieved.

The improvements are especially significant as the EA only evaluates about 1,000 candidate solution within the 20 s time limit. The EA is able to perform just as good or better than the standard plans while validating the quality of each candidate solution through the simulation in SUMO in real time.

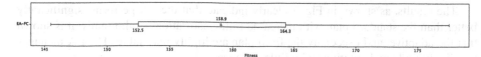

Fig. 6. Second scenario with deliberately high traffic volumes

4.2 Algorithm Robustness

The second experiment aims to examine if the EAs are able to find good solutions regardless of the traffic scenario. Beginning with the first problem scenario and linearly increasing traffic volumes up to the second problem scenario, 100 problem scenarios are generated.[3] In this experiment, the evolutionary algorithm is only run once per scenario.

Additionally, to further address the flow prediction problem, each candidate solution is evaluated multiple times on slightly different scenarios. This approach was inspired by Ferrer *et al.* [9]. Candidate solutions are evaluated once on the standard traffic scenario and then on two additional scenarios that slightly vary. This is achieved through the random flag in SUMO.

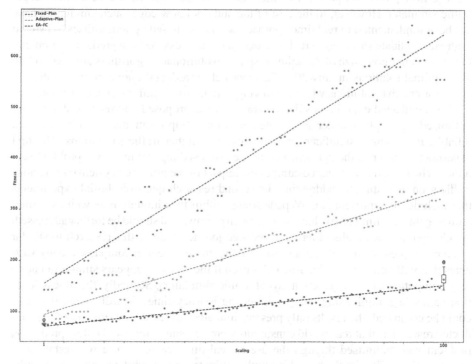

Fig. 7. Evaluating the algorithms robustness

---

[3] Due to the fact that the bus takes a different route in the two scenarios the first problem is modified, leading to different fitness values for the standard signal plans.

The results, as shown in Fig. 7 clearly indicate that the EA performs significantly better than the standard plan with increased traffic saturation. Additionally, it is shown that the adaptive, and especially the fixed plan are highly unreliable. The EA manages to reliably find good solutions with little variance.

5 Conclusion

Traffic engineers face the challenging task of developing near-optimal signal plans to ensure efficient urban mobility with steadily increasing population density. The increasing need for smarter traffic signals to prioritise public transport through the use of emerging sensors and evolutionary algorithms motivated this research.

This research seeks to answer the research questions:

1. How can an evolutionary algorithm prioritise public transportation in real time while taking the flow prediction problem and real-world traffic regulations into account?
2. How can the impact of such a system be measured?

The flow prediction problem is often addressed through the use of a microscopic traffic simulator. However, to the best of the authors knowledge, such simulators have not been implemented in real time approaches. The proposed system utilises SUMO to evaluate candidate solutions in real time in order to address the flow prediction problem. Due to the enormous size of the solution space, evolutionary algorithms are used to find near-optimal solutions in only 20 s. This research introduces a novel representation to allow for creative solutions while complying to real-world traffic signal constraints.

The conducted experiments demonstrate that the proposed approach is able to find optimised signal plans under short time constraints. Improvements could be achieved reliably, increasingly significant in scenarios with higher traffic saturations. The first experiment examines the performance of the proposed algorithm in two problem scenarios. The second experiment examines the impact of the proposed system over various traffic scenarios, directly addressing the second research question. Initial experiments that include the representation of pedestrians within the simulation as well as further reducing the time limit to 10 s have shown much promise and should be further addressed.

Comparing the results in terms of reduced journey time of this research to similar researchers presents a challenging task. Firstly, this problem encompasses many variables that will differ in existing research - even if the research appears similar in nature (e.g. computational time, junction layout, traffic simulator). Secondly, the fitness function varies (e.g. minimising delay, minimising journey time). Thirdly, even if results could be compared, the results only present simulated values. A key strength of the conducted research is that real-world constraints were accounted for and the flow prediction problem was minimised through the use of real-time traffic data, a well-established microscopic traffic simulator and multiple evaluates per candidate solution. Simply, comparing the achieved improvement in journey time does not give an indication about how the system would perform in the real-world. Nevertheless, future work should make direct comparisons between the proposed system and similar research.

On a meta-level, to the best of the authors knowledge, the conducted research proposes a truly novel approach. Some researchers have shown the vast potential of evolutionary algorithms for TSC and TSP in combination with a microscopic simulator. Other researchers demonstrated that it is also possible to make real-time adjustments under short time constraints. However, to the best of the authors knowledge, the use of evolutionary algorithms to optimise signal plans in real time through validation by a microscopic simulator has not been conducted yet. Therefore, this research addressed an important gap and proved that realistic factors do not have be neglected in order to improve signal plans in real time.

Future work will address the following issues. The proposed algorithm will be tested on additional problem scenarios to further explore its usefulness. Bigger intersections should be tackled as well as more complex layouts (e.g. bike lanes, dedicated lanes for turning traffic). A benchmark system should be developed to directly compare this approach with other research and existing real-world prioritisation systems. Additionally, a field test should be conducted to measure the performance of the proposed system in the real world. The software should be further optimised and tested on hardware that is representative of that available locally at the intersection now and in the near future. Algorithmic (e.g. population size) factors remained mostly fixed throughout this research and should also be further addressed in future work.

The weights 0.3 (A_{LV}) and 0.7 (A_B) used in the fitness function should be experimented with in future work. Furthermore, the results should be discussed in more detail with traffic engineers, as the results could include flaws that are spotted by the domain experts or could be inspirational for the traffic engineers.

Through the approach proposed in this paper, traffic engineers could gain a powerful tool to ensure the efficiency of urban mobility. On a broader level, this presents a shift in paradigm, as traffic engineers focus on optimising a system that produces an optimised signal plan, instead of spending days programming complex logic for a single intersection. The traffic engineer does not rely on historic traffic data as the proposed system adapts in real time. In addition to stationary hardware (e.g. infrared sensors), vehicle communication is on the horizon. With increasingly more real-time traffic data becoming available, systems that incorporate real-time traffic data become more appealing. In conclusion, this novel approach presents a realistic solution to tackle the task of developing near-optimal signal plans to ensure efficient urban mobility in times of steadily increasing population density.

References

1. Sumantran, V., Fine, C.H., Gonsalvez, D.J.A.: Faster, Smarter, Greener the Future of the Car and Urban Mobility. The MIT press, Cambridge (Mass.) (2017)
2. United Nations: The World's Cities in 2016. UN (2016). https://doi.org/10.18356/851989 1f-en
3. United Nations ed: Convention on Road Signs and Signals of 1968: European Agreement Supplementing the Convention ; and, Protocol on Road Markings, Additional to the European Agreement: (2006 consolidated versions). United Nations, New York (2007)
4. Shen, G., Kong, X.: Study on road network traffic coordination control technique with bus priority. IEEE Trans. Syst. Man. Cybern. **39**, 343–351 (2009). https://doi.org/10.1109/TSMCC. 2008.2005842

5. Lee, J., Shalaby, A., Greenough, J., Bowie, M., Hung, S.: Advanced transit signal priority control with online microsimulation-based transit prediction model. Transp. Res. Rec. **1925**, 10 (2005)
6. Hirulkar, P., Deshpande, R., Bajaj, P.: Optimization of traffic flow through signalized intersections using PSO. 4 (2013)
7. Zhao, D., Dai, Y., Zhang, Z.: Computational intelligence in urban traffic signal control: a survey. IEEE Trans. Syst. Man. Cybern. **42**, 485–494 (2012). https://doi.org/10.1109/TSMCC.2011.2161577
8. Manolis, D., Pappa, T., Diakaki, C., Papamichail, I., Papageorgiou, M.: Centralised versus decentralised signal control of large-scale urban road networks in real time: a simulation study. IET Intell. Transp. Syst. **12**, 891–900 (2018). https://doi.org/10.1049/iet-its.2018.0112
9. Ferrer, J., López-Ibáñez, M., Alba, E.: Reliable simulation-optimization of traffic lights in a real-world city. Appl. Soft Comput. **78**, 697–711 (2019). https://doi.org/10.1016/j.asoc.2019.03.016
10. Hunt, P.B., Robertson, D.I., Bretherton, R.D., Winton, R.I.: Scoot - A Traffic Responsive Method of Coordinating Signals. 45 (1981)
11. Lowrie, P.: The Sydney coordinated adaptive traffic system - principles, methodology, algorithms. (1982)
12. Mirchandani, P., Fei-Yue, W.: RHODES to intelligent transportation systems. IEEE Intell. Syst. **20**, 10–15 (2005). https://doi.org/10.1109/MIS.2005.15
13. Stevanovic, A.: Adaptive Traffic Control Systems: Domestic and Foreign State of Practice. Transportation Research Board, Washington, D.C (2010)
14. Sabar, N.R., Kieu, L.M., Chung, E., Tsubota, T., Maciel de Almeida, P.E.: A memetic algorithm for real world multi-intersection traffic signal optimisation problems. Eng. Appl. Artif. Intell. **63**, 45–53 (2017). https://doi.org/10.1016/j.engappai.2017.04.021
15. García-Nieto, J., Alba, E., Carolina Olivera, A.: Swarm intelligence for traffic light scheduling: application to real urban areas. Eng. Appl. Artif. Intell. **25**, 274–283 (2012). https://doi.org/10.1016/j.engappai.2011.04.011
16. Mao, T., Mihăiţă, A.-S., Cai, C.: Traffic signal control optimization under severe incident conditions using Genetic Algorithm. 14 (2019)
17. Zhang, M., Zhao, S., Lv, J., Qian, Y.: Multi-phase urban traffic signal real-time control with multi-objective discrete differential evolution. In: 2009 International Conference on Electronic Computer Technology, Macau, China, pp. 296–300. IEEE (2009). https://doi.org/10.1109/ICECT.2009.38
18. Ma, W., Liu, Y., Yang, X.: A dynamic programming approach for optimal signal priority control upon multiple high-frequency bus requests. J. Intell. Transp. Syst. **17**, 282–293 (2013). https://doi.org/10.1080/15472450.2012.729380
19. Ahmed, F., Hawas, Y.E.: An integrated real-time traffic signal system for transit signal priority, incident detection and congestion management. Transp. Res. Emerg. Technol. **60**, 52–76 (2015). https://doi.org/10.1016/j.trc.2015.08.004
20. Stevanovic, J., Stevanovic, A., Martin, P.T., Bauer, T.: Stochastic optimization of traffic control and transit priority settings in VISSIM. Transp. Res. Emerg. Technol. **16**, 332–349 (2008). https://doi.org/10.1016/j.trc.2008.01.002
21. Wittpohl, M.: Biology Inspired Prioritisation. https://gitlab.com/evostar/biology-inspired-prioritisation/. Accessed 02 Feb 2021
22. Eclipse SUMO - Simulation of Urban MObility. https://www.eclipse.org/sumo/. Accessed 20 July 2020
23. Krajzewicz, D., Bonert, M., Wagner, P.: The Open Source Traffic Simulation Package SUMO 5 (2006)

24. Segredo, E., Luque, G., Segura, C., Alba, E.: Optimising real-world traffic cycle programs by using evolutionary computation. IEEE Access. **7**, 43915–43932 (2019). https://doi.org/10.1109/ACCESS.2019.2908562

25. SUMO - SUMO Documentation. https://sumo.dlr.de/docs/SUMO.html. Accessed 20 July 2020

26. Chen, J., Xu, L.: Road-junction traffic signal timing optimization by an adaptive particle swarm algorithm. In: 2006 9th International Conference on Control, Automation, Robotics and Vision, Singapore, pp. 1–7. IEEE (2006). https://doi.org/10.1109/ICARCV.2006.345348

27. Tang, K., Boltze, M., Nakamura, H., Tian, Z.: Global Practices on Road Traffic Signal Control. Elsevier (2019). https://doi.org/10.1016/C2017-0-02878-1

28. Simulation/Traffic Lights - SUMO Documentation. https://sumo.dlr.de/docs/Simulation/Traffic_Lights.html#default_link_indices. Accessed 20 July 2020

Adaptive Covariance Pattern Search

Ferrante Neri[✉][iD]

Computational Optimisation and Learning (COL) Lab, School of Computer Science,
University of Nottingham, Nottingham, UK
ferrante.neri@nottingham.ac.uk

Abstract. Pattern search is a family of single solution deterministic optimisation algorithms for numerical optimisation. Pattern search algorithms generate a new candidate solution by means of an archive of potential moves, named pattern. This pattern is generated by a basis of vectors that span the domain where the function to optimise is defined.

The present article proposes an adaptive implementation of pattern search that performs, at run-time, a fitness landscape analysis of the problem to determine the pattern and adapt it to the geometry of the problem. The proposed algorithm, called Adaptive Covariance Pattern Search (ACPS) uses at the beginning the fundamental orthonormal basis (directions of the variables) to build the pattern. Subsequently, ACPS saves the successful visited solutions, calculates the covariance matrix associated with these samples, and then uses the eigenvectors of this covariance matrix to build the pattern. ACPS is a restarting algorithm that at each restart recalculates the pattern that progressively adapts to the problem to optimise. Numerical results show that the proposed ACPS appears to be a promising approach on various problems and dimensions.

Keywords: Numerical optimisation · Adaptive algorithms · Pattern search · Local search · Covariance matrix

1 Introduction

Over the past decades, researchers in heuristic optimisation have striven to design algorithms that display a high performance on a wide set of problems. The No Free Lunch Theorems [24] indicate that high performance and versatility are conflicting features of algorithms and hence a trade-off should be found.

Researchers attempted to achieve this aim by exploiting the information available about the optimisation problem within the design of algorithm. Since generally the information about the problem is not available a priori, modern algorithms include mechanisms to make the algorithm suitable to the specific features of the problem. We identify here two algorithmic philosophies that, albeit ideologically different, may overlap in their practical implementations.

- **fitness landscape analysis**: the optimisation problem is analysed by a method, e.g. an Artificial Intelligence tool, and the results of the analysis are used to design the algorithm, see [8,11,12,16,17]

P. A. Castillo and J. L. Jiménez Laredo (Eds.): EvoApplications 2021, LNCS 12694, pp. 178–193, 2021.
https://doi.org/10.1007/978-3-030-72699-7_12

– **adaptive algorithms**: a feedback on the algorithmic behaviour on the specific problem is collected and used to adjust the algorithm, see [18, 21]

These two categories have a different focus but are not mutually exclusive: adaptive algorithms may analyse the fitness landscape. Fitness landscape analysis approaches focus on *how* the design is performed, that is on the basis of the analysis. On the other hand, adaptive approaches focus on *when* the design is performed/adjusted that is at run-time.

Furthermore, these two approaches, albeit overlapping, do not coincide. There exists a multitude of adaptive approaches that are not based on a fitness landscape analysis. For example, the self-adaptive Differential Evolution in [1] embeds the parameters into the solutions and propagates them to other candidate solutions by exploiting their evolution. Another example is in various hyper-heuristic schemes [2, 3] where the adaptation is based on the success of the parameters and the performance associated with them.

Conversely, at the intersection between fitness landscape analysis and adaptive approaches lies, for example, the Covariance Matrix Adaptive Evolution Strategy (CMAES) [6, 7]. This popular algorithm progressively adapts a multivariate Gaussian distribution from which candidate solutions are sampled. This adaptation is performed to increase the likelihood of previously successful candidate solutions. While evolving the CMAES distribution adapts to the geometry of the problem/local optimum.

By following a similar idea but fully embracing the fitness landscape analysis philosophy, paper [14] proposes a technique to analyse the geometry of the problem. This technique samples points whose objective function values are below a threshold, then calculates the covariance matrix associated with the distribution of these points and finally calculates the eigenvectors of the covariance matrix. Following this fitness landscape analysis, the directions of the eigenvectors are used to build the pattern of a pattern search, see [22] and Sect. 2 for definition of pattern. The resulting pattern search is called Covariance Pattern Search (CPS).

The results in [14] clearly show that the pattern based on the eigenvectors of a well-estimated covariance matrix outperforms the classical pattern based on the fundamental orthonomal basis (the directions of the variables). On the other hand, the application of CPS is impractical since it requires the setting of the above-mentioned threshold parameter for each optimisation problem. This setting is performed empirically and thus requires a considerable computational effort, especially in the high dimensional case. This feature makes CPS neither versatile (over various problems) nor easily scalable.

The present paper proposes a pattern search that makes use of the intuition of [14] about the search directions but follows an adaptive structure. The proposed algorithm, namely Adaptive Covariance Pattern Search (ACPS) at the beginning of the optimisation uses the fundamental orthonormal basis and while optimising the function stores the visited successful points. These points are then used to build the associated covariance matrix. The corresponding eigenvectors are then calculated. ACPS is then restarted with the newly calculated pattern. After the restart, ACPS stores the visited successful points to build a more accurate pattern which is used after another restart. The procedure is repeated until exhaustion of the computational budget. Thus, ACPS can be seen as a restarting pattern search whose pattern changes at each restart and progressively adapts to the geometry of the local optimum.

The remainder of this article is organised in the following way. Section 2 provides the theoretical foundations of pattern search and its generalised abstraction which is then used in this study. Section 3 describes CPS and justifies the use of a basis of eigenvectors mentioned above to build the pattern. The limitations of CPS are also outlined in Sect. 3. Section 4 illustrates the proposed ACPS and provides details about its implementation and functioning. Section 5 tests the performance of ACPS and compares it against that of CPS, CMAES and a Quasi-Newtonian method. Finally, Sect. 6 presents the conclusions of this study.

2   Generalised Pattern Search

Before entering the description of the algorithms, let us introduce the notation used throughout this paper. Let us indicate with $\mathbf{x}$ an n-dimensional vector of real numbers ($\mathbf{x} \in \mathbb{R}^n$). We will refer to a numerical optimisation problem that is the minimisation of a function $f : D \to Y$ where $D \subseteq \mathbb{R}^n$ and $Y \subseteq \mathbb{R}$:

$$\min_{x \in D} f(\mathbf{x}).$$

In this study we will focus on the box constrained case ($[a_1, b_1] \times [a_2, b_2] \ldots \times \ldots [a_n, b_n]$ with $\times$ indicating the Cartesian product) which includes the unconstrained case $]-\infty, +\infty[^n = \mathbb{R}^n$.

In [22] Pattern Search has been conceptualised and interpreted as a family of direct search methods, i.e. optimisation algorithms that do not require calculations of the gradient, and indicated as Generalised Pattern Search (GPS). GPS family is characterised by two elements:

- a set of search directions (a basis of vectors) spanning the decision space D;
- a trial step vector endowed with a step variation rule.

From an initial point $\mathbf{x}$ the pattern search algorithms perturb the solution along the search directions in an iterative manner. Let us indicate with k the iteration index. Formally, the search directions are determined by two matrices. The first is a non-singular matrix, namely the *basis matrix*, and it is indicated with $\mathbf{B} \in \mathbb{R}^{n \times n}$ where $\mathbb{R}^{n \times n}$ is the set of square matrices of real numbers of order n. The second is a rectangular matrix, namely the *generating matrix*, and it is indicated with $\mathbf{G}_k \in \mathbb{Z}^{n \times p}$ where $\mathbb{Z}^{n \times p}$ is the set of matrices of relative numbers of size n by p with $p > 2n$ and rank n. The matrix $\mathbf{G}_k$ can be partitioned as:

$$\mathbf{G}_k = (\mathbf{M}_k, -\mathbf{M}_k, \mathbf{L}_K)$$

where $\mathbf{M}_k$ is a non-singular matrix of order n, $-\mathbf{M}_k$ is the opposed matrix of $\mathbf{M}_k$, and $\mathbf{L}_k$ is a n by $(p - 2n)$ matrix that contains at least the null column vector $\mathbf{o}$. The search directions are given by the columns of the matrix:

$$\mathbf{P}_k = \mathbf{B}\mathbf{G}_k = (\mathbf{B}\mathbf{M}_k, -\mathbf{B}\mathbf{M}_k, \mathbf{B}\mathbf{L}_k) \tag{1}$$

that is referred to as the *pattern*. Thus a pattern can be seen as a repository of search directions, with n of them being the direction of a basis of $\mathbb{R}^n$, n of them being the same directions but in the opposite orientation, and potentially some additional directions.

The GPS k^{th} *trial iteration* along the ith direction is the vector $\mathbf{s}_k$, defined as:

$$\mathbf{s}_k = \Delta_k \mathbf{B} \mathbf{g}_k^i \qquad (2)$$

where Δ_k is a positive real number and $\mathbf{g}_k^i$ is the ith column of the matrix $\mathbf{G}_k$. The parameter Δ_k determines the step size while $\mathbf{B} \mathbf{g}_k^i$ is the direction of the trial step.

If $\mathbf{x}_k$ is the current best solution at the iteration k, the trial point generated by means of the trial step would be:

$$\mathbf{x}^{\mathbf{t}}_k = \mathbf{x}_k + \mathbf{s}_k. \qquad (3)$$

The set of operations that yields a current best point is called the *exploratory move*. The exploratory move succeeds when a solution with better performance is detected, and fails when no update of the current best occurs. Within GPS family, various Pattern Search implementations employ different strategies, e.g. by attempting only one trial vector per step or exploring all the columns of $\Delta_k \mathbf{P}_k$. However, as explained in [22], Pattern Search implementations belong to the GPS framework only if the following hypotheses, namely the *Strong Hypotheses*, are verified.

Strong Hypotheses
Hypothesis 1: $\mathbf{s}_k$ is generated by the pattern $\mathbf{P}_k$ or, in other words, is a column vector of the matrix $\Delta_k \mathbf{P}_k$. The length is determined by the scalar Δ_k.
Hypothesis 2: If there exists a column vector $\mathbf{y}$ of $(\mathbf{BM}_k, -\mathbf{BM}_k)$ such that $f(\mathbf{x}_k + \mathbf{y}) < f(\mathbf{x}_k)$, then the exploratory move must produce a trial step $\mathbf{s}_k$ such that $f(\mathbf{x}_k + \mathbf{s}_k) < f(\mathbf{x}_k)$.
Hypothesis 3: The update of Δ_k should follow some rules. In the case of a failed exploratory move, Δ_k has to decrease, however in the case of success Δ_k must either remain the same or increase.

The pseudocode of GPS is given in Algorithm 1.

3 Covariance Pattern Search

Covariance Pattern Search (CPS) [14] is an algorithm belonging to the GPS family that performs a fitness landscape analysis of the problem to determine the matrix $\mathbf{B}$ and hence the pattern in Eq. (1). The fitness landscape analysis requires a threshold *thr* empirically set for each problem. Once this threshold has been set, a number of candidate solutions/points are sampled in the decision space D and their objective function values are calculated. The function values are compared with a threshold *thr* and those values that are below *thr* are saved

Algorithm 1. Generalized Pattern Search [22]

```
INPUT x
k ← 1
x_k ← x
while local budget condition do
    generate the trial step s_k from Δ_k P_k
    calculate x^t_k ← x_k + s_k  # Exploratory Move
    if f (x^t_k) ≤ f (x_k) then
        x_{k+1} ← x^t_k
    else
        x_{k+1} ← x_k
    end if
    k ← k + 1
    update P_k and Δ_k
end while
x ← x_{k+1}
RETURN x
```

in a data structure, while the others are discarded. The purpose of this operation is to have a sample of points whose distribution describes the geometry of the problem.

For example, Fig. 1 displays the scatter plot of points whose objective function value is below $thr = 10^8$ for the shifted and rotated ellipsoid in two dimensions as in [10].

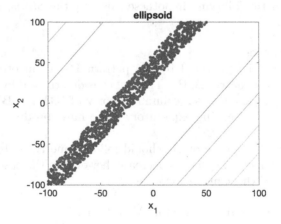

Fig. 1. Sample of points whose objective function (shifted and rotated 2D ellipsoid) is below the threshold $thr = 10^8$ (Color figure onlime)

For the sake of clarity the calculation of the ellipsoid is performed by means of the following procedure

$$\text{INPUT } x$$
$$z \leftarrow Q(x - o_s)$$
$$f \leftarrow \sum_{i=1}^{n} \left(10^6\right)^{\frac{i-1}{n-1}} z_i^2$$

where $\mathbf{Q}$ is a rotation matrix and $\mathbf{o}_s$ is a shift vector. Let us indicate with $\mathbf{V}$ the data structure where the m points whose objective function values are below thr (like the blue points in Fig. 1). These points can be interpreted as the samples of a multivariate distribution characterised by its mean vector μ and covariance matrix $\mathbf{C} = [c_{j,l}]$ where:

$$c_{j,l} = \left(\frac{1}{m}\right) \sum_{i=1}^{m} \left(\left(x_j^i - \mu_j\right)\left(x_l^i - \mu_l\right)\right).$$

Subsequently, the n eigenvectors of the matrix $\mathbf{C}$ are calculated by means of Cholesky Factorisation, see [13,19]. These eigenvectors are the columns $\mathbf{p}^i$ of a matrix $\mathbf{P} = \left(\mathbf{p}^1, \mathbf{p}^2, \dots, \mathbf{p}^n\right)$. Algorithm 2 displays the pseudocode of the Fitness Landscape Analysis.

Algorithm 2. Fitness Landscape Analysis

1: **INPUT** objective function $f(\mathbf{x})$, decision space D, and parameters thr and $samplesize$
2: $h \leftarrow 1$
3: **for** $s = 1 : samplesize$ **do**
4:     Sample (uniform distribution) a point $\mathbf{x}$ in the decision space D
5:     **if** $f(\mathbf{x}) < thr$ **then**
6:         Insert $\mathbf{x}$ into the data structure $\mathbf{V}$: $\mathbf{V}(h) \leftarrow \mathbf{x}$
7:         $h \leftarrow h + 1$
8:     **end if**
9: **end for**
10: Process the data structure $\mathbf{V}$ to calculate the mean vector μ and covariance matrix $\mathbf{C}$
11: Apply Cholesky Factorisation to extract the eigenvectors $\mathbf{P} = \left(\mathbf{p}^1, \mathbf{p}^2, \dots, \mathbf{p}^n\right)$

CPS makes use of the directions of the eigenvectors as those of the basis of the decision space to build the pattern. Simply, CPS is a GPS where Eq. (1), (2), and (3) are respectively

$$\mathbf{P}_k = \mathbf{PG}_k = \left(\mathbf{PM}_k, -\mathbf{PM}_k, \mathbf{PL}_k\right) \tag{4}$$

$$\mathbf{s}_k = \Delta_k \mathbf{Pg}_k^i \tag{5}$$

and

$$\mathbf{x}^t{}_k = \mathbf{x}_k + \mathbf{s}_k. \tag{6}$$

The choice of exploring the decision space along the directions of the eigenvectors is justified by the fact that the covariance matrix $\mathbf{C}$ can be diagonalised by means of the matrix $\mathbf{P}$. The directions of the eigenvectors can be interpreted as a new reference system characterised by a lack of correlation between pairs of variables. Consequently, the new reference system fits the geometry of the problem. This concept is broadly used in other contexts, especially in Data Science, and is closely related to Principal Component Analysis [9]. Furthermore, it was shown in [15] that, if the sampling of points in $\mathbf{V}$ describes the geometry of the basins of attraction, the directions of the eigenvectors identify the maximum and minimum directional derivative. Thus, numerical results in [14] and [15] show that CPS consistently outperforms the standard pattern search. The latter is a pattern search that explores the space along the directions of the variables, that is a pattern search whose matrix $\mathbf{B}$ of Eq. (1) is the identity matrix.

The fitness landscape analysis in Algorithm 2 has been applied to three local search schemes in [15] and has been successfully integrated in a greedy implementation of pattern search in [14]. This greedy implementation based on [23] updates the current best solution as soon as a better solution is found. Also, this implementation explore both the orientation of each direction only when a move along the first orientation failed. Algorithm 3 illustrates the implementation details of CPS as in [14].

Algorithm 3. Covariance Pattern Search according to the greedy implementation in [14]

1: **INPUT** x and matrix $\mathbf{P}$ calculated in Algorithm 2
2: $k \leftarrow 1$
3: $\mathbf{x}_k \leftarrow \mathbf{x}$
4: **while** local budget condition **do**
5:    $h \leftarrow k$
6:    **for** $i = 1 : n$ **do**
7:       $\mathbf{x}^t \leftarrow \mathbf{x}_k - \rho \cdot \mathbf{p}^i$
8:       **if** $f(\mathbf{x}^t) \leq f(\mathbf{x}_k)$ **then**
9:          $k \leftarrow k + 1$
10:         $\mathbf{x}_k \leftarrow \mathbf{x}^t$
11:       **else**
12:          $\mathbf{x}^t \leftarrow \mathbf{x}_k + \frac{\rho}{2} \cdot \mathbf{p}^i$
13:          **if** $f(\mathbf{x}^t) \leq f(\mathbf{x}_k)$ **then**
14:             $k \leftarrow k + 1$
15:             $\mathbf{x}_k \leftarrow \mathbf{x}^t$
16:          **end if**
17:       **end if**
18:    **end for**
19:    **if** $h = k$ #If no improvement occurred **then**
20:       $\rho \leftarrow \frac{\rho}{2}$
21:    **end if**
22: **end while**
23: $\mathbf{x} \leftarrow \mathbf{x}_k$
24: **RETURN** x

3.1   Limitations of Covariance Pattern Search

The main limitation of CPS is that a threshold thr must be empirically identified for each problem. A wrong choice of thr would result into a poor functioning of the algorithm. An excessively low thr value would cause an empty data structure $\mathbf{V}$ (at least $n + 1$ linearly independent vectors are needed to build the covariance matrix $\mathbf{C}$). An excessively high thr value would cause a data structure $\mathbf{V}$ that covers the entire domain and does not describe the geometry of the problem.

The choice of a proper *thr* is not only fundamental to guarantee the functioning of CPS but is also computationally expensive since it requires multiple trial and error tests. The difficulty and thus computational cost of the setting of *thr* grows with the dimensionality of the problem.

Another, albeit minor, limitation of CPS is that the algorithm is inherently a local search. The fitness landscape analysis aims at describing the geometry of a unimodal problem. Hence, CPS would likely not be usable to address multimodal problems.

4   The Proposed Adaptive Covariance Pattern Search

This paper proposes an adaptive algorithm, namely Adaptive Covariance Pattern Search (ACPS), that exploits the same mathematical principles of CPS. Unlike, CPS, the proposed ACPS does not require the setting of *thr*. Furthermore, the proposed ACPS, while is still to be considered a local search, can be successfully applied to some multimodal problems.

ACPS requires an initial solution $\mathbf{x}$, an initial exploration radius ρ, and stopping criteria on the minimum radius ρ_m and two computational budgets (maximum number of function calls), one local B_l one global B_g. The algorithm initialises the matrix $\mathbf{P}$ to the identity matrix of size n (this corresponds to the fundamental orthonormal basis of $\mathbb{R}^n$). ACPS perturbs $\mathbf{x}$ along the directions of the columns of the matrix $\mathbf{P} = (\mathbf{p}^1, \mathbf{p}^2, \ldots, \mathbf{p}^n)$. By following the logic of Algorithm 3, at the step k, for each variable i the algorithm calculates

$$\mathbf{x}^t = \mathbf{x}_k - \rho \cdot \mathbf{p}^i \tag{7}$$

and updates $\mathbf{x}_{k+1}$ to $\mathbf{x}^t$ if the trial solution $\mathbf{x}^t$ outperforms the current best solution $\mathbf{x}_k$. If the exploration in Eq. (7) is unsuccessful (the trial solution does not outperform the current best solution), ACPS attempts to explore the other orientation, that is

$$\mathbf{x}^t = \mathbf{x}_k + \frac{\rho}{2} \cdot \mathbf{p}^i, \tag{8}$$

and tests the performance of the newly calculated $\mathbf{x}^t$ before moving to the following design variable. Every time the trial solution $\mathbf{x}^t$ outperforms the current best solution $\mathbf{x}_k$, it occurs that the solution $\mathbf{x}^t$ is saved and stored in the data structure $\mathbf{V}$. If the exploration along all the n directions fail then the exploration radius ρ is halved:

$$\rho = \frac{\rho}{2}$$

The algorithm is continued until the local budget B_l is exceeded or the search radius is smaller than the minimum radius ρ_m.

When the algorithm is stopped, the covariance matrix $\mathbf{C}$ is calculated on the basis of the samples in the data structure $\mathbf{V}$ and its eigenvectors $\mathbf{p}^1, \mathbf{p}^2, \ldots, \mathbf{p}^n$ calculated by Cholesky Factorisation. Thus, the matrix $\mathbf{P} = (\mathbf{p}^1, \mathbf{p}^2, \ldots, \mathbf{p}^n)$ is updated. The initial radius ρ is initialised to its original value and the algorithm restarted on the current best solution $\mathbf{x}_k$ for up to extra B_l function calls. Also the data structure $\mathbf{V}$ is reinitialised at each restart. ACPS is stopped when the condition on the global budget B_g is exceeded. Algorithm 4 displays the functioning of the proposed ACPS.

Algorithm 4. Adaptive Covariance Pattern Search

1: **INPUT** $\mathbf{x}$ of n elements
2: $\mathbf{P} \leftarrow$ identity matrix $\mathbf{I}$ of size n
3: **while** global budget condition B_g **do**
4:    $k, l \leftarrow 1$
5:    $\mathbf{x}_k \leftarrow \mathbf{x}$
6:    # Local run
7:    **while** local budget condition B_l and $\rho > \rho_m$ **do**
8:       $h \leftarrow k$
9:       **for** $i = 1 : n$ **do**
10:          $\mathbf{x^t} \leftarrow \mathbf{x}_k - \rho \cdot \mathbf{p}^i$
11:          **if** $f\left(\mathbf{x^t}\right) \le f\left(\mathbf{x}_k\right)$ **then**
12:             $k \leftarrow k + 1$
13:             $\mathbf{x}_k \leftarrow \mathbf{x^t}$
14:             $\mathbf{V}\left(l\right) \leftarrow \mathbf{x^t}$
15:             $l \leftarrow l + 1$
16:          **else**
17:             $\mathbf{x^t} \leftarrow \mathbf{x}_k + \frac{\rho}{2} \cdot \mathbf{p}^i$
18:             **if** $f\left(\mathbf{x^t}\right) \le f\left(\mathbf{x}_k\right)$ **then**
19:                $k \leftarrow k + 1$
20:                $\mathbf{x}_k \leftarrow \mathbf{x^t}$
21:                $\mathbf{V}\left(l\right) \leftarrow \mathbf{x^t}$
22:                $l \leftarrow l + 1$
23:             **end if**
24:          **end if**
25:       **end for**
26:       **if** $h = k$ #If no improvement occurred **then**
27:          $\rho \leftarrow \frac{\rho}{2}$
28:       **end if**
29:    **end while**
30:    Locally **RETURN** x
31:    **if** the data structure $\mathbf{V}$ contains at least $n + 1$ vectors **then**
32:       Calculate the covariance matrix $\mathbf{C}$ from the samples in $\mathbf{V}$
33:       Apply Cholesky Factorisation to extract the eigenvectors $\mathbf{P} = \left(\mathbf{p}^1, \mathbf{p}^2, \ldots, \mathbf{p}^n\right)$
34:    **end if**
35:    Initialise ρ to its initial value and $\mathbf{V}$ to an empty data structure
36: **end while**
37: $\mathbf{x} \leftarrow \mathbf{x}_k$
38: **RETURN** x

The proposed ACPS in Algorithm 4 can be considered as a restarting version of CPS in Algorithm 3 where the exploration radius is re-initialised at each restart, the search directions of the matrix $\mathbf{P}$ are updated at each restart, and the starting solution $\mathbf{x}$ (input) is the output of the local search at the previous stage (before the restart).

Furthermore, the proposed ACPS embeds within the search a fitness landscape analysis similar to that presented in Algorithm 2. However, while in CPS the threshold thr is prearranged and constant, in ACPS the threshold is adaptive and integrated within the search logic. At each restart ACPS uses a different threshold that is $f(\mathbf{x}_k)$ with $\mathbf{x}_k$ starting point of that *local run* (inner while loop in Algorithm 4).

At each local run, the proposed ACPS lowers (for minimisation) the value of the threshold and progressively refines the search directions (eigenvectors) to better fit the local features of the fitness landscape.

In order to illustrate the functioning of the proposed ACPS Fig. 2 shows the trajectory of the algorithm in four consecutive local runs. With the term *trajectory* we mean the current best solutions visited by ACPS. Figure 2 refers to the shifted and rotated ellipsoid in two dimensions:

$$\textbf{INPUT } \mathbf{x}$$
$$\mathbf{z} \leftarrow \mathbf{Q}(\mathbf{x} - \mathbf{o_s})$$
$$f \leftarrow \sum_{i=1}^{2} \left(10^6\right)^{\frac{i-1}{1}} z_i^2$$

where the shift vector is

$$\mathbf{o_s} = \begin{pmatrix} -21.98 \\ 11.55 \end{pmatrix}$$

and the rotation matrix is

$$\mathbf{Q} = \begin{pmatrix} -0.6358 & -0.7718 \\ -0.7718 & 0.6358 \end{pmatrix}.$$

A random point $\mathbf{x}$ has been sampled within the domain. The objective function value of this starting point is $7.4385e + 09$.

Figure 2 shows that in the first local run the algorithm, while moving along the directions of the variables (black and red dashed lines), approaches the optimum but remains still far from it. After the restart, ACPS uses the new search directions, i.e. the eigenvectors of the covariance matrix of the distribution of samples collected during the first local run. This system of reference appears to be ineffective. We may observe that during the second local run only a marginal improvement is achieved. However, the budget spent in the second local run is not wasted: the points sampled during the second local run enable the detection of an effective reference system (eigenvectors in the third local run). During the third local run ACPS exploits the benefits of the fitness landscape analysis and quickly detects a solution close to the optimum. The results are then refined in the fourth local run where the eigenvectors are slightly corrected.

It must be observed that the proposed ACPS resembles Rosenbrock Method [20] since they both use a basis of vector which is progressively adapted during the run (Rosenbrock Method belongs to the GPS family). However, the two algorithms are radically different in the way the basis is selected and updated.

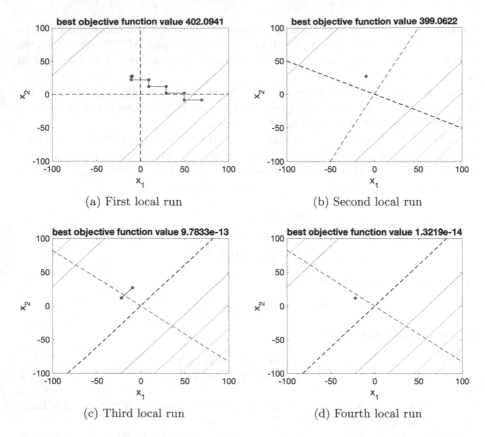

Fig. 2. Trajectory of ACPS in four consecutive local runs on a rotated and shifted ellipsoid. The red dots are current best solutions and the trajectory of the ACPS is shown as a blue solid line. The black and red dashed lines indicate the eigenvectors. The best objective function values are on the top of each figure. (Color figure online)

5   Numerical Results

In order to test and compare the performance of ACPS, a set of functions from the IEEE CEC2013 benchmark [10] have been selected and adapted. Since ACPS is a local search we selected all the unimodal problems, hence reproducing the testbed of CPS used in [14]. We also reproduced both the versions of ellipsoid presented in [14] (f_2 and f_3). The condition number of these two ellipsoids worsens with dimensionality at different speeds. In this paper, alongside bent cigar and discus we included their modified versions. Finally, in order to show that ACPS is capable, to some extent, to handle multimodal fitness landscapes, we included two simple multimodal functions from [10]. The list of the functions used in this study is displayed in Table 1. As shown in Table 1, each problem has been shifted and rotated: the variables $\mathbf{x}$ is transformed into $\mathbf{z}$. The shift vector

o_s of [10] has been used. The rotation matrices Q have been randomly generated. One matrix Q has been generated for each problem and dimensionality value.

Table 1. Objective functions used in this study

Domain
$[-100, 100]^n$

Shift and rotation
INPUT x
$z \leftarrow Q\left(x - o_s\right)$

Function name	Function calculation
Sphere	$f_1 \leftarrow \sum_{i=1}^{n} z_i^2$
Ellipsoid 1	$f_2 \leftarrow \sum_{i=1}^{n} 50 \left(i^2 z_i\right)^2$
Ellipsoid 2	$f_3 \leftarrow \sum_{i=1}^{n} \left(10^6\right)^{\frac{i-1}{n-1}} z_i^2$
Bent cigar	$f_4 \leftarrow z_1^2 + 10^6 \sum_{i=2}^{n} z_i^2$
Modified bent cigar	$f_5 \leftarrow z_1^2 + 10^6 \left(\sum_{i=2}^{n} z_i\right)^2$
Discus	$f_6 \leftarrow 10^6 z_1^2 + \sum_{i=2}^{n} z_i^2$
Modified discus	$f_7 \leftarrow 10^6 z_1^2 + \left(\sum_{i=2}^{n} z_i\right)^2$
Sum of powers	$f_8 \leftarrow \sqrt{\sum_{i=1}^{n} |z_i|^{\left(2 + 4\frac{i-1}{n-1}\right)}}$
Schwefel 2.21	$f_9 \leftarrow \max_{i=1,\ldots,n} |z_i|$
Rosenbrock	$f_{10} \leftarrow \sum_{i=1}^{n-1} \left(100 \left(z_i^2 - z_{i+1}\right)^2 + \left(z_i - 1\right)^2\right)$
Rastrigin	$f_{11} \leftarrow 10n + \sum_{i=1}^{n} \left(z_i^2 - 10\cos\left(2\pi z_i\right)\right)$

We have compared ACPS against the following three algorithms:

– Broyden–Fletcher–Goldfarb–Shanno (BFGS) algorithm [4] with an estimation of the gradient such that it may be applied to black-box problems;
– Covariance Matrix Adaptive Evolution Strategy (CMAES) [7];
– Covariance Pattern Search (CPS) [14].

The motivation behind these three competitors is the following: 1) BFGS is a Quasi-Newtonian algorithm that estimates the gradient and is here used as a benchmark algorithm; 2) CMAES is a prevalent algorithm that, like CPS and ACPS are based on theoretical considerations about multivariate distributions and the covariance matrix; 3) CPS, is a pattern search whose pattern is build according to the same principles used in ACPS. Since the difference in performance between CPS and ACPS is due to the proposed adaptation, CPS can be seen as the direct competitor of ACPS in this study. All the algorithms in this study have a comparable time complexity of $\mathcal{O}\left(n^2\right)$.

The problems in Table 1 have been considered in 10, 30 and 50 dimensions. For each problem in Table 1, dimensionality level, and algorithm in this study, 51

Table 2. Thresholds thr for CPS in 10, 30, and 50 dimensions

n	f_1	f_2	f_3	f_4	f_5	f_6	f_7	f_8	f_9	f_{10}	f_{11}
10	10^4	10^9	$5 \cdot 10^8$	$2 \cdot 10^{10}$	10^9	$2 \cdot 10^6$	10^6	10^4	10^2	$5 \cdot 10^9$	$3 \cdot 10^4$
30	$8 \cdot 10^4$	10^{12}	$2 \cdot 10^9$	10^{11}	10^9	10^6	10^6	$5 \cdot 10^5$	$1.5 \cdot 10^2$	$5 \cdot 10^{10}$	10^5
50	10^5	$5 \cdot 10^{13}$	$5 \cdot 10^9$	$2 \cdot 10^{11}$	10^{10}	$2 \cdot 10^7$	10^7	10^6	$1.5 \cdot 10^2$	10^{11}	$2 \cdot 10^5$

independent runs have been performed. For each run, the four algorithms under consideration have been run with the same initial solution. All the algorithms in this paper have been executed with a budget of $10000 \cdot n$ function calls where n is the problem dimensionality.

As reported in [14], the budget of CPS has been split in two parts: $5000 \cdot n$ function calls have been used to build the covariance matrix $\mathbf{C}$, whilst $5000 \cdot n$ function calls have been spent to execute the algorithm along the directions of its eigenvectors. In order to set the threshold thr, we used the recommended values in [14] and tuned them in order to let the algorithm achieve the best performance. Table 2 displays the thresholds used in this work.

Both CPS and ACPS have been run with an initial radius ρ equal to 10% of the domain width. As for ACPS, as mentioned above $B_g = 10000 \cdot n$. The maximum local budget B_l has been set equal to $1000 \cdot n$ and the minimum radius to restart the algorithm has been set equal to 10^{-15}. Table 3 displays the numerical results for the four algorithms under consideration and the problems in Table 1. Table 3 shows mean value and $\pm$ standard deviation over the 51 independent runs performed. Furthermore, to statistically investigate the question of whether the application of the proposed method results in performance gains, the Wilcoxon rank-sum test has been applied, see [5]. In the Tables in this section, a "+" indicates that gCPS significantly outperforms competitor, a "-" indicates that the competitor significantly outperforms gCPS, and a "=" indicates that there is no significant difference in performance.

Results in Table 3 show that CMAES, CPS, and ACPS are better suited than BFGS to address the black box problems (and hence without information on the gradient). Numerical results show that ACPS consistently displays a better performance than CPS, thus indicating the effectiveness of the proposed adaptation. Furthermore, ACPS has a performance comparable to that of CMAES. In the low dimensional case ($n = 10$), both the algorithms detect solutions very close to the optimum for the nine unimodal problems ($f_1 - f_9$) and detect the global optimum in several runs while they detect a local minumum for the two multimodal problems ($f_{10} - f_{11}$). In higher dimensions, we observe that the performance of both CMAES and ACPS deteriorates on some problems and remain excellent on others. For example, CMAES performs extremely well on $f_2 - f_4$ regardless of number of variables while ACPS deteriorates its performance as the number of dimensions increases. Conversely, ACPS handles the $f_5 - f_7$ problems better than CMAES. On average, ACPS and CMAES display a similar performance across the entire set of functions over the three numbers

Table 3. Average error avg $\pm$ standard deviation σ over 51 runs for the problems listed in Table 1: Adaptive Covariance Pattern Search (ACPS) with ACPS reference for Wilcoxon vs Covariance Pattern Search (CPS) [14], Covariance Matrix Adaptive Evolution Strategy (CMAES) [7], and Broyden–Fletcher–Goldfarb–Shanno (BFGS) algorithm [4].

	BFGS			CMAES			CPS			ACPS	
	avg	σ	W	avg	σ	W	avg	σ	W	avg	σ
10 dimensions											
f_1	1.8757e-20	2.4576e-21	+	1.6841e-15	1.2496e-15	+	7.2365e-29	9.6235e-29	+	**0.0000e+00**	0.0000e+00
f_2	1.8956e-13	4.1016e-14	+	1.5739e-15	1.1095e-15	+	1.5810e-01	5.5370e-01	+	**4.4034e-23**	6.9361e-23
f_3	6.6365e-11	2.6183e-12	+	1.7152e-15	1.0734e-15	+	1.0352e+04	2.4610e+04	+	**7.1972e-16**	1.7443e-15
f_4	4.8479e-01	1.6494e+00	+	**1.4131e-15**	1.1850e-15	-	2.0252e+04	1.3731e+04	+	2.5260e-14	1.1648e-13
f_5	1.2818e-09	2.0603e-09	+	8.8699e-15	1.0347e-14	+	3.4509e-06	5.9736e-06	+	**3.3716e-23**	1.2212e-22
f_6	3.2306e-10	5.0825e-11	+	**1.3737e-15**	1.3659e-15	=	1.9279e-12	2.4744e-12	-	8.8372e-11	4.7050e-10
f_7	3.9439e-12	7.2576e-12	+	6.6387e-15	1.0289e-14	+	5.2635e-19	1.1885e-18	+	**3.0987e-27**	1.1885e-18
f_8	1.1967e-07	4.3589e-07	+	**9.8002e-13**	8.9374e-13	-	1.7431e-05	5.0694e-06	+	4.1666e-08	6.3467e-08
f_9	7.1074e+01	2.9732e+01	+	**7.7677e-10**	2.1798e-10	-	5.7996e+00	8.9728e+00	+	1.4098e-06	7.6446e-06
f_{10}	1.1960e+00	1.8581e+00	+	7.973e-01	1.62193e+00	+	1.1752e+02	2.8670e+02	+	**5.3985e-27**	2.5363e-27
f_{11}	8.7917e+02	4.2825e+02	+	**1.6069e+01**	1.6267e+01	-	6.4207e+01	3.0468e+01	=	5.7508e+01	2.5321e+01
30 dimensions											
f_1	4.3857e-20	1.6043e-20	+	1.4429e-15	1.0251e-15	+	5.5283e-28	1.3526e-28	+	**0.0000e+00**	0.0000e+00
f_2	1.3352e-09	3.3772e-10	-	**2.9032e-15**	5.7236e-16	+	7.1932e+05	9.4686e+05	+	5.7209e-05	1.7248e-04
f_3	3.2738e-11	1.5479e-12	-	**2.0379e-15**	2.0379e-15	-	1.0276e+05	7.1458e+04	+	8.8106e-07	2.7855e-06
f_4	4.5544e+00	2.4117e+01	+	**1.3962e-15**	4.6239e-16	-	3.7216e+03	4.2577e+03	+	9.4800e-02	2.8220e-01
f_5	1.8926e-08	2.5487e-08	+	5.9103e+03	1.5913e+04	+	1.8790e-09	5.9420e-09	+	**6.2125e-24**	1.9636e-23
f_6	1.5200e-10	1.9637e-11	-	**4.1546e-15**	2.3165e-15	-	1.2576e+02	1.4733e+02	=	1.6064e+02	3.4634e+02
f_7	5.9737e-13	1.2614e-12	+	1.0770e-14	1.2033e-14	+	9.7797e-27	1.1411e-26	=	**5.3015e-27**	5.8250e-27
f_8	1.2390e-05	2.84323e-06	+	**1.5671e-11**	2.0251e-11	-	9.2850e-05	1.8269e-05	+	9.2440e-07	7.5487e-07
f_9	1.1706e+02	3.2399e+01	+	**1.3042e+00**	2.8263e+00	=	4.2458e+01	1.1286e+01	+	2.2920e+00	2.0570e+00
f_{10}	1.7275e+00	2.0093e+00	+	7.9730e-01	1.6809e+00	+	3.7031e+00	2.0897e+00	+	**3.9870e-01**	1.2607e+00
f_{11}	2.0621e+03	6.1136e+02	+	**5.0942e+01**	1.0997e+01	-	3.9956e+02	1.2392e+02	+	2.7569e+02	8.9984e+01
50 dimensions											
f_1	8.5482e-20	1.9014e-20	+	1.1890e-15	3.3954e-16	+	1.2148e-27	6.1144e-28	+	**0.0000e+00**	0.0000e+00
f_2	1.5972e-07	3.7724e-08	-	**2.1614e-14**	4.5515e-15	-	3.5727e+07	1.9921e+07	+	3.9667e+05	3.6613e+05
f_3	9.2288e-011	4.6933e-12	-	**1.3092e-15**	5.9487e-16	-	1.9244e+05	6.5138e+04	+	1.3150e+02	5.3391e+02
f_4	9.8654e-01	3.4845e+e00	-	**1.2358e-15**	5.8376e-16	-	4.6930e+03	5.8099e+03	+	1.6111e+01	3.273e+01
f_5	1.9741e-08	2.8660e-08	+	5.2536e+04	1.5800e+05	+	4.700e-03	1.4700e-02	+	**1.6298e-31**	4.3564e-31
f_6	**1.1937e-10**	7.3146e-12	+	3.0884e+04	9.7663e+04	+	1.2573e+02	1.2764e+02	+	1.0434e+02	3.3584e+02
f_7	1.5341e-13	3.2062e-13	+	1.8735e+00	4.4116e+00	+	1.3449e-26	2.7367e-26	=	**1.3501e-27**	1.8298e-27
f_8	1.1253e-05	1.8968e-06	+	**6.5703e-11**	3.2925e-11	-	1.3238e-04	1.4419e-05	+	2.3891e-06	1.2608e-06
f_9	1.2855e+02	2.7862e+01	+	**9.6761e-06**	2.8014e-05	-	6.3083e+01	1.2169e+01	+	1.8681e+01	9.8691e+00
f_{10}	1.9933e+00	2.0274e+00	+	1.1960e+00	1.9257e+00	+	1.0012e+02	2.3364e+02	+	**7.9730e-01**	1.6809e+00
f_{11}	3.3820e+03	1.0348e+03	+	1.1004e+02	1.3796e+01	+	8.2749e+02	2.0231e+02	+	**6.2442e+01**	1.9581e+01

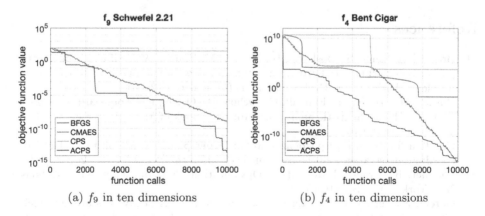

(a) f_9 in ten dimensions   (b) f_4 in ten dimensions

Fig. 3. Two examples of convergence trend (logarithmic scale), i.e. objective function values vs function calls.

of dimensions under consideration. Thus, ACPS appears to be more competitive with CMAES than CPS. Figure 3 displays two examples of convergence trend for two randomly selected runs. The "staircase" trend of ACPS can be noticed: some sharp improvements coincide with a restart and thus the identification of a new pattern.

6   Conclusion

The present paper proposes an adaptive pattern search that uses the search directions given by the eigenvectors of the covariance matrix built by means of successful visited points. The proposed ACPS is a restarting local search algorithm that at each restart adapts the search directions on the basis of the information gathered in the previous local run. Hence, ACPS progressively adapts the search directions to the problem under study.

This adaptive logic is here opposed to the fitness landscape analysis of CPS that occurs separately and prior to the optimisation. Two important advantages of ACPS with respect to CPS are: 1) ACPS does not require the setting of a threshold; 2) ACPS uses its entire computational budget to perform the optimisation, that is a budget dedicated to the fitness landscape analysis does not need to be allocated.

Numerical results show that, thanks to its adaptive logic, ACPS systematically outperforms CPS for the problems considered in this study. Thanks to its restarting logic, ACPS, albeit a local search, can successfully tackle simple multimodal optimisation problems. In ten dimensions ACPS displays a performance comparable to that of CMAES for all the problems under study. In higher dimensions (thirty and fifty), the performance of ACPS and CMAES diverge on the single problems: for some problems ACPS appears to be better suited than CMAES and for some other problems the opposite happens. Over the entire set of test problems, ACPS and CMAES display a comparable performance.

References

1. Brest, J., Greiner, S., Bošković, B., Mernik, M., Žumer, V.: Self-adapting control parameters in differential evolution: a comparative study on numerical benchmark problems. IEEE Trans. Evol. Comput. **10**(6), 646–657 (2006)
2. Burke, E.K., Hyde, M., Kendall, G., Ochoa, G., Ozcan, E., Woodward, J.: Classification of hyper-heuristic approaches. In: Handbook of Meta-Heuristics, pp. 449–468. Springer (2010)
3. Caraffini, F., Neri, F., Epitropakis, M.G.: Hyperspam: a study on hyper-heuristic coordination strategies in the continuous domain. Inf. Sci. **477**, 186–202 (2019)
4. Fletcher, R.: Practical Methods of Optimization, 2nd edn. John Wiley & Sons, New York, NY, USA (1987)
5. Garcia, S., Fernandez, A., Luengo, J., Herrera, F.: A study of statistical techniques and performance measures for genetics-based machine learning: accuracy and interpretability. Soft Comput. **13**(10), 959–977 (2008)
6. Hansen, N., Ostermeier, A.: Adapting arbitrary normal mutation distributions in evolution strategies: the covariance matrix adaptation. In: Proceedings of the IEEE International Conference on Evolutionary Computation, pp. 312–317 (1996)

7. Hansen, N., Ostermeier, A.: Completely derandomized self-adaptation in evolution strategies. Evol. Comput. **9**(2), 159–195 (2001)
8. Jana, N.D., Sil, J., Das, S.: Continuous fitness landscape analysis using a chaos-based random walk algorithm. Soft Comput. **22**(3), 921–948 (2016). https://doi.org/10.1007/s00500-016-2397-2
9. Jolliffe, I.T.: Principal Component Analysis, 2nd edn. Springer Series in Statistics, Springer (2002)
10. Liang, J., Qu, B., Suganthan, P., Hernández-DíÂaz, A.: Problem definitions and evaluation criteria for the cec 2013 special session on real-parameter optimization (01 2013)
11. Malan, K.M., Engelbrecht, A.P.: Quantifying ruggedness of continuous landscapes using entropy. In: 2009 IEEE Congress on Evolutionary Computation, pp. 1440–1447 (2009)
12. Malan, K.M., Engelbrecht, A.P.: A survey of techniques for characterising fitness landscapes and some possible ways forward. Inf. Sci. **241**, 148–163 (2013)
13. Neri, F.: Linear Algebra for Computational Sciences and Engineering. Springer, second edn. (2019)
14. Neri, F., Rostami, S.: A local search for numerical optimisation based on covariance matrix diagonalisation. In: Castillo, P.A., Jiménez Laredo, J.L., Fernández de Vega, F. (eds.) EvoApplications 2020. LNCS, vol. 12104, pp. 3–19. Springer, Cham (2020). https://doi.org/10.1007/978-3-030-43722-0_1
15. Neri, F., Zhou, Y.: Covariance local search for memetic frameworks: a fitness landscape analysis approach. In: IEEE Congress on Evolutionary Computation, CEC 2020, Glasgow, United Kingdom, July 19–24, pp. 1–8. IEEE (2020)
16. Ochoa, G., Malan, K.: Recent advances in fitness landscape analysis. In: López-Ibáñez, M., Auger, A., Stützle, T. (eds.) Proceedings of the Genetic and Evolutionary Computation Conference Companion, GECCO 2019, Prague, Czech Republic, 13–17 July 2019, pp. 1077–1094. ACM (2019)
17. Ochoa, G., Malan, K.M., Blum, C.: Search trajectory networks of population-based algorithms in continuous spaces. In: Castillo, P.A., Jiménez Laredo, J.L., Fernández de Vega, F. (eds.) EvoApplications 2020. LNCS, vol. 12104, pp. 70–85. Springer, Cham (2020). https://doi.org/10.1007/978-3-030-43722-0_5
18. Ong, Y.S., Lim, M.H., Zhu, N., Wong, K.W.: Classification of adaptive memetic algorithms: a comparative study. IEEE Trans. Syst. Man Cybern. **36**(1), 141–152 (2006)
19. Press, W.H., Teukolsky, S.A., Vetterling, W.T., Flannery, B.P.: Numerical Recipes in C (2Nd Ed.): The Art of Scientific Computing. Cambridge University Press, New York, NY, USA (1992)
20. Rosenbrock, H.H.: An automatic method for finding the greatest or least value of a function. Comput. J. **3**(3), 175–184 (1960)
21. Tirronen, V., Neri, F., Kärkkäinen, T., Majava, K., Rossi, T.: An enhanced memetic differential evolution in filter design for defect detection in paper production. Evol. Comput. **16**, 529–555 (2008)
22. Torczon, V.: On the convergence of pattern search algorithms. SIAM J. Optim. **7**(1), 1–25 (1997)
23. Tseng, L.Y., Chen, C.: Multiple trajectory search for large scale global optimization. In: Proceedings of the IEEE Congress on Evolutionary Computation, pp. 3052–3059 (2008)
24. Wolpert, D.H., Macready, W.G.: No free lunch theorems for optimization. IEEE Trans. Evol. Comput. **1**(1), 67–82 (1997)

Evaluating the Success-History Based Adaptive Differential Evolution in the Protein Structure Prediction Problem

Pedro Henrique Narloch[iD] and Márcio Dorn[(✉)][iD]

Institute of Informatics, Federal University of Rio Grande do Sul, Porto Alegre, Brazil
{pnarloch,mdorn}@inf.ufrgs.br

Abstract. Proteins are vital macro-molecules for every living organism. As the exper imental determination of protein structures is costly and time-consuming, computational methods became an interesting way to predict proteins' shape based on their amino acid sequence. Meta-heuristics have been employed in the protein structure prediction problem through the years, with different characteristics and different knowledge sources. However, these methods are heavily dependent on parameter tuning, where wrong parameters might cause poor performance. Recently, adaptive strategies were proposed to deal with parameter tuning's non-trivial task, leaving the algorithm to choose its parameters for each optimization step. Although adaptive metaheuristics are widely applied to benchmark problems, only a few were tested in the PSP problem. To contribute to the analysis of adaptive metaheuristics in the PSP problem, we explore in this work the capability of one of the CEC'14 winners: the Success-History based Adaptive Differential Evolution algorithm on the tertiary protein structure prediction problem. We tested the SHADE algorithm in eight different proteins and compared the algorithm to the other two classical non-adaptive differential evolution and the well-known self-adaptive differential evolution. Moreover, we enhanced the SHADE with domain knowledge from APL. Our results enlarge the research body in adaptive methods for the PSP problem, showing that SHADE is better than non-adaptive differential evolution approaches and competitive compared to self-adaptive differential evolution and related works.

Keywords: SHADE · Protein structure prediction · Adaptive differential evolution

1 Introduction

Protein Structure Prediction (PSP) is a challenging open problem in Structural Bioinformatics. As the problem is considered an NP-Hard problem in computer science [8], there is no known algorithm capable of finding the global optimum solution in polynomial time. In this way, bio-inspired algorithms (metaheuristics) became an attractive option for finding possible solutions for the problem in a viable computational time. Over the years, different metaheuristics

© Springer Nature Switzerland AG 2021
P. A. Castillo and J. L. Jiménez Laredo (Eds.): EvoApplications 2021, LNCS 12694, pp. 194–209, 2021.
https://doi.org/10.1007/978-3-030-72699-7_13

were applied to the problem, such as the Evolutionary Strategy [5], Genetic Algorithms, Particle Swarm Optimization [2], and Differential Evolution [13]. Although these algorithms can find viable solutions in complex search spaces, their search performance heavily depends on parameter settings that change from problem to problem [16]. In this way, adaptive methodologies seem to be a promising research direction to handle parameter tuning's challenging task. Even though they are heavily explored in benchmark competitions, few studies in the literature tried to apply and investigate adaptive metaheuristics in the PSP problem.

With this in mind, this paper has the objective of evaluating one of the state-of-art adaptive algorithms to the PSP problem: the Success-History based Adaptive Differential Evolution (SHADE) [22]. SHADE is an adaptive variant of the DE algorithm, adapting its parameters, using a history of replaced solutions during the creation of new ones, and a mutation mechanism that guides the search through the best solutions in the population. As SHADE is one of the tough competitors in the CEC competitions, it should be tested in a complex real-world problem such as the PSP. To make it comparable with other works, we enhanced SHADE with the information from the Angle Probability List (APL) [1] during the population initialization. In total, eight proteins are predicted, and comparisons are made with two non-adaptive algorithms, the canonical DE algorithm versions (best/1/bin and rand/1/bin) tested in [13], and the well known self-adaptive differential evolution (SaDE) [17] which was used with APL in [14]. All algorithms use the APL during the population initialization step. Moreover, the same population size is maintained as well as the same objective function. Overall results show that SHADE outperforms other DE approaches, showing a promising metaheuristic for the PSP problem.

This work's overall structure takes the form of four chapters, where basic concepts about the problem, the algorithms, and related works are introduced in Sect. 2. In Sect. 3, the decisions we chose to compose our approach is briefly explained, while Sect. 4 brings the discussion about the results we have obtained using SHADE. Finally, Sect. 5 contains our endings' thoughts about the method and future research.

2 Preliminaries

2.1 Protein Structure Prediction

The protein's folding process begins when the RNA reads the DNA information, translating the four nucleotide information system into 20 different molecules known as amino acids. The linear sequence of amino acids is known as the protein's primary structure. These amino acids have the same molecular structure, with an amino group NH_2, a central carbon atom C_α, and a carboxyl group $COOH$. Moreover, each amino acid has a different side-chain (R), granting them different chemical properties (such as water affinity) and sizes.

When the carboxyl group of one amino acid interacts with the amino group of a second amino acid, a molecule of water (H_2O) is lost, and a chemical bond is formed (Fig. 1a). As a consequence of the attractive and repulsive forces among the primary structure atoms, the protein starts to fold into atoms' local arrangement, forming three-dimensional patterns. This intermediate state of the folding process creates what we call a protein's secondary structure [24]. In this stage, two of the most commons structures can be observed: β—sheets and α—helixes (Fig. 1b). After stabilizing these structures by hydrogen bonding, the protein finally folds into a final three-dimensional shape, its tertiary structure. The tertiary structure is considered the protein's native state, where the molecule achieves its functional form.

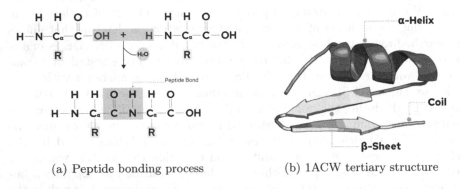

(a) Peptide bonding process   (b) 1ACW tertiary structure

Fig. 1. Fundamental concepts about protein structures. It is possible to observe the amino acid structure and how the peptide bond occurs on the left side. On the right side of the figure, the final three-dimensional shape of the protein 1ACW.

An additional classification is obtained when multiple tertiary structures interact to exert a specific biological function. This classification is called a quaternary protein structure.

To date, two experimental methods are the most used to determine the protein structures, the X-Ray Crystallography and Nuclear Magnetic Resonance (NMR). However, they are expensive and takes a long experimental time. In this way, computational approaches might be an option to help the determination of these structures since the protein structure prediction problem can be formulated as an optimization problem where the objective function to be minimized is the free energy. In order to predict the proteins tertiary structure, three mechanisms are essential [7]: (i) how to computationally represent a protein; (ii) how to evaluate the possible structure, and (iii) a search mechanism to explore the conformational search space.

Molecule Representation: Some studies have proposed different computational representations for proteins over the years, ranging from the full atom codification in an off-lattice representation to a simple 2D model. Although the 2D models have a significant aspect regarding the computational approach for the problem, they are far from encompassing these complex molecules' biological characteristics. On the other hand, the full description of the molecule can be infeasible to represent (and compute) because of the large number of atoms. In this way, the torsional angles model might be one of the most reliable representation models, where the protein representation is simplified without losing biological characteristics.

In the torsional angles representation, each amino acid contains three angles in its main-chain. The ϕ angle represents the rotation around the $N - C_\alpha$ interaction. The ψ angle speaks for the $C_\alpha - C$ bond, while the ω angle is the planar angle formed in the peptide bonding process $(N - C)$. As each amino acid contains a specific side-chain, the number of angles of each side-chain can differ. In this way, the angles χ_n represent the set of side-chain angles, ranging from 0 to 4 angles. Consequently, there is an explosion of possible shapes that a single protein can have due to the free rotation of all these angles $[-180°, +180°]$.

Energy Function: Energy functions play an essential role in evaluating different forces related to the interaction of all atoms a protein can have. In general, the energy functions can be classified into two groups, the ones who use statistics from the already known 3D structures (knowledge-based) and the ones who are purely based on physics components (physics-based) [11]. Some of the most well-known energy functions are CHARMM [3] (physics-based), AMBER [9] (physics-based), and Rosetta [18] (physics-and knowledge-based).

Angle Probability List: The prediction of protein structures from their primary structure remains an unsolved problem in Structural Bioinformatics. Since the protein structure prediction problem has a high complexity level, it is reasonable to attach some domain information to help find better solutions. In this way, the Angle Probability List was proposed by Borguesan et al. [1] based on the study of Ligabue-Braun et al. [12], where amino acids have different angle regions depending on their secondary structure (conformational preferences). All the structural information was obtained from the Protein Data Bank (PDB) with more than 11,130 high-resolution structures.

Based on all these collected structural information, a histogram matrix $(H_{aa,ss})$ of $[-180°, +180°] \times [-180°, +180°]$ for each amino acid residue (aa) and secondary structure (ss) is formed. An Angle Probability List is created with this information, with different combinations of amino acids and their dihedral angle preferences. The usage of APL as source information by metaheuristics has shown promising results [1,13], enhancing the algorithm capabilities in finding lower energies and better structures. The usage of APL is free, and a web-interface, called NIAS[1] (Neighbors Influence of Amino acids and Secondary structures) can be used [2].

2.2 Bio-Inspired Algorithms

Since the beginning of life, nature has been evolving and rising intelligent behavior characteristics in different living beings, undertaking high complexity

---

[1] http://sbcb.inf.ufrgs.br/npas.

problems. Researchers decided to abstract these behaviors, emulating them in computational models by observing nature, giving birth to the bio-inspired computing research area. The bio-inspired algorithms became a genuine option for solving complex problems, such as optimization ones, due to the limitation of classical mathematical methods regarding finding a viable computational time solution.

Differential Evolution: Storn and Price proposed the Differential Evolution algorithm during the 90s [21] to handle non-linear, non-convex multi-modal, and non-differentiable functions [6] in the continuous space. Since the first application of DE, the algorithm has been showing good results and applicability in many different fields, from simple benchmark problems to large scale global optimization with a thousand dimensions. In this way, the DE can be considered one of the most competitive and successful evolutionary algorithm (besides the popularity of GAs) [6]. Following the idea of EAs, the DE algorithm optimizes a set of possible candidates, called solutions, through four steps: initialization, mutation, crossover, and selection. In the first step, the standard **initialization** of an NP possible solutions is done randomly. The NP parameter is defined beforehand without any variation during the optimization process.

For a determined number of generations G, all individuals of the population (x_i^g) goes through a **mutation** mechanism, creating a mutated solution vector (v_i^{g+1}). The creation of v_i^{g+1} can be done in different ways. An in-depth analysis of different mutation mechanisms of DE can be found in [6]. The standard and most used mutation mechanism is known as DE/rand/1/bin (Eq. 1), where three individuals from the current population are randomly selected. The second approach is the DE/best/1/bin (Eq. 2), where the best individual is used during the mutation process. The F parameter is a mutation factor defined by user parametrization and should be tuned for each problem.

$$v_i^{g+1} = x_{r1}^g + F \cdot (x_{r2}^g - x_{r3}^g) \tag{1}$$

$$v_i^{g+1} = x_{best}^g + F \cdot (x_{r1}^g - x_{r2}^g) \tag{2}$$

The mutated individual values are then mixed with the value of the original (parent) solution in the **crossover** step, leading to a new possible solution for the problem known as trial vector (u_i). In general, the crossover decides if a dimension d receives the information from the mutant individual ($v_{i,d}$) or from the target individual ($x_{i,d}$) based on a probability, which is commonly set as a crossover rate parameter (CR). The Eq. 3 exposes the binomial crossover of the canonical DE version.

$$u_{i,d} = \begin{cases} v_{i,d} & \text{if d} = \text{d}_{rand} \text{ or rand } [0,1] \leq CR, \\ x_{i,d} & \text{otherwise} \end{cases} \tag{3}$$

After the procedure of generating new possible solutions (offspring) for the problem, these new solutions are then evaluated with the fitness function, and a

selection step decides which solutions will compose the next generation. In this case, individuals with fitness improvement are accepted to the next generation (Eq. 4).

$$x_{i,g+1} = \begin{cases} u_{i,g} & \text{if} f(u_{ig}) \leq f(x_{i,g}), \\ x_{i,g} & otherwise \end{cases} \tag{4}$$

In Algorithm 1, it is possible to exemplify the entire optimization process done by the canonical Differential Evolution algorithm in one short pseudocode.

Algorithm 1. Differential Evolution

---

g ← 0   ▷ Initial Generation
Initialize the population *pop* of solutions
Evaluate all individuals using the fitness function $f(x)$
for a determined number of generations **do**
  for each individual i in the population **do**
    Select individuals for mutation
    Create trial (u_i) based on mutation and crossover mechanism
  Create the new population pop_{g+1} based on a selection operator
  $g = g + 1$

2.3 Related Works

Thus far, several approaches were developed to solve the tertiary protein structure prediction problem [7]. Besides the vital contribution these works have made, the PSP problem still opens in Structural Bioinformatics. The development of a robust method for the problem might consider different aspects, such as search capabilities and domain knowledge integration.

Some initial insights about the problem complexity were discussed in [4,5], where the Pareto Archived Evolution Strategy (PAES) was used as a search mechanism with a bi-objective formulation, where one objective considered bonded forces. In contrast, the second one considered non-bonded interactions. Following the same concept, but with a populational-based algorithm, Venske et al. [23] proposed an Adaptive Differential Evolution Multi-Objective based on Decomposition (ADEMO/D), reaching better structures in comparison with the PAES algorithm. Besides the different search mechanisms used in these works, none of them used any problem domain knowledge.

To improve the conformational search capabilities, Borguesan et al. [1] used structural knowledge in the creation of the initial population, considering the information from an APL. Two canonical metaheuristics were used (GA and PSO) to evaluate how the search algorithms would behave. As expected, better three-dimensional structures were found, showing the positive impact that APL can have. Moreover, different mutation mechanisms of DE were evaluated in [13] with and without the same structural knowledge (APL), reinforcing the relevance of the structural information for the search mechanism. Following the trend of adding information of already known structures to the problem, a set of works started to use Contact Maps, reaching even better solutions.

Although the aggregation of different sources of information in the search mechanism was beneficial, most of the methods contain a set of parameters that need to be tunned. However, the parameter tunning is not a trivial task since it can quickly become a combinatorial problem. In this way, adaptive metaheuristics can contribute, leaving some (if not all) parameters to be defined by the algorithm. Among different adaptive methods used in benchmark problems, few of them were used in the PSP problem, such as the Self-Adaptive Differential Evolution (SaDE) [17], with the application of loop-patterns [15], with Rosetta Fragments [20], and APL [14].

In this way, there is a gap in better exploring more recent (and robust) adaptive search methods for the PSP problem using structural knowledge information. In this work, we use the SHADE algorithm enhanced with APL for the PSP problem, comparing its performance against two canonical DE algorithms and the well known SaDE algorithm, providing a larger body of analysis regarding adaptive search algorithms for the protein structure prediction problem.

3   Methodology

Exploring the conformational search is problematic since a single protein can assume many possible three-dimensional shapes. In order to predict the tertiary structure of a protein, three definitions are needed. For the (i) molecular representation, we choose the torsional angles representation, where each amino acid contains a set of angles. In our case, only the angles ϕ and ψ will be optimized, while the ω are set to $180°$ because of its planar characteristic. The χ angles are not used in this model since we are using the Rosetta `score3` energy function, where the side-chain of proteins are described as a center of mass. In this way, the solution vector has a size of $2N$, where N represents the number of amino acids.

The Rosetta score3 is provided by the Rosetta [18] modeling software, one of the most used software in high-resolution predictors. Moreover, we add a secondary structure reinforcement term to favor solutions that have matching predicted secondary structures used as input. In total, eleven terms are used, ten from the score3 equation and one additional for secondary structure:

$$E_{score3} = E_{vdW} + E_{cenpack} + E_{pair} + E_{env} + E_{cbeta} + \\ E_{rg} + E_{hs\_pair} + E_{ss\_pair} + E_{rsigma} + E_{sheet} \tag{5}$$

$$E_{SS} = \sum_{l=1}^{L} x_l \tag{6}$$

$$x_l = \begin{cases} -10, \text{ if } S_l^{predicted} = S_l^{determined} \\ +10, \text{ otherwise} \end{cases} \tag{7}$$

$$E_{PSP} = E_{score3} + E_{SS}. \tag{8}$$

where **L** is the length of the amino acid chain, $\mathbf{S}_l^{predicted}$ is the secondary structure of the lth residue from the prediction process, and $\mathbf{S}_l^{determined}$ is the secondary structure of the lth residue from the target protein. The lower the E_{SS}, the more similarity is between the secondary structures. Thus, the closer is the predicted protein from its native conformation.

To identify the formed secondary structures, an implementation of DSSP [10] by *PyRosetta* is used during the optimization process. In this way, every time that search algorithm finds a solution which the secondary structure matches with the one given as an input, a reinforcement score (Eq. 6) is assigned to the *score3* value. On the other hand, if the algorithm's perturbation does not correctly find the secondary structure, a punishment is ascribed to the solution. For single-objective approaches, the *score3* is summed with the secondary structure evaluation's fitness.

To explore the complex conformational search space, the Success-History based Adaptive Differential Evolution (SHADE), proposed by Tanabe and Fukunaga in 2003 [22], is used as a search algorithm. SHADE is an adaptive version of the Differential Evolution algorithm that uses a historical memory to adapt the DE parameters (mutation and crossover rate). Since its first participation in the Congress on Evolutionary Computation, SHADE achieved reliable results in different benchmark problems. In comparison with the original DE, SHADE can adapt the CR and F parameters according to the mean values. To do this, a historical memory M_{CR} and M_F saves a diverse set of parameters to control the parameter adaptation.

During the initialization stage of the algorithm, SHADE sets the $M_{CR,i}$ and $M_{F,i}$ to 0.5 and, in each generation, the F_i and CR_i values used by each individual x_i are generated as follows: select an index r_i randomly from $[1, H]$, where H is a user-defined parameter defining the size of the historical memory; for CR_i generate a random number from a normal distribution, where M_{CR,r_i} is the mean and 0.1 as variance. For F_i generate a random number from Cauchy distribution, where M_{CR,r_i} is the mean and 0.1 as variance. In order to control the boundaries of the parameter values, every time a CR_i outside of $[0, 1]$ is generated the limit value is assumed. For $F_i > 1$ the value is truncated to 1, while for $F_i \leq 0$ the number is generated again until it becomes feasible.

As done in another adaptive DE (JADE), the CR_i and F_i values used by successful individuals are recorded into S_{CR} and S_F variables. These values are used at the end of each generation to update the memories M_{CR} and M_F. The Eq. 9 displays the update procedure for M_{CR} while M_F is updated as exposed in Eq. 10.

$$M_{CR,k,G+1} = \begin{cases} mean_{WA}(S_{CR}) & if\ S_{CR} \neq \emptyset \\ M_{CR,k,G} & otherwise \end{cases} \tag{9}$$

$$M_{F,k,G+1} = \begin{cases} mean_{WL}(S_F) & if\ S_F \neq \emptyset \\ M_{F,k,G} & otherwise \end{cases} \tag{10}$$

where an index $k \in [1, H]$ determines the memory's position to be updated, the k value starts from 1 at the beginning of the search process, and it is incremented every time a new element is updated. When k reaches a value bigger than H, its value returns to 1. In case that the generation of all individuals fails $(S_F = S_{CR} = \emptyset)$, the memory is not updated. For M_{CR} weighted arithmetic mean is used, while the weighted Lehmer's mean used for M_F. The amount of fitness improvement is used as a weight.

Besides the parameter adaptation, SHADE also uses the current-to-$p$best/1 (Eq. 11) mutation mechanism with external archive as in JADE.

$$v_{i,g+1} = x_{i,g} + F_i \cdot (x_{pbest,g} - x_{i,g}) + F_i \cdot (x_{r1,g} - x_{r2,A}) \tag{11}$$

where $x_{pbest,g}$ is randomly selected from the top $NP \times p$ ($p \in [0, 1]$) individuals in the g-th generation, F_i the mutation factor for the individual x_i. It is possible to control the SHADE algorithm's greediness by setting the value of p, where small p-values lead to a greedier approach. The index r_1 is a random value ranging from [1, NP], and $x_{r1,g}$ is a random individual from the population in the current generation. The r_2 is a randomly selected index from the union of the current population and an external archive of solutions $(A \cup P)$. All parents $(x_{i,g})$ replaced by trial vectors $(u_{i,g})$ are preserved in this archive. The archive has the same size as the population $(|A| = |P|)$, and whenever the archive exceeds $|A|$, a random solution is dropped, creating space for the new element.

As the objective of this works is to analyze the performance of SHADE, one of the best single-objective adaptive DE versions to date, we are going to compare SHADE with three different search algorithms, two versions of the canonical DE (best/1/bin and rand/1/bin) [13] and the well-known SaDE algorithm [14]. For a fair comparison, we used the same fitness evaluation number. The APL is used to create the initial population with structural information.

Additionally to the energy function, two other metrics will be used to compare the predicted structures. The first one is the root mean square deviation (RMSD), which computes the distance in Angstroms between two structures (Eq. 12) considering the C_α atom. In this way, the closer the RMSD is from 0Å, the more similar the two compared structures are.

$$\text{RMSD}(a, b) = \sqrt{\frac{\sum_{i=1}^{n} | r_{ai} - r_{bi} |^2}{n}} \tag{12}$$

where r_{ai} and r_{bi} are the i-th C_α atom from structures a and b.

As the RMSD is very sensitive to flexible structures, such as coils, the Global Distance Test (GDT) index is the second metric we use to evaluate final structures. As in RMSD, the GDT (Eq. 13) computes the distance between C_α atoms with the difference that different positions are taken into consideration accordingly to a cutoff. With this procedure, the GDT can reduce the sensibility regarding flexible structures. The GDT index is measured in percentages, describing how close are the two compared structures. Thus, the higher the GDT percentage, the more similar the structures are.

$$GDT_{TS} = \frac{(GDT_{P1} + GDT_{P2} + GDT_{P4} + GDT_{P8})}{4} \tag{13}$$

4   Results and Analysis

To compare all four algorithms, we selected a small set of 8 proteins considering different sizes (29 to 70 amino acids) and shapes (Table 1). All these structures are available in the PDB and were used in other works [13,14,19]. In four versions, we used a population size (NP) of 100 individuals and 10^6 fitness evaluations. For the non-adaptive versions of DE, the mutation factor (F) is 0.5 with a crossover rate (CR) of 1.0. SHADE uses the same population size (100) and fitness evaluation (10^6). To statistically compare the algorithms' performance regarding structural analysis, we use Wilcoxon signed-rank test for post hoc analysis.

Table 1. Target protein sequences.

PDB ID	Size	Secondary structure	Running time
1ACW	29	$\alpha + \beta$	00 : 50 : 45
1ZDD	34	α	01 : 02 : 49
2MR9	44	α	01 : 17 : 39
2P81	44	α	00 : 44 : 25
1CRN	46	$\alpha + \beta$	01 : 37 : 32
1ENH	54	α	01 : 49 : 41
1ROP	63	α	02 : 10 : 02
1UTG	70	α	02 : 36 : 16

Table 2 summarizes the results obtained in 31 runs for each algorithm in each protein regarding the objective function we described previously. A second table (Table 3) brings the structural values of GDT, expressed in percentages (%), with maximum, mean, and standard deviation indexes. For RMSD, the values are in Angstroms (Å) with the minimum, mean, and standard deviation.

Overall, it is possible to observe that SHADE achieved better energy values in all eight proteins in comparison with the two non-adaptive DE ($DE_{rand/1/bin}$ and $DE_{best/1/bin}$). The non-adaptive results were obtained from [13]. SHADE outperforms SaDE [14] in 5 of 8 cases, ensuring the relevance of SHADE in a real-world problem as it happens with CEC benchmark problems. In this way, we might consider SHADE as the best DE version for predicting protein's tertiary structures. As is shown in Table 2, SHADE loses only in 1ZDD regarding the energy.

Table 2. Energy comparison among four DE approaches using APL. The Wilcoxon rank test directly compares SHADE with another approach. With $p - values$ lower than 0.05, we can consider that the two approaches are statistically different from each other.

PDB	Strategy	Energy			p-value
		Min	Mean	Std	
1ACW	$DE_{rand/1/bin}$ [13]	−148.18	−26.75	39.96	0.00
	$DE_{best/1/bin}$ [13]	−137.93	−85.22	36.72	0.00
	SaDE [14]	−174.37	−144.11	16.67	0.62
	SHADE	−190.65	−147.11	35.77	−
1CRN	$DE_{rand/1/bin}$ [13]	−104.85	−84.04	7.07	0.00
	$DE_{best/1/bin}$ [13]	−146.09	−104.91	16.98	0.00
	SaDE [14]	−195.71	−165.11	18.34	0.00
	SHADE	**−207.22**	**−179.75**	**14.35**	−
1ENH	$DE_{rand/1/bin}$ [13]	−342.81	−334.73	3.08	0.00
	$DE_{best/1/bin}$ [13]	−364.3	−348.53	7.86	0.00
	SaDE [14]	−376.02	−367.20	4.35	0.00
	SHADE	**−378.80**	**−372.56**	**2.98**	−
1ROP	$DE_{rand/1/bin}$ [13]	−488.1	−475.2	6.59	0.02
	$DE_{best/1/bin}$ [13]	−461.45	−448.41	6.09	0.00
	SaDE [14]	−497.09	−478.07	8.79	0.65
	SHADE	−492.01	−479.02	6.57	−
1UTG	$DE_{rand/1/bin}$ [13]	−494.43	−468.98	10.12	0.00
	$DE_{best/1/bin}$ [13]	−496.05	−476.74	9.32	0.00
	SaDE [14]	−528.54	−515.98	6.93	0.00
	SHADE	**−570.56**	**−561.00**	**5.25**	−
1ZDD	$DE_{rand/1/bin}$ [13]	−223.07	−215.01	3.77	0.00
	$DE_{best/1/bin}$ [13]	−222.07	−215.24	3.64	0.00
	SaDE [14]	**−235.4**	**−230.31**	**3.26**	0.01
	SHADE	−237.66	−228.41	2.84	−
2MR9	$DE_{rand/1/bin}$ [13]	−288.23	−254.86	12.67	0.00
	$DE_{best/1/bin}$ [13]	−272.72	−260.53	6.99	0.00
	SaDE [14]	−289.87	−280.83	3.87	0.00
	SHADE	**−307.84**	**−302.64**	**2.10**	−
2P81	$DE_{rand/1/bin}$ [13]	−239.73	−225.95	5.37	0.00
	$DE_{best/1/bin}$ [13]	−241.72	−231.95	4.69	0.00
	SaDE [14]	−257.28	−247.10	3.34	0.00
	SHADE	**−257.29**	**−251.25**	**3.33**	−

Although the energy is the objective function used for minimization, it is important to measure the quality of generated solutions by comparing them with some structural metrics that measure how close the predicted conformation is near the PDB's original structure. In this way, we used two of the most commons metrics, the RMSD and GDT. Obtained values are observed in Table 3.

Table 3. Structural comparison among four DE approaches regarding GDT (%) and RMSD (Å).

PDB	Strategy	GDT (%)				RMSD (Å)			
		Max	Mean	Std	*p-value*	Min	Mean	Std	*p-value*
1ACW	$DE_{rand/1/bin}$ [13]	64.82	41.70	8.40	0.00	2.93	7.47	1.80	0.00
	$DE_{best/1/bin}$ [13]	72.41	48.66	9.26	0.00	2.79	6.02	1.77	0.00
	SaDE [14]	82.75	59.05	10.59	0.28	2.30	4.35	1.35	0.15
	SHADE	73.79	55.81	10.77	–	2.55	4.83	1.39	–
1CRN	$DE_{rand/1/bin}$ [13]	45.21	37.69	3.95	0.00	6.35	8.20	1.16	0.22
	$DE_{best/1/bin}$ [13]	59.13	42.84	5.31	0.82	5.15	7.64	1.45	0.68
	SaDE [14]	60.86	45.73	6.44	0.03	3.77	7.13	1.67	0.07
	SHADE	62.60	42.49	6.98	–	4.61	7.78	1.46	–
1ENH	$DE_{rand/1/bin}$ [13]	45.55	36.66	4.03	0.00	6.01	9.15	1.64	0.00
	$DE_{best/1/bin}$ [13]	60.74	42.07	6.72	0.00	3.50	7.55	2.14	0.00
	SaDE [14]	74.00	49.00	9.00	0.33	2.85	6.15	2.04	0.64
	SHADE	77.03	51.44	9.18	–	3.03	5.71	1.97	–
1ROP	$DE_{rand/1/bin}$ [13]	66.42	43.07	8.01	0.45	2.70	8.03	2.45	0.37
	$DE_{best/1/bin}$ [13]	77.85	57.48	10.87	0.00	2.12	4.32	1.58	0.00
	SaDE [14]	64.00	47.00	9.00	0.30	3.16	7.25	2.65	0.40
	SHADE	61.78	44.76	8.11	–	4.15	7.39	2.33	–
1UTG	$DE_{rand/1/bin}$ [13]	40.28	32.40	3.80	0.00	5.35	9.65	2.48	0.05
	$DE_{best/1/bin}$ [13]	52.00	34.97	7.00	0.00	5.64	9.57	2.22	0.01
	SaDE [14]	55.00	38.00	7.00	0.06	5.45	8.64	2.48	0.50
	SHADE	60.85	42.76	9.16	–	4.12	8.07	3.47	–
1ZDD	$DE_{rand/1/bin}$ [13]	64.70	52.76	6.18	0.00	2.82	5.01	1.18	0.00
	$DE_{best/1/bin}$ [13]	82.35	58.45	11.02	0.00	1.84	3.89	1.13	0.00
	SaDE [14]	81.74	64.74	10.79	0.92	1.73	3.61	1.52	0.36
	SHADE	82.94	65.56	9.85	–	1.87	3.17	0.91	–
2MR9	$DE_{rand/1/bin}$ [13]	67.72	47.45	7.92	0.01	3.32	6.99	1.86	0.06
	$DE_{best/1/bin}$ [13]	65.00	47.19	8.23	0.02	3.31	6.93	1.88	0.12
	SaDE [14]	77.27	51.91	12.38	0.83	2.84	6.33	2.30	0.87
	SHADE	71.36	52.39	9.35	–	2.98	6.15	2.20	–
2P81	$DE_{rand/1/bin}$ [13]	57.72	40.72	6.56	0.00	5.48	8.36	1.63	0.50
	$DE_{best/1/bin}$ [13]	65.45	45.68	8.05	0.00	6.28	8.59	1.38	0.94
	SaDE [14]	60.91	46.88	5.83	0.00	5.68	8.27	1.36	0.23
	SHADE	66.81	50.93	7.82	–	6.86	8.81	1.13	–

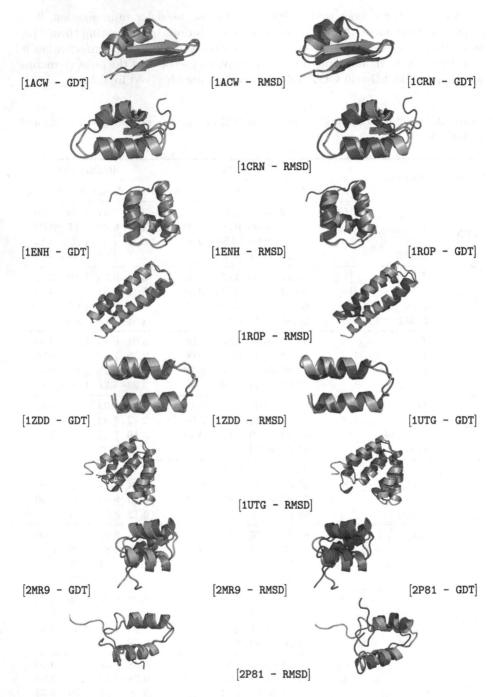

Fig. 2. Visual comparison between predicted proteins using SaDE and the native conformation. In blue the maximum GDT and in red the lowest RMSD. (Color figure online)

In general, it is possible to observe that $DE_{rand/1/bin}$ and $DE_{best/1/bin}$ are slightly worse than both self-adaptive versions of DE regarding both GDT and RMSD. This behavior can be related to how easy it is for canonical versions of DE to be stuck into local optimum, struggling to find a way out of them. In this way, algorithms that consider more individuals in their compositions and change their parameters according to their success rate can better explore the conformation search space. When we compare SHADE and SaDE, we can observe that both self-adaptive strategies achieved better predictions than the non-adaptive ones. Considering the GDT metric, SHADE only won in one protein (2P81) and lost in another (1CRN) to SaDE, while RMSD has equivalent performances in all eight cases.

In this way, it is possible to consider both SaDE and SHADE as promising algorithms for the protein structure prediction problem, considering better energies from SHADE with competitive structural analysis in comparison with SaDE. Furthermore, SHADE has the advantage of parameter adaptation, preventing the wrong definition of parameters or the challenging task of parameter tuning for each protein, which does not occur in the non-adaptive DE variants.

Finally, in Fig. 2 the predicted structures by SHADE are displayed. The green structures are the native conformation obtained in the PDB, blue are the ones with highest GDTs, while red ones are the lowest RMSDs. In some cases, the predicted structure has the highest GDT with lower RMSD. The indexes values can be found in Table 3. It is possible to observe that SHADE find similar structures in all cases, α-helixes, and β-sheets, but with some wrong predictions in the most flexible parts of proteins, the coils, and turns, harming the structural indexes. In this way, we believe that using more structural knowledge might enhance the algorithm's capability of finding better structures.

5   Conclusions

The study of proteins is one of the fundamental research problems in Biology since proteins are essential to life. Moreover, the proteins' tertiary structures have importance for drug development since these macromolecules' three-dimensional structure dictates their biological function. To date, two methods are broadly used to determine the protein structures, the NMR and X-Ray Crystallography. Even though these methods have been contributing to the study of proteins, they are expensive and time-consuming. In this way, computational approaches became interesting in the research field.

Over the last decade, different methods, systems, and search algorithms have been used to predict the proteins' tertiary structures. Despite relevant achievements by different research groups, the protein structure prediction problem is still very challenging because of its complexity. Nevertheless, the protein structure prediction represents a class of real-problems that can be used as a benchmark tool for robust search methods, testing algorithms' efficiency in complex real-world applications. In light of these facts, this work has the objective of investigating the state-of-art SHADE performance for the protein structure prediction problem.

As in benchmark tests used in different metaheuristics competitions, the SHADE algorithm was able to reach competitive results in comparison with other well-known algorithms such as the two canonical DE versions ($DE_{rand/1/bin}$ and $DE_{best/1/bin}$) [13], and the well known SaDE [14] which were already tested in the PSP problem. With the obtained results in this work, we can conclude that SHADE is a worth-study approach for the PSP problem, achieving better energy values and competitive structural indexes than other DE approaches. Future studies might consider different sources of information to be used and a multi-objective version of SHADE for the PSP problem. Moreover, bigger proteins should be considered for further analysis.

Acknowledgements. This work was supported by grants from the Fundação de Amparo à Pesquisa do Estado do Rio Grande do Sul (**FAPERGS**) [19/2551-0001906-8], Conselho Nacional de Desenvolvimento Científico e Tecnológico (**CNPq**) [*311611 / 2018-4*], Alexander von Humboldt-Stiftung (**AvH**) [*BRA 1190826 HFST* **CAPES-P**] - Germany, and was financed, in part, by the Coordenação de Aperfeiçoamento de Pessoal de Nível Superior (**CAPES**) [*Finance Code 001*] - Brazil.

References

1. Borguesan, B., e Silva, M.B., Grisci, B., Inostroza-Ponta, M., Dorn, M.: APL: an angle probability list to improve knowledge-based metaheuristics for the three-dimensional protein structure prediction. Comput. Biol. Chem. **59**, 142–157 (2015)
2. Borguesan, B., Inostroza-Ponta, M., Dorn, M.: NIAS-Server: neighbors influence of amino acids and secondary structures in proteins. J. Comput. Biol. **24**, 255–265 (2017)
3. Brooks, B.R., et al.: CHARMM: the biomolecular simulation program. J. Comput. Chem. **30**(10), 1545–1614 (2009)
4. Cutello, V., Narzisi, G., Nicosia, G.: A class of pareto archived evolution strategy algorithms using immune inspired operators for AB-initio protein structure prediction. In: Workshops on Applications of Evolutionary Computation, pp. 54–63 (2005)
5. Cutello, V., Narzisi, G., Nicosia, G.: Computational studies of peptide and protein structure prediction problems via multiobjective evolutionary algorithms. In: Multiobjective Problem Solving from Nature, pp. 93–114 (2008). https://doi.org/10.1007/978-3-540-72964-8_5
6. Das, S., Mullick, S.S., Suganthan, P.N.: Recent advances in differential evolution-an updated survey. Swarm Evol. Comput. **27**, 1–30 (2016)
7. Dorn, M., E Silva, M.B., Buriol, L.S., Lamb, L.C.: Three-dimensional protein structure prediction: methods and computational strategies. Comput. Biol. Chem. **53**, 251–276 (2014)
8. Guyeux, C., Côté, N.M.L., Bahi, J.M., Bienie, W.: Is protein folding problem really a NP-complete one? First investigations. J. Bioinf. Comput. Biol. **12**, 1350017 (2014)
9. Hornak, V., Abel, R., Okur, A., Strockbine, B., Roitberg, A., Simmerling, C.: Comparison of multiple Amber force fields and development of improved protein backbone parameters. Proteins: Struct. Funct. Bioinforma. **65**(3), 712–725 (2006)

10. Kabsch, W., Sander, C.: Dictionary of protein secondary structure: pattern recognition of hydrogen-bonded and geometrical features. Biopolymers **22**, 2577–2637 (1983)
11. Lee, J., Freddolino, P.L., Zhang, Y.: Ab initio protein structure prediction. In: Rigden, D.J. (ed.) From Protein Structure to Function with Bioinformatics, pp. 3–35. Springer, Dordrecht (2017). https://doi.org/10.1007/978-94-024-1069-3_1
12. Ligabue-Braun, R., Borguesan, B., Verli, H., Krause, M.J., Dorn, M.: Everyone is a protagonist: residue conformational preferences in high-resolution protein structures. J. Comput. Biol. **25**, 451–465 (2018)
13. Narloch, P.H., Dorn, M.: A knowledge based differential evolution algorithm for protein structure prediction. In: International Conference on the Applications of Evolutionary Computation, pp. 343–359 (2019)
14. Narloch, P.H., Dorn, M.: A knowledge based self-adaptive differential evolution algorithm for protein structure prediction. In: International Conference on Computational Science, pp. 87–100 (2019)
15. Oliveira, M., Borguesan, B., Dorn, M.: SADE-SPL: a self-adapting differential evolution algorithm with a loop structure pattern library for the PSP problem. In: IEEE Congress on Evolutionary Computation, pp. 1095–1102 (2017)
16. Parpinelli, R.S., Plichoski, G.F., Silva, R.S.D., Narloch, P.H.: A review of techniques for online control of parameters in swarm intelligence and evolutionary computation algorithms. Int. J. Bio-Inspired Comput. **13**, 1–20 (2019)
17. Qin, A.K., Suganthan, P.N.: Self-adaptive differential evolution algorithm for numerical optimization. In: 2005 IEEE Congress on Evolutionary Computation, vol. 2, pp. 1785–1791 (2005)
18. Rohl, C.A., Strauss, C.E., Misura, K.M., Baker, D.: Protein structure prediction using rosetta. Methods Enzymol. **383**, 66–93 (2004)
19. Silva, R.S., Parpinelli, R.S.: A multistage simulated annealing for protein structure prediction using rosetta. Computer on the Beach, 850–859 (2018)
20. Silva, R.S., Parpinelli, R.S.: A self-adaptive differential evolution with fragment insertion for the protein structure prediction problem. In: International Workshop on Hybrid Metaheuristics, pp. 136–149 (2019)
21. Storn, R., Price, K.: Differential evolution - a simple and efficient heuristic for global optimization over continuous spaces. J. Global Optim. **11**, 341–359 (1997)
22. Tanabe, R., Fukunaga, A.: Evaluating the performance of SHADE on CEC 2013 benchmark problems. In: 2013 IEEE Congress on Evolutionary Computation, CEC 2013, pp. 1952–1959 (2013)
23. Venske, S.M., Gonçalves, R.A., Benelli, E.M., Delgado, M.R.: ADEMO/D: an adaptive differential evolution for protein structure prediction problem. Expert Syst. Appl. **56**, 209–226 (2016)
24. Walsh, G.: Proteins: Biochemistry and Biotechnology. Wiley (2014)

Beyond Body Shape and Brain: Evolving the Sensory Apparatus of Voxel-Based Soft Robots

Andrea Ferigo[1] , Giovanni Iacca[1] , and Eric Medvet[2]([✉])

[1] Department of Information Engineering and Computer Science,
University of Trento, Trento, Italy
[2] Department of Engineering and Architecture, University of Trieste, Trieste, Italy
emedvet@units.it

Abstract. Biological and artificial embodied agents behave by acquiring information through sensors, processing that information, and acting on the environment. The sensory apparatus, i.e., the location on the body of the sensors and the kind of information the sensors are able to capture, has a great impact on the agent ability of exhibiting complex behaviors. While in nature, the sensory apparatus is the result of a long-lasting evolution, in artificial agents (robots) it is usually the result of a design choice. However, when the agents are complex and the design space is large, making that choice can be hard. In this paper, we explore the possibility of evolving the sensory apparatus of voxel-based soft robots (VSRs), a kind of simulated robots composed of multiple deformable components. VSRs, due to their intrinsic modularity, allow for great freedom in how to shape the robot body, brain, and sensory apparatus. We consider a set of sensors that allow the agent to sense itself and the environment (using vision and touch) and we show, experimentally, that the effectiveness of the sensory apparatus depends on the shape of the body and on the actuation capability, i.e., the VSR strength. Then we show that evolutionary optimizaemedvet@units.ittion is able to evolve an effective sensory apparatus, even when constraints on the availability of the sensors are posed. By extending the adaptation to the sensory apparatus, beyond the body shape and the brain, we believe that our study takes a step forward to the ambitious path towards self-building robots.

Keywords: Adaptation · Vision · CMA-ES · Morphological evolution · Embodied cognition

1 Introduction

Soft robots are deemed to be one of the key technologies for the future of mankind: compared to traditional hard robotics, they allow in fact better compliance with the environment and humans, leading to higher safety in mission-critical applications. Some of the most relevant examples of soft robots are

© Springer Nature Switzerland AG 2021
P. A. Castillo and J. L. Jiménez Laredo (Eds.): EvoApplications 2021, LNCS 12694, pp. 210–226, 2021.
https://doi.org/10.1007/978-3-030-72699-7_14

the voxel-based soft robots (VSRs) [1], and the tensegrity soft modular robots (TSMRs) [2], although other paradigms also exist [3–5]. Common to most of these robotics structures, their main features are intrinsic softness and flexibility, which allow them to perform tasks that are otherwise incredibly difficult, if not impossible, for hard robots: for instance, soft robots can perform smooth locomotion on rough terrain [6], or squeeze through tight spaces [7]. These possibilities make them ideal tools for complex robotic inspection applications, such as the exploration of hard-to-access environments [8]. In the medical domain, they have been proposed as a support for gait rehabilitation [9] and colonoscopies [10].

Another important feature of soft robots is that they are, usually, inherently prone to *modular design*. Often biologically inspired, this kind of robot can be assimilated from complex organs made of multiple components of the same kind, similar, e.g., to the myons that make up skeletal/muscle tissues. Furthermore, modularity facilitates manufacturing, redundancy, and repair [11,12].

Despite these promises, designing soft robots' morphology and controller, (sometimes referred to as the *body* and the *brain*, respectively) is especially difficult. This is mainly due to the hard-to-model dynamics of soft materials being used in the body, as well as the non-linearity of the body-brain system. This, and the current lack of analytical design strategies, make Evolutionary Algorithms (EAs), often coupled with physics-based simulations, the main tool currently available for designing soft modular robots. The importance of EAs in designing soft modular robots has been highlighted, for instance, in [13], where the authors not only found that evolutionary optimized morphologies allow different kinds of interactions with the environment, but they have also shown that morphological development can, in turn, guide evolution to more robust designs. Other recent examples of evolutionary synthesis applied to soft robots are reported in [14,15], where the authors used an EA to optimize the controller of VSRs. Overall, using EAs for soft modular robot design is clearly advantageous for a number of reasons. Artificial evolution has in fact the potential to uncover unconventional designs, difficult to anticipate for a human expert, that not only are optimized for their efficiency at the task at hand, but can also show improvements in terms of non-functional requirements, such as reduced energy consumption (thus extended lifetime), higher robustness, etc. Furthermore, evolution is able to exploit synergistic effects between body and brain that, as discussed earlier, are often too hard to model analytically.

A currently overlooked aspect in the evolutionary design of soft modular robots is the sensory apparatus, i.e., the kinds of sensors available to the controller and their position in the body. Usually, sensors are considered as given, based on expert design choices and/or physical constraints, and controllers are optimized to use the available sensors. However, *what happens if the sensory apparatus can evolve?* Or, put it in other terms, is evolution able to optimize which sensors to use, and where to position them in the body of a soft modular robot? This is our main research question. Our hypothesis is that evolving the sensory apparatus may either lead to use of fewer sensors (with respect to a manually designed sensory apparatus), or lead to more efficient use of the existing sensors, which can yield better robot performance and, potentially, better energy usage. To the best of our knowledge, the only work that addressed a similar research question are [16–18], where the sensory apparatus is evolved in different kinds of hard robots. Another work on this topic is [19], which has shown that sensor placement can alter the landscape of the controller loss function, thus guiding evolution towards better controllers. However, the context of that work was unicycle non-holonomic mobile robots. On the other hand, no prior research so far addressed this question in the domain of soft modular robots and, in particular, of VSRs. Due to intrinsic and fine-grained modularity, VSRs offer indeed great freedom in the design of the sensory apparatus.

In order to answer our question, we conduct *in silico* experiments on two kinds of VSRs, a biped and a worm, and use an EA to optimize the sensory apparatus to perform a locomotion task. In doing that, we compare the results of the evolutionary search with three baseline handcrafted sensory configurations, from low to high sensor equipment. We also evaluate the generalizability of the solutions found by the EAs on different terrains characterized by various levels of roughness and the presence of different kinds of obstacles. In a nutshell, we find that EAs are able to find sensory configurations that perform at least as well as those manually designed based on our previous knowledge, even when the number of available sensors is constrained to be smaller than that available to manual designs. This additional constraint is important as using fewer sensors decreases the complexity of the robot, thus reducing its possible points-of-failure and reducing energy use. Furthermore, we collect empirical evidence on the fact that the optimal sensory apparatus depends, in general, on the shape of the body and on the actuation capability. These results allow us to reason, qualitatively, on the link between actuation strength and sensory apparatus, and the evolutionary importance of discovering the kinds of sensors that are actually beneficial to the task.

The rest of the paper is organized as follows. In the next section, we provide the background concepts on VSRs and the sensor/controller configuration considered in this work. In Sect. 3, we describe how we represent VSRs in a way that fits evolutionary optimization. In Sect. 4, we present the experiments and discuss the results. Finally, in Sect. 5, we draw the conclusions of this work and discuss possible future research directions.

2 Background: Voxel-Based Soft Robots

Voxel-based soft robots (VSRs) are robotic agents composed of several deformable blocks (*voxels*) that can actively vary their volume in response to a control signal [20]. In this study, we consider the 2-D version of the VSRs presented in [21] along with a simulation engine tailored to optimization. We here briefly recap the main concepts of VSRs that are relevant to our study: we refer the reader to the aforecited paper and to [22] for further details.

A VSR is defined by its *morphology* and its *controller*. The morphology is itself defined by the number and placement of the voxels composing the VSR, that we call *shape*, and by the number, kind, and placement of sensors, that we call *sensory apparatus*. The controller is a law that determines, at each time step, the control signal to be applied to each voxel of the VSRs based on the readings of the sensors available in the sensory apparatus.

Shape. The shape of a VSRs is a 2-D grid of voxels where adjacent voxels are rigidly connected at their vertices (see Fig. 1). A voxel is a deformable square that is modeled, in the simulation, as a compound of masses, spring-dampers systems, and distance constraints, see [21].

A voxel changes its area depending on: (a) the control signal and (b) the external forces applied by other voxels connected to it. The control signal is a value in $[-1, 1]$ representing the request of the controller to contract or expand the voxel: -1 corresponds to maximum expansion, 1 corresponds to maximum contraction. The actuation of the control signal is modeled in the simulation as an instantaneous change of the resting length of the spring-damper systems.

The precise amount of area change depends on the parameters of the voxel model, i.e., the properties of the voxel. In this work, we assume that all the voxels have the same properties. A parameter that is particularly relevant to this work is the *maximum area change* ρ_A. Let A be the area of a voxel not subjected to external forces and with a control signal $f = 0$, then the area of the voxel not subjected to external forces and a control signal f is $A(1 - \rho_A f)$. Intuitively, ρ_A represents the "strength" of a voxel: the larger its value, the larger the area change when controlled with the same control signal.

Sensory Apparatus. The sensory apparatus of the VSR is a central point of this study and allows the VSR to perceive itself and the environment. The outcome of the perception is consumed by the controller in order to determine the values of the control signal, which in turn affects the behavior of the VSR.

The sensory apparatus of a VSR consists of zero or more sensors for each voxel of the VSR shape. Each sensor has a type, and for each voxel there can be at most one sensor of a given type. Each sensor produces, at each time step, a *sensor reading* $s \in D \subseteq \mathbb{R}^p$, D being the domain of the sensor and p being the *dimensionality* of the sensor type.

In this work, we consider four sensor types. *Area* sensors perceive the ratio between the current area of the voxel and its rest area: the domain is hence $D =]0, +\infty[$. *Touch* sensors perceive whether the voxel is touching the ground ($s = 1$) or not ($s = 0$): the domain is $D = \{0, 1\}$. *Velocity* sensors perceive the velocity of the center of mass of the voxel along the x- and y- axes integral with the voxel itself (i.e., the axes rotate with the voxel): the domain is $D = \mathbb{R}^2$. Finally, *vision* sensors perceive the distance towards close objects, as the terrain and the obstacles, within some field of view.

We designed the vision sensors for the purpose of this study and modeled them as p straight rays cast from the voxel center with angles $\alpha_1, \ldots, \alpha_p$ with respect to the positive x-axis integral with the voxel. For each i-th ray, the corresponding value s_i of the sensor reading is $\min\left(\frac{d}{d_{\max}}, 1\right)$, where d is the distance between the voxel center and the point where the ray hits the closest object and $d_{\max}$ is a parameter representing the maximum distance of sight. The domain of the vision sensors is hence $D = [0, 1]^p$. Figure 1 shows two examples of VSRs equipped with vision sensors and highlights the rays cast by those sensors.

Controller. The controller determines the value of the control signals of the VSR voxels over time. Several forms may be employed for realizing the controller. Since we are interested in studying if and how the sensory apparatus of the VSR can be evolved, we use a controller that can exploit the sensor readings. In particular, we followed the approach of [14], where the controller is a multi layer perceptron (MLP), a form of artificial neural network.

The MLP has one input for each of the values sensed by the sensors (i.e., one input for each touch sensor, two inputs for each velocity sensor, and so on), one whose value varies over time according to an input driving function, and the bias. The role of the driving function is to facilitate the emergence of dynamics useful for the task to be accomplished by the VSR [14]—we used a sinusoidal function with frequency of 1 Hz. The MLP has one output for each voxel: the value determines, at each time step, the control signal of the corresponding voxel. The input and output layers are connected through zero or more inner layers. In this work, we experimented with MLP without inner layer and we used tanh as activation function.

In this form, the controller is completely described by the weights w of the MLP. For a given VSR shape, the size $|w|$ of the weight vector depends on the sensory apparatus of the VSR.

3   Evolution of the Sensory Apparatus

We are interested in verifying if the sensory apparatus of the VSR can be optimized by means of evolutionary computation, as the shape and the controller have been showed to be. However, the controller is intrinsically connected to the sensory apparatus: in the form that we consider in this paper, the controller size is directly determined by the number and type of sensors available in the sensory apparatus. For this reason, we evolve the controller and the sensory apparatus together and propose, for this purpose, two representations according to which a numerical vector (the *genotype*) is mapped, given a shape, to a pair ⟨sensory apparatus, controller⟩ (the *phenotype*) suitable for that shape. We use a numerical vector as genotype since this enables us to use state-of-the-art evolutionary algorithms for the search. For this study, we rely on the Covariance Matrix Adaptation Evolution Strategies (CMA-ES) algorithm [23], since it has been shown to be effective for VSRs [24], as we confirmed with exploratory experimentation.

The two representations are direct, in the sense that an element of the numerical vector constituting the genotype directly determines the realization of a component of the controller and/or sensory apparatus. Both also exhibit some degree of redundancy, itself resulting in possible degeneracy of the representation [25]:

in some portion of the genotype space, several different genotypes correspond to the same phenotype.

Furthermore, both representations are specific to a given body, i.e., to a pair consisting of a shape and a *maximal sensory apparatus*. The maximal sensory apparatus determines the most complex sensory apparatus (i.e., the one with the largest number of sensors) that can be represented for that body.

The two representations differ in the possibility of further limiting the maximum number of sensors: we hence call them *Limiting* and *Unlimiting*. They work as follows. Let n_S be the overall dimensionality of the sensors of the maximal sensory apparatus and n_V the number of voxels of the shape. The genotype is defined in $\mathbb{R}^{(n_S+2)n_V}$ and directly encodes the weights $\boldsymbol{w}$ of a *maximal controller*, i.e., the MLP that takes the inputs from the maximal sensory apparatus (plus the bias and the driving function) and applies its outputs to the n_V voxels. We denote by $\boldsymbol{w}_{(s)}$ the vector of weights corresponding to the inputs of the MLP connected to the sensor s.

Unlimiting. In this representation, given a threshold $\tau_w \in \mathbb{R}^+$, the sensory apparatus corresponding to a genotype $\boldsymbol{w}$ is composed of each sensor s of the maximal sensory apparatus for which at least one weight in $\boldsymbol{w}_{(s)}$ is greater, in absolute value, than τ_w, i.e., for which $w_{s,\max} := \max_i |\boldsymbol{w}_{(s),i}| > \tau_w$. The controller is the MLP obtained by considering only the maximal controller inputs connected to the sensory apparatus obtained from the genotype. It can be seen that there is no hard limit to the complexity of the sensory apparatus that can be represented: if enough weights are large enough, the sensory apparatus is the maximal one. On the other hand, the representation allows for a sensory apparatus consisting of no sensors at all.

Limiting. In this representation, given a maximum number $n_{\text{sensors}} \in \mathbb{N}$ of sensors, the sensory apparatus corresponding to a genotype $\boldsymbol{w}$ is composed of the n_{sensors} sensors with the largest $w_{s,\max}$. The controller is set as in the Unlimiting case. It can be seen that in this case, regardless of the values in $\boldsymbol{w}$, the sensory apparatus has always the same complexity (i.e., it always consists of exactly n_{sensors} sensors). We remark, however, that weights that are very small correspond, in practice, to sensors that do not significantly impact the computation of the control signals, i.e., that are not actually used by the controller.

4   Experimental Analysis

We aimed at investigating the possibility of evolving the sensory apparatus of VSRs from different points of view. More precisely, we addressed three facets of the problem, here represented in terms of research questions:

RQ1 Are sensors beneficial to robot effectiveness? Is the benefit of sensing ability somehow diminished by greater strength? Is it dependent on the robot shape?

RQ2 Can the evolution discover an effective sensory apparatus?

RQ3 When the complexity of the evolvable apparatus is limited, what sensors are "preferred" by the evolution?

To answer these questions, we performed a number of experiments considering two VSR shapes and the task of locomotion on an uneven terrain. Concerning the shapes, we experimented with a 7×1 (x and y size of the voxel grid constituting the shape) rectangle, that we call *worm*, and a 7×4 rectangle with 3×2 missing voxels at bottom-center, that we call *biped*. Figure 1 shows the two shapes during one simulation.

Concerning the task, we considered *locomotion*, i.e., a limited time span, the *episode*, in which the robot has to travel as far as possible along the positive x direction. We measured the effectiveness of a VSR in performing locomotion as its average speed $\bar{v}_x = \frac{x(t_f) - x(0)}{t_f}$ during the episode, t_f being the episode duration and $x(t)$ being the position of the VSR center of mass at time t. Of note, locomotion is a classic task in evolutionary robotics and usually consists in making the robot run along a flat surface. On the other hand, here we used an uneven surface, since we believe that it is better suited for investigating sensing ability: robots that are able to perceive obstacles along the way should be favored with respect to robots that base their locomotion effectiveness on a regular gait not impacted by current perception [14]. Moreover, for a subset of the experiments, we measured the locomotion effectiveness $\bar{v}_x$ on two different surfaces, one used for the evolution, one after: the motivation was again to verify

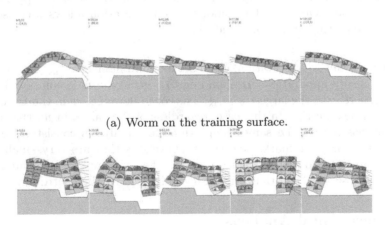

(a) Worm on the training surface.

(b) Biped on the validation surface.

Fig. 1. Frames of two VSRs (a worm and a biped, both with vision sensors) captured during two simulations. The color of each voxel encodes the ratio between its current area and its rest area: red indicates contraction, yellow no variation and green expansion; the circular sector drawn at the center of each voxel indicates the current sensed values $s(t)$ (see [21]). The rays of the vision sensors are shown in red. (Color figure online)

if the robot actually exploited the sensory apparatus for running faster on an "unknown" surface.

For all the experiments, we used CMA-ES for the optimization with default parameter settings (as indicated in [26], the main ones being the initial step size $\sigma = 0.5$ and the population size $\lambda = 4 + \lfloor 3 \log |\boldsymbol{w}| \rfloor$) and with the initial vector of means set by sampling uniformly the interval $[-1, 1]$ for each vector element. We simulated episodes lasting $t_f = 180\,\mathrm{s}$ (simulated time). For the simulation, we used the default parameters of the 2D-VSR-SIM software [21], unless otherwise specified. We made the code used for the experiments, based on JGEA (https://github.com/ericmedvet/jgea) for the evolutionary optimization part, publicly available on https://github.com/ndr09/HSMRcoevo.

4.1 RQ1: Sensor Potential Benefit

In order to answer this question, we manually designed, based on domain knowledge, three sensory apparatuses for each of the two shapes. For each resulting body, we evolved the controller with different values of ρ_A, i.e., different strengths of the bodies (see Sect. 2).

Figure 2 shows the six bodies, i.e., shapes and sensory apparatuses. For each shape, the three apparatuses are derived from a single maximal sensory apparatus that consists of a number of sensors of different types placed in the shape in order to favor the perception of a robot that moves towards the right, i.e., in the positive x direction. In particular, we placed in the maximal sensory apparatus:

– a vision sensor with three rays (with $\alpha_1 = 0°$, $\alpha_2 = -15°$, and $\alpha_3 = -30°$) on each rightmost voxel of the shape; for the worm, we also placed one vision sensor on the leftmost voxel (with $\alpha_1 = 180°$, $\alpha_2 = 195°$, and $\alpha_3 = 210°$) to compensate the limited extension of the forward front of the shape;
– a touch sensor on each voxel of the bottom row of the grid (i.e., all the voxels in the worm and the voxels corresponding to the "feet" of the biped);
– area and velocity sensors spread over the body, as shown in Fig. 2.

We then differentiated the three apparatuses based on the number of sensors that we removed from the corresponding maximal sensory apparatus. In the *Low* perception apparatus, we left just a few area sensors. In the *Medium* perception apparatus, we removed all the vision sensors. In the *High* perception apparatus, we did not remove any sensor, i.e., this apparatus is the maximal sensory apparatus and is the only one that allows the robot to "see" its surroundings. As a consequence, the number $|\boldsymbol{w}|$ of weights for the three controllers, i.e., the size of the search space from the point of view of the evolutionary optimization, was 35, 210, and 252, for the worm, and 352, 924, and 1188, for the biped, respectively for the Low, Medium, and High apparatuses.

We considered 8 values for ρ_A, evenly distributed in $[0.1, 0.8]$. For each one of the $2 \times 3 \times 8$ combinations of shape, sensory apparatus, and ρ_A, we performed 10 independent evolutionary optimizations of the controller with CMA-ES. We used the average speed $\bar{v}_x$ as fitness and we stopped the evolution after 2000 fitness evaluations.

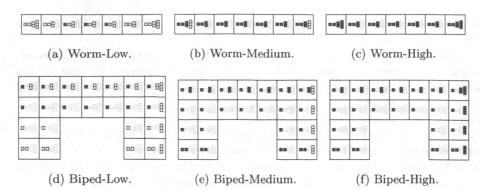

(a) Worm-Low.   (b) Worm-Medium.   (c) Worm-High.

(d) Biped-Low.   (e) Biped-Medium.   (f) Biped-High.

Fig. 2. The six bodies (shape and sensory apparatus) used in the experiments. In each voxel, sensors are represented as stacks of p squares, p being the dimensionality of the sensor (see Sect. 2). Area sensor ($p = 1$) is the first (leftmost) column; touch sensor ($p = 1$) is the second column; velocity sensor is the third ($p = 2$); vision sensor is the last ($p = 3$). The color of the sensor represents its presence in the apparatus: gray border means not present; black border means not present, but present in the maximal sensory apparatus; red fill means present. (Color figure online)

Figure 3 summarizes the results of this experiment. It shows the mean (across the 10 runs) effectiveness in locomotion (i.e., $\bar{v}_x$) of the best VSR at the last iteration of CMA-ES with the three sensory apparatuses on the two shapes for each value of ρ_A. The figure also shows the $\bar{v}_x$ that the best VSR scores on a second *validation* surface, i.e., an uneven surface different from the one used for computing the fitness (*training* surface).

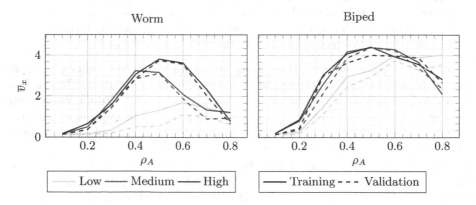

Fig. 3. Locomotion effectiveness $\bar{v}_x$ of evolved VSRs with different shapes (plot) and sensory apparatuses (line color) vs. the strength ρ_A.

Three observations can be made based on Fig. 3. First, the locomotion effectiveness depends on the robot strength. As expected, the stronger the robot, the faster in locomotion; but this holds only for values of ρ_A lower than 0.5. Instead, for $\rho_A > 0.5$, the VSRs of both shapes become less effective with greater strength: we examined the behavior of the evolved VSRs in details and found that with large ρ_A the physics model of the simulator is brought to the limit and results in voxels that contract too much, eventually making the robot difficult to control and hence ineffective.

Second, the differences in effectiveness among sensory apparatuses depend on the shape. For the worm, the more complex the sensory apparatus, the faster the robot: moreover, the three apparatuses peak at different values of strength and the Low apparatus is greatly outperformed by the Medium and High. For the biped, the differences are in general smaller: the Medium and the High apparatuses result in roughly the same peak $\bar{v}_x \approx 4.3$ for the same value of ρ_A. The gap of the Low apparatus with respect to the other two is not negligible only for values of ρ_A in the range $[0.2, 0.5]$.

Third, the difference between the effectiveness on the training and validation surfaces appears to be larger for the Low sensory apparatus—this is more apparent for the worm shape. This means that when the VSR bases its locomotion effectiveness also on the perception of the environment, it is more capable of coping with unseen environmental conditions.

We believe that these findings are important, in particular the second one, since they suggest that there is not a one-fits-all solution for the sensory apparatus. The best apparatus depends (at least) on the shape and strength of the VSR. Thus, the idea of optimizing a sensory apparatus for a specific VSR shape appears sound.

4.2   RQ2: Effectiveness of Evolved Sensory Apparatus

For answering this question, we performed a second experiment where we compared the results of the evolutionary optimization of the sensory apparatus of the two shapes, using the two representations described in Sect. 3, against the three apparatuses defined in the previous section (Low, Medium, and High). Moreover, we used the High apparatus as the maximal sensory apparatus when evolving the apparatus: the number $|w|$ of weights for the evolvable apparatuses was hence 252 and 1188, respectively for the worm and the biped.

We set the parameters of the two representations as follows. For the Limiting representation, we set $n_{\text{sensors}} = 20$ for the worm and $n_{\text{sensors}} = 30$ for the biped, i.e., approximately the number of sensors in the Medium apparatus. For the Unlimiting representation, we determined the value of the weight threshold τ_w by examining the values of the weights of the $10 + 10$ (worm and biped) evolved VSRs with the High apparatus in the previous experiment (see Fig. 4): we chose, for each shape, the value corresponding to the tenth percentile of $w_{s,\text{max}}$ (see Sect. 3), that was $\tau_w = 1.96$ for the worm and $\tau_w = 2.87$ for the biped.

We set $\rho_A = 0.3$ and we performed 10 independent evolutionary optimizations for each one of the $2 \times (3 + 2)$ configurations (two shapes and three statically defined apparatuses plus two evolvable ones). We stopped the evolution after 25 000 fitness evaluations. For the evolvable apparatuses, we initialized the

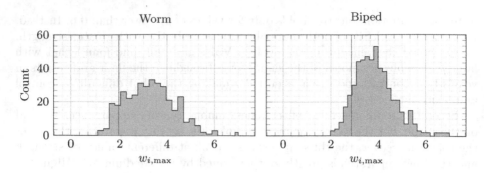

Fig. 4. Histograms of the value of $w_{s,max}$ for sensors of the VSRs evolved with the High sensory apparatus in the experiment of Sect. 4.1. The red line corresponds to the 10-th percentile. (Color figure online)

vector of means in CMA-ES to **0** instead of sampling each element $[-1, 1]$: in this way, the sensors started disabled and was up to the evolution to enable them when convenient.

Figure 5 summarizes the results of this experiment: it shows the mean fitness $\overline{v}_x$ (across the 10 runs) of the best VSR at different stages of the evolution (i.e., number of births).

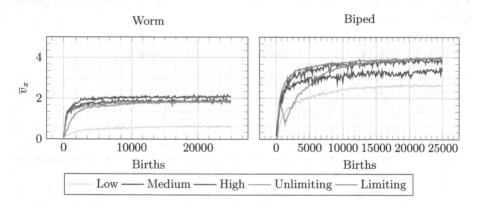

Fig. 5. Mean fitness $\overline{v}_x$ (across 10 runs) during the evolution in the second experiment.

The foremost finding that can be seen in Fig. 5 is that the evolved sensory apparatuses are not, in general, worse than the hand-designed ones. By looking in details at the value of $\overline{v}_x$ at the end of the optimizations, which is shown in Fig. 6 in the form of box plots, it can be seen that for the worm there are not significant differences between the Medium, the High, and the two evolved apparatuses, while for the biped both the evolved apparatuses and the High one outperform the others. As a further confirmation, we performed the Mann-Whitney U test (after having verified the relevant hypotheses) between pairs of samples from different apparatuses for each shape: Table 1 shows the resulting p-values.

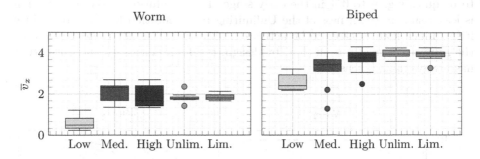

Fig. 6. Box plots of the fitness $\bar{v}_x$ at the end of the evolution in the second experiment.

Table 1. p-value of the pairwise Mann-Whitney U test performed on the $\bar{v}_x$ resulting from the second experiment (values shown in Fig. 6). Values corresponding to a significant difference (with significance level set to 0.05) are highlighted in boldface.

	Worm				Biped			
	Med.	High	Unlim.	Lim.	Med.	High	Unlim.	Lim.
Low	**0.0002**	**0.0002**	**0.0002**	**0.0002**	**0.0284**	**0.0012**	**0.0002**	**0.0002**
Med		0.5967	**0.0413**	**0.0156**		0.0821	0.0588	0.1988
High			0.4057	0.2899			0.7624	0.4497
Unlim				0.3258				0.4057

By comparing the two representations for the evolvable apparatuses it can be seen that there are no significant differences. This means that with the Limiting representation the evolution is still able to find a sensory apparatus (and the corresponding controller) that is effective in locomotion, even if the VSR can use fewer sensors.

Finally, by looking at the $\bar{v}_x$ during the evolution with Unlimiting representation, i.e., the green line in Fig. 5, it can be seen that it stays behind the Limiting representation in the early stage of the evolution. For the biped in particular, the peculiar shape of the line shows that after an initial, rapid improvement of the fitness, it then decreases up to ≈ 150 births and then starts to improve again—recall that CMA-ES does not guarantee the monotonicity of the fitness. We looked at the raw results and found that this is because of the progressive enabling of the sensors: at the beginning, the evolution pushes towards a controller that is able to run without perceiving the environment (thanks to the dynamics generated by the driving function). As sensors are discovered, they initially require the evolution to "adjust" the controller, but they later become beneficial allowing the fitness to increase again. This interpretation is supported by Fig. 7, that shows how the fraction of VSRs in the population that do not have sensors (that is initially 100 % because of the initialization of CMA-ES means to **0**) quickly goes to 0 % in the early stage of the evolution. This phenomenon is less visible in the fitness of the Unlimiting representation for the worm since it has much fewer sensors to be activated. Moreover, it is not present at all for the Limiting representation that, by design, results in a sensory apparatus that has always $n_{sensors}$ sensors.

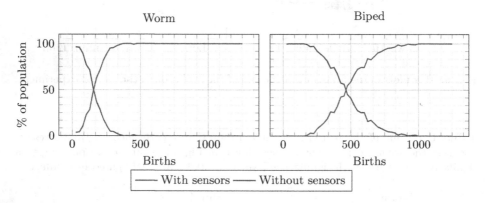

Fig. 7. Percentage of the individual of the population not using (gray) or using (red) sensors in the early stage of the evolution (up to 1250 births) with the Unlimiting representation. (Color figure online)

4.3   RQ3: Sensors Preferred by the Evolution

We attempted to answer this question in two ways. First, quantitatively, by analyzing which sensors remain not enabled (with respect to the maximal sensory apparatus) in the apparatuses evolved with the Limiting representation—we recall that, by design, the Limiting representation does not enable all the sensors. Second, qualitatively, by examining the enabling order of the sensors in the evolutionary optimizations performed with the Unlimiting—we recall that, by design, the Unlimiting representation starts with all the sensors disabled and can end with all the sensors enabled. The rationale is that the sensors that appear to be more beneficial for locomotion should be enabled more often, in the first case, and earlier, in the second case.

In order to better investigate sensor importance, we repeated the experiments of the previous section after having slightly modified the two representations. In this experiment, we allowed single dimensions of the sensors to be enabled independently: e.g., a worm could have just the front vision sensor with $\alpha_3 = -30°$ enabled, and the other dimensions ($\alpha_1 = 0°$ and $\alpha_2 = -15°$) disabled.

Table 2 shows the results corresponding to the first, quantitative analysis. It shows the number and percentage of sensors, for each type and shape, that are enabled at the end of the evolution with the Limiting representation. We considered a sensor as enabled if *at least one dimension* of the sensor was enabled.

Table 2. Number and percentage (mean across 10 runs) of sensors, for each type and shape, that are enabled at the end of the evolution with the Limiting representation, based on the number of sensors of the corresponding type that are present in the maximal sensory apparatus of the corresponding shape (first row of each shape).

		Area	Touch	Velocity	Vision
Worm	Number in maximal	7	7	7	2
	Number in evolved	5.7	5.8	6.7	2.0
	% in evolved	81.4	82.9	95.7	100.0
Biped	Number in maximal	22	4	7	4
	Number in evolved	16.4	3.4	6.8	4.0
	% in evolved	74.5	85.0	97.1	100.0

It can be seen from Table 2 that for both shapes the vision sensors result all enabled (in all runs). Velocity and touch sensors are enabled less frequently and with similar percentages in the two shapes. Finally, the area sensors appear to be the least used in both shapes. In the biped, ≈25 % of them remain not used on average: interestingly, this is also the most numerous sensor in the maximal sensory apparatus of this shape. A possible interpretation of the latter finding is that in the manually designed maximal sensory apparatus of the biped the area sensors are redundant: under the constraint posed by the Limiting representation, the evolution still finds an effective solution for locomotion (see Sect. 4.2) and hence "is aware" of this redundancy.

Concerning the qualitative analysis, we report here the detailed outcome for one of the runs with the Unlimiting representation. Figure 8 shows the sensory apparatus of the best biped (represented with the graphical notation of Fig. 2) in four salient points of the evolution, that are referred to the corresponding values of the fitness $\bar{v}_x$ and the percentage of sensor dimensions enabled with respect to the maximal sensory apparatus. Besides the beginning of the evolution, we chose as salient moments: (i) the discovery of the first sensor, (ii) the phase of maximum improvement of the fitness after the initial drop, and (iii) the first time all sensors are enabled.

Two qualitative observations can be made by looking at Fig. 8. First, in the moment of maximum improvement after the initial drop in the fitness, almost all the vision sensors are enabled, whereas the percentage of enabled sensors for

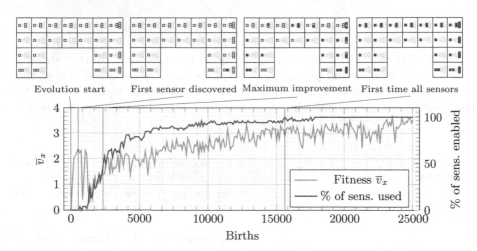

Fig. 8. The sensory apparatus of the biped in four salient moments of the evolution (see text) for one of the evolutionary runs. The plots of the VSRs are referred to the corresponding values of fitness $\bar{v}_x$ (green) and percentage of enabled sensor dimensions (gray) in the bottom plot. (Color figure online)

the other sensor types is much lower. This clue appears to support the findings discussed above (based on Table 2) about the importance of the vision sensors.

Second, the first peak value of the fitness just after the beginning of the evolution occurs at the same (evolutionary) time of the discovery of the first sensor. After that moment, the fitness rapidly decreases for some hundreds of births while other sensors are progressively enabled, until the evolution manages to "understand" how to effectively use the discovered sensors for a faster locomotion. This observation seems to be in line with what we showed in Sect. 4.2 (in particular in Fig. 7).

5   Concluding Remarks and Future Work

We have investigated how evolutionary search can be used to optimize the sensory apparatus of Voxel-based Soft Robots. To do that, we considered a locomotion task performed with two predefined shapes, a worm and a biped, and compared the results of the evolution of sensory apparatus under two genotype representations, Limiting and Unlimiting, against three manually designed sensory configurations with different levels of available sensory information. Our results confirmed the importance of Evolutionary Algorithms in soft robot design, broadening their use beyond the conventional optimization of body shape and controller. In all cases, the results of evolution were at least comparable to those of the handcrafted sensory configurations. Furthermore, we found that robots using sensors have a clear evolutionary advantage over those ones that do not use them, although different kinds of sensors have different effects on the fitness. The resulting evolutionary trends present indeed phases that indicate that evolution effectively "learns" to use the sensors that are most beneficial to the task. In practical applications, this characteristic can be used to find minimal yet efficient sensory apparatuses and thus simplify the manufacturing of the soft robots, while also reducing their points-of-failure and energy consumption.

The present work encourages a number of research directions as to what concerns, for instance, the use of alternative evolutionary paradigms, such as MAP-Elites and quality diversity algorithms [27], similar to the recent work on modular rigid robots [28]. These diversity-driven algorithms might indeed be able to explore the search space even more effectively than traditional fitness-driven EAs. Other interesting opportunities would be to include explicit energy constraints in the sensory apparatus evolution, and study the co-evolution of body (including both shape *and* sensor apparatus) and controller in VSRs.

Acknowledgments and Author Contributions. We thank Luca Zanella for the CMA-ES and Lidar sensor implementation. We gratefully acknowledge HPC-Cineca for making computing resources available. A. F.: Investigation; Software; Data curation; Visualization; Writing - original draft. G. I.: Conceptualization; Methodology; Writing - review & editing. E. M.: Conceptualization; Methodology; Software; Visualization; Writing - review & editing.

References

1. Cheney, N., MacCurdy, R., Clune, J., Lipson, H.: Unshackling evolution: evolving soft robots with multiple materials and a powerful generative encoding. In: Genetic and Evolutionary Computation Conference, pp. 167–174 (2013)
2. Zappetti, D., Mintchev, S., Shintake, J., Floreano, D.: Bio-inspired tensegrity soft modular robots. In: Mangan, M., Cutkosky, M., Mura, A., Verschure, P.F.M.J., Prescott, T., Lepora, N. (eds.) Living Machines 2017. LNCS (LNAI), vol. 10384, pp. 497–508. Springer, Cham (2017). https://doi.org/10.1007/978-3-319-63537-8_42
3. Lee, C., et al.: Soft robot review. Int. J. Control Autom. Syst. **15**(1), 3–15 (2016). https://doi.org/10.1007/s12555-016-0462-3
4. Shah, D., Yang, B., Kriegman, S., Levin, M., Bongard, J., Kramer-Bottiglio, R.: Shape changing robots: bioinspiration, simulation, and physical realization. Adv. Mater. 2002882 (2020)
5. Howison, T., Hauser, S., Hughes, J., Iida, F.: Reality-assisted evolution of soft robots through large-scale physical experimentation: a review. arXiv preprint arXiv:2009.13960 (2020)
6. Mintchev, S., Zappetti, D., Willemin, J., Floreano, D.: A soft robot for random exploration of terrestrial environments. In: International Conference on Robotics and Automation, pp. 7492–7497. IEEE (2018)
7. Cheney, N., Bongard, J., Lipson, H.: Evolving soft robots in tight spaces. In: Genetic and Evolutionary Computation Conference, pp. 935–942 (2015)
8. Hallawa, A., Iacca, G., Sariman, C., Rahman, T., Cochez, M., Ascheid, G.: Morphological evolution for pipe inspection using robot operating system (ROS). Mater. Manuf. Processes **35**(6), 714–724 (2020)
9. Song, Y.S., et al.: Soft robot for gait rehabilitation of spinalized rodents. In: International Conference on Intelligent Robots and Systems, pp. 971–976. IEEE (2013)

10. Zhang, B., Fan, Y., Yang, P., Cao, T., Liao, H.: Worm-like soft robot for complicated tubular environments. Soft Rob. **6**(3), 399–413 (2019)
11. Hiller, J., Lipson, H.: Automatic design and manufacture of soft robots. IEEE Trans. Rob. **28**(2), 457–466 (2011)
12. Lee, H., et al.: 3D-printed programmable tensegrity for soft robotics. Sci. Rob. **5**(45) (2020)
13. Kriegman, S., Cheney, N., Bongard, J.: How morphological development can guide evolution. Sci. Rep. **8**(1), 1–10 (2018)
14. Talamini, J., Medvet, E., Bartoli, A., De Lorenzo, A.: Evolutionary synthesis of sensing controllers for voxel-based soft robots. In: Artificial Life Conference, pp. 574–581. MIT Press (2019)
15. Medvet, E., Bartoli, A., De Lorenzo, A., Fidel, G.: Evolution of distributed neural controllers for voxel-based soft robots. In: Genetic and Evolutionary Computation Conference, pp. 112–120 (2020)
16. Sims, K.: Evolving virtual creatures. In: Proceedings of the 21st Annual Conference on Computer Graphics and Interactive Techniques, pp. 15–22 (1994)
17. Balakrishnan, K., Honavar, V.: On sensor evolution in robotics. In: Proceedings of the First International Conference on Genetic Programming, Citeseer, pp. 455–460 (1996)
18. Mautner, C., Belew, R.K.: Evolving robot morphology and control. Artif. Life Rob. **4**(3), 130–136 (2000)
19. Powers, J., Grindle, R., Kriegman, S., Frati, L., Cheney, N., Bongard, J.: Morphology dictates learnability in neural controllers. In: Artificial Life Conference, pp. 52–59. MIT Press (2020)
20. Hiller, J., Lipson, H.: Dynamic simulation of soft multimaterial 3D-printed objects. Soft Rob. **1**(1), 88–101 (2014)
21. Medvet, E., Bartoli, A., De Lorenzo, A., Seriani, S.:2D-VSR-SIM: a simulation tool for the optimization of 2-Dvoxel-based soft robots. SoftwareX **12**, 100573 (2020)
22. Medvet, E., Bartoli, A., De Lorenzo, A., Seriani, S.: Design, validation, and case studies of 2D-VSR-SIM, an optimization-friendly simulator of 2-D Voxel-based soft robots. arXiv preprint arXiv:2001.08617 (2020)
23. Hansen, N., Ostermeier, A.: Completely derandomized self-adaptation in evolution strategies. Evol. Comput. **9**(2), 159–195 (2001)
24. Medvet, E., Bartoli, A.: GraphEA: a versatile representation and evolutionary algorithm for graphs. In: Workshop on Evolutionary and Population-based Optimization (WEPO@AIxIA) (2020)
25. Rothlauf, F., Goldberg, D.E.: Redundant representations in evolutionary computation. Evol. Comput. **11**(4), 381–415 (2003)
26. Hansen, N.: The CMA evolution strategy: a comparing review. In: Towards a New Evolutionary Computation, pp. 75–102. Springer (2006) . https://doi.org/10.1007/3-540-32494-1_4
27. Auerbach, J.E., Iacca, G., Floreano, D.: Gaining insight into quality diversity. In: Genetic and Evolutionary Computation Conference - Companion, pp. 1061–1064 (2016)
28. Nordmoen, J., Veenstra, F., Ellefsen, K.O., Glette, K.: Quality and diversity in evolutionary modular robotics. arXiv preprint arXiv:2008.02116 (2020)

Desirable Objective Ranges in Preference-Based Evolutionary Multiobjective Optimization

Sandra González-Gallardo[1]([✉]), Rubén Saborido[2], Ana B. Ruiz[1], and Mariano Luque[1]

[1] Department of Applied Economics (Mathematics), University of Málaga, Málaga, Spain
{sandragg,abruiz,mluque}@uma.es
[2] ITIS Software, University of Málaga, Málaga, Spain
rsain@uma.es

Abstract. In this paper, we propose a preference-based Evolutionary Multiobjective Optimization algorithm, at which the preferences are given in the form of desirable ranges for the objective functions, i.e. by means of aspiration and reservation levels. The aspiration levels are values to be achieved by the objectives, while the reservation levels are objective values not to be worsen. In the algorithm proposed, the first generations are performed using a set of weight vectors to initially converge to the region of the Pareto optimal front associated with the point formed with the reservation levels. At a certain moment, these weights are updated using the nondominated solutions generated so far, to redirect the search towards the region which contains the Pareto optimal solutions with objective values among the desirable ranges. To this aim, the remaining number of generations are run using the updated weight vectors and the point formed with the aspiration levels. The computational experiment show the potential of our proposal in 2, 3 and 5-objective problems, in comparison to other state-of-the-art algorithms.

Keywords: Decision-making · Aspiration and reservation levels · Reference point · Evolutionary multiobjective optimization

1 Introduction

Multiobjective optimization problems (MOP) are problems optimizing several conflicting objectives. Usually, there is no unique optimal solution for these problems, where all objectives achieve their individual optimum at the same time. Instead, the so-called *Pareto optimal solutions* have to be found, at which no objective can be improved without degrading, at least, one of the others. All Pareto optimal solutions comprise the *Pareto optimal set* (PS) in the decision space, and the *Pareto optimal front* (PF) in the objective space.

© Springer Nature Switzerland AG 2021
P. A. Castillo and J. L. Jiménez Laredo (Eds.): EvoApplications 2021, LNCS 12694, pp. 227–241, 2021.
https://doi.org/10.1007/978-3-030-72699-7_15

Evolutionary Multiobjective Optimization (EMO) algorithms [3,4] solve MOPs by generating a set of nondominated solutions to approximate the entire PF. The obtained solutions should be as uniformly distributed as possible (diversity), and close enough to the PF (convergence). In particular, so-called *decomposition-based* EMO algorithms transform the original MOP into a set of single-objective optimization sub-problems, and select the best individuals at each generation according to these sub-problems. Within these algorithms, we find the well-known MOEA/D [16,17,23,34], NSGA-III [6,14], GWASF-GA [27] and its improved version A-GWASF-GA [10,19].

Given that all Pareto optimal solutions are equivalent in a mathematical sense, a *decision maker (DM)* expert in the problem domain has to be involved to express her/his preferences to localize the *most preferred solution (MPS)* as the final solution to the problem. The approximation found by an EMO algorithm can be useful for studying the problem itself (the degree of conflict among the objectives, their trade-offs, feasible solutions, etc.), but the task of identifying the MPS may not be easy. In order to facilitate the decision-making task inherent to the solution process, preferences are included into the algorithm procedure in the so-called *preference-based* EMO approaches [1]. Their main purpose is to approximate just the subset of solutions which correspond to the DM's preferences, the *region of interest* (ROI) [7,9,30].

Among preference-based EMO algorithms, we can mention WASF-GA [26] and its interactive version [25], at which the preferences are specified in the form of a reference point constituted by desirable aspiration levels for the objective functions. Internally, both algorithms are based on decomposition and consider a set of weight vectors to minimize an achievement scalaring function (ASF) formulated using the reference point used as preferential information. Indeed, IRA-EMO [28] has been also suggested as another interactive method based on WASF-GA, although the preferences are given in this case as desirable bounds for the objective values, i.e. as aspiration and reservation points. In IRA-EMO, an internal algorithm called Modified WASF-GA is internally used to work with both points (see [28] for further details). This approach approximates the set obtained as the union of the ROIs defined by the two points separately, using a small number of solutions at each iteration. However, when giving desirable objective bounds, the DM is only interested in the Pareto optimal solutions whose objective values are within the desirable ranges, i.e. the solutions in the intersection of the ROIs defined by the aspiration and the reservation points.

In this paper, we assume the preferences are expressed in the form of desirable ranges for the objective functions. As said, this type of preferences, in practice, determines an aspiration point formed by desirable aspiration values for the objectives, and a reservation point constituted by acceptable objective levels beyond which their values should be rejected. According to this information, the ROI to be approximated includes the Pareto optimal solutions which belong, at the same time, to the ROIs associated with both points.

To converge to this region, we propose a decomposition-based algorithm enabling the simultaneous use of an aspiration and a reservation point, and which enhances the working procedure of the Modified WASF-GA algorithm [28]. We call it *Evolutionary algorithm based on Ranges for the Objectives Functions* (EROF), and its main purpose is to directly approximate the ROI jointly defined by the two points, and not only with a few solutions, but with an enough representative approximation set.

Given that the weight vectors' distribution directly affects the performance of any decomposition-based EMO algorithm [10,13,15,19,23,29], we incorporate a procedure to re-calculate the weight vectors used based on the theoretical results published in [18,20]. In practice, once an initial approximation set is internally available, the search directions for new solutions are re-directed towards the desired ROI using both the reservation and the aspiration points.

There are several proposals to modify and adapt the weight vectors while a decomposition-based algorithm converges to the PF [13,15,19,23]. However, none of these works has been suggested to approximate a subset of the PF such as the region formed by the solutions with objective values among desirable ranges. In this sense, on the one hand, a novelty of the proposed algorithm EROF is that it is based on a preferential scheme (desirable objective function ranges) which is not very frequently used in the EMO field. Few EMO approaches have been suggested according to this scheme, such as e.g. [11,28]. On the other hand, another contribution of this paper is the procedure for the adaptation of the weight vectors based on the proposal published in [18,20] for classical MCDM methods, which has not previously incorporated to any decomposition-based EMO algorithm.

In the following, Sect. 2 introduces the main concepts and notations used in multiobjective optimization. The new algorithm is described in Sect. 3. Next, Sect. 4 describes the computational experiment carried out to show the performance of EROF. Finally, the conclusions are drawn in Sect. 5.

2   Formulation and Background Concepts

We consider *multiobjective optimization problems* (MOPs) of the form:

$$\text{minimize}\quad \{f_1(\mathbf{x}), f_2(\mathbf{x}), \ldots, f_k(\mathbf{x})\}$$
$$\text{subject to}\ \ \mathbf{x} \in S, \tag{1}$$

where $k \geq 2$ is the number of *objective functions* $f_i : S \rightarrow \mathbb{R}$ $(i = 1, \ldots, k)$, $\mathbf{x} = (x_1, x_2, \ldots, x_n)^T$ is the vector of *decision variables* in the *feasible set* $S \subset \mathbb{R}^n$. The *feasible objective region* Z belongs to the objective space $\mathbb{R}^k$ and is formed by *objective vectors* as $\mathbf{f}(\mathbf{x}) = (f_1(\mathbf{x}), f_2(\mathbf{x}), \ldots, f_k(\mathbf{x}))^T$, with $\mathbf{x} \in S$.

The degree of conflict existing among the objective functions makes it impossible to find a single optimal solution where all of the objective functions can reach their individual optima. Thus, we are interested in Pareto optimal solutions, at which no objective function can be improved without deteriorating, at least, one of the others. A solution $\mathbf{x} \in S$ is said to be *Pareto optimal* if and only if there is no other $\bar{\mathbf{x}} \in S$ such that $f_i(\bar{\mathbf{x}}) \leq f_i(\mathbf{x})$ for all $i = 1, \ldots, k$, and $f_j(\bar{\mathbf{x}}) < f_j(\mathbf{x})$ for, at least, one index j. The corresponding objective vector $\mathbf{f}(\mathbf{x})$

is referred to as a *Pareto optimal objective vector*. The set of all Pareto optimal solutions is called the *Pareto optimal set* (PS), denoted by E, and the set of all Pareto optimal objective vectors is called the *Pareto optimal front* (PF), denoted by $\mathbf{f}(E)$. In addition, given two vectors $\mathbf{z}, \bar{\mathbf{z}} \in \mathbb{R}^k$, $\mathbf{z}$ *dominates* $\bar{\mathbf{z}}$ if and only if $z_i \leq \bar{z}_i$ for all $i = 1, \ldots, k$, and $z_j < \bar{z}_j$ for, at least, one index j. In this paper, we refer as a *nondominated set* to a set of solutions whose objective vectors are not dominated by those of the rest of solutions in the set.

The so-called *ideal* and *nadir points*, denoted by $z^\star = (z_1^\star, \ldots, z_k^\star)^T$ and $\mathbf{z}^{\mathrm{nad}} = (z_1^{\mathrm{nad}}, \ldots, z_k^{\mathrm{nad}})^T$, provide lower and upper bounds for the objective function values in the PF, respectively. Formally, for every $i = 1, \ldots, k$, the ideal point is calculated as $z_i^\star = \min_{\mathbf{x} \in E} f_i(\mathbf{x}) = \min_{\mathbf{x} \in S} f_i(\mathbf{x})$. The nadir point is defined as $z_i^{\mathrm{nad}} = \max_{\mathbf{x} \in E} f_i(\mathbf{x})$, for every $i = 1, \ldots, k$.

A scheme for working with preferences of a DM is defined by a *reference point* [32], denoted by $\mathbf{q} = (q_1, \ldots, q_k)^T \in \mathbb{R}^k$. Each q_i is a desirable value for the objective function f_i appealing for the DM ($i = 1, \ldots, k$). We say that $\mathbf{q}$ is *achievable* if $\mathbf{q} \in Z + \mathbb{R}_+^k$ (where $\mathbb{R}_+^k = \{\mathbf{y} \in \mathbb{R}^k \mid y_i \geq 0 \text{ for } i = 1, \ldots, k\}$), that is, if either $\mathbf{q} \in Z$ or $\mathbf{q}$ is dominated by a Pareto optimal objective vector. Otherwise, $\mathbf{q}$ is said to be *unachievable*. In addition, we adopt the definition of the ROI associated with a reference point $\mathbf{q}$ given in [26]. When $\mathbf{q}$ is achievable, the ROI is the subset of Pareto optimal objective vectors which dominate $\mathbf{q}$, that is, the objective vectors $\mathbf{f}(\mathbf{x})$ with $\mathbf{x} \in E$ such that $f_i(\mathbf{x}) \leq q_i$, for $i = 1, \ldots, k$. If $\mathbf{q}$ is unachievable, the ROI is formed by the Pareto optimal objective vectors dominated by $\mathbf{q}$, that is, the objective vectors $\mathbf{f}(\mathbf{x})$ with $\mathbf{x} \in E$ such that $f_i(\mathbf{x}) \geq q_i$, for $i = 1, \ldots, k$.

To find the Pareto optimal solution that best satisfies the DM's expectations according to a reference point $\mathbf{q}$, we can minimize the Wierzbiki's ASF over the feasible set [32], using a vector of weights $\mu = (\mu_1, \ldots, \mu_k)^T$, with $\mu_i > 0$ for $i = 1, \ldots, k$, whose formulation is:

$$s(\mathbf{q}, \mathbf{f}(\mathbf{x}), \mu) = \max_{i=1,\ldots,k} \{ \mu_i(f_i(\mathbf{x}) - q_i) \} + \rho \sum_{i=1}^{k} \mu_i(f_i(\mathbf{x}) - q_i). \tag{2}$$

The parameter ρ is a real positive value assuring that the solution which minimizes (2) over S is always a Pareto optimal solution of the original problem (1). Actually, any Pareto optimal solution of (1) can be obtained by minimizing (2) over S and varying the reference point and/or the weight vector [21].

We consider preferences elicited as desirable ranges for the objective functions, specified by means of aspiration and reservation levels, denoted by q_i^a and q_i^r, respectively, with $z_i^\star \leq q_i^a < q_i^r \leq z_i^{\mathrm{nad}}$ ($i = 1, \ldots, k$). With this, we have an *aspiration point* $\mathbf{q}^a = (q_1^a, \ldots, q_k^a)^T$ formed by values regarded as desirable for the objective functions (i.e. values to be achieved, if possible), and a *reservation point* $\mathbf{q}^r = (q_1^r, \ldots, q_k^r)^T$ comprised of values regarded as acceptable for the DM (i.e. values above which the objective functions are not admissible).

If the DM decides to analyse solutions whose objective function values are within the desirable ranges, the area of the PF (s)he is interested in includes the Pareto optimal solutions belonging, at the same time, to the ROIs defined

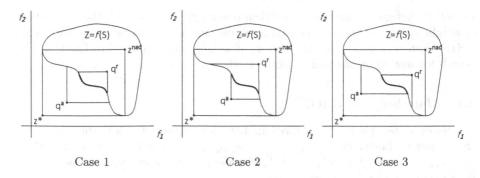

Fig. 1. Subset $R = R^a \cap R^r$ defined by $\mathbf{q}^a$ and $\mathbf{q}^r$.

separately by both the aspiration and the reservation points (denoted by R^a and R^r, respectively). This means that the ROI the DM is interested in is $R = R^a \cap R^r$. Figure 1 shows different situations for a bi-objective minimization problem, where R is the region of the PF in bold. Observe that this region is different to $R^a \cup R^r$ in the three cases. In this figure, we assume that $\mathbf{q}^a$ is unachievable and $\mathbf{q}^r$ is achievable, which is the most logical situation when the DM provides desirable ranges. In case $\mathbf{q}^a$ and $\mathbf{q}^r$ are both unachievable, $R = R^a \cap R^r = R^r$, and if both are achievable, $R = R^a \cap R^r = R^a$.

3   Desirable Objective Function Ranges as Preferences

In this work, we propose a new algorithm called *Evolutionary algorithm based on Ranges for the Objectives Functions* (EROF) to approximate the ROI defined by desirable ranges for the objective function given by a DM (or by aspiration and reservation levels), i.e. to approximate the region $R = R^a \cap R^r$. The fundamental difference with Modified WASF-GA is that the new proposal is designed to converge to this subset of Pareto optimal solutions, while Modified WASF-GA generates solutions lying in the union of the ROIs separately defined by the aspiration and the reservation points, which implies a waste of computational resources to produce solutions that the DM is not interested in.

To achieve this aim, a methodological procedure is applied in EROF to update the vectors of weights according to specified desirable ranges for the objective functions, which is supported by already existing theoretical results.

In the algorithm EROF, the way to proceed is the following. Firstly, we internally find an approximation of the ROI defined by the reservation point. Once we have this, k extreme points are calculated using the solutions of this approximation, where k denotes the number of objective functions. Next, k extreme weight vectors are calculated by projecting the aspiration point to the k extreme points, using properties of the Wierzbicki's ASF [21].

These k extreme weight vectors allow us to define a new subset of weight vectors so that the new projection directions point towards the desired ROI, the subset R. Actually, using the theoretical results given in [18, 20], the new subset of weight vectors are built as convex combinations of the inverse of the k extreme weight vectors. Finally, the new vectors of weights are employed to fine-tune the search for new solutions and converge to the region R.

3.1   Main Steps of EROF

Let us describe the EROF algorithm. Let us consider the desirable ranges of the objective functions $[q_1^a, q_1^r] \times \cdots \times [q_k^a, q_k^r]$, which define the points $\mathbf{q}^a = (q_1^a, \ldots, q_k^a)^T$ and $\mathbf{q}^r = (q_1^r, \ldots, q_k^r)^T$. We assume the more general case, i.e. $\mathbf{q}^r$ is achievable and $\mathbf{q}^a$ is unachievable.

If both points are of the same type (achievable or unachievable), the resulting subset R can be approximated by executing i.e. WASF-GA [26] using either $\mathbf{q}^a$ or $\mathbf{q}^r$ as the reference point accordingly.

In EROF, we initially need a set $W = \{\boldsymbol{\mu}^1, \ldots, \boldsymbol{\mu}^{N_\mu}\}$ with N_μ vectors of weights in $(0, 1)^k$.

Let us denote as N the population size and NG_T the total number of generations. Considering $\mathbf{q}^r$ as reference point and using the weight vectors in W, a number of generations (denoted by NG_1) are performed at first as in the original WASF-GA. The purpose of this is to internally approximate the ROI defined just by $\mathbf{q}^r$. Thus, NG_1 cannot be too small in order not to stop the algorithm too prematurely, not can it be too large so that there are still generations to improve the convergence towards R before the solution process finalizes.

After these NG_1 generations, we update the weight vectors in W using the procedure explained hereafter, based on theoretical results [18, 20], in order to orientate the projection directions onto R. This update procedure employs as input the aspiration point $\mathbf{q}^a$ and the nondominated solutions found so far. Subsequently, the remaining number of generations (denoted by NG_2, with $NG_T = NG_1 + NG_2$) are executed using the new weight vectors and the aspiration point as reference point in WASF-GA.

Let us describe the procedure designed to update the weight vectors in EROF. First, from the population generated at generation NG_1, we only consider the objective vectors that dominate the reservation point.

Let us denote them by $\{\hat{\mathbf{x}}^1, \ldots, \hat{\mathbf{x}}^{N_r}\}$ (with $N_r \leq N$) and their corresponding objective vectors by $\{\hat{\mathbf{z}}^1, \ldots, \hat{\mathbf{z}}^{N_r}\}$ (i.e. $\hat{\mathbf{z}}^j = \mathbf{f}(\hat{\mathbf{x}}^j)$, for $j = 1, \ldots, N_r$). Next, we identify the objective vector with the minimum value for each objective function f_l among these solutions ($l = 1, \ldots, k$), which we refer to as *extreme point* l and denote it by $\mathbf{q}^{m,l}$ (i.e. $\mathbf{q}^{m,l} = \hat{\mathbf{z}}^m$, where $\hat{z}_l^m = \min_{t=1,\ldots,N_r} \hat{z}_l^t$). This means that $\mathbf{q}^{m,l}$ is the objective vector with the minimum value in the component l, among the objective vectors in the current population dominating $\mathbf{q}^r$.

Now, we calculate *extreme weight vectors* by projecting the aspiration point towards the extreme points $\mathbf{q}^{m,l}$, which we name as $\boldsymbol{\mu}^{m,l} = (\mu_1^{m,l}, \ldots, \mu_k^{m,l})^T$ ($l = 1, \ldots, k$). To this aim, we distinguish between the indexes of the objective functions whose corresponding minimum value in $\mathbf{q}^{m,l}$ either improve or are equal to their aspiration levels q_l^a, and these which worsen them.

That is, for each $i = 1, \ldots, k$, the i-th component of the weight vector $\boldsymbol{\mu}^{m,l}$ is calculated as:

- If $q_i^{m,l} \leq q_i^a$, then $\mu_i^{m,l} = \frac{K^l}{\varepsilon}$.
- If $q_i^{m,l} > q_i^a$, then $\mu_i^{m,l} = \frac{K^l}{q_i^{m,l} - q_i^a}$.

The parameter ε must be a small, but numerically significant, positive real value which verifies:

$$\varepsilon \leq \min_{i=1,\ldots,k} \{q_i^r - q_i^a\}. \tag{3}$$

The parameter K^l is given by:

$$K^l = \left[\sum_{j \,|\, q_i^{m,l} > q_i^a} \frac{1}{q_j^{m,l} - q_j^a} + \sum_{j \,|\, q_i^{m,l} \leq q_i^a} \frac{1}{\varepsilon}) \right]^{-1}. \tag{4}$$

Based on the theoretical results available in [18,20], and using the weights in the set $W = \{\boldsymbol{\mu}^1, \ldots, \boldsymbol{\mu}^{N_\mu}\}$, we generate N_μ new weight vectors whose inverse components are convex combinations of the inverse components of the vectors $\boldsymbol{\mu}^{m,l}$. That is, we build the following N_μ weight vectors, denoted by $\bar{\boldsymbol{\mu}}^j = (\bar{\mu}_1^j, \ldots, \bar{\mu}_k^j)^T$ for $j = 1, \ldots, N_\mu$:

$$\bar{\mu}_i^j = \frac{1}{\sum_{l=1}^k \mu_l^j \frac{1}{\mu_i^{m,l}}}, \quad \text{for every } i = 1, \ldots, k. \tag{5}$$

As a result, we have a new set of weight vectors, which is referred to as $\bar{W} = \{\bar{\boldsymbol{\mu}}^1, \ldots, \bar{\boldsymbol{\mu}}^{N_\mu}\}$. Then, the remaining number of generations (NG_2) are performed using in WASF-GA the aspiration point $\mathbf{q}^a$ as reference point (instead of $\mathbf{q}^r$), and the new N_μ weight vectors in $\bar{W}$. Besides, the initial population used at generation $NG_1 + 1$ is the final population generated at generation NG_1.

The main steps of EROF are indicated in Algorithm 1. Note that the way of building the weight vectors in $\bar{W}$ (using $\mathbf{q}^a$ and the initial approximation found with $\mathbf{q}^r$) allows us to assure that, at the last generations, the aspiration point would be progressively projected inside the region R (in most of the cases). That is, the nondominated solutions generated will progressively converge towards the subset R in most of the cases, and this is so because of the practical meaning of minimizing the ASF (2).

4   Computational Experiments

4.1   Experimental Design

To the best of our knowledge, none of the existing reference point-based EMO algorithms (see e.g. [7,9,30]) work with aspiration and reservation points as our proposal does (in the sense that these two points define desirable lower and upper bounds for the objective function values). Note that algorithms enabling

---

Algorithm 1. EROF

Require: An aspiration point $\mathbf{q}^a$, a reservation point $\mathbf{q}^r$, weight vectors $W = \{\mu^1, \ldots, \mu^{N_\mu}\}$, the population size N, the number of generations $N_T = NG_1 + NG_2$

Ensure: A set P_{final} with nondominated solutions approximating $R = R^a \cap R^r$

1: Set $h = 0$.
2: Create an initial random population with N individuals
3: **while** $h \leq NG_1$ **do**
4:     Approximate the region of interest R^r associated with $\mathbf{q}^r$ using W
5:     Update $h = h + 1$
6: **end while**
7: Calculate $q^{m,l} = \hat{\mathbf{z}}^m$
8: Calculate the extreme weight vectors $\mu^{m,l} = (\mu_1^{m,l}, \ldots, \mu_k^{m,l})^T$, for $l = 1, \ldots, k$.
9: Generate new weight vectors $\bar{W} = \{\bar{\mu}^1, \ldots, \bar{\mu}^{N_\mu}\}$
10: **while** $h \leq N_T$ **do**
11:     Approximate the region of interest R^a associated with $\mathbf{q}^a$ using $\bar{W}$
12:     Update $h = h + 1$
13: **end while**
14: P_{final}

---

the use of several reference points, such as e.g. [7,30], could be executed using the aspiration and reservation points as two different reference points, but they would approximate the ROIs determined by the two points independently. That is, their working procedures are not designed to converge to the region $R = R^r \cap R^a$, as our algorithm does. Therefore, the existing reference point-based EMO algorithms are not valid to perform a fair comparison against EROF. In addition, we have not considered Modified WASF-GA given that this approach generates only a few nondominated solutions in $R^r \cup R^a$ (and not directly in R), as already explained. Owing to this, we have considered the EMO algorithms NSGA-III [6] and MOEA/D-DE [16] for the comparison. However, given that these algorithms approximate the whole PF, we filter the approximation sets produced to select only the nondominated solutions in the region R.

The test problems involved in our study are from the well-known families DTLZ [8], UF [35], WFG [12], and ZDT [36].These problems have been selected because they represent a wide variety of challenges for testing the capacity of EMO algorithms to approximate complicated PFs, such as these which are e.g. discontinuous, non-convex, degenerated or with objective scalability among others. They are the following ones: the 2-objective problems DTLZ1-4, DTLZ7, UF1-7, WFG1-9, ZDT1-4 and ZDT6; problems with 3 objectives DTLZ1-4, DTLZ7, UF8-10, and WFG1-9; and the 5-objective problems DTLZ1-4, DTLZ7 and WFG1-9. In DTLZ1, DTLZ2-DTLZ4, and DTLZ7 problems, we use $k + 4$, $k + 9$, and $k + 19$ decision variables (k is the number of objectives), respectively. For the WFG problems, we set the position- and distance-related parameters to $k - 1$ and 10, respectively.

Our experiment has been coded in Java using the jMetal framework [22][1]. We execute 30 independent runs for each algorithm and each test problem. The reservation and aspiration points used for each problem have been randomly generated, assuring that $z_i^* \leq q_i^a < q_i^r \leq z_i^{nad}$ ($i = 1, \ldots, k$). The population size N used is 50, 91, and 210 for the two-, three-, and five-objective problems,

---

[1] The code is available upon request to any of the authors.

respectively, and the maximum number of generations is $NG_T = 400$ in all cases. In EROF and NSGA-III, we use the SBX crossover operator [5] (distribution index $\eta_c = 30$ and probability $P_c = 0.9$), and the polynomial mutation operator [5] (distribution index $\eta_m = 20$ and probability $P_m = 1/n$, where n is the number of variables). In EROF, we execute at first 60% of the generations with $\mathbf{q}^r$, and the rest using $\mathbf{q}^a$ (i.e. $NG_1 = 240$ and $NG_2 = 160$). We have considered the experiment carried out in [10] as a reference for setting the value of NG_1, because although EROF and the algorithm proposed in this paper are different, they have some similarities in their internal procedures. In addition, we use $\varepsilon = 0.02$ in the procedure to update the weight vectors. In MOEA/D-DE, the neighborhood size used is $0.1 \cdot N$ and the probability of choosing the mate sub-problem from the neighborhood is 0.9. The crossover ratio and the scale factor are set both to 0.5 for the DE operator. For a fair comparison, all the algorithms use initially the same set of weight vectors.

The algorithms' performance has been evaluated with the hypervolume (HV) metric, which is obtained using the WFG calculation method suggested in [31] for all test problems. The HV computation requires a representative set of the true PF, and we use the representative sets available in jMetal for the problems considered. Besides, the reference point needed to calculate the HV is set as the reservation point generated for each problem. We also apply a Wilcoxon rank-sum test [33] to check if the HV achieved by EROF is significantly different to that of each of the other algorithms. For each problem, the null hypothesis is that the distribution of their HV values in the 30 runs differ by a value α, assuming that the difference is significant if the obtained p-value is lower than $\alpha = 0.05$. We use the `wilcox.test` function from the R software.[2] For estimating the magnitude of the differences between two algorithms when the comparison was significant, we use the non-parametric effect size measure Cliff's [2], denoted by δ, from the R software.[3] The effect size is small (S) for $0.147 \le \delta < 0.33$, medium (M) for $0.33 \le \delta < 0.474$, and large (L) for $\delta \ge 0.474$ [24].

4.2 Results

Table 1 shows the HV mean and standard deviation values over the 30 independent runs. For each test problem, the algorithm with the best HV mean value is highlighted in dark gray color, and the one with the second best mean value in light gray color. Indeed, we also indicate the number of problems for which the HV mean value of EROF is significantly better than ($\blacktriangle$), equal to ($\odot$)[4], or worse than ($\triangledown$) the HV mean value of the other algorithms, with a significance level $\alpha = 0.05$.

For each problem, Table 2 shows the cases when EROF is significantly better ($\blacktriangle$), equal to ($\odot$), or worse ($\triangledown$) than each of the other two algorithms (MOEA/D-DE or NSGA-III). Indeed, the p-value obtained in the Wilcoxon test and the

---

[2] https://stat.ethz.ch/R-manual/R-devel/library/stats/html/wilcox.test.html.
[3] https://cran.r-project.org/web/packages/effsize/.
[4] This means that the difference between the distributions is not significant.

Table 1. Mean and standard deviation of the HV values in 30 independent runs.

		EROF	MOEA/D-DE	NSGA-III
2 objectives	DTLZ1	$0.416715_{0.000478}$	$0.360372_{0.139663}$	$0.411875_{0.009449}$
	DTLZ2	$0.328781_{0.000034}$	$0.307486_{0.000014}$	$0.307153_{0.001569}$
	DTLZ3	$0.094957_{0.041532}$	$0.040735_{0.054714}$	$0.108502_{0.020662}$
	DTLZ4	$0.095977_{0.026090}$	$0.095327_{0.000026}$	$0.057267_{0.047558}$
	DTLZ7	$0.154441_{0.001153}$	$0.131587_{0.044615}$	$0.139624_{0.037991}$
	UF1	$0.308289_{0.148115}$	$0.442299_{0.110978}$	$0.363997_{0.129645}$
	UF2	$0.433371_{0.050775}$	$0.506668_{0.037008}$	$0.478084_{0.019651}$
	UF3	$0.304060_{0.043411}$	$0.212444_{0.078880}$	$0.147363_{0.107116}$
	UF4	$0.074124_{0.006685}$	$0.050903_{0.011187}$	$0.061170_{0.009527}$
	UF5	$0.004172_{0.017365}$	$0.001056_{0.004540}$	$0.025230_{0.037553}$
	UF6	$0.045123_{0.072917}$	$0.029894_{0.068226}$	$0.039083_{0.064534}$
	UF7	$0.107798_{0.133038}$	$0.193594_{0.139278}$	$0.111299_{0.129708}$
	WFG1	$0.002286_{0.003621}$	$0.318787_{0.040983}$	$0.133291_{0.065957}$
	WFG2	$0.297917_{0.007068}$	$0.295668_{0.000059}$	$0.296115_{0.001844}$
	WFG3	$0.565573_{0.001799}$	$0.556783_{0.000073}$	$0.555019_{0.001725}$
	WFG4	$0.184404_{0.001091}$	$0.174447_{0.003176}$	$0.186011_{0.000337}$
	WFG5	$0.079931_{0.000002}$	$0.071477_{0.000228}$	$0.072160_{0.000481}$
	WFG6	$0.094021_{0.017468}$	$0.107106_{0.014116}$	$0.086510_{0.017989}$
	WFG7	$0.132650_{0.002945}$	$0.145305_{0.000127}$	$0.148566_{0.000294}$
	WFG8	$0.075305_{0.009094}$	$0.055051_{0.004023}$	$0.058305_{0.003335}$
	WFG9	$0.266248_{0.004182}$	$0.228568_{0.061158}$	$0.249204_{0.032325}$
	ZDT1	$0.732634_{0.000247}$	$0.720652_{0.000630}$	$0.720717_{0.001006}$
	ZDT2	$0.265964_{0.000128}$	$0.258144_{0.000075}$	$0.257926_{0.000239}$
	ZDT3	$0.501230_{0.015112}$	$0.500975_{0.000191}$	$0.495078_{0.007239}$
	ZDT4	$0.648211_{0.039109}$	$0.627205_{0.115061}$	$0.665681_{0.005758}$
	ZDT6	$0.409851_{0.001310}$	$0.408858_{0.000051}$	$0.399967_{0.002633}$
			▲18 ⊙2 ▽6	▲15 ⊙4 ▽7
3 objectives	DTLZ1	$0.425849_{0.002675}$	$0.463884_{0.000744}$	$0.425900_{0.006224}$
	DTLZ2	$0.263282_{0.007957}$	$0.224681_{0.004020}$	$0.205218_{0.001390}$
	DTLZ3	$0.338282_{0.012891}$	$0.276810_{0.007114}$	$0.281478_{0.038960}$
	DTLZ4	$0.107324_{0.049162}$	$0.097622_{0.000262}$	$0.093440_{0.025405}$
	DTLZ7	$0.256389_{0.002369}$	$0.133861_{0.031475}$	$0.234979_{0.010661}$
	UF8	$0.055247_{0.053468}$	$0.083661_{0.007612}$	$0.005434_{0.011914}$
	UF9	$0.201114_{0.144337}$	$0.434271_{0.087942}$	$0.143229_{0.100497}$
	UF10	$0.058797_{0.073623}$	$0.067353_{0.081827}$	$0.048757_{0.061224}$
	WFG1	$0.063059_{0.164518}$	$0.674575_{0.138535}$	$0.182588_{0.190761}$
	WFG2	$0.910361_{0.174691}$	$0.000000_{0.000000}$	$0.760479_{0.076306}$
	WFG3	$0.132190_{0.044473}$	$0.200609_{0.000228}$	$0.153888_{0.006552}$
	WFG4	$0.381351_{0.009379}$	$0.206300_{0.011178}$	$0.273631_{0.003376}$
	WFG5	$0.167605_{0.003996}$	$0.108771_{0.003760}$	$0.162019_{0.000818}$
	WFG6	$0.088378_{0.008741}$	$0.060056_{0.018339}$	$0.084013_{0.007160}$
	WFG7	$0.393724_{0.015063}$	$0.344314_{0.005629}$	$0.321834_{0.005144}$
	WFG8	$0.091925_{0.010896}$	$0.028840_{0.002086}$	$0.048108_{0.005866}$
	WFG9	$0.084477_{0.003625}$	$0.039888_{0.007916}$	$0.035875_{0.007071}$
			▲11 ⊙2 ▽4	▲11 ⊙4 ▽2
5 objectives	DTLZ1	$0.466158_{0.045658}$	$0.320020_{0.024970}$	$0.246401_{0.008087}$
	DTLZ2	$0.176861_{0.018264}$	$0.062525_{0.011866}$	$0.018357_{0.000656}$
	DTLZ3	$0.352126_{0.044464}$	$0.080425_{0.015247}$	$0.064337_{0.027837}$
	DTLZ4	$0.029272_{0.076369}$	$0.142611_{0.039281}$	$0.020834_{0.044551}$
	DTLZ7	$0.117558_{0.006680}$	$0.081703_{0.005265}$	$0.035290_{0.023025}$
	WFG1	$0.575087_{0.194215}$	$0.669729_{0.169480}$	$0.097435_{0.100898}$
	WFG2	$0.658774_{0.336487}$	$0.000000_{0.000000}$	$0.378421_{0.083899}$
	WFG3	$0.038574_{0.000238}$	$0.011544_{0.007120}$	$0.002510_{0.001955}$
	WFG4	$0.106596_{0.071237}$	$0.012497_{0.004542}$	$0.018889_{0.002634}$
	WFG5	$0.057225_{0.079748}$	$0.012459_{0.000979}$	$0.029432_{0.001756}$
	WFG6	$0.052520_{0.060095}$	$0.001950_{0.001832}$	$0.014386_{0.001933}$
	WFG7	$0.054935_{0.046143}$	$0.000000_{0.000000}$	$0.000719_{0.000704}$
	WFG8	$0.066827_{0.113692}$	$0.010313_{0.021541}$	$0.042157_{0.010589}$
	WFG9	$0.110913_{0.074099}$	$0.024568_{0.007997}$	$0.026463_{0.004628}$
			▲9 ⊙3 ▽2	▲11 ⊙3 ▽0

Table 2. Significance and effect size (S, M, L) in 30 independent runs.

		MOEA/D-DE	NSGA-III
2 objectives	DTLZ1	▲ 5.20E-12 (L)	▲ 1.69E-17 (L)
	DTLZ2	▲ 1.69E-17 (L)	▲ 1.69E-17 (L)
	DTLZ3	▲ 1.56E-04 (L)	▽ 3.38E-02 (S)
	DTLZ4	▲ 8.48E-09 (L)	▲ 2.32E-09 (L)
	DTLZ7	▲ 3.01E-11 (L)	▲ 3.02E-11 (L)
	UF1	▽ 2.05E-06 (L)	▽ 3.14E-02 (S)
	UF2	▽ 3.46E-07 (L)	▽ 1.03E-03 (L)
	UF3	▲ 1.94E-08 (L)	▲ 1.29E-08 (L)
	UF4	▲ 2.49E-13 (L)	▲ 6.64E-08 (L)
	UF5	⊙ 9.59E-01 (-)	⊙ 9.17E-04 (M)
	UF6	⊙ 4.05E-01 (-)	⊙ 1.00E+00 (-)
	UF7	▽ 1.10E-03 (M)	⊙ 6.24E-01 (-)
	WFG1	▽ 1.44E-11 (L)	▽ 1.13E-10 (L)
	WFG2	▲ 3.51E-05 (L)	▲ 7.74E-05 (L)
	WFG3	▲ 1.69E-17 (L)	▲ 1.69E-17 (L)
	WFG4	▲ 1.69E-17 (L)	▽ 4.20E-11 (L)
	WFG5	▲ 1.69E-17 (L)	▲ 1.69E-17 (L)
	WFG6	▽ 8.01E-03 (M)	⊙ 1.73E-01 (-)
	WFG7	▽ 1.69E-17 (L)	▽ 1.69E-17 (L)
	WFG8	▲ 2.04E-12 (L)	▲ 1.67E-12 (L)
	WFG9	▲ 3.89E-13 (L)	▲ 7.41E-13 (L)
	ZDT1	▲ 1.69E-17 (L)	▲ 1.09E-17 (L)
	ZDT2	▲ 1.69E-17 (L)	▲ 1.69E-17 (L)
	ZDT3	▲ 4.84E-13 (L)	▲ 5.63E-07 (L)
	ZDT4	▲ 2.11E-03 (M)	▽ 1.76E-02 (M)
	ZDT6	▲ 4.70E-05 (L)	▲ 1.69E-17 (L)
3 objectives	DTLZ1	▽ 1.69E-17 (L)	⊙ 7.75E-01 (-)
	DTLZ2	▲ 1.69E-17 (L)	▲ 1.69E-17 (L)
	DTLZ3	▲ 1.69E-17 (L)	▲ 2.03E-16 (L)
	DTLZ4	▲ 9.46E-06 (L)	▲ 6.63E-06 (L)
	DTLZ7	▲ 1.69E-17 (L)	▲ 2.03E-16 (L)
	UF8	⊙ 9.58E-01 (-)	▲ 1.29E-03 (M)
	UF9	▽ 1.29E-08 (L)	⊙ 1.22E-01 (-)
	UF10	⊙ 6.85E-01 (-)	⊙ 9.31E-01 (-)
	WFG1	▽ 1.99E-11 (L)	▽ 3.08E-03 (M)
	WFG2	▲ 4.57E-12 (L)	▲ 3.00E-12 (L)
	WFG3	▽ 1.69E-17 (L)	▽ 2.75E-04 (L)
	WFG4	▲ 1.69E-17 (L)	▲ 1.69E-17 (L)
	WFG5	▲ 1.69E-17 (L)	▲ 2.05E-06 (L)
	WFG6	▲ 7.62E-14 (L)	⊙ 6.32E-02 (-)
	WFG7	▲ 1.69E-17 (L)	▲ 1.69E-17 (L)
	WFG8	▲ 1.69E-17 (L)	▲ 1.69E-17 (L)
	WFG9	▲ 1.69E-17 (L)	▲ 1.69E-17 (L)
5 objectives	DTLZ1	▲ 3.89E-13 (L)	▲ 1.18E-16 (L)
	DTLZ2	▲ 1.69E-17 (L)	▲ 1.69E-17 (L)
	DTLZ3	▲ 1.69E-17 (L)	▲ 3.02E-11 (L)
	DTLZ4	▽ 8.83E-08 (L)	⊙ 6.12E-02 (-)
	DTLZ7	▲ 1.69E-17 (L)	▲ 2.98E-11 (L)
	WFG1	▽ 9.06E-03 (M)	▲ 3.43E-09 (L)
	WFG2	▲ 1.95E-09 (L)	▲ 5.53E-05 (L)
	WFG3	▲ 1.69E-17 (L)	▲ 3.01E-11 (L)
	WFG4	▲ 2.12E-04 (L)	▲ 3.95E-04 (L)
	WFG5	⊙ 1.80E-01 (-)	⊙ 1.80E-01 (-)
	WFG6	⊙ 6.61E-01 (-)	⊙ 6.61E-01 (-)
	WFG7	▲ 6.25E-10 (L)	▲ 6.63E-06 (L)
	WFG8	⊙ 1.64E-01 (-)	▲ 6.68E-03 (M)
	WFG9	▲ 2.66E-04 (L)	▲ 3.54E-04 (L)

effect size for each problem (S, M or L) is also described, according to the effect size measure δ.

In relation to the two-objective problems, in general, EROF performs better than MOEA/D-DE and NSGA-III. Observe that EROF obtains the best HV mean value in 16 of the 26 problems (indicated as 16/26 hereafter), while MOEA/D-DE and NSGA-III are both the best in 5/26 problems. The Wilcoxon test reveals that EROF shows a statistically better performance in 18/26 cases in compared to MOEA/D-DE, and in 15/26 with respect to NSGA-III, with Cliff's δ effect sizes ranging from small to large but mostly large.

Concerning the problems with three objectives, EROF is also better in the general comparison, winning in 11/17 problems. In turn, MOEA/D-DE achieves the best HV mean in 6/17 problems, but NSGA-III does not win in any problem. In relation to the comparison two by two, EROF obtains significantly better results in 11/17 problems against MOEA/D-DE, and also against NSGA-III, with Cliff's δ effect sizes mostly large.

Finally, let us analyse the five-objective problems. Overall, EROF reaches the best HV mean value in 12/14 problems, MOEA/D-DE gets the best results in just 2/14 cases, while NSGA-III does not win in any problem. Regarding the Wilcoxon test, EROF achieves statistically better results in comparison to MOEA/D-DE and NSGA-III in 9/14 and 11/14 problems, respectively, with Cliff's δ effect sizes mostly large.

In these experiments, we have observed that EROF tends to perform somehow worse than the other two methods in the problems with multimodality and disconnectivity, such as the UF test problems [35].

With this computational study, the performance of our proposal has been demonstrated. Overall, EROF has outperformed the other two algorithms in most of the problems. This enables us to say that EROF seems to achieve very promising results, specially as the number of objective functions increases.

5   Conclusion

In this paper, a new preference-based EMO algorithm has been proposed which manages preferential information in the form of desirable ranges for the objective functions. The new algorithm EROF is designed to approximate the ROI of the PF formed by the Pareto optimal solutions whose objective values are within the desirable ranges.

At first, a number of generations are executed using the reservation point and an initial set of weight vectors. Next, according to the solutions generated so far and using the aspiration point, the vectors of weights are updated in order to better orientate the convergence towards the desired ROI, using theoretical results [18,20]. Finally, the rest of generations are performed using the new weight vectors and the aspiration point. In our computational study, EROF has generated very promising results in the benchmark problems.

As future research, firstly, we would like to perform a sensitivity analysis of the parameter NG_1 in the algorithm EROF. Second, we plan to investigate how the algorithm performs in higher dimension test problems, and how the search process can be better focused onto the desired ROI by dynamically adapting the vectors of weights while the algorithm converges.

Acknowledgements. This work has been supported by the Spanish Ministry of Economy and Competitiveness (project ECO2017-88883-R), and by the Andalusian Regional Ministry of Economy, Knowledge, Business and University (PAI group SEJ-532 and UMA18-FEDERJA-024). Sandra González-Gallardo is recipient of a technical research contract within "Sistema Nacional de Garantia Juvenil y del Programa Operativo de Empleo Juvenil 2014–2020 - Fondos FEDER". Rubén Saborido is recipient of a Juan de la Cierva grant (reference FJC2018-038537-I), funded by the Spanish State Research Agency.

References

1. Branke, J., Deb, K., Miettinen, K., Slowinski, R. (eds.): Multiobjective Optimization. Interactive and Evolutionary Approaches. Springer, Heidelberg (2008). https://doi.org/10.1007/978-3-540-88908-3
2. Cliff, N.: Ordinal Methods for Behavioral Data Analysis. Psychology Press (2014)
3. Coello, C.A.C., Lamont, G.B., Veldhuizen, D.A.V.: Evolutionary Algorithms for Solving Multi-Objective Problems, 2nd edn. Springer, New York (2007). https://doi.org/10.1007/978-0-387-36797-2.pdf
4. Deb, K.: Multi-objective Optimization using Evolutionary Algorithms. Wiley, Chichester (2001)
5. Deb, K.: Salient issues of multi-objective evolutionary algorithms. In: Deb, K. (ed.) Multi-objective Optimization using Evolutionary Algorithms, pp. 315–445. Wiley (2001)
6. Deb, K., Jain, H.: An evolutionary many-objective optimization algorithm using reference-point-based nondominated sorting approach, part I: solving problems with box constraints. IEEE Trans. Evol. Comput. **18**(4), 577–601 (2014)
7. Deb, K., Sundar, J., Ubay, B., Chaudhuri, S.: Reference point based multi-objective optimization using evolutionary algorithm. Int. J. Comput. Intell. Res. **2**(6), 273–286 (2006)
8. Deb, K., Thiele, L., Laumanns, M., Zitzler, E.: Scalable multi-objective optimization test problems. In: Congress on Evolutionary Computation, pp. 825–830 (2002)
9. Gong, M., Liu, F., Zhang, W., Jiao, L., Zhang, Q.: Interactive MOEA/D for multiobjective decision making. In: Conference on Genetic and Evolutionary Computation, pp. 721–728 (2011)
10. González-Gallardo, S., Saborido, R., Ruiz, A.B., Luque, M.: An improvement study of the decomposition-based algorithm Global WASF-GA for evolutionary multiobjective optimization. In: Herrera, F., et al. (eds.) CAEPIA 2018. LNCS (LNAI), vol. 11160, pp. 219–229. Springer, Cham (2018). https://doi.org/10.1007/978-3-030-00374-6_21
11. Hakanen, J., Chugh, T., Sindhya, K., Jin, Y., Miettinen, K.: Connections of reference vectors and different types of preference information in interactive multiobjective evolutionary algorithms. In: IEEE Symposium Series on Computational Intelligence (SSCI), pp. 1–8 (2016)
12. Huband, S., Hingston, P., Barone, L., While, L.: A review of multi-objective test problems and a scalable test problem toolkit. IEEE Trans. Evol. Comput. **10**(5), 477–506 (2007)

13. Ishibuchi, H., Setoguchi, Y., Masuda, H., Nojima, Y.: Performance of decomposition-based many-objective algorithms strongly depends on Pareto front shapes. IEEE Trans. Evol. Comput. **21**(2), 169–190 (2017)
14. Jain, H., Deb, K.: An evolutionary many-objective optimization algorithm using reference-point based nondominated sorting approach, part II: handling constraints and extending to an adaptive approach. IEEE Trans. Evol. Comput. **18**(4), 602–622 (2014)
15. Li, H., Landa-Silva, D.: An adaptive evolutionary multi-objective approach based on simulated annealing. Evol. Comput. **19**(4), 561–595 (2011)
16. Li, H., Zhang, Q.: Multiobjective optimization problems with complicated Pareto sets, MOEA/D and NSGA-II. IEEE Trans. Evol. Comput. **12**(2), 284–302 (2009)
17. Li, K., Deb, K., Kwong, S.: An evolutionary many-objective optimization algorithm based on dominance and decomposition. IEEE Trans. Evol. Comput. **19**(5), 694–716 (2015)
18. Luque, M.: Modified interactive Chebyshev algorithm (MICA) for non-convex multiobjective programming. Optim. Lett. **9**(1), 173–187 (2014). https://doi.org/10.1007/s11590-014-0743-9
19. Luque, M., Gonzalez-Gallardo, S., Saborido, R., Ruiz, A.B.: Adaptive GlobalWASF-GA to handle many-objective optimization problems. Swarm Evol. Comput. **54**, 100644 (2020)
20. Luque, M., Ruiz, F., Steuer, R.E.: Modified interactive chebyshev algorithm (MICA) for convex multiobjective programming. Eur. J. Oper. Res. **204**(3), 557–564 (2010)
21. Miettinen, K.: Nonlinear Multiobjective Optimization. Kluwer Academic Publishers, Boston (1999)
22. Nebro, A.J., Durillo, J.J., Vergne, M.: Redesigning the jMetal multi-objective optimization framework. In: Conference on Genetic and Evolutionary Computation, pp. 1093–1100 (2015)
23. Qi, Y., Ma, X., Liu, F., Jiao, L., Sun, J., Wu, J.: MOEA/D with adaptive weight adjustment. Evol. Comput. **22**(2), 231–264 (2014)
24. Romano, J., Kromrey, J.D., Coraggio, J., Skowronek, J., Devine, L.: Exploring methods for evaluating group differences on the NSSE and other surveys: are T-test and Cohen's d indices the most appropriate choices. In: Annual Meeting of the Southern Association for Institutional Research (2006)
25. Ruiz, A.B., Luque, M., Miettinen, K., Saborido, R.: An interactive evolutionary multiobjective optimization method: Interactive WASF-GA. In: Gaspar-Cunha, A., Henggeler Antunes, C., Coello, C.C. (eds.) EMO 2015. LNCS, vol. 9019, pp. 249–263. Springer, Cham (2015). https://doi.org/10.1007/978-3-319-15892-1_17
26. Ruiz, A.B., Saborido, R., Luque, M.: A preference-based evolutionary algorithm for multiobjective optimization: the weighting achievement scalarizing function genetic algorithm. J. Global Optim. **62**(1), 101–129 (2015)
27. Saborido, R., Ruiz, A.B., Luque, M.: Global WASF-GA: an evolutionary algorithm in multiobjective optimization to approximate the whole Pareto optimal front. Evol. Comput. **25**(2), 309–349 (2017)
28. Saborido, R., Ruiz, A.B., Luque, M., Miettinen, K.: IRA-EMO: interactive method using reservation and aspiration levels for evolutionary multiobjective optimization. In: Deb, K., et al. (eds.) EMO 2019. LNCS, vol. 11411, pp. 618–630. Springer, Cham (2019). https://doi.org/10.1007/978-3-030-12598-1_49
29. Siwei, J., Zhihua, C., Jie, Z., Yew-Soon, O.: Multiobjective optimization by decomposition with Pareto-adaptive weight vectors. In: International Conference on Natural Computation, vol. 3, pp. 1260–1264 (2011)

30. Wang, R., Purshouse, R.C., Fleming, P.J.: Whatever works best for you- a new method for a priori and progressive multi-objective optimisation. In: Purshouse, R.C., Fleming, P.J., Fonseca, C.M., Greco, S., Shaw, J. (eds.) EMO 2013. LNCS, vol. 7811, pp. 337–351. Springer, Heidelberg (2013). https://doi.org/10.1007/978-3-642-37140-0_27

31. While, L., Bradstreet, L., Barone, L.: A fast way of calculating exact hypervolumes. IEEE Trans. Evol. Comput. **16**(1), 86–95 (2012)

32. Wierzbicki, A.P.: The use of reference objectives in multiobjective optimization. In: Fandel, G., Gal, T. (eds.) Multiple Criteria Decision Making, Theory and Applications, pp. 468–486. Springer (1980). https://doi.org/10.1007/978-3-642-48782-8_32

33. Wilcoxon, F.: Individual comparisons by ranking methods. Biometrics Bull. **1**(6), 80–83 (1945)

34. Zhang, Q., Li, H.: MOEA/D: a multiobjective evolutionary algorithm based on decomposition. IEEE Trans. Evol. Comput. **11**(6), 712–731 (2007)

35. Zhang, Q., Zhou, A., Zhao, S., Suganthan, P.N., Liu, W., Tiwari, S.: Multiobjective optimization test instances for the CEC 2009 special session and competition. Technical Report (CES-487, University of Essex and Nanyang Technological University) (2008)

36. Zitzler, E., Deb, K., Thiele, L.: Comparison of multiobjective evolutionary algorithms: empirical results. Evol. Comput. **8**(2), 173–195 (2000)

Improving Search Efficiency and Diversity of Solutions in Multiobjective Binary Optimization by Using Metaheuristics Plus Integer Linear Programming

Miguel Ángel Domínguez-Ríos$^{(\boxtimes)}$, Francisco Chicano⬤, and Enrique Alba⬤

ITIS Software, Universidad de Málaga, Málaga, Spain
miguel.angel.dominguez.rios@uma.es, {chicano,eat}@lcc.uma.es

Abstract. Metaheuristics for solving multiobjective problems can provide an approximation of the Pareto front in a short time, but can also have difficulties finding feasible solutions in constrained problems. Integer linear programming solvers, on the other hand, are good at finding feasible solutions, but they can require some time to find and guarantee the efficient solutions of the problem. In this work we combine these two ideas to propose a hybrid algorithm mixing an exploration heuristic for multiobjective optimization with integer linear programming to solve multiobjective problems with binary variables and linear constraints. The algorithm has been designed to provide an approximation of the Pareto front that is well-spread throughout the objective space. In order to check the performance, we compare it with three popular metaheuristics using two benchmarks of multiobjective binary constrained problems. The results show that the proposed approach provides better performance than the baseline algorithms in terms of number of the solutions, hypervolume, generational distance, inverted generational distance, and the additive epsilon indicator.

Keywords: Multiobjective optimization · Hybrid algorithms · Integer linear programming

1 Introduction

Metaheuristics and, in particular, evolutionary algorithms have been very successful solving multiobjective optimization problems using only the information

This research is partially funded by the Spanish Ministry of Economy and Competitiveness and FEDER under contract TIN2017-88213-R (6city); Universidad de Málaga, Consejería de Economía y Conocimiento de la Junta de Andaluía and FEDER under grant number UMA18-FEDERJA-003 (PRECOG); Spanish Ministry of Science, Innovation and Universities and FEDER under contracts RTC-2017-6714-5 (Eco-IoT) and RED2018-102472-T (SEBASENet 2.0); and TAILOR ICT-48 Network (No 952215) funded by EU Horizon 2020 research and innovation programme.

© Springer Nature Switzerland AG 2021
P. A. Castillo and J. L. Jiménez Laredo (Eds.): EvoApplications 2021, LNCS 12694, pp. 242–257, 2021.
https://doi.org/10.1007/978-3-030-72699-7_16

about the fitness function and the constraint violations [18]. Most of the time, in a real context, we have more information than just the evaluation of each solution. The structure of the objective and constraint functions is usually available to be exploited.

With an increasing number of constraints, finding feasible solutions can be difficult for evolutionary computation, where, in many cases, the strategy to get feasibility is based on some kind of penalty: either in the objective function or during the selection or replacement of the solutions in the population [21]. We propose the use of integer linear programming (ILP) solvers for this purpose. The combination of metaheuristics and ILP solvers is not new. The term 'matheuristic' is also used for these hybrids [5] and a great number of papers on the topic have been published [2]. One prominent example is Construct, Merge, Solve and Adapt (CMSA), by Blum et al. [3,4]. In a matheuristic, the ILP solver is commonly used to optimize some subproblem for which an optimal solution can be found in a short time. This differs with our proposal here in which we propose the use of ILP to find a feasible solution that is also located in a region of the objective space determined by a high level strategy to find well-spread solutions (exploration). We leave the optimization to a local search (exploitation). Finding a well-located feasible solution is much easier than optimizing a constrained problem, and the ILP solver is able to do it in a very short time, improving the efficiency of the search. In short, the contributions of this work are:

- The use of ILP solvers to find feasible solutions in particular regions of the objective space very fast for linear multiobjective constrained binary optimization problems.
- The combination of ILP solvers with a high level exploration technique and an efficient local search based on delta-evaluation.
- We compare our algorithm (MultiObjective search based on integer linear programming for Feasibility and Local Search, MOFeLS), with three well-known evolutionary algorithms used in the literature: NSGA-II [9], SPEA2 [25] and MOEA/D [23]. We use 28 problem instances from two different benchmarks.

The method is able to approximate the Pareto front for multiobjective constrained binary optimization problems, including equality constraints, which are a handicap in classical metaheuristics based on bit-flip mutation.

The rest of this paper is organized as follows. In Sect. 2 we present the basic definitions required to describe our proposed algorithm, which is presented in Sect. 3. Section 4 presents the computational experiments and Sect. 5 concludes the paper.

2 Background

In this section, we present the background for this work. It is divided into two subsections: the definition of the general concepts and a general framework to solve MultiObjective Combinatorial Optimization (MOCO) problems.

2.1 Definitions

A binary linear multiobjective program of dimension p is defined as $\min_{x \in X} Cx$, where $C \in \mathbb{R}^{p \times n}$ is the objective matrix in which row i represents the coefficient vector for objective function $f_i(x)$. Vector $x \in \mathbb{B}^n$ is the binary decision vector, and $X = \{x \in \mathbb{B}^n : Ax *_{op} b\}$ is the feasible set, which is supposed to be non-empty. Here, A is an $m \times n$ matrix with the coefficients of the m constraints and $b \in \mathbb{R}^m$ is the right-hand side vector. All elements in C, A and b are real numbers. The operator vector $*_{op}$ has length m, and element i contains the sense of the i-th constraint: '$\leq$', '$\geq$' or '$=$'. The objective matrix is also expressed as $Cx = f(x) = (f_1(x), \ldots, f_p(x))$. All objective functions are considered to be minimized. If we need to maximize some objective, we use the property $max(f_i(x)) = -min(-f_i(x))$.

Given two vectors x and y, we say that y *dominates* x $(y \prec x)$, if $f_i(y) \leq f_i(x)$ $\forall i = 1, \ldots, p$, and the inequality is strict for at least one index. When a feasible solution is not dominated by any other feasible solution, we say that it is *efficient*. The image of an efficient solution x, is called a *non-dominated point*, $z = f(x)$. The set of all efficient solutions is called *efficient set*, X_E, and its image is called *Pareto front*, $PF = f(X_E)$. Due to the fact that many of the elements in X_E could lead to the same image, we are only interested in the set PF and one anti-image for each element of this set. Although it is common to use the term *efficient solution* in the decision space and *non-dominated point* in the objective space, sometimes the term *solution* is used to refer to both spaces. Given two p-dimensional vectors l and u with $l < u$, that is, $l_i < u_i, \forall i = 1, \ldots, p$, we define the *box* $[l, u] = \{x \in \mathbb{R}^p \mid l_i \leq x < u_i, \quad \forall i = 1, \ldots, p\}$.

2.2 A Framework to Solve MOCO Problems

In this section we describe a generic and exact formulation for solving MOCO problems. This framework is extracted from the work of Dächert and Klamroth [8]. Our work is based on this approach as we will see in detail in Sect. 3. The idea of the method is to maintain a set of search zones, $\mathfrak{U}$, which are p-dimensional boxes. Every box is defined by its upper bound and the lower bound is assumed to be the ideal point I of the Pareto front.

In Algorithm 1, $\mathfrak{U}$ is the set of boxes to be analyzed. Initially, the set of non-dominated solutions N is empty (Line 1) and in Line 2 the set of boxes contains the initial element, U, defined by an upper bound for the nadir point [11]. The algorithm then enters a loop until no box is left for its analysis. In each iteration of the loop it selects one box (Line 4), solves an optimization problem based on the box, and if a new non-dominated point is found, it is saved in N. Every time it finds a new non-dominated point, it updates the set $\mathfrak{U}$ accordingly (Line 7), to prevent repeated solutions in the future. Another goal of the updating procedure is to reduce the number of boxes at each iteration. More specifically, at least box B is extracted from $\mathfrak{U}$. The algorithm ends because in MOCO problems the number of non-dominated points is finite.

Algorithm 1. *General exact method for MOCO problems*

1: $N = \emptyset$
2: $\mathfrak{U} \leftarrow \{U\}$
3: **while** ($\mathfrak{U} \neq \emptyset$) **do**
4:    Select $B \in \mathfrak{U}$
5:    **if** (Model $P(B)$ *is feasible*) **then**
6:       $N = N \cup \{f(x^*)\}$
7:       Update $\mathfrak{U}$
8:    **else**
9:       $\mathfrak{U} \leftarrow \mathfrak{U} - \{B\}$
10:    **end if**
11: **end while**
12: **return** N

After a solution is found, some boxes are split into p new boxes each. The splitting process often generates redundant zones. If we have two boxes $B_1 = [I, u^1], B_2 = [I, u^2]$ with $u^1 \leq u^2$, all potential non-dominated points generated by exploring B_1 could also be generated by exploring B_2, which means that B_1 is redundant. Therefore, a filtering process should be implemented after the split. Klamroth et al. [15] proposed two different algorithms for this purpose. In this work we use one of them, called RE (*redundancy elimination*), which consists in eliminating at each iteration the dominated boxes. For more information about how this filtering process works, see [15]. At the end of the execution, Algorithm 1 returns the set N containing the complete Pareto front.

3   Algorithmic Proposal

We present our proposal, MOFeLS, in Algorithm 2, which is able to solve any binary linear multiobjective program. If the objective functions or the constraints are not linear, they can be easily linearized adding new variables for the product of two binary variables and some additional constraints. For example, the product of binary variables $x_1 x_2$ can be replaced by y and constraints $2y \leq x_1 + x_2 \leq y + 1$. The algorithm is based on the framework described in Algorithm 1, and uses an ILP solver to find a feasible solution in each iteration. Then, in the heuristic part of the algorithm, a search using a hill climber is conducted to find a local optima in the objective space. A non-dominated set of solutions N is maintained during the search. The mathematical program to solve at each iteration is the one developed by Chalmet et al. [6]. The method combines parameterization of the objective functions (weighted sum) and the ε-constraint method:

$$\min \sum_{k=1}^{p} \lambda_k f_k(x)$$
$$s.t. \quad f_k(x) \leq u_k, \quad k = 1, \ldots, p \tag{1}$$
$$x \in X.$$

If we use $\lambda_k > 0 \; \forall k = 1, \ldots, p$, and the model of Eq. (1) has a solution, then it is efficient. Vector $u = (u_1, \ldots, u_p)$ is the upper bound of the considered box. The positive weights combination does not have any influence in the feasibility of the model, and we consider $\lambda_k = 1 \; \forall k$. We denote with $P(u)$ this mathematical program.

Algorithm 2. MOFeLS

Input: *TILIM*   // Time limit for an ILP solver call
Output: N // Approximated Pareto front
1: $N = \emptyset$
2: $\mathfrak{U} = \emptyset$ // List of boxes
3: $\delta = (\delta_1, \ldots, \delta_1)$ // $0 < \delta_1 < 1$
4: Estimate bounds for the problem using linear relaxation: L_b, U_b
5: $\mathfrak{U} \leftarrow ([L_b, U_b])$
6: **while** $(\mathfrak{U} \neq \emptyset)$ **and** (**not** stopping condition) **do**
7:    $B \leftarrow$ Select box with the highest volume in $\mathfrak{U}$
8:    **if** (Solution is found for $P(B.u - \delta)$ in *TILIM* time) **then**
9:       $x \leftarrow$ Get the solution of $P(B.u - \delta)$
10:      $Slack \leftarrow$ Get the slack vector from the ILP solver
11:      $x \leftarrow Hill\_Climbing(x, Slack)$
12:      $N \leftarrow$ Filter $(N \bigcup \{(x, f(x))\})$
13:      $Update\ (\mathfrak{U}, f(x))$
14:   **else**
15:      $\mathfrak{U} \leftarrow \mathfrak{U} - \{B\}$
16:   **end if**
17: **end while**

The input parameter *TILIM* represents the maximum total time employed by the ILP solver at each call. It is fixed during the execution. At the beginning of Algorithm 2, we initialize the non-dominated set, N, and the list of boxes, $\mathfrak{U}$. The vector δ in Line 3 is necessary to guarantee that the potential new solution is not equal to the upper bound of the box, $B.u$ (see Line 8).

Before starting the loop, we need to determine the initial box. This must contains a lower and an upper bound for the Pareto front. This estimation is done by solving linear relaxations (the decision variables are continuous instead of binary) of $\min\{f_i(x)\}$ and $\max\{f_i(x)\}$. The minimum value obtained for each f_i is the i-th component of the lower bound for the ideal point. The maximum values form the upper bound of the nadir point. We have to note that for hard problems, the execution time used for this calculation could be also high, so if the parameter *TILIM* is very low, the algorithm could end without any solution. After inserting the initial box in the list $\mathfrak{U}$ (Line 5), the algorithm runs a loop while there exists a box to analyze and it does not exceed a preset limited time (stopping condition). At the beginning of the loop, the algorithm selects always the box with the highest volume (Line 7). This is efficiently implemented using heaps for the list $\mathfrak{U}$. Taking the box with the highest volume helps to increase the diversity of solutions in the objective space (spread), since it tends to select boxes where many potential solutions exist far away from other found solutions. This is just a heuristic, and it could happen that no solution is found in the box at all. But experiments show that it works well in general. The upper bound of the analyzed box is the vector u in the model, and MOFeLS then calls the ILP solver to obtain a feasible solution, always under the condition of not exceeding the *TILIM* time. The reason for introducing the *TILIM* parameter is the following: when the ILP solver takes 'long time' to calculate a feasible solution, it is probable that the box is empty (the corresponding objective space region has no solution), so we discard it and do not waste time looking for solutions that may not exist.

The possible outputs after an execution of the ILP solver[1] are:

a) An optimal solution is found.
b) A feasible suboptimal solution is found.
c) *TILIM* exceeded, but a feasible solution is found.
d) There is no solution (infeasible).
e) *TILIM* exceeded and no solution is found.
f) Problem is infeasible or unbounded.

In the cases where the output is d), e) or f), we discard that box (Line 15) and get the next one. Otherwise, we have a new feasible solution and MOFeLS calls the hill climber to improve it. Every local optimum is inserted into 𝔘 and repeated or dominated ones are discarded during the execution (Line 12). The updating procedure splits all boxes affected by the new solution found, reducing the total search space, and filtering the redundant boxes, avoiding repeated solutions in the future. For more information of how the redundancy elimination (RE) works, see [15].

Algorithm 3. *Hill_Climbing(x, Slack)*

1: Set all components of x unmarked
2: **while** (x has an unmarked component) **do**
3:    $j \leftarrow$ Select a random index of an unmarked component of x
4:    Mark x_j
5:    $(\delta_c, \Delta) \leftarrow Bit\_Flip(x, j, Slack)$
6:    **if** ($\delta_c < 0$) **then**
7:       $x_j = 1 - x_j$
8:       $Slack \leftarrow Slack + \Delta$ // Update vector *Slack*
9:       Unmark all components in x
10:   **end if**
11: **end while**
12: **return** (x)

Next, we explain an efficient strategy to reduce the computational cost in the hill climber, which starts with a feasible solution and applies local search until

---

[1] Outputs for the ILP solver CPLEX 12.6.2.

a local optimum is found. In this case, the fitness value of a solution is given by $\sum_{i=1}^{p} f_i(x)$ (see Eq. (1)). The neighborhood of a solution x is the set of solutions at Hamming distance 1 from x (one differing variable). The *Hill_Climbing* function is described in Algorithm 3. The input parameters of this function are the feasible solution x, and the slack vector $Slack = b - Ax$. This vector has one real component per constraint in the model. Every value represents the gap between the right-hand side value and the value of the constraint. These values can be extracted from the ILP solver. When the local optimum is found, the modified x is also the output. The hill climber selects every decision variable and checks if making a bit-flip (using the *Bit_Flip* function) maintains feasibility and improves the solution with a decrease in the objective cost ($\delta_c < 0$). If so, it moves to the new solution and starts again exploring the neighborhood, until no 1-bit improvement is found.

We note that in constraints of type '$\leq$' the slack value is always non-negative. In '$\geq$' constraints it is always non-positive, and for equality constraints it must be 0 for any feasible solution. We illustrate this with an example:

$$\min f(x) = (x_2 + x_3, x_3 + x_4 + 2x_5),$$

s.t.

$$x_1 + 2x_2 - 2x_3 + 7x_4 + x_5 \leq 8,$$
$$x_1 + x_2 + x_3 - x_4 + 4x_5 \geq 2, \tag{2}$$
$$x_1 + x_5 = 2,$$
$$x \in \mathbb{B}^5.$$

Suppose that the ILP solver reports the feasible solution $x = (1, 1, 0, 0, 1)$. Then, $Slack = (4, -4, 0)$ and the objective value is $f_1(x) + f_2(x) = 1 + 2 = 3$.

The *Bit_Flip* function uses delta-evaluation to efficiently compute the objective function and the constraints violation. The input parameters are the decision vector, the index of the variable to flip, and the slack vector. Its pseudocode is displayed in Algorithm 4. At the beginning, we define a vector Δ that controls the variation of $Slack$, and initialize it to the vector $(0, \ldots, 0)$. In Line 3 we get the coefficient in the objective function associated to variable x_j, that is, $\delta_c = \sum_{i=1}^{p} c_{ij}$. If this value equals 0, then no improvement in the objective function is made, regarding the value of x_j. Moreover, in the case of $\delta_c < 0$, if $x_j = 1$, and a bit-flip is done, the variable will not be in the solution, so the objective cost increases $|\delta_c|$ units, and the bit-flip should be discarded. For the same reason, if $\delta_c > 0$ and $x_j = 0$, the bit-flip is discarded. These conditions are condensed in Line 4. If $\delta_c \cdot (-1)^{x_j} < 0$, we continue checking the constraints, and change the value of δ_c to $-|\delta_c|$. That would be the improvement in objective function if the bit-flip is finally accepted. Similar arguments have been carried out for the analysis of the constraints. If one of them is violated, we return $\delta_c = 0$.

Let us illustrate this again with the example of Eq. (2). Starting from the initial solution, $x = (1, 1, 0, 0, 1)$, the objective function equals 3. We analyze

Algorithm 4. $Bit\_Flip(x, j, Slack)$

1: // Analyzing whether flipping x_j affects the objective cost
2: $\Delta = (0, \ldots, 0)$ // Variation of $Slack$ vector
3: $\delta_c \leftarrow$ Get objective coefficient cost of x_j from the ILP solver
4: **if** $(\delta_c \cdot (-1)^{x_j}) \geq 0$ **then return** $(0, (0, \ldots, 0))$
5: $\delta_c = - \mid \delta_c \mid$
6: // Analyzing constraints
7: **for** $i = 1$ **to** m **do**
8:     $d \leftarrow$ Type of the slack (1 for '$\leq$' ; -1 for '$\geq$' ; 0 for '=')
9:     **if** $(d \neq 0)$ **then**
10:         $t \leftarrow a_{ij} \cdot (-1)^{x_j}$
11:         **if** $(d \cdot Slack[i] < d \cdot t)$ **then return** $(0, (0, \ldots, 0))$
12:         $\Delta_i = -t$
13:     **else**
14:         **if** $(a_{ij} \neq 0)$ **return** $0, (0, \ldots, 0)))$
15:     **end if**
16: **end for**
17: **return** (δ_c, Δ)

---

whether a bit-flip on the second component is possible. We have $x_2 = 1$ and $\delta_c = 1$. The condition in Line 4 is false and δ_c is changed to $\delta_c = -1$ (Line 5). We continue analyzing the constraints. For the first one, $d = 1$, $t = 2 \cdot (-1) = -2$ and it holds $d \cdot Slack[1] = 1 \cdot 4 \geq -2$. The constraint is not violated (Line 11), and Δ_1 changes to $\Delta_1 = 2$. This means that the gap for that constraint will increase in two units if we finally accept the flip. In the second constraint, $Slack[2] = -4$, $d = -1$, $t = 1 \cdot (-1) = -1$ and it holds $(-1) \cdot (-4) \geq (-1) \cdot (-1)$. This constraint is not violated and Δ_2 changes to $\Delta_2 = 1$. This means that flipping the variable x_2 makes the slack on the second constraint to increase in one unit (we are nearer to the saturation of the constraint). For the last constraint, $d = 0$ (equality constraint) and $a_{ij} = 0$, so finally the function returns $(-1, (2, 1, 0))$ and the flip for x_2 is accepted. When we return to the *Hill_Climbing* function, we update the slack vector, and $Slack = (4 + 2, -4 + 1, 0 + 0) = (6, -3, 0)$. The new objective value is $3 - 1 = 2$.

4   Computational Experiments

We conduct the experimental study in this section. First, we present the instances used in this work. In the second subsection, we define the metrics we use to assess the results. In the third, we set the input parameters of all the used algorithms and, finally, we provide the numerical results.

4.1   Instances

A representative benchmark of 28 binary linear multiobjective instances are selected from two existing benchmarks in the literature. We select 20 instances[2]

---

[2] Available in http://home.ku.edu.tr/~moolibrary/.

from the work of Kirlik et al. [14], and 8 instances from multiobjective multidimensional knapsack problems.[3] We summarize them in the following:

- 10 instances of a 3-dimensional assignment problem, each with 50 agents and tasks. Every instance has 2500 variables and 100 constraints. The group of all of them is named AP.
- 10 instances of a 1-dimensional knapsack with 4 objectives. Every instance has 40 variables and one constraint. The group of all of them is named KP.
- 4 instances of a 3-dimensional knapsack problem with 3 objectives, with 100, 250, 500 and 750 variables, respectively. They are named MKP3_100, MKP3_250, MKP3_500 and MKP3_750.
- 4 instances of a 4-dimensional knapsack problem with 4 objectives, with 100, 250, 500 and 750 variables, named MKP4_100 to MKP4_750.

Multiobjective assignment problems have been selected because they have equality constraints. In addition, knapsack problems with different numbers of knapsacks and objectives are chosen because they are widely used NP-hard problems.

4.2   Quality Indicators

To evaluate the quality of the solutions [27] in our algorithm, we have decided to use a group of quality indicators that are representative [13]. The first of them is the *overall non-dominated vector generation*, which is defined as the cardinal of the elements found in the objective set, after discarding the dominated vectors,

$$\text{ONVG}(N) = |N|. \tag{3}$$

The *hypervolume* indicator is the quality measure with the highest discriminatory power among the known unary quality measures [19,26,27]. There are many software packages that calculate the hypervolume of a set, given a reference point, as in the works of Fonseca et al. [12] and While et al. [22]. Given a set of k points in the objective space, $N = \{z^1, z^2, \ldots, z^k\}$, the *hypervolume* HV is the measure of the region which is simultaneously dominated by N and bounded by a reference point $r \in \mathbb{R}^p$. It can be expressed by

$$\text{HV}(N, r) = volume\left(\bigcup_{j=1}^{k} [z^j, r]\right). \tag{4}$$

The reference point can be taken as $r_i = \max_{j=1,\ldots,k} z_i^j \; \forall i = 1, \ldots, p$. This is a good choice when we have no information about the complete Pareto front. In some cases, a positive value for each component of the reference point is added [16], in order to take into account the extreme solutions.

The *generational distance* [16] is frequently used in multiobjective evolutionary algorithms and it is defined as

---

[3] Available in https://sop.tik.ee.ethz.ch/download/supplementary/testProblemSuite/.

$$GD(N, P) = \frac{\left(\sum_{i=1}^{|N|} d_i^2\right)^{1/2}}{|N|},$$ (5)

where P is the reference set and d_i is the smallest Euclidean distance from a vector in N to the closest vector in P. The reference set we use depends on the instance. In those instances in which we have the complete Pareto front, we use the Pareto front as reference set and the metrics are more precise. For the remaining instances, the reference set consists of the union of all the outputs of the independent runs of the algorithms plus the union of the outputs of each algorithm after 40 min of computation. These unions are filtered in order to have only non-dominated points.

The *inverted generational distance* has a similar formulation to GD, but in this case we take the smallest distance for every element in P to the closest solution in N,

$$IGD(N, P) = GD(P, N).$$ (6)

The *additive epsilon indicator* gives the minimum additive factor by which the approximation set has to be translated in the objective space in order to weakly dominate the reference set [17,27]. We have scaled each objective to obtain a value in the range [0,1]. This additive epsilon indicator is defined as

$$\varepsilon_+(N, P) = \max_{x \in P} \min_{y \in N} \max_{i=1,\dots,p} \left(\frac{y_i - x_i}{r_i}\right),$$ (7)

where r_i is the range of objective i in N.

Note that all the metrics used in this paper are Pareto compliant [24].

4.3 Parameters of the Algorithms

Before the execution of the algorithms we use the *iterated racing for automatic algorithm configuration* (IRACE) [20] to tune and obtain the best parameter values for each algorithm. For MOFeLS algorithm, the *TILIM* parameter varies in the set {0.0001, 0.001, 0.01, 0.1, 0.2, 0.4, 0.6, 0.8, 1}. IRACE chose the value 0.4. For the other three metaheuristics we let IRACE to decide the best configuration between the following ranges: the number of cut points in the crossover varies from 1 to 5; the crossover probability is free in the set [0, 1]; the mutation probability is in [0, 0.5]; and the population size varies from 10 to 1000 with a step of 10. For the constrained MOEA/D algorithm [1], we also set the probability of selecting the solution in the neighborhood (solutions with close weights) or in the whole population, in the range [0, 1], and the neighborhood size varies from 2 to 20. The final configuration computed by IRACE in the three metaheuristics is shown in Table 1.

The ILP solver used in MOFeLS is CPLEX 12.6.2. We changed three CPLEX parameters. The first one, CPX_PARAM_MIPEMPHASIS, controls trade-offs between speed, feasibility, optimality, and moving bounds. Setting the value to 1, we

Table 1. Configuration of the parameters of NSGA-II, SPEA2 and MOEA/D using IRACE.

Algorithm	Number of crossover cuts	Crossover probability	Mutation probability	Population size	Neighborhood probability	Neighborhood size
NSGA-II	5	0.77	0.0009	310	–	–
SPEA2	4	0.70	0.0017	430	–	–
MOEA/D	2	0.86	0.0036	760	0.86	15

emphasize feasibility over optimality. This is done because we only use the solver to obtain a feasible solution. CPX_PARAM_INTSOLLIM sets the number of integer solutions to be found before stopping. We set this parameter to 1 (we only need one feasible solution). Finally, CPX_PARAM_TILIM sets the maximum time, in seconds, for a call to the optimizer (denoted as *TILIM* in the paper). This parameter was tuned with IRACE, as mentioned above, and it is set to 0.4.

4.4   Numerical Results

For the 28 instances considered, we execute 30 times each algorithm, using a cluster with ten machines Intel Core 2 Quad (Q9400) CPU at 2.7 GHz, a total of 4 cores each, 11 GB of memory and Ubuntu 16.04 LTS. For each run we used only 1 core, 2 GB of RAM and 30 s of computation, and reported the average values for the quality indicators. In the groups AP and KP we have also considered average values among the ten instances of each group. MOFeLS[4] is programmed using C++. For NSGA-II, SPEA2 and the constrained MOEA/D, we used the jMetal 5.8 implementation[5] (see jMetal package in [10]), conveniently modified to use a time limit as stopping condition.

When executing the three metaheuristics, only solutions which do not violate any constraint were considered, and an ulterior filtering of the points were made, avoiding repetition or domination between them. This is done off-line. We ran an exact algorithm during one week and we divided the instances into two groups: those for which we obtained the complete Pareto front using the exact algorithm and the remaining ones. In Sect. 4.2 we explained how the reference set was computed in each case. In Tables 2 and 3 we show the numerical results for these two groups of instances, respectively.

We can observe in the numerical results of Table 2 that none of the three classic metaheuristics is able to find any solution for AP. This is because those algorithms use random bit-flip mutation, and if one bit is changed, the constraints can be violated with high probability. One of the main advantage of MOFeLS is that it works well with equality constraints because the ILP solver provides a feasible solution. When the local search is not able to find an improving move due to the equality constraints, the feasible solution provided by the

---

[4] https://github.com/MiguelAngelDominguezRios/MOFeLS.
[5] https://github.com/jMetal/jMetal.

Table 2. Computational results for instances with known Pareto front. Best results are marked in bold. Undefined values are marked with hyphen.

		MOFeLS	NSGA-II	SPEA2	MOEA/D
ONVG	AP	**98.85**	0.00	0.00	0.00
	KP	**628.62**	97.40	119.46	122.41
	MKP3_100	**225.70**	40.03	42.27	94.03
HV	AP	**9.90E+07**	0.00E+00	0.00E+00	0.00E+00
	KP	**4.56E+14**	3.70E+14	3.72E+14	4.38E+14
	MKP3_100	**9.41E+11**	6.04E+11	6.52E+11	**9.41E+11**
IGD	AP	**0.54**	–	–	–
	KP	**6.57**	27.83	27.169	15.88
	MKP3_100	13.36	44.60	38.57	**12.18**
GD	AP	**1.94**	–	–	–
	KP	**0.78**	16.17	11.55	5.91
	MKP3_100	**8.55**	51.27	62.65	28.76
ε_+	AP	**0.11**	–	–	–
	KP	**0.11**	0.49	0.49	0.27
	MKP3_100	**0.22**	0.58	0.56	0.31

ILP solver is used as the final solution. For the rest of instances in the table, we observe that MOFeLS finds the best values for all the instances except in one case for IGD. Note that a lower average value in GD is preferable, meaning that the approximated front is closer to the Pareto front.

For the other group of instances, we do not have the complete Pareto fronts, and we execute during 40 min each algorithm and take as a reference set the union of these sets plus the union of the corresponding executions at 30 s. This is done for each instance. Analyzing Table 3, we see that MOFeLS has the best average number of solutions with a great difference with respect to the others. In this case, the value of the metric is just an approximation because we do not know the Pareto front. We see that MOFeLS has also the best value for HV, IGD and GD in all the cases. For the ε_+ metric, there is no clear winner and we need to do the corresponding hypothesis tests to support any conclusion. The number of solutions in MOEA/D is lower than in MOFeLS. This means that fewer solutions are closer to the reference Pareto set and this facilitates a lower value for ε_+ indicator.

To justify the well-spread of the solutions given by MOFeLS, we first define the percentage of the total hypervolume reached,

$$\text{HVR}(N, r) = \frac{\text{HV}(N, r)}{\text{HV}(PF, r)}. \tag{8}$$

We show in Table 4 the average values of HVR and IGD for every instance for which we know the Pareto front. Thus, a value close to 1 in HVR indicates a

Table 3. Computational results for instances with unknown Pareto front. Best results are marked in bold.

		MOFeLS	NSGA-II	SPEA2	MOEA/D
ONVG	MKP3_250	**438.63**	43.60	48.20	160.47
	MKP3_500	**430.33**	59.97	49.00	194.87
	MKP3_750	**283.87**	47.87	40.27	165.67
	MKP4_100	**393.03**	91.10	107.83	168.77
	MKP4_250	**546.03**	93.63	100.33	267.80
	MKP4_500	**384.50**	91.53	95.50	292.93
	MKP4_750	**307.67**	84.17	82.57	240.77
HV	MKP3_250	**5.25E+12**	2.63E+11	4.42E+11	3.79E+12
	MKP3_500	**6.31E+13**	2.02E+12	1.93E+12	1.96E+13
	MKP3_750	**1.89E+14**	4.13E+12	3.98E+12	2.48E+13
	MKP4_100	**8.06E+15**	6.5E+13	2.36E+14	2.55E+15
	MKP4_250	**2.32E+17**	1.77E+15	3.35E+15	4.12E+16
	MKP4_500	**5.57E+18**	2.08E+16	3.06E+16	3.18E+17
	MKP4_750	**1.69E+19**	4.88E+16	6.62E+16	3.56E+17
IGD	MKP3_250	**32.65**	86.43	84.88	43.47
	MKP3_500	**51.91**	132.16	176.40	110.91
	MKP3_750	**75.17**	255.64	354.76	268.28
	MKP4_100	**17.26**	39.69	32.97	19.20
	MKP4_250	**31.00**	69.93	73.86	48.40
	MKP4_500	**53.25**	129.94	175.09	126.95
	MKP4_750	**71.05**	254.02	356.08	266.17
GD	MKP3_250	**8.56**	519.09	615.60	138.02
	MKP3_500	**40.18**	1487.41	2369.15	732.73
	MKP3_750	**106.41**	3592.33	5588.16	1985.89
	MKP4_100	**31.22**	49.77	72.07	47.02
	MKP4_250	**60.16**	337.82	478.08	183.39
	MKP4_500	**280.19**	1409.77	2112.19	897.70
	MKP4_750	**396.11**	3167.34	4561.25	2008.69
ε_+	MKP3_250	0.26	0.41	0.35	**0.20**
	MKP3_500	0.19	0.33	0.27	**0.18**
	MKP3_750	0.23	0.36	0.27	**0.22**
	MKP4_100	**0.15**	0.47	0.42	0.24
	MKP4_250	**0.12**	0.44	0.40	0.30
	MKP4_500	**0.14**	0.42	0.35	0.32
	MKP4_750	**0.10**	0.33	0.24	0.24

good spread over the objective space. On the other hand, IGD measures the average distances between points in the Pareto front to the closest points in N. The more close is this value to 0, the more well-spread is the approximated Pareto front.

Table 4. Average values for HVR and IGD using MOFeLS for each instance with known Pareto front.

	HVR	IGD		HVR	IGD
AP1	0.8511	0.53	*KP1*	0.9953	9.37
AP2	0.8549	0.56	*KP2*	0.9785	6.06
AP3	0.8562	0.57	*KP3*	0.9999	4.56
AP4	0.8494	0.55	*KP4*	0.9957	8.28
AP5	0.8666	0.53	*KP5*	0.9867	7.21
AP6	0.8620	0.56	*KP6*	0.9908	6.98
AP7	0.8635	0.56	*KP7*	0.9947	6.64
AP8	0.8533	0.47	*KP8*	0.9994	5.30
AP9	0.8636	0.51	*KP9*	0.9819	6.77
AP10	0.8770	0.52	*KP10*	0.9999	4.52
MKP3_100	0.9041	13.36			

To finish our computational experiments, we do the appropriate hypothesis tests to support the conclusions. For each metric, algorithm and instance we compute the average values given by the 30 runs of the algorithm. Then, for each metric and algorithm we use the 28 samples (average of runs for each instance) as an input for the non-parametric Wilcoxon signed rank test. We compare MOFeLS with the other three using significance level $\alpha = 0.01$. All the p-values are below 10^{-5}, leading us to the conclusion that MOFeLS is the best overall algorithm for all the metrics. We also conclude, based on the results of the HVR and IGD indicators, that MOFeLS finds a well-spread set of solutions over the objective space.

5   Conclusions and Future Work

We present a hybrid algorithm able to solve binary linear constrained multiobjective problems, with good spread of the solutions over the objective space. The algorithm is able to deal with equality constraints, which is a handicap using other metaheuristics. MOFeLS provides the best approximated Pareto fronts in terms of number of solutions, hypervolume, generational distance and inverted generational distance in all the cases. For the metric ε_+, the best results are obtained by our proposed algorithm and MOEA/D. We think these preliminary results encourage the investigation of other hybrids combining exact methods and metaheuristics. In the future, it would be interesting to compare this algorithm with other matheuristics existing in the literature using additional benchmark problems. We also plan to extend the research and consider higher order objective and constraint functions (not only linear), using the advances in graybox optimization for constrained multiobjective problems [7]. We also want to analyze the behaviour of the algorithms as time progresses.

References

1. Asafuddoula, M., Ray, T., Sarker, R., Alam, K.: An adaptive constraint handling approach embedded MOEA/D. In: 2012 IEEE Congress on Evolutionary Computation, pp. 1–8. IEEE (2012)
2. Ball, M.O.: Heuristics based on mathematical programming. Surv. Oper. Res. Manage. Sci. **16**(1), 21–38 (2011)
3. Blum, C., Pereira, J.: Extension of the CMSA algorithm: an LP-based way for reducing sub-instances. In: Proceedings of the Genetic and Evolutionary Computation Conference, pp. 285–292 (2016)
4. Blum, C., Pinacho, P., López-Ibáñez, M., Lozano, J.A.: Construct, merge, solve and adapt a new general algorithm for combinatorial optimization. Comput. Oper. Res. **68**, 75–88 (2016)
5. Boschetti, M.A., Maniezzo, V., Roffilli, M., Bolufé Röhler, A.: Matheuristics: optimization, simulation and control. In: Blesa, M.J., Blum, C., Di Gaspero, L., Roli, A., Sampels, M., Schaerf, A. (eds.) HM 2009. LNCS, vol. 5818, pp. 171–177. Springer, Heidelberg (2009). https://doi.org/10.1007/978-3-642-04918-7_13
6. Chalmet, L., Lemonidis, L., Elzinga, D.: An algorithm for the bi-criterion integer programming problem. Eur. J. Oper. Res. **25**(2), 292–300 (1986). https://doi.org/10.1016/0377-2217(86)90093-7
7. Chicano, F., Whitley, D., Tinos, R.: Efficient hill climber for constrained pseudo-boolean optimization problems. In: Proceedings of the Genetic and Evolutionary Computation Conference, pp. 309–316 (2016)
8. Dächert, K., Klamroth, K.: A linear bound on the number of scalarizations needed to solve discrete tricriteria optimization problems. J. Global Optim. **61**(4), 643–676 (2014). https://doi.org/10.1007/s10898-014-0205-z
9. Deb, K., Agrawal, S., Pratap, A., Meyarivan, T.: A fast elitist non-dominated sorting genetic algorithm for multi-objective optimization: NSGA-II. In: Schoenauer, M., et al. (eds.) PPSN 2000. LNCS, vol. 1917, pp. 849–858. Springer, Heidelberg (2000). https://doi.org/10.1007/3-540-45356-3_83
10. Durillo, J.J., Nebro, A.J.: jMetal: a java framework for multi-objective optimization. Adv. Eng. Softw. **42**(10), 760–771 (2011)
11. Ehrgott, M., Tenfelde-Podehl, D.: Computation of ideal and nadir values and implications for their use in MCDM methods. Eur. J. Oper. Res. **151**(1), 119–139 (2003). https://doi.org/10.1016/S0377-2217(02)00595-7
12. Fonseca, C.M., Paquete, L., López-Ibáñez, M.: An improved dimension-sweep algorithm for the hypervolume indicator. In: Proceedings of the IEEE Congress on Evolutionary Computation, 2006. CEC 2006, pp. 1157–1163. IEEE (2006). https://doi.org/10.1109/CEC.2006.1688440
13. Jiang, S., Ong, Y.S., Zhang, J., Feng, L.: Consistencies and contradictions of performance metrics in multiobjective optimization. IEEE Trans. Cybern. **44**(12), 2391–2404 (2014). https://doi.org/10.1109/TCYB.2014.2307319

14. Kirlik, G., Sayın, S.: A new algorithm for generating all nondominated solutions of multiobjective discrete optimization problems. Eur. J. Oper. Res. **232**(3), 479–488 (2014). https://doi.org/10.1016/j.ejor.2013.08.001
15. Klamroth, K., Lacour, R., Vanderpooten, D.: On the representation of the search region in multi-objective optimization. Eur. J. Oper. Res. **245**(3), 767–778 (2015). https://doi.org/10.1016/j.ejor.2015.03.031
16. Li, M., Yao, X.: Quality evaluation of solution sets in multiobjective optimisation: a survey. ACM Comput. Surv. **52**(2), 1–38 (2019)
17. Liefooghe, A., Derbel, B.: A correlation analysis of set quality indicator values in multiobjective optimization. In: Proceedings of the Genetic and Evolutionary Computation Conference 2016, pp. 581–588 (2016)
18. Liu, Q., Li, X., Liu, H., Guo, Z.: Multi-objective metaheuristics for discrete optimization problems: a review of the state-of-the-art. Appl. Soft Comput. **93**, 106382 (2020). https://doi.org/10.1016/j.asoc.2020.106382
19. López-Ibáñez, M., Stützle, T.: Automatically improving the anytime behaviour of optimisation algorithms. Eur. J. Oper. Res. **235**(3), 569–582 (2014). https://doi.org/10.1016/j.ejor.2013.10.043
20. López-Ibáñez, M., Dubois-Lacoste, J., Cáceres, L.P., Birattari, M., Stützle, T.: The irace package: iterated racing for automatic algorithm configuration. Oper. Res. Perspect. **3**, 43–58 (2016)
21. Mezura-Montes, E., Coello Coello, C.A.: Constraint-handling in nature-inspired numerical optimization: past, present and future. Swarm Evol. Comput. **1**(4), 173–194 (2011). https://doi.org/10.1016/j.swevo.2011.10.001
22. While, L., Bradstreet, L., Barone, L.: A fast way of calculating exact hypervolumes. IEEE Trans. Evol. Comput. **16**(1), 86–95 (2012). https://doi.org/10.1109/TEVC.2010.2077298
23. Zhang, Q., Li, H.: MOEA/D: a multiobjective evolutionary algorithm based on decomposition. IEEE Trans. Evol. Comput. **11**(6), 712–731 (2007)
24. Zitzler, E., Brockhoff, D., Thiele, L.: The hypervolume indicator revisited: on the design of pareto-compliant indicators via weighted integration. In: Obayashi, S., Deb, K., Poloni, C., Hiroyasu, T., Murata, T. (eds.) EMO 2007. LNCS, vol. 4403, pp. 862–876. Springer, Heidelberg (2007). https://doi.org/10.1007/978-3-540-70928-2_64
25. Zitzler, E., Laumanns, M., Thiele, L.: SPEA2: improving the strength pareto evolutionary algorithm. TIK-report **103** (2001). https://doi.org/10.3929/ethz-a-004284029
26. Zitzler, E., Thiele, L.: Multiobjective optimization using evolutionary algorithms-a comparative case study. In: International Conference on Parallel Problem Solving from Nature, pp. 292–301. Springer (1998). https://doi.org/10.1007/BFb0056872
27. Zitzler, E., Thiele, L., Laumanns, M., Fonseca, C.M., Da Fonseca, V.G.: Performance assessment of multiobjective optimizers: an analysis and review. IEEE Trans. Evol. Comput. **7**(2), 117–132 (2003). https://doi.org/10.1109/TEVC.2003.810758

Automated, Explainable Rule Extraction from MAP-Elites Archives

Neil Urquhart[1]([✉]), Silke Höhl[2], and Emma Hart[1]

[1] School of Computing, Edinburgh Napier University, Edinburgh, UK
{n.urquhart,e.hart}@napier.ac.uk
[2] Frankfurt University of Applied Sciences, Frankfurt, Germany
s.hoehl@vgf-ffm.de

Abstract. Quality-diversity (QD) algorithms that return a large archive of elite solutions to a problem provide insights into how high-performing solutions are distributed throughout a feature-space defined by a user. They are often described as *illuminating* the feature-space, providing a qualitative illustration of relationships between features and objective quality. However, if there are 1000s of solutions in an archive, extracting a succinct set of rules that capture these relationships in a quantitative manner (i.e. as a set of rules) is challenging. We propose two methods for the automated generation of rules from data contained in an archive; the first uses Genetic Programming and the second, a rule-induction method known as CN2. Rules are generated from large archives of data produced by running MAP-Elites on an urban logistics problem. A quantitative and qualitative evaluation that includes the end-user demonstrate that the rules are capable of fitting the data, but also highlights some mismatches between the model used by the optimiser and that assumed by the user.

Keywords: Real-world · Logistics · Optimisation

1 Introduction

When solving real-world problems, the role of the automated solver is often to support a domain expert (e.g. a logistics planner) in finding a solution that meets their specific requirements. Typically, the domain expert specifies the problem instance and "owns" the final solution. It is often beneficial if the domain expert has a choice of solutions to choose from: this allows the expert to use their judgement when comparing solution characteristics and trade-offs. Quality-Diversity (QD) algorithms [13]—methods that generate an archive of high-performing but diverse solutions in a user-defined feature space—support the expert user when making these decisions by providing a large range of solutions.

However, often the size of the archives returned by QD methods can be daunting to a user, containing hundreds or even thousands of solutions. We suggest it would therefore be beneficial to be able to summarise the archive via a succinct set of policies (derived from the solutions contained within the

© Springer Nature Switzerland AG 2021
P. A. Castillo and J. L. Jiménez Laredo (Eds.): EvoApplications 2021, LNCS 12694, pp. 258–272, 2021.
https://doi.org/10.1007/978-3-030-72699-7_17

archive), which capture relationships between the problem characteristics and decision variables of interest. The derived policies should be congruent with beliefs and expert domain-knowledge of the user, thus increasing their trust in the algorithm outputs. In situations where the policies do not align with the user beliefs, then they should provide a rationale explanation to the user.

In this paper we investigate methods for automatically generating policies to explain and summarise the data generated by running a QD algorithm (MAP-Elites) on an optimisation problem in the multi-objective urban logistics domain [18]. A typical run of the technique generates 1000 s of high-quality solutions which are diverse in multiple dimensions defined by the user. In the domain considered, we deal with 9 dimensions that include for example, the emissions associated with a solution, the time taken to route and the overall cost. Based on data generated by MapElites in this domain, we compare two popular rule-generation methods (Genetic Programming [2] and CN2 [3]) inorder to answer the following research questions:

1. *Which method produces the most accurate policies in terms of describing the data?*
2. *Which method produces the least complex policies and how does this complexity relate to accuracy?*
3. *From a qualitative perspective, do the policies match user beliefs or highlight mismatches between the users' model and the implemented model?*

A domain expert is consulted in order to answer the final qualitative question.

The remainder of this paper is organised as follows, Sect. 2 provides a review of relevant previous work in order to place this work into context. The urban logistics problem and the MAP-Elites algorithm applied to it is described in Sect. 3. The two methodologies for rule extraction (CN2 and GP) are discussed in Sect. 4. The results obtained (both quantitative and qualitative) are presented in Sect. 5 and finally, Sect. 6 provides our responses to the research questions.

2   Previous Work

The Multi-dimensional Archive of Phenotypic Elites (MAP-Elites) was first introduced by Mouret *et al.* [13] and provides a mechanism for illuminating search spaces by evolving an archive of high-performing solutions mapped onto solution characteristics defined by the user. The algorithm aims to fill a multi-dimensional space defined by the features of interest and discretised into cells with the best performing solution for each cell. To date, the majority of applications of illumination algorithms have been to *design* problems [13,19] or within Evolutionary Robotics [5].

However, more recently they have been deployed in combinatorial optimisation [17] and constrained-optimisation [8]. With respect to the former, in our own previous work we have shown that MAP-Elites can be used to generate diverse solutions to a multi-objective urban logistics problem [18].

Despite the success of MAP-Elites, few of the reported applications consider the question of guiding the user towards selecting an appropriate solution from the large numbers of solutions generated, and to the best of our knowledge, none of them address the question of how to summarise or explain the data generated. An exception to the former point is recent work from [10] who develop an interactive version of MAP-Elites in which a user guides the search towards areas of interest, while an automated search procedure based on Bayesian optimisation is used by [5] to select an appropriate behaviour for a given situation in a robot application.

Generating rules from data can be tackled in multiple ways. Genetic programming (GP) has been frequently used to generate classifiers [7] and hence is selected for use. Tokinaga *et al.* [16] used GP to extract rules from a neural network to provide explanatory classifications of data. Other work used GP to generate a set of comprehensible decision rules to identify cases of bankruptcy [9]. We compare GP to a well known rule-induction algorithm CN2 [3,4] as a baseline. CN2 is designed to find a set of rules that cover the most examples in a training set with the correct classification and is known to work well even with noisy data: it has found uses in domains ranging from bio-diversity [15] to traffic accident analysis [12]. The algorithm uses entropy as a fitness measure to find a set of *IF...THEN...* rules that classify examples. This contrasts to the stochastic nature of the recombination and mutation operators used to construct rules by GP.

3 Problem Domain

3.1 The Micro Depot Routing Problem

The Micro Depot Routing Problem (MDRP) was previously described in [18] and concerns the optimal deployment of couriers for city-centre deliveries. Traditional courier deliveries have been made using vans, but this contributes to pollution and congestion. These impacts may be reduced by making deliveries using walking couriers, cycle couriers and electric vehicle couriers within city centers. As such couriers have a small capacity and limited range they are operated from micro depots (MDs). MDs are located near the city centre, but in locations which may be serviced by larger vehicles. Deliveries can be stored in depots prior to couriers making the final deliveries. We consider problems in which there are a fixed number of pre-identified MD locations: the goal is to find a solution that specifies whether an item should be delivered by a courier (and if so, from what MD, and what type of courier) and which deliveries should still be made by the large vehicle. Solutions to the problem have the following characteristics:

- Emissions: the emissions produced by the travel activities associated withe the solution
- Time: the time between leaving the central depot and the last delivery being made

- Running Cost: costs that can be apportioned to vehicle running costs and wages
- Fixed Cost: Vehicle purchase and other fixed costs
- byMD: the % of deliveries that travel via a micro-depot
- MDs in use: the number of micro-depots in use
- WalkDels: the number of deliveries carried out using walking couriers
- CycleDels: the number of deliveries carried out using cycle couriers
- EvanDels: the number of deliveries carried out using Electric Van couriers

3.2   Data Generation

This article is concerned with generating policies from data produced by running MAP-Elites on a set of micro-depot routing problems. This section describes the process by which the data that underpins the paper was generated. The five problem instances used are based on the city of Frankfurt, Germany and are described in detail in [18]. The underlying street graph is based upon Open StreetMap [11] data and delivery data is based upon information supplied by commercial CEP (Courier and Express Parcels) companies. Solutions are described by a grand-tour representing the route to be taken by the supply vehicle, and which deliveries are to be made by a courier operating from an MD. The representation is fully described in previous work [18].

MAP-Elites is used to generate multiple solutions to the problem with respect to a 9-dimensional feature-space, with each feature discretised into 5 bins, hence creating a potential archive of size 5^9. We use the MAP-Elites implementation written in Python by [13] and described in detail in our previous work [18]. MAP-Elites is run 10 times: the individual archives produced are combined into a single combined archive, retaining the single best solution found per bin. The number of solutions contained within these archives is given in Table 1.

Table 1. The number of solutions in the combined archive for each problem created by merging the archives from each of the 10 runs

Problem instance	Combined archive size
f1	1137
f2	113
f6	1523
f8	573
fCity	514

The 9 dimensional solution space created by MAP-Elites is clearly challenging to visualise. One approach is to use parallel coordinates, for example using the ElVis tool[1], visualised in Fig. 1. Each solution is represented by a polyline that

---

[1] https://commute.napier.ac.uk.

intersects the 9 axis. On each axis the solutions are normalised on a scale of 1–5. Although Fig. 1 only shows a relatively small number of solutions, it is clear that even with few solutions it can be difficult for the user to discern trends between the problem characteristics and therefore a succinct way of summarising the solutions would clearly be beneficial.

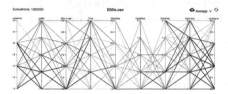

Fig. 1. A sample archive as generated by MAP-Elites, visualised using the ElVis tool. The colour of each polyline represents the overall fitness of that solution, green being the lowest and red the highest. Each axis is centered around the highest and lowest values found for that feature. (Color figure online)

4   Methods for Extracting Policies

From the perspective of an expert user (e.g. a logistics planner), four of the nine features can be considered as *outcome* variables, i.e. the user would like to know which of the other features lead to the outcome variable being classified as high or low. These four outcome variables are Emissions, Time , Running Cost and Fixed Cost: a value of low is preferred for each. A *policy*, in this context, describes a rule that links a desired outcome (e.g. low emissions) to a set of the remaining solution attributes (listed in Table 2). For example, in plain English a policy might be *"To achieve low costs, make maximum use of walking couriers and make minimal use of electric vans"*. This policy could be expressed as an *IF..THEN...* rule by CN2 (where 1 indicates low cost and 0 would indicate high cost) as shown below:

IF walkCouriers > 4 AND eVans <= 1 THEN costs =1

Alternatively, it can be expressed as a GP tree:

The goal is therefore to find a small set of policies that summarise the data, and reflect the assumptions in the underlying model. The processes used in extracting the policies as described in this section and the results as described in Sect. 5 are implemented within a Jupyter notebook which can be downloaded along with the associated Java files for FlexGP and the checker program[2].

Table 2. The solution properties of the micro depot problem

Outcome variable (Binary low/high)	Attribute (1–5)
Eissions	byMD
Time	MDsInUse
Running cost	WalkDels
Fixed cost	CycleDels
	EVanDels

4.1 Datasets

As previously described, our interest is in finding policies that are indicators of low values of emissions, time, fixed costs and running costs. The values of the other attributes can be directly inferred from the genotype. In order to find policies for each of these outcome variables we create 4 datasets (see Table 3), one for each of the outcome variables. Each data set is created by combining the outcome variable (emissions,time,fixedCost or runningCost) and the five attributes (see Table 2). As MAP-Elites algorithm has 5 bins per attribute, each of these attributes has a value in the range 1–5, indicating the bin in which it falls. The outcome variables are represented as a binary value: a solution lying in bin '1' is assigned as *"low"* while solutions lying in bins 2–5 are interpreted as *"high"*.

The outputs from Map-Elites for all problem instances are combined into each of the 4 new datasets, so that each of the 4 data sets covers all of the problem instances (see Table 3) and is concerned with a single outcome variable. The resulting data sets are unbalanced with an unequal number of low and high values of the outcome variable. We balance the data by employing *random under-sampling* which removes a random selection of examples from the majority class leaving a balanced dataset in each case.

4.2 Extraction Methodologies

We use two contrasting techniques to extract policies, CN2 and Genetic Programming. In both cases we treat the entire dataset as the training data. It is important to note that we do not need to apply the generated rules to *unseen* instances: the goal is simply to describe the existing data. Hence we use all the data as training data to generate rules and report results on the full dataset.

---

[2] https://github.com/NeilUrquhart/MAP-Elites.

Table 3. The sizes of the data sets before and after balancing.

Problem	Unbalanced (low/high)	Balanced
Emissions	1609/2251	3219
Time	535/3325	1070
Fixedcost	166/3694	332
Runningcost	35/3825	70

CN2. The CN2 rule induction algorithm [3,4] is designed to construct simple rules in the *IF <condition> THEN <classify>* format, which can then be used as the basis for policies. The CN2 algorithm is applied to each of the 4 data sets to find policies of the *IF...THEN...* format that will attempt to predict the outcome variable, as either low (1) or not low (greater then 1). Each of these rules will *cover* a number of rows within the training data. A row is *covered* by a rule if the rule can be evaluated against the values within the row and the rule output of the rule aligns with the decision variable with the row. The CN2 algorithm as a *minimum coverage* parameter, any rule that does not cover at least the specified number of rows is disregarded, which reduces the overall number of rules found. In this paper we use the CN2 algorithm as implemented within the Orange [6] data analysis framework.

Genetic Programming. Genetic Programming (GP) refers to the evolution of programs or expressions, commonly using a tree representation. As noted in Sect. 2, the use of GP to evolve classifier trees is very common. Many platforms provide implementations: here we utilise the RuleTree learner provided as part of the FlexGP Platform [1][3].

The FlexGP learner uses a two stage approach

- **Stage 1** A set of conditions are constructed which divides the attributes within the problem domain into intervals. These form conditions which are ultimately used as terminals on the evolved trees. For example, a condition used by FlexGP which specifies that attribute $X4$ must be between 1.0 and 2.3 is $\{X4\ in\ [\ 1.0\ ;\ 2.3\ ]\}$
- **Stage 2** Genetic Programming is used to evolve a Pareto front of tree based expressions, using *accuracy* and *Subtree Complexity* (as defined in [2]) as the two objectives.

The GP expressions make use of AND, OR and NOT operators which are applied to conditions defined in stage 1. An example of an expression produced by FlexGP is shown below, where $C9$ etc. are expressions created during stage 1:

(and (or (and C9 C3) C11) C2)

Substituting the full expressions gives :

---

[3] http://flexgp.github.io/gp-learners/ruletree.html.

$((((2.3 <= X4 <= 5.99$ and $1.0 <= X2 <= 1.68)$ or $2.35 <= X5 <= 5.99)$ and $3.75 <= X1 <= 5.99)$

We run flexGP for a limit of 5 min. All other parameters are as defined in [1].

4.3 Evaluating the Policies

We undertake quantitative and qualitative evaluations of the policies discovered. In order to ensure a simple and fair comparison, we construct an independent checker that enables the two methods to be compared via the same metrics. The checker takes policies in either format (CN2 or GP): for the subset of solutions covered by a rule, it returns the number of solutions in the subset for which the outcome is correctly predicted (True Positives) and number of solutions for which the outcome is incorrect (False Positives) (see Table 3). The checker calculates the precision of each rule as shown in Eq. 1.

$$precision = \frac{TruePositive}{TruePositive + FalsePositive} \tag{1}$$

A high-level of precision (which denotes the fraction of positive identifications that were actually correct) may instill user-confidence in the rule. In addition, we define *coverage* of a rule as the number of rows of data to which the condition part of a rule can be applied, i.e.

$$coverage = TruePositive + FalsePositive \tag{2}$$

The checker was written in Java and the source code made be downloaded along with the Jupyter Notebook files and data.

5 Results

Table 4 shows the best policies derived using both methods of generation, ordered by precision (as described above). The three highest scoring policies from each method are shown. It will be noticed that the GP derived policies have a consistently higher precision than their CN2 counterparts.

5.1 Policies Produced Using CN2

The policies produced using CN2, mostly have lower precision than those produced using GP. The policies are discussed below with respect to each outcome variable.

Emissions. If we examine the three emissions policies produced by CN2, we note that they all propose that large amounts of deliveries should be made via a Micro Depot (byMD $>= 4$). Policy E2 suggests that emissions are reduced with the maximal use of eVan based couriers.

Time. The three policies for time all promote the use of eVan couriers. What is significant is that none of the policies mention walking couriers—this is not surprising as they are slowest form of delivery and have the least capacity.

Running Cost. Discovering policies that capture the factors that reduce running costs was the biggest challenge of this work. In the case of CN2, only 2 policies were returned. The two policies returned have very low precision, combined with low overall coverage, suggesting that they are not of significant value.

Fixed Cost. A factor common across all three policies for lower fixed costs is byMD (% of deliveries that go via a micro-depot), suggesting that more limited use of micro-depots will lower fixed costs. Of the three policies only F2 suggests that limited use of electric vans will lower fixed costs, despite electric vans having a higher fixed cost than any other form of courier.

5.2   Policies Produced Using GP

The policies produced using GP have far higher precision and TruePositive scores than those produced by CN2.

Emissions. Of the three emissions policies produced, they exhibit the following common factors:

- CycleDels: in the range [2.3 – 6.0]
- eVanDels: in the range [2.35 – 6]

Both of the above encourage the use of cycle and electric van based couriers, which are both low emission means of deliveries. Only two of the policies mention the number of micro depots to be used suggesting that the number of micro-depots used has less influence on emissions.

Time. Three common factors run through the Time rules (T4–T6):

- WalkDels in [1.0 – 1.32]
- EVanDels in [2.5 – 6.0]
- MDSinUse in [1.64 – 4.96]

The policies suggest that time can be reduced by minimising the use of walking couriers (they are the slowest form of courier and have the lowest capacity) and encouraging the use of electric vans which are quicker than walking or cycling.

Running Cost. The running cost policies exhibit consistently high precision scores (0.78, 0.76, 0.75) but all three of the rules have a low coverage. Common factors across all three policies are:

- Low use of each courier mode is suggested
- byMD in the range [1.0 – 3.65]): i.e. between 0 and half of deliveries made via a micro depot
- MDSinUse in [1.0 – 1.04] (policies R3 and R5): i.e. use very few micro depots

These policies suggest that to minimise running costs very selective use of micro depots should be made. These policies should be viewed in the context that no policies were found that reduced running costs to 1: the only policies that could be found reduced them to 2. The overall conclusion to be drawn from this is that the use of micro depots does not lend itself to a reduction in running costs.

Fixed Cost. A consistently high precision (1) suggest that we can place a high degree of confidence in these policies, but the low coverage of these polices should be noted. Common factors across all three policies include:

- EVanDels in [1.0 – 1.05] in F5 and F6 suggests reducing the use of electric vehicles will reduce the fixed cost of the solution.
- MDSinUse in [1.0 – 1.32], byMD in [1.0 – 3.5] suggests that lower numbers of MDs to be used and no more than approximately half of the deliveries to be made via MDs

The policies show that the fixed costs are reduced through selective use of MDs and minimal use of electric vehicles.

5.3 Matching the Expectations of the Domain Expert

In order to provide a qualitative evaluation of the policies found, the authors had a domain expert state their expectations and beliefs with regards to the 4 objectives. The expectations reflect the measures that the expert would associate with reducing these objectives. Table 5 shows the expectations and how they are satisfied (or not) by the policies.

This qualitative evaluation raises a number issues of interest. Firstly the domain expert may well have a more detailed mental model of the domain than is represented in the software model. Expectation Emissions 3 is a case in point; the expert has an expectation that use of electric vehicle couriers must be reduced when reducing emissions, owing to the environmental impact of battery production. This knowledge of the impact of battery production is not included in the model and so this expectation will never be explicitly addressed (it might be satisfied, but that will be due to the solver optimising against other criterion). Some expectations such as Emissons 1, Fixed Cost 1 Time 1, Running cost 1 and Running cost 2 are satisfied by a range of policies. Where a rule satisfies multiple expectations, the rule tends to be longer and more complex.

A final observation on Table 5 suggests that the first expectation (E1, F1, T1 and R1) is more likely to be covered by the policies. The expectations are numbered in the order they were supplied by the expert: it may be that there is a form of precedence within the observations in that the earlier observations (e.g. R1) are more "obvious" than the later observations (e.g. R3).

6 Conclusions and Future Work

Based on the results described above, we provide answers to the questions posed in Sect. 1:

Which Method Produces Most Accurate Policies in Terms of Describing the Data? It is clear from Table 4 that the GP derived policies exhibit a far greater coverage and precision. This suggests that he GP derived policies are more representative of the relations that are implicit with the model that is being optimised.

Which Method Produces the Least Complex Policies and How Does This Complexity Relate to Accuracy? The styles of policies produced by FlexGP and the CN2 algorithm differ fundamentally. The policies produced by CN2 are of the *IF...THEN..* format, while FlexGP produces LISP like expressions (which can of course be converted into a tree format which may be easier for a user to interpret). A common measure of complexity of rules is their compactness, i.e. the number of nodes and leaves. If we consider the FlexGP derived policies and examine scores in relation to operators used, we note that higher scores are obtained by those policies that contain the most operators. We conclude, that in this study at least, the more complex FlexGP policies are the most accurate but this comes with the cost of greater complexity.

From a Qualitative Perspective, Do the Policies Match User Beliefs and Can They Highlight Mismatches Between the Users' Model and the Implemented Model? Table 5 shows that the initial expectations (E1, F1, T1 etc.) are covered by most methods. Most differences occur when considering the later expectations (F2, R3 etc.).

6.1 Recommendations and Future Work

In conclusion, the automated extraction of underlying policies from MAP-Elites is a worthwhile activity. QD algorithms in general are attracting a great deal of attention in recent literature due to their ability to generate large numbers of diverse but high-quality solutions. While domains that define grids in a relatively low number of dimensions can be easily and intuitively visualised, problem domains that are characterised by high-dimensions not only return very large numbers of solutions but are very to difficult to visualise. Hence, summarising the information contained within the grid concisely via a set of policies can further add to the appeal of the method.

Furthermore, the derived policies allow the algorithm-designer to determine whether the model captured by the algorithm and/or representation aligns with the requirements of the user. Comparing the extracted policies with the expectations of an expert user can highlight differences between the model assumed

Table 4. The table shows the three rules with highest precision obtained by each of the generation methods, as well as indicating coverage (i.e. true positives + false positives) for each of the four outcome variables

Characteristic	Policy	Policy ID	Source	Precision	True Positives	False Positives
Emissions	IF byMD=4.0 AND MDs in use=3.0 THEN emissions=1	E1	CN2	0.79	48	13
	IF byMD=5.0 AND EvanDels=5.0 THEN emissions=1	E2	CN2	0.76	40	16
	IF byMD>=5.0 AND MDs in use<=2.0 AND MDs in use>=2.0 AND EVanDels<=4.0 AND EvanDels>=4.0 THEN emissions=1	E3	CN2	0.67	269	132
	(and EVanDels in [2.35 - 6.0] (and CycleDels in [2.3 - 6.0] MDSinUse in [1.68 - 5.0]))	E4	GP	**0.80**	16	4
	(and EVanDels in [2.35 - 6.0] CycleDels in [2.3 - 6.0])	E5	GP	0.72	48	19
	(and (or EVanDels in [2.35 - 6.0] WalkDels in [1.64 - 4.24]) and MDSinUse in [1.68 - 5.0] CycleDels in [2.3 - 6.0]))	E6	GP	0.71	52	21
Time	IF EVanDels>=3.0 AND CycleDels>=2.0 AND EvanDels>=4.0 THEN Time=1	T1	CN2	0.64	96	55
	IF byMD=4.0 AND EvanDels=4.0 THEN Time=1	T2	CN2	0.64	96	55
	IF EVanDels>=2.0 AND byMD<=4.0 AND EvanDels>=4.0 THEN Time=1	T3	CN2	0.64	96	55
	(and (and CycleDels in [1.0 - 2.35] WalkDels in [1.0 - 1.32]) (and EVanDels in [2.5 - 6.0] MDSinUse in [1.64 - 4.96]))	T4	GP	**0.74**	65	23
	(and (and byMD in [1.2 - 4.45] MDSinUse in [1.64 - 4.96]) (and WalkDels in [1.0 - 1.32] EVanDels in [2.5 - 6.0]))	T5	GP	0.73	33	12
	(and EVanDels in [2.5 - 6.0] (and MDSinUse in [1.64 - 4.96] WalkDels in [1.0 - 1.32]))	T6	GP	0.72	71	27
Running Cost	IF byMD<=4.0 AND CycleDels<=3.0 AND byMD<=3.0 AND CycleDels<=2.0 THEN running cost=1	R1	CN2	0.55	29	24
	IF CycleDels=2.0 THEN running cost=1	R2	CN2	0.50	18	18
	(and (not (and CycleDels in [1.0 - 2.8] (and byMD in [1.0 - 3.65] EVanDels in [1.0 - 2.6]))) (or byMD in [1.0 - 3.65] (and CycleDels in [1.0 - 2.8] EVanDels in [1.0 - 2.6])) (and WalkDels in [1.0 - 1.32] MDSinUse in [1.0 - 1.04])))	R3	GP	**0.78**	7	2
	(and (or CycleDels in [1.0 - 2.8] EVanDels in [1.0 - 2.6]) byMD in [1.0 - 3.65]) (and (or byMD in [1.0 - 1.32] MDSinUse in [1.0 - 1.04]) (and WalkDels in [1.0 - 3.65] CycleDels in [1.0 - 2.8]))	R4	GP	0.76	28	9
	(and (or byMD in [1.0 - 3.65] CycleDels in [1.0 - 2.8]) (and WalkDels in [1.0 - 1.32] MDSinUse in [1.0 - 1.04]))	R5	GP	0.75	27	9
Fixed Cost	IF WalkDels<=2.0 AND byMD<=4.0 AND CycleDels>=2.0 AND CycleDels>=4.0 THEN fixed cost=1	F1	CN2	0.64	18	10
	IF byMD=3.0 AND EvanDels=2.0 THEN fixed cost=1	F2	CN2	0.59	166	115
	IF byMD<=4.0 AND CycleDels>=2.0 AND MDs in use<=2.0 THEN fixed cost=1	F3	CN2	0.50	166	165
	(and byMD in [1.0 - 3.5] (and CycleDels in [2.9 - 6.0] MDSinUse in [1.0 - 1.32]))	F4	GP	**1.00**	17	0
	(and EVanDels in [1.0 - 1.05] byMD in [1.0 - 3.5] (or (and CycleDels in [2.9 - 6.0] MDSinUse in [1.0 - 1.32]) (and WalkDels in [1.58 - 4.76] MDSinUse in [1.32 - 5.0])))	F5	GP	**1.00**	19	0
	(and EVanDels in [1.0 - 1.05] byMD in [1.0 - 3.5] (and WalkDels in [1.58 - 4.76] MDSinUse in [1.32 - 5.0]))	F6	GP	**1.00**	2	0

Table 5. The expert users' beliefs are divided into 4 categories to align with the outcome variables. Each of the generated policies are evaluated against the user beliefs. The *Satisfies* column notes the beliefs which are captured by the policy (e.g. policy E3 satisfies beliefs 1 and 2.)

	Beliefs	Policy	Satisfies
Emissions	1 low number of trucks delivering MD	E1	1
	2 low number of MD	E2	
	3 low number of EV˜	E3	1,2
	(battery's production causes emissions)	E4	1
		E5	1
		E6	1
Time	1 low number of slowest staff (walking couriers)	T1	2
	2 depending on delivery area low˜ number of EV or cycle couriers˜ (in a dense area a cycle courier is faster)	T2	2
	3 high number of parcel shops˜ (locations where people can pickup˜ their parcels instead of home delivery)	T3	
		T4	1,2
		T5	1
		T6	1
Running Cost	1 low number of MD	R1	1,2
	2 low number of expensive staff	R2	
	3 low number of expensive vehicles,˜ cheap vehicles to lower running costs,˜	R3	1,2,3
		R4	1,2,3
		R5	1,2,3
Fixed Cost	1 low number of MD	F1	
	2 low number of EV	F2	2
	3 low number of cycle couriers	F3	1
		F4	1
		F5	1,2
		F6	1,2

by the expert and the model used within optimisation. This provides an opportunity to update the optimisation model in order to move it closer to the users' expectation. In the case examined here, rules E3 and F3 might be incorporated into an updated model. More generally, the literature is increasingly focused on the question of trust between people and machines and/or algorithms: Ribeiro *et al.* note that this will be improved if the people concerned can understand the decisions that are made [14]. Hence our work takes a step in this direction. Future work should include a more in-depth comparison of rule-generation methods, for example extending the comparison to include ensemble-based classifiers. In addition, GP methods could be adapted to optimise for a weighted combination of precision, coverage and complexity.

References

1. Arnaldo, I., Veeramachaneni, K., Song, A., O'Reilly, U.: Bring your own learner: a cloud-based, data-parallel commons for machine learning. IEEE Comput. Intell. Mag. **10**(1), 20–32 (2015). https://doi.org/10.1109/MCI.2014.2369892
2. Arnaldo, I., Krawiec, K., O'Reilly, U.M.: Multiple regression genetic programming. In: Proceedings of the 2014 Annual Conference on Genetic and Evolutionary Computation, pp. 879–886 (2014)
3. Clark, P., Boswell, R.: Rule induction with CN2: some recent improvements. In: Kodratoff, Y. (ed.) EWSL 1991. LNCS, vol. 482, pp. 151–163. Springer, Heidelberg (1991). https://doi.org/10.1007/BFb0017011
4. Clark, P., Niblett, T.: The CN2 induction algorithm. Mach. Learn. **3**(4), 261–283 (1989)
5. Cully, A., Clune, J., Tarapore, D., Mouret, J.B.: Robots that can adapt like animals. Nature **521**(7553), 503 (2015)
6. Demšar, J., et al.: Orange: data mining toolbox in python. J. Mach. Learn. Res. **14**, 2349–2353 (2013). http://jmlr.org/papers/v14/demsar13a.html
7. Espejo, P.G., Ventura, S., Herrera, F.: A survey on the application of genetic programming to classification. IEEE Trans. Syst. Man Cybern. Part C (Applications and Reviews) **40**(2), 121–144 (2009)
8. Fioravanzo, S., Iacca, G.: Evaluating map-elites on constrained optimization problems. In: Proceedings of the Genetic and Evolutionary Computation Conference Companion, pp. 253–254. ACM (2019)
9. Garcia-Almanza, A.L., Alexandrova-Kabadjova, B., Martinez-Jaramillo, S.: Understanding bank failure: a close examination of rules created by genetic programming. In: 2010 IEEE Electronics, Robotics and Automotive Mechanics Conference, pp. 34–39. IEEE (2010)
10. Hagg, A., Asteroth, A., Bäck, T.: Prototype discovery using quality-diversity. In: Auger, A., Fonseca, C.M., Lourenço, N., Machado, P., Paquete, L., Whitley, D. (eds.) PPSN 2018. LNCS, vol. 11101, pp. 500–511. Springer, Cham (2018). https://doi.org/10.1007/978-3-319-99253-2_40
11. Haklay, M., Weber, P.: Open streetmap: user-generated street maps. IEEE Pervasive Comput. **7**(4), 12–18 (2008). https://doi.org/10.1109/MPRV.2008.80
12. Lavrac, N., Kavsek, B., Flach, P.A., Todorovski, L.: Subgroup discovery with CN2-SD. J. Mach. Learn. Res. **5**, 153–188 (2004)
13. Mouret, J., Clune, J.: Illuminating search spaces by mapping elites. CoRR (2015)
14. Ribeiro, M.T., Singh, S., Guestrin, C.: "why should i trust you?": explaining the predictions of any classifier. In: Proceedings of the 22nd ACM SIGKDD International Conference on Knowledge Discovery and Data Mining, KDD 2016, pp. 1135–1144. Association for Computing Machinery, New York, NY, USA (2016). https://doi.org/10.1145/2939672.2939778
15. Swe, S.M., Sett, K.M.: Approaching rules induction CN2 algorithm in categorizing of biodiversity. Int. J. Trend Sci. Res. Dev. **3**(4), 1581–1584 (2019). https://doi.org/10.5281/zenodo.3591374
16. Tokinaga, S., Lu, J., Ikeda, Y.: Neural network rule extraction by using the genetic programming and its applications to explanatory classifications. IEICE Trans. Fundam. Electron. Commun. Comput. Sci. **88**(10), 2627–2635 (2005)

17. Urquhart, N., Hart, E.: Optimisation and illumination of a real-world workforce scheduling and routing application (WSRP) via map-elites. In: Auger, A., Fonseca, C.M., Lourenço, N., Machado, P., Paquete, L., Whitley, D. (eds.) PPSN 2018. LNCS, vol. 11101, pp. 488–499. Springer, Cham (2018). https://doi.org/10.1007/978-3-319-99253-2_39
18. Urquhart, N., Höhl, S., Hart, E.: An illumination algorithm approach to solving the micro-depot routing problem. In: Proceedings of the Genetic and Evolutionary Computation Conference (2019). https://doi.org/10.1145/3321707.3321767
19. Vassiliades, V., Chatzilygeroudis, K., Mouret, J.B.: Using centroidal voronoi tessellations to scale up the multi-dimensional archive of phenotypic elites algorithm. IEEE Trans. Evol. Comput. 1 (2017)

Applications of Deep Bioinspired Algorithms

EDM-DRL: Toward Stable Reinforcement Learning Through Ensembled Directed Mutation

Michael H. Prince$^{(\boxtimes)}$, Andrew J. McGehee, and Daniel R. Tauritz

BioAI Research Group, Auburn University, Auburn, AL 36830, USA
{mhp0009,ajm0045}@auburn.edu, dtauritz@acm.org

Abstract. Deep reinforcement learning (DRL) has experienced tremendous growth in the past few years. However, training stability of agents continues to be an open research question. Here, the authors present Ensembled Directed Mutation of Deep Reinforcement Learning (EDM-DRL) - a hybridization of evolutionary computing (EC), ensemble learning, and DRL methods as a means of mitigating training instability in DRL agents. We show that our method trains more consistently than synchronous Advantage Actor Critic (A2C). We also show that by employing our novel mutation and ensemble methods, performance of DRL agents can be improved during test time without sacrificing training stability. Further, though a similar number of time steps are used, we show that the EDM-DRL algorithm uses a mere 1% or less of the network parameter updates used in A2C. Finally, we conduct an ablation study to identify components within the EDM-DRL algorithm responsible for highest contribution. Code and experimental logs are available at: https://github.com/Linked-Liszt/EDM-DRL.

Keywords: Deep reinforcement learning · Evolutionary algorithms · Ensembles · Game playing

1 Introduction

Deep reinforcement learning (DRL) has shown significant improvement over the last several years, proving its ability to competently navigate complex, high dimensional problem spaces [1]. Despite the progress, the training stability of RL agents still presents unique challenges for the field. Without the ability to train RL agents in a stable manner, the technology can only be realized *in silico* as it is too unsafe or unreliable to be applied in practical domains. Fortunately, several methods such as double Q-learning [26], prioritized experience replay [19], dueling networks [27], distributional RL [2], asynchronous advantage actor-critic (A3C) [15], multi-step bootstrapping [23,24], and Rainbow [11], which combines several of the previous, have been developed to address the issue of training instability. Though these methods have demonstrated state of the art, reproducible results, DRL training stability remains highly sensitive to choices of hyper-parameters, random seeds, and reward function design.

© Springer Nature Switzerland AG 2021
P. A. Castillo and J. L. Jiménez Laredo (Eds.): EvoApplications 2021, LNCS 12694, pp. 275–290, 2021.
https://doi.org/10.1007/978-3-030-72699-7_18

Drawing inspiration from human intelligence, the only existence proof for general intelligence, the authors hypothesize that the combination of evolution and learning may improve the state of DRL stability. Within the field of evolutionary computing (EC), several hybrid methods have been developed in order to combine the unique benefits of evolution and learning. Further, since RL problems typically require both exploration of a space and optimization of the expected reward within that space, they can certainly benefit from exploration methods which are not gradient-based, as in evolutionary algorithms (EAs). In addition, the population-based approach of EAs may offer stability to RL algorithms since, with an ensemble, various members may be able to cover each others' weaknesses at inference time. Therefore, this work explores the following research question:

How does the hybridization of EAs and DRL affect the training stability of DRL agents?

With this abstract research question in mind, the authors engage the following sub-topics in particular:

- Methods of integrating EAs and DRL which include both mutation and learning
- Comparison of ensemble methods for action selection in EDM-DRL
- Analysis of the stability of EDM-DRL as compared to its ablated components
- Analysis of stability of EDM-DRL as compared to an A2C baseline.

2   Background

RL is an area of machine learning which places agents inside of environments. These agents learn to maximize a reward signal by interacting with the environment. This work focuses on a subset of RL, referred to as DRL, which integrates deep learning and neural networks into the RL paradigm. RL and DRL have both shown much promise when applied to challenging problems in manufacturing [14] and finance [5]. DRL, in particular, has recently shown outstanding success, capable of exceeding human-level performance in the game of Go [22].

There have been significant efforts and contributions to improving the stability of RL agents during training in recent decades. Perhaps the earliest example comes from Sutton et al. in their introductory works to RL in 1988 and 1998 [23,24]. These works introduced critical concepts to the field of RL like temporal difference (TD) learning and multi-step bootstrapping for reward targets. Both have been shown to provide stability to agents under certain learning and policy conditions. The interested reader may find the more recent work by Sutton et al. an informative review on stability conditions for various forms of TD [25].

Another notable improvement, inspired by concepts in neuroscience, was the development of an experience replay mechanism in 2013 by Mnih et al. [16]. Prior to this work, DRL was unable to learn control policies directly from high dimensional sensory input such as the raw RGB pixels of an image. The addition of an experience replay buffer allows agents to uniform randomly sample and learn from experiences within a predefined history size, smoothing the reward distributions over previous behaviors.

An improvement to this work was introduced in 2015 by Schaul et al. in which the sampling of previous experiences is prioritized proportional to the TD error δ, which roughly denotes how "surprising" an action is to the agent [19]. The probability of sampling a transition is defined in Eq. 1, where $p_i > 0$ is the priority of the transition given by $|\delta_i|$, k is the transition history size, and the exponent α controls the intensity of prioritization (with $\alpha = 0$ corresponding to uniform random sampling).

$$P(i) = \frac{p_i^\alpha}{\sum_k p_k^\alpha} \tag{1}$$

Both the introduction of experience replay and prioritized experience replay have been shown to contribute significantly to the stability of RL agents during training, especially those learning from noisy reward signals. A further contribution made in 2015 by Mnih et al. was the introduction of a dual architecture (not to be confused with double Q-learning or dueling networks) where the "target" weights of a network are only periodically updated from the "online" weights, effectively avoiding overfitting to an unstable reward target [17].

Drawing inspiration from a single network with multiple streams, Wang et al. introduced the dueling network architecture in 2015 [27]. In the dueling architecture, the two streams which are aggregated together are the value stream and the advantage stream, with the prior estimating the quality (Q) of a particular state and the latter estimating the advantage gain of a particular state-dependent action. This combination of differing goals was shown to moderately improve the stability during optimization of the network.

Further improvements were introduced with the innovation of double Q-learning, first proposed in 2010 and generalized for DRL models in 2016 by van Hasselt et al. [9,26]. Double Q-learning addresses the issue of overly optimistic value estimation in Q-learning models by decoupling the evaluation and selection of actions. Two Q functions Q^A and Q^B are used to evaluate the quality of state-action pairs. However, instead of updating Q^A with Eq. 2 as in traditional Q-learning, and without loss of generality, double Q-learning uses $Q^B(s', a*)$ where Q^B is updated on a different sample of experiences than Q^A.

$$Q^A(s', a^*) = \max_a Q^A(s', a) \tag{2}$$

Another significant addition to the stability of RL agents during training was the work by Mnih et al. in 2016 on A3C [15]. A3C is in some ways similar to other multiple stream approaches. The actor is a policy based mechanism and the critic is a value based mechanism. However, the value estimations from the critic are not aggregated with other estimations in any way (as in dueling networks) nor used to update the actor's policy (as in double Q-learning). Instead the policy is updated directly through a policy gradient which aims to maximize the value estimations of the critic, which is itself independently learned. This has been shown to stabilize training of agents without the need for experience replay, allowing for on policy learning methods. In 2017, Wu et al. [28] discovered that a synchronous version of A3C, dubbed A2C, provided even more stable and efficient policy updates by waiting for all actors to finish episode roll-outs before performing the policy update. For this reason, A2C was selected as the DRL stability baseline.

More improvements to the performance of RL agents came from Bellemare et al. in their work on distributional RL in 2017 [2]. Distributional RL attempts to model expectation of reward as a discrete parameterized probability distribution. The work gives strong evidence of improvements to stability during training, especially in the case where reward signals do not follow stationary distributions. Another work in 2017 that is of note is the work by Fortunato et al. which introduced noisy networks [6]. While the work does not necessarily directly improve the stability of RL agents, it encourages exploration in tasks which require long chains of actions prior to the first reward signal without destabilizing the agent by adding intrinsic motivation signals.

In 2018, an intriguing paper by Hessel et al. was published in which several research scientists from DeepMind conducted an ablation study of several of the previously described contributions to RL [11]. Termed Rainbow, the combined algorithm was shown to be stable, generalizable, and sample efficient. Further, the work offers highly valuable insight into the individual contributions of each method to specific tasks within the Atari suite of games. An elegantly simple idea, the work strengthens the adage that the whole is greater than the sum of its parts.

Within the realm of EC, Covariance Matrix Adaptation Evolutionary Strategies (CMA-ES) has demonstrated state of the art results when optimizing functions with several local extrema and high multi-modality (e.g., shifted rastrigin) [8]. CMA-ES uses information derived from the population to dynamically adapt the distribution function used in mutation. By controlling both the step size and the "direction" of mutation, CMA-ES can more efficiently explore the problem space. Further, since CMA-ES is a population-based method with stochastic mutation, it may more easily escape deceptive gradients or suboptimal local extrema. This ability to navigate deceptive function landscapes may lend itself well to exploring highly noisy or deceptive reward landscapes in modern DRL problems.

Though the mentioned RL works all contribute significantly to the stability of RL agents, all are contributing ideas taken from mathematics, statistics, neuroscience, or deep learning. In comparison, relatively little research has been conducted on employing ideas from population dynamics, evolution, or EC to stabilize DRL training. Additionally little investigation has been done into ensembling populations in an RL setting. Some hybrid methods combining elements of EC and DRL exist [12,13,18]. However, such hybrids often merely implement existing techniques like conventional neuroevolution or Lamarckian and Baldwinian learning. Further, all the discussed related work focuses on the performance of the agent rather than having training stability as the goal. This work addresses this deficit by employing a novel combination of some of the addressed techniques with evolutionary methods and analyzing the training stability of the agents as compared against the ablated components.

3 Training Procedure

Here we propose a close integration between EC and deep learning paradigms. Our method exploits beneficial techniques common to the deep learning world, namely a shared feature extractor, as well as novel exploration techniques drawn from EC. We also exploit population-based methods by ensembling all actors at inference time during testing. This learning method is detailed in Algorithm 1 with the next sections detailing its individual components and methods.

Algorithm 1. Learning Procedure

 1: $Actors = $ INITIALIZEACTORS()
 2: $Critic = $ INITIALIZECRITIC()
 3: $FeatureExtractor = $ INITIALIZEFE()
 4: $IsUnsolved = True$
 5: $Timesteps = 0$
 6: **while** $Timesteps < MaxTimesteps$ **and** $IsUnsolved$ **do**
 7:      $Experiences = []$
 8:      $Fitnesses = []$
 9:      **for** $i, Actor \in$ ENUMERATE(ACTORS) **do**
10:          $Experiences[i], Fitnesses[i], NumSteps = $ ENVIRONMENT($Actor$)
11:          $Timesteps = Timesteps + NumSteps$
12:      **end for**
13:      $GradsFE, GradsActors, GradsCritic = $ BACKPROPAGATION($Experiences$)
14:      $FeatureExtractor = FeatureExtractor - GradsFE$
15:      $Critic = Critic - GradsCritic$
16:      $Actors = $ EVOLVE($Actors, GradsActors, Fitnesses$)
17:      $IsUnsolved = $ TESTENSEMBLE($Actors, FeatureExtractor$)
18: **end while**

3.1 Controller Structure

Our novel, hybrid controller structure is a fully connected neural network composed of the previously mentioned feature extractor, a critic network, and a population of actor networks. In contrast to other EC and RL hybrid methods, the critic network is not separate from the actor network. The model takes in a state vector representing the environment at a given time which is passed to the feature extractor for learning abstract representations. The feature extractor is a set of shared layers within the critic neural network and *all* actor networks within the population. As such, we explicitly show the separation of the critic, the feature extractor, actors, and their respective gradients in Algorithm 1. The representations learned by these layers are then passed to the population of value based actor networks, which estimate the expected reward for a given state-action pair, and the policy based critic network, which assesses the quality of the state. Finally, data from all actors, even agents which do not survive to the next generation, and data from the critic network are back-propagated through the respective networks and the shared feature extractor.

In the backward pass of the model, each actor of the generation is given a single episode to sample the environment. All the experiences are batched into a singular network update, similar to A2C. During the update, the advantage stream, or the difference between the observed value and the critic value, is back-propagated through the value network. Then, using the TD error, the critic network is updated to better predict future transitions. The accumulated gradients are then back-propagated through the feature extractor. Entropy regularization [15] is applied to encourage convergence over time.

3.2   Ensembling

Since the EDM-DRL algorithm makes use of a population of actors, it's possible to ensemble them together during test time. This ensemble is applied on line 14 of Algorithm 1. We try several ensembling methods which are influenced by the fitness of the actors. Here we define fitness as the sum of the rewards in a given episode. The first and simplest method is to allow the 1-elite actor - the member that performed best during its training episode - to select all actions during evaluation. Intuitively, this makes the assumption that reward is a near perfect representation of true performance. Alternatively, we consider modeling fitness as a probability mass function across the population by applying a softmax. The resulting action is chosen proportional to the fitness probability masses. This is a weaker assumption than the previous method, but the fittest individuals still generally choose the actions. Finally, the third method we consider is a weighted voting mechanism. Actors are assigned a number of votes proportional to their fitness. In this case, lower fitness individuals are able to overwhelm the decisions of more fit members if they are in agreement. A visualization of the weighted vote mechanism can be seen in Fig. 1.

3.3   Initialization and Termination

The parameters of every network layer, including the feature extractor, actors, and the critic, are initialized using Xavier initialization [7]. This is defined as $\mathcal{U}(-\sqrt{x}, \sqrt{x})$ where x is the number of input parameters. This type of initialization attempts to preserve the scale of the input and output activation between each layer. Each actor is initialized independently in order to encourage diversity in the population.

The algorithm is terminated on one of two conditions: solving the environment or 100k time steps, whichever is first. In the environment implementations

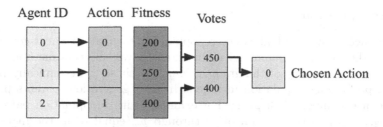

Fig. 1. The "weighted vote" mechanism. In a discrete environment, each actor selects an action. Their finesseses are accumulated. The action with the most votes is taken.

used in this work, the OpenAI gyms [4], each environment has different conditions to determine when it is "solved." In order to ensure robustness, a typical definition of "solved" is achieving a given mean reward μ across k episodes. If 100k time steps pass, the algorithm is terminated and the run is marked as unsolved. This is intentionally a significantly longer evaluation time than is needed to solve the environment as we wish to analyze failure and abnormal cases.

4   Evolution Procedure

The evolution procedure, stated in line 16 of Algorithm 1, creates the next generation of actor networks. With access to the gradients produced by back-propagation, we present a hybrid mutation method and a novel method, coined "repopulation", which replaces traditional parent and survivor selection. The base EDM-DRL method employs mutation as its sole variation operator. In a separate ablation, we experiment with adding a recombination method. In general, all the described methods try to combine and capitalize on the benefits of EC and gradient decent. They tend to be more greedy than typical EC methods through the use of gradients, but less greedy than typical DRL approaches through the use of stochastic methods and population dynamics.

Algorithm 2. Evolution Procedure

1: $Population.sort(Fitnesses)$
2: $NewPopulation = []$
3: $NewPopulation.append(Population[0])$
4: **for** $ParentIdx, ChildCount \in Enumerate(Repopulation[])$ **do**
5:    **for** $i \in Range(ChildCount)$ **do**
6:       $Child = DirectedMutation(Population[ParentIdx], Grads[ParentIdx])$
7:       $NewPopulation.append(Child)$
8:    **end for**
9: **end for**

4.1   Repopulation

We introduce a novel method, called repopulation, to create the next generation, replacing the canonical parent selection and survival selection methods. Capitalizing on the accuracy of the gradient step, we chose to systemically mutate the best performing population members. In each generation, parents produce a pre-defined number of offspring. For example, with repopulation parameters of $[p_1, p_2, \ldots, p_m]$ with the sum of p_1 through p_m equal to μ, the fittest parent produces p_1 offspring, the next produces p_2, and so on. This method, as opposed to a more traditional mating and survival selection, will cause a more greedy selection of parents which reproduce when weighted heavily on the first few members. We also add the option to guarantee *1-elite*, which is beneficial in the case that a generation G_{t+1} performs worse than generation G_t, as the 1-elite is neither mutated nor updated via the gradients. However, the 1-elite individual is re-evaluated with every new generation of offspring. This system creates a generational (μ, λ) population management model where the population size will remain static since $\mu = \lambda$. The choice of how many offspring each rank of parent is allowed to produce was hand-tuned in order to heavily bias offspring toward the most elite parents.

4.2   Mutation

Since we have access to the gradients produced by back-propagation, the mutation operator can be augmented with this information. We will call this "directed mutation." In contrast to random mutation, directed mutation is intentionally skewed to follow the previous gradient step. For each parameter in the mutated layers, a random learning rate is chosen from a defined interval, and Gaussian noise is applied to the gradient step. In addition, the size of the mutation is scaled to the size of the gradient step. In order to encourage convergence, this learning rate is multiplied by a decay rate at the end of every generation. Drawing inspiration from CMA-ES, this approach leverages the strengths of both gradients and population based methods, albeit differently. Instead of using the covariance of a population, the mutation distribution is informed by the analytical gradient. Further, rather than disallowing large gradient steps, as in trust region policy optimization and proximal policy optimization methods, we accomplish similar stability during exploration by relying on the diversity of exploration within a population [20,21]. In other words, individuals may explore unsafe regions of the reward space to their detriment, yet other members of the population may remain intact. A pseudo-code implementation of directed mutation is included in Algorithm 3. For a full visual representation, see Fig. 2.

4.3   Recombination Ablation

We also experiment with two forms of parameter-space recombination in a separate ablation, with some modification of the repopulation system. For both types of recombination, two parents are selected, and used to create a single

Algorithm 3. Directed Mutation

1: $lr = \mathcal{U}(lr\_low, \; lr\_high)$
2: **for** $param, \; grad \in \{Parameters, \; Gradients\}$ **do**
3:    $\mu = param - grad$
4:    $\sigma = mutation\_scale \cdot |param - \mu|$
5:    $param = x \sim \mathcal{N}(\mu, \sigma)$
6: **end for**

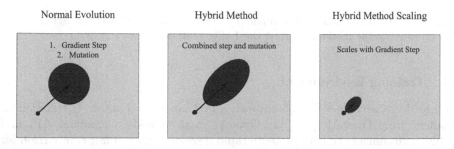

Fig. 2. Left: conventional mutation - parameters are moved randomly following a gradient step; Middle: hybrid "directed" mutation - the mutation is skewed to follow the learning step; Right: hybrid "scaled" mutation - same as the directed method but scaled to a percentage of the gradient step's magnitude.

child. The first method averages parameters from the two parent networks. The second form of recombination randomly selects individual parameters from the parents to build a full parameter set. In both cases, the parents' gradients are applied before the parameters are crossed over.

In the recombination experiments, a child actor is created through either recombination or mutation. Like the repopulation method, we greedily select the best performing members for use in recombination. In the configuration [α mutation, β (γ) recombination], the first α members are created by mutation from the best fitness member. The next β members are created through combinations of the top γ population members, denoted in parenthesis. Finally, similar to the base repopulation method, the elite member is held for the next generation.

5 Experimental Setup

This work conducts three experiments. The first experiment compares the EDM-DRL algorithm against an established baseline, the second analyzes the benefits of ensembling during test time, and the final offers an ablation study of common combinations of mutation and recombination. All experiments share the following general setup.

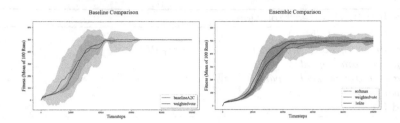

Fig. 3. On the left, EDM-DRL compared to the baseline A2C. On the right, a comparison of ensemble methods against the 1-elite method.

5.1 Training Environment

We use the "Cartpole-V1" environment, a well known and maturely tested environment from OpenAI gyms [4]. OpenAI gyms provide a common API and stable environments to help promote rapid development and fair comparison for RL algorithms. The goal of the cartpole environment is to balance a hinged pole affixed to a cart which may undergo 2D changes in motion. The agent is allowed to push the cart one unit left or right in a given time step. The agent receives a reward of positive one for each time step that the pole remains "balanced" and the cart remains within the frame. Here, "balanced" is defined as remaining within fifteen degrees of vertical center. The environment is initialized randomly with a slight tilt on the pole and offset on the cart. Version 1 of cartpole is the more challenging version as the agent must keep the pole upright and the cart on screen for 500 time steps. As mentioned previously, the definition of "solved" for this particular environment is to achieve a mean score of 475 across 100 episodes. Though this environment is certainly a toy problem, easily solved by linear, random search algorithms, it stands as a fair comparison for various agents and controllers as evidenced by its use throughout the field [1,10].

5.2 Measuring Performance and Stability

For each run, we attempt to sample the environment every 2000 time steps during training. Here a sample is defined as the mean performance of a particular agent over 100 episodes. In the A2C baseline, we are able to directly sample scores every 2000 time steps. However, due to the requirement of completing an episode prior to fitness evaluation, we are only able to sample individuals' performances following each generation. To directly and fairly compare the progress of each run at a set point, we use linear interpolation between surrounding sample points.

For each configuration, 30 unseeded runs are conducted. This gives us enough samples to compare the variation in the learning curves of each class of agent. During each run, we track the following metrics: number of runs solved in under 100k time steps, time steps until solved μ, time steps until solved σ, generations until solved μ, generations until solved σ, and the cross-run reward σ. Since this work focuses primarily on training stability, the cross-run reward standard

Mutation and Recombination Ablation

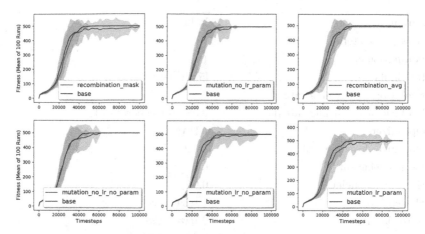

Fig. 4. Ablation of mutation and recombination methods. For readability, each ablation is shown against a base algorithm with no mutation or recombination.

deviation is of particular interest. Visually, the mean performance corresponds to the plotted line and the standard deviation corresponds to the shaded regions in Fig. 3 and Fig. 4. In addition to this variation, we also consider the standard deviation in time steps used to solve the environment as related to the agent's stability.

Since each of the configurations contain 30 runs, they can be statistically compared. In order to gauge performance, we compare time steps used to solve the environment for each run. Then we conduct an F-test to determine if the variance of each of the sets may be assumed to be equal. The logs were manually examined and were determined to follow a normal distribution. Following this, we perform a two-tailed T-test assuming the appropriate relation of variances, equal or unequal. We use a confidence level of 0.95 to determine if the differences in means are significant.

Strategy parameters are tuned using a combination of random search and hand-tuning. The parameters used in the following experiments are listed in Table 1. For each configuration, all strategy parameters remain static except for the one being ablated. For the A2C baseline, we used the hyper-parameters suggested in their respective works.

5.3 Experiments

Our algorithm draws inspiration from A2C, so it is a logical choice for benchmarking. The baseline is compared against the best found configuration of the EDM-DRL algorithm.

Then, we examine the benefits gained from allowing an ensemble approach for action selection during evaluation. We compared the softmax and weighted

Table 1. EDM-DRL strategy parameters

Parameter	Value
Base parameters	
Population size	10
Repopulation	[5,3,1] (+1 elite)
Evolutionary learning rate	5e–5
Evolutionary learning rate decay	0.98 (per generation)
Optimizer	ADAM
Optimizer learning Rate	3e–2
Value coefficient	0.5
Entropy coefficient	0.05
Shared layers	1 (size=128)
Actor layers	2 (size=128)
Value layers	1 (size=128)
Activations	ReLU
Mutation ablation parameters	
Learning rate (high bound, low bound)	[4e–5, 9e–5]
Mutation scale	0.1
Recombination ablation parameters	
Repopulation	[5 mutation , 4 (3) recomb] (+1 elite)

vote ensemble methods against a more traditional 1-elite approach. All employ their respective best found configuration.

Finally, we conduct an ablation study concerning two critical sections of the mutation and recombination algorithms. The added elements include: random selection of learning rates, application of Gaussian noise to gradient steps, mean recombination, and masking recombination. Each element is added in isolation.

6   Results and Discussion

Here we highlight the results from each of the discussed experiments. The source code and raw data for all experiments is included as supplementary material.[1] For each of the experiments we cover statistical results and graph relevant comparisons. Table 2 compares data from all of the experiments.

6.1   Comparison to A2C

As shown through statistical analysis, the A2C baseline was able to achieve solutions faster than the best configuration of our algorithm ($p = 0.0015$). However,

---

[1] https://github.com/Linked-Liszt/EDM-DRL.

Table 2. The observed results of the experiments

Algorithm	Runs	Training σ	Gen.s μ	Gen.s σ	Frames μ	Frames σ
Baseline_A2C	**30/30**	119.7	N/A	N/A	**24,560**	10,402
Weighted_vote	**30/30**	52.7	**62**	11.23	32,287	**6,627**
1elite	**30/30**	**40.4**	67	**7.9**	44,962	10,135
Softmax	29/30	60.5	73	15	44,700	13,115
Ablations						
Mutation_lr_param	30/30	66.5	62	12.5	37,560	15,384
Mutation_lr_no_param	30/30	**57.1**	65.7	14.9	33,376	6,831
Mutation_no_lr_param	30/30	57.3	62	15.6	**31,694**	**6,066**
Mutation_none	30/30	62.9	**60**	**10.1**	33,635	9,594
Mean_mating	30/30	76.6	67.9	11.0	34,093	7,134
Mask_mating	30/30	61.6	67.93	13.6	36,525	15,067

Best results in each category are bolded

the EDM-DRL algorithm is far more stable in training in general, as shown by the tighter variance, represented by the shaded areas in Fig. 3.

6.2   Ensemble Comparison

We are able to show that ensembling is an effective strategy for action selection. The weighted voting mechanism in particular outperforms the non-ensembling 1-elite strategy by a statistically significant margin ($p = 5.3e-7$) in frames used to solve the environment. This can be clearly seen in the steeper slope and greater final value of the time steps until solved μ metric, which is visualized in Fig. 3. However, the softmax ensemble method proved to be neither significantly better nor worse than the 1-elite strategy. Though these results are surprising, we speculate that the success of the weighted vote mechanism is due to the natural tendencies of a population to regress to the mean. While weaker individuals alone are less fit than a single strong individual, the combined strength of the population is able to compensate when they are in agreement.

6.3   Ablation Study

Our ablation study shows that mutation and recombination, in the current forms proposed in this work, had little positive effect on the overall performance or stability. Statistically, none of the ablated agents were better or worse than the base agent by a noteworthy margin. In particular, the mean recombination strategy is remarkably similar to the unmodified base agent. So, it stands to reason that this approach would be the least beneficial to training stability. We suspect that mutation and recombination actually injected further noise into the learning environment while not significantly destabilizing the agent. A pair-wise comparison of each ablation against an unmodified base agent is laid out in Fig. 4.

7   Conclusion

The authors have shown that using evolutionary methods may be used to create more stable DRL agents. While the ablated mutation and recombination elements of the EDM-DRL algorithm yield subpar performance, the population-based approach and repopulation mechanism detailed in this work seem to greatly benefit the stability of the EDM-DRL agent. In particular, this improvement is evidenced by the tighter standard deviation of rewards received across 30 unique runs as compared with the A2C baseline.

We observe that our algorithm is able to solve the CartPole environment using one parameter update for every 100 (up to 500 in some cases) parameter updates used in the A2C baseline. In A2C, the algorithm updates the network parameters at every time step. In contrast, EDM-DRL updates parameters only once per generation. We further demonstrate the benefits of having an ensemble of co-trained population members. The weighted voting mechanism is able to consistently perform statistically better than the 1-elite member of the population. In conventional DRL, ensembling methods are typically not practical due to the sampling inefficiency of each individual. This method mitigates such inefficiencies.

The stability of DRL agents during training remains a challenging research area for the AI community. Combined efforts over years of work have produced impressive engineering solutions which have incrementally yet profoundly improved this issue. Though in its early stages, the EDM-DRL algorithm stands to further improve upon the stability of DRL agents by hybridizing previous contributions with ideas drawn from EC.

8   Future Work

While we have interesting early results, this by no means is a comprehensive examination of the benefits that EC may offer DRL agents in terms of training stability. For example, further research may make use of more complex neural network components or architectures. The current implementation is built entirely from fully connected layers. In complex environments, particularly those which rely on raw RGB pixel input, convolutional layers would likely serve as more effective feature extractors. Memory-based units like recurrent neural networks and long-short term memory layers may also be candidates for hybridizing EC and DRL for time-series problems.

Some of the next logical steps for this work would be to explore the more complex gym environments such as the Arcade Learning Environment [3]. Further, we have observed that the discussed EDM-DRL algorithm uses significantly fewer parameter updates (by orders of magnitude) than the A2C baseline. Interesting future work may investigate whether the population based approach enables the EDM-DRL algorithm to take modified gradient steps which act as shortcuts along a purely gradient-based optimization path way.

To this end, an interesting area of research that is highly relevant to DRL is the investigation of unique exploration methods. Since DRL relies heavily on exploring the environment to gather data concerning the reward landscape, novelty search is a well suited contribution from EC which may benefit DRL agents. Particularly, the authors suggest that research into the effects novelty search may have on training stability, as opposed to performance, is worth future investigation.

Acknowledgment. The authors thank GitHub user jankrepl whose repository contained an implementation and hyper-parameter set of A2C which was critical to the development of this work. Further, the authors thank the students of Dr. Tauritz' research methods class, who served roles in reviewing and critiquing our methods.

References

1. Arulkumaran, K., Deisenroth, M.P., Brundage, M., Bharath, A.A.: Deep reinforcement learning: a brief survey. IEEE Signal Process. Mag. **34**(6), 26–38 (2017). https://doi.org/10.1109/MSP.2017.2743240
2. Bellemare, M.G., Dabney, W., Munos, R.: A distributional perspective on reinforcement learning. In: International Conference on Machine Learning, pp. 449–458. PMLR (2017)
3. Bellemare, M.G., Naddaf, Y., Veness, J., Bowling, M.: The arcade learning environment: an evaluation platform for general agents. J. Artif. Intell. Res. **47**, 253–279 (2013). https://doi.org/10.1613/jair.3912
4. Brockman, G., et al.: OpenAI Gym. arXiv preprint arXiv:1606.01540 (2016)
5. Deng, Y., Bao, F., Kong, Y., Ren, Z., Dai, Q.: Deep direct reinforcement learning for financial signal representation and trading. IEEE Trans. Neural Netw. Learn. Syst. **28**(3), 653–664 (2016). https://doi.org/10.1109/TNNLS.2016.2522401
6. Fortunato, M., et al.: Noisy Networks for Exploration. arXiv preprint arXiv:1706.10295 (2017)
7. Glorot, X., Bengio, Y.: Understanding the difficulty of training deep feedforward neural networks. In: Proceedings of the Thirteenth International Conference on Artificial Intelligence and Statistics, pp. 249–256 (2010)
8. Hansen, N., Ostermeier, A.: Adapting Arbitrary Normal Mutation Distributions in Evolution Strategies: The Covariance Matrix Adaptation. In: Proceedings of IEEE International Conference on Evolutionary Computation, pp. 312–317. IEEE (1996). https://doi.org/10.1109/ICEC.1996.542381
9. Hasselt, H.V.: Double Q-learning. In: Advances in Neural Information Processing Systems (NIPS), pp. 2613–2621 (2010)
10. Henderson, P., Islam, R., Bachman, P., Pineau, J., Precup, D., Meger, D.: Deep Reinforcement Learning that Matters. In: Proceedings of the AAAI Conference on Artificial Intelligence, vol. 32 (2018)
11. Hessel, M., et al.: Rainbow: Combining Improvements in Deep Reinforcement Learning. In: Thirty-Second AAAI Conference on Artificial Intelligence, pp. 3215–3222 (2018)
12. Khadka, S., et al.: Collaborative Evolutionary Reinforcement Learning. In: International Conference on Machine Learning, pp. 3341–3350. PMLR (2019)
13. Khadka, S., Tumer, K.: Evolution-Guided Policy Gradient in Reinforcement Learning. In: Advances in Neural Information Processing Systems (NIPS), pp. 1188–1200 (2018)

14. Li, Y., Fadda, E., Manerba, D., Tadei, R., Terzo, O.: Reinforcement learning algorithms for online single-machine scheduling. In: 15th Conference on Computer Science and Information Systems (FedCSIS 2020), pp. 277–283. IEEE (2020)
15. Mnih, V., et al.: Asynchronous Methods for Deep Reinforcement Learning. In: International Conference on Machine Learning, pp. 1928–1937 (2016)
16. Mnih, V., et al.: Playing Atari with Deep Reinforcement Learning. arXiv preprint arXiv:1312.5602 (2013)
17. Mnih, V., et al.: Human-level control through deep reinforcement learning. Nature **518**(7540), 529–533 (2015). https://doi.org/10.1038/nature14236
18. Pourchot, A., Sigaud, O.: CEM-RL: Combining Evolutionary and Gradient-Based Methods for Policy Search. arXiv preprint arXiv:1810.01222 (2018)
19. Schaul, T., Quan, J., Antonoglou, I., Silver, D.: Prioritized Experience Replay. arXiv preprint arXiv:1511.05952 (2015)
20. Schulman, J., Levine, S., Abbeel, P., Jordan, M., Moritz, P.: Trust Region Policy Optimization. In: International Conference on Machine Learning, pp. 1889–1897 (2015)
21. Schulman, J., Wolski, F., Dhariwal, P., Radford, A., Klimov, O.: Proximal Policy Optimization Algorithms. arXiv preprint arXiv:1707.06347 (2017)
22. Silver, D., et al.: Mastering the game of Go with deep neural networks and tree search. Nature **529**(7587), 484–489 (2016). https://doi.org/10.1038/nature16961
23. Sutton, R.S.: Learning to predict by the methods of temporal differences. Mach. Learn. **3**(1), 9–44 (1988)
24. Sutton, R.S., Barto, A.G.: Reinforcement Learning: An Introduction. MIT Press, Cambridge (1998)
25. Sutton, R.S., Mahmood, A.R., White, M.: An emphatic approach to the problem of off-policy temporal-difference learning. J. Mach. Learn. Res. **17**(1), 2603–2631 (2016)
26. Van Hasselt, H., Guez, A., Silver, D.: Deep Reinforcement Learning with Double Q-Learning. In: Thirtieth AAAI Conference on Artificial Intelligence (2016)
27. Wang, Z., Schaul, T., Hessel, M., Van Hasselt, H., Lanctot, M., De Freitas, N.: Dueling Network Architectures for Deep Reinforcement Learning. arXiv preprint arXiv:1511.06581 (2015)
28. Wu, Y., Mansimov, E., Grosse, R.B., Liao, S., Ba, J.: Scalable trust-region method for deep reinforcement learning using Kronecker-factored approximation. In: Advances in Neural Information Processing Systems (NIPS), pp. 5279–5288 (2017)

Continuous Ant-Based Neural Topology Search

AbdElRahman ElSaid[✉], Joshua Karns, Zimeng Lyu, Alexander G. Ororbia, and Travis Desell[✉]

Rochester Institute of Technology, Rochester, NY 14623, USA
{aae8800,tjdvse}@rit.edu, {josh,zimenglyu}@mail.rit.edu, ago@cs.rit.edu

Abstract. This work introduces a novel, nature-inspired neural architecture search (NAS) algorithm based on ant colony optimization, Continuous Ant-based Neural Topology Search (CANTS), which utilizes synthetic ants that move over a continuous search space based on the density and distribution of pheromones, strongly inspired by how ants move in the real world. The paths taken by the ant agents through the search space are utilized to construct artificial neural networks (ANNs). This continuous search space allows CANTS to automate the design of ANNs of any size, removing a key limitation inherent to many current NAS algorithms that must operate within structures of a size predetermined by the user. CANTS employs a distributed asynchronous strategy which allows it to scale to large-scale high performance computing resources, works with a variety of recurrent memory cell structures, and uses of a communal weight sharing strategy to reduce training time. The proposed procedure is evaluated on three real-world, time series prediction problems in the field of power systems and compared to two state-of-the-art algorithms. Results show that CANTS is able to provide improved or competitive results on all of these problems while also being easier to use, requiring half the number of user-specified hyper-parameters.

Keywords: Ant colony optimization · Artificial neural network · Neural architecture search

1 Introduction

Manually optimizing artificial neural network (ANN) structures has been an obstacle to the advancement of machine learning given that it is significantly time-consuming and requires a considerable level of domain expertise [1]. ANN structures are typically chosen based their reputation in existent literature or based on knowledge shared across the machine learning community.

This material is based upon work supported by the U.S. Department of Energy, Office of Science, Office of Advanced Combustion Systems under Award Number #FE0031547 and by the Federal Aviation Administration and MITRE Corporation under the National General Aviation Flight Information Database (NGAFID) award.

© Springer Nature Switzerland AG 2021
P. A. Castillo and J. L. Jiménez Laredo (Eds.): EvoApplications 2021, LNCS 12694, pp. 291–306, 2021.
https://doi.org/10.1007/978-3-030-72699-7_19

However, changing even a few problem-specific meta-parameters can lead to poor generalization upon committing to a specific topology [2,3]. To address these challenges, a number of neural architecture search (NAS) [1,4–8] and neuroevolution (NE) [9,10] algorithms have been developed to automate the process of ANN design. More recently, nature-inspired neural architecture search (NI-NAS) algorithms have shown increasing promise, including the Artificial Bee Colony (ABC) [11], Bat [12], Firefly [13], and Cuckoo Search [14] algorithms.

Ant colony optimization (ACO) [15] is another successful NI-NAS strategy that has been shown to be particularly powerful when automating the design of recurrent neural networks (RNNs). Originally, ACO for NAS was limited to small structures based on Jordan and Elman RNNs [16] or was used as a process for reducing the number of network inputs [17]. Later work proposed generalizations of ACO for optimizing the synaptic connections within RNN memory cell structures [18] and even entire RNN architectures in an algorithmic framework called Ant-based Neural Topology Search (ANTS) [19]. In the ANTS process, ants traverse a single massively-connected "superstructure", searching for optimal RNN sub-networks which connect RNN nodes both in terms of structure, i.e., all possible feed forward connections, and in time, i.e., all possible recurrent synapses that span many different time delays. This approach shares similarity to NAS methods in ANN cell and architecture design [5–7,20–24], which operate within a limited search space, generating cells or architectures with a pre-determined maximum number of nodes and edges [4].

Most NE methods, instead of operating within fixed bounds, are constructive, continually adding and removing nodes and edges during the evolutionary process (e.g., NEAT [25], CoDeepNEAT [26] and EXAMM [27]). Other strategies involve generative encoding, such as HyperNEAT [28], where a generative network is evolved, which can then be used to create architectures and assign values to their synaptic weights. Nonetheless, these approaches still require manually specifying or constraining the size or scale of the generated architecture in terms of the number of layers and nodes.

In general, constructive NAS methods often suffer from getting stuck in (early) local minima or take considerable computation time to evolve structures that are sufficiently large in order to effectively address the task at hand, especially for large-scale deep learning problems. Alternately, having to pre-specify bounds for the space of possible NAS-selected architectures can lead to poorly performing or suboptimal networks if the bounds are incorrect, requiring many runs of varying bound values. In order to address these challenges, this work introduces the novel ACO-inspired algorithm, *Continuous Ant-based Neural Topology Search (CANTS)*, which utilizes a continuous search domain that flexibly allows for the design of ANNs of any size. Synthetic continuous ant (*cant*) agents move through this search space based on the density and distribution of pheromone signals, which emulates how ants swarm in the real world, and the paths resulting from their exploration are used to construct RNN architectures. CANTS is a distributed, asynchronous algorithm, which facilitates scalable usage of high performance computing (HPC) resources, and also utilizes communal intelligence to reduce the amount of training required for candidate evolved networks. The procedure further allows for the selection of recurrent nodes from a suite of simple neurons and complex memory cells used in modern RNNs: Δ-RNN units [29], GRUs [30], LSTMs [31], MGUs [32], UGRNNs [33].

CANTS is compared to state-of-the-art benchmark algorithms used in designing RNNs for time series data prediction: ANTS [19] and EXAMM [27]. In addition to eliminating the requirement for pre-specified architecture bounds, CANTS is shown to yield results that improve upon or are competitive to ANTS and EXAMM while reducing the number of user specified hyperparameters from 16 in both EXAMM and ANTS down to 8 in CANTS. CANTS also provides an advancement to the field of ant colony optimization as it is the first algorithm capable of optimizing complex graph structures without requiring a predefined (super)structure to operate within. While ACO has been applied to continuous domain problems before [34–38], to the authors' knowledge, our algorithm is the first to simulate and apply the movements of ants through a continuous space to design unbounded graph structures.

2 Methodology

The CANTS procedure (see high-level pseudo-code in Algorithm 1) employs an asynchronous, distributed "work-stealing" strategy to allow for scalable execution on HPC systems. The work generation process maintains a population of the best-found RNN architectures and repeatedly generates candidate RNNs whenever the worker processes request them. This strategy allows workers to complete the training of the generated RNNs at whatever speed they are capable of, yielding an algorithm that is naturally load-balanced. Unlike synchronous parallel evolutionary strategies, CANTS scales up to any number of available processors, supporting population sizes that are independent of processor availability. When the resulting fitness (mean squared error over validation data) of candidate RNNs is reported to the work generator process, if the candidate RNN is better than the worst RNN in the population, then the worst RNN is removed and the candidate is added. Note that the saved pheromone placement points for the candidate are incremented in the continuous search space.

Candidate RNNs are synthesized using a search space of stacked 2D continuous planes, where each 2D plane represents a particular time step t (see Fig. 1a). The input nodes for each time step are uniformly distributed at the input edge of the search space. A synthetic continuous ant agent (or *cant*) picks one of the discrete input node positions to start at and then moves through the continuous space based on the current density and distribution of other pheromone placements. Cants are allowed to move forward on the level they are on and can move up to any plane above it. They are restricted from moving down the stack – while connections moving up the stack represent passing information from a previous time step to a future time step, the reverse would require passing unknown future data to a previous time step of the RNN which is not possible. While ants only move forward on a given plane, they are permitted to move backward when moving to a plane higher on the stack since many RNNs have recurrent connections that feed into earlier nodes in the network. This enforced

---

Algorithm 1. Continuous Ant-guided Neural Topology Search Algorithm

---

procedure $WorkGenerator$
  ▷ Construct search space with inputs at y=0 and output at y=1
  ▷ Recurrent time steps is the spaces's z axis
  $search_space = $ **new** $SearchSpace$
  for $i \leftarrow 1 \ldots max\_iteration$ **do**
    $nn_{new} \leftarrow AntsSwarm()$
    $send\_to\_worker(nn_{new}, worker.id)$
    $nn_{new}, fit \leftarrow receive\_fit\_from\_worker()$
    if $nn\_fitness < worst\_population\_member$ **then**
      $population.pop(worst\_population\_member)$
      $population.add(nn_{new})$
      $RewardPoints(nn_{new})$
procedure $Worker$
  $receive\_from\_master(nn)$
  $fitness \leftarrow train\_test\_nn(nn)$
  $send\_fitness\_to\_master(nn, fitness)$
procedure $AntsSwarm$
  ▷ Ants choose input in discrete fashion
  for $ant \leftarrow 1 \ldots no\_ants$ **do**
    $CreatePath(ant)$
  ▷ Use DBscan to cluster ants paths points
  $segments \leftarrow DBscanPaths(ants)$
  ▷ Create RNN from segments
  $rnn_{new} \leftarrow CreateRNN(segments)$ **return** rnn_{new}
procedure $CreatePath(ant)$
  ▷ Choose input in discrete fashion
  $ChooseInput(ant)$
  ▷ Create a path starting from the input
  while $ant.current\_y < 0.99$ **do**
    $r \leftarrow$ **uniform_random**$(0, pheromone\_sum - 1)$
    $ant.current\_level \leftarrow ant.climb$
    if $r > ant.exploration\_instinct$ or $search\_space[ant.current\_level]$ is not
$Empty$ **then**
      $point \leftarrow CreateNewPoint(ant.search\_radius)$
      $ant.path.insert(point)$
      $search\_space.insert(point)$
    else
      $point \leftarrow FindCenterOfMass(ant.current\_position, ant.search\_radius)$
      if $point$ not in $search\_space[ant.level]$ **then**
        $ant\_path.insert(point)$
  ▷ Choose Output in discrete fashion
  $ChooseOutput(ant)$

---

procedure *ChooseInput(ant)*
   ▷ Select input probabilistically according to pheromones
   pheromone_sum ← **sum**(*pheromones.input*)
   r ← **uniform_random**(0, *pheromone_sum* − 1)
   ant.input ← 0
   while *r* > 0 **do**:
      if *r* < *pheromones.input[ant.input]* **then**
         ant.input ← 1
         break
      else
         r ← *r* − *pheromones.input[ant.input]*
         ant.input ← *ant.input* + 1
procedure *ChooseOutput(ant)*
   ▷ Select input probabilistically according to pheromones
   pheromone_sum ← **sum**(*pheromones.output*)
   r ← **uniform_random**(0, *pheromone_sum* − 1)
   ant.input ← 0
   while *r* > 0 **do**:
      if *r* < *pheromones.input[ant.output]* **then**
         ant.output ← 1
         break
      else
         r ← *r* − *pheromones.output[ant.output]*
         ant.output ← *ant.output* + 1
procedure *DBscanPaths(ants)*
   for *ant* ← 1 . . . *num_ants* **do**
      for *point* ← 1 . . . *ant_path* **do**
         segments[ant].insert(PickPoint(point))
   return *segments*
procedure *PickPoint(point)*
   [*node, points_cluster*] ← *DBscane(point, search_space[point.level])*
   node.out_edges_weights.insert(AvrgWeights(points_cluster))
   search_space.insert(node) **return** *node*
procedure *RewardPoints(rnn)*
   for each *node* ∈ *rnn.nodes* **do**
      search_space[node].pheromone += *constant*
      search_space[node].weight ← *average_weight(node.weight, search_space[node].weight)*
      if *search_space[node].pheromone* > *PHEROMONE_THRESHOLD*
then
         search_space[node].pheromone = *PHEROMONE_THRESHOLD*

upward and (overall) forward movement ensures that cants continue to progress towards outputs and do not needlessly circle around in the search space. Figures 1 shows examples of how cants move from an input edge of the search space to the output edge, how cants explore new regions in the search space, how cants exploit previously searched areas via attraction to deposited pheromones, and how cant paths through the space are translated into a final candidate RNN.

Cant Agent Input Node and Layer Selection: Each level in the search space has a level-selection pheromone value, p_l, where l is the level. These are initialized to $p_l = 2 * l$ where the top level for the current time step is $l = 1$, the next level for the first time lag is $l = 2$ and so on. A cant selects its starting level according to the probability of starting at level l as $P(l) = \frac{p_l}{\Sigma_{l=1}^{L} p_l}$, where L is the total number of levels. This scheme encourages cants to start at lower levels of the stack at the beginning of the search. After selecting a level, the cant selects its input node in a similar fashion, based on the pheromones for each input node location on that level. When a candidate RNN is inserted into the population, the level pheromones for each level, utilized by that RNN, are incremented.

Cant Agent Movement: To balance exploration with exploitation, cants behave similarly to real-world ants by following communication clues to reach to targets.

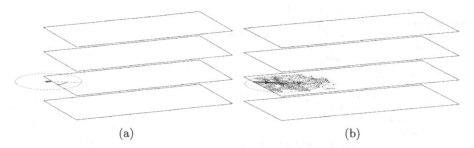

(a)   (b)

Fig. 1. Cant path selection and network construction: (a) After an cant picks a layer to start with and an input node, it decides if it will move to a new random point (exploration), or follow pheromone traces (exploitation). If the former, the cant will randomly pick a forward angle between 0° and 180° and move in that direction equal to its red sensing radius. (b) When the cant wants to use pheromone traces to determine its new point, it will first sense the pheromone traces within its sensing radius. The example cant did not change its layer, so the cant will only consider the pheromone traces in front of it and not move backwards. The ant will then calculate the center of mass of the pheromone traces within its sensing radius and then move to the center of their mass (gold sphere). (c) When the cant moves to a level above it and decides that it will use exploitation, it will consider the pheromone traces in its sensing range in all directions, which lie between the angles 0° and 360°. This way, the cant can move backwards when jumping from a layer to another, which makes a recurrent connection that goes back between hidden layers. (d) The cant moves upward to the higher level. (e) The cant will move to a new point by exploration. (f) After a series of upward and forward moves by either exploration or exploitation, when the cant has output nodes within its sensing radius, it will stop the continuous search and select an output node based on its discrete pheromone values. If there is only one output node, then the cant will directly connect its last point to the output. (g) Several cants make their path from an input to an output. (h) The cants' nodes on each level are then condensed (clustered) based on their density using DBSCAN. (i) The cant picked its input point, starting at level t_{-2}, picked a node at t_{-2} (green edge), picked a node at t_{-1} (red backward recurrent edge), picked a node at t_{-1} (green edge), picked a node at t_0 (magenta forward recurrent edge), picked a node at t_0 (green edge), picked a node at t_0 (green edge), and finally picked an output node at t_0 (green edge). (j) The final network is the final result of clustering the nodes and defining the connections between nodes in the same layer as red edges, and the connection between nodes and between layers as green forward recurrent edges or blue backward recurrent edges. The flow moves from the gray inputs at the bottom to the black outputs at the top. (Color figure online)

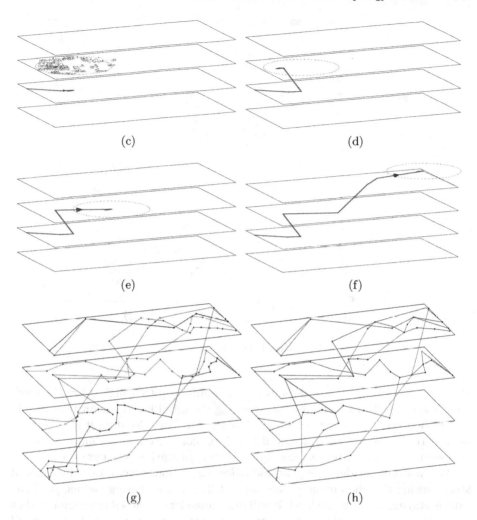

(c)

(d)

(e)

(f)

(g)

(h)

Fig. 1. (*continued*)

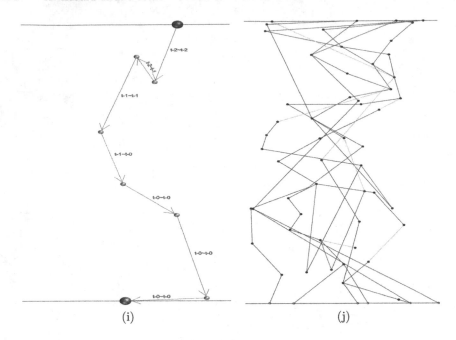

Fig. 1. (*continued*)

When a cant moves, it first decides if it will climb up to a higher (stack) level. This is done in the same manner as selecting its initial layer, except that it only selects between its current level and higher ones. After deciding if it will climb or not, the agent will then decide if it will explore or exploit. Cants randomly choose to exploit at a percentage equal to an exploitation parameter, ϵ.

When a cant decides to exploit and follow pheromone traces, *i.e.*, clues, it will start sensing the pheromone points around it, given a sensing radius, ρ. If the cant is staying on the same level, it will only consider deposited pheromones that are in front of it (*i.e.*, closer to the output nodes), otherwise, it will consider all the pheromones that are inside its sensing radius on the level it is moving to. The cant then calculates the center of mass of the pheromones in this region using the point in the space it will move to. This point is then saved by the candidate RNN (as a point to potentially increment pheromone values) if the RNN is later to be inserted into the RNN population. Since cants consider the center of mass of the pheromone values, the individual points of pheromone values are not the effective factor in cant-to-cant communication. Rather, it is the concentration of the pheromone in a region of the space that more closely aligns with how real ants move in nature.

When a cant instead decides that it will explore, it instead selects a random point that lies within the range of their sensing radius to move to. Once a cant decides if it is climbing or staying in the same level, it will generate an angle bisector that is either a random number between $[0, 1]$ if the current and next point are on the same level or $[-1, 1]$ if the current and next points are on different levels. This angle bisector is used to calculate the angle of the next movement of the cant: $\theta = angle\_bisect * PI$. The movement angle is then subsequently used to calculate the next x and y coordinates of the next position of the cant: $x_{new} \leftarrow x_{old} + \rho * cos(\theta)$, $y_{new} \leftarrow y_{old} + \rho * sin(\theta)$. These points are also saved for potential future pheromone modification.

Condensing Cant Paths to RNN Nodes: After cants choose the points in their paths from the inputs to the outputs, the points in the search space are clustered using the DBSCAN algorithm [39] to condense those points to centroids. The points of the segments of the cants' paths are then shifted to the centroids that they belong to in the search space and those new points become the nodes of the generated RNN architecture (see Figs. 1g and 1h). The node types are picked by a pheromone-based discrete local search, as is done in the discrete space ANTS. Each of these node types at the selected point will have their own pheromone values that drive probabilistic selection.

Communal Weight Sharing: In order to avoid having to retrain every newly-generated RNN from scratch, a communal weight sharing method has been implemented to allow generated RNNs to start with values similar to those of previously generated and trained RNNs. The centroid points (*i.e.*, the RNN node points in the continuous space) in CANTS retain the weights of all the outgoing edges from those nodes. Each newly-created centroid is assigned a weight value which is passed to the edges of the generated RNN. In the case where a centroid did not have any previously created centroid in its cluster, randomly initialized weights are assigned to those outgoing edges either uniformly at random between -0.5 and 0.5, or via the Kaiming [40] or Xavier [41] strategies. If there were previously-created centroids in the clustering region, the weight values assigned to the generated RNN nodes are the average of the weights of those existing centroids. The weights of a centroid are updated after an RNN is trained by calculating the averages of the original centroid weight values and all the weights of the outgoing edges of the corresponding node (after training). The updated weights can then be used to initialize new centroid weights when they lie in their cluster when DBSCAN is applied in the following iteration.

Pheromone Volatility: Pheromone decay happens on a regular basis after each iteration of optimization regardless of the performance of the generated RNN(s). The pheromones decay by a constant value and after a specific minimum threshold the point is removed from the search space. By letting points vanish, the search space removes tiny residual pheromones which might provide distraction to cant-to-cant communication as well as slow down the overall algorithm.

Pheromone Incrementation: For each successful candidate RNN, *i.e.*, each RNN that performs at least better than the worst in the population, the corresponding centroids for its RNN nodes in the search space are rewarded by increasing their pheromone values by a constant value. The values of the pheromones have a maximum limit to avoid becoming overly attractive points to the cants, which could result in premature convergence.

3 Results

This work compares CANTS to the state-of-the-art ANTS and EXAMM algorithms on three real world datasets related to power systems. All three methods were used to perform time series data prediction for different parameters, which have been used as benchmarks in prior work. Main flame intensity was used as the prediction parameter from the coal plant's burner, net plant heat rate was used from the coal plant's boiler, and average power output was used from the wind turbines. Experiments were also performed to investigate the effect of CANTS hyper-parameters: the number of cants and cant sensing radii, ϵ.

Computing Environment. The results for ANTS, CANTS, and EXAMM were obtained by scheduling the experiment on Rochester Institute of Technology's high performance computing cluster with 64 Intel® Xeon® Gold 6150 CPUs, each with 36 cores and 375 GB RAM (total 2304 cores and 24 TB of RAM). Each ANTS experiment utilized 15 nodes (540 cores), taking approximately 30 days to complete all the experiments. CANTS experiments used 5 nodes (180 cores), taking 7 days to finish all the experiments. EXAMM experiments also used 5 nodes (180 cores) and also took approximately 7 days to complete the experiments.

Datasets. The datasets used, which are derived from coal-fired power plant and wind turbine data, have been previously made publicly available on the EXAMM repository to encourage further study in time series data prediction and reproducibility[1]. The first dataset comes from measurements collected from 12 burners of a coal-fired power plant as well as its boiler parameters and the second dataset comes from wind turbine engine data from the years 2013 to 2020, collected and made available by ENGIE's La Haute Borne open data windfarm[2].

All of the datasets are multivariate and non-seasonal, with 12 (burner), 48 (boiler), and 78 (wind turbine) input variables (potentially dependent). These time series are very long, with the burner data separated into 7000 time step chunks – one for training and one for testing (per minute recordings). The boiler dataset is separated into a training set of 850 steps and test set of 211 steps (per hour recordings). The wind turbine dataset is separated into a training set of 190,974 steps and test set of 37,514 steps (each step taken every 10 min).

3.1 Number of Cant Agents

An experiment was conducted to determine the effect that the number of cant agents has on the performance of CANTS. The experiment focused on the net plant heat rate feature from the coal-fired power plant dataset. The number of ants evaluated were 10, 30, 60, 100, 150, and 210. The results, shown in Fig. 2, show that, as the number of cants are increased, the performance increases until

[1] https://github.com/travisdesell/exact/tree/master/datasets/.
[2] https://opendata-renewables.engie.com.

150 cants are used and then a decline is observed. This shows that the number of cant agents is an important hyper-parameter and requires tuning, potentially exhibiting "sweet spots" that, if uncovered, provide strong results.

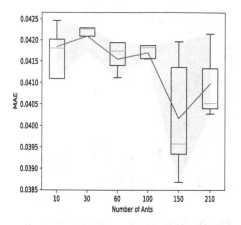 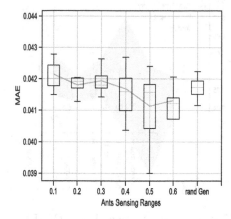

Fig. 2. CANTS w/varying # of agents.   **Fig. 3.** CANTS w/different sensing radii.

3.2 Cant Agent Sensing Radius

We next investigated the effect that the sensing radii (range) of the cant agents had on algorithm performance. Figure 3 shows that a sensing radius of 0.5 obtained better performance compared to the 0.1, 0.2, 0.3, 0.4, and 0.6 sensing radii values tested. We also evaluated the effect that using a randomly generated sensing radius per cant agent would have. For these, ϵ was randomly initialized (uniformly) via $\sim U(0.01, 0.98)$. Ultimately, we discovered that the sensing radius of 0.5 still provided the best results.

3.3 Algorithm Benchmark Comparisons

To compare the three different NAS strategies, each experiment was repeated 10 times (trials) for statistical comparison and all algorithms were set to generate 2000 RNNs per trial. For CANTS, the sensing radii of the cant agents and exploration instinct values were generated uniformly via $\sim U(0.01, 0.98)$ when the cants were created, initial pheromone values were 1 and the maximum was kept at 10 with a pheromone decay rate set to 0.05. For the DBSCAN module, clustering distance was 0.05 with a minimum point value of 2 – runs with these settings were done using 30 and 150 ants. CANTS and ANTS used a population of size 20 while EXAMM used 4 islands, each with a population of 10. ANTS, CANTS, and EXAMM all had a maximum recurrent depth of 5 and the predictions were made over a forecasting horizon of 1. The generated RNNs were each allowed 40 epochs of back-propagation for local fine-tuning (since all algorithms are mmetic). ANTS and EXAMM utilized the hyper-parameters previously reported to yield best results [19,27].

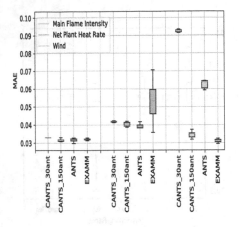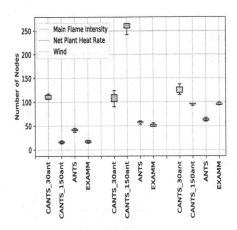

Fig. 4. Mean Average Error (MAE) ranges of best-found RNNs from each method.

Fig. 5. Number of nodes in the best found RNNs from each method.

The results shown in Fig. 4, which compare CANTS, ANTS and EXAMM in the three experiments described above (over the three datasets), report the range of mean average error (MAE) of each algorithm's best-found RNNs. While EXAMM outperformed CANTS with 30 ants, CANTS with 150 ants had a better performance than EXAMM and ANTS. CANTS was competitive with ANTS on the net plant heat rate predictions and outperformed EXAMM on this dataset. CANTS also outperformed ANTS on the wind energy dataset yet could not beat EXAMM. Potential reasons for this could be that the complexity/size of this dataset is greater and that the task is simply more difficult which results in a potentially larger search space. As CANTS allows for potentially unbounded network sizes, its search space is significantly larger than either that of ANTS or EXANM. Though ANTS outperformed CANTS on the wind dataset, CANTS is still a good competitor, especially since it has less hyper-parameters (8) to tune compared to both ANTS and EXAMM (both require at least 16). While all these reasons may be valid, the size of the search space is likely the biggest challenge. Further evidence of this is provided in Figs. 5, 6, 7, present the number of structural elements (nodes, edges, and recurrent edges, respectively) of the best-found RNN architectures using the different algorithms. The CANTS runs with 150 ants resulted in significantly more complex architectures for many of the problems, which may be an indication that CANTS can evolve better performing structure if provided more optimization iterations.

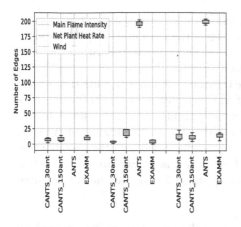

Fig. 6. Number of edges in the best-found RNNs from each algorithm.

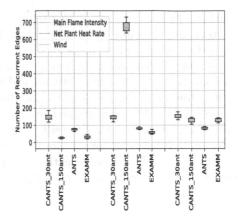

Fig. 7. Number of recurrent edges in the best-found RNNs each algorithm.

4 Discussion and Future Work

This work introduces continuous ant-based neural topology search (CANTS), a novel nature-inspired optimization algorithm that utilizes a continuous search space to conduct unbounded neural architecture search (NAS). This approach provides a unique strategy to overcome key limitations of constructive neuro-evolutionary strategies (which often prematurely get stuck at finding smaller, less performant architectures) as well as other neural architecture search strategies that require users to carefully specify the bounds limiting the neural architecture size. CANTS was experimentally evaluated for the automated design of recurrent neural networks (RNNs) to make time series predictions across three challenging real-world data sets in the power systems domain. We compared it to two state-of-the-art algorithms, ANTS (a discrete space ant colony NAS algorithm) and EXAMM (a constructive neuro-evolution algorithm). CANTS is shown to improve on or be competitive with these strategies, while also being simpler to use and tune, only requiring 8 hyper-parameters as opposed to the 16 hyper-parameters of the other two strategies.

This study presents some initial work generalizing ant colony algorithms to complex, continuous search spaces, specifically for unbounded graph optimization problems (with NAS as a target application), opening up a number of promising avenues for future work. In particular, while the search space is continuous in each two-dimensional plane (or time step) of our temporal stack, there is still the number of discrete levels that a user must specify. Therefore, a promising extension of the algorithm would be to make the search space continuous across all three dimensions, removing this parameter, and allowing pheromone placements to guide the depth of recurrent connections. This could have implications for discrete-event, continuous-time RNN models [42], which attempt to tackle a broader, more complex set of sequence modeling problems. Finally, and potentially the most interesting, is the fact that the exploitation parameter, ϵ, and the sensing radius, ρ, for each synthetic ant agent in our algorithm was held fixed (or in some cases randomly initialized) for the duration of each CANTS search. However, the ants could instead be treated as complex agents that evolve with time, learning the best exploitation and sensing parameters for the task search spaces they are applied to. This could provide far greater flexibility to the CANTS framework. Expanding this algorithm to other domains, such as the automated design of convolutional neural networks (for computer vision) or to other types of RNNs, such as those used for natural language processing, could further demonstrate the potentially broad applicability of this nature-inspired approach.

Acknowledgements. Most of the computation of this research was done on the high performance computing clusters of Research Computing at Rochester Institute of Technology [43]. We would like to thank the Research Computing team for their assistance and the support they generously offered to ensure that the heavy computation this study required was available.

References

1. Zoph, B., Le, Q.V.: Neural architecture search with reinforcement learning. arXiv preprint arXiv:1611.01578 (2016)
2. Erkaymaz, O., Özer, M., Yumuşak, N.: Impact of small-world topology on the performance of a feed-forward artificial neural network based on 2 different real-life problems. Turkish J. Electr. Eng. Comput. Sci. **22**(3), 708–718 (2014)
3. Barna, G., Kaski, K.: Choosing optimal network structure. In: International Neural Network Conference, pp. 890–893. Springer, Dordrecht (1990). https://doi.org/10.1007/978-94-009-0643-3_122
4. Elsken, T., Metzen, J.H., Hutter, F.: Neural architecture search: A survey. arXiv preprint arXiv:1808.05377 (2018)
5. Liu, H., Simonyan, K., Yang, Y.: Darts: Differentiable architecture search. arXiv preprint arXiv:1806.09055 (2018)
6. Pham, H., Guan, M.Y., Zoph, B., Le, Q.V., Dean, J.: Efficient neural architecture search via parameter sharing. arXiv preprint arXiv:1802.03268 (2018)
7. Xie, S., Zheng, H., Liu, C., Lin, L.: Snas: stochastic neural architecture search. arXiv preprint arXiv:1812.09926 (2018)
8. Luo, R., Tian, F., Qin, T., Chen, E., Liu, T.Y.: Neural architecture optimization. In: Advances in Neural Information Processing Systems, pp. 7816–7827 (2018)
9. Stanley, K.O., Clune, J., Lehman, J., Miikkulainen, R.: Designing neural networks through neuroevolution. Nature Mach. Intell. **1**(1), 24–35 (2019)
10. Darwish, A., Hassanien, A.E., Das, S.: A survey of swarm and evolutionary computing approaches for deep learning. Artif. Intell. Rev. **53**(3), 1767–1812 (2019). https://doi.org/10.1007/s10462-019-09719-2
11. Horng, M.H.: Fine-tuning parameters of deep belief networks using artificial bee colony algorithm. DEStech Transactions on Computer Science and Engineering (2017)

12. Yang, X.S.: A new metaheuristic bat-inspired algorithm. In: González, J.R., Pelta, D.A., Cruz, C., Terrazas, G., Krasnogor, N. (eds.) Nature Inspired Cooperative Strategies for Optimization (NICSO 2010). Studies in Computational Intelligence, vol. 284, pp. 65–74. Springer, Berlin (2010) https://doi.org/10.1007/978-3-642-12538-6_6

13. Yang, X.S.: Nature-Inspired Metaheuristic Algorithms. Luniver Press, London (2010)

14. Leke, C., Ndjiongue, A.R., Twala, B., Marwala, T.: A deep learning-cuckoo search method for missing data estimation in high-dimensional datasets. In: Tan, Y., Takagi, H., Shi, Y. (eds.) ICSI 2017. LNCS, vol. 10385, pp. 561–572. Springer, Cham (2017). https://doi.org/10.1007/978-3-319-61824-1_61

15. Dorigo, M., Maniezzo, V., Colorni, A.: Ant system: optimization by a colony of cooperating agents. IEEE Trans. Syst. Man Cybern. Part B (Cybernetics) **26**(1), 29–41 (1996)

16. Desell, T., Clachar, S., Higgins, J., Wild, B.: Evolving deep recurrent neural networks using ant colony optimization. In: Ochoa, G., Chicano, F. (eds.) EvoCOP 2015. LNCS, vol. 9026, pp. 86–98. Springer, Cham (2015). https://doi.org/10.1007/978-3-319-16468-7_8

17. Mavrovouniotis, M., Yang, S.: Evolving neural networks using ant colony optimization with pheromone trail limits. In: 2013 13th UK Workshop on Computational Intelligence (UKCI), pp. 16–23. IEEE (2013)

18. ElSaid, A., El Jamiy, F., Higgins, J., Wild, B., Desell, T.: Optimizing long short-term memory recurrent neural networks using ant colony optimization to predict turbine engine vibration. Appl. Soft Comput. **73**, 969–991 (2018)

19. ElSaid, A.E.R., Ororbia, A.G., Desell, T.J.: Ant-based neural topology search (ANTS) for optimizing recurrent networks. In: Castillo, P.A., Jiménez Laredo, J.L., Fernández de Vega, F. (eds.) EvoApplications 2020. LNCS, vol. 12104, pp. 626–641. Springer, Cham (2020). https://doi.org/10.1007/978-3-030-43722-0_40

20. Cai, H., Zhu, L., Han, S.: Proxylessnas: Direct neural architecture search on target task and hardware. arXiv preprint arXiv:1812.00332 (2018)

21. Guo, Z., et al.: Single path one-shot neural architecture search with uniform sampling. In: Vedaldi, A., Bischof, H., Brox, T., Frahm, J.-M. (eds.) ECCV 2020. LNCS, vol. 12361, pp. 544–560. Springer, Cham (2020). https://doi.org/10.1007/978-3-030-58517-4_32

22. Bender, G., Kindermans, P.J., Zoph, B., Vasudevan, V., Le, Q.: Understanding and simplifying one-shot architecture search. In: International Conference on Machine Learning, pp. 550–559 (2018)

23. Dong, X., Yang, Y.: One-shot neural architecture search via self-evaluated template network. In: Proceedings of the IEEE International Conference on Computer Vision, pp. 3681–3690 (2019)

24. Zhao, Y., Wang, L., Tian, Y., Fonseca, R., Guo, T.: Few-shot neural architecture search. arXiv preprint arXiv:2006.06863 (2020)

25. Stanley, K.O., Miikkulainen, R.: Evolving neural networks through augmenting topologies. Evol. Comput. **10**(2), 99–127 (2002)

26. Miikkulainen, R., et al.: Evolving deep neural networks. In: Artificial Intelligence in the Age of Neural Networks and Brain Computing, pp. 293–312. Elsevier (2019)

27. Ororbia, A., ElSaid, A., Desell, T.: Investigating recurrent neural network memory structures using neuro-evolution. In: Proceedings of the Genetic and Evolutionary Computation Conference, GECCO 2019, pp. 446–455. ACM, New York, NY, USA (2019). https://doi.org/10.1145/3321707.3321795

28. Stanley, K.O., D'Ambrosio, D.B., Gauci, J.: A hypercube-based encoding for evolving large-scale neural networks. Artif. life **15**(2), 185–212 (2009)
29. Ororbia II, A.G., Mikolov, T., Reitter, D.: Learning simpler language models with the differential state framework. Neural Computation, pp. 1–26 (2017), https://doi.org/10.1162/neco_a_01017, pMID: 28957029
30. Chung, J., Gulcehre, C., Cho, K., Bengio, Y.: Empirical evaluation of gated recurrent neural networks on sequence modeling. arXiv preprint arXiv:1412.3555 (2014)
31. Hochreiter, S., Schmidhuber, J.: Long short-term memory. Neural Comput. **9**(8), 1735–1780 (1997)
32. Zhou, G.-B., Wu, J., Zhang, C.-L., Zhou, Z.-H.: Minimal gated unit for recurrent neural networks. Int. J. Autom. Comput. **13**(3), 226–234 (2016). https://doi.org/10.1007/s11633-016-1006-2
33. Collins, J., Sohl-Dickstein, J., Sussillo, D.: Capacity and trainability in recurrent neural networks. arXiv preprint arXiv:1611.09913 (2016)
34. Socha, K., Dorigo, M.: Ant colony optimization for continuous domains. Eur. J. Oper. Res. **185**(3), 1155–1173 (2008)
35. Kuhn, L.D.: Ant colony optimization for continuous spaces. Computer Science and Computer Engineering Undergraduate Honors Theses (35) (2002)
36. Xiao, J., Li, L.: A hybrid ant colony optimization for continuous domains. Exp. Syst. Appl. **38**(9), 11072–11077 (2011)
37. Gupta, H., Ghosh, B.: Transistor size optimization in digital circuits using ant colony optimization for continuous domain. Int. J. Circuit Theor. Appl. **42**(6), 642–658 (2014)
38. Bilchev, G., Parmee, I.C.: The ant colony metaphor for searching continuous design spaces. In: Fogarty, T.C. (ed.) AISB EC 1995. LNCS, vol. 993, pp. 25–39. Springer, Heidelberg (1995). https://doi.org/10.1007/3-540-60469-3_22
39. Ester, M., Kriegel, H.P., Sander, J., Xu, X., et al.: A density-based algorithm for discovering clusters in large spatial databases with noise. Kdd. **96**, 226–231 (1996)
40. He, K., Zhang, X., Ren, S., Sun, J.: Delving deep into rectifiers: surpassing human-level performance on imagenet classification. In: Proceedings of the IEEE International Conference on Computer Vision, pp. 1026–1034 (2015)
41. Glorot, X., Bengio, Y.: Understanding the difficulty of training deep feedforward neural networks. In: Proceedings of the Thirteenth International Conference on Artificial Intelligence and Statistics, pp. 249–256 (2010)
42. Mozer, M.C., Kazakov, D., Lindsey, R.V.: Discrete event, continuous time rnns. arXiv preprint arXiv:1710.04110 (2017)
43. Rochester Institute of Technology: Research computing services (2019). https://www.rit.edu/researchcomputing/

Soft Computing Applied to Games

Playing with Dynamic Systems - Battling Swarms in Virtual Reality

Johannes Büttner[(✉)] [ID], Christian Merz[(✉)] [ID], and Sebastian von Mammen

Games Engineering, Julius-Maximilians-University, Würzburg, Germany
{johannes.buettner,sebastian.von.mammen}@uni-wuerzburg.de
christian.merz@stud-mail.uni-wuerzburg.de

Abstract. In this paper, we present a serious game with the goal to provide an engaging and immersive experience to foster the players' understanding of dynamic networked systems. Confronted with attacking swarm networks, the player has to analyse their underlying network topologies and to systematically dismantle the swarms using a set of different weapons. We detail the game design, including the artificial intelligence of the swarm, the play mechanics and the level designs. Finally, we conducted an analysis of the play performances of a test group over the course of the game which revealed a positive learning outcome.

Keywords: Swarms · Boids · Network dismantling · Serious games

1 Introduction

The complex structures of real world systems in different areas of research and engineering have long been presented as networks, e.g. in empirical studies [12], in biological systems [20], social sciences [26], or information technology [35]. Graph theory allows us to analyse the topologies of these networks, to investigate how they evolve and to reveal how we could manipulate them. According analyses considered, for instance, the robustness of power grids [13], the interplay of the world's air traffic [32], or the spreading of computer viruses [25]. Effective dismantling strategies [7], that determine which edges to cut or nodes to knock out in which order, can help to slow down or even stop according, negative spreading phenomena [1], as also witnessed during certain phases of the coronavirus pandemic [34].

Swarms [2] can be understood as networked systems whose components' interactions result in volatile topologies [22]. Due to their spatially well-presented dynamics, swarms are perceived as lively and are considered as subjects or means of artistic expression [6,23] as well as of numerous academic and commercial computer games [21]. Building on these works, we set out to harness the interactivity of swarms in a computer game as well, and highlight (parts of) the relationship between their topologies and dynamics.

J. Büttner and C. Merz—Contributed in equal parts to this work.

© Springer Nature Switzerland AG 2021
P. A. Castillo and J. L. Jiménez Laredo (Eds.): EvoApplications 2021, LNCS 12694, pp. 309–324, 2021.
https://doi.org/10.1007/978-3-030-72699-7_20

It has been questioned in the past, whether serious games, with goals other than mere entertainment [15], need to be as much fun as commercial video games [8,30]. We aimed at providing both, an insightful and fun play experience. Learning from the great success of the serious game "America's Army" [19], we designed the game as a first-person shooter (FPS) as well, tasking the player with the goal to dismantle swarms of flying robots. In [9], we presented a brief overview of the game's mechanics. We decided on a virtual reality (VR) game as it has been shown that immersion can generally foster player performance and learning results [11] and because target acquisition and pointing, the basic interaction task of an FPS, is performed significantly faster in VR, as well [18].

The remainder of this paper is structured as follows. In Sect. 2, we provide an overview of relevant research on networks, network dismantlement and networks in games. In Sect. 3, we explain the concept and design of our developed game. In Sect. 4 we present a preliminary empirical study we conducted to analyse the game's effectiveness in terms of learning about network structures and dismantling. We conclude this paper with an outlook on possible future work.

2   Related Work

Initially, we had to decide on which kinds of networks we wanted to expose to the player. Therefore, we will briefly provide an overview of widely researched network topologies before elaborating on the concept of network dismantling. We will conclude this section with a brief introduction to related computer games.

2.1   Network Topologies

Topologies describe the patterns of node interconnections in networks. Different topologies lead to different network properties. So-called *scale-free networks* have a power-law distribution of connectivity values (degrees) among their nodes, i.e. these networks consist of many nodes of low and few nodes of high degree, also referred to as hubs [3]. With the great probability of randomly choosing a single node of low degree comes robustness against loss of random nodes. However, targeted attacks against hubs can easily break scale-free networks into smaller networks [31]. A scale-free network collapses when as few as 5 to 15% of its hubs are destroyed [3]. *Star networks* with only one hub connected to all the other nodes maximally stress the discrepancy between low and high degrees, which is why we also introduce this topology in the game. This is one of the most common topologies of computer networks [29]. *Grid networks* have a matrix-like structure, where each node is connected to its fixed set of neighbours. Instead of having a small number of hubs that are primary targets for dismantling, in grid networks all the nodes have the same degree (up to the grid's borders). For our game, we focused on scale-free and grid networks as they are rather distinct.

2.2   Network Dismantling

Network dismantling is the process of finding a set of nodes whose removal from the network results in the fragmentation of the network into subcritical network components at minimal overall cost [27]. Finding the most efficient way to dismantle a network is NP-hard. For large networks this implies that there is no algorithm that can reliably find the optimal solution. But there are heuristic approaches that can efficiently find good solutions [33]. The underlying metrics of these heuristics can be the degree of a node and its betweenness centrality, with the latter achieving better results. The betweenness centrality describes the number of shortest paths between every pair of nodes of the network that run through the given node. Further efficiency improvements can be achieved when updating these values throughout the dismantling process.

2.3   Networks in Games

There are digital games that fundamentally rely on network structures. In [21] several academically motivated examples of games involving swarms were summarised and a taxonomy was suggested considering the level, target and granularity of control as well as modalities including view, interface and time of interference.

Given its indisputably adverse goal, many stores removed the game Plague Inc: Evolved [24] temporarily from their offering list. Here, favouring pathogen spread is the goal and to eradicate humanity. Although the network of air travel plays an important role here, the player is focused on driving the evolution of pathogens to be most effective. The opposite, and thus much more humane, goal is pursued in the browser game VAX [10]. The player can stop viral spread in a turn-based setup by vaccinating and quarantining persons that are at risk of infection. Despite this rare example of network dismantling in games, most of them deal with building and maintenance of networks, also in other domains such as colonization, e.g. Anno 1800 [5], or in abstract contexts as in Planarity [14], a browser game that challenges the player to unravel a planar graph.

3   The Game's Design

In the presented VR FPS, the player is approached by swarms of attacking, flying robotic units. They assault by dropping bombs or by performing heads-on kamikaze attacks. A room-scale VR experience, having ported a first prototype from the HTC Vive to the Oculus Quest head-mounted display (HMD), immerses the player in a virtual environment. There is no form of locomotion other than moving in real-life. The player can step out of the line of attack, duck for cover or shield himself. Attack is, however, the best defense in the given context and a variety of ballistic weapons are at his disposal. The player can recharge his health and ammunition, if he succeeds in clearing and picking up resource packs from the swarm robots. The continuous motion and intermittent attacks of the enemy swarm combined with the different opportunities of interaction (Fig. 1) result in a generally fast paced gameplay and open a vast space of interwoven parameters for level design. Especially the arrangement of peaks and plateaus of the pace often correspond closely with the difficulty of the game.

3.1   The Swarm

The enemy swarms move based on the boids model [28] that considers each swarm member an agent that decides on its movement based on its neighbors. Boid agents follow three simple urges, i.e. avoidance of collisions, alignment with their neighbours and separation from neighbours that come too close. For the purpose of our game, we added additional rules (Fig. 2): (a) the maintenance

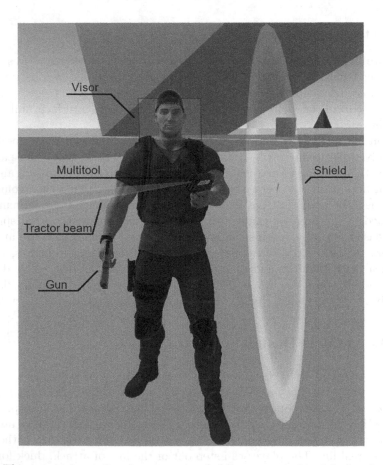

Fig. 1. This image shows the player's avatar, holding a gun in his right hand, a multitool in his left hand. The latter can emit a tractor beam to attract falling perks, put up a shield (circular, blue) and project an augmented visor field that reveals the swarms' topologies (rectangular, blue). (Color figure online)

of assigned neighbor connections in accordance with an a priori-determined network topology (Sect. 2), (b) following a given path through the environment,
and (c) avoiding collisions with objects on this path. Concerning their hostile
manoeuvres, (d) swarm agents attack the player when getting close. In addition,
(e) each agent also has a small chance to trigger an attack by its neighbors. Such
triggered attacks will not terminate until the player suffered damage or successfully shielded himself. We introduced this mechanic in order to stress the greater
influence of hubs in the network, as higher degrees of swarm agents immediately
translate to greater chances of triggering neighbor attacks, emanating greater
threats.

Due to the addition of multiple rules, for all rules R, the normalized results
r of each independent rule had to be multiplied by their respective weights w to
result in the desired direction vector d (Eq. 1).

$$d = \sum_{i=1}^{R} r_i \cdot w_i \tag{1}$$

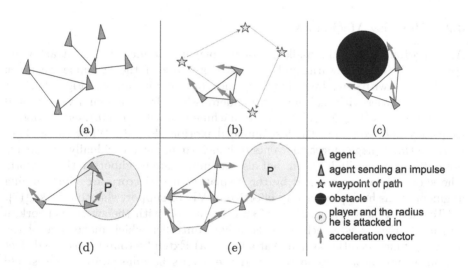

Fig. 2. (a) Boids consider pre-defined network connections, (b) follow a given path, (c)
avoid obstacles, (d) attack the player, when they are near him, and (e) can send an
impulse to their directly connected boids, which triggers an attack from them.

We designed three types of enemies with varying proximities and network
topologies (Fig. 3): (a) Tentacle agents form scale-free networks and maintain
great distances. (b) Bee-like Sting agents form grid networks and keep close
to each other. (c) There are small and large Pin agents. The large ones can
sustain large amounts of damage and are surrounded by smaller Pins to form
star networks. As stated before, targeting the hubs allows the player to fight
scale-free networks effectively. The most effective way for the player to dismantle

star-networked swarm is targeting its only hub. On the other hand, grid networks have no specific point of attack and force the player to develop a more elaborate fighting strategy.

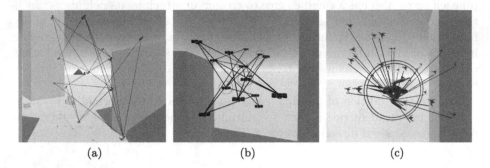

(a)   (b)   (c)

Fig. 3. (a) Tentacle bots form scale-free networks, (b) Sting bots grids, and (c) Pin bots star networks.

3.2   The Play Mechanics

An important part of the challenge for the player is to identify and attack weak spots in the enemy swarm and to make good use of the available weapons: (a) A pistol with low, $1sec$ shot frequency but infinite ammo (Fig. 4), (b) a grenade launcher with high impact, ponderous $3sec$ frequency and very limited ammo resources (Fig. 5), and (c) a sub-machine gun with high $0.125sec$ shooting frequency and, consequently, fast ammo depletion (Fig. 6). While (a) and (c) increase the damage of swarm agents to knock them out individually, (b) affects not only the primarily hit agent but also its immediate neighbors in the network. The shooting task is assisted by the display of a trajectory arc. Such aiming augmentations have proven very effective in VR to support shooting tasks [17].

To further assist the analysis of and interaction with the swarm network, a multitool (Fig. 7) is attached to the other controller which makes one of the following functionalities available at a time: (a) Extend a round *shield* to deflect swarm agents on a collision course. If the agents become aware of the shield early enough, they dodge and stop their attack. If used for too long, the shield needs to recharge. An according "energy"-bar hovers above the multitool. (b) Shoot a *tractor beam* to pull new weapons, resource packs, or swarm agents towards the player. The traction on the agents is inversely proportional to their network degrees. (c) Activate a *visor* that displays the network's edges between the swarm agents (Fig. 8). In addition, agents of high degrees are encircled. At the beginning of the game, this display is always on. But this comfort feature breaks down later in the game and the player has to activate the visor manually by holding the multitool next to his head. In this way, the player has to actively decide which multitool functionality is best in any given situation.

Fig. 4. Pistol

Fig. 5. Grenade launcher

Fig. 6. Sub-machine Gun

Fig. 7. Health and shield status float above the multitool to keep the player informed at all times.

Fig. 8. The visor augmenting the player's view with network information.

If the player's health value drops to zero, the game is over. To recover from suffered attacks, he has to pick up health packs. Resource packs are collectively carried by subsets of agents of the enemy swarm, i.e. the packs are connected to several agents and if those are taken down, loot boxes drop to the ground as well. While within reach, the player can pull the packs towards him and pick them up using the tractor beam, restoring health or ammunition. If, by accident, the player shoots any of those lootboxes (Fig. 9), they are destroyed. He, therefore, has to diligently distinguish between different nodes in the network and dismantle it carefully—in analogy to, for instance, freeing hostages in military operations, releasing non-infected persons in handling disease spread, or maintaining vital functions in economic or biological systems.

3.3 Level Design

Several tutorial levels ease the player into the game by explaining the basic interaction mechanics, effects of weapons and the required resource management. Each level of the game follows the same routine: A swarm flocks along a given path and attacks the player when in his vicinity. The player uses his tools and whits to destroy the swarm. Taking an enemy out results in a death animation of the swarm agent and text feedback with the achieved score for this takedown. When all the connections of a swarm agent are cut by knocking out its neighbours, the agent also becomes dysfunctional and falls to the ground. When the whole swarm is destroyed, the level is cleared and the player is challenged by the next of 12 levels in total. As pointed out in Sect. 2 optimally dismantling a (swarm) network is not an easy task but it ensures that (a) the player receives high scores and (b) his odds of survival rise.

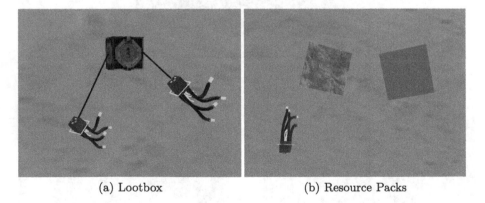

(a) Lootbox   (b) Resource Packs

Fig. 9. A lootbox (a) drops resource packs (b) when cut loose from the swarm network.

In the first level, the player can only use the multitool to learn to shield himself. It is the only level that utilizes very small enemies that are destroyed upon contact with the shield. The second level introduces the pistol, the third level the grenade launcher (and switching weapons), the fourth level the sub-machine gun, and the fifth one lootboxes. In level eight, the player's visor experiences a malfunction. Its previously always-on display of network information has to be manually activated from now on. An appropriate tutorial is provided. Level nine is special as a Pin agent in star network formation together with 30 light-weight agents occurs for the first time. Here, sustaining lots of damage and neighbor attacks become decisive mechanics. From level ten onward, the player has to battle two swarms at the same time. In level ten itself, the second swarm spawns after a $10sec$ delay, which gives the player the opportunity to focus on the first swarm but also provides for a surprise. In subsequent levels, the swarms spawn at the same time.

Figure 10 provides an overview of the level design. We organised the level progression to incrementally teach the game mechanics. Increasing the numbers of swarm individuals and swarms increases the difficulty of the game aiming at better flow and learning effects. Starting the game with a fully functioning visor shows the player the importance of the underlying network topologies. The required manual activation starting in level eight makes the player experience the lack of these crucial information and re-enforces their strategic utilization.

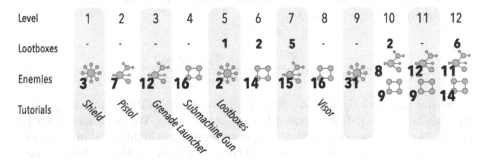

Fig. 10. Lootbox information, number of enemies and tutorials of each level. The enemies' topologies are represented symbolically as well: Star, scale-free and grid networks are first encountered in levels 1, 2, and 4, respectively.

4   Evaluating Dismantling Apprehension

In order to examine whether playing the game improves one's abilities to efficiently dismantle networks, we measured 15 players' (12 male) performances. Thirteen of the test persons were students, two of them were employed in retail. They were between 20 and 28 years of age (M = 22.5, SD = 2.23) and played games for about 11 h a week on average (M = 11.36, SD = 8.94). Three of the participants had never worn HMDs before. On average, they had used HMDs for about 40 h (M = 40.30, SD = 57.27).

We followed the following procedure: After welcoming the participants, they filled out a demographic questionnaire. Next, they were introduced to using the HMD and its controllers. The participants were advised to ask the experimenters for help, only if they could not accomplish a task by themselves. Then, the participants played the game, which lasted about $15min$. The experimenters watched the progression on a laptop and took notes. In case the participants were not able to complete all of the levels, they were not asked to replay the game. After playing, the participants were instructed to take off the HMD. Finally, they were asked by one of the experimenters, whether they had used different fighting strategies for the different opponents.

In order to evaluate the performance of the participants, we calculated two different measures, f_{bc} and f_{deg}. With increasing difficulty, both values decrease or remain steady, only if the subject's skill of dismantling networks increases. f_{bc} (Eq. 2) is the arithmetic mean of the differences of the highest betweenness centrality $max\ g(n) \in [0..1]$ yielded by node n_{max} and the betweenness centrality of the node destroyed $g(n_h)$ at discrete hit h, whereas $hits$ denotes the set of nodes hit over the course of one level.

$$f_{bc} = \frac{\sum_{h=1}^{||hits||} g(n_{max}) - g(n_h)}{||hits||} \tag{2}$$

We calculated the measure f_{deg} analogously (Eq. 3), considering the nodes' degrees $d(n)$, normalized by the maximal degree throughout a whole level, i.e. $\hat{d}(n) = d(n)/max\ d(arg\ \max_{n_h \in hits} d(n_h))$.

$$f_{deg} = \frac{\sum_{h=1}^{||hits||} \hat{d}(n_{max}) - \hat{d}(n_h)}{||hits||} \tag{3}$$

As the measures signify differences from the best possible dismantling strategy, smaller values indicate greater impact of the shots. We calculated both f_{bc} and f_{deg} because the nodes with the highest degrees are highlighted in the game, but they do not necessarily coincide with the nodes with the highest betweenness centrality. It has been shown that the latter is the better heuristic for efficiently dismantling of a network [33], but the degree is more directly observable in the game. We, therefore, investigated whether there was a difference between using f_{bc} and f_{deg} for rating the player's performance.

The topology of a swarm remains fixed until the player removes an agent/node from the swarm/network. Therefore, the measures f_{deg} and f_{bc} did not consider the time it took to take down the enemies, reaction times, weapon usage or tactics. Rather, they rate the realisation of a specific dismantling strategy, i.e. how well the player can decide which enemy should be attacked in a concrete situation. There is an optimal way to play each level, but considering the large interaction space (the states of the player and the swarm, the weapon used, the target hit, etc.), it is only of theoretical value. Therefore, the given measures only consider the optimal target at the time of a hit.

We excluded hit lootboxes from the calculations, as these nodes were not hostile. The measures were not applied to levels one and five because all the interactions in these levels were guided tutorial tasks. Level nine was excluded because it is the only network with the star topology and it does not support the analysis of performance improvements. Additionally, we calculated the correlation between the measures and the usage time of the visor ("visor up-time") by means of Pearson's correlation coefficient, starting with the proactive use of the visor in level eight.

Figure 11 shows the connectivity of swarm individuals in a given level after a given number of shots. As a result, the diagrams reveal the degree distribution established at first and how the players' shots changed the topology quantitatively over time. The initial degree distributions in grid networks peak at 3 as most agents are at the perimeter of the swarm, few are inside the grid (4 neighbours) or in the grid's corners (2 neighbours). The scale-free networks are created based on the Barabási-Albert model [4]: First, two nodes are generated and connected. Next, a new node is added to the network at a time and connected to already existing nodes with a connection probability proportional to the existing nodes' relative degrees. Statistically, this procedure results in a scale-free degree distribution. The degree distributions shown in Fig. 11 deviate in that boids with a degree of 1 cannot exist due to the game's mechanics. In addition, the initial distributions of the different levels are fixed across multiple runs to ensure a consistent game experience.

In terms of the evolution of degree distributions, one can see that levels featuring scale-free networks show higher standard deviations than those featuring grid networks. Grid networks have no immediately favourable point of attack such as the hubs in scale-free networks. Therefore, the attack strategy has a smaller influence. A plausible explanation for this difference is that the discrepancy between the players' analytical skills or knowledge is more pronounced in levels featuring scale-free networks.

In Figs. 12 and 13, the mean values with standard deviation of f_{bc} and f_{deg} are plotted in the context of the levels' difficulty. Due to the high standard deviations, there is no visible improvement or deterioration in any of the measurements throughout the game. But the difficulty of the game increases with each level due to more complex interaction mechanics, and the rising numbers of enemies and swarms as detailed in Figs. 12 and 13. In particular, we calculated the difficulty according to Eq. 4, whereas t denotes the type of the underlying network topology (weighted with 1 for star networks, 2 for grids, and 3 for scale-free and mixed swarms), n_{agents} the number of agents of the attacking swarm(s), n_{loot} the number of lootboxes in a level times the corresponding weight w_{loot} (weighted with 4) and on whether the player has to activate the visor manually, or not (encoded in variable v, weighted with 20). The values for n_{agents} and n_{loot} are shown in Fig. 10. The values and their influence on the difficulty expressed in Eq. 4 roughly correspond with the difficulty introduced by these respective game elements that we perceived during their formative development.

$$difficulty = t \cdot n_{agents} + w_{loot} \cdot n_{loot} + v \qquad (4)$$

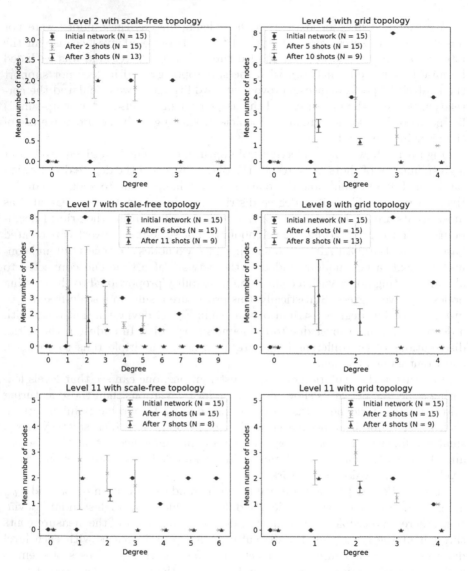

Fig. 11. Degree distribution of the mean number of nodes with the standard deviation at the initial network state, intermediate state and at the state before most players had completed the level. The left graphs show levels with scale-free networks and the right graphs show levels with grid networks.

As Hamari et al. [16] stated, an always challenging game endorses learning. The fact that there is no significant change in the calculated scores indicates that the player's performance, and therefore his knowledge about dismantling networks, improves proportionally to the rise in difficulty.

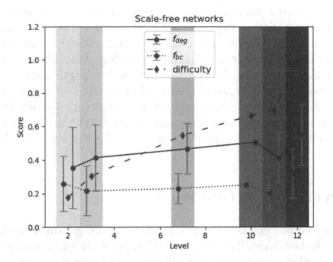

Fig. 12. Scale-free networks: Mean with standard deviation of f_{bc} and f_{deg}, and difficulty for the given levels. Intervals shaded in blue show levels featuring swarms in scale-free formation. Those in purple show levels featuring grid networks and scale-free networks. Here only scale-free networks are presented. The shades' opaqueness reflects the levels' difficulty. For clarity in the diagram, the values of the difficulty have been normalized based on the maximum difficulty value.

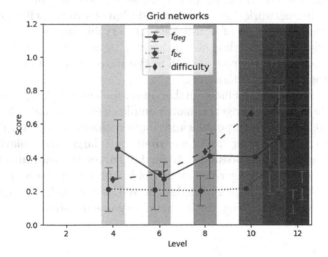

Fig. 13. Grid networks: Mean with Standard Deviation of f_{bc} and f_{deg}, and difficulty for the given levels. Intervals shaded in yellow show levels featuring swarms in grid formation. Those in purple show levels featuring grid networks and scale-free networks. Here, only grid networks are presented. The shades' opaqueness reflects the levels' difficulty. For clarity in the diagram, the values of the difficulty have been normalized based on the maximum difficulty value.

When asked about their fighting strategies, most participants pointed out differences in the behavior of the boids in the star network compared to the other formations. They reported that they focused on the central hub to destroy the network. This was validated by the game logs that show that the shots were almost exclusively on the central hub. A few participants were able to detect and specifically indicate that the Sting agents flew in closer proximity and changed directions simultaneously, whereas the tentacles flew further apart and moved more independently. One subject reported that he focused on the tentacles because they were easier to defeat. No further strategic deliberations were reported.

5   Summary and Future Work

In this paper, we presented a computer game featuring swarms as lively, interactive networked systems. The players' performances in dismantling the swarms increases with play experience. The difficulty of the levels of the game is balanced to always challenge the players to a similar extent, resulting in a desirable gaming experience and fostering the learning outcome. As the proposed performance measures do not consider the players' reactivity or resource management but only capture the gain from hitting an individual node at a time, we suggest that the players' performance improvement may be tied to an improved knowledge about network dismantling and the exposed network topologies.

As a result, the contributions of this paper include the concept of a serious game for training network dismantling, the design of swarms with fixed network formations, the integration of non-hostile, preservable nodes, various means of interaction with the networked swarm agents, as well as a flow-inducing level design that drove the gameplay, as well as the introduction of evaluation scores to measure the players' performance.

Our next steps will include further development of the game, including greater numbers of swarm agents, more complex networks and a longer overall playtime. A release through popular distribution channels is planned, especially as we hope to gain a greater size of contributors to larger-scale playtests in this way. It would open up the possibility to further survey the learning effects of the game. In this context, a longer-term study of learning apprehension and tests of explicit factual or procedural knowledge, as well as knowledge transfer could be incorporated, also considering, for instance, in-game questionnaires.

References

1. Altarelli, F., Braunstein, A., Dall'Asta, L., Wakeling, J.R., Zecchina, R.: Containing epidemic outbreaks by message-passing techniques. Phys. Rev. X **4**(2), (2014)
2. Bak, P.: How nature works: the science of self-organized criticality. Springer Science & Business Media (2013)
3. Hein, O., Schwind, M., König, W.: Scale-free networks. Wirtschaftsinformatik **48**(4), 267–275 (2006). https://doi.org/10.1007/s11576-006-0058-2

4. Barabási, A.L., Pósfai, M.: Network Science. Cambridge University Press, Cambridge (2016)
5. Blue Byte: Anno 1800 (2019). https://ubisoft.com/. Accessed 27 Mar 2020
6. Bornhofen, S., Gardeux, V., Machizaud, A.: From swarm art toward ecosystem art. Int. J. Swarm Intell. Res. (IJSIR) **3**(3), 1–18 (2012)
7. Braunstein, A., Dall'Asta, L., Semerjian, G., Zdeborová, L.: Network dismantling. Proc. Natl. Acad. Sci. **113**(44), 12368–12373 (2016)
8. Buday, R., Baranowski, T., Thompson, D.: Fun and games and boredom. GAMES FOR HEALTH: Research, Development, and Clinical Applications **1**(4), 257–261 (2012)
9. Büttner, J., Merz, C., von Mammen, S.: Horde battle iii or how to dismantle a swarm. In: 2020 IEEE Conference on Games (CoG), pp. 640–641. IEEE, Osaka, Japan (2020)
10. Campbell, E.: VAX (2014). https://vax.herokuapp.com. Accessed 23 Mar 2020
11. Cheng, M.T., She, H.C., Annetta, L.A.: Game immersion experience: its hierarchical structure and impact on game-based science learning. J. Comput. Assist. Learn. **31**(3), 232–253 (2015)
12. Costa, L.d.F., et al.: Analyzing and modeling real-world phenomena with complex networks: a survey of applications. Adv. Phys. **60**(3), 329–412 (2011)
13. Cuadra, L., Salcedo-Sanz, S., Del Ser, J., Jiménez-Fernández, S., Geem, Z.W.: A critical review of robustness in power grids using complex networks concepts. Energies **8**(9), 9211–9265 (2015)
14. Davies, J.: Planarity (2005). https://jasondavies.com/planarity. Accessed 23 Mar 2020
15. De Gloria, A., Bellotti, F., Berta, R.: Serious games for education and training. Int. J. Serious Games **1**(1) (2014). https://doi.org/10.17083/ijsg.v1i1.11
16. Hamari, J., Shernoff, D.J., Rowe, E., Coller, B., Asbell-Clarke, J., Edwards, T.: Challenging games help students learn: an empirical study on engagement, flow and immersion in game-based learning. Comput. Hum. Behav. **54**, 170–179 (2016)
17. Harvey, C., Selmanovic, E., O'Connor, J., Chahin, M.: Validity of virtual reality training for motor skill development in a serious game. In: 2018 10th International Conference on Virtual Worlds and Games for Serious Applications (VS-Games), pp. 1–8 (2018)
18. Heydn, K.A.M., Dietrich, M.P., Barkowsky, M., Winterfeldt, G., von Mammen, S., Nüchter, A.: The golden bullet: a comparative study for target acquisition, pointing and shooting. In: 2019 11th International Conference on Virtual Worlds and Games for Serious Applications (VS-Games), pp. 1–8. IEEE (2019)
19. Hitchens, M.: A survey of first-person shooters and their avatars. Game Stud. **11**(3), 96–120 (2011)
20. Liao, J.C., Boscolo, R., Yang, Y.L., Tran, L.M., Sabatti, C., Roychowdhury, V.P.: Network component analysis: reconstruction of regulatory signals in biological systems. Proc. Natl. Acad. Sci. **100**(26), 15522–15527 (2003)
21. von Mammen, S.: Self-organisation in games, games on self-organisation. In: 2016 8th International Conference on Games and Virtual Worlds for Serious Applications (VS-Games), pp. 1–8. IEEE (2016)
22. von Mammen, S., Jacob, C.: The spatiality of swarms – quantitative analysis of dynamic interaction networks. In: Proceedings of Artificial Life XI, pp. 662–669. MIT Press, Winchester, UK (2008)
23. von Mammen, S., Jacob, C.: The evolution of swarm grammars: Growing trees, crafting art and bottom-up design. IEEE Comput. Intell. Mag. **4**, 10–19 (2009)

24. Ndemic Creations: Plague Inc: Evolved (2016). https://ndemiccreations.com/. Accessed 23 Mar 2020
25. Newman, M.E., Forrest, S., Balthrop, J.: Email networks and the spread of computer viruses. Phys. Rev. E **66**(3), 035101 (2002)
26. Passos, P., Davids, K., Araújo, D., Paz, N., Minguéns, J., Mendes, J.: Networks as a novel tool for studying team ball sports as complex social systems. J. Sci. Med. Sport **14**(2), 170–176 (2011)
27. Ren, X.L., Gleinig, N., Helbing, D., Antulov-Fantulin, N.: Generalized network dismantling. Proc. Natl. Acad. Sci. **116**(14), 6554–6559 (2019)
28. Reynolds, C.W.: Flocks, herds and schools: a distributed behavioral model. SIGGRAPH Comput. Graph. **21**(4), 25–34 (1987). https://doi.org/10.1145/37402. 37406, http://doi.acm.org/10.1145/37402.37406
29. Santra, S., Acharjya, P.P.: A study and analysis on computer network topology for data communication. Int. J. Emerging Technol. Adv. Eng. **3**(1), 522–525 (2013)
30. Shen, C., Wang, H., Ritterfeld, U.: Serious games and seriously fun games. Serious games: Mechanisms and effects **48**, (2009)
31. Strogatz, S.H.: Exploring complex networks. Nature **410**(6825), 268–276 (2001). https://doi.org/10.1038/35065725, https://doi.org/10.1038/35065725
32. Verma, T., Araújo, N.A., Herrmann, H.J.: Revealing the structure of the world airline network. Sci. Rep. **4**(1), 1–6 (2014)
33. Wandelt, S., Sun, X., Feng, D., Zanin, M., Havlin, S.: A comparative analysis of approaches to network-dismantling. Sci. Rep. **8**(1), 1–15 (2018)
34. Wu, Z., McGoogan, J.M.: Characteristics of and important lessons from the coronavirus disease 2019 (covid-19) outbreak in china: summary of a report of 72 314 cases from the Chinese center for disease control and prevention. Jama (2020)
35. Yook, S.H., Jeong, H., Barabási, A.L.: Modeling the internet's large-scale topology. Proc. Natl. Acad. Sci. **99**(21), 13382–13386 (2002)

EvoCraft: A New Challenge for Open-Endedness

Djordje Grbic[1], Rasmus Berg Palm[1], Elias Najarro[1], Claire Glanois[2],
and Sebastian Risi[1,3(✉)]

[1] IT University of Copenhagen, Copenhagen, Denmark
[2] Shanghai University, Shanghai, China
[3] modl.ai, Copenhagen, Denmark

Abstract. This paper introduces EvoCraft, a framework for Minecraft designed to study open-ended algorithms. We introduce an API that provides an open-source Python interface for communicating with Minecraft to place and track blocks. In contrast to previous work in Minecraft that focused on learning to play the game, the grand challenge we pose here is to automatically search for increasingly complex artifacts in an open-ended fashion. Compared to other environments used to study open-endedness, Minecraft allows the construction of almost any kind of structure, including actuated machines with circuits and mechanical components. We present initial baseline results in evolving simple Minecraft creations through both interactive and automated evolution. While evolution succeeds when tasked to grow a structure towards a specific target, it is unable to find a solution when rewarded for creating a simple machine that moves. Thus, EvoCraft offers a challenging new environment for automated search methods (such as evolution) to find complex artifacts that we hope will spur the development of more open-ended algorithms. A Python implementation of the EvoCraft framework is available at: github.com/real-itu/Evocraft-py.

Keywords: Games · Minecraft · Interactive evolution · Automated evolution

1 Introduction

Artificial intelligence (AI) approaches have shown remarkable advances in the last couple of years, solving increasingly complex challenges. A key driver in these advances has been specific environments and competitions that allowed different approaches to be easily compared. For example, developing frameworks and learning environments, such as the StarCraft II Learning Environment [41] has spurred the development of many recent advances in the field [9,41].

A grand research challenge with relatively less progress has been the goal of open-endedness [19,32,35]. Similarly to how evolution in nature created the seemingly endless array of novel and adaptive forms, the goal in open-endedness is to create similar open-ended algorithms in artificial life simulations [1].

© Springer Nature Switzerland AG 2021
P. A. Castillo and J. L. Jiménez Laredo (Eds.): EvoApplications 2021, LNCS 12694, pp. 325–340, 2021.
https://doi.org/10.1007/978-3-030-72699-7_21

However, while current alife environments have produced a large variety of important evolutionary insights [15, 18, 22, 24, 32, 45], they are often still limited in the type of open-ended evolutionary dynamics that can emerge. Some of these alife environments are shown in Fig. 1. Compared to structures players were able to built in Minecraft (Fig. 2), current alife environments are somewhat limited in the type of behaviors or artifacts that can be discovered. Additionally, the myriad of different alife worlds that often investigate different alife aspects can make it difficult to compare approaches to each other.

In this paper, we propose to use Minecraft as the perfect environment for the study of artificial life and open-endedness in particular. Minecraft is a voxel-based environment in which the basic building blocks are different types of blocks such as wood, stone, glass, water, etc. Especially the addition of "redstone" circuit components in Minecraft (i.e. blocks that support circuits and mechanical components), has allowed players to build amazing structures, such as moving robots, fully functioning word processors, or even Atari 2600 emulators (Fig. 2). Compared to most alife domains, a major benefit of Minecraft is that everything can be built from a finite set of different and simple buildings blocks, which aligns well with the machinery of biological systems that only use a few building blocks to synthesizing the multitude of complex chemicals that form the basis of all organic life.

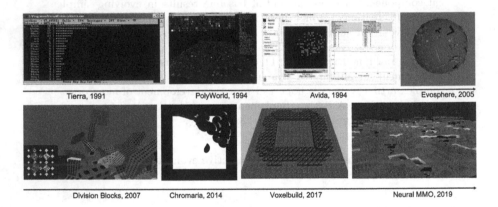

Fig. 1. A selection of existing OOE frameworks.

In this paper, we introduce the API, framework, and first results for our EvoCraft environment. EvoCraft is implemented as a mod for Minecraft that allows clients to manipulate blocks in a running Minecraft server programmatically through an API. The framework is specifically developed to facilitate experiments in artificial evolution and other optimization algorithms. We show that evolving simple artefacts, such as structures that grow towards a particular target is straightforward with our developed API. We also show that evolving a Minecraft machine that moves is a challenging problem, for which traditional fitness-based approaches fail and make little progress. We therefore argue that EvoCraft offers an exciting and challenging environment for experiments in artificial life and open-ended evolution. In addition to releasing this API, we will run EvoCraft competitions at different evolutionary and artificial life conferences, starting with GECCO 2021.

Fig. 2. Examples of human-build structures in Minecraft: A large moving robot [6], a functioning word processors [37], Atari 2600 emulator [29] and neural network digit classifier [31].

One of the ideas of open-endedness is to be surprised by its creations. While previous domains were limited in the type of structures that could be evolved, Minecraft could offer a domain in which an open-ended discovery engine could generate truly surprising artifacts.

2   Related Work

This section reviews work on environments used to study open-ended evolution and previous work that uses Minecraft to test different AI approaches.

2.1   Open-Endedness Frameworks

Researchers have explored and developed a variety of different environments to study open-endedness [2,3,5,8,15,18,22,24,32,33,38,40,45], some of which are shown in Fig. 1. One of the first examples of trying to achieve open-ended evolution in an artificial world was Tierra [24]. In Tierra programs that compete for CPU cycles evolve, being composed of machine code instructions. Avida [18] is another artificial life world, which was inspired by Tierra, but here creatures are rewarded for their ability to perform various computations. Experiments in these artificial life environments can lead to important insights into evolutionary dynamics. For example, in a landmark study Lenski et al. [13] showed how complex behaviors can evolve by building on simpler functions with digital organisms in Avida.

Other examples of such alife worlds include Geb [2], Evosphere [15] and PolyWorld [45], in which populations of creatures evolve in 3D and 2D worlds, learning to interact and fight other creatures. Another interesting example is Division Blocks [33], in which 3D creatures made out of blocks evolve to grow, shrink, exchange resources, create joints, and actuate joints.

More recently, researchers have studied in more detail what might be the necessary ingredients for open-ended dynamics to emerge. Within an alife world called Chromaria, Soros and Stanley [32], identified conditions such as that each individual must satisfy some minimum criteria before it can reproduce or that individuals should be able to decide where and how to interact with their world. If these conditions will be similar or different within the proposed EvoCraft environment is an interesting future research direction.

Recent work related to EvoCraft is the Voxelbuild virtual sandbox environment [22] (Fig. 1). In this environment, which is inspired by Minecraft, agents are evolving to build complex block structures. The environment was designed to test an important facet of open-ended evolution, which are the mechanisms behind major evolutionary transitions. The authors observe that in some evolutionary runs, these transitions occur, such as the ability for the agents to figure out how to place blocks vertically. This work shows the potential for a virtual sandbox environment to study evolution and serves as a good proof of concept for the more complex EvoCraft environment introduced in this paper.

A more recent approach, inspired by earlier multi-agent alife environments [2,15,45], is Neural MMO [38]. The Neural MMO is a multi-agent system that features a large population of agents. In contrast to previously introduced multi-agent alife environments, Neural MMO is focused on training a large number of agents through reinforcement learning approaches to forage and to engage other agents in combat. Similar to the Neural MMO, Minecraft naturally supports a large number of agents and additionally also features the ability to build structures.

While the environments presented in this section are undoubtedly useful and led to groundbreaking discoveries [13], we argue here that Minecraft offers a naturally next step to study open-endedness on a larger scale.

In addition to developing different alife environments to foster open-ended evolution, recently interest has increased in creating algorithms for more open-ended learning. For example, a class of algorithms called quality diversity (QD) methods [23], try to maximize diversity in the discovered stepping stones that can lead to more and more complex artifacts [12,17]. Algorithms such as POET [43] extend these ideas to generate both the environments and agent behaviors, creating a system for more open-ended discovery. To see the full benefits of

EvoCraft, it will likely have to be combined with one of these QD algorithms in the future, or will more likely require the development of new open-ended learning methods.

2.2 Minecraft

Minecraft has emerged as a popular testing environment for a diverse array of AI benchmarks. A popular framework for training reinforcement learning agents in Minecraft is Project Malmo [10], which gives an abstraction layer on top of Minecraft that makes it straightforward to integrate AI agents and to design and run experiments. Project Malmo and connected research efforts such as MineRL [7] (which includes a large dataset of human Minecraft demonstrations) focus on training agents operating from a first-person perspective to solve challenges such as vision, navigation, long-term planning, or interacting with other agents. In contrast, EvoCraft focuses on the idea of open-ended discovery, providing an API that allows the direct manipulation of blocks, instead of training agents to manipulate them.

The closest related challenge to ours is the Minecraft AI Settlement Generation Challenge [25, 26]. In this challenge, the goal is to write an AI program that can create interesting settlements for unseen maps. In contrast to EvoCraft, the settlement API does not support reading information back from the environment. In other words, in the settlement generation challenge, Minecraft is used to render a settlement that is generated offline based on a given map description. Instead, EvoCraft focuses on generating artifacts whose performance should be judged by the way they interact with the environment.

Others have explored to train agents in Minecraft through interactive evolution to solve simple navigation tasks [21], or created a Minecraft-like environment in which users can interactively evolve 3D building blocks and then collaboratively build larger structures [20].

In summary, EvoCraft complements the existing Minecraft APIs that are used for research in AI, by enabling real-time feedback on the position and types of blocks, and by including redstone components that allow the evolution of mechanics and circuits.

3 The EvoCraft Environment

EvoCraft is a mod for Minecraft that allows clients to manipulate blocks in a running Minecraft server programmatically through an API. A Python implementation of EvoCraft is available at: github.com/real-itu/Evocraft-py. To use the server interface with other languages, we provide interface definition files to generate clients for (almost) any programming language: github.com/real-itu/minecraft-rpc.

The API is based on the Sponge modding platform [42] that enables creating mods for Minecraft in form of Java plugins for the Minecraft server. Communication with the EvoCraft mod is based on gRPC Remote Procedure Calls (gRPC) framework which allows defining language agnostic strongly typed RPCs[1]. A gRPC specification consists of **services** and **messages**. A **service** exposes one or more **rpcs**, which are the callable endpoints and the **messages** define the inputs and outputs. A **message** is composed of other **messages** and primitive data types, e.g. strings, integers, etc. The EvoCraft RPC specification completely defines the API and serves as the primary documentation.

The initial release of the EvoCraft API has a single **service** with three **rpcs**. See Listing 1.1. The Minecraft mod implements the EvoCraft gRPC API and listens on port 5001.

```
1  service MinecraftService {
2      /** Spawn multiple blocks. */
3      rpc spawnBlocks (Blocks) returns (Empty);
4      /** Return all blocks in a cube */
5      rpc readCube (Cube) returns (Blocks);
6      /** Fill a cube with a block type */
7      rpc fillCube (FillCubeRequest) returns (Empty);
8  }
```

Listing 1.1. The EvoCraft gRPC API definition. For brevity the headers and message definitions are omitted.

Given the gRPC definition, it is possible to automatically generate clients in multiple programming languages, e.g. Python, Java, Go, etc. The initial release contains a generated python client. See Listing 1.2 for an example of using the python client.

An example of slime-block-based flying technologies, using a specific placement of pistons, blocks of redstone, observers, and slime blocks. A simple flying machine already requires a non-trivial arrangement of blocks. In Sect. 4.2 we investigate how difficult it is for evolution to discover a moving machine from scratch.

```
1  import grpc
2  import minecraft_pb2_grpc
3  from minecraft_pb2 import *
4
5  channel = grpc.insecure_channel('localhost:5001')
6  client = minecraft_pb2_grpc.MinecraftServiceStub(channel)
7
8  client.fillCube(FillCubeRequest(
9      cube=Cube(
10         min=Point(x=-10, y=4, z=-10),
11         max=Point(x=10, y=14, z=10)
12     ),
13     type=AIR
14 ))
15 client.spawnBlocks(Blocks(blocks=[
16 # Lower layer
17 Block(position=Point(x=1, y=5, z=1), type=PISTON, NORTH),
```

---

[1] https://grpc.io.

```
18  Block(position=Point(x=1, y=5, z=0),  type=SLIME, NORTH),
19  Block(position=Point(x=1, y=5, z=-1), type=STICKY_PISTON, SOUTH),
20  Block(position=Point(x=1, y=5, z=-2), type=PISTON, NORTH),
21  Block(position=Point(x=1, y=5, z=-4), type=SLIME, NORTH),
22  # Upper layer
23  Block(position=Point(x=1, y=6, z=0),  type=REDSTONE_BLOCK, NORTH),
24  Block(position=Point(x=1, y=6, z=-4), type=REDSTONE_BLOCK, NORTH),
25  # Activate
26  Block(position=Point(x=1, y=6, z=-1), type=QUARTZ_BLOCK, NORTH),
27  ]))
```

Listing 1.2. Example use of the EvoCraft python client to clear a $20 \times 10 \times 20$ working space (line 8) and spawn a minimal flying machine (line 15). See Fig. 3 for the resulting flying machine.

Fig. 3. A minimal flying machine (created by code in Listing 1.2), which perpetually moves north.

3.1   Performance

The Minecraft server runs at a fixed (maximum) update rate of 20 ticks/s. At each tick, the game state is updated and sent to the clients. If the server is overloaded such that a tick takes more than 50 ms, the tick rate drops. We perform two tests to estimate how performant the EvoCraft is on a Macbook Pro with a 2.4 GHz 8 core Intel i9 processor and 16 GB 2400 MHz DDR4 RAM. Note that the Minecraft server only uses a single core since it is single-threaded.

The first test repeatedly spawns an $N \times N \times N$ block of obsidian followed by an $N \times N \times N$ block of air for increasing values of N. When the server tick rate falls below 20 ticks/s the test is stopped. We measure the response time for the command to spawn the obsidian block, which is constant at approximately 50 ms corresponding to a single tick until 29,791 blocks corresponding to a $31 \times 31 \times 31$ cube, at which point the tick rate drops and the test is stopped (Fig. 4).

In the second test, we simultaneously spawn N minimal flying machines (Fig. 3) and let the server run for 20 s and observe the tick rate. These machines are more demanding on the tick-rate than static blocks due to the dynamic behavior. We vary N until the server tick rate falls below 20 ticks/s, which we observe happens when we spawn more than approximately 1200 flying machines.

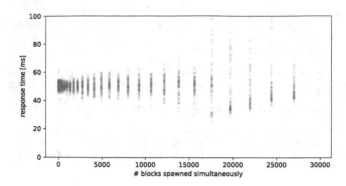

Fig. 4. Response times when spawning blocks using the EvoCraft API.

Since Minecraft runs in a single thread it is often CPU-bound on modern multi-core hardware. To overcome this limitation, multiple instances of EvoCraft can be run in parallel to scale the throughput of the simulation, although the client must balance the load manually among the environments.

3.2 Relevant Minecraft Blocks

In total, 254 blocks are available in this implementation. However, many of them do not have a specific functional role. Below we focus on some essential block types, notably redstone circuits.

Redstone Circuits –which can be thought of as kind of electrical circuits– enable to activate and control mechanisms and therefore to create machines (e.g. elevators, automatic farms, robots, CPUs, etc.), which can also be reactive to events in the environment (e.g. mob movement, item drops, etc.). Three types of elements are typically involved:

(i) A power component provides power to all or part of a circuit, may it be transmission components or adjacent mechanisms components; e.g., Redstone torch, Button, Lever, Detector rail, Pressure plate, Redstone block, etc. These items provide either short or continuous pulses, allowing mechanisms to be activated or de-activated.

(ii) A transmission component passes power from one part of the circuit to another; e.g., redstone dust, redstone repeater, redstone comparator.

(iii) A mechanism component that once activated, changes its state or something else in the environment (by producing light, moving, throwing something, etc.); e.g., Piston, Redstone lamp, Doors, Dispenser, etc.

4   Evolutionary Optimization: Baseline Approaches

Here we present some initial results on interactive (Sect. 4.1) and automated evolution (Sect. 4.2) with our API, showcasing some of its abilities.

4.1   Human in the Loop: Interactive Evolution

In interactive evolutionary computation (IEC), a human may intervene to leverage the evolutionary processes, through various forms of guidance [4,39], A major track within IEC is for the human to have some control (partial or full) over how fitness values are assigned. Consequently, IEC is particularly well suited for domains or tasks for which it is hard to explicitly define a metric or, more crucially, when criteria are inherently subjective or ill-defined (e.g. beauty, salience, complexity, open-endedness). While it is hard to narrow down an analytical expression for these attributes, humans can be arguably apt at evaluating them. Interactive evolution seems notably a promising path to explore the quest for open-endedness [28,35].

We should mention that while the promise of IEC is appealing, there are undeniable drawbacks of this approach worth mentioning such as human-bias, fuzzy behaviors, or limited exploration of the search space. Furthermore, since a large number of evaluations may be required, it may trigger what is known as 'user fatigue', possibly leading to further noise and bias in the process. Convergence behavior is, even with strong assumptions on the consistency of the user's behavior, rarely guaranteed, as it depends on the geometry of the desired phenotypic space.

For these reasons, hybrid processes using partial human interventions (and possibly proactive instead of reactive) along with other methods may be preferred instead of full human guidance and prove to be more tractable. For example, interactive evolution has been combined with novelty search to increase searching efficiency [14,44].

For the initial EvoCraft experiments in this paper, we restrict ourselves to the simplest implementation of interactive evolution. We use an evolutionary strategy [27] to evolve entities and ask a human to choose its favorite among the candidate solutions at each generation.

Artefact Encoding. The encoding is a simple feedforward multi-layer-perceptron, composed of three linear layers of 20 hidden nodes each and non-linear activations. The network is queried on a bounded spatial zone (2D or 3D box) to produce a structure. The input is composed of the relative 3D spatial coordinates and the distance to the center, which can also be symmetrized beforehand. The output is either $(N+1)$-dimensional, or $(N+7)$-dimensional if the block orientations are included in the encoding, where N is the number of block types allowed. While the first dimension determines if the queried position shall be air or matter, the following N-dimensions dictate the probability of using a certain type of block at this position. To encourage more symmetric creations, a variant of this encoding has been tested, where gaussian, tanh, sin and cos are replacing the default activations (relu and sigmoid). These activations, which resemble CPPN-network activations [34], enable more symmetric and smooth compositions. However, due to the current discretization, and the simplicity of this first encoding, the evolved shapes do not have the organicity which famously characterizes CPPN-compositions [28,34].

While the current implementation allows for the generation of structures to be stochastic via a top-k-sampling, it is currently run deterministically ($k = 1$).

IEC Setup. We use an evolutionary strategy (ES) [27] to generate a set of candidates that are presented to a human judge who has to choose one among them. Fitness is set to 1.0 for the chosen entity and 0.0 for all others. Subsequently, a new generation of candidate solutions is produced by the ES algorithm based on these fitness values. This process can be repeated ad infinitum.

The ES algorithm uses a noise modulating parameter $\sigma \sim 0.1$ and a small learning rate ~ 0.01 in order to obtain a gradual evolution so that users can make sense of the phenotypic changes produced by their choices. To speed up the evolutionary process, structures generated below a minimal size of blocks are not displayed, and their fitness is automatically set to 0.

Results. The entities evolved using IEC are shown in Fig. 5. Each row shows an evolutionary run at three stages; the left column displays the entities from the first generation and the right column the last generation. In the first three rows the user (one of the authors) was asked to choose whichever entities they found more interesting. On the other hand, for the last's row experiment, the goal was "to build a waterfall". Here the user selected over generations for entities which had water blocks. Eventually, the solutions converged to generating waterfall-like entities.

Let us underline the importance of the chosen genotype-to-phenotype encoding on the artifacts evolved, which may hinder the evolutionary road towards certain traits or artifacts while favoring others; representation learning is as crucial for open-endedness as it is for standard machine learning. The provided evolved examples (Fig. 5) serve as evidence that interactive evolution can be used to evolve interesting artifacts in a controlled manner in EvoCraft. However, the resulting evolved objects tell more about the underlying encoding representation than about the process of interactive evolution itself. The code used in the IEC experiment described here can be found in https://github.com/claireaoi/EvoCraft-interactive.

4.2   Automated Evolution

This sections presents two simple automated evolutionary experiments, which showcase how information collected from the game (e.g. the position of a particular block type) can be used to compute relevant fitness metrics.

Evolving a Tower Growing Towards a Block of Gold. In this experiment we evolve a tower structure that has to reach a golden block suspended in the sky. The tower is constructed out of a subset of all possible blocks, namely: obsidian, redstone, glass, brown mushroom, nether block, cobblestone, and slime blocks. The air blocks are not considered as a part of the tower.

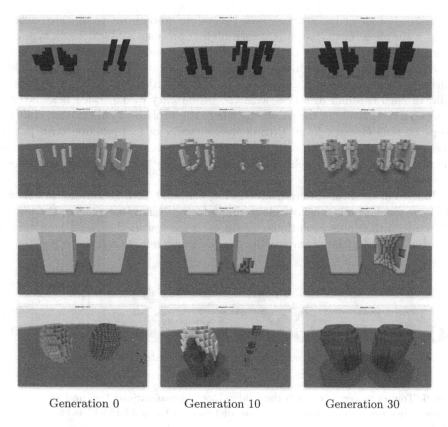

Generation 0   Generation 10   Generation 30

Fig. 5. Each row shows a different evolutionary run where the evolution of the artifacts is guided by the choice of a human experimenter. In the first three experiments, the human was asked to choose the shape they found most interesting while in the last one they were asked to produce a waterfall-like entity. Each experiment was run over 30 generations, the first being the left column and the last the right column.

We maintain a population of twenty towers and their respective targets, all existing at the same time in the same Minecraft world and being evaluated in parallel. Information on the position of the target is provided by the EvoCraft API. The distance between the closest tower block and the gold block is the tower's fitness value. The tower's initial block spawns at the base point. Each towers' target gold block is placed 10 block distances in the north direction, 10 distances in the west direction, and 10 distances in the up direction from the base point. For the next generation, we select the best 10% of the towers as parents. Two random parents are selected and merged into a child tower. There is a 5% chance that a child tower will mutate before it joins the next generation. The best tower in the current generation is copied over to the next generation unchanged.

Instead of the neural network-based encoding used above, towers are encoded using a simple ternary tree, where each node represents a block (block type and facing direction) and three edges toward children nodes represent the direction (north, west, and up) in which the child node is connected to the parent node. Initial trees are randomly generated by taking a root node and generating a child in each cardinal direction with the probability of 0.5. Each next layer is generated recursively in the same way where the probability of creating children drops by 0.05 for each level. During the crossover of two parents, both parent trees are cut at a random child node; the first parent loses the sub-tree from the random cut toward the leaf, which is replaced by a sub-tree from the second parent.

Images of the best towers from the 1st, 6th, and 13th generation are shown in Fig. 6. Evolution is quickly able to find a tower design that reaches the target. The code with simple evolutionary loop evolving towers described here can be found in https://github.com/real-itu/simple_minecraft_evolver.

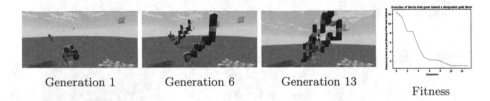

Generation 1   Generation 6   Generation 13

Fitness

Fig. 6. Towers evolving to reach the golden block at generations 1, 6, and 13. Training performance over generations (minimum distance to the gold block) is shown on the right.

Evolving a Moving Machine. To demonstrate how the API can be used to track and evolve redstone machines, we attempted to evolve a moving machine, similar to the flying one shown in Fig. 3. For this experiment, we again use the simple neural network encoding (Sect. 4.1) together with an evolutionary strategy optimizer and a population size of ten. Fitness is calculated as the change in center of mass of the evolved structure after ten seconds.

Evolution was able to find some machines that do move their center of mass slightly. However, the presented machines are not consistently moving in one direction, as the flying machine does, but spawn a combination of redstone blocks adjacent to piston blocks that push parts of the structure to a different position (Fig. 7). The minimal flying machine displaces its center of mass by 17 positions in ten seconds. So far, we were able to find machines that can push their center of mass by 0.2 block positions after which they stop, meaning we are a long way from evolving a functional flying machine.

Fig. 7. Machines evolved for moving. Two examples on the left show machines before the triggered pistons push a part of the structure. The right figure shows the same machines after the triggered pistons displace some of the blocks. Evolution failed to find a machine that can perpetually move.

5 Conclusion and Future Directions

In this paper, we presented the first version of EvoCraft, a framework that allows the evolution of artifacts in Minecraft, including circuits and mechanics. Importantly and in contrast to the existing Minecraft AI frameworks, the provided API allows to easily place and track blocks in a running Minecraft server programmatically. Compared to related challenges, such as the Minecraft Settlement Generation Challenge, EvoCraft is more about – but not exclusively focused on – the evolution of mechanical/functional artifacts. We demonstrate the usability of EvoCraft on automated and interactive evolutionary tasks.

Given the failure of purely fitness-based evolution in EvoCraft to evolve still relatively simple flying machines, a natural next step would be to try quality diversity algorithms [23]. An interesting question is if these algorithms would be able to invent stepping stones that ultimately lead to interesting artifacts such as flying and self-replicating machines, CPUs, and word processors in Minecraft (Fig. 2)? Such experiments will help us to determine which ingredients are missing from current QD methods to create a system that can produce increasingly complex artifacts in complex worlds.

While the initial experiments presented in this paper employ evolutionary optimization, EvoCraft is not restricted to such search methods. It will be interesting to see how other machine learning methods that could help in achieving open-endedness perform and compare to evolutionary approaches, such as self-play [30] or methods for procedural content generation through reinforcement learning [11]. Our framework should be able to naturally support these methods.

In addition to more powerful and exploratory search methods, another important next direction is to explore and develop different genetic encodings for EvoCraft. In this paper, we showed results with two different but relatively simple encodings. The field of generative and developmental systems [36] has produced many encodings such as neural cellular automata [16] or CPPNs [34] that could extend the diversity of artifacts we can evolve. Additionally, we imagine that encodings that can build a library of interesting building blocks (e.g. a moving part, a CPU register, etc.) will be essential to allow truly open-ended innovation in Minecraft.

Important future work also includes extending the API in the next generation of the framework. For example, while we can simulate multiple individuals in the same Minecraft world, in the future we plan to add the ability to also parallelize evolution across multiple different Minecraft servers.

Acknowledgments. We thank Christoph Salge, Raluca D. Gaina, and Sam Devlin for helpful discussions on Minecraft. This project was partially supported by a Sapere Aude: DFF-Starting Grant (9063-00046B) and by the Danish Ministry of Education and Science, Digital Pilot Hub and Skylab Digital.

References

1. Bedau, M.A., et al.: Open problems in artificial life. Artif. Life **6**(4), 363–376 (2000)
2. Bedau, M.A., Snyder, E., Packard, N.H.: A classification of long-term evolutionary dynamics. In: Artificial Life VI, pp. 228–237 (1998)
3. Bohm, C., Hintze, A.: Mabe (modular agent based evolver): a framework for digital evolution research. In: Artificial Life Conference Proceedings 14, pp. 76–83. MIT Press (2017)
4. Breukelaar, R., Emmerich, M., Bäck, T.: On interactive evolution strategies. In: Rothlauf, F., et al. (eds.) EvoWorkshops 2006. LNCS, vol. 3907, pp. 530–541. Springer, Heidelberg (2006). https://doi.org/10.1007/11732242_51
5. Chan, B.W.C.: Lenia-biology of artificial life. arXiv preprint arXiv:1812.05433 (2018)
6. Cubehamster: Controllable Two Legged Walking Attack Robot - Colossus (2015). https://youtu.be/GPbE6fnNfSA, Accessed 17 Nov 2020
7. Guss, W.H., et al.: Minerl: a large-scale dataset of minecraft demonstrations. arXiv preprint arXiv:1907.13440 (2019)
8. Harrington, K., Pollack, J.: Escalation of memory length in finite populations. Artif. Life **25**(1), 22–32 (2019)
9. Jaderberg, M., et al.: Population based training of neural networks. arXiv preprint arXiv:1711.09846 (2017)
10. Johnson, M., Hofmann, K., Hutton, T., Bignell, D.: The malmo platform for artificial intelligence experimentation. In: IJCAI, pp. 4246–4247 (2016)
11. Khalifa, A., Bontrager, P., Earle, S., Togelius, J.: Pcgrl: Procedural content generation via reinforcement learning. arXiv preprint arXiv:2001.09212 (2020)
12. Lehman, J., Stanley, K.O.: Evolving a diversity of virtual creatures through novelty search and local competition. In: Proceedings of the 13th Annual Conference on Genetic and Evolutionary Computation, pp. 211–218 (2011)
13. Lenski, R.E., Ofria, C., Pennock, R.T., Adami, C.: The evolutionary origin of complex features. Nature **423**(6936), 139–144 (2003)
14. Löwe, M., Risi, S.: Accelerating the evolution of cognitive behaviors through human-computer collaboration. In: Proceedings of the Genetic and Evolutionary Computation Conference, vol. 2016, pp. 133–140 (2016)
15. Miconi, T., Channon, A.: A virtual creatures model for studies in artificial evolution. In: 2005 IEEE Congress on Evolutionary Computation, vol. 1, pp. 565–572. IEEE (2005)
16. Mordvintsev, A., Randazzo, E., Niklasson, E., Levin, M.: Growing neural cellular automata. Distill **5**(2), e23 (2020)

17. Mouret, J.B., Clune, J.: Illuminating search spaces by mapping elites. arXiv preprint arXiv:1504.04909 (2015)
18. Ofria, C., Wilke, C.O.: Avida: a software platform for research in computational evolutionary biology. Artif. Life **10**(2), 191–229 (2004)
19. Packard, N., et al.: An overview of open-ended evolution: editorial introduction to the open-ended evolution ii special issue. Artif. Life **25**(2), 93–103 (2019)
20. Patrascu, C., Risi, S.: Artefacts: minecraft meets collaborative interactive evolution. In: 2016 IEEE Conference on Computational Intelligence and Games (CIG), pp. 1–8. IEEE (2016)
21. González de Prado Salas, P., Risi, S.: Collaborative interactive evolution in Minecraft. In: Proceedings of the Genetic and Evolutionary Computation Conference Companion, pp. 127–128 (2018)
22. Pugh, J.K., Soros, L.B., Frota, R., Negy, K., Stanley, K.O.: Major evolutionary transitions in the voxelbuild virtual sandbox game. In: Artificial Life Conference Proceedings 14, pp. 553–560. MIT Press (2017)
23. Pugh, J.K., Soros, L.B., Stanley, K.O.: Quality diversity: a new frontier for evolutionary computation. Front. Rob. AI **3**, 40 (2016)
24. Ray, T.S.: An approach to the synthesis of life. Artif. Life **II**(11), 371–408 (1991)
25. Salge, C., Green, M.C., Canaan, R., Togelius, J.: Generative design in minecraft (gdmc) settlement generation competition. In: Proceedings of the 13th International Conference on the Foundations of Digital Games, pp. 1–10 (2018)
26. Salge, C., et al.: The AI settlement generation challenge in minecraft. KI-Künstliche Intelligenz **34**(1), 19–31 (2020)
27. Salimans, T., Ho, J., Chen, X., Sidor, S., Sutskever, I.: Evolution Strategies as a Scalable Alternative to Reinforcement Learning. ArXiv e-prints arXiv:1703.03864 (2017)
28. Secretan, J., et al.: Picbreeder: a case study in collaborative evolutionary exploration of design space. Evol. Comput. **19**(3), 373–403 (2011)
29. SethBling: 1fps Atari 2600 Emulator in Vanilla Minecraft 1.13 (2019). https://youtu.be/mq7T5_xH24M. Accessed 17 Nov 2020
30. Silver, D., et al.: Mastering chess and shogi by self-play with a general reinforcement learning algorithm. arXiv preprint arXiv:1712.01815 (2017)
31. SirBeNet: r/Minecraft - [::] Neural network for handwritten digit recognition implemented in vanilla (2020). https://www.reddit.com/r/Minecraft/comments/ak22ur/neural_network_for_handwritten_digit_recognition, Accessed 17 Nov 2020
32. Soros, L., Stanley, K.: Identifying necessary conditions for open-ended evolution through the artificial life world of chromaria. In: Artificial Life Conference Proceedings 14, pp. 793–800. MIT Press (2014)
33. Spector, L., Klein, J., Feinstein, M.: Division blocks and the open-ended evolution of development, form, and behavior. In: Proceedings of the 9th Annual Conference on Genetic and Evolutionary Computation, pp. 316–323 (2007)
34. Stanley, K.O.: Compositional pattern producing networks: a novel abstraction of development. Genet. Program. Evolvable Mach. **8**(2), 131–162 (2007)
35. Stanley, K.O., Lehman, J., Soros, L.: Open-endedness: the last grand challenge you've never heard of. While open-endedness could be a force for discovering intelligence, it could also be a component of AI itself (2017)
36. Stanley, K.O., Miikkulainen, R.: A taxonomy for artificial embryogeny. Artif. Life **9**(2), 93–130 (2003)
37. Steamed, K.: Minecraft Redstone Computer Word Processor (2014). https://youtu.be/g_ULtNYRCbg, Accessed 17 Nov 2020

38. Suarez, J., Du, Y., Isola, P., Mordatch, I.: Neural mmo: a massively multiagent game environment for training and evaluating intelligent agents. arXiv preprint arXiv:1903.00784 (2019)
39. Takagi, H.: Interactive evolutionary computation: fusion of the capabilities of EC optimization and human evaluation. Proc. IEEE **89**(9), 1275–1296. https://doi.org/10.1109/5.949485, http://ieeexplore.ieee.org/document/949485/
40. Taylor, T.J.: From Artificial Evolution to Artificial Life. Ph.D. thesis, School of Informatics, College of Science and Engineering, University of Edinburgh (1999). http://hdl.handle.net/1842/361
41. Vinyals, O., et al.: Starcraft ii: a new challenge for reinforcement learning. arXiv preprint arXiv:1708.04782 (2017)
42. Volunteers: Sponge (2020). https://github.com/SpongePowered
43. Wang, R., Lehman, J., Clune, J., Stanley, K.O.: Paired open-ended trailblazer (poet): Endlessly generating increasingly complex and diverse learning environments and their solutions. arXiv preprint arXiv:1901.01753 (2019)
44. Woolley, B.G., Stanley, K.O.: A novel human-computer collaboration: combining novelty search with interactive evolution. In: Proceedings of the 2014 conference on Genetic and evolutionary computation - GECCO 2014, pp. 233–240. ACM Press. https://doi.org/10.1145/2576768.2598353, http://dl.acm.org/citation.cfm?doid=2576768.2598353
45. Yaeger, L.: Computational genetics, physiology, metabolism, neural systems, learning, vision, and behavior or poly world: Life in a new context. In: Sante Fe Insitute Studies in the Sciences of Complexity Proceedings, vol. 17, pp. 263–263. Addison-Wesley Publishing (1994)

A Profile-Based 'GrEvolutionary' Hearthstone Agent

Alejandro Romero García and Antonio M. Mora García(⊠) (iD)

Department Signal Theory, Telematics and Communications, University of
Granada, Granada, Spain
algebro96@correo.ugr.es, amorag@ugr.es

Abstract. In the last few years, the Hearthstone AI international Competition has
been gaining fame among the scientific community. Several different entries have
been presented using varied approaches. One of the best, EVA, was based on a
Greedy approach combined with an Evolutionary Algorithm. However, almost all
the proposals were designed to work in a general way, i.e. for any of the possible
heroes. This generalisation presents a flaw, since the exclusive cards per hero are
not really exploited, nor their potential different behaviour profiles. This paper
follows a similar philosophy to EVA, also hybridizing Greedy + Evolutionary
algorithms, but having in mind three different, and extended among the community, archetypes or profiles: Aggro, Control and Midrange. Thus, three different
behaviours have been optimized aiming to create a more specialized agent able to
use an Artificial Intelligence engine depending on the hero to play with. To prove
the value of the approach several experiments have been conducted, comparing the
evolved agents with EVA in many different matches using three different heroes.
The results show an improvement over EVA for the three profile-based agents, as
well as an excellent performance when combined with a MonteCarlo Tree Search
approach.

Keywords: Digital collectible card games · Hearthstone · Hearthstone AI
Competition · SabberStone · Artificial Intelligence · Evolutionary algorithms ·
Profile-based optimisation

1 Introduction

Hearthstone is a famous and widely extended Digital Collectible Card Game (DCCG),
which in 2018 reached 100 million players confronting in online matches. It is still very
active nowadays, so it has become a very interesting and challenging environment for
the design and development of autonomous agents (bots) able to play the game, and
even being competitive. In this regard an International Hearthstone AI Competition has
arisen [18], as well as some simulators, such as Sabberstone [17], to develop and test
the implemented bots.

Many different techniques were applied in the entries presented to past editions of the
Hearthstone AI Competition. However, the most successful approaches were focused

© Springer Nature Switzerland AG 2021
P. A. Castillo and J. L. Jiménez Laredo (Eds.): EvoApplications 2021, LNCS 12694, pp. 341–356, 2021.
https://doi.org/10.1007/978-3-030-72699-7_22

on two main techniques. Thus, a significant percentage of competitors implemented Greedy algorithms, or combinations of them with Backtracking or Lookahead techniques [16]. On the other hand, agents applying techniques based on Monte Carlo Tree Search (MCTS) [4] or variations on it, were also very numerous and many of them finished on the first positions of the ranking.

With regard to the competition track '*User-created decks*' there is a big difference in the number of entries applying Greedy and MCTS approaches, so it is strongly favourable to the first, being almost the totality of agents presented based on greedy variations.

This paper is focused on the design and implementation of an approach to that specific track of the Hearthstone AI Competition. Thus, we have chosen a Greedy technique due to its simplicity and effectiveness on that track.

This implementation has been improved by means of an Evolutionary Algorithm (EA) [1], which has been applied to optimise the parameters (thresholds and weights) considered in the decision rules that guide the bot's behaviour. This kind of approach was already used in previous entries, such as EVA [9], which reached second place in 2018 competition and the same position in 2019. However, EVA follows a generalistic behaviour, i.e. a common set of decision rules for all the 9 heroes - which have different sets of cards to use - in the game.

The *GrEvolutionary (Greedy + Evolutionary)* agent proposed here, on the contrary, has been designed to bear in mind different behaviours according the three main profiles or *archetypes*, namely:

- **Aggro:** a clearly offensive profile in which the main objective is to reduce the opponent character's (hero) health with every single card, if possible. The aim is to win the game as soon as possible.
- **Control:** a defensive profile, in which the player tries to avoid damage in the first turns to get to the last turns alive and then to use high-power cards to finish the combat.
- **Midrange:** an intermediate profile between the two previous. The aim is to control at the very beginning and get aggressive after half of the game turns. It uses cards with a good relationship between attack, defense and cost.

It is important to note that these archetypes refer to the decks (the set of cards) a player can compose according to the selected character/hero. Thus, the same hero could play following one of these profiles or another, but the unique cards related to the hero mainly promote one of these behaviours.

This way, the proposed approach will apply an EA to evolve (optimise) the weights of the decision rules considered by the greedy algorithm, composing a different set of values per profile. Since the aim is to obtain specialised behaviours adapted to manage specific decks, depending on the hero that the bot controls.

The agent has been tested in several experiments conducted following the competition rules inside the same simulator used in that championship, called Sabberstone. Thus, it has been compared with EVA, as a reference approach which obtained very good results in the last editions of the competition.

The rest of the paper is structured as follows. Next section presents some preliminary concepts and background on the Hearthstone game, the competition and the Evolutionary Algorithms applied here. Then Sect. 3 analyses related work and other agents. The

Profile-based GrEvolutionary approach is described in Sect. 4. Conducted experiments and obtained results are shown and analysed in Sect. 5. Finally, Sect. 6 poses some conclusions and identifies some future lines of work.

2 Background

2.1 Hearthstone, AI Competition and Sabberstone

Hearthstone: Heroes of Warcraft is a multiplayer digital collectible card game (DCCG), developed by Blizzard Entertainment company. It is a turn-based card game confronting two opponents, who can choose a hero among 9 different classes and define specific decks of thirty cards (some of them common and some others exclusive of each hero) before fighting. The cards of the deck appear in the game randomly, and the players use their limited mana crystals (which are increased every turn) to cast spells, equip weapons or summon minions to attack their rival, with the goal to reduce the opponent's health to zero in order to defeat him.

Figure 1 shows a capture of one match, where it can be seen the heroes fighting, their corresponding minions, the remaining cards and one card which is being played. It should be noticed that every card has associated two values: attack in red color and defense in yellow color, and also each of them has an associated cost in number of mana crystals (number in blue). This means a hero must own at least this number of mana in order to play that card.

Fig. 1. Image of a Hearthstone match (Blizzard Ent.). Player's hero is on the bottom (visible cards) and the enemy on the top part (hidden cards). Minions on the upper part of the board belongs to the enemy and those on the bottom to our player. (Color figure online)

Hearthstone is a *zero-sum*, *non-deterministic*, and *imperfect information* game [26], since one player wins at the expense of the other, the cards are extracted randomly from the deck, and the player cannot see the opponent's cards, so he/she can not predict his/her actions. Moreover, given the great amount of different cards (more than 2000 are collectable by the players), the amount of possibilities become gigantic.

Thus, the game is an excellent testbed for the implementation of autonomous agents. For this reason, some years ago the Hearthstone AI Competition was launched [18]. It is an international championship which tries to find the best AI implementation. There are two different tracks: 'Premade Decks' (specific Aggro, Control and Midrange decks must be used), and 'User-defined decks' (the agent can define its own set of cards to beat the opponents).

The competition is run using a simulator named Sabberstone [17]. It is a Hearthstone simulator, written in C#.Net Core. It is the most accurate simulator of the game, since it implements cards' effects as they are described in the Advanced Hearthstone Rulebook [19]. It is also expandable as new game cards are launched. The aim of this simulator is to provide an easy way to AI developers to implement and test autonomous agents for Hearthstone.

2.2 Evolutionary Algorithms

EAs are methods inspired in the natural evolution of the species [1]. Thus, they evolve populations of individuals encoding potential solutions for a problem. An EA normally follows a process of selection of the best individuals, recombination of their genetic material (the parameter values they encode) and mutation of some of them, aiming to create an offspring which combined with previous parents will define a new population of better individuals on average. This process is repeated a number of generations (iterations) until a stop criterion is met. In order to perform the selection and replacement it is mandatory to define an evaluation or fitness function which should assign a value indicating the goodness of an individual.

EAs have been widely applied to solve a huge amount of optimisation problems, including the improvement of behavioural AI engines [7–9, 21], as in the present work.

3   State of the Art

Digital collectible card games, and specifically Hearthstone has become one of the main dominions for research in the last years, due to its success together with the arising of open simulators/frameworks, such as Metastone [5] or Sabberstone [17], which have simplified the implementation and test of autonomous agents for playing the game, or the automatic creation and validation of decks.

The latter line has been studied inside Hearthstone in works such as [11], where different decks were defined by means of an EA trying to find the best combination of cards for different heroes among 700. Bhatt et al. in [2] conducted a similar study on deckbuilding by means of Evolutionary Strategies, but focused on the analysis of the game from the player balancing point of view, i.e. testing if it is possible to build unbeatable decks for the rest of players. García-Sánchez et al. [10] presented another study in the same line using EAs, however it was focused on the design part, trying to promote the game balancing and analysing possible unbalanced cards in the decks when an expansion for the game is launched. Also related to the creation of decks, Góes et al.

[12] proposed a method based on creativity when defining decks to perform combos (combinations of cards aiming for a higher effect).

However, the main research line in this domain is definitely the design and implementation of autonomous agents to play the game, strongly boosted by the arising of the aforementioned Hearthstone AI Competition. Around 30 entries have been submitted every year and some of them have derived into published papers. The present work is also focused on the generation of an agent for that competition.

There are several different works related to Hearthstone agents. For instance Bursztein in [3] described a very competitive approach based on statistical analyses or Grad [14], who presented an agent using Neural Networks. However the majority of proposals are variations of Monte Carlo Tree Search (MCTS). Santos et al. [24] proposed a standard approach, Swiechowski et al. [25] improved MCTS to handle imperfect information in this game, whereas Zhang and Buro [27] combined that technique with Neural Networks.

Following a simpler technique, García-Sánchez et al. proposed in [9] a Greedy agent, named as EVA. It considers 21 different attributes or factors extracted from the game, which are based on differences between states during a match. They defined a valuation function that computes the differences between the current state of the game, and every possible state resulting from choosing each possible action at a time. To this end, they use the 21 values considered in its valuation function. The algorithm is simple, but the evaluation function was defined by expert players and combines many factors. Moreover there are a set of weights associated with these factors which were optimised by means of an EA. This agent finished in second position in 2018 and 2019 competitions.

We take in this study EVA as a reference, because it is essentially a Greedy approach like the bot proposed here, based also on an evaluation function which considers many factors from the game state, and which reached very good rank in the past competitions. Thus, our aim in this study is starting from this 'simple' proposal and analyse the influence of the incorporation of archetypes into the optimisation process, defining specific profile-based mechanisms. We argue that this design will lead to create more competitive agents than those designed to attain a general behaviour (as EVA), i.e. not taking into account the class of the hero to play with, neither the archetype of the decks. The proposed agent is described in the following section.

4 GRETIVE: Our GrEvolutionary Agent

4.1 Agent General Description

The proposed Hearthstone bot, named GRETIVE, is composed of a set of decision rules, following a greedy strategy in order to decide the best card or cards to play in every turn depending on the available mana crystals.

Thus this decision is based on a simulation of playing each available and feasible card in the hand of our hero. So, the simulation, run in Sabberstone, offers as output the state of the board once the card would be used, i.e. the final hero and enemy's minions, as well as their status (both for heroes and minions). Given this information, several variables are extracted from the board concerning remaining health, potential attack points, spells, taunts, etc. These factors are multiplied by a set of weights, which assigns a relative relevance to each of them and all of them summed to obtain a *"preference value"* for that decision. Once all the possible plays have been evaluated, GRETIVE will perform the one with the best preference value. The formula used to compute that value is shown in Eq. 1.

$Pref\_Value = w1 \cdot OwnMinionTotalAttackw + w2 \cdot EnemyMinionTotalAttack$

$+ w3 \cdot OwnMinionTotalHealth + w4 \cdot EnemyMinionTotalHealth + w5 \cdot OwnMinionTotalHealthTaunt$

$+ w6 \cdot EnemyMinionTotalHealthTaunt + w7 \cdot OwnHeroArmor + w8 \cdot EnemyHeroArmor$

$+ w9 \cdot OwnHeroHealth + w10 \cdot EnemyHeroHealth$

$$(1)$$

It is important to note that weights could be positive, negative or even 0 (thus removing the corresponding factor).

As it can be inferred, the decisions strongly depend on the set of weights, whose value should be set carefully. Most of the entries in the competition were based on a fixed set of weights, looking for a general good behaviour independent of the hero and the deck itself. However, as previously stated, GRETIVE will optimise these weights by means of a profile-based Evolutionary Algorithm. Thus, the proposed approach consists of optimizing the set of weights in search of an improvement in the agent's game strategy, assuming a specific style of play, based on any of the game archetypes mentioned above. By means of the adaptation function, it is sought to promote not only the victory, but also that the agent pursues a specific technique to achieve a given game result.

4.2 Profile-Based EA

We have implemented a Genetic Algorithm (GA) [20] with a Generational approach [13]. Each **individual** is represented as a vector of ten floating point values, representing the weights *[w1,...,w10]* used in Eq. 1. Each one of these weights, which can be positive or negative, corresponds to a quantifiable feature of the game, which allows to value and compare different states of a match, and used at the time of determining the next action to be performed by the agent, based on the result obtained from valuing the states derived from each candidate action.

An **elitist Selection Strategy** has been applied, where the individuals who have the worst suitability rating are eliminated to make room for new individuals as a result of the crossing of those with better scores. The scheme of the selection and **replacement** process is shown in Fig. 2. For every five random individuals, two are removed from the population (those with lower scores), two are selected for reproduction (the best ones), and their two descendants will replace the two eliminated. The remaining individual will survive and pass to the next generation.

A standard **single-point crossover operator** has been applied [15], so an intermediate position in the chromosomes will be chosen, and the first part of one individual (vector) will be joined with the second part of the other, and then the two remaining parts are joined. **Non-Uniform mutation** [23] has been implemented for the variation of individuals. Thus a small percentage of the population is chosen and at least one gene (weight) of those individuals is significantly altered.

Aiming for the Profile-based optimisation, **three different fitness functions** have been defined. They are described in the following section.

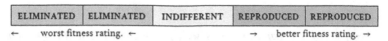

| ELIMINATED | ELIMINATED | INDIFFERENT | REPRODUCED | REPRODUCED |

←   worst fitness rating. ←   →   better fitness rating. →

Fig. 2. Selection strategy of the implemented EA 2/5 of the population are eliminated and later replaced by the new individuals generated by crossover of the best 2/5 parts, which are chosen as parents.

4.3 Profile-Based Evaluation Functions

The **evaluation** of an individual is done through a succession of simulated games in which the individual applies its current weights to the different selections required for the actions on the game. To do this, a **profile-based evaluation function** is applied, i.e. the fitness value will be computed considering different factors, depending on the target behaviour or strategy we want to optimise for the agent. Thus, it will measure in a quantitative way how well the individual has played and how much it has adapted to the expected behaviour.

It is important to note that considering the *uncertainty* or noise present in non-deterministic games optimisation [22], as Hearthstone is, every individual will be re-evaluated in the following generation, aiming to discover if it is really a good or a bad one regarding its achievement. Moreover the evaluation will consist in performing 40 different matches, aiming to evaluate as accurately as possible the quality of every individual, i.e. trying to avoid a good valuation for a really bad agent or the other way round, due to luck or bad luck in the matches respectively. The rival on all these matches will be a User-defined Aggro Greedy approach for a Warrior class (the initial agent created by the authors for the competition), and the individual will use the class of hero which is being optimised, i.e. the one corresponding to the archetype.

Before presenting the fitness functions Table 1 shows the terms/variables used in all of them, for the sake of clarity. They are referred to the state of the game/board at the end of every single match.

First, the **fitness function for the Aggro Profile** is as follows:
If the individual wins:

$$F_{AG} = 180 - 7 \cdot GT + PH + PA + 2 \cdot SPMA + 3 \cdot (PB - EB) \quad (2)$$

If the individual loses:

$$F_{AG} = -130 + 5 \cdot GT - 10 \cdot (EH + EA) - 3 \cdot SEMA + 5 \cdot SPMA - EB \quad (3)$$

These equations aim to promote an 'aggressive behaviour' for the agent, i.e. trying to deal damage to the opponent quickly (in a few turns), with a large number of minions, or simply focusing on harm to the opponent.

In the case of the **Control Profile**, the **fitness function** is defined as:
If the individual wins:

$$F_{CT} = 150 + GT + 2 \cdot (PH + PA) + 2 \cdot SPMA + 2 \cdot (SPMH + SPMTH) - 4 \cdot SEMA \quad (4)$$

If the individual loses:

$$F_{CT} = -200 + 10 \cdot GT - 4 \cdot (EH + EA) + 5 \cdot SPMA + 2 \cdot (PB + SPMTC + SPMTH) - 6 \cdot SEMA \quad (5)$$

This function tries to encourage late victories, while it focuses on the elimination of enemy's minions by avoiding damage, control of the board, and playing powerful cards in later rounds of the game. Thus, Taunt in the minions is very relevant, because it obligates the enemy to attack them first; in addition, the remaining health of minions is also important in order to better defend our hero.

Table 1. Considered values to evaluate the performance of the agent (individual), 'p' refers to the player and 'e' to the enemy. Profiles are 'a' for aggro, 'c' for control, and 'm' for midrange.

Acronym	Values	Description	Profile
GT	Game_Turn	The amount of player turns passed in the game	A - C - M
[P/E]H	X_Health	The remaining amount of health this player has at the end	A - C -M
[P/E]A	X_Armor	The remaining amount of armor (damage that can be received before starting to lose health)	A - C -M
S[P/E]MA	SUM_X_Minion_Attack	Summation of the attack of all the minions the player owns	A - C -M
[P/E]B	X_BoardZone	The amount of minion units that the player owns	A
S[P/E]MH	SUM_X_Minion_Health	Summation of the health of all minions that the player owns	C
S[P/E]MTH	....-WithTaunt_Health	Summation of the health of all minions with taunt ability that the player owns	C
S[P/E]MTC	....-WithTaunt_Cost	Summation of the mana cost of all minions with taunt ability that the player owns	C

Finally, the **fitness function for the Midrange Profile** is defined as:
If the individual wins:

$$F_{MR} = 180 - 3 \cdot GT + 3 \cdot (PH + PA) + 2 \cdot SPMA \quad (6)$$

If the individual loses:

$$F_{MR} = -120 + 5 \cdot GT - 5 \cdot (EH + EA) - 5 \cdot SEMA + 3 \cdot SPMA \quad (7)$$

This evaluation function is among the behaviours of previous decks. It aims at promoting the victory in an intermediate stage of the game, controlling the board completely at the beginning and passing through very efficient cards (in terms of cost/power) to a totally aggressive attitude. Hero's health is more important here as well as the minions' attack.

In the following section, this algorithm is tested in some experiments.

5 Experiments and Results

In order to validate the proposal, we have conducted several experiments. First of all, in the following section the considered configuration for the EA execution is shown as well as the description of the experiments performed. After this, the obtained results for three specific profiles are presented, including some graphs and tables to prove the correct working of the EA in each case. Then, the best agents obtained are compared with EVA agent, in order to test the value of the method in terms of performance against a competitive entry for the Hearthstone AI Competition. Finally, an agent combining our obtained results with a MCTS approach is tested.

5.1 Experimental Setup

The first part of the experiments is focused on study of the optimisation process (i.e. the EA performance). To this end the configuration presented in Table 2 has been considered.

Table 2. Parameters used in the EA for the experiments

Parameter	Value
Generations	30
Population	30 individuals
Evaluation	40 matches against Human-defined Aggro Warrior
Crossover probability	40% (2/5 population)
Mutation probability	10% individuals 1 gene per individual
Mutation rate	Between 0.2 and 0.8

The evaluations involve 36000 simulations per run. This is the base of our approach, since the profile-based fitness functions are applied over those simulation results. In every evaluation, the predefined decks per hero are considered, since the hero class will lead to a profile or predominant strategy using their exclusive cards (per class).

The experiments have been performed in a computer with CPU Intel Core i7-7700K (4.2 GHz), 16 GB RAM, SSD, Windows 10 Pro, able to run a generation in 120 s and one execution complete in around 1 h. And another PC with CPU Intel Core i5–4690 (3.5 GHz), 8 GB RAM, HDD, Windows 8.1 Pro, which finishes each run in 90 min.

5.2 Profile-Based Optimisation

Firstly, we conducted several optimization runs, considering the most adequate archetypes per class of hero. Thus, we performed the improvement of weights for the main used profiles according to the most common deck types presented in the Hearthstone Advanced Rulebook [19]. The optimized profiles are labelled with 'Yes' in Table 3.

Now, we analyse the EA performance in ten runs for each of the three most representative Class-Profile pairs, marked in the table in dark grey.

Table 3. Profiles/archetypes that have been optimized for each hero class. Those marked in dark grey are the most representative

Hero class	Strategy profile (Archetype)		
	Aggro	Control	Midrange
Druid	–	Yes	Yes
Hunter	Yes	–	–
Mage	–	Yes	Yes
Paladin	Yes	Yes	Yes
Priest	–	–	Yes
Rogue	Yes	Yes	–
Shaman	–	Yes	–
Warlock	Yes	–	Yes
Warrior	Yes	–	Yes

It is important to note that the results can be evaluated considering two factors:

- *Fitness*: is the value obtained by every agent/individual during the EA evolution for the corresponding evaluation function. Thus, Aggro profile will be computed using Eqs. 2 and 3, Control profile with Eqs. 4 and 5, and Midrange profile with Eqs. 6 and 7.
- Win Rate (W.R.): is the percentage of wins (in [0,1]) reached by every agent/individual in the 40 matches performed to evaluate it during the evolution.

Figures 3, 4 and 5 show the EA optimization results on average of the ten runs. Figure 3 shows the performance of the EA when optimizing Aggro profile agents. As it can be seen, both the fitness and the win rates follow a growing distribution, which can be seen clearer looking at the trend lines. This is the desirable tendency for an optimization algorithm, i.e. the population is being improved every generation. Moreover, even if the reference value for optimization is the fitness, the win rate graphs show a pretty similar behaviour, so the evaluation functions seem to be correctly defined, since high values on fitness correspond to higher Win Rates, which is, in turn, the main objective of any agent (i.e. 'to win as much as possible').

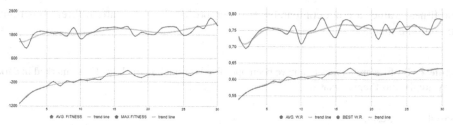

Fig. 3. Aggro profile results. Fitness and Win Rate evolution on average of ten different runs. Best/Maximum values and Average values are represented in the graphs.

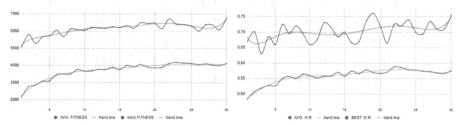

Fig. 4. Control profile results. Fitness and Win Rate evolution on average of ten different runs. Best/Maximum values and Average values are represented in the graphs.

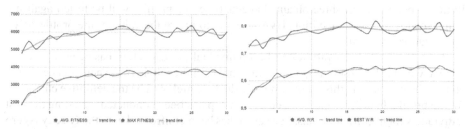

Fig. 5. Midrange profile results. Fitness and Win Rate evolution on average of ten different runs. Best/Maximum values and Average values are represented in the graphs.

Figures 4 and 5 show similar results then previous ones, with a clear growing tendency and congruent fitness and win rate graphs. However, it is remarkable the high similarity of the graphs in Fig. 5, both, the best and average values of fitness and win rate, follow almost identical distributions, which can be understood as a very accurate definition of the evaluation function for Midrange profile with regard to the corresponding win rate of the generated agents.

Numerical results are presented in Table 4. They are an average of the ten runs per profile-based optimization. As it can be seen Aggro strategy is the most risky one, since it shows the highest variation between good individuals (high fitness value) and bad ones, having an average negative fitness, even though the reached win rates are very good. Midrange is the profile which reaches the best win rates. Anyway, we should remind that the fitness values are not comparable between profiles, as there are different functions to compute them.

Table 4. Profiles/archetypes that have been optimized for each hero class. Those marked in dark grey are the most representative.

Profile	Results						
	Stat. param.	Max fit.	Min fit.	Avg. fit.	Best w.r.	Worst w.r.	Avg. w.r.
Aggro	Avg	1943.2	−2361.1	−59.3	0.75	0.45	0.61
	Std.Dev	234.1	581.3	334.8	0.02	0.05	0.02
Control	Avg	6139.9	1126.5	3712.6	0.70	0.40	0.55
	Std.Dev	370.8	699.7	488.4	0.03	0.03	0.02
Midrange	Avg	5871.7	802.9	3448.2	0.78	0.46	0.63
	Std.Dev	365.5	741.2	451.3	0.02	0.04	0.02

5.3 GRETIVE Agent Performance

In this experiment, the three obtained agents (one per profile) will be tested against a tough rival from the competition, EVA. We aim to prove the value of the profile-based optimization proposal.

First of all, for every profile, the best individual per execution has been selected as the one with the highest fitness value and win rate in the whole run. Then, it is needed to choose the best among this set of best individuals, which will be the definitive champion for the profile. In order to elect it, a championship has been conducted including the best individuals for the different runs. Each agent has been confronted with the Greedy Aggro Warrior opponent used during the evolution in 200 matches, being each of them player 1 and player 2 in 100 combats alternatively. It is important to note that being player 1 means to do the first action, which could be very relevant for the match development.

The winner of this championship was the one with the highest win rate against the common rival. Thus, after this process, there is an Aggro-Champion, Control-Champion and Midrange-Champion, named respectively GRETIVE-AG, GRETIVE-CT and GRETIVE-MR.

Each champion has been confronted with EVA agent using the same hero class, i.e. Hunter for matches GRETIVE-AG vs EVA, Shaman for GRETIVE-CT vs EVA, and Druid for GRETIVE-MR vs EVA. 2000 matches have been conducted in each case, playing 1000 as player 1 our agent and 1000 as player 1 EVA. The obtained results are presented in Table 5.

Looking at the results we can notice the high impact that the position in the matches has, much more for similar and tough rivals as EVA and our three bots seem to be.

It can be seen in the win rate column that our agents are able to win EVA in a higher amount of matches than this agent. GRETIVE-CT is the one with the best performance.

Table 5. Percentage of victories obtained by every profile-based agent against eva agent, being player 1 and player 2. Total win rate per agent.

Results against EVA			
Agent	Victories as player 1	Victories as player 2	Total win rate
GRETIVE-AG	64.9%	36.8%	50.85%
GRETIVE-MR	65.3%	39.8%	52.55%
GRETIVE-CT	65.8%	41.9%	53.85%

Anyway, the differences with EVA are not high, but we should take into account that EVA reached second position in the last two Hearthstone AI Competitions, among 30 entries each time. Thus, this leads us to think that our agents could also reach a good position in the rank. In addition, due to some limitations on the simulator, we have not been able to use our own defined deck per profile, including the most advantageous cards per hero class aiming for a clear archetype strategy. Instead, we have run the matches just using the aleatory decks generated by the simulator for the heroes' classes. We are convinced that the performance of the agents would be higher using our own decks.

Finally, we also want to remark that the total amount of turns performed in these confrontations have been around 16000 for GRETIVE-AG matches, around 18500 for GRETIVE-MR combats and more than 20000 for GRETIVE-CT matches. This also demonstrates that the profile-based agents are behaviouring as expected, being Aggro the fastest in winning, Control the slowest and Midrange in the middle of them.

5.4   GRETIVE + MCTS Agent Performance

Finally, a 'definitive' agent has been implemented considering the combination of the optimised weights obtained after the evolutionary process and a Lookahead approach [16] for MTCS. This agent does not follow a greedy strategy to select the next action, but a multilevel scan is performed, so the results obtained according to each combination of successive actions are taken into consideration. Thus, several additional moves/actions are evaluated per every possible action at a step.

This agent, named as *GRETIVE-MCTS* has been compared against EVA and our greedy approach *GRETIVE-AG*, using classes Warrior and Hunter - usual Aggro archetypes -. A test has been executed following the match allocation algorithm provided by the HS AI Competition organizers [18], i.e. a round robin approach.

Thus, each agent has been confronted using each one of the two heroes (same profile) against each one of the other agents (using respectively also one of those heroes), 8 matches as player 1 and 8 matches as player 2. So this means a total of 192 confrontations, 128 per agent. Win rate results are shown in Table 6, where the MCTS variation proves its value against the greedy approaches, outperforming them.

A GRETIVE-MCTS approach was created for the HS AI Competition 2020, named GRETIVE-Comp. It was able to choose dynamically the set of optimized weights (to use in the decision process) before the match, according to the most appropriate profile for the hero to play with. This agent was ranked 3rd in that competition.

Table 6. Results of round robin confrontations following HS AI Competition rules. Total win rate per agent from 8 matches as player 1 and 8 matches as player 2.

Agent	Total win rate	Detail
GRETIVE-MCTS	73%	94 out of 128 victories
EVA	46%	59 out of 128 victories
GRETIVE-AG	35%	45 out of 128 victories

6   Conclusions and Future Work

This paper presents a proposal for the creation of autonomous agents to be competitive players in the Digital Collectible Card game Hearthstone. To this end, we have started from a Greedy behavioural engine able to decide the best card to play at every moment, and have applied an Evolutionary Algorithm (EA) to optimize the weights (relevance) of the game factors considered to make this decision (such as the health of our own hero, or the attack of our minions in the board, for instance).

This EA is based on the so-called *profiles*, which are archetypes or strategies frequently followed by many players in the game. Each of these profiles involves normally not only a way of play, but also the use of specific types of cards, which also depend on the hero that the player is controlling. Thus, there are three different evaluation functions in the EA, related to profiles Aggro (aggressive), Control (conservative) and Midrange (medium).

The three optimized agents, one per profile, have been tested in a confrontation of 2000 matches against one agent of the state of the art named EVA. It is also a Greedy algorithm designed by expert players which was optimized by means of an EA, but aiming for a general behaviour (independent of the hero). EVA finished in second position in Hearthstone International Competition [18] in 2018 and 2019. The results of these matches show an improvement with regard to EVA, getting a higher win rate than this agent in the three cases (our three agents).

The difference is not very big, but these results lead us to think that our proposal is working, and the obtained agents are quite competitive. Anyway, the agents have been tested with default decks, so in the near future we will try to test them again composing specific decks for each of the archetypes.

We also aim to improve the competition agent, so it would be able to change the strategy during the game, according to the current deck, enemy's deck, or even the cards in hand.

In addition, the evaluation functions used in the EA can be improved, considering additional information from the matches, such as the cemetery (i.e. cards used during the match).

Finally, the Greedy algorithm used as the agents behavioural engine could be also enhanced, including a search/decision in several levels (analysing more than one possible action at a time), looking for combinations of cards, since 'combos' are very powerful and effective in this game.

Acknowledgements. This work has been supported in part by projects B-TIC-402-UGR18 (FEDER and Junta de Andalucía), RTI2018–102002-A-I00 (Ministerio Español de Ciencia, Innovación y Universidades), and project TIN2017–85727-C4-{1–2}-P (Ministerio Español de Economía y Competitividad).

References

1. Bäck, T.: Evolutionary Algorithms in Theory and Practice. Oxford University Press, New York (1996)
2. Bhatt, A., Lee, S., de Mesentier Silva, F., Watson, C.W., Togelius, J., Hoover, A.K.: Exploring the hearthstone deck space. In: Dahlskog, S., et al. (eds.) Proceedings of the 13th International Conference on the Foundations of Digital Games, FDG 2018, Malmö, Sweden, 07–10 August 2018, pp. 18:1–18:10. ACM (2018)
3. Bursztein, E.: I am a legend: Hacking hearthstone using statistical learning methods. In: IEEE Conference on Computational Intelligence and Games, CIG 2016, Santorini, Greece, September 20–23, 2016, IEEE, pp. 1–8 (2016)
4. Chaslot, G.M.J.B., Winands, M.H.M., Uiterwijk, J.W.H.M., van den Herik, H.J., Bouzy, B.: Progressive strategies for Monte-Carlo tree search. New Math. Natural Comput. **4**(3), 343–359 (2008)
5. Demilich1, MetaStone - A Hearthstone simulator (2015). https://github.com/demilich1/met astone. Accessed 25 Mar 2020
6. Dockhorn - Bot downloads. https://dockhorn.antares.uberspace.de/wordpress/bot-dow nloads. Accessed 25 Mar 2020
7. Esparcia-Alcázar, A.I., Moravec, J.: Fitness approximation for bot evolution in genetic programming. Soft Comput. **17**(8), 1479–1487 (2013)
8. Fernández-Ares, A., García-Sánchez, P., Mora, A.M., Castillo, P.A., Merelo J.J.: There Can Be only One: Evolving RTS Bots via Joust Selection. In: Squillero G., Burelli P. (eds) EvoApplications 2016. LNCS, vol. 9597, pp. 541–557. Springer, Cham (2016). https://doi.org/https://doi.org/10.1007/978-3-319-31204-0_35
9. García-Sánchez, P., Tonda, A.P., Fernández-Leiva, A.J., Cotta, C.: Optimizing Hearthstone agents using an evolutionary algorithm. Knowl. Based Syst. vol. 188 (2020)
10. García-Sánchez, P., Tonda, A.P., García, A.M., Squillero, G., Merelo Guervós, J.J.: Automated playtesting in collectible card games using evolutionary algorithms: a case study in Hearthstone. Knowl.-Based Syst. **153**, 133–146 (2018)
11. García-Sánchez, P., Tonda, A.P., Squillero, G., Mora, A.M., Merelo Guervós, J.J.: Evolutionary deckbuilding in Hearthstone. In: IEEE Conference on Computational Intelligence and Games, CIG 2016, Santorini, Greece, September 20–23, IEEE, pp. 1–8 (2016)
12. Góes, L.F.W., et al.: Honingstone: building creative combos with honing theory for a digital card game. IEEE Trans. Comput. Intell. AI Games **9**(2), 204–209 (2017)
13. Goldberg, D.E.: Genetic Algorithms in search, optimization and machine learning. Addison Wesley (1989)
14. Grad, L.: Helping AI to play Hearthstone using neural networks. In: 2017 Federated Conference on Computer Science and Information
15. Gwiazda, T.D.: Genetic Algorithms Reference Vol.1 Crossover for single-objective numerical optimization problems, Tomasz Gwiazda Books, Lomianki (2006)

16. Haralick, R.M., Elliot, G.L.: Increasing tree search efficiency for constraint satisfaction problems. Artif. Intell. **14**, 263–313 (1980)
17. HearthSim, SabberStone - Hearthstone simulator. https://hearthsim.info/sabberstone/. Accessed 25 Mar 2020
18. Hearthstone AI Competition. https://www.is.ovgu.de/Research/HearthstoneAI.html. Accessed 25 Mar 2020
19. Hearthstone, Gamepaedia - Advanced Rulebook. https://hearthstone.gamepedia.com/Advanced_rulebook. Accessed 25 Mar 2020
20. Herrera, F., Lozano, M., Verdegay, J.: Tackling real-coded genetic algorithms: operators and tools for behavioural analysis. Artif. Intell. Rev. **12**, 265–319 (1998)
21. Kim, T.S., Na, J.C., Kim, K.J.: Optimization of an autonomous car controller using a self-adaptive evolutionary strategy. Int. J. Adv. Rob. Syst. **9**(3), 73 (2012)
22. Mora, A.M., Fernández-Ares, A., Merelo, J.J., García-Sánchez, P., Fernandes, C.M.: Effect of noisy fitness in real-time strategy games player behaviour optimisation using evolutionary algorithms. J. Comput. Sci. Technol. **27**(5), 1007–1023 (2012)
23. Neubauer, A.: A theoretical analysis of the non-uniform mutation operator for the modified genetic algorithm. In:: Proceedings of the IEEE International Conference on Evolutionary Computation. IEEE Press, Indianapolis, IN, USA (1997)
24. Santos, A., Santos, P.A., Melo, F.S.: Monte Carlo tree search experiments in hearthstone. In: IEEE Conference on Computational Intelligence and Games, CIG 2017, New York, NY, USA, 22–25 August 2017, pp. 272–279. IEEE (2017)
25. Swiechowski, M., Tajmajer, T., Janusz, A.: Improving Hearthstone AI by combining MCTS and supervised learning algorithms In: 2018 IEEE Conference on Computational Intelligence and Games, CIG 2018, Maastricht, the Netherlands, 14–17 August, pp. 1–8. IEEE (2018)
26. Thomas, L.C.: Games, Theory and Applications. Mineola New York: Dover Publications. p. 19 (2003)
27. Zhang, S., Buro, M.: Improving hearthstone AI by learning high-level rollout policies and bucketing chance node events. In: IEEE Conference on Computational Intelligence and Games, CIG 2017, New York, NY, USA, 22–25 August 2017, IEEE, pp. 309–316 (2017)

Machine Learning and AI in Digital Healthcare and Personalized Medicine

Modelling Asthma Patients' Responsiveness to Treatment Using Feature Selection and Evolutionary Computation

Alejandro Lopez-Rincon[1]([✉]), Daphne S. Roozendaal[1], Hilde M. Spierenburg[1], Asta L. Holm[1], Renee Metcalf[1], Paula Perez-Pardo[1], Aletta D. Kraneveld[1], and Alberto Tonda[2][iD]

[1] Division of Pharmacology, Utrecht Institute for Pharmaceutical Sciences, Faculty of Science, Utrecht University, Universiteitsweg 99, 3584 CG Utrecht, The Netherlands
a.lopezrincon@uu.nl
[2] UMR 518 MIA, INRAE, Université Paris-Saclay, Paris, France
alberto.tonda@inrae.fr

Abstract. For several medical treatments, it is possible to observe transcriptional variations in gene expressions between responders and nonresponders. Modelling the correlation between such variations and the patient's response to drugs as a system of Ordinary Differential Equations could be invaluable to improve the efficacy of treatments and would represent an important step towards personalized medicine. Two main obstacles lie on this path: (i) the number of genes is too large to straightforwardly analyze their interactions; (ii) defining the correct parameters for the mathematical models of gene interaction is a complex optimization problem, even when a limited number of genes is involved. In this paper, we propose a novel approach to creating mathematical models able to explain patients' response to treatment from transcriptional variations. The approach is based on: (i) a feature selection algorithm, set to identify a minimal set of gene expressions that are highly correlated with treatment outcome, (ii) a state-of-the-art evolutionary optimizer, Covariance Matrix Adaptation Evolution Strategy, applied to finding the parameters of the mathematical model characterizing the relationship between gene expressions and patient responsiveness. The proposed methodology is tested on real-world data describing responsiveness of asthma patients to Omalizumab, a humanized monoclonal antibody that binds to immunoglobulin E. In this case study, the presented approach is shown able to identify 5 genes (out of 28,402) that are transcriptionally relevant to predict treatment outcomes, and to deliver a compact mathematical model that is able to explain the interaction between the different genes involved.

Keywords: Omalizumab · Machine learning · Evolutionary computation · Asthma · Mathematical model

© Springer Nature Switzerland AG 2021
P. A. Castillo and J. L. Jiménez Laredo (Eds.): EvoApplications 2021, LNCS 12694, pp. 359–372, 2021.
https://doi.org/10.1007/978-3-030-72699-7_23

1   Introduction

When patients are treated with medical drugs, it is possible to observe a variation in their gene expression. Such transcriptional variation can potentially be correlated with the responsiveness to treatment, and this relationship can be described through a system of Ordinary Differential Equations (ODE).

Such a model would be important not only to explain the differences in treatment outcome, but also to provide indications to medical personnel on how to improve the therapy. For example, if a gene is shown to be overexpressed in non-responsive patients, with respect to responsive patients, doctors might devise a new therapy, combining the current treatment with substances that lower the expression of that particular gene.

Nevertheless, obtaining such an ODE system is not a straightforward process. The genes potentially correlated to drug response number in the tens of thousands, with possible complex interconnections in expression levels. Not only that, but even when a limited number of genes is identified, finding satisfying values of the parameters for the ODE system describing their interactions is a complex optimization problem that cannot be tackled through gradient-based techniques.

In this paper, we propose a novel methodology to obtain compact mathematical models describing the correlation between gene expression levels and responsiveness to treatment. The methodology combines a technique for feature selection [19,20], able to identify a small set of genes highly correlated with treatment outcome, and a state-of-the-art evolutionary optimizer [15] in order to find good values for the ODE system characterizing their interaction.

The presented approach is tested on real-world data from N=40 patients affected by moderate-to-severe asthma, treated with the recent anti-IgE drug Omalizumab (30 responsive and 10 non-responsive). The results show that the methodology is effective in identifying 5 genes that are highly correlated with responsiveness to treatment, and it is able to deliver an ODE system that can reliably describe their interaction, explaining the responsiveness of patients to the Omalizumab treatment.

2   Background

In this section, we introduce the minimal notions that are necessary to introduce the scope of our work.

2.1   Feature Selection

In machine learning (ML), feature selection (FS) is defined as the process of identifying the features of a data set in order to obtain a minimal, informative subset. Features may not be part of this subset for two main reasons: they might be unrelated to the underlying nature of the problem, just adding noise; they might be heavily correlated with other features, adding no relevant information for the task. Applications range from face recognition [31] to medicine [35], and approaches can be divided into two categories [12]: filters that score features according to a criterion (often a statistical test); and recursive procedures (forward or backwards) that attempt to reduce the features to a small set of non-redundant ones [8,18].

In the scope of this work, we focus on recursive FS algorithms, in particular Recursive Ensemble Feature Selection (REFS). The method is a variation of Recursive Feature Elimination (RFE) [13] that scores the features in a 10-fold cross-validation scheme, using 8 different classifiers: gradient boosting, passive aggressive classifier, logistic regression, Support Vector Machine classifier (SVC), random forest, Stochastic Gradient Descent (SGD), ridge classifier and bagging. The lowest scoring features are removed from the analysis and the process is repeated until the overall classification accuracy drops below a given threshold. The use of an ensemble of classifiers reduces the effects of the inherent bias in each ML algorithm, thus delivering a more objective feature ranking. This technique has been applied successfully for problems involving both mRNA [20] and miRNA [19], featuring number of variables ranging from 1,046 to 54,675.

2.2   Omalizumab Treatment for Asthma Patients

Omalizumab is the first humanized monoclonal antibody that binds to immunoglobuline E (anti-IgE) prescribed to patients with moderate-to-severe allergic asthma who do not respond to inhaled corticosteroids and long-acting $\beta 2$-agonist bronchodilators. Omalizumab works by specifically binding free serum IgE [29], which characterizes allergic asthma. IgE binds to high affinity receptors (FcϵRI) expressed on effector cells such as basophils and mast cells, but also on other immune cells like eosinophils, thereby triggering an inflammatory cascade through the release of inflammatory mediators [14]. By binding to the Fc region of IgE and forming IgE-antibody complexes, Omalizumab prevents the binding of allergen specific IgE to FcϵRI and the subsequent inflammatory allergy reaction [29]. Consequently, FcϵRI expression is reduced, leading to less immune activation. Furthermore, Omalizumab decreases eosinophil numbers found in the airway of asthmatic patients, although the mechanism through which this effect is achieved is not entirely understood [29]. Eosinophils and their derived proinflammatory mediators are major contributors to airway inflammation and damage [26]. Omalizumab's ability to combat long-term airway remodeling is still under investigation [14].

It is important to understand the mechanism of action of Omalizumab treatment and to research the differences in responsiveness. Potential transcriptional variations between responders (R) and non-responders (NR) to Omalizumab can function as predictive biomarkers in the future. A recent study by Upchurch et al. 2020, with accession number GSE134544 at gene expression omnibus (GEO) [30] investigated whole blood transcriptomes of moderate-to-severe asthma patients (N = 40; 30 responders (R) and 10 non-responders (NR)), over the course of

Omalizumab treatment. Blood was collected at day 0, 7, 42, 98, 182 where the treatment started at day 7, and day 0 marks one week before the treatment.

Total RNA was isolated from whole blood, and all samples passing quality control were then amplified, (biotin-)labelled and hybridized to Illumina HT-12 V4 BeadChips (Illumina). Subsequent differential gene expression analysis was performed using Welch's T-test for comparisons between R and NR, and transcriptional changes within each group were assessed using a paired T-test. However, direct comparisons between R and NR did not provide sufficient gene lists after multiple testing corrections. Therefore, whole blood mRNA signature differences between groups were characterized using a gene cluster strategy, or modular-level type analysis adopted from studies by Chaussabel et al. [7] and Banchereau et al. [3]. Hierarchical clustering of genes revealed 8 similarly expressed transcript clusters in R and NR (i.e. protein synthesis (1); T cell/NK cell/ cytotoxicity (2); hematopoiesis (3); cell cycle control/proliferation (4); T cell regulation and activation (5); monocytes (6); glucose metabolism (7) and inflammation (8)). Of these, cluster 2 and 7 in R were reported to be higher, while clusters 3 and 8 were higher in NR, suggesting that clusters 2, 3, 7 and 8 can be used as predictors of response to Omalizumab treatment. These clusters, combined, contain a total of 1,776 genes.

Due to the unpredictability of an asthma patient's responsiveness to Omalizumab, there have been multiple studies into finding a reliable biomarker that can act as a predictor. A recent study [16] reported that interleukin (IL)-9, IL-13, IL-25, IL-33 and thymic stromal lymphopoietin (TSLP) levels were significantly higher in R compared to NR. Most R were of a high type-2 cytokine endotype whereas only one NR was [16]. Data from the INNOVATE trial of Omalizumab for severe persistent asthma [17] was analyzed by [5], and this study found that of the biomarkers recorded by INNOVATE, only baseline total IgE levels were a predictor of efficacy. However, pooled analysis showed that treatment was effective in some cases irrespective of IgE levels. It was concluded that the most meaningful measure of responsiveness was the physician's overall assessment [5]. An extensive look into gene expression relating to asthma patients vs controls in different tissue types, disease severity and response to allergens and corticosteroid treatment in several datasets reported multiple gene signatures and pathways [1]. Although this may prove useful in explaining Omalizumab response, it revealed no significant gene overlap.

3   Proposed Approach

We present a new approach to obtain compact, human-readable mathematical models to explain responsiveness to treatment in patients. The methodology first applies feature selection to identify a small set of relevant genes, and then uses state-of-the-art evolutionary optimization to find the parameters of an ODE system that describes the relationship between gene expression levels and patient's responsiveness to treatment.

3.1 Feature Selection

In a first step, our objective is to select the most meaningful genes to correctly predict and model patients' responsiveness to treatment. We apply the REFS algorithm, which uses the feedback of an ensemble of classifiers to rank each feature depending on its usefulness for the process of classification. Then, the lowest-scoring features are removed, and the classification/ranking is repeated, until the average classification accuracy falls below a user-defined threshold.

3.2 Mathematical Modeling

Once a small subset of the genes is identified, we create a mathematical model that interconnects the gene expression given the values at different time points. While other solutions to model the correlation between the gene expression values and responsiveness are possible, like black-box machine learning, white-box models are preferred by practitioners, as they are commonly considered more interpretable. We assume to have whole blood mRNA expression at different points in time available, and we will consider the average value for R and NR over all samples at each point in time, for each category of patients. Thus, the mathematical model we propose is a system of ordinary differential equations (ODEs) in the form of Eq. 1:

$$\frac{dg_0}{dt} = -k_0 u(t) + \alpha_0 e^{-\beta_0 t},$$
$$...,$$
$$\frac{dg_n}{dt} = -k_n u(t) + \alpha_n e^{-\beta_n t},$$
$$u(t) = K_{g_0} g_0 + ... + K_{g_n} g_n, \tag{1}$$

where g_0 to g_n will be the most important genes, k_i, α_i, β_i and K_{g_i} are coefficients calculated by each gene and $u(t)$ is an unknown function that interconnects the gene expression of all the genes, as to consider a relationship between all the variables.

Then, to solve the model, we use Euler's numerical method which transforms system 1 into:

$$g_0^t = g_0^{t-1} + \triangle t \frac{dg_0}{dt},$$
$$...,$$
$$g_n^t = g_n^{t-1} + \triangle t \frac{dg_n}{dt},$$
$$u(t) = K_{g_0} g_0^t + ... + K_{g_n} g_n^t. \tag{2}$$

$u(t)$ models the interconnection between different gene expressions, that we hypothesize exists to avoid trivial assumptions of independence. As the problem is not treatable resorting to classical gradient-based techniques, it is necessary to use state-of-the-art stochastic optimization, such as CMA-ES [15], to find satisfying values for k_i, α_i, β_i and K_{g_i}.

Given the measurement of gene expressions at different instants $t = \{t_0, ..., t_N\}$, from Eq. 2 we can define the cost function to be minimized by CMA-ES as:

$$error = \sum_{i=0}^{n} |g_{CRi}^t - g_{Ri}^t| + |g_{CNRi}^t - g_{NRi}^t| \tag{3}$$

where g_{CRi}^t is the average gene i expression calculated at time t for R, g_{Ri}^t is the average gene i expression measured t time t for responders, g_{CNRi}^t is the average gene i expression calculated at time t for non-responders and g_{NRi}^t is the average gene i expression measured t time t for non-responders.

4 Experimental Evaluation

All the necessary code for the experiments has been developed in Python, using the scikit-learn package [25] for machine learning, and the cma package for CMA-ES. The code is hosted on the open GitHub repository:[1]

4.1 Data

Moderate-to-severe asthma patients were prescribed Omalizumab, based on the manufacturer's dosing table. Patient blood was collected at day 0, 7, 42, 98, 182 where the treatment started at day 7 with Omalizumab in 40 patients: 30 R and 10 NR. For each patient, for each sample, for each instant of time, the dataset contains information about 28,402 gene expression levels. All data was used as provided, at GEO accession code GSE134544 [30].

4.2 Feature Selection

Running the REFS algorithm previously described 10 times, we identified a set of 5 features (out of 28,402). This compact set can predict the Omalizumab responsiveness in patients with a mean accuracy of 0.975 in a 10-fold cross-validation, considering the binary classification problem (R/NR) with all classifiers in the REFS ensemble. As the REFS process is stochastic, it was iterated 10 times and the feature set corresponding to the highest peak in accuracy was selected (see Fig. 1). From the figure, it is interesting to notice how using all 28,402 features actually provides a lower mean classification accuracy (0.703). Classification algorithms, usually exploiting optimization heuristics, often show a lower performance when asked to explore a larger feature search space.

The resulting most significant features uncovered by the presented algorithms are $ILMN\_3286286$; $ILMN\_1775520$; $ILMN\_1656849$; $ILMN\_1781198$ and $ILMN\_1665457$ (Fig. 2). Details of the Illumina probes are further specified in Table 1.

To further validate the selected features, we computed the area under the curve (AUC) and receiver operating characteristic (ROC) curve in a 10-fold

---

[1] https://github.com/steppenwolf0/modelingEvolutionaryComputation.

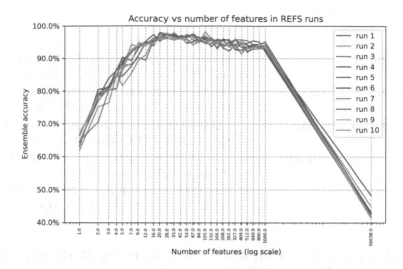

Fig. 1. The results of 10 runs of the REFS algorithm for the classification of Omalizumab responsiveness in allergic asthma patients. The x axis cuts at 5 variables, in correspondence with the highest peak.

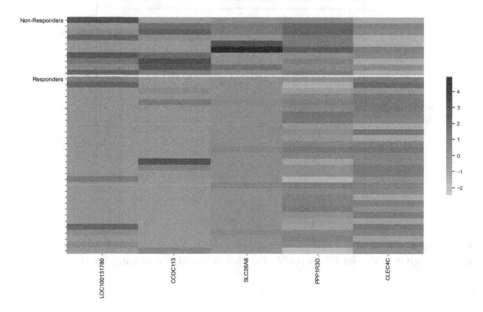

Fig. 2. Heatmap for the normalized gene expression for the 5 selected genes in all of the samples. Interestingly, samples of the two classes can be visually separated by just looking at the different normalized gene expression of the samples in the two groups.

Table 1. Information on the selected features to predict the responsiveness of the Omalizumab treatment.

Illumina probe	Corresponding gene	Sequence
ILMN_3286286	LOC100131780	GAGATTGCGAAACTGGACAAACTGCTGA ACCTGGACAGGGGCCAGGGCTG
ILMN_1775520	CCDC113	GGACATGAGAACATATTTCCAAGACAGA GGATTCTATGGGGACGGGTCAC
ILMN_1656849	SLC26A8	TGGGCGTATTGGGTTTGGGCTTCATTGC CACTTACCTTCCGGAGTCTGCA
ILMN_1781198	PPP1R3D	GGCCTTCACTGCTACGCCCCTGGCCCCA AAACAGAGAGCAAGACAGTTGT
ILMN_1665457	CLEC4C	GTGGTTCCAGTTGAAGGTCTGGTCCATG GCAGTCGTATCCATCTTGCTCC

cross-validation, using just the selected features, testing all classifiers in the REFS ensemble. The best AUC, 0.99, was obtained using Passive Aggressive classifier. This result is considered as an excellent diagnostic accuracy (AUC 0.9-1.0) by specialists of the field [21,27].

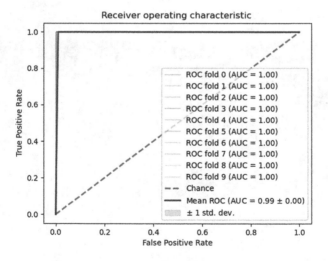

Fig. 3. ROC Curve in a 10-fold cross validation using Passive Aggressive classifier (the most effective in the REFS ensemble for this particular problem) for the 5 selected genes.

4.3 Mathematical Modeling

Considering we find 5 gene expressions to be the most meaningful, and using the template defined in Eq. 1, we can write the specific model linking gene expression levels to responsiveness to Omalizumab as:

$$\frac{dg_0}{dt} = -k_0 u(t) + \alpha_0 e^{-\beta_0 t},$$

$$\frac{dg_1}{dt} = -k_1 u(t) + \alpha_1 e^{-\beta_1 t},$$

$$\frac{dg_2}{dt} = -k_2 u(t) + \alpha_2 e^{-\beta_2 t},$$

$$\frac{dg_3}{dt} = -k_3 u(t) + \alpha_3 e^{-\beta_3 t},$$

$$\frac{dg_4}{dt} = -k_4 u(t) + \alpha_4 e^{-\beta_4 t},$$

$$u(t) = K_{g_0} g_0 + K_{g_1} g_1 + K_{g_2} g_2 + K_{g_3} g_3 + K_{g_4} g_4, \tag{4}$$

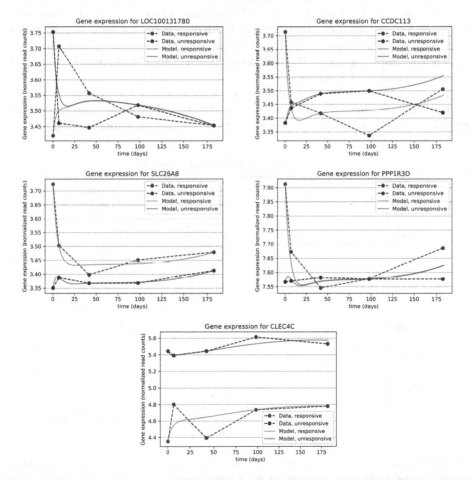

Fig. 4. Genes expression modeling and measured values for the 5 selected features at $t = 0, 7, 42, 98, 182$.

where we will need to find 20 parameters. We run CMA-ES with a $\sigma = 0.01$ and $\lambda = 1000$ with default stop conditions. Using CMA-ES with the cost function in Eq. 3, with $\Delta t = 0.25$, we find the following values; $k_0 = 0.5313, k_1 = 0.6440, k_2 = 0.4899, k_3 = 0.5504, k_4 = -0.4702, \alpha_0 = -0.0001, \beta_0 = -0.0168, \alpha_1 = -0.0386, \beta_1 = 0.9277, \alpha_2 = -0.0071, \beta_2 = 0.0733, \alpha_3 = -0.0176, \beta_3 = 0.1422, \alpha_4 = 0.0029, \beta_4 = 0.0079, K_{g_0} = 0.2598, K_{g_1} = 0.1078, K_{g_2} = 0.8069, K_{g_3} = -0.5708, K_{g_4} = 0.0565$ with an $error = 1.6036$ as the best of 20 runs.

As a baseline comparison, we also tested the `scipy` [32] implementation of the Nelder-Mead optimization algorithm [11], currently considered among the state-of-the-art for gradient-free optimization, for 20 runs. The best run of the Nelder-Mead algorithm yields a solution with $error = 4.3143$, of lower quality than that of CMA-ES.

From the results in Fig. 4, we can see that the model approximates considerably the behaviour of the genes, given the parameters and the initial values only; with a clear exception of $LOC100131780$. Although the increase of responders and decrease of non-responders functions are reflected, the amplitude does not match, therefore suggesting the necessity of increasing the degree of the answer or a more precise ODE solver.

Finally, from function $u(t)$ reported in Fig. 5, it is possible to notice that, just from its initial value $u(0)$, it is already possible to differentiate responders from non-responders, predicting the outcome of the treatment before its beginning.

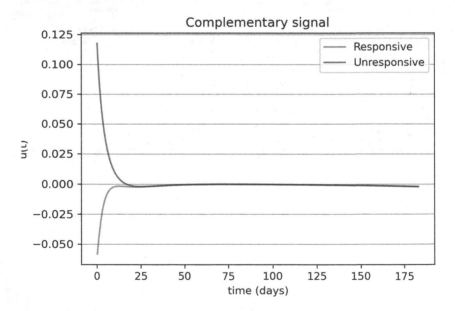

Fig. 5. Complementary signal $u(t) = K_{g_0}g_0 + K_{g_1}g_1 + K_{g_2}g_2 + K_{g_3}g_3 + K_{g_4}g_4$ that interconnects the expression values of all of the genes.

5   Discussion and Conclusions

Severe-to-moderate asthma patients appear to respond differently to the biological anti-IgE treatment Omalizumab. Total mRNA sequencing of whole blood from R and NR of Omalizumab treatment can help appreciate the differences at a transcriptional level. In this study, the GSE134544 dataset (that was recently published by Upchurch et al. [30]), was analyzed with the use of machine learning-based REFS. This novel study reveals 5 genes that are highly relevant in predicting Omalizumab responsiveness in asthma patients. In addition, we created a mathematical model to approximate the interdependence of the most significant genes to explain the effect of Omalizumab treatment using evolutionary computation.

Investigating gene function corresponding to the 5 mRNA (Table 1) predictors found in this study may illuminate new pathways involved in allergic asthma and the mechanism of Omalizumab resistance. For example, CCDC113 is vital for ciliogenesis and when knocked down, causes a reduction in cilium formation [10] which is previously related to severe asthma [28]. Also, this gene was found to be overexpressed in asthma patients as compared to controls [24], and in NR as compared to R.

CLEC4C is a marker for plasmacytoid dendritic cells (pDCs) subtypes [22, 23], which both have been implicated in driving acute asthma exacerbations [6, 33] and have shown to have a tolerogenic effect in asthma by inducing Treg cell differentiation [33]. CLEC4C is overexpressed in R when comparing against NR. PPP1R3D, a gene that codes for a subunit of PP1 (protein phosphatase 1) [2] regulates protein serine/threonine phosphatase activity and was found to be a causal key driver for acute peanut allergic response [34]. Genes coding for other subunits of PP1 have been shown to be upregulated in asthmatic patients (PPP1R16A) or, more specifically, in corticosteroid resistant patients (PPP1R15A) [1]. This gene is underexpressed in R, when compared against NR.

More unexpected in its relation to Omalizumab responsiveness in severe-to-moderate asthma is SLC26A8, which is most commonly associated with sperm motility and mutations that can cause male infertility [9]. It was also found to be upregulated in patients with severe asthma as compared to healthy controls [4]. Lastly, LOC100131780 is proprietary of Illumina and we, unfortunately, could not find a perfect gene match for this probe. The sequence did, however, overlap partially with DNAI1, which codes for dynein axonemal intermediate chain 1. The gene is strongly linked to primary ciliary dyskinesia (DNAI1 - Dynein Intermediate Chain 1, Axonemal - Homo Sapiens (Human) - DNAI1 Gene & Protein), which can cause respiratory infections and breathing problems (NHLBI).

An attempt to understand transcriptional variations between responders and non-responders on Omalizumab treatment was made by Upchurch et al. 2020, who recently analyzed changes in 8 gene clusters. In Omalizumab responders, the T cell/natural killer (NK) cell/cytotoxicity gene cluster and the glucose metabolism gene cluster were higher, whereas gene clusters involved in hematopoiesis and inflammation appeared to be higher in non-responders. 19 genes of the 8th (inflammatory) gene cluster were specifically annotated in their paper [30]; however, none of these genes corresponded with the 5 most relevant genes we found with our methodology.

By setting a goal of predicting responsiveness instead of investigating transcriptional changes, the amount of data and complexity are reduced, since only the pre-testing time point needs to be considered. Using REFS provides the benefit of illuminating possible gene interactions without bias, as opposed to using a single algorithm or performing significance tests and clustering up- or down-regulated genes on the basis of known pathway function. The overall benefit of machine learning over basic statistics is that it is able to find predictive patterns which do not rely on assumptions about the data-generating system. Furthermore, it avoids the problem of eliminating significant mRNAs by not needing to take into account false discovery rate (FDR correction). Therefore, the technique used in this paper greatly reduced the number of meaningful mRNAs (5) compared to Upchurch et al. 2020 (1,776).

Further clinical testing and a replication dataset could reveal whether the 5 mRNAs proposed in this paper can reliably predict moderate-to-severe asthma patients' response to Omalizumab treatment on a larger scale. Implementing this sort of pre-treatment testing can both reduce the cost of asthma treatment, as Omalizumab is a relatively expensive drug, and prevent unnecessary and unproductive treatment time. Although currently, we limit our study to Omalizumab, it could be applied to similar studies.

This study not only proposes 5 specific genes that are transcriptionally relevant to predict Omalizumab responsiveness in moderate-to-severe asthma patients, but also puts forward a novel technique that aims to reduce the necessary information to the smallest set of whole blood mRNAs. The presented methodology elucidates the power of machine learning versus more general univariate/multivariate statistical analysis strategies.

References

1. Alrashoudi, R.H., Crane, I.J., Wilson, H.M., Al-Alwan, M., Alajez, N.M.: Gene expression data analysis identifies multiple deregulated pathways in patients with asthma. Biosci. Rep. **38**(6), (2018)
2. Armstrong, C.G., Browne, G.J., Cohen, P., Cohen, P.T.: Ppp1r6, a novel member of the family of glycogen-targetting subunits of protein phosphatase 1. FEBS Lett. **418**(1–2), 210–214 (1997)
3. Banchereau, R., et al.: Personalized immunomonitoring uncovers molecular networks that stratify lupus patients. Cell **165**(3), 551–565 (2016)
4. Bigler, J., et al.: A severe asthma disease signature from gene expression profiling of peripheral blood from u-biopred cohorts. Am. J. Respir. Crit. Care Med. **195**(10), 1311–1320 (2017)
5. Bousquet, J., et al.: Predicting and evaluating response to omalizumab in patients with severe allergic asthma. Respir. Med. **101**(7), 1483–1492 (2007)
6. Chairakaki, A.D., et al.: Plasmacytoid dendritic cells drive acute asthma exacerbations. J. Allergy Clin. Immunol. **142**(2), 542–556 (2018)
7. Chaussabel, D., et al.: A modular analysis framework for blood genomics studies: application to systemic lupus erythematosus. Immunity **29**(1), 150–164 (2008)

8. Chien, Y., Fu, K.S.: On the generalized karhunen-loève expansion (corresp.). IEEE Trans. Inf. Theory **13**(3), 518–520 (1967)
9. Dirami, T., et al.: Missense mutations in slc26a8, encoding a sperm-specific activator of CFTR, are associated with human asthenozoospermia. Am. J. Hum. Genetics **92**(5), 760–766 (2013)
10. Firat-Karalar, E.N., Sante, J., Elliott, S., Stearns, T.: Proteomic analysis of mammalian sperm cells identifies new components of the centrosome. J. Cell Sci. **127**(19), 4128–4133 (2014)
11. Gao, F., Han, L.: Implementing the nelder-mead simplex algorithm with adaptive parameters. Comput. Optim. Appl. **51**(1), 259–277 (2012)
12. Guyon, I., Elisseeff, A.: An introduction to variable and feature selection. J. Mach. Learn. Res. **3**, 1157–1182 (2003)
13. Guyon, I., Weston, J., Barnhill, S., Vapnik, V.: Gene selection for cancer classification using support vector machines. Machine learning **46**(1–3), 389–422 (2002)
14. Hamelmann, E.: The rationale for treating allergic asthma with anti-ige. Eur. Respir. Rev. **16**(104), 61–66 (2007)
15. Hansen, N., Ostermeier, A.: Completely derandomized self-adaptation in evolution strategies. Evol. Comput. **9**(2), 159–195 (2001). https://doi.org/10.1063/1.2713540
16. Huang, Y.C., Weng, C.M., Lee, M.J., Lin, S.M., Wang, C.H., Kuo, H.P.: Endotypes of severe allergic asthma patients who clinically benefit from anti-ige therapy. Clin. Exp. Allergy **49**(1), 44–53 (2019)
17. Humbert, M., et al.: Benefits of omalizumab as add-on therapy in patients with severe persistent asthma who are inadequately controlled despite best available therapy (gina 2002 step 4 treatment): Innovate. Allergy **60**(3), 309–316 (2005)
18. Lewis, P.: The characteristic selection problem in recognition systems. IRE Trans. Inform. Theory **8**(2), 171–178 (1962)
19. Lopez-Rincon, A., Martinez-Archundia, M., Martinez-Ruiz, G.U., Schoenhuth, A., Tonda, A.: Automatic discovery of 100-mirna signature for cancer classification using ensemble feature selection. BMC Bioinform. **20**(1), 480 (2019)
20. Lopez-Rincon, A., et al.: Machine learning-based ensemble recursive feature selection of circulating mirnas for cancer tumor classification. Cancers **12**(7), 1785 (2020)
21. Mandrekar, J.N.: Receiver operating characteristic curve in diagnostic test assessment. J. Thorac. Oncol. **5**(9), 1315–1316 (2010)
22. Murray, L., Xi, Y., Upham, J.W.: Clec4c gene expression can be used to quantify circulating plasmacytoid dendritic cells. J. Immunol. Methods **464**, 126–130 (2019)
23. Murray, L.M., Yerkovich, S.T., Ferreira, M.A., Upham, J.W.: Risks for cold frequency vary by sex: role of asthma, age, tlr7 and leukocyte subsets. Eur. Respir. J. (2020)
24. Pandey, G., et al.: A nasal brush-based classifier of asthma identified by machine learning analysis of nasal RNA sequence data. Sci. Rep. **8**(1), 1–15 (2018)
25. Pedregosa, F., et al.: Scikit-learn: machine learning in python. J. Mach. Learn. Res. **12**, 2825–2830 (2011)
26. Possa, S.S., Leick, E.A., Prado, C.M., Martins, M.A., Tibério, I.F.L.C.: Eosinophilic inflammation in allergic asthma. Front. Pharmacol. **4**, 46 (2013)
27. Šimundić, A.M.: Measures of diagnostic accuracy: basic definitions. Ejifcc **19**(4), 203 (2009)
28. Thomas, B., et al.: Ciliary dysfunction and ultrastructural abnormalities are features of severe asthma. J. Allergy Clin. Immunol. **126**(4), 722–729 (2010)

29. Thomson, N.C., Chaudhuri, R.: Omalizumab: clinical use for the management of asthma. Clinical Medicine Insights: Circulatory, Respiratory and Pulmonary Medicine 6, CCRPM-S7793 (2012)

30. Upchurch, K., et al.: Whole blood transcriptional variations between responders and non-responders in asthma patients receiving omalizumab. Clinical & Experimental Allergy (2020)

31. Vignolo, L.D., Milone, D.H., Scharcanski, J.: Feature selection for face recognition based on multi-objective evolutionary wrappers. Expert Syst. Appl. 40(13), 5077–5084 (2013)

32. Virtanen, P., et al.: SciPy 1.0 Contributors: SciPy 1.0: fundamental algorithms for scientific computing in python. Nature Methods 17, 261–272 (2020). https://doi.org/10.1038/s41592-019-0686-2

33. Vroman, H., Hendriks, R.W., Kool, M.: Dendritic cell subsets in asthma: impaired tolerance or exaggerated inflammation? Front. Immunol. 8, 941 (2017)

34. Watson, C., et al.: Integrative transcriptomic analysis reveals key drivers of acute peanut allergic reactions. Nat. Commun. 8(1), 1–13 (2017)

35. Zhou, Z., Li, S., Qin, G., Folkert, M., Jiang, S., Wang, J.: Multi-objective based radiomic feature selection for lesion malignancy classification. IEEE J. Biomed. Health Inform. (2019)

Bayesian Networks for Mood Prediction Using Unobtrusive Ecological Momentary Assessments

Margarita Rebolledo[1]([envelope]), A. E. Eiben[2], and Thomas Bartz-Beielstein[1]

[1] Institute for Data Science, Engineering and Analytics, TH Köln, Cologne, Germany
{margarita.rebolledo,thomas.bartz-beielstein}@th-koeln.de
[2] Department of Computer Sciences, Vrije Universiteit Amsterdam,
Amsterdam, Netherlands
a.e.eiben@vu.nl

Abstract. Depression affects an estimated 300 million people around the globe. Early detection of depression and associated mental health problems constitutes one of the best prevention methods when trying to reduce the disease's incidence. Information collected by tracking smartphone use behaviour and using ecological momentary assessments (EMA) can be used together with machine learning techniques to identify patterns indicative of depression and predict its appearance, contributing in this way to its early detection. However many of these techniques fail to identify the importance and relationships between the factors used to reach their prediction outcome. In this paper we propose the use of Bayesian networks (BN) as a tool to analyse and model data collected using EMA and smartphone measured behaviours. We compare the performance of BN against results obtained using support vector regression and random forest. The comparison is done in terms of efficacy, efficiency, and insight. Results show that no significant difference in efficacy was found between the models. However, BN presented clear advantages in terms of efficiency and insight given its probability factorization, graphical representation and ability to infer under uncertainty.

Keywords: Bayesian networks · Modelling · Ecological momentary assessments · Interpretability

1 Introduction

Depression and other associated mental health disorders can have disturbing effects on every life aspect of people suffering from it. According to the world health organization an estimated 300 million people were suffering from depression in 2015. It is also the largest contributor to global disability. Prevention and early recognition can reduce the incidence of depression and mitigate the negative impacts associated with this disorder.

Several studies have linked the influence of smartphones in the development and intensity of depression and anxiety symptoms [8]. However, they can also

© Springer Nature Switzerland AG 2021
P. A. Castillo and J. L. Jiménez Laredo (Eds.): EvoApplications 2021, LNCS 12694, pp. 373–387, 2021.
https://doi.org/10.1007/978-3-030-72699-7_24

work as a tool for early recognition of depressive indicators. One possible approach is through the use of ecological momentary assessments (EMA) to help
evaluate the current mental state of the user. EMA methods allow the collection
of psychological phenomena in real-time and within a subject's natural environment to avoid retrospective biases. One common data collection method is self-
assessment questions through the user's mobile phone. Another less obstructive
approach is making use of software monitoring or embedded smartphone sensors to follow the user's activities and behaviors. The identification of certain
patterns could lead to the early detection of depressive symptoms.

Bayesian networks (BN) is a probabilistic graphical model that represents the
conditional dependencies between a set of variables. They are especially useful
when dealing with restricted amounts of data and in aiding human decision making. According to a recent review of BN use in healthcare [14], its implementation
in psychological and psychiatric disorders make up the fourth-largest group of
applications. However, this number still lags when considering other machine
learning approaches and more work still needs to be done to bring more attention to this modelling method. Some works focusing on the implementation of
BN in the field of depression include [15], where possible causal relationships
between obsessive-compulsive disorder and depression were disclosed. In [6] an
ontology model together with BN is used to infer the probability of becoming
depressed. Other works have also used smartphone sensing to monitor and study
depression and similar mental health disorders [1,9,21]. Different machine learning methods have been implemented for mood prediction. In [10] an autoencoder
is used to fill missing data and provide a robust mood prediction. Deep learning
is also implemented in [20] to classify mood readings deviating from common
relaxed characteristics. In [7] random forest is used for mood prediction using
digital log data. L2-regression and support vector machines are used to predict
medical regression using PHQ-9 data in [9].

In a background study [4] different machine learning techniques were tested
on EMA to predict the mood of users. Their focus was on predicting the current
mood of individual participants based on their smartphone measurements. They
concluded that machine learning techniques support vector regression (SVR) and
random forest (RF), which incorporate all data about a participant, performed
better. However, they stated that more work should focus on finding the most
relevant attributes influencing the short-term mood of the participants.

The aim of this work is to expand on the findings in [4] and implement BN
as a quick to perform and easy to interpret model to predict the current mood
of the user. Given the intrinsic properties of BN new information about the
attributes that most influence the mood and their conditional dependencies can
be gained. This information can be presented to users for them to have a better
understanding of their patterns, be used by medical professionals to provide
better insight into personalized and general patterns and behaviors that can
influence mood, or, be used as a base to design more comprehensive experiments
that allow discovering possible causal relationships between variables. In short,
the present study seeks to answer the following questions:

RQ-1 How would BN compare to SVR and RF in terms of efficiency, efficacy, and insight when modelling each participant individually?

RQ-2 How would BN compare to SVR and RF in terms of efficiency, efficacy, and insight when generating a general model for all participants?

The paper is structured in the subsequent manner. Section 2 explains the data available for the model building. In Sect. 3 the different methods used to model the data are presented. Experiments are conducted on Sect. 4 and their results are discussed on Sect. 5. Final thoughts and future work are given in Sect. 6.

2 Data

The data set presented here was first described in [2] and used in [4]. The data originates from a pilot study where 27 university students self-monitored their mood for a time frame of 6 weeks. During this time each participant would be prompted by a cellphone application to input their current mood on a scale from 1 to 10, 10 being the best, five times a day. Additional to logging the mood self-assessment information, the mobile application also recorded other different EMA in the background. Information about the duration and frequency of calls, SMS, screen on/off events, applications used, number of images taken with the camera, and activity were recorded. A total of 55 parameters make up the initial data set. An overview of all variables is presented in Table 1.

Table 1. Mood prediction data set. The attributes names correspond to one or more attributes collecting similar information. The number of variables in each group is given in n_Variables.

Attribute name	Explanation	n_Variables	Range
Id	Participant's identification code	1	[1–27]
mood (Target)	Mood scored by the user	1	[1–10]
callc1c - callc5c	Number of calls to top 5 contacts	5	[0–1]
callc1d - callc5d	Duration of calls to top 5 contacts	5	[0–1]
smsc1c - sms5c	Number of SMS to top 5 contacts	5	[0–1]
accelerometer.high	Percentage of high activity time	1	[0–1]
screen.duration	Standardized total screen-on events	1	[−3,3]
screen.n	Standardized frequency screen-on event	1	[−3,3]
app.a1c - app.a5c	Top 5 Apps usage frequency	5	[0–1]
app-a1d - app.a5d	Top 5 Apps usage duration	5	[0–1]
appCat.n	Apps use frequency	11	[0–1]
appCat.sum	Apps usage duration	11	[0–1]
image.n	Number of images taken	1	[0–1]
mood.l1	Standardized mood of yesterday	1	[−3–3]
mood.l2	Standardized mood of day before yesterday	1	[−3–3]

The target variable *mood* is a daily average. Only days with at least one rating of mood are included in the data set. As a result, participants have a different number of effective samples going from 26 up to 40. Variables related to calls, SMS, images taken, and Apps duration and frequency of use were summarized daily and normalized within participants. The variable accelerometer.high represents the percentage of time during the day in which the participant's activity surpassed a threshold of 10 m/s^2. Lastly, variables mood.l1, mood.l2, screen.duration and screen.n are transformed to the standard normal distribution. That is, 99.97% of their values fall between −3 and 3. For more in-depth information about the different variables please refer to [2].

As an additional preprocessing step, variables with near zero variance were removed from the data set. Variables for which the ratio between the frequency of its most common value to its second most common value was less than 15 were removed.

In the end, the data set used to build the models presented in the following sections contains a total of 24 predictors, excluding target and id variables, and 595 observations across all participants are available.

3   Methods

3.1   Bayesian Networks

BN [12,16] are probabilistic models based on directed acyclic graphs (DAG). A DAG structure is given by $\mathcal{G} = (\mathbf{V}, A)$ where $\mathbf{V}$ is the node and A is the arc set. Nodes represent the random variables of interest $\mathbf{V} = \{X_1, X_2, ..., X_n\}$, and arcs represent informational or causal dependencies among the variables. They are quantified as conditional probabilities for each node given its parent nodes. The DAG defines a factorization of the global probability distribution of $\mathbf{V}$ into local probability distributions, one for each node. The local distribution for a random variable $P(X_i)$ is given as the conditional distribution of X_i and its parents Π_{X_i} as $P(X_i|\Pi_{X_i})$. In other words, the local distribution of a node is independent of other nodes given its parents. Following the same method, the global probability distribution of the network defined by $\mathcal{G}$ is

$$P(X_1, ..., X_n) = \prod_i^n P(X_i|\Pi_{X_i})   \tag{1}$$

where n is the number of nodes. Any probability of interest can be computed from this joint probability.

In order to learn the BN model from the data two steps are required: structure learning and parameter learning. Structure learning entails finding the DAG encoding the dependence structure of the nodes given the data, $P(\mathcal{G}|D)$, where D is the data. This can be guided by expert knowledge if available. In parameter learning, the parameters Θ, that define the local distributions for each node are estimated. As already mentioned, these distributions are independent and as such the Θ can be computed as

$$P(\Theta|\mathcal{G}, D) = \prod_{i=1}^{n} P(\Theta_i|\Pi_{X_i}, D) \tag{2}$$

Three main approaches for structure learning are possible: constraint-based, score-based, and hybrid [19].

Constraint-based approaches implement conditional independence tests, such as Fischer's Z test, to discover the dependence structure of the data. In score-based approaches, general-purpose optimization techniques like hill-climbing or Tabu search are used to generate candidate DAGs. Each candidate receives a score reflecting its goodness-of-fit which the optimization algorithm tries to maximize. Finally, hybrid algorithms combine both approaches sequentially by first selecting a network skeleton using constraint-based algorithms and then maximizing its score.

Finally, assumptions need to be done about the distribution followed by $\mathbf{X}$. In general, if the data set contains continuous parameters it is assumed that $\mathbf{X}_i$ follows a multivariate normal distribution and that the relationship with its parents is linear. These networks are known as Gaussian BNs and are the type used in this work.

For the implementation of BN we used the *bnlearn* R package [18]. The network structure is learned via the score-based hill-climbing search by maximizing the Bayesian information criterion (BIC).

3.2 Support Vector Regression

Support vector regression (SVR) [3] is a generalization of the well known support vector machines (SVM) for classification. In the classification case SVM finds the optimal hyperplane separating different categories. In the general case SVR introduces an ε-insensitive region, called ε-tube. The regression is then formulated as an optimization problem where a convex ε-insensitive loss function needs to be minimized to find the flattest tube that contains most of the training data samples. The optimization problem is solved using numerical optimization algorithms. For non-linear functions, the data can be mapped into a higher dimensional space using a kernel function.

To follow the implementation in [4], we implemented SVR on the *kernlab* R package [11]. The SVR was defined as an epsilon regression with epsilon and the cost of constraint violation set to 0.5. The radial kernel was used with hyperparameters values calculated internally by the included heuristic sigest.

3.3 Random Forest

Random Forest (RF) [5] is a well-known type of non-linear multiple regression. It is an ensemble method that groups several weak learners (decision trees) and combines them to generate a strong learner (a forest). For each decision tree, an input is split into smaller subsets until it no longer brings an improvement to the model response. Another quality of RF is their computation of relative variable importance by measuring the mean decrease in mean square error (MSE) that each parameter generates.

Following the implementation in [4], the number of trees for our models is set to 500 and the number of variables sampled at the splits is set internally by the model. The random forest model is implemented using the R package randomForest [13].

4   Experiments

Two types of experiments are carried out: in the first experimental case each user's data is modeled separately and results will apply only to the specific user. For the second experiment type, the data of all users is combined to build a general model. This will allow examining whether for this data set it is possible to use knowledge of other individuals to improve the prediction of *mood*. The results of the different models on both experiments are compared in terms of efficiency, efficacy, and insight.

The *efficacy* of the models is evaluated in terms of MSE and stability. The average MSE after 10 cross-validations runs is taken as the final MSE of the model. To determine whether a significant difference between the different model's MSE is present the Kruskal-Wallis rank-sum test is used. If the test is positive, a post-hoc test according to Conover [17], for pairwise multiple comparisons, checks for differences in each algorithm pair. The comparisons are further used to rank the algorithms from 1 (best) to 3. The second efficacy measure corresponds to the stability of the model. To control no large changes occur in the prediction given slight changes in the input data, we define stability as the difference between the minimum and maximum result in the model across the 10 cross-validation runs.

The *efficiency* of the models is given as the wall clock time in seconds required to build the models on one machine.

Lastly, the *insight* is understood as the model interpretability. We define interpretability as the informativeness and intelligibility of the model. A model is informative when it allows to explore the data and provide assistance to a human decision maker. Intelligibility is defined as how intuitive the understanding of the model is.

4.1   Individual Models

The first round of experiments is focused on predicting the current *mood* using only the data available for each of the participants. On the one hand, this ensures a completely personalized analysis and acknowledges the differences between each user, but on the other hand, this suffers from a lack of sufficient data samples that some participants presented.

The model validation was done through 10 fold cross-validation. Each participant's data was partitioned into training and testing sets with ratio 85/15. The wall clock time in seconds required by each algorithm to finish all 10 cross-validation runs across all 27 participants is taken. Table 2 presents the results obtained for MSE, time, stability, and rank for the case of individual models. It is clear that all models present the same level of performance, indicated by them all obtaining the same best rank by the post-hoc test. Their only significant difference is the time required to build the model.

Table 2. Individual model results. MSE corresponds to the average across the 10 cross-validation runs and 27 participants. The time in seconds is measured as the total time taken for the 10 repetitions of the 27 models. The rank is assigned after following a post-hoc test according to Conover [17] and rated from 1 (best) to 3.

	SVM	BN	RF
MSE	0.41	0.47	0.39
Stability	1.00	0.87	0.81
Time	30	9	13
Rank	1	1	1

To give a qualitative measure of interpretability the models should be examined individually. As an illustration example, we will use the model for the participant with *id* "AS14.0".

Neither SVR or RF offer an understandable visual depiction of their model structure. The higher dimensionality kernel representation is prohibiting for the case of SVR and the high number of trees in RF is restrictive for the complete representation of the model. In the case of BN the visual representation of the model is more straightforward thanks to its DAG structure.

Figure 1 shows the network learned from user "AS14.01". The arrows' direction indicate the conditional dependencies of the data. For this specific model, *mood* is conditionally dependent of it parents *app.a5c* and *screen.n* such that $P(mood) = P(mood|app.a5c, screen.n)$. The gray shaded nodes depict the Markov blanket of *mood*, or in other words, the subset of variables that have all the information required to compute the probability of the variable of interest according to the joint probability factorization explained in the section above. Also of interest is the arc strength which gives a measure of confidence for each arc. Strength is measured as the decrease in the network score that would be caused by the arcs removals. If it is of interest the network could be reduced using this information. The arc's thickness in Fig. 1 represents the arc's strength, in this case, thicker arcs have a higher confidence level.

A similar functionality to the arcs' strength is given by RF measure of importance. Here the decrease of accuracy, as measured by the MSE, when a variable is removed from the model is taken as the importance of the variable. The parameters importance according to the random forest model of user "AS14.01" is

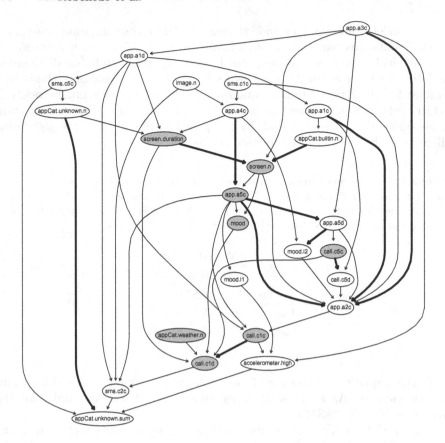

Fig. 1. Learned Bayesian network for user *id* "AS14.01". Arrows represent the conditional probability dependencies of each node. The arcs thickness corresponds to the arc's importance in the network according to their BIC score. The target node *mood* and the nodes conforming its Markov blanket are gray shaded. In this model it can be seen that *screen.n* influences the value of *mood* while *sms.c2c* has no relationship with it.

shown in Fig. 2. It is interesting to note that parameters with higher importance are not all included in the Markov blanket of the BN model.

As a final characteristic of BN that largely impact their interpretability is their ability of inference under uncertainty. It is possible to investigate the effects of new evidence using the information encoded in the BN and compute the maximum posterior density, or simply put, the probability of a given combination of events on a node. If we are interested in finding the probability that for user "AS14.01" a *mood* higher than 6 happens if the *screen.duration* value is higher than 2 (higher than the mean) and the *app.a5c* is lower than 0.03 (lower than the mean) then the probability of *mood* will be $P(mood > 6|screen.duration > 2 \cup app.a5c < 0.03) = 0.96$. This probability decreases if we consider a lower value of *screen.duration* $P(mood > 6|screen.duration < 2 \cup app.a5c < 0.03) = 0.9$.

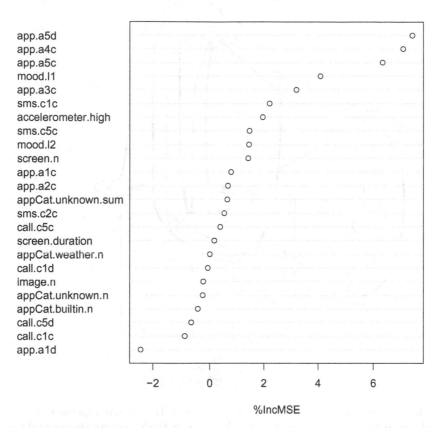

Fig. 2. Random forest importance measure for user *id* "AS14.01". The importance is measured as the decrease of accuracy (MSE) in out of bag samples when the variable is excluded from the model.

This ability of 'what if' queries greatly increase the amount of information that can be obtained from the model

To illustrate the variability between the networks obtained from different participants, we present the learned Bayesian network for user "AS14.31" in Fig. 3. Markov blanket and arc strength are visualized as previously explained. We can see that variables part of the Markov blanket for user "AS14.01", as is the case with *call.c5c*, are considered here conditional independent. Predicted values for these variables are taken from their assumed prior distributions.

4.2 General Model

In the case that behaviors between participants do not differ considerably, it should be possible to combine all the information the data can give and use it to predict *mood*.

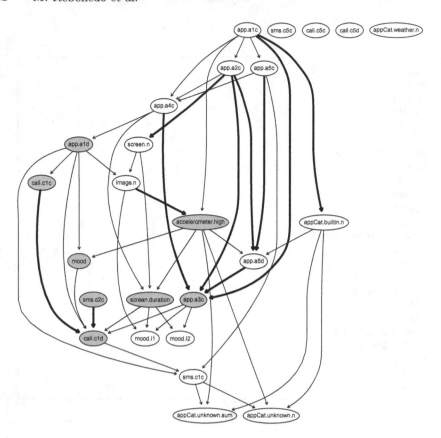

Fig. 3. Learned Bayesian network for user *id* "AS14.31". Arrows represent the conditional probability dependencies of each node. The arcs thickness corresponds to the arc's importance in the network according to their BIC score. The target node *mood* and the nodes conforming its Markov blanket are gray shaded. In this model it can be seen that *app.a1d* influences the value of *mood* while *call.c5c* has no relationship with it.

The same procedure as for the individual models was followed to build the general model. The data is partitioned into test and training sets, and the model was validated using 10 cross-validation runs.

As an initial approach, the models were built omitting any personal information given here by the *id* parameter. Results indicate that despite counting with more data samples no reasonably conditional dependence was established for the *mood* parameter. A look into the performance of all three models indicates that no improvement was seen in the MSE.

The model was build again including the *id* parameter. In this case, the model is able to identify conditional dependencies for *mood*. Results for this general model can be seen in Table 3. Also in this case the models do not present any improvement in performance and no significant difference between them. However, the time saving achieved by BN is notable.

Table 3. Results for the general model. MSE corresponds to the average across the 10 cross-validation runs. The time in seconds is measured as the total time taken for the 10 repetitions. The rank is assigned after following a post-hoc test according to Conover [17] and rated from 1 (best) to 3.

	SVM	BN	RF
MSE	0.45	0.44	0.41
Stability	0.41	0.34	0.38
Time	22	2	25
Rank	1	1	1

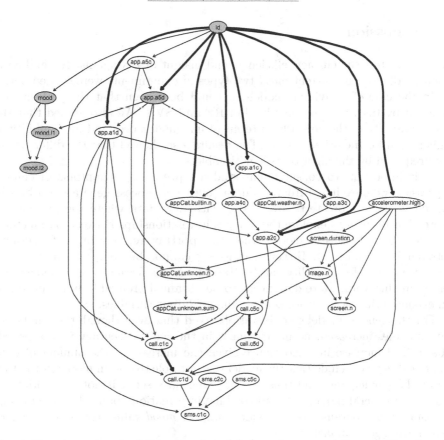

Fig. 4. Bayesian network of the general model. Arrows represent the conditional probability dependencies of each node. The arc's thickness corresponds to the arc's importance in the network according to their BIC score. The target node *mood* and the nodes conforming its Markov blanket are gray shaded. It can be seen that many of the most important dependencies relate to *id*, and *mood* is also conditionally dependent of it. On the other side, there is total independence from *sms.c5c*.

Similar to the individual models' case, the structure of the general model can be observed in Fig. 4. As previously explained, the thicker arcs represent the ten connections with the highest confidence level. As it can be seen in the figure most of them are related to the *id*.

A look into RF measure of importance also shows that *id* is by far the most important parameter influencing the MSE. Taking into account that the model efficacy did not improve with the addition of more data samples and that the identification parameter seems to be of great importance to the understanding of the model, it can be assumed that the prediction of mood using all the participants is not a good idea for this data set.

5   Discussion

In order to test the efficacy, efficiency, and insight of BN against RF and SVR when predicting the current *mood* two types of experiments were carried out.

In the case of individual models, it could be proven that the performance achieved by BN is at the same level of RF and SVR. We also argued that the interpretability of the network, in terms of informativeness and intelligibility, is higher than for the other models. The results also showed that the difference in time required by the algorithms is noticeable.

It is important to consider that students presenting symptoms of clinical depression were excluded from the data collection process generating a bias in the *mood* data. More tests are needed with new data where the presence of depression is given to explore the changes in relationships between parameters.

BN are probabilistic models that can portray relationships of causality between its parameters. However, causality cannot be confirmed and only a conjectural case for causality can be started when referring to the models presented in this work. More data needs to be obtained preferably from controlled experiments that account for confounding or latent variables.

For the general model case, it was observed that even though the number of data samples increased, no improvement in the model accuracy was observed. The lack of increase in performance given the increase in the number of data points led us to conclude that the model was not able to obtain more information about the participants and thus for the given data set it is not appropriate to generate a general model that can combine information about all patients. The addition of new parameters or a wider range of *mood* values could be necessary to achieve a good model.

The similarity in the performance of the tested models make criteria such as interpretability an important concept to define according to the end purpose of the model. In a scenario of medical studies where analysis should be personalized for each patient, it is beneficial to have a model that allows the medical professional to understand the flow of data and its conditional dependencies to plan experiments and better analyze results.

6 Conclusion

The use of unobtrusively collected EMA via smartphone as a way to predict the current mood of the user through BN is studied in this work. To answer our research questions we compared the efficacy, efficiency, and insight of BN against the already tested models SVR and RF. The efficacy is measured in terms of MSE and stability. The wall-clock time measures the efficiency and the level of insight is measured in terms of interpretability. Two types of experiments were carried out on the data in order to answer our research questions.

RQ-1 How would BN compare to SVR and RF in terms of efficiency, efficacy, and insight when modelling each participant individually? In our first experiment, one model per participant was build and the performance of the models was evaluated using cross-validation. The results showed that no significant difference in performance was found between the models. In terms of speed and interpretability BN presented clear advantages. Interpretability is defined as the informativeness and intelligibility of a model. In Fig. 1, it was easy to identify which of the parameters had an influence on the outcome of *mood* based on the arc connections present between the nodes and the visual representation of its Markov blanket. At the same time, it was easy to represent the conditional probabilities with the most importance in the model.

RQ-2 How would BN compare to SVR and RF in terms of efficiency, efficacy, and insight when generating a general model for all participants? For the second type of experiment one general model was implemented. Results were consistent in terms of performance between the three models. Also here the gains in interpretability and speed were noticeable for BN. However, it was clear given the lack of performance improvement that the amount and quality of data may be insufficient to build such a general model and neither of the tested methods presented a considerable improvement.

BN as a tool to graphically model the conditional dependencies between variables do not present any loss in performance against SVR or RF. On the other hand, it was shown that BN bring benefits in terms of efficiency and insight given its probability factorization, graphical representation, and ability to infer under uncertainty. These advantages would make its implementation as informative models in mobile devices realizable. A conceivable application would be a weekly presentation of the built model to inform the user of their behavioral trends.

In future work, we would like to make use of another important feature of BN that allows the inclusion of expert knowledge into the model. In this way, relationships between already studied parameters can be included and inference and reasoning capabilities of the model can be improved. More work is also needed using a more comprehensive data set in order to achieve a more robust understanding of the influence certain behaviors have on the mood. It is necessary to evaluate the inclusion of new measurable variables in the data collection, such as sleep duration and patterns. Feature selection and feature engineering to define the parameters to be modeled remain as an open possibility that needs to be explored.

References

1. Aledavood, T., Torous, J., Triana Hoyos, A.M., Naslund, J.A., Onnela, J.P.,Keshavan, M.: Smartphone-based tracking of sleep in depression, anxiety, and psychotic disorders. Current Psychiatry Rep. **21**(7), 49 (2019).https://doi.org/10. 1007/s11920-019-1043-y

2. Asselbergs, J., Ruwaard, J., Ejdys, M., Schrader, N., Sijbrandij, M., Riper, H.: Mobile phone-based unobtrusive ecological momentary assessment of day-to-day mood: An explorative study. J. Med. Int. Res. **18**(3), e72–e72 (2016). https://doi. org/10.2196/jmir.5505

3. Awad, M., Khanna, R.: Support Vector Regression, pp. 67–80. Apress, Berkeley, CA (2015). https://doi.org/10.1007/978-1-4302-5990-9_4

4. van Breda, W., Pastor, J., Hoogendoorn, M., Ruwaard, J., Asselbergs, J., Riper, H.: Exploring and comparing machine learning approaches for predicting mood over time. In: Chen, Y.-W., Tanaka, S., Howlett, R.J., Jain, L.C. (eds.) Innovation in Medicine and Healthcare 2016. SIST, vol. 60, pp. 37–47. Springer, Cham (2016). https://doi.org/10.1007/978-3-319-39687-3_4

5. Breiman, L.: Random forests. Mach. Learn. **45**(1), 5–32 (2001). https://doi.org/ 10.1023/A:1010933404324

6. Chang, Y.S., Fan, C.T., Lo, W.T., Hung, W.C., Yuan, S.M.: Mobile cloud-based depression diagnosis using an ontology and a Bayesian network. Future Gener. Comput. Syst. **43-44**, 87–98 (2015).https://doi.org/10.1016/j.future.2014.05.004, http://www.sciencedirect.com/science/article/pii/S0167739X1400137X

7. Cho, C.H., Lee, T., Kim, M.G., In, H.P., Kim, L., Lee, H.J.: Mood prediction of patients with mood disorders by machine learning using passive digital phenotypes based on the circadian rhythm: prospective observational cohort study. J. Med. Int. Res. **21**(4), e11029 (2019). https://doi.org/10.2196/11029, http://www.ncbi.nlm. nih.gov/pubmed/30994461

8. Elhai, J.D., Dvorak, R.D., Levine, J.C., Hall, B.J.: Problematic smartphone use: a conceptual overview and systematic review of relations with anxiety and depression psychopathology. J. Affect. Disord. **207**, 251– 259 (2017). https://doi. org/10.1016/j.jad.2016.08.030, http://www.sciencedirect.com/science/article/pii/ S0165032716303196

9. Farhan, A.A., et al.: Behavior vs. introspection: refining prediction of clinical depression via smartphone sensing data. In: 2016 IEEE Wireless Health (WH), pp. 1–8 (2016). https://doi.org/10.1109/WH.2016.7764553

10. Jaques, N., Taylor, S., Sano, A., Picard, R.: Multimodal autoencoder: a deep learning approach to filling in missing sensor data and enabling better mood prediction. In: 2017 Seventh International Conference on Affective Computing and Intelligent Interaction (ACII), pp. 202–208 (2017). https://doi.org/10.1109/ACII.2017. 8273601

11. Karatzoglou, A., Smola, A., Hornik, K., Zeileis, A.: kernlab - an S4 package for kernel methods in R. J. Stat. Softw. **11**(9), 1–20 (2004). http://www.jstatsoft.org/ v11/i09/

12. Korb, K.B., Nicholson, A.E.: Bayesian Artificial Intelligence. CRC Press, Boca Raton (2010)

13. Liaw, A., Wiener, M.: Classification and regression by random forest. R News **2**(3), 18–22 (2002). https://CRAN.R-project.org/doc/Rnews/

14. McLachlan, S., Dube, K., Hitman, G.A., Fenton, N.E., Kyrimi, E.: Bayesian networks in healthcare: distribution by medical condition. Artif. Intell. Med. **107**, 101912 (2020).https://doi.org/10.1016/j.artmed.2020.101912, http://www.sciencedirect.com/science/article/pii/S0933365720300774

15. McNally, R., Mair, P., Mugno, B., Riemann, B.: Co-morbid obsessive-compulsive disorder and depression: a Bayesian network approach. Psychol. Med. **47**(7), 1204 (2017). https://www.mcnallylab.com/wp-content/uploads/McNally-Mair-Mugno-Riemann-2017-Psychological-Medicine.pdf

16. Pearl, J.: Probabilistic Reasoning in Intelligent Systems: Networks of Plausible Inference. Morgan Kaufmann Publishers Inc., San Francisco (1988)

17. Pohlert, T.: The pairwise multiple comparison of mean ranks package (pmcmr) (2014). http://CRAN.R-project.org/package=PMCMR. Accessed 12 Jan 2016

18. Scutari, M.: Learning Bayesian networks with the bnlearn R package. J. Stat. Softw. **35**(3), 1–22 (2010). https://doi.org/10.18637/jss.v035.i03, https://arxiv.org/pdf/0908.3817.pdf

19. Scutari, M., Graafland, C.E., Gutiérrez, J.M.: Who learns better Bayesian network structures: accuracy and speed of structure learning algorithms. Int. J. Approximate Reasoning **115**, 235–253 (2019). https://doi.org/10.1016/j.ijar.2019.10.003, http://www.sciencedirect.com/science/article/pii/S0888613X19301434

20. Spathis, D., Servia-Rodriguez, S., Farrahi, K., Mascolo, C., Rentfrow, J.: Passive mobile sensing and psychological traits for large scale mood prediction. In: Proceedings of the 13th EAI International Conference on Pervasive Computing Technologies for Healthcare. pp. 272–281. PervasiveHealth 2019, Association for Computing Machinery, New York, NY, USA (2019). https://doi.org/10.1145/3329189.3329213

21. Wahle, F., Kowatsch, T., Fleisch, E., Rufer, M., Weidt, S.: Mobile sensing and support for people with depression: a pilot trial in the wild. JMIR Mhealth Uhealth **4**(3), e111 (2016). https://doi.org/10.2196/mhealth.5960,http://www.ncbi.nlm.nih.gov/pubmed/27655245

A Multi-objective Multi-type Facility Location Problem for the Delivery of Personalised Medicine

Andreea Avramescu[1]([⊠])[iD], Richard Allmendinger[1][iD],
and Manuel López-Ibáñez[1,2][iD]

[1] Alliance Manchester Business School, University of Manchester,
Manchester M15 6PB, UK
andreea.avramescu@manchester.ac.uk
[2] School of Computer Science, University of Málaga, 29071 Málaga, Spain

Abstract. Advances in personalised medicine targeting specific sub-populations and individuals pose a challenge to the traditional pharmaceutical industry. With a higher level of personalisation, an already critical supply chain is facing additional demands added by the very sensitive nature of its products. Nevertheless, studies concerned with the efficient development and delivery of these products are scarce. Thus, this paper presents the case of personalised medicine and the challenges imposed by its mass delivery. We propose a multi-objective mathematical model for the location-allocation problem with two interdependent facility types in the case of personalised medicine products. We show its practical application through a cell and gene therapy case study. A multi-objective genetic algorithm with a novel population initialisation procedure is used as solution method.

Keywords: Personalised medicine · Biopharmaceuticals · Supply chain · Facility location-allocation · Evolutionary multi-objective optimisation

1 Introduction

Personalised medicine, or precision medicine (PM), has been defined in numerous ways and there is no standard understanding behind the new healthcare mantra [28]. In this paper, we focus on the Advanced Therapies Medicinal Products (ATMPs), i.e., the biopharmaceutical products that have been created as a result of the development of PM. ATMPs use tissue, genes, or cells to treat progressive diseases, such as cancer and rare disorders. They have the ability to overcome the generally accepted fact that the current drugs are not useful for the entire population, with some estimates pointing to a 60% efficiency rate [13]. In 2019, there were 42 ATMPs with commercial authorisation [11] and more than 2000 clinical trials in Europe [29]. These numbers may triple by 2030 [26].

PM's development was enhanced by the completion of the Human Genome Project [19] and our subsequent ability to sequence a person's DNA set through

© Springer Nature Switzerland AG 2021
P. A. Castillo and J. L. Jiménez Laredo (Eds.): EvoApplications 2021, LNCS 12694, pp. 388–403, 2021.
https://doi.org/10.1007/978-3-030-72699-7_25

a simple procedure [38]. The medical field has made considerable progress concerning PM treatments and their ability to cure progressive diseases. In contrast, little research has been conducted in regard to the way these products should be manufactured and delivered. Using a high level of stratification and low global demand, the continuous, off-the-shelf, and mass production of traditional drugs is shifting towards a batch and on-demand model. Additionally, biopharmaceutical companies work with new technologies under highly regulated markets. As a result ATMPs research followed a sparse approach that analysed different supply chain echelons independently without creating a holistic model.

The lack of optimisation models that take into account the specific requirements of ATMPs mean that decisions at strategical and operational levels are taken using existing pharmaceutical models. The current approach for the commercialisation of ATMPs has led to major challenges for some companies, such as the cases of Provenge [18] and ChondroCelect [1], or to lower quality treatments, such as the case of Kymriah [5]. Additional consequences for the patients also include limited availability. The high costs and complex manufacturing processes, together with the requirement for timely delivery in a cold supply chain,[1] restrict these medicines to be used only as a last resort.

The goal of this paper is to contribute towards the creation of more specialised optimisation models capable of tackling the inherent complexities associated with the delivery of PM. Accordingly, we propose a multi-objective optimisation (MOO) model to find the location of two types of facilities required as part of the supply chain, that minimises the cost and delivery time and maximises the demand covered while satisfying a number of constraints. Subsequently, we use a customised MOO algorithm to solve the problem. Our proposed algorithm is based on NSGA-II [9] but uses customised strategies for the population initialisation, mating and mutation of solutions, considering the dependency of one facility type on the other. Finally, we also propose an algorithm based on states proximity to obtain the demand allocation per hospital.

The rest of this paper is organised as follows. Section 2 outlines the theoretical background and highlights the relevant literature. Section 3 describes the supply chain and introduces the proposed mathematical model for the given problem. Sections 4 and 5 describe the data and methodological approach, while the results are presented in Sect. 6. The paper ends with a summary of the main findings and suggestions for future work.

2   Related Work

PM lies at the core of multiple supply chains in the pharmaceutical and healthcare industries. Therefore, the relevant theoretical background encompasses different topics. Using living cells, its delivery process shares common characteristics with the substances of human origin; while the research on the supply chains that support biopharmaceuticals are helpful in optimising the manufacturing aspect. As a service-oriented supply chain, key social requirements within

---

[1] A temperature-controlled supply chain that maintains a product viable through decreases in temperature.

healthcare are equity and fairness in access to medications and preventing drug shortages [22]. The guarantee of perfect demand coverage or the maximisation of available backup assistance in case of disruptions are among the most common objectives. The societal impact was assessed through the cost-effectiveness of the products and the ability to create an affordable healthcare system for both the society and the patient. Such objectives are extensively reviewed by Pirabán et al. [25] in the context of blood supply chains, and models of multiple healthcare supply chains are further outlined by Ahmadi-Javid et al. [2].

Most of the products (e.g. blood and pharmaceuticals) within the above mentioned supply chains are part of the essential and emergency medical system and are protected by fundamental human rights [7]. This is not the case for ATMPs and access to breakthrough therapies is not guaranteed. The high uncertainty in evidence regarding the efficiency at big scale as an outcome of the low number of products approved and their short time-frame on the market, combined with the products' complex and inefficient supply chains, makes numerous regulatory bodies reluctant to approve such therapies [15]. While capable of revolutionising treatment through a patient-centric approach, the requirements of PM are believed to widen the gap in access to healthcare [37]. To solve some of these problems, a scenario-based bi-objective facility-location problem formulation was proposed in [36]. The paper aimed to maximise the net present value, and minimise the average response time for patients. Nevertheless, to the best of our knowledge, the main constraints of the PM supply chain, concerning the product shelf-life and fragility, have not been addressed before from an operations research perspective.

Facility location-allocation is a well-known class of NP-hard problems [14]. Therefore, solving the problems using exact solution methods is only feasible when the decision space is small [14]. For real-world scenarios, different meta-heuristics have been applied, such as local search heuristics, and various variants of Genetic Algorithms (GAs) [4]. The applications of GAs to this problem type [27,39] and to some of its extensions [3,17] are prominent. When discussing the number of objectives, for bi- and multi-objective problems, the Non-dominated Sorting Genetic Algorithm (NSGA-II) [9] has been applied to problems such as uncapacitated facility location problem [34], hub location [12] and hub maximal covering under uncertainty [40], warehouse location [6], gas field location [35], location of public facilities in places prone to natural hazards [10], and hospital waste management networks [21].

3   Problem Description

In this paper we focus on the autologous supply chain of an ATMP [24] (Fig. 1) i.e., the donor is the patient itself and, after being processed, the cells need to be returned to the same hospital from where they were collected. Thus, each patient's cells correspond to one *order* that needs to be processed. The process starts with material collection from the donor at a hospital that has FACT (Foundation for the Accreditation of Cellular Therapy) authorisation. The collected

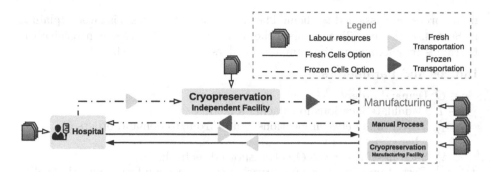

Fig. 1. ATMPs supply chain network flow with three modes of production, separate and integrated cryopreservation facilities.

product is then transported to a manufacturing facility where it is genetically modified. Using living cells, the entire process from hospital collection until the cells are returned to the patient must be shorter than the cells' shelf-life; between a few hours and a few days depending on each product type. Otherwise, it is common that cells are frozen at an independent cryopreservation facility and the transportation is done under cryogenic temperatures. Freezing the material extends the preservation time-frame relaxing altogether the time constraints. In this paper, we consider the shelf-life to become redundant once the cells are cryopreserved. This scenario is realistic since we assume that once the cells are processed they are automatically returned to the patient without any long-term storage in-between.

3.1 Mathematical Model

Starting from the above problem description, we aim to find an optimal location of manufacturing and cryopreservation facilities and allocate each patient's cells, typically from hospitals, accordingly. We start with a predefined set of locations L, that can be any geographical point where a facility can be placed, and a set of orders O. Each order has associated a known geographical location, typically a hospital. We know the travel time between any two candidate locations, and between candidate locations and hospitals denoted as t_{ij}, where $i, j \in L \cup O$. For simplicity, in this paper, we calculate t_{ij} by dividing the distance between any two locations or orders, $i, j \in L \cup O$, by the average car driving speed in the USA. We model the PM supply chain as an MOO problem (see next page).

Objective (1) minimises the average delivery time per patient. As each order corresponds to one patient and has hospitals as starting point, the objective minimises the travel time from order o to its assigned manufacturing facility located at i, possibly via a cryopreservation facility located at j if $z_o = 1$. Objective (2) minimises the total cost of the supply chain, i.e., the cost of opening manufacturing and cryopreservation facilities, which is independent of the orders assigned to them, and the cost of operating the facilities, which depends on how many orders are assigned to them. The calculation of the costs is later explained in Sect. 4. Objective (3) maximises the number of patients that can receive the therapies by maximising the number of orders being processed.

Indices and Parameters

$o \in O$ Demand orders.

$i \in L$ Candidate locations for placing a facility.

t_{ij} Travel time between locations L and from/to demand orders O, where $i, j \in L \cup O$.

γ_o^f Shelf-life if order $o \in O$ is transported as fresh.

f_i^C, f_i^M Cost of opening a cryopreservation (C) or a manufacturing (M) facility at location $i \in L$.

e_i^M, e_i^C Operating (M) or cryopreservation (C) cost of a facility placed at location $i \in L$.

Decision Variables

y_{oi}^M, y_{oi}^C 1 if order o is allocated to a manufacturing (M) or a cryopreservation (C) facility placed at location $i \in L$, 0 otherwise.

x_i^M, x_i^C 1 if a manufacturing (M) or a cryopreservation (C) facility is placed at candidate location $i \in L$, 0 otherwise.

z_o 1 if order $o \in O$ is delivered as frozen, 0 otherwise.

Objectives

$$\min \sum_{o \in O} \sum_{i \in L} \left(y_{oi}^M \cdot ((1 - z_o) t_{oi} + t_{io}) + z_o y_{oi}^C \cdot \left(t_{oi} + \sum_{j \in L} (t_{ij} \cdot y_{oj}^M) \right) \right) \quad (1)$$

$$\min \sum_{i \in L} \left(f_i^M \cdot x_i^M + e_i^M \cdot \left(\sum_{o \in O} y_{oi}^M \right) + f_i^C \cdot x_i^C + e_i^C \cdot \left(\sum_{o \in O} y_{oi}^C \right) \right) \quad (2)$$

$$\max \sum_{o \in O} \sum_{i \in L} y_{oi}^M \quad (3)$$

Constraints

$$2 \cdot (1 - z_o) \sum_{i \in L} (t_{oi} \cdot y_{oi}^M) + z_o \sum_{i \in L} t_{oi} \cdot y_{oi}^C \leq \gamma_o^f \quad \forall o \in O \quad (4)$$

$$\sum_{i \in L} x_i^M \geq 1 \quad (5)$$

$$\sum_{i \in L} y_{oi}^M \leq 1 \quad \forall o \in O \quad (6)$$

$$\sum_{i \in L} y_{oi}^C \leq z_o \quad \forall o \in O \quad (7)$$

$$y_{oi}^M \leq x_i^M \quad \forall o \in O, \forall i \in L \quad (8)$$

$$y_{oi}^C \leq x_i^C \quad \forall o \in O, \forall i \in L \quad (9)$$

$$x_i^C + x_i^M \leq 1 \quad \forall i \in L \quad (10)$$

$$y_{oi}^M, y_{oi}^C, x_i^M, x_i^C, z_o \in \{0, 1\} \quad (11)$$

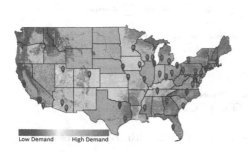

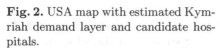

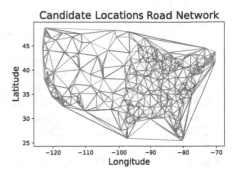

Candidate Locations Road Network

Fig. 2. USA map with estimated Kymriah demand layer and candidate hospitals.

Fig. 3. USA road network connections between the 1000 candidate locations.

The most important constraints in the PM supply chain are time constraints ensuring that each order is delivered within its respective shelf-life (4). Constraint (5) ensures that at least one manufacturing facility is placed, otherwise orders cannot be processed. Constraint (6) does not allow orders to be assigned to more than one manufacturing facility. In the case of (7), the order is only assigned to a cryopreservation facility if the order is cryopreserved. Constraints (8) and (9) limit orders to be assigned only to open facilities. Finally, we restrict that no more than one facility can be placed at each location (10).

4   Data

We test the proposed model using publicly available data of a personalised medicine product, Kymriah, manufactured and distributed by the biopharmaceutical company Novartis. Kymriah is a genetically engineered autologous cell therapy that first obtained market authorisation and the breakthrough therapy designation by the Food and Drug Administration (FDA) in August 2017 [8]. While the product has recently obtained authorisation to expand their targeted patients, the demand data was calculated using only the designation for B-cell precursor acute lymphoblastic leukaemia (ALL) that is refractory or relapsed (r/r) in paediatric patients in the USA. The data was obtained from the IICC-3 (International Incidence of Childhood Cancer [32]) and supplemented with expert opinions. It is estimated that about 80% of all paediatric ALL cases are caused by B-precursor [30] and in paediatric patients about 20% of these will be r/r [33]. Due to the above differences, as well as the usage of a different production mode, a comparison with the current Kymriah distribution is not possible.

The list of candidate hospitals that can accept patients for Kymriah was obtained from the official Novartis data and matched against the FACT accredited hospitals (Fig. 2). The demand at state level was then distributed using a random allocation to the hospitals within the same state until the entire capacity of those was filled. The remaining demand was then allocated randomly to

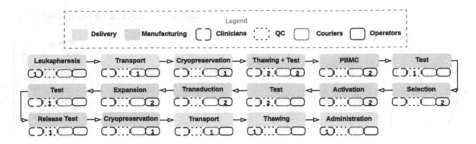

Fig. 4. Cell and gene therapy traditional sequence of tasks with required resources.

a hospital in one of the neighbouring states that still had capacity remaining. If there was no available hospital in a neighbouring state, then the allocation was moved to hospitals within the second level neighbouring states. The candidate locations for both manufacturing and cryopreservation facilities (L) are the 1 000 largest cities of the USA; their network is presented in Fig. 3.

The data for the manufacturing tasks was obtained using the Biosolve Process software [31]. Finally, the hourly wage for the labour resources was obtained for each individual state from the U.S. Bureau of Labor Statistics. This data is used later to calculate the total cost for the PM supply chain (see Eq. 2), which comprises the cost of opening manufacturing and cryopreservation facilities, and the operation cost. The operation cost was defined as the total cost for manufacturing and transportation, and calculated using a standard manual production setup [20]. The exact staff allocation for each task is shown in Fig. 4.

5   Methodology

We consider two MOO algorithms to solve the PM supply chain problem defined in Sect. 3.1: Multi-Objective Random Search (MORS) and a modified version of NSGA-II [9]. The performance of MORS shall serve as baseline.

Before we explain both MOO algorithms, we describe a procedure (Algorithm 1) for determining the allocation of orders to manufacturing and/or cryopreservation facilities based on the shelf-life. An order can only be allocated to a manufacturing facility at a particular location (without cryopreservation) if the travel time from the order to the location is smaller than half its shelf-life. Similarly, an order can only be allocated to a cryopreservation facility at a

---

Algorithm 1. Shelf-life Radius

Require: L, O, γ_o^f, t_{oi}
1: **for** $i \in L$ **do**
2:     $R_i^{\mathrm{M}} \leftarrow \{o \in O \mid t_{oi} < \gamma_o^f/2\}$
3:     $R_i^{\mathrm{C}} \leftarrow \{o \in O \mid t_{oi} < \gamma_o^f\}$
4: **end for**
5: **return** $R_i^{\mathrm{M}}, R_i^{\mathrm{C}}, i \in L$

Algorithm 2. Initial Population

Require: L; N (population size)
1: $P \leftarrow \varnothing$
2: **while** TRUE **do**
3:     $M \leftarrow$ randomly selected subset of L
4:     $C_{\text{full}} \leftarrow$ ProgressiveCoverage(M)   ▷ See Algorithm 3
5:     **for** $k = 1$ **to** $|C_{\text{full}}|$ **do**
6:         $C \leftarrow \{c_1, \ldots, c_k\} \subseteq C_{\text{full}}$ ▷ First k elements
7:         $s \leftarrow \{x_i^{\text{M}} = 1 \; \forall i \in M, \, x_j^{\text{C}} = 1 \; \forall j \in C\}$ ▷ Create partial solution
8:         $P \leftarrow P \cup \{s\}$
9:         **if** $|P| = N$ **then**
10:            **return** P
11:        **end if**
12:    **end for**
13: **end while**

Algorithm 3. Progressive Coverage

Require: $M \subset L$; $R_i^{\text{M}}, R_i^{\text{C}} \; \forall i \in L$
1: $C_{\text{full}} \leftarrow \varnothing$
2: $O_{\text{coverage}} \leftarrow \bigcup_{i \in M} R_i^{\text{M}}$ ▷ R_i^{M} calculated by Algorithm 1
3: $\overline{O} \leftarrow O \setminus O_{\text{coverage}}$ ▷ Uncovered orders
4: $\overline{L} \leftarrow L \setminus M$ ▷ Available locations
5: **while** $\overline{O} \neq \varnothing$ **do**
6:     $I^* \leftarrow \arg\max_{i \in \overline{L}} |R_i^{\text{C}} \cap \overline{O}|$ ▷ R_i^{C} calculated by Algorithm 1
7:     $i^* \leftarrow \arg\max_{I^*} |R_i^{\text{C}}|$
8:     $C_{\text{full}} \leftarrow C_{\text{full}} \cup \{i^*\}$
9:     $\overline{O} \leftarrow \overline{O} \setminus R_{i^*}^{\text{M}}$
10:    $\overline{L} \leftarrow \overline{L} \setminus i^*$
11: **end while**
12: **return** C_{full}

---

particular location if the travel time from the order to the location is smaller than its shelf-life (once the order is cryopreserved, the shelf-life constraint is deactivated). We apply this procedure once prior to running an MOO algorithm to calculate, for each location $i \in L$, which orders in O could be assigned to a manufacturing facility in location i without cryopreservation (line 3) and which orders could be assigned to a cryopreservation facility in that location (line 2). That is, $R_i^{\text{M}}, R_i^{\text{C}} \subseteq O$ are the orders that can be safely assigned to either a manufacturing facility (without cryopreservation) or a cryopreservation facility located in $i \in L$.

Following the allocation described above, we can now apply an MOO algorithm to tackle the PM supply chain problem. The NSGA-II approach considered here differs from the standard one [9] in the initialisation, mutation and crossover operators, while it maintains the non-dominated sorting procedure coupled with crowding distance, and binary tournament selection. Our NSGA-II follows Algorithm 2 to create an initial population of size 500. The goal of our initialisation is to ensure that we have a mix of solutions representing different configurations in terms of the number of manufacturing and cryopreservation facilities, and their coverage levels. By replacing the random initialisation with this approach, the algorithm is able to reach better solutions in less iterations. We use prior knowledge of the shelf-life and the radius of each facility to find a minimum number of cryopreservation facilities that can cover the demand. For placing the cryopreservation facilities, we employ the progressive coverage procedure outlined in Algorithm 3. It is important to note that since having a manufacturing facility is a mandatory requirement for an order to be processed, we prioritise the placement of this facility type, and construct the cryopreservation around it. For this, we use an iterative approach (Algorithm 3) to place the cryopreservation facilities: Looking at all orders that are not within the radius of any placed manufacturing facility (M), a cryopreservation facility is positioned at the candidate location (I^*) that can safely cover the most orders with no coverage (line 6). If several candidate locations cover an equal number of uncovered orders, then the location i^* with the maximum number of potentially assigned orders would be selected (line 7). This approach was preferred in order to increase the resilience of the supply chain in case of disruptions of any manufacturing facilities. The process is repeated until the demand from all orders is covered. This results in multiple solutions also containing cryopreservation facilities with different coverage levels for each potential assignment of manufacturing facilities.

Our NSGA-II creates new solutions using crossover and mutation operators. As the cryopreservation facilities depend on having an assigned manufacturing facility, the crossover ignores the former and considers only the latter type of facilities. If there is a common manufacturing location, this facility is inherited by the child, while the non-identical ones are inherited with a probability of 0.5 from either parent. As orders cannot be covered without being processed, solutions without manufacturing facilities are not allowed. For each solution, the mutation is applied randomly to a solution as follows. With probability of 0.1, a manufacturing facility is added or removed at random. It is not allowed to remove a manufacturing facility if it is the only one in the solution. A second mutation, applied with probability of 0.8 follows the network of candidate locations (Fig. 3) and allows a manufacturing facility to be moved at random only in one of the adjacent locations on the map. The allocation of orders to facilities is done after each mutation, each order being assigned to the closest facility.

If not otherwise stated, any results shown were obtained by running our two MOO approaches for 20 independent runs, each consisting of 800 generations (using a population size of 500).[2]

---

[2] Code for both MOO algorithms is available at doi: 10.5281/zenodo.4495163.

6   Results

We have tested the current case study by constraining the problem to three levels of coverage. The restrictions imposed either a minimum 50% or 80% coverage, and a third scenario with no coverage restriction (i.e. no minimum number of orders). The non-dominated solutions generated by NSGA-II and MORS are presented in Figs. 5 and 6 for two levels of minimum coverage. The three objectives (time, cost, and coverage) are represented on the plot axes, while the colour scheme corresponds to the number of manufacturing facilities placed within each solution.

Several patterns can be observed from Figs. 5 and 6. An increase in the coverage of orders leads to an increase in the cost but has no direct impact on the delivery time. This is influenced by the cryopreservation facilities which allow an order to be covered even though the total distance travelled increases. The average delivery time and the cost are negatively correlated. This is a result of the higher costs of manufacturing facilities compared to cryopreservation facilities. A higher number of manufacturing facilities in a solution corresponds to a lower average delivery time, higher costs, and higher coverage. The best-known non-dominated solutions obtained by MORS is similar in terms of slope and tendency of the trade-offs between the objectives, but MORS is not able to find good trade-off solutions between the cost and time objectives. Unlike NSGA-II, MORS does not use Algorithm 3 to optimise the number of cryopreservation locations. For this reason, MORS is more likely to find extreme solutions by selecting both manufacturing and cryopreservation facilities at random regardless of the coverage.

Table 1 shows the best values from all 20 runs for each of the objectives for the three coverage scenarios. These are only extreme examples and the more realistic trade-off solutions are shown in Figs. 5 and 6. When the coverage was not constrained, NSGA-II found better solutions for both cost and time objectives. Both algorithms found solutions that covered the entire demand. Because there were multiple solutions that had no uncovered demand, the second order sorting when selecting the solution was done by cost. With respect to a minimum of 50% or 80% coverage, MORS returned a better minimum cost but the difference was negligible when benchmarking with the covered demand and delivery time. For minimum delivery time, NSGA-II found better solutions than MORS together with a better coverage, but had overall worse total cost. Similar to the no coverage restriction scenario, both algorithms found solutions that covered the entire demand.

To exemplify one of the solutions in relation to the Kymriah case study, we have filtered the solutions of both algorithms to match the current Novartis' location. Kymriah is currently manufactured at the Morris Plains, USA. Among our final solutions, NSGA-II had 68 unique solutions that had placed at least a manufacturing facility within a 50 km radius of the above location for the 80% coverage restriction, 31 for the 50%, and 30 when no coverage restriction was imposed (MORS returned 28, 21, and 14 solutions respectively). The best solution in terms of coverage, breaking ties according to average delivery time,

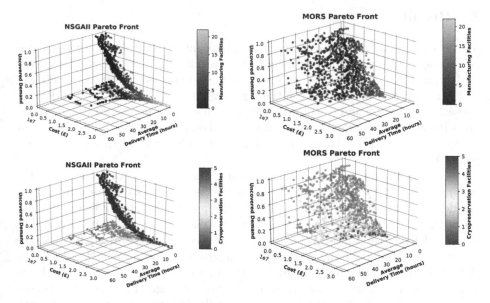

Fig. 5. Non-dominated solutions obtained by NSGA-II (*left*) and MORS (*right*) when there are no coverage restrictions. The same solutions are shown in the top and bottom plots. The only difference is the colour that shows the number of manufacturing and cryopreservation facilities, respectively.

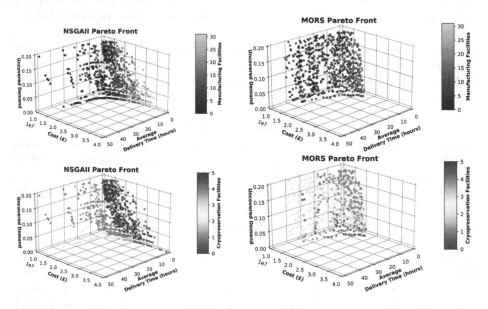

Fig. 6. Non-dominated solutions obtained by NSGA-II (*left*) and MORS (*right*) when there is a minimum of 80% coverage restriction. The same solutions are shown in the top and bottom plots. The only difference is the colour that shows the number of manufacturing and cryopreservation facilities, respectively.

Table 1. Comparison of extreme solutions identified by NSGA-II and MORS for different coverage restrictions.

No coverage restrictions

	NSGA - II					MORS				
	Uncovered demand	Average delivery time	Total cost	Configuration		Uncovered demand	Average delivery time	Minimum cost	Configuration	
Minimum cost	98%	6 h	£934,848	Manufacturing	1	93%	15.6 h	£1,648,944	Manufacturing	1
				Cryopreservation	0				Cryopreservation	1
Minimum average delivery time	95%	40 min	£2,336,130	Manufacturing	2	75%	56 min	£8,322,743	Manufacturing	6
				Cryopreservation	0				Cryopreservation	1
Maximum coverage	0%	21.7 h	£12,969,249	Manufacturing	1	0%	21 h	£12,914,729	Manufacturing	1
				Cryopreservation	2				Cryopreservation	3

50% coverage restrictions

	NSGA - II					MORS				
	Uncovered demand	Average delivery time	Total cost	Configuration		Uncovered demand	Average delivery time	Minimum cost	Configuration	
Minimum cost	50%	5 h	£8,029,810	Manufacturing	2	50%	27.7 h	£7,114,973	Manufacturing	1
				Cryopreservation	0				Cryopreservation	1
Minimum average delivery time	16%	1.7 h	£20,631,568	Manufacturing	22	31%	3 h	£18,116,561	Manufacturing	10
				Cryopreservation	0				Cryopreservation	1
Maximum coverage	0%	21.6 h	£12,677,729	Manufacturing	1	0%	23.4 h	£13,238,729	Manufacturing	1
				Cryopreservation	2				Cryopreservation	3

80% coverage restrictions

	NSGA - II					MORS				
	Uncovered demand	Average delivery time	Total Cost	Configuration		Uncovered demand	Average delivery time	Minimum cost	Configuration	
Minimum cost	19%	30 h	£10,866,954	Manufacturing	1	20%	23.5 h	£10,443,065	Manufacturing	1
				Cryopreservation	1				Cryopreservation	2
Minimum average delivery time	3.6%	36 min	£34,589,842	Manufacturing	6	16%	1.7 h	£19,083,259	Manufacturing	9
				Cryopreservation	0				Cryopreservation	1
Maximum coverage	0%	2.6 h	£28,047,023	Manufacturing	1	0%	20 h	£12,969,729	Manufacturing	1
				Cryopreservation	2				Cryopreservation	3

was returned by NSGA-II and the entire solution representation is shown in Fig. 7.

The total cost of this solution is £32,850,481 with an average delivery time of approximately one hour. The solution has 6 manufacturing facilities, one of them placed at the current Kymriah location, and 2 cryopreservation facilities. Given the higher number of hospitals on the eastern half of the USA, there were considerably more manufacturing facilities placed here compared to the western side. This distribution leads to a lower average delivery time, but the overlapping of manufacturing radiuses indicates that it is possible to reduce the cost by gradually increasing the time objective. Finally, because we assume that the orders are assigned only from existing hospitals, there are areas of the USA uncovered. Since there is a possibility for hospitals within those areas to obtain FACT authorisation, the demand coverage would be reduced. In terms of resiliency, this configuration has a high back-up coverage in case of possible disruptions to one of the production sites, as all hospitals are within the shelf-life radius of a cryopreservation facility. Nevertheless, given the unbalanced distribution of hospitals between the two facilities, one of the facilities might become overloaded and the solution infeasible should capacity constraints be taken into consideration.

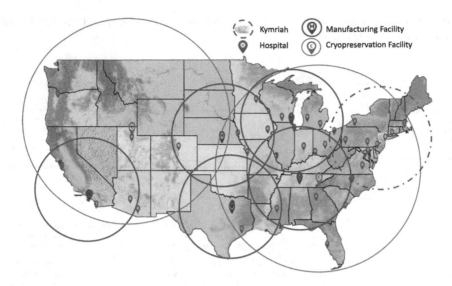

Fig. 7. USA map with the demand layer, hospitals (order locations), manufacturing (shelf-life radius in purple) and cryopreservation (shelf-life radius in green) facilities. The dashed circle corresponds to the radius of the current location of Kymriah. (Color figure online)

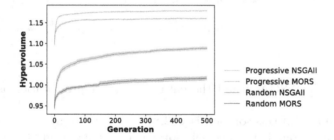

Fig. 8. Algorithms performance comparison between NSGA-II and MORS using the two different initialisation procedures, progressive (Algorithm 3) or random.

Finally, we want to analyse the convergence behaviour of the two MOO algorithms. For this, Fig. 8 shows the average hypervolume (HV) and the corresponding 95% confidence interval obtained by our NSGA-II and MORS. It is apparent that our NSGA-II is able to achieve significantly higher HV values than MORS when compared with the same initialisation procedure. However, the algorithms using the progressive coverage initialisation (Algorithm 3) perform better overall than those applying a random initialisation, which shows that the proposed initialization is critical. Moreover, even though both algorithms are faster at the beginning, NSGA-II continues to improve, which indicates that better solutions can be obtained using a higher number of generations.

7   Conclusion and Future Research

Progressing the field of PM has essential implications. Breakthrough therapies are creating possibilities to treat life-endangering diseases for which no other treatment is feasible. Nevertheless, existing research in logistics and supply chain management does not provide sufficient knowledge that can sustain the commercialisation of personalised healthcare. Novel formulations that integrate different supply chains, together with continuous theoretical development of the PM products' requirements are essential.

We have presented a multi-objective mathematical model for a PM supply chain, and analysed the performance of two MOO algorithms. A novel initialisation procedure considering progressive coverage of cryopreservation was also proposed and found to be superior to the random one for both algorithms. The model captured trade-offs between cost, delivery time, and demand coverage in facility location-allocation, and was validated for three scenarios representing constraints on different coverage levels. Broadly translated, our findings indicate that the operations research field has the potential to help biopharmaceutical companies offer timely and costly products, thus making revolutionary therapies more widely available.

The current study can be continued in various ways. For instance, the thawing necessary after freezing the product increases the risk of damaging the material [16,23]. Thus, future research considering cryopreservation methods with variable shelf-life might extend the current research towards a more resilient and safe supply chain. Maintaining the cells viable is crucial as the possibility of replacements is minimal. The autologous process involves patients with advanced stage diseases and the poor health condition might preclude another apheresis procedure. Finally, the novelty of the products and the uncertain global demand require the implementation of stochastic models.

Acknowledgements. We thank Biopharm Services for their assistance with this project. Biopharm provided us with extensive datasets and invaluable feedback on the research. Their contribution has significantly increased the quality and accuracy of this paper. M. López-Ibáñez is a "Beatriz Galindo" Senior Distinguished Researcher (BEAGAL 18/00053) funded by the Ministry of Science and Innovation of the Spanish Government.

References

1. Abou-El-Enein, M., Elsanhoury, A., Reinke, P.: Overcoming challenges facing advanced therapies in the EU market. Cell Stem Cell **19**(3), 293–297 (2016)
2. Ahmadi-Javid, A., Seyedi, P., Syam, S.S.: A survey of healthcare facility location. Comput. Oper. Res. **79**, 223–263 (2017)
3. Ardjmand, E., Weckman, G.R., Park, N., Taherkhani, P., Manjeet, S.: Applying genetic algorithm to a new location and routing model of hazardous materials. Int. J. Prod. Res. **53**, 916–928 (2015)

4. Basu, S., Sharma, M., Ghosh, P.S.: Metaheuristic applications on discrete facility location problems: a survey. Opsearch **52**(3), 530–561 (2014). https://doi.org/10.1007/s12597-014-0190-5

5. Bersenev, A., Kili, S.: Management of 'out of specification' commercial autologous CAR-T cell products. Cell Gene Therapy Insights **4**(11), 1051–1058 (2018)

6. Bhattacharya, R., Bandyopadhyay, S.: Solving conflicting bi-objective facility location problem by NSGA II evolutionary algorithm. Int. J. Adv. Manuf. Technol. **51**(1–4), 397–414 (2010)

7. Burkholder, T.W., Hill, K., Hynes, E.J.C.: Developing emergency care systems: a human rights-based approach. Bull. World Health Organ. **97**(9), 612–619 (2019)

8. CBER: Kymriah (tisagenlecleucel) (2017). https://www.fda.gov/vaccines-blood-biologics/cellular-gene-therapy-products/kymriah-tisagenlecleucel. Accessed 20 Sept 2020

9. Deb, K., Pratap, A., Agarwal, S., Meyarivan, T.: A fast and elitist multi-objective genetic algorithm: NSGA-II. IEEE Trans. Evol. Comput. **6**(2), 182–197 (2002)

10. Doerner, K.F., Gutjahr, W.J., Nolz, P.C.: Multi-criteria location planning for public facilities in tsunami-prone coastal areas. OR Spectrum **31**(3), 651–678 (2008)

11. Eder, C., Wild, C.: Technology forecast: advanced therapies in late clinical research, EMA approval or clinical application via hospital exemption. J. Market Access Health Policy **7**(1), 1600939 (2019)

12. Eghbali, M., Abedzadeh, M., Setak, M.: Multi-objective reliable hub covering location considering customer convenience using NSGA-II. Int. J. Syst. Assur. Eng. Manage. **5**(3), 450–460 (2013). https://doi.org/10.1007/s13198-013-0189-y

13. Ermak, G.: Emerging medical technologies. World Scientific (2016)

14. Farahani, R.Z., SteadieSeifi, M., Asgari, N.: Multiple criteria facility location problems: a survey. Appl. Math. Model. **34**, 1689–1709 (2010)

15. Gonçalves, E.: Advanced therapy medicinal products: value judgement and ethical evaluation in health technology assessment. Eur. J. Health Econ. **21**(3), 311–320 (2020). https://doi.org/10.1007/s10198-019-01147-x

16. Hanley, P.J.: Fresh versus frozen: effects of Cryopreservation on CAR T Cells. Mol. Therapy **27**(7), 1213–1214 (2019), ISSN 15250024

17. Hiassat, A., Diabat, A., Rahwan, I.: A genetic algorithm approach for location-inventory-routing problem with perishable products. J. Manuf. Syst. **42**, 93–103 (2017)

18. Jarosławski, S., Toumi, M.: Sipuleucel-t (Provenge) - Autopsy of an Innovative Paradigm Change in Cancer Treatment: Why a Single-Product Biotech Company Failed to Capitalize on its Breakthrough Invention. BioDrugs **29**(5), 301–307 (2015)

19. Lander, E.S., Linton, L.M., Birren, B.: Initial sequencing and analysis of the human genome. Nature **409**(6822), 860–921 (2001)

20. Lopes, A.G., Noel, R., Sinclair, A.: Cost analysis of vein-to-vein CAR T-cell therapy: automated manufacturing and supply chain. Cell Gene Therapy Insights **6**(3), 487–510 (2020)

21. Medaglia, A.L., Villegas, J.G., Rodríguez-Coca, D.M.: Hybrid biobjective evolutionary algorithms for the design of a hospital waste management network. Journal of Heuristics **15**(2), 153–176 (2009)

22. Nematollahi, M., Hosseni-Motlagh, S.M., Heydari, J.: Economic and social collaborative decision-making on visit interval and service level in a two-echelon pharmaceutical supply chain. J. Clean. Prod. **142**, 3956–3969 (2017)

23. Panch, S.R., et al.: Effect of cryopreservation on autologous chimeric antigen receptor T-Cell characteristics. Mol. Therapy **27**(7), 1275–1285 (2019), ISSN 15250024

24. Papathanasiou, M.M., Stamatis, C., Lakelin, M., Farid, S., Titchener-Hooker, N., Shah, N.: Autologous CAR T-cell therapies supply chain: challenges and opportunities? Cancer Gene Ther. **27**(10–11), 799–809 (2020)
25. Pirabán, A., Guerrero, W.J., Labadie, N.: Survey on blood supply chain management: models and methods. Comput. Oper. Res. **112**, 104756 (2019)
26. Quinn, C., Young, C., Thomas, J., Trusheim, M.: Estimating the Clinical Pipeline of Cell and Gene Therapies and Their Potential Economic Impact on the US Healthcare System. Value Health **22**(6), 621–626 (2019)
27. Rahmani, A., Mirhassani, S.: A hybrid Firefly-Genetic Algorithm for the capacitated facility location problem. Inf. Sci. **283**, 70–78 (2014)
28. Redekop, W.K., Mladsi, D.: The faces of personalized medicine: a framework for understanding its meaning and scope. Value Health **16**(6), (2013)
29. Alliance for Regenerative Medicine: Clinical Trials in Europe: Recent Trends in ATMP Development. Technical report ARM, October 2019
30. Sexauer, A., Sandlund, J.T., Marcus, K.J.: Paediatric Leukemia and Lymphoma. In: Gunder's & Tepper's Clinical Radiation Oncology, pp. 1468–1476, Elsevier (2020)
31. Sinclair, A., Monge, M.: Measuring Manufacturing Cost and Its Impact on Organizations. BioProcess International, p. 36–44 (2010)
32. Steliarova-Fourcher, E., Colombet, M., Ries, L., Moreno, F., Dolya, A., Bray, F., et. al.: International incidence of childhood cancer, 2001–2010: a population based registry study. Lancet Oncol. **18**(6), 719–731 (2017)
33. Sun, W., Malvar, J., Sposto, R., Verma, A., et al.: Outcome of children with multiply relapsed B-cell acute lymphoblastic leukemia: a therapeutic advances in childhood leukemia & lymphoma study. Leukemia **32**(11), 2316–2325 (2018)
34. Villegas, J.G., Palacios, F., Medaglia, A.L.: Solution methods for the bi-objective (cost-coverage) unconstrained facility location problem with an illustrative example. Ann. Oper. Res. **147**(1), 109–141 (2006)
35. Wang, B., Liang, Y., Zheng, T., Yuan, M., Zhang, H.: Multi-objective site selection optimization of the gas-gathering station using nsga-ii. Process Saf. Environ. Prot. **119**, 350–359 (2018)
36. Wang, X., Kong, Q., Papathanasiou, M.M., Shah, N.: Precision healthcare supply chain design through multi-objective stochastic programming. 13th International Symposium on Process Systems Engineering (PSE 2018) Computer Aided Chemical Engineering, p. 2137–2142 (2018)
37. Weiss, D., Rydland, H.T., Øversveen, E., Jensen, M.R., Solhaug, S., Krokstad, S.: Innovative technologies and social inequalities in health: A scoping review of the literature. PLoS One **13**(4), e0195447 (2018)
38. Wilson, B., Nicholls, S.G.: The Human Genome Project, and recent advances in personalized genomics. Risk Management and Healthcare Policy, p. 9–20 (2015)
39. Yang, L., Jones, B.F., Yang, S.H.: A fuzzy multi-objective programming for optimization of fire station locations through genetic algorithms. Eur. J. Oper. Res. **181**(2), 903–915 (2007)
40. Ebrahimi Zade, A., Sadegheih, A., Lotfi, M.M.: A modified NSGA-II solution for a new multi-objective hub maximal covering problem under uncertain shipments. J. Ind. Eng. Int. **10**(4), 185–197 (2014). https://doi.org/10.1007/s40092-014-0076-4

Evolutionary Computation in Image Analysis, Signal Processing and Pattern Recognition

RDE-OP: A Region-Based Differential Evolution Algorithm Incorporation Opposition-Based Learning for Optimising the Learning Process of Multi-layer Neural Networks

Seyed Jalaleddin Mousavirad[1]([✉]), Gerald Schaefer[2], Iakov Korovin[3],
and Diego Oliva[4,5]

[1] Department of Computer Engineering, Hakim Sabzevari University, Sabzevar, Iran
[2] Department of Computer Science, Loughborough University, Loughborough, UK
[3] Southern Federal University, Taganrog, Russia
[4] IN3 - Computer Science Dept., Universitat Oberta de Catalunya, Castelldefels, Spain
[5] Depto. de Ciencias Computacionales, Universidad de Guadalajara, Guadalajara, Mexico

Abstract. Learning in multi-layer neural networks (MLNNs) involves finding appropriate weights and biases and is a challenging and important task since the performance of MLNNs is directly dependent on the weights. Conventional algorithms such as back-propagation suffer from difficulties including a tendency to get stuck in local optima. Population-based metaheuristic algorithms can be used to address these issues. In this paper, we propose a novel learning approach, RDE-OP, based on differential evolution (DE) boosted by a region-based scheme and an opposition-based learning strategy. DE is a population-based metaheuristic algorithm which has shown good performance in solving optimisation problems. Our approach integrates two effective concepts with DE. First, we find, using a clustering algorithm, regions in search space and select the cluster centres to represent these. Then, an updating scheme is proposed to include the clusters in the current population. In the next step, our proposed algorithm employs a quasi-opposition-based learning strategy for improved exploration of the search space. Experimental results on different datasets and in comparison with both conventional and population-based approaches convincingly indicate excellent performance of RDE-OP.

Keywords: Neural networks · Differential evolution · Clustering · Opposition-based learning

1 Introduction

Artificial neural networks (ANNs) are popular pattern recognition techniques to tackle complex classification and regression problems in various domains such as

P. A. Castillo and J. L. Jiménez Laredo (Eds.): EvoApplications 2021, LNCS 12694, pp. 407–420, 2021.
https://doi.org/10.1007/978-3-030-72699-7_26

food quality [34] and medicine [17] due to their learning capability and generalisation ability [25,26]. In particular in recent years, ANNs have attracted a lot of attention in both academia and industry [32].

Multi-layer neural networks (MLNNs) are one of the most common ANN structures, where each connection has a weight, indicating its strength. Learning in MLNNs involves finding appropriate weights so as to minimise the error between the actual and predicted outputs. Conventional algorithms such as gradient-based approaches are conventionally employed for MLNN learning but suffer from drawbacks such a tendency to get stuck in local optima of the search space.

Population-based metaheuristic (PBMH) algorithms such as particle swarm optimisation (PSO) [37], differential evolution (DE) [39], and human mental search (HMS) [31], can overcome these limitations. Various PBMH algorithms have been used for MLNN learning including PSO [13,28,33], artificial bee colony [15], grey wolf optimiser [2,20], and dragonfly algorithm [18], among others.

Differential evolution [39] is an effective PBMH algorithm that has shown excellent performance in solving various optimisation problems [11,24,30]. It is based on three main operators: mutation for generating mutant vectors based on differences among individuals, crossover for combining the mutant vector with its parent, and selection for selecting a better individual. [14] proposes a DE algorithm for MLNN learning and compares it with gradient-based methods, showing DE to obtain better performance. In [38], an adaptive DE algorithm is proposed for MLNN learning with experiments on a parity problem, indicating good performance in finding the optimal weights. [7] combines adaptive Cauchy DE with self-adaptive DE, showing satisfactory performance on solving MLNN learning problems. In one of the most recent works, [29] employs a DE algorithm improved by opposition-based learning.

In this paper, we propose a novel DE algorithm, RDE-OP, for MLNN training based on differential evolution incorporating a clustering algorithm and opposition-based learning. The clustering algorithm selects a region and acts similar to a multi-parent crossover in the region, while RDE-OP employs a population updating scheme to include the cluster centres in the current population. In addition, opposition-based learning (OBL) [40] is incorporated in the algorithm to further improve its efficacy. For this, we use a variant of OBL called quasi-based OBL [36] which is more effective than standard OBL. The encoding strategy uses a one-dimensional array to store the weight and bias terms, while the objective function is based on the classification error. Experimental results on different datasets and in comparison with both conventional and population-based approaches convincingly indicate excellent performance of RDE-OP.

The remainder of this paper is organised as follows. Section 2 briefly explains some background on MLNNs and DE. Section 3 first introduces the main components of RDE-OP and then details its workings. Section 4 assesses RDE-OP on some benchmark classification problems and compares its performance to various other algorithms. Finally, Sect. 5 concludes the paper.

2   Background

2.1   Multi-layer Neural Networks

Multi-layer neural networks (MLNNs) are a type of ANN consisting of simple components called neurons. Each single neuron performs a minor task and they collaborate to perform complex tasks in machine learning. Generally, an MLNN has three types of layers, input, output, and hidden layers. While one hidden layer is sufficient to solve each problem, there is no specific rule to determine an optimal number of neurons in the hidden layer [14]. Figure 1 shows the general architecture of an MLNN. Here, w_{nh}^l is the weight between the n-th neuron of the $l - 1$-th layer and the h-th neuron of the l-th layer, and b_h^l is the bias for the l-th neuron of the l-th layer. Finding appropriate weights and bias terms is crucial since there is a high dependency between the weights and the efficacy of the network. It is however also a rather challenging task.

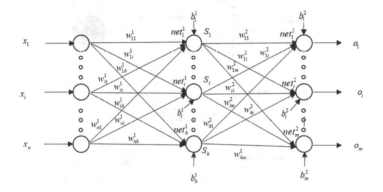

Fig. 1. General architecture of an MLNN.

2.2   Differential Evolution

Differential evolution (DE) [39] is a well-established and effective PBMH for complex optimisation problems [9,11,27]. It is based on three main operators, mutation, crossover, and selection.

The mutation operator creates a mutant vector $v_i = (v_{i,1}, v_{i,2}, ..., v_{i,D})$ $i = 1, ..., N_P, j = 1, ..., D)$ for each target vector as

$$v_i = x_{r1} + F(x_{r2} - x_{r3}), \tag{1}$$

where x_{r1}, x_{r2}, and x_{r3} are three distinct randomly selected individuals, and F is a scaling factor.

The crossover operator generates a trial vector $u_i = (u_{i,1}, u_{i,2}, ..., u_{i,D})$ based on the mutant vector v_i and the target vector x_i as

$$u_{i,j} = \begin{cases} v_{i,j} & \text{if } rand(0,1) \leq CR \text{ or } j == j_{rand} \\ x_{i,j} & \text{otherwise} \end{cases}, \tag{2}$$

where CR is the crossover rate, and j_{rand} is a random number between 1 and the population size N_p.

The selection operator is a greedy operator to carry the better individual of the trial and target individuals into the next iteration.

3 RDE-OP Algorithm

In this paper, we propose a novel algorithm, RDE-OP, for optimising the learning process of MLNNs based on an improved DE algorithm. The general framework of RDE-OP is shown in Fig. 2. In the following, we first describe the main components of RDE-OP and then explain the proposed algorithm.

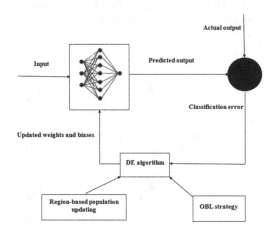

Fig. 2. General framework of RDE-OP approach.

3.1 Region Construction

After selection, RDE-OP constructs regions based on a clustering algorithm on the current population. For this, we use the well known k-means algorithm [19]. Each cluster corresponds to a region, and the number of clusters is set to a random number between 2 and $\sqrt{N_P}$. The cluster centres can be seen as representative of their clusters but also a type of multi-parent crossover because they are the means of all individuals located in a cluster.

3.2 Population Update

Inspired by [6] and a generic population-based algorithm (GPBA) proposed in [10], RDE-OP employs a population updating strategy to enhance the efficacy of the algorithm. GPBA has four general rules to solve optimisation problems. Population-updating in RDE-OP is based on a GPBA strategy governed by:

– **Selection:** randomly select some individuals from the current population. This corresponds to selecting initial seeds in the k-means algorithm.
– **Generation:** create m individuals (set A). RDE-OP generates the new individuals based on the k-means clustering algorithm so that each cluster centre is considered as a new individual.
– **Replacement:** choose m individuals (set B) from the population for replacement. RDE-OP selects m randomly selected individuals.
– **Update:** from the combination set $A \cup B$, select the m best individuals as $\bar{B}$. The new population is then obtained as $(P - B) \cup \bar{B}$.

3.3   Clustering Period

RDE-OP periodically performs clustering to exploit the search space more effectively similar to the mechanism proposed in [6,8]. It is crucial to select a clustering period so that DE has time to form stable clusters. Consequently, we employ a parameter C_P that determines the clustering period.

3.4   Quasi Opposition-Based Learning

RDE-OP employs a quasi opposition-based learning strategy for further improvement. The opposite number of x is formulated as

$$\bar{x}_i = a_i + b_i - x_i, \tag{3}$$

where a and b are the lower and upper bounds of the search space, and i is the i-th dimension of x. We use quasi-opposition numbers [36] as an efficient scheme defined as

$$\check{x}_i = rand \left[\frac{a_i + b_i}{2}, a_i + b_i - x_i \right], \tag{4}$$

where $rand[m, n]$ generates a uniform random number between m and n. Quasi-opposition numbers have a higher chance to converge to the solution compared to standard opposite number [36].

In order to enable higher exploration, RDE-OP employs the quasi-opposition learning strategy both for the initialisation step and after region construction and update. In the initialisation step, RDE-OP first generates a population Pop uniform randomly. Then, a new population $OPop$ based on quasi-opposition learning is created using Eq. (4). Eventually, RDE-OP selects the N_P best individuals from the combination of Pop and $OPop$ as the initial population.

After region-based population update, RDE-OP generates a new population based on quasi-opposition learning with a probability (jumping rate) J_r between 0 and 0.4 [36]. Then, the N_P best individuals among the union of the current population and the quasi-opposition-based population determines the new population.

It is worth noting that the opposition of each individual is computed dynamically. In other words, the maximum and minimum values of the individuals are employed to generate the opposite individual as

$$\check{x}_{i,j} = min_j^p + max_j^p - x_{i,j} \quad i = 1, 2, ..., N_p \quad j = 1, 2, ..., D, \tag{5}$$

where D is the dimensionality, N_p is the population size, and min_j^p and max_j^p are the minimum and maximum of the population in the j-th dimension.

3.5   Encoding Strategy

We employ a real-valued encoding strategy with a vector representing the weights and biases. Each individual includes two main parts, the connection weights between neurons, and the bias for each neuron. Figure 3 illustrates a typical MLNN with one hidden layer and the corresponding individual.

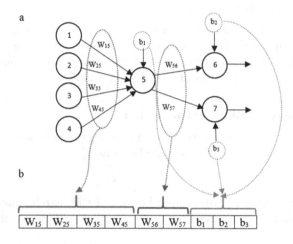

Fig. 3. (a) an MLNN with 4-1-2 structure (b) the corresponding individual.

3.6   Objective Function

We use an objective function based on classification error defined as

$$E = \frac{100}{P} \sum_{p=1}^{P} \xi(x_p), \tag{6}$$

with

$$\xi(x_p) = \begin{cases} 1 & \text{if } o_p \neq d_p \\ 0 & \text{otherwise} \end{cases}, \tag{7}$$

where d_p and o_p are the desired and predicted output, respectively, of input x_p, the p-th of P test samples.

3.7 Algorithm

Our proposed RDE-OP algorithm, which combines DE with a region-based strategy and a quasi opposition-based learning strategy, is presented, in the form of pseudo-code, in Algorithm 1.

Input : D: dimensionality, L_i/U_i: lower/upper bound, Max_{NFC}: max. no. of function evaluations, N_P: population size, J_r: jumping rate, C_P: clustering period.

Output: x^*: the best individual

// quasi opposition-based initialisation

Generate initial population Pop randomly based on representation in Section 3.5

for $i \leftarrow 0$ to N_P do

    for $j \leftarrow 0$ to D do

        $OPo\breve{p}(i,j) = rand\left[\frac{L(i,j)+U(i,j)}{2}, L_{i,j} + U_{i,j} - Pop(i,j)\right]$

    end

end

Evaluate the objective function for each population based on Eq. (6)

Select the N_P best individuals from the union of Pop and $OPop$ as the initial population.

$iter \leftarrow 1$

while $NFC < MAX_{NFC}$ do

    for $i \leftarrow 1$ to N_P do

        Select x_{i1}, x_{i2}, and x_{i3} randomly from current population with $x_{i1} \neq x_{i2} \neq x_{i3}$

        $v_i = x_{i1} + F(x_{i2} - x_{i3})$

        for $j \leftarrow 0$ to D do

            if $rand_j[0,1] < C_R$ or $j == j_{rand}$ then

                $u_{i,j} = v_{i,j}$

            else

                $u_{i,j} = x_{i,j}$

            end

        end

        Calculate objective function value of u_i based on Eq. (6)

        if $f(u_i) < f(x_i)$ then

            $x_i \leftarrow u_i$

        end

    end

    // region construction and update

    if $iter$ modulo $C_P == 0$ then

        Randomly generate k as a random number between 2 and $\sqrt{N_P}$

        Perform k-means clustering and select the cluster centres as individuals of set A

        Select k individuals randomly from the current population as set B

        From the combination of $A \cup B$, select the best k individuals as $\bar{B}$

        Select the new population as $(P - B) \cup \bar{B}$.

    end

    // opposition-based generation jumping

    if $rand(0,1) < J_r$ then

        for $i \leftarrow 1$ to N_p do

            for $j \leftarrow 0$ to D do

                $Opop(i,j) = rand\left[\frac{min_j^p + max_j^p}{2}, min_j^p + max_j^p - Pop(i,j)\right]$

           end

           Calculate objective function value of $Opop_i$ based on Eq. (6)

        end

    end

    Select the N_p best individuals from $\{Pop, Opop\}$ as the current population

    $iter = iter + 1$

end

$x^* \leftarrow$ the best individual in the population

Algorithm 1: RDE-OP algorithm in the form of pseudo code.

4   Experimental Results

To assess our proposed RDE-OP algorithm, we perform a set of experiments on some well-known clinical classification benchmark datasets with diverse characteristics from the UCI repository[1].

Since in this paper we do not focus on the optimal network structure, we follow the approach from [25,32] to set the number of neurons in the hidden layer as $2N + 1$, where N is the number of inputs. The lower and upper bounds for all algorithms are set to –10 and +10, respectively. We use 10-fold cross-validation, where the dataset is divided into 10 partitions, one partition for testing and 9 as training data, and the process repeated 10 times so that each fold is used for testing once. We report statistical results (over the folds) of obtained classification accuracy, including mean, standard deviation, median, minimum, and maximum as well as rankings (based on the mean).

We compare our algorithm with five conventional algorithms, including gradient descent with momentum backpropagation(GDM) [35], gradient descent with adaptive learning rate backpropagation (GDA) [5], gradient descent with momentum and adaptive learning rate backpropagation (GDMA) [41], one-step secant backpropagation (OSS) [4], and Bayesian regularisation backpropagation(BR) [12], and five, mostly recent, PBMH-based learning algorithms, namely ABC [15], GWO [20], DA [18], WOA [1], and SSA [3]. Since our algorithm is based on DE, we also compare RDE-OP with two DE-based learning algorithms, standard DE and QODE [29].

For all PBMHs, the number of function evaluations and population size are set to 25,000 and 50, respectively, while other parameter settings are given in Table 1.

The Wisconsin Breast Cancer (WBC) dataset is a binary classification problem with 699 samples and 9 features. MLNNs of structure 9–19-1 are trained and consequently the number of decision variables is 210. Table 2 gives the results on the dataset for all algorithms. As we can see from there, RDE-OP is top ranked, followed by GWO and QODE. In comparison to DE and QODE, RDE-OP decreases the classification error by more than 54% and 24%, respectively, confirming the effectiveness of RDE-OP. Also, and as expected, the conventional algorithms perform the worst.

The Pima Indian Diabetes (PID) dataset is a challenging dataset with 768 samples, 2 classes, and 8 features. MLNNs of structure 8–17-1 are trained and consequently the number of decision variables is 210. From Table 3, RDE-OP is again placed in first rank, followed by QODE. RDE-OP improves the mean error rate by more than 14%/3% compared to DE/QODE.

The Liver Disorder (LD) dataset is a clinical dataset comprising 7 features, 345 samples, and 2 classes. MLNNs of structure 6–13-1 are trained and thus, the number of weights and biases for optimisation is 105. From Table 4, we can observe that RDE-OP is ranked second behind QODE. While QODE thus yields

---

[1] https://archive.ics.uci.edu/ml/index.php.

Table 1. Parameter settings for the experiments

Algorithm	Parameter	Value
ABC [16]	Limit	$n_e \times$- dimensionality of problem
	n_o	50% of the colony
	n_e	50% of the colony
	n_s	1
GWO [23]	No parameters	
DA [21]	No parameters	
WOA [22]	b	1
SSA [3]	No parameters	
DE [39]	Scaling factor	0.5
	Crossover probability	0.9
QODE [29]	Scaling factor	0.5
	Crossover probability	0.9
	Jumping rate	0.3
RDE-OP	Scaling factor	0.5
	Crossover probability	0.9
	Jumping rate	0.3
	Clustering period	10

Table 2. 10CV classification results on WBC dataset.

Algorithm	Mean	Std.dev.	Median	Min.	Max.	Rank
GDM	92.99	7.60	97.06	77.94	98.53	11
GDA	95.90	2.04	95.62	92.65	98.55	10
GDMA	90.47	5.94	91.30	80.88	97.06	13
OSS	96.34	2.21	97.06	92.65	100.00	9
BR	91.81	3.82	92.71	84.06	95.65	12
ABC	97.95	1.03	98.53	95.59	98.55	4
GWO	98.10	1.39	98.53	95.59	100.00	2
DA	97.51	1.83	97.79	95.59	100.00	6
WOA	97.07	1.96	97.08	94.12	100.00	8
SSA	97.80	2.42	98.53	92.65	100.00	5
DE	97.36	2.06	97.10	94.12	100.00	7
QODE	98.10	0.99	98.53	97.06	100.00	3
RDE-OP	98.82	1.67	100.00	95.59	100.00	1

Table 3. 10CV classification results on PID dataset.

Algorithm	Mean	Std.dev.	Median	Min.	Max.	Rank
GDM	67.98	13.03	71.43	37.66	77.92	12
GDA	75.91	4.52	77.92	68.83	80.52	9
GDMA	73.20	6.74	74.68	59.74	81.58	11
OSS	76.58	4.30	75.97	71.43	85.53	8
BR	75.89	5.37	76.62	67.11	85.71	10
ABC	78.26	4.45	78.95	71.43	84.42	3
GWO	67.45	2.79	67.98	62.34	71.43	13
DA	77.85	5.40	77.92	65.79	85.71	4
WOA	76.95	3.65	77.27	72.37	83.12	6
SSA	77.34	6.50	75.32	70.13	93.51	5
DE	76.94	4.97	77.12	69.74	84.42	7
QODE	79.55	4.95	81.17	71.05	88.31	2
RDE-OP	80.21	5.73	81.17	67.53	88.31	1

Table 4. 10CV classification results on LD dataset.

Algorithm	Mean	Std.dev.	Median	Min.	Max.	Rank
GDM	59.47	15.05	62.31	29.41	76.47	12
GDA	58.24	6.53	57.35	50.00	68.57	13
GDMA	60.66	13.99	61.76	40.00	85.29	11
OSS	64.89	8.01	66.68	52.94	76.47	9
BR	70.71	6.93	67.65	64.71	85.71	5
ABC	70.75	6.47	70.00	62.86	80.00	4
GWO	73.01	9.74	72.48	52.94	85.29	3
DA	70.42	7.01	69.58	58.82	82.86	6
WOA	62.87	6.40	62.31	50.00	71.43	10
SSA	69.85	7.78	68.11	61.76	82.86	7
DE	67.81	8.21	67.14	58.82	82.86	8
QODE	76.82	9.46	73.95	64.71	91.18	1
RDE-OP	75.63	6.45	77.14	58.82	82.35	2

slightly better mean accuracy, the standard deviation of RDE-OP is much lower, indicating superior robustness.

The Blood Transfusion Service Center (BTSC) dataset is a binary clinical dataset with 748 samples and 4 features. Here, as is evident from Table 5, RDE-OP obtains the highest mean classification accuracy followed by ABC and SSA. RDE-OP decreases the classification error by more than 6% and 5% compared

Table 5. 10 CV classification results on BTSC dataset.

Algorithm	Mean	Std.dev.	Median	Min.	Max.	Rank
GDM	77.27	3.08	77.33	72.00	82.67	11
GDA	77.40	2.06	77.18	74.67	81.33	10
GDMA	74.07	4.33	75.17	66.67	81.33	13
OSS	76.87	1.63	77.33	72.97	78.67	12
BR	79.55	3.08	79.86	74.67	85.33	9
ABC	80.62	4.06	80.54	73.33	88.00	2
GWO	80.08	3.14	80.54	74.67	84.00	6
DA	79.94	4.52	79.19	74.67	89.33	7
WOA	80.48	3.07	81.22	75.68	84.00	4
SSA	80.61	2.65	80.54	77.03	84.00	3
DE	79.81	4.48	80.00	72.00	89.33	8
QODE	80.09	2.24	80.00	77.33	83.78	5
RDE-OP	81.14	3.30	80.67	77.03	86.67	1

to DE and QODE, respectively. As for all other datasets, the conventional algorithms perform worst.

The Vertebral Column (VC) dataset has 310 samples and 6 biomedical features located in the 2 classes. From Table 6, we can see that RDE-OP yields the second rank here. QODE is ranked first with a higher mean accuracy compared to RDE-OP, the latter however has a much lower standard deviation, indicating better robustness.

Table 6. 10 CV classification results on VC dataset.

Algorithm	Mean	Std.dev.	Median	Min.	Max.	Rank
GDM	76.13	9.15	74.19	64.52	90.32	12
GDA	80.65	5.27	80.65	67.74	87.10	10
GDMA	72.90	17.62	80.65	41.94	93.55	13
OSS	80.97	8.93	83.87	67.74	93.55	9
BR	84.52	6.94	87.10	74.19	96.77	5
ABC	82.90	5.70	82.26	74.19	93.55	6
GWO	81.94	7.93	82.26	67.74	93.55	7.5
DA	81.94	5.31	79.03	77.42	90.32	7.5
WOA	79.03	10.99	80.65	61.29	93.55	11
SSA	85.81	7.16	87.10	70.97	93.55	3
DE	85.16	5.31	85.48	77.42	93.55	4
QODE	88.39	8.76	90.32	70.97	100.00	1
RDE-OP	86.77	4.42	87.10	77.42	93.55	2

Table 7 aggregates the results on the various datasets in terms of average and overall ranks. As can be seen from there, RDE-OP is overall top ranked and by a wide margin. The average/overall rank of DE is 6.8 indicating that our proposed algorithm provides a significant improvement with average rank of 1.4. It also clearly outperforms QODE, the second-best algorithm, for which an average rank of 2.4 is obtained.

Table 7. Overall and average ranks.

	GDM	GDA	GDMA	OSS	BR	ABC	GWO	DA	WOA	SSA	DE	QODE	RDE-OP
Average rank	11.6	10.4	12.2	9.4	8.2	7.6	6.3	6.1	7.8	4.6	6.8	2.4	1.4
Overall rank	12	11	13	10	9	7	5	4	8	3	6	2	1

5   Conclusions

Learning is one of the most challenging aspects of multi-layer neural networks (MLNNs). Most MLNN learning algorithms adjust the weights based on gradient descent, and thus suffer from some difficulties such as getting trapped in local optima.

In this paper, we have proposed a novel learning algorithm, RDE-OP, for finding optimal weights in MLNNs based on a differential evolution algorithm which is boosted by a region-based strategy and a quasi opposition-based learning scheme. In an extensive set of experiments on clinical classification datasets, we have convincingly demonstrated that RDE-OP outperforms other algorithms including both conventional methods and PBMHs.

In future work, we intend to extend our approach to find other parameters in MLNNs including activation functions and architectures. Also, our algorithm can be employed for deep learning networks, with some modifications so that to be able to handle the very large number of parameters without much increase in computational complexity.

Acknowledgements. This paper is published due to the financial support of the RFBR under research project 18-29-03225.

References

1. Aljarah, I., Faris, H., Mirjalili, S.: Optimizing connection weights in neural networks using the whale optimization algorithm. Soft Comput. **22**(1), 1–15 (2018)
2. Amirsadri, S., Mousavirad, S.J., Ebrahimpour-Komleh, H.: A Levy flight-based grey wolf optimizer combined with back-propagation algorithm for neural network training. Neural Comput. Appl. **30**(12), 3707–3720 (2018)
3. Bairathi, D., Gopalani, D.: Salp swarm algorithm (SSA) for training feed-forward neural networks. In: Bansal, J.C., Das, K.N., Nagar, A., Deep, K., Ojha, A.K. (eds.) Soft Computing for Problem Solving. AISC, vol. 816, pp. 521–534. Springer, Singapore (2019). https://doi.org/10.1007/978-981-13-1592-3_41

4. Battiti, R.: First-and second-order methods for learning: between steepest descent and newton's method. Neural Comput. **4**(2), 141–166 (1992)
5. Beale, H.D., Demuth, H.B., Hagan, M.: Neural network design. Pws, Boston (1996)
6. Cai, Z., Gong, W., Ling, C.X., Zhang, H.: A clustering-based differential evolution for global optimization. Appl. Soft Comput. **11**(1), 1363–1379 (2011)
7. Choi, T.J., Ahn, C.W.: Adaptive Cauchy differential evolution with strategy adaptation and its application to training large-scale artificial neural networks. In: International Conference on Bio-Inspired Computing: Theories and Applications, pp. 502–510 (2017)
8. Damavandi, N., Safavi-Naeini, S.: A hybrid evolutionary programming method for circuit optimization. IEEE Trans. Circ. Syst. I Regul. Pap. **52**(5), 902–910 (2005)
9. Das, S., Konar, A.: Automatic image pixel clustering with an improved differential evolution. Appl. Soft Comput. **9**(1), 226–236 (2009)
10. Deb, K.: A population-based algorithm-generator for real-parameter optimization. Soft Comput. **9**(4), 236–253 (2005)
11. Fister, I., Fister, D., Deb, S., Mlakar, U., Brest, J.: Post hoc analysis of sport performance with differential evolution. Neural Comput. Appl. **32**, 1–10 (2018)
12. Foresee, F.D., Hagan, M.T.: Gauss-newton approximation to bayesian learning. Int. Conf. Neural Networks **3**, 1930–1935 (1997)
13. Gudise, V.G., Venayagamoorthy, G.K.: Comparison of particle swarm optimization and backpropagation as training algorithms for neural networks. In: IEEE Swarm Intelligence Symposium, pp. 110–117 (2003)
14. Ilonen, J., Kamarainen, J.K., Lampinen, J.: Differential evolution training algorithm for feed-forward neural networks. Neural Process. Lett. **17**(1), 93–105 (2003)
15. Karaboga, D., Akay, B., Ozturk, C.: Artificial bee colony (ABC) optimization algorithm for training feed-forward neural networks. In: International Conference on Modeling Decisions for Artificial Intelligence, pp. 318–329 (2007)
16. Karaboga, D., Basturk, B.: A powerful and efficient algorithm for numerical function optimization: artificial bee colony (ABC) algorithm. J. Global Optim. **39**(3), 459–471 (2007)
17. Khastavaneh, H., Ebrahimpour-Komleh, H.: Neural network-based learning kernel for automatic segmentation of multiple sclerosis lesions on magnetic resonance images. J. Biomed. Phys. Eng. **7**(2), 155 (2017)
18. Khishe, M., Safari, A.: Classification of sonar targets using an MLP neural network trained by dragonfly algorithm. Wireless Pers. Commun. **108**(4), 2241–2260 (2019)
19. MacQueen, J.: Some methods for classification and analysis of multivariate observations. In: 5th Berkeley Symposium on Mathematical Statistics and Probability, pp. 281–297 (1967)
20. Mirjalili, S.: How effective is the grey wolf optimizer in training multi-layer perceptrons. Appl. Intell. **43**(1), 150–161 (2015)
21. Mirjalili, S.: Dragonfly algorithm: a new meta-heuristic optimization technique for solving single-objective, discrete, and multi-objective problems. Neural Comput. Appl. **27**(4), 1053–1073 (2016)
22. Mirjalili, S., Lewis, A.: The whale optimization algorithm. Adv. Eng. Softw. **95**, 51–67 (2016)
23. Mirjalili, S., Mirjalili, S.M., Lewis, A.: Grey wolf optimizer. Adv. Eng. Softw. **69**, 46–61 (2014)
24. Mousavirad, S.J., Asilian Bidgoli, A., Rahnamayan, S.: Tackling deceptive optimization problems using opposition-based DE with center-based Latin hypercube initialization. In: 14th International Conference on Computer Science and Education (2019)

25. Mousavirad, S.J., Bidgoli, A.A., Ebrahimpour-Komleh, H., Schaefer, G.: A memetic imperialist competitive algorithm with chaotic maps for multi-layer neural network training. Int. J. Bio-Inspired Comput. **14**(4), 227–236 (2019)
26. Mousavirad, S.J., Bidgoli, A.A., Ebrahimpour-Komleh, H., Schaefer, G., Korovin, I.: An effective hybrid approach for optimising the learning process of multi-layer neural networks. In: International Symposium on Neural Networks, pp. 309–317 (2019)
27. Mousavirad, S.J., Ebrahimpour-Komleh, H.: Multilevel image thresholding using entropy of histogram and recently developed population-based metaheuristic algorithms. Evol. Intell. **10**(1–2), 45–75 (2017)
28. Mousavirad, S.J., Jalali, S.M.J., Sajad, A., Abbas, K., Schaefer, G., Nahavandi, S.: Neural network training using a biogeography-based learning strategy. In: International Conference on Neural Information Processing (2020)
29. Mousavirad, S.J., Rahnamayan, S.: Evolving feedforward neural networks using a quasi-opposition-based differential evolution for data classification. In: IEEE Symposium Series on Computational Intelligence (2020)
30. Mousavirad, S.J., Rahnamayan, S., Schaefer, G.: Many-level image thresholding using a center-based differential evolution algorithm. In: Congress on Evolutionary Computation (2020)
31. Mousavirad, S.J., Schaefer, G., Ebrahimpour-Komleh, H.: The human mental search algorithm for solving optimisation problems. In: Hassanien, A.-E., Taha, M.H.N., Khalifa, N.E.M. (eds.) Enabling AI Applications in Data Science. SCI, vol. 911, pp. 27–47. Springer, Cham (2021). https://doi.org/10.1007/978-3-030-52067-0_2
32. Mousavirad, S.J., Schaefer, G., Jalali, S.M.J., Korovin, I.: A benchmark of recent population-based metaheuristic algorithms for multi-layer neural network training. In: Genetic and Evolutionary Computation Conference Companion, pp. 1402–1408 (2020)
33. Mousavirad, S.J., Schaefer, G., Korovin, I.: An effective approach for neural network training based on comprehensive learning. In: International Conference on Pattern Recognition (2020)
34. Mousavirad, S., Akhlaghian, F., Mollazade, K.: Classification of rice varieties using optimal color and texture features and BP neural networks. In: 7th Iranian Conference on Machine Vision and Image Processing, pp. 1–5 (2011)
35. Phansalkar, V., Sastry, P.: Analysis of the back-propagation algorithm with momentum. IEEE Trans. Neural Netw. **5**(3), 505–506 (1994)
36. Rahnamayan, S., Tizhoosh, H.R., Salama, M.M.: Quasi-oppositional differential evolution. In: IEEE Congress on Evolutionary Computation, pp. 2229–2236 (2007)
37. Shi, Y., Eberhart, R.: A modified particle swarm optimizer. In: IEEE International Conference on Evolutionary Computation, pp. 69–73 (1998)
38. Slowik, A.: Application of an adaptive differential evolution algorithm with multiple trial vectors to artificial neural network training. IEEE Trans. Ind. Electron. **58**(8), 3160–3167 (2010)
39. Storn, R., Price, K.: Differential evolution-a simple and efficient heuristic for global optimization over continuous spaces. J. Global Optim. **11**(4), 341–359 (1997)
40. Tizhoosh, H.R.: Opposition-based learning: a new scheme for machine intelligence. In: International Conference on Computational Intelligence for Modelling, Control and Automation and International Conference on Intelligent Agents, Web Technologies and Internet Commerce, vol. 1, pp. 695–701 (2005)
41. Yu, C.C., Liu, B.D.: A backpropagation algorithm with adaptive learning rate and momentum coefficient. Int. Joint Conf. Neural Netw. **2**, 1218–1223 (2002)

Estimation of Grain-Level Residual Stresses in a Quenched Cylindrical Sample of Aluminum Alloy AA5083 Using Genetic Programming

Laura Millán[1] , Gabriel Kronberger[2]([⊠]) , J. Ignacio Hidalgo[3] ,
Ricardo Fernández[1] , Oscar Garnica[3] , and Gaspar González-Doncel[1]

[1] Department of Physical Metallurgy, Centro Nacional de Investigaciones Metalúrgicas (CENIM) C.S.I.C., Av. de Gregorio Del Amo, 8, 28040 Madrid, Spain
{mglauri,ric,ggd}@cenim.csic.es
[2] Josef Ressel Center for Symbolic Regression, University of Applied Sciences Upper Austria, Softwarepark 11, 4232 Hagenberg, Austria
gabriel.kronberger@fh-hagenberg.at
[3] Adaptative and Bioinspired System Group, Universidad Complutense de Madrid, Profesor José García Santesmases, 9, 28040 Madrid, Spain
{hidalgo,ogarnica}@ucm.es

Abstract. Residual stresses are originated during manufacturing processes of metallic materials, so its study is important to avoid catastrophic accidents during component service. There are two main types of residual stresses, according to the length scale; macroscopic and microscopic. While the determination of tmacroscopic ones is almost a routine analysis, determining the microscopic stress of individual grains remains a pending task. In this paper, we present an approach using genetic programming to obtain the micro residual stresses in grains of a quenched cylindrical sample of aluminium alloy AA5083. The microstructure of this alloy is formed by grains with different orientation and stress. To obtain the stress of each grain we estimate the values of the micro residual stresses for each crystallographic orientation using information from neutron and electron back-scattered diffraction experiments. This information includes orientation maps of a normal section to the cylinder axes (individual orientations) and the dimensions of each grain. We assume that the micro residual stresses of each grain can be expressed as a function based on these variables and use genetic programming to find this expression.

Keywords: Microscopic residual stress · Microstructure · Diffraction · Symbolic regression · Genetic programming

Supported by FEDER.

P. A. Castillo and J. L. Jiménez Laredo (Eds.): EvoApplications 2021, LNCS 12694, pp. 421–436, 2021.
https://doi.org/10.1007/978-3-030-72699-7_27

1 Introduction

It is not surprising that, from time to time, the media report accidents occurring in industrial facilities or factories of different kinds, and even in homes and places of residence. They are accidents of a very different nature, such as the rupture of pipes or tanks that collapse due to corrosion and/or fatigue problems, and the breakage of components before the end of their life cycle due to the generation of cracks that propagate in an uncontrolled and sudden way. Attention in these accidents is generally focused on the economic cost they entail and, above all, on the human factor when, as in many cases, they are accidents with tragic consequences. Usually there is a technical problem behind the accident, such as a poor design, an inappropriate manufacturing procedure or material selection. Undoubtedly, the detailed analysis of these failures and the knowledge of their cause have served, and still serve, to advance in new designs and improve the performance of new components. A reliable diagnosis requires a complete data history of the materials, their use conditions, their microstructural characteristics, etc. Unfortunately, this information is not always available.

Therefore, it is still common to resort to tolerance margins that alleviate the ignorance of these factors in anticipation of their possible relevance during the component's service life. This is the area where the residual stresses can play a crucial role. These stresses are generally present in materials and components. They are originated in the different stages of their manufacturing process. Residual stresses are generated whenever there is a non-homogeneous dimensional change (deformations and/or expansions). The different residual stresses in materials are distinguished in the dimensional scale at which they are manifested. In the case of macroscopic stresses (M-RS), they can be determined without great complexity. However, there are other stresses, the microscopic ones, which magnitude is still unknown, but their influence on the problems described above may also be relevant. To understand the origin of microscopic stresses, it is necessary to delve deeper into the materials' microstructure. These microscopic stresses are classified into intergranular (type II) and intragranular (type III). The microscopic stresses of type II (or m-RS), which are of interest in this research, vary between neighbouring grains as a consequence of the different degree of plastic (and elastic) deformation that a grain has suffered with respect to its neighbours during a given metallurgical process (e.g., rolling). This study is focused on determining these m-RSs.

This aim of this work is to develop a methodology for mapping m-RS, particularly in aluminium alloys components. The procedure applies a genetic programming (GP) approach to neutron diffraction data acquired from large European facilities. Our proposal is based on analyzing the peak displacements and broadening and the corresponding material microstructure, determined by EBSD (Electron Back-Scatter Diffraction). GP is applied for searching an expression which relates the diffraction pattern with the micro-structural parameters of the grains by predicting the peak displacement as a function of the micro-structural parameters. We use GP to produce a mathematical formula to establish this unknown link. Parameter optimization methods such as simulated annealing [9] or evolution strategies [2] cannot be used to solve this problem as we do not have a parametric model. Instead we aim to identify this model using GP.

The rest of the paper is organized as follows. Section 2 discusses previous related work. Section 3 explains the methods used to collect the data and the description of the GP implementation details. Section 4 contains the results. Finally, Sect. 5 summarizes the main result and describes the work in progress.

2   Related Work

Regarding the use of evolutionary computation for solving materials problems, genetic algorithms have been employed for optimizing other thermo-mechanical processes such as friction stir welding (FSW) in AA2014 and AA6061 samples [13]. Furthermore, neural networks trained using evolutionary algorithms can model the mechanical properties of the materials [8].

Our group has shown the presence of m-RS in welded samples [4]. In particular, we analyzed the unstressed lattice spacing to determine the residual stresses in a FSW plate of an age-hardenable aluminum alloy. We have shown that m-RS can be estimated from the total stress by subtracting the M-RS contribution. The first step is to know the lattice parameter value in the free stress state (denoted as d_0^{hkl}). This parameter is necessary to determine the strain as the differences between the relaxed and the strained grains. Diffraction methods and the application of evolutionary algorithms allowed us to estimate this d_0^{hkl} value. In particular, we could reproduce the M-RS profile across welds using evolutionary algorithms [7]. However, there is still a long way to develop a whole methodology to calculate them.

The average m-RS of AA2014 aluminum alloy was estimated in a more recent work [5] where age hardenable alloy was used. However, a methodology for mapping the m-RS of all grains that form the poly-crystal has not been developed yet. In other hand, the thermo-mechanical treatments can generate precipitates of different nature depending on the alloying elements. These precipitates are aggregates that appear in the microstructure and a have different composition from the initial aluminum grains. Its presence modifies the microstructure, distorts the crystalline lattice, and can alter the material's properties. So the m-RS of the original aluminum grains can be altered by the presence of these precipitates. However, a thorough study of the microstructure generated with the thermo-mechanical treatment was not carried out. Nonetheless, estimating an average value of the m-RS was an important contribution of [5].

Recently, our group improved the stress equilibrium method for determining the M-RS [11] considering the differences in the inner and outer microstructures, and the tri-axial stress state. In addition, we solved the problem of the precipitates using a non-hardenable alloy. In this work, we propose to continue this way and combine all the methods mentioned above using GP for obtaining a value of m-RS of each ones of these grains. Besides, more robust m-RS values are expected with this alloy. To the best of our knowledge, this is the first approximation to identify m-RS at the grain level.

3 Methodology

A sample of AA5083 aluminium alloy, which composition appears in Table 1, was chosen for this study. It is a commercial single phase alloy, *i.e.*, it has a microstructure formed by a large number of grains with similar composition. Each one is characterized by its size and orientation. Each grain is surrounded by a group of neighbor grains that can have the same or different orientation. There are four principal crystallographic orientations of Miller Index (*hkl*): 111, 200, 220, and 311. These Indexes, indicate the crystal direction of the corresponding group of grains which is parallel to the cylinder axes direction. It is important to emphasize that grains with different orientation present different mechanical behaviour under the action of an external uniaxial force (crystal anisotropy). This causes the generation of m-RS when the material undergoes a thermo-mechanical process that generates (non-homogeneous) plastic deformation. The radial and hoop directions present a different grain orientation with respect to the axial, i.e., the extrusion direction. Therefore, the elastic deformation among neighbors is not homogeneous. Besides, the grains are deformed according to their crystallographic orientation during the extrusion process resulting in a fiber texture. In extrusion, the most populated orientations are for 111 and 200 directions, while the 220 and 311 are the least favoured. Moreover, it is important to note that the material also undergoes frictional stresses with the extrusion die, so the outer microstructure must be different from the inner one. Consequently, this treatment induces a certain microstructural gradient in the material. Additionally, the quenching step generates m-RS in the individual grains. Therefore, the orientation, size, and distribution of these grains are factors that influence the m-RS to which they develop.

Table 1. Chemical composition of aluminium samples

Element	Weight (%)
Si	0.20
Fe	0.30
Cu	0.04
Mn	0.70
Mg	4.70
Cr	0.09
Zn	0.03
Ti	0.01
Al	Matrix

The electron back-scattered diffraction (EBSD) method allows measuring different micro-structural variables, principally individual grain orientations. Additionally, neutron diffraction (diffraction peaks) provides information on the overall residual stress of materials; In particular of the m-RS state of a large collective of grains with common crystallographic orientation through the peak position and width. There are four high-intensity peaks: 111, 200, 220, and 311, which correspond to the preferred orientations (texture) the material. The lattice spacing, $d_{x_i}^{hkl}$, is used to calculate the stress. The lattice spacing is the distance between two parallel crystalline planes of atoms that have the same orientation. It is assumed here that if the m-RS of the individual grains depends on the microstructure, there should be a mathematical function that relates these stresses with the microstructural parameters. Taking into account the mechanical behavior of the grains, this function should be the same for grains with the same orientation.

We formulate the goal of finding this mathematical expression for this mapping function as a symbolic regression problem and use GP to solve it. The independent variables for the model are the microstructural parameters provided by the EBSD. The dependent variable is the lattice spacing value, $d_{x_i}^{hkl}$, for each grain as a surrogate for the m-RS (see Sect. 3.2). However, it is impossible to measure m-RS for the individual grains but only the (measured) diffraction peak provided by a large number of grains. Thus, we cannot use the usual supervised learning approach. Instead, we calculate a predicted diffraction distribution from the individual predicted $d_{x_i}^{hkl}$ values and try to minimize the difference between the measured and the predicted distribution. Thus the symbolic regression model obtained through GP allows us to estimate the m-RS state for each grain from the microstructural parameters.

3.1   EBSD Technique

This technique, Electron Back-Scattered Diffraction (EBSD), allows determining the orientation of individual grains, as well as their size/shape. The incident beam collides with the ordered atoms of the polycrystalline sample. The interation causes the beam to diffract and reach a detector that picks up two bands. These bands correspond to a crystallographic orientation of the material. The separation between them is related to the lattice spacing between the atoms' planes. The detector records all the bands and it compares them with theoretical patterns of crystalline systems. Finally, it transforms the experimental pattern into a representation of points that offer information about the microstructure of the material [6].

We used an extruded AA5083 sample. The cylindrical sample (40 mm in diameter and 16.6 mm high) was extracted from the original bar. This sample was heated at 530 °C for 3 h to allow the ordering of the grains after the machining. Subsequently, it was cooled in the air for 24 h. Then three cubes with 4 mm^3 were removed from the center, to 6 mm, and from the outside to 12 mm along the radial direction. The process is shown in Fig. 1.

The EBSD measurements were made on the axial face of the cubes. This requires a previous preparation of the surface to be observed. Therefore, an initial roughing was then done to eliminate the roughness coming from the cuts

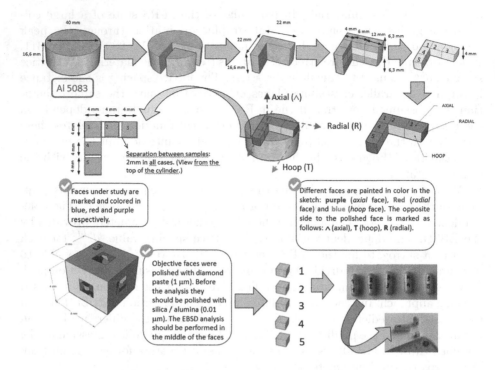

Fig. 1. Simplified description of cubes processing.

Fig. 2. Map of individual the grains orientations obtained by EBSD for the center position of the sample. The normal to the observed surface is parallel to the cylinder axes

[12]. For this, a sequential sanding of each of the faces was done with silicon carbide sieves. Subsequently, the faces of each sample were polished with diamond paste in suspension to eliminate the remaining imperfections. Finally, the EBSD measurements were conducted at the Centrum výzkumu Řež (Czech Republic) Previous to the measurements, a final polishing with colloidal silica suspension was conducted. [15].

The EBSD provides a map of grains represented by the Fig. 2. It shows the microstructure on the axial face in the center of the sample resulting from the above thermo-mechanical treatment. Each colour corresponds to a different orientation of the grains. The presence of components 111 and 200 (blue and red colours) is more frequent, if is compared to the 220 grains (green colour). In addition, the 220 grain are isolated, while 111 and 200 grains appear forming groups. A similar pattern is observed for the 311 grains in pink colour. From this, it follows that the microstructure, and therefore, the m-RS stresses, are dependent on the thermo-mechanical treatment to which the material is subjected. Then, it is proposed that there must be a pattern of the ordering of the grains depending on the treatment that generates these m-RSs.

Besides, EBSD measurements provides a complete list of the number of grains, areas and diameters of each of them, number of neighboring grains, aspect ratio, slope, and crystallographic orientation for each cube. These parameters are present for each grain and have an associated m-RS value dependent on their mechanical behaviour. Therefore, there must be a function that relates them and is fulfilled for all grains of the same orientation.

3.2 Neutron Diffraction

Neutron diffraction allows determining with high accuracy the lattice spacing, $d_{x_i}^{hkl}$, of different lattice planes (hkl) which is the requirement to calculate the level of strain (and stress) developed within grains. Due to their high penetration capacity measurements can be made in the interior of materials, for which a superficial preparation of the material is not required. The neutron beam penetrates into the material and interacts with the atoms of the crystal lattice. The neutrons undergo diffraction by the crystal lattice and reach a detector that registers their Time Of Flight (TOF). This time is reflected in a diffractogram or diffraction pattern. In Fig. 3a, the high-intensity peaks (in y axis) correspond to the four mentioned texture components. And their positions in the x-axis are the lattice spacings. These experimental lattice spacings, $d_{x_i}^{hkl}$, are related with the stress, which the grains undergo. Thus, it will allow us to calculate the m-RS for each orientation.

The experiment was conducted on the FSD instrument at The Frank Laboratory of Neutron Physics in Dubna (Russia). The sample was a cylinder (25 mm in diameter and 60 mm high) extracted from the 40 mm diameter extruded bar of 5083 aluminum alloy. This sample geometry was chosen to facilitate stress calculations. The sample was heated at 530 °C for 3 h and quenched in water to generate residual stresses. Stresses are generated at the macro- and microscopic scales. The cylindrical sample was situated in two configurations, horizontal and vertical position, to acquire diffraction data from the axial, radial and hoop direction. All values were taken at different positions, $i = \{0, 3.5, 7, \text{and } 10\}$ mm with respect to the center of the sample. The instrument provided the measurements in TOF units [3]. The conversion to lattice spacing was made using the detectors parameters and the expression:

$$d_{x_i}^{hkl} = \frac{(N + D_0) \cdot \tau}{C \cdot L \cdot sin(\theta))} \tag{1}$$

where

- $d_{x_i}^{hkl}$ is the experimental lattice spacing for each hkl component at position i on the axis x.
- C is a constant which value is 505 556
- D_0 is spectrum delay
- τ is channel width
- L is the total flight path between the Fourier chopper and the detector
- θ is the Bragg angle
- N is the number of channels that the neutrons pass through

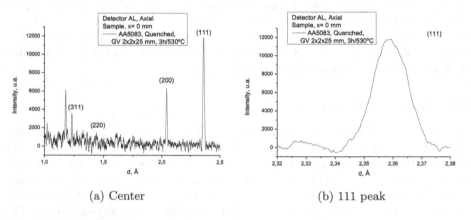

(a) Center   (b) 111 peak

Fig. 3. Intensity distributions with respect to its lattice spacing in the axial direction along the diameter of the quenched sample.

As it was mentioned, the GP implementation aims to relate each grain of the list obtained by EBSD, with a lattice spacing value, $d_{x_i}^{hkl}$. Thus, we have to give stress distributions (similar to the experimental peaks profiles) are described by an expression which terms were the microstructural parameters provides by the EBSD technique. In order to simplify the problem, we assume the following approximations:

- For a first analysis, only the 111 orientation peak was selected, due to its mechanical behaviour and that these grains were more clearly identified, from the list elaborated with the EBSD technique. Therefore, it is assumed that the stress distribution is produced by 755 grains in this case.

- The simulation will study the axial face of the cube number one, i.e., the centre position from the initial cylinder.
- All 111 grains in the EBSD list must contribute proportionally to the profile observed in Fig. 3b. This implies that the equation of the lattice spacing predicted must be the same despite the grain (i.e., we assume that grains have approximately equal participation in the diffraction peak).
- We consider the influence of the diffraction measurement instrument neglected.

In this way, the formula found using the symbolic regression model allows us calculating the lattice spacing, $d_{x_i}^{hkl}$, from the parameters described in Sect. 3.1. Those values will be used to obtain the total stress, $\sigma_{x_0}^{T,hkl}$, for each grain. The process for calculating these total stresses is described in the following steps.

First, the stress equilibrium method explained in [11], was used to obtain the macroscopic stress, M-RS, and the free-stress lattice spacing, d_0^{hkl}, for all orientations. The results were already discussed in [11].

Then, we obtain the strain, $\epsilon_{x_i}^{hkl}$, of each grain, from the values of the free-stress and predicted lattice spacing:

$$\epsilon_{x_i}^{hkl} = \frac{d_{x_i}^{hkl} - d_0^{hkl}}{d_0^{hkl}} \tag{2}$$

where

- $\epsilon_{x_i}^{hkl}$ is the strain suffered by the grains with hkl orientation in x axis
- $d_{x_i}^{hkl}$ is the experimental lattice spacing of grains with hkl orientation in x axis
- d_0^{hkl} is the free stresses lattice spacing grains with hkl orientation

By substituting these strain values in the following equation, the total (T) stresses (σ) at i position are obtained:

$$\sigma_{x_i}^{T,hkl} = E^{hkl} \epsilon_{x_i}^{hkl} \tag{3}$$

where

- $\sigma_{x_i}^{T,hkl}$ is the total stress for i position and hkl texture component (orientation) in x axis
- E^{hkl} is the Elastic Modulus and is constant for each hkl orientation.

Finally, the M-RS calculated previously was uses to obtain the m-RS, considering that the total stress is the sum of the macro and microscopic stresses.

$$\sigma_{x_i}^{T,hkl} = \sigma_{x_i}^{M} + \sigma_{x_i}^{m,hkl} \tag{4}$$

where

- $\sigma_{x_i}^{m,hkl}$ is the micro stress for i position and hkl texture component in the x axis.
- $\sigma_{x_i}^{M}$ is the Macro stress for i position in the x axis.

3.3   Genetic Programming

We use GP with the probabilistic tree creator (PTC2) [10] to initialize the population and gender-specific selection, where the first parent is selected with probability proportional to its fitness and the second parent is selected randomly [14]. All children are produced via sub-tree crossover and optional random mutation of function or terminal symbols. Only children with fitness equal or better than both parents are added to the next generation (offspring selection) [1]. Strict offspring selection, where children must be better than both parents, ensures sufficient selection pressure even with rather low pressure in parent selection [1]. The best individual is kept as elite.

Table 2 shows all GP parameters we have used. In preliminary experiments we observed that the specific parameter values used do not impact the results greatly. We have tried several different population sizes as well as tree size limits. In the end we have chosen parameter values that we know to work robustly for many different problem instances and a maximum tree size that ensures that the resulting model is still readable. In our experiments we visualized the curve shown in Fig. 5 for the best model so far in the GP run. We consistently observed that GP quickly (within a few minutes) converged to a curve which was close to the target curve. The measurements are noisy and the fit of the GP model was frequently good enough even after a few minutes of runtime. For the experiments we increased the number of generations to result in a runtime of approximately one hour. We have not tried to optimize these parameter values as the problem can be consistently solved using the parameters we have chosen and this is not a study about optimizing the efficiency of GP for this type of problem.

Table 2. The parameter values used for GP

Parameter	Value
Function set	+, -, *, log(x), exp(x)
Terminal set	Variables: grain area, number of neighbouring grains, aspect ratio, slope random constants
Tree creation	PTC2
Population size	500
Max. generations	1000
Max. tree size	50 nodes
Max. tree height	12 levels
Mutation probability	15%
Crossover probability	100%
Selection	Male: fitness-proportional
	Female: random
Offspring selection	Strict
Fitness function	Absolute differences between intensity distributions (see below)

The fitness function is specific to this application as we use GP to predict a quantity that is not directly measurable, the lattice spacing of grains. Instead, we need to estimate an intensity distribution from the predicted lattice spacing and match this distribution to the measured distribution from diffraction measurement. We assume that the measured distribution is a sum of individual peaks – one for each grain – each of which can be approximated by Gaussian bell-curves with small variance. Consequently, we calculate the estimated spectrum from the predicted lattice spacing via a convolution. The pseudo-code in Algorithm 1 shows the convolution procedure for a given symbolic regression model $m()$ for the discretized distribution.

Algorithm 1: Algorithm for calculating the estimated intensity distribution from a model for predicting lattice spacing values.

Input: Symbolic regression model m(), dataset for grains' characteristics measured using EBSD, dataset $\mathcal{D}$ for actual lattice spacing measured using neutron diffraction

Output: Estimate of the number of grains for each lattice spacing value $d_{x_i}^{khl}$

deviation $\leftarrow 10^{-4}$

scaling_factor $\leftarrow \frac{1}{\text{deviation} \cdot \sqrt{2 \cdot \pi}}$

foreach *grain g = (area, numNeighbours, aspectRatio, slope)* **do**

    $d_{x_i}^{pred} \leftarrow m(g)$ /* Predicted lattice spacing value */

    foreach $d_{x_i} \in \mathcal{D}$ **do**

        intensity$[d_{x_i}]+ = $ scaling_factor $\cdot \frac{\exp(-0.5 \cdot (d_{x_i} - d_{x_i}^{pred})^2}{\text{deviation}^2}$

    end

end

In our runs, we experimented with different variance values and found $1 \cdot 10^{-4}$ to work well. After the convolution, we calculate the sum of absolute intensity differences for the estimated and the measured distribution. The negative sum of absolute differences is used as the fitness function to be maximized.

For the implementation and experiments, we used HeuristicLab[1] an open-source environment for heuristic optimization, which includes an implementation of GP and symbolic regression. The custom fitness function is implemented using scripting functionality of HeuristicLab.

4   Experimental Results

Thirty GP runs were executed on an Intel Core i5 processor with 8 GB RAM, running under Windows 10. On average approximately 920 000 solutions were evaluated requiring on 39.9 minutes. Results are shown in Fig. 4. Each solution gives a distribution of the grains that fits the diffraction profile. The figure

---

[1] https://dev.heuristiclab.com.

summarizes the results of all the 30 distributions. The red line is the real profile of the 111 peak, which is the target of this paper. In the Fig. 4, the x axis indicates the position in the lattice spacing, $d_{x_i}^{hkl}$, where the neutron beam diffracted with 111 grains. y axis represents the number of grains 111 assigned by GP to each lattice spacing value $d_{x_i}^{hkl}$. Each box plot groups the assignment corresponding to each of the thirty executions. A line inside of each box indicates the average of these thirty values and the bar its standard deviation. The error values with respect to the target distribution were analysed, and the distribution with the minor differences with respect to the actual profile was selected and appears in Fig. 5.

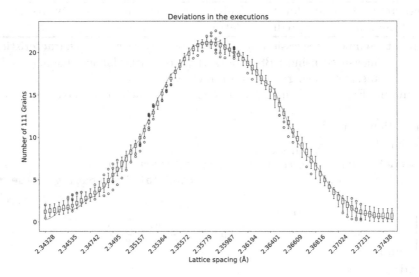

Fig. 4. Deviations in the executions of GP and the measured intensities.

A partial dependence plot as shown in Fig. 6 can be used to visualize the dependency of the predicted $d_{x_i}^{hkl}$ from the input parameters for the model. The numbers on top of the plots are the parameter values set for area, l, aspect ratio and slope (the x-position is shown with the vertical red dotted line). The plots show that the model is smooth and grain area, as well as slope, have a positive correlation with $d_{x_i}^{hkl}$, while the number of neighbours I is negatively correlated. The dependency from the aspect ratio is non-linear.

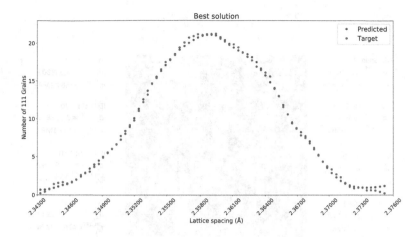

Fig. 5. Best solution found by GP for the distribution of 111 grains

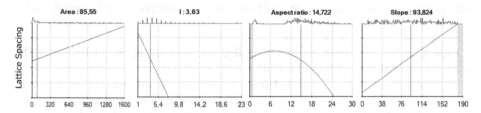

Fig. 6. The partial dependence plot shows the dependency of the model for the lattice spacing location $d_{x_i}^{hkl}$ from the grain parameters.

The corresponding expression of the best solution appears simplified in the following equation[2]:

$$
\begin{aligned}
d_{x_i}^{hkl} &= 3.49151 \cdot 10^{-10} A_n S_n \left(-0.91242 I_n + 0.28228 S_n - 8.02763\right) + \\
&+ 2.36180 + 6.04821 \cdot 10^{-10} - 5.96236 \cdot 10^{-5} I_n^2 - 0.00020 A R_n - \\
&- 3.65400 \cdot 10^{-7} \left(-0.63851 A R_n - 8.51731\right) \left(46.76401 A R_n^2 - 0.63851 A R_n\right) \\
&\quad \left(2.69392 I_n + 0.28386 S_n - 41.05772\right)
\end{aligned}
$$

$$(5)$$

where,

- A_n is the area for n grain
- I_n is the number of neighbors grains for n grain
- AR_n is the Aspect Ratio for n grain
- S_n is the is the Slope for n grain

Furthermore, the micro-structural parameter that appears most frequently is the aspect ratio. This is a reasonable fact since the compression or traction of a grain depends on the stress to which it is linked. This indicates that this method

---

[2] Output has to be scaled linearly to the range of the diffraction measurement.

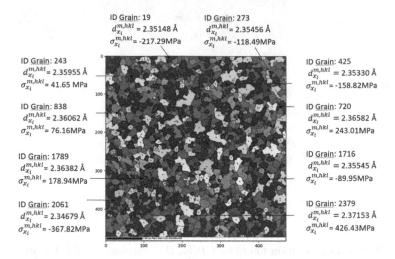

Fig. 7. Selection the grains 111 with its lattice spacing obtained with GP and its m-RS

is robust and the expression can be applied for calculating the m-RS using the micro-structural parameters of EBSD.

The values of the micro-structural parameters for all the 111 grains were replaced in the expression obtained, and its m-RS was calculated using the equations described in Sect. 3.2. Some of the values obtained are shown in Fig. 7. In order to know if this solution is physically feasible, we can analyse if the stresses assigned to each grain are coherent with other variables.   In this sense, it is known that the Elastic Modulus E^{xyz}, for each of the four families of grains are: $E^{111} = 75.5\,\text{GPa}$, $E^{200} = 63.2\,\text{GPa}$, $E^{220} = 72.0\,\text{GPa}$, and $E^{311} = 69.0\,\text{GPa}$. Those values inform us about the hardness of the grains, being the 111 grains the hardest and the 200 the softest. Taking into account these considerations, we can see in Fig. 7 that grains 111 surrounded by themselves have more tension as occurs in grains ID.2379 or ID.1789. However, if the neighbours grains are more soft, like 200 or 311 grains, for example, in grain ID.2061. However, in some cases, this is not true. This is, for instance, the case of grain ID.273 (in the right top of Fig. 7). This appears to be due to their size; larger grains present less stress than smaller grains. Therefore, in some grains, the influence of both factors can be observed. This fact seems to agree with the *dhkl* expression obtained by GP, where the aspect ratio and the number of neighbours are the most frequent terms. Consequently, this model determines the values of m-RS according to what could theoretically be expected.

5   Conclusions

This paper proposes a method to estimate the micro residual stresses in a quenched cylindrical sample of AA5083 aluminum alloy using GP. This is the first time that m-RS are numerically estimated at the grain level to the best of our knowledge. This cannot be solved directly using a usual supervised learning approach and requires a custom GP fitness function to link microstructural parameters of grains to the peak profile acquired via neutron diffraction.

The low error value between the predicted and the target peak profile demonstrated the validity and quality of the method. The approach has given values of $d_{x_i}^{hkl}$ inside the expected range. However, the identified expression is only valid for one lattice direction. Consequently, as a next step, the combination of the peak profiles for all directions as well as the micro-structural data corresponding to other positions along the diameter of the sample shall be used to identify a more general model for m-RS of grains. We hypothesize that the same GP approach can be generalized easily for this task. The results of the m-RS will be compared to the micro-structural characteristics in a later study. Apparently, GP indicates that the number and type of neighbouring grains and the aspect ratio are the most important factors influencing the m-RS values in 111 grains. Future work should necessarily include a complete view of all the orientations and other materials.

Acknowledgments. This work has been supported by Madrid Regional Government-FEDER grants Y2018/NMT-4668 (Micro-Stress- MAP-CM) and MAT2017-83825-C4-1-R. Thanks are also due to the FLNR-JINP for the beam time allocated on FSD instrument and to the Centrum Výzkumu Řež, in Prague, for the EBSD map and the micro-structural analysis.

References

1. Affenzeller, M., Winkler, S., Wagner, S., Beham, A.: Genetic Algorithms and Genetic Programming: Modern Concepts and Practical Applications. 1st edn, Chapman & Hall/CRC, Boca Raton (2009)
2. Bäck, T., Hoffmeister, F., Schwefel, H.P.: A survey of evolution strategies. In: Proceedings of the fourth international conference on genetic algorithms. Citeseer (1991)
3. Bokuchava, G., Papushkin, I.: Neutron time-of-flight stress diffractometry. J. Surface Invest. X-ray Synchrotron Neutron Tech. **12**(1), 97–102 (2018)
4. Cioffi, F., et al.: Analysis of the unstressed lattice spacing, d0, for the determination of the residual stress in a friction stir welded plate of an age-hardenable aluminum alloy-use of equilibrium conditions and a genetic algorithm. Acta Materialia **74**, 189–199 (2014)
5. Fernández, R., Ferreira-Barragáns, S., Ibáñez, J., González-Doncel, G.: A multi-scale analysis of the residual stresses developed in a single-phase alloy cylinder after quenching. Mater. Des. **137**, 117–127 (2018). https://doi.org/10.1016/j.matdes.2017.10.013
6. Grajales, D.H.M.: Principios y aplicaciones de la técnica de difracción de electrones retro-proyectados (ebsd, electron back-scattering diffraction). Informador técnico **74**, (2010)
7. Hidalgo, J.I., Fernández, R., Colmenar, J.M., Cioffi, F., Risco-Martín, J.L., González-Doncel, G.: Using evolutionary algorithms to determine the residual stress profile across welds of age-hard enable aluminum alloys. Appl. Soft. Comput. **40**, 429–438 (2016)

8. Karak, S.K., Chatterjee, S., Bandopadhyay, S.: Mathematical modelling of the physical and mechanical properties of nano-Y2O3 dispersed ferritic alloys using evolutionary algorithm-based neural network. Powder Tech. **274**, 217–226 (2015)
9. Kirkpatrick, S., Gelatt, C.D., Vecchi, M.P.: Optimization by simulated annealing. Science **220**(4598), 671–680 (1983)
10. Luke, S.: Two fast tree-creation algorithms for genetic programming. IEEE Trans. Evol. Comput. **4**(3), 274–283 (2000). https://doi.org/10.1109/4235.873237
11. Millán, L., Bokuchava, G., Fernández, R., Papushkin, I., González-Doncel, G.: Further insights on the stress equilibrium method to investigate macroscopic residual stress fields: case of aluminum alloys cylinders. J. Alloys Compd. **861**, 158506 (2020)
12. Romero, M.: Determinación de la textura en aleaciones de aluminio aa-3003 con temple h14 a través de la técnica ebsd
13. Vijayan, D., Abhishek, P.: Multi objective process parameters optimization of friction stir welding using nsga-ii. In: IOP Conference Series: Materials Science and Engineering, vol. 390, p. 012087 (2018)
14. Wagner, S., Affenzeller, M.: SexualGA: gender-specific selection for genetic algorithms. In: Proceedings of the 9th World Multi-Conference on Systemics, Cybernetics and Informatics (WMSCI), vol. 4, pp. 76–81 (2005)
15. Zhang, R., et al.: The influence of grain size and grain orientation on sensitization in aa5083. Corrosion **72**(2), 160–168 (2016)

EDA-Based Optimization of Blow-Off Valve Positions for Centrifugal Compressor Systems

Jacob Spindler[1,2], Rico Schulze[1], Kevin Schleifer[1], and Hendrik Richter[2]([✉]) [ID]

[1] AviComp Controls GmbH, Leipzig, Germany
jacob.spindler@stud.htwk-leipzig.de,
{rico.schulze,kevin.schleifer}@avicomp.com
[2] HTWK University of Applied Sciences, Leipzig, Germany
hendrik.richter@htwk-leipzig.de

Abstract. Designing actuators is an important part of automation technology and indispensable for the operation of plants in process industry. This also applies to valves which are important actuators of compressor systems. Compressor systems have a high degree of complexity due to the interconnection of many different components. Often simulation environments are used to test already designed actuators. In this study we show how a digital twin of a compressor system in combination with an Estimation of Distribution (EDA) algorithm can be used to facilitate the valve design. In addition, the installation position in the plant is determined in order to achieve a desired operating behaviour during an emergency shutdown.

Keywords: EDA-based optimization · Control valve placement · Compressor system simulation

1 Introduction

Proper operation of technological processes depends largely on actuators. This also applies to compressor systems for which valves are the most important type of actuators. Valves are used for adjusting the mass flow and the pressure conditions in the process. Their design must ensure that the process works properly in different operating modes. These operating modes include various stationary operating points, load changes, startups and shutdowns as well as emergency shutdowns (ESD). An improperly designed valve may be the cause for serious malfunctions, damages to the compressor, or even a complete breakdown.

The work reported in this paper was triggered by a troubleshooting study in an industrial application of a centrifugal compressor. In this study it was noticed that due to an improperly designed valve, an entire compressor-turbine unit exhibited reverse shaft rotation during an ESD. Such a reverse rotation can cause severe damages to various parts of the compressor-turbine unit. In a first step of the troubleshooting study, it was identified that the installation of

© Springer Nature Switzerland AG 2021
P. A. Castillo and J. L. Jiménez Laredo (Eds.): EvoApplications 2021, LNCS 12694, pp. 437–452, 2021.
https://doi.org/10.1007/978-3-030-72699-7_28

additional blow-off valves (BOVs) could be a reasonable countermeasure. The question that needed to be answered was how the valves should be designed and where they should be installed to eliminate reverse shaft rotation. For answering these questions, we use a simulation model of a compressor system and apply an EDA for the selection and placement of additional BOVs to achieve a desired speed response.

The application of nature-inspired metaheuristics for answering analysis and design questions of centrifugal compressors is well established. Examples are the optimization of the compressor's casing and wheel by coupling metaheuristic algorithms with computational fluid dynamics simulations [12], genetic algorithms for blade design [16] and multipoint shape optimisation [17]. See also the use of evolutionary algorithms for the geometry optimization of the compressor diffuser [4,5], or ring cavity optimization using a PSO [11], or instability detection using artificial immune systems [15]. The topic of this paper, design and placement of BOVs using evolutionary computation methods received little attention so far.

The paper is structured as follows. In the next section we give a brief introduction to compressor systems and the main components in such systems. Then we describe the underlying optimization problem and present a suitable solution approach. We then introduce the EDA and explain the setup of the fitness function. In Sect. 4 we present the simulation results and end with conclusions, a summary of the results and a pointer at further questions.

2   Compressor Systems

Compressor systems are an important part of many technological processes. They serve as fluid feeds and transfer units as well as pressure increasing components. Compressors are an integral part of transport vehicles, e.g. in form of turbochargers or as a compressor unit in airplane engines. Small compressor units are also used in refrigerators and cooling systems. In the process industry, rotating compressors are an essential part of plants providing continuous gas flows and pressures. The main areas of application cover natural gas extraction and transportation, gas processing in the petrochemical and metallurgical industry as well as air feeding in wastewater treatment plants. In addition, industrial plants frequently use compressors as a central generating system for auxiliary pneumatics.

A compressor system consists of several technological components, such as the compressors unit itself, vessels, valves, filters, heat exchangers, motors or turbines. All components are interconnected with pipes. Each functional component has a specific affect on the thermo- and fluiddynamic state of the fluid. Control valves, for example, perform control and safety-critical tasks to ensure continuous plant operation. Since both the compressor unit and the control valve are objects of the EDA-based optimization presented in this paper, in the following these components are discussed in more detail.

2.1   Rotating Compressor

Rotating compressors are turbomachines which transfer kinetic energy to a continuous fluid flow and thus achieve an increase in pressure and temperature. In general, there are two different designs: axial and centrifugal compressors [9,10,18]. The designs differ in the way the fluid is passed through the machine. In contrast to the axial design, the centrifugal design radially redirects the fluid in order to achieve higher pressure ratios per stage. This results in different areas of application as the axial compressor can transport larger flow rates, while the centrifugal compressor can achieve higher pressure. Figure 1 shows an example of a centrifugal compressor and the necessary peripheral assemblies.

Fig. 1. Example of a compressor on a mounting plate, equipped with measuring instruments

Important parts of a compressor include the suction line (inlet, optionally equipped with variable guide vanes), the impeller with rotor and stator blades, the diffuser (vaned or non-vaned), the discharge line (outlet) and the compressor housing. During operation of a centrifugal compressor, a fluid is sucked through the suction pipe and axially guided to the impeller which is mounted on a rotating shaft. The impeller is designed to deflect the flow and discharge it radially. As a result, the fluid experiences an acceleration and thus an increase in kinetic energy. A diffuser is installed downstream of the impeller. This causes a reduction in speed and yields an increase in pressure and temperature [10]. How much energy the compressor transfers to the fluid is described by performance maps. These maps represent the steady-state relationship between the specific energy transfer (head) and the flow rate of the fluid (see Fig. 2). The head is an enthalphy difference depending on gas composition, pressures and temperatures. In order to modify a given operating point, the rotational speed as well as the inflow and outflow angle of the fluid can be varied. For this reason, compressors can be equipped with speed-regulating devices or variable guide vanes.

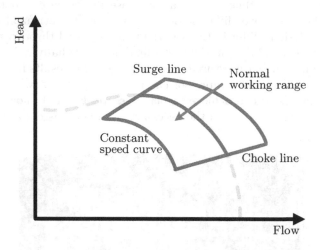

Fig. 2. Schematic drawing of a typical compressor map.

Stable compressor operation is only guaranteed within a certain working range. The range is limited by the surge line and restricts operation to a minimum flow. If the flow drops below a critical value the energy transfer is discontinued by rapidly growing aerodynamic instabilities. This leads to fast oscillating fluid flows and pressures which trigger rotating stall or compressor surge. These phenomena severely decrease performance, damage the compressor and thus eventually lead to a complete breakdown. The stable range is further limited by the choke or stonewall line. This line represents the maximum stable flow rate through the compressor. Using specific extrapolation methods, a compressor map can be expanded to additionally describe the unstable operation in dynamic simulations.

2.2   Control Valve and Other Components

Control valves are actuators designed to control flow rate and pressure. This is done by changing the valve opening. Opening the valve causes a reduced flow resistance and thus increases the flow rate. The flow resistance is quantified by the so-called flow coefficient K_v. If a valve is fully open, the maximum flow coefficient K_{vs} is obtained [7]. The flow coefficient K_v is an important design parameter. The required valve set point is determined by a process controller, which passes the control signal to the valve positioner, who puts the valve to the prescribed position. The relationship between valve set point and flow coefficient is represented by the valve characteristics. The two most common shapes of characteristic in compressor systems are the linear and the equal percentage characteristic. For more details refer to [7,19].

Further significant design parameters are the opening and the closing speed of the valve. These parameters determine how fast a valve can perform the opening and closing process. Usually the required opening and closing speed result from the related technical process and its operating modes. Especially for safety-critical plant components, it may be necessary to seal off a part of a plant rapidly or to quickly provide more fluid flow. The later effect is very important to prevent the compressor operating point from exceeding the surge limit. To guarantee a certain minimum flow, most compressor systems are equipped with bypass control valves (BPVs) which recirculate partly the compressed fluid from discharge to suction side. Some compressor systems use BOVs instead, which vent the fluid from discharge side to atmosphere.

In addition to the compressor itself and different types of valves, further components such as turbines, pipes, vessels, heat exchangers, motors and expander units have to be modeled for simulation based studies. All component models must satisfy the laws of conservation of energy, mass and momentum to represent the real-world behaviour. Given reasonable simplifications, this results in ordinary nonlinear differential equations. In addition to fluid dynamics, thermodynamic state variables are calculated using real gas models such as Peng-Robinson or Soave-Redlich-Kwong [14].

3 Problem Analysis and Solution Finding

In this section the analyzed compressor system is presented. Then, we explain the dynamic simulation model we use and discuss the requirements for the EDA. Finally, we present the fitness function.

3.1 System and Problem Description

The compressor system under investigation consists of four centrifugal compressor stages and provides compressed air to an upstream process (see Fig. 3). Between the compressor stages there are several large vessels for buffering and tube bundle heat exchangers for reducing the air temperature. The discharge side of the last stage is equipped with a check valve that separates the system from the upstream process. In addition, a BOV is installed acting as anti-surge valve. The compressor stages are driven by a condensing steam turbine with a nominal output of 12.000 kW. The drive shaft is connected to the 1st and 2nd stage via a coupling. The 3rd and 4th compressor stages are mounted to a second shaft, which is coupled to the drive shaft by a gearbox.

As mentioned above, an accidental effect occurred during an emergency shutdown (ESD) triggered by a malfunction in a neighboring system. During this ESD, the drive shaft exhibits a reversed rotation which causes increased radial vibrations and axial displacements. Due to small mechanical tolerances, this causes damages to bearings and gas labyrinths, couplings and gears as well as to the impellers themselves. These damages mean significant repair and downtime costs. Hence, reverse rotation is a safety-critical behaviour for the compressor and needs to be avoided.

For developing solution strategies avoiding reversed shaft rotations, simulation models are particularly suitable as these models provide flow and state variables which are not (or only with significant effort) measurable in a real compressor. The simulation results give important insights into the sequence of events eventually leading to reversed shaft rotations. Such models can be fitted to measured data by parameter tuning. Measurement data from different steady-states and dynamic processes have been used for validation. Based on several ESD simulations, two main causes for reverse rotations could be identified. First of all, the existing BOV was not large enough. In addition, the vessels and heat exchangers installed were to large. This has increased the total compressor system volume. Both causes contribute to a slower blow-off. Hence, the air cannot be discharged from the system fast enough which leads to a flow reversal in the first two stages. A high braking torque was generated at the shaft and finally caused a strong braking of the entire machine unit until the direction of rotation was reversed.

Therefore, it needs to be ensured that the air in the system can be discharged faster. A suitable measure is the installation of further BOVs. Seven possible installation positions were identified, which are located upstream and downstream of each compressor stage (see Fig. 3 where the valves are depicted in green). However, finding the most suitable position and design of the valve is far from being obvious. This is due to the fact that the installation of additional BOVs leads to a structural change of the system and thus affects its behaviour in other operating modes.

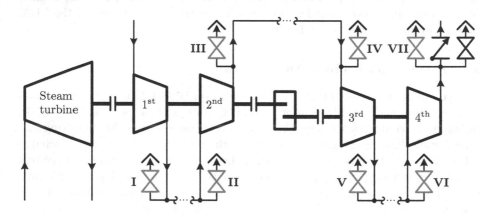

Fig. 3. Schematic drawing of the investigated system with possible additional BOVs.

3.2   Dynamic Simulation Model

We employed a simulation model based on principles of computational fluid dynamics [10, 17] for calculating the flows and thermodynamic states of gases. The model also shows the interaction of the gas with the physical structures of the considered technical components. It simulates the underlying nonlinear differential equations and their dynamics as well as their input and output behaviour. It is implemented using a proprietary framework in MATLAB/

Simulink. This framework provides a series of blocks that represent the plant components of the real system. Each block has a uniform set of input and output variables, but different state variables. Typical state variables are the density and temperature of a vessel or the mass flow of a pipe or rotating compressor. To adapt the model to real measured data it is possible to change the parameterization of these equations. Important parameters include pipe lengths and vessel volumes, friction and heat transfer coefficients, but also component-specific design conditions. Due to the variable interconnections of blocks and the large number of interconnected blocks in a model (about 40 in this study) as well as the different parameterizations, we obtain a very complex set of equations.

Furthermore, the structure of the model is changed by adding additional BOVs at predefined positions, while the parameterization changes due to different valve designs, such as K_{vs}-value, characteristic and opening speed. This means that there is no fixed input and output behaviour and therefore it cannot be handled with conventional optimization methods and tools.

3.3 Requirements for the Algorithm

As shown above, the model-based optimization task presented here consists of finding the optimal installation positions and designs of the BOVs. All these parameters can only be set in discrete values. For the position only integer values between 1 (I) and 7 (VII) are allowed, see Fig. 3. The availability of valves also restricts the design parameters. Thus valves are only available in steps of the K_{vs}-values. The same applies to the opening speed. The characteristics of a valve can be either linear or equal percentage. Thus, we have a combinatorial optimization problem for which classical optimization algorithms such as derivative based methods most likely are not suitable. In comparison, metaheuristic methods are well suited to solve this kind of problem in combination with a simulation for evaluating the fitness [1,2,8].

For each solution candidate a numerical simulation of the complete compressor model is necessary. The parameterization of the model, at which position a valve is located and how it is parameterized, is linked to the parameter values of an individual. During the simulation the shaft rotating speed is calculated and can subsequently be used to evaluate the fitness function. The numerical effort for a simulation is very high due to the complexity of the system. Thus, we needed an algorithm which requires as few fitness evaluations as possible to find a solution. Therefore we decided to use the Estimation of Distribution Algorithm (EDA). It has already been used in other complex applications like in [20] and [6] to determine the positions of sensors.

The idea behind an EDA is to describe possible solutions not by explicit solution candidates but by a probabilistic model. In [13] it is described that EDAs are basically divided into two types, population-based EDAs and incremental EDAs. We use an incremental EDA, more precise an population-based incremental learning (PBIL) algorithm, as described by Beluja in [3], see Algorithm 1 for the description as pseudocode. The algorithm provides a probabilistic model and samples solution candidates from it. Then we perform a fitness evaluation for all individuals and the model is adjusted based on the best solution. After that a mutation operator is executed on the model, which is controlled by the mutation strength (ms). The algorithm has a higher mutation strength at the beginning, which is reduced after a defined number of generations.

```
t := 1;
// Initialize model P
for i := 1 to l do
|   P^t[i] = 0.5;
end
while not termination do
    Ind := sampleIndividualsFromProbModel(P^t);
    simOut := simulateAllIndividuals(Ind);
    Fit := evaluateFitness(simOut);
    BestInd := selectBestIndividual(Ind, Fit);
    // Update the probabilistic model
    P^{t+1} = (1 - lr) * P^t + lr * BestInd;
    P^{t+1} = (1 - ms) * P^{t+1} + ms * rand(0or1);
    if all(P^{t+1} > 0.9 or P^{t+1} < 0.1) then
    |   termination := True;
    end
    t := t+1;
end
```

Algorithm 1: Pseudocode for EDA (PBIL)

The parameters of the individuals allow only discrete values, thus a binary representation is suitable. An individual consists of 4 n-bit long binary strings for each valve it represents. This means that if an individual represents 2 valves, there are 8 n-bit long binary strings, see Table 1. The length of the binary strings

Table 1. Structure of the probabilistic model P for one and two control valves, shifted distribution in the model for two valves and one possible solution candidate sampled from the model

	Parameter	Model P	Individual	Parameter values
One valve	Position	0.5 0.5 0.5	0 0 1	I
	K_{vs}-value	0.5 0.5 0.5 0.5 0.5	1 1 0 0 1	$650m^3/h$
	Opening speed	0.5 0.5 0.5 0.5 0.5	0 0 0 0 1	$5\%/s$
	Characteristic	0.5 0.5	0 1	linear
Two valves	Position 1	0.5 0.5 0.5	0 1 0	III
	K_{vs}-value 1	0.5 0.5 0.5 0.5 0.5	0 1 0 0 0	$600m^3/h$
	Opening speed 1	0.5 0.5 0.5 0.5 0.5	0 1 1 0 0	$40\%/s$
	Characteristic 1	0.5 0.5	1 0	equal
	Position 2	0.9 0.1 0.1	1 0 0	VII
	K_{vs}-value 2	0.1 0.1 0.1 0.1 0.9	0 0 0 0 1	$250m^3/h$
	Opening speed 2	0.9 0.9 0.1 0.1 0.1	1 1 0 0 0	$80\%/s$
	Characteristic 2	0.1 0.9	0 1	linear

depends on the parameter it represents, e.g. the binary string for the position in this study is 3-bit long.

Each of the p_i in the vectors describe whether the bit on the ith-position in the string is 0 or 1. The advantage of this algorithm is that all p_i can be set to 0.5 and thus assume an uniform distribution over all solutions. But with a priori information about the solution these probabilities can be shifted. The algorithm terminates as soon as the termination criterion is met. For this purpose, it was specified that all probabilities p_i in P^t must be larger than 0.9 or smaller than 0.1.

3.4   Fitness Function

The installation of further BOVs should ensure that the direction of shaft rotation is no longer reversed. In order to make a statement about how well an individual has solve this task, it is necessary to define a fitness function. For this purpose, a target speed curve f_{set} with normal direction of rotation during shutdown is defined. The task of the algorithm is to find a solution that minimizes the distance between the simulated speed curve $f_{sim}(t)$ and the target speed curve $f_{set}(t)$ for $t_{ESD} \leq t \leq t_{end}$, where t_{ESD} is the simulation time at which the ESD occurs and t_{end} is the time where the simulation is stopped. To make sure that individuals with the undesired speed behaviour are not used to update the model, the area which is covered by the speed in the negative range is integrated and added to the fitness as a penalty term (Pt_1) by

$$f_{neg}(t) = \min(0(t), f_{sim}(t)), \quad 0(t) = 0, \forall t \tag{1}$$

$$Pt_1 = \int_{t_{ESD}}^{t_{end}} |f_{neg}(t)| dt. \tag{2}$$

Since during a shutdown further undesirable effects can occur in the compressor system, e.g. surge, the output pressures of all compressor stages are also examined for the calculation of the fitness function value. Compressor surge is reflected by strong oscillations of the discharge pressure p_{out}. For the fitness function the positive increase in the normalized discharge pressure of all compressor stages n is summed up (Pt_2):

$$dp_i(t) = \max\left(0(t), \frac{dp_{out}(t)}{dt}\right) \tag{3}$$

$$Pt_2 = \frac{1}{n} \sum_{i=1}^{n} \int_{t_{ESD}}^{t_{end}} dp_i(t) dt. \tag{4}$$

The two penalty terms are provided with weighting factors and added to the squared distance of $f_{sim}(t)$ and $f_{set}(t)$:

$$Fit = \int_{t_{ESD}}^{t_{end}} (f_{sim}(t) - f_{set}(t))^2 dt + w_1 \cdot Pt_1 + w_2 \cdot Pt_2. \tag{5}$$

4 Results

In this section we show numerical results of the EDA-based compressor optimization which minimizes the fitness function (5). For this purpose the algorithm is tested with four different configurations. For each configuration, five runs were executed. All runs were performed on the same hardware using a I9-9900K CPU. The Algorithm is implemented in MATLAB and the Parallel Computing Toolbox is used to parallelize the simulations. Some settings of the algorithm are identical for all runs, including the learning rate, the number of generations of the exploration phase, the mutation strength while exploration and exploitation, the reference speed curve and the weighting factors for the fitness function, see also Table 2. The target speed curve was designed in such a way that 45 s after the shutdown 60% of the nominal speed is obtained. The simulation time for

Table 2. General configuration of algorithm for all runs

Parameter	Value
lr	0.1
NumExp	25
ms_{explor}	0.1
$ms_{exploit}$	0.01
Reference speed curve $f_{set}(t)$	$2.7125 * t^{(-0.3685)}$, $\forall\{t \in \mathbb{R}, 15\,\text{s} \leq t \leq 60\,\text{s}\}$
w_1	1/100
w_2	3

each individual was 60 s. During the first 15 s a stationary operating point was simulated to ensure that all state variables are in a steady state. Afterwards the shutdown was performed. The search space consists of the following parameters: position, K_{vs}-value, opening speed and characteristics of the valve. They are limited according to Table 3.

Table 3. Limits of the search space and the resulting number of possible settings

Parameter	Limits	Number of possible values
Position	$x \in \mathbb{N}, \text{I} \leq x \leq \text{VII}$	$n_{pos} = 7$
K_{vs}-value	$250\,\text{m}^3/\text{h} + 25\,\text{m}^3/\text{h} * k, 0 \leq k \leq 16$	$n_{Kvs} = 17$
Opening speed	$5\%/\text{s} + 5\%/\text{s} * k, 0 \leq k \leq 15$	$n_{Open} = 16$
Characteristic	$x \in \mathbb{N}, 1 \leq x \leq 2$	$n_{Chara} = 2$

The possible positions result from the plant conditions, see Sect. 3.1. The discretization of the K_{vs}-values and opening speeds are a consequence of available real control valves. The valve characteristic is either linear or equal percentage. These restrictions of the search space mean a combinatorial optimization problem for which the number of all possible solutions can be calculated by $\frac{n_{Pos}!}{(n_{Pos}-k)!k!} \cdot (n_{Kvs} \cdot n_{Open} \cdot n_{Chara})^k$, where k is the number of valves. This yields 3.808 possible solutions for one valve and 6.214.656 solutions for two valves, which cannot be solved by enumaration within a reasonable amount of time.

For the different configurations the following specifications were made. In configuration 1, each individual represents one valve and the initial state of P^t is 0.5 for all p_i. The number of individuals per generation is 16, this also applies to configurations 2–3. In configuration 2 it is set that each individual represents two valves, again the initial state of P^t was 0.5 for each p_i. In configuration 3 each individual also represents two valves, but here the probabilistic model at the end of configuration 1 run 1 was used as search bias for one of the valves. Configuration 4 is similar to Configuration 2, but the number of individuals

Table 4. Results of algorithm for different configurations

	Run 1		Run 2		Run 3		Run 4		Run 5	
Configuration 1:										
Fitness:	54,23		54,23		54,23		64,69		54,23	
Time [h]:	3,02		2,11		2,88		1,47		1,36	
Number of generations:	74		50		73		37		34	
Position:	VII		VII		VII		VII		VII	
K_{vs}-value [m³/h]:	525		525		525		475		525	
Opening speed [%/s]:	15		15		15		65		15	
Characteristic:	Equal		Equal		Equal		Equal		Equal	
Configuration 2:										
Fitness:	20,33		15,81		16,09		16,65		16,81	
Time [h]:	4,53		7,3		3,8		5,52		4,16	
Number of generations:	110		181		95		137		104	
Positions:	V	VII	IV	VII	III	VII	III	VII	IV	VII
K_{vs}-values [m³/h]:	300	650	450	625	525	625	575	575	475	625
Opening speeds [%/s]:	65	20	20	5	20	5	65	10	70	5
Characteristics:	Linear	Equal	Equal	Linear	Equal	Linear	Linear	Equal	Linear	Linear
Configuration 3:										
Fitness:	16,18		16,18		16,18		16,18		16,18	
Time [h]:	3,52		2,65		3,84		2,9		3,08	
Number of generations:	86		65		94		71		75	
Positions:	III	VII	III	VII	III	VII	III	VII	III	VII
K_{vs}-values [m³/h]:	550	550	550	550	550	550	550	550	550	550
Opening speeds [%/s]:	40	10	40	10	40	10	40	10	40	10
Characteristics:	Linear	Equal	Linear	Equal	Linear	Equal	Linear	Equal	Linear	Equal
Configuration 4:										
Fitness:	20,26		23,55		20,26		20,26		15,58	
Time [h]:	5,99		5,22		4,91		6,13		5,93	
Number of generations:	78		69		62		81		80	
Positions:	V	VII	III	VII	V	VII	V	VII	III	VII
K_{vs}-values [m³/h]:	300	650	600	425	300	650	300	650	525	550
Opening speeds [%/s]:	75	20	20	15	75	20	75	20	60	10
Characteristics:	Linear	Equal	Equal	Equal	Linear	Equal	Linear	Equal	Equal	Equal

per generation was increased from 16 to 32. These numerical experiments were chosen in order to better investigate the convergence behaviour of the algorithm and to be able to make a statement about how a practical approach for solving the problem might look like. Table 4 summarizes the results.

All runs with the configuration 1 result in a valve at position VII. There are 4 valves with exactly the same design parameters. Only run 4 yields a valve with a smaller K_{vs}-value and a higher opening speed finally leading to worse fitness value compared to the other runs. The results with configuration 2 are more diverse. The algorithm found solutions with different positions and designs of the valves. But a valve at position VII is always part of the solution. However, the fitness values do not differ substantially from each another.

In Configuration 3 we used the probabilistic model obtained for configuration 1 run 1 for one of the valves. This more or less determines the position and the design of this valve. The algorithm still has the possibility to change the model by updating and mutation during the calculation. This can be seen in the results. In comparison to configuration 1 run 1, the design of the valve at position VII changes only slightly from $525 \, m^3/h$ and $15\%/s$ opening speed to $550 \, m^3/h$ and $10\%/s$. The characteristics remain identical. Furthermore it can be seen that the runs all give exactly the same position combinations and designs as results.

As already described, the number of individuals per generation was doubled for configuration 4. The underlying idea was to increase the diversity in each generation. The results obtained here can best be compared with configuration 2, since in both cases the initial state of P^t was uniformly distributed. It can be seen that different results are obtained. However, the algorithm converged to only 3 instead of 5 different results. In addition, fewer generations are needed. Interestingly, the fitness values of runs 1–4 are slightly worse than in configuration 2, only run 5 had a better fitness.

The time the algorithm takes to calculate a solution is strongly dependent on the number of generations needed. It varies from an average of 5.26 h for configuration 2 to 6.22 h for configuration 3, taking into account that with this setting a solution with one valve has been calculated beforehand. Configuration 4 required an average of 5.64h to find a solution. The fitness values of each configuration are rather similar and the standard deviation is also very small.

Since the different solutions have very similar fitness function values despite their different parameterizations, it can be assumed that the fitness space is rather flat over a large parameter range. In order to verify and visualize this assumption, we may use an approximation of the fitness landscape, see Fig. 4. The figure shows any combination of the valve positions, which is plotted on the X-axis and the corresponding K_{vs}-values of the valves on the Y-axis. The opening speeds and the characteristics of the valves are not taken into account. Thus, the plot can be interpreted as approximating a 2D-slice through the fitness landscape. By reducing the dimensionality of the problem, it can happen that for certain combinations of positions and K_{vs}-values more than one fitness value applies. In Fig. 4 only the minimal fitness values of the combinations are shown. The plot was created for run 2 of configuration 2, which was

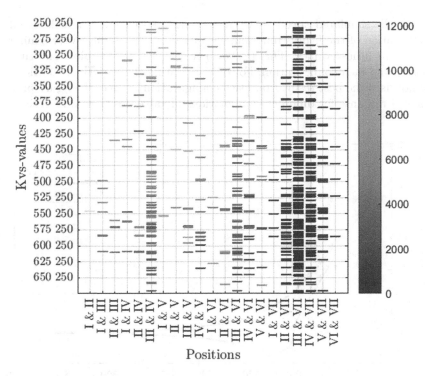

Fig. 4. Approximated fitness landscape for all individuals from run 2 with configuration 2.

chosen because most of the fitness evaluations were performed in this run. Thus, we do not sample the whole search space and only have an approximation of the landscape.

From this figure we may derive some assumptions about the search and convergence behaviour of the algorithm. It can be seen that during the run fitness function evaluations were performed for all position combinations and a substantial number of different valve designs. Positions with very high fitness values (which are not desirable as we solve a minimization problem) are less densely sampled (I&II) than positions with an above average fitness, e.g. (III&VII). Furthermore, it can be seen that almost all combinations with a valve at position VII have a very low fitness value (which is desirable) over a large range of K_{vs}-values. The position of the valves therefore has the biggest influence on the operating behaviour of the system and the actual design is a fine tuning of the desired operating behaviour. From Table 4 it can be deduced that it is very likely that the valves at positions III&VII or IV&VII produce best results. However, it cannot be excluded that there are some isolated solutions with a very low fitness in the non-sampled areas of the search space, but we think this is rather unlikely. The lowest fitness value is achieved with configuration 4 run 5. However, all fitness values of configurations 2–4 are very low. Since the distance between the simulated speed curve and a target speed curve is calculated for the evaluation of the fitness function, the speed curves are also very similar for very similar fitness values. This is shown in Fig. 5. For this plot, one run was selected from each configuration. For demonstrating the variety of solutions, we have not used the best result from each configuration. Hence, the figure presents the speed response for different combinations of valve positions and design.

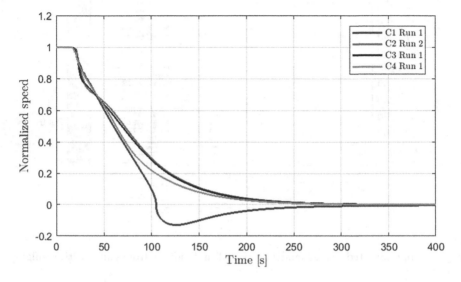

Fig. 5. Normalized speed curve after optimization for selected runs from Table 4

It turns out that the results of configuration 1 are not sufficient to solve the problem of changing the direction of rotation, see the blue curve in Fig. 5, which has a negative normalized speed for a certain time interval and thus a reversal of the direction of rotation approx. 90 s after the ESD. As expected, the speed curves from configurations 2–4 show a very similar behaviour, despite the different positions and designs of the valves. For the practical application, based on the speed curves alone, no statement can be made about which solution is better than the other. In order to select a specific solution, other aspects have to be considered, which will be discussed in the following section.

5   Conclusions

We have shown that it is possible to use a simulation model in combination with an EDA to solve a real-world troubleshooting scenario in a complex compressor system. We identified positions and designs of additional blow-off valves that eliminate reverse shaft rotation during an emergency shutdown. The algorithm was configured in different ways and the convergence behaviour was studied. It has been demonstrated that the extension of the system by a single valve is not sufficient to avoid reverse shaft rotation. At least two valves are necessary. The different runs of the algorithm showed that the algorithm converges to various local optima and accordingly outputs different positions with different valve designs as results. We have also observed that the biggest influence on the system behaviour comes from the positions of the valves. Combinations with valves at the outlet of the system, i.e. parallel to the already existing blow-off, achieve particularly low fitness values. Especially for valves at the positions III&VII and IV&VII we obtain good results. For these valve positions the influence of the valve design is less prominent, very good fitness values are achieved over a large K_{vs}-value range. As mentioned before, it cannot be excluded that in the thinly sampled areas of the search space there are also solutions with a very low fitness. But from an application point of view it is better if the fitness value shows a small sensitivity to the design of the valves. From the results obtained it can be deduced that an iterative search is best suited for the practical application of the algorithm. First, a solution with one valve should be sought. If the calculated valve does not solve the problem, the obtained valve configuration model $P^{t=end}$ of this run can be used to bias the search for two valves. This procedure shows a stable convergence behaviour, see for instance Table 4 configuration 3.

The approach we presented can be extended in several ways. The current implementation of the algorithm is a simple single-objective optimization with user-defined weighting factors. However, a number of other constraints can be imposed on the solution. These include the cost of the valves, the cost of installation in the plant and system-related requirements for the practical design of the valves. As a system-related requirement, it could be formulated that valves in positions with high system pressures preferably have a small K_{vs}-value to reduce the noise of the blow-off. If additionally these points are considered, it would make sense to reformulate the problem and carry out a multi-objective optimization. A comparison of different multi-objective optimization algorithms might be useful at this stage. Furthermore, only a specific emergency shutdown event was investigated here. If a system is also operated in other steady-state operating points, also an emergency shutdown from these points should be included in the optimization task to ensure that the reversal of the shaft's direction of rotation is completely eliminated.

References

1. Amaran, S., Sahinidis, N.V., Sharda, B., Bury, S.J.: Simulation optimization: a review of algorithms and applications. Ann. Oper. Res. **240**(1), 351–380 (2015). https://doi.org/10.1007/s10479-015-2019-x
2. Bekker, J., Oliver, Y.: Using the population-based incremental learning algorithm with computer simulation: Some applications. S. Afr. J. Industr. Eng. **19**, 53–72 (2008)
3. Baluja, S.: Population-Based Incremental Learning: A Method for Integrating Genetic Search Based Function Optimization and Competitive Learning. Technical Report. Carnegie Mellon University, USA (1994)

4. Benini, E. Toffolo, A., Lazzaretto, A.: Centrifugal compressor of a 100 kW micro-turbine: Part 1 - Experimental and numerical investigations on overall performance. In: Proceedings ASME Turbo Expo 2003, pp. 691–698 (2003)
5. Benini, E., Toffolo, A., Lazzaretto, A.: Experimental and numerical analyses to enhance the performance of a microturbine diffuser. Exp. Thermal Fluid Sci. **30**, 427–440 (2006)
6. Carnero, M., Hernandez, J., Sánchez, M.: Optimal sensor location in chemical plants using estimation of distribution algorithms. Ind. Eng. Chem. Res. **57**, 12149–12164 (2018)
7. DIN EN 60534: Industrial process control valves; Part 1: Control valve terminology and general considerations. Beuth-Verlag, Berlin (2005)
8. Fu, M.C., Glover, F., April, J.: Simulation optimization: A review, new developments, and applications. In: Proceedings - Winter Simulation Conference, pp. 83–95 (2005)
9. Gambini, M., Vellini, M.: Preliminary design of radial inflow turbines. Turbomachinery. STME, pp. 199–253. Springer, Cham (2021). https://doi.org/10.1007/978-3-030-51299-6_5
10. Lüdtke, K.H.: Process Centrifugal Compressors: Basics, Function, Operation, Design. Application. Springer, Berlin (2004) https://doi.org/10.1007/978-3-662-09449-5
11. Ma, S.B., Afzal, A., Kim, K.Y.: Optimization of ring cavity in a centrifugal compressor based on comparative analysis of optimization algorithms. Appl. Therm. Eng. **138**, 633–647 (2018)
12. Mehrnia, S., Miyagawa, K., Kusaka, J., Nakamura, Y.: Radial turbine optimization under unsteady flow using nature-inspired algorithms. Aerospace Sci. Technol. **103**, 105903 (2020)
13. Du, K.-L., Swamy, M.N.S.: Estimation of distribution algorithms. Search and Optimization by Metaheuristics, pp. 105–119. Springer, Cham (2016). https://doi.org/10.1007/978-3-319-41192-7_7
14. Poling, B. E., Prausnitz, J. M., O'Connell, J. P.: Properties of Gases and Liquids. McGraw-Hill Education, New York (2001)
15. Schulze, R., Dietel, F., Jäkel, J., Richter, H.: An artificial immune system for classifying aerodynamic instabilities of centrifugal compressors. Int. J. Comput. Intell. Appl. **11**, 1250002 (2012)
16. Sugimura, K. Kobayashi, H. Nishida, H.: Design optimization and experimental verification of centrifugal compressors with curvilinear element blades. In: Proceedings of ASME Turbo Expo 2012: Turbine Technical Conference and Exposition, pp. 779–791 (2012)
17. Tüchler, S., Chen, Z., Copeland, C.D.: Multipoint shape optimisation of an automotive radial compressor using a coupled computational fluid dynamics and genetic algorithm approach. Energy **165A**, 543–561 (2018)
18. VDI 2045 Part 2: Acceptance and performance tests on turbo compressors and displacement compressors; theory and examples (1993)
19. VDI 2173: Fluidic characteristic quantities of control valves and their determination (2007)
20. Wang, J., Wang, Z., Ma, X., Feng, G., Zhang, C.: Locating sensors in complex engineering systems for fault isolation using population-based incremental learning. Energies **13**, 310–324 (2020)

3D-2D Registration Using X-Ray Simulation and CMA-ES

Tianci Wen[1]([✉])(iD), Radu P. Mihail[2](iD), and Franck P. Vidal[1](iD)

[1] School of Computer Science and Electronic Engineering, Bangor University, Bangor, UK
{t.wen,f.vidal}@bangor.ac.uk
[2] Department of Computer Science, Valdosta State University, Georgia, USA
rpmihail@valdosta.edu

Abstract. Radiographs of the hand are useful in diagnosing and staging diseases such as rheumatoid arthritis (RA) and other musculoskeletal diseases. Radiographs are projections of the 3D anatomy, with the useful information such as pose and pathology becoming lost in the process. We propose a 3D hand pose recovery method for radiographs of hands using a novel hybrid image registration method. Our pose recovery pipeline consists of aligning a simulated X-ray (digitally reconstructed radiograph) of an articulated phantom mesh model to a real hand radiograph using Covariance Matrix Adaptation Evolution Strategy. Early results demonstrate that our approach works well. Further inquiry is required to evaluate the applicability of our registration approach to other articulated musculoskeletal anatomy.

Keywords: 2D–3D registration · X-ray simulation · Artificial evolution · Evolutionary computing · CMA-ES · DRRs

1 Introduction

Computational methods of disease tracking and progression prediction based on the analysis of medical imagery is receiving heightened attention in recent years. Chronic diseases of the human musculoskeletal system caused by autoimmune processes lead to progressive, irreversible anatomical changes over time. In the case of rheumatoid arthritis (RA), a chronic inflammatory disorder with largely unknown pathogenesis, patients often present to the clinician with swelling of the hands. If left untreated, the disease progresses in distinct stages, from joint pain, swelling, stiffness to cartilage loss, bone erosion, deformities and total loss of joint function [15].

Plain radiographic imaging (X-rays) of the hands is done routinely for diagnostic and tracking purposes, as routine care for RA patients. Since hand radiographs are relatively inexpensive and low-risk, they provide clinicians with baselines, and visible changes over time. The rate of disease progression is modulated by treatment and lifestyle choices, but distinct deformations have been

© Springer Nature Switzerland AG 2021
P. A. Castillo and J. L. Jiménez Laredo (Eds.): EvoApplications 2021, LNCS 12694, pp. 453–468, 2021.
https://doi.org/10.1007/978-3-030-72699-7_29

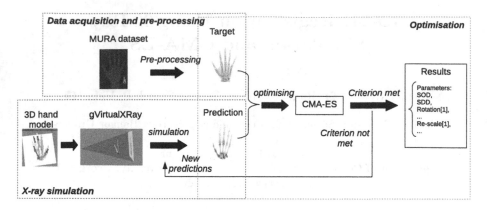

Fig. 1. Registration pipeline based on X-ray simulation and CMA-ES. (Color figure online)

documented [17,19]. Typical deformities include boutonnière, swan-neck, hitch-hiker's thumb and claw toe, Other, less obvious changes include bone erosions, induced by the inflammation of the synovial membrane, as shown in Fig. 2.

Radiographs are projections of 3D structures, hence much information is lost. The anatomy of the hand varies among different individuals, e.g. the ratio of the lengths of the long bones is not always consistent. Using this observation and the ability to speedily create digitally reconstructed radiographs (DRRs), we propose a method to register a 3D mesh model of a hand to Posterior Anterior (PA) view hand radiograph.

Anomaly detection in hand radiographs is important for disease staging and monitoring. Our registration method is a pre-processing step for algorithms that modify the mesh model using domain-specific knowledge to better track disease-induced changes without expensive volumetric scans that clinicians may not be equipped with or are cost-prohibitive. Time-series, patient-specific information regarding the progression of a disease is critical for treatment planning and drug effectiveness monitoring.

Our main contribution consists of a novel registration method of a highly articulated and anatomically correct 3D mesh model, hereby referred to as the phantom model, to a real radiograph using a DRR software (https://sourceforge.net/p/gvirtualxray/) [21,22]. Our proposed optimisation process (inside green box in Fig. 1) consists of using an evolutionary algorithm to solve for the articulated 3D pose of the virtual hand that best fits the real radiograph. Similar works on 3D/2D registration using Evolutionary Algorithms (EAs) are presented by Gomez et al. [8,9]. We use Covariance Matrix Adaptation Evolution Strategy (CMA-ES) [12] from Pymoo [3] as the numerical optimisation algorithm. This paper is based on previous work where synthetic data were used [25]. The paper is organised as follows: Sect. 2 provides an overview of related work, Sect. 3 describes our method, including the data used and data pre-processing, Sect. 4

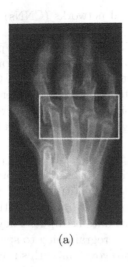

(a)

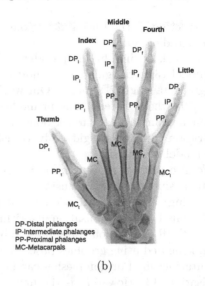

(b)

Fig. 2. a) Erosions induced by RA inflammatory processes visible around the red asterisks. Image source [19]. b) Naming of hand fingers and bones. Source: The MURA dataset.

describes our results as well as quantitative and qualitative evaluation, Sect. 5 provides conclusions and describes future work.

2   Background

Medical image registration is important for pathology modeling, treatment and surgery planning, diagnosis and prognosis, among other tasks. Work in this area has focused on all imaging modalities, including projective (X-rays) and volumetric, either from computed tomography (CT) or magnetic resonance imaging (MRI), and a combination 2D to 3D and 3D to 3D registration. The medical image literature is vast, and we refer the interest reader to several review papers [1, 23, 24].

Registration of DRRs of articulated objects to real radiographs is scarcely investigated. Related work in this area falls into several categories: 2D radiograph to 3D volumetric scan registration [5, 7], biplanar radiograph to model registration [2, 4, 14].

Kanhonou et al. [14] propose a method for automatic registration of phantom tibia and femur to biplanar radiographs for pathology detection using rigid transformations as the optimisation variables. Englander et al. [4] propose a vision-based method for in-vivo registration of phantom tibia and femur models to high-speed biplanar radiographs to study Anterior Cruciate Ligament (ACL) length and strain during dynamic activity. Aubert et al. [2] propose a spine reconstruction method using deep convolutional neural networks (CNNs) from biplanar radiographs.

Our work fits in a hybrid paradigm: the registration of a DRR from a phantom model (3D triangular mesh model) using simulated radiography to a real radiograph (a single 2D image). Our work aligns most closely with that of Gong et al. [10] who register phantom models in DRRs to fluoroscopy imagery for treatment planning in complex bone fractures. In contrast with [10] where the registration involves a rigid body transform, we register a highly articulated mesh model of a hand.

We also propose an automatic method for the registration of a hand phantom to a single radiograph using rigid transformations (translation, rotation and scaling) as the optimisation variables. Due to the repetitive use of DRR calculations by the optimisation algorithm, an extremely fast implementation is needed. DRR calculation codes often rely on CT scans data as input. They can be implemented using graphics processing unit (GPU) programming to speedup computations [6]. Polygon meshes can be converted into voxel data; this is called voxelisation [13]. However, as the hand model is deformed by the optimisation algorithm for each DRR, this approach will be far too costly and can actually be avoided. The alternative is to use a fast X-ray simulation model that can support polygon meshes [16]. It can be efficiently implemented on GPU using real-time Computer Graphics (CG) techniques. This approach is the most suitable one in our application context as real-time CG techniques are designed for polygon meshes. The Virtual X-ray Imaging Library on GPU (gVirtualXRay) provides an open-source implementation that can run on laptops, desktop computers, and large supercomputers. gVirtualXRay is a C++ library to simulate X-ray imaging [22]. It also provides a Python 3 wrapper that we used to prototype our framework in this study.

3   Methodology

3.1   The MURA Dataset

The MURA dataset, freely available on GitHub at https://stanfordmlgroup. github.io/competitions/mura/, contains 40,561 musculoskeletal radiographs from 14,863 clinical studies of 12,173 different patients [18]. It focus on upper extremities of human body, including elbow, finger, forearm, hand, humerus, shoulders and wrist. Each radiograph is manually labelled as normal or abnormal. 15 radiographs (Fig. 3) are selected to test the performance of our approach (Sect. 4.1), which only require a single radiograph.

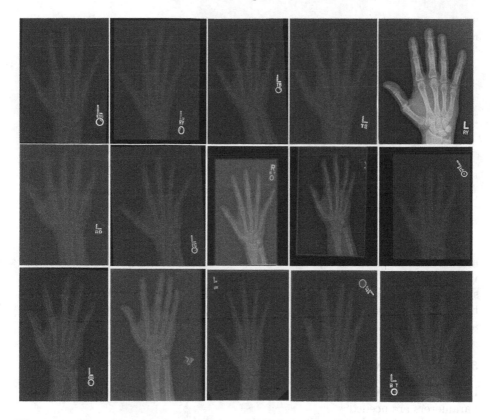

Fig. 3. 15 selected hand radiographs from MURA dataset. Images are numbered from image 1 (top left) to image 15 (bottom right). Top row: image 1–5, middle row: image 6–10, and bottom row: image 11–15.

Unlike typical medical images such as Digital Imaging and Communications in Medicine (DICOM) [11], radiographs in the MURA dataset are in Portable Network Graphics (PNG) format which a lot of information is missing (Table 1). To adapt data to use in our experiments, those radiographs are pre-processed to improve the structural difference between the object and other areas. More discussion about image pre-processing in Sect. 3.2.

3.2 Image Pre-processing

Although the MURA dataset was created for the purpose of abnormality detection, it is also useful for testing the performance of our registration framework. We focus on hand radiographs with PA views. We manually pre-processed 15 different radiographs as follow: i) each radiograph is cropped so that only the hand part remains, ii) the left or right marker is removed and the area surrounding the hand is "cleaned" (to have same pixel values), iii) the skin around finger is removed as much as possible, iv) the radiographs, which are negative images,

Table 1. Information needed to simulate X-ray radiographs that are present in typical medical imaging file formats such as DICOM but missing in the PNG files from the MURA dataset.

Properties	PNG	DICOM
X-ray tube voltage	Plausible energy beam	Known
Quantisation	8-bit	16-bit
source-to-object distance (SOD)	Need to estimate	Known
source-to-detector distance (SDD)	Need to estimate	Known
Pixel spacing (mm)	Need to estimate	Known
Object location	Need to estimate	Known
Object orientation	Need to estimate	Known

are inverted to match the positive images generated by X-ray simulation, and v) all images are re-scaled to the same size of simulated X-ray images. Corresponding images are shown in Fig. 4. In each image, we define the name of each finger (from left to right): thumb, index finger, middle finger, the fourth finger and little finger, as shown in Fig. 2.

3.3   GVirtualXRay

In order to simulate an X-ray image (inside blue box of Fig. 1), some input parameters are needed:

- An incident energy beam,
- A 3D object to scan, including its geometry, position, and orientation.
- A virtual X-ray detector, including its pixel resolution, pixel spacing, and orientation.
- The source-to-object distance (SOD),
- The source-to-detector distance (SDD).

All these parameters must be set before a DRR can be generated. Some of them can be set once for all, such as the incident energy beam, the detector's resolution and orientation, and pixel spacing. As mentioned above, the actual values are unknown due to the use of PNG files instead of DICOM files in the MURA dataset. We used plausible values. The registration consists in tuning all the other parameters.

3.4   Optimisation

CMA-ES [12] is a widely used optimisation algorithm which provides a great baseline result. Other optimisation algorithms could be used for further evaluations of our approaches such as multi-objective optimisation algorithms [20]. CMA-ES is a special evolution strategy with adaption of covariance matrix.

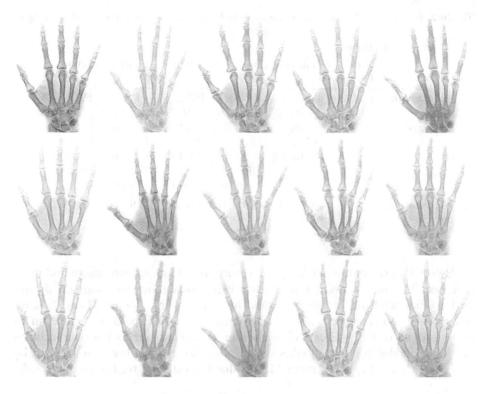

Fig. 4. 15 selected hand radiographs from the MURA dataset after pre-processing. Images are numbered from Image 1 (top left) to Image 15 (bottom right). Top row: Images 1–5, middle row: Images 6–10, and bottom row: Images 11–15.

It is used to solve complex problems that require derivative-free optimisation. An evolution strategy is inspired by biological evolution. The idea is: initialising individuals (a set of solutions), recombination and mutation is used to create new individuals, best individuals are then selected based on their fitness value to become the parents of next generation of individuals. This process is repeated until satisfactory results (set termination criterion) are found. In Evolution Strategies (ES), new individuals are created by sampling from the probability distribution. In CMA-ES, however, sampling is achieved through the use of a covariance matrix of the distribution. This gives CMA-ES great advantages in the ill-conditioned problems which small changes of input variables result in large change of output. The optimisation process is shown in Fig. 1 (green box).

Table 2. Rotation and re-scaling parameters to be optimised and corresponding ranges.

Parameters	Bones					
	Whole hand	Thumb	Index	Middle	Fourth	Little
Rotation range (degrees)	[-20, 20]	MC_t: $[-10, 10]$ $[-20, 0]$ PP_t: $[-10, 10]$	PP_i: $[-10, 10]$ $[-20, 0]$ IP_i: $[-20, 0]$ DP_i: $[-20, 0]$	PP_m: $[-10, 10]$ $[-20, 0]$ IP_m: $[-20, 0]$ DP_m: $[-20, 0]$	PP_f: $[-10, 10]$ $[-20, 0]$ IP_f: $[-20, 0]$ DP_f: $[-20, 0]$	PP_l: $[-10, 10]$ $[-20, 0]$ IP_l: $[-20, 0]$ DP_l: $[-20, 0]$
Rescaling ratio	-	$[0.9, 1.1]$	$[0.9, 1.1]$	$[0.9, 1.1]$	$[0.9, 1.1]$	$[0.9, 1.1]$

Before thoptimisation, all images are normalised to have zero-mean and unit-variance. This is to prevent that some features becoming too dominant during optimisation while other features would be less relevant. We use Mean absolute error (MAE) to construct the objective function, i.e. as the fitness function to be minimised by CMA-ES. MAE is the sum of absolute errors between samples and then divided by total number of samples (Eq. 1). The best number can be achieved is zero. Typically, lower MAE value indicates better optimising result.

$$\text{MAE}(\mathbf{Y}, \hat{\mathbf{Y}}) = \frac{1}{w \times h} \sum_{j}^{h} \sum_{i}^{w} \left| \hat{\mathbf{Y}}(i, j) - \mathbf{Y}(i, j) \right| \qquad (1)$$

where $\mathbf{Y}$ is the target image, $\hat{\mathbf{Y}}$ is the predicted image, w and h are width and height of target and predicted images, respectively.

Our registration problem is considered to be complex both in terms of number of parameters and the corresponding data range. There are 38 parameters that need to be optimised including 2 distance parameters: SOD and SDD. SOD is a ratio of SDD with a value between 0.7 and 0.95. By using ratios, we make sure that the distance between the source and the object, is always less than the distance between the source and the detector. SDD ranges between 10 and 1000 centimetres. There are 22 rotating angles and 14 rescaling factors, which are shown in Table 2. The rotation range is determined based on the modelling of rotations of the real hand except the whole hand, which is determined by a priori knowledge of the PA pose but adding some degrees of complexity. There are no constraint handlers implemented in our framework since our work is still at preliminary stage. Further improvements of registration results would certainly involves modelling restrictions among parameters.

Table 3. Registration results for 15 different target images along with corresponding metric values.

Image number & Metrics	Target	Prediction	Error map	Number of objective function calls
1 & MAE=0.3937 ZNCC=0.7060				2050
2 & MAE=0.3497 ZNCC=0.7378				1964
3 & MAE=0.4060 ZNCC=0.7264				1934
4 & MAE=0.3953 ZNCC=0.7051				2056
5 & MAE=0.4398 ZNCC=0.6603				2050
6 & MAE=0.3947 ZNCC=0.7179				2056
7 & MAE=0.4029 ZNCC=0.7012				2055
8 & MAE=0.3765 ZNCC=0.7202				1886
				Continued on next page

(continued)

Table 3. (*continued*)

Image number & Metrics	Target	Prediction	Error map	Number of objective function calls
9 & MAE=0.4356 ZNCC=0.6130				2119
10 & MAE=0.4790 ZNCC=0.6503				2308
11 & MAE=0.4167 ZNCC=0.7094				2186
12 & MAE=0.4073 ZNCC=0.7156				1817
13 & MAE=0.3903 ZNCC=0.7218				2016
14 & MAE=0.4464 ZNCC=0.6535				1898
15 & MAE=0.4206 ZNCC=0.7409				2027

4 Results

There are two ways to assess the effectiveness of our method in solving the registration problem. In any case, several runs must be performed to gather statistically meaningful data. In Sect. 4.1, we selected 15 different radiographs and tested our method once on each of the radiographs. The emphasis is on **data and simulation variability: For different input images, does the algorithm always provide outputs of similar quality?** In Sect. 4.2, we selected the images of the worse, median and best registrations of Sect. 4.1. The registration is then repeated 15 times for these three images. The emphasis is on **optimisation algorithm variability: For a given input image, does the algorithm always provide a similar output?** We also aim to determine if some images harder to register than others.

4.1 Data and Simulation Variability

Here, we aim to determine if the algorithm always provide outputs of similar quality on different input images. 15 registrations using 15 different real X-ray images were performed, i.e. one registration per image, due to computational demand (about 4 h per registration on a single Intel Core i5-8400 (2.80GHz) central processing unit (CPU) and a single NVIDIA GeForce GTX 1070 Ti GPU). The 15 pre-processed images that we used are shown in Fig. 4. MAE is used to compare target and predicted images during registration because it is relatively faster to compute. Zero mean normalised cross correlation (ZNCC) is used for visual analysis of the predicted images after registration. It is a measurement of similarity between two images. Since it is hard to interpret the value of MAE, ZNCC is very helpful to analyse the performance of the registrations.

To compute ZNCC, the target and predicted images are normalised first, which is subtracting all pixels by the mean value and divided by standard deviation. Normalised target and predicted images are then multiplied. Finally, all values are added and divided by total number of pixels (see Eq. 2). ZNCC primarily concentrates on template matching and completely different images might have very high scores.

$$\text{ZNCC}\left(\hat{\mathbf{Y}}, \mathbf{Y}\right) = \frac{1}{w \times h} \sum_{j}^{h} \sum_{i}^{w} \frac{\left(\hat{\mathbf{Y}} - \overline{\hat{\mathbf{Y}}}\right)\left(\mathbf{Y} - \overline{\mathbf{Y}}\right)}{\sigma_{\hat{\mathbf{Y}}} \sigma_{\mathbf{Y}}} \tag{2}$$

where $\overline{\mathbf{Y}}$ and $\overline{\hat{\mathbf{Y}}}$ are mean pixel value of target and predicted images, and $\sigma_{\mathbf{Y}}$ and $\sigma_{\hat{\mathbf{Y}}}$ are standard deviation of the pixel values in target and predicted images.

ZNCC ranges from -1 to 1, where i) the value is close to 1, the two images are highly similar which implies high level of correlation, ii) the value is 0, two images are extremely different which implies there is no correlation, iii) the value is -1, one image is the negative of the other image which implies they are anti-correlated or inversely correlated.

Table 3 lists results from 15 registrations. By looking at predictions and associated error maps, there are 6 registrations that successfully recovered all 5 fingers, where ZNCC is all above 0.7. There are 6 registrations that successfully recovered 4 fingers, where ZNCC is all above 0.7 except image 14. There are 3 registrations that recovered 1 finger, where ZNCC is all below 0.7. It is clear from

Table 3 that Images 5, 9, 10 and 14 are visually worse than the other images. This trend is not necessarily visible in Fig. 5 (bar chart of the MAE for each registration). However, Fig. 5 clearly show two groups: Images 5, 9, 10 and 14 exhibit a significantly lower ZNCC than the other images.

Results demonstrate that our approaches perform well. However, there are some problems that need to be addressed in future researches:

1. Some fingers are not within images. For example, Registration 4, 12 and 14 have the middle finger extended outside the image space. Registration 10 has middle finger and fourth finger extended outside the image space.
2. In 3 registrations (5, 9 and 10) only the thumb is recovered, the middle finger is matched with the target's index finger, the fourth finger is matched with the target's middle finger, and the little finger is matched with the target's fourth finger.
3. A finger is overlapped with another finger. In Registration 4 and 8, the little finger is overlapped with the fourth finger. In Registration 9, the index finger is overlapped with middle finger.

4.2 Optimisation Algorithm Variability

Here, we aim to determine if the algorithm always provides outputs of similar quality on the same input image. We selected the best, median and worse results from the previous subsection, i.e. Images 2, 3, and 10. We perform another 14 registrations on each image and included their previous results (i.e. a total of 15 results per image) to test the variability of the algorithm, CMA-ES, when the input data is the same. Then we compute the mean and standard deviations (STDEVs) of MAE, ZNCC and number of calls to objective function over the 15 runs. The data is summarised in Table 4. It shows that CMA-ES provides registrations of consistent quality, both in terms of MAE and ZNCC, for Images 2

Table 4. Results for 15 registrations on Images 2, 3 and 10.

Image number	MAE (mean ± STDEV)	ZNCC (mean ± STDEV)	Number of objective function calls (mean ± STDEV)
2 (best run in Table 3)	0.3460 ± 0.0055	0.7426 ± 0.0074	2105 ± 189
3 (median run in Table 3)	0.4076 ± 0.0019	0.7227 ± 0.0035	1954 ± 132
10 (worse run in Table 3)	0.4701 ± 0.0218	0.6597 ± 0.0184	2137 ± 162

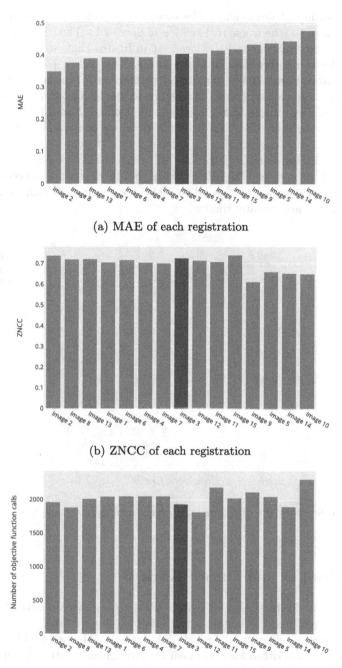

(a) MAE of each registration

(b) ZNCC of each registration

(c) Number of objective function calls of each registration

Fig. 5. Bar charts for quantitative results shown in Table 3. All data is sorted on MAE and the median result is highlighted in red.

and 3 (low standard deviations). However, the standard deviations are much higher for Image 10 (the worse registration of Sect. 4.1). The MAE is higher than for the other two images, and the lower. It indicates that, somehow, Image 10 is a lot harder to register than Images 2 and 3. The scatter plot in Fig. 6 shows the MAE (circles) and ZNCC (triangles) plotted as a function of the number of generations. Green and purple marks are aligned and form horizontal lines: CMA-ES produces consistent registrations for Images 2 and 3. Blue marks are scattered over the plot: CMA-ES does not produce consistent registrations for Image 10.

CMA-ES can produce registrations of good quality consistently for some images. For other images, CMA-ES may fail. Further research is needed to comprehend what makes Image 10 hard to register compared to Images 2 and 3 as the three images are visually similar.

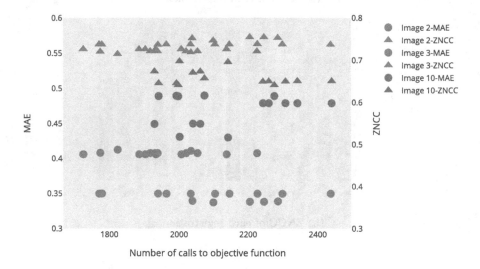

Fig. 6. Scatter plots of results for 15 registrations on Image 2, 3 and 10.

5   Conclusions and Future Work

We have shown the feasibility of using DRRs to register an articulated phantom model to real hand radiographs without visible pathology. Our registration framework heavily relies on numerical optimisation. We used CMA-ES, a popular evolutionary algorithm for non-linear or non-convex continuous optimisation problems. Performing the registration on different X-ray images showed that results were not always of the same quality. However, CMA-ES produces similar results with low variability during 15 runs on the same image. This demonstrate that the stochastic nature of CMA-ES is not a concern in our case. It also indicates that some images are harder than others to register.

In the future, we will use this work as an initialisation step in a pipeline that tweaks the geometry of a phantom model to match the pathology seen in real radiographs, such as those afflicted by RA. This will allow clinicians access to clean (already segmented) volumetric rendering of pathological skeletal anatomy without the high doses of ionising radiation typically associated with CT scans, or where there is no access to volumetric scans.

We are also planning to address some of the problems discussed in previous section:

- We can pad white spaces (same pixel values as background) around images to make them bigger. The alternative way is to impose constraints on parameters where fingers are not allowed to extend outside images.
- There are some images (e.g. Image 5) where fingers are mis-matched or overlapped. We can look into multi-objective optimisation algorithms with both MAE and ZNCC as objectives. ZNCC is very helpful for shape matching. The algorithm are working by minimising MAE and maximising ZNCC in the same time.

References

1. Andrade, N., Faria, F.A., Cappabianco, F.A.M.: A practical review on medical image registration: from rigid to deep learning based approaches. In: 2018 31st SIBGRAPI Conference on Graphics, Patterns and Images (SIBGRAPI), pp. 463–470. IEEE (2018)
2. Aubert, B., Vazquez, C., Cresson, T., Parent, S., de Guise, J.A.: Toward automated 3D spine reconstruction from biplanar radiographs using CNN for statistical spine model fitting. IEEE Trans Med Imaging **38**(12), 2796–2806 (2019)
3. Blank, J., Deb, K.: Pymoo: multi-objective optimization in python. IEEE Access **8**, 89497–89509 (2020)
4. Englander, Z.A., Martin, J.T., Ganapathy, P.K., Garrett, W.E., DeFrate, L.E.: Automatic registration of MRI-based joint models to high-speed biplanar radiographs for precise quantification of in vivo anterior cruciate ligament deformation during gait. J. Biomech. **81**, 36–44 (2018)
5. Esteban, J., Grimm, M., Unberath, M., Zahnd, G., Navab, N.: Towards fully automatic X-ray to CT registration. In: International Conference on Medical Image Computing and Computer-Assisted Intervention. pp. 631–639. Springer (2019)
6. Folkerts, M., Jia, X., Gu, X., Choi, D., Majumdar, A., Jiang, S.:MO-FF-A4-05: implementation and evaluation of various DRR algorithms on GPU. Med. Phys. **37**(6Part6), 3367-3367 (2010)
7. Gao, C., Liu, X., Gu, W., Killeen, B., Armand, M., Taylor, R., Unberath, M.: Generalizing spatial transformers to projective geometry with applications to 2D/3D registration. arXiv preprint arXiv:2003.10987 (2020)
8. Gómez, O., Ibáñez, O., Valsecchi, A., Bermejo, E., Molina, D., Cordón, O.: Performance analysis of real-coded evolutionary algorithms under a computationally expensive optimization scenario: 3D–2D comparative radiography. Appl. Soft Comput. **97**, (2020)
9. Gómez, O., Ibanez, O., Valsecchi, A., Cordón, O., Kahana, T.: 3D-2D silhouette-based image registration for comparative radiography-based forensic identification. Pattern Recogn. **83**, 469–480 (2018)

10. Gong, R.H., Stewart, J., Abolmaesumi, P.: Multiple-object 2-D-3-D registration for noninvasive pose identification of fracture fragments. IEEE Trans. Biomed. Eng. **58**(6), 1592–1601 (2011)
11. Graham, R.N., Perriss, R.W., Scarsbrook, A.F.: DICOM demystified: a review of digital file formats and their use in radiological practice. Clin. Radiol. **60**(11), 1133–1140 (2005)
12. Hansen, N., Ostermeier, A.: Completely derandomized self-adaptation in evolution strategies. Evol. Comput. **9**(2), 159–195 (2001)
13. Huang, J., Yagel, R., Filippov, V., Kurzion, Y.: An accurate method for voxelizing polygon meshes. In: Kaufman, A.E., Yagel, R., Lorensen, W.E. (eds.) Proceeding of the 1998 IEEE Symposium on Volume Visualization, VVS 1998, Research Triangle Park, NC, USA, 19–20 October 1998, pp. 119–126. ACM/IEEE Comput Soc (1998)
14. International Journal of Computer Assisted Radiology and Surgery Registration and motion analysis. **9**(1), 31–34 (2014). https://doi.org/10.1007/s11548-014-1017-9
15. Neumann, E., Lefèvre, S., Zimmermann, B., Gay, S., Müller-Ladner, U.: Rheumatoid arthritis progression mediated by activated synovial fibroblasts. Trends Mol. Med. **16**(10), 458–468 (2010)
16. N. Freud, P.Duvauchelle, Létang, J.M., D.Babot: Fast and robust ray casting algorithms for virtual X-ray imaging. Nuclear Instruments and Methods in Physics Research Section B: Beam Interactions with Materials and Atoms 248(1), 175–180 (2006)
17. Illustrated Handbook of Rheumatic and Musculo-Skeletal Diseases. Springer, Cham (2019). https://doi.org/10.1007/978-3-030-03664-5_9
18. Rajpurkar, P., et al.: Mura: Large dataset for abnormality detection in musculoskeletal radiographs. arXiv preprint arXiv:1712.06957 (2017)
19. Schett, G.: Erosive arthritis. Arthritis Res. Therapy **9**(1), 1–6 (2007)
20. Valsecchi, A., Bermejo, E., Damas, S., Cordón, O.: Metaheuristics for Medical Image Registration. In: Martí, R., Pardalos, P.M., Resende, M.G.C. (eds.) Handbook of Heuristics, pp. 1079–1101. Springer, Cham (2018). https://doi.org/10.1007/978-3-319-07124-4_56
21. Vidal, F.P., Garnier, M., Freud, N., Létang, J.M., John, N.W.: Simulation of X-ray attenuation on the GPU. In: Proceedings of Theory and Practice of Computer Graphics 2009, pp. 25–32. Eurographics Association, Cardiff, UK, Jun 2009
22. Vidal, F.P., Villard, P.-F.: Development and validation of real-time simulation of X-ray imaging with respiratory motion. Comput. Med. Imaging Graph. **49**, 1–15 (2016)
23. Viergever, M.A., Antoine Maintz, J., Klein, S., Murphy, K., Staring, M., Pluim, J.P.: A survey of medical image registration-under review. Med. Image Anal. **33**, 140–144 (2016)
24. Wang, M., Li, P.: A review of deformation models in medical image registration. J. Med. Biol. Eng. **39**(1), 1–17 (2019)
25. Wen, T., Mihail, R., Al-maliki, S., Létang, J.M., Vidal, F.P.: Registration of 3D triangular models to 2D X-ray projections using black-box optimisation and X-ray simulation. In: Computer Graphics and Visual Computing (CGVC), pp. 105–113. The Eurographics Association (2019)

Lateralized Approach for Robustness Against Attacks in Emotion Categorization from Images

Harisu Abdullahi Shehu[1]([✉])[ID], Abubakar Siddique[1][ID], Will N. Browne[1][ID], and Hedwig Eisenbarth[2][ID]

[1] School of Engineering and Computer Science, Victoria University of Wellington, 6012 Wellington, New Zealand
{harisushehu,abubakar.siddique,will.browne}@ecs.vuw.ac.nz
[2] School of Psychology, Victoria University of Wellington, 6012 Wellington, New Zealand
hedwig.eisenbarth@vuw.ac.nz

Abstract. Deep learning has achieved a high classification accuracy on image classification tasks, including emotion categorization. However, deep learning models are highly vulnerable to adversarial attacks. Even a small change, imperceptible to a human (e.g. one-pixel attack), can decrease the classification accuracy of deep models. One reason could be their homogeneous representation of knowledge that considers all pixels in an image to be equally important is easily fooled. Enabling multiple representations of the same object, e.g. at the constituent and holistic viewpoints provides robustness against attacking a single view. This heterogeneity is provided by lateralization in biological systems. Lateral asymmetry of biological intelligence suggests heterogeneous learning of objects. This heterogeneity allows information to be learned at different levels of abstraction, i.e. at the constituent and the holistic level, enabling multiple representations of the same object.

This work aims to create a novel system that can consider heterogeneous features e.g. mouth, eyes, nose, and jaw in a face image for emotion categorization. The experimental results show that the lateralized system successfully considers constituent and holistic features to exhibit robustness to unimportant and irrelevant changes to emotion in an image, demonstrating performance accuracy better than (or similar) to the deep learning system (VGG19). Overall, the novel lateralized method shows a stronger resistance to changes (10.86–47.72% decrease) than the deep model (25.15–83.43% decrease). The advances arise by allowing heterogeneous features, which enable constituent and holistic representations of image components.

Keywords: Adversarial attacks · CK+ · Emotion categorization · Facial expression · Lateralization · Learning Classifier Systems (LCS) · sUpervised Classifier System (UCS) · VGG19.

© Springer Nature Switzerland AG 2021
P. A. Castillo and J. L. Jiménez Laredo (Eds.): EvoApplications 2021, LNCS 12694, pp. 469–485, 2021.
https://doi.org/10.1007/978-3-030-72699-7_30

1   Introduction

Emotion categorization, based on facial expression, plays an important role in human-computer interaction [1]. Nowadays, there is a growing demand for robots in hotels and retail stores to interact with customers. However, these robots need to understand human emotions in this close-proximity situation. It helps to improve their interaction with the customers to achieve an enhanced customer experience [2]. The term emotion categorization is used here as we contend that humans can superficially express an emotional state that is different from the one that they are experiencing internally.

Deep Learning (DL) based systems have widely been used for image classification [3], including emotion categorization. These systems have demonstrated limited competency by achieving high performance on many state-of-the-art datasets as well as having won many challenges set up by the data science community such as the ImageNet challenge [4]. However, their homogeneous representation of knowledge has made them vulnerable to adversarial attacks, i.e. deliberate changes to the image in an attempt to fool the classifier [5]. For instance, a small modification made to the test or train data might mislead the model to misclassify the input object [6].

On the other hand, biological intelligence supports heterogeneity. It has been hypothesized that lateral asymmetry of the vertebrate brains enables the processing of information at different levels of abstraction, i.e. at a constituent level and holistic level [7]. For instance, the left hemisphere processes sensory input at the constituent (elementary) level, whereas, the right hemisphere processes the same signal at a higher level of abstraction, up to the top holistic level. This heterogeneity concept has recently been shown beneficial at handling noisy data in artificial visual classification systems [8].

The main goal of this work is to create a lateralized system, inspired by the lateralization in biological intelligence, for emotion categorization that will be robust against image changes. As the lateralized approach is considered to be heterogeneous, we anticipate that the novel system will lead to obtaining a much higher accuracy than a homogeneous DL based system when obfuscate changes are made to an image. This is because an emotion, such as happy, may be visible in individual features (e.g. eyes, mouth, jaw) plus their higher-order relationships rather than simply pixel colors (e.g. on a cheek or foreground in an image). Since a constituent or a holistic feature may exhibit robustness against a specific change, these features could be combined, at different levels of abstraction, to obtain overall robustness against a variety of changes. One half of the system will consider the constituent features, whereas, the other half will handle the higher level holistic features. Subsequently, constituent level likelihood and holistic level likelihood will be computed by utilizing constituent and holistic features, respectively. Finally, these likelihoods will be utilized at different levels of abstraction to predict the emotional category of the given image.

The holistic level derived its prediction from a deep model whereas the constituent level derived its prediction from a deep model, as well as a sUpervised learning classifier systems (UCS) to reduce the spread in the average skill of a predictive model, in order to improve the overall accuracy of the system. We will compare the performance of the lateralized system with the performance of a typical DL algorithm before and after changes are made to the images. VGG19 [9] was chosen as the benchmark approach as it is the latest among other VGG models and also because it is a well tested standard model.

The rest of the paper is organized as follows: Sect. 2 provides the required background knowledge from computer vision and machine learning. It also includes the state-of-the-art relevant techniques that have been investigated for emotion categorization. Section 3 presents the lateralized system, its critical components, and the learning mechanism. The robustness of the developed lateralized approach against attacks is evaluated in Sect. 4. Section 5 provides a further explanation of the obtained results. It also explains the decision-making process of the novel system. Finally, Sect. 6 concludes the paper and hints at further studies.

2   Background

The goals of this section are two-fold: first, to review the relevant techniques that have been investigated for emotion categorization in images; and second, to provide the required background knowledge from machine learning and computer vision techniques.

2.1   Computer Vision

This section presents a brief introduction to the attacks that will be applied on the data set to evaluate the robustness of the categorization techniques. It also includes the feature extraction techniques that will be utilized in this work.

Modification Attacks. An adversarial attack is any change made to an input image with the intention to mislead a classifier to misclassify the input image. An adversarial attack can be targeted, which aims to mislead the classifier to misclassify an input to a specific/target class, or non-targeted, which aims to fool the classifier to misclassify an input image but does not specify to which class should the input be misclassified. DeepFool is one of the commonly used and well-recognized methods to generate adversarial attacks [17]. It is a simple and accurate perturbation method designed to fool a deep network model. The algorithm repeatedly applies a small change/perturbation to the original image until the newly produced image, which is known as the perturbed image, is predicted incorrectly by the deep model. This work will apply three types of adversarial attacks, i.e. (i) an enhanced version of DeepFool based adversarial attack (named Distractor Attack), (ii) sunglasses based adversarial attack (named Wrapper Attack), and a combination of distractor attack and wrapper attack (named Hybrid Attack) (see Sect. 4).

Features. The histogram oriented gradient (HOG) is one of the commonly used features in computer vision problems [18]. The HOG descriptor utilizes the occurrence of gradient orientation for the detection of complex objects. This utilization of the local gradient makes the HOG features invariant to light conditions, geometric transformation, and color variation. These features assist the lateralized system to accurately classify images based on facial expressions.

2.2 Machine Learning

This section provides an overview of the relevant deep learning and evolutionary machine learning (i.e. learning classifier systems) techniques.

Deep Learning. Inspired by the neural connections that exist in the human brain, deep learning (DL) is a methodology of extracting higher-level features from unstructured or raw data [19]. VGG19 is one of the commonly used DL models for classification problems [20] [21]. According to the VGG paper, representation depth is beneficial for classification accuracy. As such, VGG19 is chosen to be used to obtain the constituent and holistic level prediction in the novel lateralized system as it has the latest (19) weight layers among other VGG models such as the VGG16 with 16 weight layers.

Learning Classifier Systems. Learning Classifier Systems (LCSs) are a rule-based learning method developed to solve complex problems. They combine a learning component with a genetic algorithm (GA) to perform either supervised, unsupervised, or reinforcement learning. In this research, the sUpervised Classifier System (UCS) [23] is used to predict emotion categories of the constituent level likelihood in the attention phase. UCS is chosen to be used because we know the actual label of the constituent parts and also because the representation of rules in the UCS are straightforward for a human to understand [22].

2.3 Related Work

A large number of techniques have been developed for emotion categorization from images. Convolutional deep networks based techniques have been commonly used for emotion categorization. Recently, a convolutional neural network (CNN) based system is created to classify six basic plus neutral emotions of the facial action coding system [10]. Initially, a face in an image was detected using the Viola-Jones algorithm [11]. Subsequently, the face area was cropped to eliminate the surrounding unimportant data. These cropped images were converted to grayscale and facial features were extracted by using the edge detection technique. Finally, these extracted features were used as input problem instances for the CNN model. This system achieved a performance accuracy of 79.8% on the FER2013 dataset [12]. However, an optimization technique, which might provide an improvement on the accuracy, had not been applied on the CNN. Therefore, the achieved accuracy might be improved with the application of an optimization technique.

Another attempt was made to create a deep CNN based framework for emotion classification in real-time [13]. The proposed network consisted of four separate modules, each of which had multiple layers. The generalizability was achieved by using images from various sources, e.g. a mixture of movie snapshots, emotion datasets such as JAFFE [14], personal photos, and publicly available images from the internet. Not only was the developed application fast, but also the detected emotion per frame in the real-time feed was accurate at almost 96%.

Sokolov et al. [15] proposed a CNN-based system, similar to ResNet [16], to categorize facial expressions by using cross-platform data in real-time. Emotions were estimated in the arousal-valence scale, i.e. how valence or aroused a person is. The developed system achieved a classification accuracy of 63.01%. Considering that the system was developed to categorize emotion based on two different classes (high/low valence or high/low arousal), the achieved accuracy is a little bit better than random guessing. As such, questions remain as to whether it will perform well on the six basic (or the six basic plus neutral) emotional expressions.

Recently, a lateralized system was created for the classification of cats and dogs [8]. The developed system considered the constituents and holistic features of the given image. The lateralized system outperformed other state-of-the-art deep models by 2.15%–25.84%. The study was conducted based on an artificial visual recognition system to classify cats and dogs. However, it is unknown if such lateralized systems can accurately work as an emotion categorization system since different facial features might have different contributions to different emotions, e.g. the importance of mouth shape to happy compared with fear.

Deep learning algorithms have been used to categorize emotion from images [10,13,15]. However, feeding deep models directly with face images considers the color distribution within pixels by representing all pixels in an image to be equally important. This is anticipated to make these techniques vulnerable to even a small change made to the images. Besides, different people might have a slightly different way of expressing the same emotion depending on their cultural background. This work will create a lateralized system that will be robust against changes to the pixels in an image to categorize emotion.

3   Lateralized System

The overall classification scheme of the novel lateralized system, shown in Fig. 1 is similar to a standard supervised learning system except that the prediction can be generated by two phases, i.e. context phase and attention phase. The context phase is developed by using deep models, whereas, the attention phase is developed by using UCSs. Both the phases identify, extract, and utilize constituent and holistic features to make predictions. These techniques are explained below.

3.1   Context Phase

The context phase consists of six deep models (VGG19). Five deep models are used to obtain the constituent level predictions, i.e. prediction about the face, jaw, eyes, mouth, and nose. One reason for doing this is to enable us to move away from end-to-end learning so as to improve performance by testing important feature groups as we know that certain emotional features are innately recognized [24].

The prediction is the probability that a part belongs to a candidate emotion category (class). For this purpose, a face in the given image is initially detected by utilizing the Haar cascade classifier [25]. Subsequently, the position of each constituent part is obtained by using *dlib* (an open-source c++ library for ML) [26]. These position values are used to segment the respective parts. The segmented images are given to the respective deep models and predictions are computed for each emotion category. These prediction values of each category are summed to obtain the vote for that category, e.g. the prediction values of face, jaw, eyes, mouth, and nose for category anger are added to obtain the anger vote.

$$CP = \sum_{i=1}^{n} P_i \tag{1}$$

where CP is the overall prediction that a constituent part belongs to a specific category, P_i represents the probability of each constituent part for that category, and n is the number of total constituent parts. Finally, the CP of each category are compared and the category with highest vote is considered as a constituent level likelihood (CLL), as given below.

$$CLL = \max_{x \in [1,...,m]} CP(x) \tag{2}$$

where m is the number of emotion categories.

Moreover, a deep model is used to obtain the holistic level prediction, i.e. the prediction of the whole image. The resultant highest prediction value for an emotion category is considered as a holistic level likelihood (HLL), as given below.

$$HLL = \max_{x \in [1,...,m]} P(x) \tag{3}$$

where P is the prediction value.

The system analyses the feedback received from the context phase. If the CLL and HLL predict the same category, the system makes the final prediction with confidence and generates an inhibit signal to the attention phase to stop processing. However, if the CLL and HLL predict different categories, the system generates an excite signal to the attention phase to do further analysis. The pseudo-code of the technique developed for the context phase is presented in Algorithm 1.

Algorithm 1. Algorithm adopted by the context phase

1: Initilize
2: $L_{t_i} \leftarrow$ List of images
3: $Prediction_{list} \leftarrow [\,]$
4: **repeat**
5:     **for** Image i in L_{t_i} **do**
6:         $Image_{copy} \leftarrow Original_{image}$
7:         Detect Face($Image_{copy}$) % *Detect face in the image.*
8:         Locate ROI($Image_{copy}$) % *Locate the position of region of interest (ROI) such as face, jaw, eyes, nose, mouth, in the image*
9:         Crop ROI($Image_{copy}$) % *Get a cropped copy of each ROI*
10:        $L_{roi} \leftarrow$ List of ROIs
11:        **for** each ROI in L_{roi} **do**
12:            $P_{roi} =$ getPrediction(ROI) % *Prediction of each constituent part from its associated Deep Model. Returns probability*
13:        **end for**
14:        **for** each CP in all emotion categories **do** % *For each constituent part (CP)*
15:            **for** each P_i in P_{roi} **do**
16:                CP_{cat} +=P_i % *Overall prediction that a constituent part belongs to a specific category*
17:            **end for**
18:        **end for**
19:        $CLL =$ argmax(CP_{cat}) % *The category with highest constituent prediction is considered as a constituent level likelihood (CLL).*
20:        $Prediction_{Holistic} =$ getPrediction($Original_{image}$) % *get a holistic level prediction from a DL model*
21:        $HLL =$ argmax($Prediction_{Holistic}$) % *The category with highest holistic prediction is considered as a holistic level likelihood (HLL).*
22:        **if** (CLL and HLL Predict the Same Category) **then**
23:            Add CLL and HLL
24:            MakeFinalPrediction ()
25:            GenerateInhibitSignal() % *Generate inhibit signal to stop further processing at the attention phase.*
26:        **else**
27:            GenerateExciteSignal() % *Generate excite signal to do further processing at the attention phase.*
28:        **end if**
29:    **end for**
30: **until** $i ==$ len(L_{t_i}) % *all test images are processed*

3.2 Attention Phase

The attention phase consists of six UCSs. Five of the UCSs are used to obtain constituent level predictions about the parts, i.e. face, jaw, nose, eyes, and mouth. This phase utilizes the segmented images generated for each part during the context phase. The HOG features are computed for the segmented images. The resultant features are used as input instances for the respective UCS to obtain the constituent level prediction for each part. Here, the prediction is the probability

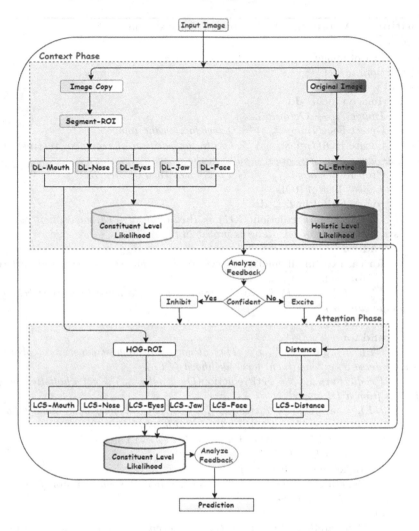

Fig. 1. Flow chart of the laterized system

that each constituent part belongs to a specific category. It is computed by dividing the votes that favor a specific category by the total votes in the UCS prediction array. Subsequently, the respective constituent level prediction values for each category are added to obtain the overall prediction probability for that category (see Eq. 1). Moreover, we identify the facial landmark[1] using *dlib* [2, 26]. Subsequently, we compute the distance of each (x, y) landmark coordinate from the center of the face, assuming the tip of the nose to be the center. These distances are the holistic level features that represent the relationship between constituents (parts). The sixth UCS is used to obtain the holistic level prediction

---

[1] The facial landmark is a set of coordinates that cover the whole face.

Algorithm 2. Algorithm adopted by the attention phase

Check Inhibit Signal() % *Stops if receive inhibit signal*
$L_{roi} \leftarrow$ List of ROIs % *List of ROI from the Context Phase*
for each ROI in L_{roi} **do**
    HOG_{ROI} = Compute HOG() % *Compute HOG Feature of each constituent part*
    P_{roiUCS} = getPredictionFromUCS(HOG_{ROI}) % *Prediction of each constituent part from its associated UCS model*
end for
for each CP in all emotion categories **do** % *For each constituent part (CP)*
    for each P_i in P_{roiUCS} **do**
        CP_{cat} += P_i % *Overall prediction that a constituent belongs to a specific category*
    end for
end for
CLL_{UCS} = argmaxCP_{cat} % *The category with the highest constituent prediction is considered as the CLL from UCS.*
Face = DetectFace($Image_{copy}$)
Detect FacialLandmark(Face) % *Detect (x, y) landmark coordinates from the face*
$Dist$ = ComputeDistance() % *Get the distance of each landmark coordinate from the center(tip of the nose)*
$Prediction_{Holistic}$ = getPredictionFromUCS($Dist$) % *Get holistic level prediction from UCS*
HLL_{UCS} = argmax($Prediction_{Holistic}$) % *The category with highest holistic prediction is considered as a holistic level likelihood (HLL).*
Normalize CLL_{UCS} and HLL_{UCS}
Add (CLL_{UCS}, HLL_{UCS}, CLL, and HLL) % *Add all the perceptions from the context phase and the attention phase.*
MakeFinalPrediction ()

---

by using these distances as an input instance. Subsequently, the computed UCS-based constituent level and holistic level prediction values are normalized. These values are added to the corresponding CLL and HLL values from the context phase to obtain the overall prediction probability for each category. Finally, the category with the maximum probability value is predicted. The pseudo-code of the technique developed for the attention phase is presented in Algorithm 2.

4   Experimental Work

4.1   Data Set

This work is designed to evaluate the robustness of the lateralized approach in emotion categorization. This is achieved by conducting experiments on one of the commonly used data set, i.e. CK+ [27]. The data set contains facial expressions of 201 adult participants. Each participant's posed emotions are recorded in the form of a video that has a varied number of image frames, i.e. 10 to 60 frames. This work uses 3368 images of six basic expressions [28] plus neutral expression.

These images are extracted from the last-half frames of the videos by using the technique developed by Shehu et al. [29]. The sample expression images are shown in Fig. 2.

Anger   Disgust   Fear   Happy   Neutral   Sad   Surprise

Fig. 2. Sample of six basic plus neutral expressions extracted from the CK+ database, the majority of the images are grayscale.

4.2   Experimental Setup

The learning methodology of the context phase is developed by using state-of-the-art VGG19 deep models. These models are trained for 200 epochs. To avoid overfitting, the learning rate is reduced by 10% after $80, 100, 120$ and 160 epochs, and 5% after 180 epochs. The learning methodology of the attention phase is developed by using UCSs. The configuration settings of the UCS are the same as used by the majority of the researchers [30,31], except for the population size which is set to 10000 as this has shown to give a high performance result. The UCS is coded with upper and lower bound representation and configured as follows: Genetic Algorithm's (GA) threshold $\theta_{ga} = 20$; Crossover probability of $\chi = 0.8$; Crossover type = "two point"; Probability of mutating an allele $\mu = 0.04$; Deletion threshold $\theta_{del} = 20$; Subsumption threshold $\theta_{sub} = 20$, Subsumption accuracy $\epsilon_0 = 0.99$, Initial fitness $f_i = 0.01$; Fitness reduction $\alpha = 0.1$; GA parent selected strategy (s) = tournament; Fraction included in tournament $\tau = 0.4$; Learning rate $\beta = 0.2$; finally, the UCSs is set to run over 500000 iterations to ensure convergence. The HOG features are computed with the following parameters: Window size = (64, 64), block size = (16, 16), cell size = (16, 16), window sigma = 4, normalization type = 0, L2-normalization threshold = $2.1x10^{-15}$, number of levels = 64, window stride = (8, 8), and location = (10, 20).

4.3   Experiments

For all the experiments, the expression images are randomly divided into 80% and 20% train and test images, respectively. The novel lateralized system is trained by using the original train images only. The adversarial attacks are applied only to the test images. The performance accuracy of the novel system is evaluated by using the test images, whereas the robustness of the novel lateralized approach is evaluated by using the adversarial images.

Three types of adversarial attacks are applied to the test images, i.e. (i) Distractor Attack, (ii) Wrapper Attack, and (iii) Hybrid Attack as shown in Fig.

3. The distractor attack is generated by using the DeepFool with the following settings: overshoot $= 0.02$, CenterCrop $= 224$, mean $= [0.516, 506, 0.496]$, std $= [0.375, 0.365, 0.355]$, $max\_iteration = 1$. The wrapper attack is applied by first detecting the landmark coordinates of the left and right eyes and then adding sunglasses on top of the eyes. However, the width of the sunglasses is reduced to 90% so as not to cover the entire face. The Hybrid attack is the combination of both the distractor attack and the wrapper attack.

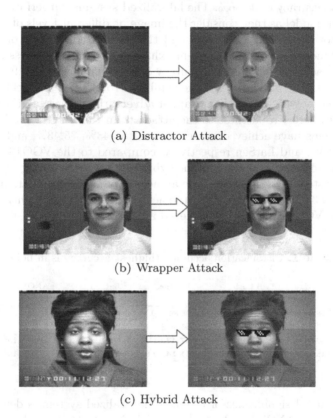

(a) Distractor Attack

(b) Wrapper Attack

(c) Hybrid Attack

Fig. 3. Sample original images and the resultant adversarial images after applying distractor, wrapper, and hybrid attacks.

Three variants of the lateralized approach are evaluated, i.e. (i) Lateral All, (ii) Lateral Anecdotal, and (iii) Lateral Sense. *Lateral All* (LatAll) utilizes the constituent level and holistic level predictions obtained from all the parts, i.e. eyes, mouth, nose, jaw, and face. *Lateral Anecdotal* (LatAne) utilizes the predictions obtained from the top three parts, i.e. mouth, jaw, and face. These three parts are selected as they anecdotally contribute to emotion. *Lateral Sense* (Lat-Sen) utilizes the predictions obtained from three sensing parts, i.e. eyes, nose, and mouth. These parts are selected as they are believed to be used by humans for the expression of their emotions [32]. In reporting the statistical test, the letters a, b, c, and d are used to indicate if the result is significantly different compared to the VGG19 model. The same letter infers that there is no significant difference whereas different letters show that there is a significant difference.

The experimental results show that all the variants of the lateralized approach obtained a performance accuracy better than or equal to the conventional DL model (VGG19), see Table 1. For original test images (none attack), Lat-Sen obtained a classification accuracy of 99.14%, whereas the VGG19 model obtained an accuracy of 98.86%. The lateralized systems outperformed the conventional DL model as they consider the image at different levels of abstraction. For distractor adversarial images, two of the lateralized systems outperformed the VGG19 model. The LatAll system exhibited strong robustness against the distractor attack and achieved an accuracy of 88%, whereas VGG19 obtained an accuracy of 73.71%. Similarly, LatAne exhibited robustness and achieved a classification accuracy of 86.86%. For wrapper adversarial images, all the lateralized system shows better robustness to the attack than the VGG19 model. The lateralized systems have achieved an accuracy of 87.43%, 75.43%, and 59.71% for LatAne, LatAll, and LatSen respectively, compared to the VGG19 model that achieved an accuracy of 36.43%. As the hybrid attack is the strongest attack, the lateralized systems could only achieve an accuracy of 51.14% (LatAne), 49.14% (LatAll), and 34.29% (LatSen). Yet, the achieved accuracy is higher when compared to the VGG19 model that achieved an accuracy of only 15.43%.

Table 1. Classification accuracy (highest accuracy is in bold).

Atttack	VGG19	LatAll	LatAne	LatSen	ANOVA	
					F	p
None	$98.86 \pm 0.2^{*a}$	$98.86 \pm 1.9^{*a}$	$98.86 \pm 0.1^{*a}$	$\mathbf{99.14 \pm 2.3^{*a}}$	30.03	< .001
Distractor	$73.71 \pm 0.2^{*a}$	$\mathbf{88.0 \pm 6.6^{*b}}$	$86.86 \pm 3.8^{*c}$	$73.71 \pm 6.7^{*a}$	2.04×10^{29}	< .001
Wrapper	$36.57 \pm 0.2^{*a}$	$75.43 \pm 13.0^{*b}$	$\mathbf{87.43 \pm 11.3^{*c}}$	$59.71 \pm 16.1^{*d}$	2.39×10^{30}	< .001
Hybrid	$15.43 \pm 0.2^{*a}$	$49.28 \pm 8.6^{*b}$	$\mathbf{51.14 \pm 9.8^{*c}}$	$47.14 \pm 10.2^{*d}$	5.20×10^{30}	< .001

The statistical significance of the novel lateralized system is determined by applying one-way ANOVA and post hoc comparison tests (see Table 1). Initially, a one-way ANOVA was conducted to determine the significance of interaction between the groups. Here, we have three groups, i.e. (i) VGG19-LatAll, (ii) VGG19-LatAne, (iii) VGG19-LatSen); and four scenarios, i.e. None (original images), distractor, wrapper, and hybrid. A significant interaction was found between these groups (all $p < .001$).

Similarly, a post hoc comparison of a two-sample t-test with *Bonferroni correction* was performed on the obtained experimental results and no significant difference was found for the original images. However, the experimental results for all the lateralized systems after the attack (except the LatSen system for distractor images) were found to be significantly higher than for VGG19 at the $\alpha = .017$.

4.4   Interpretation of Decisions

The decision-making process of the novel lateralized system is interpretable as we can read the rules generated by the LCS. The analysis of predictions obtained for original and adversarial images reveals the reasons behind the robustness against adversarial attacks. The constituent and holistic models at the context phase may generate wrong predictions for adversarial images. In the majority of such cases, the constituent and holistic models predict different classes. Consequently, the system considers that it is not confident to predict the class of the given image and generates an excite signal to the attention phase to do further analysis. After receiving the feedback from the attention phase, the system combines all the predictions and confidently predicts the class of the given adversarial image.

For example, during the classification process of an original image '*Img-org*' (see Fig. 4a)), the holistic level deep model predicted its class as 100% happy. The constituents level deep models predicted the mouth as 99.99% happy and 0.01% anger, the nose as 99.99% happy and 0.01% disgust, and the eyes as 99.61% happy and 0.39% surprise. Since all the holistic and constituents level models were predicting the same class (see Eqs. 2 and 3), the lateralized system predicted the class of the given original image as happy and generated an inhibit signal to the attention phase to stop further processing of the image.

The image '*Img-adv*' was generated by applying a hybrid adversarial attack to the *Img-org*, see Fig. 4b). The holistic level deep model predicted its class as 99.90% disgust and 0.10 sad. However, the constituents level deep models predicted the mouth of the image as 99.68% happy and 0.32% anger, the nose as 99.99% disgust and 0.01% fear, and the eyes as 49.91% sad, 44.68% happy, and 5.41% disgust. In this case, the holistic and constituents level deep models were at odd with each-others. Consequently, the system generated an excite signal to the attention phase for further analysis. Subsequently, the CLL (144.36 happy) was computed by using the Eqs. 2 and the HLL value (99.90% disgust) was computed by using Eq. 3.

At the attention phase, the holistic level UCS models predicted the class of the given image as 72.73% disgust and 27.27% anger. Similarly, the constituent level UCS model predicted it as a 100% happy mouth. All the other constituent level UCS models were not able to predict their respective parts (could not find a matching rule). These prediction values were normalized and the winner class prediction probability was shared with the system. Subsequently, the returned value was added with the CLL and HLL values computed at the context phase. Finally, the lateralized system predicted the given image class as a happy class with a likelihood of 169.36.

5   Discussion

This work is designed to provide robust solutions for emotion categorization against adversarial images. The novel lateralized system considers the given image instance at the constituents level and the holistic level simultaneously. This empowers the novel system to effectively counter the disruptive patterns

 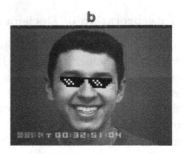

Fig. 4. a) Happy expression, original image (*Img-org*). b) Happy expression, adversarial image after hybrid attack ('*Img-adv*)

generated by the adversarial attacks. An adversarial attack needs to successfully challenge all the constituents and holistic patterns to fool the novel lateralized system.

The classification accuracy achieved by all the variants of the lateralized systems is better than or equal to the state-of-the-art VGG19 model. The experimental results demonstrated that the novel system successfully exhibited robustness against the majority of the adversarial attacks. In worse case, the classification accuracy of the novel system (LatAne) was 51.14% against the hybrid attack. It is understandable because hybrid is such a strong adversarial attack that the VGG19 model could not resist it and obtained a very low classification accuracy, i.e. 15.43% (close to random guess). Moreover, the statistical tests show that the improvement in the performance accuracy of the lateralized system is statistically significant.

The decision-making process of the novel lateralized system is interpretable. During the analysis of the results, it is revealed that the lateralized system may wrongly predict some of the constituents or holistic parts but the overall prediction made by the novel system is correct. Moreover, the utilization of inhibit and excite signal assists the novel system to achieve performance efficiency and makes it a more lateralized system rather than an ensemble system. All this suggests that it is worthy to create lateralized classification systems to achieve robustness against noisy and irrelevant real-world data.

In-spite of that, it is also important to keep in mind that these improvements have the negative consequences of increasing the computational costs. While it took an average of 2 hrs/run for the VGG19 model in the holistic level to train on an 8 GB Graphical Processing Unit (GPU) device GeForce RTX 2080ti with CUDA version 10.2, an average of 2 hrs is required to train each of the five deep models in the context phase, i.e. an approximate 10 hrs on a single machine (GPU slot). The UCS at the attention phase was run on grid computing, so there is no accurate estimate of time. However, on average, it took about 4–5 hrs for each UCS model to run completely. It is noted that this work did not optimize for time.

6   Conclusion

The novel system successfully exhibited robustness against adversarial attacks by applying lateralization. The ability to simultaneously consider the parts of the face (constituents level) and the whole face (holistic level) empowers the lateralized system to correctly classify emotions. The utilization of inhibit and excite signals enable the novel system to efficiently classify original images and pay more attention to the noisy and corrupt images. Consequently, the novel system made correct decisions for badly corrupt images and exhibited robustness against strong adversarial attacks. The novel lateralized system outperformed the state-of-the-art VGG19 model by 15−36% point.

Even though the novel lateralized system achieved a significantly better classification accuracy as compared to VGG19, it could not resist the strong adversarial attack (classification accuracy 51.14%). The future work will improve the lateralized method to exhibit robustness against such strong adversarial attacks.

References

1. Brave, S., Nass, C.: Emotion in human-computer interaction. Human-comput. Inter. Fundamentals **20094635**, 53–68 (2009)
2. Shehu H.A., Browne W.N., Eisenbarth H.: An adversarial attacks resistance-based approach to emotion recognition from images using facial landmarks. In: 2020 IEEE International Conference on Robot and Human Interactive Communication (2020)
3. Zoph, B., Vasudevan, V., Shlens, J., Le, Q.V.: Learning transferable architectures for scalable image recognition. In: 2018 IEEE/CVF Conference on Computer Vision and Pattern Recognition, Salt Lake City, UT, 2018, pp. 8697–8710. https://doi.org/10.1109/CVPR.2018.00907
4. Russakovsky, O., et al.: Imagenet large scale visual recognition challenge. Int. J. Comput. Vis.n 115(3), 211–252 (2015)
5. Madry, A., Makelov, A., Schmidt, L., Tsipras, D., Vladu, A.: Towards deep learning models resistant to adversarial attacks. arXiv preprint arXiv:1706.06083 (2017)
6. Heaven, D.: Why deep-learning AIs are so easy to fool. Nature **574**(7777), 163–166 (2019)
7. Grimshaw, G.M., Carmel, D.: An asymmetric inhibition model of hemispheric differences in emotional processing. Front. Psychol. **5**, 489 (2014)
8. Siddique, A., Browne, W.N., Grimshaw, G.M.: Lateralized learning for robustness against adversarial attacks in a visual classification system. In: Proceedings of the 2020 Genetic and Evolutionary Computation Conference, pp. 395–403, June 2020
9. Simonyan, K., Zisserman, A.: Very deep convolutional networks for large-scale image recognition (2014). arXiv preprint arXiv:1409.1556
10. Babajee, P., Suddul, G., Armoogum, S., Foogooa, R.: Identifying human emotions from facial expressions with deep learning. In: 2020 Zooming Innovation in Consumer Technologies Conference (ZINC). Novi Sad, Serbia 2020, pp. 36–39 (2020). https://doi.org/10.1109/ZINC50678.2020.9161445
11. Happy, S.L., Member, S., Routray, A.: Automatic facial expression recognition using features of salient facial patches. IEEE Trans. Affective Comput. **6**, 1–12 (2015)

12. Goodfellow, I.J., et al.: Challenges in Representation Learning: A Report on Three Machine Learning Contests. In: Lee, M., Hirose, A., Hou, Z.-G., Kil, R.M. (eds.) ICONIP 2013. LNCS, vol. 8228, pp. 117–124. Springer, Heidelberg (2013). https://doi.org/10.1007/978-3-642-42051-1_16
13. Pathak, K.M., Yadav, S., Jain, P., Tanwar, P., Kumar, B.: A facial expression recognition system to predict emotions. In: 2020 International Conference on Intelligent Engineering and Management (ICIEM), London, United Kingdom, 2020, pp. 414–419 (2020). https://doi.org/10.1109/ICIEM48762.2020.9160229
14. Lyons, M.J., Akamatsu, S., Kamachi, M., Gyoba, J., Budynek, J.: The Japanese female facial expression (JAFFE) database. In: Proceedings of Third International Conference on Automatic Face and Gesture Recognition, pp. 14–16, April 1998
15. Sokolov, D., Patkin, M.: Real-time emotion recognition on mobile devices. In: IEEE International Conference on Automatic Face & Gesture Recognition (FG 2018), pp. 787–787 (2018). https://doi.org/10.1109/FG.2018.00124
16. He, K., Zhang, X., Ren, S., Sun, J.: Deep residual learning for image recognition. In: Proceedings of the IEEE Computer Society Conference on Computer Vision and Pattern Recognition. 770–778 (2015). https://doi.org/10.1109/CVPR.2016.90
17. Moosavi-Dezfooli, S. M., Fawzi, A., Frossard, P.: Deepfool: a simple and accurate method to fool deep neural networks. In: Proceedings of the IEEE Conference on Computer Vision and Pattern Recognition, pp. 2574–2582 (2016)
18. Dalal, N., Triggs, B.: Histograms of oriented gradients for human detection. In: 2005 IEEE Computer Society Conference on Computer Vision and Pattern Recognition (CVPR'05), vol. 1, pp. 886–893. IEEE, June 2005
19. Goodfellow, I., Bengio, Y., Courville, A.: Deep Learning. MIT press, Cambridge (2016)
20. Mateen, M., Wen, J., Song, S., Huang, Z.: Fundus image classification using VGG-19 architecture with PCA and SVD. Symmetry 11(1), 1 (2019)
21. Oloko-Oba, M., Viriri, S.: Pre-trained convolutional neural network for the diagnosis of tuberculosis. In: Bebis, G., et al. (eds.) ISVC 2020. LNCS, vol. 12510, pp. 558–569. Springer, Cham (2020). https://doi.org/10.1007/978-3-030-64559-5_44
22. Dam, H.H., Abbass, H.A., Lokan, C., Yao, X.: Neural-based learning classifier systems. IEEE Trans. Knowl. Data Eng. 20(1), 26–39 (2008). https://doi.org/10.1109/TKDE.2007.190671
23. Bernadó-Mansilla, E., Garrell-Guiu, J.M.: Accuracy-based learning classifier systems: models, analysis and applications to classification tasks. Evolutionary Comput. 11(3), 209–238 (2003)
24. Addabbo, M., Longhi, E., Marchis, I.C., Tagliabue, P., Turati, C.: Dynamic facial expressions of emotions are discriminated at birth. PloS one 13(3), e0193868 (2018)
25. Viola, P., Jones, M.: Rapid object detection using a boosted cascade of simple features. In: Proceedings of the IEEE Computer Society Conference on Computer Vision and Pattern Recognition 1, (2001). https://doi.org/10.1109/cvpr.2001.990517
26. Dlib Python API Tutorials [Electronic resource] - Access mode. http://dlib.net/python/index.html
27. Lucey, P., Cohn, J.F., Kanade, T., Saragih, J., Ambadar, Z., Matthews, I.: The extended Cohn-Kanade dataset (CK+): a complete dataset for action unit and emotion-specified expression. In: 2010 IEEE Computer Society Conference on Computer Vision and Pattern Recognition - Workshops, CVPRW 2010, pp. 94–101 (2010)
28. Ekman, P., Friesen, W.V.: Constants across cultures in the face and emotion. Journal of personality and social psychology 17(2), 124 (1971)

29. Shehu, H.A., Browne, W., Eisenbarth, H.: Emotion categorization from video-frame images using a novel sequential voting technique. In: Bebis, G., et al. (eds.) ISVC 2020. LNCS, vol. 12510, pp. 618–632. Springer, Cham (2020). https://doi.org/10.1007/978-3-030-64559-5_49

30. Siddique, A., Iqbal, M., Browne, W.N.: A comprehensive strategy for mammogram image classification using learning classifier systems. In: IEEE Congress on Evolutionary Computation (CEC), pp. 2201–2208. IEEE (2016)

31. Nguyen, T.B., Browne, W.N., Zhang, M.: Online feature-generation of code fragments for XCS to guide feature construction. In: IEEE Congress on Evolutionary Computation (CEC), pp. 3308–3315 (2019)

32. Moore, K.L., Dalley, A.F., Agur, A.M.R.: Moore's clinical anatomy. United States of America: Lippincott Williams & Wilkins. pp. 843–980 (2010). ISBN 978-1-60547-652-0

Evolutionary Machine Learning

Improved Crowding Distance in Multi-objective Optimization for Feature Selection in Classification

Peng Wang[1]([✉])[iD], Bing Xue[1][iD], Jing Liang[2][iD], and Mengjie Zhang[1][iD]

[1] School of Engineering and Computer Science, Victoria University of Wellington, Wellington, New Zealand
{wangpeng,bing.xue,mengjie.zhang}@ecs.vuw.ac.nz
[2] School of Electrical Engineering, Zhengzhou University, Zhengzhou, China
liangjing@zzu.edu.cn

Abstract. Feature selection is an essential preprocessing step in data mining and machine learning. A feature selection task can be treated as a multi-objective optimization problem which simultaneously minimizes the classification error and the number of selected features. Many existing feature selection approaches including multi-objective methods neglect that there exists multiple optimal solutions in feature selection. There can be multiple different optimal feature subsets which achieve the same or similar classification performance. Furthermore, when using evolutionary multi-objective optimization for feature selection, a crowding distance metric is typically used to play a role in environmental selection. However, some existing calculations of crowding metrics based on continuous/numeric values are inappropriate for feature selection since the search space of feature selection is discrete. Therefore, this paper proposes a new environmental selection method to modify the calculation of crowding metrics. The proposed approach is expected to help a multi-objective feature selection algorithm to find multiple potential optimal feature subsets. Experiments on sixteen different datasets of varying difficulty show that the proposed approach can find more diverse feature subsets, achieving the same classification performance without deteriorating performance regarding hypervolume and inverted generational distance.

Keywords: Feature selection · Multi-objective optimization · Crowding distance

1 Introduction

Real-world machine learning problems often have a large number of features because of the development of technology in data collection. The irrelevant or redundant features may have negative impacts on the classification performance. Therefore, feature selection is proposed to reduce the number of features and

© Springer Nature Switzerland AG 2021
P. A. Castillo and J. L. Jiménez Laredo (Eds.): EvoApplications 2021, LNCS 12694, pp. 489–505, 2021.
https://doi.org/10.1007/978-3-030-72699-7_31

improve the quality of the feature set by eliminating irrelevant and redundant features [11].

Feature selection is a process to find a small number of features while maintaining or even improving the classification accuracy [10]. Feature selection is a difficult task due to three main reasons. (1) The size of search space increases exponentially with respect to the number of original features. (2) The complex interactions between features increase the difficulty of addressing feature selection problems. For example, two individual relevant features, which retain similar information towards the class, may produce redundancy when they are chosen together. Two weakly relevant features, including little information about the class, could become very useful when they are selected together. When some features, cooperating with each other (i.e., complementary features), are chosen together, the classification performance of a learning algorithm can be improved [14]. (3) Feature selection can be considered as a multi-objective problem. The two objectives, minimizing the number of selected features and maximizing the classification accuracy (or minimizing the error rate), are usually in conflict [20].

Compared with some traditional feature selection methods (e.g., floating selection methods [15]), Evolutionary Computation (EC) approaches, including Genetic Algorithm (GA) [6] and Particle Swarm Optimization (PSO) [9], have a strong global search ability. More importantly, EC approaches are especially suitable for multi-objective feature selection, since evolutionary multi-objective optimization (EMO) approaches, such as Non-dominated Sorting based Multi-objective GA II (NSGAII) [3] and Multi-objective PSO (MOPSO) [1], can obtain a set of non-dominated solutions for feature selection. EMO techniques have shown promise for addressing feature selection problems [5,13,19] due to their population based search mechanism.

The existence of redundant and interactive features results in multiple optimal feature subsets (i.e., solutions) in a dataset. However, many existing feature selection methods miss some potential optimal feature subsets since these methods do not specifically design a strategy to keep all those different solutions with the same performance during evolution. In real-world scenarios, when an optimal feature subset is found, the cost of collecting some features (e.g., lifetime) can be too expensive, making the subset quite difficult to use. If multiple optimal solutions with different features selected are obtained, users can choose one which they prefer. For example, for the Breast Cancer Wisconsin (Original) data [4], Yue et al. [22] observed that using subset $\{F_1, F_2, F_7\}$ and subset $\{F_2, F_3, F_7\}$ can achieve the same classification accuracy of 97.81%. However, users may prefer the subset $\{F_1, F_2, F_7\}$ since the feature F_1 (Clump Thickness) is easier to be collected than F_3 (Uniformity of Cell Shape).

Although EMO-based feature selection methods can obtain a set of Pareto-optimal solutions of feature selection (see Fig. 1), these methods still lose some optimal feature subsets (e.g., S_3 or S_4 in Fig. 1). The missed feature subsets may show better classification performance than the obtained solutions on a test set [18]. Generally, an EMO-based feature selection algorithm usually consists of several main components. The first one is the evaluation criterion, which is responsible for evaluating candidate feature subsets. The second one is represented by environmental selection strategies, which are able to balance the convergence and the diversity of a population.

Feature selection approaches can be separated into two main categories based on the evaluation criterion: filter and wrapper methods. In filter methods, a feature subset is assessed by certain statistical measures such as distance and correlation without using any learning algorithm. However, wrapper methods evaluate a feature subset by a specific learning algorithm, e.g., K-Nearest Neighbour (KNN) [2]. The classification accuracy of a wrapper method is typically better than that of a filter method, since wrapper methods use a learning algorithm to directly evaluate the goodness of the selected features. Therefore, a wrapper approach is utilized in this work to evaluate the candidate feature subsets.

Apart from the fitness function, an environmental selection strategy also plays an important role in a feature selection approach. The aim of environmental selection is to evaluate all parents and offspring by a predefined selection criterion, and preserve the feature subsets having better measures of selection criterion into the next generation [7]. However, many existing environmental selection strategies fail to take the multiple feature subsets with the same performance and duplicated solutions (multiple different individuals result in the same feature subset) into account. Therefore, this work aims to improve the performance of an EMO-based feature selection method by proposing a novel environmental selection method which simultaneously considers the selected features in the search space and the objective values in the objective space.

1.1   Goals

The overall goal of this work is to develop a new calculation of crowding metrics to help an EMO-based feature selection method to find more diverse optimal feature subsets without deteriorating the feature selection performance. In order to achieve this goal, the proposed environmental selection strategy is specifically designed for feature selection to preserve good feature subsets while deleting duplicated solutions. The proposed strategy will be examined and compared against eight EMO-based feature selection algorithms on sixteen datasets. Specifically, we will investigate:

1. whether the proposed crowding distance calculation method and the special crowding distance in [23] can assist EMO-based feature selection methods to find more diverse optimal feature subsets than that of the standard crowding distance calculation in [3], and
2. whether integrating new environmental selection strategy can enhance the exploration ability of an EMO-based feature selection method, and
3. whether using the proposed framework can shorten the running time of a feature selection method.

2   Background

2.1   Multi-objective Optimization

Multi-objective Optimization Problems (MOPs) need to optimize multiple conflicting objectives simultaneously. A minimization MOP can be stated as follows:

$$\begin{cases} \min \; \boldsymbol{f}(\boldsymbol{x}) = (f_1(\boldsymbol{x}), f_2(\boldsymbol{x}), \ldots, f_m(\boldsymbol{x}))^{\mathrm{T}} \\ \boldsymbol{x} \in \Omega \end{cases} \tag{1}$$

where Ω stands for the feasible region of $\boldsymbol{x}$, and $\boldsymbol{x} = (x_1, x_2, \ldots, x_d)$ means the
decision variable vector. $\boldsymbol{f}$ includes m objective functions. For an MOP, Pareto-
dominance relationship [3] is used to obtain Pareto-optimal solutions. Suppose
two feasible solutions are $\boldsymbol{x}_1$ and $\boldsymbol{x}_2$, $\boldsymbol{x}_1$ is said to dominate $\boldsymbol{x}_2$ (i.e., $\boldsymbol{x}_1 \prec \boldsymbol{x}_2$)
if and only if $f_i(\boldsymbol{x}_1) \leq f_i(\boldsymbol{x}_2)$ ($\forall\, i \in \{1, 2, \ldots, m\}$), and there exists at least one
$j \in \{1, 2, \ldots, m\}$ such that $f_j(\boldsymbol{x}_1) < f_j(\boldsymbol{x}_2)$. A solution $\boldsymbol{x}^*$ is Pareto-optimal
solution, on condition that it is not dominated by any $\boldsymbol{x} \in \Omega$. Pareto Front (PF)
is a set of all the Pareto-optimal solutions.

2.2   Crowding Distance

The concept of Crowding Distance (CD) was firstly proposed in [3], which
gives an estimate of the density of solutions surrounding the target solution.
In NSGAII, if both two non-dominated solutions belong to the same PF, the
algorithm prefers the solution locating in a region with a smaller number of
nearby solutions (i.e., a less crowded region) in the objective space. This strategy enables the algorithm to evolve towards a widely distributed PF. Therefore,
this CD measure has been applied to many EMO algorithms (e.g., NSGAII and
MOPSO) to address different kind of optimization problems including feature
selection.

   To solve multimodal MOPs, Yue et al. [23] developed a CD measure. The
proposed Special CD (termed SCD) in [22,23] considers both the objective and
the search spaces. Assuming the i-th solution $\boldsymbol{x}_i$ is located in the PF $\boldsymbol{R}$, the
calculation of the CD value of $\boldsymbol{x}_i$ in SCD in the objective space c_i^{obj} is the same
as NSGAII. However, unlike the boundary-point metric assignment in NSGAII,
the CD value of the solutions locating in the boundary of the PF in the objective
space in SCD is set to 1. Meanwhile, the CD value of $\boldsymbol{x}_i$ in the search space c_i^{sea}
is calculated including the following main steps. First, $\forall\, j \in \{1, \ldots, D\}$ (D is the
dimension of the search space), a CD value of $\boldsymbol{x}_i$ in the j-th decision variable
$c_{i,j}^{sea}$ is calculated as shown in Eq. (2).

$$c_{i,j}^{sea} = \begin{cases} 2(\frac{x_{i+1,j} - x_{i,j}}{x_j^{max} - x_j^{min}}) & \text{if } x_{i,j} = x_j^{min} \\ 2(\frac{x_{i,j} - x_{i-1,j}}{x_j^{max} - x_j^{min}}) & \text{else if } x_{i,j} = x_j^{max} \\ \frac{x_{i+1,j} - x_{i-1,j}}{x_j^{max} - x_j^{min}} & \text{otherwise} \end{cases} \tag{2}$$

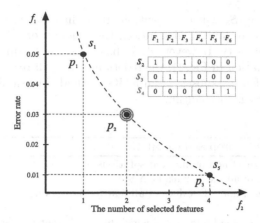

Fig. 1. The PF of a feature selection problem. The f_1 and f_2 are the classification error rate and the number of selected features, respectively. Supposing the three points are the PF of this feature selection problem with six features. 1 and 0 mean the selected and the unselected features, respectively. As shown, point p_2 can map to three different feature subsets. Using features F_1 and F_3 or features F_2 and F_3 or features F_5 and F_6 can achieve the same 97% classification accuracy.

where all solutions in $\boldsymbol{R}$ are sorted according to the values of the j-th decision variable in a descending order. In Eq. (2), $x_j^{max} = \max_{\boldsymbol{x} \in R}\{x_j\}$ and $x_j^{min} = \min_{\boldsymbol{x} \in R}\{x_j\}$. Then, when all the $c_{i,j}^{sea}$ are obtained, $c_i^{sea} = (\sum_{j=1}^{D} c_{i,j}^{sea})/D$.

The average values c_{avg}^{sea} and c_{avg}^{obj} are obtained as follows: $c_{avg}^{sea} = (\sum_{i=1}^{|\boldsymbol{R}|} c_i^{sea})/|\boldsymbol{R}|$ and $c_{avg}^{obj} = (\sum_{i=1}^{|\boldsymbol{R}|} c_i^{obj})/|\boldsymbol{R}|$. Finally, the crowding distance value c_i of $\boldsymbol{x}_i$ is calculated using Eq. (3).

$$c_i = \begin{cases} max\{c_i^{obj}, c_i^{sea}\} & \text{if } c_i^{obj} > c_{avg}^{obj} \text{ or } c_i^{sea} > c_{avg}^{sea} \\ min\{c_i^{obj}, c_i^{sea}\} & \text{otherwise} \end{cases} \tag{3}$$

3   The Proposed Crowding Distance Calculation Method

Generally, an environmental selection strategy plays a crucial role in most EMO methods, which needs to take both the convergence of population to the PF and the distribution of the solutions into account [12]. In principle, the crowding metrics can be utilized to play a role in environmental selection. However, both CD in NSGAII and SCD in MO_Ring_PSO_SCD [23] have limitations when addressing feature selection problems because they cannot consider the multiple optimal feature subsets and the duplicated solutions. A detailed description of their limitations is given below.

In Fig. 1, following the calculations of CD in NSGAII, the CD metric of S_3 is 0 since its neighbors (S_2 and S_4) have the same objective values. Then, during the environmental selection process, if only three individuals can enter the next generation, S_3 will be wiped off. If S_3 includes the same features as S_2 or S_4, i.e., S_3 is a duplicated solution, the deletion of S_3 will not influence the population diversity. However, if S_3 has different features from S_2 or S_4 (as shown the situation in Fig. 1), the deletion of S_3 will result in missing some potential optimal feature subsets of an EMO method. The similar situations will also occur in the SCD mechanism.

Algorithm 1: The proposed calculation of CD

Input: NS: A set of non-dominated solutions
NS_fit: Fitness of all individuals in NS
Output: NS_cd: Final CD values of all feature subsets in NS

1 **begin**
2   NS_uni: Feature subsets in NS which have different fitness values
3   NS_re: $NS \backslash NS\_uni$
4   NS_uni_fit: Fitness values of subsets in NS_uni
5   NS_re_fit: Fitness values of subsets in NS_re
6   // Calculate the crowding metrics of feature subsets in NS_uni, and store in NS_uni_cd
7   **for** $i = 1$ *to* $size(NS\_re)$ **do**
8   **for** $j = 1$ *to* $size(NS\_uni)$ **do**
9   **if** $NS\_re(i)$ *has the same features as* $NS\_uni(j)$ **then**
10                 $NS\_re\_cd(i) = 0$
11   **end**
12   **if** $NS\_re(i)$ *has different features with* $NS\_uni(j)$ **and** $NS\_re\_fit(i)$ $= NS\_uni\_fit(j)$ **then**
13                 $NS\_re\_cd(i) = NS\_uni\_cd(j)$
14   **end**
15   **end**
16   **end**
17     $NS\_cd = NS\_uni\_cd \cup NS\_re\_cd$
18 **end**

To overcome such undesirable situations, this paper proposes a new CD calculation, which is shown in Algorithm 1. It contains the following three principles:

1. The final CD values of the duplicated feature subsets should be 0 so that the duplicated feature subsets are firstly removed,
2. The subsets which have different features while achieving the same classification performance will have the same CD value,
3. Preserve the feature subsets who have large final CD metrics as well as the feature subsets sitting in the boundary of the PF.

Algorithm 1 mainly include three steps to calculate the final CD values. First, after obtaining a set of non-dominated solutions for feature selection, the feature subsets are divided into two parts, NS_uni and NS_re. The objective values of all feature subsets in NS_uni are different from each other. The remaining feature subsets are kept in NS_re (Line 3). Second, the CD values of the solution in NS_uni are calculated based on the CD calculation in NSGAII or the SCD calculation in [23] (Line 6). The final step is to calculate the CD values of the feature subsets in NS_re (Lines 7 to 16), which is the most critical step. The selected features and the objective values of the solutions in NS_re are compared with that of the solutions in NS_uni one by one. If a i-th subset in NS_re ($NS\_re(i)$) has exactly the same features as the j-th subset in NS_uni ($NS\_uni(j)$), the CD value of $NS\_re(i)$ is set to 0 (Lines 7 to 11) since $NS\_re(i)$ is a duplicated feature subset. If $NS\_re(i)$ has different features with $NS\_uni(j)$ while achieves the same objective values as $NS\_uni(j)$, the CD value of $NS\_re(i)$ is set to the same value as the CD value of $NS\_uni(j)$ (Lines 12 to 16) since both feature subsets are equally important.

According to the proposed CD calculation, during the environmental selection process, the feature subsets which have larger CD indicators will have higher priority to enter the next generation or to be kept in an external archive. Noted that the proposed CD calculation method in theory can be used in any EMO approach that uses CD during the evolutionary process. Moreover, the proposed CD calculation approach is flexible, since different existing CD calculation methods can be used in the proposed method (i.e., in Line 6 of the Algorithm 1). In this paper, when the standard CD calculation method [3] is used in Line 6 of the Algorithm 1, the proposed method is termed ICD. When SCD [23] is utilized in Line 6 of the Algorithm 1, the proposed method is named ISCD. Line 6 is to assign CD metrics to the feature subsets which have different fitness values between each other, which can maintain the diversity of population in the objective space. Meanwhile, Lines 7 to 16 of the Algorithm 1 can increase the diversity of feature subsets in the search space, since these steps are to find and keep potential good feature subsets. Furthermore, the proposed CD calculation method also does not limited to solve feature selection problems, but can be used in problems similar to features election, such as portfolio selection [24] and sparse reconstruction [21].

4   Experiment

4.1   Baseline EMO Approaches

In order to examine the performance of the improved CD calculation method, two common multi-objective feature selection algorithms, NSGAII [3] and MOPSO [1], are used in the experiments. In NSGAII, a fast non-dominated sorting technique is employed to rank the combination of generated offspring and parents to different non-dominated levels. The non-dominated solutions in the same level are further ranked based on their CDs. The top-ranked solutions will enter the next generation. Different from NSGAII, MOPSO utilizes an external archive to store non-dominated solutions during evolution. When the size of archive set is larger than the population size, CD will play a role of truncation operator.

Adding or removing one or more candidate solutions from the external archive set of MOPSO depends on the dominance relationship and CD, respectively.

In this paper, the two algorithms, **NSGAII** and **MOPSO**, use the standard CD calculation shown in [3]. **NSGAII-SCD** and **MOPSO-SCD** mean that NSGAII and MOPSO respectively used SCD in their methods. NSGAII and MOPSO with the proposed ICD strategy are named **NSGAII-ICD** and **MOPSO-ICD**, respectively. When NSGAII and MOPSO employ ISCD, the two algorithms are called **NSGAII-ISCD** and **MOPSO-ISCD**, respectively.

Table 1. The information of datasets

Number	Dataset	# Features	# Classes	# Instances
1	Wine	13	3	178
2	Zoo	16	7	101
3	SPECT	22	2	267
4	WBCD	30	2	569
5	Ionosphere	34	2	351
6	Sonar	60	2	208
7	Movementlibras	90	15	360
8	Hillvally	100	2	606
9	Musk1	166	2	476
10	Multiple Features (pix)	240	10	2000
11	Arrhythmia	279	16	452
12	Madelon	500	2	4400
13	CNAE	856	9	1080
14	SRBCT	2308	4	83
15	Leukemia	5147	2	72
16	DLBCL	7050	2	77

4.2 Objective Functions and Representation

The objective functions are to minimize the classification error rate and the number of selected features simultaneously, as shown in Eq. (4).

$$\min\{ f_1 = \text{Error Rate} = \frac{FP+FN}{TP+TN+FP+FN}, f_2 = \text{Frate} = \frac{\#Features}{\#\text{All Features}}\} \quad (4)$$

where FP, FN, TP, and TN are the false positives, false negatives, true positives, and true negatives, respectively. $\#Features$ means the number of selected features. KNN is used as the classifier to calculate the classification Error Rate.

The representation of an individual in NSGAII or a particle in MOPSO is a vector with real value encoding. The dimensionality of each vector is equal to the number of features of one dataset, where a threshold θ is employed to decide whether one feature is selected or not. If the corresponding value of a vector is larger than the threshold θ, the feature will be chosen, and otherwise not chosen. During the evaluation process, the classification performance is obtained only based on the selected features.

4.3 Datasets and Parameter Settings

In this work, NSGAII and MOPSO methods are compared on sixteen different datasets of varying difficulty from the UCI Machine Learning Repository [4]. The selected datasets have different numbers of classes, features and instances. The information of datasets can be seen in Table 1.

For all the eight methods, the population size is equal to the number of features of one dataset, but limited to 300 due to limited memory for computation as suggested in [16]. The maximum number of iterations is 100 and the threshold θ is set to 0.6 [13]. Each algorithm has 30 independent runs. K in KNN classifier is set to 5 so that KNN can avoid noise instances while still maintain its efficiency [13].

4.4 Performance Indicators

Two indicators are adopted to compare the performance of different algorithms on obtaining multiple feature subsets with the same objective values, which are Probability (PR) and Average Number (AN), as shown in Eq. (5) and Eq. (6), respectively.

$$PR = \frac{\sum_{i=1}^{NR} SF(i)}{NR} * 100\% \tag{5}$$

where NR means the total number of independent runs (30 in this work). In the i-th run of an algorithm, if there are multiple feature subsets with the same objective values in the obtained set of non-dominated solutions, SF will be set to 1. Otherwise, it is set to 0.

$$AN = \frac{\sum_{i=1}^{NR} TS(i)}{NR} \tag{6}$$

where TS is the total number of feature subsets in the non-dominated solutions with more than one feature subsets which achieve the same objective values in the i-th run of an algorithm. If and only if $SF(i) = 1$, $TS(i)$ will be larger than 0. When $SF(i) = 0$, $TS(i)$ will be also equal to 0. AN is the average number of TS of an algorithm across the NR runs.

A larger AN means an algorithm can find more feature subsets with the same objective values in a single run. The larger the PR, the more runs an algorithm can find multiple solutions with the same objective values.

Here is an example to calculate PR and AN. If the obtained PF by an algorithm is shown in Fig. 1, TS and SF of this run will be three and one, respectively. The reason is that the algorithm can find three different feature subsets, $\{F_1, F_3\}$, $\{F_2, F_3\}$ and $\{F_5, F_6\}$, sitting in the same point (p_2) in the objective space. If point p_3 in Fig. 1 can map to two different feature subsets (i.e., another two different feature subsets can achieve the same 99% classification accuracy), TS will change to five while SF will stand still. Following these calculations, the PR and AN of an algorithm can be obtained.

To compare the convergence and the diversity of the eight multi-objective feature selection algorithms, another two commonly used indicators, the Hypervolume (HV) [17] and the Inverted Generational Distance (IGD) [8] indicators, are also employed. Generally, the calculation of HV requires a reference point which is set to $(1, 1)$ in this paper. To calculate IGD, the "true PF" is usually required beforehand, but it is unknown in feature selection. To overcome this issue, the "true PF" is estimated by the non-dominated solutions obtained from the union of all feature subsets produced by the 30 independent runs of the eight methods. The larger the HV or the lower the IGD, the better the method. For feature selection in classification, users generally pay more attention to the test performance of an algorithm, which is more important than the training performance. Therefore, the HV and IGD of the test results are given.

Table 2. The PR and AN of the four NSGAII algorithms

Dataset	NSGAII		NSGAII-ICD		NSGAII-SCD		NSGAII-ISCD	
	PR	AN	PR	AN	PR	AN	PR	AN
Wine	0%	0	0%	0	0%	0	0%	0
Zoo	13.3%	0.3	**86.7%**	**1.8**	53.3%	1.2	80%	1.7
SPECT	56.7%	1.9	**76.7%**	2.2	33.3%	0.9	73.3%	**2.3**
WBCD	0%	0	**10%**	**0.2**	10%	0.2	6.7%	0.1
Ionosphere	0%	0	0%	0	**3.3%**	**0.1**	3.3%	0.1
Sonar	0%	0	**40%**	**0.9**	13.3%	0.3	26.7%	0.6
Movementlibras	3.3%	0.1	**43.3%**	**1.0**	33.3%	0.9	40%	0.9
Hillvally	3.3%	0.1	16.7%	0.4	**40%**	**0.8**	30%	0.6
Musk1	13.3%	0.5	66.7%	2.0	**86.7%**	**4.0**	73.3%	2.1
Multiple	66.7%	1.8	**73.3%**	2.8	**73.3%**	**3.0**	63.3%	1.9
Arrhythmia	6.7%	0.1	40%	1	43.3%	1.2	**53.3%**	**1.5**
Madelon	6.7%	0.2	**60%**	**1.5**	33.3%	1.1	56.7%	1.4
CNAE	16.7%	0.3	**30%**	**0.7**	23.3%	0.5	10%	0.2
SRBCT	20%	0.4	20%	0.6	23.3%	**0.7**	**26.7%**	0.6
Leukemia	3.3%	0.1	6.7%	0.1	13.3%	0.3	**16.7%**	**0.4**
DLBCL	3.3%	0.1	13.3%	0.3	10%	0.2	**16.7%**	**0.4**
Rank	3.65	3.75	**2.03**	2.09	2.25	2.13	2.06	**2.03**

Table 3. The PR and AN of the four MOPSO algorithms

Dataset	MOPSO		MOPSO-ICD		MOPSO-SCD		MOPSO-ISCD	
	PR	AN	PR	AN	PR	AN	PR	AN
Wine	0%	0	**6.7%**	**0.3**	**6.7%**	**0.3**	**6.7%**	**0.3**
Zoo	23.3%	1.1	40%	**4.2**	**53.3%**	3.5	**53.3%**	**4.2**
SPECT	16.7%	0.7	30%	**3**	**36.7%**	0.9	30%	1.4
WBCD	6.7%	0.3	16.7%	0.8	13.3%	0.6	**30%**	**1.5**
Ionosphere	3.3%	0.1	**6.7%**	**0.3**	3.3%	0.1	3.3%	0.1
Sonar	20%	0.8	36.7%	**3.0**	40%	2.2	**43.3%**	**3.0**
Movementlibras	23.3%	1.6	**60%**	**4.4**	26.7%	1.8	50%	**4.4**
Hillvally	26.7%	1.6	33.3%	2.2	**46.7%**	2.3	36.7%	**2.5**
Musk1	53.3%	3.7	76.7%	13.7	**83.3%**	12.2	80%	**20.4**
Multiple	50%	3.9	**63.3%**	5.4	50%	4.8	56.7%	**6.6**
Arrhythmia	26.7%	4.2	**56.7%**	**4.5**	**56.7%**	4.4	30%	1.8
Madelon	23.3%	1.5	33.3%	1.6	**46.7%**	**3.8**	36.7%	3.0
CNAE	0%	0	**13.3%**	0.5	10%	**0.7**	**13.3%**	0.5
SRBCT	6.7%	0.3	**20%**	0.8	6.7%	0.3	13.3%	**0.9**
Leukemia	6.7%	0.3	**10%**	**0.4**	3.3%	0.1	**10%**	**0.4**
DLBCL	0%	0	3.3%	0.1	0%	0	**13.3%**	**0.5**
Rank	3.78	3.75	1.97	**1.84**	2.41	2.75	**1.84**	1.66

5 Experimental Results

For the test results of HV and IGD, a statistical significance test, Wilcoxon test with a significance level of 0.05, is utilized to compare the performance between two methods. The symbol "↑" or "↓" represents that an algorithm achieved significantly better or worse classification performance than another one, and "o" means there is no significant difference between two methods. Due to page limit, the full results of HV and IGD are omitted. Tables 4 and 5 present the sum of "↑", "o" and "↓" between a pair of algorithms. For example, 0/14/2 (HV) in Table 4 means that NSGAII-ICD achieves similar HV as NSGAII on fourteen datasets, while worse HV than NSGAII on two datasets.

Figures 2 and 3 present a visual intuition about the obtained training and testing PFs from the eight algorithms. More specifically, 30 sets of feature subsets achieved by each approach from the 30 runs are combined into one union set where only the non-dominated solutions are kept and shown. In each sub-figure of Figs. 2 and 3, the two values within a bracket represent the number of original features and the training or testing classification error by using all features of one dataset. The vertical and horizontal axes are Error Rate (f_1) and Frate (f_2), respectively. Three datasets are chosen as representatives of small (SPECT), medium (CNAE), and large (DLBCL) datasets.

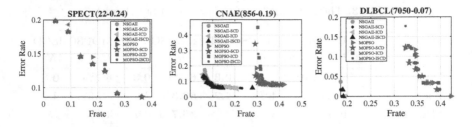

Fig. 2. The obtained PFs of eight algorithms on the training sets.

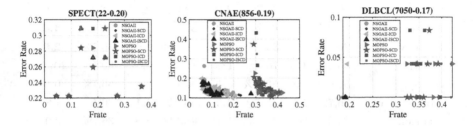

Fig. 3. The obtained PFs of eight algorithms on the test sets.

5.1 Performance on ICD

Tables 2 and 3 present the results of PR and AN of the eight EMO-based feature selection methods on the training sets of the sixteen datasets. They also provide the rankings of different algorithms (in the last row) with the Friedman Test based on PR and AN, respectively. In this paper, ICD uses the standard CD [3] to assign the CD metrics of the feature subsets which have different fitness values between each other (i.e., the NS_uni in Algorithm 1).

As shown in Tables 2 and 3, NSGAII-ICD and MOPSO-ICD respectively achieve significantly larger PR and AN values than NSGAII and MOPSO on

Table 4. The results of Wilcoxon test between the four NSGAII based feature selection algorithms

Algorithm	NSGAII	NSGAII-ICD	NSGAII-SCD
NSGAII-ICD	0/14/2 (HV) 0/14/2 (IGD)		
NSGAII-SCD	3/11/2 (HV) 2/12/2 (IGD)	5/11/0 (HV)5/11/0 (IGD)	
NSGAII-ISCD	0/14/2 (HV) 0/12/4 (IGD)	0/16/0 (HV) 0/16/0 (IGD)	0/13/3 (HV) 0/11/5 (IGD)

Table 5. The results of Wilcoxon test between the four MOPSO based feature selection algorithms

Algorithm	MOPSO	MOPSO-ICD	MOPSO-SCD
MOPSO-ICD	0/16/0 (HV) 1/15/0 (IGD)		
MOPSO-SCD	2/14/0 (HV) 1/15/0 (IGD)	0/15/1 (HV)0/16/0 (IGD)	
MOPSO-ISCD	1/15/0 (HV) 1/15/0 (IGD)	0/16/0 (HV)1/15/0 (IGD)	1/14/1 (HV) 1/14/1 (IGD)

most datasets. In terms of NSGAII-ICD and NSGAII, the largest difference on PR and AN is in the Zoo dataset where NSGAII-ICD can find the multiple feature subsets achieving the same classification performance almost in each run (86.7%) while NSGAII only has a small ratio value (13.3%). The rankings of NSGAII-ICD are higher than NSGAII both on PR and AN. However, the superiority of NSGAII-ICD to NSGAII on other two indicators, HV and IGD, is not significant. In Table 4, NSGAII-ICD achieves similar HV and IGD as NSGAII on fourteen datasets while even being significantly worse of HV and IGD on the Wine dataset.

The similar trend can also be seen between MOPSO and MOPSO-ICD in Table 3. Compared with MOPSO, MOPSO-ICD obtains greater values of PR and AN on all the datasets. The most significant improvement on AN is a result of improvement on the Musk1 dataset where MOPSO-ICD gets 3 times more AN than MOPSO. Moreover, the rankings of MOPSO-ICD (1.97 and 1.84) are higher than MOPSO (3.78 and 3.75) among the four MOPSO algorithms on PR and AN respectively. However, the results on HV and IGD in Table 4 show that there is no significant difference between MOPSO-ICD and MOPSO. Meanwhile, only on the Sonar dataset does MOPSO-ICD achieve a significantly better IGD value than MOPSO.

The results show that using the proposed ICD mechanism to assign crowding metrics of individuals or particles can help an EMO algorithm to find more diverse feature subsets with the same classification performance. However, the performances of HV and IGD are not significantly improved since the shapes of the fronts are similar on one dataset among the four NSGAII or the four MOPSO based feature selection algorithms especially in Fig. 3.

5.2   Performance on ISCD

ISCD employs SCD [23] to calculate the CD metrics of feature subsets in the NS_uni in Algorithm 1.

Now we will analyze the other two pairs of methods, NSGAII-SCD and NSGAII-ISCD, MOPSO-SCD and MOPSO-ISCD, respectively. According to the results in Table 2, NSGAII-ISCD shows the best performance among the four NSGAII algorithms. More specifically, NSGAII-ISCD gets higher values both on PR and AN than NSGAII-SCD on seven datasets, while loses advantage on five datasets, including the WBCD, Hillvally, Musk1, Multiple and Leukemia datasets. Meanwhile, NSGAII-ISCD is significantly worse than NSGAII-SCD both on HV and IGD on the Zoo, Musk1 and DLBCL datasets.

In Table 3, on more than half of the datasets, the higher values of both PR and AN are shown by MOPSO-ISCD rather than MOPSO-SCD. It is interesting to note that MOPSO-ISCD achieves significantly better HV and IGD results than MOPSO-SCD on the Multiple dataset while significantly worse HV and IGD results than MOPSO-SCD on the SPECT dataset.

The results show that the SCD mechanism working under the proposed method can find more diverse feature subsets without deteriorating the performance regarding HV and IGD.

Table 6. The obtained multiple feature subsets with the same classification accuracy

Dataset	Subset	Accuracy
Wine	$\{F_4, F_7, F_{10}\}$ $\{F_1, F_7, F_{10}\}$	91.1%
	$\{F_1, F_2, F_4, F_7, F_9, F_{10}\}$ $\{F_1, F_2, F_4, F_7, F_{10}, F_{12}\}$	94.3%
Zoo	$\{F_1, F_2, F_9\}$ $\{F_1, F_9, F_{12}\}$	85.8%
	$\{F_4, F_5, F_8, F_9\}$ $\{F_2, F_4, F_5, F_8\}$	90.0%
SPECT	$\{F_1\}\ \{F_{13}\}\ \{F_{15}\}\ \{F_{17}\}$	80.2%
	$\{F_1, F_{13}, F_{16}, F_{17}, F_{20}, F_{22}\}$ $\{F_1, F_{12}, F_{13}, F_{17}, F_{20}, F_{22}\}$	88.7%
Sonar	$\{F_{12}, F_{17}\}$ $\{F_{12}, F_{23}\}$	77.4%
	$\{F_2, F_6, F_9, F_{12}, F_{17}, F_{31}, F_{37}, F_{44}, F_{50}, F_{54}\}$ $\{F_2, F_6, F_{11}, F_{12}, F_{17}, F_{31}, F_{37}, F_{44}, F_{50}, F_{54}\}$	84.9%
Musk1	$\{F_{31}, F_{36}, F_{67}, F_{105}, F_{114}, F_{115}, F_{126}, F_{137}, F_{153}\}$ $\{F_{31}, F_{36}, F_{105}, F_{114}, F_{115}, F_{126}, F_{130}, F_{137}, F_{153}\}$	98.7%
	$\{F_1, F_5, F_{18}, F_{31}, F_{36}, F_{38}, F_{55}, F_{66}, F_{103}, F_{114}, F_{115}, F_{125}, F_{128}, F_{160}, F_{161}\}$ $\{F_1, F_5, F_{18}, F_{31}, F_{36}, F_{38}, F_{55}, F_{67}, F_{103}, F_{114}, F_{115}, F_{128}, F_{154}, F_{160}, F_{161}\}$	99.1%
Madelon	$\{F_{49}, F_{56}, F_{106}, F_{154}, F_{319}, F_{337}, F_{379}, F_{443}, F_{476}, F_{494}\}$ $\{F_{49}, F_{106}, F_{154}, F_{183}, F_{319}, F_{379}, F_{443}, F_{476}, F_{482}, F_{494}\}$	90.7%

5.3   Further Analysis on the Obtained Solutions

In Table 6, some examples are given on the obtained multiple feature subsets with the same classification accuracy by NSGAII-ISCD and MOPSO-ISCD in a single run. Due to the page limit, the selected feature subsets on six datasets, which are easy to display, are selected as representatives. The patterns are similar on the other ten datasets.

In Table 6, multiple different subsets obtained by NSGAII-ISCD or MOPSO-ISCD do achieve the same classification accuracy on different datasets. More specifically, for the Zoo dataset, both subset $\{F_4, F_5, F_8, F_9\}$ and $\{F_2, F_4, F_5, F_8\}$ can achieve the classification accuracy of 90.0%. As described in UCI Repository [4], the feature F_2 of Zoo is 'Feathers', and the feature F_9 is 'Backbone'. Obviously, the information of F_2 is easier to be collected than that of F_9. If only four features are allowed to be selected, most users would prefer subset $\{F_2, F_4, F_5, F_8\}$ to $\{F_4, F_5, F_8, F_9\}$. The similar situations also can be seen in other datasets. Additionally, on the Musk1 dataset, the four different feature subsets in Table 6, can almost achieve the same classification accuracy of 100%.

These examples demonstrate that improving the environmental selection strategies enable an algorithm to provide a user with multiple feature subsets which have the same or similar classification accuracy. Therefore, the user can choose the subset with low feature collection costs.

5.4   Computational Costs

Table 7 presents the average computational time (in minutes) of the eight methods on the sixteen datasets. All the eight algorithms can finish one run within

Table 7. Computation time (in minutes) of the eight methods

Dataset	NSGAII	NSGAII-SCD	NSGAII-ICD	NSGAII-ISCD	MOPSO	MOPSO-SCD	MOPSO-ICD	MOPSO-ISCD
Wine	0.3	0.2	0.3	0.3	0.2	0.3	0.3	0.3
Zoo	0.4	0.3	0.3	0.3	0.3	0.3	0.3	0.3
SPECT	0.5	0.5	0.5	0.5	0.5	0.6	0.6	0.5
WBCD	1.0	1.0	1.1	1.0	1.1	0.9	0.9	1.1
Ionosphere	0.8	0.9	0.8	1.0	0.9	1.0	0.9	1.0
Sonar	1.8	1.8	1.5	1.7	1.4	1.8	1.4	1.4
Movementlibras	3.8	3.7	3.6	3.2	3.3	2.7	2.7	3.2
Hillvally	8.0	7.6	7.3	6.4	6.5	7.2	6.6	6.3
Musk1	22.6	22.9	27.3	23.6	28.8	33.9	28.4	28.8
Multiple	72.1	85.1	75.9	86.9	96.8	98.9	117.3	94.0
Arrhythmia	29.2	22.6	26.5	22.8	14.0	14.2	14.1	16.1
Madelon	156.8	175.6	155.2	155.0	351.4	417.9	416.1	354.4
CNAE	116.5	113.2	113.5	137.9	145.0	171.5	142.2	172.2
SRBCT	53.9	65.6	65.4	68.6	14.7	12.5	14.3	12.5
Leukemia	90.2	111.3	120.8	93.3	20.7	20.7	20.9	20.9
DLBCL	141.7	160.4	118.8	167.1	35.5	27.5	27.7	33.2

8 minutes when the number of features is smaller than 100. The main reason of consuming longer time on large datasets is that all the eight algorithms are wrapper approaches where most of their time is spent on fitness evaluations.

Although compared with NSGAII or MOPSO, NSGAII-ICD or MOPSO-ICD have extra steps regarding the analysis of the selected features and the objective values during evolution, NSGAII-ICD or MOPSO-ICD is still computationally cheap. Even, on the DLBCL dataset, NSGAII-ICD and MOPSO-ICD spend shorter time than NSGAII and MOPSO, respectively. The reason is that ICD is fast. However, the computational time of NSGAII-SCD and MOPSO-SCD is longer on most of the large datasets than that of NSGAII and MOPSO, respectively. This is because SCD requires the calculation of crowding metrics for each dimension in the search space. When combining the proposed framework with SCD, NSGAII-ISCD and MOPSO-ISCD respectively spend shorter time than NSGAII-SCD and MOPSO-SCD on almost half of the datasets and spend similar time on the other half. The main reason is that ICD takes 0 as the final crowding metrics of the duplicated solutions rather than calculating based on each dimension.

6 Conclusions

This paper aimed to develop a new CD calculation method to calculate crowding metrics during environmental selection for finding multiple optimal feature subsets without deteriorating their overall performance. This goal has been achieved by assigning equally important crowding metrics to those different feature subsets with the same classification performance while assigning 0 to the duplicated solutions. The proposed method was examined by incorporating it into two popular EMO approaches, NSGAII and MOPSO, and compared with standard crowding distance, and SCD from [23] i.e. forming eight different EMO-based feature selection algorithms on sixteen datasets. The results showed that by using the proposed CD method, NSGAII and MOPSO based feature selection algorithms choose a smaller number of features while still achieve better classification accuracy than using all features (see Figs. 2 and 3). More importantly, the results showed that the proposed CD calculation method can make an EMO-based feature selection method produce multiple diverse feature subsets with the same classification performance, but the training time is not been shortened.

In the future, we will develop some novel strategies to further decrease the number of the duplicated feature subsets during the evolutionary process.

References

1. Coello, C.C., Lechuga, M.S.: Mopso: A proposal for multiple objective particle swarm optimization. In: 2002 IEEE Congress on Evolutionary Computation, vol. 2, pp. 1051–1056 (2002)
2. Cover, T., Hart, P.: Nearest neighbor pattern classification. IEEE Trans. Inf. Theory **13**(1), 21–27 (1967)
3. Deb, K., Agrawal, S., Pratap, A., Meyarivan, T.: A fast elitist non-dominated sorting genetic algorithm for multi-objective optimization: NSGA-II. In: Schoenauer, M. (ed.) PPSN 2000. LNCS, vol. 1917, pp. 849–858. Springer, Heidelberg (2000). https://doi.org/10.1007/3-540-45356-3_83
4. Dua, D., Graff, C.: UCI machine learning repository (2017). http://archive.ics.uci.edu/ml
5. Hamdani, T.M., Won, J.-M., Alimi, A.M., Karray, F.: Multi-objective feature selection with NSGA II. In: Beliczynski, B., Dzielinski, A., Iwanowski, M., Ribeiro, B. (eds.) ICANNGA 2007. LNCS, vol. 4431, pp. 240–247. Springer, Heidelberg (2007). https://doi.org/10.1007/978-3-540-71618-1_27
6. Harik, G.R., Lobo, F.G., Goldberg, D.E.: The compact genetic algorithm. IEEE Trans. Evol. Comput. **3**(4), 287–297 (1999)
7. He, Z., Yen, G.G.: Many-objective evolutionary algorithms based on coordinated selection strategy. IEEE Trans. Evol. Comput. **21**(2), 220–233 (2016)
8. Ishibuchi, H., Masuda, H., Tanigaki, Y., Nojima, Y.: Modified distance calculation in generational distance and inverted generational distance. In: Gaspar-Cunha, A., Henggeler Antunes, C., Coello, C.C. (eds.) EMO 2015. LNCS, vol. 9019, pp. 110–125. Springer, Cham (2015). https://doi.org/10.1007/978-3-319-15892-1_8
9. Kennedy, J., Eberhart, R.: Particle swarm optimization. In: Proceedings of ICNN 1995-International Conference on Neural Networks, vol. 4, pp. 1942–1948. IEEE (1995)
10. Liu, H., Motoda, H.: Feature Extraction, Construction and Selection: A Data Mining Perspective, vol. 453, Springer, Boston (1998)
11. Liu, H., Motoda, H., Setiono, R., Zhao, Z.: Feature selection: an ever evolving frontier in data mining. In: Feature Selection in Data Mining, pp. 4–13 (2010)
12. Liu, Y., Gong, D., Sun, J., Jin, Y.: A many-objective evolutionary algorithm using a one-by-one selection strategy. IEEE Trans. Cybern. **47**(9), 2689–2702 (2017)
13. Nguyen, B.H., Xue, B., Andreae, P., Ishibuchi, H., Zhang, M.: Multiple reference points-based decomposition for multiobjective feature selection in classification: static and dynamic mechanisms. IEEE Trans. Evol. Comput. **24**(1), 170–184 (2019)

14. Nguyen, H.B., Xue, B., Andreae, P., Zhang, M.: Particle swarm optimisation with genetic operators for feature selection. In: 2017 IEEE Congress on Evolutionary Computation, pp. 286–293 (2017)
15. Pudil, P., Novovičová, J., Kittler, J.: Floating search methods in feature selection. Pattern Recogn. Lett. **15**(11), 1119–1125 (1994)
16. Tran, B., Xue, B., Zhang, M.: Variable-length particle swarm optimization for feature selection on high-dimensional classification. IEEE Trans. Evol. Comput. **23**(3), 473–487 (2018)
17. While, L., Hingston, P., Barone, L., Huband, S.: A faster algorithm for calculating hypervolume. IEEE Trans. Evol. Comput. **10**(1), 29–38 (2006)
18. Xu, H., Xue, B., Zhang, M.: A duplication analysis based evolutionary algorithm for bi-objective feature selection. IEEE Trans. Evol. Comput. https://doi.org/10.1109/TEVC20203016049
19. Xue, B., Zhang, M., Browne, W.N.: Particle swarm optimization for feature selection in classification: a multi-objective approach. IEEE Trans. Cybern. **43**(6), 1656–1671 (2012)
20. Xue, B., Zhang, M., Browne, W.N., Yao, X.: A survey on evolutionary computation approaches to feature selection. IEEE Trans. Evol. Comput. **20**(4), 606–626 (2015)
21. Yue, C., Liang, J., Qu, B., Han, Y., Zhu, Y., Crisalle, O.D.: A novel multiobjective optimization algorithm for sparse signal reconstruction. Signal Process. **167**, (2020)
22. Yue, C., Liang, J., Qu, B., Yu, K., Song, H.: Multimodal multiobjective optimization in feature selection. In: 2019 IEEE Congress on Evolutionary Computation, pp. 302–309 (2019)
23. Yue, C., Qu, B., Liang, J.: A multiobjective particle swarm optimizer using ring topology for solving multimodal multiobjective problems. IEEE Trans. Evol. Comput. **22**(5), 805–817 (2017)
24. Zhang, X., Fang, L., Hipel, K.W., Ding, S., Tan, Y.: A hybrid project portfolio selection procedure with historical performance consideration. Expert Syst. Appl. **142**, (2020)

Deep Optimisation: Multi-scale Evolution by Inducing and Searching in Deep Representations

Jamie Caldwell[1]([✉])[ID], Joshua Knowles[2], Christoph Thies[1], Filip Kubacki[1],
and Richard Watson[1]

[1] Agents, Interaction and Complexity (AIC) Research Group,
Southampton University, Southampton SO17 1BJ, UK
`j.r.caldwell@soton.ac.uk`
[2] Invenia Labs, Cambridge CB2 1AW, UK

Abstract. The ability of evolutionary processes to innovate and scale up over long periods of time, observed in nature, remains a central mystery in evolutionary biology, and a challenge for algorithm designers to emulate and explain in evolutionary computation (EC). The Major Transitions in Evolution is a compelling theory that explains evolvability through a multi-scale process whereby individuality (and hence selection and variation) is continually revised by the formation of associations between formerly independent entities, a process still not fully explored in EC. Deep Optimisation (DO) is a new type of model-building optimization algorithm (MBOA) that exploits deep learning methods to enable multi-scale optimization. DO uses an autoencoder model to induce a multi-level representation of solutions, capturing the relationships between the lower-level units that contribute to the quality of a solution. Variation and selection are then performed within the induced representations, causing model-informed changes to multiple solution variables simultaneously. Here, we first show that DO has impressive performance compared with other leading MBOAs (and other rival methods) on multiple knapsack problems, a standard combinatorial optimization problem of general interest. Going deeper, we then carry out a detailed investigation to understand the differences between DO and other MBOAs, identifying key problem characteristics where other MBOAs are afflicted by exponential running times, and DO is not. This study serves to concretize our understanding of the Major Transitions theory, and why that leads to evolvability, and also provides a strong motivation for further investigation of deep learning methods in optimization.

Keywords: Model-Building Optimisation Algorithms · Deep autoencoder · Multi-scale search · Problem structure

1 Introduction

Deep Optimisation (DO) is a recent addition to the class of Model-Building Optimisation Algorithm (MBOA) that exploits deep learning concepts [3].

© Springer Nature Switzerland AG 2021
P. A. Castillo and J. L. Jiménez Laredo (Eds.): EvoApplications 2021, LNCS 12694, pp. 506–521, 2021.
https://doi.org/10.1007/978-3-030-72699-7_32

MBOAs are a class of black-box optimisation techniques inspired by the process of variation and selection in natural evolution. Variation defines the solution neighbourhood, and selection defines the path a search trajectory takes in that neighbourhood. MBOAs work by adapting the solution neighbourhood using a machine learning model to capture relationships within a distribution of promising solutions. These relationships form a compressed representation of the search space allowing selection to find higher quality solutions. Exploiting problem structure in this way has been successful in multiple problem domains. MBOAs share similarities with the well-known Variable Neighbourhood Search method [6], where a fixed set of neighbourhoods are manually defined prior to searching in them. However, in MBOAs, and specifically DO, a compression of a neighbourhood is induced from solutions found in a larger neighbourhood, providing a new and intelligent space to search in.

State-of-the-art (SOTA) MBOAs [16,20], however, do not use a neural network model. The MBOAs that do are generally limited to a single layer and produce uncompetitive results [5,17]. A summary of MBOAs using neural networks can be found in [18]. DO differs from these approaches in two important ways. First, DO constructs a deep representation of the solution by recursively transforming the solution representation. Each layer is constructed using solutions that are locally optimal relative to the neighbourhood defined by the preceding layer. Second, previous MBOAs that use a neural network model generate complete solutions from the model—Model-Informed Generation (MIG). In contrast, DO improves a solution by explicitly searching in a latent representation of the solution—Model-Informed Variation (MIV).

DO, like other MBOAs, is inspired by the processes of biological evolution. However, whereas other methods aim to model the structure of allelic associations in a population of individuals at a single level of biological organisation, DO is inspired by evolutionary processes operating over multiple levels of organisation. So called, Evolutionary Transitions in Individuality (ETIs), observed in biology [26], have the characteristic that multiple individuals at one level of organisation form associations that result in a new evolutionary unit at a higher level of organisation [19,25]. For example, unicellular life transitioned into multicellular organisms—and these are not merely cooperative relationships among coevolving unicellular organisms but new evolutionary units. These new units allow combinations of units from the previous layer to be combined and selected together, enabling evolution to move through solution space at a new level of representation. In DO, solution variables are encoded into a compressed latent space. Variation in this latent space is decoded back to the solution space, producing large organised variation. By using MIV, in an iterative selection process (local search in the latent space), DO represents the process of variation and selection acting on high-order evolutionary units. Each subsequent layer recodes again, in the analogue of successive hierarchical transitions in individuality [25].

Alternative methods that use machine learning to improve optimisation include: learning a heuristic for a set of problem instances [1,9,28]; using a surrogate model to approximate the fitness function [22]; adapting the learning function to bias future search [2,7]; embedding a machine learning model within the model of a combinatorial problem [10] and using machine learning to select a suitable solver [21]. The use of deep reinforcement learning algorithms for combinatorial optimisation is a popular approach [14]. Deep reinforcement learning is used to learn a policy that performs an action on a given state to improve the solution. This policy can then be used on multiple instances from the same problem class. Unlike DO, and in general MBOAs, these methods don't use the model to recode the neighbourhood of a search space.

In this paper, we investigate what type of problem characteristics DO can overcome that other MBOAs cannot. We first evaluate the performance of SOTA-MBOAs and DO on the multi-dimensional Knapsack problem, and show that DO can find solutions that SOTA-MBOAs cannot. We then explore types of problem characteristics, by using a synthetic problem construction, to distinguish the capabilities of SOTA-MBOAs and DO.

2   Model-Building Optimisation Algorithms

A fitness landscape is defined by the solutions neighbourhood and the fitness differences between neighbouring solutions. The characteristics of the landscape present challenges that an algorithm must overcome to find a superior solution efficiently. We are interested in methods that explore the fitness landscape in order to find a globally optimum solution despite these challenges.

MBOAs explore the landscape using processes inspired by natural evolution. Generally, MBOAs apply a hill-climber selection, i.e., a candidate solution is only replaced by an alternative solution with greater fitness. An MBOA overcomes challenges in the landscape by adapting the neighbourhood of a solution using a machine learning model. The model captures relationships between variables from a distribution of promising solutions. These relationships are then exploited to reorganise the neighborhood of a solution. An MBOA then continuous its search by exploring in the new and induced neighbourhood.

Exploring the neighborhood induced by the model can be done in one of two ways, MIG and MIV. For instance, for a binary problem, suppose that in a distribution of promising solutions we observe that two particular solution variables frequently take the same value as each other (i.e., "00" or "11"). We then desire a model that represents this relationship. In MIG, the model generates 00 and 11 more often than 01 or 10. In MIV, the model represents 00 and 11 as neighbours even though they are not neighbours in original space. Further, we expect differences between model capacities to have a significant impact on the adaptation that an MBOA can exhibit. In this paper we compare DO to the SOTA-MBOAs LTGA and hBOA, that differ both in their model capacities and model exploitation methods.

Linkage Tree Genetic Algorithm (LTGA). [20] uses agglomerative clustering to construct a hierarchical tree compression of the linkage information. The linkage information is provided by the dependency structure matrix (DSM), representing the variation of information between two clusters, populated from a distribution of promising solutions. Each variable is initially considered a separate cluster. After each clustering step, the DSM is updated to include the clustering. The outcome is a tree data-structure of linkage-sets, with each set representing a compression of lower-order linkage-sets.

New solutions are generated by applying a type of MIV method to the candidate solutions called optimal-mixing: As a generalised analogue of crossover in sexual recombination, the constructed linkage-set determines which variables to exchange between solutions. The model thus represents the structure of dependencies between variables, not the values assigned to variables. Values are constructed from a random solution drawn from the population. As such, the variation applied to a solution is dependent on the population and linkage-set. Each linkage-set is utilised by traversing the tree with each beneficial exchange being kept. This is applied to all solutions in a population. A new model is then constructed using the new distribution of solutions.

Hierarchical Bayesian Optimisation Algorithm (hBOA). [15] uses a Bayesian network to represent variable dependencies in a distribution of promising solutions. The construction process uses a greedy algorithm that adds directed edges to an empty graph based on how much it improves the Bayesian information criterion—a pairwise metric that accounts for the likelihood function and model complexity. The model construction requires both learning the linkage structure and conditional probabilities. Learning high-order interactions causes an exponential increase in the number of parameters. hBOA limits this by representing regularities in conditional probabilities using decision trees.

New solutions are generated by sampling the model to generate a complete solution (MIG). Restricted tournament replacement (RTR) is then used for solution replacement. Specifically, the solution, within a subset of the population, that is the nearest neighbour (Hamming distance) to the generated solution is used for competition. The solution with greater fitness is retained. As such, this process is functionally related to searching in a redefined neighbourhood. MIG is repeated to generate a new distribution of solutions. A new model is then constructed using the new distribution of solutions.

Deep Optimisation (DO). [3] constructs a deep autoencoder model using a layerwise procedure. The autoencoder model consists of an encoder (E) and decoder (D) network that transforms an input to a latent representation (H) and then back to the original input representation. Specifically, $S_r = D(E(S))$, where S and S_r is a solution and solution reconstruction respectively.

The algorithm is presented in Algorithm 1. A population is first initialised. Local variation and selection are applied in the solution representation, generating a distribution of promising candidate solutions. An autoencoder with a single hidden layer is then trained using the distribution of solutions as the training set. The parameters of the encoder and decoder are updated using back-propagation to minimise the error between the input solution and reconstructed solution. Dropout is used during training, to encourage a latent representation that captures the relationships between the variables.

Algorithm 1: Deep Optimisation

Initialize: Population of Solutions;
Initialize: Single layered Autoencoder model;
while *Model Depth < Maximum Depth* **do**
    for *Solution in Population* **do**
        while *Optimizing Solution* **do**
            └ Apply variation and selection to Solution using MIV

    `// apply transition`
    Train autoencoder using the population as training set
    └ Add hidden layer to the autoencoder model

Search then continues at the new latent representation using the learned model – this is the first 'transition'. Specifically, each solution in the population is updated using MIV in the following manner. A solution is encoded to produce a latent representation, H. A local change is then made to the latent representation, producing H'. Both representations are then decoded and binarized, to produce S_r and S'_r respectively. A new model-informed variant, S', is constructed from S using $S' = S + (S'_r - S_r)$. Intuitively, this approximates $S' = S'_r$ but avoids the requirement that the autoencoder reconstruction is perfect. If S' is fitter than S then S' is kept; otherwise, S is retained. MIV of this form is iterated to accumulate further improvements if available. We refer to this as 'local search in the latent space'. When applied to all solutions in the population this produces a distribution of solutions that are locally optimal relative to neighbourhood of the latent representation. A new hidden layer is then added to the model and trained, updating the parameters for both layers, using the new distribution of solutions. This is the second transition. This process is repeated through multiple transitions, applying local search in the latent representation of solutions and then training a new layer added on to the autoencoder. When the model has multiple layers, MIV can be applied at any layer.

DO, as the other MBOAs, performs best by prioritising simpler models over more complex models. In hBOA and LTGA this parsimony pressure is implicit in the model construction. DO enables this to be explicitly controlled using L1 and L2 regularisation. LTGA and hBOA differ both in the model type (linkage trees and Bayesian networks) and the way in which the model is used (MIV or MIG). In DO we can vary the model depth and the use of MIV or MIG independently. For simplicity, this paper reports DO results for MIV only. We summarise the three key differences between LTGA, hBOA and DO:

– Model capacity – LTGA uses a tree data structure whereas hBOA and DO use a graph data structure. LTGA only learns the linkage information. hBOA and DO learn the linkage information and the value assignments.

- Model construction method – LTGA and hBOA use pairwise statistics. DO uses a reconstruction error.
- Model exploitation method – LTGA and hBOA use their models in different ways to implicitly adapt the neighbourhood of the search process. DO explicitly searches in multiple levels of redefined neighbourhoods.

3   Multi-dimensional Knapsack Problem (MKP)

We first evaluate the performance of MBOAs and DO on exploiting problem structure from an applied problem. We use benchmark MKP instances from [4]. Results for a simple genetic algorithm (GA), LTGA and dBOA (hBOA = dBOA + RTR) are provided [13]. This paper adds results for DO and DO limited to a single hidden layer (DO_1). Further, we included results found by a single-bit local search (LS) and a 2-bit local search (2bLS), allowing for item swaps, to illustrate the performance improvement made by the models.

The objective of MKP is to assign a set of items that maximises the combined value while within the m knapsack dimensions. Formally, MKP is expressed as

$$\text{maximize} \quad \sum_{j=0}^{N} p_j x_j \quad , \tag{1}$$

$$\text{subject to} \quad \sum_{j=0}^{N} w_{ji} x_j \le c_i, \quad i = 1, \ldots, m \quad , \tag{2}$$

$$x_j \in \{0, 1\} \quad , \quad j \subset N \quad , \tag{3}$$

where p_j is the value of item j, N is the number of available items, x_j is a binary assignment determining if item j is selected, w_{ij} is the size of item j in dimension i and c_i is the total capacity of the knapsack in dimension i. The instances were constructed in the following way. The dimension size for each item w_{ij} was generated from a discrete uniform distribution $U(0, 1000)$. The capacity of each dimension c_i was calculated as $c_i = \alpha \sum_{j=1}^{N} w_{ij}$ where α is called the tightness ratio. Instances with a smaller tightness ratio and or higher knapsack dimension are generally considered more complex. Comparison is made using an instance size of $N = 100$, knapsack dimensions (m) of 5, 10 and 30 and tightness ratios (α) of 0.25 and 0.75.

All algorithms, except DO, use a repair operator to overcome the problem challenge of infeasible solutions. Given an infeasible solution, the repair operator iteratively removes individual items, in the order of lowest to highest utility, calculated by $u_j = p_j/(\sum_{i=0}^{m} r_{ij})$, until no constraints are violated. Then, items are iteratively added, in the order of highest to lowest utility, to the solution until an item addition violates a constraint. When this occurs, the item is not assigned and the repair is terminated. DO uses no repair operator and stays only within the feasible region; if a variation to a solution violates a constraint, it is rejected rather than repaired. Whilst comparing DO with MBOAs utilising a domain-specific repair operator appears to handicap DO, it is sufficient to demonstrate both the applicability of DO and its ability to exploit problem structure in applied problems.

All algorithms use a population size of 1000 and run until the population converges. The population of dBOA and LTGA are initialised using LS to improve the signal of good variable combinations. For DO, LS and 2bLS all solution variables are initialised with 0's (an empty knapsack). The average best solution gap found for 10 instances of a problem type m, α are reported in Table 1.

Table 1. Performance evaluation on MKP instances

		% Gap from optimum fitness						
m	α	LS	2bLS	GA	dBOA	LTGA	DO_1	DO
5	0.25	14.69	6.79	0.67	0.56	**0.19**	0.65	0.30
10	0.25	15.44	6.03	NA	1.33	0.75	1.43	**0.63**
30	0.25	14.91	4.70	NA	1.74	1.43	1.18	**0.65**
5	0.75	5.02	1.69	0.48	0.13	0.19	0.16	**0.05**
10	0.75	5.66	1.42	0.75	0.37	0.40	0.16	**0.07**
30	0.75	6.03	0.84	1.08	0.49	0.49	0.26	**0.11**
	Model	NA	NA	NA	Bayesian network	Linkage tree	AE 1D	AE 6D

The comparison between LS and 2bLS show a significant improvement when a variation operator can swap items in and out of the knapsack rather than only add items. This indicates the usefulness of domain-specific operators. The simple GA using a repair operator outperforms LS. hBOA, LTGA and DO all find superior solutions compared to the basic methods. Significantly, the results show that DO appears to provide good results compared to other MBOAs, with greatest performance observed in the most complex cases (large m). This shows that DO is able to exploit more structure from the population that other MBOAs cannot. Further, by comparing DO with DO_1, the results show that a deep model is required to exploit this structure.

It is not clear, in these randomly generated MKP instances, what type of problem structure DO is able to exploit that other MBOAs cannot. Martins et al. [12] found that LTGA can be improved by including a 2-point mutation, a repair operator and diversity maintenance. Similar to that used in the original paper [4]. However, this is not to say the model cannot improve optimisation. Using these additional domain-specific operators is a method for reducing the apparent problem complexity. Due to the random construction of these instances, the random structure may not be well suited for MBOAs. However, the results presented here are a comparison of the models used in MBOAs. Whilst improvements can be made to LTGA, hBOA and DO in the form of utilising domain-specific methods, for these results, the model is the primary method (or only method in the case of DO) that improves a candidate solution. Thus, an MBOA's performance can, we suggest, be improved by using a deep model.

It is important for us to understand why DO can exploit structure that the other MBOAs, using different models, cannot. Our main contribution, therefore, is to provide this understanding by using a synthetic problem construction to explore different problem challenges.

4   Exploring Characteristics of Problem Difficulty

In this section, we investigate the types of problem structure that distinguish the capabilities of LTGA, hBOA and DO. Specifically, to identify problem characteristics that cause a polynomial vs exponential time complexity differentiation between the MBOAs. Results thus far have failed to provide such a distinction [20]. MBOAs share the concept of adapting the neighbourhood of a solution to enhance search. Therefore, we focus on investigating the differences between the type of neighbourhood compression a model can perform (differences in model capacity and construction) and the differences between the methods used to exploit information from the model to inform search. We do this because an MBOA may be capable of accurately reorganising a solution's neighbourhood (sufficient model capacity), but cannot efficiently exploit the information to explore it. Conversely, an MBOA may be capable of efficiently exploring the neighbourhood of a solution, but the model cannot learn it. To explore these functionalities separately, we construct a synthetic optimisation problem that separates the complexity of reorganising a solutions neighbourhood (induction) and the type of search to perform in the reorganised neighbourhood (model exploitation). We achieve this by separating the fitness map $F: S \rightarrow F$ into two: a solution to higher-level binary representation (R) map $C: S \rightarrow R$ and a higher-level representation to fitness map $E: R \rightarrow F$; detailed in Eq. 4,

$$F(S) = E(R) = E(C(S)) \ . \tag{4}$$

The problem requires maximising F. The E map (environment) defines how variables in R combine to provide fitness contributions and, subsequently, provides the signal to find higher quality solutions. The types of E mappings investigated here are relatively straightforward, i.e., a globally optimal solution can be found in polynomial time using a hill-climber or an MBOA when $S = R$ (when C is an identity map). The C map (compression) defines the complexity of the neighbourhood reorganisation an MBOA must perform to see the signal for combining variables (provided by the E map). The C maps used here perform a compression that allows each unit in R to vary independently given a suitable change to S, i.e., local variation in R is the same as local variation in a bit-string. What makes this problem construction useful is that the change at S, informed by the model of an MBOA, required to make a single-unit change at R can be defined independently from how these changes are used to find higher-order solutions. This problem construction enables us to attribute the performance differences between MBOAs to specific problem characteristics related to either the reorganisation of the neighbourhood of a solution, by changing C, or the ability to explore the reorganised solution neighbourhood, by changing E.

4.1   Solution to Representation Mapping (C)

To ensure that C is learnable as the problem size increases, we construct a compression map using a concatenation of building-blocks (BBs)—a familiar construction used for evaluating the performance of MBOAs. Each BB maps a disjoint set of solution variables (S_m) to representation variables R_m as detailed in Eq. 5,

$$R = C(S) = [R_1, \ldots, R_m] = [bb(S_1), \ldots, bb(S_m)] \quad , \tag{5}$$

where bb is a BB mapping and m is the number of BBs. In this paper, a BB performs a compression from 4 solution units to 2 binary representation units. The compression represents a subset of 4 solutions (of size 4), that we call partial-solutions (PS), from a possible set of 16 solutions. Each PS is represented by a unique binary code at R_m. A Combination in S_m that is not a PS is represented at R_m by null values. The E map only rewards non-null values in R. Therefore, in finding a PS to a BB, the PS must be substituted with an alternative PS to avoid deleterious fitness changes.

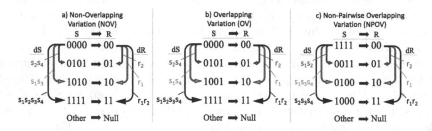

Fig. 1. A BB of size 4 contains 4 partial solutions each represented by a unique binary code at R. Alternative combinations are represented by nulls. A multi-unit variation dS in S is required to make a local variation dR in R. The types of multi-unit variations explored are (a) non-overlapping, (b) overlapping and (c) non-pairwise overlapping.

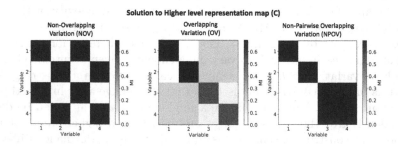

Fig. 2. The mutual information within a BB for each compression mapping (C) type.

The PS set controls the compression complexity of a BB. We synthetically determine this to induce different types of higher-order variations required in S to make a local change in R. The types explored in this paper are Non-Overlapping Variation (NOV), Overlapping Variation (OV) and Non-Pairwise Overlapping Variation (NPOV). Figure 1 illustrates, for each variation set type (BB mapping), the variation required in S, dS, to make a change in R. The NOV set presents the baseline complexity. The collection of variations in S that make a local change in R, i.e., from $R = [0,0]$ to $R = [1,0]$ or $R = [0,1]$ use variation operators, dS, that share no linkage information—all dS sets that perform a local change in R are disjoint. For OV, the collection of variation operators that produce a local variation in R share linkage information—all dS sets that perform a local change in R are not disjoint. In the example illustrated in Fig. 1.b, variable s_4 is shared between the variation operators that perform a local change at R. Note, our construction of overlapping problem structure differs from others [23,27]. Finally, the NPOV set contains overlapping linkage and, more importantly, the linkage cannot be identified using pairwise statistics. Specifically, the differences between solutions, and consequently the variation operator that moves between PSs, appear univariate using pairwise statistics—a property called pairwise independent functions [11]. In the example illustrated in Fig. 1.c this is true for variables s_1, s_2 and s_3. variable s_4 is used to maintain a consistent BB size across BB types and thus takes the same value as variable s_3 (does not add to the complexity).

Figure 2 presents the mutual-information between a pair of variables for each BB type. In the case of $C = $ NOV, linkage information does not overlap. For, $C = $ OV, linkage information does overlap. For $C = $ NPOV, variables s_1, s_2 and $s_3 s_4$ appear independent yet two variables must change simultaneously to avoid a deleterious fitness effect. A problem instance uses the same BB mapping for all BB. Therefore, the complexity of C is attributed to the particular characteristics of a BB mapping, i.e., if an algorithm can learn a BB mapping, learning more of the same only increases the complexity of separating the building-blocks. The optimal PS to use in each BB is a function of the dependencies between building-blocks, controlled separately by E. Therefore, an MBOA must first compress the search space to PSs and then vary between them to find higher-order solutions.

4.2   Representation to Fitness Mapping (E)

The E map defines how PSs, and therefore units in R, interact to provide a higher-order solution. The PSs are easily found by rewarding only non-null values in R. Specifically, all E maps have the contribution defined in Eq. 6,

$$F = \sum_{i=0}^{m} f(R_i), \quad f(R_i) = \begin{cases} 0, & \text{if } R_i = \text{null} \\ 1, & \text{otherwise} \end{cases} \tag{6}$$

To ensure that the complexity of C is present throughout the search process, and require an MBOA to learn C accurately, we separate R into two sets, R_1 and R_2. Each set contains only a single representation unit from each BB; thus each set contains m units. Both sets are used to calculate the fitness of the solution. This separation in the representation ensures that all PSs can be the correct PS to use in each BB at all stages of the search. Therefore, the C map's complexity does not get reduced during optimisation.

The baseline E mapping, called Generating Combinations (GC), does not contain higher-level dependencies. Search requires an MBOA to only combine a PS one at a time with the majority in the solution. Consequently, the signal that leads to a globally optimal solution can be identified from a distribution of randomly generated solutions that conserve PSs. Thus all MBOAs, regardless of the differences between the methods used to exploit information, can efficiently follow a signal to higher-order solutions. Thus the mapping evaluates an MBOAs capability to learn C. The fitness (Eq. 7), is a summation of the Hamming weight ($H()$) distance of each R set from the middle hamming weight of a subset ($m/4$). The separation of R_1 and R_2 produces a problem containing four global optima; each one containing the same PS for all BBs,

$$F = F + |H(R_1) - \frac{m}{4}| + |H(R_2) - \frac{m}{4}| \quad . \tag{7}$$

Interesting cases for MBOAs arise when a subset of low-order components can form high-order components, such as the case of hierarchical problem structure. Here we use the same hierarchical construction used in [24] as all MBOAs can overcome this characteristic when C is the identity map. This is because higher-order combinations can be efficiently identified by generating a distribution of solutions using the lower-level combinations. Therefore, this mapping evaluates an MBOA's capability to represent combinations of the variation operators at multiple scales of organisation. We name this mapping Hierarchically Generating Combinations (HGC). The hierarchical dependencies are represented by a binary tree containing $D = log_2(2m)$ layers. Each layer l contains 2^{D-l} parent nodes. Each node (r_l) represents an additive combination (A) of two child nodes (r_{l-1}^i, r_{l-1}^j) from the layer below. A parent node represents the common value if the child nodes contain the same value (excluding nulls), otherwise it represents a null. This compression is provided in Eq. 8. A parent node with a non-null value is assigned a fitness benefit. The total fitness, Eq. 9, is the sum of all fitness contributions from all parent nodes,

$$r_{l+1}^i = A(r_l^i, r_l^j), \quad A(r_i, r_j) = \begin{cases} r_i, & \text{if } r_i = r_j \\ \text{null}, & \text{otherwise} \end{cases}, \tag{8}$$

$$F = F + \sum_{l=0}^{D} \sum_{i=0}^{2^{D-l}} f(r_l^i), \quad f(r_i) = \begin{cases} 0, & \text{if } r_i = \text{null} \\ 1, & \text{otherwise} \end{cases} . \tag{9}$$

The hierarchical linkage is shuffled for each instance to ensure that overlapping variation operators are present at all scales of variations.

The last type we explore is when higher-order components are not found by combining lower-order components. Rather they are found by searching in the space of lower-order components. Therefore, this mapping evaluates an MBOA's

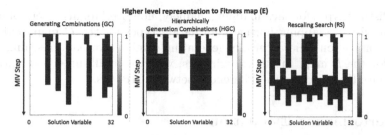

Fig. 3. An example of a solution trajectory, from a random solution (start of MIV) to a globally optimal solution (end of MIV) for each E map when $C = \text{NOV}$.

capability to exploit information from the model and search in the learnt representation (reorganised neighbourhood), hence we name this mapping Rescaling Search (RS). This characteristic is created by defining a unique path (UP) to the global solution. The location on the path is provided by coordinates: The Hamming weight of each R subset is used as coordinates for a 2D fitness mapping:

$$F = F + UP[H(R_1), H(R_2)] \quad . \tag{10}$$

The mapping contains a monotonically increasing slope function that takes any solution towards the start of the path at coordinates $(R_1, R_2) = (m, m/2)$. The path proceeds to coordinates $(m, 0) \rightarrow (0,0) \rightarrow (0, m) \rightarrow (m, m)$, where (m, m) is the global optimum. Each step along the path increases the fitness, and thus deviations from the path cause a deleterious fitness. Using R_1 and R_2 ensures that local variations in R must be performed. A non-local change would cause a change to the other coordinate, causing a deviation from the path. Note, the path length scales polynomially with respect to the problem size and is easy to follow via local search in R, thus differentiating it from the long path problem [8].

Figure 3 presents examples of solution trajectories, from a random solution initialisation (start of MIV steps) to a globally optimal solution (end of MIV steps) for each E map type. In these examples, $C = \text{NOV}$. For $E = \text{GC}$, search first identifies PSs and then continuous by substituting individual PS. In the case $E = \text{HGC}$, search is repeatedly rescaled to higher-orders of organisation, where the last adaptive variation makes a simultaneous change to half of the solution variables. For, $E = \text{RS}$, search cycles through multiple PS for each BB to find the global optimum. Note for $E = \text{RS}$ all PSs are used to search for the global optimum, but not necessarily used in the global optimum.

The combination of maps C and E create a complex fitness landscape relative to S. The capability of an MBOA to reorganise the neighbourhood of a solution, by capturing relationships using the model, is evaluated by differences in the C map. The capability of an MBOA to exploit the information from the model, to explore the reorganised neighbourhood, is evaluated by differences in the E map. The synthetic construction ensures that if an MBOA does not accurately reorganise and search within the neighbourhood, it will take exponential time to find a globally optimal solution. Thus a scaling analysis will suitably demonstrate if an MBOA can or cannot overcome the problem characteristics. We have created three distinct types for each mapping, namely: non-overlapping; overlapping and non-pairwise overlapping linkage information types for the C map, and generating combinations, hierarchically generating combinations and rescaling search types for the E map. In our experiments, we explore all nine combinations to investigate the performance differences between MBOAs.

5   Performance Evaluation

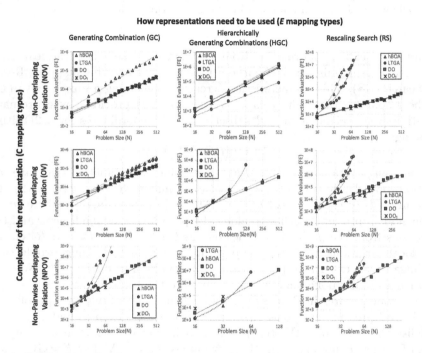

Fig. 4. DO is the only algorithm to show polynomial scaling for all experiments. C maps: non-overlapping (row 1 [r_1]), overlapping (r_2), and non-pairwise overlapping (r_3); and E maps: generating combinations (column 1 [c_1]), hierarchically generating combinations (c_2) and rescaling search (c_3).

In this section, we assess the performance of LTGA, hBOA and DO and DO_1 on all combinations of complexity and environment maps (Fig. 4). The data points present the average number of function evaluations performed to find the global optimum solution in up to 10 independent runs (for runs with greater than 10^7 function evaluations, three independent runs are performed). The population size is set such that within all independent runs, a global optimum is found. The population is initialised using local search such that the distribution contained all PSs (removing potential challenges associated with finding the PSs). Algorithms are terminated if a global solution is not found within 10^9 function evaluations, and therefore no data point is provided. An advantage of LTGA and hBOA is that they do not have additional parameters to tune. A disadvantage is that this does not admit control over the inductive bias. DO, like other neural network methods, has several tuneable parameters. These values were selected from preliminary results on a small sample of problems. Specifically, hidden layer compression $= 0.8$ (maximum layers used was 9), dropout rate: 0.2, epochs: 400, learning rate $= 0.002$. Regularisation parameters in the range L1 $= [1 \times 10^{-3} : 1 \times 10^{-5}]$, L2 $= [2 \times 10^{-3} : 2 \times 10^{-6}]$.

The MBOA distinctions we conclude from these experiments are:

1. A deep representation, and the ability to search in deep representations, are required when generating hierarchical combinations of OV operators (see Fig. 4.$r_{[2,3]}c_2$) and representing NPOV operators (see Fig. 4.r_3)—distinguishing the capability of deep representations from shallow representations.
2. LTGA and hBOA fail to perform local search in the neighbourhood defined by the model, DO is successful here (see Fig. 4.c_3)—distinguishing the model exploitation capability of DO from LTGA and hBOA.
3. LTGA fails to learn and exploit overlapping variation operators and requires exponential time complexity as the size of overlap increases, hBOA and DO are successful here (see Fig. 4.r_2c_2)—distinguishing the induction capability of DO and hBOA from LTGA.
4. hBOA and LTGA fail to learn NPOV operators causing exponential scaling as the number of operators increases, DO is successful here (see Fig. 4.r_3)—distinguishing the induction capability of DO from LTGA and hBOA

As previously hypothesised, LTGA fails when variation operators share linkage (overlap). LTGA does not fail when overlapping linkage is small, (see Fig. 4.r_2c_1). However, when variation operators need to be rescaled to higher-orders ($E = $ HGC), the failure of LTGA to capture overlap in C creates failure at higher-level search (see Fig. 4.r_2c_2). The models of hBOA and DO use a graph data structure and are capable of representing overlap. DO$_1$ also failed here (DO$_1$ generally fails abruptly rather than showing exponential scaling) implying that hierarchical overlapping dependencies require a deep representation. Both LTGA and hBOA fail on problems containing NPOV operators (see Fig. 4.r_3). This is due to the models inability to compress the solution space as evidenced by the failure in the baseline environment ($E = $ GC, see Fig. 4.r_3c_1). Further, DO$_1$ also fails here, indicating this set of variation operators require a deep model to represent. LTGA and hBOA fail when $E = $ RS (see Fig. 4.c_3). As failure occurs in the baseline compression map ($C = $ NOV), for which we know all algorithms can represent (evidenced by Fig. 4.r_1c_1), this failure is due to the way models are used to inform search. Specifically, LTGA and hBOA fail to perform local search using the model. On the other hand, DO is capable of explicitly searching in the compressed neighbourhood of all C maps (Fig. 4.c_3).

Here we have identified problem challenges that differentiate the performance of MBOAs from DO. Further research is required to understand if MKP instances contain the problem challenges identified here and if these challenges are responsible for the performance differences between DO and MBOAs in MKP.

6 Conclusion

In this paper, we investigated the optimisation capabilities of emulating the process of Major Transitions in Individuality via DO. DO showed an impressive performance when compared to State-Of-The-Art (SOTA) methods on MKP instances (even without using a problem-specific repair operator). Further, we investigate the types of problem structure that differentiate the performance between SOTA methods. We identified that overlapping variation, non-pairwise overlapping variation and local search in the reorganised neighbourhood are distinct problem characteristics that DO can solve that neither hBOA nor LTGA can solve. The results showing DO outperforming DO_1 (i.e., using only a single hidden layer) demonstrate that a deep representation is necessary to capture the problem structure correctly. The results from this paper suggest that simple evolutionary processes (local search), when operating at multiple scales, can provide optimisation capabilities that outperform SOTA MBOAs. This demonstrates that the intuitive links between multi-scale evolution and deep learning [25] can be exploited for optimisation, suggesting further investigation into how other advanced tools available for deep learning can be applied to MBOAs.

Acknowledgements. We acknowledge financial support from the EPSRC Centre for Doctoral Training in Next Generation Computational Modelling grant EP/L015382/1.

References

1. Bello, I., Pham, H., Le, Q.V., Norouzi, M., Bengio, S.: Neural combinatorial optimization with reinforcement learning. arXiv preprint arXiv:1611.09940 (2016)
2. Boyan, J., Moore, A.W.: Learning evaluation functions to improve optimization by local search. J. Mach. Learn. Res. **1**(Nov), 77–112 (2000)
3. Caldwell, J., Watson, R.A., Thies, C., Knowles, J.D.: Deep optimisation: Solving combinatorial optimisation problems using deep neural networks. arXiv preprint arXiv:1811.00784 (2018)
4. Chu, P.C., Beasley, J.E.: A genetic algorithm for the multidimensional knapsack problem. J. Heuristics **4**(1), 63–86 (1998)
5. Churchill, A.W., Sigtia, S., Fernando, C.: A denoising autoencoder that guides stochastic search. arXiv preprint arXiv:1404.1614 (2014)
6. Hansen, P., Mladenović, N., Pérez, J.A.M.: Variable neighbourhood search: methods and applications. Ann. Oper. Res. **175**(1), 367–407 (2010)
7. Hopfield, J.J., Tank, D.W.: "neural" computation of decisions in optimization problems. Biol. Cybern. **52**(3), 141–152 (1985)
8. Horn, J., Goldberg, D.E., Deb, K.: Long path problems. In: Davidor, Y., Schwefel, H.-P., Männer, R. (eds.) PPSN 1994. LNCS, vol. 866, pp. 149–158. Springer, Heidelberg (1994). https://doi.org/10.1007/3-540-58484-6_259
9. Khalil, E., Dai, H., Zhang, Y., Dilkina, B., Song, L.: Learning combinatorial optimization algorithms over graphs. In: Advances in Neural Information Processing Systems, pp. 6348–6358 (2017)
10. Lombardi, M., Milano, M., Bartolini, A.: Empirical decision model learning. Artif. Intell. **244**, 343–367 (2017)

11. Martins, J.P., Delbem, A.C.: Pairwise independence and its impact on estimation of distribution algorithms. Swarm Evol. Comput. **27**, 80–96 (2016)
12. Martins, J.P., Fonseca, C.M., Delbem, A.C.: On the performance of linkage-tree genetic algorithms for the multidimensional knapsack problem. Neurocomputing **146**, 17–29 (2014)
13. Martins, J.P., Neto, C.B., Crocomo, M.K., Vittori, K., Delbem, A.C.: A comparison of linkage-learning-based genetic algorithms in multidimensional knapsack problems. In: 2013 IEEE Congress on Evolutionary Computation, pp. 502–509. IEEE (2013)
14. Mazyavkina, N., Sviridov, S., Ivanov, S., Burnaev, E.: Reinforcement learning for combinatorial optimization: A survey. arXiv preprint arXiv:2003.03600 (2020)
15. Pelikan, M., Goldberg, D.E.: Hierarchical bayesian optimization algorithm. In: Pelikan, M., Sastry, K., CantúPaz, E. (eds.) Scalable Optimization via Probabilistic Modeling. Studies in Computational Intelligence, vol. 33, pp. 63–90. Springer, Berlin (2006). https://doi.org/10.1007/978-3-540-34954-9_4
16. Pelikan, M., Goldberg, D.E., Tsutsui, S.: Hierarchical bayesian optimization algorithm: toward a new generation of evolutionary algorithms. In: SICE 2003 Annual Conference (IEEE Cat. No. 03TH8734), vol. 3, pp. 2738–2743. IEEE (2003)
17. Probst, M.: Denoising autoencoders for fast combinatorial black box optimization (2015)
18. Santana, R.: Gray-box optimization and factorized distribution algorithms: where two worlds collide (2017)
19. Smith, J.M., Szathmáry, E.: The Major Transitions in Evolution. Oxford University Press, Oxford (1997)
20. Thierens, D., Bosman, P.A.: Hierarchical problem solving with the linkage tree genetic algorithm. In: Proceedings of the 15th Annual Conference on Genetic and Evolutionary Computation, pp. 877–884 (2013)
21. Volpato, R., Song, G.: Active learning to optimise time-expensive algorithm selection (2019)
22. Vu, K.K., D'Ambrosio, C., Hamadi, Y., Liberti, L.: Surrogate-based methods for black-box optimization. Int. Trans. Oper. Res. **24**(3), 393–424 (2017)
23. Wang, S.M., Wu, J.W., Chen, W.M., Yu, T.L.: Design of test problems for discrete estimation of distribution algorithms. In: Proceedings of the 15th Annual Conference on Genetic and Evolutionary Computation, pp. 407–414 (2013)
24. Watson, R.A., Hornby, G.S., Pollack, J.B.: Modeling building-block interdependency. In: Eiben, A.E., Bäck, T., Schoenauer, M., Schwefel, H.-P. (eds.) PPSN 1998. LNCS, vol. 1498, pp. 97–106. Springer, Heidelberg (1998). https://doi.org/10.1007/BFb0056853
25. Watson, R.A., Szathmáry, E.: How can evolution learn? Trends Ecol. Evol. **31**(2), 147–157 (2016)
26. West, S.A., Fisher, R.M., Gardner, A., Kiers, E.T.: Major evolutionary transitions in individuality. Proc. Nat. Acad. Sci. **112**(33), 10112–10119 (2015)
27. Yu, T.L., Sastry, K., Goldberg, D.E.: Linkage learning, overlapping building blocks, and systematic strategy for scalable recombination. In: Proceedings of the 7th Annual Conference on Genetic and Evolutionary Computation, pp. 1217–1224. GECCO 2005 (2005)
28. Zhang, W., Dietterich, T.G.: Solving combinatorial optimization tasks by reinforcement learning: a general methodology applied to resource-constrained scheduling. J.of Artif. Intell. Res. **1**, 1–38 (2000)

Evolutionary Planning in Latent Space

Thor V. A. N. Olesen[1], Dennis T. T. Nguyen[1], Rasmus B. Palm[1],
and Sebastian Risi[1,2(✉)]

[1] IT University of Copenhagen, Copenhagen, Denmark
[2] modl.ai, Copenhagen, Denmark

Abstract. Planning is a powerful approach to reinforcement learning
with several desirable properties such as sampling efficiency. However,
it requires a world model, which is not readily available in many real-
life problems. In this paper, we propose to learn a world model that
enables *Evolutionary Planning in Latent Space* (EPLS). We use a Variational Auto Encoder (VAE) to learn a compressed latent representation of individual observations and extend a Mixture Density Recurrent
Neural Network (MDRNN) to learn a stochastic, multi-modal forward
model of the world used for planning. We use the Random Mutation Hill
Climbing (RMHC) algorithm to find a sequence of actions that maximize
expected reward in this learned model of the world. We demonstrate how
to build a world model by bootstrapping it with rollouts from a random
policy and iteratively refining it with rollouts from an increasingly accurate planning policy using the learned world model. After few iterations,
our planning agents exceed standard model-free reinforcement learning
approaches, which demonstrates the viability of our approach. Code to
reproduce the experiments is available at https://github.com/two2tee/
WorldModelPlanning and videos at https://youtu.be/3M39QgeF27U.

Keywords: World models · Evolutionary planning · Iterative
training · Model-based reinforcement learning

1 Introduction

Planning by searching for action sequences that maximize expected reward is a
powerful approach to reinforcement learning problems, which has recently lead
to breakthroughs in complex domains such Go, Shogi, Chess, and Atari games
[21–23]. To plan, the agent needs access to a model of the world which it can
use to simulate the outcome of actions, to determine which course of action is
best. Planning using a model of the world also allows you to introspect what the
agent is planning and why it thinks certain actions are preferable. It even allows
you to add constraints or change the objective at runtime.

In games, these world models are readily available and given by the rules of
the game. However, for many real-world problems like driving a car, they are
not available.

T. V. A. N. Olesen and D. T.T. Nguyen—Contributed equally

© Springer Nature Switzerland AG 2021
P. A. Castillo and J. L. Jiménez Laredo (Eds.): EvoApplications 2021, LNCS 12694, pp. 522–536, 2021.
https://doi.org/10.1007/978-3-030-72699-7_33

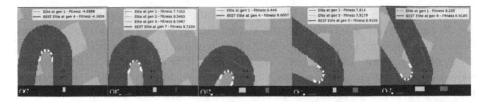

Fig. 1. Planed trajectories using evolutionary planning in the latent space of a learned world model.

In problems where a world model is not available, one can instead use model-free reinforcement learning, which learns a policy that directly maps from the environment state to the actions that maximize expected reward. However, these approaches often require many samples from the real environment, which is often expensive to obtain when learning the statistical relationship between states, actions, and rewards. That is especially true if the environment requires complex sequences of actions to observe any rewards.

Alternatively, a *learned* world model is used to find an optimal policy, which is the approach taken in this paper. This is known as model-based reinforcement learning. Learning a model of the world requires fewer samples of the environment than learning a policy directly from the state space since it can use supervised learning methods to predict the environment state transitions, regardless of the reward signal being sparse or not. Several models have been proposed for learning world models [6, 8, 21].

In this paper, we propose an extension to the Mixture Density Recurrent Neural Network (MDRNN) model [6], which makes it suitable for planning, and demonstrate how to do evolutionary planning in latent space by using the learned world model. See Fig. 1 for examples of planned trajectories and Fig. 2 for an overview of the proposed method.

We further show how to iteratively improve the world model by using the existing world model to do the planning and using the planned policy to sample better rollouts of the environment, which, in turn, are used to train a better world model. This process is bootstrapped by using an initial random policy. Given few iterations, we obtain results that outperform standard model-free approaches, demonstrating the viability of the approach.

2   Related Work

2.1   Planning

In planning, an agent uses a model of the world to predict the consequences of its actions and select an optimal action sequence accordingly. Planning is a powerful technique that has recently lead to breakthroughs in complex domains such as Go, Chess, Shogi, and Atari [21–23].

Monte-Carlo Tree Search (MCTS) is a state-of-the-art planning algorithm for discrete action spaces, which iteratively builds a search tree that explores the most promising paths using a fast, often stochastic, rollout policy [3].

Rolling Horizon Evolutionary Algorithms (RHEA) encode individuals as sequences of actions and uses evolutionary algorithms to search for optimal trajectories. *Rolling Horizon* (RH) refers to how the first action in a plan is executed before the plan is reevaluated and adjusted, looking one step further into the future and slowly expanding the horizon [5,10,11,18]. RHEA naturally handles continuous action spaces. Tong et al. [24] show how to learn a prior for RHEA by training a value and policy network. The value network reduces the required planning horizon by estimating the rewards of future states. The policy network helps initialize the population of planning action trajectories to narrow the search scope to a near-optimal local action policy-subspace. In our approach, we use a randomly initialized set of planning trajectories and improve them iteratively through evolution.

Random Mutation Hill-Climb (RMHC) is a simple and effective type of evolutionary algorithm that repeats the process of randomly selecting a neighbour of a best-so-far solution and accepts the neighbour if it is better than or equal to the current best-so-far solution. This local search method starts with a solution and iteratively tries to improve it by taking random steps or restarting from another region in the policy space.

Planning approaches that rely on imperfect models may plan non-optimal trajectories. The authors of [17] suggest incorporating uncertainty estimation into the forward model to improve the agent. In general, planning under uncertainty has been extensively studied [2,12,16].

2.2 Learning World Models

If a world model is unavailable, it is learned from environment observations. Using such a model to find a policy is generally known as model-based Reinforcement Learning (RL).

World Models [6] introduces a stochastic recurrent world model learned from environment observations under an initially random policy. The model uses a Variational Auto-Encoder (VAE) to encode pixel inputs into a low dimensional latent vector. A recurrent neural network (RNN) is trained to predict sequences of latent states using a Gaussian Mixture Model to capture the uncertain and multi-modal nature of the environment. Notably, the authors do not use this world model for planning, but rather for training a simple single-layer linear policy network.

In *MuZero* [21], the authors do planning with a learned model in video and board games by using tree-based search (MCTS) to enable imitation learning with a policy network.

In *PlaNet* [8], the authors have shown it is possible to do online planning in latent space using an adaptive randomized algorithm on a recurrent state-space model (SSM) with a deterministic and stochastic component and a multi-step prediction objective. *PlaNet* [8] is the approach that is most similar to the work presented here (i.e., online planning on a learned model). However, it uses a rather complicated dynamics model and planning algorithm. In *Dreamer* [7], the authors use the *PlaNet* world model but no longer do online planning. Instead, their Dreamer agent uses an actor-critic approach to learn behaviors that consider rewards beyond a horizon. Namely, they learn an action model and value model in the latent space of the world model. Thus, their approach is similar to *World Models* [6] where they plan on a learned model by training a policy inside the simulated environment with backpropagation and gradient descent, instead of evolution. The novel part is using a value network to estimate rewards beyond a finite imagination horizon. Also, *World Models* [6] does not show how to do planning on a fully learned model, since the reward signal is not learned in their model. Finally, MuZero [21] relies on extensive training data and access to unrealistic GPU resources, which may not be feasible in practice.

In another related approach, *Neural Game Engine* [1], the authors show how to learn accurate forward models from pixels that can generalize to different size game levels. However, their methods currently only work on grid-based world games. The authors argue it does not work as a drop-in replacement for the kind of world models we need in real-life environments. For this purpose, the authors recommend looking into some of the previously presented methods that learn a latent dynamics model with a 2D state-space model (SSM) like shown in PlaNet and Dreamer that both use a Recurrent State Space Model (RSSM).

3   Approach

We use a model-based RL approach to solve a continuous reinforcement learning control task. We achieve this through online evolutionary planning on a learned model of the environment. Our solution combines a world model [6] with rolling horizon evolutionary planning [18]. See Fig. 2 for an overview.

Similar to the original world model [6], our model uses a visual sensory component (V) to compress the current state into a small latent representation. The memory component (M) is extended to predict the next latent state, the expected reward, and whether the environment terminates. In the original world model, the decision-making component uses a simple learned linear model that maps latent and hidden states directly to actions at each time step. In contrast, EPLS uses a random mutation hill-climbing (RMHC) algorithm as the decision-making component that exploits M to do online planning in latent space.

3.1   Learning the World Model

The **visual component** (V) is implemented as a convolutional variational autoencoder (ConvVAE), which learns an abstract, compressed representation $z_t \in \mathbb{R}^{64}$ of states (i.e., frames) $s_t \in \mathbb{R}^{64 \times 64 \times 3}$ using an encoder and decoder as shown in Fig. 3.

The VAE encoder is a neural network that outputs a compressed representation of a state s (i.e., frame) using a deep convolutional neural network (DCNN)

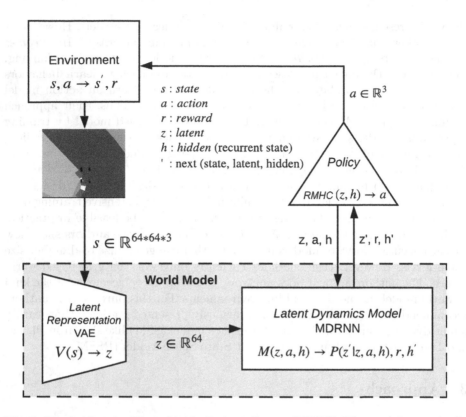

Fig. 2. Evolutionary Planning in Latent Space (EPLS). The raw observation is compressed by V at each time step t to produce a latent vector z_t. RMHC does planning by repeatedly generating, mutating, and evaluating action sequences $a_0, ..., a_T$ in the learned world model, M where T is the horizon. The learned world model, M, receives an action a_t, latent vector z_t and hidden state h_t and predicts the simulated reward r_t, next latent vector z_{t+1}, and next hidden state h_{t+1}. The predicted states are used with the next action as inputs for M to let the agent simulate the trajectory in latent space. The first action of the plan with the highest expected total reward in the simulated environment is executed in the real environment.

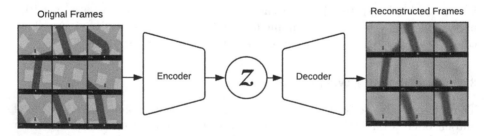

Fig. 3. Flow diagram of a Variational Autoencoder (VAE). The VAE learns to encode frames into latent vectors by minimizing the pixel-wise difference between input frames and reconstructed frames (i.e., L2 or MSE) generated by decoding the latent vectors.

of four stacked convolutional layers and non-linear relu activations to compress the frame and two fully-connected (i.e., dense) layers that encode the convolutional output into low dimensional vectors μ_z and σ_z:

$$encoder : s \in \mathbb{R}^{64 \times 64 \times 3} \rightarrow \mu_z \in \mathbb{R}^{64}, \sigma_z \in \mathbb{R}^{64} . \tag{1}$$

The means μ_z and standard deviations σ_z are used to sample a latent state z from a multivariate Gaussian with diagonal covariance:

$$z \in \mathbb{R}^{64} \sim \mathcal{N}(z|\mu_z, \sigma_z) . \tag{2}$$

The decoder is a neural network that learns to decode and reconstruct the state (i.e., frame) s given the latent state z using a deep CNN of four stacked deconvolution layers:

$$decoder : z \in \mathbb{R}^{64} \rightarrow s' \in \mathbb{R}^{64 \times 64 \times 3} . \tag{3}$$

Each convolution and deconvolution layer uses a stride of two. Convolutional and deconvolutional layers use relu activations. The output layer maps directly to pixel values between 0 and 1. The VAE is trained with the standard VAE loss [13].

We extend the **memory component** (M) of [6] to output an expected reward r and a binary terminal signal τ to obtain a fully learned world model that supports planning entirely in latent space. M is an LSTM with 512 hidden units, which jointly models the next latent state z_t, reward r_t, and whether or not the environment terminates, τ_t,

$$p(z_t, r_t, \tau_t|h_{t-1}) = p(z_t|h_{t-1})p(r_t|h_{t-1})p(\tau_t|h_{t-1}) . \tag{4}$$

The LSTM hidden state h_t depends on the previous hidden state h_{t-1}, the current action a_t, and the current latent state z_t such that $h_t = \text{LSTM}(z_t, a_t, h_{t-1})$.

Most complex environments are stochastic and multi-modal so $p(z_t|h_{t-1})$ is approximated as a mixture of Gaussian distribution (MD-RNN). The output of the MDRNN are the parameters π, μ, σ of a parametric Gaussian mixture model where π represents mixture probabilities:

$$p(z_t|h_{t-1}) = \sum_{k=1}^{5} \pi_k \mathcal{N}(z_t|\mu_k, \sigma_k) , \tag{5}$$

where π, μ and Σ are linear functions of h_{t-1} and each mixture component is a multivariate Gaussian distribution with diagonal covariance.

We model the reward r using a Gaussian with a fixed variance of one such that

$$p(r_t|h_{t-1}) = \mathcal{N}(r_t|\mu_t^\tau, 1) , \tag{6}$$

where μ_t^τ is a linear function of h_{t-1}. Finally we model the terminal state τ using a Bernoulli distribution,

$$p(\tau_t|h_{t-1}) = p^{\tau_t}(1-p)^{1-\tau_t} , \tag{7}$$

where $p = \text{sigmoid}(f(h_{t-1}))$ is the sigmoid of a linear function of h_{t-1}.

We train M by minimizing the negative log-likelihood of $p(z_t, r_t, \tau_t | h_{t-1})$ for observed rollouts of the environment,

$$\mathcal{L} = -\log p(z_t, r_t, \tau_t | h_{t-1}) = \text{MSE}(r_t, \hat{r}_t) + \text{BCE}(\tau_t, \hat{\tau}_t) + \text{GMM-NLL}(z_t, \hat{z}_t), \quad (8)$$

where MSE is the mean squared error, BCE is the binary cross-entropy, GMM-NLL is the negative log likelihood of a gaussian mixture model, and $\hat{z}, \hat{r}, \hat{\tau}$ are the observed latent states, rewards and terminals. The learnable weights and biases in the different neural network-based modules are all initialized uniformly by default in PyTorch: $U(-\sqrt{(k)}, \sqrt{(k)})$ with $k = \frac{1}{in\_features}$ where $in\_features$ is the size of each input sample.

3.2 Evolutionary Planning in Latent Space

Once the world model is trained, it can enable planning (Fig. 4). We use Random Mutation Hill Climbing (RMHC), which is a simple evolutionary algorithm. RMHC works by iteratively mutating and evaluating individuals, and letting the elite be the starting point in the next round of mutation. We use RMHC to find a sequence of actions that maximize the expected reward as predicted by the world model. The action sequence length, also known as the horizon, determines how far into the future the agent plans. Finally, shift buffering is used to avoid repeating the entire search process from scratch at every time step [4]. In short, after each planning step, we pop the first action of the action sequence and add a new random action to the end of the action sequence. This modified plan is then the starting point for the next planning step.

4   Experiments

We test our approach on the continuous control `CarRacing-v0` domain [14], built with the Box2D physics engine. At every trial, the agent's driving abilities are evaluated on a randomly generated track (where randomness affects the number of track tiles, its layout, and car starting position). Reaching a high score requires the agent to plan how to make each turn with continuous actions, which makes it a suitable test domain for our evolutionary latent planning approach. The environment yields a reward of -0.1 each time step and a reward of $+1000/N$ for each visited track tile where N is the total number of tiles in the track. While it is not necessarily difficult to drive slowly around a track, reaching a high reward is difficult for many current RL methods [6].

Since the environment gives observations as high dimensional pixel images, these are resized to 64×64 pixels before being used as observations in our world model. Pixels are stored as three floating-point values between 0 and 1 that represent each of the RGB channels. The dimension of our latent space is 64 since this yielded better reconstructions than using 32 as in [6]. Actions contain three numeric components that represent the degree of steering, acceleration, and braking.

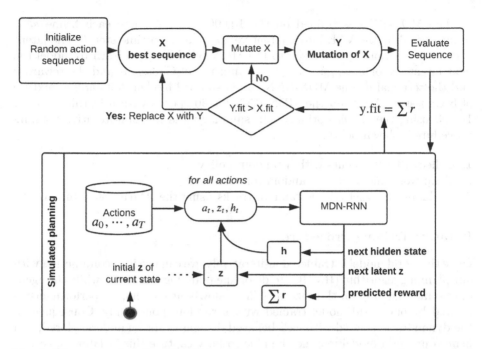

Fig. 4. Planning details. RMHC initializes a random sequence of actions sampled from the environment and mutates it repeatedly across generations. Each plan is evaluated in latent space using the simulated environment where the fitness metric is the total undiscounted expected reward associated with executing the planning trajectory in latent space.

Capturing Rollouts. The MDN-RNN and VAE models are trained in a supervised manner, and rely on access to a representative dataset of environment rollouts for training and testing. Each sample is a rollout in the environment and consists of a sequence of (state, action, reward, terminal) tuples. States, rewards, and terminals are produced by the environment when given an action. Initially, we use a random policy in the environment and record states, rewards, actions, and terminals in T steps. We use $T = 500$ in the non-iterative procedure and $T = 250$ in the iterative procedure. We found that using $T = 250$ was sufficient while speeding up the iterative training procedure.

Non-iterative Training Procedure. The non-iterative training procedure follows the same approach as presented in the original world model work [6]. To train the VAE and MDN-RNN, we first collect a dataset of 10,000 rollouts using a random policy to explore the environment where we record the random action a_t executed and the generated observations. The dataset is used to train the VAE so it can learn an abstract and compressed representation of the environment. The VAE is trained for 50 epochs with a learning rate of $1e - 4$ using the *Adam* optimizer.

The MDN-RNN is trained on the 10,000 rollouts where each frame s_t is preprocessed by the VAE into a latent vector z_t at each time step t. The latent vectors and actions a_t are given to the MDN-RNN for it to learn to model the next latent vector $p(z_{t+1}|a_t, z_t, h_t)$ as a mixture of Gaussians and the reward r and the terminal d. The MDN-RNN consists of 512 hidden units and a mixture of 5 Gaussians. We train the MDN-RNN for 60 epochs with a learning rate of $1e-3$ using the *Adam* optimizer. In summary, the full non-iterative training procedure is shown below:

1. Collect 10,000 rollouts with a random policy
2. Train world model using random rollouts.
3. Evaluate the agent on 100 random tracks using the RMHC planning policy.

Iterative Training Procedure

Once the world model is trained non-iteratively, we can use it in conjunction with our planning algorithm (RMHC) to do online planning. However, while the agent may somewhat stay on the road and drive slowly at corners, its performance is limited by our world model trained with a random policy only. Consequently, the dynamics associated with well-behaved driving might be underexplored, and hence our world model may not be able to fully capture this in latent space.

To address this, we used an iterative training procedure as suggested in [6], in which we iteratively collect rollouts using our agent's planning policy and improve our world model (and thus our planning) using the new rollouts. Intuitively, we expect planning with the learned world model to yield a better policy than with a random model. The new rollouts generated during planning are stored in a replay buffer to overcome *catastrophic forgetting* by retaining both old and new rollouts, which allows the MDN-RNN to learn from both past and new experiences. We collect 500 rollouts per iteration. The iterative training procedure is as follows:

1. Train MDN-RNN and VAE non-iteratively to obtain baseline model
2. Collect rollouts using RMHC planning policy and add them to the replay buffer
3. Train the world model using rollouts in replay buffer.
4. Evaluate the agent on 100 random tracks using RMHC planning policy.
5. Go back to (2) and repeat for I iterations or until the task is complete

For both approaches, we found that training the VAE using 10k random rollouts was sufficient in representing different scenarios of the car racing environment across all our experiments. We used RMHC with a horizon of 20, and the action sequence was evolved for ten generations at every time step t with shift buffering.

5   Results

5.1   Non-iterative Training

The MDN-RNN serves as a predictive model of future latent z vector that the VAE may produce and the reward r that the environment is expected to produce. Thus the rollouts used to train the MDN-RNN may affect its predictive ability and how well it represents the real environment during online planning. For this reason, we trained two MDN-RNNs by using the non-iterative training procedure to obtain a random model and an expert model. The random model is trained on 10,000 random rollouts and acts as our baseline model for all iteratively-trained models. The expert model trains on 5,000 random rollouts and 5,000 expert rollouts. The expert rollouts are collected with the pre-trained agent in *World Models* [6]. The random rollouts allow the MDN-RNN to learn the consequences of bad-driving behavior, and the expert rollouts allow it to learn the positive reward signal associated with expert-driving. The expert model is a reference model used for comparison that helps determine how well an agent may perform when the MDN-RNN is trained on a well-representative dataset.

Using the random model, the agent did learn to drive unsteadily around the track and sometimes plan around sharp corners. However, the agent only managed to achieve a mean score of 356.20 ± 176.69 with the highest score of 804. In contrast, using the expert model, the agent managed to obtain a mean score of 765.17 ± 102.18 with the highest score of 900. The expert rollouts improved the MDN-RNN's ability to capture the dynamics of the environment, which significantly improved the agent's performance (Fig. 5).

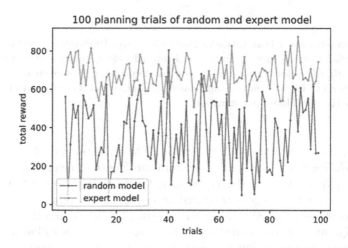

Fig. 5. Total rewards in 100 trials with MDN-RNN trained on 10,000 rollouts using random policy vs. an MDN-RNN trained on 5000 random and 500 expert rollouts. The latter yields a much higher total reward due to the dataset containing a rollouts that exhibit both random and well-behaved driving.

5.2   Iterative Training

Since we cannot rely on access to pre-trained expert rollouts, we have implemented an iterative training procedure that allows the agent to improve its performance over time by learning from its own experiences. Namely, we generate rollouts by online planning with the RMHC evolutionary policy search method, which iteratively improve our world model. We investigate if the random baseline model can improve by using a small number of only 500 rollouts and a sequence length of 250 experiences trained over ten epochs and five iterations. Figure 6 shows the mean total rewards after each of the five iterations.

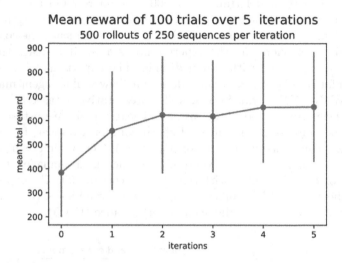

Fig. 6. Mean total rewards and standard deviations over 100 trials across five iterations. The 0th iteration represents the mean total reward before iterative training, but after training on 10,000 rollouts obtained from a random policy. Notice, using 500 rollouts (Experiment A) yields a faster training time and a better result compared to experiment B that uses 10.000 rollouts per iteration.

Already after a single training iteration, the agent managed to get a mean score of 557.87 ± 244.97 and peaked at iteration 5 with a mean score of 656.82 ± 226.67. Despite not beating the expert model, we saw improvements throughout the iterations, and the agent managed to occasionally complete the game by scoring a total reward of 900 during benchmarks. While the first iteration yielded the most significant improvement in total average reward, the following iterations still improved. The great improvement seen in the first iteration might be due to the MDN-RNN learning the dynamics of more well-behaved driving from the agent's planning policy, which ultimately mitigates the errors made by the initially random model.

Investigating Different Planning Horizons and Generations. The benchmarks from iterative training show how refining the world model can affect the agent's planning capabilities. Given the best iterative model found after five training iterations, it is interesting to see how different horizon lengths and max generations affect the agent's ability to plan with the iterative model and the RMHC policy search method.

Both planning parameters are adjusted independently and individually to see how they affect planning. However, we must keep in mind that the horizon length and the maximum number of generations are very likely to be highly correlated. Thus, one should also conduct experiments where both parameters are adjusted together. Figure 7 shows how typical parameter values used for evolutionary planning [15] affect the average total reward obtained by planning with RMHC on a model trained with five iterations across 100 trials.

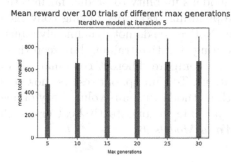 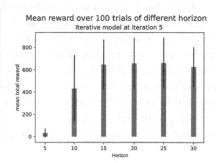

Fig. 7. Left: max planning generations vs. mean rewards with a horizon of length 20. Right: Horizon planning length vs. mean reward with a max generation of 10. While a minimum number of generations and horizon length are necessary for the agent to plan well, increasing these values further does not increase the performance of the agent.

The baseline number of generations is 10. Reducing this to 5 shows a decrease in mean total reward, achieving a score of 473.53 ± 280.18. This reduction is likely due to the agent having less planning time so it is unable to converge to a better trajectory in a local policy subspace. Increasing the number of generations to 15 increases the mean reward to 707.79 ± 195.44, which is not surprising since it gives the agent more planning time. However, increasing the number of generations further did not improve the results. Presumably, this may imply that the agent has converged to a locally optimal trajectory in the simulated environment after being evolved 15 generations.

The results when varying the horizon are shown in Fig. 7, right. The baseline horizon length is 20. Reducing this value to 5 resulted in poor planning and yielded a mean score of 31.91 ± 40.54. Seemingly, a short horizon exploits a more certain near future but does not bring much information for long-term planning of a trajectory associated with well-behaved driving. Consequently, this kind of short-sighted agent may not act in time before driving into the grass. As we increase the horizon from 5 to 20, the mean score increases. The agent receives more information about the car's trajectory, which allows it to plan accordingly. However, a horizon beyond 20 does not help the agent, which is likely due to the increased uncertainty caused by planning too far into the future. The further the agent plans ahead, the more uncertain the trajectory becomes, which makes it less relevant to the current situation that the agent must act upon. This is a problem in most model-based RL approaches, which may be addressed by having a separate network predict state values beyond the planning horizon [7].

In conclusion, the iterative training procedure significantly improved our random baseline model and showed improvement after only one iteration (Table 1). Additionally, increasing the maximum number of generations to 15 and a horizon of 20 used in our RMHC policy search approach improved the total average reward obtained across 100 random tracks (Fig. 7). However, increasing the parameter values more than this yields diminishing returns, and a slight decrease in total reward. This may be due to the model's inability to predict far into the future when using a high horizon or the planning trajectory having converged when using a large number of generations. Notice, we do not dynamically adjust the horizon and number of generations during iterative training but keep them fixed during all five iterations. Instead, we compare different combinations of parameters across whole runs of five iterations. To sum up, our results show it is possible to beat traditional model-free RL methods with an evolutionary online planning approach, although we are not yet able to consistently beat or match the learned expert model presented in *World Models* [6].

6   Discussion and Future Work

While the agent reaches a decent score, it does fail occasionally. It usually happens when the agent is unable to correct itself due to loss of friction during turns at sharp corners with high speed. Compared to the expert model that enacts conservative driving-behavior, the current iterative model prefers more risky driving at high speed. Possibly, the expert policy has learned to slow down at corners,

Table 1. CarRacing-v0 approaches with mean scores over 100 trials. Our approaches are shown in bold.

Methods	Mean scores
DQN [19]	343 ± 18
Non-iterative random model	$\mathbf{356 \pm 177}$
A3C (Continuous) [9]	591 ± 45
Iterative model (5 iterations, 15 gen., 20 horizon)	$\mathbf{708 \pm 195}$
Non-iterative - expert model	$\mathbf{765 \pm 102}$
World model [6]	906 ± 21
Deep neuroevolution [20]	903 ± 72

which helps maximize the reward. On the other hand, our planning agent does not seem to have explored sufficient rollouts of this kind to make the MD-RNN learn to associate higher rewards with slower driving when approaching corners.

Another issue occurs when the agent approaches the right corners. In many cases, the agent can complete right corners though there are times where the agent does not know whether to turn or not. In these scenarios, the agent usually brakes or slows down while trying to navigate the race track in a sensible direction. This phenomenon is likely due to the right turns being underrepresented in the generated tracks that are biased towards containing mainly left turns. Consequently, the MDN-RNN is unable to represent right turns in the simulated environment compared to other frequently occurring segments of the track. Arguably, both issues are resolved by running more iterative training iterations. However, it also depends on how often the issues arise in the generated rollouts. Interestingly, the issues occurred more often in the random model compared to the iterative model, which indicates that the iterative training procedure can help improve the world model.

Acknowledgments. We would like to thank Mathias Kristian Kyndlo Löwe for helping us with computational infrastructure. A special thanks go to Corentin Tallec and his team for providing the PyTorch open-source implementation of *World Models* [6]. We also thank Simon Lucas, Chris Bamford, and Alexander Dockhorn for helpful suggestions. This project was supported by a Sapere Aude: DFF-Starting Grant (9063-00046B) and by the Danish Ministry of Education and Science, Digital Pilot Hub, and Skylab Digital.

References

1. Bamford, C., Lucas, S.: Neural game engine: Accurate learning of generalizable forward models from pixels. arXiv preprint arXiv:2003.10520 (2020)
2. Blythe, J.: An overview of planning under uncertainty. In: Wooldridge, M.J., Veloso, M. (eds.) Artificial Intelligence Today. LNCS (LNAI), vol. 1600, pp. 85–110. Springer, Heidelberg (1999). https://doi.org/10.1007/3-540-48317-9_4
3. Browne, C.B., et al.: A survey of monte carlo tree search methods. IEEE Trans. Comput. Intell. AI Games **4**(1), 1–43 (2012)
4. Gaina, R.D., Devlin, S., Lucas, S.M., Perez-Liebana, D.: Rolling horizon evolutionary algorithms for general video game playing. arXiv preprint arXiv:2003.12331 (2020)
5. Gaina, R.D., Lucas, S.M., Pérez-Liébana, D.: Population seeding techniques for rolling horizon evolution in general video game playing. In: 2017 IEEE Congress on Evolutionary Computation (CEC), pp. 1956–1963. IEEE (2017)
6. Ha, D., Schmidhuber, J.: World models. arXiv preprint arXiv:1803.10122 (2018)
7. Hafner, D., Lillicrap, T., Ba, J., Norouzi, M.: Dream to control: Learning behaviors by latent imagination. arXiv preprint arXiv:1912.01603 (2019)
8. Hafner, D., et al.: Learning latent dynamics for planning from pixels. In: International Conference on Machine Learning, pp. 2555–2565. PMLR (2019)
9. Jang, S., Min, J., Lee, C.: Reinforcement car racing with A3C (2017)

10. Justesen, N., Mahlmann, T., Risi, S., Togelius, J.: Playing multiaction adversarial games: online evolutionary planning versus tree search. IEEE Trans. Games **10**(3), 281–291 (2017)

11. Justesen, N., Risi, S.: Continual online evolutionary planning for in-game build order adaptation in StarCraft. In: Proceedings of the Genetic and Evolutionary Computation Conference, pp. 187–194 (2017)

12. Kahn, G., Villaflor, A., Pong, V., Abbeel, P., Levine, S.: Uncertainty-aware reinforcement learning for collision avoidance. arXiv preprint arXiv:1702.01182 (2017)

13. Kingma, D.P., Welling, M.: Auto-encoding variational bayes. arXiv preprint arXiv:1312.6114 (2013)

14. Klimov, O.: Carracing-v0 (2016). https://gym.openai.com/envs/CarRacing-v0/

15. Lucas, S.M., et al.: Efficient evolutionary methods for game agent optimisation: Model-based is best. arXiv preprint arXiv:1901.00723 (2019)

16. Michie, D.: Game-playing and game-learning automata. In: Advances in Programming and Non-numerical Computation, pp. 183–200. Elsevier (1966)

17. Ovalle, A., Lucas, S.M.: Bootstrapped model learning and error correction for planning with uncertainty in model-based RL. arXiv preprint arXiv:2004.07155 (2020)

18. Perez, D., Samothrakis, S., Lucas, S., Rohlfshagen, P.: Rolling horizon evolution versus tree search for navigation in single-player real-time games. In: Proceedings of the 15th Annual Conference on Genetic and Evolutionary Computation, pp. 351–358 (2013)

19. Prieur, L.: Deep-q learning for Box2D racecar RL problem (2017). https://goo.gl/VpDqSw

20. Risi, S., Stanley, K.O.: Deep neuroevolution of recurrent and discrete world models. In: Proceedings of the Genetic and Evolutionary Computation Conference, pp. 456–462 (2019)

21. Schrittwieser, J., et al.: Mastering atari, go, chess and shogi by planning with a learned model. arXiv preprint arXiv:1911.08265 (2019)

22. Silver, D., et al.: Mastering the game of go with deep neural networks and tree search. Nature **529**(7587), 484–489 (2016)

23. Silver, D., et al.: Mastering chess and shogi by self-play with a general reinforcement learning algorithm. arXiv preprint arXiv:1712.01815 (2017)

24. Tong, X., Liu, W., Li, B.: Enhancing rolling horizon evolution with policy and value networks. In: 2019 IEEE Conference on Games (CoG), pp. 1–8. IEEE (2019)

Utilizing the Untapped Potential of Indirect Encoding for Neural Networks with Meta Learning

Adam Katona[1]([⊠]), Nuno Lourenço[2], Penousal Machado[2], Daniel W. Franks[1], and James Alfred Walker[1]

[1] Department of Computer Science, University of York, York, UK
{ak1774,daniel.franks,james.walker}@york.ac.uk
[2] CISUC, Department of Informatics Engineering,
University of Coimbra, Coimbra, Portugal
{naml,machado}@dei.uc.pt

Abstract. Indirect encoding is a promising area of research in machine learning/evolutionary computation, however, it is rarely able to achieve performance on par with state of the art directly encoded methods. One of the most important properties of indirect encoding is the ability to control exploration during learning by transforming random genotypic variation into an arbitrary distribution of phenotypic variation. This gives indirect encoding a capacity to learn to be adaptable in a way which is not possible for direct encoding. However, during normal objective based learning, there is no direct selection for adaptability, which results in not only a missed opportunity to improve the ability to learn, but often degrading it too. The recent meta learning algorithm MAML makes it possible to directly and efficiently optimize for the ability to adapt. This paper demonstrates that even when indirect encoding can be detrimental to performance in the case of normal learning, when selecting for the ability to adapt, indirect encoding can outperform direct encoding in a fair comparison. The indirect encoding technique Hypernetwork was used on the task of few shot image classification on the Omniglot dataset. The results show the importance of directly optimizing for adaptability in realizing the powerful potential of indirect encoding.

Keywords: Indirect encoding · Evolvability · Meta learning · Neuroevolution · Hypernetwork · HyperNEAT

1 Introduction

Most deep learning research is done with the natural representation of neural networks, where each weight in the network directly maps on to a separate parameter in the representation. We call this a direct encoding. On the other hand, in an indirect encoding the weights do not directly map on to the representation, and instead, we apply a transformation to the representation to

© Springer Nature Switzerland AG 2021
P. A. Castillo and J. L. Jiménez Laredo (Eds.): EvoApplications 2021, LNCS 12694, pp. 537–551, 2021.
https://doi.org/10.1007/978-3-030-72699-7_34

produce the weights. In Evolutionary Computation (EC), this transformation is commonly referred to as the genotype-phenotype mapping.

Direct encoding seems to work well and we can successfully train models with as many as 175 billion parameters [4]. As such, direct encoding dominates practically all benchmark problems. Natural evolution on the other hand uses indirect encoding. It is debatable whether evolution is as successful a problem solver because it uses indirect encoding or despite it. There could be many reasons why nature ended up with indirect encoding, be it biological limitations or because indirect encoding provides benefits. However, when designing our learning algorithms, we are faced with the decision of using either. This raises the question: Is there any advantage in using an indirect encoding?

1.1 The Potential of Indirect Encoding

In this work we argue that indirect encoding is worthy of our attention because it has two interesting properties, which direct encoding lacks:

1. Indirect encoding can control the exploration during learning by making changes in promising directions more sensitive and changes in less promising directions insensitive.
2. Indirect encoding can reuse parameters multiple times, making it possible to learn regular structures.

Controlling Exploration. Indirect encoding is capable of controlling exploration during learning by modifying the type of variation mutations can cause. This is possible since the genotype-phenotype map has the ability to transform random genotypic variation to an advantageous distribution of phenotypic variation [31].

A simple example which is often used to demonstrate this property is how nature encodes development plans for symmetric bodies [17,19]. Because of the way the developmental program for the body is encoded, it is easier for evolution to change the length of both limbs together, then to change them separately, which is probably a useful way to explore possible space of body configurations.

A similar concept that describes the same phenomena is developmental canalization. Indirect encoding has the ability to entrench certain phenotypic features, making them difficult to change, the same way water can dig a canal, making the path of future flow more stable. A great example of how canalization can emerge in artificial evolution is given in [17]. In their experiments, developmental canalization made certain good quality variation more common, increasing the ability to innovate.

One of the most successful algorithms that controls its own exploration is Covariance Matrix Adaptation Evolution Strategy (CMA-ES) [14]. CMA-ES uses an exploration strategy of adapting the covariance matrix of a multivariate Gaussian distribution in a way that more promising directions are explored more. By using indirect encoding we can allow the algorithm to automatically discover exploration strategies instead of manually inventing and incorporating them into our algorithms.

Reusing Parameters. Another important property of indirect encoding is the ability to reuse parameters multiple times. We argue that this is actually a similar property to controlling exploration, since having many separate parameters that always change together, or having one parameter which is reused many times achieves similar results.

Indirect encoding allows the reuse of information to build regular and modular structures [16, 25]. We already know how beneficial some structures are, for example the convolution is reusing the convolutional kernel weights many times at different locations in the image, which makes learning vision tasks efficient. By using indirect encoding we open the possibility to discover such useful structures automatically, even when using a fully connected architecture [8].

The Vision of Indirect Encoding. By using an indirect encoding, we can allow our algorithms to automatically discover different modular architectures, and exploration strategies, instead of manually inventing and coding them. The vision of automatically discovering these kinds of representations with the ability to learn effectively for many kinds of problems is extremely alluring [25].

Richard Sutton's bitter lesson argument [30] postulates that general methods which scale well with computation eventually always outperform methods for which the AI researchers build in extra handcrafted knowledge. For this reason, researchers should concentrate their main efforts on studying general and scalable methods. We hypothesise that utilising indirect encoding will allow us to discover efficient learning systems automatically in a data-driven way in the spirit of Sutton's argument.

1.2 The Difficulties with Indirect Encoding

As we discussed in the previous section, indirect encodings have a powerful capability to control their own exploration during training. Since the ability to improve further has no effect on current fitness, greedy algorithms are not expected to select for representations which result in good exploration strategies. Because there are many more bad exploration strategies than good ones, if there is no selection for the ability to adapt, the exploration strategy will just drift, causing indirect encoding to most likely hurt learning performance. This leads to the main hypothesis of this paper.

Hypothesis. Greedy learning algorithms are unlikely to make full use of the capabilities of indirect encoding.

We do not suggest however that it is impossible to make use of indirect encoding capabilities without selecting for the ability to adapt, only that it is much more difficult. Several researchers in the field of evolution of evolvability [1, 20, 31] argue that evolvability can emerge without selection in an unsupervised way. Huizinga et al. [17] showed that developmental canalization can emerge in a divergent search like environment.

Much effort was given to algorithms which instead of selecting for individuals with the ability to improve their fitness, select for the ability to generate diverse behaviour in their offspring [10,19]. These algorithms capture a different aspect of evolvability which might be able to utilize the capabilities of indirect encoding just as well.

In the rest of the section, we evaluate our hypothesis in the context of past results with indirect encoding.

HyperNEAT. HyperNEAT [26] is one of the most well known indirect encoding techniques for neuroevolution. There are several demonstrations of how Hyper-NEAT outperforms direct encoding in different domains [3,7,11], especially if the task is more regular [6]. These results seemingly contradict our hypothesis, since HyperNEAT does not directly select for the ability to adapt. We argue however, that this is not the case for three reasons.

First, HyperNEAT uses innovation protection. Innovation protection was originally introduced in NEAT [27], and it keeps innovative genes in the gene pool even if they have a poor performance. The justification for it is that when we change the topology, fitness likely decreases first until the weights of the new structural elements can be fine-tuned. However, innovation protection also helps to protect individuals that are better at evolving, since it provides them with a few generations to prove their ability to improve. This means that HyperNEAT is actually indirectly selecting for the ability to adapt. More experiments are necessary to evaluate whether HyperNEAT would perform well without innovation protection, but this is beyond the scope of this paper.

Second, the baselines for these results were using some version of NEAT such as plain NEAT, Fixed Topology NEAT (FT-NEAT) or Perceptron NEAT (P-NEAT). While NEAT might be a good algorithm to evolve the small query networks for HyperNEAT, it might not be an ideal baseline for the larger directly encoded networks. NEAT changes parameters one by one, recent results suggest that techniques which modify many weights at the same time perform much better for large networks, like CMA-ES [15], GA [29] and ES [22]. When we compare the performance of HyperNEAT to these more efficient baselines, on the task of learning to play Atari games, direct encoding seems to have the advantage in most games [22].

Finally, HyperNEAT experiments are typically using relatively small networks. Choromanska et al. [5] showed that as the network size increases, the number of bad quality local optima are diminishing exponentially. The problem of local optima, which is a very important factor in the case of small networks, is less important for large networks. For this reason, the results obtained in many HyperNEAT experiments are not necessarily expected to generalize to large scale networks.

Differentiable Pattern Producing Network. One of the most impressive achievements of indirect encoding is the demonstrated ability to invent convolution from scratch using a fully connected architecture [8]. The DPPN (Differentiable Pattern Producing Network) is a differentiable version of the CPPN (Compositional Pattern Producing Network) [24] used in HyperNEAT. In this work, the authors run experiments with three different settings. In the Darwinian setting, individuals were evaluated on their ability to solve the task without further adaptation. In the case of the Baldwinian setting, individuals were allowed to learn further by using gradient descent, resulting in selection for the ability to adapt. In the case of the Lamarckian setting, the situation is the same as with Baldwinian evolution with the additional feature of inheriting the learned weights as well. In the case of the Darwinian setting, without selection for the ability to adapt, the task was not solved successfully, not a single digit was recognisable in the image reconstruction task. When they used Baldwinian or Lamarckian evolution however performance was much better, and convolution-like fully connected weights were generated. This experiment supports our hypothesis that selection for the ability to learn is crucial in realizing the full capabilities of indirect encoding.

Hypernetworks. A recent indirect encoding technique called Hypernetworks [13] can achieve near state of the art performance on sequence modelling tasks. This result was achieved with dynamic Hypernetworks, where a recurrent network is enhanced with the new ability to modify its own weights during inference, based on the current input and state of the network. The simpler static Hypernetwork does not change the capabilities of the network, only the way the parameters are represented, making the comparison between direct and indirect encoding easy. When using static Hypernetworks to generate the weights of a convolutional network, the results on an image classification task are worse than direct encoding. This result however was obtained by using around an order of magnitude less parameter for the indirect encoding. We show in Sect. 3.4. That we achieve similar results when using Hypernetworks with the same number of parameters, indirect encoding cannot outperform direct encoding on an image classification task with greedy learning.

2   Background

In this paper we combine ideas from the fields of Deep Learning and Evolutionary Computation, so we use the terminology from both fields to describe similar concepts. For example, we use the terms evolvability and the ability to adapt which are similar concepts, both are concerned with potential yet unrealized improvements, but imply a different underlying algorithm. The situation is the same with the phrases "selecting for" or "optimizing for".

2.1   Indirect Encoding for Neuroevolution

There is a vast literature covering indirect network encoding. The field of artificial embriogeny is concerned with these techniques, a great review is available by [28]. Relatively few of these techniques were constructed with modern deep learning scale in mind (millions or billions of connections). In this section, we discuss two families of techniques, which were shown to be viable for these large networks.

One family of methods to indirectly encode the weights of a neural network is to use query function and a substrate [26]. The query function is a parameterized function; typically a small neural network [24], which maps the coordinates of a source and a target neuron to a single weight between the source and target neuron. These coordinates for the neurons come from the substrate, which is often manually crafted by placing each neuron in 2D or 3D space, or it can also be learned [21]. A conceptual diagram of how this kind of encoding can represent weights can be seen in Fig. 1.

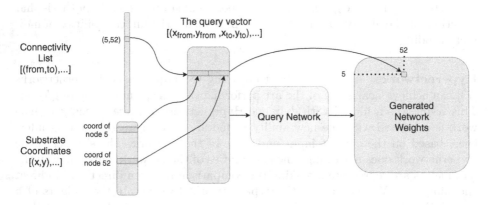

Fig. 1. Query networks: In the case of query networks, each node in the neural network is assigned a coordinate in space, which is called the substrate (this example shows a 2D space with coordinates x and y). For each connection, a query vector is assembled from the coordinates of the source and target neurons. The weight for each connection is determined by evaluating the query vector with the query network, which is a small neural network. To generate the whole network as many forward passes are necessary as there are connections in the network. Yellow blocks represent the learned parameters, blue blocks represent fixed or generated values, and the red blocks show an example of how a single weight is generated (Color figure online)

To calculate the weights of the whole network, we need to query this network as many times as many weights there is. For a large network, this could mean millions of queries, which could become prohibitively expensive. This is especially problematic in cases when we only use the network a few times before updating, like supervised learning, and less problematic in control or reinforcement learning problems, where we use the network hundreds or thousands of times before updating it. This is only an issue during training since during inference time the network does not change anymore. Luckily the size of the query network is typically very small, and due to the large number of queries, they can effectively utilize the GPU.

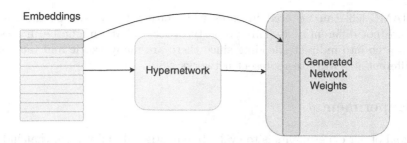

Fig. 2. Hypernetworks: Each embedding is transformed into a chunk of weights by the Hypernetwork [13]. Yellow blocks represent the learned parameters, the blue block represents the generated weights, and the red blocks show an example of how a single embedding is transformed into a chunk of generated weights. See Fig. 4 on how a Hypernetwork can be used as part of a larger model (Color figure online)

Another family of methods is to simply transform an embedding space to the weight space. The first method to use this technique for large neural networks is Hypernetworks [13] which uses a simple linear projection as transformation. A conceptual diagram of how this kind of encoding can represent weights can be seen in Fig. 2. The learned parameters are a set of embeddings and the parameters of the projection network. Each embedding is then used to generate a separate part of the network. This separation into smaller chunks is required to keep the size of the transformation manageable. Another side effect of this separation, which motivated the invention of the technique is that there is a kind of information sharing between these chunks, since they are projected from the same subspace.

2.2   MAML

In this work, we use the meta learning algorithm MAML [9] as an algorithm which can optimize for the ability to adapt. The goal of MAML is to find initial parameters that allow for fast adaptation for many different tasks. It consists of 2 different kinds of updates. There is a so-called fine-tuning step, which is a normal gradient step that changes the parameters θ so the training task $\mathcal{D}_i^{tr}$ loss is lower, as seen in Eq. 1. Then there is the meta update, which updates the initial or meta parameters, so fine-tuning can achieve good generalization performance on the test tasks $\mathcal{D}_i^{ts}$. Calculating the meta gradient requires us to differentiate through a gradient step (see Eq. 2), which means we also need to calculate second order gradients.

$$\theta' = \theta - \alpha \nabla_\theta \mathcal{L}(\theta, \mathcal{D}_i^{tr}) \tag{1}$$

$$\mathcal{L}_{meta} = \sum_{task\ i} \mathcal{L}(\theta', \mathcal{D}_i^{ts}) = \sum_{task\ i} \mathcal{L}(\theta - \alpha \nabla_\theta L(\theta, \mathcal{D}_i^{tr}), \mathcal{D}_i^{ts}) \tag{2}$$

In this work, we used the gradient based version of MAML because both our models and the task are differentiable. The evolutionary version of the algorithm

ES MAML [23] can be used in cases when either the model or the task or both are not differentiable. This property of ES MAML might be interesting for research into indirect encoding since there are many exotic and interesting nondifferentiable ways to represent networks [28].

3 Experiment

The goal of our experiments is to evaluate our original hypothesis, that indirect encoding is unlikely to be beneficial in case of greedy learning, but can lead to better performance when the ability to adapt is selected.

We used two kinds of vision tasks, simple image classification on the FashionMNIST [32] dataset for greedy learning and few shot classification on the Omniglot [18] dataset for meta learning. The problem setting of few shot image classification is shown in Fig. 3.

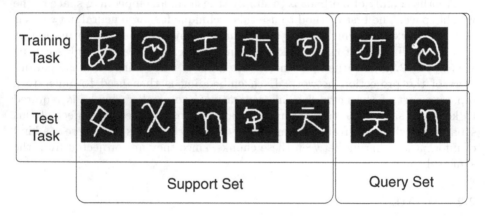

Fig. 3. Few shot learning problem. The goal of MAML is to find model parameters that can be fine-tuned given the few examples in the support set (in this example 5 way 1 shot, there are 5 different classes with 1 example from each), so they can accurately classify the images in the query set. The training tasks created by randomly sampling 5 out of the 1200 training classes. The performance is evaluated on the test tasks, which are created by sampling 5 out of the 400 test classes.

We used fully connected networks because convolutional networks are already very good at vision tasks and we wanted to leave room for improvement. Because the two dataset uses the same resolution 28 by 28 we could use the same networks without any modification for both tasks.

3.1 Fair Comparison

To determine whether indirect encoding is beneficial for learning, we need to establish a baseline with direct encoding. To make the comparison fair, we used approximately the same number of parameters to encode the exact same networks with both direct and indirect encoding. We used 4 different sized networks, which are summed up in Table 1.

Table 1. Dimensions of the networks, and the number of parameters used in both direct and indirect encoding. The table also shows the hyperparameters used for indirect encoding.

	Hidden dims	Direct parameters	Indirect parameters	$[z_{dim1}, N_{in1}, N_{out1}]$	$[z_{dim2}, N_{in2}, N_{out2}]$
Tiny	[32,16]	25,829	25,977	[14,2,2]	[16,2,2]
Small	[64,32]	52,677	51,237	[14,4,4]	[16,2,2]
Medium	[128,64]	109,445	107,229	[30,4,4]	[16,2,2]
Large	[256,128,64,64]	247,621	244,837	[56,4,4]	[32,4,4]

For indirect encoding, we generated the weights of the first two hidden layers (the vast majority of parameters), the biases and the rest of the weights were encoded directly, as shown in Fig. 4. The authors of the original Hypernetwork paper used a single Hypernetwork to generate the weights of all layers. They argue that this constrained the system to share some commonality between the layers, which resulted in decreased performance [13]. This would especially be the case for fully connected networks since the intermediate fully connected representations lack the common structure that the intermediate representations of convolutional networks have. For this reason, we used separate Hypernetworks for the two generated layers.

3.2   Implementation Details

We used the same formulation of the Hypernetwork as in [13], instead of a simple projection, 2 matrix multiplications are used to project the embeddings into weights. First, the embeddings with size z_{dim} are projected into the shape N_{in} by z_{dim}. The second projection then projects the result of the previous projection into the shape $[N_{out}, N_{in}, unit_{dim}]$. Where $unit_{dim}$ is the size of the smallest chunk of weights generated. N_{out}, N_{in} are hyperparameters controlling how much weights should be generated from a simple embedding. Doing the projection this way is equivalent to a simple large projection but uses way fewer parameters because the weights of the second matrix are reused many times. We choose $unit_{dim}$ to be the number of connections a single neuron has in the generated layer.

Initializing weights is an important aspect of training neural networks to avoid the vanishing or exploding gradient problem. Normally we would want to initialize our weight in a way that the magnitude of the activations throughout the network stays constant. This can be achieved by initializing each layer so their gain is one [12]. Normally in a fully connected layer, the variance of the

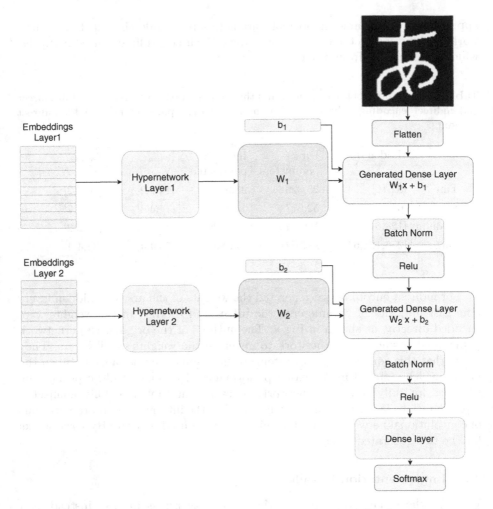

Fig. 4. The indirect architecture used in the experiments. The yellow boxes are learned parameters, the blue boxes are generated parameters and the gray boxes are functions. The direct encoding uses the same architecture, but the two dense layers are represented normally. (Color figure online)

activations in a layer depends on the variance of the inputs, the variance of the weights, and the number of neurons in the previous layer as shown in Eq. 3.

$$Var(a_l) = n_{l-1} * Var(W_l) * Var(a_{l-1}) \tag{3}$$

In the case of Hypernetworks however we use one network to generate the weights of another network. We initialized the Hypernetwork in a way that will result in the generated layer to have a gain of one. In the case of Hypernetworks, because the matrix weights in the second projection are reused multiple times, we need to use the number of neurons contributing to a single weight, which is the number of embeddings, z_{dim} (Eq. 5). In the following equations, W_1 is the first matrix and W_2 is the second matrix in the Hypernetwork.

$$Var(a_1) = z_{dim} * Var(W_1) * Var(a_0) \tag{4}$$

$$Var(a_2) = z_{dim} * Var(W_2) * Var(a_1) \tag{5}$$

$$Var(a_2) = z_{dim} * Var(W_2) * z_{dim} * Var(W_1) * Var(a_0) \tag{6}$$

Let the gain of the Hypernetwork be equal to the required variance of the generated layer for it to have a gain of one, and provide the additional constraint of $Var(W_1) = Var(W_2)$

$$Var(a_2)/Var(a_0) := 1/n_{generated\ fan\ in} \tag{7}$$

$$Var(W) = \sqrt{\frac{1}{n_{generated\ fan\ in} * z_{dim} * z_{dim}}} \tag{8}$$

The source code for all of our experiments are available at https://github.com/adam-katona/indirect_encoding_maml.

3.3 Greedy Learning Experiment

To evaluate the effect of indirect encoding on performance in the case of a greedy learning algorithm, we used the FashionMNIST dataset for image classification. The networks were trained with gradient descent. The batch size was 64, we used the Adam optimizer with a learning rate of 0.001. Each run was repeated 20 times, test results are show in Fig. 5 and in Table 2.

Indirect encoding achieves slightly but consistently worse test accuracies for all network sizes. For all but the tiny network the difference is significant (p<0.01, Mann-Whitney U test). These are similar result reported in [13], showing the inability of greedy learning to benefit from the capabilities of indirect encoding, supporting our original hypothesis.

Table 2. Median test accuracies (out of 20 runs) achieved on the FashionMNIST dataset.

	Direct	Indirect
Tiny	**0.8723**	0.8718
Small	**0.8840**	0.8817
Medium	**0.8903**	0.8862
Large	**0.8937**	0.8904

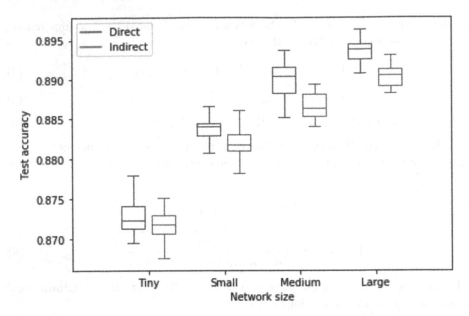

Fig. 5. Greedy learning results: Final test accuracy on the FashionMNIST dataset. Without selecting for adaptability, the direct encoding slightly but consistently outperforms indirect encoding in a fair comparison. The difference is significant for the small, medium and large networks (p<0.01, Mann-Whitney U test)

3.4　Meta Learning Experiment

To evaluate the performance of indirect encoding when we are optimizing for the ability to adapt, we run experiments with few shot learning on the Omniglot dataset. We use 5 way 1 shot learning. We followed the procedure described in [9]. We used 1200 characters for training and 400 for testing. We augmented the characters by applying multiples of 90° rotations. We used batch normalization in the same way as in the original MAML implementation, only using batch statistics and not accumulating running statistics. We used a learnable per step, per parameter learning rate for the fine-tuning update, as proposed in [2]. We used cosine annealing meta learning rate schedule, as proposed in [2]. We used a meta batch size of 32. We used the Adam optimizer and the initial meta learning rate of 0.005 using cosine annealing learning rate scheduler with a restart period of 3000 meta batches. We trained each model for 50000 iterations (meta batches). We used a single adaptation step while training, and used three while evaluating performance on the test tasks, the same way as done in the original MAML paper [9].

Each run was repeated 8 times, test results are show in Fig. 6 and in Table 3. For the tiny, small, and medium networks, indirect encoding achieved higher accuracies. For the small and medium sizes the difference is significant (p<0.01, Mann-Whitney U test). For the large network, indirect encoding has slightly lower accuracy than direct encoding.

The result with the large network is surprising since for all other network configurations indirect encoding had the advantage. For the large network we added 2 additional directly encoded layers. We suspect that there is some kind of interesting interactions between the direct and indirect layers which hinders performance.

Table 3. Median test accuracies (out of 8 runs) achieved on 5-way, 1-shot learning on the Omniglot dataset.

	Direct	Indirect
Tiny	0.739	**0.754**
Small	0.775	**0.806**
Medium	0.818	**0.839**
Large	**0.875**	0.872

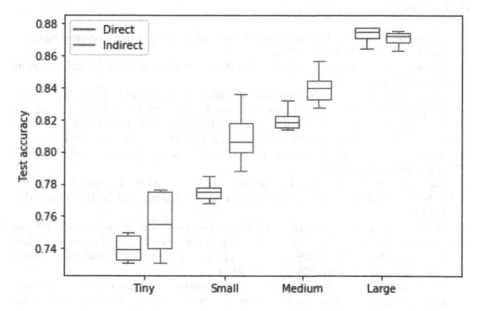

Fig. 6. Meta learning results: Final test accuracies after the third gradient step on the test tasks of 5-shot, 1-way image classification. When adaptability is selected, the indirect encoding outperforms the direct encoding in a fair comparison for most network sizes, except when networks are large.

4   Conclusion

We proposed the hypothesis that greedy learning is unlikely to benefit from the capabilities of indirect encoding, and selecting for the ability to adapt is necessary. We verified the previously demonstrated [13] results that the indirect encoding technique Hypernetworks achieves lower accuracy when trained on an image classification task compared to direct encoding. We then showed that when the ability to adapt is selected with MAML, Hypernetworks can outperform direct encoding on an image classification task. Our results suggest that optimizing for the ability to adapt is indeed of key importance when learning with indirect encoding. More experiments are needed in different domains to verify whether the hypothesis holds in a more general setting. We hope that our results will motivate other researchers to explore the exciting possibilities of utilizing meta learning to realize the powerful potential of indirect encoding.

Acknowledgement. This work was supported by the EPSRC Centre for Doctoral Training in Intelligent Games & Game Intelligence (IGGI) [EP/L015846/1] and the Digital Creativity Labs funded by EPSRC/AHRC/Innovate UK [EP/M023265/1]. This work was partially supported by Society for the Promotion of Evolutionary Computation in Europe and its Surroundings (SPECIES).

References

1. Altenberg, L., et al.: The evolution of evolvability in genetic programming. Adv. Genet. Program. **3**, 47–74 (1994)
2. Antoniou, A., Edwards, H., Storkey, A.: How to train your MAML. arXiv preprint arXiv:1810.09502 (2018)
3. Assunção, F., Lourenço, N., Machado, P., Ribeiro, B.: Using GP Is NEAT: evolving compositional pattern production functions. In: Castelli, M., Sekanina, L., Zhang, M., Cagnoni, S., García-Sánchez, P. (eds.) EuroGP 2018. LNCS, vol. 10781, pp. 3–18. Springer, Cham (2018). https://doi.org/10.1007/978-3-319-77553-1_1
4. Brown, T.B., et al.: Language models are few-shot learners. arXiv preprint arXiv:2005.14165 (2020)
5. Choromanska, A., Henaff, M., Mathieu, M., Arous, G.B., LeCun, Y.: The loss surfaces of multilayer networks. In: Artificial Intelligence and Statistics, pp. 192–204 (2015)
6. Clune, J., Ofria, C., Pennock, R.T.: How a generative encoding fares as problem-regularity decreases. In: Rudolph, G., Jansen, T., Beume, N., Lucas, S., Poloni, C. (eds.) PPSN 2008. LNCS, vol. 5199, pp. 358–367. Springer, Heidelberg (2008). https://doi.org/10.1007/978-3-540-87700-4_36
7. Clune, J., Ofria, C., Pennock, R.T.: The sensitivity of HyperNEAT to different geometric representations of a problem. In: Proceedings of the 11th Annual Conference on Genetic and Evolutionary Computation, pp. 675–682 (2009)
8. Fernando, C., et al.: Convolution by evolution: differentiable pattern producing networks. Proc. Genet. Evol. Comput. Conf. **2016**, 109–116 (2016)
9. Finn, C., Abbeel, P., Levine, S.: Model-agnostic meta-learning for fast adaptation of deep networks. arXiv preprint arXiv:1703.03400 (2017)
10. Gajewski, A., Clune, J., Stanley, K.O., Lehman, J.: Evolvability ES: scalable and direct optimization of evolvability. In: Proceedings of the Genetic and Evolutionary Computation Conference, pp. 107–115 (2019)
11. Gauci, J., Stanley, K.O.: A case study on the critical role of geometric regularity in machine learning. In: AAAI, pp. 628–633 (2008)

12. Glorot, X., Bengio, Y.: Understanding the difficulty of training deep feedforward neural networks. In: Proceedings of the Thirteenth International Conference on Artificial Intelligence and Statistics, pp. 249–256 (2010)
13. Ha, D., Dai, A., Le, Q.V.: Hypernetworks. arXiv preprint arXiv:1609.09106 (2016)
14. Hansen, N., Ostermeier, A.: Adapting arbitrary normal mutation distributions in evolution strategies: the covariance matrix adaptation. In: Proceedings of IEEE International Conference on Evolutionary Computation, pp. 312–317. IEEE (1996)
15. Hausknecht, M., Lehman, J., Miikkulainen, R., Stone, P.: A neuroevolution approach to general atari game playing. IEEE Trans. Comput. Intell. AI Games 6(4), 355–366 (2014)
16. Huizinga, J., Clune, J., Mouret, J.B.: Evolving neural networks that are both modular and regular: hyperneat plus the connection cost technique. In: Proceedings of the 2014 Annual Conference on Genetic and Evolutionary Computation, pp. 697–704 (2014)
17. Huizinga, J., Stanley, K.O., Clune, J.: The emergence of canalization and evolvability in an open-ended, interactive evolutionary system. Artif. Life 24(3), 157–181 (2018)
18. Lake, B., Salakhutdinov, R., Gross, J., Tenenbaum, J.: One shot learning of simple visual concepts. In: Proceedings of the Annual Meeting of the Cognitive Science Society, vol. 33 (2011)
19. Mengistu, H., Lehman, J., Clune, J.: Evolvability search: directly selecting for evolvability in order to study and produce it. Proc. Genet. Evol. Comput. Conf. 2016, 141–148 (2016)
20. Pigliucci, M.: Is evolvability evolvable? Nat. Rev. Genet. 9(1), 75–82 (2008)
21. Risi, S., Stanley, K.O.: Enhancing ES-hyperneat to evolve more complex regular neural networks. In: Proceedings of the 13th Annual Conference on Genetic and Evolutionary Computation, pp. 1539–1546 (2011)
22. Salimans, T., Ho, J., Chen, X., Sidor, S., Sutskever, I.: Evolution strategies as a scalable alternative to reinforcement learning. arXiv preprint arXiv:1703.03864 (2017)
23. Song, X., Gao, W., Yang, Y., Choromanski, K., Pacchiano, A., Tang, Y.: ES-MAML: Simple hessian-free meta learning. arXiv preprint arXiv:1910.01215 (2019)
24. Stanley, K.O.: Compositional pattern producing networks: a novel abstraction of development. Genet. Program. Evolvable Mach. 8(2), 131–162 (2007)
25. Stanley, K.O., Clune, J., Lehman, J., Miikkulainen, R.: Designing neural networks through neuroevolution. Nat. Mach. Intell. 1(1), 24–35 (2019)
26. Stanley, K.O., D'Ambrosio, D.B., Gauci, J.: A hypercube-based encoding for evolving large-scale neural networks. Artif. Life 15(2), 185–212 (2009)
27. Stanley, K.O., Miikkulainen, R.: Evolving neural networks through augmenting topologies. Evol. Comput. 10(2), 99–127 (2002)
28. Stanley, K.O., Miikkulainen, R.: A taxonomy for artificial embryogeny. Artif. Life 9(2), 93–130 (2003)
29. Such, F.P., Madhavan, V., Conti, E., Lehman, J., Stanley, K.O., Clune, J.: Deep neuroevolution: Genetic algorithms are a competitive alternative for training deep neural networks for reinforcement learning. arXiv preprint arXiv:1712.06567 (2017)
30. Sutton, R.: The bitter lesson. Incomplete Ideas (blog), March 13, 12 (2019)
31. Watson, R.A., Szathmáry, E.: How can evolution learn? Trends Ecol. Evol. 31(2), 147–157 (2016)
32. Xiao, H., Rasul, K., Vollgraf, R.: Fashion-MNIST: a novel image dataset for benchmarking machine learning algorithms. arXiv preprint arXiv:1708.07747 (2017)

Effective Universal Unrestricted Adversarial Attacks Using a MOE Approach

Alina Elena Baia[ID], Gabriele Di Bari[ID], and Valentina Poggioni[✉][ID]

University of Perugia, Perugia, Italy
valentina.poggioni@unipg.it

Abstract. Recent studies have shown that Deep Leaning models are susceptible to adversarial examples, which are data, in general images, intentionally modified to fool a machine learning classifier. In this paper, we present a multi-objective nested evolutionary algorithm to generate universal unrestricted adversarial examples in a black-box scenario. The unrestricted attacks are performed through the application of well-known image filters that are available in several image processing libraries, modern cameras, and mobile applications. The multi-objective optimization takes into account not only the attack success rate but also the detection rate. Experimental results showed that this approach is able to create a sequence of filters capable of generating very effective and undetectable attacks.

Keywords: Universal adversarial attacks · Evolutionary algorithms · Multi-objective optimization · Deep learning

1 Introduction

Deep learning (DL) has witnessed a significant progress over the last decade and it has been effectively applied to a variety of applications in different machine learning domains achieving state-of-the-art performance. The great success of DL models, both in academia and industry, made them object of attacks. People started investigating the vulnerability and security aspects of such models since attacks pose significant risks and challenges for real-world security-sensitive systems such as medical diagnosis, voice controllable systems, and autonomous driving. Recent studies have shown that Deep Neural Networks, despite their superior performance, are remarkably vulnerable to adversarial attacks, creating severe security issues at the time of deployment of such systems.

The attacking techniques, at the highest level, are classified in *per-instance attacks* and *universal attacks*. In the first class we can find all those systems that generate a different perturbation for each image; in that case a separate optimization process has to run for each image in order to find the corresponding adversarial image [5,9,13,16,24,25,28]. On the other hand, in the second class

© Springer Nature Switzerland AG 2021
P. A. Castillo and J. L. Jiménez Laredo (Eds.): EvoApplications 2021, LNCS 12694, pp. 552–567, 2021.
https://doi.org/10.1007/978-3-030-72699-7_35

we can find all those systems able to find a unique universal perturbation that, when applied to 'any' image, can fool the classification system; these systems are called universal because they are essentially image-agnostic [10,15,17,23].

Moreover, the adversarial attacks follow the typical classification used in security sectors that distinguish white-box attacks, i.e. attacks having access to the target network model and underlying training policy, from black-box ones in which the parameters and the underlying architecture are unknown to the attacker.

If we consider the type of the applied perturbations, the attacks can be classified as restricted or unrestricted. In the restricted case, the modifications applied to the original image are usually small and bounded by a L_p-norm distance measure, forcing the adversarial image x^* to be as close as possible to the original one. On the contrary, unrestricted attacks use large perturbations without L_p-bounded constraints that manipulate the image in order to create photo-realistic adversarial examples. In this case the objective is not to limit the modifications on pixels but limit the human perception that a modification has been applied [24].

From the point of view of the expected results, the attacks are further distinguished in *untargeted*, when the aim is to simply generate a misclassification, and *targeted*, when the misclassification is driven towards a specified target class.

In this scenario, the robustness of DNN against adversarial examples has gained significant attention in the last few years, and several approaches and systems able to detect adversarial attacks have been proposed and developed. Some of them follow the *adversarial training* approach increasing the network robustness by means of adversarial examples in the training process [14,16,28,30], while others propose ad-hoc trainable techniques like distillation [22], perturbation rectifying [1] or feature squeezing [32].

In a black-box scenario, traditional approaches rely on gradient estimation or on training a substitute network and transfer the generated examples to the targeted model [6,19,20], but alternative, gradient-free optimization techniques, mostly based on evolutionary algorithms, have been recently introduced [2,18,26,31]. Among this group, techniques using Multi-Objective optimization recently reached interesting results and are quickly emerging [8,27].

The majority of the proposed attacks are performed and optimized to add small random perturbations to the pixel values. However, these artificial modifications are often not semantically meaningful and can create unnatural-looking images that are easily detectable. For this reason, researchers start exploring new types of threats models that can significantly change an input while maintaining the semantics.

Such methods require either access to the targeted network architecture [35] or additional resources like pretrained networks to perform image segmentation [24], colorization and style transfer [4]. In some cases, it is necessary to train neural networks from scratch in order to find the adversarial perturbations [25].

In our work, we decided to focus on generating non-targeted unrestricted universal adversarial attacks in a black-box scenario, since the limited knowledge and ability of the attacker is more similar to a real-world scenario, making the attack itself more challenging but its applicability more practical.

We propose a gradient-free method based on nested evolutionary algorithms and multi-objective optimization that, given a set of commonly-used image filters, finds an optimal image-agnostic sequence of them that, when applied to an image is hardly detectable and causes the classifier to misclassify the image. The standard universal L_p-bounded attacks are transformed into universal unrestricted attacks and a multi-objective evolutionary approach is used to build a process able to optimize, at the same time, the attack success rates and the attack detection rate.

By using well-known filters already available in several image processing libraries and in modern cameras and widely used in social media (e.g. Instagram), we aim to reduce the awareness towards the applied modification.

The method provides two optimization stages. The first stage utilizes a genetic algorithm in order to identify the optimal sequence of filters, whereas the second one optimizes the parameters of each selected filter. For this stage we investigated three optimization strategies: genetic algorithm, evolutionary strategy and a random approach with tournament.

To find a successful adversarial filter configuration, a population of candidate solutions is evolved and the solution quality is assessed by means of a fitness value. Our goal is to select filter sequences that will not alter the shape and semantics of images while maximizing the attack success rate on the target model. Moreover, since many deployed deep learning models are protected by defense methods, we want to find an attack able to bypass such mechanisms. Thus, we choose to incorporate the feedback given by the defenses methods directly into the fitness function used for the filters optimization.

Given the conflicting nature of the above-mentioned objectives and motivated by the success of multi-objective evolutionary algorithms (MOEA) in other applications [3,36], we propose to model our method as a multi-objective optimization problem. We employ the non-dominated sorting genetic algorithm II (NSGA-II) for the selection process.

The experimental results demonstrates the effectiveness of our method when tested against one of the most highly rated detection frameworks, namely Feature Squeezing [32]. Our algorithm is able to bypass such defense in most of the cases, having a detection rate smaller than 5% on the testing set while achieving good results in term of attack success rate.

2   Related Works

Over the years, many methodologies have been proposed for generating adversarial examples in both white-box and black-box settings.

Szegedy et al. [28] were the first to introduce the concept of adversarial examples by analyzing the properties of neural networks that make these models susceptible to adversarial attacks. The authors used box-constrained L-BFGS to calculate the perturbation needed to get the image misclassified. Based on this work, Goodfellow et at. [9] explained that the linear part of the high-dimensional model is to blame for their sensitivity to small changes in the input. They also introduced a fast method for generating adversarial examples (FGSM). In the following years, a variety of other attack algorithms have been proposed, both in the white-box [5,16,21] and black-box scenario [6,15,20].

Most of the proposed works on adversarial examples have been focusing on finding small perturbations that can change the predictions of a classifier: in some cases it is sufficient to change just one pixel [26] or inject a random quasi-imperceptible-perturbation [15]. Due to the urgency of taking counter-measures, several detection and defense methods have been introduced to overcome such vulnerabilities. Therefore, nowadays, these types of adversarial images are easily detectable by applying denoising filters or by adversarial training [33]. For this reason, many researchers have been shifting their attention to unrestricted adversarial attacks that employ large and visible perturbations but have the advantage that the resulting images are still looking natural and non-suspicious to the human eye.

Hosseini et al. [12] were one of the first to analyze the effectiveness of unrestricted adversarial examples on deep learning models. They proposed to randomly change the hue and saturation values of an image while maintaining the shape of the objects. The authors in [24] address the limitations of [12] which was found to produce unnatural colors by employing priors on color perception. Other works propose to craft malicious inputs by applying image-enhancement filters obtained by means of neural networks [25] or via gradient descent optimization [35]. Pretrained colorization models and texture style transfer methods have also been successfully utilized without norm constraints on the perturbations [4].

Our idea is to use well known filters that are available in several libraries and mobile applications used extensively every day to enhance photos and images. The power of this application relies on the natural presence of these filters in almost all the images we can find everywhere and this essentially makes them transparent to the human perception. Clearly, the filters have to be "gently" applied otherwise the resulting image could become unrealistic, for example with supersaturated colors, but in general they cannot alter the image semantic.

In the world of adversarial attacks, recent studies have proposed the use of evolutionary algorithms to overcome the limitations imposed by the methods relying on gradient computation/estimation as well as the long training time necessary in the generative approaches. The main benefit is that a population-based optimization algorithm does not require gradient computation nor a differentiable objective function. Furthermore, the gradient-free nature of such methods makes the attacks more robust to gradient masking and obfuscation defenses. Several works which employ a variety of evolutionary algorithms such as Differential Evolution, Genetic Algorithm, and Particle Swarm Optimization have been presented. All of them evolve a population of feasible solutions, according to a fitness function. They make use of similar strategies: the new candidate solutions are obtained by applying small random perturbations to the initial population and the fitness of each population individual is evaluated to find a successful example [2,18,26,31]. Moreover, two very recent papers introduced the idea to use multi-objective evolutionary algorithm to produce image perturbations trying, at the same time, to maximize the attack success rate and minimize the perturbation size [8,27]. Differently from them, we propose to include in the optimization process, alongside the maximization of the attack rate, the minimization of the detection rate of defence methods in order to produce attacks that will be intrinsically successful. To the best of our knowledge there are no other works that take into consideration the detection rate while crafting the attack.

3   Image Filters

We employed Instagram inspired image filters to perform the attacks. The filters were implemented using Python3 and the Pillow, OpenCV and Numpy libraries. We chose five of the most popular Instagram filters, specifically Clarendon, Juno, Reyes, Gingham and Lark. Each filter has distinct characteristics and effects given by different level of contrast, saturation, brightness, shadows, etc.:

- Clarendon adds light to bright areas darkness to dark areas, slightly increasing saturation and contrast while keeping the mid-tones rather warm and cooling down shadows and highlights.
- Juno only manipulates the contrast and the vividness of an image by intensifying the yellows and reds making these colors pop out more than the blues.
- Reyes adds a subtle old-time look by reducing the saturation and by brightening up the photos.
- Gingham also gives a dusty-vintage feel to the image. It significantly lowers the highlights and the saturation. To complete the look it applies a white soft lens effect which draws the attention to the center of the images and creates an elegant and dreamy atmosphere.
- Lark increases the exposure making the photo brighter and reduces the vibrance. Moreover, it also accentuates blues and greens while desaturating the reds.

For each filter there are two parameters that the evolutionary algorithm has to tune: *intensity* α and *strength* s.

The α manipulates the intensity of the filter, i.e. for Clarendon α determines how much the dark areas are light, while for Juno the quantity of yellows and reds that has to be applied, whereas for Gingham that parameter indicates the intensity of the vintage effect. Following the same logic, for Lark α controls the increment and decrement of the photo exposure. For the sake of clarity, in Table 1 the effects of the α parameter for each filter is reported.

Regarding the *strength*, it is the parameter of the convex interpolation among the original image x and the manipulated image x^*, which is calculated as follows:

$$strength(x, x^*, s) = (1.0 - s) \cdot x + s \cdot x^* \qquad (1)$$

thus, if $s = 0$ the output image of the filter is the original image, while with $s = 1$ the filter returns the manipulated image x^*.

Table 1. Effects of filters with different α values

	Original	$\alpha = 0.5$	$\alpha = 0.65$	$\alpha = 0.8$	$\alpha = 1.0$	$\alpha = 1.3$	$\alpha = 1.5$
Clarendon							
Juno							
Reyes							
Gingham							
Lark							

4   Problem Formulation and Backgrounds

Given an input image $x \in X \subset \mathbb{R}^d$ and its corresponding label y, let F be a neural network classifier that (correctly) predicts the class label for the input image $x : F(x) = y$. An adversarial attacks attempts to modify the input image x adding a perturbation δ into an adversarial image $x^* = x + \delta$ such that the classifier was mislead into making a wrong prediction, i.e. $F(x^*) \neq F(x)$. In general the objective is to find the smallest perturbation $\delta \in \mathbb{R}^d$ able to cause the misclassification and this is obtained limiting the perturbation size, $||\delta||_p \leq \epsilon$, where $|| \cdot ||_p$ denotes the L_p norm defined as

$$||x||_p = \sqrt[p]{\sum_{i=1}^{n} x_i^p}, \qquad x = (x_1, ..., x_n) \tag{2}$$

In case of *per-image* approaches, a different δ is found for each image and it is necessary to run the training process for each attack. On the other hand, in case of *universal* approaches the objective is to find *only one* such δ able to fool F for *almost all* the data points available in X, that is

$$F(x + \delta) \neq F(x), \qquad \text{for almost all } x \in X \tag{3}$$

4.1   Multi-Objective Problem

In multiobjective optimization, the aim is to solve problems of the type[1]:

$$\text{minimize } \boldsymbol{f}(\boldsymbol{x}) := [f_1(\boldsymbol{x}), f_2(\boldsymbol{x}), \ldots, f_k(\boldsymbol{x})] \tag{4}$$

---

[1] Without loss of generality, we will assume only minimization problems.

subject to:

$$g_i(\boldsymbol{x}) \leq 0 \quad i = 1, 2, \ldots, m \tag{5}$$

$$h_i(\boldsymbol{x}) = 0 \quad i = 1, 2, \ldots, p \tag{6}$$

where $\boldsymbol{x} = [x_1, x_2, \ldots, x_n]^T$ is the vector of decision variables, $f_i : \mathbb{R}^n \to \mathbb{R}$, $i = 1, \ldots, k$ are the objective functions and $g_i, h_j : \mathbb{R}^n \to \mathbb{R}$, $i = 1, \ldots, m$, $j = 1, \ldots, p$ are the constraint functions of the problem.

Definition 1. Given two vectors $\boldsymbol{x}, \boldsymbol{y} \in \mathbb{R}^k$, we say that $\boldsymbol{x} \leq \boldsymbol{y}$ if $x_i \leq y_i$ for $i = 1, \ldots, k$, and that $\boldsymbol{x}$ **dominates** $\boldsymbol{y}$ (denoted by $\boldsymbol{x} \prec \boldsymbol{y}$) if $\boldsymbol{x} \leq \boldsymbol{y}$ and $\boldsymbol{x} \neq \boldsymbol{y}$.

Definition 2. We say that a vector of decision variables $\boldsymbol{x} \in \mathcal{X} \subset \mathbb{R}^n$ is **non-dominated** with respect to $\mathcal{X}$, if there does not exist another $\boldsymbol{x}' \in \mathcal{X}$ such that $\boldsymbol{f}(\boldsymbol{x}') \prec \boldsymbol{f}(\boldsymbol{x})$.

Definition 3. We say that a vector of decision variables $\boldsymbol{x}^* \in \mathcal{F} \subset \mathbb{R}^n$ ($\mathcal{F}$ is the feasible region) is **Pareto-optimal** if it is nondominated with respect to $\mathcal{F}$.

Definition 4. The **Pareto Optimal Set** $\mathcal{P}^*$ is defined by:

$$\mathcal{P}^* = \{\boldsymbol{x} \in \mathcal{F} | \boldsymbol{x} \text{ is Pareto-optimal}\}$$

Definition 5. The **Pareto Front** $\mathcal{PF}^*$ is defined by:

$$\mathcal{PF}^* = \{\boldsymbol{f}(\boldsymbol{x}) \in \mathbb{R}^k | \boldsymbol{x} \in \mathcal{P}^*\}$$

When solving multi-objective optimization problems (MOPs), the aim is to obtain the Pareto optimal set from the set $\mathcal{F}$. Thus, given a MOP, the goal of a Multi-Objective Evolutionary Algorithm (MOEA) is to produce a good approximation of its Pareto front. One of the most widely used MOEAs for problems having only two or three objectives is the Nondominated Sorting Genetic Algorithm-II (*NSGA-II*) [7]. This MOEA solves a MOP using nondominated sorting and a crowding-comparison operator that acts as its density estimator.

5   Approach and Algorithm

We propose a nested-evolutionary algorithm for generating universal unrestricted adversarial examples in a black-box scenario. Given a sequence of image filters as input, the algorithm returns the best image-agnostic filter configuration which, applied to the images from the dataset, greatly increases the classification error of the target model.

The method consists of two evolutionary nested algorithms: the outer algorithm is in charge of finding the sequence of filters to use, while the inner algorithm has to choose the parameter values.

The population is composed by sequences of parameterized filters that are applicable to images and transform them in possibly malign images.

Given a set $S = \{f_1, f_2, \cdots f_m\}$ of m image filters, the outer algorithm geno-type (with length l) is encoded as a list of integers representing the corresponding filters in S. Similarly, the inner algorithm genotype is represented by a list containing the parameters used for each selected filter.

The associated phenotype, applied to a set of images, generates the adversarial examples by applying the selected sequence of filters, with their corresponding optimized parameters, to legitimate images.

5.1 Outer Algorithm

For the outer optimization step we employ a genetic algorithm: a population of N candidate solutions is iteratively evolved towards better solutions. In order to breed a new generation, population members are randomly selected and the crossover and mutation operations are performed. The quality of the candidates is evaluated based on their fitness values.

Initial population: it is generated by randomly selecting l filters from the set S of available filters and their parameters are initialized with default values equal to 1.

Crossover: a standard one-point crossover is used to generate new off-springs from randomly selected members. Each child is guaranteed to inherit some genetic information from both parents, including the optimized parameters.

Mutation: it is applied by substituting a filter with another one based on a mutation probability. The substituent filter is initialized with random parameter values. This way we also ensure a complete mutation of the parameters.

Selection: at the end of each iteration, we choose the N best individuals from the set of 2N candidates (parents and offsprings) according to their fitness values. This process is repeated until the algorithm exhausts the allowed number of epochs.

5.2 Inner Algorithm

For the inner algorithm we propose and evaluate three different optimization strategies: a genetic algorithm (GA), a $(1, \lambda)$ evolutionary strategy (ES) and a random-based approach with tournament (in Algorithm 1, defined as follows: $optimizer_O$, where $O \in \{ \text{`GA'}, \text{`ES'}, \text{`Tournament'} \}$).

The genetic algorithm of the inner optimization has the same structure and operators as the outer GA, except that its task is to evolve a population of lists of parameters for every individual from the outer algorithm.

Alternatively to GA, we propose to optimize the parameters by using $(1, \lambda)$ evolution strategy with $\lambda = 5$. ES iteratively updates a search distribution by following the natural gradient towards higher expected fitness. In our case, for each list of parameters we compute a batch of N samples by perturbing the original individual. A gradient towards a better solution is estimated using the fitness values of the N samples. This gradient is then used to update the original individual. The entire process is repeated until a stopping criterion is met.

Finally, the random-based method is implemented as a 2-way competition. Given a solution inherited from the outer algorithm, a new individual is generated by randomly changing the parameters values of the original solution. The two candidates compete against each other in a tournament and the winner is passed on to the next generation.

5.3 Evaluation

The last part of our algorithm is about how the evaluation is performed. A candidate sequence of filters $\bar{y}$, and its own optimized parameters $\bar{n}$, is decoded as the phenotype b which is evaluated by querying the target neural network. We modeled the fitness function as a multi-objective problem which accounts for both the attack success rate as well as the detection mechanism bypassing rate. The goal is to give the attacker the ability to bypass detection mechanisms. We believe this to be a powerful feature of our method given that the field of adversarial machine learning lacks such approaches.

Let F the target neural network, x_i the i-th image of the original dataset X and X* the set of perturbed images x_i^* obtained by applying the sequence of filters we want to evaluate to all the images in X, we define

- the *Attack Success Rate ASR* as

$$ASR(X, X^*) = \frac{1}{n} \sum_{i=0}^{n} F(x_i) \neq F(x_i^*) \qquad (7)$$

where n is the size of the dataset X and X^*
- the *Detection Rate DR* as

$$DR(X^*) = \frac{1}{n} \sum_{i=0}^{n} D(x_i^*) \qquad (8)$$

where D is the chosen detector (e.g. feature squeezing), which returns 1 if the image is detected as an attack, 0 otherwise.

Accordingly, we can define multi-objective problem of our interest as

$$minimize \, \mathcal{F}(X, X^*) = \{1.0 - ASR(X, X^*), DR(X, X^*)\} \qquad (9)$$

which is managed by means of the *non_dominated_sorting* and *crowding_distance* procedures of the NSGA-II technique [7]. The general structure of the proposed algorithm is illustrated in Algorithm 1.

6 Experiments and Discussion

6.1 Experimental Setup

We evaluate the proposed method by attacking the convolutional neural network proposed by Papernot et al. in [22] and used also in [5] to prove the effectiveness of their attack. The model is composed of a series of 2 convolutional layers having

---

Algorithm 1: General structure of the nested evolutionary algorithm for generating adversarial examples

---

Input: Dataset D, population size N, epochs E

Extract the K batches $B_1, \ldots, B_K$ from D ;

Initialize population P of N individuals;

Evaluate each individual of P by the two fitness ASR and DR;

for $e = 0$ **to** E **do**

    for $i = 1$ **to** K **do**

        Offsprings $= \{\emptyset\}$;

        for $i = 1$ **to** N **do**

            Select randomly $parent_1$,$parent_2$ from P ;

            $\overline{p}_1 \leftarrow encode_1(parent_1)$;

            $\overline{p}_2 \leftarrow encode_1(parent_2)$;

            $y_i = \mathrm{crossover}(\overline{p}_1, \overline{p}_2)$;

            $\overline{y}_i = \mathrm{mutation}(y_i)$;

            $n_i \leftarrow encode_2(\overline{y}_i)$;

            $\overline{n}_i = \mathrm{optimizer}_O(n_i)$;

            Offsprings $\leftarrow (\overline{y}_i, \overline{n}_i)$;

        end

        foreach $(\overline{y}_i, \overline{n}_i) \in$ Offsprings **do**

            $b \leftarrow$ decode $(\overline{y}_i, \overline{n}_i)$;

            Evaluate the fitness ASR and DR on batch B_i ;

        end

        $P = \mathrm{selection}(P, \text{Offsprings})$;

    end

end

return: best image-agnostic filter configuration;

---

64 3×3 filters paired with ReLU activation function and a max-pooling layer, 2 convolutional layers with 128 3×3 filters with ReLU followed by a another max-pooling layer, 2 fully connected layers with ReLU and a softmax layer used for the final classification. This network was trained using the CIFAR-10 dataset which is a very popular benchmark image dataset consisting in 50000 training and 10000 testing colour images with a resolution of 32×32, belonging to 10 different classes. Dropout was used in order to prevent overfitting, and momentum and parameter decay were employed to guarantee model convergence.

For these preliminary experiments, we choose to adopt the *Feature Squeezing* detection method [32] as detection method in the fitness function used during the optimization process since it is one of the most popular and low-cost techniques that has been proven to achieve high detection rates (over 85% for CIFAR-10 and Imagenet dataset) against different famous state-of-the-art attacks.

The hyperparameters default values used to conduct the experiments were fixed as follows, where not differently specified: number of filters = 5, mutation probability = 0.5, batch size = 100, population size = 10 for the outer algorithm, epochs = 3. For the inner algorithms we set the population size equal to 5 and the number of generations was fixed to 3. To perform the detection we used the combination of features squeezers reported in [32] to work best for CIFAR-10 images: reduction to 5-bit depth, a local median smoothing and a non-local mean smoothing, and threshold to find the illegitimate images set to 1.7547^2.

Dataset

We used the CIFAR-10 testing set for training our algorithm and evaluating its effectiveness. The set was divided in two subsets: the first 200 images were used for the filter configuration optimization process and the remaining 9800 images were used for testing the adversarial attack. The optimization subset of images was chosen relatively small in order to measure the power of the universal attack.

Selection of the training epochs, number of filters and parameters range

Several experiments were carried out in order to estimate the best trade-off between the performance of the proposed method and computation time. We tested all three inner optimization algorithms (GA, ES and Tournament) with the default parameters configuration except for the number of epochs which was set to 10. We analyzed their attack success rate (ASR), feature squeezing detection rate (DR) and computation time. We observed that they all had similar performance-time behaviour. We decided to stick to 3 epochs since it was producing good results while keeping the computational time fairly low. Figure 1 illustrates the attack and detection rate curve with respect to the number of epochs with ES inner optimizer.

Moreover, we also wanted to investigate the importance of choosing different numbers of filters for creating the adversarial configuration. The minimum filters selection was set to 3 while the maximum is the cardinality of set S of available filters. We adopted the policy of no-repeating filters, meaning that a filter can be picked only once inside a certain configuration. We calculated the attack rate of our algorithm by using all three inner optimization methods. Table 2 shows that using 5 filters has the best outcome in terms of attack success rate.

In our implementation filters can be applied using different features parameters similar to how Instagram allows users to control the effect of filters by manually adjusting their intensities within a certain range. The parameters of each filter can vary between a fixed range of values. The minimum and maximum values of each interval were found by performing a quality analysis on the modified images with the above mentioned filters and diverse parameters values. This analysis allowed to restrict the search space in order to further reduce the training time. In order to evaluate the universality of our attack we applied the optimized filter configuration to each image in the testing set and computed the detection rate defined as follows:

$$FSDR = \frac{\sum_{i=0}^{m} D(\widehat{x}_i)}{|\widehat{X}|}, \qquad \widehat{x} \in \widehat{X} \tag{10}$$

---

[2] https://github.com/mzweilin/EvadeML-Zoo/blob/master/ Reproduce_FeatureSqueezing.md.

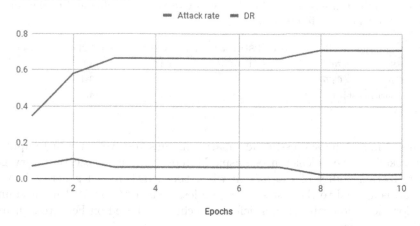

Fig. 1. Attack rate and FSDR wrt Epochs with ES optimizer.

Table 2. Evaluation of attack success rate (ASR) with respect to the number of filters.

Optimizer	Number of filters	ASR %
ES	3	46.5
ES	4	43.5
ES	**5**	**70**
GA	3	58.5
GA	4	52
GA	**5**	**68.5**
Tournament	3	41.5
Tournament	4	45.5
Tournament	**5**	**61**

where D corresponds to the features squeezing detector which returns 1 if the image is identified as illegitimate and 0 otherwise, $\widehat{X}$ represents the set of successful adversarial examples, and $m = |\widehat{X}|$ is the cardinality of $\widehat{X}$.

In Table 3 we report the attack success rate and the detection rate for both training and testing subsets with the default hyperparameters values, which were found to work best.

First of all, from these results, we can note that, even if the attack success rate is lower than the ones obtained by other methods in literature (also greater than 90% in some cases), these values should be fairly compared to the ones obtained by the other methods excluding the attacks that would be blocked by a defense mechanism. Considering that Xu et al. evaluated Feature Squeezing method with respect to 11 different attacks on three different datasets and reported for CIFAR-10 an overall detection rate of 84.5% [32], our attack is very effective

Table 3. Attack success rate (ASR) and Feature Squeezing Detection Rate (FSDR) with different optimizers on Carlini CNN and CIFAR-10 training and testing subsets, epochs = 3, number of filters = 5.

Optimizer	ASR % train set	FSDR % train set	ASR % test set	FSDR % test set
ES	70	2.1	63.7	3.5
GA	68.5	2.9	63.8	3.4
Tournament	61	5.7	56.3	4.5

because among the successful adversarial images just very few attempts will be blocked by the defense mechanism. Moreover, we can observe a very good generalization ability of the model: when the attack model generated by our method is applied to the test set, we lose less than 10% for ASR maintaining a very low detection rate when a defense mechanism based on Feature Squeezing method is applied.

6.2 Generated Images

Table 4 shows some successful adversarial examples generated by applying the filter configurations with their respective optimized parameters found by the proposed algorithm on the unseen images from the testing subset.

Table 4. Successful adversarial attacks on CIFAR-10 testing subset. On the left: original image; On the right: successful adversarial example.

Optimizer	Successful adversarial examples on the testing set
ES	
GA	
Tournament	
Label names	airplane : 0 automobile : 1 bird : 2 cat : 3 deer : 4 dog : 5 frog : 6 horse : 7 ship : 8 truck : 9

For each adversarial example we attached the original image and we also indicate the classification labels before and after the modification. It is very interesting to note that the solutions found by our method, i.e. the applied perturbations, are very uniform across the image and no unnatural patterns or high-frequency areas can be noticed.

7   Conclusions and Future Works

The experimental results show that the multi-objective method with detection feedback is able to produce successful adversarial examples while keeping the detection rate low. Even though the attack success rate is lower with respect to other state-of-the-art methods (restricted & unrestricted) we have the advantage of not being caught by detection methods. This indicates the potential of the proposed attack whose goal is not only to force the classifier to mispredict but also to evade possible defenses.

Nonetheless, there is a wide room for improvement. We intend to continue this study since the topic of multi-objective evolutionary attacks opens up an interesting research direction. We also plan to run more experiments on more complex models and to test the universality of our attacks across multiple neural networks architectures. Moreover, considering the availability of multi-objective evolutionary methods like MOEA/D [34] able to take into account more than two objective functions, we want to further improve our algorithm in order to include in the fitness function the three components: attack success rate, detection rate and image control. Differently from all the other approaches, our idea is to manage the image perturbations and control it by using no-reference image quality assessment like NIMA [29] or Frechet Inception Distance (FID) [11] instead of the L_p-norms.

References

1. Akhtar, N., Liu, J., Mian, A.: Defense against universal adversarial perturbations. In: 2018 IEEE/CVF Conference on Computer Vision and Pattern Recognition, pp. 3389–3398 (2018)
2. Alzantot, M., Sharma, Y., Chakraborty, S., Zhang, H., Hsieh, C.J., Srivastava, M.B.: Genattack. In: Proceedings of the Genetic and Evolutionary Computation Conference (Jul 2019)
3. Baioletti, M., Coello, C.A.C., Di Bari, G., Poggioni, V.: Multi-objective evolutionary GAN. In: Proceedings of the 2020 Genetic and Evolutionary Computation Conference Companion, pp. 1824–1831. GECCO 2020, Association for Computing Machinery, New York, NY, USA (2020)
4. Bhattad, A., Chong, M.J., Liang, K., Li, B., Forsyth, D.: Unrestricted adversarial examples via semantic manipulation. In: ICLR (2020)
5. Carlini, N., Wagner, D.: Towards evaluating the robustness of neural networks. In: 2017 IEEE Symposium on Security and Privacy (SP), pp. 39–57 (2017)

6. Chen, P., Zhang, H., Sharma, Y., Yi, J., Hsieh, C.J.: Zoo: zeroth order optimization based black-box attacks to deep neural networks without training substitute models. In: Proceedings of the 10th ACM Workshop on Artificial Intelligence and Security (2017)

7. Deb, K., Pratap, A., Agarwal, S., Meyarivan, T.: A fast and elitist multiobjective genetic algorithm: NSGA-II. IEEE Trans. Evol. Comput. **6**(2), 182–197 (2002)

8. Deng, Y., Zhang, C., Wang, X.: A multi-objective examples generation approach to fool the deep neural networks in the black-box scenario. In: 2019 IEEE Fourth International Conference on Data Science in Cyberspace (DSC), pp. 92–99. IEEE (2019)

9. Goodfellow, I.J., Shlens, J., Szegedy, C.: Explaining and harnessing adversarial examples. CoRR abs/1412.6572 (2015)

10. Hayes, J., Danezis, G.: Learning universal adversarial perturbations with generative models. In: 2018 IEEE Security and Privacy Workshops (SPW), pp. 43–49. IEEE (2018)

11. Heusel, M., Ramsauer, H., Unterthiner, T., Nessler, B., Hochreiter, S.: Gans trained by a two time-scale update rule converge to a local nash equilibrium. In: Guyon, I., et al. (eds.) Advances in Neural Information Processing Systems, vol. 30, pp. 6626–6637. Curran Associates, Inc. (2017). https://proceedings.neurips.cc/paper/2017/file/8a1d694707eb0fefe65871369074926d-Paper.pdf

12. Hosseini, H., Poovendran, R.: Semantic adversarial examples. CoRR abs/1804.00499 (2018). http://arxiv.org/abs/1804.00499

13. Kurakin, A., Goodfellow, I.J., Bengio, S.: Adversarial examples in the physical world. arXiv abs/1607.02533 (2017)

14. Kurakin, A., Goodfellow, I., Bengio, S.: Adversarial machine learning at scale. arXiv preprint arXiv:1611.01236 (2016)

15. Moosavi-Dezfooli, S.M., Fawzi, A., Fawzi, O., Frossard, P.: Universal adversarial perturbations. In: 2017 IEEE Conference on Computer Vision and Pattern Recognition (CVPR), pp. 86–94 (2017)

16. Moosavi-Dezfooli, S.M., Fawzi, A., Frossard, P.: Deepfool: a simple and accurate method to fool deep neural networks. In: 2016 IEEE Conference on Computer Vision and Pattern Recognition (CVPR), pp. 2574–2582 (2016)

17. Mopuri, K.R., Ganeshan, A., Babu, R.V.: Generalizable data-free objective for crafting universal adversarial perturbations. IEEE Trans. Pattern Anal. Mach. Intell. **41**(10), 2452–2465 (2018)

18. Mosli, R., Wright, M., Yuan, B., Pan, Y.: They might not be giants: Crafting black-box adversarial examples with fewer queries using particle swarm optimization. arXiv abs/1909.07490 (2019)

19. Narodytska, N., Kasiviswanathan, S.: Simple black-box adversarial attacks on deep neural networks. In: 2017 IEEE Conference on Computer Vision and Pattern Recognition Workshops (CVPRW), pp. 1310–1318 (2017)

20. Papernot, N., McDaniel, P., Goodfellow, I.J., Jha, S., Celik, Z.Y., Swami, A.: Practical black-box attacks against machine learning. In: Proceedings of the 2017 ACM on Asia Conference on Computer and Communications Security (2017)

21. Papernot, N., McDaniel, P., Jha, S., Fredrikson, M., Celik, Z.Y., Swami, A.: The limitations of deep learning in adversarial settings. In: 2016 IEEE European Symposium on Security and Privacy (EuroS&P), pp. 372–387 (2016)

22. Papernot, N., McDaniel, P., Wu, X., Jha, S., Swami, A.: Distillation as a defense to adversarial perturbations against deep neural networks. In: 2016 IEEE Symposium on Security and Privacy (SP), pp. 582–597 (2016)

23. Mopuri, K.R., Uppala, P.K., Babu, R.V.: Ask, acquire, and attack: data-free UAP generation using class impressions. In: Ferrari, V., Hebert, M., Sminchisescu, C., Weiss, Y. (eds.) ECCV 2018, Part IX. LNCS, vol. 11213, pp. 20–35. Springer, Cham (2018). https://doi.org/10.1007/978-3-030-01240-3_2

24. Shahin Shamsabadi, A., Sanchez-Matilla, R., Cavallaro, A.: ColorFool: semantic adversarial colorization. In: 2020 IEEE/CVF Conference on Computer Vision and Pattern Recognition (CVPR) (June 2020)

25. Shamsabadi, A.S., Oh, C., Cavallaro, A.: EdgeFool: an adversarial image enhancement filter. In: ICASSP 2020–2020 IEEE International Conference on Acoustics, Speech and Signal Processing (ICASSP) (May 2020)

26. Su, J., Vargas, D.V., Sakurai, K.: One pixel attack for fooling deep neural networks. IEEE Trans. Evol. Comput. **23**, 828–841 (2019)

27. Suzuki, T., Takeshita, S., Ono, S.: Adversarial example generation using evolutionary multi-objective optimization. In: 2019 IEEE Congress on Evolutionary Computation (CEC), pp. 2136–2144. IEEE (2019)

28. Szegedy, C., et al.: Intriguing properties of neural networks. CoRR abs/1312.6199 (2014)

29. Talebi, H., Milanfar, P.: NIMA: neural image assessment. IEEE Trans. Image Process. **27**, 3998–4011 (2018)

30. Tramèr, F., Kurakin, A., Papernot, N., Goodfellow, I., Boneh, D., McDaniel, P.D.: Ensemble adversarial training: attacks and defenses. In: 6th International Conference on Learning Representations, ICLR 2018 (2018)

31. Vidnerová, P., Neruda, R.: Vulnerability of classifiers to evolutionary generated adversarial examples. Neural Netw. Off. J. Int. Neural Netw. Soc. **127**, 168–181 (2020)

32. Xu, W., Evans, D., Qi, Y.: Feature squeezing: Detecting adversarial examples in deep neural networks. arXiv abs/1704.01155 (2018)

33. Yuan, X., He, P., Zhu, Q., Li, X.: Adversarial examples: attacks and defenses for deep learning. IEEE Trans. Neural Netw. Learn. Syst. **30**(9), 2805–2824 (2019)

34. Zhang, Q., Li, H.: MOEA/D: a multiobjective evolutionary algorithm based on decomposition. IEEE Trans. Evol. Comput. **11**(6), 712–731 (2007). https://doi.org/10.1109/TEVC.2007.892759

35. Zhao, Z., Liu, Z., Larson, M.: Adversarial color enhancement: Generating unrestricted adversarial images by optimizing a color filter. arXiv: Computer Vision and Pattern Recognition (2020)

36. Zhou, A., Qu, B.Y., Li, H., Zhao, S.Z., Suganthan, P.N., Zhang, Q.: Multiobjective evolutionary algorithms: a survey of the state of the art. Swarm Evol. Comput. **1**(1), 32–49 (2011)

Improving Distributed Neuroevolution Using Island Extinction and Repopulation

Zimeng Lyu$^{(\boxtimes)}$, Joshua Karns, AbdElRahman ElSaid, Mohamed Mkaouer, and Travis Desell

Rochester Institute of Technology, Rochester, NY 14623, USA
zimenglyu@mail.rit.edu, josh@mail.rit.edu, aae8800@rit.edu, mwmvse@rit.edu, tjdvse@rit.edu

Abstract. Neuroevolution commonly uses speciation strategies to better explore the search space of neural network architectures. One such speciation strategy is the use of islands, which are also popular in improving the performance of distributed evolutionary algorithms. However, islands may experience stagnation, which prevents their convergence towards better solutions and can result in wasted computation. This work evaluates utilizing an island extinction and repopulation mechanism to avoid premature convergence using Evolutionary eXploration of Augmenting Memory Models (EXAMM), an asynchronous island based neuroevolution algorithm that progressively evolves recurrent neural networks (RNNs). In island extinction and repopulation, all members of the worst performing island are erased periodically and repopulated with mutated versions of the global best RNN. This island based strategy is additionally compared to NEAT's (NeuroEvolution of Augmenting Topologies) speciation strategy. Experiments were performed using two different real-world time series datasets (coal-fired power plant and aviation flight data). With statistical significance, results show that in addition to being more scalable, this island extinction and repopulation strategy evolves better global best genomes than both EXAMM's original island based strategy and NEAT's speciation strategy. The extinction and repopulation strategy is easy to implement, and can be generically applied to other neuroevolution algorithms.

Keywords: NeuroEvolution · Neural architecture search · Extinction · Repopulation · Recurrent neural networks · Time series prediction

1 Introduction

Neuroevolution (NE), or the evolution of artificial neural networks (ANNs), has been widely applied as a neural architecture search strategy for a variety of

This material is based upon work supported by the U.S. Department of Energy, Office of Science, Office of Advanced Combustion Systems under Award Number #FE0031547 and by the Federal Aviation Administration and MITRE Corporation under the National General Aviation Flight Information Database (NGAFID) award.

P. A. Castillo and J. L. Jiménez Laredo (Eds.): EvoApplications 2021, LNCS 12694, pp. 568–583, 2021.
https://doi.org/10.1007/978-3-030-72699-7_36

machine learning problems, including image classification, natural language processing, reinforcement learning and time series data prediction [23,32]. As the complexity of the tasks ANNs are trained to solve increases, manually designing the network becomes impossible, especially when they may need to be optimized for multiple criteria such as cost, latency, power consumption, and accuracy. NE provides a way to evolve ANNs in large and high dimensional space without prior knowledge, searching through the growing number of ANN building blocks, such as activation functions, memory cells, convolutional filter, and feature map types, while at the same time determining network topology.

NE algorithms tend to be computationally expensive in that candidate neural networks need to be trained or otherwise evaluated to determine their fitness. Because of this, most NE algorithms are distributed in order to make progress more quickly. The use of islands, as a common strategy in distributed evolutionary algorithms, has been shown to potentially provide significant speedup beyond distribution, as islands can evolve independently with smaller populations as different species more quickly, with the periodic transfer best found solutions [1]. However, if we look into how species evolve, we find that different species converge and evolve at different speeds. Some species show premature convergence and can become stuck at local optima. In this work, we take inspiration from *extinction* and *repopulation* mechanisms, which have shown to speed up evolution and speciation in the real world [25] as well as in EAs [11,15,20,37] and apply them to distributed NE algorithms.

This work presents a novel extinction and repopulation strategy that repopulates poorly performing islands by first removing all the genomes in the island and then repopulating it with random mutations of the global best genome. Experiments explore how the frequency of extinction and the number of random mutations applied to the global best genome affect the island based evolution strategy. This was done using the Evolutionary eXploration of Augmenting Memory Models (EXAMM) [26] algorithm that evolves deep Recurrent Neural Networks (RNN) for time series data prediction. We further implemented NEAT's speciation strategy in EXAMM, so it could be fairly compared as a benchmark. To test the robustness of this strategy, we used two real world, non-seasonal, large scale time series data sets from aviation data and a coal-fired power plant. Results show that the new extinction and repopulation based strategies outperform baseline EXAMM and NEAT's speciation strategy with statistical significance.

2   Related Work

According to the history of biological evolution, extinction plays an important role in the process of evolution [7,8,25]. It will erase the species that are not suited for their niches and create opportunities for new species to emerge. Similarly in EAs, research conducted by Greenwood et al. [11] and Krink et al. [20] show that applying mass extinction can enhance the performance in evolutionary search. A mass extinction mechanism was also shown to significantly improve hybrid particle swarm optimizer model performance [39], and more recently, Lehman *et al.* proved using extinction events is an effective mechanism for divergent search algorithms [21].

In addition to extinction, the biological concepts of migration and repopulation are also applied in EAs to improve performance. Grefenstette *et al.* have investigated replacing a percentage of the population with randomly generated individuals [12]. De Falco *et al.* take the inspiration of biological invasion and migrate genomes into other subpopulations to compete with native genomes [4]. Hernandez *et al.* replace a fraction of the population with selective repopulation [15], and Wan *et al.* take genomes generated from "elite clusters" to randomly replace individuals in the population [37].

In terms of speciation for NE, NEAT (Evolving Neural Networks through Augmenting Topologies) [31] presented one of the first speciation strategies for NE, where genomes speciate by tracking historical genes and measuring the distance between new genomes and an existing species. This has been extended with Natural Evolution Speciation for NEAT (NENEAT) [18], which replaces NEAT's speciation with a cladistic strategy, where all the genomes in the same species share a subset of nodes. Trujillo *et al.* speciate evolutionary robotics in the behavior space [35], whereas NEAT and NENEAT speciate genomes in topology space. Hadjiivanov *et al.* also investigated a complexity-based speciation strategy, which groups genomes by their number of hidden neurons [13].

Other than strategies to divide genomes into different species, evolutionary rules such as mutation, crossover, weight initialization, and distance functions, can be used to drive speciation and improve EA performance. Verbancsics *et al.* investigated the effect of crossover and mutation on the NE speciation strategies [36]. Mathias *et al.* explored the use of extinction for path finding GAs in a continuous environment [24]. Sun *et al.* applied a variable length gene encoding to avoid the network depth constraint for solving complex problems [34]. Krčah *et al.* modified NEAT's fitness evaluation rule by changing the capacity of species dynamically [19]. Lastly, instead of using objective functions to measure the fitness of a genome, Lehman *et al.* instead drove search using behavior novelty [22].

In contrast to these strategies, the extinction and repopulation presented in this paper is easily adaptable to any NE or EA method utilizing islands, and does not require fitness modifications or the calculation of expensive distance metrics, which in many cases need to be evaluated against all other individuals or species within the population, which can significantly degrade performance in a distributed EA. In fact, when comparing to NEAT's speciation strategy, this issue became apparent as we were limited in the number of processors we could scale to (see Sect. 4.4). The strategy is also easier to use and tune, only requiring users to specify the frequency of extinction and repopulation events.

3   Methodology

3.1   Evolutionary eXploration of Augmenting Memory Models

This work utilizes the Evolutionary eXploration of Augmenting Memory Models (EXAMM) neuroevolution algorithm [26] to explore the extinction and repopulation of islands. EXAMM evolves progressively larger RNNs through a series of mutation and crossover (reproduction) operations. Mutations can be edge-based: *split edge, add edge, enable edge, add recurrent edge,* and *disable edge* operations, or work as higher-level node-based mutations: *disable node, enable node, add node, split node* and *merge node*. The type of node to be added is selected uniformly at random from a suite of simple neurons and complex memory cells: Δ-RNN units [27], gated recurrent units (GRUs) [2], long short-term memory cells (LSTMs) [16], minimal gated units (MGUs) [40], and update gate RNN cells (UGRNNs) [3]. This allows EXAMM to select for the best performing recurrent memory units. EXAMM also allows for *deep recurrent connections*, which enables the RNN to directly use information beyond the previous time step. These deep recurrent connections have proven to offer significant improvements in model generalization, even yielding models that outperform state-of-the-art gated architectures [5]. EXAMM has both a multithreaded implementation and a Message Passing Interface (MPI) implementation for distributed use on high performance computing resources. To the authors' knowledge, these capabilities are not available in other neuroevolution frameworks capable of evolving RNNs, which is the primary reason EXAMM was selected for this work.

EXAMM uses an asynchronous island based evolution strategy with a fixed number of islands n, each with an island capacity m. During the evolution process, islands go through two phases: *initialized,* and *filled.* During the *initialization* phase, each island starts with one seed genome, which is the minimal possible feed-forward neural network structure with no hidden layers, with the input layer fully connected to the output layer. Worker processes repeatedly request genomes to evaluate from the master process using a work stealing approach.

On receiving a genome, the worker then evaluates its *fitness,* calculated as mean squared error (MSE) on a validation data set after being trained by stochastic back propagation through time (BPTT). When reported back to the master process, if the island is not full, it is inserted into the island, or if the *fitness* is better than the worst genome in that island, it will replace the worst genome. The master generates new genomes from islands in a round-robin manner, by doing one random mutation on randomly selected genomes from an island until that island reaches its maximum capacity m, and its status becomes *filled.* When all islands are *filled,* they repopulate through inter-island crossover, intra-island crossover and mutation operations. *Intra-island crossover* selects two random genomes from the same island, and the child gets inserted back to where its parents come from. *Inter-island crossover* selects the first parent at random from the target island, and the second parent is the best genome from another randomly selected island. As islands are distinct sub-populations and evolve independently, the only chance for the islands to exchange genes is through *inter-island crossover*.

The weights of the seed genome, generated during the *initialization* phase, are initialized uniformly at random between -0.5 and 0.5, or by the Kaiming [14] or Xavier [9] strategies. After this, RNNs, generated through mutation or crossover, reuse parental weights, allowing the RNNs to train from where the parents left off, *i.e.*, *"Lamarckian" weight initialization*. Mutation operations may add new nodes or/and edges that are not present in the parent, and these are initialized using a normal distribution of the average μ and variance σ^2 of the best parent's weights. During crossover, in the case where an edge or node exists in both parents, the child weights are generated by recombining the parents' weights. Given a random number $-0.5 <= r <= 1.5$, a child's weight w_c is set to $w_c = r(w_{p2} - w_{p1}) + w_{p1}$, where w_{p1} is the weight from the more fit parent, and w_{p2} is the weight from the less fit parent. This allows the child weights to be set along a gradient calculated from the weights of the two parents, allowing for informed exploration of the weight space of the two parents.

3.2   EXAMM Island Repopulation and Extinction

While investigating the performance of the EXAMM algorithm, it was observed that islands do not converge at the same speed, and some are stagnant. A naive approach to repopulation would be to erase the prematurely converged island and restart from scratch, however, given that the other islands will have well-developed genomes, it might be impossible for the restarted island to ever catch up. Further, it would involve re-examining the preliminary regions of the search space. Taking inspiration from nature, most new species are not directly evolved from a single-celled organism. In common cases, a group of organisms evolves in a certain direction to adapt to a new niche, and eventually new species emerge. With this as motivation, we utilize the idea of immigrating existing genomes to the worst island for repopulation. In addition, we opt for using mutations on these immigrating genomes to bring innovation through the evolution process, allowing them to potentially further explore new niches.

Using our proposed strategy, the EXAMM island repopulation strategy has now three phases: *initialization*, *filled*, and *repopulation*. The *initialization* phase is the same as original EXAMM. However, after all the islands become *filled*, we introduce periodic extinction mechanisms to the worst performing island. At the time of an extinction mechanism, all the islands are ranked based on their best genome's fitness, and all the genomes in the worst island are removed. Then this depopulated island moves into the *repopulation* phase. During this phase, new genomes for the island are generated by randomly performing m mutations on the global best genome until the island is full and goes back to *filled* status. To handle the asynchronous RNN evaluation in EXAMM, when a worker processes return trained RNNs generated from before the extinction mechanism, they are not added to the repopulating island and instead immediately removed. Through this, these periodic extinction mechanisms encourage further diversity in the entire population.

To repopulate an island, there are two ways EXAMM uses to find and erase the worst performing island: 1) the worst island can be repopulated at any extinction event, and 2) if an island becomes the worst island again after being repopulated, it has to wait for e other extinction events before it can become extinct and be repopulated again. The difference between the two strategies is that the second gives the newly repopulated island more time to evolve. As a repopulated island might need more time to evolve and find new well performing genomes, if the extinction mechanisms keep erasing the worst island regardless of its recent repopulation, the same island might end up being repeatedly repopulated. On the other hand, mutated global best genomes can perform better or worse than the original ones, especially when more than one mutation are applied together. If an island has not caught up with the rest of the population by the next extinction mechanism, it may have become stagnant in different local optima.

3.3 NEAT Speciation

To compare to a benchmark strategy, we utilized the speciation strategy from the popular Neuro-Evolution of Augmenting Topologies (NEAT) [31]. Newer versions of NEAT, such as HyperNeat [33] were not used because they cannot easily be applied to recurrent neural networks, especially those with modern memory cells. Further, HyperNEAT still utilizes NEAT's speciation strategy to generate its compositional pattern producing networks as opposed to a different strategy. Instead of using an island strategy, NEAT organizes genomes into small sub-populations, or species. New genomes are inserted into the first species in which the distance δ between the new genome and a random genome inserted from last generation is less than threshold δ_t. The distance is calculated using a distance function, δ:

$$\delta = \frac{C_1 E}{N} + \frac{C_2 D}{N} + C_3 \overline{W} \tag{1}$$

where E and D are the excess and disjoint genes between two genomes, and $\overline{W}$ is the weight difference of matching genes. $c1$, $c2$, and $c3$ are hyperparameters adjusting the weight of those factors and N is the number of genes in the larger genome.

NEAT does not limit the number of species or the species capacity. The species size is controlled by *explicit fitness sharing* [10]. A genome's adjusted fitness f_i' is calculated by:

$$f_i' = \frac{f_i}{\sum_{j=1}^{n} sh(\delta(i,j))} \tag{2}$$

When distance between two genomes i and j exceeds a threshold δ_t, sh is set to 0, sh is 1 otherwise [30]. Genomes who have a high adjusted fitness f_i' are removed. If the best fitness of a species does not improve in 15 generations, this species loses the ability to reproduce. If the entire population does not improve for 20 generations, then only the top 2 species are allowed to reproduce.

4 Results

4.1 Data Sets

Two datasets were utilized to test the varying speciation strategies.[1] The first comes from a coal-fired power plant, and the second comes from a selection of 10 flights worth of data from the National General Aviation Flight Information Database (NGAFID). Both datasets are multivariate, with 12 and 31 parameters, respectively, non-seasonal, and the parameter recordings are not independent. Furthermore, they are very long – the aviation time series range from 1 to 3 hours worth of per-second data, while the power plant data consists of 10 days worth of per-minute readings. *Main flame intensity* was chosen as the prediction parameter from the coal data set, and *pitch* was chosen as the prediction parameter from the flight data set.

4.2 Hyperparameter Settings

Each EXAMM run used 10 islands, each with a maximum capacity of 10 genomes. EXAMM was then allowed to evolve and train 20,000 genomes (RNNs) through its neuroevolution process. New RNNs were generated via mutation at a rate of 70%, intra-island crossover at a rate of 20%, and inter-island crossover at a rate of 10%. 10 out of EXAMM's 11 mutation operations were utilized (all except for *split edge*), and each was chosen with a uniform 10% chance. EXAMM generated new nodes by selecting from simple neurons, Δ-RNN, GRU, LSTM, MGU, and UGRNN memory cells uniformly at random. Recurrent connections could span any time-skip generated randomly between $\mathcal{U}(1, 10)$.

In related work, EXAMM has been shown to significantly outperform standard NEAT [6]. We attribute this to the fact that EXAMM can create nodes from a library of recurrent memory cells, has additional node level mutations, uses a Lamarckian/epigenetic weight inheritance strategy, and trains RNNs via stochastic gradient descent and back propagation through time (BPTT). On the other hand, NEAT only deploys edge-level mutations and has a rather simple evolutionary strategy to assign weights to networks. Additionally, NEAT was not designed for large scale parallelism, and uses a synchronous strategy for iteratively generating new populations. Due to this, we implemented NEAT's speciation strategy within the EXAMM framework to compare the speciation strategies without confounding effects from other algorithmic details.

NEAT typically generates 150 genomes per generation, and if a species has not improved its best fitness within 15 generations, it will be disabled and not allowed to procreate. It will further disable the entire population except for the top 2 species if the whole population has not found a new best fitness within 20 generations. To convert NEAT's generation based strategy to EXAMM's asynchronous strategy, which does not have explicit generations, species were instead

---

[1] These data sets are made publicly available at EXAMM GitHub repository: https://github.com/travisdesell/exact/tree/master/datasets/ for reproduction of these results.

disabled if they did not improve after 2250 new genomes were inserted (the same number of total genomes as 15 generations of 150 genomes), and all species except the top 2 were disabled if the best found fitness did not improve after 3000 genomes were inserted. The hyperparameters used for NEAT's speciation strategy were $c_1 = 1$, $c_2 = 1$, $c_3 = 0.4$, and the fitness threshold was set to $\delta_t = 0.6$ for the coal dataset, and $\delta_t = 0.4$ for the flight dataset. The c_1, c_2 and c_3 hyperparameters are the standard NEAT values, however the δ_t values were hand tuned to ensure good speciation. The NEAT runs were highly sensitive to δ_t and we found higher values resulted in all genomes clustering to the same species, and lower values resulted in each genome having its own species.

For both EXAMM and NEAT, all RNNs were locally trained for 10 epochs via stochastic gradient descent (SGD) and using back propagation through time (BPTT) [38] to compute gradients, all using the same hyperparameters. RNN weights were initialized by EXAMM's Lamarckian strategy (described in [26]), which allows child RNNs to reuse parental weights, significantly reducing the number of epochs required for the neuroevolution's local RNN training steps. SGD was run with a learning rate of $\eta = 0.001$ and used Nesterov momentum with $\mu = 0.9$. For the memory cells with forget gates, the forget gate bias had a value of 1.0 added to it (motivated by [17]). To prevent exploding gradients, gradient scaling [28] was used when the norm of the gradient exceeded a threshold of 1.0. To combat vanishing gradients, gradient boosting (the opposite of scaling) was used when the gradient norm was below 0.05. These parameters have been selected as they were recommended in previous papers about the EXAMM algorithm.

4.3 Experimental Design

Due to the stochastic nature of our experiments, we performed 20 repeats for each NEAT and EXAMM experiment on the coal and flight data sets. For EXAMM, we compared the baseline strategy (islands without extinction mechanism) to the two variations of the extinction strategy, one allowing repeated repopulations and the other not. For these strategies, extinction frequencies of 1000 and 2000 generated genomes were evaluated, and during the repopulation process, we allowed the global best genome (at the time of the extinction mechanism) to be mutated m times, with $m = 0$, 2, 4, or 8, before being inserted into the repopulated island. This resulted in a total of 680 experiments, 20 for NEAT, 20 for baseline EXAMM, and 320 for the 2 extinction strategies, 2 extinction frequencies, and 4 mutation values for each of the 2 datasets. For the experiments which disallowed repeated extinction for $e = 2$ events.

Various experiments were performed to get an understanding of how the frequency of extinction mechanism affected performance, $i.e.$, did having more frequent extinction mechanisms prevent repopulated islands from catching up and improving on the global best solution? Additionally, the two extinction strategies allowed us to determine the impact of allowing islands to be repeatedly made extinct, to see if they needed even more time to become well performing. Finally, modifying the mutation rates was done to provide an idea of how much exploration needed to be performed when repopulating the islands, to allow them to find new potentially better areas in the search space.

4.4 Computing Environment

Results were gathered using Rochester Institute of Technology's research computing systems. This system consists of 2304 Intel® Xeon® Gold 6150 CPU 2.70 GHz cores and 24 TB RAM, with compute nodes running the RedHat Enterprise Linux 7 system. All EXAMM baseline and EXAMM speciation strategies experiments utilized 180 cores. Since the NEAT speciation strategy is implemented in the EXAMM framework, and the EXAMM master process is responsible for generating and inserting genomes, whereas worker processes are only responsible for stochastic back propagation training and evaluate the fitness of genomes, all the genome distances and explicate fitness sharing evaluations were done in the master process. Utilizing NEAT's speciation strategy presented a speed bottleneck at the master process when using a larger number of cores. Therefore, the NEAT runs were limited to 72 cores, as adding additional cores did not improve runtime.

4.5 Repopulation Strategy Evaluation

Figures 1 and 2 present the performance across the 20 repeated experiments for NEAT speciation and the EXAMM variations. The solid line shows the average of the global best genomes across the 20 experiments, and the filled in area shows the range between the min and max. The test results show that the EXAMM extinction and repopulation strategies perform better than baseline EXAMM algorithm across all tests, with the NEAT speciation strategy performing worse than baseline EXAMM. On average, in three of the coal plant test cases and two of the four flight test cases, 2 mutations resulted in the best performing genomes. For the other test cases, applying 4 or 8 mutations found the best performing genomes, and all those test cases come from non-repeated repopulations for both datasets, which proves that innovations need more time to evolve and become better. The results also suggest that adding some, but not too much variance to the global best genome for island repopulation allowed the strategies to best find new regions of the search space to improve performance.

As a further investigation, Table 1 presents Mann–Whitney U test p-values comparing the best genomes of the 20 repeats from the various strategies to the best genomes from the 20 repeats of baseline EXAMM. p-values in bold represent statistically significant differences with $\alpha = 0.05$, showing that the results of the varying mutation strategies have a statistically significant difference from EXAMM, which similarly has a statistically significant difference from NEAT speciation.

Table 1 also provides more detail about the best, average and worst global best genome fitness at the end of the 20 repeated tests for each experiment. From this we can see that in the average cases having a faster extinction frequency

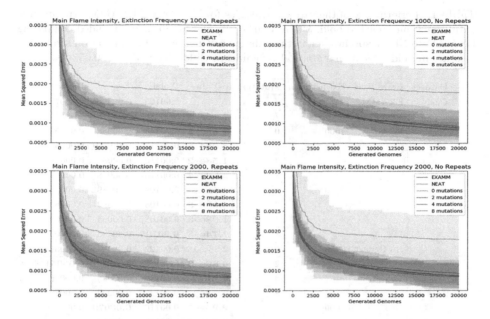

Fig. 1. Convergence rates (in terms of best MSE on validation data) for NEAT speciation and the EXAMM extinction and repopulation strategies predicting *main flame intensity* from the coal fired power plant dataset.

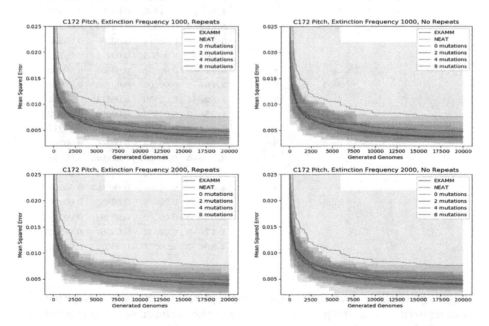

Fig. 2. Convergence rates (in terms of best MSE on validation data) for NEAT speciation and the EXAMM extinction and repopulation strategies predicting *pitch* from the c172 flight dataset.

Table 1. Performance of the various strategies for the varying EXAMM experiments, with best values marked bold. Mann–Whitney U test p-values are included comparing EXAMM to NEAT speciation and the different extinction and repopulation strategies. p-values in bold indicate a statistically significant difference with $\alpha = 0.05$.

Dataset	Erase Rule	Extinct Freq	Mutation	p-Value	Worst	Avg	Best
Coal	EXAMM	/	/	/	0.00125	0.00099	0.00072
	NEAT	/	/	**7.15e−8**	0.00238	0.00178	0.00115
	Repeat	1000	0	**4.55e−2**	0.00123	0.00088	0.00054
			2	**8.05e−5**	0.00117	**0.00079**	0.00059
			4	**1.58e−2**	0.00116	0.00086	0.00054
			8	**2.06e−2**	0.00123	0.00088	0.00067
		2000	0	5.68e−2	0.00109	0.00089	0.00053
			2	**1.28e−3**	0.00108	0.00082	0.00062
			4	**1.98e−3**	0.00108	0.00084	0.00060
			8	**7.74e−3**	**0.00105**	0.00086	0.00064
	No Repeat	1000	0	2.28e−1	0.00122	0.00093	0.00057
			2	**4.89e−3**	0.00120	0.00083	**0.00051**
			4	6.32e−2	0.00126	0.00089	0.00056
			8	2.20e−1	0.00132	0.00094	0.00070
		2000	0	**9.99e−5**	0.00116	**0.00079**	0.00057
			2	**3.28e−3**	0.00107	0.00084	0.00058
			4	7.39e−2	0.00112	0.00091	0.00065
			8	**3.82e−2**	0.00118	0.00090	0.00064
C172	EXAMM	/	/	/	0.00765	0.00480	0.00316
	NEAT	/	/	**1.3e−6**	0.01725	0.00755	0.00473
	Repeat	1000	0	**5.72e−3**	0.00526	0.00404	0.00229
			2	**3.31e−5**	0.00514	0.00360	0.00236
			4	**2.56e−3**	0.00523	0.00401	0.00282
			8	**5.72e−3**	0.00538	0.00401	0.00242
		2000	0	**2.16e−3**	0.00606	0.00385	0.00223
			2	**1.52e−4**	0.00556	0.00371	0.00234
			4	**1.28e−2**	0.00584	0.00399	0.00252
			8	**1.04e−2**	0.00621	0.00411	0.00216
	No Repeat	1000	0	**3.70e−5**	0.00513	0.00366	0.00281
			2	**3.70e−5**	**0.00497**	**0.00355**	0.00240
			4	**4.18e−4**	0.00672	0.00382	0.00266
			8	**4.64e−5**	0.00554	**0.00355**	0.00258
		2000	0	**5.07e−4**	0.00539	0.00387	0.00257
			2	**3.02e−3**	0.00590	0.00398	0.00246
			4	**1.17e−3**	0.00643	0.00381	**0.00163**
			8	**4.89e−3**	0.00577	0.00411	0.00300

of 1000 generally provided the best results, providing more evidence that performing extinction and repopulation improves the performance of neuroevolution strategy. Interestingly, the strategy which allowed islands to not be repeatedly erased provided slightly better results in the best case for both the coal and flight data.

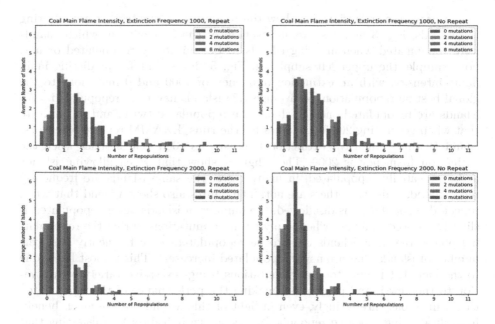

Fig. 3. The average number of times islands were repopulated across the repeated and no repeated experiments using the various EXAMM repopulation strategies on Coal dataset.

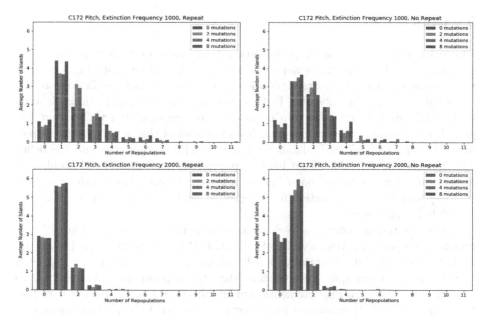

Fig. 4. The average number of times islands were repopulated across the repeated and no repeated experiments using the various EXAMM repopulation strategies on C172 dataset.

To provide more insight into how the repopulation strategies were affecting the islands, Fig. 3 and 4 shows an average of the frequency in which islands were repopulated when allowing islands to be repeatedly repopulated or not. For example, the upper left subplot in Fig. 3 shows that for predicting main flame intensity, with an extinction frequency of 1000 and 0 mutations to the global best on repopulation, on average 1.25 islands never are repopulated, 3.75 islands are repopulated once, 3 islands are repopulated twice, and so on. Note that when generating 20,000 genomes for the runs, EXAMM removes the worst island 19 times when the extinction frequency is 1000, and 9 times when the extinction frequency is 2000. These figures show that when allowing islands to be repeatedly repopulated, in many cases, the same islands are frequently repopulated, while the others are not. The figures also show a trend that when repeated repopulation is disallowed, the number of islands never repopulated is slightly reduced. Further, when applying more mutations during the repopulating phase, the same islands tend to be repopulated more frequently (*i.e.*, the number of islands that are never repopulated increases). This is most likely due to the fact that having too many mutations brings excessive variety or innovation to the new island population, making the performance of the repopulated island unstable. Interestingly, even in light of this we did not see much benefit from disallowing repeated repopulation (as shown in Tables 1), suggesting that if a repopulated island does not quickly find new better genomes, it does not have a good chance of finding better results if given more time to evolve.

5   Conclusion

This work investigates a novel speciation strategy based on extinction and repopulation mechanisms for island based evolutionary algorithms, applying it to neuroevolution of recurrent neural networks for time series data prediction on two challenging real-world data sets. In this strategy, the worst performing islands periodically experience extinction events and are repopulated with either the global best genome or mutations of it. Two versions of this strategy were implemented, one which allowed islands to be repeatedly repopulated and the other which prevented an island from being repopulated until a specified number of extinction events occurred on other islands. We investigated versions of this strategy with varying extinction frequencies, as well as numbers of mutations to the global best genome.

These mutation strategies were incorporated into the Evolutionary eXploration of Augmenting Memory Models (EXAMM) neuroevolution project, along with NEAT's speciation strategy as a benchmark comparison to a well-known neuroevolution technique. Results show that the repopulation strategy led to statistically significant improvements over baseline EXAMM, which in turn had large and statistically significant improvements over NEAT's speciation strategy. The repopulation strategies were also found to be more scalable than NEAT's strategy which requires determining the distance of each new genome to all others in the population to perform speciation. While the number of mutations applied to the global genome during repopulation was not significantly correlated with the best performance, in general a lower number (2 or 4) provided the best results. Having more mutations brought more innovation, but was also more unstable, leading to repopulated islands being repeatedly erased. Allowing islands to be repeatedly repopulated had advantages and disadvantages, where repeated repopulation would remove "bad" genomes more quickly, but preventing repeat repopulations protected innovations, giving the repopulated islands more time to evolve. In general, both strategies (allowing and disallowing repeated repopulation) provided statistically significant improvements over not using extinction and repopulation, but interestingly, neither significantly outperformed the other.

This work explored how a different number of mutations combined with different island extinction rules affected the repopulation process. Future work will involve examining other types of island extinction mechanisms, for example erasing multiple islands during an extinction, or controlling extinction mechanisms based on how much an island has improved over a period of time. Other options for repopulation can also be investigated beyond using the global best genome. Future work also includes investigating how to use varying forms of crossover to improve the repopulation algorithm's performance, which will include examining various crossover rules for repopulation, changing genome encoding methods, and redesigning the distance evaluation function. Lastly, it was particularly interesting that preventing and allowing repeated extinction both provided similar improvements, but neither outperformed the other. Developing a strategy that can make use of the best qualities of both may lead to further performance improvements. It should also be noted that while this work was examined in the context of neuroevolution algorithms, it could also be applied to any evolutionary strategy utilizing islands.

Acknowledgements. Most of the computation of this research was done on the high performance computing clusters of Research Computing at Rochester Institute of Technology [29]. We would like to thank the Research Computing team for their assistance and the support they generously offered to ensure that the heavy computation this study required was available.

References

1. Alba, E., Tomassini, M.: Parallelism and evolutionary algorithms. IEEE Trans. Evol. Comput. **6**(5), 443–462 (2002)
2. Chung, J., Gulcehre, C., Cho, K., Bengio, Y.: Empirical evaluation of gated recurrent neural networks on sequence modeling. arXiv preprint arXiv:1412.3555 (2014)
3. Collins, J., Sohl-Dickstein, J., Sussillo, D.: Capacity and trainability in recurrent neural networks. arXiv preprint arXiv:1611.09913 (2016)
4. De Falco, I., Della Cioppa, A., Maisto, D., Scafuri, U., Tarantino, E.: Biological invasion-inspired migration in distributed evolutionary algorithms. Inf. Sci. **207**, 50–65 (2012)

5. Desell, T., ElSaid, A., Ororbia, A.G.: An empirical exploration of deep recurrent connections using neuro-evolution. In: The 23nd International Conference on the Applications of Evolutionary Computation (EvoStar: EvoApps 2020), Seville, Spain, April 2020

6. ElSaid, A.E.R., Ororbia, A.G., Desell, T.J.: Ant-based neural topology search (ANTS) for optimizing recurrent networks. In: Castillo, P.A., Jiménez Laredo, J.L., Fernández de Vega, F. (eds.) EvoApplications 2020. LNCS, vol. 12104, pp. 626–641. Springer, Cham (2020). https://doi.org/10.1007/978-3-030-43722-0_40

7. Fuqua, L.M., Bralower, T.J., Arthur, M.A., Patzkowsky, M.E.: Evolution of calcareous nannoplankton and the recovery of marine food webs after the cretaceous-paleocene mass extinction. Palaios **23**(4), 185–194 (2008)

8. Gallala, N., Zaghbib-Turki, D., Arenillas, I., Arz, J.A., Molina, E.: Catastrophic mass extinction and assemblage evolution in planktic foraminifera across the Cretaceous/Paleogene (K/PG) boundary at Bidart (SW France). Mar. Micropaleontol. **72**(3–4), 196–209 (2009)

9. Glorot, X., Bengio, Y.: Understanding the difficulty of training deep feedforward neural networks. Aistats **9**, 249–256 (2010)

10. Goldberg, D.E., Richardson, J., et al.: Genetic algorithms with sharing for multimodal function optimization. In: Genetic algorithms and their applications: Proceedings of the Second International Conference on Genetic Algorithms, Hillsdale, NJ, pp. 41–49. Lawrence Erlbaum (1987)

11. Greewood, G., Fogel, G.B., Ciobanu, M.: Emphasizing extinction in evolutionary programming. In: Proceedings of the 1999 Congress on Evolutionary Computation-CEC99 (Cat. No. 99TH8406), vol. 1, pp. 666–671. IEEE (1999)

12. Grefenstette, J.J., et al.: Genetic algorithms for changing environments. In: PPSN, vol. 2, pp. 137–144. Citeseer (1992)

13. Hadjiivanov, A., Blair, A.: Complexity-based speciation and genotype representation for neuroevolution. In: 2016 IEEE Congress on Evolutionary Computation (CEC), pp. 3092–3101. IEEE (2016)

14. He, K., Zhang, X., Ren, S., Sun, J.: Delving deep into rectifiers: surpassing human-level performance on ImageNet classification. In: Proceedings of the IEEE International Conference on Computer Vision, pp. 1026–1034 (2015)

15. Hernández, A., Botello, S., et al.: Repairing normal EDAs with selective repopulation. Appl. Math. Comput. **230**, 65–77 (2014)

16. Hochreiter, S., Schmidhuber, J.: Long short-term memory. Neural Comput. **9**(8), 1735–1780 (1997)

17. Jozefowicz, R., Zaremba, W., Sutskever, I.: An empirical exploration of recurrent network architectures. In: International Conference on Machine Learning, pp. 2342–2350 (2015)

18. Knapp, J.S., Peterson, G.L.: Natural evolution speciation for neat. In: 2019 IEEE Congress on Evolutionary Computation (CEC), pp. 1487–1493. IEEE (2019)

19. Krčah, P.: Effects of speciation on evolution of neural networks in highly dynamic environments. In: Hamadi, Y., Schoenauer, M. (eds.) LION 2012. LNCS, pp. 425–430. Springer, Heidelberg (2012). https://doi.org/10.1007/978-3-642-34413-8_39

20. Krink, T., Thomsen, R.: Self-organized criticality and mass extinction in evolutionary algorithms. In: Proceedings of the 2001 Congress on Evolutionary Computation (IEEE Cat. No. 01TH8546), vol. 2, pp. 1155–1161. IEEE (2001)

21. Lehman, J., Miikkulainen, R.: Enhancing divergent search through extinction events. In: Proceedings of the 2015 Annual Conference on Genetic and Evolutionary Computation, pp. 951–958 (2015)

22. Lehman, J., Stanley, K.O.: Abandoning objectives: evolution through the search for novelty alone. Evol. Comput. **19**(2), 189–223 (2011)
23. Liu, Y., Sun, Y., Xue, B., Zhang, M., Yen, G.: A survey on evolutionary neural architecture search. arXiv preprint arXiv:2008.10937 (2020)
24. Mathias, H.D., Ragusa, V.R.: An empirical study of crossover and mass extinction in a genetic algorithm for pathfinding in a continuous environment. In: 2016 IEEE Congress on Evolutionary Computation (CEC), pp. 4111–4118. IEEE (2016)
25. Newman, M., Roberts, B.W.: Mass extinction: evolution and the effects of external influences on unfit species. Proc. Royal Soc. London. Ser. B: Biol. Sci. **260**(1357), 31–37 (1995)
26. Ororbia, A., ElSaid, A., Desell, T.: Investigating recurrent neural network memory structures using neuro-evolution. In: Proceedings of the Genetic and Evolutionary Computation Conference. GECCO 2019, pp. 446–455. ACM, New York, NY, USA (2019). https://doi.org/10.1145/3321707.3321795
27. Ororbia II, A.G., Mikolov, T., Reitter, D.: Learning simpler language models with the differential state framework. Neural Comput. 1–26 (2017). https://doi.org/10. 1162/neco_a_01017, pMID: 28957029
28. Pascanu, R., Mikolov, T., Bengio, Y.: On the difficulty of training recurrent neural networks. In: International Conference on Machine Learning, pp. 1310–1318 (2013)
29. Rochester Institute of Technology: research computing services (2019). https:// doi.org/10.34788/0S3G-QD15, https://www.rit.edu/researchcomputing/
30. Spears, W.: Speciation using tag bits. Handbook of Evolutionary Computation (1995)
31. Stanley, K., Miikkulainen, R.: Evolving neural networks through augmenting topologies. Evol. Comput. **10**(2), 99–127 (2002)
32. Stanley, K.O., Clune, J., Lehman, J., Miikkulainen, R.: Designing neural networks through neuroevolution. Nat. Mach. Intell. **1**(1), 24–35 (2019)
33. Stanley, K.O., D'Ambrosio, D.B., Gauci, J.: A hypercube-based encoding for evolving large-scale neural networks. Artif. Life **15**(2), 185–212 (2009)
34. Sun, Y., Xue, B., Zhang, M., Yen, G.G.: Evolving deep convolutional neural networks for image classification. IEEE Trans. Evol. Comput. **24**, 394–407 (2019)
35. Trujillo, L., Olague, G., Lutton, E., Fernández de Vega, F.: Discovering several robot behaviors through speciation. In: Giacobini, M., et al. (eds.) EvoWorkshops 2008. LNCS, vol. 4974, pp. 164–174. Springer, Heidelberg (2008). https://doi.org/ 10.1007/978-3-540-78761-7_17
36. Verbancsics, P., Stanley, K.O.: Evolving static representations for task transfer. J. Mach. Learn. Res. **11**(May), 1737–1769 (2010)
37. Wan, J., Chu, P., Jiao, Y., Li, Y.: Improvement of machine learning enhanced genetic algorithm for nonlinear beam dynamics optimization. Nucl. Instrum. Meth. Phys. Res. Sect. A: Accelerators, Spectrometers, Detectors Associated Equipment **946**, 162683 (2019)
38. Werbos, P.J.: Backpropagation through time: what it does and how to do it. Proc. IEEE **78**(10), 1550–1560 (1990)
39. Xie, X.F., Zhang, W.J., Yang, Z.L.: Hybrid particle swarm optimizer with mass extinction. In: IEEE 2002 International Conference on Communications, Circuits and Systems and West Sino Expositions, vol. 2, pp. 1170–1173. IEEE (2002)
40. Zhou, G.-B., Wu, J., Zhang, C.-L., Zhou, Z.-H.: Minimal gated unit for recurrent neural networks. Int. J. Autom. Comput. **13**(3), 226–234 (2016). https://doi.org/ 10.1007/s11633-016-1006-2

An Experimental Study of Weight Initialization and Lamarckian Inheritance on Neuroevolution

Zimeng Lyu[✉], AbdElRahman ElSaid, Joshua Karns, Mohamed Mkaouer, and Travis Desell[✉]

Rochester Institute of Technology, Rochester, NY 14623, USA
{zimenglyu,aelsaid,josh}@mail.rit.edu,
{mwmvse,tjdvse}@rit.edu

Abstract. Weight initialization is critical in being able to successfully train artificial neural networks (ANNs), and even more so for recurrent neural networks (RNNs) which can easily suffer from vanishing and exploding gradients. In neuroevolution, where evolutionary algorithms are applied to neural architecture search, weights typically need to be initialized at three different times: when the initial genomes (ANN architectures) are created, when offspring genomes are generated by crossover, and when new nodes or edges are created during mutation. This work explores the difference between the state-of-the-art Xavier and Kaiming methods, and novel Lamarckian weight inheritance for weight initialization during crossover and mutation operations. These are examined using the Evolutionary eXploration of Augmenting Memory Models (EXAMM) neuroevolution algorithm, which is capable of evolving RNNs with a variety of modern memory cells (e.g., LSTM, GRU, MGU, UGRNN and Delta-RNN cells) as well as recurrent connections with varying time skips through a high performance island based distributed evolutionary algorithm. Results show that with statistical significance, the Lamarckian strategy outperforms both Kaiming and Xavier weight initialization, can speed neuroevolution by requiring less backpropagation epochs to be evaluated per genome, and that the neuroevolutionary process provides further benefits to neural network weight optimization.

Keywords: Neuroevolution · Neural architecture search · Weight inheritance · Weight initialization · Lamarckian evolution

This material is based upon work supported by the U.S. Department of Energy, Office of Science, Office of Advanced Combustion Systems under Award Number #FE0031547 and by the Federal Aviation Administration and MITRE Corporation under the National General Aviation Flight Information Database (NGAFID) award.

Electronic supplementary material The online version of this chapter (https://doi.org/10.1007/978-3-030-72699-7_37) contains supplementary material, which is available to authorized users.

P. A. Castillo and J. L. Jiménez Laredo (Eds.): EvoApplications 2021, LNCS 12694, pp. 584–600, 2021.
https://doi.org/10.1007/978-3-030-72699-7_37

1   Introduction

Neuroevolution (NE), or the use of evolutionary algorithms (EAs) for neural architecture search (NAS) and training, has seen a significant growth in popularity due to the challenges of designing deep neural networks [17,27]. While some approaches to NE, such as indirect encoding, *e.g.*, HyperNEAT [28], where the genomes are used to generate the architecture and assign weights; or fitness estimation, *e.g.*, [2,3] where genome fitness is estimated without training the networks, most modern NE algorithms involve a direct encoding approach, where a neural network's architecture and weights are directly represented as *genomes* that can be evolved by crossover and mutation operations.

In direct encoding, the initialization of network weights is critical, especially for deep neural networks (DNNs) [21], as it has been shown that poor weight initialization quickly leads to gradient vanishing and exploding problems [11]. The Xavier [11] and Kaiming weight initialization [12] methods have been a great success in reducing issues for DNNs and are now the de facto standard for training DNNs, however, these methods do not take into account extra information available during NE. For example, during mutation, a child genome is generated by randomly modifying a previously trained parent genome, and during crossover, a child genome is generated utilizing two (or more) previously trained parental genomes. These parental distributions and weight values and distributions contain valuable information that can be used to better initialize child genome weights, and this process is known as *Lamarckian* [6,23,24] or sometimes *Epigenetic* [7] weight initialization.

Unfortunately, many NE algorithms still use an outdated uniform random initialization for initial populations [9,19,26,29], with a few exceptions that use Xavier [1,23] or Kaiming [7] initialization. Among recent state-of-the-art NAS works, few used the Kaiming or Xavier methods, such as ENAS [22] which uses Kaiming, but others such as NSGA-NET [18] and Progressive NAS [16], still use uniform random weight initialization.

In Evolutionary Algorithms (EAs), using Lamarckian weight inheritance means that offspring inherit weights from their parents through mutation or crossover. Some studies suggest that Lamarckian weight inheritance can reduce the number of backpropagation (BP) epochs to train neural networks [7,15] and lead to better performing neural networks, but to the best of authors' knowledge, Lamarckian weight inheritance has not been rigorously compared to the modern Xavier and Kaiming weight initialization methods.

The main contribution of this work is to provide an experimental analysis of Lamarckian weight inheritance methods (one for crossover and another for mutation) to Xavier and Kaiming initialization. This study was done in the context of evolving deep recurrent neural networks (RNNs) for time series data prediction using three challenging real world data sets. Results are promising, showing that with statistical significance the Lamarckian strategies outperform Xavier and Kaiming weight initialization, and further can reduce the amount of BP epochs used to train the neural networks, allowing more time to be spent on architectural evolution. Additionally, the neuroevolutionary process is shown to provide additional benefits to the selection of weights, as it is shown that when the best found architectures are retrained, even for a large number of epochs, in most cases, they do not surpass the performance of the networks with the evolved weights.

2   Weight Initialization and Inheritance

2.1   Xavier and Kaiming Weight Initialization

Xavier weight initialization [11] was designed for DNNs with symmetrical activation functions such as $tanh$ and $softsign$. The weights in each layer are generated using a uniform distribution:

$$W \sim \mathcal{U}[-\frac{\sqrt{6}}{\sqrt{f_{in} + f_{out}}}, \frac{\sqrt{6}}{\sqrt{f_{in} + f_{out}}}] \tag{1}$$

where f_{in} and f_{out} are fan in and fan out of the layer.[1]

Kaiming weight initialization [12] was designed for non-symmetrical activation functions such as ReLUs. The weights in each layer are generated with a normal distribution, and the fan in, f_{in}:

$$W \sim N(0, 1) * \frac{\sqrt{2}}{f_{in}} \tag{2}$$

2.2   Lamarckian Weight Inheritance

The Lamarckian strategies investigated in this work were first introduced by Desell et al. for NE of convolutional neural networks (CNNs) and later used for recurrent neural networks [7,19]. While Prellberg and Kramer also investigated Lamarckian weight inheritance for CNNs, their strategy was a simpler version where Lamarckian inheritance was only done on crossover, and mutated components were re-initialized randomly [23].

For direct encoding NE algorithms, after the initial genomes' weights are initialized, new genomes are created either via crossover, where two or more parents are recombined into a child genome, or by mutation where a single parent has one or more random modifications made.

For crossover, given a more fit and less fit parent, child genome weights are initialized as follows. When the same architectural component (e.g., node, edge or layer) exists in both parents[2], the weights and biases for that component are generated using a stochastic line search recombining weights or biases from those

---

[1] Fan in is the number of input signals that feed into the layer, fan out is the number of output signals that come out of the layer.

[2] Components are identified as being the same by having the same *innovation number*, which is uniquely created by the neuroevolution process when an architectural component is added to a genome, and are inherited by children on crossover and mutation, as in the NEAT algorithm [26].

in the parents' components. Given a random number $r \sim \mathcal{U}[-0.5, 1.5]$, a child's weight w_c is set to:

$$w_c = r(w_{p2} - w_{p1}) + w_{p1} \tag{3}$$

where w_{p1} is the weight from the more fit parent, and w_{p2} is the weight from the less fit parent (note the same r value is used for *all* child weights). This allows the child weights to be set along a gradient calculated from the weights of the two parents, performing an informed exploration of the weight space between and around the two parents. In the case where the component only exists in one parent, the same weights and biases are copied to the child.

For mutations, new components are added to the parent neural network architecture, so it is not possible to directly utilize weights from the parent. Instead, statistical information about the weight distributions of the parents can be used. Weights and biases for new components generated during mutations are instead initialized using a normal distribution around the mean μ_p and variance σ_p^2 of the parent's weights:

$$W \sim N(\mu_p, \sigma_p^2) \tag{4}$$

while the other weights are directly copied from the parent. This network-aware approach using the statistical distribution of a network's weights has also been shown to speed transfer learning, lending further credence to this approach [10].

3   Methodology

This work utilizes the Evolutionary eXploration of Augmenting Memory Models (EXAMM) neuroevolution algorithm [19] to explore the different weight initialization and inheritance strategies. EXAMM evolves progressively larger RNNs through a series of mutation and crossover (reproduction) operations. When nodes are added their type is selected uniformly at random from a suite of simple neurons and complex memory cells: Δ-RNN units [20], gated recurrent units (GRUs) [4], long short-term memory cells (LSTMs) [13], minimal gated units (MGUs) [30], and update gate RNN cells (UGRNNs) [5]. This allows EXAMM to select the best performing recurrent memory units. EXAMM also allows *deep recurrent connections*, which enable the RNN to directly use information beyond the previous time step. These deep recurrent connections have proven to offer significant improvements in model generalization, even yielding models that outperform state-of-the-art gated architectures [8]. EXAMM has both a multithreaded implementation and an MPI implementation for distributed use on high performance computing resources. To the authors' knowledge, these capabilities are not available in other neuroevolution frameworks capable of evolving RNNs, which is the primary reason EXAMM was selected for this work.

EXAMM uses an asynchronous island based evolution strategy with a fixed number of islands n, each with an island capacity m. During the evolution process, islands go through two phases: *initialization*, and *filled*. During the *initialization* phase, each island starts with one seed genome, which is the minimal possible feed-forward neural network structure with no hidden layers, with the input layer fully connected to the output layer. Worker processes repeatedly request genomes to evaluate from the master process using a work-stealing approach.

On receiving a genome the worker then evaluates its *fitness*, calculated as mean squared error (MSE) on a validation data set after stochastic back propagation training. When reported back to the master process, if the island is not full, it is inserted into the island; otherwise, if the *fitness* is better than the worst genome on that island, it will replace the worst genome. The master generates new genomes from islands in a round-robin manner, by doing a random mutation on randomly selected genomes from an island until that island reaches maximum capacity m, and its status becomes *filled*. When all islands are *filled*, they repopulate through inter-island crossover, intra-island crossover and mutation operations. *Intra-island crossover* selects two random genomes from the same island, and the child gets inserted back to where its parents come from. *Inter-island crossover* selects the first parent at random from the island the child will be inserted into, and the second parent is the best genome from another randomly selected island. As islands are distinct sub-populations and otherwise evolve independently, the only chance for the islands to exchange genes is through *inter-island crossover*.

4   Results

Data Sets: This work utilized three real-world data sets for predicting time series data with RNNs.[3] The first comes from data collected from 12 burners of a coal-fired power plant, the second is the wind turbine engine data from 2013 to 2020, collected and made available by ENGIE's La Haute Borne open data windfarm[4], and the third comes from a selection of 10 flights worth of data from the National General Aviation Flight Information Database (NGAFID). All of the datasets are multivariate (with 12, 88, and 31 parameters, respectively), non-seasonal, and the parameter recordings are not independent. Furthermore, they are very long. The power plant data consists of 10-days worth of per-minute data, the wind turbine data consists of readings every 10 min from 2013 to 2020, and the aviation time series range from 1 to 3 h worth of per-second data. *Main flame intensity* was chosen as the output parameter for the coal dataset and *average active power* was selected as output parameter for the wind turbine data set. The aviation dataset was used to predict 4 engine output parameters, *E1 CHT1, E1 CHT2, E1 CHT3, E1 CHT4*.

Results were gathered using Rochester Institute of Technology's research computing systems. This system consists of 2304 Intel® Xeon® Gold 6150 CPU 2.70 GHz cores and 24 TB RAM, with compute nodes running the RedHat Enterprise Linux 7 system. Each experiment utilized 72 cores.

---

[3] These data sets are made publicly available at EXAMM GitHub repository: https://github.com/travisdesell/exact/tree/master/datasets/.

[4] https://opendata-renewables.engie.com.

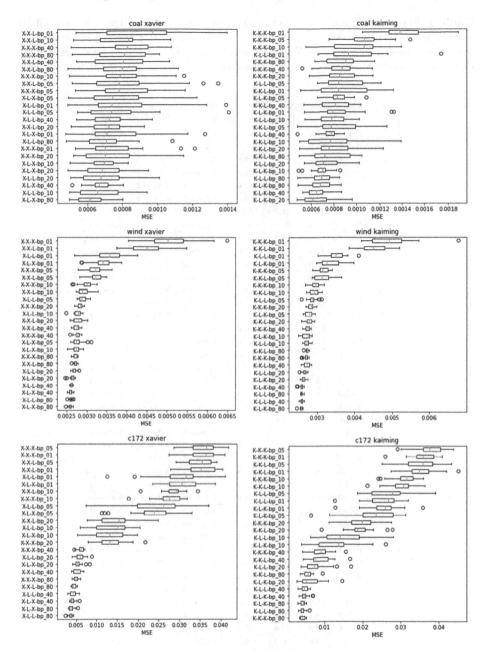

Fig. 1. Convergence rates (in terms of best MSE on validation data) with Xavier, Kaiming weight initialization predicting *main flame intensity* from the coal fired power plant dataset, *average active power* for the wind turbine dataset, and *E1 CHT1, E1 CHT2, E1 CHT3, E1 CHT4* for the aviation dataset. Weight initialization and inheritance type are labeled by *initial genome strategy-crossover strategy-mutation strategy*, so *e.g.*, *K-L-K* would use Kaiming for the initial genomes, Lamarckian on crossover operations, and Kaiming for components generated by mutation.

Table 1. Statistics of best genomes over 20 repeats on the coal dataset. Weight initialization and inheritance type are labeled by *initial genome strategy-crossover strategy-mutation strategy*, so *e.g.*, *K-L-K* would use Kaiming for the initial genomes, Lamarckian on crossover operations, and Kaiming for components generated by mutation.

BP Epochs	Type	Avg Node	Avg Edge	Avg Rec Edge	Worst MSE	Avg MSE	Best MSE
1	K-K-K	17.1	41.6	38.0	1.89e−3	1.42e−3	1.05e−3
	K-L-K	29.8	118.2	55.6	1.74e−3	9.84e−4	6.60e−4
	K-L-L	23.3	90.0	64.0	1.33e−3	8.40e−4	5.36e−4
	K-K-L	16.7	41.0	49.8	1.32e−3	8.83e−4	5.03e−4
	X-X-X	16.6	39.4	47.0	*1.21e−3*	*7.51e−4*	5.30e−4
	X-L-X	23.4	92.3	65.8	1.39e−3	8.18e−4	4.87e−4
	X-L-L	21.8	81.7	75.1	1.27e−3	7.85e−4	*4.75e−4*
	X-X-L	16.4	39.6	54.9	1.40e−3	9.11e−4	5.32e−4
5	K-K-K	16.1	34.5	28.3	1.47e−3	1.07e−3	7.58e−4
	K-L-K	21.9	73.2	47.6	1.21e−3	8.88e−4	6.56e−4
	K-L-L	20.0	62.5	35.5	*1.08e−3*	8.36e−4	6.52e−4
	K-K-L	15.9	31.9	22.0	1.26e−3	8.16e−4	*4.75e−4*
	X-X-X	15.6	31.7	19.9	1.16e−3	8.21e−4	5.29e−4
	X-L-X	18.4	52.0	27.6	1.41e−3	*7.70e−4*	5.42e−4
	X-L-L	18.9	56.6	36.9	1.23e−3	7.73e−4	4.89e−4
	X-X-L	16.2	33.4	26.6	1.34e−3	8.22e−4	5.11e−4
10	K-K-K	16.1	34.0	20.9	1.39e−3	9.89e−4	5.51e−4
	K-L-K	22.9	71.0	33.6	1.02e−3	7.80e−4	5.45e−4
	K-L-L	21.6	66.1	32.0	8.54e−4	6.90e−4	*4.87e−4*
	K-K-L	15.7	30.1	17.7	1.39e−3	7.78e−4	4.95e−4
	X-X-X	16.4	32.0	15.8	1.15e−3	8.06e−4	4.97e−4
	X-L-X	18.4	51.2	23.1	9.41e−4	*6.78e−4*	4.96e−4
	X-L-L	19.9	58.0	34.5	*8.33e−4*	6.90e−4	5.01e−4
	X-X-L	16.0	30.3	15.5	1.08e−3	7.79e−4	5.18e−4
20	K-K-K	16.4	30.9	11.5	1.14e−3	8.62e−4	5.80e−4
	K-L-K	20.9	58.0	25.0	1.02e−3	7.37e−4	5.38e−4
	K-L-L	18.2	43.6	17.4	9.60e−4	*6.57e−4*	**4.72e−4**
	K-K-L	15.8	28.1	10.2	1.22e−3	8.11e−4	4.95e−4
	X-X-X	16.5	30.6	11.6	1.15e−3	7.27e−4	5.19e−4
	X-L-X	18.3	42.3	18.8	1.01e−3	6.96e−4	5.04e−4
	X-L-L	21.6	61.0	25.2	9.50e−4	6.93e−4	4.88e−4
	X-X-L	16.4	30.9	9.7	*9.25e−4*	7.12e−4	5.06e−4
40	K-K-K	15.9	25.9	7.5	1.13e−3	8.47e−4	5.18e−4
	K-L-K	19.4	46.9	15.5	8.90e−4	7.57e−4	*4.77e−4*
	K-L-L	19.1	43.7	15.1	8.67e−4	*6.55e−4*	5.26e−4
	K-K-L	15.8	26.2	7.6	1.04e−3	8.09e−4	5.34e−4
	X-X-X	15.9	26.6	6.5	1.08e−3	8.34e−4	5.06e−4
	X-L-X	18.1	37.1	12.1	9.69e−4	7.25e−4	5.37e−4
	X-L-L	17.8	34.9	13.4	*8.05e−4*	6.72e−4	5.12e−4
	X-X-L	15.6	26.2	6.5	1.07e−3	7.79e−4	5.36e−4
80	K-K-K	15.3	22.4	4.3	1.15e−3	8.71e−4	6.32e−4
	K-L-K	17.8	34.8	9.1	8.48e−4	6.78e−4	*4.75e−4*
	K-L-L	17.7	35.0	8.8	8.62e−4	6.76e−4	4.81e−4
	K-K-L	15.7	23.7	3.1	1.05e−3	7.64e−4	4.93e−4
	X-X-X	14.9	20.9	3.9	1.01e−3	7.93e−4	5.13e−4
	X-L-X	17.0	30.8	7.0	1.08e−3	6.97e−4	4.79e−4
	X-L-L	16.8	30.4	6.5	**8.02e−4**	**6.19e−4**	4.95e−4
	X-X-L	15.4	23.0	5.7	1.12e−3	7.82e−4	4.88e−4

Table 2. Statistics of best genomes over 20 repeats on the wind dataset. Weight initialization and inheritance type are labeled by *initial genome strategy-crossover strategy-mutation strategy*, so *e.g.*, *K-L-K* would use Kaiming for the initial genomes, Lamarckian on crossover operations, and Kaiming for components generated by mutation.

BP Epochs	Type	Avg Node	Avg Edge	Avg Rec Edge	Worst MSE	Avg MSE	Best MSE
1	K-K-K	95.0	123.0	7.2	6.76e−3	4.95e−3	4.19e−3
	K-L-K	101.3	170.2	24.2	4.11e−3	3.51e−3	3.02e−3
	K-L-L	95.0	151.8	33.3	3.98e−3	*3.37e−3*	2.98e−3
	K-K-L	93.7	121.1	5.5	5.20e−3	4.55e−3	3.85e−3
	X-X-X	95.1	126.9	6.6	6.50e−3	5.07e−3	4.04e−3
	X-L-X	99.2	170.2	27.6	4.26e−3	3.57e−3	*2.69e−3*
	X-L-L	94.3	154.1	33.5	*3.86e−3*	3.38e−3	2.86e−3
	X-X-L	96.0	132.1	8.6	5.48e−3	4.50e−3	3.75e−3
5	K-K-K	94.0	121.1	9.5	3.40e−3	3.17e−3	2.88e−3
	K-L-K	98.7	158.1	24.9	3.12e−3	2.87e−3	*2.58e−3*
	K-L-L	96.2	139.8	25.5	*2.94e−3*	*2.77e−3*	2.62e−3
	K-K-L	94.5	124.8	10.8	3.66e−3	3.16e−3	2.87e−3
	X-X-X	94.5	126.0	11.2	3.62e−3	3.21e−3	2.78e−3
	X-L-X	98.7	154.8	20.5	3.09e−3	2.90e−3	2.75e−3
	X-L-L	95.3	140.3	23.4	3.12e−3	*2.77e−3*	2.60e−3
	X-X-L	93.6	119.3	10.9	3.50e−3	3.23e−3	2.82e−3
10	K-K-K	93.7	119.4	10.2	3.18e−3	2.94e−3	2.68e−3
	K-L-K	100.3	159.6	22.2	*2.86e−3*	2.72e−3	2.61e−3
	K-L-L	96.4	140.8	22.6	*2.86e−3*	*2.71e−3*	*2.49e−3*
	K-K-L	93.5	116.7	10.8	3.13e−3	2.91e−3	2.71e−3
	X-X-X	94.0	121.2	9.4	3.26e−3	2.98e−3	2.63e−3
	X-L-X	97.7	147.1	16.4	2.90e−3	2.77e−3	*2.49e−3*
	X-L-L	95.5	132.9	22.2	2.91e−3	2.72e−3	2.51e−3
	X-X-L	93.2	114.9	9.9	3.28e−3	2.92e−3	2.72e−3
20	K-K-K	93.3	115.2	7.3	3.00e−3	2.83e−3	2.69e−3
	K-L-K	100.3	156.0	18.1	2.75e−3	2.65e−3	2.52e−3
	K-L-L	95.9	130.8	18.9	2.74e−3	*2.63e−3*	2.53e−3
	K-K-L	92.5	110.5	9.2	2.93e−3	2.78e−3	2.58e−3
	X-X-X	93.7	117.0	7.3	2.94e−3	2.82e−3	2.68e−3
	X-L-X	98.5	145.1	13.5	2.81e−3	2.68e−3	2.59e−3
	X-L-L	95.6	128.2	16.9	*2.71e−3*	*2.63e−3*	*2.46e−3*
	X-X-L	92.9	112.4	6.8	3.02e−3	2.79e−3	2.58e−3
40	K-K-K	93.3	115.0	5.2	2.84e−3	2.74e−3	2.61e−3
	K-L-K	101.5	155.2	18.9	*2.65e−3*	2.59e−3	2.51e−3
	K-L-L	94.5	118.2	13.4	*2.65e−3*	*2.58e−3*	*2.46e−3*
	K-K-L	91.8	104.5	5.7	2.85e−3	2.73e−3	2.57e−3
	X-X-X	92.8	110.8	4.8	2.87e−3	2.76e−3	2.58e−3
	X-L-X	98.2	138.8	12.2	2.66e−3	2.61e−3	2.57e−3
	X-L-L	95.4	124.7	14.6	2.67e−3	2.60e−3	2.51e−3
	X-X-L	92.3	108.1	4.9	2.87e−3	2.74e−3	2.60e−3
80	K-K-K	91.5	101.5	4.0	2.78e−3	2.70e−3	2.58e−3
	K-L-K	97.4	131.6	11.2	2.65e−3	2.59e−3	2.55e−3
	K-L-L	94.2	114.8	9.3	**2.62e−3**	**2.57e−3**	**2.45e−3**
	K-K-L	90.8	98.7	4.4	2.80e−3	2.73e−3	2.64e−3
	X-X-X	92.3	106.4	3.0	2.78e−3	2.71e−3	2.60e−3
	X-L-X	97.4	131.1	8.9	2.66e−3	2.59e−3	2.51e−3
	X-L-L	94.0	112.7	10.2	2.66e−3	2.58e−3	2.48e−3
	X-X-L	91.0	98.8	4.0	2.78e−3	2.71e−3	2.62e−3

Table 3. Statistics of best genomes over 20 repeats on the c172 dataset. Weight initialization and inheritance type are labeled by *initial genome strategy-crossover strategy-mutation strategy*, so *e.g.*, *K-L-K* would use Kaiming for the initial genomes, Lamarckian on crossover operations, and Kaiming for components generated by mutation.

BP Epochs	Type	Avg Node	Avg Edge	Avg Rec Edge	Worst MSE	Avg MSE	Best MSE
1	K-K-K	46.1	243.7	8.9	4.08e−2	3.60e−2	2.58e−2
	K-L-K	43.0	206.5	8.9	*3.20e−2*	*2.53e−2*	*1.26e−2*
	K-L-L	41.8	196.7	12.3	3.60e−2	2.54e−2	1.28e−2
	K-K-L	42.7	205.3	6.9	4.50e−2	3.52e−2	2.73e−2
	X-X-X	53.8	324.4	16.3	4.09e−2	3.54e−2	2.74e−2
	X-L-X	40.2	181.8	9.2	4.10e−2	2.97e−2	*1.26e−2*
	X-L-L	46.9	249.7	11.2	3.87e−2	3.08e−2	2.36e−2
	X-X-L	53.2	319.4	16.4	4.04e−2	3.56e−2	2.79e−2
5	K-K-K	39.2	167.8	3.1	4.37e−2	3.75e−2	2.91e−2
	K-L-K	41.0	185.3	10.1	3.91e−2	2.69e−2	1.87e−2
	K-L-L	39.7	172.4	8.4	*3.13e−2*	*2.28e−2*	*6.45e−3*
	K-K-L	39.1	162.8	4.2	4.32e−2	3.54e−2	2.50e−2
	X-X-X	39.1	161.2	3.4	4.19e−2	3.60e−2	2.86e−2
	X-L-X	39.6	172.8	10.7	3.70e−2	2.41e−2	7.35e−3
	X-L-L	40.1	182.1	11.1	3.30e−2	2.36e−2	1.13e−2
	X-X-L	40.5	175.2	3.6	3.90e−2	3.48e−2	2.91e−2
10	K-K-K	39.0	167.0	4.7	3.61e−2	3.11e−2	2.40e−2
	K-L-K	40.7	190.3	17.1	2.80e−2	1.52e−2	6.21e−3
	K-L-L	39.7	177.2	16.4	2.59e−2	1.33e−2	*3.82e−3*
	K-K-L	38.4	157.7	3.8	3.65e−2	3.02e−2	2.12e−2
	X-X-X	38.9	163.9	5.2	3.19e−2	2.74e−2	1.77e−2
	X-L-X	40.0	183.2	17.9	2.05e−2	1.35e−2	5.90e−3
	X-L-L	40.5	193.9	20.4	*1.99e−2*	*1.30e−2*	5.27e−3
	X-X-L	38.8	161.9	3.5	3.45e−2	2.86e−2	2.05e−2
20	K-K-K	38.8	164.0	7.2	2.75e−2	1.96e−2	1.12e−2
	K-L-K	40.3	184.2	14.9	1.69e−2	7.69e−3	3.69e−3
	K-L-L	40.2	182.3	15.2	1.46e−2	6.53e−3	*2.61e−3*
	K-K-L	38.5	160.7	6.0	2.77e−2	1.92e−2	9.17e−3
	X-X-X	38.8	165.8	8.9	2.18e−2	1.37e−2	7.83e−3
	X-L-X	40.0	180.3	16.4	8.78e−3	5.92e−3	3.95e−3
	X-L-L	40.1	181.9	17.9	*8.33e−3*	*5.46e−3*	4.18e−3
	X-X-L	40.0	178.7	8.6	2.49e−2	1.51e−2	7.68e−3
40	K-K-K	38.5	161.1	7.0	1.56e−2	8.87e−3	4.15e−3
	K-L-K	39.3	171.6	10.7	6.31e−3	4.66e−3	*2.92e−3*
	K-L-L	39.4	171.3	11.5	6.93e−3	4.68e−3	3.22e−3
	K-K-L	38.2	158.2	7.0	1.68e−2	8.69e−3	4.23e−3
	X-X-X	39.1	167.6	7.8	7.15e−3	6.13e−3	4.47e−3
	X-L-X	40.0	178.7	11.4	5.86e−3	4.21e−3	2.97e−3
	X-L-L	40.0	179.5	9.1	*5.81e−3*	*4.17e−3*	3.40e−3
	X-X-L	39.0	168.3	7.9	6.83e−3	5.24e−3	3.92e−3
80	K-K-K	37.1	146.2	4.8	5.12e−3	4.18e−3	3.28e−3
	K-L-K	38.4	159.5	6.5	5.94e−3	4.17e−3	3.00e−3
	K-L-L	37.7	152.2	6.7	5.09e−3	4.22e−3	2.87e−3
	K-K-L	36.9	142.7	4.7	9.40e−3	5.63e−3	3.50e−3
	X-X-X	36.9	144.2	4.5	6.08e−3	4.91e−3	4.05e−3
	X-L-X	38.0	155.5	6.5	**4.33e−3**	**3.68e−3**	**2.45e−3**
	X-L-L	38.9	164.4	5.8	5.38e−3	3.83e−3	3.03e−3
	X-X-L	37.8	152.6	5.0	5.32e−3	4.44e−3	3.76e−3

Each EXAMM run used 10 islands, each with a maximum capacity of 10 genomes. New RNNs were generated via mutation at a rate of 70%, intra-island crossover at a rate of 20%, and inter-island crossover at a rate of 10%. 10 out of EXAMM's 11 mutation operations were utilized (all except for *split edge*), and each was chosen with a uniform 10% chance. EXAMM generated new nodes by selecting from simple neurons, Δ-RNN, GRU, LSTM, MGU, and UGRNN memory cells uniformly at random. Recurrent connections could span any time-skip generated randomly between $\mathcal{U}(1, 10)$. Backpropagation (BP) through time was run with a learning rate of $\eta = 0.001$ and used Nesterov momentum with $\mu = 0.9$. For the memory cells with forget gates, the forget gate bias had a value of 1.0 added to it (motivated by [14]). To prevent exploding gradients, gradient scaling [21] was used when the norm of the gradient exceeded a threshold of 1.0. To combat vanishing gradients, gradient boosting (the opposite of scaling) was used when the gradient norm was below 0.05. These parameters have been selected by hand-tuning during the prior experience.

Effect of Weight Inheritance on RNN Training Time: Our hypotheses were that *i)*, utilizing Lamarckian weight inheritance would provide performance improvements over Xavier and Kaiming initialization, and *ii)*, it could potentially allow for networks to be effectively evolved using fewer BP epochs per genome. To provide a comprehensive exploration, we set up experiments where the initial genomes initialized weights with the Xavier and Kaiming strategies (as the Lamarckian strategies could not yet be used). In these experiments, we tested the combinations of the two Lamarckian strategies with the initial weight inheritance strategy. Note that when Lamarckian weight inheritance is used for crossover and Xavier for weight inheritance, this is identical to the Lamarckain strategy used by [23], so their strategy was also investigated.

BP epochs of 1, 5, 10, 20, 40 and 80 per genome generated were examined. To have a fair comparison between the test cases, the total number of BP epochs for each search was held fixed at 200k for each test. This resulted in the total number of genomes generated during evolution for the tests being 200k, 40k, 20k, 10k, 5k and 2.5k respectively. In total, for each initial weight strategy (Kaiming and Xavier) there were 72 different experiments done with different BP epochs and strategies for crossover and mutation weight initialization for the coal fired power plant, wind turbine, and aviation datasets. All the experiments were repeated 20 times, allowing the Mann–Whitney U-test for statistical significance.

Figure 1 presents box plots of the best genome fitness from 20 repeats of each of the experiments using Xavier and Kaiming weight initialization and their combinations with the Lamarckian strategies. These results are summarized in Tables 1, 2 and 3, which present the best, average, and worst global best genome mean average error (MAE) at the end of the 20 repeated tests for each experiment performed on coal, wind, and aviation datasets. The best performing experiments are highlighted in bold and italics for each number of BP epochs, and the overall best experiment is highlighted in bold.

In the average case, for all three datasets, all but one best performing genomes were found using Lamarckian weight inheritance on crossover, and further all but one of the best cases utilized Lamarckian weight inheritance for crossover. Only one case used Xavier for weight initialization, inheritance for crossover and

Table 4. Mann–Whitney U test p-values comparing Kaiming and Xavier weight initialization and inheritance strategies for the three datasets. p-values in bold indicate a statistically significant difference with $\alpha = 0.05$. Weight initialization and inheritance type are labeled by *initial genome strategy-crossover strategy-mutation strategy*, so *e.g.*, *K-L-K* would use Kaiming for the initial genomes, Lamarckian on crossover operations, and Kaiming for components generated by mutation.

Cessna 172 - Kaiming

BP Epochs	Type	K-K-K	K-L-K	K-L-L	K-K-L
1	K-K-K	/	0.0000	0.0000	0.1427
	K-L-K	0.0000	/	0.4302	0.0000
	K-L-L	0.0000	0.4302	/	0.0000
	K-K-L	0.1427	0.0000	0.0000	/
5	K-K-K	/	0.0000	0.0000	0.0702
	K-L-K	0.0000	/	0.0283	0.0000
	K-L-L	0.0000	0.0283	/	0.0000
	K-K-L	0.0702	0.0000	0.0000	/
10	K-K-K	/	0.0000	0.0000	0.1897
	K-L-K	0.0000	/	0.2285	0.0000
	K-L-L	0.0000	0.2285	/	0.0000
	K-K-L	0.1897	0.0000	0.0000	/
20	K-K-K	/	0.0000	0.0000	0.3676
	K-L-K	0.0000	/	0.1042	0.0000
	K-L-L	0.0000	0.1042	/	0.0000
	K-K-L	0.3676	0.0000	0.0000	/
40	K-K-K	/	0.0000	0.0000	0.3474
	K-L-K	0.0000	/	0.4516	0.0000
	K-L-L	0.0000	0.4516	/	0.0000
	K-K-L	0.3474	0.0000	0.0000	/
80	K-K-K	/	0.4946	0.4946	0.0001
	K-L-K	0.4946	/	0.2714	0.0000
	K-L-L	0.4946	0.2714	/	0.0000
	K-K-L	0.0001	0.0000	0.0000	/

Cessna 172 - Xavier

BP Epochs	Type	X-X-X	X-L-X	X-L-L	X-X-L
1	X-X-X	/	0.0010	0.0008	0.4516
	X-L-X	0.0010	/	0.4409	0.0006
	X-L-L	0.0008	0.4409	/	0.0006
	X-X-L	0.4516	0.0006	0.0006	/
5	X-X-X	/	0.0000	0.0000	0.1824
	X-L-X	0.0000	/	0.2452	0.0000
	X-L-L	0.0000	0.2452	/	0.0000
	X-X-L	0.1824	0.0000	0.0000	/
10	X-X-X	/	0.0000	0.0000	0.1971
	X-L-X	0.0000	/	0.3375	0.0000
	X-L-L	0.0000	0.3375	/	0.0000
	X-X-L	0.1971	0.0000	0.0000	/
20	X-X-X	/	0.0000	0.0000	0.1552
	X-L-X	0.0000	/	0.0739	0.0000
	X-L-L	0.0000	0.0739	/	0.0000
	X-X-L	0.1552	0.0000	0.0000	/
40	X-X-X	/	0.0000	0.0000	0.0015
	X-L-X	0.0000	/	0.3474	0.0024
	X-L-L	0.0000	0.3474	/	0.0002
	X-X-L	0.0015	0.0024	0.0002	/
80	X-X-X	/	0.0000	0.0000	0.0090
	X-L-X	0.0000	/	0.3676	0.0000
	X-L-L	0.0000	0.3676	/	0.0006
	X-X-L	0.0090	0.0000	0.0006	/

Coal - Kaiming

BP Epochs	Type	K-K-K	K-L-K	K-L-L	K-K-L
1	K-K-K	/	0.0000	0.0000	0.0000
	K-L-K	0.0000	/	0.0360	0.1366
	K-L-L	0.0000	0.0360	/	0.3575
	K-K-L	0.0000	0.1366	0.3575	/
5	K-K-K	/	0.0036	0.0000	0.0429
	K-L-K	0.0036	/	0.0057	0.1308
	K-L-L	0.0000	0.0057	/	0.0010
	K-K-L	0.0429	0.1308	0.0010	/
10	K-K-K	/	0.0024	0.0001	0.0033
	K-L-K	0.0024	/	0.0120	0.3779
	K-L-L	0.0001	0.0120	/	0.1427
	K-K-L	0.0033	0.3779	0.1427	/
20	K-K-K	/	0.0137	0.0006	0.1552
	K-L-K	0.0137	/	0.0234	0.1427
	K-L-L	0.0006	0.0234	/	0.0077
	K-K-L	0.1552	0.1427	0.0077	/
40	K-K-K	/	0.0072	0.0001	0.2047
	K-L-K	0.0072	/	0.0004	0.0994
	K-L-L	0.0001	0.0004	/	0.0005
	K-K-L	0.2047	0.0994	0.0005	/
80	K-K-K	/	0.0003	0.0001	0.0360
	K-L-K	0.0003	/	0.4302	0.1366
	K-L-L	0.0001	0.4302	/	0.0903
	K-K-L	0.0360	0.1366	0.0903	/

Coal - Xavier

BP Epochs	Type	X-X-X	X-L-X	X-L-L	X-X-L
1	X-X-X	/	0.1754	0.3779	0.0158
	X-L-X	0.1754	/	0.2896	0.0666
	X-L-L	0.3779	0.2896	/	0.0481
	X-X-L	0.0158	0.0666	0.0481	/
5	X-X-X	/	0.1617	0.1824	0.3474
	X-L-X	0.1617	/	0.4409	0.2538
	X-L-L	0.1824	0.4409	/	0.2896
	X-X-L	0.3474	0.2538	0.2896	/
10	X-X-X	/	0.0077	0.0077	0.3474
	X-L-X	0.0077	/	0.2367	0.0249
	X-L-L	0.0077	0.2367	/	0.0158
	X-X-L	0.3474	0.0249	0.0158	/
20	X-X-X	/	0.2625	0.3375	0.4730
	X-L-X	0.2625	/	0.4409	0.2896
	X-L-L	0.3375	0.4409	/	0.3575
	X-X-L	0.4730	0.2896	0.3575	/
40	X-X-X	/	0.0053	0.0002	0.1552
	X-L-X	0.0053	/	0.0455	0.1617
	X-L-L	0.0002	0.0455	/	0.0266
	X-X-L	0.1552	0.1617	0.0266	/
80	X-X-X	/	0.0283	0.0004	0.3277
	X-L-X	0.0283	/	0.0283	0.0266
	X-L-L	0.0004	0.0283	/	0.0002
	X-X-L	0.3277	0.0266	0.0002	/

(*continued*)

Table 4. (*continued*)

Wind - Kaiming

BP Epochs	Type	K-K-K	K-L-K	K-L-L	K-K-L
1	K-K-K	/	0.0000	0.0000	0.0158
	K-L-K	0.0000	/	0.0509	0.0000
	K-L-L	0.0000	0.0509	/	0.0000
	K-K-L	0.0158	0.0000	0.0000	/
5	K-K-K	/	0.0000	0.0000	0.2538
	K-L-K	0.0000	/	0.0072	0.0000
	K-L-L	0.0000	0.0072	/	0.0000
	K-K-L	0.2538	0.0000	0.0000	/
10	K-K-K	/	0.0000	0.0000	0.2896
	K-L-K	0.0000	/	0.4623	0.0000
	K-L-L	0.0000	0.4623	/	0.0000
	K-K-L	0.2896	0.0000	0.0000	/
20	K-K-K	/	0.0000	0.0000	0.0739
	K-L-K	0.0000	/	0.0429	0.0005
	K-L-L	0.0000	0.0429	/	0.0001
	K-K-L	0.0739	0.0005	0.0001	/
40	K-K-K	/	0.0000	0.0000	0.3882
	K-L-K	0.0000	/	0.4946	0.0000
	K-L-L	0.0000	0.4946	/	0.0000
	K-K-L	0.3882	0.0000	0.0000	/
80	K-K-K	/	0.0000	0.0000	0.1824
	K-L-K	0.0000	/	0.2285	0.0000
	K-L-L	0.0000	0.2285	/	0.0000
	K-K-L	0.1824	0.0000	0.0000	/

Wind - Xavier

BP Epochs	Type	X-X-X	X-L-X	X-L-L	X-X-L
1	X-X-X	/	0.0000	0.0000	0.0024
	X-L-X	0.0000	/	0.0266	0.0000
	X-L-L	0.0000	0.0266	/	0.0000
	X-X-L	0.0024	0.0000	0.0000	/
5	X-X-X	/	0.0000	0.0000	0.3575
	X-L-X	0.0000	/	0.0008	0.0000
	X-L-L	0.0000	0.0008	/	0.0000
	X-X-L	0.3575	0.0000	0.0000	/
10	X-X-X	/	0.0000	0.0000	0.0405
	X-L-X	0.0000	/	0.0818	0.0008
	X-L-L	0.0000	0.0818	/	0.0001
	X-X-L	0.0405	0.0008	0.0001	/
20	X-X-X	/	0.0000	0.0000	0.1197
	X-L-X	0.0000	/	0.0133	0.0057
	X-L-L	0.0000	0.0133	/	0.0001
	X-X-L	0.1197	0.0057	0.0001	/
40	X-X-X	/	0.0000	0.0000	0.3084
	X-L-X	0.0000	/	0.2452	0.0000
	X-L-L	0.0000	0.2452	/	0.0000
	X-X-L	0.3084	0.0000	0.0000	/
80	X-X-X	/	0.0000	0.0000	0.2124
	X-L-X	0.0000	/	0.1306	0.0000
	X-L-L	0.0000	0.1366	/	0.0000
	X-X-L	0.2124	0.0000	0.0000	/

mutation in coal dataset that achieved the average best when the BP epochs was 1. All other best and average cases used Lamarckian weight initialize for crossover, mutation or both. Generally, the more epochs used in BP training in EXAMM, the better the validation MSE. In all of the three datasets the average global best results come from BP epoch 80. The global best genome in coal dataset is found when using 20 BP epochs, whereas the global best genomes in the other two datasets are all found using 80 epochs.

Further strengthening these results on the benefit of the Lamarckian strategy, Table 4 presents Mann-Whitney U tests of statistical significance comparing the varying weight initialization tests against each other for each number of BP epochs. For the wind turbine data, we see very strong statistical significance in most cases, highlighting that the improvements from the Lamarckian strategy. While the statistical significance is less strong in some cases on the coal dataset, interestingly the statistical significance increases with the number of BP epochs utilized perhaps due to the fact more training time enables quicker convergence to local or global minima.

For the coal and wind turbine dataset, increasing the number of BP epochs does not significantly improve the validation MSE. It means utilizing Lamarckian weight inheritance provides the ability to reduce the number of BP epochs required for training, which in turn allows for more time to be spent evolving the RNN architectures. However, the C172 dataset results generally improve when using more BP epochs, perhaps due to the added complexity of having multiple output parameters.

Table 5. EXAMM best MSE and best genome retrain best MSE, the better result is marked in bold for the same dataset and same weight initialization and weight inheritance type. Weight initialization and inheritance type are labeled by *initial genome strategy-crossover strategy-mutation strategy*, so *e.g.*, *K-L-K* would use Kaiming for the initial genomes, Lamarckian on crossover operations, and Kaiming for components generated by mutation.

BP Epochs	Type	Coal – EXAMM Best MSE	Coal – Retrain Best MSE	Wind – EXAMM Best MSE	Wind – Retrain Best MSE	C172 – EXAMM Best MSE	C172 – Retrain Best MSE	Coal – EXAMM Avg MSE	Coal – Retrain Avg MSE	Wind – EXAMM Avg MSE	Wind – Retrain Avg MSE	C172 – EXAMM Avg MSE	C172 – Retrain Avg MSE
1	K-L-K	**6.601e-4**	1.106e-3	3.016e-3	**2.769e-3**	1.264e-2	**1.285e-3**	**9.839e-4**	5.197e-2	**3.515e-3**	6.745e-2	**2.528e-2**	7.750e-2
	K-L-L	5.358e-4	**5.170e-4**	2.982e-3	**2.645e-3**	1.279e-2	**1.055e-3**	**8.395e-4**	6.032e-2	**3.371e-3**	4.936e-2	2.538e-2	**1.389e-2**
	K-K-L	**5.033e-4**	7.330e-4	3.850e-3	**2.837e-3**	2.726e-2	**1.085e-3**	**8.828e-4**	1.667e-2	**4.554e-3**	4.265e-2	**3.525e-2**	5.049e-2
	X-L-K	**4.875e-4**	1.159e-3	**2.687e-3**	2.730e-3	1.257e-2	**1.482e-3**	**8.184e-4**	4.842e-2	**3.573e-3**	5.481e-2	**2.965e-2**	1.186e-1
	X-L-L	**4.753e-4**	1.208e-3	**2.858e-3**	3.081e-3	2.361e-2	**1.569e-3**	**7.845e-4**	2.124e-1	**3.381e-3**	1.012e-1	**3.082e-2**	1.063e-1
	X-X-L	**5.321e-4**	1.494e-3	3.750e-3	**2.590e-3**	2.788e-2	**1.839e-3**	**9.112e-4**	3.213e-2	**4.502e-3**	4.077e-2	**3.562e-2**	1.497e-1
5	K-L-K	6.561e-4	**5.190e-4**	**2.581e-3**	2.644e-3	1.865e-2	**1.492e-3**	**8.882e-4**	5.872e-3	**2.869e-3**	1.033e-2	**2.693e-2**	4.403e-2
	K-L-L	**6.524e-4**	7.460e-4	2.624e-3	**2.547e-3**	2.497e-2	**1.451e-3**	**8.361e-4**	1.816e-2	**2.774e-3**	1.114e-2	**2.277e-2**	5.902e-2
	K-K-L	**4.754e-4**	5.130e-4	2.869e-3	**2.680e-3**	2.497e-2	**1.648e-3**	**8.165e-4**	3.798e-2	**3.155e-3**	3.662e-3	**3.544e-2**	6.933e-2
	X-L-X	**5.415e-4**	8.040e-4	2.752e-3	**2.730e-3**	7.350e-3	**1.255e-3**	**7.704e-4**	5.240e-2	**2.898e-3**	1.876e-2	**2.411e-2**	5.466e-2
	X-L-L	**4.890e-4**	5.520e-4	**2.598e-3**	2.675e-3	1.128e-2	**1.354e-3**	**7.728e-4**	8.748e-2	**2.770e-3**	1.674e-2	**2.355e-2**	9.598e-2
	X-X-L	**5.107e-4**	6.400e-4	2.823e-3	**2.693e-3**	2.913e-2	**1.773e-3**	**8.217e-4**	4.371e-3	**3.229e-3**	1.831e-2	**3.478e-2**	1.426e-1
10	K-L-K	5.447e-4	**4.860e-4**	**2.608e-3**	2.631e-3	6.208e-3	**1.389e-3**	**7.801e-4**	9.670e-3	**2.720e-3**	8.780e-3	**1.516e-2**	8.258e-2
	K-L-L	**4.871e-4**	5.650e-4	**2.492e-3**	2.596e-3	3.818e-3	**1.049e-3**	**6.903e-4**	4.617e-3	**2.706e-3**	6.111e-3	**1.328e-2**	7.331e-2
	K-K-L	**4.950e-4**	5.880e-4	2.711e-3	**2.628e-3**	2.121e-2	**1.710e-3**	**7.784e-4**	5.204e-3	**2.913e-3**	6.102e-3	**3.022e-2**	5.077e-2
	X-L-X	**4.958e-4**	5.210e-4	**2.491e-3**	2.640e-3	5.895e-3	**1.737e-3**	**6.777e-4**	3.834e-3	**2.769e-3**	4.701e-3	**1.354e-2**	1.335e-1
	X-L-L	**5.008e-4**	5.500e-4	**2.514e-3**	2.642e-3	5.270e-3	**1.785e-3**	**6.900e-4**	2.797e-2	**2.725e-3**	3.883e-3	**1.295e-2**	1.565e-1
	X-X-L	**5.180e-4**	5.970e-4	2.724e-3	**2.650e-3**	2.055e-2	**1.720e-3**	**7.887e-4**	3.139e-3	**2.916e-3**	2.970e-3	**2.856e-2**	1.019e-1
20	K-L-K	5.381e-4	**4.880e-4**	**2.517e-3**	2.593e-3	3.691e-3	**1.175e-3**	**6.574e-4**	3.532e-3	**2.653e-3**	3.144e-3	**6.533e-3**	7.914e-2
	K-K-L	**4.720e-4**	5.610e-4	**2.532e-3**	2.611e-3	2.607e-3	**1.181e-3**	**8.109e-4**	4.018e-2	**2.626e-3**	3.727e-3	**1.922e-2**	4.841e-2
	X-L-X	**4.947e-4**	6.200e-4	**2.576e-3**	2.655e-3	9.174e-3	**1.649e-3**	**6.956e-4**	5.459e-3	**2.775e-3**	2.978e-3	**2.978e-2**	4.296e-2
	X-L-L	**5.040e-4**	5.190e-4	**2.589e-3**	2.630e-3	3.947e-3	**2.138e-3**	**6.929e-4**	5.919e-2	**2.681e-3**	3.376e-3	**5.465e-3**	2.547e-2
	X-X-L	**4.877e-4**	5.060e-4	**2.462e-3**	2.634e-3	4.185e-3	**1.114e-3**	**7.118e-4**	3.719e-3	**2.626e-3**	3.336e-3	**1.508e-2**	5.384e-2
	—	**5.056e-4**	7.820e-4	**2.577e-3**	2.641e-3	7.675e-3	**1.870e-3**	**7.569e-4**	5.389e-2	**2.785e-3**	3.099e-3	**4.663e-3**	4.319e-2
40	K-L-K	**4.772e-4**	4.810e-4	**2.513e-3**	2.630e-3	2.915e-3	**1.919e-3**	**6.550e-4**	5.689e-3	**2.586e-3**	6.016e-3	**4.679e-3**	8.081e-2
	K-L-L	**5.261e-4**	5.770e-4	**2.456e-3**	2.597e-3	3.221e-3	**1.521e-3**	**8.090e-4**	1.831e-2	**2.577e-3**	3.921e-3	**8.687e-3**	6.318e-2
	K-K-L	5.340e-4	**5.120e-4**	**2.566e-3**	2.626e-3	4.230e-3	**1.497e-3**	**7.254e-4**	2.680e-3	**2.727e-3**	3.139e-3	**4.211e-3**	3.815e-2
	X-L-X	5.374e-4	**4.940e-4**	**2.565e-3**	2.647e-3	2.973e-3	**1.812e-3**	**6.718e-4**	1.878e-3	**2.612e-3**	3.142e-3	**4.167e-3**	3.480e-2
	X-L-L	**5.120e-4**	5.130e-4	**2.513e-3**	2.630e-3	3.400e-3	**1.468e-3**	**7.795e-4**	3.615e-2	**2.602e-3**	5.542e-3	**5.235e-3**	3.657e-2
	X-X-L	**5.361e-4**	5.660e-4	**2.603e-3**	2.637e-3	3.917e-3	**1.399e-3**	**6.778e-4**	2.883e-3	**2.745e-3**	2.889e-3	**4.172e-3**	3.241e-2
80	K-L-K	**4.749e-4**	5.650e-4	**2.553e-3**	2.615e-3	3.001e-3	**1.213e-3**	**6.758e-4**	3.917e-3	**2.586e-3**	2.911e-3	**4.219e-3**	3.761e-2
	K-L-L	4.812e-4	**4.800e-4**	**2.452e-3**	2.616e-3	2.867e-3	**1.599e-3**	**7.639e-4**	3.025e-2	**2.574e-3**	2.978e-3	**5.633e-3**	3.731e-2
	K-K-L	**4.928e-4**	5.820e-4	2.644e-3	**2.608e-3**	3.495e-3	**1.776e-3**	**6.974e-4**	2.595e-3	**2.725e-3**	3.025e-2	**3.683e-3**	3.050e-2
	X-L-X	**4.790e-4**	4.990e-4	**2.510e-3**	2.621e-3	2.450e-3	**1.695e-3**	**6.186e-4**	2.436e-3	**2.595e-3**	3.044e-2	**3.695e-3**	3.044e-2
	X-L-L	**4.954e-4**	5.010e-4	**2.478e-3**	2.641e-3	3.033e-3	**1.196e-3**	**6.883e-4**	3.026e-2	**2.580e-3**	3.307e-3	**3.832e-3**	4.158e-2
	X-X-L	**4.883e-4**	6.460e-4	2.623e-3	**2.619e-3**	3.765e-3	**1.604e-3**	**7.825e-4**	3.064e-3	**2.707e-3**	3.016e-3	**4.443e-3**	2.450e-2

Effect of Evolution on Genome's Weight Performance: Further tests were done to see if Lamarckian weight inheritance and the neuroevolutionary process provided any other benefits over training RNNs for long periods of time. The best RNN architectures from each of the 20 repeats from all the experiments were retrained with their weights reinitialized with both the Kaiming and Xavier methods. Those architectures were then retrained for a long time (3000 epochs), and the best and average validation MSE of the retrained results were compared with the best and average validation MSE results.

Table 5 shows the best and average EXAMM validation results compared to the best and average retrained results for all the experiment types across all three datasets. In the best case, for the coal and wind dataset, almost all of the results at the end of EXAMM outperform the retrained RNNs, and in the cases where it does not the results are quite close. The C172 data proved more challenging here and outperformed the final EXAMM results, which may indicate that it would benefit from even longer training epochs when generating genomes. Additionally, when the BP epochs were 40, EXAMM performed the best on both the coal and wind dataset, which shows that utilizing Lamarckian strategies can provide strong results using fewer epochs, and also that the neuroevolutionary process is providing additional benefits, as even when these networks are retrained for a very long period of time, they still perform worse than the ones with evolved weights.

In the average case, EXAMM strongly outperforms the retrained networks for all the datasets in all but one case. This shows that EXAMM's Lamarckian weight inheritance method typically evolves genomes that do not require further training, as opposed to other neural architecture search strategies which first find the architecture and then need to train it for a significant period of time.

5 Conclusions

This work is an experimental study on the effects of weight initialization and weight inheritance in neuroevolution. It compares the well known Kaiming and Xavier weight initialization strategies to two Lamarckian weight inheritance strategies, once based on recombining parental weights during crossover, and another using statistical information of parental weights to assign new weights in mutation operations. This is done in the context of the Evolutionary eXploration of Augmenting Memory Models (EXAMM) neuroevolution algorithm, which progressively evolves and trains RNNs for time series data prediction using a direct encoding strategy. Experiments were done using three large scale real world time series data sets, one generated from a coal fired power plant, one from a wind turbine, and one from aviation flight.

A comprehensive suite of tests was run, finding with statistical significance that the Lamarckian strategies outperform Xavier and Kaiming weight initialization for generating new RNNs through EXAMM. Further, these Lamarckian strategies are also shown to be able to reduce the number of backpropagation epochs required to train the generated neural networks, allowing the neuroevolution algorithm to be able to perform more architectural evolution. These results validate a commonly held view that Lamarckian weight inheritance strategies can improve the performance of neuroevolution algorithms [7,19,23], which to the authors knowledge has not been rigorously compared to state-of-the-art Xavier and Kaiming weight initialization.

Further, the weights found during the neuroevolution process with Lamarckian weight inheritance were found to provide better results than when the best found evolved architectures were retrained from random Xavier or Kaiming initializations for a large number of epochs. This highlights that the Lamarckian evolutionary process is providing additional benefit to the selection of weights and how the weight search space is traversed, showing that in most cases, the networks and weights generated by EXAMM and Lamarckian weight inheritance do not require further training, unlike many other neural architecture search strategies which first find an architecture and then need to continue to train it for a longer period of time.

The Lamarckian strategies presented are generic and can be applied to any direct encoding neuroevolution algorithm. Future work will expand these results to convolutional neural networks as well as recurrent neural networks used for natural language processing tasks (which tend to have wider but shallower architectures). Furthermore, this weight initialization and inheritance strategy can also be applied to and tested on other NE algorithms. Given these results as motivation, investigating new Lamarckian strategies to further enhance performance will also be done.

Acknowledgements. Most of the computation of this research was done on the high performance computing clusters of Research Computing at Rochester Institute of Technology [25]. We would like to thank the Research Computing team for their assistance and the support they generously offered to ensure that the heavy computation this study required was available.

References

1. Aly, A., Weikersdorfer, D., Delaunay, C.: Optimizing deep neural networks with multiple search neuroevolution. arXiv preprint arXiv:1901.05988 (2019)
2. Camero, A., Toutouh, J., Alba, E.: Low-cost recurrent neural network expected performance evaluation. arXiv preprint arXiv:1805.07159 (2018)
3. Camero, A., Toutouh, J., Alba, E.: A specialized evolutionary strategy using mean absolute error random sampling to design recurrent neural networks. arXiv preprint arXiv:1909.02425 (2019)
4. Chung, J., Gulcehre, C., Cho, K., Bengio, Y.: Empirical evaluation of gated recurrent neural networks on sequence modeling. arXiv preprint arXiv:1412.3555 (2014)
5. Collins, J., Sohl-Dickstein, J., Sussillo, D.: Capacity and trainability in recurrent neural networks. arXiv preprint arXiv:1611.09913 (2016)
6. Deb, K., Pratap, A., Agarwal, S., Meyarivan, T.: A fast and elitist multiobjective genetic algorithm: NSGA-II. IEEE Trans. Evol. Comput. **6**(2), 182–197 (2002)
7. Desell, T.: Accelerating the evolution of convolutional neural networks with node-level mutations and epigenetic weight initialization. In: Proceedings of the Genetic and Evolutionary Computation Conference Companion, pp. 157–158. ACM (2018)

8. Desell, T., ElSaid, A., Ororbia, A.G.: An empirical exploration of deep recurrent connections using neuro-evolution. In: The 23nd International Conference on the Applications of Evolutionary Computation (EvoStar: EvoApps 2020), Seville, Spain, April 2020
9. ElSaid, A., El Jamiy, F., Higgins, J., Wild, B., Desell, T.: Optimizing long short-term memory recurrent neural networks using ant colony optimization to predict turbine engine vibration. Appl. Soft Comput. **73**, 969–991 D(2018)
10. ElSaid, A., Karns, J., Lyu, Z., Krutz, D., Ororbia, A., Desell, T.: Improving neuroevolutionary transfer learning of deep recurrent neural networks through network-aware adaptation. In: Proceedings of the 2020 Genetic and Evolutionary Computation Conference, pp. 315–323 (2020)
11. Glorot, X., Bengio, Y.: Understanding the difficulty of training deep feedforward neural networks. In: Proceedings of the Thirteenth International Conference on Artificial Intelligence and Statistics, pp. 249–256 (2010)
12. He, K., Zhang, X., Ren, S., Sun, J.: Delving deep into rectifiers: surpassing human-level performance on ImageNet classification. In: Proceedings of the IEEE International Conference on Computer Vision, pp. 1026–1034 (2015)
13. Hochreiter, S., Schmidhuber, J.: Long short-term memory. Neural Comput. **9**(8), 1735–1780 (1997)
14. Jozefowicz, R., Zaremba, W., Sutskever, I.: An empirical exploration of recurrent network architectures. In: International Conference on Machine Learning, pp. 2342–2350 (2015)
15. Ku, K.W., Mak, M.W.: Exploring the effects of Lamarckian and Baldwinian learning in evolving recurrent neural networks. In: Proceedings of 1997 IEEE International Conference on Evolutionary Computation (ICEC'97), pp. 617–621. IEEE (1997)
16. Liu, C., et al.: Progressive neural architecture search. In: Proceedings of the European Conference on Computer Vision (ECCV), pp. 19–34 (2018)
17. Liu, Y., Sun, Y., Xue, B., Zhang, M., Yen, G.: A survey on evolutionary neural architecture search. arXiv preprint arXiv:2008.10937 (2020)
18. Lu, Z., et al.: NSGA-Net: neural architecture search using multi-objective genetic algorithm. In: Proceedings of the Genetic and Evolutionary Computation Conference, pp. 419–427 (2019)
19. Ororbia, A., ElSaid, A., Desell, T.: Investigating recurrent neural network memory structures using neuro-evolution. In: Proceedings of the Genetic and Evolutionary Computation Conference. GECCO 2019, pp. 446–455. ACM, New York, NY, USA (2019). https://doi.org/10.1145/3321707.3321795
20. Ororbia II, A.G., Mikolov, T., Reitter, D.: Learning simpler language models with the differential state framework. Neural Comput. 1–26 (2017). https://doi.org/10.1162/neco_a_01017, pMID: 28957029
21. Pascanu, R., Mikolov, T., Bengio, Y.: On the difficulty of training recurrent neural networks. In: International Conference on Machine Learning, pp. 1310–1318 (2013)
22. Pham, H., Guan, M.Y., Zoph, B., Le, Q.V., Dean, J.: Efficient neural architecture search via parameter sharing. arXiv preprint arXiv:1802.03268 (2018)
23. Prellberg, J., Kramer, O.: Lamarckian evolution of convolutional neural networks. In: Auger, A., Fonseca, C.M., Lourenço, N., Machado, P., Paquete, L., Whitley, D. (eds.) PPSN 2018. LNCS, vol. 11102, pp. 424–435. Springer, Cham (2018). https://doi.org/10.1007/978-3-319-99259-4_34
24. Real, E., et al.: Large-scale evolution of image classifiers. arXiv preprint arXiv:1703.01041 (2017)

25. Rochester Institute of Technology: Research computing services (2019). https://doi.org/10.34788/0S3G-QD15, https://www.rit.edu/researchcomputing/
26. Stanley, K., Miikkulainen, R.: Evolving neural networks through augmenting topologies. Evol. Comput. **10**(2), 99–127 (2002)
27. Stanley, K.O., Clune, J., Lehman, J., Miikkulainen, R.: Designing neural networks through neuroevolution. Nat. Mach. Intell. **1**(1), 24–35 (2019)
28. Stanley, K.O., D'Ambrosio, D.B., Gauci, J.: A hypercube-based encoding for evolving large-scale neural networks. Artif. Life **15**(2), 185–212 (2009)
29. Zhang, Q., Li, H.: MOEA/D: a multiobjective evolutionary algorithm based on decomposition. IEEE Trans. Evol. Comput. **11**(6), 712–731 (2007)
30. Zhou, G.B., Wu, J., Zhang, C.L., Zhou, Z.H.: Minimal gated unit for recurrent neural networks. Int. J. Autom. Comput. **13**(3), 226–234 (2016)

Towards Feature-Based Performance Regression Using Trajectory Data

Anja Jankovic[1(✉)], Tome Eftimov[2], and Carola Doerr[1]

[1] Sorbonne Université, CNRS, LIP6, Paris, France
anja.jankovic@lip6.fr
[2] Computer Systems Department, Jožef Stefan Institute, Ljubljana, Slovenia

Abstract. Black-box optimization is a very active area of research, with many new algorithms being developed every year. This variety is needed, on the one hand, since different algorithms are most suitable for different types of optimization problems. But the variety also poses a meta-problem: which algorithm to choose for a given problem at hand? Past research has shown that per-instance algorithm selection based on exploratory landscape analysis (ELA) can be an efficient mean to tackle this meta-problem. Existing approaches, however, require the approximation of problem features based on a significant number of samples, which are typically selected through uniform sampling or Latin Hypercube Designs. The evaluation of these points is costly, and the benefit of an ELA-based algorithm selection over a default algorithm must therefore be significant in order to pay off. One could hope to by-pass the evaluations for the feature approximations by using the samples that a default algorithm would anyway perform, i.e., by using the points of the default algorithm's trajectory. We analyze in this paper how well such an approach can work. Concretely, we test how accurately trajectory-based ELA approaches can predict the final solution quality of the CMA-ES after a fixed budget of function evaluations. We observe that the loss of trajectory-based predictions can be surprisingly small compared to the classical global sampling approach, if the remaining budget for which solution quality shall be predicted is not too large. Feature selection, in contrast, did not show any advantage in our experiments and rather led to worsened prediction accuracy. The inclusion of state variables of CMA-ES only has a moderate effect on the prediction accuracy.

Keywords: Exploratory landscape analysis · Automated algorithm selection · Black-box optimization · Performance regression · Feature selection

1 Introduction

In many real-world optimization challenges, we encounter optimization problems which are too complex to be explicitly modeled via mathematical functions, but which nonetheless need to be assessed and solved, more often than not requiring

© Springer Nature Switzerland AG 2021
P. A. Castillo and J. L. Jiménez Laredo (Eds.): EvoApplications 2021, LNCS 12694, pp. 601–617, 2021.
https://doi.org/10.1007/978-3-030-72699-7_38

significant computational resources to do so. Explicit problem modeling is also an issue when the relationship between decision variables and solution quality cannot be established other than by simulations or experiments. A standard example for the latter is the design of (deep) neural networks. *Black-box optimization algorithms (BBOA)* are algorithms designed to solve problems of the two types above. BBOA are usually iterative procedures, which actively steer the search by using information obtained from previous iterations, with the goal to eventually converge towards an estimated optimal solution. In each generation, a number of solutions candidates are generated and undergo evaluation.

Classically, BBOA were manually designed, based on users' experience. A plethora of algorithmic components exist from which users can choose to build their own algorithms, and the number of these components is growing every year. Even though the basic underlying principles of these components can be considered similar in nature, their performances on different problem instances can greatly vary. An important and challenging task is thus to select the most appropriate and efficient algorithm when presented with a new, unknown problem instance. This research problem, formalized as the *algorithm selection problem (ASP)* [33], is one of *the* core questions that evolutionary computation aims to answer. The algorithm selection problem is classically tackled by relying on expert knowledge of both the problem instance and the algorithm's strengths and weaknesses. In recent years, however, due to the significant progress in the machine learning (ML) field, there has been a shift towards an *automated* selection [16,18,20,27] and configuration [3] of algorithms based on supervised learning approaches. The idea behind these approaches is in utilizing ML techniques to design and to train models to accurately predict the performance of different black-box algorithms on previously unseen problem instances, with the goal to use these performance predictions to select and to configure the best algorithm for the problem at hand, respectively. In order to apply supervised learning, problem instances need to be represented in a convenient way via numerical values. That is, we need to quantify relevant characteristics of a problem instance through appropriate measures. These measures are referred to as *features*. In the terminology used in evolutionary computation (EC), features are hence aimed at describing the *fitness landscape* of a problem instance.

Fitness landscape analysis has a long tradition in EC. For practical use in black-box optimization, however, the fitness landscape properties can only be described via an informed guessing strategy. Concretely, we can only approximate the fitness landscapes, through the samples that we have evaluated and to which a solution quality has been assigned. Research addressing efficient ways to characterize problem instances via feature approximations is subsumed under the umbrella term *exploratory landscape analysis (ELA)* [24]. Common research questions in ELA concern the number of samples needed to accurately approximate feature values, the design and the selection of features that are descriptive and easy to approximate, and the possibility to use feature values to transfer learned policies from some instances to previously unseen ones.

A drawback of existing ELA-approaches are the resources needed to extract and to compute the feature values, the time required to train the models, and a lack of explainability. In this work, we focus on the first issues, the feature extraction. Most ELA-based studies perform a three-step selection/configuration: in the first step a number of search points are sampled (commonly using uniform sampling, Latin Hypercube Designs, or quasi-random sampling [32]), evaluated, and then plugged into a feature computation algorithm such as the R tool *flacco* [21]. In the second step the model for the classification or regression task is built and an algorithm and/or its configuration is suggested. In the third step, this algorithm is then run on the problem instance under consideration. Clearly, the effort for steps 1 and 2 cannot be neglected, and can have a decisive influence on the usefulness of a per-instance algorithm selection/configuration approach, as its effort needs to pay off compared to the performance of a default solver. Even when neglecting the computational overhead of this approach and focusing on function evaluations only as performance measure (as is commonly done in evolutionary computation [12]), the evaluations needed for completing step 1 need to be taken into account. Much research has been done on determining a suitable number of samples, and typical recommendations vary between $30d$ [2] and $50d$ samples [19], where d denotes the dimension of the problem. This is hence a considerable investment.

Of course, one could use these samples to *warm-start* the optimization heuristics, e.g., by initiating them in good regions and/or by calibrating their search behavior based on the information obtained from the samples used to compute the features.

A charming, yet straightforward alternative would be to integrate the first step of the ELA-based approach described above into the optimization routine, by computing the features based on the search points that a default algorithm would anyway perform. That is, one would use the search trajectory of such a default algorithm to predict and then to select and/or to configure a solver *on the fly*, once or even several times during the optimization process.

Similar to parameter control [1,8,17], such a dynamic selection would not only allow to *identify* an efficient algorithm for the given problem instance, but could also benefit from *tracking* the best choice while the optimization process (and the best response to its needs) evolves. Such a dynamic algorithm selection can therefore be seen as an ELA-based variant of hyper-heuristics [5]. The approach has previously been used in the context of constrained optimization, with the goal to have a dynamic, ELA-guided selection of a suitable constraint handling technique; see [23] for examples and further references.

A key challenge in applying dynamic ELA-based algorithm selection is the fact that the feature values can vary drastically between different sampling strategies [32]. Since the distribution of points sampled on different problem instances can differ quite drastically even when using the same algorithm, it is not clear, a priori, if or how suitable ML models can be trained. This challenge was confirmed in [15], where it was shown that the landscape which an algorithm sees locally during the optimization process (i.e., the partial landscape it is aware of at each step of the optimization process) usually differs a lot from the global fitness landscape of the problem it is solving.

Our Results. With the long-term goal to obtain well-performing dynamic ELA-based algorithm selection and configuration techniques, we analyze in this work a first, rather cautious task: ELA-based performance prediction using the trajectory samples of the algorithm under investigation. More precisely, we consider the Covariance Matrix Adaptation Evolution Strategy (CMA-ES [13]), and we aim at predicting its solution quality (measured as target precision, i.e., the difference to an optimal solution in quality space) after a fixed budget of function evaluations. Concretely, we use the first 250 samples evaluated by the CMA-ES and we aim at predicting its performance after additional 250 evaluations, doing so for 20 independent CMA-ES runs. The performance regression is done via a random forest model which takes as input the features computed from the trajectory data and which outputs an estimate for the final solution quality.

We then take into account that problem characteristics cannot only be described via classic ELA features, but that internal states of the search heuristics can also be used to derive information about the problem instance at hand. Such approaches have in the past been used, for example, for local surrogate-modelling [31]. We analyze the accuracy gains when using the same state information as in [31], that is, the values of the CMA-ES internal variables that mainly carry information about the current probability distribution from which the CMA-ES samples candidates for the new generation. In our experiments, the advantage of using this state information over using ELA-features only, however, is only marginal. Concretely, the average difference between true and predicted solution quality decreases from 14.4 to 12.1 when adding the state variables as features (where the average error reported here is taken over all 24 benchmark problems from the BBOB suite of the COCO platform [12], and over all performed CMA-ES runs).

We observe in the experiments above that some CMA-ES runs are drastic outliers in terms of performance, at times with the target precision differing from the target precision of all the other runs by up to 10 orders of magnitude. We therefore also consider an intentionally more "friendly" setting, in which we analyze the regression quality only for the run achieving median performance on a given problem instance. Conclusions for combining trajectory-based and state variable features remain almost identical to those stated above.

We then compare these median trajectory-based predictions to the classical approach using globally sampled features. Here, we pessimistically assume that the samples were computed for free. That is, we couple 2 separate sets of the global feature values approximated from 250 and 2000 uniformly sampled points each to the target precision achieved by the CMA-ES after 500 function evaluations. Interestingly, the difference in prediction accuracy compared to our trajectory-based predictions is rather small. The global predictions still remain, however, more accurate, with an average absolute prediction error of 4.7 vs. 6.2 for the trajectory approach (where again the average is taken over all 24 BBOB functions).

Furthermore, we also use this median setting to analyze the influence of feature selection on prediction accuracy. Different state-of-the-art methods were applied, using a transfer learning scenario, to select features estimated to be the most important and to have highest discriminative power. Here again, the differences in prediction accuracy were small, with feature selection surprisingly leading to an overall slightly worsened solution quality than the full feature portfolio.

As suggested in [16], all our experiments are based on two independently trained models: one which aims to predict target precision after 500 evaluations, and one which predicts the logarithm of this target precision. While the former is better in guessing the broader "ball park", the latter is more suitable for fine-grained performance prediction, i.e., when the expected performance of the algorithm is very good. As in [16], we also build a combined regression, which uses either one of the two models, depending on whether the predicted performance is better or worse than a certain threshold. The optimal thresholds differ quite drastically between different feature sets. However, a sensitivity analysis reveals that their influence on overall performance is rather small. Also, the ranking of the different feature portfolios remains almost unaffected by the choice of the threshold. In line with the results in [16], the combined models perform consistently better than any of the two standalone ones, albeit slightly.

2 Supervised ML for Performance Regression

The Experimental Setup. When it comes to landscape-aware performance prediction, supervised machine learning techniques such as regression and classification have been studied in a variety of settings. Regression models, unlike classification ones, have an advantage of keeping track of the magnitude of differences between performances of different algorithms, as they measure concrete values for performances of all algorithms from the portfolio.

Among different supervised learning regressors in the literature, such as support vector machines, Gaussian processes or ridge regression to name a few, it has been empirically shown that random forests outperform other models in terms of prediction accuracy [14]. A random forest is an ensemble-based meta-estimator that works by fitting multiple decision trees on subsamples of the original data set, then uses averaging as a way to control overfitting. In our experimental setup, we used an off-the-shelf random forest regressor from the Python *scikit-learn* package [29], without parameter tuning and using 1000 estimators.

We restricted this work to a single heuristic, the Covariance Matrix Adaptation Evolution Strategy (CMA-ES [13]). The CMA-ES works by iteratively sampling a new population of candidate solutions from a shifted multivariate normal distribution, choosing the best offspring of the current population based on their respective fitness values, and then updating the parameters of the probability distribution according to the best candidates. For the purpose of our work, we used its standard version, available in the Python *pycma* package [11], which uses a fixed population size and no restarts during the optimization process.

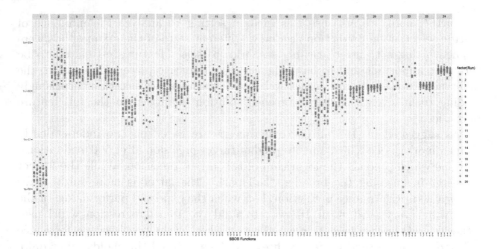

Fig. 1. Target precision achieved by the CMA-ES with a budget of 500 function evaluations, for each of the first five instances of all 24 BBOB functions. Differently colored and shaped points represent 20 independent CMA-ES runs.

As our benchmark, we used the first five instances of all 24 noiseless *BBOB* functions of the *COCO* platform [12], an environment for comparison of algorithm performance in continuous black-box optimization. The different instances of each function are generated by translating and rotating the function in the objective space. These transformations do not affect the performance of CMA-ES, but they do influence some of the feature values, especially those which are not transformation-invariant [35] (for the invariant features, the boundary handling can have an effect on the feature values). We focus on dimension $d = 5$ here.

For our first experiments, we perform 20 independent runs of the CMA-ES on these 120 problem instances, while keeping track of the search trajectories and the internal state variables of the algorithm itself. Throughout this work, we fix the budget of 500 function evaluations, after which we stop the optimization and record the target precision of the best found solution within the budget. In order to predict those recorded target precisions after 500 function evaluations, we compute the trajectory-based landscape features using the first 250 sampled points and their evaluations from the beginning of each trajectory, and couple them with the values of the internal CMA-ES state variables extracted at the 250th function evaluation.

Figure 1 summarizes the target precision achieved by CMA-ES in each of the 20 runs. We see that the results are more or less homogeneous across different runs and across different instances of the same problem. However, we also observe several outliers, e.g., for functions 7 (outlier for all instances), function 10 (instance 4), function 12 (instance 1). It is important to keep in mind that the randomness of these performances are entirely caused by the randomness of the algorithm itself – the problem instance does not change between different runs.

For landscape feature computation, we use the R package *flacco* [21]. Following suggestions made in [3,20] we restrict ourselves to those feature sets that do not require additional function evaluations for computing the features. Namely, in this work we use 2 original ELA feature sets (*y-Distribution* and *Meta-Model*), as well as *Dispersion, Nearest-Better Clustering* and *Information Content* feature sets. This gives us a total of 38 landscape features per problem instance. In addition, we follow up on an idea previously used in [31] and consider a set of internal CMA-ES state variables as features:

- Step-size: its value indicates how large is the approximated region from which the CMA-ES samples new candidate solutions.
- Mahalanobis mean distance: represents the measure of suitability of the current sampled population for model training from the point of view of the current state of the CMA-ES algorithm.
- C evolution path length: indicates the similarity of landscapes among previous generations.
- σ evolution path ratio: provides information about the changes in the probability distribution used to sample new candidates.
- CMA similarity likelihood: it is a log-likelihood of the set of candidate solutions with respect to the CMA-ES distribution and may also represent a measure of the set suitability for training.

As suggested in [16], and using the elements described above, we establish two separate regression approaches. One model is trained to predict the actual, true value of the target precision data (we refer to it as the *unscaled model* in the remainder of the paper), while the other predicts the logarithm of the target precision data (the *log-model*). It is important to note that the target precision measure intuitively carries the information about the order of magnitude of the actual distance to the optimum, i.e., the *distance level* to the optimum, which is effectively computed as the log-target precision. For instance, if an algorithm reaches a target precision of 10^{-3} for one problem instance and 10^{-7} for another, it means that the algorithm found a solution which is 4 distance levels closer to the optimum in the latter scenario. Moreover, to reduce variability, we estimate both models' prediction accuracy through performing a 5-fold *leave-one-instance-out* cross-validation, making sure to train on 4 out of 5 instances per BBOB function, test on the remaining instance and combine the results over the rounds.

Results. Adopting our two regression models, we trained them separately in the following three scenarios: using as predictor variables the landscape features only, using the internal CMA-ES state variables only, and using the combination of the two. We trained the random forests 3 independent times and took a median of the 3 runs to ensure the robustness of the results.

Figure 2 highlights the absolute prediction errors per BBOB function using two regression models, the unscaled and the log-one, when trained with 3 different feature sets: using only the trajectory landscape data, only the CMA-ES state variable data, and the combination of the two. For the majority of the functions, using the combination of the trajectory data and the state variable data seems to help in improving the performance prediction accuracy, compared to the scenarios which use only one of those two feature sets.

FID	Unscaled model			Log model		
	SV	ELA	ELA+SV	SV	ELA	ELA+SV
1	4.6	2.6	1.9	0.1	0.0	0.0
2	60.4	64.2	63.7	65.4	58.0	57.1
3	6.4	5.4	5.2	10.1	7.2	6.9
4	9.0	7.0	6.9	12.4	8.7	8.6
5	86.4	6.6	26.2	5.5	4.6	4.5
6	9.1	9.4	4.0	1.1	0.5	0.6
7	6.5	1.0	0.8	0.9	0.7	0.7
8	6.8	1.8	1.7	1.7	1.2	1.2
9	9.2	1.1	1.0	0.9	0.7	0.7
10	126.2	171.1	125.1	125.9	119.7	114.8
11	37.2	12.7	23.9	6.8	5.4	5.6
12	15.2	101.8	24.5	15.3	14.3	13.0
13	9.8	5.6	5.1	4.1	3.9	3.7
14	4.8	2.5	1.1	0.4	0.1	0.0
15	8.8	10.7	5.5	9.6	6.9	6.5
16	4.7	4.8	5.0	0.8	1.7	1.7
17	6.4	1.9	1.8	1.4	0.7	0.7
18	7.8	2.4	2.3	2.7	2.3	2.3
19	11.7	2.3	1.6	2.9	0.5	0.5
20	4.6	0.5	0.6	1.4	0.6	0.6
21	3.8	3.5	3.7	3.5	3.6	3.6
22	10.1	9.0	8.6	9.1	8.6	8.6
23	13.4	1.8	2.0	2.6	0.8	0.8
24	9.4	5.2	5.1	14.9	8.3	8.5

Fig. 2. Absolute prediction errors for both regression models aggregated per BBOB function in 3 different scenarios depending on the feature set used. The *SV* column stands for the CMA-ES state variables, the *ELA* for the landscape features, and the third one is the combination of both.

We also confirm that the log-model is indeed better at predicted fine-grained target precision (e.g., in the case of F1 (sphere function) or F6 (linear slope function), we know that those functions do not require many function evaluations to converge to the global optimum, and their recorded target precision values are already quite small as they are very near the optimal solution). On the other hand, the unscaled model performs better where the target precision values are higher (e.g., for the functions such as F3, F15 (two versions of Rastrigin function), and also F24 (Lunacek bi-Rastigin), which are all highly multimodal, the number of function evaluations in our budget was not nearly enough to allow for finding a true optimum).

We also notice that using only the state variables for the unscaled model does not suffice for an accurate prediction in the most cases. The reverse situation is nevertheless also possible: we see that for F12, using only the state variables yields the best accuracy in the unscaled model. Furthermore, there are also exceptions where using only the landscape data results in a higher accuracy than using the combined features (e.g., F11 for both models, F5 for the unscaled model).

3   Comparison with Global Feature Values

We then proceeded to compare the differences in the prediction accuracy from the sets described in the Sect. 2 with the prediction accuracy using the global feature data, both alone and combined with the same CMA-ES state variable data as above. To be able to perform a fair comparison, for the trajectory data we selected from the 20 executed CMA-ES runs those runs with the median target precision value per problem instance and their corresponding features and re-trained the unscaled and the log-model. Global features-wise, both models were also trained using features computed from 2000 and 250 globally uniformly sampled points (the median value of 50 independent feature computations) for each function and instance.

	Unscaled model							Log model						
FID	SV	ELA	ELA +SV	GLOB2k	GLOB2k +SV	GLOB250	GLOB250 +SV	SV	ELA	ELA +SV	GLOB2k	GLOB2k +SV	GLOB250	GLOB250 +SV
1	4.4	2.2	2.0	0.9	1.3	1.8	2.0	0.29	0.00	0.00	0.00	0.00	0.00	0.00
2	31.2	17.4	16.7	18.5	17.9	18.9	17.7	38.89	31.56	31.06	25.65	26.58	28.98	30.20
3	8.3	5.2	5.5	1.6	2.6	3.6	4.9	10.14	7.08	6.97	4.93	5.69	8.33	8.80
4	9.3	3.5	3.8	2.9	3.7	3.9	4.6	11.78	4.45	4.99	3.59	4.87	7.64	8.31
5	1.7	1.4	1.0	1.3	1.1	1.2	0.9	7.16	8.19	8.17	4.97	5.22	5.93	6.21
6	5.0	6.7	6.1	1.4	1.6	2.5	2.5	0.66	1.45	1.33	0.23	0.25	0.30	0.34
7	3.8	4.9	4.7	13.1	12.9	4.0	3.2	0.68	0.31	0.33	2.42	2.05	1.00	1.01
8	3.2	1.6	1.9	1.9	2.2	1.8	2.0	0.98	0.98	0.96	0.81	0.76	0.91	0.71
9	3.2	1.1	0.7	0.5	0.4	1.0	0.8	0.73	0.26	0.27	0.45	0.38	0.40	0.41
10	37.0	24.4	24.3	19.5	19.3	24.8	26.9	37.98	30.84	31.48	29.15	29.94	28.75	30.17
11	14.4	8.6	10.2	2.6	3.0	6.4	8.4	2.18	5.18	5.36	3.09	3.52	2.57	3.05
12	2.2	24.9	20.2	2.3	2.5	4.4	3.7	4.55	1.76	1.40	3.43	3.57	3.65	3.55
13	9.7	2.2	3.6	2.4	2.4	3.2	4.8	1.95	1.62	1.70	1.73	1.81	1.49	1.65
14	2.8	0.7	0.6	3.5	3.5	5.5	5.4	0.45	0.00	0.00	0.05	0.06	0.23	0.25
15	5.5	3.6	3.5	4.3	5.5	5.6	5.8	7.23	7.48	6.23	6.04	6.57	8.23	8.40
16	2.8	5.6	5.5	0.6	1.1	0.5	1.1	0.35	4.26	4.08	0.27	0.33	0.21	0.23
17	3.3	1.3	1.2	2.4	2.2	3.3	2.8	0.89	0.26	0.25	0.27	0.30	0.27	0.27
18	3.3	0.9	1.0	3.0	2.7	3.6	3.0	0.44	0.34	0.27	0.29	0.25	0.39	0.41
19	18.1	2.7	3.5	1.4	2.3	1.4	3.2	2.91	0.24	0.27	0.43	0.53	0.40	0.43
20	3.3	5.8	5.7	0.2	1.1	0.6	1.9	1.27	0.67	0.80	0.67	0.93	0.64	0.75
21	3.1	1.9	2.6	4.1	3.6	2.9	3.0	3.27	3.16	3.15	3.96	3.98	4.11	3.96
22	7.2	7.0	7.0	9.1	9.2	9.6	9.3	7.87	7.45	7.45	7.66	7.85	7.61	7.66
23	6.9	3.0	3.6	0.2	0.9	0.5	2.5	2.53	1.11	1.19	0.61	0.63	0.65	0.68
24	6.7	4.0	4.2	1.5	2.4	2.2	3.3	12.65	8.35	9.22	4.41	7.24	8.07	9.87

Fig. 3. Absolute prediction errors for both regression models for the median trajectory-based prediction (the first 3 columns of each block) and the median global feature prediction (the middle two columns of each block represent the errors when using the 2000-sample features, and the last two columns correspond to using the 250-sample features).

Figure 3 shows the absolute errors in prediction when the trajectory-based approach is compared with the results using the global features. The highest accuracy is reported in cases when only the global landscape features were used, across almost all problems, with 2000-sample features yielding the best results. Here, we do not observe a huge improvement when combining the global landscape features with the state variable data. It seems that the number of samples used to compute the features can be crucial in reducing the errors in prediction, as global sampling could be linked to a potential higher discriminative power of

Table 1. Number of ELA and state variable features for each selected feature portfolio. Details are available in Table 3.

	Boruta	swfb	rfe	cor0.5	cor0.75	cor0.9
# selected ELA features	37	1	7	4	9	15
# selected state variable features	2	0	0	3	3	5

features thus computed. Again, for certain functions such as F2 and F10 (both of which are different variants of the ellipsoidal function), we observe an overall low accuracy.

4   Sensitivity Analyses

Feature Selection. To provide a sensitivity analysis based on the features used for the performance regression, we performed feature selection in the scenario of transfer learning, i.e., between different supervised tasks, where the features selected for the problem classification task have been evaluated on the performance regression task.

To do this, we have explored four state-of-the-art feature selection techniques: *Boruta* [22] is a feature selection and ranking algorithm based on random forests algorithm, which only selects features that are statistically significant. *Recursive feature elimination (rfe)* [10] learns a model assessing different sets of features by recursively eliminating features per loop until a good model is learnt. It requires an ML algorithm for evaluation, and here we use a random forest. *Stepwise forward and backward selection (swfb)* [7] tries to fit the best regression model by iteratively selecting and removing features. In our experiments, we used it in both directions simultaneously. *Correlation analysis with different threshold values (cor)* [4] is based on the correlation analysis done only using the features (i.e., excluding the target). The result is a feature set where highly correlated features are omitted. In our case, we tested three different correlation thresholds: 0.50, 0.75, and 0.90. Note that while the first three feature selection methods require a supervised ML task, the last one is completely unsupervised and does not depend on the target.

Our experimental design has been done using stratified 5-fold cross-validation. For a fair feature selection, we used the aforementioned methods on each training fold separately, then selected the intersection of the features returned by each training fold in the end. These features are further evaluated in the performance regression task.

Table 1 summarizes how many features were selected per portfolio, from the whole set of 38 ELA landscape features and 5 CMA-ES state variable features.

Combined Selector Model and Sensitivity Analysis

As common in ML, we measure the regression accuracy in terms of *Root Mean Squared Error* (RMSE). Table 2 summarizes the RMSE values for the different feature portfolios when using (1) the unscaled model, (2) the scaled model, and (3) a combination of unscaled and the log-model (see last three rows of Table 2). The threshold τ at which the predictive model changes is optimized for each feature portfolio individually, the obtained thresholds are summarized at the top of Table 2. That is, we select the prediction of the log-model when the predicted precision (according to the log-model) is smaller than the threshold value τ, and we use the prediction of the unscaled model otherwise. Note that the optimal threshold value τ varies significantly between the different feature portfolios.

Table 2. RMSE values of the combined selector in three scenarios: when the prediction is based on the search trajectory landscape features and state variables (first 3 columns), on global features (next 4 columns), and finally on selected feature portfolios (last 6 columns).

FID	min_tp	max_tp	SV	ELA	ELA +SV	GLOB2k	GLOB2k +SV	GLOB250	GLOB250 +SV	boruta	cor 0.5	cor 0.75	cor 0.9	rfe	swfb
						Best threshold τ									
			1.336	3.99	4.742	14.497	9.46	0.694	2.605	3.63	1.813	4.901	1.717	7.388	20
1	0	0	0.43	0	0	0	0	0	0	0	0	0	0	0	0.21
2	9.25	87.47	44.69	25.47	24.46	24.49	23.65	28.96	27.98	25.16	36.78	35.28	34.62	24.51	53.85
3	10.34	14.63	9.73	6.62	7.02	5.62	6.25	4.43	9.39	6.73	8.08	7.7	5.63	7.95	8.82
4	10.29	14.53	11.86	5.08	5.08	4.81	5.73	5.1	7.49	5.18	9.26	6.71	5.59	7.53	8.41
5	8.53	11.34	4.59	8.24	8.15	6.02	5.52	1.48	1.06	8.21	2.36	6.76	4.91	4.52	7.74
6	0.04	0.11	0.78	3.87	2.15	0.24	0.27	0.33	0.37	4.46	1.02	1.19	1.65	0.89	1.43
7	0.13	1.83	3.84	0.36	0.39	4.49	4.07	4.62	1.13	0.42	0.86	0.6	0.65	0.67	7.94
8	1.22	2.59	3.02	1.06	1.1	1.25	1.22	2.03	0.84	0.95	2.02	0.93	1.04	1.42	4.88
9	0.68	1.36	3.05	0.34	0.34	0.59	0.53	0.77	0.48	0.33	0.52	0.26	0.29	0.86	3.47
10	8.44	84.69	43.33	32.06	32.85	21.39	23.16	29.29	33.35	32.13	42.18	32.73	35.01	29.64	47.68
11	4.97	8.83	17.48	10.37	12.63	3.46	2.99	8.26	10.18	11.17	25.11	21.61	20.86	2.43	4.77
12	2.53	6.32	4.76	19.34	15.89	4.03	4.16	5.76	4.13	19.45	4.38	2.31	9.69	19.32	3.56
13	1.09	5.92	13.62	2.07	2.13	2.29	2.32	3.51	2.21	2.11	2.45	2.04	5.37	2.03	3.5
14	0	0	1.65	0.01	0.01	0.07	0.08	1.89	0.37	0.01	0.61	0	0	0	5.18
15	8.49	12.93	7.44	6.79	6.66	6.08	6.81	6.24	8.12	5.77	7.07	6.11	5.88	6.73	9.12
16	0.18	0.83	0.87	6.31	5.85	0.32	0.35	0.25	0.25	6.45	0.48	4.42	4.77	2.43	1.21
17	0.03	0.64	2.63	0.36	0.33	0.32	0.33	0.28	0.31	0.38	4.25	0.41	0.38	0.27	2.75
18	0.16	0.69	1.54	0.34	0.34	0.33	0.3	4.96	0.45	0.34	0.54	0.28	0.3	0.54	1.24
19	0.75	1.19	18.75	0.34	0.36	0.65	0.67	1.66	0.49	0.38	9.95	0.59	0.5	0.46	8.54
20	1.7	1.79	3.77	0.76	0.84	0.99	1.17	0.99	0.93	0.69	3.2	1.22	3.16	1.77	5.16
21	0	8.12	4.86	4.55	4.52	5.02	5.02	5.2	4.95	4.53	4.72	4.84	4.83	4.83	3.72
22	0	25.48	12.04	11.91	11.91	11.9	11.91	12.88	11.94	11.91	11.89	11.93	11.7	11.92	5.34
23	1.99	2.35	7.49	3.67	3.61	0.69	0.77	0.64	0.91	3.72	7.89	2.73	4.53	2.46	3.04
24	15.73	20.73	10.06	4.76	4.94	5.15	6.52	2.95	4.29	4.81	11.13	9.49	7.22	7.43	11.65
Overall RMSE, combined			15.05	10.41	10.25	7.74	7.92	9.48	10.05	10.43	13.66	11.67	11.86	9.77	15.73
Overall RMSE, unscaled			15.08	11.18	10.88	9.21	9.30	9.58	10.19	11.16	14.11	11.80	12.00	10.93	17.03
Overall RMSE, log			15.63	13.05	13.21	11.46	11.88	12.05	12.87	13.14	14.65	13.89	14.29	12.61	15.73

When comparing all the different portfolios (initial trajectory-based, global and selected trajectory-based ones), the good performance of the global feature sets is not surprising. Differences from the initial trajectory-based predictions are marginal for sets such as *boruta*, *cor0.75* and *cor0.9*, whereas *swbf* and *cor0.5* perform constantly worse than *ELA+SV*. Using the *rfe* set, on the other hand, led to better results than using the original feature set. *SV* alone does not achieve good accuracy, but its contribution to ELA-only feature portfolio is around 3% at the best threshold for the combined model, which is $\tau = 4.901$. The absolute errors per instance are plotted in Fig. 4.

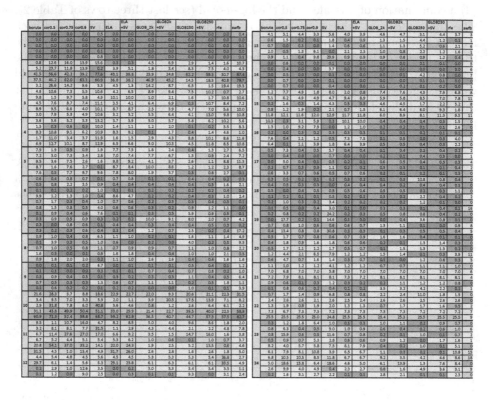

Fig. 4. Absolute prediction errors of the combined models using portfolio-specific optimal thresholds τ.

Table 3. Feature portfolios.

Feature	# sets	boruta	swfb	rfe	cor0.5	cor0.75	cor0.9
ela_distr.skewness	4	x	x	x			x
ela_distr.kurtosis	4	x		x	x	x	
ela_distr.number_of_peaks	4	x			x	x	x
ela_meta.lin_simple.adj_r2	2	x					x
ela_meta.lin_simple.intercept	1	x					
ela_meta.lin_simple.coef.min	2	x					x
ela_meta.lin_simple.coef.max	2	x		x			
ela_meta.lin_simple.coef.max_by_min	3				x	x	x
ela_meta.lin_w_interact.adj_r2	1	x					
ela_meta.quad_simple.adj_r2	2	x		x			
ela_meta.quad_simple.cond	4	x			x	x	x
ela_meta.quad_w_interact.adj_r2	3	x		x			x
disp.ratio_mean_02	1	x					
disp.ratio_mean_05	1	x					
disp.ratio_mean_10	1	x					
disp.ratio_mean_25	1	x					
disp.ratio_median_02	2	x					x
disp.ratio_median_05	1	x					
disp.ratio_median_10	1	x					
disp.ratio_median_25	1	x					
disp.diff_mean_02	1	x					
disp.diff_mean_05	1	x					
disp.diff_mean_10	1	x					
disp.diff_mean_25	1	x					
disp.diff_median_02	3	x				x	x
disp.diff_median_05	1	x					
disp.diff_median_10	1	x					
disp.diff_median_25	1	x					
nbc.nn_nb.sd_ratio	2	x					x
nbc.nn_nb.mean_ratio	1	x					
nbc.nn_nb.cor	2	x					x
nbc.dist_ratio.coeff_var	3	x				x	x
nbc.nb_fitness.cor	2	x		x			
ic.h.max	3	x				x	x
ic.eps.s	1	x					
ic.eps.max	1	x					
ic.eps.ratio	4	x		x		x	x
ic.m0	3	x				x	x
step_size	4	x			x	x	x
mahalanobis_dist	2				x		x
c_evol_path	3				x	x	x
sigma_evol_path	2					x	x
cma_simil_lh	2	x					x

5   Conclusions and Future Work

We analyzed in this paper the accuracy of predicting the CMA-ES solution quality after given budget based on the features computed from the samples on the CMA-ES search trajectory using two complementary regression models, the unscaled and the log-model. Adding information obtained from the CMA-ES internal state variables does not improve the prediction accuracy drastically compared to the trajectory-based data only. Those results were then contrasted to the regression using the global features, where using the latter ones, especially those computed using a higher number of samples, yielded a consistently better accuracy.

Next, we tested whether we would achieve further gains in accuracy through feature selection. Although the overall results are comparable to the ones from initial trajectory-based portfolios, several selected feature sets resulted in worse accuracy than in the initial approach. We ultimately pointed out the advantages of using our combined selector model over relying separately on predictions of the standalone unscaled or log-model across all different feature portfolios in all 3 scenarios.

In terms of **future work,** we plan on continuing this research by considering the following questions and tasks:

(0) Performance prediction of **other solvers**: How accurately can we use trajectory-based features of one algorithm to predict the performance of another algorithm? In this work, we have only tried to predict performance for the same algorithm from whose trajectory the feature values have been computed. A next step would be to test if models for configuring the same algorithm can be trained. When this is successful, transfer learning from one algorithm to another one can be considered.

(1) How can we more efficiently capture the **temporal component**, i.e., the information which sample was evaluated *when* during the search? Using such longitudinal data, both in terms of extracted feature values and in terms of state variable evolution could possibly be done using recurrent neural networks [36].

(2) **Combining global and trajectory-based sampling:** In our work, we only considered the case in which *either* global sampling *or* trajectory-based sampling is used. The accuracy of the models based on global sampling was better than that of the trajectory-based features. Even if we keep in mind that this comparison was unfair in that we provided the global feature values "for free", the results nevertheless suggest that a combination of global and trajectory-based feature computations could be worthwhile to investigate. How we can optimally balance the budget between global sampling, trajectory-based sampling, and remaining optimization budget is a challenging question in this context.

(3) **Warm-starting** the CMA-ES such that it starts the optimization process with the covariance matrix and other parameters that are extrapolated from the (uniformly or otherwise) distributed global samples might significantly improve the overall accuracy, as the CMA-ES will have a better overview of the whole problem instance "from the get-go". A similar approach has been suggested in [25] when switching from a Bayesian optimization algorithm to CMA-ES.

(4) **Feature selection and ranking:** Instead of using transfer learning for feature selection between two different supervised ML tasks, feature selection within the same supervised task has not been considered in this paper. We also plan on making better use of variable importance estimations provided by feature ranking algorithms such as those based on ensemble of predictive clustering trees [30] and those based on ReliefF and RReliefF [34].

(5) **Feature design:** The work [6] suggests several algorithm-specific features for the SOO tree algorithm [26]. Such specific features can much more explicitly capture the characteristics of the algorithm-problem instance interaction. It could be worthwhile to study whether, possibly in addition to the longitudinal data mentioned in (1), such specific features can be identified for other common solvers, such as the CMA-ES.

(6) **Feature portfolio:** We note that our work above is based on the features available in the *flacco* package [21]. Since the design of *flacco*, however, several new feature sets have been suggested. Another straightforward way to extend our analyses would be in the inclusion of these feature sets, with the hope to improve the overall regression accuracy. In this respect, we find in particular the Search Trajectory Networks suggested in [28] worth investigating.

(7) **Representation learning of landscapes:** The feature data will be additionally explored by applying representation learning methods that automatically learn new data representations by reducing the dimension of the data, automatically detecting correlations, and removing bias and redundancies presented in the feature data. The work presented in [9] showed that linear matrix factorization representations of the ELA features values significantly detects better correlation between different problem instances.

(8) **Hyperparameter tuning of regression models:** Last, but not least, we are planning to explore algorithm portfolio that consists of different regression methods in order to find the most suitable one, together with finding its best hyperparameters for achieving better performance. In this study, we have used random forest for regression without tuning its parameters, since we have been interested in the contribution of different feature portfolios.

Acknowledgments. This research benefited from the support of the Paris Ile-de-France region and of a public grant as part of the Investissement d'avenir project, reference ANR-11-LABX-0056-LMH, LabEx LMH. This work was also supported by projects from the Slovenian Research Agency: research core funding No. P2-0098 and project No. Z2-1867. We also acknowledge support by COST Action CA15140 "Improving Applicability of Nature-Inspired Optimisation by Joining Theory and Practice (ImAppNIO)".

References

1. Aleti, A., Moser, I.: A systematic literature review of adaptive parameter control methods for evolutionary algorithms. ACM Comput. Surv. **49**, 56:1–56:35 (2016)

2. Belkhir, N., Dréo, J., Savéant, P., Schoenauer, M.: Surrogate assisted feature computation for continuous problems. In: Festa, P., Sellmann, M., Vanschoren, J. (eds.) LION 2016. LNCS, vol. 10079, pp. 17–31. Springer, Cham (2016). https://doi.org/10.1007/978-3-319-50349-3_2

3. Belkhir, N., Dréo, J., Savéant, P., Schoenauer, M.: Per instance algorithm configuration of CMA-ES with limited budget. In: GECCO, pp. 681–688. ACM (2017)

4. Benesty, J., Chen, J., Huang, Y., Cohen, I.: Pearson correlation coefficient. In: Noise Reduction in Speech Processing, pp. 1–4. Springer (2009). https://doi.org/10.1007/978-3-642-00296-0_5

5. Burke, E.K., et al.: Hyper-heuristics: a survey of the state of the art. J. Oper. Res. Soc. **64**, 1695–1724 (2013)

6. Derbel, B., Liefooghe, A., Vérel, S., Aguirre, H., Tanaka, K.: New features for continuous exploratory landscape analysis based on the SOO tree. In: FOGA, pp. 72–86. ACM (2019)

7. Derksen, S., Keselman, H.J.: Backward, forward and stepwise automated subset selection algorithms: frequency of obtaining authentic and noise variables. Br. J. Math. Stat. Psychol. **45**(2), 265–282 (1992)

8. Doerr, B., Doerr, C.: Theory of parameter control mechanisms for discrete black-box optimization: provable performance gains through dynamic parameter choices. In: Theory of Evolutionary Computation: Recent Developments in Discrete Optimization, pp. 271–321. Springer (2020). https://doi.org/10.1007/978-3-030-29414-4_6

9. Eftimov, T., Popovski, G., Renau, Q., Korosec, P., Doerr, C.: Linear matrix factorization embeddings for single-objective optimization landscapes. In: SSCI, pp. 775–782. IEEE (2020)

10. Granitto, P.M., Furlanello, C., Biasioli, F., Gasperi, F.: Recursive feature elimination with random forest for PTR-MS analysis of agroindustrial products. Chemom. Intell. Lab. Syst. **83**(2), 83–90 (2006)

11. Hansen, N., Akimoto, Y., Baudis, P.: CMA-ES/pycma on Github. https://github.com/CMA-ES/pycma (2019)

12. Hansen, N., Auger, A., Ros, R., Mersmann, O., Tušar, T., Brockhoff, D.: COCO: a platform for comparing continuous optimizers in a black-box setting. Optim. Meth. Softw. **36**, 1–31 (2020)

13. Hansen, N., Ostermeier, A.: Completely derandomized self-adaptation in evolution strategies. Evol. Comput. **9**(2), 159–195 (2001)

14. Hutter, F., Xu, L., Hoos, H.H., Leyton-Brown, K.: Algorithm runtime prediction: methods and evaluation. Artif. Intell. **206**, 79–111 (2014)

15. Jankovic, A., Doerr, C.: Adaptive landscape analysis. In: GECCO, Companion Material, pp. 2032–2035. ACM (2019)

16. Jankovic, A., Doerr, C.: Landscape-aware fixed-budget performance regression and algorithm selection for modular CMA-ES variants. In: GECCO, pp. 841–849 (2020)

17. Karafotias, G., Hoogendoorn, M., Eiben, A.: Parameter control in evolutionary algorithms: trends and challenges. IEEE Trans. Evol. Comput. **19**, 167–187 (2015)

18. Kerschke, P., Kotthoff, L., Bossek, J., Hoos, H., Trautmann, H.: Leveraging TSP solver complementarity through machine learning. Evol. Comput. **26**(4), 597–620 (2018)

19. Kerschke, P., Preuss, M., Wessing, S., Trautmann, H.: Low-Budget Exploratory Landscape Analysis on Multiple Peaks Models. In: GECCO, pp. 229–236 (2016)

20. Kerschke, P., Trautmann, H.: Automated algorithm selection on continuous black-box problems by combining exploratory landscape analysis and machine learning. Evol. Comput. **27**(1), 99–127 (2019)

21. Kerschke, P., Trautmann, H.: Comprehensive feature-based landscape analysis of continuous and constrained optimization problems using the R-package flacco. In: Bauer, N., Ickstadt, K., Lübke, K., Szepannek, G., Trautmann, H., Vichi, M. (eds.) Applications in Statistical Computing. SCDAKO, pp. 93–123. Springer, Cham (2019). https://doi.org/10.1007/978-3-030-25147-5_7

22. Kursa, M.B., Jankowski, A., Rudnicki, W.R.: Boruta-a system for feature selection. Fundamenta Informaticae **101**(4), 271–285 (2010)

23. Malan, K.M.: Landscape-aware constraint handling applied to differential evolution. In: Fagan, D., Martín-Vide, C., O'Neill, M., Vega-Rodríguez, M.A. (eds.) TPNC 2018. LNCS, vol. 11324, pp. 176–187. Springer, Cham (2018). https://doi.org/10.1007/978-3-030-04070-3_14

24. Mersmann, O., Bischl, B., Trautmann, H., Preuss, M., Weihs, C., Rudolph, G.: Exploratory Landscape Analysis. In: GECCO, pp. 829–836. ACM (2011)

25. Mohammadi, H., Le Riche, R., Touboul, E.: Making EGO and CMA-ES complementary for global optimization. In: Dhaenens, C., Jourdan, L., Marmion, M.-E. (eds.) LION 2015. LNCS, vol. 8994, pp. 287–292. Springer, Cham (2015). https://doi.org/10.1007/978-3-319-19084-6_29

26. Munos, R.: Optimistic optimization of a deterministic function without the knowledge of its smoothness. In: Advances in Neural Information Processing Systems, pp. 783–791 (2011)

27. Muñoz, M.A., Sun, Y., Kirley, M., Halgamuge, S.K.: Algorithm selection for black-box continuous optimization problems: a survey on methods and challenges. Inf. Sci. **317**, 224–245 (2015)

28. Ochoa, G., Malan, K.M., Blum, C.: Search trajectory networks of population-based algorithms in continuous spaces. In: Castillo, P.A., Jiménez Laredo, J.L., Fernández de Vega, F. (eds.) EvoApplications 2020. LNCS, vol. 12104, pp. 70–85. Springer, Cham (2020). https://doi.org/10.1007/978-3-030-43722-0_5

29. Pedregosa, F., et al.: Scikit-learn: machine learning in Python. JMLR **12**, 2825–2830 (2011)

30. Petković, M., Kocev, D., Džeroski, S.: Feature ranking for multi-target regression. Mach. Learn. **109**(6), 1179–1204 (2020)

31. Pitra, Z., Repický, J., Holena, M.: Landscape analysis of Gaussian process surrogates for the covariance matrix adaptation evolution strategy. In: GECCO, pp. 691–699. ACM (2019)

32. Renau, Q., Doerr, C., Dreo, J., Doerr, B.: Exploratory landscape analysis is strongly sensitive to the sampling strategy. In: Bäck, T., et al. (eds.) PPSN 2020. LNCS, vol. 12270, pp. 139–153. Springer, Cham (2020). https://doi.org/10.1007/978-3-030-58115-2_10

33. Rice, J.R.: The algorithm selection problem. Advances in Computers, vol. 15, pp. 65–118. Elsevier (1976)

34. Robnik-Šikonja, M., Kononenko, I.: Theoretical and empirical analysis of ReliefF and RReliefF. Mach. Learn. **53**(1–2), 23–69 (2003)

35. Skvorc, U., Eftimov, T., Korosec, P.: Understanding the problem space in single-objective numerical optimization using exploratory landscape analysis. Appl. Soft Comput. **90**, (2020)

36. Zhao, J., et al.: Learning from longitudinal data in electronic health record and genetic data to improve cardiovascular event prediction. Sci. Rep. **9**(1), 1–10 (2019)

Demonstrating the Evolution of GANs Through t-SNE

Victor Costa[✉], Nuno Lourenço, João Correia, and Penousal Machado

CISUC, Department of Informatics Engineering, University of Coimbra,
Coimbra, Portugal
{vfc,naml,jncor,machado}@dei.uc.pt

Abstract. Generative Adversarial Networks (GANs) are powerful generative models that achieved strong results, mainly in the image domain. However, the training of GANs is not trivial, presenting some challenges tackled by different strategies. Evolutionary algorithms, such as COEGAN, were recently proposed as a solution to improve the GAN training, overcoming common problems that affect the model, such as vanishing gradient and mode collapse. In this work, we propose an evaluation method based on t-distributed Stochastic Neighbour Embedding (t-SNE) to assess the progress of GANs and visualize the distribution learned by generators in training. We propose the use of the feature space extracted from trained discriminators to evaluate samples produced by generators and from the input dataset. A metric based on the resulting t-SNE maps and the Jaccard index is proposed to represent the model quality. Experiments were conducted to assess the progress of GANs when trained using COEGAN. The results show both by visual inspection and metrics that the Evolutionary Algorithm gradually improves discriminators and generators through generations, avoiding problems such as mode collapse.

Keywords: Neuroevolution · Coevolution · Generative Adversarial Networks

1 Introduction

Generative Adversarial Networks (GANs) [12] gained relevance in the past years for producing impressive results in the context of images. The GAN model uses adversarial training to achieve strong discriminative and generative components. The typical model is comprised of two neural networks: a generator and a discriminator. These networks compete in a unified training process where the generator uses its neural network to produce samples and the discriminator tries to classify these samples as fake or real (i.e., drawn from the input dataset). Although the discriminator trained by a GAN also represents an important outcome of the training process, GANs are mostly used as a generative model to produce innovative samples based on an input distribution.

© Springer Nature Switzerland AG 2021
P. A. Castillo and J. L. Jiménez Laredo (Eds.): EvoApplications 2021, LNCS 12694, pp. 618–633, 2021.
https://doi.org/10.1007/978-3-030-72699-7_39

Despite the progress regarding generative models, the training of GANs is challenging and is affected by some well-known issues, such as the vanishing gradient and mode collapse [6,10]. Therefore, a trial-and-error approach is usually applied to obtain the expected results, making the training of GANs an uncertain process. The vanishing gradient and the mode collapse problems are related to the balance between the discriminator and the generator. Vanishing gradient occurs when the discriminator or generator becomes much more powerful than the other, leading to stagnation of training. Mode collapse occurs when the generator captures only a small fraction of the input distribution.

Several improvements were proposed for the initial GAN model. These proposals aim not only to improve the GAN training but also to produce more realistic results, focusing on two aspects of GANs: loss functions and architectural mechanisms of the neural networks. Therefore, more efficient loss functions and architectural improvements were proposed, such as WGAN [2], BEGAN [5], LSGAN [21], SN-GAN [23], StyleGAN [16], and DCGAN [24]. However, stability issues in GAN training are still present.

Neuroevolution is an approach used to design and optimize neural networks through the application of evolutionary algorithms [22,28,33]. These algorithms are based on the evolutionary mechanism found in nature, evolving a population of individuals through selective pressure, leading to the discovery of efficient solutions for a certain problem [27]. Recently, a combination of evolutionary algorithms and GANs were proposed to improve the original model. Progress was made in both the resulting quality of the outcome and the stability of the GAN training. Methods such as E-GAN [31], Pareto GAN [11], Lipizzaner [1], Mustangs [30], and COEGAN [7,9] use different approaches to apply Evolutionary Algorithms on the training of GANs.

Coevolutionary GAN (COEGAN) [7,9] combines neuroevolution and coevolution on the orchestration of the GAN training. Namely, competitive coevolution is used to design the algorithm in order to produce evolutionary pressure and overcome the stability issues affecting the training of GANs. The authors showed through experimental analysis that the method was able to discover efficient models for GANs in different datasets [7].

We propose in this paper a new method to evaluate the progress of GANs during the training process. Therefore, we design an evaluation method that uses t-distributed Stochastic Neighbour Embedding (t-SNE) [20] to visualize and quantify the performance of discriminators and generators during the evolutionary process. For this, we use the feature space produced by discriminators to analyze images produced by generators and drawn from the input dataset. The t-SNE algorithm was fed with this feature space in order to distribute those images in a two-dimensional grid. A metric based on the Jaccard index in the resulting t-SNE maps was proposed to quantify the performance achieved by GAN models.

This evaluation method was applied to analyze the evolution of discriminators and generators in COEGAN. The experiments evidenced that the distribution of samples produced by our evaluation method is able to create a consistent visualization of the evolutionary process in COEGAN. The results provide additional evidence of the evolution of generators and discriminators achieved by COEGAN.

The remainder of this paper is organized as follows: Sect. 2 introduces t-SNE, GANs, and neuroevolution, presenting state-of-the-art works using these concepts; Sect. 3 summarizes the COEGAN algorithm; Sect. 4 presents the method proposed in this work to evaluate the progress of discriminators and generators; Sect. 5 displays the experimental results of COEGAN using our evaluation method; finally, Sect. 6 presents our conclusions and future work.

2   Background and Related Works

In this section, we present the concepts used in this work to develop the evaluation method and apply it in Evolutionary Algorithms. Therefore, we will introduce concepts of neuroevolution and GANs. We will also describe works proposed to use Evolutionary Algorithms in the training of GANs. Finally, we describe the t-SNE algorithm and show works using it to represent and evaluate data distributions.

2.1   Neuroevolution

Evolutionary Algorithms find inspiration in nature to design mechanisms based on biological evolution [27]. Several strategies to apply these evolution mechanisms were proposed in the literature, offering new perspectives to solve a variety of problems. In general, Evolutionary Algorithms use a population of potential solutions to solve a defined problem, using variation operators and selective pressure to adapt individuals toward the target. Thus, each solution is an individual represented through an abstraction called genotype. The genotype transformation derives the concrete solution, called phenotype.

Neuroevolution is the application of Evolutionary Algorithms to the evolution of neural networks. In this case, the genotype represents an abstraction for the implementation of a neural network. This representation can be direct, i.e., all nodes and connections of the neural architecture are encoded [22,28], or indirect, i.e., rules are specified to derive the concrete implementation of neural networks, such as in structured grammatical evolution [3,19].

Weights, topology, and hyperparameters can be evolved through neuroevolution [33]. Thus, the manual process used by researchers to discover efficient models can be transformed into an automatic process. It is important to note that the training of neural networks is a time-consuming task, impacting the performance of neuroevolution algorithms.

NeuroEvolution of Augmenting Topologies (NEAT) [28] is a well-known model that uses neuroevolution in the evolution of both weights and topologies of neural networks. The genotype is a direct representation of the neural network, where NEAT defines two lists for the genome of individuals: a list of neurons and a list of connections between these neurons. A further expansion of

NEAT was proposed to enable larger search spaces in DeepNEAT and CoDeep-NEAT [22]. In these models, the genes composing a genome are abstractions of entire layers, enabling the representation of deep neural networks. Deep neural networks became popular and achieved strong performance in several tasks. Thus, the need for automation became relevant to improve progress on deeper models [22].

2.2 Generative Adversarial Networks

In Generative Adversarial Networks (GANs) [12], two neural networks are used in an adversarial way in a unified training process. These networks are represented by one generator and one discriminator. The discriminator is trained with some input dataset and has to classify samples as originated from this dataset (i.e., real samples) or samples produced by the generator (i.e., fake samples). Thus, the discriminator outputs a probability of each sample belonging to the input dataset. On the other hand, the generator receives a probability distribution as input and transforms this input into fake samples similar to the input dataset. These fake samples are also used as input to the discriminator to evaluate their quality. This adversarial model leads to the creation of strong generative and discriminative models, taking advantage of these adversarial characteristics to progressively improve their performance. Generators trained by GANs produce high-quality results without losing the characteristics of the input data.

Figure 1 describes the interaction between discriminators and generators in a GAN when using a dataset such as Fashion MNIST [32].

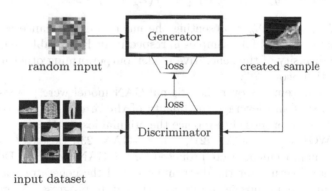

Fig. 1. Interaction between the components of a GAN during the training process.

The GAN training algorithm works iteratively. At each iteration, backpropagation is applied for training the discriminator and the generator with their respective loss functions in order to update their network parameters. The loss function of the discriminator ($\mathcal{L}_D^{GAN}$) is defined as follows:

$$\mathcal{L}_D^{GAN} = -\mathbb{E}_{x \sim p_d}[\log D(x)] - \mathbb{E}_{z \sim p_z}[\log(1 - D(G(z)))]. \tag{1}$$

For the generator, the non-saturating version of the loss function ($\mathcal{L}_G^{GAN}$) is defined by:

$$\mathcal{L}_G^{GAN} = -\mathbb{E}_{z \sim p_z}[\log(D(G(z)))]. \tag{2}$$

In Eq. (1), p_d represents the input dataset and x represents its samples. In Eq. (1) and Eq. (2), p_z is the distribution used for the generator, z is the latent space drawn from p_z, G is the generator, and D represents the discriminator.

GANs lead to relevant progress for generative models. However, the training of GANs is challenging, and stability issues frequently affect the process. Two common issues that impact training are the vanishing gradient and the mode collapse problem. The vanishing gradient occurs when the capacities of the generator and the discriminator are not in equilibrium, making one of them too powerful when compared to the other. Thus, the gradient does not properly improve the performance and the training progress stagnates. The mode collapse issue occurs when the generator fails to capture the input distribution used on training. In this case, samples created by the generator will partially represent this distribution. For example, the mode collapse occurs in a digits dataset when only some digits are represented in the set of created samples.

The Fréchet Inception Distance (FID) [14] is frequently used to evaluate the performance of GANs. FID uses the outcome of the last hidden layer in Inception Net [29] (trained on ImageNet [25]) to transform images from the input dataset and created by generators into a feature space. This feature space is interpreted as a continuous multivariate Gaussian, and the mean and covariance of the two resulting Gaussians are used to calculate the Fréchet distance as:

$$FID(x,g) = ||\mu_x - \mu_g||_2^2 + Tr(\Sigma_x + \Sigma_g - 2(\Sigma_x \Sigma_g)^{1/2}), \tag{3}$$

with μ_x, Σ_x, μ_g, and Σ_g representing the mean and covariance estimated for the input dataset x and fake samples g, respectively. FID is able to quantify the quality and diversity of the generative model, outperforming other metrics such as the Inception Score [26].

Several improvements over the original GAN model were proposed to minimize these issues and leverage the quality of the results. In this context, new loss functions were proposed to replace the original losses (Eq. (1) and Eq. (2)), such as in WGAN [2], LSGAN [21], and SN-GAN [23]. Besides loss functions, architectural improvements were proposed for the GAN model. In DCGAN [24], a reference architecture for the discriminator and the generator was proposed. In [15], the authors propose a predefined strategy to progressively grow a GAN during the training process. SAGAN [34] uses self-attention modules to model the relationship between spatial regions of the input sample.

These alternative loss functions and architectural improvements minimize some problems and produce better results, but issues still affect the training of GANs [2,13,26]. Besides, efficient models designed for a specific task are not guaranteed to work properly in other tasks. Thus, the discovery of efficient models and hyperparameters is not trivial, requiring recurrent empirical validation depending on the underlying problem.

2.3   Evolutionary Algorithms and GANs

Recently, Evolutionary Algorithms were proposed to train and evolve GANs. These solutions make use of different mechanisms of evolutionary computation not only to minimize stability problems in GANs but also to produce better outcomes concerning the quality of created samples.

E-GAN [31] proposes a variation operator that switches the loss functions of generators. The architectures of generators and the discriminator are fixed and based on DCGAN [24]. In [11], neuroevolution was used in combination with Pareto set approximations to evolve GANs. In this case, the architecture is not fixed and evolves through generations. Lipizzaner [1] uses spatial coevolution to train GANs. The architectures of generators and discriminators are fixed. A mixture of weights is used to compose generators through an evolution strategy based on their spatial neighborhood. In Mustangs [30], the Lipizzaner model was extended to combine the E-GAN dynamic loss function with the spatial coevolution mechanism from Lipizzaner. COEGAN [7,9] designs an algorithm that combines competitive coevolution and neuroevolution with the GAN training process. We provide an overview of the method in Sect. 3. A comparison between these algorithms can be seen in [8].

2.4   t-SNE

t-distributed Stochastic Neighbour Embedding (t-SNE) [20] is a technique used to produce a map (two or three dimensions) that represents the data distribution. Therefore, t-SNE is useful to provide the visualization of complex distributions by revealing the structure of the data. t-SNE was applied in a variety of problems from different fields [4,18]. It was also used to visualize the distribution of images produced by GANs in [35].

The t-SNE algorithm works iteratively. A set of pairwise affinities is calculated for the input data and the solution is randomly initialized using a probabilistic distribution. At each iteration, the gradient is calculated based on the Kullback-Leibler divergence between the high-dimensional input space and the corresponding lower-dimensional representation. The gradient is used to update the solution. After all iterations, t-SNE outputs the final solution, representing points in a two or three-dimensional grid for the input data.

The number of iterations and perplexity are two important parameters for the t-SNE algorithm. Perplexity defines how the neighborhood of each data point is handled. The range [5, 50] is recommended for perplexity. The number of iterations limits the number of steps used to update the final solution.

Principal Components Analysis (PCA) can be used as a preprocessing step to reduce the dimensionality of the data, suppress noise, and achieve a faster computation [18,20]. For example, PCA was used to reduce the dimensionality of the data to 30 and 50 in [20] and [18], respectively.

3   COEGAN

Coevolutionary Generative Adversarial Networks (COEGAN) algorithm combines neuroevolution and competitive coevolution on the training and evolution of GANs [7,9]. COEGAN was initially inspired by NEAT [28] and DeepNEAT [22] to develop a representation for neural networks. Nevertheless, COEGAN adapts the evolutionary model to the context of GANs. In this section, we describe the fundamental aspects of the algorithm. More details of the algorithm can be found in [7,9].

In COEGAN, a population of discriminators and another of generators are used in a competitive coevolution setup. At each generation, generators and discriminators are paired for the application of the original GAN training algorithm, using backpropagation to learn internal weights and bias of neural networks. COEGAN can be used with different pairing strategies. One simple strategy is the *all vs. all* pairing, which defines all possible pairs between generators and discriminators in the current population. Another possibility is to take only the best individuals for pairing. This strategy defines the *all vs. k-best* pairing, using the top *k* individuals from each population for the GAN training. For performance reasons, each pair in COEGAN is trained with a limited set of data at each generation. However, COEGAN reuses the weights and bias of individuals in the breeding process, resembling a transfer learning mechanism to obtain a full representation of the input distribution. The fitness of each individual is derived from the results of these matches between generators and discriminators.

3.1   Representation

In COEGAN, individuals use a genotype composed of a sequential array of genes. These genes are directly transformed into sequential layers in a neural network and can represent a linear (fully connected), convolution, or deconvolution (transpose convolution) layer. Each type of gene has internal parameters, such as the activation function and the number of output features, that are subject to the variation operators. Some internal parameters are dynamically defined at the phenotype transformation phase, making use of the setup of the genome to form a valid neural network for the application of backpropagation. Therefore, the number of input channels, stride, and kernel size are parameters adjusted based on the configuration of the previous layer for convolution layers.

Figure 2 illustrates the genotypes of a discriminator and a generator. In Fig. 2(a), the discriminator contains a convolutional section with two layers, followed by a linear section of a single output layer. This output layer returns the probability of samples to be real or fake. In Fig. 2(b), the generator starts with a linear layer followed by two deconvolutional layers. The last layer returns synthetic samples with the same characteristics (i.e., shape and number of color channels) as samples from the input dataset.

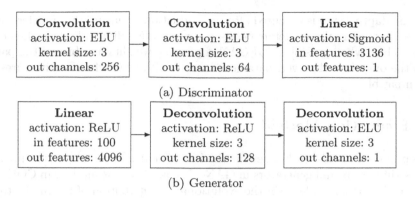

(a) Discriminator

(b) Generator

Fig. 2. Example of genotypes of a discriminator and a generator. The discriminator contains two convolution layers and one linear layer. The generator has one linear and two deconvolution layers. The parameters are listed for each gene (e.g., activation type, kernel size, and the number of channels).

3.2 Fitness

COEGAN uses specific fitness functions for discriminators and generators. The fitness of discriminators is based on the loss function of the original GAN model (Eq. (1)). The fitness of generators is based on the FID score (Eq. (3)). These fitness functions were chosen to produce selection pressure on the evolution of better individuals.

3.3 Selection

The selection mechanism in COEGAN is based on the speciation originally proposed on NEAT [28]. In COEGAN, a distance function based on the genome similarity is used to subdivide each population into species. Thus, individuals with similar neural networks have a tendency to belong to the same group. On the other hand, individuals modified by mutation can form new species, making use of speciation to protect their innovation.

In the selection phase, COEGAN uses the speciation strategy to select individuals for asexual reproduction. Individuals from each population are selected in proportion to the average fitness of their species. Tournament is also applied inside each species to finally determine the survivors.

3.4 Variation Operators

COEGAN uses only mutations as variation operators. Three types of mutations were defined with the purpose of adding, removing, and modifying layers. The addition operator randomly initializes a new layer and inserts it into the genotype. The removal operator randomly removes a layer from the genotype. The change operator modifies the internal attributes of a randomly selected gene (e.g., the activation function, number of channels, and number of features).

An adaptive step is executed after reproduction to ensure the transference of the learned internal parameters between compatible individuals through generations. Thus, when possible, COEGAN copies the weights and bias of the parent into the offspring. However, parameters are reinitialized when architectures are incompatible.

4   Evaluation Method

We proposed in this work a new method to visualize and evaluate the progress of discriminators and generators in GANs. We applied this method in COEGAN to provide further evidence of the evolutionary contribution of the model to the creation of strong generators and discriminators. Nevertheless, this method can also be applied in regular GANs (e.g., the original GAN model or WGAN).

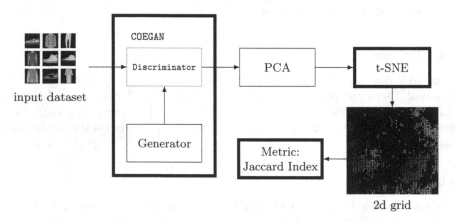

Fig. 3. Overview of the evaluation method proposed in this work to analyze the progress of generators and discriminators in GANs.

Figure 3 presents an overview of the evaluation method. We initially train COEGAN with the input dataset. After training, we use snapshots of the best discriminators and generators from different generations to visualize the performance through t-SNE. For the t-SNE calculation, we provide to discriminators samples from the input dataset and samples created by generators, using the output of the last hidden layer to construct a high-dimensional features matrix. To improve the performance, we apply Principal Components Analysis (PCA) to reduce the number of features and use the resulting matrix to fed t-SNE.

This matrix contains data from the input dataset and also from all evaluated generators. Thus, the resulting data of all inputs are jointly used for creating a lower-dimensional representation of the data through the t-SNE algorithm. Then, the output of t-SNE is transformed into a two-dimensional grid that spatially distributes the input images. This grid represents a map revealing the distribution of samples according to their inner characteristics. Thus, we can visualize problems such as mode collapse by inspecting the grid and ensuring that the distribution of samples is not concentrated in a single region. We can also visually compare the distribution of samples from the input dataset with samples from the generator to assess the completeness of the generative model. Furthermore, by using discriminators to transform images into a feature space, we also assess their capacity to classify samples.

Besides these visualizations, we also propose a metric to quantify the performance of the model. For this, given a map M^G of samples produced by a generator (in a specific generation) and a map M^d produced by the input dataset, we calculate the Euclidean distances $D_{(i,j)}$ between all samples in M^G and M^d:

$$\mathcal{D}_{i,j} = \|M_i^G - M_j^d\|. \tag{4}$$

Samples in M^G and M^d are not perfectly equal and distances in $\mathcal{D}_{i,j}$ are not zeroed. Thus, we use these distances to define a threshold for the similarity between samples. A global threshold τ is defined by the median of the minimum distances in $\mathcal{D}_i$ for maps M^G related to the last generation. This threshold defines the set of samples in M_G with corresponding samples in M_d as:

$$\mathcal{I}^G = \{M_i^G | \exists j, D_{i,j} < \tau\}. \tag{5}$$

The set $\mathcal{I}^G$ contains the samples in M_G that were successfully approximated by a sample in M_d, evidencing that this part of the input distribution was captured by the model. Thus, we consider this set as the intersection between these two grids and calculate the Jaccard index as:

$$J^G = \frac{|\mathcal{I}^G|}{|M^G \cup M^d|} \tag{6}$$

In this work, we use Eq.(6) to quantify the quality of models. A high J^G indicates that the generator was able to capture the input distribution successfully. On the other hand, a perfect score in this metric indicates that the generative model is not able to produce innovative samples.

5   Experiments

Experiments were conducted to assess the evolution of generators and discriminators in COEGAN using the evaluation method proposed in this work. The Fashion MNIST dataset was used in COEGAN training to gauge the characteristics of the proposed evaluation method.

5.1   Experimental Setup

Table 1 describes the parameters used in COEGAN, chosen based on previous experiments [7,9]. We train COEGAN for 100 generations in a population of generators and discriminators of 10 individuals using the *all vs. all* pairing strategy.

Table 1. Experimental parameters

Evolutionary parameters	Value
Number of generations	100
Population size (generators and discriminators)	10, 10
Probabilities (add, remove, change)	30%, 10%, 10%
Output channels range	[32, 512]
Tournament k_t	2
FID samples	5000
Genome Limit	4
Species	3
GAN parameters	Value
Batch size	64
Batches per generation	10
Optimizer	Adam
Learning rate	0.003
Evaluation parameters	Value
PCA dimensions	50
t-SNE Perplexity	30
t-SNE Iterations	1000
Samples per model	1000

The probabilities for mutations to add, remove, or change genes are 30%, 10%, and 10%, respectively. The genome was limited to four genes, representing a network of four layers in the maximum allowed setup. Only convolution and transpose convolution were used as options when creating new layers. This setup was sufficient to discover efficient solutions in the experiments with Fashion MNIST. We use three species in each population of generators and discriminators. The FID score was applied with 5000 samples to evaluate generators.

For each training pair where the GAN training is applied, we use 10 batches of 64 images and the Adam optimizer [17] with 0.003 as the learning rate.

In Table 1, we also list the parameters used in the evaluation method. PCA was applied to reduce the dimensionality of the data to 50. For the t-SNE algorithm, 30 and 1000 were used as perplexity and number of iterations, respectively. We use 1000 samples for each model and from the input dataset to obtain the two-dimensional map through t-SNE.

5.2   Results

First, we show the results of a single execution of COEGAN using the parameters defined in Table 1. Figure 4 presents the resulting map of images after the application of t-SNE with the feature map of the best discriminator at the last generation. In Figs. 4(a), 4(b), and 4(c), we can see the distribution of samples created by the best generators at generation 5, 10 and 100, respectively.

Figure 4(d) represents the distribution of the input dataset. Initially, at generation 5, samples are concentrated in a compact region of the grid, indicating that the distribution was not successfully captured yet. The distribution of samples improves at generation 10. At the final generation, we can see that the distribution of samples is similar to the input dataset. Therefore, Figs. 4(c) and 4(d) presents similar structure regarding the two-dimensional grid. Furthermore, the distribution of samples shows that the mode collapse issue does not affect the GAN model in this experiment.

We use the outcome of t-SNE to extract some metrics to quantify and represent the observations we made by visual inspection. For this, we calculate the distances between each sample created at generations 5, 10, and 100 with the samples from the input dataset.

We show in Fig. 5 examples of created samples and their respective nearest and farthest samples from the input dataset concerning the t-SNE map. We can see that the t-SNE map, calculated through the features trained for discriminators, is able to aggregate images based on the similarity. Thus, the neighborhood of a sample in the t-SNE grid contains images with similar characteristics.

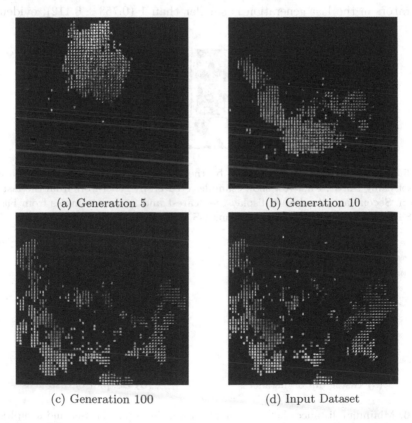

(a) Generation 5

(b) Generation 10

(c) Generation 100

(d) Input Dataset

Fig. 4. Two-dimensional grid revealing the distribution of images after applying t-SNE for generations 5 (a), 10 (b), 100 (c), and for the input dataset (d).

Figure 6 shows the distribution of the minimum distances between each generated sample in the last generation and samples from the input dataset. This distribution is used to calculate the threshold for the next step. In this case, we use the value of the median (0.0394) as the threshold.

This threshold is applied to get the intersection between the map of the input dataset and maps of generations 5, 10, and 100. We use the number of samples in this intersection to calculate the metric to quantify the progress of the model.

Figure 7 shows the Jaccard index (Eq. 6) between created samples and the input dataset for generators and discriminators at generations 5, 10, and 100 for ten executions. The results evidenced that discriminators in all three generations were able to identify poor samples produced by generators in generation 5. This is evidenced by the low Jaccard index, revealing that samples do not have strong similarities with the input dataset. For samples created at generation 10, we can see that more evolved discriminators are slightly more capable of identifying fake samples. Finally, all three discriminators were able to successfully distribute samples when evaluated with samples created at the final generation. Besides, more evolved discriminators are better on the distribution of samples, leading to better results concerning the proposed metric. As expected, the metric for generators in the last generation is smaller than 1 (0.753 ± 0.112), evidencing

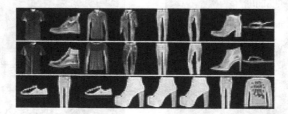

Fig. 5. Comparison of samples created by the generator and samples from the input dataset using t-SNE. First row shows samples created by generators from the last generation. Second and third rows display the nearest and farthest samples from Fashion MNIST using distances from the resulting t-SNE grid.

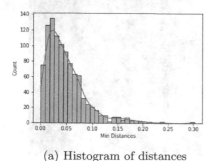

(a) Histogram of distances

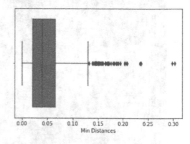

(b) Boxplot of distances

Fig. 6. Minimum distances between samples from the input dataset and samples created by generators at the last generation.

that generators are not only capable of capturing the input distribution but also to produce innovative samples.

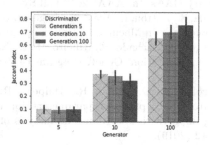

Fig. 7. Average Jaccard index (10 executions) for generators when comparing created samples with samples drawn from the input dataset.

6   Conclusions

In this paper, we propose a new evaluation method to assess the progress of generators and discriminators in Generative Adversarial Networks (GANs). For this, we propose a method based on t-SNE to visually inspect the quality of discriminators and generators in GANs. Furthermore, a metric based on the Jaccard index between t-SNE maps was designed to quantitatively represent the aspects of the model.

This evaluation method was applied to a GAN trained by an Evolutionary Algorithm to validate our proposal. COEGAN combines competitive coevolution and neuroevolution on the evolution of GANs and is capable of avoiding stability issues on training, using selective pressure to guide the progress of generators and discriminators. Therefore, we use this model in experiments to show the evolution of discriminators and generators through our evaluation method, providing further evidence of the evolutionary aspects of COEGAN.

Results demonstrate both by visual inspection and the proposed metric that COEGAN is able to gradually evolve GANs, avoiding problems such as mode collapse. We also show that the use of t-SNE proposed in this work can aggregate similar samples and provide their efficient distribution in a two-dimensional grid.

For future work, we intend to expand the experiments to analyze the results in more complex datasets, such as CelebA and CIFAR10. Furthermore, we expect to incorporate new mechanisms proposed for GANs into an Evolutionary Algorithm to assess the contributions of them when evaluated with our method.

Acknowledgments. This work is partially funded by the project grant DSAIPA/DS/0022/2018 (GADgET), by national funds through the FCT - Foundation for Science and Technology, I.P., within the scope of the project CISUC - UID/CEC/00326/2020 and by European Social Fund, through the Regional Operational Program Centro 2020. We also thank the NVIDIA Corporation for the hardware granted to this research.

References

1. Al-Dujaili, A., Schmiedlechner, T., Hemberg, E., O'Reilly, U.M.: Towards distributed coevolutionary GANs. In: AAAI 2018 Fall Symposium (2018)
2. Arjovsky, M., Chintala, S., Bottou, L.: Wasserstein generative adversarial networks. In: International Conference on Machine Learning, pp. 214–223 (2017)
3. Assunção, F., Lourenço, N., Machado, P., Ribeiro, B.: DENSER: deep evolutionary network structured representation. Genet. Program Evolvable Mach. **20**(1), 5–35 (2019)
4. Belkina, A.C., Ciccolella, C.O., Anno, R., Halpert, R., Spidlen, J., Snyder-Cappione, J.E.: Automated optimized parameters for t-distributed stochastic neighbor embedding improve visualization and analysis of large datasets. Nature Commun. **10**(1), 1–12 (2019)
5. Berthelot, D., Schumm, T., Metz, L.: BEGAN: boundary equilibrium generative adversarial networks. arXiv preprint arXiv:1703.10717 (2017)
6. Brock, A., Donahue, J., Simonyan, K.: Large scale GAN training for high fidelity natural image synthesis. In: International Conference on Learning Representations (2019)
7. Costa, V., Lourenço, N., Correia, J., Machado, P.: COEGAN: Evaluating the coevolution effect in generative adversarial networks. In: Proceedings of the Genetic and Evolutionary Computation Conference, pp. 374–382. ACM (2019)
8. Costa, V., Lourenço, N., Correia, J., Machado, P.: Neuroevolution of generative adversarial networks. In: Iba, H., Noman, N. (eds.) Deep Neural Evolution. NCS, pp. 293–322. Springer, Singapore (2020). https://doi.org/10.1007/978-981-15-3685-4_11
9. Costa, V., Lourenço, N., Machado, P.: Coevolution of generative adversarial networks. In: Kaufmann, P., Castillo, P.A. (eds.) EvoApplications 2019. LNCS, vol. 11454, pp. 473–487. Springer, Cham (2019). https://doi.org/10.1007/978-3-030-16692-2_32
10. Fedus, W., Rosca, M., Lakshminarayanan, B., Dai, A.M., Mohamed, S., Goodfellow, I.: Many paths to equilibrium: GANs do not need to decrease a divergence at every step. In: International Conference on Learning Representations (2018)
11. Garciarena, U., Santana, R., Mendiburu, A.: Evolved GANs for generating pareto set approximations. In: Proceedings of the Genetic and Evolutionary Computation Conference, GECCO 2018, pp. 434–441. New York, ACM (2018)
12. Goodfellow, I., et al.: Generative adversarial nets. In: NIPS. Curran Associates, Inc. (2014)
13. Gulrajani, I., Ahmed, F., Arjovsky, M., Dumoulin, V., Courville, A.C.: Improved training of wasserstein GANs. In: Advances in Neural Information Processing Systems, pp. 5769–5779 (2017)
14. Heusel, M., Ramsauer, H., Unterthiner, T., Nessler, B., Hochreiter, S.: GANs trained by a two time-scale update rule converge to a local nash equilibrium. In: Advances in Neural Information Processing Systems, pp. 6629–6640 (2017)
15. Karras, T., Aila, T., Laine, S., Lehtinen, J.: Progressive growing of GANs for improved quality, stability, and variation. In: International Conference on Learning Representations (2018)
16. Karras, T., Laine, S., Aila, T.: A style-based generator architecture for generative adversarial networks. arXiv preprint arXiv:1812.04948 (2018)
17. Kingma, D.P., Ba, J.: Adam: A method for stochastic optimization. In: International Conference on Learning Representations (ICLR) (2015)

18. Kobak, D., Berens, P.: The art of using t-SNE for single-cell transcriptomics. Nature Commun. **10**(1), 1–14 (2019)
19. Lourenço, N., Pereira, F.B., Costa, E.: SGE: a structured representation for grammatical evolution. In: Bonnevay, S., Legrand, P., Monmarché, N., Lutton, E., Schoenauer, M. (eds.) EA 2015. LNCS, vol. 9554, pp. 136–148. Springer, Cham (2016). https://doi.org/10.1007/978-3-319-31471-6_11
20. Maaten, L.V.D., Hinton, G.: Visualizing data using t-SNE. J. Mach. Learn. Res. **9**, 2579–2605 (2008)
21. Mao, X., Li, Q., Xie, H., Lau, R.Y., Wang, Z., Smolley, S.P.: Least squares generative adversarial networks. In: 2017 IEEE International Conference on Computer Vision (ICCV), pp. 2813–2821. IEEE (2017)
22. Miikkulainen, R., et al.: Evolving deep neural networks. arXiv preprint arXiv:1703.00548 (2017)
23. Miyato, T., Kataoka, T., Koyama, M., Yoshida, Y.: Spectral normalization for generative adversarial networks. In: International Conference on Learning Representations (2018)
24. Radford, A., Metz, L., Chintala, S.: Unsupervised representation learning with deep convolutional generative adversarial networks. arXiv preprint arXiv:1511.06434 (2015)
25. Russakovsky, O., et al.: Imagenet large scale visual recognition challenge. Int. J. Comput. Vision **115**(3), 211–252 (2015)
26. Salimans, T., Goodfellow, I., Zaremba, W., Cheung, V., Radford, A., Chen, X.: Improved techniques for training GANs. In: Advances in Neural Information Processing Systems, pp. 2234–2242 (2016)
27. Sims, K.: Evolving 3d morphology and behavior by competition. Artif. Life **1**(4), 353–372 (1994)
28. Stanley, K.O., Miikkulainen, R.: Evolving neural networks through augmenting topologies. Evol. Comput. **10**(2), 99–127 (2002)
29. Szegedy, C., Vanhoucke, V., Ioffe, S., Shlens, J., Wojna, Z.: Rethinking the inception architecture for computer vision. In: Proceedings of the IEEE Conference on Computer Vision and Pattern Recognition, pp. 2818–2826 (2016)
30. Toutouh, J., Hemberg, E., O'Reilly, U.M.: Spatial evolutionary generative adversarial networks. arXiv preprint arXiv:1905.12702 (2019)
31. Wang, C., Xu, C., Yao, X., Tao, D.: Evolutionary generative adversarial networks. arXiv preprint arXiv:1803.00657 (2018)
32. Xiao, H., Rasul, K., Vollgraf, R.: Fashion-MNIST: a novel image dataset for benchmarking machine learning algorithms. arXiv preprint arXiv:1708.07747 (2017)
33. Yao, X.: Evolving artificial neural networks. Proc. IEEE **87**(9), 1423–1447 (1999)
34. Zhang, H., Goodfellow, I., Metaxas, D., Odena, A.: Self-attention generative adversarial networks. arXiv preprint arXiv:1805.08318 (2018)
35. Zhang, H., et al.: StackGAN++: realistic image synthesis with stacked generative adversarial networks. IEEE Trans. Pattern Anal. Mach. Intell. **41**(8), 1947–1962 (2018)

Optimising Diversity in Classifier Ensembles of Classification Trees

Carina Ivaşcu$^{(\boxtimes)}$, Richard M. Everson⬩, and Jonathan E. Fieldsend⬩

University of Exeter, Exeter, UK
{ci233,R.M.Everson,J.E.Fieldsend}@exeter.ac.uk

Abstract. Ensembles of predictors have been generally found to have better performance than single predictors. Although diversity is widely thought to be an important factor in building successful ensembles, there have been contradictory results in the literature regarding the influence of diversity on the generalisation error. Fundamental to this may be the way diversity itself is defined. We present two new diversity measures, based on the idea of ambiguity, obtained from the bias-variance decomposition by using the cross-entropy error or the hinge-loss. If random sampling is used to select patterns on which ensemble members are trained, we find that generalisation error is negatively correlated with diversity at high sampling rates; conversely generalisation error is positively correlated with diversity when the sampling rate is low and the diversity high. We use evolutionary optimisers to select the subsets of patterns for predictor training by maximising these diversity measures on training data. Evaluation of their generalisation performance on a range of classification datasets from the literature shows that the ensembles obtained by maximising the cross-entropy diversity measure generalise well, enhancing the performance of small ensembles. Contrary to expectation, we find that there is no correlation between whether a pattern is selected and its proximity to the decision boundary.

Keywords: Ensembles · Classification · Diversity · Cross-entropy · Hinge-loss

1 Introduction

A principal concern of supervised machine learning is to ensure a predictor demonstrates good *generalisation*. A predictor is considered to have the ability to generalise, if it has a good performance in predicting on unseen data drawn from the same process that it was trained on [1,2]. Ensembles are collections of predictors, each of which is trained on a different subset of patterns or features. Some ensemble methods such as bagging [3] or boosting [4] have been seen to be very successful in pattern classification tasks [5], and ensembles have been proven in general to predict better than a single predictor [6,7].

Electronic supplementary material The online version of this chapter (https:// doi.org/10.1007/978-3-030-72699-7_40) contains supplementary material, which is available to authorized users.

ⓒ Springer Nature Switzerland AG 2021
P. A. Castillo and J. L. Jiménez Laredo (Eds.): EvoApplications 2021, LNCS 12694, pp. 634–648, 2021.
https://doi.org/10.1007/978-3-030-72699-7_40

In this paper we consider classification of patterns $\mathbf{x}_n$, $n = 1, \ldots, N$ into two classes, the positive and the negative class. Each of the M members of the ensemble yields a score $y_{in} \equiv y_i(\mathbf{x}_n)$, $i = 1, \ldots, M$ indicating how likely it is that $\mathbf{x}_n$ belongs to the positive class, and the ensemble score $Y_n \equiv Y(\mathbf{x}_n)$, which may be converted to a decision by thresholding is, in general, the weighted average of the constituent predictor scores [8]:

$$Y_n \equiv Y(\mathbf{x}_n) = \sum_{i=1}^{M} c_i y_{in} \tag{1}$$

where c_i are the non-negative weights assigned to the constituent ensemble members, $\sum_i^M c_i = 1$. Here we assume throughout that the ensemble members carry equal weight so that $c_i = 1/M$ for all i. When the constituent classifiers produce a hard decision and the weights are equal this amounts to the often used majority voting.

Various methods for assigning the classifier weights have been developed in [9–12]. Linear combinations have been mathematically investigated in [13, 14], together with nonlinear methods utilising rank-based information in [15], belief-based methods in [16–18] and voting schemes in [19,20]. Here, however, we assume that the predictors are equally weighted and focus on the choice of patterns on which the ensemble members are trained.

Clearly, an accurate ensemble requires accurate members. However, Krogh and Vedelsby [21] have proven that an ensemble with good generalisation performance consists of members which disagree in their predictions [22]. As a result, diversity and accuracy are key factors in building successful ensembles.

Although the role of diversity has long been recognised, many ways of quantifying the diversity of an ensemble have been proposed. Kuncheva and Whitaker [23] empirically compared different diversity measures in order to assess the impact that diversity has on an ensemble's generalisation performance. However, their results could not support the influence of diversity on the overall performance of the ensembles. This aspect was partially explained in [24], which showed that different diversity measures have different degrees of correlation with generalisation error. It was also shown that there tends only to be high (negative) correlation between diversity and generalisation error when diversity is low and generalisation error is high; as diversity increases the correlation with generalisation error decreases [24]. We explore this aspect in more detail below.

In [21] Krogh and Vedelsby introduced a new diversity measure based on the ambiguity decomposition of regression ensembles and the bias-variance decomposition. The ambiguity term is obtained by subtracting the ensemble error from the average error of the predictors. Since the ambiguity is necessarily positive, this property shows the usefulness of the ensembles, since the ensemble error is lower than the average error of the classifiers. The ambiguity measures how much the predictions of the ensemble members differ from the ensemble prediction and as a result can be considered a type of diversity. Chen [24] defined another ambiguity measure in a similar fashion as to [21], but for classifiers and using the 0–1 loss. In his work, Chen demonstrated that out of all the diversity measures tested (Q-statistics, Kappa statistics, Correlation coefficient, Disagreement, Entropy, Kohavi-Wolpert variance, the measure of difficulty, generalised diversity, coincident failure diversity), the ambiguity measure had the highest correlation with the generalisation error [24]. In this paper we use the term *ambiguity* to refer to a measure of ensemble diversity.

Here we further explore the connection between ensemble diversity and generalisation error. Following [21,24], we define and characterise new ambiguity measures appropriate for the log loss and hinge loss. We investigate empirically the relationship between the ambiguity and the generalisation error. This leads to an evolutionary algorithm for the direct maximisation of the ensemble ambiguity, and thus generalisation error, by optimisation of the patterns that each ensemble member is trained on.

The principal contributions of our work are as follows:

1. the derivation of a cross-entropy-based ambiguity measure for ensemble diversity;
2. the derivation of a hinge-loss-based ambiguity measure for ensemble diversity;
3. the empirical assessment of the ambiguity/generalisation error trade-off on a number of widely used classification data sets, using decision trees ensembles;
4. the exploration of the effect of ensemble sampling rates on this trade-off;
5. the exploration of the direct *maximisation* of ensemble ambiguity via an evolutionary optimisation of the training patterns to maximise generalisation performance.

In the next section we present different diversity measures for ensembles using log and hinge losses. Section 4 presents an evolutionary algorithm for the optimisation of the cross-entropy diversity. Section 5 illustrates the performance of the evolutionary optimiser on a range of classification problems. Section 6 presents the conclusions and the future work.

2   Ambiguity Measures

Extending the idea of quantifying diversity in regression ensembles [21], Chen [24] defined a new classifier ensemble diversity measure in terms of how diverse the outputs of the constituent classifiers are compared with the ensemble prediction. Following this line, we define new diversity measures as the difference between the average error of the individual classifiers forming the ensemble and the ensemble error; that is we define the ambiguity through the simple relation:

$$\text{Ensemble error} \quad = \quad \text{Average error} \quad - \quad \text{Ambiguity} \tag{2}$$

In line with [24], we call these measures of diversity *ambiguity measures*.

We first review the ambiguity for the 0–1 loss [24], before defining new ambiguities for the log loss and hinge loss.

2.1 Ambiguity Measure for 0–1 Loss

Here we assume that the targets, the true classes against which the classifiers are trained, are $t_n \in \{-1, +1\}$, $n = 1, \ldots, N$. Then the ensemble prediction for patterns $\mathbf{x}_n$ is

$$Y_n = \text{sign}\left(\sum_{i=1}^{M} c_i y_i(\mathbf{x}_n)\right) \tag{3}$$

and the error or loss for the ensemble classifying $\mathbf{x}_n$ is thus

$$L_{01}(Y_n \cdot t_n) = \begin{cases} 0 & \text{if } Y_n \cdot t_n \geq 0 \\ 1 & \text{if } Y_n \cdot t_n < 0. \end{cases} \tag{4}$$

We denote the outputs of the ensemble members when classifying patterns $\mathbf{x}_n$ by $\mathcal{Y}_n = \{y_{in} = y_i(\mathbf{x}_n)\}_{i=1}^{M}$. Then, using (2), the corresponding ambiguity in the ensemble when classifying a single $(\mathbf{x}_n, t_n)$ pair is thus [24]:

$$\text{amb}_{01}(\mathcal{Y}_n) = \frac{1}{2}\sum_{i=1}^{M}(\frac{1}{M}Y_n - c_i y_{in})t_n. \tag{5}$$

The ambiguity of the ensemble for a dataset of N patterns is just the ambiguity for each pattern averaged over the N patterns.

$$\text{amb}(\mathcal{Y}) = \frac{1}{N}\sum_{n=1}^{N}\text{amb}(\mathcal{Y}_n) \tag{6}$$

for the 0–1 loss and the other losses which we consider. It can be shown that (see Supplementary Material) the 0–1 ambiguity is zero if and only if all the ensemble members agree on the classification of a pattern, that is $\text{amb}_{01}(\mathcal{Y}_n) = 0 \Leftrightarrow y_{in} = y_{jn} \; \forall 1 \leq i, j \leq M$. We note, however, that $\text{amb}_{01}(\mathcal{Y}_n) < 0$ if $Y_n \neq t_n$ so that the ambiguity is negative if the ensemble classification is incorrect.

2.2 Ambiguity Measure for Log Loss

The cross-entropy error or log loss measures the discrepancy between the output of the classifier and the true class when the classifier produces an output between 0 and 1 which may be interpreted as a posterior probability; for convenience we denote the classes as 0 and 1, $t_n \in \{0, 1\}$. We can express the loss for the ith classifier on the nth pattern as:

$$L_{log}(y_{in}, t_n) = -[t_n \log(y_{in}) + (1 - t_n)\log(1 - y_{in})] \tag{7}$$

where y_{in} is the probability prediction of the ith classifier for the nth pattern belonging to the positive class. The error made by the ensemble for the nth pattern is therefore quantified as:

$$L_{log}(Y_n, t_n) = -[t_n \log(Y_n) + (1 - t_n)\log(1 - Y_n)]. \tag{8}$$

Again defining the ambiguity as the difference between the average loss of each member of the ensemble and the ensemble loss we obtain the cross-entropy ambiguity for a single pattern:

$$\text{amb}_{CE}(\mathcal{Y}_n) = \sum_{i=1}^{M} c_i L_{log}(y_{in}, t_n) - L_{log}(Y_n, t_n). \tag{9}$$

Using Eqs. (7), (8) and (9), we obtain:

$$\text{amb}_{CE}(\mathcal{Y}_n) \triangleq t_n \log\left(\frac{\sum_{i=1}^{M} c_i y_{in}}{\prod_{i=1}^{M} y_{in}^{c_i}}\right) + (1 - t_n) \log\left(\frac{\sum_{i=1}^{M} c_i(1 - y_{in})}{\prod_{i=1}^{M}(1 - y_{in})^{c_i}}\right). \tag{10}$$

Note that for any t_n only one of the terms will not be zero, so $\text{amb}_{CE}(\mathcal{Y}_n)$ is the logarithm of the ratio between the arithmetic and geometric means of the proximity of the classifiers' outputs to the desired targets. The cross entropy ambiguity for many patterns is just the ambiguity averaged over patterns (6).

We note Woodhouse [25] shows that the ratio of the arithmetic mean to the geometric mean is equivalent to a cross-entropy quantifying the amount of information added in an image processing problem. In addition in [26] the ratio of the arithmetic to geometric mean is used to measure homogeneity.

Using the inequality between arithmetic and geometric means, namely that the arithmetic mean is greater than or equal to the geometric mean, it can be seen that $\text{amb}_{CE}(\mathcal{Y}_n) \geq 0$ for any input pattern. It can also be shown that $\text{amb}_{CE}(\mathcal{Y}_n) = 0$ if and only if all the constituent classifiers agree, $y_{in} = y_{jn}$ $\forall 1 \leq i, j \leq M$.

2.3 Ambiguity Measure for Hinge Loss

Following the same route, an ambiguity measure can be obtained appropriate for the hinge loss. The hinge-loss is defined as:

$$L_H(y_{in}, t_n) = \max(0, 1 - t_n y_{in}). \tag{11}$$

Here y_{in} is the ith classifier score for the nth pattern and t_n is the target, where it is convenient to label the targets as $\{\pm 1\}$. The ambiguity measure obtained for the hinge loss is obtained by straightforward substitution, resulting in the following:

$$\text{amb}_{HL}(\mathcal{Y}_n) = \sum_{i=1}^{M} c_i \max(0, 1 - t_n y_{in}) - \max\left(0, \sum_{i=1}^{M} c_i(1 - t_n y_{in})\right). \tag{12}$$

As for amb_{CE}, the hinge loss ambiguity is non-negative: $\text{amb}_{HL}(\mathcal{Y}) \geq 0 \,\forall \mathcal{Y}$. However, while it is easy to verify that if all the component classifiers have the same score ($y_{in} = y_{jn}$ for all $1 \leq i, j \leq M$) then $\text{amb}_{HL}(\mathcal{Y}_n) = 0$, the converse is not true. This occurs when

$$1 - t_n y_{in} \geq 0 \,\forall i \in \{1, \ldots, M\}. \tag{13}$$

Inequality (13) can be satisfied when one of the component classifiers predicts incorrectly the class ($\exists i \in \{1, \ldots, M\} \, t_n y_{in} < 0$), whereas the others classify correctly the class, but with a score in absolute value lower or equal to 1 ($\forall j \in \{1, \ldots, M\}, j \neq i, t_n y_{jn} > 0$ and $|y_{jn}| \leq 1$). Proofs for the formulae of the ambiguity measures and their properties are presented in the Supplementary Material.

3   Correlation Between Ambiguity and Generalisation Error

Previous studies have investigated the relationship between diversity (measured in a variety of ways) and the error/loss [23,24]. A negative correlation between generalisation error and ambiguity has been reported [24]. However, it is clear that this cannot be true across the entire range of ambiguity because it would imply that choosing the ensemble with the maximum diversity would minimise the generalisation error, but a maximally diverse ensemble (with no predictive power) could be constructed from learners that make random predictions. We therefore empirically investigate the relationship between the ambiguity measured on a *training* data set and the error/loss on a test data set (approximating the generalisation error).

Bagging was used in order to control the diversity by sampling different independent samples to train the classifiers in the ensemble. We use 30 sampling rates in the range [0.01, 1]. For each sampling rate an ensemble of decision trees, forming a random forest [3] was trained on the sampled patterns. From the 2000 available observations, 1000 were drawn at random and used for training, while the remaining 1000 for evaluating the generalisation error; the roles of the training and testing sets were then swapped and the corresponding ambiguities and losses calculated. This process was repeated 50 times and the ambiguities and errors averaged over the resulting 100 instances.

We used the GMM5 dataset [27] which comprises two-dimensional features generated by a Gaussian mixture model with 5 components (an extension of the 4-component model of [28]) allowing a large quantity of data to be synthesised and the Bayes error rate to be calculated exactly.

Figure 1 shows the variation of the generalisation error with the diversity of the ensemble measured on the training dataset for each of the ambiguity measures discussed. The first column of panels in Fig. 1 corresponds to a small ensemble of $M = 5$ trees the second column shows the variation for a large ensemble of $M = 100$ trees. Although there is considerable variation between the curves for the different ambiguity measures, they all display common characteristics. At high sampling rates the ambiguity and test error are negatively correlated, as also reported by [24]. In this regime, as the sampling rate increases member classifiers are trained on increasingly similar views of the data and therefore diversity decreases. Since the average error per classifier is approximately constant (because adding more data does not appreciably increase their accuracy), Eq. (2) shows that the ensemble error increases.

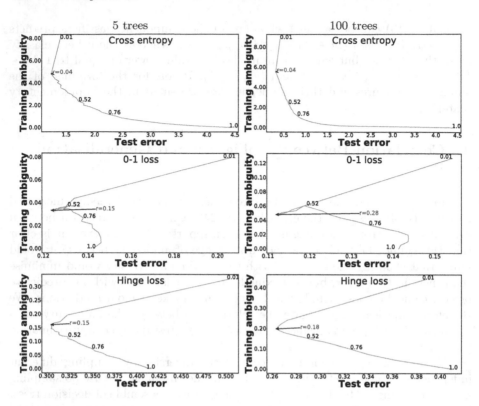

Fig. 1. Curves of the three types of ambiguities versus the corresponding losses that were derived from the ambiguity measures detailed in Sect. 2. The test error versus the training ambiguity was plotted for different sampling rates for ensembles formed of 5 trees (left column) and 100 tress (right column) for the GMM5 dataset. The first row shows the behaviour of the test cross entropy versus the training cross entropy ambiguity, in the second row the test 0–1 loss versus its corresponding training ambiguity is plotted, respectively the behaviour of the hinge loss is presented in the third row of panels. The optimal sampling rate (r) is indicated by an arrow. (Color figure online)

Decreasing the sampling rate means that the members of the ensemble are trained on different views of the data, leading to increasing diversity/ambiguity and therefore a smaller ensemble error cf. (2). However, as the sampling rate is reduced to even lower levels, each component classifier is trained on a very small number of patterns and therefore starts to become inaccurate. In (2) the average error increases more rapidly than the diversity and the result is that the ensemble error begins to rise again. Unfortunately, determining the sampling rate that yields the best generalisation error is not straightforward or susceptible to *a priori* analysis. In Sect. 4 we therefore describe an evolutionary algorithm to determine this rate.

The same pattern is apparent for both small ($M = 5$, Fig. 1 left column) and large ($M = 100$, Fig. 1 right column) ensembles, although the larger ensemble achieves a lower generalisation error. This generalisation error is very close to the Bayes error (0.11 misclassification rate) for this data set. It might be expected that the optimum sampling rate would be at least $1/M$, so that each classifier in the ensemble is trained on N/M examples and each example is used on average in the training of at least one classifier. However, as the panels in Fig. 1, the optimum sampling rate is well below $1/M$, meaning that some of the data is not used at all by the ensemble. This indicates the significant role played by diversity: to achieve best generalisation performance it is better to ensure diversity by exposing classifiers to very different views of the data than to better train them by providing more data.

Although only shown here for the GMM5 dataset we emphasise that very similar relationships between ambiguity and generalisation error were observed on a number of additional datasets (Table 1). We also repeated the experiments using sampling with replacement, but bagging without replacement in general yielded lower generalisation errors.

We also investigated the variation of generalisation error with the number M of classifiers forming the ensemble. This was achieved by generating ensembles with 2 to 100 members and training them, as before, with samples at a given rate. This was repeated 20 times for each ensemble size and sampling rate. The average (test) cross entropy error plotted against size of ensemble and sampling rate is shown in the panel of Fig. 2 for the Sonar data set (Table 1, [29, 30]). This figure plainly shows the benefit of a large ensemble: the optimum generalisation error with a large ensemble is obtained over a wide range of sampling rates. The average training cross entropy ambiguity is plotted against size of ensemble and sampling rate in the right panel of Fig. 2. These two figures together show the relationship between generalisation error and training ambiguity; high ambiguities yield lower test errors, provided the sampling rate is not too small. However, these two plots show the difficulty of predicting from the training ambiguity the optimal rate that will yield the lowest generalisation error.

4   An Evolutionary Algorithm to Optimise Ambiguity

As we have shown, provided that the sampling rate is not too low, the generalisation error is reduced for ensembles with high diversity. We therefore use an evolutionary algorithm to maximise the ambiguity of an ensemble of classifiers by selecting the patterns, that is the particular training examples, on which the constituent optimisers are trained. Pseudocode for the algorithm is presented in Algorithm 1.

We use ensembles of M classifiers, each of which is trained on a fraction ρ of the N available training patterns. In common with standard bagging ensembles, each of the classifiers is trained on all the available features. The patterns on which each classifier is trained is represented by a string of N 0s and 1s, where a 1 indicates that the corresponding pattern is used to train the classifier, so that there are exactly $\lceil \rho N \rceil$ 1s in each string and $[\cdot]$ indicates rounding to the nearest integer. The strings representing the training patterns are initialised

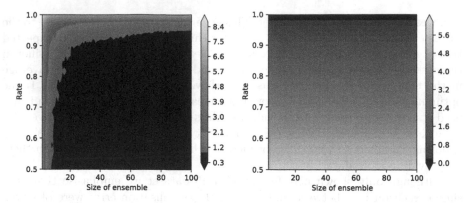

Fig. 2. The figure in the left of the panel represents the cross entropy generalisation error versus the size of the ensemble and the sampling rate. On the right hand side the training ambiguity derived from the cross entropy versus the size of the ensemble and the sampling rate is plotted. The plots were obtained for the Sonar data. (Color figure online)

using stratified random sampling without replacement so that the class ratios are preserved.

A single ensemble is evolved through mutation. Between 1 and M strings are mutated in one of two ways, chosen with equal probability (line 3 in Algorithm 1). Then a type of mutation is chosen with equal probability (line 5):

1. A proportion up to $\frac{N}{2}$ of 1s and 0s are flipped at random. This is performed in a stratified manner to preserve the class ratio and so as to maintain the sampling rate as ρ (line 6).
2. The current string is discarded and replaced with a new string chosen in the same way as the initialisation, preserving the class ratio and the sampling rate (line 8).

Following mutation the N_{pop} members with the largest ambiguity are retained to proceed into the next generation. In case of equality, the forest with the lower error will be preferred (line 10).

5   Experiments

We ran our algorithm on six standard classification datasets from the UCI Machine Learning Repository: Australian, Cancer, Liver, Heart, Sonar, Ionosphere [31] and an additional synthetic dataset GMM5 [28,32]. Table 1 summarises the dataset characteristics.

Since the result shown in Fig. 2 show that for large ensembles, the generalisation error is small for sufficiently low sampling rates, we concentrate on small ensembles. We used ensembles of $M = 5$ trees, which were implemented by using the `DecisionTreeClassifier` function from the sklearn library [33] in Python and the ambiguity measure $\text{amb}_{CE}(\cdot)$ derived from the log loss (10).

Algorithm 1. Evolutionary algorithm for evolving a diverse ensemble

Input: $X = \{\mathbf{x}_n\}_{n=1}^{N}$ ▷ training data
Input: $t = \{t_n\}_{n=1}^{N}$ ▷ targets
Input: M ▷ number of trees
Input: g ▷ number of generations
Input: ρ.   ▷ sampling rate
Output: $\mathcal{T}$ ▷ evolved forest

1:   $\mathcal{T} \leftarrow initialize(X, t, M)$ ▷ generate a random ensemble/forest
2: **for** $i = 1 \rightarrow g$ **do**
3:     $m \leftarrow random(1, M)$ ▷ choose m trees to be changed
4:     $indices \leftarrow indicesToChange(M, m)$ ▷ choose the indices of the m trees
5:     **if** $U(0, 1) < 0.5$ **then**
6:        $\mathcal{T}' \leftarrow mutate(\mathcal{T}, indices, \rho)$ ▷ mutation type 1
7:     **else**
8:        $\mathcal{T}' \leftarrow genNewTrees(\mathcal{T}, indices, \rho)$ ▷ mutation type 2
9:     **end if**
10:    **if** $(\mathrm{amb}_{CE}(\mathcal{T}') > \mathrm{amb}_{CE}(\mathcal{T}))$ **or**
       $(\mathrm{amb}_{CE}(\mathcal{T}') = \mathrm{amb}_{CE}(\mathcal{T})$ **and** $L_{log}(\mathcal{T}', t) < L_{log}(\mathcal{T}, t))$ **then**
11:       $\mathcal{T} \leftarrow \mathcal{T}'$
12:    **end if**
13: **end for**
14: **return** $\mathcal{T}$

Table 1. Dataset characteristics

Datasets	Patterns	Features
GMM5	1000	2
Australian	690	14
Cancer	569	10
Liver	345	6
Heart	270	75
Sonar	208	60
Ionosphere	351	34

Evolutionary Algorithm. Data was partitioned into the following stratified parts as follows: one half for the test data, a quarter of the data for the training and the remaining quarter for the validation data. The evolutionary algorithm was run using the training data and the resulting ensemble evaluated on the validation data. The forest with the sampling rate that yields the lowest validation error was evaluated on the test data to assess the algorithm's performance.

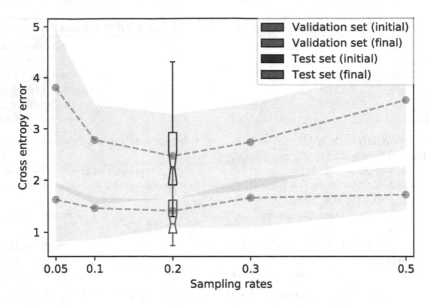

Fig. 3. Example results on the Liver dataset, using an evolutionary algorithm to optimise the cross-entropy ambiguity. (Color figure online)

Figure 3 shows example results obtained on the Liver dataset. The optimisation was repeated 30 times for each sampling rate and the figure shows the mean and interquartile range of the cross entropy generalisation error.

We compared the ensemble's validation error for the initial generation with the optimised ensemble's validation error, for the following sampling rates: 0.05, 0.1, 0.2, 0.3, 0.5. The (upper) green dashed line in Fig. 3 corresponds to the mean of the 30 runs for the initial population, whereas the (lower) purple dashed line represents the mean for the final population. Shading indicates the interquartile range. The (upper) blue box plot corresponds to the test error for the initial populations, whereas the (lower) red box plots represents the test error for the corresponding final populations. These box plots were generated just for the sampling rate that yielded the lowest average validation error.

We also performed non-parametric statistical tests to assess the significance of the results. We used the Wilcoxon signed rank two-tailed test, $p = 0.05$. In Table 2 the mean test error of the initial ensemble for the sampling rate that yielded the smallest validation error is shown, along with the mean test error of the corresponding final evolved ensemble. The values in the parenthesis correspond to the 25th quartile and 75th quartiles. These results show that, in general, the EA performs significantly better than the random sampling from the initial population, and never worse. The ambiguity optimised ensembles have lower test errors on average than the initial ensemble across all test problems.

Table 2. Results on datasets, mean over 30 runs given (lower and upper quartile in brackets). Bold mean value indicates significant difference (Wilcoxon signed rank two-tailed test, $p = 0.05$).

Datasets	Initial cross entropy	Final cross entropy
GMM5	1.32 (0.82, 1.75)	**0.73** (0.6003, 0.852)
Australian	1.35 (1.11, 1.52)	1.26 (0.92, 1.39)
Cancer	0.63 (0.35, 0.74)	**0.421** (0.32, 0.45)
Liver	2.41 (1.91, 2.92)	**1.37** (0.98, 1.61)
Heart	1.76 (1.195, 2.17)	**1.32** (0.94, 1.55)
Sonar	2.19 (1.52, 2.953)	**1.21** (0.91, 1.52)
Ionosphere	1.32 (0.97, 1.57)	**1.01** (0.83, 1.195)

What Patterns Are Selected? In our evolutionary algorithm we evolved the patterns that were selected in each tree. As such it would be interesting to see which patterns were actually chosen, and if they have any particular properties. In order to gain an understanding of which are the selected patterns, we analyse a two dimensional case.

A preliminary experiment was to plot the evolved patterns from the final generations of the evolutionary algorithm with their frequency of appearance. We performed this experiment just for the GMM5 dataset, because the distribution of these data are known and we have access to the posterior probabilities. We characterised the patterns according to their distance from the decision boundary. In order to determine how far a pattern is from the decision boundary, we calculated the maximum posterior probability of the pattern belonging to each of the two classes. The patterns belonging to the decision boundary have a minimum maximum posterior probability of 0.5. We averaged the number of appearances for the patterns from the final generation throughout the 30 runs. On the x-axis of Fig. 4 the maximum of the posterior probability for both classes for each pattern is represented in 20 bins. On the y-axis, the proportion of occurrences is plotted. The short horizontal lines (green) represent the medians of the number of occurrences for the patterns belonging to each of the 20 bins. This plot was obtained from the results of the evolutionary algorithm for the $\rho = 0.1$ sampling rate. Our results suggest that for this particular problem there is no preference for choosing some patterns during the optimisation, and that there is no correlation between whether a pattern is selected and its proximity to the decision boundary. This is contrary to what might be expected *a priori*—that is that points closer to the class boundary might be preferred as they give more information for bracketing the boundary.

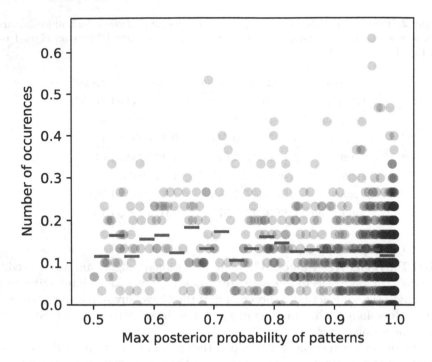

Fig. 4. Frequency of patterns selected by the evolutionary algorithm at the final generation for the gmm5test dataset, for the 0.1 sampling rate. On the x-axis is the maximum posterior probability of a pattern belonging to each of the two classes. The y-axis represents the average proportion each pattern was selected over the 30 runs of the evolutionary algorithm. The values from the x-axis have been divided into 20 bins. The short horizontal lines represent the medians of the number of occurrences of the patterns belonging to each bin. (Color figure online)

6   Conclusion

In this paper we introduced two ambiguity measures using the bias-variance decomposition and the cross-entropy error or the hinge loss. Together with the ambiguity corresponding to the 0–1 loss, we established the properties of these new diversity measures. We evolved the training patterns of the classifiers in order to maximise the ambiguity obtained from the cross-entropy (amb_{CE}) and our results show that the evolved ensemble generally has a better generalisation error than the initial ensemble. Hence, our results support the influence that the diversity has on minimising generalisation error. Also the ambiguity measure obtained by using the cross-entropy error satisfies all the required properties of a diversity measure (being always positive and being zero if and only if the predictions of the classifiers are all the same). This property is not present in the ambiguity obtained by using the 0–1 loss (see [24]), which we find can be negative.

Our results show that if random sampling is used to select patterns on which ensemble members are trained, we find that generalisation error is negatively correlated with diversity at high sampling rates; conversely generalisation error is positively correlated with diversity when the sampling rate is low and the diversity high.

Also, we found that there is no correlation between whether a pattern is selected and its proximity to the decision boundary (at least for the problem we considered where we had direct access to the posterior probabilities and therefore could determine the 'true' decision boundary precisely).

Our experiments were based on random forests. Therefore a possible extension of our work would be to use other types of ensembles and classifiers. In addition, other methods of inducing diversity, such as selection of features and different models, could be investigated.

In our experiments the weights c_i of the classifiers were equal, as a result our future work will aim to optimise the weights of the classifiers in order to maximise ambiguity, without compromising the average error. Also some patterns have different ambiguities, so future work will focus on how to effectively select the most ambiguous patterns.

References

1. Bishop, C.: Pattern Recognition and Machine Learning. Springer, New York (2006)
2. Duda, R.O., Hart, P.E., Stork, D.G.: Pattern Classification, 2nd edn. Wiley, New York (2001)
3. Breiman, L.: Bagging predictors. Mach. Learn. **24**, 123–140 (1996)
4. Freund, Y., Schapire, R.E.: A short introduction to boosting. J. Japanese Soc. Artif. Intell. **14**(5), 771–780 (1999)
5. Tang, E.K., Suganthan, P.N., Yao, X.: An analysis of diversity measures. Mach. Learn. **65**, 247–271 (2006)
6. Tumer, K., Ghosh, J.: Error correlation and error reduction in ensemble classifiers. Connection Sci. **8**, 385–404 (1996)
7. Brown, G., Wyatt, J., Harris, R., Yao, X.: Diversity creation methods: a survey and categorisation. Inf. Fusion **6**, 5–20 (2005)
8. Tumer, K., Ghosh, J.: Error correlation and error reduction in ensemble classifiers. Connect. Sci. **8**, 385–404 (1996)
9. Benediktsson, J., Sveinson, J., Ersoy, O., Swain, P.: Parallel consensual neural networks with optimally weighted outputs. Proc. World Congr. Neural Netw. **III**, 129–137 (1994)
10. Hashem, S., Schmeiser, B.: Approximating a function and its derivatives using mse-optimal linear combination of trained feedforward neural networks. Proc. Joint Conf. Neural Netw. **I**, 617–620 (1993)
11. Jacobs, R.A., Jordan, M.I., Nowlan, S.J., Hinton, G.E.: Adaptive mixtures of local experts. Neural Comput. **3**, 78–88 (1991)
12. Lincoln, W., Skrzypek, J.: Synergy of clustering multiple back propagation networks. Adv. Neural Inf. Proc. Syst. **2**, 650–657 (1990)
13. Tumer, K., Ghosh, J.: Theoretical foundations of linear and order statistics combiners for neural pattern classifiers. Technical Report TR-95-02-98, Computer and Vision Research Center, University of Texas, Austin (1995)

14. Tumer, K., Ghosh, J.: Analysis of decision boundaries in linearly combined neural classifiers. Pattern Recogn. **29**(2), 341–348 (1996)
15. Ho, T.K., Hull, J.J., Srihari, S.N.: Decision combinations in multiple classifier systems. IEEE Trans. Pattern Anal. Mach. Intell. **16**(1), 66–76 (1994)
16. Rogova, G.: Combining the results of several neural networks classifiers. Neural Netw. **7**(5), 777–781 (1994)
17. Yang, J.-B., Singh, M.G.: An evidential reasoning approach for multiple-attribute decision making with uncertainty. IEEE Trans. Syst. Man Cybern. **24**(1), 1–19 (1994)
18. Xu, L., Kryzyzak, A., Suen, C.Y.: Methods of combining multiple classifiers and their applications to handwriting recognition. IEEE Trans. Syst. Man Cybern. **22**(3), 418–435 (1992)
19. Hansen, L.K., Salamon, P.: Neural networks ensembles. IEEE Trans. Pattern Anal. Mach. Intell. **12**(10), 993–1000 (1990)
20. Battiti, R., Colla, A.M.: Democracy in neural nets: Voting schemes for classification. Neural Netw. **7**(4), 691–709 (1994)
21. Krogh, A., Vedelsby, J.: Neural network ensembles, cross validation and active learning. Neural Inf. Process. Syst. **7**, 231–238 (1995)
22. Chandra, A., Yao, X.: Multi-objective ensemble construction, learning and evolution. In PPSN Workshop Multi-objective Problem Solving from Nature. In: Part 9th International Conference Parallel Problem Solving from Nature: PPSN-IX, pp. 9–13 (2006)
23. Kuncheva, L., Whitaker, C.J.: Measures of diversity in classifier ensembles and their relationship with the ensemble accuracy. Mach. Learn. **51**, 181–207 (2003)
24. Chen, H.: Diversity and Regularization in Neural Network Ensembles. PhD thesis, University of Birmingham (2008)
25. Woodhouse, I.H.: The ratio of the arithmetic to the geometric mean: a cross-entropy interpretation. IEEE Trans. Geosci. Remote Sens. **39**(1), 188–189 (2001)
26. Chen, C.C., Sen, P.K., Wu, K.Y.: Robust permutation tests for homogeneity of fingerprint patterns of dioxin congener profiles. Environmetrics **23**, 285–294 (2012)
27. Fieldsend, J.E., Bailey, T.C., Everson, R.M., Krzanowski, W.J., Partridge, D., Schetinin, V.: Bayesian inductively learned modules for safety critical systems. Comput. Sci. Stat. **35**, 110–125 (2003)
28. Ripley, B.D.: Neural networks and related methods for classification (with discussion). J. Royal Stat. Soc. Ser. B **56**(3), 409–456 (1994)
29. Gorman, R.P., Sejnowski, T.J.: Analysis of hidden units in a layered network trained to classify sonar targets. Neural Netw. **1**, 75–89 (1988)
30. UCI Machine Learning Repository. Connectionist bench (sonar, mines vs. rocks) data set. https://archive.ics.uci.edu/ml/datasets/Connectionist+Bench+(Sonar,+Mines+vs.+Rocks)
31. Dua, D., Graff, C.: UCI machine learning repository (2017)
32. Krzanowski, W.J., Fieldsend, J.E., Bailey, T.C., Everson, R.M., Partridge, D., Schetinin, V.: Confidence in classification: a Bayesian approach. J. Classif. **23**(2), 199–220 (2006)
33. Pedregosa, F., et al.: Scikit-learn: machine learning in Python. J. Mach. Learn. Res. **12**, 2825–2830 (2011)

WILDA: Wide Learning of Diverse Architectures for Classification of Large Datasets

Rui P. Cardoso[1]([⊠]), Emma Hart[2], David Burth Kurka[1,2], and Jeremy Pitt[1,2]

[1] Imperial College London, London, UK
{rui.cardoso,d.kurka,j.pitt}@imperial.ac.uk
[2] Edinburgh Napier University, Edinburgh, UK
e.hart@napier.ac.uk

Abstract. In order to address scalability issues, which can be a challenge for Deep Learning methods, we propose Wide Learning of Diverse Architectures—a model that scales horizontally rather than vertically, enabling distributed learning. We propose a distributed version of a quality-diversity evolutionary algorithm (MAP-Elites) to evolve an architecturally diverse ensemble of shallow networks, each of which extracts a feature vector from the data. These features then become the input to a single shallow network which is optimised using gradient descent to solve a classification task. The technique is shown to perform well on two benchmark classification problems (MNIST and CIFAR). Additional experiments provide insight into the role that diversity plays in contributing to the performance of the repertoire.

Keywords: Diversity · MAP-elites · Machine learning · Ensemble

1 Introduction

Deep Learning (DL) techniques have revolutionised the field of Machine Learning (ML) in recent years, providing high-performing neural network models for solving a number of complex tasks such as Computer Vision (CV) and Natural Language Processing (NLP). However, the best performing networks often have very large numbers of layers and millions of parameters, exhibiting a type of scaling that has mostly been vertical. Some DL algorithms run for days [18,19]. Amongst other things, this raises important questions regarding the environmental sustainability of DL methods [16]. As an alternative, *distributed* learning techniques have been proposed as a way of enacting *horizontal* scaling [22]. Often such methods involve training an *ensemble* of networks whose results can be aggregated in some manner. This has the obvious advantage that the ensemble can be trained in parallel, with the added benefit not only that ensembles are often much more accurate than the individual classifiers they encompass [3], but also that the individual members of ensembles do not themselves have to be complex or high-performing [6].

© Springer Nature Switzerland AG 2021
P. A. Castillo and J. L. Jiménez Laredo (Eds.): EvoApplications 2021, LNCS 12694, pp. 649–664, 2021.
https://doi.org/10.1007/978-3-030-72699-7_41

In this paper, we propose an algorithm called WILDA (Wide Learning of Diverse Architectures) that integrates ML and Evolutionary Computation (EC) to train a classification model applicable to the type of datasets used in DL. WILDA falls under the broad paradigm of Wide Learning (WL) [12,15,23] as a viable complementary alternative to DL. The approach first trains an ensemble of low-complexity artificial neural networks (ANNs), each of which extracts a feature vector from each data point. In a second phase, the features extracted from the ensemble are then aggregated in a single shallow model to solve the classification task. It is well understood that a necessary condition for good ensemble performance is that its members are both *accurate* and *diverse* [3]: although the former can be addressed through judicious training of each member in the ensemble using standard ML methods, the latter provides more challenge. To address this, we turn to a relatively recent class of algorithms from EC known as *quality diversity* (QD) algorithms [14]. These algorithms return an archive of diverse, high-quality solutions to a problem in a single run, where diversity is defined by the user with respect to features of interest. Here, we exploit the QD approach to generate an ensemble of shallow neural networks which are *architecturally diverse* yet each optimised with respect to the classification task. The features extracted from each network in the first phase are then used in the second phase to train a single shallow network to output the final classification. The resulting architecture is easily parallelised and quickly trained, unlike a typical DL model, which often uses a complex model on a single machine. Running the full method takes around 50 min.

The major contribution of the work is to describe the novel WILDA algorithm, which exploits the latest developments in EC to generate an ensemble of networks which are diverse w.r.t their *hyperparameters* and uses ML methods to optimise their *parameters*. The main goal is to develop a general model that can be easily applied to large datasets without specialisation and executed on standard computer architectures. As such, we do not expect to obtain state-of-the-art results that compete with methods that are specialised to specific datasets and extensively tuned. Instead, we aim to show that the method produces reasonable results without any specialisation to a dataset and gain insight into the factors that influence the performance of the method.

2   Background

Deep neural networks typically consist of large numbers of stacked layers of neurons. Layers can be different *types*, for example convolutional, dense, or pooling [8], and each layer can have a variable number of neurons. Network design is thus an optimisation problem, and as such, Evolutionary Algorithms (EAs) have naturally been applied to this task. For example, the evolutionary-algorithm-based Automatic Evolving CNN (AE-CNN) algorithm [19] achieves high performance on the CIFAR-10 dataset, however consuming 22 d of computational time on three Graphics Processing Units (GPUs). Using a surrogate model with an EA considerably reduces this time [18], but still requires 8 GPU days. Genetic Programming (GP) is employed by Suganuma et al. [17] to evolve a CNN, again for image processing, showing promising results although resulting in networks with over 1.5 million learnable weights.

The above approaches all use an EA to evolve a single high-performing network. In contrast, *ensemble methods* consist of building a set of models and then aggregating their outputs to form a collective prediction, rather than relying on the predictions made by a single model [3]. Although the use of ensembles is well known in classical ML, it is less used in DL. An ensemble method for image classification using deep networks [5] has been shown to provide excellent performance; the networks within the ensemble contain up to 152 layers each, contrasting to classical ML ensemble approaches which tend to consist of multiple but low-complexity models (e.g. Random Forest [1]).

The *diversity* of an ensemble is crucial to its performance [3] and hence is a key factor in its design. The relatively recent paradigm of *quality diversity* (QD) [14] algorithms within the EA field—which aim to find a maximally diverse but high-performing collection of individuals for a given optimisation task—thus appears ideally suited to this goal. Specifically of interest to this paper is the ability of QD methods to produce a diverse repertoire of optimised solutions in a single run. The methods have received much attention in the Evolutionary Robotics (ER) literature to evolve behaviourally or structurally diverse robots [2,10] but much less attention elsewhere[1]. A single example within ML [20] uses a QD algorithm (Novelty Search) as an approach to unsupervised feature learning in a method that continually accumulates features that make novel discriminations amongst a training set (with no regard to the classification task), showing that after generating approximately 3000 features, a simple two-layer network performed well compared to other shallow architectures. In this paper, for the first time we propose to use the MAP-Elites algorithm [10] to evolve a set of optimised architectures that are diverse w.r.t to their structure, as explained in the next sections.

3   Methodology

WILDA (Wide Learning of Diverse Architectures) uses a two-step approach to classification in which a diverse ensemble of shallow ANNs is trained in the first step (Sect. 3.2) and the features extracted by the ensemble are used in the second step (Sect. 3.4) to train a small feedforward ANN to provide the final result. This is based on the conjecture that a set of diverse features can be extracted from an architecturally diverse repertoire of ANNs, which can then be used to efficiently train a single shallow network in the aggregation phase. The process can be summarised as follows:

1. Apply MAP-Elites to discover a *set* of neural network classifiers which are architecturally diverse, each optimised for accuracy using gradient descent (Sect. 3.1, Algorithm 2)

---

[1] With the exception of a handful of papers in the combinatorial optimisation domain, for example [21].

2. Repeat step 1 r times, and then merge the r sets into a single archive (Sect. 3.3)
3. Extract a single feature from each network in the merged archive for each data point (Sect. 3.2)
4. For each data point, concatenate the features extracted in step 3 to form a single input vector (Sect. 3.4)
5. Train a single shallow network to output the desired classification using the input vectors from step 4 as input (Algorithm 5)

WILDA uses a hybrid method that combines an evolutionary approach (MAP-Elites [10]) with a traditional ML approach (gradient descent) for training each ANN (Algorithm 1). MAP-Elites (Multi-dimensional Archive of Phenotypic Elites) explores a low-dimensional projection of the space of *hyperparameters* which describe the architecture of the networks and returns an archive of structurally diverse networks. A gradient descent procedure optimises the *parameters* of each ANN discovered. The MAP-Elites algorithm can be run simultaneously on multiple nodes, resulting in n_nodes archives at the end of the feature-extraction phase. These archives are merged before running the aggregation phase, which provides the final classification. We first give an overview of the MAP-Elites algorithm before describing each phase in detail.

Algorithm 1. WILDA algorithm (high-level view)

---
procedure WILDA
    for $n = 1 \rightarrow$ n_nodes **do**
        $MAP_n \leftarrow$ MapElites()   ▷ generate n archives of diverse networks
    end for
    $mergedMap \leftarrow$ merge($MAPs$)   ▷ merge n archives into a single archive
    $features \leftarrow$ extractFeatures($data$, $mergedMap$)   ▷ for each data point, extract a feature vector from each network in the archive
    $aggregatedModel \leftarrow$ trainShallowNetwork($features$)   ▷ train single network to classify data
end procedure

3.1   MAP-Elites

Fundamentally different to a traditional search algorithm, the MAP-Elites algorithm provides a holistic view of how high-performing solutions are distributed throughout a feature space [10]. The method creates an archive of high-performing solutions at each point in a space defined by dimensions of variation chosen by a user, according to characteristics of a solution that are of interest. The resulting archive enables the user to gain specific insight into how combinations of characteristics of solutions correlate with performance. As the approach encourages diversity, it has often been shown to be more capable of fully exploring a search space, outperforming state-of-the-art search algorithms which are given a single objective, and can be particularly helpful in overcoming deception [14].

The standard algorithm is given in Algorithm 2. This is adapted for our purposes as follows. A solution consists of a PyTorch [13] representation of an ANN. We select three dimensions to characterise an architecture, namely the number of convolutional layers, the number of dense layers, and the maximum size (number of outputs) of any dense layer in the network, which together comprise the featureDescriptor. The algorithm begins by generating random solutions which are mapped to a grid that is discretised in each dimension into a fixed number of cells (representing possible values of each feature). The grid thus contains $|C| \times |D| \times |S|$ cells, where these values represent the total number of values permitted for the convolutional, dense and size dimensions, respectively. Following an initialisation phase, solutions are randomly selected from the grid, after which a *variation* operator is applied to generate new solutions. Child solutions are evaluated according to a performance metric and then mapped back to the grid according to their descriptor: a child solution replaces an existing solution in any cell if it is better according to its performance metric or may simply occupy an empty cell. The search process aims to fill the entire grid with solutions, each of which represents the best performing solution for a given feature descriptor. The precise implementation of each of the above steps is described in the next section.

Algorithm 2. MAP-Elites Algorithm, taken directly from [10]

---

procedure MAP-ELITES ALGORITHM
    $(\mathcal{P} \leftarrow \emptyset, \mathcal{X} \leftarrow \emptyset)$
    for $iter = 1 \rightarrow max\_iterations$ **do**
        if $iter < initialise\_iterations$ **then**
            $x' \leftarrow$ randomSolution()
        else
            $x \leftarrow$ randomSelection($\mathcal{X}$)
            $x' \leftarrow$ randomVariation(x)
        end if
        $b' \leftarrow$ featureDescriptor(x')
        $p' \leftarrow$ performance(x')
        if $\mathcal{P}(b') = \emptyset$ or $\mathcal{P}(b') < p'$ **then**
            $\mathcal{P}(b') \leftarrow p'$
            $\mathcal{X}(b') \leftarrow x'$
        end if
    end for
    return feature-performance map ($\mathcal{P}$ and $\mathcal{X}$)
end procedure

3.2   Feature-Extraction Phase

During the extraction phase, MAP-Elites attempts to find a set of diverse ANN architectures, each of which is optimised on a subset of the data towards solving a classification task of interest. At the end of this phase, a feature vector is extracted from each network for each data point, corresponding to the output of the second-to-last layer of each network as explained below.

Network Representation. An individual uses a list representation to describe a variable-length sequence of convolutional layers followed by a variable-length sequence of dense layers. Each layer has a random number of neurons, selected from a list of discrete values. Each dense layer uses a hyperbolic tangent [11] activation function. The last hidden layer is designated as the *feature layer*: the output of this layer is a binary vector which represents a feature extracted by the network to be used in the second phase (Sect. 3.4). As a result, this layer always has a fixed number of neurons, *feature_size*, set by the user according to the desired size of the feature vector. Finally, an output layer is added which provides the classification of the data point.

Variation Operators. Three new individuals are generated at each iteration by the *crossover* and *mutation* operators. Two children are generated by applying *crossover* to a pair of randomly selected individuals. The third child is generated by applying *mutation* to a single randomly selected parent. Crossover randomly picks two individuals, selects random crossover points among their dense layers, and swaps them accordingly. Mutation randomly picks a mutation point among the dense layers of an individual and either adds or removes a layer at that position. Note that crossing over two sequences of dense layers or removing a layer from such a sequence will, in the general case, require changing the input and/or output sizes of layers at the crossover/mutation point; when adding a layer at a mutation point, its size is given by the output and input sizes of the previous and following layer, respectively. For simplicity, crossover and mutation only operate over the dense layers of an ANN; since convolutional layers tend to have a non-decreasing number of channels, these operations would require modifying all layers beyond the crossover/mutation point, defeating their purpose [8]. However, as the convolutional layers generated in the initialisation process will be paired with different combinations of dense layers as a result of these two operations, this still ensures a diverse search process.

Performance Evaluation. To evaluate each individual, the single network encoded by the individual is *trained* for a fixed number of iterations (eval_iters) on a sample training set using a standard gradient descent procedure which minimises cross-entropy loss [11]. Its classification accuracy is then calculated on a sample test set, and this value assigned as its fitness, as described in Algorithm 3. The sample train and test sets are drawn randomly from the training data at each iteration; they are both 20% the size of the complete training data, which encompasses 60000 examples in the two datasets we tested (MNIST and CIFAR-10). For this reason, each node uses 12000 examples at each evaluation and may therefore only ever have a partial view of the data required to solve the task.

3.3   Distribution of Computation

As described in the introduction, one of the goals of WL is to be able to distribute the computation over multiple nodes to enable the model to be run in parallel. One approach to achieving this would be to segment the $|C| \times |D| \times |S|$ grid into sub-partitions and run each sub-partition on a separate node. However, here we adopt an approach described in [4], which proposes a fully distributed implementation of MAP-Elites designed to be run on a robot swarm. In this approach, each node runs its own instance of the MAP-Elites Algorithm 4. At the end of the extraction phase, all the maps returned are merged into a single map referred to in the QD literature as a global map of elites. In previous work [4], we evaluated multiple options for performing the merge step which inform our choice of two strategies:

1. merging without overlap: for each cell in the map, select the highest-performing ANN model found in that cell from any of the **n_nodes** individual maps returned
2. merging with overlap: for each cell in the map, return all of the ANNs found in that cell across all **n_nodes** maps. This means that a maximum of **n_nodes** $\times$ $|C| \times |D| \times |S|$ neural networks is returned

In both cases, the maximum number of models passed to the learning phase via the global map is N, where N is the size of the map (i.e. $|C| \times |D| \times |S|$). When merging without overlap, the procedure returns a maximum of N networks, maximising diversity. On the other hand, the merge with overlap procedure can return $>> N$ networks. In this case, the procedure selects the top N networks according to their fitness metric. This strategy can return multiple networks which map to the same cell, therefore favouring the quality of solutions over their diversity.

Algorithm 3. Calculating the fitness of an individual neural network and adding it to the map of elites

---

procedure TRAIN_AND_EVAL(m, $sample\_train$, $sample\_test$, ME)
    $c, l, s \leftarrow$ architectural features of m
    train(m, $sample\_train$)
    if $ME[c, l, s] = \emptyset$ **OR**
        accuracy(m, $sample\_test$) $> ME[c, l, s]$.fitness **then**
        $ME[c, l, s] \leftarrow m$
    end if
end procedure

Algorithm 4. Training loop for each node in the extraction phase

---
create empty map of elites ME
draw $sample\_train$ and $sample\_test$ from training set $\mathcal{D}$
for $initial\_size$ **do**
    $m \leftarrow$ generate random ANN model
    train_and_eval($m, sample\_train, sample\_test, ME$)
end for
for $extraction\_epochs$ **do**
    draw $sample\_train$ and $sample\_test$ from training set $\mathcal{D}$
    draw individuals x, y from map of elites ME
    $x', y' \leftarrow$ crossover(x, y)
    train_and_eval($x', sample\_train, sample\_test, ME$)
    train_and_eval($y', sample\_train, sample\_test, ME$)
    draw individual z from map of elites ME
    $z' \leftarrow$ mutate(z)
    train_and_eval($z', sample\_train, sample\_test, ME$)
end for

3.4 Learning/Aggregation Phase

The learning phase uses the information learnt by the ANNs contained in the repertoire resulting from the first phase to train a single model to solve the classification task. This single model is a fixed-structure shallow ANN that has a single intermediate layer with **n_hidden_agg** neurons and a hyperbolic tangent activation function. The node where this model is trained is called the *root node*. Note that, even though there is a global merged repertoire at the end of the feature-extraction phase, as described in Sect. 3.3, this repertoire contains only references to the models which were generated and trained in separate nodes and each of these models will still be running in its corresponding node.

Algorithm 5. Learning phase of the procedure for the **root node**

$all\_MEs \leftarrow$ gather_all_maps()   ▷ Root node receives all repertoires
$global\_ME \leftarrow$ merge(all_MEs).   ▷ Repertoires merged into a global map
send $global\_ME$ to the other nodes   ▷ Global map known by all nodes
initialise model M
for $learning\_epochs$ **do**
    for batched $data$ and $labels$ **do**
        $all\_features \leftarrow$ gather_all_features($data$)   ▷ Each node sends its feature
                                             vector extracted from $data$
        concatenate $all\_features$ into intermediate representation $\underline{f}$
        M.train_step $\left(\underline{f}, labels\right)$
    end for
end for

The phase begins with an extraction step: each data point in the training set is passed through each of the n networks contained in the merged map from the previous phase. This returns n binary vectors, each representing a feature (as described in Sect. 3.2), which are concatenated to form the input layer of the new model. This model is then trained with a standard gradient descent procedure by minimising cross-entropy loss. Algorithm 5 shows pseudocode for the learning phase specific to the root node and Algorithm 6 shows pseudocode for all nodes.

Algorithm 6. Learning phase of the procedure for all nodes (including root node)

---

send(ME, root)   ▷ Sends own repertoire to root node
$global\_ME \leftarrow$ receive(root)   ▷ Receives global map from root node
$own\_models \leftarrow$ get_own_models($global\_ME$)
for $learning\_epochs$ **do**
    for batched $data$ **do**
        $own\_features \leftarrow$ get_features($own\_models, data$)
        send($own\_features$, root)   ▷ Sends feature vector to root node
    end for
end for

---

4   Experiments

Experiments have been conducted to: (1) evaluate the performance of WILDA as a classifier on two datasets providing varying levels of challenge; (2) explore the effects of encouraging diversity vs. quality within an ensemble; (3) explore the influence of the size of the ensemble used to execute the centralised learning step.

Two well-known benchmark datasets are used: MNIST [8] and CIFAR-10 [7]. MNIST is a set of 60000 hand-written digits, while the CIFAR-10 dataset consists of 60000 32×32 colour images in 10 classes, with 6000 images per class. MNIST is known to be relatively straightforward for ANN architectures, while the latter poses a significant challenge to "off-the-shelf" models; state-of-the-art DL models for CIFAR-10 require significant customisation and tuning. Four sets of experiments are conducted as described below.

As a baseline for comparing the quality of the ensemble-based solutions from WILDA, we use a single shallow ANN, trained in a similar fashion to the aggregated single-layer model used in the learning phase of the algorithm (Sect. 3.4). This ANN is the one that has achieved the best performance after a run of the feature-extraction phase 3.2. Note that this is not a true "baseline" in the sense that we do not choose a random or otherwise uninformed architecture, but rather one that has been found to be the best. This is because we wish to understand the benefits of the ensembles built by our diversity driven approach; outperforming individual neural networks with the highest fitness values is therefore a more interesting challenge. Out of interest, the shallow network trained with diverse features mentioned in Sect. 2 [20] achieves an accuracy of 98.75% on MNIST, while a shallow CNN is reported to obtain 75.86% on CIFAR-10 in [9]. The relevant parameter values are set as per Table 1, which lists all the parameter values that are used throughout the experiments. All experiments, including the runs of the feature-extraction phase to get the baseline results, are repeated 30 times in order to evaluate statistical significance. Two-tailed Mann-Whitney significance tests are applied to compare experimental results, and noted as significant if the resulting p-value is < 0.01.

Table 1. Parameter settings

Parameter	Description	Value(s)
n_nodes	Number of distributed nodes	8
initialise_iterations	Number of ANNs in the initial maps	20
C	set of possible # of convolutional layers	{1, 2}
D	set of possible # of dense layers	{2, 3, 4}
S	set of possible values for layer size	{100, 110, 120, 130, 140, 150, 170}
max_iterations	Number of iterations in the extraction phase	30
eval_iters	Number of iterations in gradient-descent training in extraction phase	5
feature_size	Size of binary vector produced by last hidden dense layer in extraction phase	100
aggregation_iters	Number of iterations in the learning phase	10
n_hidden_agg	Number of neurons in the intermediate layer of the centralised model (learning phase)	50
merge	Strategy used to merge the maps of elites evolved by each node	*with/without overlap*
n_models	Maximum number of models to use in the learning phase (≤ the size of the map)	48

4.1 Comparison of Different Merge Strategies

This set of experiments compares the two merge strategies (Sect. 3.2) to understand how the construction of the merged archive impacts the performance of the aggregated model. For reference, a full run of WILDA with the parameters of Table 1 takes around 50 min on the machine upon which the algorithm was tested. Recall that the two strategies represent different trade-offs between diversity and quality of the solutions. The size of the maps evolved by each node, as well as the global map, is $2 \times 3 \times 8 = 48$; this is also the maximum number of ANN models used in the learning phase (n_models).

Table 2 presents the median test set accuracy for the two merge strategies and compares them to the baseline. Recall that the architecture of the baseline network is that of the best network found in a run of the feature-extraction phase, as explained earlier in this section. Both methods significantly outperform the baseline individual best network for both datasets ($p \ll 0.01$). There is no significant difference between the two merge strategies, however. A possible reason for this is that these two merge strategies actually lead to similar global maps of elites. On the one hand, each node might be finding high-performing ANNs in different regions of their individual maps, thus leading to few overlaps at a same cell when merging. On the other, it is possible that networks which are mapped to the same cell are still significantly diverse. Further investigation is required to answer these questions. We also include for interest the result obtained by Szerlip et al. [20] from first evolving 3000 divergent discriminative features, but note that the training procedure used in that paper differs from ours, which runs a two-phase procedure that first trains on a small training set before shifting to the full example set, using a single-layer network to classify. Our evolved ensemble of features obtained from 48 diverse networks outperforms both the single high-performing learner and the previously obtained result.

Table 2. Median test set accuracy for the two merge strategies considered

	MNIST	CIFAR-10
Baseline	0.9899	0.646
Merge without overlap	0.99175	0.6982
Merge with overlap	0.9919	0.6983
Divergent discriminative feature accumulation [20]	0.9875	n/a

4.2 Investigating the Role of Architectural Diversity

The global map of elites which is constructed from the individual maps and used in the aggregation phase is essentially an ensemble of the best ANNs found for different types of architecture. This naturally raises the question of how useful it is to promote *architectural diversity* amongst the networks in the ensemble, and how the performance of such a diverse ensemble compares with ensembles which do not have *architectural* diversity, but are diverse in terms of their optimised *weights* due to training on different samples of the dataset. Thus, we compare the performance of architecturally diverse ensembles evolved by WILDA with two kinds of ensembles that lack architectural diversity:

- an ensemble of networks in which every individual has the *best* architecture found in the extraction phase but is trained using a different sample of the training data

– an ensemble of networks in which each individual has the *worst* architecture found in the extraction phase but is trained using a different sample of the training data

Table 3 shows the accuracy results for ensembles trained with a fixed set of architectures (the best and worst architectures found in the extraction phase). All differences are significant compared to both the baseline and to both merge strategies ($p \ll 0.01$). It is clear that ensembles that do not have architectural diversity perform significantly worse than the results obtained by WILDA on both datasets. They also show that the fixed-architecture ensembles perform significantly worse than the baseline case. This is perhaps surprising given that the baseline case uses a feature vector from a single network obtained from the extraction phase. It appears that combining the predictions made by the best architecture trained on different subsets of the data leads to overall poorer performance than training an individual network on all of the data. This could be a particular characteristic of our procedure for aggregating the features extracted from the data by the ANNs in the ensemble during the learning phase, as described in Sect. 3.4. However, it is a clue that the ensembles may be accumulating and reinforcing prediction errors when there is a lack of architectural diversity, i.e. errors made on the same data or on data from which similar features have been extracted. The performance of an ensemble depends on the *diversity of errors* made by each of its learners [3]; the results of this section enable us to suggest that promoting architectural diversity among the ANNs in the repertoires built during the extraction phase of the algorithm drives diversity of features extracted from the data and diversity of prediction errors, which in turn leads to higher test set accuracy. This observation is of the utmost importance in informing future research into how to increase the performance of the diverse ensembles evolved by WILDA.

Table 3. Median test set accuracy for ensembles without architectural diversity

	MNIST	CIFAR-10
Ensemble of instances of the best architecture	0.98685	0.62835
Ensemble of instances of the worst architecture	0.97815	0.557

4.3   Investigation of the Influence of Ensemble Size

After constructing the merged map, one question that arises is how to use it to solve the task. We can simply pick the single best-performing architecture, as per the baseline case, or use an ensemble selected from the map. This raises the question of how many networks to include in the ensemble. This set of experiments assesses the relevance of fine-tuning the number of ANN models used in the ensemble by comparing the test set performance of ensembles of different sizes. We vary **n_models** (the size of the ensemble) in the range {10, 20, 30, 40, 48}, selecting the best **n_models** ANNs in each experiment. All the other parameters are fixed as per Table 1.

Figure 1 presents the performance results when only the **n_models** top-performing models from the global map of elites are used in the learning phase. In all cases the algorithm significantly outperforms the baseline and changing this parameter only produces small variations in accuracy. For MNIST, using only 10 models outperforms all other cases. The difference is statistically significant when compared with cases using 30 or more models. These observations suggest that using fewer models in the learning phase leads to better performance on the MNIST dataset. This could be because the simplicity of MNIST leads to smaller error diversity among different learners, which would cause the reinforcement of errors in larger ensembles. On the other hand, using only 10 models leads to significantly worse performance on the CIFAR-10 dataset than all other cases. This disparity in the observations for both datasets suggests that the choice of number of models that brings optimal performance is domain-dependent and must therefore be fine-tuned to the problem being tackled.

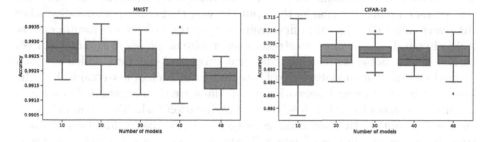

Fig. 1. Test set accuracy for each number of models added to the ensemble in the learning phase

4.4 Search Space Illumination

Figure 2 shows an example of how the extraction phase of WILDA, which runs a version of MAP-Elites, can *illuminate* the search space of architectures. For each combination of number of dense layers and maximum size of any dense layer, the diagram shows the fitness (accuracy on sample test set)—averaged out along the other dimension, which is the number of convolutional layers—of the best-performing ANNs on the CIFAR-10 dataset which map to that cell after merging all individual maps into a global map *without overlap* (Sect. 3.2). Note that more runs of the extraction phase would be required in order to draw conclusions about which architecture leads to the best performance.

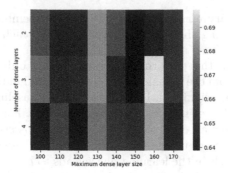

Fig. 2. Illuminating the architectures' search space for the CIFAR-10 dataset - the colour shading indicates the accuracy of the best network found for each cell

5   Conclusions and Future Work

We have presented an innovative diversity-driven distributed algorithm dubbed WILDA for training classification models within a WL paradigm. The basic idea is to extract a representation for the input in a way that scales horizontally rather than vertically. The algorithm first trains a repertoire of *architecturally diverse* ANNs in parallel: each node constructs a repertoire of high-performing, architecturally diverse networks, accessing different subsets of the data, which are then merged together into a global map of elite networks, each of low complexity. The features extracted by each network from the data are then aggregated and fed to a centralised model which will solve the classification task. The approach relies on the assumption that networks constructed with diverse architectures and trained on diverse samples of data will extract diverse features from a dataset, ultimately improving classification.

The overriding goal of the paper is to show that a general method that is easily distributed and does not require either vast amounts of computational power or expert knowledge to design a network is capable of reasonable performance. Experimental results show that this technique performs well on the MNIST and CIFAR-10 datasets and that a diverse ensemble performs better than the best individual model found in the extraction phase. We also show that architectural diversity is key to improving performance: ensembles using fixed architectures have been found to perform worse than an individual model, likely due to the accumulation and reinforcement of the same kind of errors. The results suggest that architectural diversity promotes error diversity, which in turn increases the performance of the ensembles evolved by the algorithm. Note that only basic tuning of the method was conducted and there remains considerable scope for improvement, for instance in investigating greater ranges of values for each of the dimensions over which diversity is defined, or adding additional dimensions of diversity within MAP-Elites; both would lead to an increase in the size of the map and therefore a larger potential space of networks.

We note that the algorithm can also be a useful tool for exploring and illuminating the space of hyperparameters in that it exposes correlations between the characteristics of different architectures and their performance. Moreover, we believe that the WL paradigm can complement current DL techniques, particularly when addressing issues of scaling and distribution. Finally, further work will focus on using QD methods to explicitly create an archive of diverse features, rather than implicitly relying on diverse architectures to do so.

References

1. Breiman, L.: Random forests. Mach. Learn. **45**(1), 5–32 (2001)
2. Cully, A., Clune, J., Tarapore, D., Mouret, J.B.: Robots that can adapt like animals. Nature **521**(7553), 503 (2015)
3. Dietterich, T.G.: Ensemble methods in machine learning. In: Kittler, J., Roli, F. (eds.) MCS 2000. LNCS, vol. 1857, pp. 1–15. Springer, Heidelberg (2000). https://doi.org/10.1007/3-540-45014-9_1
4. Hart, E., Steyven, A.S.W., Paechter, B.: Evolution of a functionally diverse swarm via a novel decentralised quality-diversity algorithm. In: Proceedings of the Genetic and Evolutionary Computation Conference, GECCO '18, pp. 101–108. ACM, New York (2018)
5. He, K., Zhang, X., Ren, S., Sun, J.: Deep residual learning for image recognition. In: Proceedings of the IEEE Conference on Computer Vision and Pattern Recognition, pp. 770–778 (2016)
6. Hong, L., Page, S.E.: Groups of diverse problem solvers can outperform groups of high-ability problem solvers. Proc. Natl. Acad. Sci. **101**(46), 16385–16389 (2004). https://doi.org/10.1073/pnas.0403723101
7. Krizhevsky, A.: Learning Multiple Layers of Features from Tiny Images. University of Toronto, Science Dept, Technical report (2009)
8. LeCun, Y., Bottou, L., Bengio, Y., Haffner, P.: Gradient-based learning applied to document recognition. Proceedings of the IEEE (1998)
9. McDonnell, M.D., Vladusich, T.: Enhanced image classification with a fast-learning shallow convolutional neural network. In: Proceedings of the International Joint Conference on Neural Networks (2015). https://doi.org/10.1109/IJCNN.2015.7280796
10. Mouret, J.B., Clune, J.: Illuminating search spaces by mapping elites. arXiv preprint arXiv:1504.04909 (2015)
11. Murphy, K.P.: Machine learning: a probabilistic perspective (2012)
12. Pandey, G., Dukkipati, A.: To go deep or wide in learning? (2014)
13. Paszke, A., et al.: Automatic differentiation in PyTorch. In: Advances in Neural Information Processing Systems 32 (2019)
14. Pugh, J.K., Soros, L.B., Stanley, K.O.: Quality diversity: a new frontier for evolutionary computation. Front. Robot. AI **3**, 40 (2016)
15. Shafaei-Bajestan, E., Baayen, R.H.: Wide learning for auditory comprehension. In: Proceedings of the Interspeech 2018, pp. 966–970 (2018). 10.21437/Interspeech.2018-2420. http://dx.doi.org/10.21437/Interspeech.2018-2420
16. Strubell, E., Ganesh, A., McCallum, A.: Energy and policy considerations for deep learning in NLP. arXiv preprint arXiv:1906.02243 (2019)

17. Suganuma, M., Shirakawa, S., Nagao, T.: A genetic programming approach to designing convolutional neural network architectures. In: Proceedings of the Genetic and Evolutionary Computation Conference, pp. 497–504 (2017)
18. Sun, Y., Xue, B., Zhang, M., Yen, G.G.: Automatically designing CNN architectures using genetic algorithm for image classification. arXivpreprint arXiv:1808.03818 (2018)
19. Sun, Y., Xue, B., Zhang, M., Yen, G.G.: Automatically designing CNN architectures using genetic algorithm for image classification. arXiv preprint arXiv:1808.03818 (2018)
20. Szerlip, P.A., Morse, G., Pugh, J.K., Stanley, K.O.: Unsupervised feature learning through divergent discriminative feature accumulation. In: Proceedings of the National Conference on Artificial Intelligence (2015)
21. Urquhart, N., Hart, E.: Optimisation and illumination of a real-world workforce scheduling and routing application (wsrp) via map-elites. In: International Conference on Parallel Problem Solving from Nature, pp. 488–499. Springer (2018)
22. Xing, E.P., Ho, Q., Xie, P., Wei, D.: Strategies and Principles of Distributed Machine Learning on Big Data (2016). https://doi.org/10.1016/J.ENG.2016.02.008
23. Zagoruyko, S., Komodakis, N.: Wide residual networks (2016)

Evolving Character-Level DenseNet Architectures Using Genetic Programming

Trevor Londt(✉)(iD), Xiaoying Gao(iD), and Peter Andreae(iD)

School of Engineering and Computer Science, Victoria University of Wellington, Wellington, New Zealand
{trevor.londt,xgao,peter.andreae}@ecs.vuw.ac.nz

Abstract. Densely Connected Convolutional Networks (DenseNet) have demonstrated impressive performance on image classification tasks, but limited research has been conducted on using character-level DenseNet (char-DenseNet) architectures for text classification tasks. It is not clear what DenseNet architectures are optimal for text classification tasks. The iterative task of designing, training and testing of char-DenseNets is a time consuming task that requires expert domain knowledge. Evolutionary deep learning (EDL) has been used to automatically design CNN architectures for the image classification domain, thereby mitigating the need for expert domain knowledge. This study demonstrates the first work on using EDL to evolve char-DenseNet architectures for text classification tasks. A novel genetic programming-based algorithm (GP-Dense) coupled with an indirect-encoding scheme, facilitates the evolution of performant char-DenseNet architectures. The algorithm is evaluated on two popular text datasets, and the best-evolved models are benchmarked against four current state-of-the-art character-level CNN and DenseNet models. Results indicate that the algorithm evolves performant models for both datasets that outperform two of the state-of-the-art models in terms of model accuracy and three of the state-of-the-art models in terms of parameter size.

Keywords: Character-level DenseNet · Evolutionary deep learning · Genetic programming · Text classification

1 Introduction

Natural language processing (NLP) has benefited significantly from the application of deep learning [1] techniques in recent years [2–5]. In particular, the task of text classification has gained impressive performance increases. Long short-term memory (LSTM) [6] models have traditionally been the architecture of choice for text classification tasks. However, transformer [7] models and convolutional neural networks (CNN) [2,3,8] outperform LSTM's for text classification tasks. While transformer models dominate the leaderboards, they have the disadvantage of containing massive numbers of parameters. CNN's are generally not

© Springer Nature Switzerland AG 2021
P. A. Castillo and J. L. Jiménez Laredo (Eds.): EvoApplications 2021, LNCS 12694, pp. 665–680, 2021.
https://doi.org/10.1007/978-3-030-72699-7_42

encumbered by these limitations and have demonstrated excellent success for text classification tasks.

There are two approaches when using CNNs for text classification: word-level (word-CNN) and character-level CNNs (char-CNN). Word-level approaches generally outperform character-level approaches [2]. However, word-level approaches require a pre-trained word-model such as word2vec [9] or GloVe [10]. This requirement is a similar limitation as seen with transformer models. Further, an additional disadvantage of word-level CNNs is that they require the input text to be pre-processed by removing stop words, stemming words, removing punctuation and dealing with out of vocabulary words. Each of these operations increases the likelihood of the input text being corrupted or important discriminating information being inadvertently removed. There is also the potential problem of not having a pre-trained word-model available for a particular language. Char-CNNs require no pre-trained word or language models. Also, char-CNNs require no pre-processing of the input text data, mitigating any potential errors introduced through incorrect pre-processing. The disadvantage of char-CNNs is that they are, in general, less accurate than word-level CNNs. Research has shown that adding depth to a char-CNN does not result in breakthrough performance improvements, as shown in the image classification domain. DenseNet [11] is a network architecture that has shown good performance in the image domain and has recently shown promising results in the text classification domain [8]. However, the results have still not demonstrated breakthrough level improvements. Research focused on using DenseNets for text classification is limited, with little to no further research conducted to determine what hyperparameters or DenseNet topologies could further improve classification performance.

Designing, training and testing a deep network architecture is not a trivial task. A network topology has a learning bias, and its performance is dependant on the quality of chosen hyperparameters. The selection of these properties is based on trial and error or the practitioners' experience. Evolutionary deep learning (EDL) is an evolutionary computation technique that aims to locate performant network architectures for a particular task automatically. An evolutionary-inspired search algorithm coupled with the backpropagation [12] algorithm is used to locate, train and evaluate a population of candidate network architectures. Each candidate architecture is encoded in a genotype, contained in the population. Each genotype is decoded to a phenotype which represents a trainable candidate architecture. EDL reduces the need for expert domain knowledge and the need for a trial and error approach. To the best of our knowledge, EDL has never been used to locate candidate char-DenseNets for text classification tasks.

Genetic programming (GP) [13] is an evolutionary-inspired algorithm that evolves a population of programs represented by tree structures. The task of manually constructing a neural network can be considered as a sequence of program steps taken to construct a neural network from scratch up to a performant state. These sequence of steps are the equivalent of a computer program (genotype) that when executed, constructs a neural network (phenotype). This property makes GP an appropriate algorithm to evolve neural network architectures.

1.1   Goal

The goal of this work is to use GP with the backpropagation algorithm to evolve performant character-level DenseNet architectures for text classification tasks automatically. This goal is achieved through the following objectives:

1. Introduce an appropriate indirect-encoding for representing char-DenseNet architectures that can be used in a GP-based algorithm.
2. Evaluate the proposed algorithm over two well-known text classification datasets, one being of small size and the other of large size, to determine the ability of the algorithm to generalise over different text classification tasks.
3. Benchmark the performance of the best-evolved models against current state-of-the-art char-CNN and char-DenseNet models.

2   Background

2.1   Character-Level Convolutional Neural Networks

Zhang et al. [2] demonstrated that char-CNNs are an effective approach for text classification. The approach implemented a modular design and used the back-propagation [12] algorithm, via stochastic gradient descent [14], for network training. A temporal convolutional module was used for convolutional operations with their large model (Large Char-CNN) using 1024 feature maps and their small model (Small Char-CNN) using 256 feature maps. Max-pooling allowed networks deeper than six layers. ReLU [15] was used for non-linearity, and two fully connected layers provided the classifier component of their network. Each character in the input text sequence was converted to a one-hot-vector. Each vector was then stacked to produce a matrix of vectors representing the text sequence. Text sequences were limited to a maximum of 1014 characters. Longer text sequences were truncated, and shorter sequences were padded. The authors created eight datasets to evaluate their model. The model was shallow at only six layers. Their work showed that char-CNNs perform well over large datasets but underperform on smaller datasets when compared to traditional machine learning methods.

Motivated by the performance increases gained by adding depth to a network as evidenced in image classification tasks, Conneau et al. [3] introduced their *very deep convolutional neural network* (VDCNN) model. Introducing the concept of a *convolutional block*, consisting of a convolutional layer, a batch normalisation layer and a ReLU activation function. Their model stacked these convolutional blocks in sequential order one after the other. Further, their model implemented ResNet [16] links to allow their model to be extended to a depth of 29 layers. Their model outperformed all current state of the art char-CNNs and demonstrated the importance of adding depth to char-CNNs. However, their model could not be extended beyond 29 layers without degrading the model's classification accuracy.

Le et al. [8] conducted a study to understand the role of depth for both char-CNNs and word-CNNs. Their model was inspired by the DenseNet [11] model used for image classification tasks. Using the same hyperparameters as in [2,3] and introducing the concept of a *Dense block*, where each block consisted of multiple convolutional blocks stacked in sequential order with all convolutional blocks densely connected. Their model was able to outperform VDCNN on some datasets. Their research showed that DenseNet architectures have promising potential for text classification tasks. An interesting finding is that, again, adding depth to their model resulted in only minor improvements. The authors conclude that char-CNNs must be deep to be effective and that the problem of improving char-CNNs is not yet well understood. It is not known what other char-CNN architectures may perform better.

2.2   Related Work

Evolutionary deep learning (EDL) is a challenging and popular research task, particularly in the image classification domain. However, there is little to no research conducted on evolving CNNs for text classification tasks. There is no research work directly related to evolving char-DenseNets; however, Liang et al. [17] conducted research work for evolving LSTM-based architectures for text classification. Their algorithm, LEAF, can evolve performant network architectures and hyperparameters concurrently for image and text classification tasks. The LEAF algorithm consists of an algorithm-layer, systems-layer and problem-domain subsystem where each component is responsible for different aspects of the algorithm. The problem-domain layer is supported by both the algorithm-layer and systems-layer. CoDeepNEAT [18] is the underlying algorithm for the algorithm-layer, which is responsible for evolving the topology and hyperparameters of the candidate networks. It should be noted that networks were encoded as graphs structures. CoDeepNEAT makes use of components such as LSTM, convolutional and fully connected layers, where each selected component represents a node in the network topology. Concerning text classification, their algorithm was only evaluated on the Wikipedia comment toxicity dataset [19]. It is noted that although the LEAF algorithm is the most well-known algorithm for evolving architectures for text classification tasks, it is not specifically designed to evolve char-CNN architectures.

3   The Proposed Method

The proposed method, GP-Dense, is a genetic programming-based algorithm that evolves GP trees representing executable programs that can construct trainable char-DenseNet architectures. The genotypes (GP trees) consists of executable program symbols, each representing an action to be performed in the construction of a neural network. Decoding a genotype to a phenotype involves the process of executing the program symbols in the genotype resulting in a structurally valid and trainable neural network. The overall workflow of GP-Dense is presented below in Algorithm 1.

The algorithm begins by assigning a unique seed for the current experiment run. Then a population of randomly generated genotypes of varying depth is created. Each genotype is decoded to a phenotype and uploaded to the graphics processing unit (GPU). Each phenotype is trained and evaluated on the validation set to determine its fitness. The top fittest corresponding genotypes are added to the elite population. Tournament selection is used to generate a population of selected genotypes. Crossover and mutation operations are applied to the selected individuals resulting in a new population of offspring genotypes. The elite genotypes are then added to the new population. This process is repeated until a maximum number of generations has been attained, after which the fittest genotype is retrained on the full training set for an extended period of epochs and evaluated on the test set to determine its final fitness.

Algorithm 1: GP-DenseNet.

---

1 **begin**;
2   *seed* ← Assign next seed from list;
3   *population* ← genotypes with specified depth range;
4 **while** *not maximum generations* **do**
5   **foreach** *genotype* ∈ *population* **do**
6   GPU ← *phenotype* ← *decode(genotype)*;
7   *evaluate(genotype, reduced train. set, val. set)*;
8   **end foreach**
9   *elite* ← fittest from population;
10   *selected* ← *tournament(population)*;
11   *offspring population* ← *crossover(selected)*;
12   *population* ← *mutate(offspring population)*;
13   *limit(population ∪ elite)*;
14 **end while**
15 *fittest* ← *population*;
16 *evaluate(fittest, full train. set, test set)*;
17 **end**;

3.1   Encoding Network Architecture

An appropriate genotype encoding is required to represent neural network architectures in order for evolutionary algorithms to operate on them. There are two encoding paradigms: direct and indirect encodings. Direct encoding approaches explicitly state the components and structure of the network architecture. For example, the genotype could contain convolutional layers, max-pooling and activation functions, where the position of these components is directly related to their position in the phenotype structure. A significant drawback of this approach is that evolutionary operators such as the crossover operation could result in an offspring architecture with a broken topology that is no longer a valid feed-forward neural network. Indirect encodings contain the information on how to build a neural network architecture starting from a valid base network architecture. This information can take the form of executable program symbols. For example, a program symbol can represent adding depth to the network.

Evolutionary operations, such as crossover operations, have little potential to create invalid offspring networks as the selected program symbols are designed to always return a valid network topology. Indirect encodings are a natural fit for genetic programming algorithms.

Gruau et el. [20] created the well known *cellular encoding* scheme for evolving multilayer perceptrons. Cellular encoding is inspired by the division of biological cells, as seen in nature. By using a set of operations on cells (nodes in the network), the encoding can represent an extensive range of network topologies from shallow to deep and narrow to wide. We propose the use of a reduced set of cellular encoding operations to evolve char-DenseNet architecture where each cell in the network represents a *dense block* [8].

Input and Classifier Layer: Each character of the input text sequence is encoded as a n-dimensional vector using a lookup table that contains embeddings of a fixed alphabet. Therefore, an input text sequence of length l will be encoded into a matrix of dimension $n \times l$. The classifier layer of the ancestor network is defined as in [3], containing a k-max pooling layer followed by three fully connected layers using ReLU [15] activation functions and softmax outputs in the final layer.

Dense Blocks (Cell): A dense block (cell), as represented in Fig. 1, consists of multiple convolutional blocks as in [3]. Each convolutional block consists of a batch normalisation layer, ReLU [15] activation function and convolutional layer. The output channels from each convolutional block are transported to the input channels of every following convolutional block in a feed-forward manner. All preceding input channels to a convolutional block are concatenated together. Densely connected blocks have been shown to increase classification performance and mitigate the vanishing gradient problem [11]. Each dense block is followed by a transitional layer, as implemented in [8], containing a 1×3 convolution and a 1×2 local max-pooling layer.

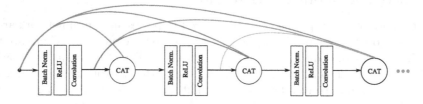

Fig. 1. Internal configuration of a dense block (cell).

GP Function Set: Two operations are used from Gruau et el's. [20] cellular encoding: SEQ and PAR. The SEQ program symbol is a sequential split operation. The operation is provided with a *mother* cell that is duplicated into a new *child* cell. The mother and child cell are then connected to each other in a feed-forward sequential manner from the mother to the child. The PAR program symbol is also provided with a mother cell and produces a duplicate child cell. However, the two cells are then connected in parallel, still in a feed-forward manner. In this work, we treat a dense block as a cell. We introduce a third operation called the END operation. This operation is a *no operation* symbol and is used to terminate the execution of a branch of the GP tree currently being traversed.

Terminal Set and Decorator Set: Two sets are defined: *Dense block parameter* terminals (DBT) and *Training parameter* decorators (TPD). The DBT set consists of integers in the range from 1 to 10. This terminal set defines the number of convolutional blocks contained in a dense block (cell). DBT is used on all dense blocks (cells). The TPD consists of real values in the range 0.0 to 0.5 and represents the probability of a dense block being dropped during a batch training cycle. This function serves as a dropout feature to prevent the neural network from over-relying on a particular feature learned from the input data. If a dense block has a dropout value of 0.5, then during every second batch of training data, the dense block will be bypassed in the neural network. Each symbol in a GP tree can be *decorated* with a value from the TPD terminal set to control the dense block dropout operation during the training cycle of the neural network. A probability value is used to determine if a dense block (cell) is to be decorated with the drop out feature or not. To the best of the authors' knowledge, this is the first work to include a CNN training hyperparameter in the genotype of an evolutionary algorithm.

3.2   Decoding Network Architecture

The decoding of a genotype to its corresponding phenotype is demonstrated in Fig. 2. The GP-Dense algorithm uses a depth-first traversal approach when decoding a genotype. GP-Dense always starts with a *ancestor network* containing one dense block containing two convolutional blocks with an initial 32 input and output channels. In step I, the *ancestor* network is represented by the symbol DB. The root symbol, represented by the first letter S (SEQ) of the GP tree, is executed. Step II displays the outcome. The phenotype now has two dense blocks, the original dense block and a child dense block that contains five convolutional blocks. The ancestor dense block will now be operated on by the left branch of the preceding symbol in the genotype and the child block by the right branch of the preceding genotype symbol. Step III represents the neural network after the P (PAR) symbol has been executed. Note that the PAR symbol operates on the ancestor dense block that was created by the previous genotype symbol. This ancestor dense block is now referred to as the *mother* dense block and the new dense block as the child dense block. The mother and the child are now connected in parallel. The next symbols is an S (SEQ) and the output is shown in step IV. The following symbol is the END symbol which performs no operation but traces back up the GP tree as indicated by the green arrows in step IV. Step V presents the neural network after executing the S (SEQ) symbol connected to the right branch of the root cell in the genotype. This operation results in the mother dense block connected to a new child dense block, containing two convolutional blocks, in sequential order. Note that the child dense block is decorated with the real value of 0.2, which represents a dropout function applied to the child dense block.

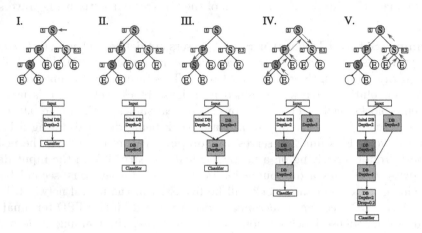

Fig. 2. Decoding genotype to phenotype. S = SEQ, P = PAR, E = END, DB = Dense Block, D = Decorator

3.3 Evolutionary Operators

Tournament selection is used to select k randomly selected genotypes from the population to build a breeding pool. Single point crossover is used in this work. A random point in the GP tree of each genotype is selected, and the subtrees of each genotype are exchanged at that point. This operation results in two offspring genotypes. The chosen mutation operation is uniform. A selected genotype is mutated in a random position in its GP tree structure by attaching a small randomly generated subtree at that point. The chosen crossover and mutation operations are well-researched variants and are chosen for their simplicity. Future research will focus on novel crossover and mutation operations.

4 Experiment Design

4.1 Peer Competitors

There are no related EDL algorithms with which to benchmark the proposed method. To mitigate this problem, the best evolved models from the proposed algorithm are benchmarked against current state of the hand-crafted character-level models: Le et al.'s [8] char-DenseNet model, Zhang et al.'s [2] Small-Char-CNN and Large-Char-CNN models and Conneau et al.'s [3] VDCNN model. All the benchmark models are pure character-level models, meaning that there is no data augmentation or text pre-processing conducted.

4.2   Benchmark Datasets

Two datasets from the work of Zhang et al. [2] are selected for this research work as listed in Table 1. The AG News dataset is the smallest of the datasets selected and is regarded as a challenging dataset to classify. The second chosen dataset is the Yelp Review Full dataset which is considered a large text dataset. This dataset is particularly difficult to model as the current best accuracies level are typically still below 65%. Each dataset is split as shown in Table 1. These values are based on the split ratio as in [2,3].

Table 1. Datasets by training, validation and test splits.

Dataset	No. classes	No. train	No. validation	No. test
AG News	4	112,852	7,148	7,600
Yelp Review Full	5	603,571	46,429	50,000

Table 2 lists the statistics of the instances in each dataset. The AG News dataset consists of text sentences of 236 characters on average. Zhang et al.'s [2], Conneau et al.'s [3] and Le et al.'s [8] models all use a temporal length of 1014 characters. This implies redundant padding and wasted convolutional operations. Therefore, this work uses a maximum sentence length of 256 characters when evolving models for the AG News dataset and 512 characters for the Yelp Reviews Full dataset.

Table 2. Sentence statistics.

Dataset	Mean	Minimum	Maximum
AG News	236 ± 66	100	1,012
Yelp Review Full	732 ± 664	10	5,849

4.3   Parameter Settings

Table 3 lists the parameter settings for the experiment. Thirty runs of the algorithm are conducted for each dataset. Each run is assigned a single unique seed. Candidate architectures are trained for 10 epochs to mitigate the problem of long training times. The values for the learning rate, momentum and batch size are the same as in [2,3]. Stochastic gradient descent is used for the network optimiser as used in [2]. Each population run consists of 20 individuals and is evolved over 20 generations. Elitism, crossover and mutation rate settings are values found in the literature [13]. The mutation growth depth is set to a low value to ensure that only small changes are made to the genotype so as not to significantly alter the phenotype. The maximum tree depth is set to a value of 17 and is considered best practice [13]. The objective is to maximise the candidate architectures validation accuracy.

Table 3. Parameter settings.

Parameter	Value
Run count, seed	30, Unique per Run
Epochs, batch size	10, 128 [2,3]
Initial learning rate, momentum	0.01, 0.9 [3]
Learning schedule	Halve every 3 epochs [2]
Weight initialisation	Kaiming [2,3,21]
Training data usage	0.25
Alphabet	Same as in [2,3]
Max sentence length	256 (AG News) 512 (Yelp)
Kernel size, stride, padding	3,1,1 [3]
Number of generations	20
Population size, elitism size	20, 0.1
Crossover prob and type, mut. prob. and type	0.5 Single, 0.1, Unif
Mutation growth, size	Grow, [1,3]
Tournament selection Size	3
Initial, max tree depth	[1,10], 17 [13]
Fitness gunction	Max (val. acc.) [2,3]
Probability dropout applied to cell	0.1

5   Results and Discussions

The validation accuracies of all the models evolved by the GP-Dense algorithm over the AG News and Yelp Reviews Full dataset are presented in Fig. 3.

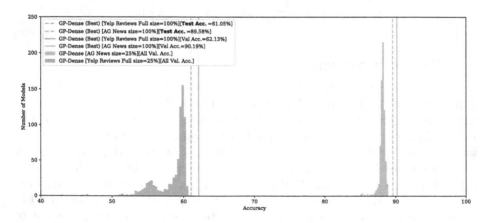

Fig. 3. Distribution of validation accuracy for evolved architectures.

The distribution in orange represents the validation accuracies attained over the Yelp Reviews Full dataset, and the distribution in blue represents those attained over the AG News dataset. It is noted that these validation accuracies are attained using only 25% of each dataset. Both distributions are left-skewed, indicating that GP-Dense has managed to maintain populations of models with similar good validation accuracies and only a few of lower quality. It can be observed that GP-Dense attained a maximum validation accuracy of 62.13% for the Yelp Reviews Full dataset and 90.19% for the AG News dataset. These values are achieved when retraining the best-evolved models for each dataset using 100% of the training set. Evaluating each of the best fully trained models yields test accuracies of 61.05% for Yelp Reviews Full and 89.59% for the AG News dataset. Figure 4 presents the combined validation performance of all evolved models over each generation for 30 runs. GP-Dense converges to a maximum validation accuracy early in the evolutionary process and maintains this position through to the end of the evolutionary process. There are scatterings of low-quality models that appear in each generation. An analysis of these models indicates that they are the result of crossover and mutation operations that resulted in low-performance models.

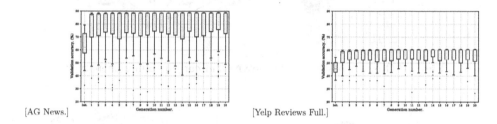

[AG News.]   [Yelp Reviews Full.]

Fig. 4. GP-dense performance over generations.

The distribution of the number of SEQ and PAR operations that are contained in the genotypes of all evolved models is presented in Fig. 5. There is no evidence that the evolutionary process favoured either operation over the other.

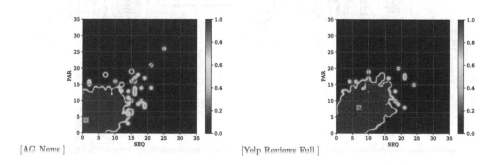

[AG News]   [Yelp Reviews Full]

Fig. 5. Density of number of SEQ vs PAR operations.

Each of the best-evolved models is highlighted by a lime green square. The best-evolved model from AG News contained 4 PAR operations and 1 SEQ operation in its genotype, indicating that the phenotype is wide and shallow. The best model evolved for Yelp Reviews Full contained 7 PAR operations and 8 SEQ operations, indicating that the phenotype is likely to be deep and relatively wide. The fittest genotype and corresponding phenotype evolved for the AG News dataset is presented in Fig. 6. Note that the phenotype has eight dense blocks connected in parallel. It can also be observed that the deepest path in the network is eight convolutional layers deep. The networks depth is comparable to Zhang et al.'s [2] original char-CNN network.

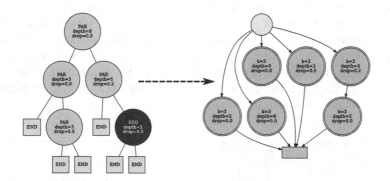

Fig. 6. AG News: best evolved genotype and corresponding phenotype.

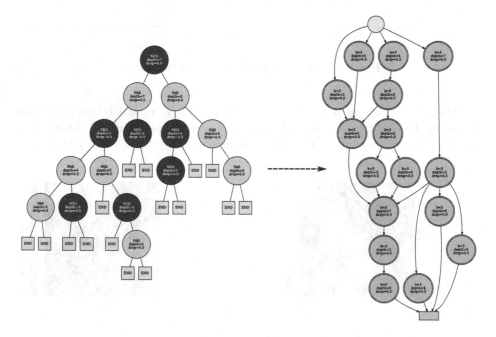

Fig. 7. Yelp Reviews Full: Best evolved genotype and corresponding phenotype.

The fittest genotype and corresponding phenotype for the Yelp Reviews Full dataset set are presented in Fig. 7. This network is significantly deeper at 34 convolutional layers deep. The network is comparable to the depth of VDCNN [3] at 29 convolutional layers.

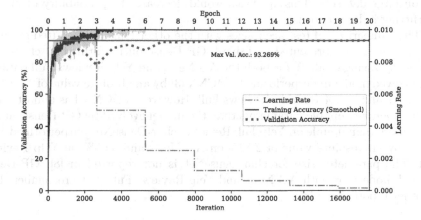

Fig. 8. Training response of best evolved model for AG News dataset.

The training response for the fittest phenotype evolved over the AG News dataset is presented in Fig. 8. The model converged within six epochs, highlighting the evolutionary pressure applied by GP-Dense to evolve models that converge within ten epochs. The validation accuracy degraded after the third epoch. However, after halving the learning rate, the validation accuracy increased again. The same behaviour is seen when the learning rate halved again at the sixth epoch. Further reducing the learning rate stabilised the validation accuracy.

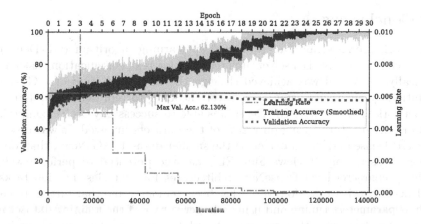

Fig. 9. Training response of best evolved model for Yelp Reviews full dataset.

Figure 9 presents the training response of the fittest evolved phenotype over the Yelp Reviews Full dataset. Halving the learning rate every three epochs did not provide any benefit in improving the accuracy of the model. The model began overfitting after the tenth epoch. This observation suggests that GP-Dense may need to evolve a candidate model for longer than ten epochs when training on large datasets. This approach would decrease the probability of models overfitting in later epochs.

The comparison of test accuracies with the other four hand-crafted state-of-the-art models are presented in Table 4. GP-Dense outperformed all char-CNN models by Zhang et al. [2] for both the AG News and Yelp Reviews Full dataset. The evolved model underperformed VDCNN [3] by an absolute value of 1.69% on AG News and 3.67% for Yelp Reviews Full. However, VDCNN has almost triple the number of trainable parameters than the model evolved by GP-Dense on AG News more than double on Yelp Full Reviews. char-DenseNet outperformed GP-Dense by an absolute value of 2.52% on AG News and 3.05% on Yelp Reviews Full. The parameter size for char-DenseNet is not reported in [8]. GP-Dense evolved models for both AG News and Yelp Reviews Full that are smaller than all other reported models.

Table 4. Test accuracies attained.

Model or Algorithm	AG News	Params	Yelp Reviews	Params
Large Char-CNN (Zhang et al. [2])	87.18	˜15	60.38	˜15
Small Char-CNN (Zhang et al. [2])	84.35	˜11	59.16	˜11
VDCNN-29 (Conneau et al. [3])	91.27	˜17	**64.72**	˜17
char-DenseNet (Le et al.) [8]	**92.10**	–	64.10	–
GP-Dense Best (ours)	89.58	˜**4**	61.05	˜**7**

6   Conclusions

This work proposed an evolutionary deep learning algorithm (GP-Dense) to evolve character-level DenseNet architectures for text classification tasks automatically. This goal was achieved through the implementation of a GP-based evolutionary algorithm using an indirect encoding to represent candidate neural network architectures. GP-Dense was able to successfully evolve competitive network architectures using only 25% of the datasets involved. It was observed that GP-Dense performed better on the smaller dataset, AG News, than on the larger dataset, Yelp Reviews Full. EDL has the potential to perform well on evolving character-level DenseNet architectures for text classification tasks as evidenced by this work. However, it has been demonstrated that further research such as parameters tuning and using a larger subset of the training dataset may be required to ensure that performant architectures can be evolved for larger datasets.

References

1. Goodfellow, I., Bengio, Y., Courville, A.: Deep Learning. The MIT Press, Cambridge (2016)
2. Zhang, X., Zhao, J., LeCun, Y.: Character-level convolutional networks for text classification. In: Proceedings of the 28th International Conference on Neural Information Processing Systems, NIPS 2015, vol. 1, pp. 649–657. MIT Press, Cambridge (2015)
3. Conneau, A., Schwenk, H., Barrault, L., Lecun, Y.: Very deep convolutional networks for text classification. In: Proceedings of the 15th Conference of the European Chapter of the Association for Computational Linguistics: Volume 1, Long Papers, Valencia, Spain, pp. 1107–1116. Association for Computational Linguistics (April 2017). https://www.aclweb.org/anthology/E17-1104
4. Collobert, R., Weston, J., Bottou, L., Karlen, M., Kavukcuoglu, K., Kuksa, P.: Natural language processing (almost) from scratch. J. Mach. Learn. Res. **12**(76), 2493–2537 (2011). http://jmlr.org/papers/v12/collobert11a.html
5. Yang, Z., Dai, Z., Yang, Y., Carbonell, J., Salakhutdinov, R.R., Le, Q.V.: XLNet: generalized autoregressive pretraining for language understanding. In: Wallach, H., Larochelle, H., Beygelzimer, A., d' Alché-Buc, F., Fox, E., Garnett, R. (eds.) Advances in Neural Information Processing Systems, vol. 32, pp. 5753–5763. Curran Associates, Inc. (2019). https://proceedings.neurips.cc/paper/2019/file/dc6a7e655d7e5840e66733e9ee67cc69-Paper.pdf
6. Hochreiter, S., Schmidhuber, J.: Long short-term memory. Neural Comput. **9**(8), 1735–1780 (1997)
7. Devlin, J., Chang, M., Lee, K., Toutanova, K.: BERT: pre-training of deep bidirectional transformers for language understanding. In: Burstein, J., Doran, C., Solorio, T. (eds.) Proceedings of the 2019 Conference of the North American Chapter of the Association for Computational Linguistics: Human Language Technologies, NAACL-HLT 2019, Minneapolis, MN, USA, 2–7 June 2019, Volume 1 (Long and Short Papers), pp. 4171–4186. Association for Computational Linguistics (2019). https://doi.org/10.18653/v1/n19-1423
8. Le, H.T., Cerisara, C., Denis, A.: Do Convolutional Networks need to be deep for text classification? In: AAAI Workshop on Affective Content Analysis. New Orleans, United States (February 2018)
9. Church, K.W.: Word2Vec. Nat. Lang. Eng. **23**(1), 155–162 (2017)
10. Pennington, J., Socher, R., Manning, C.: GloVe: global vectors for word representation. In: Proceedings of the 2014 Conference on Empirical Methods in Natural Language Processing (EMNLP), Doha, Qatar, pp. 1532–1543. Association for Computational Linguistics (October 2014). https://www.aclweb.org/anthology/D14-1162
11. Huang, G., Liu, Z., Van Der Maaten, L., Weinberger, K.Q.: Densely connected convolutional networks. In: 2017 IEEE Conference on Computer Vision and Pattern Recognition (CVPR), pp. 2261–2269 (2017)
12. Rumelhart, D.E., Hinton, G.E., Williams, R.J.: Learning Representations by Back-Propagating Errors, pp. 696–699. MIT Press, Cambridge (1988)
13. Koza, J.R.: Genetic Programming: On the Programming of Computers by Means of Natural Selection. MIT Press, Cambridge, MA, USA (1992)
14. De Sa, C., Feldman, M., Ré, C., Olukotun, K.: Understanding and optimizing asynchronous low-precision stochastic gradient descent. In: 2017 ACM/IEEE 44th Annual International Symposium on Computer Architecture (ISCA), pp. 561–574 (2017)

15. Hara, K., Saito, D., Shouno, H.: Analysis of function of rectified linear unit used in deep learning. In: 2015 International Joint Conference on Neural Networks (IJCNN), pp. 1–8 (2015)
16. He, K., Zhang, X., Ren, S., Sun, J.: Deep residual learning for image recognition, CoRR abs/1512.0 (2015)
17. Liang, J., Meyerson, E., Hodjat, B., Fink, D., Mutch, K., Miikkulainen, R.: Evolutionary neural automl for deep learning. In: Proceedings of the Genetic and Evolutionary Computation Conference, GECCO 2019, pp. 401–409. Association for Computing Machinery, New York (2019). https://doi.org/10.1145/3321707.3321721
18. Miikkulainen, R., et al.: Evolving deep neural networks (2017)
19. Wulczyn, E., Thain, N., Dixon, L.: Wikipedia talk labels: personal attacks (2017). https://figshare.com/articles/dataset/Wikipedia_Talk_Labels_Personal_Attacks/4054689
20. Gruau, F.: Neural Network Synthesis Using Cellular Encoding and the Genetic Algorithm. Ph.D. Thesis (1994)
21. Kaiming, H., Xiangyu, Z., Shaoqing, R., Jian, S.: Delving deep into rectifiers: surpassing human-level performance on imagenet classification Kaiming. Biochem. Biophys. Res. Commun. **498**(1), 254–261 (2018)

Transfer Learning for Automated Test Case Prioritization Using XCSF

Lukas Rosenbauer[1]([⊠]), David Pätzel[2], Anthony Stein[3], and Jörg Hähner[2]

[1] BSH Hausgeräte GmbH, Im Gewerbepark B10, 93059 Regensburg, Germany
lukas.rosenbauer@bshg.com
[2] University of Augsburg, Eichleitner Street 30, 86159 Augsburg, Germany
{david.paetzel,joerg.haehner}@informatik.uni-augsburg.de
[3] University of Hohenheim, Garbenstr. 9, 70599 Stuttgart, Germany
anthony.stein@uni-hohenheim.de

Abstract. With the rise of test automation, companies start to rely on large amounts of test cases. However, there are situations where it is unfeasible to perform every test case as only a limited amount of time is available. Under such circumstances a set of crucial tests has to be compiled. Recent research has shown that *reinforcement learning* methods such as *XCSF classifier systems* are well-suited for this task. This work investigates whether reusing knowledge of XCSF-based agents is beneficial for prioritizing test cases and subsequently selecting test suites in terms of performance. We developed a simplistic population transformation and evaluate it in a series of experiments. Our evaluation shows that XCSF may indeed benefit from transfer learning for this use case.

Keywords: Automated testing · Evolutionary machine learning · Transfer learning · XCSF classifier system

1 Introduction

Testing plays an important role in software development and thus has a high impact on a project's total development costs [9]. For that reason, research has focused on several aspects of testing as documented in the survey of Yoo and Harman [26]. The software validation use case we investigate comes from *continuous integration* (CI). CI is a common practice in software development where source code of individual programmers is merged frequently into a common code base, thus avoiding large software forks that become hard to integrate. This way, quality can be ensured more easily. Typical CI tools such as Jenkins [1] automatically download source code and then build, test, and deploy it. Each run of the resulting pipeline is called a *CI cycle*.

Our work focuses exclusively on the test stage during which all kinds of tests may run (e. g. integration tests or even full system tests). Tests can vary in their execution time as well as in their effectiveness of finding errors. Over the course

© Springer Nature Switzerland AG 2021
P. A. Castillo and J. L. Jiménez Laredo (Eds.): EvoApplications 2021, LNCS 12694, pp. 681–696, 2021.
https://doi.org/10.1007/978-3-030-72699-7_43

of a project's lifetime it might not always be reasonable to run all tests due to time constraints [4]. For example, the software verification method of *smoke testing* aims at deciding whether further testing is useful or whether the software should be rejected outright. In such cases, a subset of tests has to be selected; one approach to this is to prioritize them based on their duration and capability of detecting faults. At that, long tests that pass are undesirable (i. e., should receive a low priority) whereas short tests that are likely to fail should receive a high priority. Based on the prioritization and the available execution time, a test schedule can be created. The task of determining such a prioritization and based on that finding a close-to-optimal test suite is referred to as the *adaptive test case selection problem* (ATCS) [20].

Recent research has shown that *reinforcement learning* (RL) is suitable for ATCS [20]. Spieker et al. designed a neural network–based agent capable of creating effective test schedules based on the aforementioned metadata. Subsequent studies applied *learning classifier systems* (LCS) to the problem, in the process showing that these are not only suitable for this problem but that a solution based on the *XCSF classifier system* is actually superior to the neural network–based solution [18,19].

LCSs are a family of evolutionary rule-based machine learning algorithms that can be applied to a variety of machine learning disciplines including RL [23]. LCS such as the aforementioned XCSF develop a population of rules for various different states (here test cases).

Previous research with the RL interpretation of ATCS focused to our knowledge solely on training an agent from scratch for individual software projects. However, within this use case, states solely rely on CI metadata which is independent from the specific type of software (e. g. whether it is a web application or a car). Thus, one might argue that an LCS tries to develop general project-independent rules. Hence a reuse of a rule population for a new project might be beneficial. This leads to the hypothesis that we are examining in this work:

Hypothesis. *XCSF benefits from the reuse of previously trained classifier population in terms of performance for ATCS.*

Accordingly, the contributions of this paper can be summarized as follows:

- To our knowledge we are the first to apply transfer learning to test case prioritization which we achieve by introducing a novel population transformation for XCSF.
- We extend the evaluation of XCSF for ATCS [17] by examining a new dataset.

Thus our work belongs to the field of *transfer learning* (TL) which focuses on the application of previously acquired knowledge to related problems [22].

The paper is structured as follows: In Sect. 2 we discuss related work. This is followed by a detailed description of ATCS (Sect. 3). In Sect. 4 we describe the used LCS which is a derivative of XCSF [24]. We proceed with an elaboration of our knowledge transformation in Sect. 5. Afterwards we present the results of a series of experiments and statistical analysis that verify our approach (Sect. 6).

We close this work with a discussion of future work and a summarizing conclusion (Sect. 7).

2   Related Work

The reduction of a test suite's size has been investigated from several different angles as documented in the survey of Marijan and Gotlieb [11].

There are researchers that concentrate on coverage-based criteria. For example, McMaster and Memon's approach intends to find a minimal number of tests that cover all encountered call stack depths [12] whereas Jeffrey and Gupta [7] approximate a minimal test suite which maximizes code coverage.

The aforementioned techniques focus on different coverage criteria. However, there are also methods that target fault detection and exploit historical data to accomplish this [8,14,15]. Using RL for prioritizing test cases and then reducing the number of tests in the suite by having a fixed time budget was first used by Spieker et al. [20]. They successfully compared their approach against traditional techniques such as random or greedy selections. From an architectural perspective, their approach allows easy integration into existing systems.[1]

This work makes use of TL, a paradigm where knowledge of a previous, related problem is reused [22]. TL routines already exist for artificial neural networks (e. g. [5,22]). For example it is common for object recognition tasks to reuse a network that has been pre-trained for the well-known ImageNet challenge. Such networks are publically available in the widespread deep learning library keras.[2] However, TL only received little research attention in the LCS community. A first study has been performed by Iqbal et al. [6] who developed a rule extraction method for the *XCS classifier system* (XCS); their technique identifies a subset of the rules part of a solution for low-dimensional binary problems which may be useful for higher dimensional problems of the same problem family. In another work, Li et al. [10] develop transformations for the classifiers' conditions for certain binary problems (e. g. multiplexers) that make it possible to reuse them in other contexts. However, our problem does not fit to the aforementioned approaches (as the structure of our state space and action space differs) which gives rise to a need of new form of TL for LCS.

3   Problem Description

For the sake of consistency, we follow the notation as introduced by Rosenbauer et al. [17,19].

---

[1] For example, Netflix has decided to use RL based system to prioritize and select test cases (last accessed 16. November 2020): https://netflixtechblog.com/lerner-using-rl-agents-for-test-case-scheduling-3e0080211198.

[2] See here (last accessed 16. November 2020): https://keras.io/guides/transfer_learning/.

There is a fixed time budget C available for each CI cycle i. A test case T's estimated duration is given by $d(T)$. The task is to assign a rank $\mathrm{rk}_i(T)$ to each test which corresponds to its priority. This is done at the beginning of each CI cycle. Note it is possible that two test cases get assigned the same rank (meaning ranks are not unique).

After assigning ranks to all tests, a schedule is created which relies on the ranks as well as the available time budget C as follows:

1. The available tests are sorted by their ranks in descending order.
2. Tests are scheduled from the beginning of the sorted list as long as the esti-mated overall duration does not exceed the budget C.
3. If it is not possible to schedule all tests having equal rank, the remaining time budget is filled up with randomly chosen tests of that rank.
4. The resulting schedule, or, test suite, $\mathcal{TS}_i$ can be seen as a list; we denote the index of test T in that list as $l_k(T)$.

After the test suite's execution, the results can be inspected. Let $\mathcal{TS}_i^{\mathrm{f}}$ be the test cases of $\mathcal{TS}_i$ that failed. Furthermore, let $\mathcal{TS}_i^{\mathrm{t,f}}$ be the set of failed tests if all available tests would have been executed. Thus the *percentage of failures found* p_i can be computed as follows:

$$p_i = \frac{|\mathcal{TS}_i^{\mathrm{f}}|}{|\mathcal{TS}_i^{\mathrm{t,f}}|}. \tag{1}$$

A commonly used metric to examine a test prioritization's quality is the *nor-malized average percentage of faults detected* (NAPFD) [16]:

$$\mathrm{NAPFD}(\mathcal{TS}_i) = p_i - \frac{\sum_{T \in \mathcal{TS}_i^{\mathrm{f}}} l_k(T)}{|\mathcal{TS}_i^{\mathrm{f}}| \cdot |\mathcal{TS}_i|} + \frac{p_i}{2 \cdot |\mathcal{TS}_i|}. \tag{2}$$

Its values range from 0 to 1 with a high value being desired. Its advantage over p_i itself is that it takes the prioritization into account (by depending on the l_ks). If many passing test cases receive high priorities, i. e., have a low index l_k in the schedule list, then the NAPFD metric decreases. Vice versa, if the schedule contains a large number of failing tests with high priorities (i. e., low indexes l_k), then this results in a higher NAPFD value. It is worth mentioning that NAPFD is a rather academic measure since it requires the knowledge of p_i which is in practice unknown.

NAPFD is the key metric to optimize in the *adaptive test case selection problem* (ATCS) which is defined as follows:

$$\begin{aligned} \max \quad & \mathrm{NAPFD}(\mathcal{TS}_i) \\ \text{subject to} \quad & \sum_{T \in \mathcal{TS}_i} d(T) \leq C \\ & \mathcal{TS}_i \subseteq \mathcal{T}_i \end{aligned} \tag{3}$$

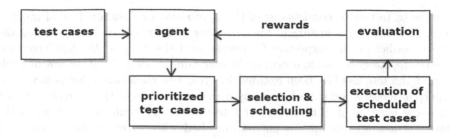

Fig. 1. Workflow for solving ATCS using RL.

where T_i denotes the entire set of all available tests of the CI cycle i. Hence for ATCS the goal is to find an subset TS_i from T_i which has a execution time lower than C and maximizes NAPFD.

The workflow of RL interpretation of ATCS is described in Fig. 1. In the following we describe the state space, action space and reward functions which are known in literature [19,20].

NAPFD cannot be used as a reward function due to its dependence on p_i. If we would use it then we have to execute all tests to compute p_i which is what should be avoided in this use case. Thus Spieker et al. [20] have proposed the following reward functions for a test case T (a state):

– *failure count reward*
$$r_i^{\text{fc}}(T) = |TS_i^{\text{f}}| \tag{4}$$

– *time rank reward*
$$r_i^{\text{trk}}(T) = |TS_i^{\text{f}}| - v_i(T) \cdot \sum_{\substack{t_k \in TS_i^{\text{f}}, \\ \text{rk}(T) < \text{rk}(t_k)}} 1 \tag{5}$$

where $v_i(T)$ denotes the binary verdict of a test case T in CI cycle i. A "1" corresponds to "test passed" or "test not executed due to time restriction". A "0" means "test failed". In the following, we denote the reward received at time t simply as $r(t)$.

The failure count reward gives each test case the same reward, namely, the number of failed tests of the current schedule. The time rank reward is more fine-grained as it rewards test cases individually and also takes the prioritization into account as it punishes a passed test by the number of failed tests having a lower priority; furthermore, passed tests with a low rank receive a relatively high reward. It is worth mentioning that there exists a third reward function called *test case failure* reward that we leave out in this work since a previous study showed that the other two reward functions lead to better results for LCSs [17] (a similar observation can be made for the neural network of Spieker et al. [20]).

The state space S corresponding to ATCS can be described as follows:

$$S := [0, C] \times \{0, 1\}^k \times [0, 1]. \tag{6}$$

A state (a test case) consists out of the *approximated duration* (a real number in $[0, C]$), the *testing history* (a binary vector of length k, each entry being the tests's verdict of the respective CI cycle), and the *time of the last execution relative to the entire testing history* (a real number in $[0, 1]$, if we are in cycle 10 and the test has last been excuted in cycle two then this value is 0.8). The hyperparameter k indicates how many previous verdicts of the current test case the agent is aware of. If there are not k test outcomes available yet (e. g., at the start of training), the missing entries are filled with zeroes. State vectors have the dimension $k + 2$; we denote the state at time t by $\mathbf{s}(t)$.

The action space A is $\mathbb{R}$ as each agent maps a test case described by the current state $\mathbf{s}(t)$ to a scalar rank which reflects its priority. We define $a(t)$ as the action chosen at time t.

It should be noted that the RL interpretation of ATCS differs from the traditional *temporal difference learning* (TD) scenario. There sequences of states, actions, and rewards usually occur in the following order:

$$\mathbf{s}(1), a(1), r(1), \mathbf{s}(2), a(2), r(2), \ldots \tag{7}$$

However, for ATCS, all available tests are ranked (i. e., a state observed and an action executed) first one by one. After that, a corresponding schedule is executed based on whose outcome rewards are distributed (see Fig. 1). Hence here we observe the following sequence:

$$\mathbf{s}(1), a(1), \mathbf{s}(2), a(2), \ldots, \mathbf{s}(n), a(n), r(1), r(2), \ldots, r(n) \tag{8}$$

In the ATCS RL problem, an episode corresponds to a single CI cycle with the terminal state being the last available test case of the cycle. Furthermore, the length of an episode as well as the states encountered are determined by the available tests and not by the agent's actions. It is also worth mentioning that the learning environment for the ATCS problem can be considered non-stationary, i. e., it does not stay constant throughout the episodes. This is due to the fact that, between two cycles, the software to be tested or the available tests may change.

4   XCSF

Learning Classifier Systems (LCSs) comprise a family of evolutionary, rule-based machine learning algorithms. In this work, we focus on the XCSF classifier system [24] that is designed to be a general purpose function approximator. An XCSF consists of a population of rules, a locally acting learning mechanism for them, as well as a globally acting evolutionary algorithm that optimizes the rules' localization, i. e., the subspace of S each rule covers. A rule participates in the decision process if a certain set of rule-specific conditions is fulfilled by the given state (e. g., a condition could assert that an attribute lies within a certain interval). One such rule is called a *classifier* cl. Each classifier has several learning parameters which determine its influence in the system's collective decisions making process.

Rosenbauer et al. [17] used XCSF to approximate a state-value function $V(\cdot)$ for the following policy π:

$$\pi(\mathbf{s}) = \hat{V}(\mathbf{s}) \tag{9}$$

where $\hat{V}(\cdot)$ is an approximation of $V(\cdot)$. This policy follows a simple heuristic: If a test case (i. e., a state) has a high value then it should have a high priority. $\hat{V}(\cdot)$ estimates the reward that will be received if that policy is applied. Thus this RL approach can also be seen as a form of regression which makes XCSF well-suited for it.

Each classifier cl of the proposed XCSF-based agent models a linear *prediction function* cl.$p(\mathbf{s})$ (the rule's estimation of $V(\mathbf{s})$) as follows:

$$\text{cl.}p(\mathbf{s}) = w_0 + \sum_{i=1}^{k+2} w_i \cdot \mathbf{s}_i \tag{10}$$

where w_i are real-valued weights which are initialized randomly and $k+2$ denotes the state space's dimension (cf. (6)).

A classifier tracks how often the rule has been applied which is called its *experience*. Additionally, it keeps record of its prediction accuracy relative to the prediction accuracies in its local niche (i. e., of other, overlapping, rules); this is called its *fitness* cl.F. Another quality parameter of a classifier is the prediction error cl.ϵ which is the mean absolute error estimate of its prediction function.

In order to make a prediction for a state $\mathbf{s}(t)$, XCSF searches the rule population for classifiers whose conditions are satisfied by $\mathbf{s}(t)$ in a process known as *matching*. The resulting classifiers are collected in the so-called *match set M*. If the match set is too small, then new classifiers that match the given point are created at random, a technique called *covering*. Based on the classifiers within M, XCSF computes the estimation of the function at $\mathbf{s}$ (in our case, the estimation of the value function):

$$\hat{V}(\mathbf{s}) = \frac{\sum_{cl \in M} \text{cl.}p(\mathbf{s}) \cdot \text{cl.}F}{\sum_{cl \in M} \text{cl.}F}. \tag{11}$$

In the LCS community, this value is usually called the *system prediction*. In the investigated scenario, it corresponds to the action to be chosen next since we follow the policy described by (9).

Provided an observed function value r for a place $\mathbf{s}$ (here reward and state), XCSF uses a gradient-based update rule for the prediction functions cl.$p(\mathbf{s})$ (cf. (10)) which is known as the *modified delta rule* [24]:

$$\Delta w_i = \frac{\eta}{\|\tilde{\mathbf{s}}\|^2}(r - \text{cl.}p(\mathbf{s}))\tilde{\mathbf{s}}_i \tag{12}$$

where $\|\cdot\|$ denotes the Euclidean norm and η is the learning rate. The weights of $cl.p(\cdot)$ are updated by adding Δw_i. The vector $\tilde{\mathbf{s}}$ is the same as the state vector $\mathbf{s}$ but extended with a leading 1 to fit the intercept weight w_0, i. e.,

$$\tilde{\mathbf{s}} = (1, \mathbf{s}_1, \mathbf{s}_2, ..., \mathbf{s}_{k+2})^T, \tag{13}$$

and r denotes the reward received for the chosen action in **s**. Due to spatial restrictions, we have to assume a certain degree of familiarity with XCSF's learning mechanism. Hence, for the remaining learning parameters of the classifiers $cl \in M$ such as $cl.F$ and $cl.\epsilon$ we refer the reader to [24, 25].

Rosenbauer et al. [17] deviated from the vanilla XCSF by incorporating *experience replay* (ER) into the system. In doing so, they exploited a novel result by Stein et al. [21] who showed that ER can improve learning efficiency and overall performance for certain classes of problems. ER saves past experiences of the form $(\mathbf{s}(t), r(t))$ in a buffer from which, at the end of each CI cycle, a batch of a fixed size is drawn. For each of the drawn states, a match set is computed based on which the usual XCSF update takes place.

XCSF periodically applies to its match set a *steady-state niche genetic algorithm* (GA) that is used to optimize the classifiers' conditions. It tries to find an optimal partitioning of the state space S. It selects two parent classifiers from the match set M (with the probability to be selected being proportionate to their fitness values, $cl.F$) and creates offspring by applying mutation and crossover on their conditions.

The population of XCSF has a fixed capacity. If the population contains too many classifiers after new classifiers have been introduced to it (i. e., by the GA or by the covering mechanism), XCSF deletes classifiers at random but proportional to their quality. We call this mechanism *pruning*.

5   Transfer Learning

TL is a branch of machine learning developing techniques for reusing trained models for similar problems. For example, a common transfer learning approach for artificial neural networks is to redesign the output layer of an already trained model and then only briefly retrain it on some data from the new problem [5].

Li et al. [10] as well as Iqbal et al. [6] performed first attempts of TL in the context of XCS. Their approaches are limited to binary state spaces and merely deal with how to adapt the knowledge when the state space is changed. Since the state space of the ATCS RL problem is

- non-binary and
- solely depends on fairly general CI metadata that is independent from the specific software being tested, meaning that the state space does not change upon transfer,

a different transformation is required to apply TL to this setting. Our approach is to simply reset certain classifier quality parameters (experience, numerosity, fitness and prediction error) to their initial default values (see Algorithm 1). We transform the entire population and hence reuse all classifiers.

Both the fitness and experience values have a large impact on which classifiers are deleted and which ones are kept whenever the population is being pruned. By resetting them, we enable the system to quickly get rid of rules detrimental to the new scenario although having been good for the previous one. If a previous

---

Algorithm 1: Classifier conversion. Notation adapted from Butz et al. [3].

---

   input : classifier cl
   output: transformed classifier
1 cl.experience = 0
2 cl.numerosity = 1
3 cl.fitness = f_I
4 cl.ϵ = ϵ_I
5 return cl

---

rule turns out to be appropriate for the new scenario as well, it will regain high fitness values quickly. We coin an XCSF that includes this mechanism *XCSF-TL*.

It is worth stressing that we do not adapt the classifier's prediction weights since we use the same action space and these prediction functions are used to compute the actions. Hence we regard them as the main knowledge of the population that we explicitly intend to keep. Furthermore, our approach is not necessarily exclusively linked to ATCS but might also be applied to other problems where the state and action space stay the same between two problem instances.

Our method expects that the dimensionality of the state space of the receiving XCSF and the sending XCSF is the same. The dimensionality of the state space may seem to be variable (it has a dimensionality of $k + 2$, see (6)) but empirical results for both the neural network based [20] and LCS-based approaches [17–19] indicate that for each kind of RL approach, there is a certain testing history length k yielding good results. Thus, we assume an arbitrary but fixed k for ATCS for each considered dataset and neglect a change of dimensionality.

6 Evaluation

To evaluate our system, we use four different industrial datasets. Three of them were originally examined by Spieker et al. [20]. The first two (*ABB paint control* and *ABB IOF/ROL*) are from a Scandinavian robot company whereas the third is the *Google shared dataset of test results* (GSDTSR). The last, novel, dataset SMBV1 is from a dishwasher project of BSH Hausgeräte GmbH which is a German manufacturer for various home appliances. An overview of the datasets' structure is provided in Table 1.

We compare our approach to the XCSF of Rosenbauer et al. [17]. For the new dataset we also include the neural network of Spieker et al. [20] (for the other datasets it has already been demonstrated that the XCSF approach is the better choice [17]). For these two agents we can rely on the original implementation and hyperparameters. We also made ours publicly available.[3]

Within these experiments we aim at evaluating the effects of our TL approach for XCSF. In order to create a ceteris paribus environment we adopt the XCSF modeling and hyperparameters from Rosenbauer et al. [17]. Thus we can observe

---

[3] Available here: https://github.com/LagLukas/transfer_learning.

Table 1. Examined datasets.

	Paint control	IOF/ROL	GSDTSR	SMBV1
CI cycles	312	320	336	40
Test cases	114	2,086	5,555	1,632
Verdicts	25,594	30,319	1,260,617	165,073
Failed	19.36%	28.43%	0.25%	0.58%

the effects of incorporating our population transformation in an isolated way
since both LCS solely differ from each other in that one uses TL and the other
not. For the sake of completeness we revisit the aforementioned modeling and
hyperparameters.[4]

For the problem setting in this work, and according to the used definition of
the state space S, classifiers' conditions are a mix of interval-based parts (for the
real-valued numbers the state vector $\mathbf{s}(t)$) and ternary encoded parts (for the
binary numbers of the state vector). For the GA a roulette wheel selection based
on the classifiers' fitness is used. For the crossover of the ternary conditions
a one-point crossover is employed and for the intervals and weights of $cl.p(\cdot)$
an arithmetic one is implemented. For the mutation of the ternary conditions
Rosenbauer et al. [17] followed Butz et al. [3] (i. e., iterate over the bits and
flip each with a probability of $\frac{1}{m}$ where m is the number of bits) and for the
interval-based conditions and weights of $cl.p(\cdot)$ a random mutation is applied
(i. e., choosing an entirely random interval). They also do not perform any form
of subsumption. The ER buffer has a maximum capacity of 12 000 and we draw
batches of size 2 000. Further, updates using ER are performed every third cycle.
The initial weights of $cl.p(\cdot)$ during covering and mutation are drawn uniformly
at random from $[-10, 10]$.

Rosenbauer et al. [17] chose an appropriate value for the history length k
by means of conducting a preliminary hyperparameter study. They evaluated
$k \in \{2, 3, ..., 10\}$ on the paint control dataset using the time rank reward. At
that, XCSF achieved the best results for a value of $k = 6$. We performed the same
study and confirmed this value. Thus we use it for XCSF-TL in the succeeding
experiments.

We have run our experiments for 30 i. i. d. repetitions and present the averaged results. Since the datasets contain the results of all the test cases for the
respective number of CI cycles, we are able to measure the performance of the
methods in terms of the NAPFD metric while still simulating the actual use case
by only providing the agent with the results of the tests that it chose to run.

Our first question deals with the choice of the base dataset for our transfer learning approach. A common practice in natural language processing and
computer vision is to reuse a trained model that performed reasonably well on

---

[4] $\eta = 0.1$, $N = 2000$, $\alpha = 0.15$, $\beta = 0.15$, $\nu = 5$, $\theta_{GA} = 25$, $\mu = 0.025$ (for the real-
valued parts), $\epsilon_I = 0$, $F_I = 0$, $\theta_{del} = 20$, $\theta_{sub} = 20$, $\chi = 0.75$, $\epsilon_0 = 0.01$, $P_\# = 0.33$
(notation of Butz et al. [3]).

a large dataset [2,13]. This would point to the usage of the GSDTSR dataset since it is the largest and the previous LCSs performed well on it [19]. We examined this hypothesis by using each available dataset as a training basis for XCSF and by applying the pretrained model on the other remaining datasets. We displayed the averaged NAPFD values achieved in Table 2 (using the time rank reward). On the SMBV1 dataset, all pretrained models perform similar. On the other datasets, the model pretrained on the GSDTSR dataset works best. Thus results show that, on average, the GSDTSR dataset is the best choice. We confirmed this by applying a series of one-sided Wilcoxon tests whose p-values were below our significance level of 0.05 for both the paint control and the IOF/ROL datasets. On the SMBV1 dataset we used a two-sided Wilcoxon test whose p-value indicated that the agents indeed perform equally (again using a significance level of 0.05). Hence in the following experiments we are using the model pretrained on the GSDTSR dataset.

Table 2. Average NAPFD $\pm\sigma$ achieved for different datasets as knowledge bases. The columns correspond to the examined pretrained model and the rows to the examined dataset.

$applied\,to \backslash^{pretrained\,on}$	Paint control	IOF/ROL	GSDTSR	SMBV1
Paint control	–	0.78 ± 0.26	0.79 ± 0.27	0.78 ± 0.26
IOF/ROL	0.5 ± 0.32	–	0.51 ± 0.34	0.48 ± 0.32
GSDTSR	0.69 ± 0.17	0.74 ± 0.17	–	0.66 ± 0.2
SMBV1	0.5 ± 0.0	0.5 ± 0.0	0.5 ± 0.0	–

Now we switch our focus to a comparison with the model without TL [17]. We consider the paint control, IOF/ROL and SMBV1 dataset (since we used the GSDTSR for pretraining the model).

We display the quotient of the NAPFD values of XCSF-TL and the base version in Table 3. There we can see that the usage of TL boosts the performance by up to 5.5%. Furthermore, we cannot observe negative effects in any of the nine experimental set ups. The lowest performance increase can be observed for the SMBV1 dataset when trained using the time rank reward. There, TL improves the performance only by about 0.01%. Nonetheless, the experimental results are in favor of our hypothesis. We once more perform additional statistical tests to examine our hypothesis since the averaged NAPFD values contain a certain level of variance. We again use one-sided Wilcoxon tests and test the hypothesis that the XCSF without TL is superior to XCSF-TL. The p-values are shown in Table 4. We once more used a significance level of 0.05 and all p-values are below it. We can reject all null hypotheses and thus infer that XCSF benefits from TL on the considered datasets.

We also intend to give an overview about the corresponding time series of each agent and not only about aggregated results. Thus we plotted the averaged NAPFD values for each CI cycle, agent, and dataset in Figs. 2 to 4. Note, that

Table 3. NAPFD ratio between the XCSF-TL and the XCSF of Rosenbauer et al. [17].

	Paint control	IOF/ROL	SMBV1
Failcount	1.0121	1.0550	1.0264
Time rank	1.0341	1.0210	1.0001

Table 4. p-values for the null hypothesis that TL is detrimental for the performance in terms of NAPFD.

	Paint control	IOF/ROL	SMBV1
Failcount	1.46e-29	4.86e-73	2.29e-524
Time rank	1.28e-87	6.91e-24	0.001346

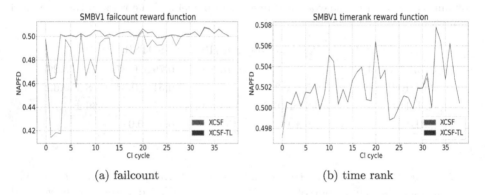

(a) failcount   (b) time rank

Fig. 2. Averaged achieved NAPFD values for the SMBV1 dataset.

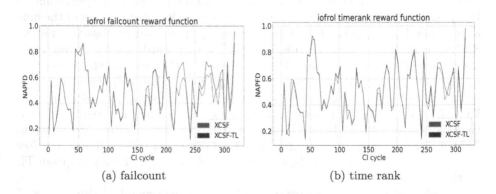

(a) failcount   (b) time rank

Fig. 3. Averaged achieved NAPFD values for the IOF/ROL dataset.

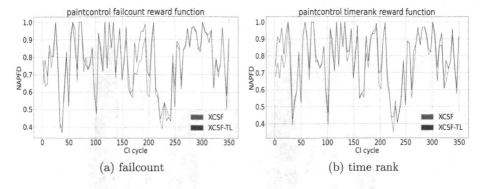

(a) failcount   (b) time rank

Fig. 4. Averaged achieved NAPFD values for the paintcontrol dataset.

there is a certain variance in performance due to the changes in the underlying environment (e.g. due to new software errors or fixed ones).

In Fig. 2 we can observe close to no effect of TL for the time rank reward. We can only see a small performance increase at the start and around CI cycle 32. For the other cycles the performance is equal. However, for the failcount reward we can clearly recognize the advantage of TL in terms of NAPFD. The vanilla XCSF needs about 35 CI cycles to catch up.

For the IOF/ROL dataset (Fig. 3) we can see no performance boost at the start of the experiment. However, TL dampens occuring performance breakdowns, especially for the failcount reward (e.g. for CI cycles between 200 and 250). The same effects appear even more distinct on the paint control scenario (Fig. 4).

In general, the visual evaluation fits our statistical one. The Wilcoxon test filters out values of equal performance and only considers data points where the observations differ. In the majority of these differing data points our TL approach has higher NAPFD values which explains the p-values below the significance level.

Table 5. Mean achieved NAPFD $\pm\sigma$.

	Neural network	XCSF	XCSF-TL
Failcount	0.47066 ± 0.03048	0.48717 ± 0.02418	0.50007 ± 0.00863
Time rank	0.45947 ± 0.03088	0.50193 ± 0.00228	0.50197 ± 0.00224

On the paint control, IOF/ROL, and GSDTSR datasets, the LCS based agents are superior to the neural network approach of Spieker et al. [19]. For the SMBV1 dataset we yet only demonstrated that XCSF-TL is statistically the better choice than XCSF [17]. However, we also intend examine whether LCSs are a better choice than the neural network of Spieker et al. [20]. In order to do so

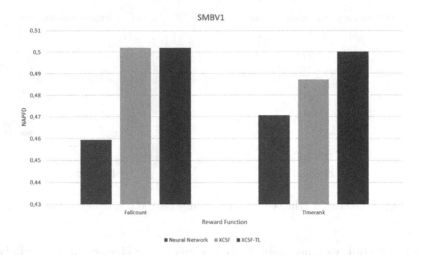

Fig. 5. Comparison with the artificial neural network of Spieker et al. [20].

we plotted the average NAPFD achieved in Fig. 5 and the concrete numbers plus minus the standard deviation in Table 5. On average, both LCSs are superior to the neural network; it is worth mentioning however that the difference of XCSF and XCSF-TL for the failcount reward is only marginal (in the plot not even visible). Besides, there is a certain variance in the results and thus we once more rely on statistical tests to verify the observation that the two LCS are the better choice for this dataset. Indeed, the corresponding one-sided Wilcoxon tests indicate significance (using a significance level of 0.05) which leads to the conclusion that LCSs are the better choice for this dataset as well.

7   Conclusions and Future Work

We examined the *adaptive test case selection* (ATCS) problem, i. e. the problem of compiling an optimal test suite for a certain software project, by *reinforcement learning* (RL). Recent research focused on the development of RL agents that efficiently find crucial tests. We investigated whether the knowledge of a trained agent can be *reused* beneficially for other software projects (i. e., other, but similar domains). We developed an easy to implement knowledge transformation for the *XCSF classifier system* and demonstrated promising performance increases of up to 5% when compared to the version not taking previous knowledge into account. Thereby we provided a first proof of concept that transfer learning can be applied to test case prioritization using RL.

A possible first improvement to our simplistic approach is based on the following observation: Before retraining on the new domain, all the classifiers' fitness parameters are being set to the same value. This has the unintended side effect that XCSF's system prediction may change in areas of the input space where more than one classifier matches. The reason for this is that XCSF uses the classifiers' fitness parameter not only as a quality estimate for the GA but also as a mixing weight. And while we mean to reset the classifiers' quality estimates to speed up retraining, we probably do not want to set all of the mixing weights to the same value as this unnecessarily distorts the system prediction (i. e., turning it into an *unweighted* average). Nevertheless, for simplicity's sake, we left introducing an additional explicit mixing weight parameter which, like the classifier's weight vector, is not changed upon population transfer, for future work.

References

1. Jenkins: The Definitive Guide. O'Reilly, Beijing (2011)
2. Baevski, A., Edunov, S., Liu, Y., Zettlemoyer, L., Auli, M.: Cloze-driven Pretraining of Self-attention Networks. CoRR abs/1903.07785 (2019). http://arxiv.org/abs/1903.07785
3. Butz, M.V., Wilson, S.W.: An algorithmic description of XCS. In: Luca Lanzi, P., Stolzmann, W., Wilson, S.W. (eds.) IWLCS 2000. LNCS (LNAI), vol. 1996, pp. 253–272. Springer, Heidelberg (2001). https://doi.org/10.1007/3-540-44640-0_15
4. Dustin, E., Rashka, J., Paul, J.: Automated Software Testing: Introduction, Management, and Performance. Addison-Wesley Longman Publishing Co., Inc, USA (1999)
5. Géron, A.: Hands-on Machine Learning with Scikit-Learn and TensorFlow: Concepts, Tools, and Techniques to Build Intelligent Systems. O'Reilly Media, Sebastopol (2017)
6. Iqbal, M., Browne, W.N., Zhang, M.: Reusing building blocks of extracted knowledge to solve complex, large-scale boolean problems. IEEE Trans. Evol. Comput. **18**(4), 465–480 (2014)
7. Jeffrey, D., Gupta, N.: Improving fault detection capability by selectively retaining test cases during test suite reduction. IEEE Trans. Softw. Eng. **33**(2), 108–123 (2007)
8. Kim, J.M., Porter, A.: A history-based test prioritization technique for regression testing in resource constrained environments. In: Proceedings of the 24th International Conference on Software Engineering, ICSE 2002, pp. 119–129 (2002)
9. Lazic, L., Mastorakis, N.: Cost effective software test metrics. World Sci. Eng. Acad. Soc. (WSEAS) **7**(6), 599–619 (2008)
10. Li, X., Yang, G.: Transferable XCS. In: Proceedings of the Genetic and Evolutionary Computation Conference 2016, GECCO 2016, pp. 453–460, Association for Computing Machinery, New York, NY, USA (2016)
11. Marijan, D., Gotlieb, A., Sen, S.: Test case prioritization for continuous regression testing: an industrial case study. In: 2013 IEEE International Conference on Software Maintenance, pp. 540–543 (2013)
12. McMaster, S., Memon, A.M.: Call stack coverage for test suite reduction. In: 21st IEEE International Conference on Software Maintenance (ICSM 2005), pp. 539–548 (2005)
13. Mohamed, E., Sirlantzis, K., Howells, G.: Application of transfer learning for object detection on manually collected data. In: Bi, Y., Bhatia, R., Kapoor, S. (eds.) IntelliSys 2019. AISC, vol. 1037, pp. 919–931. Springer, Cham (2020). https://doi.org/10.1007/978-3-030-29516-5_69

14. Noguchi, T., Washizaki, H., Fukazawa, Y., Sato, A., Ota, K.: History-based test case prioritization for black box testing using ant colony optimization. In: 2015 IEEE 8th International Conference on Software Testing, Verification and Validation (ICST), pp. 1–2 (2015)

15. Park, H., Ryu, H., Baik, J.: Historical value-based approach for cost-cognizant test case prioritization to improve the effectiveness of regression testing. In: 2008 Second International Conference on Secure System Integration and Reliability Improvement, pp. 39–46 (2008)

16. Qu, X., Cohen, M.B., Woolf, K.M.: Combinatorial interaction regression testing: a study of test case generation and prioritization. In: 2007 IEEE International Conference on Software Maintenance, pp. 255–264 (2007)

17. Rosenbauer, L., Stein, A., Pätzel, D., Hähner, J.: XCSF with experience replay for automatic test case prioritization. In: 2020 IEEE Symposium Series on Computational Intelligence (SSCI) (2020)

18. Rosenbauer, L., Stein, A., Maier, R., Pätzel, D., Hähner, J.: XCS as a reinforcement learning approach to automatic test case prioritization. In: Proceedings of the 2020 Genetic and Evolutionary Computation Conference Companion, GECCO 2020, pp. 1798–1806, Association for Computing Machinery, New York, NY, USA (2020)

19. Rosenbauer, L., Stein, A., Pätzel, D., Hähner, J.: XCSF for automatic test case prioritization. In: Proceedings of International Joint Conference on Computational Intelligence (2020)

20. Spieker, H., Gotlieb, A., Marijan, D., Mossige, M.: reinforcement learning for automatic test case prioritization and selection in continuous integration. In: Proceedings of the 26th ACM SIGSOFT International Symposium on Software Testing and Analysis, ISSTA 2017, pp. 12–22. Association for Computing Machinery, New York, NY, USA (2017)

21. Stein, A., Maier, R., Rosenbauer, L., Hähner, J.: XCS Classifier System with Experience Replay. In: Proceedings of the 2020 Genetic and Evolutionary Computation Conference, GECCO 2020, pp. 404–413. Association for Computing Machinery, New York, NY, USA (2020)

22. Torrey, L., Shavlik, J.: Transfer learning. Handbook of Research on Machine Learning Applications (2009)

23. Urbanowicz, R.J., Browne, W.N.: Introduction to Learning Classifier Systems, 1st edn. Springer, Berlin (2017)

24. Wilson, S.: Classifiers that approximate functions. Natural Comput. 1, 1–2 (2002)

25. Wilson, S.W.: Classifier fitness based on accuracy. Evol. Comput. 3(2), 149–175 (1995)

26. Yoo, S., Harman, M.: Regression testing minimization, selection and prioritization: a survey. Softw. Test. Verif. Reliab. 22(2), 67–120 (2012)

On the Effects of Absumption for XCS with Continuous-Valued Inputs

Alexander R. M. Wagner[✉] and Anthony Stein

Department of Artificial Intelligence in Agricultural Engineering and
Computational Science Lab (CSL), University of Hohenheim,
Garbenstraße 9, 70599 Stuttgart, Germany
{a.wagner,anthony.stein}@uni-hohenheim.de

Abstract. The rule-based *XCS Classifier System* (XCS) aims at forming classifiers which are as general as possible to achieve an optimal
performance level. A too high generalization pressure may lead to over-
general classifiers degrading the performance of XCS. To date, no method
exists for *XCS for real-valued input spaces* (XCSR) to handle over-general
classifiers ensuring an accurate population. The *Absumption* mechanism
and the *Specify* operator, both developed for XCS with binary inputs,
provide a promising basis for over-generality handling in XCSR. This
paper introduces adapted versions of Absumption and Specify by proposing different identification and specialization strategies for the application in XCSR. To determine their potential, the adapted techniques will
be evaluated in different classification problems, i.e., common benchmarks and real-world data from the agricultural domain, and in a multi-
step problem.

Keywords: Learning classifier systems · XCS classifier system ·
Absumption · Over-general classifiers · Agricultural data

1 Introduction

The most widely studied *Learning Classifier System* (LCS) in terms of formal
theoretical analysis [18] and empirical evaluation is currently the *XCS Classifier
System* (XCS) [29]. It represents an evolutionary rule- and accuracy-based online
machine learning technique characterized by an inherent generalization pressure
hypothesized to result in accurate and maximally-general rules. Yet, an excessive
generalization pressure can reduce the system performance of XCS under certain
circumstances [2,11,13] due to the formation of over-general classifiers. By using
intervals in the continuous real-valued input space to describe a classifier condition, the *XCS for real-valued input spaces* (XCSR) [27] theoretically permits
infinite variations in one dimension of the condition, unlike the traditional XCS
with binary inputs just allowing 3 different states. Thus, the concepts of generalization and over-generalization differ significantly in traditional XCS and XCSR,
whereas XCSR is characterized by a considerably increased complexity due to
the large number of variations. Until now, no solution has been proposed for the

© Springer Nature Switzerland AG 2021
P. A. Castillo and J. L. Jiménez Laredo (Eds.): EvoApplications 2021, LNCS 12694, pp. 697–713, 2021.
https://doi.org/10.1007/978-3-030-72699-7_44

problem of identifying and handling over-general classifiers in XCSR guaranteeing an accurate population during the learning phase. In contrast, for traditional XCS, the *Absumption* mechanism [16] and the *Specify* operator [12] have been proposed offering a basis for XCSR. Since both methods aim at solving the same problem, we refer to them as *Over-Generality Handling* (OGH) in this paper.

This work is part of our overarching aspiration to deal with the still unsolved issue of over-generalization in XCS when applied to real-valued problem spaces, cf. e.g., [20]. We focus on XCS(R) as it forms the basis for many descended systems such as UCS [3], ExSTraCS [25] or XCSF [28]. We also deem the capability of XCS to learn complete $X \times A \to P$ mappings as a crucial feature in our pursuit of readying robust and reliable online learning systems allowing for interpretability but also self-reflection of the evolved knowledge [19,21].

The contributions of this work are: (1) The evaluation of the application of Absumption and of Specify to gain insights into their impact on the learning performance of XCSR. (2) The introduction of identification and specialization strategies for OGH in real-valued problem spaces. (3) A comparative study of the use of Absumption and of Specify in XCSR, applied to several well-known toy problems (single- and multi-step), and agricultural real-world classification tasks.

We proceed with a brief overview of approaches to remove inappropriate classifiers in LCS in Sect. 2 followed by necessary background information on XCS and OGH in Sect. 3. Section 4 introduces the adapted versions of the OGH approaches for XCSR (or short XCS in the remainder) including new specialization and identification strategies. In Sect. 5 the results of empirical studies on various classification tasks and on a multi-step problem are reported. We conclude with a short summary and a description of future work in Sect. 6.

2 Related Work

Early on, over-generalization was part of the research in the field of XCS [13], but so far only procedures for traditional XCS with binary inputs have been developed. The Absumption method [16], underlying ASCS [17], is the most recent procedure especially designed for single-step problems. The Specify operator [12] was introduced to handle the problem of over-general classifiers in multi-step problems. In addition, further specialization mechanisms in other LCSs have been developed: For the ALECSYS Classifier System, the *Mutespec* operator [9] was introduced to handle over-general classifiers. Furthermore, ACS2 [6] applies a specialization mechanism not intended to identify over-general classifiers. In the field of Pittsburgh-style LCSs, rule specialization methods have also been introduced, such as the so-called memetic operators in BioHEL [8]. In addition to approaches for rule specialization, further methods exist to remove unnecessary or inappropriate rules from the population to form an optimal solution. In [29], *condensation* was proposed. Another method represents the *compaction* algorithm [30], extended by *closest classifier matching* in [5].

3   Background

This section briefly provides the necessary background for OGH and XCS. However, a certain familiarity with temporal difference learning in general and XCS in particular is assumed due to space constraints. For a more detailed introduction, the reader is referred to [23] and [7,27].

3.1   Real-Valued XCS in a Nutshell

The evolutionary rule-based machine learning system XCS [26,29] belongs to the family of Michigan-style LCSs, attributed to Holland [10]. Since XCS heavily relies on a niche-relative variant of Holland's *genetic algorithm* (GA) employing the rule's accuracy as fitness, it also represents the origin of the family of

---

Algorithm 1: XCS learning loop, adapted from [7]

---

1   Observe environmental state σ_t at time t
2   Create match set $[M] \subseteq [P]$ for σ_t with $[M] := \{cl_i \mid \sigma_t \in cl_i.C\}$
3   Create PA from $[M]$ with $PA(a) = \dfrac{\sum_{cl \in [M] \mid cl.a=a} cl.p * cl.F}{\sum_{cl \in [M] \mid cl.a=a} cl.F}$
4   **if** $U_{[0,1]} < \epsilon$ **then**
5   $\quad$ Select random action, i.e., $a_{exec} = \text{rand}(A)$
6   **else**
7   $\quad$ Select best action, i.e., $a_{exec} = \text{argmax}_a PA(a)$
8   **end if**
9   Create action set $[A] \subseteq [M]$ with $[A] := \{cl_i \mid cl_i.a = a_{exec}\}$
10 Execute a_{exec} on and observe reward r_t from the environment
11 **if** $[A]_{t-1} \neq \emptyset$ **then**
12 $\quad$ $P \leftarrow r_{t-1} + \gamma \cdot \text{argmax}_a PA(a)$
13 $\quad$ Update each $cl \in [A]_{t-1}$ using P by means of Widrow-Hoff delta rule
14 $\quad$ **if** $t - \dfrac{\sum_{cl \in [A]_{t-1}} cl.num * cl.ts}{\sum_{cl \in [A]_{t-1}} cl.num} > \theta_{GA}$ **then**
15 $\quad\quad$ Run GA on $[A]_{t-1}$ considering σ_{t-1}
16 $\quad$ **end if**
17 **end if**
18 **if** *end of episode* **then**
19 $\quad$ $P \leftarrow r_t$
20 $\quad$ Update each $cl \in [A]$ using P by means of Widrow-Hoff delta rule
21 $\quad$ **if** $t - \dfrac{\sum_{cl \in [A]} cl.num * cl.ts}{\sum_{cl \in [A]} cl.num} > \theta_{GA}$ **then**
22 $\quad\quad$ Run GA on $[A]$ considering σ_t
23 $\quad\quad$ $[A]_{t-1} \leftarrow \emptyset$
24 $\quad$ **end if**
25 **else**
26 $\quad$ $[A]_{t-1} \leftarrow [A]$
27 $\quad$ $r_{t-1} \leftarrow r_t$
28 $\quad$ $\sigma_{t-1} \leftarrow \sigma_t$
29 **end if**

---

accuracy-based LCSs [24]. Operating as an online learning system continuously updating its learned model, XCS is capable of adapting to changes in its environment while in use, representing an important factor for reliable use under real-world conditions. The evolutionary learning approach of XCS constitutes a particular strength in adapting to the environment enabling XCS to learn dynamic goals. As proposed by Wilson's *generalization hypothesis* [26], XCS aims to construct a complete, accurate and maximally-general state-action map, more formally defined as $X \times A \to P$. The set of all possible environmental states σ_t is called *input space* X. The *action space* A represents all possible actions and P denotes the *payoff space*. In XCS the state-action map is represented by a population $[P] := \{cl_i\}_{i \in \mathbb{N}}$ of rules or classifiers, usually just called *cl* and defined as $cl := (C, a, p, \epsilon, F)$. $cl.C \subseteq X$ defines a subset of X matched by *cl*, whereas the action advocated by *cl* is $cl.a \in A$. $cl.p$ denotes the *payoff prediction* of *cl*. The use of local learning in XCS by means of classifiers facilitates both the interpretability and the reflection of the acquired knowledge, e.g., whether knowledge gaps or contradictions exist. In $cl.\epsilon$, an estimate of the absolute *prediction error* is stored. $cl.F$ represents the *fitness* of *cl*, estimating the niche-relative accuracy of the payoff prediction of *cl*. Furthermore, additional book-keeping parameters are maintained in XCS: the number of performed reinforcements of a *cl* is stored in $cl.exp$ and the number of successful subsumption operations in $cl.num$. To control the GA invocation, a timestamp parameter $cl.ts$ is updated each time a *cl* was a candidate for the GA.

Algorithm 1 presents a detailed description of a single pass of the main learning loop of XCS. As long as the defined termination criteria are not satisfied, e.g., a maximum number of learning steps, the loop is repeated. When applied to single-step problems, i.e., classification, the actions are usually selected by alternating explore and exploit steps instead of an ϵ-greedy approach. $U_{[0,1]}$ draws a value uniformly at random from the given interval. The basic structure of XCS features a great flexibility regarding possible tasks, also reflected in the good extensibility of XCS. Thus, many extensions to XCS have already been introduced to expand its application range, cf. e.g., [25,27,28].

3.2   Generalization and Over-Generalization in XCS

Based on Wilson's description in [26], a system uses generalization whenever it treats different situations in the same way, if these situations lead to equivalent after-effects for the system when performing the same action. A major problem for LCS is the unintended formation of over-general classifiers, i.e., a classifier just capable of advocating the correct action for a subset of its condition [11]. These classifiers are capable of degrading the performance of a system, as they may result in the selection of an incorrect action and propagate incorrect information. Since over-general classifiers match incompatible niches, they possess an oscillating prediction due to being only locally accurate. This usually causes them to be inaccurate. As conjectured by Wilson's *Generalization Hypothesis* [26], explaining the process of evolving accurate and maximal-general classifiers in XCS, over-general classifiers should be removed from the population due to their inaccuracy. However, sometimes the counteracting fitness signal is not sufficient, leading to over-general classifiers caused by the generalization pressure present in XCS. If the oscillation of the classifier prediction is small enough, inaccurate classifiers may be considered accurate due to the error threshold hyperparameter ϵ_0 enabling XCS to tolerate small oscillations [11]. Thus, as described in [13], an over-general classifier must be observed at all or often enough by XCS to cause sufficient oscillation of the prediction for the classifier to be recognized as inaccurate. We refer to this problem as *unequally observed environmental niches*, which can be caused by *non-uniform sampling* or *unequally sized niches*. The problem of unequally sized niches can also occur in environments with equally sized niches if different types of niches are not or not almost equally contained in a classifier. Another problem causing XCS to consider over-general classifiers as accurate is the issue of *indistinguishable payoff levels* of different environmental niches associated with multi-step problems [2]. This issue can arise due to the application of a discounted reward or the presence of *dominant* classifiers, i.e., over-general classifiers resulting in a misleading fitness signal. In comparison to binary inputs, these problems are generally more serious for real-valued inputs, since the number of possible observations in the possibly continuous input space is substantially increased. On the other hand, in each dimension of a condition, an infinite number of variations of the intervals are theoretically possible. For a more detailed description of generalization and over-generalization in the context of XCS, we refer the reader to [2,11,13] and [4].

4   Over-Generality Handling for Real-Valued XCS

To address the challenge of over-generality in real-valued problem spaces by identifying and suitably handling over-general classifiers, we design two *Over-Generality Handling* (OGH) approaches, one based on the *Absumption* mechanism in [16] and the other based on the *Specify* operator in [12]. If OGH is enabled, it is invoked subsequently to the reinforcement in each iteration of XCS's main loop. First, we will introduce the basic structure and the identification strategies of both approaches, as the specialization strategies, creating more specific versions of an identified over-general classifier, are shared between both variants of OGH.

As shown in Algorithm 2, the adapted version for real-valued problem spaces uses a more generic basic structure compared to the original Absumption [16], i.e., both the identification and the specialization strategy employed are exchangeable. Based on the *REA* ratio of an over-general classifier cl_{og}, Absumption decides, whether a cl_{og} in $[overG]$ is removed from the population or decomposed into more specific versions. REA is the ratio of cl_{og}'s experience to the dimensionality of its condition, i.e., an indicator of useful information contained in cl_{og}. The threshold value is set to 1 as described in [16]. Thus, if the REA of cl_{og} is at least 1, the specialization strategy applied decomposes cl_{og} into an amount of more specific versions defined by $cl_{og}.num$.

The first strategy we propose for detecting over-general classifiers, called *Inconsistency*, is based on the mechanism proposed in [16]. It utilizes the idea

---

Algorithm 2: Absumption for real-valued XCS

Input: $[A]$:= classifiers in action set
           $[P]$:= classifier population
1 $[overG]$:= detect over-general classifiers in $[A]$ by identification strategy
2 **forall** cl_{og} in $[overG]$ **do**
3 | **if** *REA* of cl_{og} < 1 **then**
4 | | remove cl_{og} from $[P]$
5 | **else**
6 | | $[spec]$:= create more specific versions of cl_{og} by specialization strategy
7 | | remove cl_{og} from $[P]$ and $[A]$
8 | | add all classifiers from $[spec]$ to $[P]$ and $[A]$
9 | **end if**
10 **end forall**

---

of over-general classifiers matching incompatible niches by tracking the *number of positive rewards* (NPR) and the *number of negative rewards* (NNR). If $NPR * NNR > 0$ is valid for a classifier, it is considered to be over-general. As Inconsistency can only be applied to single-step problems, we introduce the second identification strategy, *Prediction Deviation Variance*. This strategy performs the identification based on the increased prediction oscillation of an over-general classifier. In this strategy, for each classifier cl, the absolute deviation $|cl.p - r_t|$, where r_t denotes the current reward at time t, is tracked in a FIFO-buffer within cl, denoted as $cl.dev$. cl is only checked for over-generality by this strategy if $cl.exp > \theta_{OGCIdent}$ applies. If the variance of the absolute deviations in $cl.dev$ is more than twice the average deviation variances of the entire population, cl is regarded as over-general. This condition was determined in preliminary experiments and does not claim to be optimal, but showed good results.

Specify for real-valued XCS is based on the version for binary inputs in [12], already employing an identification strategy applicable in single- and multi-step problems. The process of Specify for real-valued XCS is shown in Algorithm 3. This OGH approach uses an indirect mechanism to detect over-general classifiers based on the condition $\epsilon_{[A]} \geq 2 * \epsilon_{[P]}$ proposed in [12].

We propose two specialization strategies returning the required amount of more specific versions of an identified classifier cl_{id} utilizing the center point c of cl_{id}'s hyperrectangular condition $cl_{id}.C = (\boldsymbol{l}^{cl_{id}}, \boldsymbol{u}^{cl_{id}})$, i.e., $c_i = l_i^{cl_{id}} + (u_i^{cl_{id}} - l_i^{cl_{id}})/2$ for $i = 1...n$. The first method is the *New Condition Specialization* (NCS) strategy. A new classifier cl_{new} is generated by computing the so-called interval predicate (l_i, u_i) of condition $cl_{new}.C$ for each dimension $i = 1...n$ as follows: $l_i = \max\{l_i^*, c_i - U_{[0,r_0)}\}$ and $u_i = \min\{u_i^*, c_i + U_{[0,r_0)}\}$. l_i^* and u_i^* denote the minimum and maximum bounds of the problem space for dimension i, respectively. In $U_{[0,r_0)}$, the given standard spread parameter r_0 is excluded. The other attributes of cl_{new} are initialized with the attribute values of cl_{id}, except $cl_{new}.exp = 0$ and $cl_{new}.num = 1$. However, as a simple and fast strategy, it does not guarantee the creation of $cl_{new}.C$ inside $cl_{id}.C$. This drawback is solved by the *Inside Condition Specialization* (ICS) strategy, where $(\boldsymbol{l}, \boldsymbol{u})$ of $cl_{new}.C$ are determined differently: $l_i = \max\{l_i^{cl_{id}}, l_i^*, c_i - U_{[0,r_0)}\}$ and $u_i = \min\{u_i^{cl_{id}}, u_i^*, c_i + U_{[0,r_0)}\}$. Thus, $cl_{new}.C$

Algorithm 3: Specify for real-valued XCS

Input:	$[A]$:= classifiers in action set
	$[P]$:= classifier population

1 **if** *average experience in* $[A] \geq \theta_{OGCIdent}$ **then**

2 $\quad \epsilon_{[A]} := \dfrac{\sum_{cl \in [A]} cl.\epsilon}{\sum_{cl \in [A]} cl.num}$

3 $\quad \epsilon_{[P]} := \dfrac{\sum_{cl \in [P]} cl.\epsilon}{\sum_{cl \in [P]} cl.num}$

4 $\quad$ **if** $\epsilon_{[A]} \geq 2 * \epsilon_{[P]}$ **then**

5 $\quad\quad$ cl := ϵ-proportionate selection of one classifier in $[A]$

6 $\quad\quad$ cl_{spec} := create one more specific version of cl by specialization strategy

7 $\quad\quad$ add cl_{spec} to $[P]$

8 $\quad$ **end if**

9 **end if**

is fully contained inside $cl_{id}.C$, as the constraints $l_i^{cl_{id}} \leq l_i$ and $u_i \leq u_i^{cl_{id}}$ are satisfied. The other attributes of cl_{new} are initialized analogously to NCS.

5   Evaluation

In this section the results of a variety of experiments are summarized we carried out to evaluate the impact of Absumption- and Specify-based OGH on the performance on XCS with real-valued inputs. We performed experiments with XCS on two multi-step problems and on six single-step problems, i.e., classification tasks. These tasks comprise three well-known toy problems and three real-world data sets from the agricultural domain, as the authors' research is concerned with the usage of AI in agricultural applications. Typically, other types of modern LCSs, e.g., ExSTRaCS [25] or BioHEL [1], are preferred for classification tasks and for mining of data sets. However, we have chosen XCS as it enables reliable learning at runtime, i.e., online, in systems facing real-world conditions, due to creating a complete $X \times A \rightarrow P$ mapping. We intend to show OGH improving the ability of XCS to generate accurate complete mappings and, thus, to reliably perform classification tasks and stream mining of online real-world data. Furthermore, OGH is designed to be easily applicable to any system descended from XCS.

All experiments have been repeated for 30 i.i.d. runs with individual random seeds. The repetition means and the observed standard deviations of the conducted experiments are given in Table 1 and Table 2 below. In all conducted experiments, the performance of XCS was evaluated using 4 metrics: (1) The average reward achieved at the end of the learning period. (2) The system error, i.e., the average error of system prediction in relation to the actual reward received. (3) The average number of macro classifiers or the average size of the population, indicated by $||[P]||$ (4) The average volume of classifier conditions in $[P]$, i.e. the average classifier generality. In the evaluation experiments, both a configuration with the Specify-based and with the Absumption-based

OGH approach have been evaluated and are set in contrast to standard XCS as baseline. For statistical evaluation, we analyzed the experimental results by means of different statistical tests for significance: A standard *ANOVA* paired with a *Tukey-HSD* post-hoc test was conducted to test for statistically significant differences if a test for *homoscedasticity* was positive. Otherwise, we employed the robust *Welch-ANOVA* in combination with a *Games-Howell* post-hoc test. Figure 1 shows plots of the learning curves of the compared configurations over the entire learning period along with the standard deviation in form of error bars. As commonly done in the LCS literature, the learning progress of the single-step problems is shown in form of reward achieved and system prediction error. For the multi-step problems, the learning progress is depicted by means of required steps to the goal.

5.1   Results in Benchmark Problems

First, we performed an evaluation of three well-known benchmark problems, as their known problem structure facilitates an analysis with respect to specific characteristics and provides the basis for comparison with results from the literature: (1) *Real k-multiplexer problem* (RMP) [27], (2) *Checkerboard problem* (CBP) [22], and (3) *Mario* classification problem [19]. RMP poses a challenging problem of real-valued binary classification with properties like feature interaction (*epistasis*) and multiple niches with same actions (*heterogeneity*) [25]. For each dimension x_i, with $i = 1, ..., k$, the input space of RMP is defined in the interval $0.0 \leq x_i < 1.0$. A threshold θ specifies the two partitions of the bit values in each dimension. In this paper we applied RMP with $\theta = 0.5$ and $k = 6$, denoted as 6-RMP. CBP is a well-known benchmark for LCS, designed to provide an increased complexity compared to RMP [22]. The underlying problem is to predict a multidimensional checkerboard pattern consisting of black and white areas. In this paper, we used a variant of CBP with 3 dimensions and 3 divisions per dimension denoted as CBP(3,3). Mario is a two-dimensional real-valued multi-class classification problem in the form of a 16×16 pixel art of Super Mario. Unlike CBP it features seven different actions, comprising the various colors, and allows for different levels of generalization in the niches, e.g., the blue trousers compared to the yellow knobs. Analogously to RMP, the input space of CBP and Mario is also defined in the interval $0.0 \leq x_i < 1.0$ for each dimension x_i.

A single repetition of an experiment was run over 100,000 alternating explore/exploit steps. In each step, the input space of the benchmark problems was sampled using a uniform distribution. We applied a binary reward scheme for each of the benchmark problems. Each correctly predicted action of a sampled situation led to a reward of 1000, otherwise 0. The intervals of a classifier condition were encoded by the unordered bound hyperrectangular representation [22]. The configuration and hyperparameters of OGH were determined in preliminary experiments. In all benchmark problems, we applied the specialization strategy NCS for both OGH approaches and the *Inconsistency* identification strategy of Absumption. For Specify, $\theta_{OGCIdent}$ was set to 10 for

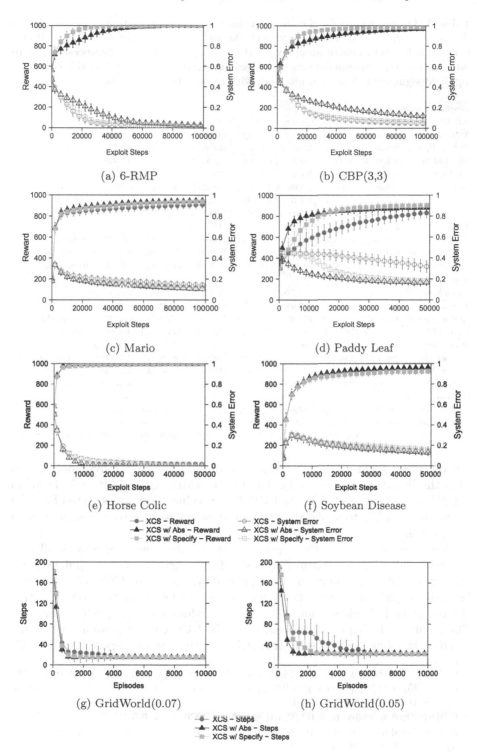

Fig. 1. Learning curve plots of the conducted experiments.

Table 1. Overall results for classification tasks, i.e., reward, system error, population size and generality. All entries represent the means ± 1 SD of the 30 repetitions. Letters in brackets denote groups with statistically significant differences, i.e., a p-value $< \alpha = 0.05$. Arrows indicate an increase or decrease in a metric and bold entries highlight significant improvements, both with respect to the baseline.

Benchmark problems				
6-RMP	Reward	Sys. Err.	$\|[P]\|$	Generality
XCS w/ Abs	935.07↓ ± 9.92 (B)	119.73↑ ± 14.56 (A)	408.62↑ ± 23.95 (A)	0.00067↓ ± 0.00006 (C)
XCS w/ Specify	968.10↑ ± 3.97 (A)	77.88↑ ± 6.67 (B)	323.96↑ ± 11.89 (B)	0.00113↓ ± 0.00004 (B)
Standard XCS	967.96 ± 6.07 (A)	65.82 ± 10.43 (C)	279.93 ± 17.03 (C)	0.00118 ± 0.00007 (A)
CBP(3,3)	Reward	Sys. Err.	$\|[P]\|$	Generality
XCS w/ Abs	899.39↓ ± 6.72 (B)	209.16↑ ± 7.35 (A)	1103.25↑ ± 20.99 (A)	0.00363↑ ± 0.00003 (A)
XCS w/ Specify	936.25↑ ± 4.27 (A)	130.47↑ ± 6.05 (B)	765.16↑ ± 14.75 (B)	0.00356↑ ± 0.00011 (B)
Standard XCS	935.61 ± 5.57 (A)	119.05 ± 7.85 (C)	689.61 ± 17.99 (C)	0.00312 ± 0.00010 (C)
Mario	Reward	Sys. Err.	$\|[P]\|$	Generality
XCS w/ Abs	**907.33**↑ ± 2.45 (A)	**156.24**↓ ± 2.69 (C)	3544.48↑ ± 26.96 (A)	0.00557↓ ± 0.00014 (C)
XCS w/ Specify	**891.98**↑ ± 3.80 (B)	**169.79**↓ ± 3.62 (B)	3291.98↑ ± 24.87 (B)	0.00709↓ ± 0.00019 (B)
Standard XCS	866.50 ± 5.28 (C)	190.84 ± 4.98 (A)	2690.30 ± 31.56 (C)	0.00939 ± 0.00034 (A)
Real-world problems				
Paddy Leaf	Reward	Sys. Err.	$\|[P]\|$	Generality
XCS w/ Abs	**828.09**↑ ± 4.57 (A)	**217.95**↓ ± 4.61 (C)	4416.52↑ ± 29.31 (A)	0.00117↓ ± 0.00003 (C)
XCS w/ Specify	**808.03**↑ ± 12.38 (B)	**277.43**↓ ± 10.34 (B)	3145.65↑ ± 57.59 (B)	0.00661↓ ± 0.00882 (B)
Standard XCS	688.16 ± 34.67 (C)	398.29 ± 29.64 (A)	1711.14 ± 145.73 (C)	0.01855 ± 0.00334 (A)
Horse Colic	Reward	Sys. Err.	$\|[P]\|$	Generality
XCS w/ Abs	**990.89**↑ ± 0.66 (A)	**31.93**↓ ± 1.89 (B)	5102.72↓ ± 26.60 (B)	2.75×10^{-11}↓ ±1.42×10^{-11}(A)
XCS w/ Specify	984.18↓ ± 2.73 (B)	54.26↑ ± 5.03 (A)	5139.62↑ ± 26.87 (A)	3.54×10^{-11}↓ ±1.50×10^{-11}(A)
Standard XCS	984.83 ± 2.42 (B)	54.00 ± 4.72 (A)	5104.23 ± 28.37 (B)	3.63×10^{-11} ±1.53×10^{-11}(A)
Soybean Disease	Reward	Sys. Err.	$\|[P]\|$	Generality
XCS w/ Abs	**895.71**↑ ± 6.41 (A)	**187.89**↓ ± 14.02 (B)	21471.02↓ ± 33.76 (B)	6.05×10^{-17}↑ ±5.06×10^{-17}(A)
XCS w/ Specify	866.61↓ ± 10.25 (B)	208.64↑ ± 12.65 (A)	21987.54↑ ± 33.79 (A)	5.34×10^{-17}↓ ±4.48×10^{-17}(A)
Standard XCS	871.53 ± 8.83 (B)	200.99 ± 12.28 (A)	21470.48 ± 28.94 (B)	5.46×10^{-17} ±3.11×10^{-17}(A)

6-RMP and to 50 for CBP(3,3) and Mario. We adopted further hyperparameters from the literature, which can be found for 6-RMP[1], CBP(3,3)[2] and Mario[3] in [22,27] and [19], respectively. For CBP(3,3), a value of 0.5 was selected for r_0 in deviation from [22] to artificially create a tendency of XCS to over-generalize in this problem.

According to Table 1, the application of Absumption or Specify in all considered problems is accompanied by a significant increase of the population size and by a significant reduction of the generality, except for CBP(3,3). This can be easily explained by the underlying concept of OGH, as the decomposition of over-general classifiers can lead to many redundant over-specific classifiers. The significantly improved generality in CBP(3,3) can be possibly attributed to OGH enabling XCS to solve the problem from the over-specific side, facili-

---

[1] 6-RMP: $N = 800$, $\alpha = 0.1$, $\beta = 0.2$, $\delta = 0.1$, $\nu = 5$, $\theta_{mna} = 2$, $\theta_{GA} = 12$, $\theta_{del} = 20$, $\theta_{sub} = 20$, $\epsilon_0 = 10$, $\chi = 0.8$, $\mu = 0.04$, $p_{ini} = 10.0$, $\epsilon_{ini} = 0.0$, $F_{ini} = 0.01$, $\epsilon_{red} = 0.25$, $F_{red} = 0.1$, $m_0 = 0.1$, $r_0 = 1.0$.

[2] CBP(3,3): Analogous to 6-RMP, except: $N = 2000$, $r_0 = 0.5$.

[3] Mario: Analogous to 6-RMP, except: $N = 7000$, $\beta = 0.3$, $\theta_{mna} = 6$, $\theta_{GA} = 30$, $\theta_{del} = 50$, $\theta_{sub} = 50$, $r_0 = 0.1$.

tating the formation of accurate classifiers with increased generality. Regarding the reward and system error metrics, in case of 6-RMP and CBP, XCS benefits neither from Specify nor from Absumption. Compared to standard XCS, the application of Specify results in a non-significantly different reward value and an increased system error. In contrast, the application of Absumption reduces the reward value and leads to the highest system error of all configurations. One possible explanation of the results is the basic structure of these problems posing a challenge to OGH. The equally sized niches with strictly defined boundaries require the intervals of a classifier condition to be accurately inside a niche in order for a classifier not to be regarded as over-general. Due to the random decomposition of identified over-general classifiers, it cannot be guaranteed that newly created conditions will be contained inside a niche. Especially for Absumption, this effect seems to have a major impact, as the strict evaluation of inaccuracies and their subsequent treatment seem to reduce the learning speed, as shown in the learning curve diagrams in Fig. 1a and 1b. For Specify, this problem seems less affecting, which may be due to the indirect identification of at most one over-general classifier per iteration. It would therefore be of interest to realize a more focused specialization pressure by OGH, which will be subject of future research. In Mario, the results are quite different, as this problem enables different generalizations and is known to lead to over-general classifiers due to its more inconsistent underlying structure consisting of unequal-sized niches. Both OGH approaches increase the performance of XCS and lead to a significant improvement of the reward and the system error metrics compared to the standard configuration. Special attention is drawn to Absumption, which significantly outperforms all other configurations in the aforementioned metrics. This is also reflected in the learning curves of Mario (cf. Fig. 1c) showing a significantly increased learning speed by OGH, especially by Absumption. Thus, OGH seems to enable a significant refinement of the learned model of a problem affected by over-general classifiers, resulting in increased accuracy and performance.

To summarize, in our experiments, the application of OGH in XCS mainly provides significant improvements regarding the system error and reward metrics for problems characterized by the formation of over-general classifiers and no significant benefits for other problems. It is also associated with an increase in population size and, in most cases, a decrease in generality in our experiments.

5.2 Results in Real-World Problems

In addition, an evaluation with real-world data was performed to assess the effects of OGH when applied to XCS in real-world settings. Since the authors are conducting research on the use of AI in agricultural applications, three available data sets covering different agricultural domains were selected for evaluation: (1) *Paddy Leaf*, (2) *Horse Colic* and (3) *Soybean Disease*. The Paddy Leaf[4] data set from Kaggle represents a multi-class classification task based on the

---

[4] https://www.kaggle.com/torikul140129/paddy-leaf-images-aman (05.11.2020).

average RGB values of 6000 paddy leaf pictures used to perform nitrogen fertilizer recommendation. The data set is balanced and consists of 3 real-valued attributes, indicating the average color channel values of red, green and blue present in a picture, and 4 different labels. The task of the Horse Colic[5] data set from the UCI repository is a binary classification, whether a lesion of a horse suffering from a colic was surgical or not based on different health attributes. The data set is unbalanced and consists of 368 instances with 21 different health attributes, either real-valued, integer-valued or boolean, and a total of 30% missing attribute entries. In case of missing entries, each attribute has been assigned a default value not being within the value range of the respective attribute. The last data set is Soybean Disease[6] from the UCI repository. The task is to classify 19 different soybean diseases from 35 integer-valued marker attributes also containing missing entries, handled analogously to the Horse Colic data set. The data set consists of 683 instances and is highly unbalanced. W.l.o.g., we normalized the attributes to the range $[0, 1]$ for all data sets.

A single repetition of an experiment was run over 50,000 alternating explore/exploit steps. In each step, an instance is drawn uniformly at random from the used data set with replacement. We also applied a binary reward scheme, i.e., a reward of 1000 for each correctly predicted action, i.e., class, otherwise 0. For the evaluation experiments with real-world data sets, a standard parameterization[7] of XCS was used. The conditions were encoded by unordered bound hyperrectangular representation. θ_{mna} was set depending on the number of available classes: In Paddy Leaf it was set to 4, in Horse Colic to 2 and in Soybean Disease to 19. Due to the high number of attributes and available classes in Soybean Disease, $N = 25,000$ to increase the population size. The experiments for the 3 real-world data sets shared the same configuration for OGH: The specialization strategy ICS was employed by both approaches, the *Inconsistency* identification strategy was applied in Absumption and, for Specify, $\theta_{OGCIdent}$ was set to 50.

Considering the results in Table 1, the application of Absumption results in significant performance improvements regarding the reward and system error metrics in all conducted experiments. It leads to a significant increase in learning performance and superior results compared to the other configurations. As shown in the learning curve plots in Figs. 1d, 1e and 1f, Absumption also causes a faster and more accurate learning of the problems, which is most evident in Paddy Leaf. Specify also leads to advantages in Paddy Leaf in terms of faster learning and a significant improvement of the reward and system error metrics, however, less pronounced compared to Absumption. In the other data sets, Specify does not yield any advantage, possibly due to the just indirect identification of over-general classifiers. Compared to the benchmark problems, only in one real-world data set, i.e., Paddy Leaf, OGH shows a significant increase in

---

[5] https://data.world/uci/horse-colic (05.11.2020).

[6] https://data.world/uci/soybean-large (05.11.2020).

[7] Analogous to 6-RMP, except: $N = 6400$, $\theta_{GA} = 48$, $\theta_{del} = 50$, $\theta_{sub} = 50$, $\epsilon_0 = 1.0$, $\epsilon_{red} = 1.0$, $m_0 = 0.5$, $r_0 = 1.0$.

population size and a significant reduction in generality. Similarly to the benchmark problems, this can be attributed to the underlying concept of OGH and is more pronounced in the case of Absumption. For the other two data sets, Specify causes a significantly increased population size, unlike Absumption. This can be attributed to the direct identification of over-general classifiers by Absumption, only performing necessary decompositions, which is not guaranteed in the case of Specify. Regarding generality, there are no significant differences between the configurations in Horse Colic and Soybean Disease.

In summary, for real-world data sets, the application of OGH, especially Absumption, in XCS causes significant improvements of the reward and system error metrics in our experiments. The increase in population size and decrease in generality due to OGH was less pronounced in our experiments. Based on the results, we expect OGH also provides advantages beyond the agricultural domain for problems featuring characteristics comparable to the applied data sets, such as unbalanced data or missing entries. However, we left this for future work.

5.3   Results in Multi-step Problems

To preliminarily evaluate the potential of OGH for multi-step problems, we conducted experiments in two differently configured variants of the *GridWorld* environment, which is based on the *Puddles* environment introduced in [14]. The problem space of GridWorld is two dimensional and each dimension x_i is defined in the interval $0.0 \leq x_i < 1.0$. In GridWorld, the task to be learned is to reach the goal in position $(1, 1)$ in as few steps as possible. In each episode the agent starts in a random position within the environment except the goal. The agent is allowed to move within the environment with a given step size in four directions, i.e., left, right up and down. For each step taken, the agent receives a negative reward or punishment of -0.5, except the step leading to the goal, resulting in a reward of 0. The environment also contains so-called puddles leading to an additional punishment of -2 for each puddle the agent is in. An episode ends either if the goal has been reached or if 200 steps have been taken.

In our experiments, we applied a step size of 0.07 and 0.05 denoted as GridWorld (0.07) and GridWorld (0.05), respectively. Each repetition of the experiments was run over 10,000 episodes. As a fixed number of episodes is defined for the repetitions, the configurations and repetitions differ in the number of steps. Thus, the results of the metrics already used in the single-step experiments are determined over the first 205,000 steps and 285,000 steps for GridWorld (0.07) and GridWorld (0.05), respectively. In addition to these metrics, the performance of XCS is evaluated over the entire repetition run using the steps to goal metric, which calculates as the 100-episode mean steps required to reach the goal. XCS only used explore steps in combination with an ϵ-decay action selection regime, parameterized as follows: $\epsilon = 1.0$, $\epsilon_{fin} = 0.02$ and a decay fraction of 10% of the episodes, i.e., in the reported experiments the ϵ was decayed from 1.0 to 0.02 over the first 1000 episodes. GridWorld (0.07) and GridWorld (0.05) shared the same parameterization[8], based on the settings for Puddles (0.1) in [14]. The conditions of the classifiers were encoded by unordered bound hyperrectangular representation. The classifiers employed a computed prediction using *recursive least squares* [15] with a parameterization of $\lambda_{RLS} = 1.0$ and $\delta_{RLS} = 1.0$. The settings of OGH were determined in preliminary experiments: For both experiments, the specialization strategy ICS was applied for both OGH approaches, for Specify a $\theta_{OGCIdent}$ of 100 was set and Absumption employed the *Prediction Deviation Variance* identification strategy with a FIFO-buffer size of 200.

Table 2. Overall results of conducted multi-step experiments, i.e., reward, system error, population size, generality and steps to goal. Entries are defined analogously to Table 1.

GridWorld (0.07)	Reward	Sys. Err.	|[P]|	Generality	Steps
Determined over	First 205,000 steps				Entire run
XCS w/Abs	− **0.536** ↑ (A)	**3.10** ↓ (C)	5120.70 ↑ (A)	0.00328 ↓ (C)	**20.04** ↓ (B)
	± 0.003	± 0.08	± 77.08	± 0.00017	± 0.32
XCS w/Specify	− **0.538** ↑ (A)	**4.28** ↓ (B)	3627.34 ↑ (B)	0.02234 ↓ (B)	**21.32** ↓ (B)
	± 0.005	± 0.74	± 65.95	± 0.00682	± 1.37
Standard XCS	− 0.549 (B)	5.27 (A)	2873.86 (C)	0.03807 (A)	23.80 (A)
	± 0.007	± 1.32	± 221.72	± 0.01423	± 6.37
GridWorld (0.05)	Reward	Sys. Err.	|[P]|	Generality	Steps
Determined over	First 285,000 steps				Entire run
XCS w/Abs	− **0.534** ↑ (A)	**4.14** ↓ (C)	5306.61 ↑ (A)	0.00300 ↓ (C)	**29.41** ↓ (C)
	± 0.003	± 0.17	± 129.26	± 0.00018	± 1.09
XCS w/Specify	− **0.537** ↑ (B)	**6.00** ↓ (B)	3600.12 ↑ (B)	0.03148 ↓ (B)	**33.60** ↓ (B)
	± 0.003	± 0.92	± 150.25	± 0.00961	± 3.80
Standard XCS	− 0.543 (C)	8.01 (A)	2510.71 (C)	0.05421 (A)	42.95 (A)
	± 0.004	± 1.56	± 326.01	± 0.01368	± 7.86

As can be seen from Table 2, XCS using OGH significantly outperforms the standard configuration in terms of the steps to goal, reward and system error metrics in both configurations of GridWorld. Analogously to Mario and the real-world problems, Absumption significantly surpasses Specify in terms of the aforementioned metrics, except for the reward and system error metrics in GridWorld (0.07). The learning curve of GridWorld (0.05) in Fig. 1h shows a faster reduction of the required steps by the OGH approaches compared to the standard configuration, with Absumption being clearly superior to Specify. In GridWorld (0.07) (cf. Fig. 1g) the difference between OGH and the standard configuration is less pronounced, since GridWorld (0.07) already seems to be well solvable by the standard configuration. The significant improvement of the steps to goal, the reward and the system error metrics indicates the application of both Specify and Absumption in GridWorld enables XCS to evolve a more accurate model of the underlying problem faster. Absumption provides

---

[8] Analogous to 6-RMP, except: $N = 10,000$, $\gamma = 0.95$, $\theta_{mna} = 4$, $\theta_{GA} = 50$, $\theta_{del} = 50$, $\theta_{sub} = 50$, $\epsilon_0 = 0.005$, $m_0 = 0.25$, $r_0 = 0.5$.

additional benefits since it is superior to Specify. In terms of population size and generality, both OGH approaches cause a significant increase in population size and a significant decrease in generality. Once again, this can be attributed to the underlying concept of OGH, the decomposition of over-general classifiers. The intensified occurrence of this effect in Absumption can be explained by the direct identification of over-general classifiers, resulting in more classifiers being decomposed per iteration of XCS compared to Specify.

In conclusion, the use of OGH and especially Absumption results in significantly improved steps to goal, reward and system error metrics in our experiments in multi-step environments, indicating faster learning of an accurate model. However, due to the mode of operation of OGH, these advantages are accompanied by an increase in population size and a decrease in generality in our experiments.

6   Conclusion

We presented two *Over-Generality Handling* (OGH) approaches adapted for *XCS with real-valued inputs* (XCSR), one based on the Absumption mechanism and one based on the Specify operator. The presented approaches provide promising means to deal with the challenge of over-general classifiers arising in XCS-based systems designed for real-valued inputs. This is particularly evident in reinforcement learning settings that demand for long-action chains and only provide sparse reward signals. To enable the use of OGH in XCSR, two specialization strategies were introduced enabling a decomposition of over-general classifiers into more specific ones in real-valued problem space. A new identification strategy for over-general classifiers was proposed to enable the application of Absumption in multi-step problems. To fathom the potential of OGH, the Absumption- and Specify-based OGH was evaluated in multi-step problems and in single-step problems, i.e., classification tasks based on common benchmark problems and on real-world data sets. The presented results of the conducted empirical studies showed the application of OGH results in considerable improvements in benchmark problems, tending towards the formation of over-general classifiers, in our experiments. Regarding the considered real-world data sets from the agricultural domain, especially the Absumption-based OGH caused significant improvements. In the evaluated multi-step problems, the application of OGH in general and Absumption in particular led to a significant performance increase of XCSR. Moreover, it turned out the underlying concept of OGH can result in an increased number of specific classifiers during the learning phase.

The overall goal we strive for is to enhance XCS's ability of learning in environments driving the system to suffer from over-generalization, i.e., *reinforcement learning* problems. Thus, our future research will aim at enabling a more focused specialization pressure in real-valued problem spaces, both in terms of a more precise localization of incompatible niches and a more systematic decomposition of over-general classifiers. The results in 6-RMP and CBP motivate an investigation of whether OGH has difficulties with such tasks in general, or whether the results are due to a possibly too unfocused specialization pressure. Furthermore, we will evaluate OGH on additional and also larger real-world data sets.

References

1. Bacardit, J., Burke, E.K., Krasnogor, N.: Improving the scalability of rule-based evolutionary learning. Memet. Comput. **1**(1), 55–67 (2009)
2. Barry, A.M.: The stability of long action chains in XCS. Soft Comput. **6**(3), 183–199 (2002)
3. Bernadó-Mansilla, E., Garrell-Guiu, J.M.: Accuracy-based learning classifier systems: models, analysis and applications to classification tasks. Evol. Comput. **11**(3), 209–238 (2003)
4. Butz, M.V., Kovacs, T., Lanzi, P.L., Wilson, S.W.: How XCS evolves accurate classifiers. In: Proceedings of GECCO 2001. GECCO 2001, pp. 927–934. Morgan Kaufmann Publishers Inc., San Francisco, CA, USA (2001)
5. Butz, M.V., Lanzi, P.L., Wilson, S.W.: Function approximation with XCS: hyperellipsoidal conditions, recursive least squares, and compaction. IEEE T Evolut. Comput. **12**(3), 355–376 (2008)
6. Butz, M.V., Stolzmann, W.: An algorithmic description of ACS2. In: Lanzi, P.L., Stolzmann, W., Wilson, S.W. (eds.) IWLCS 2001. LNCS (LNAI), vol. 2321, pp. 211–229. Springer, Heidelberg (2002). https://doi.org/10.1007/3-540-48104-4_13
7. Butz, M.V., Wilson, S.W.: An algorithmic description of XCS. In: Luca Lanzi, P., Stolzmann, W., Wilson, S.W. (eds.) IWLCS 2000. LNCS (LNAI), vol. 1996, pp. 253–272. Springer, Heidelberg (2001). https://doi.org/10.1007/3-540-44640-0_15
8. Calian, D.A., Bacardit, J.: Integrating memetic search into the BioHEL evolutionary learning system for large-scale datasets. Memet. Comput. **5**(2), 95–130 (2013)
9. Dorigo, M.: Genetic and non-genetic operators in ALECSYS. Evol. Comput. **1**(2), 151–164 (1993)
10. Holland, J.H., Reitman, J.S.: Cognitive systems based on adaptive algorithms. In: Pattern-Directed Inference Systems, pp. 313–329. Academic Press (1978)
11. Kovacs, T.: Towards a theory of strong overgeneral classifiers. In: FOGA 6, pp. 165–184. Morgan Kaufmann, San Francisco (2001)
12. Lanzi, P.L.: A study on the generalization capabilities of XCS. In: Proceedings of ICGA 1997, pp. 418–425 (1997)
13. Lanzi, P.L.: An analysis of generalization in the XCS classifier system. Evol. Comput. **7**(2), 125–149 (1999)
14. Lanzi, P.L., Loiacono, D., Wilson, S.W., Goldberg, D.E.: XCS with computed prediction in continuous multistep environments. In: IEEE CEC 2005, vol. 3, pp. 2032–2039, September 2005
15. Lanzi, P.L., Loiacono, D., Wilson, S.W., Goldberg, D.E.: Generalization in the XCSF classifier system: analysis, improvement, and extension. Evol. Comput. **15**(2), 133–168 (2007)
16. Liu, Y., Browne, W.N., Xue, B.: Absumption to complement subsumption in learning classifier systems. In: Proceedings of GECCO 2019, pp. 410–418. ACM, New York, NY, USA (2019)
17. Liu, Y., Browne, W.N., Xue, B.: Absumption and subsumption based learning classifier systems. In: Proceedings of GECCO 2020, pp. 368–376. ACM, New York, NY, USA (2020)

18. Pätzel, D., Stein, A., Hähner, J.: A survey of formal theoretical advances regarding XCS. In: Proceedings of GECCO 2019, pp. 1295–1302. Association for Computing Machinery, New York, NY, USA (2019)

19. Stein, A., Maier, R., Hähner, J.: Toward curious learning classifier systems: combining XCS with active learning concepts. In: Proceedings of GECCO 2017, pp. 1349–1356. ACM, New York, NY, USA (2017)

20. Stein, A., Maier, R., Rosenbauer, L., Hähner, J.: XCS classifier system with experience replay. In: Proceedings of GECCO 2020, pp. 404–413. ACM, New York, NY, USA (2020)

21. Stein, A., Menssen, S., Hähner, J.: What about interpolation? A radial basis function approach to classifier prediction modeling in XCSF. In: Proceedings of GECCO 2018, pp. 537–544. ACM, New York, NY, USA (2018)

22. Stone, C., Bull, L.: For real! XCS with continuous-valued inputs. Evol. Comput. 11(3), 299–336 (2003)

23. Sutton, R.S., Barto, A.G.: Reinforcement Learning: An Introduction. MIT press (2018)

24. Urbanowicz, R.J., Moore, J.H.: Learning classifier systems: a complete introduction, review, and roadmap. J. Artif. Evol. App. 2009, 1:1–1:25 (2009)

25. Urbanowicz, R.J., Moore, J.H.: ExSTraCS 2.0: description and evaluation of a scalable learning classifier system. Evol. Intell. 8(2), 89–116 (2015)

26. Wilson, S.W.: Generalization in the XCS classifier system. In: Proceedings of GP 1998. Morgan Kaufmann, Madison, Wisconsin, USA (1998)

27. Wilson, S.W.: Get real! XCS with continuous-valued inputs. In: Lanzi, P.L., Stolzmann, W., Wilson, S.W. (eds.) IWLCS 1999. LNCS (LNAI), vol. 1813, pp. 209–219. Springer, Heidelberg (2000). https://doi.org/10.1007/3-540-45027-0_11

28. Wilson, S.W.: Classifiers that approximate functions. Nat. Comput. 1(2), 211–234 (2002)

29. Wilson, S.W.: Classifier fitness based on accuracy. Evol. Comput. 3(2), 149–175 (1995)

30. Wilson, S.W.: Compact rulesets from XCSI. In: Lanzi, P.L., Stolzmann, W., Wilson, S.W. (eds.) IWLCS 2001. LNCS (LNAI), vol. 2321, pp. 197–208. Springer, Heidelberg (2002). https://doi.org/10.1007/3-540-48104-4_12

A NEAT Visualisation of Neuroevolution Trajectories

Stefano Sarti[(✉)] and Gabriela Ochoa

University of Stirling, Scotland, UK
{stefano.sarti,gabriela.ochoa}@stir.ac.uk

Abstract. NeuroEvolution of Augmenting Topologies (NEAT) is a system for evolving neural network topologies along with weights that has proven highly effective and adaptable for solving challenging reinforcement learning tasks. This paper analyses NEAT through the lens of Search Trajectory Networks (STNs), a recently proposed visual approach to study the dynamics of evolutionary algorithms. Our goal is to improve the understanding of neuroevolution systems. We present a visual and statistical analysis contrasting the behaviour of NEAT, with and without using the crossover operator, when solving the two benchmark problems outlined in the original NEAT article: XOR and double-pole balancing. Contrary to what is reported in the original NEAT article, our experiments without crossover perform significantly better in both domains.

Keywords: Neuroevoltuion · NEAT · Search Trajectory Networks

1   Introduction

NeuroEvolution of Augmenting Topologies (NEAT) is an algorithmic system that belongs to the category of topology and weight evolving artificial neural networks. NEAT strengthens the analogy between genetic algorithms and natural evolution by both optimising and complexifying the solutions simultaneously. Starting from a population of simple neural networks (without hidden units), NEAT incrementally grows them to produce more complex structures, while preserving the simplest amongst the complexified configurations. Other features of NEAT include speciation to protect innovation, genome's historical markings to facilitate recombination, and fitness sharing to ensure diversity. NEAT outperformed the best fixed-topology neuroevolution methods on a challenging pole balancing task [12]. Thereafter, NEAT has proven to be an effective and adaptable system with several applications such as dynamically evolving agents and content for video games [4,13], generating complex musical compositions [5], evolving reaction networks in synthetic biochemical systems [3], prediction in geosciences [14] and generating trading signals for financial markets [7].

Besides standard comparative performance studies, there is a lack of tools to analyse and explain the dynamic behaviour of neuroevolution systems and their variants. This article contributes to fill this gap by bringing a recent visualisation

© Springer Nature Switzerland AG 2021
P. A. Castillo and J. L. Jiménez Laredo (Eds.): EvoApplications 2021, LNCS 12694, pp. 714–728, 2021.
https://doi.org/10.1007/978-3-030-72699-7_45

and analysis tool, Search Trajectory Networks (STNs), to the realm of neuro-volution. The concept of STNs was proposed in a recent conference paper [9], where the authors modelled the dynamics of two population-based algorithms when solving synthetic continuous benchmark functions. STNs are a data-driven, graph-based model of search trajectories where nodes represent a given state of the search process and edges represent search progression between consecutive states. Once a system is modelled as a graph (network) it can be visualised and analysed with the plethora of powerful analytical and visualisation tools provided by the science of complex networks [8].

The main contributions of this article are to:

- Adapt STNs to model incremental and variable length genotypes such as those in NEAT
- Offer, for the first time, a network-based visual analysis of neuroevolution trajectories
- Revisit the issue of the role of crossover in neuroevolution systems

The rest of the article is organised as follows. Section 2 describes the STN model and how to adapt it to deal with NEAT trajectories. Section 3 describes the experimental setup, including the benchmark functions, algorithm variants and parameter values. Our results are presented and discussed in Sect. 4, while Sect. 5 summarises our main findings and suggestions for future work.

2   Search Trajectory Networks

We start with some relevant definitions and follow with our proposal to store NEAT genotypes so they can be used as nodes in the graph-based STN model. Moreover, we describe the sampling process to generate the models.

2.1   Definitions

In order to define a network model, we need to specify the nodes and edges. The relevant definitions are given below.

Representative Solution. A solution to the neuroevolution task at a given time step that represents the status of the search algorithm. As NEAT is a population based algorithm, we selected the best solution in the population at the given iteration as the representative solution.

Location. A subset of solutions that results from a predefined partitioning of the search space. Each solution in the search space is an element of one and only one location. Each location is assigned a representative objective value. The distinction between *solutions* and *locations* is required because in continuous domains, such as neuroevolution, the number of candidate solutions is infinite in principle. Therefore we require a coarsening or partition of the search space, which is achieved by controlling the parameters' (weights, bias) numerical precision.

Search Trajectory. Given a sequence of representative solutions in the order in which they are encountered during the search process, a search trajectory is defined as a sequence of locations formed by replacing each solution with its corresponding location.

Node. A location in a search trajectory of the search process being modelled. The set of nodes is denoted by N.

Edges. Edges are directed and connect two consecutive locations in the search trajectory. Edges are weighted with the number of times a transition between two given nodes occurred during the process of sampling and constructing the STN. The set of edges is denoted by E.

Search Trajectory Network (STN). A STN is a directed graph STN = $G(N, E)$, with node set N, and edge set E as defined above.

2.2   Mapping NEAT Genotypes to Locations

Due to NEAT's dynamic nature, genotypes which encode both topologies and connections weights, can grow or shrink through generations. This makes the representation of NEAT search states hard to consistently map to the location signatures required for STNs modelling. STNs use said signatures as node identifiers to construct the aforementioned graph models. Therefore, it is important to capture and map all necessary information of a location in the NEAT search space.

To overcome this challenge, we propose using the Python object serialisation facilities, as provided by the `pickle` module function `dumps`. *Pickling* is the process whereby a Python object is converted into a byte stream. Our proposal is to serialise NEAT genomes and use the resulting byte streams as location signatures. Since the signatures are unique and contain all the genotypic information, they provide a faithful representation for the STNs nodes.

Figure 1 illustrates the details of the mapping process. NEAT genotypes encode both nodes and connections. Each node has an identifying id (key). Each connection can be either enabled or disabled. Connectionism tells us that for every node there is a bias and every connection has a weight. We extract this information from the genotype and separate them; focusing on the flow of information from nodes acted upon by other nodes. We then use this information to construct a pseudo-phenotypical vector representation (NN Representation in Fig. 1). The mapping is completed by passing this vector representation to the `pickle.dumps` function which enables us to create a flattened, compressed representation of the genotype as a byte stream.

Before the data is extracted and mapped, the numerical precision of the weights and bias values needs to be reduced. The goal is to partition the search space, and thus reduce the number of possible locations. This allows having manageable visual representations, as it was done for the continuous benchmark functions studied in [9] where a solution precision parameter was used to partition the continuous search space into equal-sized discrete portions. In the

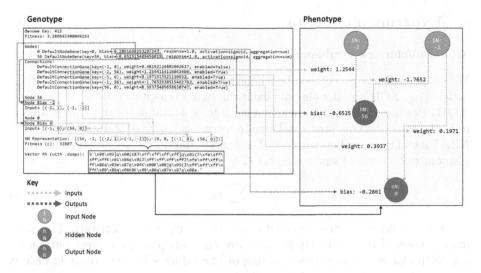

Fig. 1. Mapping NEAT genotypes to location signatures using Python object seriali-sation (`pickle.dumps`).

experiments reported in this paper, the partition is achieved by rounding off to $1e-0$ the numeric values in the genotype (weights and biases, as they are bounded in the range $[-30,30]$, see Table 1), and to $1e-4$ for the fitness values.

2.3   Sampling and STN Model Construction

One strength of the STN model is that it does not require any additional sampling methods. Instead, the models are constructed from data gathered while running the evolutionary or metaheuristic algorithms under study. In this paper, the STNs were generated for two NEAT variants (with and without crossover) on two benchmark problems: XOR and double-pole balancing with velocities (DPV). For each problem, an STN was constructed by aggregating all the unique nodes and edges encountered across five independent runs of each NEAT variant. Section 3 gives details on the benchmark functions and parameter settings used.

We also constructed the **merged STN** model of the two NEAT variants. The merged STN model for a given instance is obtained by the graph union of the two individual graphs for that instance. More formally, let $\text{STN}_A = G(N_A, E_A)$ and $\text{STN}_B = G(N_B, E_B)$ be the STNs of algorithm variants A and B for a given instance. We then construct $\text{STN}_{\text{merged}}$ as the union of the two graphs. Specifically, $\text{STN}_{\text{merged}} = G(N_A \cup N_B, E_A \cup E_B)$. The merged graph contains the nodes and edges that are present in at least one of the algorithm graphs. Attributes are kept for the nodes and edges indicating whether they were visited by both algorithms or by one of them only.

3   Experimental Setup

3.1   Benchmark Problems

We considered the two classic benchmark tasks outlined in the original NEAT article [12]; XOR and double pole balancing with velocities (DPV).

XOR. Because XOR is not linearly separable, a neural network requires hidden units to solve it. This structural requirement makes XOR suitable for testing NEAT's ability to evolve structure. The fitness function is measured as the complement of the sum of squared errors (Eq. 1).

$$\mathcal{F} = 4.0 - \sum_i \left(e_i - a_i\right)^2 \tag{1}$$

Here e_i and a_i are the expected and actual outputs, respectively. The maximum expected output is 4.0, as these are the four possible correct output for the XOR domain. Any values equating or exceeding a fitness threshold of 3.98 are considered to have solved the problem.

DPV. The pole balancing domain is well known in the reinforcement learning literature. We considered the double-pole balancing with velocity inputs, where two poles are connected to a moving cart by a hinge and the neural network must apply force to keep the poles balanced for as long as possible within the boundaries of the track. The Runge-Kutta fourth-order method is used to implement the system dynamics. The criteria for success on this task is keeping both poles balanced for 100,000 time steps (approx. 30 min of simulated time). Fitness is measured as the number of time steps that both poles remain balanced (Eq. 2).

$$\mathcal{F} = 1.0 - \frac{\log t_{max} - \log t_{eval}}{\log t_{max}} \tag{2}$$

Here t_{max} denotes the maximum expected number of time-steps (100,000 in our experiments), and t_{eval} the actual number of steps during which the controller was able to maintain a balanced state of the pole within the specified limits of $\pm 36°$, within the boundaries of ± 2.4 meters of the middle of track.

This particular implementation [10] uses logarithmic scales because most trials fail approximately in the initial 100 steps. Since the solving criteria is 100,000 steps, a logarithmic scale ensures a better distribution of scores. The second term in Eq. 2 is the loss function, in the range of [0,1]. The fitness function $\mathcal{F}$ is the complement of the loss score. Hence, fitness scores are in the [0,1] range, with best performing values tending to 1.0. Any values that equate or exceed 0.98 are considered to have solved the domain (fitness threshold).

3.2   Algorithms and Parameters

In terms of the search algorithm variants, we obtained inspiration from the *ablations* study conducted in [12] to identify how each of NEAT's components help to deliver its enhanced performance. The ablations isolate key properties of NEAT to assess whether removing them causes a significant decrease in performance. Four ablations were studied in [12], non-growth, random initialisation (instead of minimal initialisation), non-speciation and non-mating.

Here, we consider the non-mating ablation. That is, we measured the performance of NEAT with and without using the recombination (crossover) operator. The experiments use the same parameter values as in the original paper [12], the principal ones are listed in Table 1.

Table 1. NEAT parameter values used on each domain.

Parameter	XOR	DPV
Population size	150	1000
Total generations	100	1000
Fitness threshold	3.989	0.989
Bias range	$[-30, 30]$	$[-30, 30]$
Weight range	$[-30, 30]$	$[-30, 30]$
Input nodes	2	6
Output nodes	1	1

The experiments were conducted with the Python implementation of NEAT, neat-python [6]. For each domain and algorithm variant, 30 runs were conducted in order to correctly apply statistical tests.

4   Results

We start with a statistical analysis, supported by a non-parametric test (Mann-Whitney), contrasting the performance of the two NEAT variants (with and without crossover) when solving the two benchmark problems. This is followed by a detailed analysis contrasting the search dynamics using the STN model.

4.1   Performance Analysis

For each algorithm variant and benchmark function, 30 runs were executed with the parameter settings outlined in Table 1. Table 2 summarises the success rate, average number of evaluations to reach a solution and average quality of solution reached for both domains. As results indicate, the no crossover NEAT variant has a slightly higher success rate, and is noticeably more efficient as it reaches a solution with lower evaluations on average. Furthermore, the mean best fitness is calculated on successful runs at the stage when solution is reached. This is slightly higher for the variant without recombination, proving that this type of system produces better solutions on average. This overall observation is more marked for the DPV problem. This is in sharp contrast with the results reported in the original NEAT article [12], where the non-mating ablation study indicated that the use of crossover improves NEAT performance.

Table 2. Performance metrics.

	XOR		DPV	
	Crossover	No Crossover	Crossover	No Crossover
Evaluations (avg)	8,815.90	7,708.69	241,750.01	73,933.33
Evaluations (std)	2,760.28	2,199.09	227,395.80	74,380.52
Best fitness (avg)	3.9919	3.9924	0.99900	0.99947
Best fitness (std)	0.0060	0.0061	0.0030	0.0028
Success rate	73.3%	76.6%	93.3%	100%

In order to observe the dynamic behaviour of the two NEAT variants, Figures 2 and 3 show the average performance (best fitness) curves with error-bands (standard deviation), on the two benchmark problems respectively. The oscillating behaviour in the average fitness across generations, particularly observable in Figure 3 is expected, as for our experiments elitism was not considered. This means that at each generation, the best-performing individual may differ from the best-performing individual at the previous generation. The algorithm, however, tracks the best overall solution obtained across the run, which is then returned at the end of the run.

Given the aforementioned results, we proceed to assess for significance using the Mann-Whitney test; setting a *p-value* of 0.05. The system of hypothesis was formulated as follows.

- H_0: NEAT without crossover has similar distributions as the system with crossover.
- H_1: The two NEAT variants have significantly different distributions. Hence NEAT without crossover performs significantly better.

Table 3 displays the results related to the quality of the solution reached (effectiveness) both at midpoint (test 1) and endpoint (test 2). Moreover, we test for the evaluations required to reach solution (efficiency). As results indicate, H_0 is rejected in most cases as tested distributions differ, producing a p-value lower than 0.05, with the exception of XOR, tested at endpoint which shows no significance.

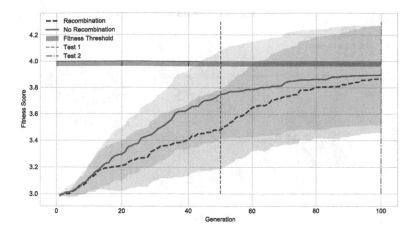

Fig. 2. Average best fitness with standard deviations across generations for the two NEAT variants on the XOR domain.

Table 3. Significance testing.

	XOR	DPV
Effectiveness midpoint test	$p = 0.00178$	$p = 0.00502$
Effectiveness endpoint test	$p = 0.32071$	$p = 0.00360$
Efficiency test	$p = 0.03911$	$p = 0.00007$

In Figure 4 and 5 these findings are substantiated by visualising the distribution of the number of evaluations to reach a solution (left plot) and the best fitness sampled at run midpoint (right plot), on the two domains respectively.

In Figure 4 we observe that in the system without crossover, the distribution of values for efficiency testing (evaluations required to reach a solution) are concentrated much lower, than its counterpart.

The second plot on the right, represents the distributions of fitness values halfway through the runs. Visibly, the system without crossover, exhibits a bimodal distribution with some values concentrating between 3.4 and 3.5, similarly as the variant with recombination. Although, in the system without crossover, greater density can be observed higher towards the upper whisker (between 3.85 and 4.0).

Comparably, Figure 5 depicts tested values for the DPV domain. In relation to the plotted efficiency (left plot), we observe that in the no crossover system, a greater and narrower density of values resides much lower in the evaluations. The distribution of values in the crossover system is similar to its counterpart, yet it shows wider variance with greater upper and lower bounds.

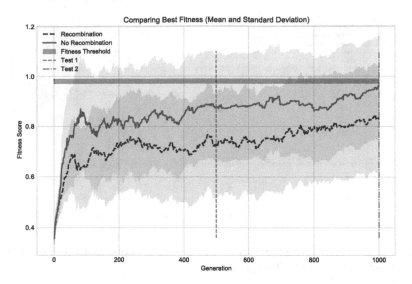

Fig. 3. Average best fitness with standard deviations across generations for the two NEAT variants on the DPV domain.

Distributions of fitness values tested at midpoint show similar spreads between the two systems. Bi-modality can be observed in both systems, in similar ways, although less accentuated in the no crossover system. Higher density can be witnessed in the crossover system at lower values, between 0.5 and 0.7. For the system without recombination, a much higher concentration is visible around higher values, between 0.9 and 1.0. Further confirming the improved performance of this system.

4.2   STNs Analysis

When networks are of moderate size, visualisation is a powerful tool allowing us to appreciate structural features which can be difficult to infer studying only network metrics. Node-edge diagrams, used here, are the most common visual representation of a network. Node-edge diagrams assign nodes to points in the 2-dimensional Euclidean space, and connect adjacent nodes by lines. If the graphs are directed, arrowheads are used to indicate the direction of connections. Nodes are then drawn on top of the edges using simple geometric shapes (such as circles or squares). Typically, the most important attributes of nodes and edges are assigned to visual properties (such as size and colour) of the shapes and lines; for instance, the area of a circle can be made proportional to the degree of the node in order to highlight hubs (i.e. highly connected nodes).

The graph visualisations in this paper were produced with the `igraph` library [2] of the R programming language. We visualised the merged STN models using the Reingold-Tilford [11] layout algorithm, which is specially suited for drawing trees (graphs without layout cycles). It generates a layout where

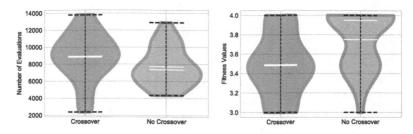

Fig. 4. Distribution (across 30 runs) of the number of evaluations to reach a solution (left plot) and the best genomes fitness values at the middle of the run for the two NEAT variants on the XOR domain.

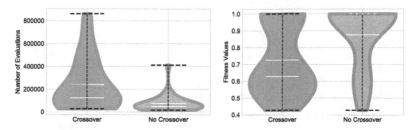

Fig. 5. Distribution (across 30 runs) of the number of evaluations to reach a solution (left plot) and the best genomes fitness values at the middle of the run for the two NEAT variants on the DPV domain.

vertices are organised into layers based on their geodesic distance (path length) from a chosen root vertex, which in our case are the start of trajectories. The algorithm also strives to minimise the number of edge crossings and to make the layout as narrow as possible.

Figures 6 and 7 illustrate the merged STN models for XOR and DPV, respectively. Nodes and edges are decorated to highlight relevant features of the search dynamics. Node sizes are proportional to their incoming weighted degree, which indicates to what extend nodes are revisited and thus attract the search process. The no crossover NEAT variant is visualised in red while the crossover variant in blue. Five trajectories were used to generate the STN for each algorithm variant, which start from the same five random seeds. This can be appreciated by the five start nodes highlighted in yellow and of larger size. All the visualised trajectories end in a different solution (fitness value above the respective threshold for each domain), which is visualised with the dark grey enlarged nodes. For both domains, trajectories from start to solution nodes are clearly shorter on average for the no crossover variant. This is more noticeable for the DPV domain (Fig. 7) where the blue trajectories (NEAT with crossover), are consistently larger.

The XOR merged STN of Figure 6, shows a larger number of nodes where the two algorithm variants overlap (visualised in light grey). The five initial nodes in yellow are shared by both algorithms, after this some grey shared nodes occur at the early stages of the search process (first steps of the search trajectory).

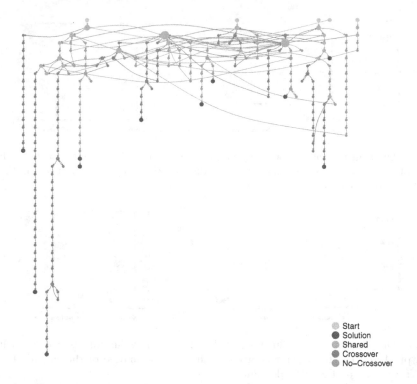

Start
Solution
Shared
Crossover
No–Crossover

Fig. 6. Merged STN for XOR. The nodes and edges visited by each NEAT variant are identified with different colours. Light grey nodes indicate locations visited by both variants. Node sizes are proportional to their incoming degree. The start of trajectories and the nodes achieving the fitness threshold (solutions) are also highlighted in different colours and of slightly larger size. (Color figure online)

This is consistent with the incremental grow of the NEAT genotypes, the early structures are more likely to be similar. The number of shared nodes is smaller for the more complex DPV domain (Figure 7), which can be explained by the larger genotypes for this task. Interestingly, we can observe a large shared node in the DPV domain (grey node around the top middle of the image), which is visited by the 3rd no crossover (red) trajectory and also traversed by three of the crossover (blue) trajectories. Recall that the size of nodes is proportional to their incoming degree. We hypothesise that this shared node is a good but sub-optimal configuration that tends to attract the search process with crossover.

In order to support the visual STN analysis, Table 4 reports the following network metrics for each domain:

– Nodes: The number of nodes, which corresponds to the number of unique locations visited by each variant.
– Edges: The number of edges, which corresponds to the number of unique search transitions between locations.

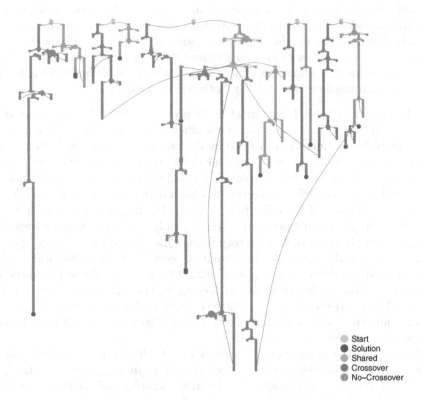

Fig. 7. Merged STN for DPV. The nodes and edges visited by each NEAT variant are identified with different colours. Light grey nodes indicate locations visited by both variants. Node sizes are proportional to their incoming degree. The start of trajectories and the nodes achieving the fitness threshold (solutions) are also highlighted in different colours and of slightly larger size. (Color figure online)

Table 4. STN structural metrics.

	XOR		DPV	
	Crossover	No Crossover	Crossover	No Crossover
Nodes	173	112	954	320
Edges	186	121	1018	345
Path length (avg)	34	20	137.38	44.34
Path length (std)	13.72	8.59	58.56	23.08
Shared nodes	27		12	
Shared edges	7		5	

- Path length: Average path length (with standard deviation) from start to solution nodes. The length of a path is the number of edges it contains.
- Shared nodes: The number of shared nodes in the STN model, which corresponds to the number of locations visited by both NEAT variants.
- Shared edges: The number of shared edges, which corresponds to the number of search transitions traversed by both NEAT variants.

The metrics in Table 4, confirm that the no crossover NEAT variant produces much shorter trajectories and thus more efficient search on both domains. The larger number of unique nodes visited by the crossover variant on both domains, indicate that crossover brings increased diversity to the evolutionary process. However, in the two domains explored, this diversity does not translate into a more efficient or more effective search. For both domains and algorithm variants, the number of edges is of similar magnitude to the number of nodes, indicating little trajectory overlap across runs; that is, only a few nodes are revisited by different runs. Instead, each trajectory follows mostly a different path, specially after the few early stages of the search process, and all trajectories end up in a successful different configuration with fitness value above the threshold. This observation can be confirmed by looking at the STN plots (Figs. 6 and 7) where all the trajectories end in different dark nodes (solutions). This occurs because numerous differing neural network topologies and weight combinations can produce similar good performance.

In terms of the number of nodes visited by both algorithm variants (shared nodes), this is relatively small in both domains (in comparison to the total number of nodes), being smaller for the more complex pole balancing domain. This is primarily due to the large variety of topologies being produced by the NEAT algorithm.

5   Conclusions

We have adapted a recent graph-based optimisation analysis and visualisation tool, Search Trajectory Networks (STNs) [9], to study the behaviour of a neuroevolution system (NEAT) [12]. To the best of our knowledge, this is the first time a neuroevolution system is visualised using this technique. Our proposal considers object serialisation in Python, combined with partitioning (rounding off) the genotypic numerical search space, in order to manage the complexity of NEAT growing genotypes.

We revisited the issue of the usefulness of crossover in neuroevolution systems. Contrary to what was reported in the original NEAT article [12] and to our surprise, the results indicate that crossover slows down the evolutionary process. We observe this, both in a standard statistical performance analysis of the NEAT variants with and without crossover, and with the recent STN analysis. The NEAT trajectories with crossover, explored the search space more widely, thus bringing diversity to the search process. This diversity, however, does not translate into improved performance. Without crossover, NEAT trajectories towards a solution are shorter and direct; thus the process is more efficient.

NEAT without crossover is also more effective, producing higher best fitness values in our experiments. This finding is consistent with an earlier observation by Angeline et al. [1] who demonstrated that neuroevolution of topologies does not need crossover to work, and indeed suggested that crossover does more harm than good.

When contrasting the structure of the STN models of NEAT against those of the classical optimisation benchmark functions studied in [9], we observed that NEAT search spaces contain multiple alternative nodes that achieved the desired fitness threshold. Therefore, there is little overlap of the neuroevolution trajectories when progressing towards good solutions. This happens because numerous differing neural network topologies and weight combinations can produce similar behaviours. This is in contrast with the search trajectories of synthetic optimisation benchmark functions, which tend to converge towards the portion of the search space containing the global optimum, or towards a small number of suboptimal solutions attracting the search process.

Future work will explore the role of crossover in other neuroevolution settings. For example, is crossover useful when solving more challenging tasks using NEAT? What about the role of crossover in other neuroevolution systems? Furthermore, we plan to augment the STN modelling technique with additional metrics and visual decorators, which may offer supplementary instruments to analyse and understand more complex systems. In this research, object serialisation has proven to be a powerful mapping technique, that has extended the potential reach of STNs. We hope that bringing such tools to neuroevolution and metaheuristcs, will contribute to their understanding and explainability, as well as guiding the way towards improving their performance. The hope is that increasing STN adoption will further improve its analytical powers.

References

1. Angeline, P.J., Saunders, G.M., Pollack, J.B.: An evolutionary algorithm that constructs recurrent neural networks. IEEE Trans. Neural Nctw. **5**(1), 54 65 (1994)
2. Csardi, G., Nepusz, T.: The igraph software package for complex network research. InterJ. Complex Syst. **1695**, 1–9 (2006)
3. Dinh, H., Aubert, N., Noman, N., Fujii, T., Rondelez, Y., Iba, H.: An effective method for evolving reaction networks in synthetic biochemical systems. IEEE Trans. Evol. Comput. **19**(3), 374–386 (2015)
4. Hastings, E., Guha, R., Stanley, K.: Automatic content generation in the galactic arms race video game. IEEE Trans. Comput. Intell. AI Games **1**(4), 245–263 (2009)
5. Hoover, A., Stanley, K.: Exploiting functional relationships in musical composition. Connect. Sci. **21**(2–3), 227–251 (2009)
6. McIntyre, A., Kallada, M., Miguel, C.G., da Silva, C.F.: NEAT-Python. https://github.com/CodeReclaimers/neat-python
7. Nadkarni, J., Ferreira Neves, R.: Combining neuroevolution and principal component analysis to trade in the financial markets. Expert Syst. Appl. **103**, 184–195 (2018)
8. Newman, M.E.J.: Networks: An Introduction. Oxford University Press, Oxford; New York (2010)

9. Ochoa, G., Malan, K.M., Blum, C.: Search trajectory networks of population-based algorithms in continuous spaces. In: Castillo, P.A., Jiménez Laredo, J.L., Fernández de Vega, F. (eds.) EvoApplications 2020. LNCS, vol. 12104, pp. 70–85. Springer, Cham (2020). https://doi.org/10.1007/978-3-030-43722-0_5

10. Omelianenko, I.: Hands-On Neuroevolution with Python. Packt Publishing, Limited (2019)

11. Reingold, E.M., Tilford, J.S.: Tidier drawings of trees. IEEE Trans. Softw. Eng. SE-7(2), 223–228 (1981)

12. Stanley, K.O., Miikkulainen, R.: Evolving neural networks through augmenting topologies. Evol. Comput. 10(2), 99–127 (2002)

13. Stanley, K., Bryant, B., Miikkulainen, R.: Real-time neuroevolution in the NERO video game. IEEE Trans. Evol. Comput. 9(6), 653–668 (2005)

14. Wang, G., Cheng, G., Carr, T.: The application of improved neuroevolution of augmenting topologies neural network in marcellus shale lithofacies prediction. Comput. Geosci. 54, 50–65 (2013)

Evaluating Models with Dynamic Sampling Holdout

Celio H. N. Larcher Jr$^{(\boxtimes)}$ and Helio J. C. Barbosa

Laboratório Nacional de Computação Científica, Petrópolis, RJ, Brazil
{clarcher,hcbm}@lncc.br

Abstract. Automated Machine Learning (Auto-ML) is a growing field where several techniques are being developed to address the question of how to automate the process of defining machine learning pipelines, using diverse types of approaches and with relative success, but still, being far from solved. Among these still unsolved questions, the computational cost is one of the major issues. In this context, evaluating a model takes a lot of time and resources, and yet that is still a step that has not received much attention in the Auto-ML literature.

In this sense, this work revisits the Auto-CVE (Automated Coevolutionary Voting Ensemble) and proposes a new method for model evaluation: the dynamic sampling holdout. When compared to the regular Auto-CVE with cross-validation and the popular TPOT (Tree-based Pipeline Optimization Tool) algorithm, Auto-CVE with dynamic holdout shows competitive results in both predictive performance and computing time.

Keywords: Auto-ML · Machine learning · Evolutionary algorithms

1 Introduction

The demand for machine learning (ML) solutions is growing exponentially nowadays, mainly due to the fact that there is much more data and computational power available.

In addition, there is a trend to make the ML process more accessible to newcomers. A large part of the job of an ML practitioner is to perform repetitive tasks such as train a model, test its performance, adjust the parameters, etc. Automated Machine Learning (Auto-ML) arises from the idea of automating as much as possible the whole process. Tackling the tasks of model selection and hyper-parameter optimization, Auto-ML allows the ML practitioner to focus on more specialized tasks such as preparing the data or analyzing the results.

One key aspect of Auto-ML approaches is the computational cost. Evaluating a machine learning model can be an expensive task. As the amount of data grows, the use of brute-force procedures that try all possibilities of parameters and algorithms (traditional grid-search by example) becomes prohibitive. In this sense, the use of metaheuristics is one of the trends in Auto-ML. Two of the most promising solutions in the Auto-ML field nowadays are based on metaheuristics: Auto-SKLearn [8] uses a Bayesian Optimization approach, while TPOT [15]

© Springer Nature Switzerland AG 2021
P. A. Castillo and J. L. Jiménez Laredo (Eds.): EvoApplications 2021, LNCS 12694, pp. 729–744, 2021.
https://doi.org/10.1007/978-3-030-72699-7_46

uses a Genetic Programming implementation. The P4ML is another example, but with a heuristic procedure [9].

Despite the different forms of exploring the search space of ML techniques, all these Auto-ML proposals evaluate their models through cross-validation.

In fact, the two most traditional ML approaches are cross-validation and holdout procedures. Although being much less time consuming, the holdout procedure is usually avoided in Auto-ML given the high uncertainty in its measure, which can easily overfit the search procedure. This overfitting potential makes cross-validation almost mandatory for low to mid-sized databases and turns the already costly Auto-ML process into an even more expensive one.

Some initiatives to mitigate this problem consist in using a Successive Halving strategy to best allocate resources as in Hyperband [13], and reducing the dataset size through sampling [4]. In another direction, the work of Lévesque [12] proposes the use of holdout with a reshuffling procedure, changing training and test samples after each model evaluation, and shows how that can be used to avoid overfitting when combined with Bayesian Optimization.

With the intent of making the Auto-ML procedure cheaper, this paper revisits the Auto-CVE proposed in [11], looking for more efficient ways to evaluate its individuals. Specifically, this work proposes a new method, dynamic sampling, to evaluate models through holdout in an evolutionary procedure (in a way analogous to that in [12]), seeking to avoid overfitting, but still evaluating all individuals with the same sampling.

Despite the work of Lévesque [12], this is the first time, to the best of the authors' knowledge, that this type of procedure is applied to an Auto-ML proposal (especially an evolutionary one).

The remaining text is organized as follows: Sect. 2 presents three relevant concepts: pipelines, models and ensembles; Sect. 3 explains the overfitting problem in Auto-ML systems; Sect. 4 shows the proposed modifications into the Auto-CVE algorithm in order to apply the dynamic sampling approach; Sect. 5 shows some results obtained with the proposed approach and compares them to those obtained by the previous Auto-CVE and the TPOT algorithm, and, finally, Sect. 6 gives some conclusions and suggests possible future works.

2   Pipelines, Models and Ensembles

Machine learning pipeline is an expression used to represent a set of operations applied to a dataset in order to process the data and obtain some results. Besides the core ML procedure, these operations include all the pre-processing steps, such as scaling techniques, feature selection, dimensionality reduction, encoding, etc. In addition, the definition of a pipeline will include the choice of all parameters used in each of these operators. The Fig. 1 shows an example of a pipeline.

When the pipeline is trained with some data, it produces a model of the problem, from which it is possible to obtain predictions based on what was previously observed in the training phase. Despite the mentioned difference between

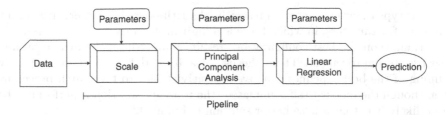

Fig. 1. Example of a pipeline where the data is initially rescaled, then it is projected into another feature-space via principal component analysis, and at the end, some target value is predicted using the linear regression algorithm.

pipelines and models, the terms pipeline and individual model (model with a single pipeline) will be used interchangeably here.

This work focuses on the supervised learning paradigm, where a subset of samples with an already known response is used to train an algorithm and, based on the relationship learned from those samples and responses, a model capable of generalizing the information to unknown instances is expected to be found.

Based on the supervised learning paradigm, the pipeline definition used here is a sequence of an optional pre-processing step (which can transform the data via Principal Component Analysis, or even add more features such as applying a polynomial expansion in the features), an optional feature selection algorithm, and a mandatory classification method at the end. Furthermore, the processed dataset is scaled before being fed to an algorithm that requires it.

Ensembles are the combination of individual models in order to enhance the performance in the machine learning task. The main idea is that when using a set of techniques, the limitations of each one are compensated by the abilities of others. In this sense, to obtain an ensemble with good performance, it is required that the components (individual models) (i) present good performance themselves (at least better than chance) and (ii) present enough diversity (they make different mistakes when making their predictions) [6].

Also, in order to combine the response of the individual models, this work uses the traditional voting scheme, particularly the proportional vote. In this procedure, all models in the ensemble receive the same input data and predict their output. After that, all these outputs are combined to predict the output of the ensemble: for classification tasks, the class which receives more "votes" is predicted, while in regression problems, the mean result is used.

3   Overfitting in Auto-ML

In a similar way to the training procedure, model selection is another step in which overfitting can occur when building an ML solution. That happens because, in a systematic search for better configurations, the obtained results can be biased given the sampling procedure itself, with a pipeline presenting good results just because the sample distribution is propitious.

This type of event is mostly present in algorithms with a larger variance and number of parameters, in which there is a high probability that good predictive performance on the best configurations results mainly from the metric variance towards its improvement. Then, the use of a fixed dataset and the successive refining of the best pipelines can give a positivist bias to the search procedure, even though the metric itself is unbiased (the more exploration is performed, the more likely it is that a false better solution is found) [2].

In this sense, it is possible to see how an intensive search procedure through a large variety of complex models (the Auto-ML context) can easily interpret noise as indicative of good performance. In a thorough analysis, it is highly probable that the procedure can find irregularities in the search space (given its huge size) that indicate false performance gains. As a result, without any mechanism that validates the performance in other ways than using a fixed data sample, it turns out that the search procedure optimizes over the data sample itself, instead of seeking for the best model in the real distribution.

Some methodologies to mitigate this problem are: using cross-validation (reducing the metric variance); splitting an additional subset exclusively to choose the best model after the search procedure (reducing the bias effect on the search procedure); searching for stable optimal solutions (in which nearby solutions have a good fit too); combining several models in ensembles (reducing the effect of individual errors); and re-sampling the dataset across the search procedure; being an attention point to Auto-ML techniques [7,12].

4   Auto-CVE with Dynamic Sampling

In this section, the Auto-CVE (Automated Coevolutionary Voting Ensemble) with dynamic sampling is presented, a modification of the technique shown in [11] in order to use holdout as evaluation procedure. In the Auto-CVE, the population of components is evolved by means of a Context-Free Genetic Programming (CFGP) [18] implementation, while a Genetic Algorithm (GA) is applied in the population of ensembles, with these two strategies interacting with each other. The ensemble strategy chosen is the voting ensemble with a proportional vote, and each individual of the population of ensembles corresponds to a different voting ensemble. The Algorithm 1 gives an overview of the technique.

The proposed procedure is based on the multi-population coevolutionary workflow: the populations are initialized randomly, and the evolution proceeds with each population advancing one step per generation.

The fitness function that evaluates each ensemble is given by the performance of the ensemble itself. In contrast, the fitness function that evaluates the population of components, is given by the mean performance of the component across the ensembles it is part of (or the performance of the component itself when it is not part of any ensemble).

The first and main change to the standard Auto-CVE is in the way the performance of each component is measured. Where cross-validation used to be the choice, now a holdout procedure is applied with the training and test sets changed after each generation. The Fig. 2 shows a scheme of how this works.

Algorithm 1. Coevolutionary procedure with dynamic sampling evaluation

1: **function** Auto-CVE
2:    $P_0^E \leftarrow$ initPopulation(), $P_0^C \leftarrow$ initPopulation();
3:    $G \leftarrow 0$;
4:    **while** stop criteria **do**
5:       $P_{G+1}^C \leftarrow$ nextGenComponent(P_G^C, P_G^E);
6:       $P_{G+1}^E \leftarrow$ nextGenEnsemble(P_{G+1}^C, P_G^E);
7:       $G \leftarrow G + 1$;
8:    **end while**
9:    fitPredictCV(P_{last}^C);
10:   **for** $i = 1 \dots N$ **do**
11:      $P_{G+i+1}^E \leftarrow$ nextGenEnsemble(P_{last}^C, P_{G+i}^E);
12:   **end for**
13:   $e \leftarrow$ best element in P_{last}^E;
14:   **return** $e(P_{last}^C)$;
15: **end function**

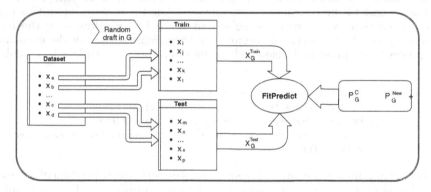

Fig. 2. Scheme representing the evaluation through holdout with dynamic sampling.

In the dynamic sampling, a random draft is made after each generation, which splits the dataset into training and test sets as it is usually done in hold-out. All individuals already in the population of components (P_G^C) and the new individuals created in this generation (P_G^{new}) are reevaluated/evaluated using these two sets so that every comparison between individuals is made under the same condition. At the same time, every generation is evaluated with a distinct sample, which ensures that any evaluation bias relative to the test set sampling procedure will be restricted to the respective generation.

With this procedure, it is expected that the evaluation time is reduced and, at the same time, overfitting is avoided in the run [12]. Besides, even if some good solutions can be lost, it is expected that, in the long run, the populations as a whole converge to better and more generalizable configurations.

After the coevolutionary procedure, a single evaluation with the cross-validation procedure is performed in order to avoid the high variance of holdout within a generation in the choice of the final model. Besides, a small number of additional generations of the ensemble population are performed to adjust these individuals under the new information.

In the end, the procedure returns the best ensemble found in the population of ensembles, composed of the chosen elements of the population of components.

The explanation of the evolution process used in each population is given in the following subsections.

4.1   Evolution of Components

The implemented CFGP procedure is intended to optimize a component population where each individual (component) is a pipeline (a sequence of operations and hyper-parameters) as defined previously. The grammar used is based on the TPOT list of operations, but with the context component added. The inclusion of context to the grammar allows one to define the order of operators prior to the execution, which reduces the search space by including only the most promising combinations [17]. A fragment of the grammar used in the evolutionary procedure is presented below, while the operators are displayed in Table 1.

```
<pipeline> ::= <add_features> "->" <classifier>
             | <add_features> "->" <selector> "->" <classifier>
             | <scaler> "->" <preprocessing> "->" <classifier>
             | <scaler> "->" <preprocessing> "->" <selector> "->" <classifier>
             | <classifier>
```

In this grammar segment, it is possible to observe the composition of the solutions based on the previously adopted definition of pipelines. The non-terminal <pipeline> is the starting symbol and, following that, there are three possibilities to build a solution: (i) a single classifier; (ii) a classifier preceded by the addition of some features and an optional selector; (iii) and a classifier preceded by some pre-processing procedure and an optional selector. Furthermore, if the operator demands, the dataset is scaled before its use.

Besides the structure of a pipeline and the operators, a list of the possible hyper-parameter values for each technique is also present in the grammar, allowing CFGP to perform both model selection and hyper-parameter search.

Another difference to TPOT is that in the grammar defined here, recursion is not employed. In contrast, TPOT uses recursion as a way to create new attributes in a "stacker-like" procedure, which increases the complexity of the pipelines built. This lack of recursion means that the pipelines in Auto-CVE are simpler (with less capability), with more complex models arising from the combination of these pipelines into ensembles. Note that the TPOT pipelines are ensembles by themselves, contrasting with the definition of pipeline used here.

The Auto-CVE implementation of CFGP aims at the generation of performative and diverse components. Towards that, a niching scheme, deterministic crowding [14], is added to the algorithm. In this scheme, after the generation

Table 1. List of all operators used in the Auto-CVE with the respective non-terminal. The TPOT/ZeroCount and TPOT/OneHotEncoder operators are custom implementations of the TPOT framework, the XGBClassifier belongs to the XGBoost [3] library while all other operators come from scikit-learn [16] library.

<classifier>		
GaussianNB	LinearSVC	RandomForestClassifier
BernoulliNB	LogisticRegression	GradientBoostingClassifier
MultinomialNB	DecisionTreeClassifier	XGBClassifier
KNeighborsClassifier	ExtraTreesClassifier	
<scaler>		
MaxAbsScaler	RobustScaler	StandardScaler
MinMaxScaler		
<preprocessing>		
Binarizer	FeatureAgglomeration	FastICA
Normalizer	Nystroem	PCA
PolynomialFeatures	RBFSampler	
<add_features>		
TPOT/ZeroCount	TPOT/OneHotEncoder	
<selector>		
SelectFwe	RFE	VarianceThreshold
SelectPercentile	SelectFromModel	

of a pool of new solutions, each solution of the current generation is compared with the closest one present in this pool (based on some distance criterion) and, among them, the one with the best fitness remains in the next generation.

In this sense, the predicted response in the test set is used to compute a measure of distance, given by the inverse of a simple similarity function: each match between the response of two individuals counts as 1 (independent of the correctness), while different answers count as 0. A greedy procedure is then applied to find the minimum distance between the solutions in the current generation and the pool of new solutions: this procedure iterates through solutions of the current generation (in random order) and, for each solution in this set, it finds the closest one in the pool of new solutions, removing both solutions of their pools (selection without replacement). These two chosen solutions are then elected to compete. The Algorithm 2 shows the procedure implemented in the CFGP.

In this algorithm, the parents of the next generation are selected by randomly pairing solutions in the current generation, which guarantees that all current generation solutions are selected exactly once to be submitted to the evolutionary operators (line 2).

After selection and before breeding, the individuals are checked in order to improve the efficiency of the evolutionary process. To this end, the mutation operator is applied to every invalid individual and to each pair of selected individuals with the same sequence of operators and hyper-parameters (lines 5–11).

Algorithm 2. A single generation of the components population.

1: **function** NEXTGENCOMPONENT(P^C, P^E)
2:     Parents ← randomPairing(copy(P^C));
3:     P^C_{new} ← ∅;
4:     **for each** (p_1,p_2) ∈ Parents **do**
5:         **if** $p_1//p_2$ is invalid **then**
6:             $p_1//p_2$ ← mutationComponents($p_1//p_2$);
7:         **end if**
8:         c_1 ← p_1, c_2 ← p_2;
9:         **if** $c_1 = c_2$ **then**
10:             $c_1//c_2$ ← mutationComponents($c_1//c_2$);
11:         **end if**
12:         $sort_{cross}$ ← random(0,1), $sort_{mut}$ ← random(0,1);
13:         **if** $sort_{cross} < rate_{cross}$ **then**
14:             (c_1, c_2) ← crossoverComponents(c_1,c_2);
15:         **end if**
16:         **if** $sort_{mut} < rate_{mut}$ **then**
17:             $c_1//c_2$ ← mutationComponents($c_1//c_2$);
18:         **end if**
19:         **if** $c_1//c_2 = p_1$ **or** $c_1//c_2 = p_2$ **then**
20:             $c_1//c_2$ ← mutationComponents($c_1//c_2$);
21:         **end if**
22:         P^C_{new} ← $P^C_{new} \cup \{c_1, c_2\}$;
23:     **end for**
24:     fitPredict(P^C_{new});
25:     **for each** $p_{old} \in P^C$ **do** /*Random order*/
26:         p_{new} ← arg min$_{p \in P^C_{new}}$ (distance(p, p_{old}));
27:         P^C_{new} ← $P^C_{new} - \{p_{new}\}$;
28:         P^C_{temp} ← copy(P^C);
29:         $P^C_{temp}[i_{p_{old}}]$ ← p_{new};
30:         evaluate(P^C,P^E);
31:         evaluate(P^C_{temp},P^E);
32:         **if** $p_{old\,score} < p_{new\,score}$ **then**
33:             $P^C[i_{p_{old}}]$ ← p_{new};
34:         **end if**
35:     **end for**
36:     **return** P^C;
37: **end function**

$p_1//p_2(c_1//c_2)$ means that the operation is applied in parallel to both $p_1(c_1)$ and $p_2(c_2)$

The procedures of mutation and crossover are performed as usually done in CFGP. Mutation deletes a random subtree and randomly reconstructs it, while crossover searches for two subtrees with the same non-terminal and swaps them between the solutions (lines 12–18).

Also, if a new individual has the same sequence of operators and hyperparameters as one of its parents, a mutation operation is applied to prevent a clone from entering the population (lines 19–21).

The training and testing steps (procedure fitPredict in line 24) are performed through a holdout procedure, changing the training and test sets after each generation (as commented above). The predicted vector, which is used to compute the similarity and evaluate the ensembles, comes from the response of the model in the test set and is, as well, changed after each generation.

The evaluation is performed with each solution in the current generation paired with the closest one in the pool of new solutions (greedy procedure). The distance between solutions in these two sets is computed as described before, and the solutions with more proximity/similarity in predicted response are chosen to compete (line 26). Finally, for each pair of competing solutions, the one with the higher score is selected to be in the next generation while the other is discarded (lines 32–34).

The score is computed as the mean performance of the solution among all ensembles in which the pipeline is included. If there is no ensemble, the performance of the pipeline by itself is considered. The score is computed considering the old and the new solution as possible solutions of the ensemble (lines 28–31).

Note that the most expensive operation, the function *fitPredict* (in which the pipelines are trained and evaluated), is performed just once, with the ensemble performance computed using the predicted vector of the solution.

The initialization is a simple random process using the standard procedure for CFGP: in each individual, the generation procedure follows the grammar with each production rule chosen randomly until all branches end with a terminal.

4.2   Evolution of Ensembles

As mentioned before, the Auto-CVE uses the voting ensemble procedure. In this sense, an individual is represented as a binary vector where the value 1 in the i-th position means that the i-th pipeline is used in that ensemble, while the value 0 means the opposite. Then, each vector of an ensemble has a size equal to the number of individuals present in the population of components.

The evolution is performed by a Genetic Algorithm, as mentioned before. The Algorithm 3 shows the evolutionary procedure implemented.

This procedure resembles the evolution used in the population of components. As before, the evaluation step is performed pairing the current population and the pool of new solutions, guided by the lower distances between solutions. The comparison is made with the score proportional to the measure defined in the execution and, as a second criterion, the solution with fewer components is maintained in the next generation. The response of each ensemble is computed considering the majority response among all active components for each test sample (in case of a tie, the class with lower label value is chosen as default in scikit-learn [16]).

The distance of these ensembles is defined as the inverse of a similarity measure given by the number of common components, divided by the maximum number of used components among the compared solutions. Then, as an example, if a solution has 5 activated bits (value 1) and another has 3, with 2 of these bits activated in the same position in both solutions, then the similarity between

---

Algorithm 3. A single generation of the ensemble population.

1: **function** NEXTGENENSEMBLE(P^C, P^E)
2:     Parents ← randomPairing(copy(P^E));
3:     P^E_{new} ← ∅;
4:     **for each** (p_1,p_2) ∈ Parents **do**
5:         c_1 ← p_1, c_2 ← p_2;
6:         **if** $c_1 = c_2$ **then**
7:             $c_1//c_2$ ← mutationEnsemble($c_1//c_2$);
8:         **end if**
9:         $sort_{cross}$ ← random(0,1), $sort_{mut}$ ← random(0,1);
10:        **if** $sort_{cross} < rate_{cross}$ **then**
11:            (c_1, c_2) ← crossoverEnsemble(c_1,c_2);
12:        **end if**
13:        **if** $sort_{mut} < rate_{mut}$ **then**
14:            $c_1//c_2$ ← mutationEnsemble($c_1//c_2$);
15:        **end if**
16:        **if** $c_1//c_2 = p_1$ **or** $c_1//c_2 = p_2$ **then**
17:            $c_1//c_2$ ← mutationEnsemble($c_1//c_2$);
18:        **end if**
19:        P^E_{new} ← $P^E_{new} \cup \{c_1, c_2\}$;
20:    **end for**
21:    evaluate(P^C,P^E_{new});
22:    **for each** p_{old} ∈ P^E **do** /*Random order*/
23:        p_{new} ← arg min$_{p \in P^E_{new}}$ (distance(p, p_{old}));
24:        P^E_{new} ← $P^E_{new} - \{p_{new}\}$;
25:        **if** $p_{old\,score} < p_{new\,score}$ **or** ($p_{old\,score} == p_{new\,score}$ **and** $p_{old_{length}} > p_{new_{length}}$) **then**
26:            $P^E[i_{p_{old}}]$ ← p_{new};
27:        **end if**
28:    **end for**
29:    **return** P^E;
30: **end function**

$p_1//p_2(c_1//c_2)$ means that the operation is applied in parallel to both p_1(c_1) and p_2(c_2)

---

these solutions is computed considering these two bits as numerator divided by the maximum amount of components ($max(3,5) = 5$), with the distance being: $distance = \frac{1}{similarity} = \frac{1}{\frac{2}{5}} = \frac{5}{2}$.

The crossover and mutation operators have some adaptations compared to the traditional GA. In the crossover, the "cutting" area is restricted to that between the leftmost and rightmost 1 value within the two solutions combined. For the mutation operator, the procedure is divided into two steps: firstly, there is a random choice about whether the mutation procedure will add or remove a component. After that, a random choice of which position to be mutated is performed: a random 0/1 bit is flipped (if a component is to be added/removed).

The initialization is made through a simple random process: the probability of an individual receiving the value 1 in the i-th position is 10% while receiving the value 0 is 90%. The choice of a small probability for the value 1 aims at generating small ensembles in the initial population, since (i) these tend to be preferable due to the lower complexity and (ii) that in the initial generations, it is important to have an adequate estimate of the effective role of each component, which can be hidden in larger ensembles.

5   Experiments

To verify the performance of Auto-CVE with dynamic sampling, a set of experiments was conducted comparing this technique with the Auto-CVE using cross-validation (same procedure presented here but removing the last few extra steps of evolution in the ensemble population), and with a popular framework in the Auto-ML field, the TPOT [15]. The same set of ML operators is used in all techniques, coming from the scikit-learn [16] and the XGBoost [3] libraries and following the default list of methods currently used in the TPOT. The choice of the same set of operators was made to ensure that any difference in performance between the techniques is not caused by the presence or absence of any operator.

The parameters used in the Auto-CVE are obtained through experimentation and can be divided into two sets, one for each population: in the components population, the mutation rate is 0.9, crossover rate is 0.9, and population size is 50; while in the ensembles population, the mutation rate is 0.1, crossover rate is 0.9, and population size is 50. Also, after evolution, 10 extra steps are performed in the ensemble population alone in the Auto-CVE with dynamic sampling.

For each training and testing step in each pipeline, a limit of 60 s is set. Any individual exceeding this limit is considered invalid. The value of k used in the cross-validation procedure is 5, which results in 5×60 seconds for the 5-fold cross-validation procedure. In holdout, 70% of the dataset is used for training a pipeline and 30% to get its performance (as there is only one training and test step, 60 s is the maximum time spent in one pipeline). The 60-second time limit on both Auto-CVE versions and a 5-fold setting are chosen to follow the default TPOT configuration of 5 min for a 5-fold cross-validation.

In TPOT, the default parameters are used. Besides, the stop criterion is reached with 100 generations or 90 min of execution for all three techniques.

All code of the Auto-CVE approach can be found at https://github.com/celiolarcher/AUTOCVE, while datasets and scripts are available at https://github.com/celiolarcher/autocve_experiments.

The Auto-CVE, in its current version, is applied only to classification tasks (although it can be easily extended to regression); as a result, only classification datasets were tested here. The instances are obtained from the benchmark presented by Balaji & Allen [1] proposed for the comparison of Auto-ML approaches. A subset of 15 of the classification datasets in [1] was selected, observing the maintenance of some diversity of characteristics among them. In this sense, the datasets have between 5 and 1.301 features and between 500 and 96.320 samples, distributed in binary and multiclass classification tasks. All samples with a null value in the target feature are dropped before the optimization procedure as none of the three techniques can handle this case.

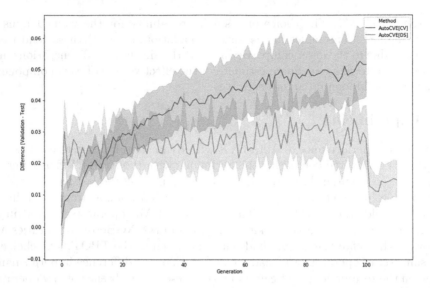

Fig. 3. Overfitting measure (difference between inner validation score and test score) by generation with confidence interval of 95%, grouped by the mean across all executions of Auto-CVE with cross-validation (Auto-CVE[CV]) and Auto-CVE with dynamic sampling holdout (Auto-CVE[DS]). The last 10 steps in Auto-CVE[DS] are performed just in the ensemble population and after a cross-validation procedure (as described in Sect. 4).

A list of the datasets with the respective *id* attributed in the benchmark follows: BREAST-W/15, DIABETES/37, VOWEL/307, IRISH/451, ANALCAT-DATA AUTHORSHIP/458, ANALCATDATA DMFT/469, GAS-DRIFT/1476, MADELON/1485, MICRO-MASS/1515, ADULT/1590, CYLINDER-BANDS/6332, NUMERAI28.6/23517, LED-DISPLAY-DOMAIN-7DIGIT/40496, TEXTURE/40499, CLIMATE-MODEL-SIMULATION-CRASHES/40994.

In each dataset, 10 runs are made to verify the performance. Besides, for every run, a test subsample of 30% maintained out of the optimization procedure to be used only to evaluate the final model provided by the techniques. As a performance metric, this work uses the balanced accuracy [10]. The experiments were performed on a Ryzen 7 1700 processor with 16 GB of ram running a Linux system, with all the 16 threads employed in the optimization procedure.

Firstly, a comparison between the two versions of Auto-CVE is made to verify the occurrence of overfitting in the evolutionary process. To this end, the best ensemble found in each generation accordingly with the internal evaluation procedure was also evaluated with the test subsample (maintained out of the optimization procedure), and the difference between these two measures is defined as the amount of overfitting of this model. The Fig. 3 shows a comparison between the two Auto-CVE evaluation methods, with the mean overfitting measure grouped by generation for all executions.

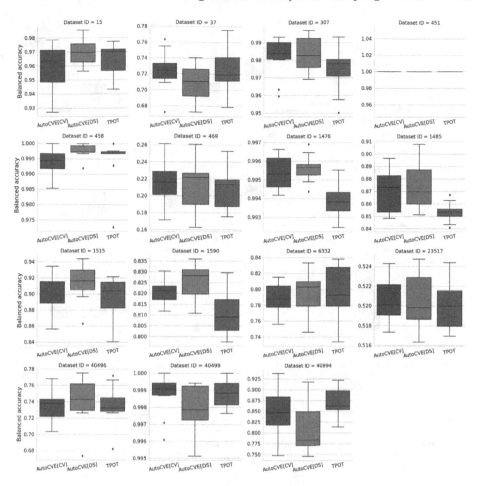

Fig. 4. Boxplot with the balanced accuracy obtained by Auto-CVE with cross-validation (Auto-CVE[CV]), Auto-CVE with dynamic sampling holdout (Auto-CVE[DS]) and TPOT through 10 runs for each dataset.

As it can be seen, the holdout method indeed has a higher bias by generation (early generations) than cross-validation, but, as dynamic sampling strategy is applied, the bias is maintained at the same level during all evolution. For cross-validation, although the bias is very small in early generations, its value potentially grows up, being eventually higher than in holdout with dynamic sampling. These observations indicate that the holdout with dynamic sampling can indeed be a viable choice for Auto-ML techniques and even be a better choice than cross-validation when a large number of models are evaluated (given the increase of bias in the long run). Also, the choice of performing cross-validation at the end of the procedure is welcome, given that it reduces the bias in a few generations.

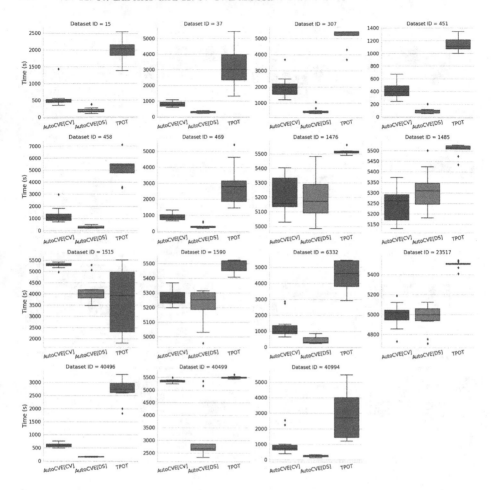

Fig. 5. Boxplot with the time consumed in seconds by Auto-CVE with cross-validation (Auto-CVE[CV]), Auto-CVE with dynamic sampling holdout (Auto-CVE[DS]) and TPOT through 10 runs for each dataset.

To verify how the dynamic sampling holdout changes the overall result of the techniques, Figs. 4 and 5 show the balanced accuracy performance and time consumed in the optimization procedure across the mentioned datasets. As it can be seen, the balanced accuracy for the three techniques is relatively similar. Auto-CVE with dynamic sampling (Auto-CVE[DS]) has a better mean performance in 7 datasets, while Auto-CVE with cross-validation (Auto-CVE[CV]) has a better mean performance in 5 datasets and TPOT has a better mean performance in 2, but with no large differences in the mean performance between them. Another factor is that both Auto-CVE variants show consistent performance, with low standard deviation across the datasets.

This analysis indicates that the Auto-CVE[DS] is competitive, reaching results close to both Auto-CVE[CV] and TPOT and, in several cases, better.

In addition, the execution time shows a large difference between these techniques: Auto-CVE with dynamic sampling holdout (Auto-CVE[DS]) is, in the majority of the executions, faster than both Auto-CVE with cross-validation (Auto-CVE[CV]) and TPOT. The instances where the execution time is similar are those in which the maximum time budget is reached for the tree techniques (named 1476, 1485, 1515, 1590, 23517, and some executions of the 40499) with Auto-CVE[CV] and TPOT probably stopping with fewer generations.

Finally, the Friedman's test was applied to the experiment results, following the procedure proposed in Demšar [5] to compare multiple algorithms over multiple datasets. The test results fail to reject the null hypothesis, indicating that there is no statistical evidence to confirm any difference between the performance of these techniques (p = 0.13 > 0.05). This test result goes towards the analysis that the performance of these techniques are close, even though the result is not conclusive.

In summary, both performance and time analysis show an impressive result towards the use of dynamic sampling, since Auto-CVE[DS] can reach similar performance to both Auto-CVE[CV] and TPOT, but with (sometimes orders of magnitude) less time consumed. Of course, a more in-depth study is still needed using a larger group of datasets (which was not possible here given the required computer time).

6   Conclusions and Future Works

This work revisits the Auto-CVE work [11], proposing a new method to evaluate models (the most expensive step). The dynamic sampling holdout makes it possible to evaluate models faster and mitigates the occurrence of overfitting, which is the biggest issue when using the regular holdout.

Through a set of experiments, it is shown that the use of a dynamic sampling holdout made it possible to maintain the level of performance of the Auto-CVE and reach these results in less time than when using the regular Auto-CVE with cross-validation. Also, a lower mean overfitting estimate of the returned model is achieved compared with the regular Auto-CVE.

This behavior is much more clear when the results are observed against the TPOT: the Auto-CVE with dynamic sampling is several orders of magnitude faster and achieves similar predictive capacity.

As future work, one possibility is using this dynamic sampling holdout in other Auto-ML techniques to investigate if the impact is similar. Besides, the use of this version of Auto-CVE with other, more complex, ensemble approaches, such as weighted voting and stacking, is a point to explore considering that the challenge of avoiding overfitting with those structures can be more significant.

References

1. Balaji, A., Allen, A.: Benchmarking Automatic Machine Learning Frameworks. CoRR abs/1808.0 (2018)
2. Cawley, G.C., Talbot, N.L.: On over-fitting in model selection and subsequent selection bias in performance evaluation. JMLR **11**, 2079–2107 (2010)
3. Chen, T., Guestrin, C.: XGBoost: A Scalable Tree Boosting System. In: Proceedings of KDD 2016, vol. 19, pp. 785–794 (2016)
4. DeCastro-García, N., Castañeda, Á.L.M., García, D.E., Carriegos, M.V.: Effect of the Sampling of a Dataset in the Hyperparameter Optimization Phase over the Efficiency of a Machine Learning Algorithm. Complexity 2019, pp. 1–16 (February 2019)
5. Demšar, J.: Statistical comparisons of classifiers over multiple data sets. JMLR **7**, 1–30 (2006)
6. Dietterich, T.G.: Ensemble methods in machine learning. In: Kittler, J., Roli, F. (eds.) MCS 2000. LNCS, vol. 1857, pp. 1–15. Springer, Heidelberg (2000). https://doi.org/10.1007/3-540-45014-9_1
7. Fabris, F., Freitas, A.A.: Analysing the overfit of the auto-sklearn automated machine learning tool. In: Nicosia, G., Pardalos, P., Umeton, R., Giuffrida, G., Sciacca, V. (eds.) LOD 2019. LNCS, vol. 11943, pp. 508–520. Springer, Cham (2019). https://doi.org/10.1007/978-3-030-37599-7_42
8. Feurer, M., Eggensperger, K., Falkner, S., Lindauer, M., Hutter, F.: Auto-Sklearn 2.0: The Next Generation. arXiv abs/2007.0, 1–18 (2020)
9. Gil, Y., et al.: P4ML: A phased performance-based pipeline planner for automated machine learning. In: Proceedings of ICML 2018, AutoML Workshop (2018)
10. Guyon, I., et al.: Design of the 2015 ChaLearn AutoML challenge. In: Proceedings of IJCNN 2015, pp. 1–8. IEEE (July 2015)
11. Larcher, Jr., C.H.N., Barbosa, H.J.C.: Auto-CVE: a coevolutionary approach to evolve ensembles in Automated Machine Learning. In: Proceedings of GECCO 2019, pp. 392–400 (2019)
12. Lévesque, J.C.: Bayesian Hyperparameter Optimization: Overfitting, Ensembles and Conditional Spaces. Ph.D. thesis, Université Laval (2018)
13. Li, L., Jamieson, K., DeSalvo, G., Rostamizadeh, A., Talwalkar, A.: Hyperband: Bandit-based configuration evaluation for hyperparameter optimization. In: Proceedings of ICLR 2017, pp. 1–15 (2016)
14. Mahfoud, S.W.: Crowding and preselection revisited. In: Parallel Problem Solving From Nature, pp. 27–36. North-Holland (1992)
15. Olson, R.S., Moore, J.H.: TPOT: A tree-based pipeline optimization tool for automating machine learning. In: Proceedings of ICML 2016, AutoML Workshop, pp. 66–74 (2016)
16. Pedregosa, F., et al.: Scikit-learn: machine learning in python. JMLR **12**, 2825–2830 (2011)
17. de Sá, A.G.C., Pinto, W.J.G.S., Oliveira, L.O.V.B., Pappa, G.L.: RECIPE: a grammar-based framework for automatically evolving classification pipelines. In: Genetic Programming, pp. 246–261 (2017)
18. Whigham, P.A.: Grammatically-based genetic programming. In: Proceedings of the Workshop on Genetic Programming: From Theory to Real-World Applications, vol. 16, pp. 33–41 (1995)

Parallel and Distributed Systems

Event-Driven Multi-algorithm Optimization: Mixing Swarm and Evolutionary Strategies

Mario García-Valdez[1]([✉])[iD] and Juan J. Merelo[2][iD]

[1] Tijuana Institute of Technology, Tijuana, Baja California, Mexico
mario@tectijuana.edu.mx
[2] University of Granada, Granada, Spain
jmerelo@ugr.es

Abstract. Researchers in nature-inspired optimization have recently proposed multi-population asynchronous algorithms that split the evolutionary process between different search paradigms working in collaboration. These algorithms execute the optimization strategy by reading streams of messages containing solution populations from message queues. After searching for a small number of iterations, new evolved populations are generated and sent back to a queue. Current research suggests that when we have many population-processing algorithms communicating in parallel, parameters intensifying exploration or exploitation in each population strike a dynamic that balances the two, exploring and exploiting simultaneously, maintaining an overall diversity, and improving the search. In this work, we propose a simple reactive migration, population-generation, and processing method for the asynchronous processing of multi-population, multi-strategy algorithms that achieves an improvement over homogeneous configurations. We evaluate this method by comparing a heterogeneous ensemble of multi-populations against a homogeneous solution consisting of a Genetic Algorithm (GA) and Particle Swarm Optimization (PSO) populations, using five problems from the noiseless BBOB toolbox for the optimization of continuous functions. Results show that compared with other asynchronous homogeneous population-based algorithms, this method offers better performance concerning the maximum number of evaluations needed to find a solution and the number runs where it found it.

Keywords: Heterogeneous multi-population algorithms · Genetic algorithms · Cloud-native systems

1 Introduction

The class of algorithms generically denominated nature-inspired [44], which include evolutionary (EAs) and swarm intelligence (SI) algorithms [2,22], have a lot of characteristics in common. Together with others like PBIL (Population

© Springer Nature Switzerland AG 2021
P. A. Castillo and J. L. Jiménez Laredo (Eds.): EvoApplications 2021, LNCS 12694, pp. 747–762, 2021.
https://doi.org/10.1007/978-3-030-72699-7_47

Based Incremental Learning) [3] and EDAs (Estimation of Distribution algorithms) [23] use (or generate, in the case of EDA) a set of (initially) random candidate solutions to produce a new set of candidates considering each candidate solutions' fitness.

Additionally, EAs and PSOs share another characteristic, besides the fact that they act on populations: they can use the same data structures to represent members of the population. Besides there is a certain equivalence in the variation operators, with, for instance, mutation in GAs being roughly equivalent to random motion, but they are different enough to perform search in different ways. The fact that they use the same data structures means that you can apply them in turns, or simply start calling a "chromosome" a "particle" or the other way round, without any conversion, and keep working with it with any of the algorithms. We will get back to this a bit later. They also face common challenges: Since all population members have to be evaluated to obtain a fitness or score that will be used to select them (or not), a disadvantage of this kind of algorithms is that they can be computationally expensive: every candidate solution needs to be evaluated, and the different strategies to efficiently explore the search space might eventually lead to lots of evaluations.

This fact, together with the a priori ease of simultaneous evaluation of different segments of the population, have spawned proposals of some form of parallelization from the start [31] to decrease their execution time, at least in the area of evolutionary algorithms. One of the earliest parallelization methods was the island model, which led to increased performance [14,16]. The idea was to divide the population into smaller segments that interacted with each other. Since then, other researchers have borrowed the concept and found other advantages besides a reduced execution time; these include avoiding an early convergence while maintaining the global population's diversity [24]. We are going to call these kinds of methods, multi-population algorithms [28]. The relative isolation in which the Algorithm manages populations, together with the synchronous or asynchronous communication, helps increase the global diversity since each population searches over a different area, at least between communications [26,43]. In some cases, even a multi-population based algorithm is able to scale better due to these interactions and the operation's parallelism [1].

These initial procedures replicate the same parameters (and, implicitly, the same algorithm) in all segments (often called *demes*) in which the population is divided. But this is not really mandatory: Having many populations offers researchers many configuration choices and additional challenges when designing scalable algorithms. Designers must choose the number of populations and their size, the type of communication among them, each population's search area, the search strategy, its parametrization, and, of course, the actual algorithm that every segment is running. In the literature, we can find several heterogeneous mixed-algorithm multi-population methods that integrate variations of population-based algorithms, and often, these have a better performance than algorithms using a single-population or homogeneous multi-populations [33,43].

In this paper, we will focus in this aspect, with multiple populations running with distinct parameters and optimization algorithms.

Mixed-algorithm parallel methods put an additional burden on the tuning of parameters for each population, since the space of free parameters (and its possible interactions) blows up; some parameters influence the solution's accuracy while others affect the convergence speed of individual algorithms, tipping the balance between exploring or exploiting the solution space. Moreover, current literature shows that having a higher number of populations communicating in parallel evens out the effect on exploration and exploitation in each individual population [26,42]. We can add some heterogeneity by just altering each population's parameters, but in this work, we are interested in evaluating the compensating effect that heterogeneous, mixed-algorithm search strategies have. Having multiple search strategies can further improve the heterogeneous effect because different methods explore the search space differently. For instance, a PSO method creates new candidate solutions by moving towards promising candidates, while a GA interchanges portions of solutions with better fitness. This line of research can bring light to the type of benefits this type of mixing can bring to the field. Our hypothesis here is that expanding the search space exploration capabilities of the algorithm by mixing different algorithms might on one hand reduce the need to fine-tune single-algorithm parameters, and, on the other hand, get better results than single-algorithm methods by leveraging synergies between the exploration and exploitation capabilities of the algorithms involved. Our objective is to prove that the advantage of heterogeneous configurations resides not only in the increased scalability but also in the search performance. Therefore, in this paper, we have implemented an asynchronous multi-population algorithm version, using a message queue for inter-process communication (in a way similar as the one used in [29]) and a reactive migration procedure.

We compare three heterogeneous configurations using a randomized parameter technique, since our intention is to get close to minimal or no configuration parameters. We experimented with all populations using a GA or PSO search strategies versus an ensemble multi-population with both GA and PSO algorithms, using as a benchmark the separable functions of the BBOB noiseless testbed [21]. We compare the options by measuring the average running time (aRT) as the number of functions (#FEs), in order to prove the advantage of this kind of heterogeneous configurations.

The organization of the paper is as follows: First, in Sect. 2 we present the relevant state of the art. In Sect. 3, we describe in detail the framework used in this work. Section 4 describes the design of the empirical evaluation we designed to assess the effectiveness of the method, and in Sect. 5, we report and discuss the results. Finally, we present conclusions and offer future work suggestions in Sect. 6.

2 State of the Art

Designing a population-based algorithm always relies on achieving a good exploration-exploitation balance via the clever use of selection and variation operators [4]. In pursuit of that objective, it is important to keep diversity high [45], but different algorithms have different mechanisms for increasing diversity (exploration) or decreasing it (exploitation). PSO has two constants that rule in which direction the *particle* is going to move: either randomly (exploration) or in the direction of the best particle (exploitation); evolutionary algorithms use mutation and, to a certain point, crossover for exploration and crossover and selection procedures for exploitation. Since these mechanisms are fundamentally different, mixing different algorithms might be considered a win-win situation by way of performing exploitation in several different directions, implying, at the same time, exploration, which will be able to get closer to the solution as well as generate new possibilities as has been indicated previously in the introduction.

This is what the first papers to propose such a hybrid algorithm, by Robinson et al. [38] leveraged, explicitly playing on this fact, and also on what we might call diversity of local minima, by running an algorithm on a population until it became stagnated, and then switching to the other one. This was done apparently only once, but eventually the mixture of the two algorithms was able to obtain better results in the design of a kind of antenna called "horn" than any of them separately, although they report that the best value was obtained by the algorithm that started as a PSO and terminated as an evolutionary one.

Another kind of hybrid was proposed independently by Shi et al. [40], citing the "local optimum" problem, that is, the same one as before; it mixes both algorithms testing in different configurations: "parallel" and "serial" testing which configuration works better and is able to avoid that. Their results on benchmark functions are mixed; In general, however, a well-designed evolutionary or PSO algorithm will not fall in that local optimum; it is certainly true that, within a certain evaluation budget, neither might be able to find that global optimum. However, it is probably that they mean that, since exploitation of better-than-average solutions is done by the two algorithms in different directions, a hybrid algorithm might help the single-algorithm version to escape that.

This better exploitation capability was used by Grimaldi et al. [15], with the objective of solving electromagnetic problems. What they do is to split the population into two different populations which will be processed by an EA and a PSO algorithm; the new individuals generated are merged in a single population, which is then split all over again in the next iteration. This guarantees that none of the two algorithms is getting stuck, since the individuals will be randomly subjected to one or the other on every generation.

Later on, Esmin et al. [7] leveraged to design their algorithms; this idea was later extended by Li et al. [25]; in this work, chromosomes/particles represent Support Vector Machines, which are optimized to find the most representative features of gene expression data sets. PSO and EAs are applied serially: 10 iterations of each, after which the finalization criterion is examined; first PSO, then EA. Separate EA and PSO are tested against this hybrid algorithm, finding improvements of a few percent points in the accuracy over classification of the whole dataset. This marginal, but significant, improvement is essentially the kind of results that should be expected. While improvements in diversity always boost the results by allowing the algorithms to find better solutions, an order-of-magnitude difference is not usually achieved, since both algorithms, by themselves, have good mechanisms for global exploration.

Other methods have later been suggested: Pandi et al. [34] suggest a combination of swarm intelligence and another algorithm denominated harmony search; Lien et al. [27] combine particle swarm optimization with bee colony algorithms, while Zhao et al. [46] combine the latter with evolutionary algorithms.

Some authors have proposed the combination of search methods for continuous function optimization, in particular for the black-box optimization benchmark. PSO it is often chosen for the combination, García-Nieto et al. [11] combined PSO with Differential Evolution. El-Abd and Kamel proposed a PSO hybrid [6] with a Estimation of Distribution Algorithm (EDA), that works by sampling an independent univariate Gaussian distribution based on the best half of the swarm. They choose with a certain probability, whether to update the particle using the normal PSO equations or to sample the particle using the estimated distribution.

Hybrid algorithms are still able to perform beyond the state of the art: Gulia et al. [17] mix ant colony optimization, which is a swarm intelligence algorithm, and EAs, to select software testing cases. ACO and EA are used serially, with GA acting to refine the test suite initially selected by the ant algorithm. A very recent article [39] compares how different hybrid algorithms, including GA-PSO hybrids, are applied to software reliability problems.

The state of the art is, then, use swarm intelligence and evolutionary algorithms coupled to a population to which they are applied either one after the other, or splitting the population so that every one is applied to a part. This is, however, not done in a parallel and asynchronous way, or decoupling population and algorithms and applying them in a non-deterministic and mostly parameter-free way. This is what we are going to do in this paper.

3   Proposed Method

As we have mentioned before, when designing efficient multi-population algorithms, we need to consider additional issues [28], including the number and size of populations, how they interact or communicate between them, and the search strategy in each. We have considered these requirements and, Considering these requirements, in this paper, we propose a cloud-native hybrid-algorithm, multi-population solution. In this model, populations are the primary data structures, and we package them as messages that are part of a continuous stream flow from one computing node, that performs a kind of algorithm, to the next. To achieve this "continuous stream," everything must happen asynchronously without. Computing nodes running an algorithm "wake up" when they receive a message, with no idle time between the processing of messages arriving from the stream.

We implemented this streaming functionality by using a message queue system, we show the architecture in Fig. 1. The main components of the architecture

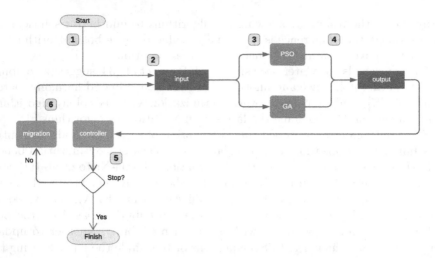

Fig. 1. General scheme of the architecture of this method. Please refer to text for the explanation of the different numbers.

are producers and consumers of messages. There are two queues, one labeled `input`, which mainly holds populations that are going to be evolved, and the other called `output` which is where algorithm nodes send their population messages. In a queue, *push* and *pop* operations are shown as arrows entering or leaving the box. The `controller` process manages the migration of individuals from one population to the other and keeps track of the algorithm's iterations. In this case, there are two search strategies `PSO` and `GA`, these as red boxes. The stream of messages follows the path explained next:

1. As a first step, a specified number of populations is created. At first populations are just data, that includes randomly created individuals. Each populations has its corresponding metadata section with the algorithm's parameters.
2. The setup process pushes each population on to the `input` queue, this queue in turn is consumed by all the `stateless_functions` executing the search algorithms.
3. These functions have the task of executing the optimization algorithm, taking the population's current state and running a certain number of iterations. When creating a population message, the setup function randomly selects an optimization algorithm and parameters. These parameters are part of the population's metadata read by the stateless functions executing the algorithm. In the current configuration, all types of algorithms have the same probability of being chosen.
4. Once a stateless function finishes the iterations, the population state is pushed to the `output` queue; when the computing node is done with a population, it draws another one from the queue.

5. The `controller` logs the metadata of each population pulled from the `output` queue, it stops the algorithm when reaching a certain solution or when completing all the iterations.
6. If not, it sends the incoming messages to a "migration" function, responsible for mixing the populations. This function generates new populations, that again are pushed to the `input` queue closing the loop. Although this steps corresponds roughly to the classical *migration*, since it mixes different populations, it is actually a selection procedure, since it ranks the individuals of the mixed population and selects the best half, eventually generating three new populations. Without this step, there would be no real parallel algorithm; populations would be sequentially processed by different algorithms, though.

This message queue pattern is a common component of highly scalable reactive architectures; one of the reasons for this scalability is the use of stateless functions. Stateless functions do not need to read, keep, or modify data outside of the scope of the method, it will have no side effects reading inputs and producing an output, mapping input to output as it were. Suppose we implement population-based optimization algorithms using stateless functions. In that case, the system can handle one or many copies pulling work at the same time. This architecture has been implemented successfully for developing cloud-native multi-population algorithms, using serverless functions [12], and concurrent programming [30].

To have a stateless version of a population-based algorithm, we only need to skip the step of creating a random population. Instead, the function receives the population as a parameter along with the required parameters. After several iterations (specified in the parameters), the function returns the current state of the population, with additional data describing the local execution. This data is necessary to log the #FE and current fitness values.

As the controller is pulling population messages from the output queue, it waits until the message queue contains three valid populations to trigger an event handled by the `population_mixer` function, which uses as an argument a list containing the three populations. This design has the advantage of following the reactive paradigm while not needing to keep a buffer in memory or external storage. A disadvantage is that it only migrates between populations that have arrived sequentially from the message queue, but we could mitigate this with a larger buffer and in fact populations do not need to arrive to the buffer in the same order they were created or processed, so this shouldn't, in principle, contribute to any loss of diversity. The output queue composition depends on two factors: The number or ratio between each type of algorithm and the amount of time required to finish the required number of iterations specified for each population. For instance, if the implementation of a PSO algorithm could finish faster than a GA implementation for the same number of iterations, or if we have more functions executing a particular algorithm, we will have more messages from one of the algorithms in the output queue.

We will use this set up to perform a series of experiments destined to measure the performance of this hybrid algorithm. We will do this next.

4   Experimental Setup

In this section, we present the experimental setup needed to verify if a multi-population algorithm, using asynchronous heterogeneous populations with a migration procedure, has better performance than a single homogeneous algorithm method, needing fewer function evaluations to reach a solution.

For the experiment, we use five benchmark separable functions ($f_1 to f_5$) from the Continuous Noiseless BBOB testbed, which is part of the Comparing Continuous Optimizers (COCO) framework [19]. Although there are not many real-world problems that are entirely separable, we want to focus on these five separable functions as a primary benchmark for testing the performance of a hybrid multi-population algorithm. And there is interest in solving such problems using more general methods [5, 41].

These functions are real-parameter, single-objective, and are usually employed as benchmarks. We have tested with fifteen instances of each function, each one having a distinct optimum value. The BBOB testbed uses these 15 instances over 2, 3, 5, 10, 20, and 40 dimensions. With the maximum number of function evaluations (#FEs) increasing with dimension (D), using the expression $10^5 \cdot D$ (i.e. for $D = 2$, #FEs is 200, 000). To test our proposal, we compare the aRT between a multi-population ensemble, and standalone versions of GA and PSO algorithms.

The stateless GA function is implemented using DEAP [9], while the PSO algorithm uses EvoloPy [8]. These libraries are free software written in Python, and easily deployable in our framework or in the cloud. We show the parameters for each algorithm in Table 1; these were obtained by following a method proposed by García et al. in [13] and have been also used in [10]. We randomly (within the range shown in the table) set mutation and crossover probabilities for the GA with the goal of having more diverse populations and less parameters to tune. We did not follow the same tactic for PSO, as we choose the same parameters as those proposed by El-Abd and Kamel in the PSO implementation for the BBOB benchmark [6]. We have not changed these settings during the experiments, and we have only provided the population size and number of generations as parameters.

Table 1. DEAP GA and EvoloPy PSO parameters

GA		PSO	
Selection	Tournament size = 12	V_{max}	6
Mutation type	Gaussian $\mu = 0.0$, $\sigma = 0.5$, indbp = 0.05	W_{max}	0.9
Probability of mutation	[0.1, 0.3]	W_{min}	0.2
Crossover type	Two-point	C_1	2
Probability of crossover	[0.2, 0.6]	C_2	2

To run the experiments, we have deployed the Docker application with 8 worker containers hosting the stateless version of the GA and PSO algorithms described earlier, and a total of 10 populations. This setup is similar, and in fact precedes, the one published in [10]. Table 2 shows the parameters we have used (from [10]). The proportion of populations using the GA algorithm against the PSO is given by the parameter *GA-PSO Ratio*. We have used the standard number of instances in the BBOB benchmark [19], 15 and f_1 to f_5. The list of dimensions that we have tested is in the *Dimensions* parameter; for every dimension, we must specify the number of populations; together with the number of generations and population size for each population. Finally, we have defined how many complete loops the algorithm will perform. The product of these parameters gives us a maximum #FEs. For example, for $D = 2$, the #FEs is $200,000$ (see first column in Table 2).

Table 2. Parameters used in the experiments, for ten populations and eight workers.

Dimension	2	3	5	10	20	40
Generations	40	25	28	50	66	80
Population size	50	60	60	70	100	125
Populations	10	10	10	10	10	10
Iterations	10	20	30	30	30	40

We have deployed the container-based application in a PC with an AMD Ryzen9 3900x with a 12-core CPU, 24 threads, and 16 GB RAM. We used Docker version 19.03.3, and `docker-compose` version 1.21.0, in Ubuntu Linux 18.04, and Python 3.7.5 code. Container images and Docker compose file are available at (https://hub.docker.com/mariosky), and (https://github.com/mariosky/EvoSwarm). The experiments were performed with COCO [19] version bbob.v15.03 written in Python. The plot shown below was generated using COCO version 2.3.2.

5   Results

Our main intention here is to show how the combination of two kinds of population-based algorithms is able to outperform single-algorithm versions of the same method. We will run the BBOB benchmarks for the five selected functions. These functions, even if they are not the full range of BBOB benchmarks, are a sufficiently diverse set and are able to find differences in performance between the two single-algorithm methods and the mixed algorithm we are focusing on this paper. These functions have also been used in [10], which can also be used for comparison.

Figure 2 shows the classical COCO comparison, which is related to the #FE needed to reach target values Δf. Line colors indicate the average of FEs for targets reached at least one time, a red circle (without a number on top) means that

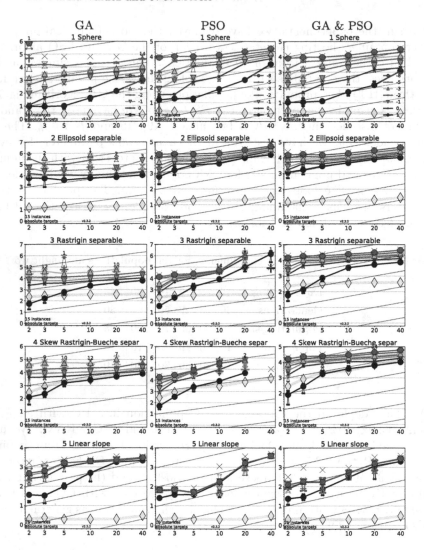

Fig. 2. Running time needed to reach Δf (y, in $\log_{10}$ scale, divided by dimension) vs. dimension (x). Lines: average runtime (aRT); (+): median runtime of successful runs to reach the most difficult target that was reached at least once; (×): maximum number of evaluations in any trial. Notched boxes: interquartile range with median of simulated runs. Please note that y in the same row, generated automatically by COCO, can be different.

the algorithm, reached on all instances, the most difficult target 10^{-8}; a number on the top indicates how many times the target was reached. For instance, you can see numbers in f_2 to f_5 for the evolutionary algorithm, implying there are, in fact, few cases where the target was reached, for instance, just 1 for dimension = 10, $\delta_f = 10^{-3}$ and f_2. Values of targets $\Delta f = 10^k$ are given in the legend of the first

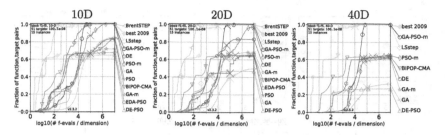

Fig. 3. Bootstrapped empirical cumulative distribution of the number of objective function evaluations divided by dimension (FEvals/DIM) for the functions used in this paper.

function, k values are $[-8, -5, -3, -2, -1, 0, 1]$. Each column presents the results for GA, PSO, and GA&PSO methods. In general, and in this framework, the GA (on the left column) hardly reaches even the 10^{-5} target in functions ($f_1 - f_4$), and achieved the worst performance in 20 and 40 dimensions. However, it's quite competitive for f_5 where it reaches the 10^{-8} target on all dimensions, but it has the highest runtime on lower dimensions. As indicated in [21], this results shows a characteristic of the algorithm, that is to adapt the size of changes in individual solutions and also be able to get out of a local optimum; a GA is able to perform reasonably well (and definitely better than in functions f_1 to f_4). Nonetheless, multi-population PSO (on the middle), in general, achieves a better performance than the GA, reaching all targets in f_1 and f_2 functions; however it needs a high number of evaluations. On the higher dimensions of functions f_3 and f_4, PSO is not able to reach most difficult target (10^{-8}); but for dimensions 2, 3, and 5 of f_5 achieves the best runtime.

Finally, the PSO&GA multi-population algorithm, shown in the right column see Fig. 2, reaches the most difficult 10^{-8} target for all functions ($f_1 - f_5$) scaling well to higher dimensions, even on f_3 and f_4, which are usually considered difficult functions [20]. Please bear in mind that the scale of the y axis, corresponding to the number of evaluations, has a smaller span in this column, in some cases two orders of magnitude less than for the single-algorithm methods, thus showing a more robust, and consistently higher, performance.

These results are also competitive when compared against other GA and PSO implementations of past BBOB workshops. Figure 4 shows how the aRT scales against dimensions to reach the most difficult target ($\Delta f = 10^{-8}$) in all functions. We chose two types of representative algorithms, first, Evolutionary an Swarm based and not population-based. We chose a simple binary GA algorithm of Nicolau [32], the PSO algorithm by El-Abd and Kamel [6], an EDA and PSO hybrid [6], Differential Evolution (DE) with adaptive encoding [37] by Pošík and Klemš, the hybrid DE-PSO by García-Nieto et al. [11], and the BIPOP-CMA-ES algorithm [18] by Hansen, this last algorithm has the best overall ($f_1 - f_2$) performance on the BBOB-2009 benchmark, as it could solve 23, 22 and 20 functions out of 24 in dimensions 10, 20 and 40, respectively. The

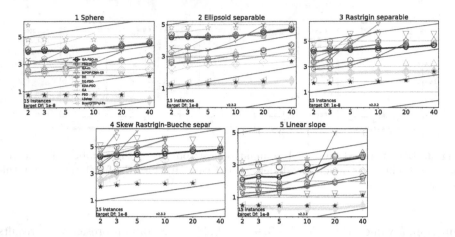

Fig. 4. Average running time (in #FEs as log_{10} value) normalized by dimension for target function value 10^{-8} (y) per dimension (x). Black stars mark significantly better results. Legend: ○:GA-PSO-m, ◇:PSO-m, ⋆:GA-m, ▽:BIPOP-CMA-ES, ◯:DE, △:DE-PSO, ⬠:EDA-PSO, ⚬:GA, ⋎:PSO, ◇:LSstep, ◁:BrentSTEP

algorithm uses two interlaced restart strategies, one with an increasing population size and one with varying small population sizes using a covariance matrix adaptation evolution strategy (CMA-ES). We also compare with two methods that are not population-based, but univariate solvers generalized for the optimization of separable functions, the line-search algorithm LSStep by Pošík [35], and the Hybrid Brent-STEP by Pošík and Baudiš [36]. The performance for the Brent-STEP algorithm is the best for this group of functions, finding all targets with less FEs.

We can see that the number of evaluations of GA-PSO-m tends to be higher in most cases, but on the other hand, it could solve all functions while others could not. This fact is in accordance with our hypothesis that a having a combination of methods, gives as a result an exploration that keeps diversity in balance with exploitation. It can take more evaluations, but it explores other areas of the search space, avoiding local minima in more cases. As expected, the BIPOP-CMA-ES algorithm has the best running time on functions f_1, f_2 and f_5 and reaches three targets at search dimensions 20 and 40. It is worth to notice the performance of the DE algorithm, having the best running time on lower dimensions of f_3 and f_4. Figure 3 highlights the performance of our proposal in search space of dimensions 10, 20, and 40. The figure shows the fraction of functions-target pairs by the number of FEs. In this case, an algorithm that requires less FEs to reach all targets will have more area under the curve. For higher dimensions, the GA-PSO multi-population gives competitive results by reaching all targets within budget. The Brent-STEP algorithm did not provide results for 40D.

6 Conclusions, Discussion and Future Lines of Work

A common element of different population based metaheuristics, namely, the population itself, has made the application of different algorithms relatively easy by decoupling the algorithms from the population. In [10] we showed how this could be used in a cloud native framework; this paper scales back the functionality showing a more basic mixed-algorithm, stateless and concurrent implementation that combines off-the-shelf open source libraries to create a higher level optimization framework that can be easily deployed locally or on the cloud. The fact that populations and evolution (or any other kind of change) are totally decoupled and the processing of every population is stateless enables the creation create a mixture of processing algorithms that work asynchronously (and possibly concurrently) and in a way that's totally independent of each other. More methods can be added to the mix by simply adding another stateless function that listens to the population queue and writes back to it.

We have tested this combination of algorithms on the BBOB benchmark functions, obtaining results that are better than those obtained by any of them separated. This confirms results obtained by previous authors in hybrid algorithms, except that, in this case, the architecture is different and there are improvements all across the tested functions; besides, results are better than results that have been published for other algorithms, including a hybrid one, making the hybrid PSO/GA a firm contender in the function optimization arena. It is interesting to note that this is done despite mixing both algorithms in a totally random way, so that it's really impossible to know whether an individual population will be processed by a GA or PSO, or how many cycles of each has undergone. The migration process, however, guarantees a mixing of results and is probably the key to the ultimate success of the algorithm proposed here.

We can conclude, then, than our experiments prove that the mixed-algorithm method is able to outperform single-algorithm methods in the same setup, reaching success more often, and needing less evaluations; this effectively overcomes the excessive exploration that might occur in PSO and the excessive exploitation that sometimes GA suffer.

As future lines of work, we will try to add different population-based, data-compatible algorithms to the mix, to see what kind of results they obtain and what could possible be the best possible mix; this will be needed to prove that it's this specific combination of algorithms, and not simply the fact that the algorithms are different, the key to its performance. An extensive study on the real effects of the mix of algorithms should also be performed, with a theoretical basis if possible, using the size of the basins of attractions, the evolution of entropy in every population, or how different algorithms move along the fitness landscape. This will help us understand how diversity is maintained by the combination of methods and random parameters, which will help us to propose new ways to adapt this diversity to the state of the search.

Acknowledgments. We would like to thank the anonymous reviewers for their helpful suggestions and corrections. This work received support from projects DeepBio (TIN2017-85727-C4-2-P) and TecNM (11356).

References

1. Alba, E.: Parallel evolutionary algorithms can achieve super-linear performance. Inf. Process. Lett. **82**(1), 7–13 (2002). Evolutionary Computation
2. Back, T.: Evolutionary Algorithms in Theory and Practice: Evolution Strategies, Evolutionary Programming, Genetic Algorithms. Oxford University Press, Oxford (1996)
3. Baluja, S.: Population-based incremental learning. a method for integrating genetic search based function optimization and competitive learning. Technical report, Carnegie-Mellon University, Pittsburgh PA, Department of Computer Science (1994)
4. Črepinšek, M., Liu, S.H., Mernik, M.: Exploration and exploitation in evolutionary algorithms: a survey. ACM Comput. Surv. (CSUR) **45**(3), 1–33 (2013)
5. Doerr, B., Sudholt, D., Witt, C.: When do evolutionary algorithms optimize separable functions in parallel? In: Proceedings FOGA XII, pp. 51–64 (2013)
6. El-Abd, M., Kamel, M.S.: Black-box optimization benchmarking for noiseless function testbed using an EDA and PSO hybrid. In: Proceedings of the 11th Annual Conference Companion on Genetic and Evolutionary Computation Conference: Late Breaking Papers, pp. 2263–2268 (2009)
7. Esmin, A.A.A., Lambert-Torres, G., Alvarenga, G.B.: Hybrid evolutionary algorithm based on PSO and GA mutation. In: 2006 Sixth International Conference on Hybrid Intelligent Systems (HIS 2006), pp. 57. IEEE (2006)
8. Faris, H., Aljarah, I., Mirjalili, S., Castillo, P.A., Merelo-Guervós, J.J.: EvoloPy: an open-source nature-inspired optimization framework in Python. In: IJCCI (ECTA), pp. 171–177 (2016)
9. Fortin, F.A., Rainville, F.M.D., Gardner, M.A., Parizeau, M., Gagné, C.: DEAP: evolutionary algorithms made easy. J. Mach. Learn. Res. **13**, 2171–2175 (2012)
10. García Valdez, M., Merelo Guervós, J.J.: A container-based cloud-native architecture for the reproducible execution of multi-population optimization algorithms. Future Gener. Comput. Syst. **116**, 234–252 (2021). https://doi.org/10.1016/j.future.2020.10.039. http://www.sciencedirect.com/science/article/pii/S0167739X20330235
11. García-Nieto, J., Alba, E., Apolloni, J.: Noiseless functions black-box optimization: evaluation of a hybrid particle swarm with differential operators. In: Proceedings of the 11th Annual Conference Companion on Genetic and Evolutionary Computation Conference: Late Breaking Papers, pp. 2231–2238 (2009)
12. García-Valdez, J.M., Merelo-Guervós, J.J.: A modern, event-based architecture for distributed evolutionary algorithms. In: Proceedings of the Genetic and Evolutionary Computation Conference Companion, pp. 233–234 (2018)
13. García-Valdez, M., Merelo, J.: Benchmarking a pool-based execution with GA and PSO workers on the BBOB noiseless testbed. In: Proceedings of the Genetic and Evolutionary Computation Conference Companion, pp. 1750–1755 (2017)
14. Gorges-Schleuter, M.: Explicit parallelism of genetic algorithms through population structures. In: Schwefel, H.-P., Männer, R. (eds.) PPSN 1990. LNCS, vol. 496, pp. 150–159. Springer, Heidelberg (1991). https://doi.org/10.1007/BFb0029746

15. Grimaldi, E.A., Grimaccia, F., Mussetta, M., Pirinoli, P., Zich, R.: Genetical swarm optimization: a new hybrid evolutionary algorithm for electromagnetic applications. In: 2005 18th International Conference on Applied Electromagnetics and Communications, pp. 1–4. IEEE (2005)
16. Grosso, P.: Computer simulations of genetic adaptation: parallel subcomponent interaction in multilocus model. Ph.D. dissertation, University of Michigan (1985)
17. Gulia, P., et al.: Hybrid swarm and GA based approach for software test case selection. Int. J. Electr. Comput. Eng. **9**, 4898–4903 (2019). (2088–8708)
18. Hansen, N.: Benchmarking a BI-population CMA-ES on the BBOB-2009 function testbed. In: Proceedings of the 11th Annual Conference Companion on Genetic and Evolutionary Computation Conference: Late Breaking Papers, pp. 2389–2396 (2009)
19. Hansen, N., Auger, A., Mersmann, O., Tusar, T., Brockhoff, D.: COCO: a platform for comparing continuous optimizers in a black-box setting. arXiv preprint arXiv:1603.08785 (2016)
20. Hansen, N., Auger, A., Ros, R., Finck, S., Pošík, P.: Comparing results of 31 algorithms from the black-box optimization benchmarking BBOB-2009. In: Proceedings of the 12th Annual Conference Companion on Genetic and Evolutionary Computation, pp. 1689–1696. ACM (2010)
21. Hansen, N., Finck, S., Ros, R., Auger, A.: Real-parameter black-box optimization benchmarking 2009: noiseless functions definitions. Ph.D. thesis, INRIA (2009)
22. Kennedy, J.: Swarm intelligence. In: Zomaya, A.Y. (ed.) Handbook of Nature-Inspired and Innovative Computing, pp. 187–219. Springer, Boston (2006). https://doi.org/10.1007/0-387-27705-6_6
23. Bengoetxea, E., Larrañaga, P., Bloch, I., Perchant, A.: Estimation of distribution algorithms: a new evolutionary computation approach for graph matching problems. In: Figueiredo, M., Zerubia, J., Jain, A.K. (eds.) EMMCVPR 2001. LNCS, vol. 2134, pp. 454–469. Springer, Heidelberg (2001). https://doi.org/10.1007/3-540-44745-8_30
24. Li, C., Nguyen, T.T., Yang, M., Yang, S., Zeng, S.: Multi-population methods in unconstrained continuous dynamic environments: the challenges. Inf. Sci. **296**, 95–118 (2015)
25. Li, S., Wu, X., Tan, M.: Gene selection using hybrid particle swarm optimization and genetic algorithm. Soft. Comput. **12**(11), 1039–1048 (2008)
26. Li, X., Ma, S., Wang, Y.: Multi-population based ensemble mutation method for single objective bilevel optimization problem. IEEE Access **4**, 7262–7274 (2016)
27. Lien, L.C., Cheng, M.Y.: A hybrid swarm intelligence based particle-bee algorithm for construction site layout optimization. Expert Syst. Appl. **39**(10), 9642–9650 (2012)
28. Ma, H., Shen, S., Yu, M., Yang, Z., Fei, M., Zhou, H.: Multi-population techniques in nature inspired optimization algorithms: a comprehensive survey. Swarm Evol. Comput. **44**, 365–387 (2019)
29. Merelo Guervós, J.J., García-Valdez, J.M.: Introducing an event-based architecture for concurrent and distributed evolutionary algorithms. In: Auger, A., Fonseca, C.M., Lourenço, N., Machado, P., Paquete, L., Whitley, D. (eds.) PPSN 2018. LNCS, vol. 11101, pp. 399–410. Springer, Cham (2018). https://doi.org/10.1007/978-3-319-99253-2_32
30. Merelo-Guervós, J.J., Laredo, J.L.J., Castillo, P.A., Valdez, M.G., Rojas-Galeano, S.: Improving the algorithmic efficiency and performance of channel-based evolutionary algorithms. In: Proceedings of the Genetic and Evolutionary Computation Conference Companion, pp. 320–321 (2019)

31. Mühlenbein, H., Gorges-Schleuter, M., Krämer, O.: Evolution algorithms in combinatorial optimization. Parallel Comput. **7**(1), 65–85 (1988)
32. Nicolau, M.: Application of a simple binary genetic algorithm to a noiseless testbed benchmark. In: Proceedings of the 11th Annual Conference Companion on Genetic and Evolutionary Computation Conference: Late Breaking Papers, pp. 2473–2478 (2009)
33. Nseef, S.K., Abdullah, S., Turky, A., Kendall, G.: An adaptive multi-population artificial bee colony algorithm for dynamic optimisation problems. Knowl.-Based Syst. **104**, 14–23 (2016)
34. Pandi, V.R., Panigrahi, B.K.: Dynamic economic load dispatch using hybrid swarm intelligence based harmony search algorithm. Expert Syst. Appl. **38**(7), 8509–8514 (2011)
35. Pošík, P.: BBOB-benchmarking two variants of the line-search algorithm. In: Proceedings of the 11th Annual Conference Companion on Genetic and Evolutionary Computation Conference: Late Breaking Papers, pp. 2329–2336 (2009)
36. Pošík, P., Baudiš, P.: Dimension selection in axis-parallel brent-step method for black-box optimization of separable continuous functions. In: Proceedings of the Companion Publication of the 2015 Annual Conference on Genetic and Evolutionary Computation, pp. 1151–1158 (2015)
37. Pošík, P., Klemš, V.: Benchmarking the differential evolution with adaptive encoding on noiseless functions. In: Proceedings of the 14th Annual Conference Companion on Genetic and Evolutionary Computation, pp. 189–196 (2012)
38. Robinson, J., Sinton, S., Rahmat-Samii, Y.: Particle swarm, genetic algorithm, and their hybrids: optimization of a profiled corrugated horn antenna. In: IEEE Antennas and Propagation Society, AP-S International Symposium (Digest), vol. 1, pp. 314–317, February 2002. https://doi.org/10.1109/APS.2002.1016311
39. Sangeeta, S.: Comprehensive analysis of hybrid nature-inspired algorithms for software reliability analysis. J. Stat. Manag. Syst. **23**(6), 1037–1048 (2020)
40. Shi, X., Lu, Y., Zhou, C., Lee, H., Lin, W., Liang, Y.: Hybrid evolutionary algorithms based on PSO and GA. In: The 2003 Congress on Evolutionary Computation 2003. CEC 2003, vol. 4, pp. 2393–2399. IEEE (2003)
41. Swarzberg, S., Seront, G., Bersini, H.: Step: the easiest way to optimize a function. In: Proceedings of the First IEEE Conference on Evolutionary Computation. IEEE World Congress on Computational Intelligence, pp. 519–524. IEEE (1994)
42. Tanabe, R., Fukunaga, A.: Evaluation of a randomized parameter setting strategy for island-model evolutionary algorithms. In: 2013 IEEE Congress on Evolutionary Computation (CEC), pp. 1263–1270. IEEE (2013)
43. Wu, G., Mallipeddi, R., Suganthan, P.N., Wang, R., Chen, H.: Differential evolution with multi-population based ensemble of mutation strategies. Inf. Sci. **329**, 329–345 (2016)
44. Yang, X.S.: Nature-Inspired Optimization Algorithms. Elsevier, Amsterdam (2014)
45. Yuan, B., Gallagher, M.: On the importance of diversity maintenance in estimation of distribution algorithms. In: Proceedings of the 7th Annual Conference on Genetic and Evolutionary Computation, pp. 719–726 (2005)
46. Zhao, H., Pei, Z., Jiang, J., Guan, R., Wang, C., Shi, X.: A hybrid swarm intelligent method based on genetic algorithm and artificial bee colony. In: Tan, Y., Shi, Y., Tan, K.C. (eds.) ICSI 2010. LNCS, vol. 6145, pp. 558–565. Springer, Heidelberg (2010). https://doi.org/10.1007/978-3-642-13495-1_68

TensorGP – Genetic Programming Engine in TensorFlow

Francisco Baeta[✉], João Correia, Tiago Martins, and Penousal Machado

CISUC, Department of Informatics Engineering, University of Coimbra,
Coimbra, Portugal
{fjrbaeta,jncor,tiagofm,machado}@dei.uc.pt

Abstract. In this paper, we resort to the TensorFlow framework to investigate the benefits of applying data vectorization and fitness caching methods to domain evaluation in Genetic Programming. For this purpose, an independent engine was developed, TensorGP, along with a testing suite to extract comparative timing results across different architectures and amongst both iterative and vectorized approaches. Our performance benchmarks demonstrate that by exploiting the TensorFlow eager execution model, performance gains of up to two orders of magnitude can be achieved on a parallel approach running on dedicated hardware when compared to a standard iterative approach.

Keywords: Genetic Programming · Parallelization · Vectorization · TensorFlow · GPU computing

1 Introduction

Genetic Programming (GP), which targets the evolution of computer programs, is known to require large amounts of computational resources since all individuals in the population need to be executed and tested against the objective. As a result, fitness evaluation is generally regarded as the most computationally costly operation in GP for most practical applications [1]. Despite this, GP is beyond doubt a powerful evolutionary technique, capable of tackling every problem solvable by a computer program without the need for domain-specific knowledge [2]. Furthermore, although computationally intensive by nature, GP is also "embarrassingly parallel" [3].

Previous works on accelerating fitness evaluation in GP mainly focus on two techniques: the caching of intermediate fitness results and the vectorization of the evaluation domain. The first method aims to save the results of code execution from parts of a program to avoid re-executing this code when evaluating other individuals. On the other hand, the second method evaluates the full array of fitness cases simultaneously by performing a tensor operation for each function within an individual.

The last decade saw the exponential growth of computing power proposed by Gordon Moore back in 1965 [4] start to break down. As we start meeting the limits of physics, a paradigm shift towards multi-core computing and parallelization

© Springer Nature Switzerland AG 2021
P. A. Castillo and J. L. Jiménez Laredo (Eds.): EvoApplications 2021, LNCS 12694, pp. 763–778, 2021.
https://doi.org/10.1007/978-3-030-72699-7_48

becomes inevitable. Namely, with the rise of parallel computing, devices such as the Graphics Processing Units (GPUs) have become ever more readily available [5]. Tensor operations are highly optimised on GPUs as they are necessary for the various stages of the graphical rendering pipeline. Therefore, it makes sense to couple the data vectorization approach with such architectures.

In this work, we resort to the TensorFlow plataform in order to investigate the benefits of applying the aforementioned approaches to the fitness evaluation phase in GP, as well as comparing performance results across different types of processors. With this purpose, a novel and independent GP engine was developed: TensorGP. Other engines such as KarooGP [6] already take advantage of TensorFlow's capabilities to speed program execution. However, our engine exploits new TensorFlow execution models, which are shown to benefit the evolutionary process. Moreover, we intend on extending the application of TensorGP outside the realm of classical symbolic regression and classification problems by providing support for different types of functions, including image specific operators.

The remainder of this paper is organised as follows. Section 2 provides a compilation of related work. Section 3 presents the framework. Section 4 lays the experimental setup and analyzes benchmarking results. Finally, Sect. 5 draws final conclusions and points towards future work.

2   Related Work

Because GP individuals usually share highly fit code with the rest of the population and not only within themselves [7], techniques to efficiently save and reuse the evaluation of such code have been of special interest to research around GP. In specific, Handley [8] first implemented a method of fitness caching by saving the computed value by each subtree for each fitness case. Furthermore, Handley represented the population of parsed trees as a Directed Acyclic Graph (DAG) rather than a collection of separate trees, consequently saving memory by not duplicating structurally identical subtrees.

However, because system memory is finite, the caching of intermediate results must obey certain memory constraints. In this regard, Keijzer [9] proposed two cache update and flush methods to deal with fixed size subtree caching: a first method using a postfix traversal of the tree to scan for nodes to be added to or deleted from the cache and a second method that implemented a variant of the DAG approach. Even if we rule out the amount of memory used, hit-rates and search times are still a grave concern. Wong and Zhang [10] developed a caching mechanism based on hash tables to estimate algebraic equivalence between subtrees, which proved efficient in reducing the time taken to search for common code by reducing the number of node evaluations. Besides, caching methods are particularly useful in scenarios with larger evaluation domains and where code re-execution is more time-consuming. As an example, Machado and Cardoso [11] applied caching to the evolution of large-sized images (up to 512 by 512 pixels) in the NEvAr evolutionary art tool.

Another common way to accelerate GP is to take advantage of its potential for parallelization. Various works have explored the application of parallel hardware such as Central Processing Units (CPUs) with Single Instruction Multiple Data (SIMD) capabilities [12–14], GPU-based architectures [15–18] and even Field Programmable Gate Arrays (FPGAs) [19] to fitness evaluation within the scope of GP. However, arguably the most promising speedups still come from GPUs as they are the most widely available throughput-oriented architectures. Namely, Cano et al. [15] verified speedups of up to 820 fold for certain classification problems versus a standard iterative approach by massively parallelizing the evaluation of individuals using the NVIDIA Compute Unified Device Architecture (CUDA) programming model.

One common way to abstract this parallelization process is to vectorize the set of operations performed over the fitness domain, effectively reducing the running time of a program to the number of nodes it contains [9]. Some interpreted languages such as Matlab, Python and Perl already support vectorized operations in an attempt to reduce computational efforts. In particular, TensorFlow [20] is a numerical computation library written in Python that provides an abstraction layer to the integration of this vectorization process across different hardware. Staats et al. [6] demonstrated the benefits of using TensorFlow to vectorized GP fitness data in both CPU and GPU architectures, achieving performance increases of up to 875 fold for certain classification problems. The engine that the authors developed, KarooGP, is still used to tackle many symbolic regression and classification problems [21–23]. However, KarooGP does not take advantage of recent additions to TensorFlow execution models.

3 TensorGP

TensorGP takes the classical approach of most other GP applications and expands on it by using TensorFlow to vectorize operations, consequently speeding up the domain evaluation process through the use of parallel hardware. Moreover, TensorFlow allows for the caching of intermediate fitness results, which accelerates the evolutionary process by avoiding the re-execution of highly fit code. TensorGP is implemented in Python 3.7 using the TensorFlow 2.1 framework and is publicly available on GitHub [1].

In this section, we describe the implementation details of the incorporated GP features, as well as the efforts of integrating some of these features with the TensorFlow platform.

3.1 Genotype to Phenotype

As the name implies, TensorGP works with tensors. In essence, a tensor is a generalization of scalars (that have no indices), vectors (that have exactly one index), and matrices (that have exactly two indices) to an arbitrary number

---

[1] TensorGP repository available at https://github.com/AwardOfSky/TensorGP.

of indices [24]. We start by describing the process of executing an individual in TensorGP. Figure 1 demonstrates our engine's translation pipeline from genotype to phenotype.

In its simplest form, each individual in GP can be represented as a mathematical expression. TensorGP follows a tree-based approach, internally representing individuals as a tree graph. This implies a first translation phase from string to tree representation, which is only performed at the beginning of the evolutionary process in case the initial population is not randomly generated.

TensorFlow can either execute in an eager or graph-oriented mode. When it comes to graph execution, TensorFlow internally converts the tree structure into a graph before actually calculating any values. This is done in order to cache potential intermediate results from subtrees, effectively generalizing our tree graph structure to a DAG. On the other hand, the eager execution model allows for the immediate execution of vectorized operations, eliminating the overhead of explicitly generating the intermediate DAG of operations.

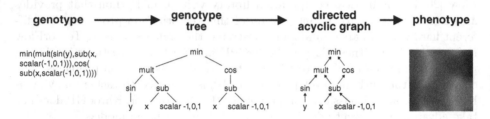

Fig. 1. Genotype to phenotype translation phases in TensorGP.

Even though graph-oriented execution enables many memory and speed optimizations, there are heavy performance costs associated with graph building. TensorFlow eager execution mode aims to eliminate such overheads without sacrificing the benefits furnished by graphs [25]. Because the individuals we are evolving are constantly changing from generation to generation, we would be inclined to think that eager mode would be a good fit for tensor execution. For this reason, in Sect. 4, we include some performance comparisons between both these TensorFlow execution modes.

Finally, the last translation phase goes through the entire genotype data to produce a phenotype, which will be the target of fitness assessment. Because the domain of fitness data points to be evaluated is fixed for all operations, the vectorization of this data is made trivial using a tensor representation. Generally speaking, our phenotype is a tensor, which can be visually represented as an image for a problem with 3 dimensions, as seen in the last stage of Fig. 1. In this example, the first two dimensions correspond to the width and height of the image, while the third dimension encodes information regarding the RGB color channels. The resulting tensor phenotype is obtained by chaining operators, variables and constants that make part of the individual. These variables and constants are also tensors, which occupy a range of $[-1, 1]$ for the example given. With the aid of TensorFlow primitives, we can apply an operation to all domain points at the same time while seamlessly distributing computational efforts amongst available hardware.

3.2 Primitive Set

To provide a general-purpose GP tool and ease evolution towards more complex solutions, the primitive set implemented goes beyond the scope of simple mathematical and logic operators. This way, we attempt to provide sufficiency through redundancy of operators for as many problems as possible. Some image specific operators are also included to facilitate the application of TensorGP to image evolution domains (such as evolutionary art). One of such operators, and perhaps the most intriguing, is the *warp*. The *warp* operator is commonly used to deform images and is defined as a transformation that maps every element of a tensor to a different coordinate. This mapping is done according to an array of tensors with a size equal to the number of dimensions of the problem. Each of these tensors dictate where elements will end up within a given dimension.

Operators must also be defined for all possible domain values, which in some cases means implementing protection mechanisms for certain cases. Table 1 enumerates the different types of operators and respective special cases. All operators are applied to tensors and integrated into TensorGP through composition of existing TensorFlow functions. While the main math and logic operators can be implemented with a simple call to the corresponding TensorFlow function, more complex operators may imply chaining multiple functions. For instance, while TensorFlow possesses a plethora of operators to cater to our vectorization needs, it lacks a *warp*-like operator. Therefore, to implement it, we need to express the whole transformation process as a composition of existing TensorFlow functions.

Besides the specified protective mechanism, there are noteworthy implementation details for some operators. As an example, when calculating trigonometric operators, the input argument is first multiplied by π. The reasoning behind this is that most problem domains are not defined in the $[-\pi, \pi]$ range, but are otherwise normalised to either $[0, 1]$ or $[-1, 1]$. As a matter of fact, $[-1, 1]$ this is the standard domain range used in TensorGP. This makes it so that the argument to the trigonometric operators is in the $[-\pi, \pi]$ range, which covers the whole output domain for these operators.

3.3 Features

TensorGP was implemented with ease of use in mind. To demonstrate some of its functionality, the following paragraphs describe the main features of the presented engine.

When a GP run is initiated on TensorGP, a folder is created in the local file system with the aim of logging evolution data. In each generation, the engine keeps track of depth and fitness values for all individuals. When the run is over,

Table 1. Description of implemented TensorGP operators.

Type	Subtype	Operator (engine abbreviation)	Arity	Functionality
Mathematical	Arithmetic	Addition (add)	2	$x + y$
		Subtraction (sub)	2	$x - y$
		Multiplication (mult)	2	$x \times y$
		Division (div)	2	x/y 0 if denominator is 0
	Trigonometric[a]	Sine (sin)	1	$\cos(x\pi)$
		Cosine (cos)	1	$\sin(x\pi)$
		Tangent (tan)	1	$\tan(x\pi)$
	Others	Exponentional (exp)	1	e^x
		Logarithm (log)	1	$\log x$ -1 if $x < 0$
		Exponentiation (pow)	2	x^y 0 if x and y equal 0
		Minimun (min)	2	$min(x, y)$
		Maximun (max)	2	$max(x, y)$
		Average (mdist)	2	$(x + y)/2$
		Negative (neg)	1	$-x$
		Square Root (sqrt)	2	$\sqrt{x}$ 0 if $x < 0$
		Sign (sign)	1	-1 if $x < 0$ 0 if x equals 0 1 if $x > 0$
		Absolute value (abs)	1	$-x$ if $x < 0$ x if $x \geq 0$
		Constrain (clip)[b]	3	ensure $y \leq x \leq z$ or $max(min(z, x), y)$
		Modulo (mod)	2	x mod y remainder of division
		Fractional part[b] (frac)	1	$x - \lfloor * \rfloor x$
Logic	Conditional	Condition (if)	3	if x then y else z
	Bitwise[c]	OR (or)	2	logic value of $x \vee y$ for all bits
		Exclusive OR (xor)	2	logic value of $x \oplus y$ for all bits
		AND (and)	2	logic value of $x \wedge y$ for all bits
Image	Transform	Warp (warp)	n	Transform data given tensor input[d]
	Step	Normal (step)	1	-1 if $x < 0$ 1 if $x >= 0$
		Smooth (sstep)	1	$x^2(3 - 2x)$
		Perlin Smooth (sstepp)	1	$x^3(x(6x - 15) + 10)$
	Color	Distance (len)	2	$\sqrt{x^2 + y^2}$
		Linear Interpolation (lerp)	3	$x + (y - x) \times frac(z)$

[a] Input argument in radians, [b] These are mostly support operators [c] Transformation to integer is needed, [d] More details in Subsect. 3.2

a visualzation for the depth and fitness values of individuals across generations is automatically generated along with a CSV file with experimental data.

Besides, TensorGP keeps an updated state with all the important parameters and evolution data. With each new generation, the engine updates this file with information regarding evolution status. When it is time to resume the experiment, the engine simply loads the corresponding configurations from the file of that experiment, gathering the latest generational data.

Although the default engine behavior is to generate the initial population according to a given (or otherwise random) seed, the user can choose to specify a custom initial population by passing a text file containing string-based programs to the engine.

Currently, there are two stop criteria implemented: the generation limit (which the engine defaults to) and acceptable error. In the acceptable error method, the experiment comes to an end if the best-fitted individual achieves a fitness value specified by the user. The conditional check for this value is made differently depending on whether we are dealing with a minimization or maximization problem, which leads to the next main feature.

It is possible to define custom operators for the engine. The only requirement for the implementation of any operator is that it must returns a tensor generated with TensorFlow and have $dims = []$ as one of the input arguments (in case the tensor dimensions are needed). Along with the implementation, the user is required to register the operator by adding an entry to the function set with the corresponding operator name and arity.

4   Benchmark Experimentation

In this section, we describe the experimentation performed with the objective of investigating how TensorGP fares against other common GP approaches. To attain this goal, execution times were extracted and compared for a symbolic regression task across different domain sizes. First, a tree evaluation experiment is implemented where we isolate the tensor evaluation phase and execute a batch of populations within a controlled environment. Next, we extend on this experiment by including the evolutionary process with the intent of testing a more typical GP scenario.

4.1   Experimental Setup

All experiments concern the symbolic regression problem of approximating the polynomial function defined by:

$$f(x,y) = \frac{1}{1+x^{-4}} + \frac{1}{1+y^{-4}} \tag{1}$$

This function is also known as Pagie Polynomial and is commonly used in GP benchmarks due to its reputation for being challenging [26]. Because the domain of this problem is two-dimensional, we represent it using a rank 2 tensor.

Table 2. Experimental GP parameters.

Parameter	Value
Runs	5
Maximum tree depth	12
Population size	50
Generation method	Ramped-Half-and-Half
Objective	Minimize RMSE from Pagie Polynomial
Test cases	6 (2^{2n}, for n in $[6, 11]$)

Table 2 enumerates the parameters used for both the tree evaluation and evolutionary experiments. Regarding problem size, all experiments encompass the same array of 6 test cases, evaluating a two-dimensional domain that exponentially increases in size. The first test case evaluates a 64 by 64 grid of data points, thus involving a total of 4,096 evaluations. In each subsequent test case, the length of the grid doubles, effectively quadrupling the number of points to evaluate. This grid of values, represented in TensorGP by a rank-2 tensor, keeps increasing until the length of each side of the tensor is 2,048 (over 4 million evaluation points).

Larger domains were not tested mainly due to VRAM limitations of the GPU used during the experiments. Moreover, the same set of populations were used for all test cases, where each population contains 50 individuals generated with the Ramped-Half-and-Half method and 12 for maximum allowed depth.

While the first experiment only saw the execution of the aforementioned population batch, in the evolutionary run we let the individuals evolve for 50 generations for all test cases. Both experiments use the minimization of the Root Mean Squared Error (RMSE) metric as a fitness evaluation function.

In total, six approaches were considered. Four of these approaches concern TensorGP implementations, testing both graph and eager execution modes when running in the GPU versus CPU. The other two approaches implement serial GP evaluation methods: one resorting to the DEAP framework and another one using a modified version of the engine that evaluates individuals with the *eval* Python function instead of TensorFlow.

DEAP is a commonly used EC framework written in Python and offers a powerful and simple interface for experimentation [27]. We have chosen to include comparisons to this framework because it represents the standard for iterative domain evaluation in research and literature around GP. Moreover, DEAP is easy to install and allows for the prototyping of controlled environments within a few lines of code.

Furthermore, we also include our own serial baseline. The purpose is to compare achievable timings for an iterative approach that does not use third-party software. We do this by passing the expression of an individual to the Python *eval* method so we can run it. In order to eliminate the overhead of parsing code, *eval* is called only once by plugging in a lambda defined expression of the individual. For future reference, this approach will be referred to as EVAL.

Table 3. Hardware and software specifications used for all experiments.

Component	Specification
CPU	Intel® Core™ i7-6700 (3.40 GHz)
GPU	NVIDIA GeForce GTX 1060 3 GB
RAM	2 × 8 GB @2,666 MHz
Operative system	Windows 10
Execution environment	Command prompt

The software and processing hardware used for the execution of these experiments is defined in Table 3.

Because the experimental results presented in the next subsection encompass a wide range of values covering multiple orders of magnitude, our best bet for graphical representation is to use a logarithmic scale as it would be otherwise impossible to distinguish between timings.

4.2   Results

The first experiment compares average execution times amongst all considered approaches. Figure 2 shows the average time taken for the evaluation of all 5 populations in all test cases. We can conclude that both EVAL and DEAP results are similar, following a linear increase in evaluation time with an increase in evaluation points.

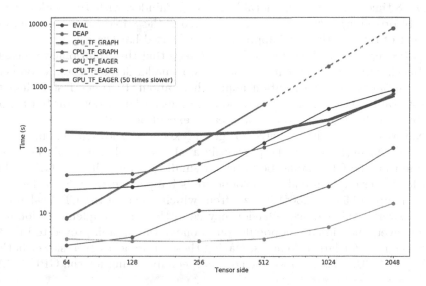

Fig. 2. Time (in seconds) comparison of different approaches for raw tree evaluation across domain sizes. (Color figure online)

Table 4. Standard deviation (STD) and average (AVG) of timing values (in seconds) across domain sizes for the tree evaluation experiment.

		EVAL	DEAP	TF graph (GPU)	TF graph (CPU)	TF eager (GPU)	TF eager (CPU)
64^2	**AVG**	8.35	8.05	23.14	39.81	3.82	3.04
4,096	**STD**	0.22	0.20	0.56	0.84	0.22	0.08
128^2	**AVG**	33.13	31.78	25.89	42.00	3.54	4.07
16,384	**STD**	0.82	0.89	0.50	1.07	0.13	0.11
256^2	**AVG**	132.28	126.93	32.97	60.22	3.53	10.90
65,536	**STD**	3.36	3.50	0.77	1.66	0.13	0.11
512^2	**AVG**	531.15	522.53	128.75	109.53	3.83	11.37
262,144	**STD**	12.76	13.97	2.79	2.92	0.19	0.92
$1,024^2$	**AVG**	DNF	DNF	446.90	252.23	5.92	26.23
1,048,576	**STD**	DNF	DNF	8.94	21.27	0.23	1.06
$2,048^2$	**AVG**	DNF	DNF	879.74	775.54	14.20	107.42
4,194,304	**STD**	DNF	DNF	31.78	58.38	0.37	4.74

DNF stands for "Did Not Finish".

Because there is no domain vectorization, the direct relation between elements and time taken comes as no surprise. It is worth noting that because of time constraints, results corresponding to the dashed lines in the two largest tensors sizes were not run but instead predicted by following the linear behavior from previous values.

Analysing results for TensorFlow eager execution mode, we see that even though the CPU is faster for the smallest test case, this trend fades rapidly for larger problems domains. In fact, for 16,384 elements (128^2), the GPU is already marginally faster than the CPU. This margin widens with an increase in tensor side, resulting in GPU evaluation over a 4 million point domain ($2,048^2$) being almost 8 times faster as seen in Table 4. As a reminder, with TensorFlow we are already providing operator vectorization, hence the 8 fold increase is merely a product of running the same approach on dedicated hardware.

Moreover, we can also confirm the hypothesis that the evolutionary process in GP benefits from eager execution. For the two smaller domain sizes, we observed that the slowest eager execution approach is about 10 times faster than the fastest graph execution one. This trend continues for larger domains but the gap shortens to about 8 times (in favor of eager execution).

Nevertheless, results gathered for graph execution show rather unexpected behavior. As suggested by the previously analyzed results, it would be safe to assume that the CPU would be faster for small domains with the GPU taking over for larger ones. In reality, the opposite is happening: the GPU is faster for domains up to 65,536 (256^2) in size, from which point on the CPU takes over. The answer to this strange behavior may lie in the graph implementation used. Fitting every individual of a population in one session graph proved to take too much memory for larger domains, making these approaches even slower both in GPU and CPU. This need for memory is specially taxing for the GPU VRAM (which is only 3 GB compared to the available 16GB for system memory) that did not even finish some test cases while trying to include the entire population in a single graph.

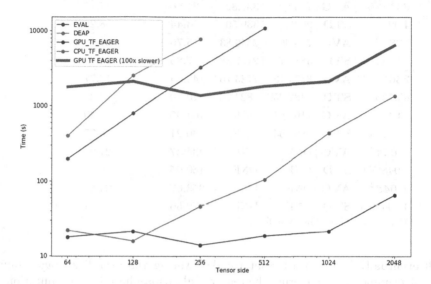

Fig. 3. Time (in seconds) comparison of different approaches for a full evolutionary run across domain sizes. (Color figure online)

For this reason, and to be consistent with all domain sizes, we decided to test these graph execution approaches by opening a session graph for each individual instead of evaluating the entire population in a single graph. Still, we can safely conclude that both graph execution approaches are slower than their eager equivalents. The red bold line, in Fig. 2, is intended as a visualization aid that represents a 50 times performance threshold over our fastest approach (TensorFlow eager on GPU) for approaches above the line.

For the evolutionary experiment, however, only four of the considered approaches were used: the iterative ones (DEAP and EVAL) and the ones that concern TensorFlow execution in eager mode (both in CPU and GPU). Graph execution was omitted as it was demonstrated to be systematically slower than their eager equivalents.

Figure 3 shows the total run time for all considered approaches. Probably the most noticeable aspect of these results is that they appear to be less linear when compared to those regarding raw tree evaluation. This happens because, even though we are using a fix population batch for each test case, evolution might be guided towards different depths for different initial populations. If the best-fitted individual happens to have a lower depth value, the rest of the population

Table 5. Standard deviation (STD) and average (AVG) timing values (in seconds) across domain sizes for the evolutionary experiment.

		EVAL	DEAP	TF eager (CPU)	TF eager (GPU)
64^2	**AVG**	196.87	397.82	21.86	17.77
4,096	**STD**	96.26	339.50	13.44	8.29
128^2	**AVG**	795.36	2546.83	15.76	21.19
16,384	**STD**	381.71	2127.38	7.85	11.99
256^2	**AVG**	3274.13	7783.76	45.64	13.77
65,536	**STD**	2482.256	5824.78	20.79	7.39
512^2	**AVG**	11052.16	DNF	104.96	18.49
262,144	**STD**	3887.54	DNF	30.21	8.75
$1,024^2$	**AVG**	DNF	DNF	434.37	21.21
1,048,576	**STD**	DNF	DNF	160.05	9.98
$2,048^2$	**AVG**	DNF	DNF	1353.67	64.54
4,194,304	**STD**	DNF	DNF	679.56	32.51

DNF stands for "Did Not Finish".

will eventually lean towards that trend, lowering the overall average population depth and thus rendering the tensor evaluation phase less computationally expensive. The opposite happens if the best-fitted individual is deeper, resulting in more computing time. This explains the relatively higher standard deviations presented in Table 5 and the non-linear behavior across problem sizes (*e. g.* the test case for size 65,536 (256^2) runs faster than the two smaller domains for TensorFlow running on GPU).

Still regarding TensorFlow results, from the two first test cases, we can not identify a clear preference towards CPU or GPU as, for these domain sizes, the GPU memory transfer overhead is in par with the lack of CPU parallelization power. Nonetheless, for test cases larger than 65,536 (256^2), a clear preference towards GPU starts to be evident, with an average speedup of over 21 times for a problem with 4 over million points ($2,048^2$).

Perhaps the most unexpected results are the test cases for the DEAP framework, which are consistently slower than the EVAL baseline. In tree evaluation, we saw that domain calculation is slightly faster in DEAP than in our baseline. However, DEAP uses dynamic population sizes during evolution which might slow down the run. It is also worth mentioning that only the basic genetic operators and algorithms were used for DEAP. A more extensive experimentation with the evolutionary capabilities of this framework would most likely reveal a more optimal set of genetic operators and parameters that could prove faster than EVAL. Even so, that is not the aim of this work and so we shall compare TensorFlow timings against our baseline, which follows the same iterative principle.

In turn, EVAL proves to be slower than any of the TensorFlow approaches for all considered test cases, with an average verified speedup of almost 600 times over GPU_TF_EAGER for the 512^2 test case (262,144 points).

We can take the red line in Fig. 3 line as a visualization aid for approaches two orders of magnitude slower. For both iterative approaches, tests cases corresponding to higher problem sizes were not completed as they proved to be too time-consuming. Besides, based on previous results, performance margins would only maintain an increasing tendency.

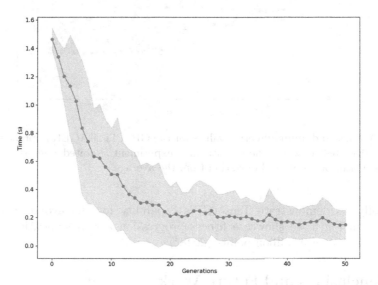

Fig. 4. Average evaluation time (in seconds) cross generations for the 64 tensor side test case (4,096 points) with the GPU_TF_EAGER approach regarding the evolutionary experiment. Painted regions above and below represent one standard deviation from the average.

The results shown for the GPU in TensorFlow are fast, maybe even too fast. Indeed, with the evolutionary process thrown in the mix, it would be safe to assume that the speed up between iterative and vectorized approaches would shorten, even if marginally, as the genetic operators are run exclusively on CPU. However, This seems to not be the case.

In fact, speedups are higher when compared to tree evaluation experiments. Previous results with 512 tensor side (262,144) for TensorFlow GPU against EVAL regarding raw tree evaluation shows a speedup of almost 140 times, which is a far cry from the aforementioned nearly 600 times confirmed with evolution. This can be explained by the caching of intermediate results that TensorFlow performs, leading to a pronounced decrease in evaluation time after the first few initial generations, as observed in Fig. 4. These results further make the case for expression evolution with TensorFlow in eager mode.

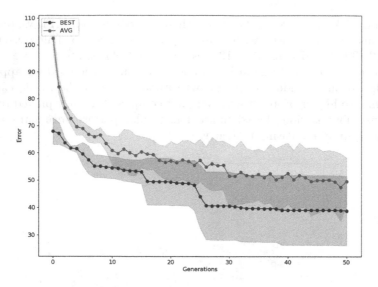

Fig. 5. Average and minimum error values for the GPU_TF_EAGER approach regarding the 2048^2 test case for the evolutionary experiment. Painted regions above and below represent one standard deviation from the average.

Finally, to demonstrate TensorGP's capability for the evolution of large domains, in Fig. 5 we showcase fitness progression across generations for the test case with over 4 million points (2048^2).

5   Conclusions and Future Work

In this work, we propose different approaches to ease the computational burden of GP by taking advantage of its high potential for parallelism. Namely, we investigate the advantages of applying data vectorization to the fitness evaluation phase using throughput-oriented architectures such as the GPU. To accomplish this, we employed the TensorFlow numerical computation library written in Python, to develop a general-purpose GP engine capable of catering to our vectorization needs – TensorGP.

Experimental results with our engine show that performance gains of up to 600 fold are attainable for the approximation of large evaluation domains in regards to the Pagie Polynomial function. Furthermore, we demonstrate the benefits of TensorFlow's eager execution model over graph execution for the caching of fitness results throughout generations. Nevertheless, our test results for smaller domains seem to still make the case for more latency-oriented programming models such as the CPU. Therefore, modern-day GP seems to be best suited for heterogeneous computing frameworks like TensorFlow that are device-independent.

Upon completion of this work, some possibilities are to be considered for future endeavours. We believe that the implementation of a preprocessing phase to simplify the mathematical expressions of individuals could greatly improve TensorGP's performance. Additionally, we consider the elimination of overhead incurred by operator composition and protection mechanisms through the integration of device specific code with TensorFlow. Moreover, with the incorporation of image specific operators in our engine, the exploration of evolutionary art is an appealing work path. Finally, the time comparison study amongst different approaches could be extended by including different GP frameworks, possibly under less strict evolutionary setups.

Acknowledgements. This work is funded by national funds through the FCT - Foundation for Science and Technology, I.P., within the scope of the project CISUC - UID/CEC/00326/2020 and by European Social Fund, through the Regional Operational Program Centro 2020 and by the project grant DSAIPA/DS/0022/2018 (GADgET). We also thank the NVIDIA Corporation for the hardware granted to this research.

References

1. Giacobini, M., Tomassini, M., Vanneschi, L.: Limiting the number of fitness cases in genetic programming using statistics. In: Guervós, J.J.M., Adamidis, P., Beyer, H.-G., Schwefel, H.-P., Fernández-Villacañas, J.-L. (eds.) PPSN 2002. LNCS, vol. 2439, pp. 371–380. Springer, Heidelberg (2002). https://doi.org/10.1007/3-540-45712-7_36
2. Poli, R., Langdon, W.B., McPhee, N.F., Koza, J.R.: A field guide to genetic programming. Lulu. com (2008)
3. Andre, D., Koza, J.R.: Parallel genetic programming: a scalable implementation using the transputer network architecture. In: Advances in Genetic Programming, pp. 317–337. MIT Press (1996)
4. Moore, G.E., et al.: Cramming more components onto integrated circuits (1965)
5. Arenas, M., Romero, G., Mora, A., Castillo, P., Merelo, J.: GPU parallel computation in bioinspired algorithms: a review. In: Kołodziej, J., Khan, S., Burczyński, T. (eds.) Advances in Intelligent Modelling and Simulation. SCI, vol. 422, pp. 113–134. Springer, Heidelberg (2012). https://doi.org/10.1007/978-3-642-30154-4_6
6. Staats, K., Pantridge, E., Cavaglia, M., Milovanov, I., Aniyan, A.: TensorFlow enabled genetic programming. In: Proceedings of the Genetic and Evolutionary Computation Conference Companion, pp. 1872–1879. ACM (2017)
7. Keijzer, M.: Efficiently representing populations in genetic programming. In: Advances in Genetic Programming, pp. 259–278. MIT Press (1996)
8. Handley, S.: On the use of a directed acyclic graph to represent a population of computer programs. In: Proceedings of the First IEEE Conference on Evolutionary Computation. IEEE World Congress on Computational Intelligence, pp. 154–159. IEEE (1994)
9. Keijzer, M.: Alternatives in subtree caching for genetic programming. In: Keijzer, M., O'Reilly, U.-M., Lucas, S., Costa, E., Soule, T. (eds.) EuroGP 2004. LNCS, vol. 3003, pp. 328–337. Springer, Heidelberg (2004). https://doi.org/10.1007/978-3-540-24650-3_31
10. Wong, P., Zhang, M.: Scheme: caching subtrees in genetic programming. In: 2008 IEEE Congress on Evolutionary Computation (IEEE World Congress on Computational Intelligence), pp. 2678–2685. IEEE (2008)

11. Machado, P., Cardoso, A.: Speeding up genetic programming. In: Proceedings of the 2nd International Symposium AI and Adaptive Systems, CIMAF, vol. 99, pp. 217–222 (1999)
12. Chitty, D.M.: Fast parallel genetic programming: multi-core CPU versus many-core GPU. Soft. Comput. **16**(10), 1795–1814 (2012)
13. Burlacu, B., Kronberger, G., Kommenda, M.: Operon C++ an efficient genetic programming framework for symbolic regression. In: Proceedings of the 2020 Genetic and Evolutionary Computation Conference Companion, pp. 1562–1570 (2020)
14. de Melo, V.V., Fazenda, Á.L., Sotto, L.F.D.P., Iacca, G.: A MIMD interpreter for genetic programming. In: Castillo, P.A., Jiménez Laredo, J.L., Fernández de Vega, F. (eds.) EvoApplications 2020. LNCS, vol. 12104, pp. 645–658. Springer, Cham (2020). https://doi.org/10.1007/978-3-030-43722-0_41
15. Cano, A., Zafra, A., Ventura, S.: Speeding up the evaluation phase of GP classification algorithms on GPUs. Soft. Comput. **16**(2), 187–202 (2012)
16. Chitty, D.M.: A data parallel approach to genetic programming using programmable graphics hardware. In: Proceedings of the 9th Annual Conference on Genetic and Evolutionary Computation, pp. 1566–1573. ACM (2007)
17. Cano, A., Ventura, S.: GPU-parallel subtree interpreter for genetic programming. In: Proceedings of the 2014 Annual Conference on Genetic and Evolutionary Computation, pp. 887–894. ACM (2014)
18. Augusto, D.A., Barbosa, H.J.: Accelerated parallel genetic programming tree evaluation with OpenCL. J. Parallel Distrib. Comput. **73**(1), 86–100 (2013)
19. Koza, J.R., Bennett, F., Hutchings, J.L., Bade, S.L., Keane, M.A., Andre, D.: Evolving sorting networks using genetic programming and the rapidly reconfigurable Xilinx 6216 field-programmable gate array. In: Conference Record of the Thirty-First Asilomar Conference on Signals, Systems and Computers (Cat. No. 97CB36136), vol. 1, pp. 404–410. IEEE (1997)
20. Abadi, M., et al.: TensorFlow: a system for large-scale machine learning. In: 12th USENIX Symposium on Operating Systems Design and Implementation (OSDI 2016), pp. 265–283 (2016)
21. Cavaglia, M., Staats, K., Gill, T.: Finding the origin of noise transients in LIGO data with machine learning. arXiv preprint arXiv:1812.05225 (2018)
22. Fu, X., Ren, X., Mengshoel, O.J., Wu, X.: Stochastic optimization for market return prediction using financial knowledge graph. In: 2018 IEEE International Conference on Big Knowledge (ICBK), pp. 25–32. IEEE (2018)
23. Matousek, R., Hulka, T., Dobrovsky, L., Kudela, J.: Sum epsilon-tube error fitness function design for GP symbolic regression: preliminary study. In: 2019 International Conference on Control, Artificial Intelligence, Robotics & Optimization (ICCAIRO), pp. 78–83. IEEE (2019)
24. Rowland, T., Weisstein, E.W.: Tensor. From MathWorld–A Wolfram Web Resource. http://mathworld.wolfram.com/Tensor.html
25. Agrawal, A., et al.: TensorFlow Eager: a multi-stage, Python-embedded DSL for machine learning. arXiv preprint arXiv:1903.01855 (2019)
26. Pagie, L., Hogeweg, P.: Evolutionary consequences of coevolving targets. Evol. Comput. **5**(4), 401–418 (1997)
27. Fortin, F.A., De Rainville, F.M., Gardner, M.A.G., Parizeau, M., Gagné, C.: DEAP: evolutionary algorithms made easy. J. Mach. Learn. Res. **13**(1), 2171–2175 (2012)

Applications of Nature-Inspired Computing for Sustainability and Development

A Novel Evolutionary Approach for IoT-Based Water Contaminant Detection

Claudio De Stefano, Luigi Ferrigno, Francesco Fontanella$^{(\boxtimes)}$, Luca Gerevini,
and Mario Molinara

Department of Electrical and Information Engineering (DIEI),
University of Cassino and Southern Lazio, Cassino, FR, Italy
{destefano,ferrigno,fontanella,m.molinara,luca.gerevini}@unicas.it

Abstract. Nowadays, the problem of pollution in water is a very serious issue to be faced and it is really important to be able to monitoring it with non-invasive and low-cost solutions, like those offered by smart sensor technologies. In this paper, we propose an improvement of an our innovative classification system, based on geometrical cones, to detect and classify pollutants, belonging to a given set of substances, spilled into waste water. The solution is based on an ad-hoc classifier that can be implemented aboard the Smart Cable Water (SCW) sensor, based on SENSIPLUS technology developed by Sensichips s.r.l. The SCW is a smart-sensor endowed with six interdigitated electrodes, covered by specific sensing materials that allow detecting between different water contaminants. In order to develop an algorithm suitable to apply the "edge computing" paradigm we first compress the input data from a 10-dimensional space to a 3-D space by using the PCA decomposition techniques. Then we use an ad-hoc classifier to classify between the different contaminants in the transformed space. To learn the classifier's parameters we used the evolutionary algorithms. The obtained results have been compared with the old classification system and other, more classical, machine learning approaches.

Keywords: IoT · Evolutionary algorithms · Water contaminant detection · Smart sensors

1 Introduction

Nowadays, about 23% of diseases worldwide, are associated with the presence of pollutants in air and water. For this reason, many researchers working in the machine learning field are focusing their attention on the development of tools for automatic contaminant detection in water and air. In particular, water pollution is a worldwide concern, also regarding drinkable tap water [25]: World Health Organization has estimated that about two billion people worldwide is plagued by this problem. Drinking water quality is usually monitored in laboratory-based analyses, performed by expert professionals. Because of the time required, this approach does not allow the prevention of environmental disasters. Since in most

© Springer Nature Switzerland AG 2021
P. A. Castillo and J. L. Jiménez Laredo (Eds.): EvoApplications 2021, LNCS 12694, pp. 781–794, 2021.
https://doi.org/10.1007/978-3-030-72699-7_49

cases water is contaminated during dispatching, an effective and responsive water requires a large number of distributed measurement systems. Nowadays these systems are available and guarantee good a performance, in terms of accuracy and reliability. However, the usage of these systems on a large scale is limited by their high costs. In this context, low-cost microsensors for capillary monitoring would be very useful. They should combine low costs with a good measurement accuracy, as well as good reliability, even for low levels of pollution. These requirements could allow a large diffusion of water monitoring also in poor and developing countries. Furthermore, these systems would allow the development of systems endowed with sensing, elaboration and communication capabilities, according to the Internet of Things (IoT) and Edge Computing paradigms [1,24], to perform on-field early analysis and detection. These paradigms need Artificial Intelligence (AI) and Machine Learning (ML) techniques to analyze and exploit effectively the information contained in the huge volume of data generated [2,5,6].

In this context, in a previous paper [13], we presented a novel IoT-ready system for water pollutant detection and classification, based on the multi-sensor microcontroller SENSIPLUS®. In the proposed system, input data were projected into a 3-D space and then classified using simple geometrical models: cones centered at the origin of the transformed 3-D reference system. The classification adopted a one-versus-all strategy: given the cone Γ learned to detect the contaminant γ, the points internal to Γ are labeled as belonging to γ, whereas the external ones were labeled as belonging to one of the other contaminants to be detected. We chose that model because it could be implemented even with the very few computational resources present on the SENSIPLUS® microcontroller. To find the optimal values of the cone parameters we used an evolutionary algorithm, where a chromosome consisted of four real values representing the cone parameters to be optimized.

In this paper, we propose a further development of the approach just mentioned. In particular, we have changed the classification model: each contaminant is now represented by a straight line passing for the origin of the transformed 3-D reference system and each point is assigned to its nearest axis, according to the Euclidean distance. This approach implement a multiclass classifier in a straightforward manner, thus avoiding the problems of the one-versus-all strategy, e.g. labeling conflicts between cones or N distinct, and independent, training steps for the model parameters, where N is the number of classes (contaminants in our case). The proposed approach also allow us to simplify the classification model: in a 3-D space a straight line passing for the origin is represented by three parameters (four in the case of cones). Finally, we used the same evolutionary algorithm adopted in previous approach mentioned above.

The remainder of the paper is organized as follows: Sect. 2 discusses the related work; Sect. 3 presents the system architecture, while Sect. 4 details the evolutionary algorithm we used to learn the parameters of the classification model; Sect. 5 shows the experimental results. Some conclusions are eventually left to Sect. 6.

2   Related Work

Nowadays, many research activities have been addressing the problem of pollution monitoring by using the emerging sensing technologies, as well as the new possibilities of data analysis offered by Artificial Intelligence and Machine Learning [3,4,15,17]. Among the others, in [7] the authors used Artificial Neural Network and Principal Component Regression techniques to estimate nitrate concentration in groundwater, whereas a pattern recognition solution based on partial least square discriminant analysis (PLS-DA) was presented in [15]. More recently, also Deep Learning (DL) architectures have been used to detect and classify chemicals in seawater [7,14,15].

Principal Component Analysis (PCA) is a feature reduction technique that tries as much as possible to reduce the loose of the information contained in the original data. It is most often used as a preprocessing step for feature reduction before classification and never used to develop an ad-hoc classifier as is the case of our approach. Indeed, in [21] the authors used PCA to reduce the number of features to provide as an input to a neural network, trained to detect tumors in gene expression microarray data. In [19], instead, the authors found that PCA achieved allowed a Support Vector Machine (SVM) to achieve satisfactory results with less computational efforts in a fault classification problems in challenging industrial processes. Finally, similar approaches have also been used for face recognition [16] and intrusion detection problems [26].

EAs are proven effective search tools in solving many real-world problems, especially when characterized by large and on-linear search spaces [8–10,12]. They have been also used to optimize the performance of PCA by suitably selecting or modifying the principal components provided by standard algorithm. In particular, in [20], in a hyperspectral image classification problem, the authors used a GA to select the best feature subset to provide in input to PCA. In [27], instead, used a GA to find the optimal PCA components in an application where PET images were used to identify dementia syndromes. Finally, [22] used a PCA-based GA for human face recognition.

Therefore, EAs have been widely used to improve the results of the PCA procedure but, to the best of our knowledge, they have never been used to learn the parameters of a classification model in the feature space provided by the PCA as is the case of the approach presented here.

3   System Architecture

In our system, input sensors data are classified in two steps. Firstly, we use PCA to transform input data into 3-D points. The aim of this transformation is twofold: (i) simplify the original data by identifying a few uncorrelated features maximizing data variability; (ii) to set up a simple classification model that can be implemented with very few hardware resources. Secondly, transformed data are classified by simple geometrical models: straight lines passing for the origin of the transformed 3-D reference system. The PCA-based transformation and the classification model implemented are described in the following subsections.

3.1   Data Transformation

As mentioned in the Introduction, our main goal is to build an *ad-hoc* classification system that can be implemented aboard low-cost sensors. For this reason, it is necessary to try to simplify as much as possible the space dimensionality in order to reduce the overall system's computational complexity.

To this aim, we applied a PCA decomposition to the input data to project them from a ten-dimensional space to a 3-D space. This data transformation allowed us to design a simple and lightweight classification model that can be implemented with very few hardware resources. PCA decomposition has been performed via the eigen-decomposition of the covariance matrix [18].

3.2   The Classification Model

Once projected into the 3-D space, input data are passed to the multi-class classifier, modeling C classes (C is the number of contaminants to recognize). Each contaminant, except for Synthetic Waste Water (SWW) is represented by a line passing through the origin of the xyz reference system (see Fig. 1(a)). Each line r is defined by three parameters (l, m, n) as described below. A point in the 3-D transformed space is then labeled as belonging to the class associated to its nearest line. As concerns the classification of the SWW, as we chose to do in our old system, we have used a sphere (in other words a threshold on the distance from the origin). In particular, if a given point P falls inside the chosen sphere, then it is labeled as belonging to SWW (see Fig. 1). We chose this solution because the points of the SWW are concentrated all around the origin (see Fig. 1(b)) and thus using a line to classify it, as for the others contaminants, drastically reduce the overall performances.

We chose to change from our old classification model based on C geometrical cones Γ to the new one based on C lines r in order to further decrease the computational complexity of our system. Indeed in the new classification model we have to compute only $C \times 3$ multiplications and sums, while in the old one, in addition to these operations, if a point P falls within the volume of more than one cone (say n) we have to compute $n \times 3$ additional multiplications and sums. Furthermore, in the proposed classification model we cannot have "undefined" point (see below for a detailed explanations if this aspect).

As mentioned above, a point P in the 3-D space has been assigned according to a two-steps procedure: (i) distances between P and each of the C lines were computed; (ii) P is labeled with the label of the nearest line. To find the distance between a point P and a line r we start from the parametric equation in the 3-D space of the line:

$$r : \begin{cases} x_r = x_0 + lt \\ y_r = y_0 + mt \quad \text{with } t \in \mathbb{R} \implies v_r = (l, m, n) \\ z_r = z_0 + nt \end{cases} \tag{1}$$

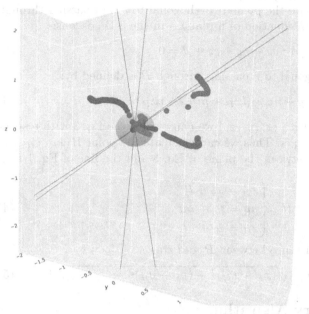

(a) Entire Model 3-D View.

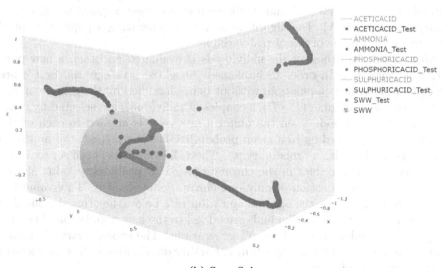

(b) Sww Sphere

Fig. 1. Line-based model 3D view.

where (x_0, y_0, z_0) are the Cartesian coordinates of a point of the line r (that in our case is the origin of the reference system), while (l, m, n) are the components with respect to the base $\{i, j, k\}$ of a parallel vector to r.

At this point we compute the plane α orthogonal to r and passing through P as follows. The Cartesian equation of a plane α in the 3-D space is:

$$\alpha : ax + by + cz + d = 0 \tag{2}$$

And thus the plane orthogonal to r passing through P is defined by:

$$lx + my + nz - (lx_P + my_P + nz_P) = 0 \tag{3}$$

Now substituting (x, y, z) with (x_r, y_r, z_r) we can resolve the Eq. 3 with respect to the parameter t of the Eq. 1. Thus we can calculate the point $H(x_H, y_H, z_H)$ given by the intersection between the plane of Eq. 3 and the line of Eq. 1 that results in:

$$H : \begin{cases} x_H = x_0 + lt \\ y_H = y_0 + mt \\ z_H = z_0 + nt \end{cases} \tag{4}$$

Finally we compute the distance between P and r as:

$$d(P, r) = d(P, H) = \sqrt{(x_P - x_H)^2 + (y_P - y_H)^2 + (z_P - z_H)^2} \tag{5}$$

4   The Evolutionary Algorithm

To find the optimal parameters for the C lines in the 3-D space representing the contaminants to be detected and distinguished, we used a generational evolutionary algorithm (EA). The algorithm starts by generating a population of P individuals, each made of $3 \times C$ real variables.

Afterwards, the fitness of the individuals is evaluated and then a new population is generated. In order to implement an elitist strategy, the best e are just copied in the new population, without being modified by the genetic operators[1]. Then the remaining $(P - D)/2$ couples of individuals are selected by using the tournament method. Then the uniform crossover is applied to each of the selected couples, according to a given probability factor p_c. Next, the mutation operator is applied with a probability p_m. The value of p_m has been set to $3 \times C$, i.e. the number of variables in the chromosome. This probability value allows, on average, the modification of only one chromosome element. This value has been suggested in [23] as the optimal mutation rate below the error threshold of replication. Finally, these individuals are added to the new population. The process just described is repeated for N_g generations. The evolutionary algorithm implemented is described in Algorithm 1. Further details about the evolutionary algorithm can be found in [11].

Given a training set $\mathcal{T}$, the fitness of an individual I was computed as detailed in Algorithm 2.

---

[1] Note that this strategy ensures that the best individuals found along the evolutionary process are not lost.

Algorithm 1: Evolutionary algorithm

---

input: list of parameters (Table 1), a data set $\mathcal{T}$
output: best individual found

begin
    randomly *initialize* a population of $\mathcal{P}$ individuals;
    evaluate the fitness of each individual;

    $g = 0$;
    while $g < N_g$ **do**
        copy the best e individuals in the new population;
        for $i = 0$ to $\mathcal{P}/2 - e$ **do**
            select a couple of individuals;
            replicate the selected individuals;
            if flip(p_c) **then**
                apply the crossover operator on the selected individuals;
            if flip(p_m) **then**
                perform the mutation on the offspring;
        evaluate the fitness of each individual;
        replace the old population with the new one;
        update the best individual found so far;
        $g = g + 1$;

    return the best individual found;
end

The function flip(p) returns the value 1 with a probability p and the value 0 with a probability $(1 - p)$.

---

5   Experimental Results

To test the effectiveness of our system we took into account four contaminants (acetic acid, phosphoric acid, sulphuric acid, ammonia) as well as SWW. The dataset contained ten data acquisitions per contaminant, each consisting of 1,600 samples. From each acquisition we removed the first 600 samples: the first half to allow sensors to stabilize, the remaining half to build the baseline. Finally, the last 1,000 samples have been used to build up our dataset. So, for each contaminant we got 10,000 samples. To evaluate the classification performance of our system we used the ten-fold cross-validation strategy.

Since the nature of the physical quantities measured by the aboard sensors of our system is different, they have different value ranges. For this reason we performed a data normalization with respect to the baseline.

In particular, the 1,000 samples of each acquisition used to build our dataset have been divided by the respective baseline, computed on the first 600 samples as follows:

$$n = \frac{x_i}{b_i} - 1.0 \qquad \forall \quad i \in [1, 2, ..., 10] \tag{6}$$

Algorithm 2: Fitness function

---

input: A dataset T consisting of N_T points in the 3-D space, an individual I representing C lines
output: Accuracy achieved by I on T

begin
   $N_c = 0$;
   for $i = 1$ to N_T **do**
      compute the distance between $P_i \in T$ and each of the lines of I
      assign P_i to the nearest line r_n
      if $label(P_i) == label(r_n)$ **then**
         $N_c = N_c + 1$;

   return N_c/N_T ;
end

---

where x_i represents the set of last 1,000 samples of the i-th acquisition, b_i is the baseline of that given acquisition, and n is the output set, consisting of the normalized samples. Furthermore, to centering our data in the origin, we subtract 1.0 to the obtained value. This operation was performed over all the acquisitions used to build our dataset.

We split the dataset built as just mentioned into two sets: a training set containing the 90% of the samples of all substances except the SWW, and a test set consisting of the remaining samples as well as the SWW samples. Summarizing, the training set consists of 36,000 samples (9,000 for each substance), whereas the test set contains 5,000 samples (1,000 per contaminant plus the 1,000 SWW samples). We chose to add only 1,000 samples (one acquisition) at time of SWW, in the test set, in order to maintain the data balanced.

The training set was used to compute the individuals' fitness of the EA outlined in Sect. 4. For each fold, we performed twenty runs and at the end of each run, the twelve real values (three parameters per contaminant, see Eq. 3) encoded by the individual with the best fitness were stored as the solution provided by that run. To set the parameters of the EA, we performed some preliminary trials. These parameters were used for all the experiments described below and are shown in Table 1.

To evaluate the effectiveness of the proposed approach, we performed two sets of experiments. In the first we compared the results of our system with those achieved by the previously presented system, whereas in the second the results achieved were compared with those of four well-known and widely-used classification algorithms. Figure 2 shows the confusion matrix obtained on the test data by our system (line-based, LB in the following) and the previous one (cone-based, CB in the following). From the figure we can see that the proposed LB system outperforms the CB system for the acetic acid.

Table 1. Evolutionary algorithm parameters.

Parameter	Symbol	Value
Population size	P	100
Number of generations	N_g	500
Elitism	e	2
Tournament size	t	5
Crossover probability	p_c	0.6
Mutation probability	p_m	0.08
Mutation range	m_r	0.1

Table 2. Percentages of contaminants.

Contaminant	w.r.t undef	w.r.t. contam
Acetic Acid	44.5	89.0
Ammonia	15.5	31.0
Phosphoric Acid	34.5	71.0
Sulphuric Acid	5.5	11.0
Sww	0.0	0.0

It is worth noting that in the CB system an unseen point was labeled as belonging to the class of the contaminant γ if it fell within the related cone Γ. In the case a point didn't fall inside any of the learned cones, it was labeled as "undefined", i.e. the system wasn't able to identifying the contaminant polluting the water, but only to warn that water is polluted. Therefore, the confusion matrix for the CB system was computed excluding the undefined points. Table 2 shows the data related to these points: how they are shared among the contaminants as well as SWW (second column); for each contaminant the percentage of samples labeled as undefined (third column). From the table we can observe that most of the acetic acid samples were labeled as undefined by the CB system, whereas in the LB system these samples have been labeled with an accuracy of 99%. The second most undefined contaminant is the phosphoric acid (71%). Also in this case the new LB system achieved an accuracy of 97%. Finally, also 31% of ammonia samples were left undefined by the CB system, whereas the LB system achieved an accuracy of 99%.

Summarizing, the proposed system has been able to correctly identify most of the contaminants polluting the water, whereas the CB system, although has achieved similar classification performance on the labeled system (except for the acetic acid), has produced a significant number of undefined samples.

To further test the effectiveness of our approach, we compared its results with those achieved by four well-known and widely-used classification algorithms, namely Decision Tree (DT), Neural Networks (NN), Support Vector Machines, and Convolutional Neural Network (CNN). The values of the parameters used in

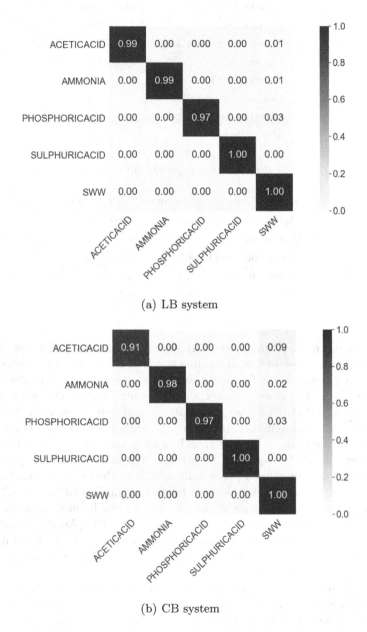

(a) LB system

(b) CB system

Fig. 2. Confusion matrices. The element M(i,j) represents the fraction of samples belonging to the i-th class assigned to the j-th class.

Table 3. Values of the classifier parameters used in the experiments. Note that as for the number of hidden neurons of the NN we applied, it derives from the following formula: (#features + #classes)/2.

Classifier	Parameter	Value
DT	Confidence factor	0.25
	Minimum #instances per leaf	2
NN	Learning rate	0.3
	Momentum	0.2
	Hidden Neurons	6
	Epochs	500
SVM	Kernel	RBF
	C	1.0
	γ	0.5

the experiments are shown in Table 3, except for the CNN. For the latter classifier we used a single convolutional layer with 64 unidimensional 3 × 1 kernels. We added two fully connected layers, after a batch normalization layer, with 256 hidden neurons intervaled with a dropout fixed to 0.5. As activation function for the fully connected layers we chose respectively, relu and softmax functions. For the sake of a fair comparison we used the ten-fold cross-validation strategy to evaluate the classification performance of these classifiers.

Comparison results are shown in Table 4, and include those achieved by the CB system. From the table it can be observed that the proposed line-based approach outperforms the four state-of-art classifiers used fro the comparison, as well as the previous presented cone-based system, confirming its effectiveness.

Table 4. Comparison results.

Classifier	Accuracy
DT	82.75
NN	84.88
SVM	89.56
CNN	83.59
CB system	*96.50*
LB system	**99.06**

6   Conclusions and Future Work

Pollution of drinkable water is a worldwide concern, with two billion people currently plagued by this problem. Therefore, it is crucial to find reliable and low-cost technologies for a continuous and diffused monitoring of water.

In a previous paper we presented an IoT-ready system for water pollutant detection and classification, based on the multi-sensor microcontroller SENSIPLUS®. That system used a simple geometrical model in a 3-D space that could be implemented with very few computational resources. In this paper, we presented a further development of that approach. This development allowed us to further simplify the classification model, in such a way to make the evolutionary computation based training process more effective, as well as reducing the amount of computational resources needed to implement the system.

The experiments were performed on a large dataset containing data from four contaminants. The obtained results proved that the new approach outperforms the old one, as well as some state-of-the-art classification algorithms.

Future work will focus on two aspects. Firstly, different techniques for the input data transformation step, e.g. Linear discriminant Analysis (LDA). Secondly, we will use a variable-length chromosome. This should allow us to individuate sub-clusters of points belonging to the same contaminant.

Acknowledgments. The research leading to these results has received funding from the European Union's Horizon 2020 research and innovation programme under grant agreement SYSTEM No. 787128. The authors are solely responsible for it and that it does not represent the opinion of the Community and that the Community is not responsible for any use that might be made of information contained therein.

The authors gratefully acknowledge Sensichips s.r.l. for the support during the experimental phases.

This work was also supported by MIUR (Minister for Education, University and Research, Law 232/216, Department of Excellence).

References

1. Atzori, L., Iera, A., Morabito, G.: The internet of things: a survey. Comput. Netw. **54**(15), 2787–2805 (2010)
2. Bernieri, A., Ferrigno, L., Laracca, M., Molinara, M.: An SVM approach to crack shape reconstruction in eddy current testing. In: 2006 IEEE Instrumentation and Measurement Technology Conference Proceedings, pp. 2121–2126 (2006)
3. Betta, G., Cerro, G., Ferdinandi, M., Ferrigno, L., Molinara, M.: Contaminants detection and classification through a customized IoT-based platform: a case study. IEEE Instrum. Measur. Mag. **22**(6), 35–44 (2019)
4. Bruschi, P., et al.: A novel integrated smart system for indoor air monitoring and gas recognition. In: 2018 IEEE International Conference on Smart Computing (SMARTCOMP), pp. 470–475, June 2018
5. Cerro, G., Ferdinandi, M., Ferrigno, L., Laracca, M., Molinara, M.: Metrological characterization of a novel microsensor platform for activated carbon filters monitoring. IEEE Trans. Instrum. Meas. **67**(10), 2504–2515 (2018)

6. Cerro, G., Ferdinandi, M., Ferrigno, L., Molinara, M.: Preliminary realization of a monitoring system of activated carbon filter RLI based on the sensiplus® microsensor platform. In: 2017 IEEE International Workshop on Measurement and Networking (M N), pp. 1–5 (Sep 2017)
7. Charulatha, G., Srinivasalu, S., Uma Maheswari, O., Venugopal, T., Giridharan, L.: Evaluation of ground water quality contaminants using linear regression and artificial neural network models. Arab. J. Geosci. 10(6), 1–9 (2017). https://doi.org/10.1007/s12517-017-2867-6
8. Cilia, N.D., De Stefano, C., Fontanella, F.: Novel mutation operators of a variable-length representation for EC-based feature selection in high-dimensional data. In: Huang, D.-S., Bevilacqua, V., Hussain, A. (eds.) ICIC 2020. LNCS, vol. 12463, pp. 53–63. Springer, Cham (2020). https://doi.org/10.1007/978-3-030-60799-9_5
9. Cilia, N.D., De Stefano, C., Fontanella, F., Scotto di Freca, A.: Variable-length representation for EC-based feature selection in high-dimensional data. In: Kaufmann, P., Castillo, P.A. (eds.) EvoApplications 2019. LNCS, vol. 11454, pp. 325–340. Springer, Cham (2019). https://doi.org/10.1007/978-3-030-16692-2_22
10. Cilia, N., De Stefano, C., Fontanella, F., Raimondo, S., Scotto di Freca, A.: An experimental comparison of feature-selection and classification methods for microarray datasets. Information (Switzerland) 10(3) (2019)
11. Cordella, L.P., De stefano, C., Fontanella, F.: Evolutionary prototyping for handwriting recognition. Int. J. Pattern Recogn. Artif. Intellig. 21(01), 157–178 (2007)
12. De Stefano, C., Fontanella, F., Folino, G., di Freca, A.S.: A bayesian approach for combining ensembles of GP classifiers. In: Sansone, C., Kittler, J., Roli, F. (eds.) MCS 2011. LNCS, vol. 6713, pp. 26–35. Springer, Heidelberg (2011). https://doi.org/10.1007/978-3-642-21557-5_5
13. De Stefano, C., Ferrigno, L., Fontanella, F., Gerevini, L., Scotto di Freca, A.: A novel PCA-based approach for building on-board sensor classifiers for water contaminant detection. Pattern Recogn. Lett. 135, 375–381 (2020). https://doi.org/10.1016/j.patrec.2020.05.015
14. Dean, S.N., Shriver-Lake, L.C., Stenger, D.A., Erickson, J.S., Golden, J.P., Trammell, S.A.: Machine learning techniques for chemical identification using cyclic square wave voltammetry. Sensors 19(10) (2019)
15. Desmet, C., Degiuli, A., Ferrari, C., Romolo, F.S., Blum, L., Marquette, C.: Electrochemical sensor for explosives precursors' detection in water. Challenges 8(1), 10 (2017)
16. Faruqe, M.O., Hasan, M.A.M.: Face recognition using PCA and SVM. In: 2009 3rd International Conference on Anti-counterfeiting, Security, and Identification in Communication, pp. 97–101, August 2009
17. Ferdinandi, M., et al.: A novel smart system for contaminants detection and recognition in water. In: 2019 IEEE International Conference on Smart Computing (SMARTCOMP), pp. 186–191, June 2019
18. Halko, N., Martinsson, P.G., Tropp, J.A.: Finding structure with randomness: probabilistic algorithms for constructing approximate matrix decompositions. SIAM Rev. 53(2), 217–288 (2011)
19. Jing, C., Hou, J.: SVM and PCA based fault classification approaches for complicated industrial process. Neurocomputing 167, 636–642 (2015)
20. Liu, Y., Gu, Y., Ye, Z.: Hyperspectral feature extraction using selective PCA based on genetic algorithm with subgroups. In: 1st International Conference on Innovative Computing, Information and Control - Volume I (ICICIC'06), vol. 3, pp. 652–656, August 2006

21. Lotfi, E., Keshavarz, A.: Gene expression microarray classification using PCA-BEL. Comput. Biol. Med. **54**, 180–187 (2014)
22. Mahmud, F., Haque, M.E., Zuhori, S.T., Pal, B.: Human face recognition using PCA based genetic algorithm. In: 2014 International Conference on Electrical Engineering and Information Communication Technology, pp. 1–5, April 2014
23. Ochoa, G.: Error thresholds in genetic algorithms. Evol. Comput. **14**(2), 157–182 (2006)
24. Shi, W., Dustdar, S.: The promise of edge computing. Computer **49**(5), 78–81 (2016)
25. Whelton, A.J., et al.: Residential tap water contamination following the freedom industries chemical spill: Perceptions, water quality, and health impacts. Environ. Sci. Technol. **49**(2), 813–823 (2015)
26. Xu, X., Wang, X.: An adaptive network intrusion detection method based on PCA and support vector machines. In: Li, X., Wang, S., Dong, Z.Y. (eds.) ADMA 2005. LNCS (LNAI), vol. 3584, pp. 696–703. Springer, Heidelberg (2005). https://doi.org/10.1007/11527503_82
27. Yong Xia, Wen, L., Eberl, S., Fulham, M., Feng, D.: Genetic algorithm-based PCA eigenvector selection and weighting for automated identification of dementia using FDG-pet imaging. In: 2008 30th Annual International Conference of the IEEE Engineering in Medicine and Biology Society, pp. 4812–4815, August 2008

Evolutionary Algorithms for Roughness Coefficient Estimation in River Flow Analyses

Antonio Agresta[1] , Marco Baioletti[2] , Chiara Biscarini[1] ,
Alfredo Milani[2] , and Valentino Santucci[1](✉)

[1] University for Foreigners of Perugia, Perugia, Italy
{antonio.agresta,chiara.biscarini,valentino.santucci}@unistrapg.it
[2] Department of Mathematics and Computer Science,
University of Perugia, Perugia, Italy
{marco.baioletti,alfredo.milani}@unipg.it

Abstract. Management and analyses of water resources is of paramount importance in the implementation of water related sustainable development goals. Hydraulic models are key in flood forecasting and simulation applied to a river flood analysis and risk prediction and an accurate estimation of the roughness is one of the main factors in predicting the discharge in a stream. In practical implementation roughness can be represented by the prediction of the well known Manning's coefficient necessary for discharge calculation. In this paper we design an objective function that measures the quality of a given configuration of the Manning's coefficient. Such an objective function is optimised through several evolutionary approaches, namely: (1+1)-ES, CMA-ES, Differential Evolution, Particle Swarm Optimization and Bayesian Optimization. As case of study, a river in the central Italy was considered. The results indicate that the model, consistent with the classical techniques adopted in the hydraulic engineering field, is applicable to natural rivers and is able to provide an estimation of the roughness coefficients with a satisfactory accuracy. A comparison of the performances of the five evolutionary algorithms is also proposed.

Keywords: Evolutionary algorithms · River flow analysis · Estimating Manning's coefficient

1 Introduction

Hydraulic sciences plays a relevant role in supporting the implementation of the sustainable development goals launched by United Nation Organisation, since they are crucial in assessing the impacts of climate changes and the sustainable management of water sources and environment.

© Springer Nature Switzerland AG 2021
P. A. Castillo and J. L. Jiménez Laredo (Eds.): EvoApplications 2021, LNCS 12694, pp. 795–811, 2021.
https://doi.org/10.1007/978-3-030-72699-7_50

In fact, hydraulic models are fundamental to properly predict floods and more in general to set up water management [17,30], to organize river regulation [9,21,27], sediment transport [10], to help developing flood protection systems [16], to generate simulations in order to construct flooding maps and many others purposes [11,24,29]. Hydraulic computations of flow involve roughness coefficients, which represent the resistance to flood flows in channels and flood plains. The Mannings's equation (cite Manning in 1889) is an empirical equation that applies to uniform flow in open channels and is a function of the roughness coefficient (n) selected from standard reference, tables [20] or calculated from field measurements, the estimation of a Manning's coefficient can affect computational results [8].

With the aid of computational and numerical techniques, a precise assessment of the Manning's coefficient in open channels represents an important achievement in terms of modelling and study of possible solutions to prevent and fix flood generated disasters.

The parameters typically used in hydraulic engineering models are divided into physical parameters and empirical parameters. Physical parameters describe the physical properties of materials and they are usually constants, while empirical parameters, due to the complexity and the variability of specific elements characterizing the hydraulic engineering (e.g. the roughness of channel surface, the bed material, vegetation, channel alignment and irregularities, channel shape and size, stage and discharge, suspended sediment load and bed sediment loads) need to be calculated through mathematical models [2]. Among these, the Manning's roughness coefficient, usually denoted by n, is often uncertain and this led researchers to find empirical formulas to estimate as correctly as possible the value of n [4].

Determining the n value is a critical and complex task in the hydraulics of open channel flows: this value changes in time and space, and depends on the multiple factors such as the geometric, geomorphological, and hydraulic parameters of water current and river beds [5].

With these premises, in the present work we propose an evolutionary approach to the estimation of the Manning's roughness coefficients for different cross-sections of a river. We design a black-box optimization problem by introducing an objective function that, by encapsulating all the hydraulic methodologies, takes in input a vector of Manning's coefficients and returns a loss score.

Internally, the objective function runs an hydraulic simulation procedure by considering the inputted Manning's coefficients and returns the expected depth of the river in a particular station, then this depth is compared with the true depth observed at that station and their absolute difference is returned as the loss score of the Manning's coefficients in input.

Interestingly, this black-box formulation allows to estimate the roughness coefficients by adopting any evolutionary algorithm or, more in general, any meta-heuristic proposed in the literature for numerical optimization problems.

As case of study we selected data from a river reach in the central Italian region of Umbria, namely the river "Paglia", during the flood event of the year

2012. Then, experiments were held by considering five popular Evolutionary Algorithms (EAs) from the literature, namely: the evolution strategy (1+1)-ES [6], the Differential Evolution (DE) scheme [28], the Particle Swarm Optimization (PSO) algorithm [18], the Covariance Matrix Adaptation Evolution Strategy (CMA-ES) [14], and the Bayesian Optimization (BO) algorithm [12].

The rest of the paper is organized as follows. Section 2 describes the hydrologic context, while Sect. 3 introduces the objective function. Section 4 briefly recalls the five EAs considered. Experiments are described in discussed in Sect. 5. Finally, conclusions are drawn in Sect. 6 where future lines of research are also depicted.

2 The Hydrologic Problem

The hydrodynamic analysis of river flows was performed using the free software HEC-RAS, created by The U.S. Army Corps of Engineers [1].

The hydrographic framework chosen as a test case is the river Paglia with a basin of 1187 km^2 that includes three Italian regions, Toscana, Umbria and Lazio, and an average flow rate of 11.3 m^3/s.

2.1 The Mathematical Formulation and Programming Settings

HEC-RAS is used to calculate water surface profiles and energy grade lines in 1D/2D, steady and unsteady state, and gradually varied flow analysis.

In the present study, HEC-RAS has been employed to perform one dimensional, steady, hydraulic calculation for a river flow.

The model employed to perform calculations is based on the steady 1D case which is described by the simple energy Eq. (1):

$$z_1 + h_1 + \alpha_1 \frac{v_1^2}{2g} = z_2 + h_2 + \alpha_2 \frac{v_2^2}{2g} + h_e, \tag{1}$$

where: z is the bottom elevation, h is the depth, v is the mean velocity in the channel cross-section, α is called the St. Venant coefficient and plays the role of the correction factor, including the effect of velocity profile non-uniformity, while g is the well known acceleration of gravity.

It is worthwhile to note that Eq. (1) is provided for gradually-varying flow, when the assumption of hydrostatic pressure distribution may be suitable.

As for the specific program implementation, HEC-RAS, version 5.0.7 (the latest at time of writing) allows to set the geometric data of the river directly from geo-referenced files. Once the geometry is set, upstream and downstream boundary conditions are to be properly implemented.

Cross section coordinates were defined by entering the river station and elevation points from left to right bank in sequence along the river.

Twenty cross sections were allocated over the river reach as represented in Fig. 1.

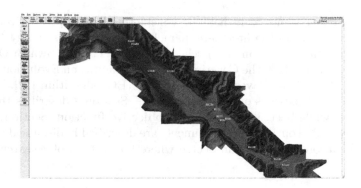

Fig. 1. HEC-RAS: Paglia's DEM file with the cross sections selected

After the geometry is defined, data of discharge were defined for the calculation process finalizing the model creation.

The actual 1D, steady model in HEC-RAS uses empirical Manning's equation, in the form of Eq. (2), to supply the relationship between the river discharge,
hydraulic resistance, river geometry, and the friction energy loss. In the case of
a change in channel geometry, energy losses are assessed using coefficients of
contraction or expansion multiplied by the change in velocity head. Head loss
between two sections is computed from Eq. (3), while the water surface is calculated from the energy Eq. (4) [1].

$$Q = KS_f^{1/2}, \tag{2}$$

$$h_e = LS_f + C \left(\frac{\alpha_1 v_1^2}{2g} + \frac{\alpha_2 v_2^2}{2g} \right), \tag{3}$$

$$h = Z + y + \frac{\alpha v^2}{2g}. \tag{4}$$

In Eqs. (2) Q is the flow rate or discharge and K is the conveyance of the
channel. Moreover, in Eq. (3) S_f is the energy slope, g is the acceleration due to
gravity, h_e is the energy head loss, C is the expansion or contraction coefficient,
α_1 and α_2 are the velocity weighting coefficients, while v_1 and v_2 the average
velocities. Finally, in Eq. (4) h is the water surface level above a specified datum,
Z is the bed elevation, y is the depth of flow, α is the kinetic energy correlation
coefficient, and v is the average velocity. The subscripts 1 and 2 denote two
different cross-sections in the same channel reach. The basic assumption is that
the cross-section number 1 is located upstream of the cross-section number 2. L
is defined as the distance weighted reach length and it is calculated as follows:

$$L = \frac{L_{lob}\bar{Q}_{lob} + L_{ch}\bar{Q}_{ch} + L_{rob}\bar{Q}_{rob}}{\bar{Q}_{lob} + \bar{Q}_{ch} + \bar{Q}_{rob}}, \tag{5}$$

where the subscripts lob, ch, rob stand respectively for left overbank, main channel, and right overbank. The quantity $(\bar{Q}_{lob} + \bar{Q}_{ch} + \bar{Q}_{rob})$ represents the

arithmetic average of the flows between sections for the left overbank, the main channel and the right overbank.

Variable h_e, as before mentioned, describes friction losses due to bed and banks influence on flowing water and plays a fundamental role, as it includes effects of channel contraction and extension. If the depth is known in one cross-section, on this basis, the depth may be also determined in the second cross-section. To calculate the distribution of the depth along the channel, its value must be known in one cross-section immediately upstream. So it becomes clear that this cross-section is the inlet or outlet boundary of the channel reach. Hence, the condition is frequently called "boundary condition", but it is rather a hydraulic term than strict mathematical language.

The kinematic energy terms, as well as friction losses, depend on the magnitude of the flow, exactly the discharge Q. The influence of floodplains is included in the calculation of the St. Venant coefficients and calculation of weighted distance between cross-sections.

In order to determine the total conveyance and the velocity coefficient for a cross section, HEC-RAS approach requires the flow to be subdivided into sections whose velocities can be considered uniformly distributed.

The approach followed is to subdivide the flow in the overbank areas using the input cross section value break points (locations where n-values change) as the basis for subdivision. Conveyance is calculated within each subdivision from the Manning's Eq. 2.

The empirical correlation between the Manning's equation and the Manning's coefficient is given by the conveyance coefficient for subdivision, K which can be expressed by:

$$K = \frac{1.486}{n} AR^{2/3}, \qquad (6)$$

where n is the Manning's roughness coefficient, A is the flow area and R is the hydraulic radius (area/wetted perimeter), all to be intended for each subdivision.

The program sums up all the incremental conveyances in the overbanks to obtain a conveyance for the left overbank and the right overbank. The main channel conveyance is normally computed as a single conveyance element. The total conveyance for the cross section is obtained by summing the three subdivision conveyances (left, channel, and right).

One can opt for a single Manning's n for each section (*lob*, *ch* or *rob*) or for multiple selection for a single section. In this work, as anticipated, 20 cross sections have been identified and a single n has been set for each segment, hence $3n$ values for each cross section, for a total of 60 Manning's roughness coefficients.

In order to evaluate the Manning's n values to be inserted in HEC-RAS, the standard tabulated values from the classic work of Chow [20], as in Fig. 2.

2.2 The Selected Test Case

Without any lack of generality for the scope of our study, as already introduced, a one-dimensional steady flow hydraulics computation was performed and a

Type of Channel and Description	Minimum	Normal	Maximum
Natural streams - minor streams (top width at floodstage < 100 ft)			
1. Main Channels			
a. clean, straight, full stage, no rifts or deep pools	0.025	0.030	0.033
b. same as above, but more stones and weeds	0.030	0.035	0.040
c. clean, winding, some pools and shoals	0.033	0.040	0.045
d. same as above, but some weeds and stones	0.035	0.045	0.050
e. same as above, lower stages, more ineffective slopes and sections	0.040	0.048	0.055
f. same as "d" with more stones	0.045	0.050	0.060
g. sluggish reaches, weedy, deep pools	0.050	0.070	0.080
h. very weedy reaches, deep pools, or floodways with heavy stand of timber and underbrush	0.075	0.100	0.150
2. Mountain streams, no vegetation in channel, banks usually steep, trees and brush along banks submerged at high stages			
a. bottom: gravels, cobbles, and few boulders	0.030	0.040	0.050
b. bottom: cobbles with large boulders	0.040	0.050	0.070

3. Floodplains			
a. Pasture, no brush			
1. short grass	0.025	0.030	0.035
2. high grass	0.030	0.035	0.050
b. Cultivated areas			
1. no crop	0.020	0.030	0.040
2. mature row crops	0.025	0.035	0.045
3. mature field crops	0.030	0.040	0.050
c. Brush			
1. scattered brush, heavy weeds	0.035	0.050	0.070
2. light brush and trees, in winter	0.035	0.050	0.060
3. light brush and trees, in summer	0.040	0.060	0.080
4. medium to dense brush, in winter	0.045	0.070	0.110
5. medium to dense brush, in summer	0.070	0.100	0.160
d. Trees			
1. dense willows, summer, straight	0.110	0.150	0.200
2. cleared land with tree stumps, no sprouts	0.030	0.040	0.050
3. same as above, but with heavy growth of sprouts	0.050	0.060	0.080
4. heavy stand of timber, a few down trees, little undergrowth, flood stage below branches	0.080	0.100	0.120
5. same as 4. with flood stage reaching branches	0.100	0.120	0.160

Fig. 2. Manning's n for channels

specific reach, taken as testing geographical framework, was selected. Data were collected from the hydrographic service of the Umbria Region[1].

The river Paglia originates from the Amiata mountain, an extinct volcano at 1738 m above sea level and, proceeding from upstream to downstream, the river enters in the Orvieto plain as in Fig. 3.

The characteristics of the materials present along the riverbed are mainly graveled and rocky throughout its course, with short grassy banks depending on the seasons. The entire basin is generally characterized by materials with low permeability, about 75%, and its slope is averaged at 4.8% up to its confluence with the canal Subbisone, its first stretch, then a steeper one of 7% between this confluence and the Mount Rubiaglio, and finally, the stretch of our interest, sloping at about 3.3%.

In order to perform a validation for the optimization procedure, data have been collected from a specific event that happened in the selected area. During the night between November 11th and 12th 2012, a massive rain fall has been registered by pluviometers, with a peak discharge of 307 mm registered at the gauging station positioned at the location of Orvieto Scalo.

The gauging spot of Orvieto Scalo corresponds with the cross section labeled with "12850", as in Fig. 4.

The event under analysis produced a considerable increase in the hydrometric levels, generating overflows that caused damages in many towns and villages in the surrounding area. A peak discharge was registered of $Q = 2200$ m^3/s, a value that was employed, in our work, as the upstream boundary condition.

3   The Objective Function

The objective function is designed as a loss function where the variables to optimize are the Manning's coefficients at the different cross-sections of the considered river reach. As described in Sect. 2.2, we have 20 cross-sections and, for

---

[1] Available at https://www.regione.umbria.it/ambiente/servizio-idrografico.

Fig. 3. Satellite and DEM representation of the simulated overflow event

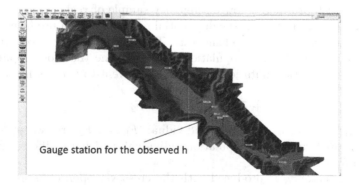

Gauge station for the observed h

Fig. 4. HEC-RAS: Particular of the cross section corresponding to the gauge station

each cross-section, three Manning's coefficients are considered (left bank, central channel, right bank). Hence, a solution to our optimization problem is real vector $x \in \mathbb{R}^{60}$. Furthermore, every vector's component is bounded to the suitable range of $[0.025, 0.2]$.

The objective function proceeds as follows: (i) uses the vector x of Manning's coefficients in order to setup an HEC-RAS simulation, (ii) runs the HEC-RAS simulation $HR(x)$ which returns the expected depth of the water at the gauge station deployed along the river, and (iii) computes and returns the absolute difference between the simulated depth $HR(x)$ and the true depth h_{obs} observed at the gauge station.

Formally, the goal is to find the vector of Manning's coefficients $x \in \mathbb{R}^{60}$ that minimizes the objective function

$$f(x) = |HR(x) - h_{obs}|, \tag{7}$$

with the constraints that $x_i \in [0.025, 0.2]$ for $1 \le i \le 60$.

The ideally optimal vector of Manning's coefficients is the one with a loss score of 0, thus 0 is a lower bound for $f(x)$.

4   Evolutionary Algorithms

In this section we describe the meta-heuristics employed for the optimization problem described in Sect. 3.

4.1   Differential Evolution

Differential Evolution (DE) is a population based evolutionary metaheuristic designed for continuous optimization, originally proposed in [28].

The DE population is composed by N d-dimensional vectors $\{x_1, \ldots, x_N\}$ and can be initialized using different strategies, the most common way is to sample the search space. In this work we chose to use the Scrambled Hammersley procedure which produces a low discrepancy sample of vectors.

The key operator of DE is the differential mutation which produces a mutant vector v_i for each population element x_i. The mutant vector is computed as a linear combination of some population elements. One the most popular strategy for the differential mutation operator is "current-to-best" scheme which is defined as

$$v_i = x_i + F_1 \cdot (x_{best} - x_i) + F_2 \cdot (x_{r_1} - x_{r_2}),$$

where x_{best} is the best population individual, F_1 and F_2 are two scale factors, and x_{r_1}, x_{r_2} are two random population individuals which are different from each other and from x_i.

A target vector y_i is produced with the crossover operator applied to each population element x_i and the corresponding mutant vector v_i. The most used crossover operator is the uniform crossover: the j-th component of y_i, for $j = 1, \ldots, d$, is computed as

$$y_{i,j} = \begin{cases} v_{i,j} & \text{if } r_j < CR \text{ or } j = \bar{j} \\ x_{i,j} & \text{otherwise}, \end{cases}$$

where CR is the crossover ratio, r_j is a random number in $[0,1]$ and $\bar{j}$ is a random index in $\{1, \ldots, d\}$.

At the end of each iteration, the fitter between y_i and x_i is kept in the population for the next iteration.

For further details see [3,7,25]. In our experimentation, the paramters have been set as follows: $N = 30$, $F_1 = F_2 = 0.8$, while CR is randomly chosen in $[0,1]$ before every crossover application.

4.2 Particle Swarm Optimization

Particle Swarm Optimization (PSO) is one of the most famous metaheuristic based on swarm intelligence principle, firstly proposed in [18]. PSO maintains a population of N elements, each of them has a position x_i in the search space and a velocity v_i, which is also a d-dimensional vector.

Population individuals are connected by undirected links, which are used to propagate information among the population.

As in DE, the population is evolved during a given number of iterations. At each iteration, for $j = 1, \ldots, d$ and for $i = 1, \ldots, N$, the component j of the velocity of the element i is updated by means of the following formula

$$v_{i,j} \leftarrow v_{i,j} + c_1 r_{1,j}(lb_{i,j} - x_{i,j}) + c_2 r_{2,j}(pb_{i,j} - x_{i,j}),$$

where c_1 and c_2 are the *social* and the *cognitive coefficients*, respectively, and $r_{1,j}$ and $r_{2,j}$ are random number in $[0,1]$.

The vector lb_i is the best element among those connected to x_i (the *local best*), while pb_i is the best position ever reached by x_i in all the previous iterations (the *personal best*).

After having computed the new velocity vectors, each position is simply updated as $x_i \leftarrow x_i + v_i$.

The most common choice for the connection schema among the population elements is the complete graph: in this setting, lb_i is the best population element (called *global best*).

Other details about PSO can be found in [7,26]. In our experimentation: the population size N was set to 30, while all the other parameters were set as their default values in Nevergrad library [22].

4.3 (1+1)-ES

Evolution strategies [6] are evolutionary algorithms which evolve a population of μ individuals by producing a set of λ children by means of genetic operators recombination, mutation and selection.

The simplest form of evolutionary strategy is (1+1)-ES in which the population contains one element x and, at each generation, one child y is produced by means of a mutation operator based on a Gaussian distribution with mean 0 and a given variance σ. Formally, $y_j = x_j + N(0, \sigma_j^2)$, for $j = 1, \ldots, d$. If y is fitter than x, then x will be replaced by y in the next iteration.

In our experiments, the algorithm starts with the vector x^0 located at the center of the search space, i.e. $x_j^0 = L_j + \frac{U_j - L_j}{2}$, for each $j = 1, \ldots, d$, where L_j and U_j are, respectively, the lower and the upper bounds for dimension j. Moreover, we set $\sigma_j = \frac{U_j - L_j}{5}$.

4.4 CMA-ES

One of the most successful form of evolution strategies is the Covariance Matrix Adaptation evolution strategy (CMA-ES) [14].

CMA-ES is an iterative process which updates a mean vector m, the step size σ, and a covariance matrix C. At each iteration g, λ samples $x_1^{(g)}, \ldots, x_\lambda^{(g)}$ are generated with the multivariate normal distribution $N(m, \sigma^2 C)$.

m is then updated as the weighted average of μ fittest samples $x_{1:\lambda}^{(g)}, \ldots, x_{\mu:\lambda}^{(g)}$

$$\mu^{(g)+1} = \sum_{i=1}^{\mu} w_i x_{i:\lambda}^{(g)}$$

One of the most used method to update C is the Rank-μ-update, where the new value of C is computed as

$$C^{(g+1)} = C^{(g)\,1/2} [I + c_\mu \sum_{i=1}^{\lambda} w_i (z_{i:\lambda}^{(g)} z_{i:\lambda}^{(g)'})] C^{(g)\,1/2},$$

where c_μ is a smoothing coefficient, $z_{i:\lambda}^{(g)} = C^{(g)-1/2} y_{i:\lambda}^{(g)}$ and $y_{i:\lambda}^{(g)} = \frac{x_{i:\lambda}^{(g)} - m^{(g)}}{\sigma^{(g)}}$, for $i = 1, \ldots, \lambda$.

Another method is Rank-one-update, where an evolution path p_C is updated at each iteration with the formula

$$p_C^{(g+1)} = (1 - c_C) p_C^{(g)} + \sqrt{c_C(2 - c_C)} \frac{m^{(g+1)} - m^{(g)}}{\sigma^{(g)}}$$

and then C is updated as

$$C^{(g+1)} = (1 - c_1) C^{(g)} + c_1 p_C^{(g+1)} p_C^{(g+1)'}$$

Finally, σ is updated using a process called cumulative step-size adaptation (CSA). To accomplish this task, another evolution path p_σ is used. p_σ is updated with the following formula

$$p_\sigma^{(g+1)} = (1 - c_\sigma) p_\sigma^{(g)} + \sqrt{c_\sigma(2 - c_\sigma)} C^{(g)-1/2} \frac{m^{(g+1)} - m^{(g)}}{\sigma^{(g)}}.$$

Then σ is updated as

$$\sigma^{(g+1)} = \sigma^{(g)} \exp\left(\frac{c_\sigma}{d_\sigma} \left(\frac{||p_\sigma^{(g+1)}||}{E||N(0, I)||} - 1 \right) \right).$$

In our experimentation, λ was set to 30, while all the other parameters were set to their default value in the Nevegrad library [22].

4.5 Bayesian Optimization

Bayesian Optimization (BO) [12] is used on optimization problems where the computation of the fitness function is time demanding, as the case described in this paper. This kind of approach is called "surrogate methods".

In BO, a probabilistic model, usually a Gaussian Process, is used to forecast the fitness function of any point of the search space and then to sample the most promising element.

More precisely, a Gaussian process (GP) is defined with mean function $\mu(x)$ and a covariance function (or kernel) $\Sigma(x, x')$ and it is built up by choosing an initial set of points $x_1, \ldots, x_n$ and their corresponding fitness values $f(x_1), \ldots, f(x_n)$.

The GP can be used to compute the distribution of $f(x)$ given the values $f(x_1), \ldots, f(x_n)$, for all $x \in \mathbb{R}^d$.

An acquisition function is used to find the point x_{n+1} whose fitness value can be maximal. One of the most frequently employed acquisition function is based on the expected improvement, which correspond to select the point $x_{n+1} \in \mathbb{R}^d$ such that $E([f(x_{n+1}) - f^*]^+)$ is maximal, where $f^* = \max\{f(x_1), \ldots, f(x_n)\}$

Then, the fitness value $f(x_{n+1})$ is evaluated and x_{n+1} and $f(x_{n+1})$ are used to update the parameters of the GP.

BO proceeds in this way until a given number of fitness evaluation is reached. In our experimentation, the number of initial samples considered was set to 30, while all the other parameters were set to their default values in the Nevergrad library [22].

5   Experiments

In order to analyze the proposed methodology, we have held an experimental comparison among the five Evolutionary Algorithms (EAs) described in Sect. 4 by considering the objective function introduced in Sect. 3. Moreover, the effectiveness of any single algorithm is also compared with that of the standard approach described in Sect. 2.1.

The implementations of the selected algorithms available in the recently proposed Python's library Nevergrad [22,23] (version 0.4.2, the latest one at time of writing) were adopted. All the experiments have been carried out on a machine equipped with an Intel Xeon E5-2650v4 clocking at 2.20 GHz, 128 GB of RAM and running Windows 10.

It is worthwhile to note that: (i) the Windows operating system was necessary in order to run the HEC-RAS simulation required by the objective function evaluation, and (ii) the communication between the Python's code and the HEC-RAS simulation was realized through the well known COM interface for inter-process communications [13].

Each one of the five EAs was executed 25 times on the case study described in Sect. 2 and every execution terminates when the computational budget of 600 s is exhausted. In terms of number objective evaluations, considering that a single evaluation lasts around two seconds on the available machine, every algorithm performed around 300 objective evaluations.

Moreover, in order to analyze the experimental results from different point-of-views, for every single execution we registered both the final objective value achieved and the full optimization trajectory.

In Table 1, we provide all the statistics about the best solutions obtained by the five EAs in all their executions. The algorithms are ordered by average objective value. Moreover, in the last line of the table we provide the objective value achieved by the standard methodology (a clearly deterministic method, so only one value is provided) described in Sect. 2.1. Best results are in bold.

Table 1. Statistics about the final objective values observed in the experiments.

Algorithm	Final Objective Values			
	Average	Minimum	Maximum	St.Dev.
(1+1)-ES	$< 10^{-5}$	0	**0.00005**	$< 10^{-5}$
DE	0.00147	0.00004	0.00665	0.00211
CMA-ES	0.00167	0.00013	0.00355	0.00139
BO	0.01364	0.00538	0.02898	0.00807
PSO	0.03719	0.00199	0.08304	0.03013
Std Method	1.63000			

From Table 1 it is possible to see that all the five EAs largely outperform the standard approach in any single execution. Since the objective value is the estimation error in meters, the accuracy gain obtained by the proposed automatic methodology is of more than 1.5 m with respect to the standard approach, while BO, the worst average error of all tested evolutionary algorithms, obtains an error of less than 3.8 cm.

Regarding the comparison among the five EAs, it is interesting to note that (1+1)-ES clearly outperforms all the other competitors. This is possibly motivated by the small budget of evaluations allowed (due to the time complexity of the objective function) and the fact that (1+1)-ES evolves a single solution and not a population as the other methods. Moreover, the worst objective value obtained by (1+1)-ES differs from the theoretically optimal value of 0 by only 10^{-5}.

Moreover, we statistically validated the comparisons among the EAs by running a Kolmogorov-Smirnov statistical test [15] for each pair of EAs. By considering a significance threshold of 0.01, in Fig. 5 we provide an heatmap to be interpreted as follows: an entry is red if the algorithm indicated in the column is significantly better than that indicated in the row, an entry is blue if the row's algorithm is significantly better than that column's algorithm, while the gray color indicates no significant difference.

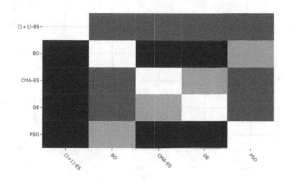

Fig. 5. Results of the Kolmogorov-Smirnov tests.

Observing Fig. 5, it is clear that (1+1)-ES significantly outperforms all the other competitors. Moreover, DE and CMA-ES do not show significant differences in terms of effectiveness and both outperform the PSO and BO.

The empirical probability density functions of the final objective values obtained by the executions of any single algorithm are depicted in the violin-plot of Fig. 6. This plot clearly confirms the main observation: (1+1)-ES is by a large amount the algorithm to go for the problem at hand under the considered budget. Furthermore, no execution of BO was competitive with respect to (1+1)-ES, CMA-ES and DE, probably because the dimension of the search space (60) is too large for BO. Regarding the robustness: (1 | 1)-ES is the most robust algorithm, while PSO shows the largest variance. Since PSO is known to suffer of premature convergence to local optima [19], an high variance may indicate the presence of a considerable amount of local optima in the fitness landscape associated to the objective function.

Finally, Fig. 7 depicts the convergence behaviours of the five algorithms averaged over the different executions. By recalling that the population-based algorithms were set with a population size of 30, an interesting observation here is to note that (1+1)-ES, after the first 30 evaluations, is the most effective algorithm. Then, (1+1)-ES is able to keep the gap till the end of the execution. However, Fig. 7 also shows that, with a larger budget, it is likely that both DE and CMA-ES will be able to match the same effectiveness of (1+1)-ES.

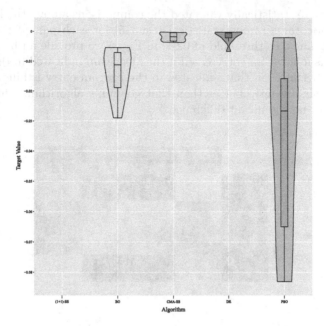

Fig. 6. Empirical probability density functions of the final objective values registered by the executions of each algorithm.

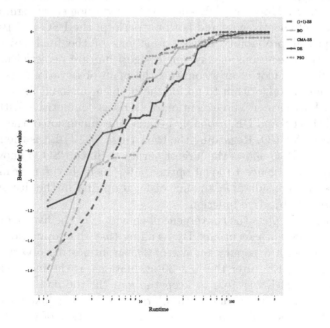

Fig. 7. Average convergence behaviours (abscissa is in log-scale).

6   Conclusion and Future Work

Hydraulic computation of flow is largely involved in modeling and preventing flood disasters depending on the conformation and features of channels, river and flood plains. The accuracy of the flow computational results is strictly connected with the estimate of Manning's roughness coefficients for different cross-sections of the rivers. Although deterministic methods exist for estimating Manning's coefficient, they exhibit a low accuracy. In this work a black-box approach is proposed, which allows to formulate Manning's roughness coefficient estimation problem as an optimization process, which tries to minimize the estimation error of a river depth by varying the coefficient value. Evolutionary algorithms, using the error estimation as a blackbox objective function, have been applied; they cover different classes of metaheuristics including DE, PSO, (1+1)-ES, CMA-ES and BO. The algorithms have been tested using a real dataset, from a case study of a river in central Italy, and compared with a standard deterministic methodology used in hydraulic computation literature. Results show that the application of evolutionary metaheuristics always outperforms by orders of magnitude the traditional methodology. The simple (1+1)-ES is the most performing metaheuristic, obtaining errors of less than 10^{-5} m in river depth estimation with respect to more than 1.5 m of the deterministic method.

The proposed approach is quite promising, future works will aim to confirm the performances by its application to other datasets, also considering multiple gauge stations deployed along the river. It must be pointed out that the proposed black-box formulation for Manning's coefficient estimation is quite general, since it allows to apply any meta-heuristic for numerical optimization problem to roughness coefficients estimation. Therefore, a systematic experimentation of other metaheuristic approaches is planned, as well as considering the extensions of the black box approach to the estimation of other hydraulic flow parameters.

Acknowledgement. This work was partially supported by the following research grants: (i) Università per Stranieri di Perugia – Progetto di ricerca *Artificial Intelligence for Education, Social and Human Sciences*; (ii) Università per Stranieri di Perugia – *Finanziamento per Progetti di Ricerca di Ateneo—PRA 2020*; (iii) PRIN project *PHRAME: Phraseological Complexity Measures in learner Italian*.

References

1. HEC-RAS, User Manual, Davis Version 4.0
2. Atanov, G.A., Evseeva, E.G., Meselhe, E.A.: Estimation of roughness profile in trapezoidal open channels. J. Hydraulic Eng. **125**(3), 309–312 (1999)
3. Baioletti, M., Milani, A., Santucci, V.: Variable neighborhood algebraic differential evolution: An application to the linear ordering problem with cumulative costs. Inf. Sci. **507**, 37–52 (2020)
4. Becker, L., Yeh, W.W.G.: Identification of parameters in unsteady open channel flows. Water Resour. Res. **8**(4), 956–965 (1972)
5. Becker, L., Yeh, W.W.G.: Identification of multiple reach channel parameters. Water Resour. Res. **9**(2), 326–335 (1973)

6. Beyer, H.G., Schwefel, H.P.: Evolution strategies - A comprehensive introduction. Nat. Comput. **1**(1), 3–52 (2002)
7. Brabazon, A., O'Neill, M., McGarraghy, S.: Natural Computing Algorithms, 1st edn. Springer, Cham (2015)
8. Di Francesco, S., Zarghami, A., Biscarini, C., Manciola, P.: Wall roughness effect in the lattice Boltzmann method. In: AIP Conference Proceedings, vol. 1558, pp. 1677–1680. American Institute of Physics (2013)
9. Di Francesco, S., Biscarini, C., Manciola, P.: Numerical simulation of water free-surface flows through a front-tracking lattice Boltzmann approach. J. Hydroinformatics **17**(1), 1–6 (2015)
10. Di Francesco, S., Biscarini, C., Manciola, P.: Characterization of a flood event through a sediment analysis: the Tescio river case study. Water **8**(7), 308 (2016)
11. Drake, J., Bradford, A., Joy, D.: Application of HEC-RAS 4.0 temperature model to estimate groundwater contributions to Swan Creek, Ontario, Canada. J. Hydrol. **389**(3), 390–398 (2010)
12. Frazier, P.I.: A tutorial on bayesian optimization. Preprint arXiv:1807.02811 (2018)
13. Gray, D.N., Hotchkiss, J., LaForge, S., Shalit, A., Weinberg, T.: Modern languages and Microsoft's component object model. Commun. ACM **41**(5), 55–65 (1998)
14. Hansen, N., Ostermeier, A.: Completely derandomized self-adaptation in evolution strategies. Evol. Comput. **9**(2), 159–195 (2001)
15. Hollander, M., Wolfe, D.A., Chicken, E.: Nonparametric statistical methods, vol. 751. Wiley (2013)
16. Horritt, M., Bates, P.: Evaluation of 1D and 2D numerical models for predicting river flood inundation. J. Hydrol. **268**(1), 87–99 (2002)
17. Kachiashvili, K.: Software realization problems of mathematical models of pollutants transport in rivers. Adv. Eng. Softw. **40**(10), 1063–1073 (2009)
18. Kennedy, J., Eberhart, R.: Particle swarm optimization. In: Proceedings of IEEE International Conference on Neural Networks, vol. 4, pp. 1942–1948 (1995)
19. Larsen, R.B., Jouffroy, J., Lassen, B.: On the premature convergence of particle swarm optimization. In: Proceedings of 2016 Eur. Control Conference, pp. 1922–1927 (2016)
20. Perry, B.: Open-channel hydraulics. Science **131**(3408), 1215–1215 (1960)
21. Pinar, E., et al.: Artificial neural network approaches for prediction of backwater through arched bridge constrictions. Adv. Eng. Softw **41**(4), 627–635 (2010)
22. Rapin, J., Teytaud, O.: Nevergrad - A gradient-free optimization platform (2018). https://GitHub.com/FacebookResearch/Nevergrad
23. Rapin, J., Bennet, P., Centeno, E., Haziza, D., Moreau, A., Teytaud, O.: Open source evolutionary structured optimization. In: Proceedings of the 2020 Genetic and Evolutionary Computation Conference Companion, pp. 1599–1607 (2020)
24. Rodriguez, L.B., Cello, P.A., Vionnet, C.A., Goodrich, D.: Fully conservative coupling of HEC-RAS with MODFLOW to simulate stream-aquifer interactions in a drainage basin. J. Hydrol. **353**(1), 129–142 (2008)
25. Santucci, V., Baioletti, M., Di Bari, G., Milani, A.: A binary algebraic differential evolution for the MultiDimensional two-way number partitioning problem. In: Liefooghe, A., Paquete, L. (eds.) EvoCOP 2019. LNCS, vol. 11452, pp. 17–32. Springer, Cham (2019). https://doi.org/10.1007/978-3-030-16711-0_2
26. Santucci, V., Milani, A., Caraffini, F.: An optimisation-driven prediction method for automated diagnosis and prognosis. Mathematics **7**(11), 1051 (2019)
27. Shen, D., Jia, Y., Altinakar, M., Bingner, R.L.: GIS-based channel flow and sediment transport simulation using CCHE1D coupled with AnnAGNPS. J. Hydraul. Res. **54**(5), 567–574 (2016)

28. Storn, R., Price, K.: Differential evolution - a simple and efficient heuristic for global optimization over continuous spaces. J. Global Optim. **11**(4), 341–359 (1997)
29. Violante, C., Biscarini, C., Esposito, E., Molisso, F., Porfido, S., Sacchi, M., et al.: The consequences of hydrological events on steep coastal watersheds: the Costa d'Amalfi, eastern Tyrrhenian Sea. IAHS Publ. **327**, 102 (2009)
30. Zischg, A.P., Mosimann, M., Bernet, D.B., Röthlisberger, V.: Validation of 2D flood models with insurance claims. J. Hydrol. **557**, 350–361 (2018)

EA-Based ASV Trajectory Planner for Pollution Detection in Lentic Waters

Gonzalo Carazo-Barbero, Eva Besada-Portas$^{(\boxtimes)}$ (ID), José M. Girón-Sierra (ID),
and José A. López-Orozco (ID)

Universidad Complutense de Madrid, 28040 Madrid, Spain
{gocarazo,ebesada,gironsi,jalo}@ucm.es

Abstract. This paper presents a new planner based on Evolutionary Algorithms (EAs) to optimize the trajectory of an Autonomous Surface Vehicle (ASV), equipped with a probe, that has to determine the location of a pollutant in lentic water bodies (e.g. reservoirs, dams). To achieve it, our planner 1) exploits the information provided by a simulator that determines the pollutant distribution based on the water currents and 2) is supported by an EA that optimizes the mission duration, the ASV trajectory length and the measurements taken by its probe in highly polluted areas. The current version of the planner also ensures that the trajectories are feasible from the ASV and water body perspective, and solves this constrained multi-objective problem as a mono-objective one that linearly combines the constraint and objective functions. The preliminary results over different scenarios show that the planner can already determine overall good solutions, but that needs to be modified (e.g. using a multi-objective intended EA) to improve them further.

Keywords: Water pollution · Modelling and simulation · Autonomous Surface Vehicles · Trajectory optimization · Evolutionary algorithms

1 Introduction

Fresh water is a fragile resource, threatened by pollution and scarcity, which must be frequently monitored to guarantee that its healthiness and purity is adequate for its consumption, for recreational uses, and for the conservation and protection of the environment. The availability of quality inland water bodies is reduced by their misuse and by environmental factors, including the extreme floods and droughts caused by climate change. The importance of the problem makes *water availability and its management* a goal of the United Nations 2030 Agenda for Sustainable Development [4] and it is already considered by European water regulations [2], which indicate, among other things, the dangerous substances that must be monitored (and when necessary, reduced), as well as their monitoring frequency.

This work has been supported by the Spanish National Societal Challenges Program, through the AMPBAS project (RTI2018-098962-B-C21).

P. A. Castillo and J. L. Jiménez Laredo (Eds.): EvoApplications 2021, LNCS 12694, pp. 812–827, 2021.
https://doi.org/10.1007/978-3-030-72699-7_51

To achieve part of the monitoring requirements of the regulations, early warning networks, with geographically distributed probes capable of automatically and frequently taking measurements of different water parameters, are used to alert the water authorities about the detection of new pollution episodes [15]. Despite their success, since they can only take measurements on the strategic points where the probes were placed, they cannot determine, as the European Water Directive recommends, the space-time distribution of the pollutants.

To perform a dynamic monitoring (i.e. at mobile points of the water body), Autonomous Surface Vehicles (ASVs), which are self-driving boats equipped with the required water probes, can be used and sent to the "best" locations to take the measurements. In fact, the water monitoring possibilities offered by ASVs have attracted the attention of companies and institutions that are already marketing or using some platforms especially designed for this purpose [13,14]. However, these platforms have not yet solved all the monitoring issues, since to make them autonomous, it is necessary to develop a complete solution that – incorporating advanced location, perception, planning, guidance, navigation and control techniques – deploys and controls the movement of the ASVs [10].

This paper is focused in the development of a new approach for pre-planning the trajectory of an ASV in order to optimize pollutant detection missions. To do it, we define an optimization problem and solve it with an Evolutionary Algorithm (EA). Previous works of water monitoring missions with ASVs have followed similar approaches with different purposes. To name a few, we select the following. When no information about the pollutant distribution is available, ASV water monitoring can be set up as a coverage problem and solved with Genetic Algorithms [6,7]. Otherwise, when the information to be gathered in the regions of interest is relevant, it can be set up as an information gain problem and solved with Ant Colony Optimization (ACO, [18]) and Particle Swarm Optimization [17]. An alternative monitoring problem, solved in [16] with ACO, arises when an operator decides which are the points of interest, and the planner has to find the best path to visit them. Finally, many trajectory planners for water monitoring with autonomous underwater vehicles can be found in the comprehensive state-of-the-art presented in [11], and many other applications of EAs to water resources engineering are reviewed in [9].

Our approach differs from the previous (i.e. from [6,7,16–18]), as our planner is being designed to take into consideration the results of a physical simulator that determines where the pollutant might be placed (concentrated and distributed) during the ASV monitoring mission. In more detail, the preliminary version of our planner that is presented in this paper simultaneously optimizes, using an EA, the mission duration, the ASV trajectory length and the measurements taken from the ASV in highly polluted areas of the water body.

Besides introducing the problem and the pollution simulator in Sect. 2, the paper describes the main characteristics of the planner in Sect. 3, presents and analyzes the results obtained over different polluting scenarios in Sect. 4, and draws conclusions and introduces future research lines in Sect. 5.

2   Problem Description

This section characterizes the main elements of the problem. In particular, it presents the problem elements and most relevant variables, the physical model used to simulate the pollution evolution, and the scenarios of the test cases.

2.1   Problem Elements and Variables

We consider a scenario where a single ASV, equipped with an adequate vertically movable probe, has to explore *efficiently* a body of lentic water (e.g. reservoir or dam) where a pollutant has appeared.

To achieve it, on one side we have a planner that determines a 3 Dimensional (3D) trajectory $(s(t) = [s_x(t), s_y(t), s_z(t)])$, where $(s_x(t), s_y(t))$ indicates the ASV location on the water body and $(s_x(t), s_y(t), s_z(t))$ the probe 3D location within the water body (i.e. we consider that the probe and ASV share the horizontal coordinates $(s_x(t), s_y(t))$ and that the probe is submerged at depth $s_z(t)$). On the other side, we have a pollution simulator that is capable of determining, for N_p pollutant particles, their 3D locations $(p^k(t) = [p_x^k(t), p_y^k(t), p_z^k(t)]$ with $k \in [1, ..., N_p])$, taking into account the initial pollutant locations $p^k(t_0)$ and the steady state velocity of the water flow $u_{ss}(w) = [u_{ss,x}(w), u_{ss,y}(w), u_{ss,z}(w)]$ at any location $w = [x, y, z]$ of the water body. Finally, our planner will try to identify ASV and probe 3D trajectories $(s(t) = [s_x(t), s_y(t), s_z(t)])$ that, starting and ending at fixed locations $(s(t_0)$ and $s(t_e))$, are short and good to observe a high number of polluting particles and to reduce the mission time $(t_e - t_0)$.

Besides, and for notation purposes, $\dot{s}(t)$ and $\ddot{s}(t)$ stand for the ASV and probe velocity and accelerations, $u_p(t) = \dot{p}^k(t)$ for the pollutants velocity, and $u(w, t) = [u_x(w, t), u_y(w, t), u_z(w, t)]$ for the velocity of the non-stationary water flow. Finally, in some cases the variable's dependencies will be dropped to shorten the expressions.

2.2   Pollutant Distribution Simulation

In order to pre-estimate the evolution of the distribution of the pollutants in the water body, we perform simulations of the physical models that define their behavior. Although these models are pollutant dependent, they all consider the effect of the water currents in the pollutant distribution. For this reason, in the preliminary version of our planner we only consider this effect and postpone the modelling of others (such as biological growth, pollutant diffusion or decantation) for future versions of the simulator.

To simulate the pollutant displacement we assume that our pollutant behaves as a set of particles and divide the model in two parts: the water fluid dynamics, unaffected by the pollutant, and the transport of the particles, whose main driving forces are precisely the water currents. Moreover, since the model is one-way coupled, the fluid dynamics can be simulated first, without considering the particle transport, in order to obtain the currents required to simulate, in a second stage, the particles' displacement. Besides, the physical domain of the simulation, which represents the space occupied by the water, must also be defined, since it affects the water currents.

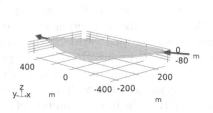
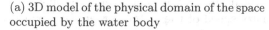

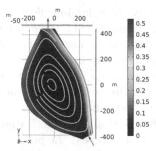

(a) 3D model of the physical domain of the space occupied by the water body

(b) Solution of the fluid flow

Fig. 1. Water body domain and fluid flow solution

The Physical Domain is given in the form of a CAD model (an STL file in this case) with multiple faces. In the examples of this paper, we use the model displayed in Fig. 1a, whose top face represents the water surface, its bottom face is the reservoir bed, and the side faces are the water input and output (as marked by the arrows). This reservoir has a surface area of 3.17×10^5 m^2, a volume of 1.32×10^7 m^3, and reaches a maximum depth of 100 m under the surface.

Fluid Dynamics are modeled with the Navier-Stokes Eq. (1) for incompressible fluids and the continuity Eq. (2), where ρ_f and ν are respectively the fluid's density and kinematic viscosity. Besides, the term $\frac{\partial u}{\partial t}$ represents the local fluid accelera-tion, $(u \cdot \nabla) u$ the convective acceleration, $-\frac{1}{\rho_f} \nabla p$ an internal acceleration due to the pressure gradient, F any external accelerations such as that of gravity or elec-tromagnetic forces, and $\nu \nabla^2 u$ the viscous diffusion of momentum [8].

$$\frac{\partial u}{\partial t} + (u \cdot \nabla) u = -\frac{1}{\rho_f} \nabla p + F + \nu \nabla^2 u \tag{1}$$

$$\nabla \cdot u = 0 \tag{2}$$

Solving these equations is non-trivial, so the common practice is to simulate them numerically. Although different numerical techniques[1] can be implemented to perform the simulation of this part of the model, we have decided to simplify this process using the commercial software COMSOL Multiphysics [1].

In particular, to simulate the water dynamics of the reservoir of this paper, we assume that the flow is laminar and in steady state, which is reasonable for rela-tively small time frames and slow moving water. So, within COMSOL we create a

---

[1] Each of them has advantages and disadvantages. For instance, the Finite Differ-ence Method (FDM) is simple to understand and does not require to transform the model into a variational formulation, but its implementation in irregular meshes such as the one used in our case is exceedingly difficult. Alternatively, the Finite Elements Method (FEM) and Finite Volumes Method (FVM), which are often used in problems involving fluid mechanics, are harder to understand but can use irreg-ular meshes easily. However, all of them often present convergence problems in the calculation process due to the non-linearity of the Navier-Stokes equation.

steady state, laminar flow (single phase fluid) model, import the reservoir geometry from the STL file and set the fluid material to water. Next, we respectively configured the water surface and bed with a sliding and non-sliding boundary condition, impose on the input face a laminar inflow rate[2] of $100\,\mathrm{m^3/s}$, and set on the output face a null pressure without any backflow. Finally, in order to speed up and facilitate the convergence of the simulation, we use six meshes, which range from "extremely coarse" to "fine", start solving the problem with the coarsest mesh (after setting to zero its initial condition) to obtain the initial condition of the next mesh, and repeat the process until the desired refinement level is obtained. After this process, we obtain the stationary speed of the water flow $u_{ss}(w)$, which is partially represented in Fig. 1b, where the colors show the magnitude of the flow velocity (in m/s) on the reservoir surface and the white stripes represent the flow lines (i.e. the trajectory that a water element takes). Both inform that there is a current flowing directly from the inlet to the outlet, that a vortex is created in the slow-moving region of the reservoir (creating an opportunity for particles to get trapped there instead of promptly exiting the domain), and that there is water transfer between the main current and the vortex (so given sufficient time all the water, and particles within, are recycled).

Particle Transport. After obtaining $u_{ss}(w)$, we can simulate the transport of the particles. To do it, we use the force balance Eq. (3) obtained from [5], where ρ_p is the particle's density, g is the gravitational acceleration vector, d_p is the particle diameter, the operator $\frac{d}{dt} = \frac{\partial}{\partial t} + (u_p \cdot \nabla)$ is the time derivative along the trajectory of a particle, and $\frac{D}{Dt} = \frac{\partial}{\partial t} + (u_{ss} \cdot \nabla)$ is the convective derivative along the path of the fluid[3].

$$\left(1 + \frac{1}{2}\frac{\rho_f}{\rho_p}\right)\frac{du_p}{dt} = \left(1 + \frac{\rho_f}{\rho_p}\right)g + \frac{18\nu\rho_f}{d_p^2\rho_p}(u_{ss} - u_p) + \frac{3}{2}\frac{\rho_f}{\rho_p}\frac{Du_{ss}}{Dt} \qquad (3)$$

The numerical technique used to solve this model is a time-stepping explicit integration that we have implemented in MATLAB [3]. In each iteration, the new particle acceleration $\frac{du_p}{dt}$ is obtained using the previous time step velocities u and u_p, and then, the new particle velocity is obtained using the explicit Euler Method. The same method is then used once more to integrate over time and obtain the position p^k of each particle. The top boundary of the domain allows for horizontal sliding and sinking, but prevents the particles from coming out of the water, while the rest of the domain faces are non-sliding boundaries (implying that the particles that reach them, remain at this position).

---

[2] As water is incompressible and the domain volume does not change, the outflow is forced to have the same magnitude as the inflow.

[3] The first of these accelerations is used in a Lagrangian frame of reference to obtain the velocity of a particle over time, while the second is calculated from the fluid flow in its Eulerian description at the position of the particle. Besides, Eq. (3) is also valid for a non-stationary flow, substituting $u_{ss}(w)$ by $u(w, t)$.

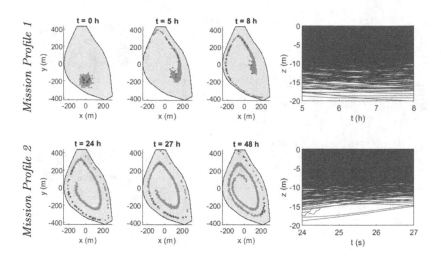

Fig. 2. Particle distribution A

2.3 Scenarios Under Study

Using the solution of the fluid flow shown in Fig. 1b, different scenarios can be set up by changing the initial distribution of the particles $(p^k(t_0))$ or by modifying the mission profile, defined by the initial and ending ASV and probe locations $(s(t_0)$ and $s(t_e))$, the initial mission time t_0 and the maximum time duration. With both possibilities, we set up the following two particles distributions (A & B) and mission profiles (1 & 2), and combine them to obtain the four scenarios that will be used as test cases (A1, A2, B1 & B2) in Sect. 4.

Particle Distribution A has 1000 initial particles sampled according to a gaussian distribution[4] centered at $[0, -200, -5]$ m with standard deviation $[25, 25, 5]$ m. The pollutant location evolution is shown in Fig. 2, where the six graphics on the left show the horizontal particle distribution $p^k(t)$ at the time indicated in the graph, and the two graphics on the right show the particles depth between the time lapse indicated at their abscissas axis. The graphics show how the pollutant gets distributed around the reservoir center as the time passes and how the depth of the particles changes slowly in both directions (up and down), since the fluid flow, which is loosely followed by the particles, is mostly horizontal due to the reservoir geometry.

Particle Distribution B has 1000 initial particles sampled according to a gaussian distribution centered at $[-26, 8, -1]$ m with a standard deviation of $[25, 25, 5]$ m. The pollutant location evolution is represented in Fig. 3, which shows that the majority of the particles are kept in the vortex. The vertical

---

[4] Particles outside the water body are re-sampled to make them start at valid locations.

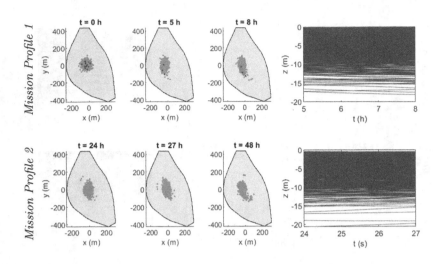

Fig. 3. Particle distribution B.

variation of their position is even less noticeable in this case since the fluid flow in this region of the reservoir is slowest, and still mostly horizontal.

Mission Profile 1 has equal initial and final ASV locations at $s(t_0) = s(t_e) = [200, -300, -0.25]$ m, an initial mission time $t_0 = 5$ h and a maximum mission duration $T_{max} = 3$ h. Hence, the pollutants get distributed according to the particle trajectories defined between $t = 5$ h and $t = 8$ h, which correspond to the three graphics at the top right of Fig. 2 and 3.

Mission Profile 2 has different initial and final ASV locations at $s(t_0) = [-15, 300, -1]$ m and $s(t_e) = [220, -320, -2.2]$ m, an initial mission time $t_0 = 24$ h and a maximum mission duration $T_{max} = 3$ h. Hence, the pollutants get distributed according to the particle trajectories defined between $t = 24$ h and $t = 27$ h, corresponding to three of the graphics at the bottom of Fig. 2 and 3.

3   EA-Based ASV's Trajectory Planner

This section presents the main characteristics of our planner, which has been implemented in Matlab. It starts describing the codification of the decision variables (in our case the ASV trajectory), continues introducing the objective and constraint functions used to evaluate them, and ends presenting the EA that finds overall good ASV and probe trajectories.

3.1   Trajectory Encoding

Spline curves are a common and compact way of encoding smooth trajectories followable by different types of vehicles. From the family of these curves [12], we have decided to use a spline that: 1) has C^2 continuity, 2) goes through the nodes that define it, and 3) lets setting as parameters the position and first two derivatives of its ending points. The first requirement guarantees that the position, velocity and acceleration of the spline are continuous and can be followed by the ASV. The second condition makes it easier for the optimization algorithm to check if the ASV trajectory is contained in the water body. Finally, the third requirement provides control over the starting and ending position, velocity and acceleration of the ASV, letting the user set them to specific values according to each mission.

A straightforward way to accomplish these requirements is to use the spline $s(t)$ defined with Eq. (4), which is formed by N_f polynomial functions $f_i(t)$, of third degree in the interior segments ($i \in \{2, ..., N_f - 1\}$) and of fourth degree in the first and last segments ($i \in \{1, N_f\}$).

$$s(t) = \begin{cases} f_1(t) & \text{for } t \in [t_0, t_1], \\ \vdots & \vdots \\ f_{N_f}(t) & \text{for } t \in [t_{N_f-1}, t_{N_f}], \end{cases} \tag{4}$$

In order to meet the requirements, these polynomials must hold:

On the interior segments (i.e. $\forall i \in \{2, \ldots, N_f - 1\}$): $f_{i-1}(t_i) = f_i(t_i) = c^i$, $\dot{f}_{i-1}(t_i) = \dot{f}_i(t_i)$, $\ddot{f}_{i-1}(t_i) = \ddot{f}_i(t_i)$, where $c^i = [c_x^i, c_y^i, c_z^i]$ stands for the i-th control point of the spline. This implies that c^i fixes the spline location at t_i, while its corresponding speed and acceleration are established by the continuity conditions.

On the exterior segments: $f_1(t_0) = s(t_0)$, $\dot{f}_1(t_0) = \dot{s}(t_0)$, $\ddot{f}_1(t_0) = \ddot{s}(t_0)$, $f_{N_f}(t_{N_f}) = s(t_e)$, $\dot{f}_{N_f}(t_{N_f}) = \dot{s}(t_e)$, $\ddot{f}_{N_f}(t_{N_f}) = \ddot{s}(t_e)$. This implies that the initial and ending location, speed and acceleration are fixed to the values imposed in the mission.

Hence, when codifying the 3D probe trajectory with a spline of N_p segments, the decision variables of the EA will be $N_p - 1$ intermediate control points c^i and its associated time steps t_i. Besides, as we also want to optimize the mission duration, the final time t_e also becomes a decision variable. So, our EA manipulates vectors with $4 \cdot (N_f - 1) + 1$ continuous decision variables. Finally, although $s(t)$ is a continuous function over time, the EA evaluates some criteria that use it at periodic time steps (i.e. at $t \in \{t_0 : T_s : t_e\}$, with $t_j = t_0 + j \cdot T_s$ and $T_s = \sup(\frac{t_e - t_0}{5000}, \frac{t_e - t_0}{2L})$, where L is the length of $s(t)$ calculated by the objective function OF_2 that we will introduce in next section).

3.2   Evaluation Criteria

This section presents the Constraint and Optimization Functions (CFs and OFs) used to evaluate the $s(t)$ that the EA propose for exploring efficiently the water body. It also explains how to efficiently compute some of them.

Constraints. To evaluate the ASV trajectories we consider 4 CFs:

- *Maximal mission duration:* $\text{CF}_1 = t_e - t_0 - T_{mission} \leq 0$
  This ensures that the UAV performs its mission in the allowed time.
- *Maximal ASV velocity:* $\text{CF}_2 = \sup(\|\dot{s}(t)\|) - v_{max} \leq 0, \forall t \in \{t_0 : T_s : t_e\}$
  This constraint ensures that the spline can be followed by the ASV. The
  maximum velocity is obtained by sampling the derivative of the spline at
  periodic time steps (i.e. $\forall t \in \{t_0 : T_s : t_e\}$)
- *Maximal ASV acceleration:* $\text{CF}_3 = \sup(\|\ddot{s}(t)\|) - a_{max} \leq 0, \forall t \in \{t_0 : T_s : t_e\}$
  As the previous, this function makes the spline followable by the ASV and is
  evaluated at periodically spaced time steps.
- *Spatial domain constraint:* $\text{CF}_4 = \left(\sum_{l=1:2:N_{inter}} \int_{t_{l-1}}^{t_l} \|\dot{s}(t)\| \, dt \right) \leq 0$

This function, where t_l stands for the time instants with intersections between
$s(t)$ and the boundaries of the spatial domain, measures the length of $s(t)$
outside the spatial domain. To define this domain, we select a smaller area
than the corresponding to the water body surface to ensure a navigation
margin with the reservoir shores. We also limit the vertical displacement of
the probe $s_z(t)$ to the range $[-10,0]$ m. The resulting volume, $G(x,y,z) \leq 0$,
delimits the spatial domain that $s(t)$ can traverse without restrictions applying. To evaluate the spatial domain constraint, we can find the intersections
of $s(t)$ with this volume by solving $G(s_x(t), s_y(t), s_z(t)) = 0$ in the time interval $[t_0, t_e]$. Although this equation can have multiple solutions, if we assume
that the starting and ending points of the spline ($s(t_0)$ and $s(t_e)$), defined by
the user, are inside the domain, the number of intersections N_{inter}, if any,
must be even. In order to find all of them, we use a technique inspired by the
bisection method, but instead of checking a single interval at once, we subdivide the time interval in many sub-intervals and look for sign changes in
the resulting vector. This subdivision is repeated in any intervals containing
a sign change[5] until the accuracy of the solution reaches the desired value.
Finally, the integral used to calculate the length of each trajectory section is
evaluated with Matlab `integral` function[6].

Optimization Criteria. Our planner considers 3 OC:

- *Minimize the mission duration:* $\min \text{OF}_1 = (t_e - t_1)$
  Its purpose is to free the ASV as soon as possible to let it perform other
  missions and/or save energy.

---

[5] As the only requirement for using this solver is to have a different sign inside and
outside of the domain function, any mathematical function that meets that criterion
(including those with non-continuous images such as boolean functions) is valid. In
other words, our way of proceeding simplifies immensely the definition of domains
with irregular geometry.

[6] We tested that it is quicker and more accurate to do it with Matlab than with our
own trajectory discretization.

- *Minimize the total trajectory length:* $\min \mathrm{OF}_2 = \left(\int_{t_0}^{t_e} \|\dot{\mathbf{s}}(t)\| \, dt \right)$

  Its purpose is to avoid, whenever possible, useless displacements of the ASV. Again, we use Matlab `integral` function to calculate this OF[7].
- *Maximize the amount of observed particle trajectories:*

$$\max \mathrm{OF}_3 = \left[\sum_{k \in \{1...N_p\}} H \left(\sum_{d \in \{x,y,z\}} \frac{\left(p_d^k(t) - s_d(t)\right)^2}{r_d^2} \leq 1 \right) \right],$$

where $H(\cdot) = 1$ if there $\exists t \in \{t_0 : T_s : t_e\}$ where the inequality holds and $H(\cdot) = 0$ otherwise, and $\mathbf{r} = [5,5,1]$ m. The purpose of this function is to count the amount of trajectory particles that at any t can be observed from the probe, which is modeled as an ellipsoidal ideal sensor whose semi-axes are given by $\mathbf{r}$. Hence, it is responsible of making the ASV and probe trajectory traverse the polluted regions.

Evaluation Function. Considering the previous restrictions and optimization criteria, the EA has to tackle a constrained multi-objective problem. In the preliminary version of the planner presented in this paper, we convert it into a mono-objective problem with the following equation that performs a weighted addition of the constraints violations and objective functions, where $w_{cons,r}$ and $w_{obj,r}$ respectively stand for the weights of the constraints and of the objective.

$$\mathrm{EV} = \sum_{r=1}^{4} w_{cons,r} \cdot \max(\mathrm{CF}_r, 0) + w_{obj,1}\mathrm{OF}_1 + w_{obj,2}\mathrm{OF}_2 - w_{obj,3}\mathrm{OF}_3 \quad (5)$$

As usual, selecting those weights is not trivial and can have a big impact in the obtained results. For that reason, we will analyze their effects in Sect. 4.

3.3 Evolutionary Algorithm

The EA that performs the optimization of the problem described in the previous sections has the usual steps of a Genetic Algorithm. In the following, we explain its main features.

- *Population Initialization.* To generate each solution (trajectory) of the population, we sample the values of the interior control points $\mathbf{c}^i$ and their times t_i, as well as the initial and ending times t_0 and t_e from a uniform distribution. More in detail, c_x^i and c_y^i are sampled from the range given by the extremes of the reservoir geometry, c_z^i from $[-10, 0]$ m and t_0, all t_i and t_e from $[t_0^{mission}, t_0^{mission} + T_{max}]$, where $t_0^{mission}$ is the starting time of the mission and T_{max} its maximal duration. Next, we sort and slide the entire time vector ($t_q = t_q - t_0 + t_0^{mission}$, with $q = \{0, 1, \ldots, N_f - 1, e\}$) to make t_0 equal to the starting mission time $t_0^{mission}$.

---

[7] In this case, we are forced to use the Matlab function, as OF_2 determines the value of L, which is required to perform the proportional trajectory discretization.

- *Parents Selections.* We linearly map the Evaluation Function (EV) values calculated with Eq. (5) for all the population to the range $[0.1, 0.5]$. In particular, the biggest value (worst case) is mapped to 0.1, while the smallest value (best case) is mapped to 0.5. Next, we use the mapped values in the roulette selection method to pick pair of parents.
- *Crossover.* For each pair of parents, we first decide if they are directly copied as children or undergo a mating step, sampling a value from the uniform in $[0, 1]$ and testing if its value is bigger than the probability of crossover. To cross the mating pairs, we sample two cutting points indexes m and n from a uniform integer distribution in the range $[1, N_f - 1]$; define three Index Ranges $\text{IR}_1 = \{1 : min(m, n)\}$, $\text{IR}_2 = \{min(m, n) : max(m, n)\}$ and $\text{IR}_3 = \{max(m, n) : N_f - 1\}$; and create two children whose control points c^i belong to the control points with IR_1 and IR_3 of one parent and to the control point with IR_2 of the other. Afterwards, we sort the values of the time vector, and if it has repeated time values (that will make the spline matrix singular), one of them is averaged with the previous[8].
- *Mutation.* For the no-mating children of the previous step, we decide whether each decision variable mutates, independently of the others, testing if a value sampled from a uniform distribution in range $[0, 1]$ is smaller than the probability of mutation. Each mutating decision variables is *added* a value that is sampled, independently, from the uniform distribution in the range $[-20, 20]$ m for the mutating c_x^i or c_y^i, in $[-2, -2]$ m for c_z^i, and in $[-600, 600]$ s for t_i and t_e. After the mutation, the time vector is sorted and slid to make $t_0 = t_0^{mission}$.
- *Immigrants*: In each generation (EA iteration) a few new solutions are created with the procedure used to initialize the population and introduced in the new population.
- *Population Recombination.* The initial population of the next generation is formed by the new solutions (created with the crossover, mutation and immigrant operators) and by a fraction of the previous best (elitist) solutions.
- *Stop Condition.* The algorithm ends when a) the maximum number of generations has been reached or b) when the EV value of the best solution has converged during a given number of generations.

The different parameters of the algorithm and the results obtained with them are presented in the following section.

4   Results

This section presents and discusses the preliminary results obtained by different configurations of our planner over the four scenarios (A1, A2, B1 & B2) introduced in Sect. 2. In the following we explain the configurations, indicate how the comparative analysis has been performed, and discuss the results.

---

[8] In this case we do not need to slide the time vectors since the t_0 of both parents always equals the initial mission time $t_0^{mission}$.

4.1   Planner Configurations

In order to configure the planner's behavior we have to select multiple parameters discussed in Sect. 3. As presenting an extensive study of the influence of those parameters is out of the scope of this paper, we have fixed the majority of them to the values presented in Table 1 and show what happens when we change the value of $w_{obj,2}$ to create the configurations presented in Table 2.

Table 1. Planner parameters fixed during the study cases

Mission		Optimization		EA	
Maximal ASV speed (v_{max} in m/s)	1	Spline segments (N_f)	10	Population size	50
				Crossover probability	40%
Maximal ASV acceleration (a_{max} in m/s)	0.1	Weight $w_{cons,1}$	10^{20}	Mutation probability	5%
		Weight $w_{cons,2}$	10^{20}	Immigrants	5
		Weight $w_{cons,3}$	10^{20}	Elitist solutions	5
Maximal mission duration (T_{max} in h)	3	Weight $w_{cons,4}$	10^{20}	Stop generation	500
		Weight $w_{obj,1}$	1	Convergence count	30%
		Weight $w_{obj,3}$	10^4	Conv. Tolerance	10^{-6}

Table 2. Planner configurations under test

Changing parameter	Configuration identifier		
	V1	V2	V3
$w_{obj,2}$	10	10^2	10^3

Among the selected values is worth noting the following. N_f is set to an intermediate value to allow $s(t)$ to adapt to the scenario without increasing the number of decision variables unnecessarily. Constraints weights values $w_{cons,r}$ are a lot higher than the objective ones $w_{obj,r}$ to ensure that unfeasible solutions have a worse EV than feasible solutions. Objective function weights $w_{obj,r}$ take into consideration both the range of values of each OF and its importance. Hence, by changing only $w_{obj,2}$ we modify the relative importance of the three OFs. EVs of the configurations with different $w_{obj,2}$ are not directly comparable, as the same solution (with given CF_r and OF_r) has different EV. Finally, as the population size at every generation is 50, and the new generation populations are formed by 5 old elite solutions and 5 immigrants, 40 children are selected.

4.2   Comparative Analysis

To analyze the performance of the different configurations of the planner, we run them over each scenario 25 times. Besides, for each run, we store: 1) the best solution returned by the planner at the end (the generation number will depend on the convergence of the run) and 2) the values of the constraint functions (CF_r) and objective functions (OF_r) of the the best solution found so far in each generation. Next, for the 25 runs of each configuration of the planner and each generation of the EA:

– We count the number of runs where the best solution of the EA does not fulfill the constraints to determine if certain configurations are able to obtain feasible solutions sooner than others. This information is summarized, for each scenario, in the red-green images of Fig. 4, which represent in each cell, the number of runs where the best solutions does not yet fulfill the constraints at a given generation (abscissa axis) and given configuration (in the ordinate axis). We use green to identify the cases (configuration and generations) where the best solution of all the runs is feasible, and a red scale to account for the number of runs with unfeasible solutions.

– We obtain the mean value[9] of each OF independently to determine if their average behavior, represented, grouped by scenario, in the shaded error bar graphics[10] of Fig. 4, is the expected one (i.e. the particle count grows while the mission time and ASV trajectory length decrease) and if a certain configuration is better than another[11].

– Finally, in Fig. 5 we also display a representative solution obtained by one of the configurations of the planner for each scenario. In the top row of graphics: we mark the water body allowed domain in violet; we draw the trajectories of the pollutant particles placed within the allowed domain, using red lines up to the moment that they are observable by the ASV and green lines afterwards; and we represent the ASV trajectory provided by the planner with black lines, marking its control points with black circles and the regions of the trajectory where the ASV traverses unobserved particles with blue lines[12]. The graphics at the bottom row represent, using the same lines and colors as in the graphics at the top, the vertical trajectories of the probe and of the particles that fall within the $[-10, 0]$ m allowed depth of the probe[13]. Finally, the captions at each column of graphics indicate the scenario and the planner configuration used to obtain the represented solution.

4.3 Discussion

The red-green constraint graphs in Fig. 4 show that for Scenarios A1 and A2, configuration V2 finds feasible solutions in all the runs sooner than the others, while for B1 and B2, the best is V1. Besides, analyzing the red scale in detail, at least half of the runs of all configurations find feasible solutions during the first

---

[9] To obtain this average, for those runs that have finished earlier than in 500 iterations we extend the last obtained value to the remaining iterations up to 500.

[10] The center line of each shade represents the corresponding mean value while the shade width over/under the mean is the standard deviation.

[11] We avoid drawing the mean value over 25 runs of the EV of the best solution for each configuration and iteration, since the EV values of one configuration are not comparable with the values of others, due to the change of value in $w_{obj,2}$.

[12] In fact, in the graphics in top row, the green lines of the particle trajectories appear after a blue section in the ASV horizontal trajectory.

[13] Particle vertical trajectories do not become green only for having the probe at its corresponding height, because it is also necessary to have the ASV located over them.

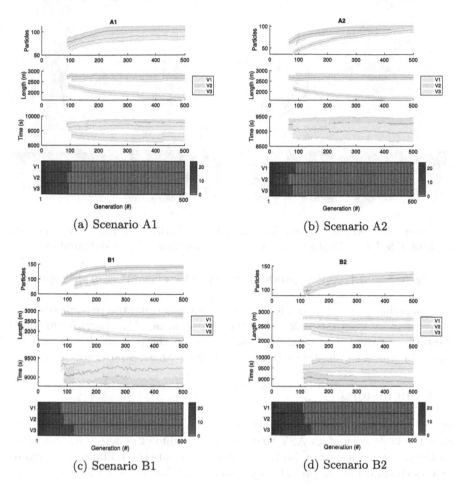

(a) Scenario A1   (b) Scenario A2

(c) Scenario B1   (d) Scenario B2

Fig. 4. Evolution of the constraint and objective functions

50 generations. Regarding the shaded error bar graphics, the best configuration for the trajectory particle count (i.e. those with the highest values) are usually V1 and V2, while the best ones for the ASV trajectory length (i.e. those with the smallest values) is usually V3. This behaviour is expected, as V3 has the highest value of $w_{cons,2}$, making the reduction of the ASV trajectory length relatively more important than observing new particles. Besides, we can not identify a best configuration regarding the mission duration (i.e. one with the lowest value), because it is different for each scenario. Finally, the variability of the quality of the solutions is scenario dependent and usually wider in the duration time (probably, because $w_{cons,1}$ is too low to make OF_1 compete against OF_2 and OF_3). In short, we can not conclude that there is a better overall configuration for the constraints, objective functions and/or scenarios.

Solutions presented in Fig. 5 show that a big part of the ASV horizontal trajectories does not traverse the particle trajectories (especially in A1, B1 & B2). Hence, although Fig. 4 suggests that the EA has usually converged in

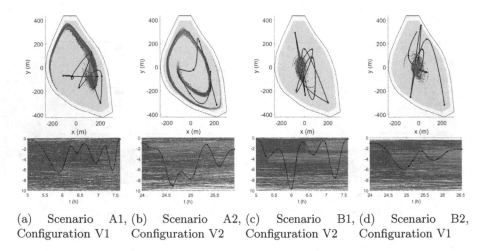

(a)   Scenario   A1, (b)   Scenario   A2, (c)   Scenario   B1, (d)   Scenario   B2,
Configuration V1   Configuration V2   Configuration V2   Configuration V1

Fig. 5. Selected solutions provided by different configurations of the planner

500 generations, there is room for improvement regarding the particle count and ASV trajectory length. Besides, the depth distribution of the particles makes the adaptation of the probe height almost useless in the presented scenarios (and hence, the approach should be tested over others where it becomes meaningful).

5   Conclusions

This paper presents the preliminary version of an EA-based planner that optimizes the trajectory of an ASV that has to determine the actual distribution of a pollutant in a lentic water body. To efficiently locate the pollutant, the planner exploits the information provided by a simulator that models the water dynamics and pollutant transportation, and uses an EA that simultaneously optimizes the mission duration, the ASV trajectory length and the chances to detect the pollutant, while ensuring the ASV safety and manoeuvrability.

The results presented in this paper show that there is a plenty of room for improvement in the future versions of the planner. Regarding its pollutant simulator, we want to enrich it we new models that consider specific behaviors of certain pollutants and use it to perform Monte Carlo simulations of the particles distribution. Both improvements would let our planner identify ASV trajectories that are good for the probable distribution of certain pollutants. Regarding its supporting EA, we are thinking of using a variant better intended for constrained multi-objective problems, developing a problem specific initialization step (that produces better organized trajectories and samples the initial control points in polluted regions of the water body), performing the optimization in two stages (first horizontally and later vertically), and carrying out systematic studies of the effects of the parameters and of the new versions in many different scenarios.

Finally, we want to highlight that in spite of the envisioned improvements, the current version of the planner is working and sets up a valid infrastructure that already incorporates simple versions of its elements.

References

1. COMSOL Multiphysics. https://www.comsol.com/. Accessed 15 Oct 2020
2. European Commission water related directives. https://ec.europa.eu/environment/water/index_en.htm. Accessed 15 Oct 2020
3. MATLAB. https://www.mathworks.com/. Accessed 15 Oct 2020
4. United Nations 2030 Agenda for Sustainable Development. https://sdgs.un.org/goals. Accessed 15 Oct 2020
5. Aparicio-Medrano, E.: Physical aspects explaining cyanobacteria scum formation in natural systems. Ph.D. thesis, Eindhoven (2014)
6. Arzamendia, M., Gregor, D., Reina, D.G., Toral, S.L., Gregor, R.: Evolutionary path planning of an autonomous surface vehicle for water quality monitoring. In: International Conference on Developments in e-Systems Engineering (2016)
7. Arzamendia, M., Gregor, D., Reina, D., Toral, S.: An evolutionary approach to constrained path planning of an autonomous surface vehicle for maximizing the covered area of Ypacarai lake. Soft. Comput. **23**, 1723–1734 (2019)
8. Bistafa, S.R.: On the development of the Navier-Stokes equation by Navier. Revista Brasileira de Ensino de Física **40**(2), 1–12 (2017)
9. Janga-Reddy, M., Nagesh-Kumar, D.: Evolutionary algorithms, swarm intelligence methods, and their applications in water resources engineering: a state of the art review. H2Open J. **3**(1), 135–188 (2020)
10. Liua, Z., Zhanga, Y., Yua, X., Yuana, C.: USVs: an overview of developments and challenges. Ann. Rev. Control **41**, 71–93 (2016)
11. Panda, M., Das, B., Subudhi, B., Pati, B.B.: A comprehensive review of path planning algorithms for autonomous underwater vehicles. Int. J. Autom. Comput. **17**, 321–352 (2020)
12. Ravankar, A., Ravankar, A., Kobayashi, Y., Hoshino, Y., Peng, C.: Path smoothing techniques in robot navigation: state-of-the-art, current and future challenges. Sensors **18**, 3170 (2018)
13. Shuo, J., Yonghui, Z., Wen, R., Kebin, T.: The unmanned autonomous cruise ship for water quality monitoring and sampling. In: International Conference on Computer Systems, Electronics and Control (2017)
14. Siyang, S., Kerdcharoen, T.: Development of unmanned surface vehicle for smart water quality inspector. In: International Conference on Electrical Engineering/Electronics, Computer, Telecommunications and Information Technology (2016)
15. Storey, M., van der Gaag, B., Burns, B.: Advances in on-line drinking water quality monitoring and early warning systems. Water Res. **42**(2), 741–747 (2011)
16. Xia, G., Han, Z., Zhao, B., Liu, C., Wang, X.: Global path planning for unmanned surface vehicle based on improved quantum ant colony algorithm. Math. Probl. Eng. **2019**, 1–30 (2019)
17. Xiong, C., Zhou, H., Lu, D., Zeng, Z., Lian, L., Yu, C.: Rapidly-exploring adaptive sampling tree*: a sample-based path-planning algorithm for unmanned marine vehicles information gathering in variable ocean environments. Sensors **20**, 2515 (2020)
18. Xiong, C., Chen, D., Lu, D., Zeng, Z., Lian, L.: Path planning of multiple autonomous marine vehicles for adaptive sampling using voronoi-based ant colony optimization. Robot. Auton. Syst. **115**, 90–103 (2019)

Author Index

Agresta, Antonio 795
Alba, Enrique 242
Aljarah, Ibrahim 146
Allmendinger, Richard 50, 388
Andreae, Peter 665
Avramescu, Andreea 388

Baeta, Francisco 763
Baia, Alina Elena 552
Baioletti, Marco 795
Barbosa, Helio J. C. 729
Bartz-Beielstein, Thomas 373
Besada-Portas, Eva 812
Birattari, Mauro 130
Biscarini, Chiara 795
Browne, Will N. 469
Büttner, Johannes 309

Caldwell, Jamie 506
Carazo-Barbero, Gonzalo 812
Cardoso, Rui P. 649
Castillo, Pedro A. 146
Chicano, Francisco 242
Correia, João 81, 618, 763
Costa, Victor 618

De Stefano, Claudio 781
DeHaan, Kristian 97
Desell, Travis 291, 568, 584
Di Bari, Gabriele 552
Doerr, Benjamin 17
Doerr, Carola 17, 601
Domínguez-Ríos, Miguel Ángel 242
Dorn, Márcio 194
Dreo, Johann 17

Eftimov, Tome 601
Eiben, A. E. 373
Eisenbarth, Hedwig 469
Ellefsen, Kai Olav 34
ElSaid, AbdElRahman 291, 568, 584
Everson, Richard M. 634

Ferigo, Andrea 210
Fernández, Ricardo 421
Ferrigno, Luigi 781
Fieldsend, Jonathan E. 634
Fontanella, Francesco 781
Franks, Daniel W. 537

Gao, Xiaoying 665
García, Alejandro Romero 341
García, Antonio M. Mora 341
García-Valdez, Mario 747
Garnica, Oscar 421
Gerevini, Luca 781
Girón-Sierra, José M. 812
Glanois, Claire 325
Glette, Kyrre 3, 34
González-Doncel, Gaspar 421
González-Gallardo, Sandra 227
Grbic, Djordje 325

Hähner, Jörg 681
Hart, Emma 258, 649
Hidalgo, J. Ignacio 421
Höhl, Silke 258
Holm, Asta L. 359

Iacca, Giovanni 210
Iskandar, Andrew 50
Ivaşcu, Carina 634

Jankovic, Anja 601

Kajihara, Sho 65
Karns, Joshua 291, 568, 584
Katona, Adam 537
Khurma, Ruba Abu 146
Knowles, Joshua 506
Korovin, Iakov 407
Kraneveld, Aletta D. 359
Kronberger, Gabriel 421
Kubacki, Filip 506
Kuckling, Jonas 130
Kurka, David Burth 649

Larcher Jr, Celio H. N.   729
Liang, Jing   489
Londt, Trevor   665
López-Ibáñez, Manuel   388
López-Orozco, José A.   812
Lopez-Rincon, Alejandro   359
Lourenço, Nuno   537, 618
Luque, Mariano   227
Lyu, Zimeng   291, 568, 584

Machado, Penousal   537, 618, 763
Martins, Tiago   763
McGehee, Andrew J.   275
Medvet, Eric   210
Merelo, Juan J.   747
Merz, Christian   309
Metcalf, Renee   359
Mihail, Radu P.   453
Milani, Alfredo   795
Millán, Laura   421
Mkaouer, Mohamed   568, 584
Molinara, Mario   781
Mousavirad, Seyed Jalaleddin   407

Najarro, Elias   325
Narloch, Pedro Henrique   194
Neri, Ferrante   178
Nguyen, Dennis T. T.   522
Noor, Md Asaduzzaman   113
Nordmoen, Jørgen   3
Nygaard, Tønnes F.   3

Ochoa, Gabriela   714
Olesen, Thor V. A. N.   522
Oliva, Diego   407
Ororbia, Alexander G.   291

Palm, Rasmus B.   522
Palm, Rasmus Berg   325
Pätzel, David   681
Pereira, Vitor   81
Perez-Pardo, Paula   359
Pitt, Jeremy   649
Plötz, Per-Arno   162
Poggioni, Valentina   552
Prince, Michael H.   97, 275

Rebolledo, Margarita   373
Renau, Quentin   17
Richter, Hendrik   437
Risi, Sebastian   325, 522
Rocha, Miguel   81
Roozendaal, Daphne S.   359
Rosenbauer, Lukas   681
Ruiz, Ana B.   227

Saborido, Rubén   227
Sabri, Khair Eddin   146
Samuelsen, Eivind   3
Santucci, Valentino   795
Sarti, Stefano   714
Sato, Hiroyuki   65
Schaefer, Gerald   407
Schleifer, Kevin   437
Schulze, Rico   437
Shehu, Harisu Abdullahi   469
Sheppard, John W.   113
Siddique, Abubakar   469
Sousa, Tiago   81
Spierenburg, Hilde M.   359
Spindler, Jacob   437
Stein, Anthony   681, 697
Stensby, Emma Hjellbrekke   34

Takadama, Keiki   65
Tauritz, Daniel R.   97, 275
Thies, Christoph   506
Tonda, Alberto   359

Urquhart, Neil   162, 258

van Pelt, Vincent   130
Vidal, Franck P.   453
von Mammen, Sebastian   309

Wagner, Alexander R. M.   697
Walker, James Alfred   537
Wang, Peng   489
Watson, Richard   506
Wen, Tianci   453
Wittpohl, Milan   162

Xue, Bing   489

Zhang, Mengjie   489